LORD JESUS CHRIST

LORD JESUS CHRIST

*Devotion to Jesus
in Earliest Christianity*

LARRY W. HURTADO

WILLIAM B. EERDMANS PUBLISHING COMPANY
GRAND RAPIDS, MICHIGAN / CAMBRIDGE, U.K.

Wm. B. Eerdmans Publishing Co.
255 Jefferson Ave. S.E., Grand Rapids, Michigan 49503 /
P.O. Box 163, Cambridge CB3 9PU U.K.

Printed in the United States of America

08 07 06 05 04 03   7 6 5 4 3 2 1

Library of Congress Cataloging-in-Publication Data

Hurtado, Larry W., 1943-
Lord Jesus Christ: devotion to Jesus in earliest Christianity / Larry W. Hurtado.
p.   cm.
Includes bibliographical references and index.
ISBN 0-8028-6070-2 (cloth: alk. paper)
1. Jesus Christ — History of doctrines — Early church, ca. 30-600.
2. Jesus Christ — Cult — History.   I. Title.

BT198.H87   2003
232'.8'09015 — dc21
2003048048

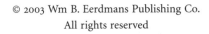

www.eerdmans.com

To
the EHCC
Scholarship, friendship,
a sense of humor, Highland irrigation

Contents

CONTENTS

Preface

A few words of clarification are in order at the outset. This is not a New Testament Christology, not a history of early Christianity, and not a history of early Christian doctrines. It is a historical analysis of the beliefs and religious practices that constituted devotion to Jesus as a divine figure in earliest Christianity. It is about the role of the figure of Jesus in the religious life and thought of earliest Christians.

As I explain in the introduction, so far as I know, this is the first book of quite this kind (in focus, scope, and depth) since Wilhelm Bousset's classic from 1913, *Kyrios Christos.* (At the end of the considerable effort involved in producing this one, I can see more readily why such a work has not been attempted!) This is not, however, a revised edition of that influential volume. Perhaps I should say, instead, that this book has been inspired and shaped in some ways by *Kyrios Christos.* But I offer here my own historical analysis of the emergence and early development of devotion to Jesus; and mine is very different from his. I admire Bousset's enormous learning. But I think he was seriously wrong on some rather important matters. His great erudition I do not question, but I am not so confident of his judgments.

Also, of course, things have moved on quite a lot since 1913. There are important additions to the body of primary data (such as the Nag Hammadi cache), and the oceanic body of relevant scholarly publications has brought major changes in approaches and conclusions on a number of matters.

This was always going to be a big book. But it is much bigger, and took much longer to write, than I had expected at the outset. Whoever asks readers to accommodate a book as big as this owes them an explanation. I can offer one. (But whether the writing of any book, large or small, is *justified,* ah, that is left for its readers to decide.) Basically, this book is unavoidably large because of its chronological scope, the mass of evidence considered, and its depth of treatment of matters.

But I have endeavored to write for a wide readership. It is, I hope, a book that is sufficiently important that scholars in relevant fields *ought* to read it, and yet also a book written accessibly enough that anyone else seriously interested in this subject would be *able* to read it. I have transliterated Greek, Aramaic, and Hebrew words, and have often used footnotes to provide explanatory material for those less well acquainted with the issues and data. When I placed a previous manuscript of mine in his hands and posited a similar aim for it, the late John Hollar (a trenchant and supportive editor to many in my field) replied that it was a pretty tall order. But, after reading that manuscript, John and other readers of that and other publications have encouraged me to think that it is feasible to combine serious discussion and accessibility. So, with some confidence I offer this big tome, to serious "lay" readers as well as scholars, to "take it up and read."

Because it is intended to help (re)shape scholarly opinion, this book is fitted out with the apparatus of scholarship. Whether they are scholars and students in the subjects discussed here or "general readers" with a serious interest in the origins of Christianity, I write for those who are not particularly intimidated by footnotes or put off reading books that have them. I give my readers credit as those who appreciate having available adequate references to the primary data and the rich body of relevant scholarly publications. Moreover, I believe in transparent scholarship. So you can see the basis for the analysis that I provide.

Also, I engage here many controversial matters, and I have not declined to "call 'em the way I see 'em." So I have provided the sort of engagement with scholarship that critical readers have a right to expect in a book intended to be taken seriously. Those readers who may not be so concerned with such matters but essentially want to follow the analysis offered here will find, I trust, that my discussion is sufficiently readable as well as buttressed.

A number of friends and colleagues in the scholarly guild have read portions of the manuscript in earlier stages as it was being written, generously giving time to provide me with comments (in some cases, very extensive), both critical and encouraging: Dale Allison, Darrell Bock, David Capes, April DeConick, Peter Hayman, Alan Kirk, John Kloppenborg Verbin, Ian McDonald, Carey Newman, Paul Owen, James Robinson, Marianne Meye Thompson, Catrin Williams, and David Wright. Very deliberately I chose people of a variety of viewpoints, each of whom, however, is an expert in the subject(s) of the chapter(s) he or she kindly read. For some chapters I was able to have the services of two or more of these colleagues, benefiting from their various points of view. On a number of matters they alerted me to evidence and publications that I had missed, gave me suggestions to strengthen my arguments, and also candidly indicated their disagreements, and where they didn't find my arguments persuasive. I am enormously grateful to them all. Even when I have been unable to accede to their views, their criticism has enabled me to identify places where I hope that I have made a better job of presenting my own views. Whatever its remaining flaws (which, no doubt, reviewers will be prompt to identify!), this is a better book than it would have been thanks to these scholars.

Behind the nearly three years of writing this book are nearly twenty years of research and other publications in its subject matter. Grants in support of the research from the Social Sciences and Humanities Research Council of Canada, a research leave grant from the Arts and Humanities Research Board (UK), and sabbatical leaves from the University of Manitoba and the University of Edinburgh were crucial. I gratefully acknowledge the investment of all these bodies in my research.

The team at Eerdmans have been wonderfully supportive and patient in the considerable delay between my earlier hopes and the completion of this work. Their enthusiasm for the project has been constant. I am grateful to colleagues in New College (the School of Divinity) who have been so encouraging, and also considerate of the demands of this big project. My wife, Shannon, has lovingly endured my preoccupation with this drawn-out task, patiently listening to me muse about this or that issue, while she was herself finishing her Ph.D. thesis in history!

On a sadder note, one of those friends to whom this book is dedicated, Don Juel, did not live to see it in finished form. I admire Don's scholarship, and I am privileged to have known him personally. He will be missed greatly by all who knew him. I treasure an e-mail message from him, sent in the final days of his long and difficult bout with illness, in which he expressed his enjoyment of friendships and a moving confidence in the Faithfulness, to whom he entrusted himself. In the same spirit, then, not really "good-bye," but *"Au revoir,"* Don!

Edinburgh,
27 March 2003

Abbreviations

Academic Abbreviations

AB	Anchor Bible Commentary Series
ABD	*Anchor Bible Dictionary,* ed. D. N. Freedman, 6 vols. (New York: Doubleday, 1992)
AGJU	Arbeiten zur Geschichte des antiken Judentums und des Urchristentums
AJT	*American Journal of Theology*
ANF	Ante-Nicene Fathers, ed. Alexander Roberts and James Donaldson, 10 vols. (1885; reprint, Peabody, Mass.: Hendrickson, 1994)
ANRW	*Aufstieg und Niedergang der römischen Welt,* ed. H. Temporini and W. Haase (Berlin: De Gruyter, 1978-)
ANTF	Arbeiten zur neutestamentlichen Textforschung
ASTI	*Annual of the Swedish Theological Institute*
ATANT	Abhandlungen zur Theologie des Alten und Neuen Testaments
ATR	*Anglican Theological Review*
BAGD	W. Bauer, W. Arndt, F. W. Gingrich, and F. W. Danker, eds., *A Greek-English Lexicon of the New Testament and Other Early Christian Literature,* 3rd ed.
BBET	Beiträge zur biblischen Exegese und Theologie
BDF	F. Blass, A. Debrunner, and R. W. Funk, eds., *A Greek Grammar of the New Testament* (Chicago: University of Chicago Press, 1961)
BHT	Beiträge zur historischen Theologie
BIOSCS	*Bulletin of the International Organization for Septuagint and Cognate Studies*
BJS	Brown Judaic Studies
BR	*Biblical Research*
BZ	*Biblische Zeitschrift*

BZAW	Beihefte zur *Zeitschrift für die alttestamentliche Wissenschaft*
BZHT	Beiträge zur historischen Theologie
CBET	Contributions to Biblical Exegesis and Theologie
CBQ	*Catholic Biblical Quarterly*
CBQMS	Catholic Biblical Quarterly — Monograph Series
CCSA	Corpus Christianorum, Series Apocrypha
CH	*Church History*
CHB	*Cambridge History of the Bible*, vol. 1, ed. P. R. Ackroyd and C. F. Evans (Cambridge: Cambridge University Press, 1975)
ConBNT	Coniectanea biblica, New Testament
CR	*Critical Review of Books in Religion*
CRBS	*Currents in Research: Biblical Studies*
CRINT	Compendia rerum iudaicarum ad novum testamentum
DJG	*Dictionary of Jesus and the Gospels*, ed. J. B. Green et al. (Downers Grove, Ill.: InterVarsity, 1992)
DLNTD	*Dictionary of the Later New Testament and Its Developments*, ed. R. P. Martin and Peter H. Davids (Downers Grove, Ill.: InterVarsity, 1997)
DPL	*Dictionary of Paul and His Letters*, ed. G. F. Hawthorne et al. (Downers Grove, Ill.: InterVarsity, 1993)
Ebib	Etudes bibliques
EDNT	*Exegetical Dictionary of the New Testament*, ed. H. Balz and G. Schneider, 3 vols. (Grand Rapids: Eerdmans, 1990-93)
EEC	*Encyclopedia of Early Christianity*, ed. Everett Ferguson, 2nd ed., 2 vols. (New York: Garland, 1997)
EECh	*Encyclopedia of the Early Church*, ed. Angelo Di Berardino (New York: Oxford University Press, 1992)
ESCJ	Studies in Christianity and Judaism/Études sur le christianisme et le judaïsme
ET	English translation
ETL	*Ephemerides theologicae lovanienses*
ExpT	*Expository Times*
FFNT	Foundations and Facets: New Testament
FRLANT	Forschungen zur Religion und Literatur des Alten und Neuen Testaments
HDR	Harvard Dissertations in Religion
HNT	Handbuch zum Neuen Testament
HR	*History of Religions*
HTR	*Harvard Theological Review*
HTS	Harvard Theological Studies
HUCA	*Hebrew Union College Annual*
ICC	International Critical Commentary
Int	*Interpretation*

Academic Abbreviations

JBL	*Journal of Biblical Literature*
JECS	*Journal of Early Christian Studies*
JJS	*Journal of Jewish Studies*
JR	*Journal of Religion*
JRH	*Journal of Religious History*
JSJ	*Journal for the Study of Judaism*
JSJSup	Journal for the Study of Judaism — Supplements
JSNT	*Journal for the Study of the New Testament*
JSNTSup	Journal for the Study of the New Testament — Supplement Series
JSPSup	Journal for the Study of the Pseudepigrapha — Supplements
JSSR	*Journal for the Scientific Study of Religion*
JTS	*Journal of Theological Studies*
LCL	Loeb Classical Library
LQF	Liturgische Quellen und Forschungen
LTP	*Laval théologique et philosophique*
LXX	Septuagint
MBT	Münsterische Beiträge zur Theologie
MHT	J. H. Moulton, W. F. Howard, and N. Turner, *A Grammar of New Testament Greek,* 4 vols. (Edinburgh: T. & T. Clark, 1908-79)
MM	J. H. Moulton and G. Milligan, eds., *The Vocabulary of the Greek New Testament* (1930)
MT	Masoretic text
NHLE	*The Nag Hammadi Library in English,* ed. James M. Robinson, 3rd rev. ed. (New York and Leiden: Brill, 1988)
NHMS	Nag Hammadi Monograph Series
NHS	Nag Hammadi Studies
NICNT	New International Commentary on the New Testament
NIDNTT	*New International Dictionary of New Testament Theology,* ed. Colin Brown, 3 vols. (Grand Rapids: Zondervan, 1975-78)
NIGTC	New International Greek Testament Commentary
NKZ	*Neue kirchliche Zeitschrift*
NovT	*Novum Testamentum*
NovTSup	Novum Testamentum, Supplements
NRSV	New Revised Standard Version
NTA	*New Testament Apocrypha,* ed. W. Scheemelcher, 2 vols. (Louisville: Westminster John Knox; Cambridge: James Clarke, 1991)
NTAbh	Neutestamentliche Abhandlungen
NTF	Neutestamentliche Forschungen
NTOA	Novum Testamentum et Orbis Antiquus
NTS	*New Testament Studies*
NTTS	New Testament Tools and Studies
OCD	*Oxford Classical Dictionary,* ed. Simon Hornblower and Antony Spawforth, 3rd ed. (Oxford: Oxford University Press, 1996)

OTP	*Old Testament Pseudepigrapha,* ed. J. H. Charlesworth, 2 vols. (Garden City, N.Y.: Doubleday, 1983-85)
P.Oxy.	Oxyrhynchus Papyri
PTR	*Princeton Theological Review*
PTS	Patristische Texte und Studien
RevB	*Revue biblique*
RHE	*Revue d'histoire ecclésiastique*
RHPR	*Revue d'histoire et de philosophie religieuses*
RHR	*Revue de l'histoire des religions*
RSR	*Recherches de science religieuse*
SANT	Studien zum Alten und Neuen Testament
SBLDS	Society of Biblical Literature Dissertation Series
SBLEJL	Society of Biblical Literature Early Judaism and Its Literature
SBLMS	Society of Biblical Literature Monograph Series
SBLSP	Society of Biblical Literature Seminar Papers
SBS	Stuttgarter Bibelstudien
SBT	Studies in Biblical Theology
SBTss	Studies in Biblical Theology, second series
SC	Sources chrétiennes
SD	Studies and Documents
SecCent	*Second Century*
SFSHJ	South Florida Studies in the History of Judaism
SJLA	Studies in Judaism in Late Antiquity
SJT	*Scottish Journal of Theology*
SNT	Studien zum Neuen Testament
SNTSMS	Society for New Testament Studies Monograph Series
SPap	*Studia papyrologica*
SPB	Studia postbiblica
SR	*Studies in Religion/Sciences religieuses*
ST	*Studia theologica*
STDJ	Studies on the Texts of the Desert of Judah
SUNT	Studien zur Umwelt des Neuen Testaments
SVTP	Studia in Veteris Testamenti pseudepigrapha
TB	*Tyndale Bulletin*
TBl	*Theologische Blätter*
TDNT	*Theological Dictionary of the New Testament,* ed. G. Kittel and G. Friedrich, 10 vols. (Grand Rapids: Eerdmans, 1964-76)
TJT	*Toronto Journal of Theology*
TRu	*Theologische Rundschau*
TS	*Theological Studies*
TSAJ	*Texte und Studien zum antiken Judentum*
TTS	Trier Theologische Studien
TU	Theologische Untersuchungen

VC	Vigiliae christianae
VCSup	Vigiliae christianae Supplements
VT	Vetus Testamentum
WBC	Word Biblical Commentaries
WMANT	Wissenschaftliche Monographien zum Alten und Neuen Testament
WUNT	Wissenschaftliche Untersuchungen zum Neuen Testament
ZKG	Zeitschrift für Kirchengeschichte
ZKT	Zeischrift für katholische Theologie
ZNW	Zeitschrift für die neutestamentliche Wissenschaft
ZTK	Zeitschrift für Theologie und Kirche

Classical Sources

1 Apoc. Jas.	1 Apocalypse of James
1 Apol.	Justin Martyr, 1 Apology
2 Apol.	Justin Martyr, 2 Apology
1 Clem.	1 Clement
2 Clem.	2 Clement
1QapGenar	Genesis Apocryphon, Qumran
4QEnast^{b}ar	4QAstronomical Enoch (4Q209)
1QH	Hymns Scroll (Hodayot), Qumran
1QS	Rule of the Community, Qumran
11QMelch	Melchizedek text, Qumran
11QPs	Psalms Scroll, Qumran
11QtgJob	11QTargum of Job (11Q10)
Abr.	Philo, De Abrahamo (On the Life of Abraham)
Acts Pet.	Acts of Peter
Acts Thom.	Acts of Thomas
Adv. haer.	Irenaeus, Adversus haereses (Against Heresies)
Adv. Marc.	Tertullian, Adversus Marcionem
Ant.	Flavius Josephus, Jewish Antiquities
Ap. Jas.	Apocryphon of James
Ap. John	Apocryphon of John
Apoc. Abr.	Apocalypse of Abraham
Asc. Isa.	Ascension of Isaiah
Barn.	Epistle of Barnabas
b. Sanh.	Babylonian Talmud, Tractate Sanhedrin
CD	Cairo (Genizeh text of the) Damascus Document
Conf. ling.	Philo, De confusione linguarum (On the Confusion of Languages)
Decal.	Philo, De decalogo
Dem.	Irenaeus, Demonstration (Epideixis)
Dial.	Justin Martyr, Dialogue with Trypho
Dial. Sav.	Dialogue of the Savior

Did.	*Didache*
Ep. Apos.	*Epistle of the Apostles (Epistula Apostolorum)*
Ep. Pet. Phil.	*Letter of Peter to Philip*
Exc. Theod.	*Excerpta ex Theodoto (Excerpts from Theodotus)*
GJohn	Gospel of John
Gos. Phil.	*Gospel of Philip*
Gos. Thom.	*Gospel of Thomas*
Gos. Truth	*Gospel of Truth*
Haer.	Tertullian, *De praescriptione haereticorum (Prescription against Heretics)*
HE	Eusebius, *Historia ecclesiastica (Church History)*
Herm. Sim.	*Hermas, Similitude(s)*
Herm. Vis.	*Hermas, Vision(s)*
Ign. *Eph.*	Ignatius, *Letter to the Ephesians*
Ign. *Magn.*	Ignatius, *Letter to the Magnesians*
Ign. *Philad.*	Ignatius, *Letter to the Philadelphians*
Ign. *Poly.*	Ignatius, *Letter to Polycarp*
Ign. *Rom.*	Ignatius, *Letter to the Romans*
Ign. *Smyrn.*	Ignatius, *Letter to the Smyrnaeans*
Ign. *Trall.*	Ignatius, *Letter to the Trallians*
IGos. Thom.	*Infancy Gospel of Thomas*
Leg. alleg.	Philo, *Legum allegoriae (Allegorical Interpretation)*
Mart. Pol.	*Martyrdom of Polycarp*
Migr. Abr.	Philo, *De migratione Abrahami (The Migration of Abraham)*
m. Sanh.	Mishnah, Tractate *Sanhedrin*
m. Tamid	Mishnah, Tractate *Tamid*
Pan.	Epiphanius, *Panarion (Haereses)*
PJ	*Protevangelium (Infancy Gospel) of James*
Pol. *Phil.*	Polycarp, *Letter to the Philippians*
Pss. Sol.	*Psalms of Solomon*
Quaest. Gen.	Philo, *Quaestiones et Solutiones in Genesim et Exodum*
Ref.	Hippolytus, *Refutatio omnium haeresium*
Sib. Or.	*Sibylline Oracles*
Somn.	Philo, *De somnis (On Dreams)*
Soph. Jes. Chr.	Sophia of Jesus Christ
Spec. leg.	Philo, *De specialibus legibus (Special Laws)*
Strom.	Clement of Alexandria, *Stromateis*
Thom. Cont.	*Book of Thomas the Contender*
T. Mos.	*Testament of Moses*
Treat. Res.	*Treatise on the Resurrection*
Trim. Prot.	*Trimorphic Protennoia*
Vir. illus.	Jerome, *On the Lives of Illustrious Men*
Vit. Mos.	Philo, *De Vita Mosis (Life of Moses)*

Introduction

The indisputable centrality of the figure of Jesus in early Christian devotion is the premise for this book, and my aim is to offer a new historical description and analysis of this remarkable phenomenon. Indeed, the key distinguishing 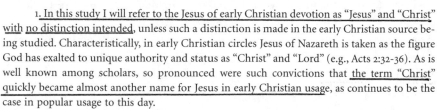 feature of the early Christian circles was the prominent place of Jesus Christ in their religious thought and practice.[1] There certainly were plenty of other religious groups worthy of note in the Roman period, and even some that shared a number of important features with early Christianity. There were, for example, other movements and groups that recruited converts across ethnic lines, offering intimate fellowship, initiation rituals, and sacred meals with a deity.[2] There were philosophical movements to which the early Christian groups can be likened in their concern to define and promote ethics.[3] But despite the similarities

1. In this study I will refer to the Jesus of early Christian devotion as "Jesus" and "Christ" with no distinction intended, unless such a distinction is made in the early Christian source being studied. Characteristically, in early Christian circles Jesus of Nazareth is taken as the figure God has exalted to unique authority and status as "Christ" and "Lord" (e.g., Acts 2:32-36). As is well known among scholars, so pronounced were such convictions that the term "Christ" quickly became almost another name for Jesus in early Christian usage, as continues to be the case in popular usage to this day.

2. The classic study by A. D. Nock, *Conversion: The Old and the New in Religion from Alexander the Great to Augustine of Hippo* (Oxford: Oxford University Press, 1933), is still essential reading.

3. E. A. Judge, "The Early Christians as a Scholastic Community," *JRH* 1 (1961): 4-15, 125-37. A. J. Malherbe, *Moral Exhortation, a Greco-Roman Sourcebook* (Philadelphia: Westminster, 1986), discusses the moral/ethical traditions of the Roman era. For discussions of early Christian ethics that take these traditions as context, see W. A. Meeks, *The Moral World of the First Christians*, Library of Early Christianity (Philadelphia: Westminster, 1986); J. I. H. McDonald, *The Crucible of Christian Morality* (London: Routledge, 1998); and Troels Engberg-Pedersen, *Paul and the Stoics* (Louisville: Westminster John Knox, 2000).

with other religious movements and groups of the Roman period, all the various forms of early Christianity (whatever their relationship to what came to be
known as "orthodox" or "catholic" Christianity) can be identified as such by
the importance they attached to the figure of Jesus.

Moreover, an exalted significance of Jesus appears astonishingly early in
Christian circles. Well within the first couple decades of the Christian movement (i.e., ca. 30-50 C.E., to make at this point in the discussion a deliberately
modest chronological claim) Jesus was treated as a recipient of religious devotion and was associated with God in striking ways. In fact, as we will see later in
this study, we probably have to posit a virtual explosion of devotion to Jesus toward the earlier end of this short period.[4] I have proposed that in this development we have what amounts to a new and distinctive "mutation" or variant
form of the monotheistic practice that is otherwise characteristic of the Jewish
religious matrix out of which the Christian movement sprang.[5] In this book my
aim is to offer a full-scale analysis of the origin, development, and diversification of devotion to Christ in the crucial first two centuries of the Christian
movement (ca. 30-170 C.E.).

In the following chapters I have basically three main points to make. First,
as I have already mentioned, a noteworthy devotion to Jesus emerges phenom-
enally early in circles of his followers, and cannot be restricted to a secondary
stage of religious development or explained as the product of extraneous
forces. Certainly the Christian movement was not hermetically sealed from the
cultures in which it developed, and Christians appropriated (and adapted for
their own purposes) words, conceptual categories, and religious traditions to
express their faith. But devotion to Jesus was not a late development. So far as
historical inquiry permits us to say, it was an immediate feature of the circles of
those who identified themselves with reference to him.

Second, devotion to Jesus was exhibited in an unparalleled intensity and
diversity of expression, for which we have no true analogy in the religious environment of the time. There is simply no precedent or parallel for the level of
energy invested by early Christians in expressing the significance of Jesus for

---

4. "At the beginning there was not a 'quite rapid development,' but an 'explosion.'"
Martin Hengel and Anna Maria Schwemer, *Paul between Damascus and Antioch: The Un-
known Years* (Louisville: Westminster John Knox, 1997), 283-84, in critique of Wilhelm
Bousset's characterization of early devotion to Jesus. See also Hengel's programmatic essay,
"Christology and New Testament Chronology," in *Between Jesus and Paul* (London: SCM
Press, 1983), 30-47.

5. See, e.g., L. W. Hurtado, *One God, One Lord: Early Christian Devotion and Ancient Jewish Monotheism*, 2nd ed. (Edinburgh: T. & T. Clark, 1998; 1st ed., Philadelphia: Fortress, 1988);
Hurtado, "First Century Jewish Monotheism," *JSNT* 71 (1998): 3-26.

them in their religious thought and practice. The full pattern of devotion to Jesus that we examine in this book is not one example of a class of analogous religious phenomena in comparable groups, but is instead truly remarkable in the history of religions, justifying (indeed, requiring) a special effort to understand it in historical terms. Toward that end I propose a model of the historical forces and factors that shaped and propelled early devotion to Jesus, which is the particular focus of the next chapter.

3 The third thesis is that this intense devotion to Jesus, which includes reverencing him as divine, was offered and articulated characteristically within a firm stance of exclusivist monotheism, particularly in the circles of early Christians that anticipated and helped to establish what became mainstream (and subsequently, familiar) Christianity. That is, with notable exceptions that will be discussed in a later chapter, these early believers characteristically insisted on the exclusive validity of the God of the Scriptures of Israel, rejecting all the other deities of the Roman world; and they sought to express and understand Jesus' divine significance in relation to this one God. In their religious thought, that is, in the ways they defined and portrayed Jesus in their teachings, they characteristically referred to him with reference to God (e.g., as God's "Son," "Christ/Messiah," "Word," "Image"). In their devotional practices as well (for example, in their patterns of prayer and worship), they characteristically sought to express a rather full veneration of Jesus in ways that also affirmed the primacy of God "the Father."

To be sure, there are indications that maintaining this close linkage and distinction of Jesus and God was not easy. In some forms of early "popular" Christianity, Jesus almost seems to have eclipsed "the Father." In other cases a monotheistic concern may not have featured at all, as appears to be so in the so-called gnostic systems of multiple divine beings and emanations. But the religious thought and devotional practice that were most characteristic in the first two centuries, and that came to mark Christian tradition subsequently, express reverence for Jesus within the context of an exclusivist commitment to the one God of the Bible.

Christ-Devotion

Now, as a further introductory step, I want to define the phenomena that form the subject of the investigation. "Devotion" is my portmanteau word for the beliefs and related religious actions that constituted the expressions of religious reverence of early Christians. For a number of years now I have proposed the term "Christ-devotion" in preference to "Christology" to refer to the range of phenomena we shall consider here.[6] "Christology" has been used for study of Christian *beliefs* about the figure of Jesus, the *doctrine(s)* and *concepts* involved, and the wording used by Christians to express them. To be sure, these things all form part of the present investigation. But to do full justice to the way in which Jesus figures in early Christian circles requires us to take account of additional matters as well, some of which have not always been given adequate attention.

To cite one particularly important matter, there is the place of Jesus in the patterns of worship characteristic of early Christian groups. At an astonishingly early point, in at least some Christian groups, there is a clear and programmatic inclusion of Jesus in their devotional life, both in honorific *claims* and in devotional *practices*. In addition, Jesus functioned in their ethical ideals and demands, in both interpersonal and wider social spheres.

As another kind of evidence, already within the early period addressed in this book we can even find initial attempts to register piety and devotion to Jesus in phenomena that signify an emergent *material* and *visual* culture. For instance, this can be seen in the way Christian manuscripts were prepared, specifically, the so-called *nomina sacra*, sacred abbreviations of key terms that refer to God and to Jesus.[7]

By "Christ-devotion" and "devotion" to Jesus, thus, I mean the significance and role of the figure of Jesus Christ in both the religious life and thought of those forms of Christianity observable to us within the first two centuries. In particular, we shall focus on the ways in which early Christians referred and related to Jesus that seem to constitute treating him as a "divine" figure, or at least a figure of unique significance in God's plan. So this book is neither a "New Testament Christology" (in the sense of an organized presentation of all the expressions of christological beliefs in the New Testament) nor simply a survey of all christological beliefs of the historical period under review here. Instead, the particular "story" I try to tell in this historical study concerns the ways that Jesus functions as divine in the religious life of Christian groups of the first two centuries, when and how this is exhibited in beliefs and other expressions of their faith, and what historical forces probably shaped devotion to Jesus in this period.

---

6. E.g., L. W. Hurtado, "Christ-Devotion in the First Two Centuries: Reflections and a Proposal," *TJT* 12, no. 1 (1996): 17-33.

7. L. W. Hurtado, "The Origin of the *Nomina Sacra:* A Proposal," *JBL* 117 (1998): 655-73.

Explanations

As to why and how Jesus came to be held and treated as messianic and a divine figure among early Christians, two major approaches can be mentioned as particularly influential, with both of which I take issue. Among Christians of more naive orientation (this can include otherwise sophisticated people who have simply not been made aware of the issues) and among some anticritical Christian apologists, there is often the view that Jesus was regarded as divine simply because he was in fact the Messiah and divine Son of God and made both his messiahship and his divinity clear to his disciples during his ministry. Consequently, in this view, there is no historical process to investigate and nothing particularly difficult to understand historically about Christ-devotion in the early period. The early Christian claims about Jesus may be difficult for non-believers to accept for various reasons, but the explanation of how and why early Christians promoted such high views of Jesus as are attested in the New Testament and other early Christian writings is thought to be simple: the truth of Jesus' messiahship and divinity was revealed by Jesus himself, and so naturally was taken up from the beginning in Christian beliefs and religious practice. In effect, in this view it is either puzzling or downright inappropriate (especially in the view of anticritical apologists) to apply historical analysis to the Christ-devotion of early Christianity and seek to explain how it developed. In the anticritical expressions of this viewpoint, it is held that the theological and religious validity of traditional Christian devotion to Christ would be called into question if it were really treated as a historical phenomenon.[8]

The other influential approach arose in large part in reaction against this naive and ahistorical view. Though the roots of modern historical-critical study of the Bible lie in eighteenth-century Deism, for our purposes the key period is the late nineteenth century and early decades of the twentieth, when the so-called *religionsgeschichtliche Schule* (history-of-religions school of thought) sought to set Christian origins thoroughly within the history of the Roman era.[9] These scholars devoted particular attention to the questions of how Jesus

---

8. The term "anticritical apologists" is not intended as pejorative, but rather as a fair reflection of the rejection of critical inquiry espoused by some in the past and present. This obviously does not include scholars who engage in critical investigation and argue on historical grounds that the christological claims in the New Testament have a strong basis in Jesus' own self-understanding and claims. Whatever one judges to be the merits of this position, they seek seriously to engage other scholars, addressing the evidence and methods of modern scholarship.

9. W. G. Kümmel, *The New Testament: The History of the Investigation of Its Problems*, trans. S. M. Gilmour and H. C. Kee (Nashville: Abingdon, 1972), esp. 206-324; Gerd Lüdemann and Martin Schröder, *Die religionsgeschichtliche Schule in Göttingen: Eine Dokumentation*

came to be so central in early Christianity and how early Christian devotion to Jesus developed in the period prior to the classical creedal statements about Christ and the Trinity of the fourth century and later.

The history-of-religions scholars insisted that the divine status of Jesus in early Christianity was the result of a thoroughly historical process and was thus in principle subject to the same sort of historical investigation that one would apply to any other historical phenomenon. This investigation demanded the utmost of scholars in becoming thoroughly familiar with all the early Christian sources and with the whole of the wider Roman era, especially the religious environment of the time. The great scholars of this school of thought demonstrated impressive (and today almost unmatchable) breadth of learning and competence in the languages and texts of the ancient world.

But in this *religionsgeschichtliche Schule* the whole impressive effort of historical investigation had the effect (and likely, the intention) of demonstrating that the emergence of devotion to Christ as a divine figure was essentially a simple and really rather unremarkable process of syncretism. Essentially, devotion to Jesus as divine resulted from the influence of "pagan" religion of the Roman era upon "Hellenistic" Christians supposedly more susceptible to such influence than were "Palestinian" Jewish Christians.

I will have more to say about this particular view of things later. For now, I limit myself to making one ironic point. Though the history-of-religions scholars took issue with the naive or precritical view and insisted that the devotion to Christ reflected in early Christian sources could be approached as a historical phenomenon, their view of the historical process behind this phenomenon was practically as simplistic as the view they opposed. In their own way they too wound up claiming (though for very different reasons, to be sure) that the emergence and development of Christ-devotion in early Christianity was neither very remarkable nor difficult to understand. Presented as one particular example of the deification of heroes and the emergence of new gods rampant in the Roman world, early Christ-devotion was to be understood simply as resulting from the impact of this "pagan" religious environment upon an originally purer Christian movement in which ideas of Jesus' divinity could not have appeared.

(Göttingen: Vandenhoeck & Ruprecht, 1987); Carsten Colpe, *Die religionsgeschichtliche Schule: Darstellung und Kritik ihres Bildes vom gnostischen Erlösermythus* (Göttingen: Vandenhoeck & Ruprecht, 1961). On the Deist origins of biblical criticism, see now Jonathan Z. Smith, *Drudgery Divine* (Chicago: University of Chicago Press, 1990). As illustration of the continuing influence of the old *religionsgeschichtliche Schule*, see, e.g., Kurt Rudolph, "Early Christianity as a Religious-Historical Phenomenon," in *The Future of Early Christianity: Essays in Honor of Helmut Koester*, ed. B. A. Pearson (Minneapolis: Fortress, 1991), 9-19.

I wish to take issue in this book with both of these views, which in varying forms continue to be influential. On the one hand, I agree with the history-of-religions school that Christ-devotion can be approached as a historical phenomenon. Whatever stance one takes on the religious validity of the devotion to Jesus reflected in the various early Christian sources, this devotion manifested itself within history and therefore, in principle, can be investigated in the ways we inquire about any other historical person, event, or movement. We may or may not have sufficient historical understanding of the time and sufficient understanding of how religious movements originate to develop a plausible analysis of the particular historical process involved in the emergence of Christ-devotion. I believe that we can, as I hope to show in this book. But whatever the particular merits of my own proposals, in principle the effort to understand devotion to Jesus historically is valid.

But, on the other hand, both the naive view and the familiar history-of-religions view are wrong in portraying early devotion to Jesus as basically simple, unremarkable, and not difficult to understand. For several reasons I contend that Christ-devotion is an utterly remarkable phenomenon, and that it is also the result of a complex of historical forces and factors. Here are some major features that justify us in seeing early devotion to Jesus as remarkable.

(1) It began amazingly early, and was already exhibiting signs of routinization by the time of the letters of Paul (i.e., by ca. 50 C.E.), which means that the origins of cultic veneration of Jesus have to be pushed well back into the first two decades of the Christian movement. (2) Devotion to Jesus was by no means confined to this or that conventicle but seems to have spread with impressive rapidity across the Christian movement, though there were also variations in its expression. (3) Although at a certain high level of generalization one can draw some comparisons with other Roman-era groups and movements, we have no full analogue in the Roman world, which makes the task of historical explanation particularly difficult (the more so to the degree that historical "explanation" is seen to rest upon analogy). To cite one key matter, we have no other Roman-era example of a religious movement with similar ties to the Jewish religious tradition of exclusivistic monotheism and with a devotional pattern that involved so thoroughly a second figure in addition to God.[10] (4) Devotion to Jesus was central in early Christian groups and of enormous significance for the historical development of Christianity.

As already indicated, I contend that the historical process was not simple but complex, involving not one factor but the interaction of several important factors or forces. One of my major aims in the long research and reflection that

---

10. Hurtado, *One God, One Lord*, passim.

has led to this book has been to develop an understanding of these historical factors and forces and to make them explicit for others to judge. In the next chapter I describe the historical process and propose the key factors involved.

Before we proceed further toward analyzing Christ-devotion as a historical phenomenon, however, it may be helpful to note a relevant (and in my view misguided) assumption shared by both the pre/anticritical and the history-of-religions approaches. It is worth identifying because it continues to be influential in both popular and scholarly circles. This is the notion that the validity of a religious belief or practice is called into question if it can be shown to be a truly historical phenomenon, and the product of historical factors and forces that we can attempt to identify and analyze. D. F. Strauss, the controversial biblical scholar of the early nineteenth century, is credited with a much-repeated epigram: "The true criticism of a dogma is its history."[11] Although the epigram more explicitly expresses the assumption in a form that would be more congenial to history-of-religions scholars than to anticritical apologists, both approaches to early Christ-devotion seem to have assumed something like this, and then took sharply divergent actions with diametrically opposed aims.

Wishing to preserve the religious and theological validity of traditional christological claims, the anticritical view attempted to deny or minimize as far as possible the historically conditioned nature of early Christ-devotion. On the other hand, the history-of-religions scholars were convinced that their demonstration of the historically conditioned nature of early Christ-devotion proved that it was no longer to be treated as theologically valid or binding for modern Christians. In both views the assumption is the same: if something can be shown to have arisen through a historical process, then it cannot be divine "revelation" or have continuing theological validity.

It is not my aim in this book to consider the continuing theological validity of the patterns of devotion to Jesus that we shall examine here. I simply want to make two points. First, the assumption that seems to have lain behind the historical-critical work of the history-of-religions school, and the anticritical efforts of apologists as well, is of dubious validity (or at least is not compelling). There is no obvious reason why, in principle, divine revelations could not come through thoroughly historical processes involving people and events of particular times and places and conditioned by particular cultures. To claim divine revelations in particular historical events or people requires a case to be made,

---

11. E.g., the saying is attributed to Strauss in M. Hengel, *The Son of God: The Origin of Christology and the History of Jewish-Hellenistic Religion*, trans. John Bowden (London: SCM Press; Philadelphia: Fortress, 1976), 6.

of course, and on appropriate grounds that would have to be weighed. But our being able to show that given people and events were parts and results of historical processes does not mean that these same historically conditioned people and events are thereby discredited as divine revelations that have some sort of continuing validity. To assume otherwise is shallow philosophical thinking.

Second, the misguided assumption I am criticizing here has obviously worked mischief in scholarship. It has driven anticritical apologists (sometimes with impressive trappings of scholarship) to strive to avoid or minimize the force of the evidence that early Christ-devotion was a historical phenomenon, and it has led a good deal of historical-critical scholarship to opt for some simplistic historical analyses in the interest of opposing traditional Christian beliefs. In short, on both sides opposing religious and theological concerns were promoted on the basis of a shared but fallacious assumption.

So I wish to make it clear that, in approaching Christ-devotion as a historical phenomenon that can in principle be analyzed in the ways that historians study other historical phenomena, *I do not intend thereby either to refute or to validate the religious and theological meaning of early devotion to Jesus.* I have my views of traditional christological claims and readers will have theirs. To come clean, I confess to being guilty of Christian faith (though, Christians being what we are, not every other one will be satisfied with my version of Christian faith!). But I do not believe that the religious validity of a Christian christological conviction necessarily rests upon the time or manner of its appearance in history.

Thus, for example, I do not think it is necessary for Jesus to have thought and spoken of himself in the same terms that his followers thought and spoke of him in the decades subsequent to his crucifixion in order for the convictions of these followers to be treated as valid by Christians today. A good many may disagree, both among those who assert and among those who oppose traditional Christian beliefs. Most Christians will likely think that some degree of continuity between what Jesus thought of himself and what early Christians claimed about him is at least desirable and perhaps necessary for these claims to have religious validity. My object in this book, however, is not to engage in these theological questions. I only wish to indicate briefly why I contend that the historical analysis of early devotion to Jesus can be, and should be, pursued without the level of theological anxiety with which it has been resisted by some, and also without what I regard as the simplistic zeal for theological reformation with which it has sometimes been pursued by some others. So far as I am aware, the conclusions I urge in this study do not rest upon a personally felt need that they should be so, or a fear that if they are wrong there are automatically profound consequences for Christian faith.

໋ We all have motivations for our research that extend beyond mere curiosity. Among other things, they can include professional advancement, academic notoriety and influence, religious faiths, and even antagonisms against particular religious faiths (e.g., often what seem to be "postreligious" stances that can sometimes be pursued with the zeal of the stereotypical missionary!). These motivations usually help to explain our interests in particular historical topics, and they can help to provide the energy for the effort required in historical research. Along with our other characteristics, they help make us the various people that we are, and we do not need to be embarrassed about them. But true historical criticism means primarily to be self-critical, to try to be conscious of one's motivations and personal concerns and critical of one's assumptions, perhaps especially those that one might be most inclined to take for granted. Historical study is a "discipline," both because it demands expertise in relevant languages and sources and also because it involves disciplined use of critical analysis and skills in putting the data together into plausible, preferably persuasive, pictures of events, people, and processes. Right down to the present, the history of critical inquiry into Christian origins is littered with attempts to make this or that historical picture serve this or that religious aim. This is understandable, but the subject of this book is sufficiently intriguing in its own right to warrant and reward disciplined study, and sufficiently important in historical terms to make it worth every effort to produce as complete and accurate a picture of things as we can.

Unlike Bousset (and some of the latter-day scholars mentioned in this chapter), however, I do not present this portrayal of early Christ-devotion in the service of some critique of traditional Christian beliefs or some revisionist theological aim. Elsewhere I have noted that Bousset's views were obviously colored by and in service to his own theological preferences.[12] A recently published study by Karsten Lehmkühler has now demonstrated this thoroughly, tracing the theological influences and aims taken up in the historical studies of the *religionsgeschichtliche Schule*.[13]

To cite one crucial matter, Lehmkühler shows that in *Kyrios Christos* Bousset's firm distinction between a supposedly original ethicizing piety of Jesus (and the primitive "Palestinian" community of Jesus followers) and the "Christ cult" of the "Hellenistic" Christian community was theologically driven. This distinction permitted him to posit an ideal, original Christian pi-

---

12. Hurtado, *One God, One Lord,* 10-11, 135 nn. 34-35.
13. Karsten Lehmkühler, *Kultus und Theologie: Dogmatik und Exegese in der religionsgeschichtliche Schule,* Forschungen zur systematischen und ökumenischen Theologie 76 (Göttingen: Vandenhoeck & Ruprecht, 1996).

ety with which he could more comfortably associate himself as a liberal Protestant of his time.[14]

Of course, liberal Protestantism of the very early twentieth century is not the only religious point of view that can distort one's historical analysis. Each of us may have preferences among the various forms of early Christian piety and beliefs. But it is simplistic and imperils sound historical analysis to think we can promote our own theological or piety preference by identifying it with some "original" form of Christianity. Just as in biological evolution, so in religious traditions, original or earlier forms of life or religious expression are not necessarily better. The primary motivation for the research presented in the present book is curiosity about a fascinating central feature of a notable new religious movement which appeared in the Roman era, diversified and grew rapidly to become now the largest religious tradition in the world. What form of Christian piety and belief is, or ought to be, preferred and triumphant in the present and future will not (and should not) be decided by historical claims about which forms were earliest and what historical processes generated them.

A New *religionsgeschichtliche Schule?*

On the back cover of the American edition of my 1988 book *One God, One Lord: Early Christian Devotion and Ancient Jewish Monotheism,* Professor Martin Hengel endorsed the study as reflecting "the results of scholarly experts in many countries who are in some way forming a new *'religionsgeschichtliche Schule.'"* Taking a cue from this comment, Jarl Fossum presented a paper at the 1991 meeting of the Society of Biblical Literature entitled "The New *Religionsgeschichtliche Schule:* The Quest for Jewish Christology," in which he attempted to sketch some features of the research being carried out by a number of current scholars interested in historical analysis of early Christ-devotion.[15]

To be sure, there is a recent and continuing body of newer scholarly studies focused on the emergence of devotion to Jesus, and the scholars involved have all been shaped very much in interaction with one another's work.[16] But

14. Lehmkühler, 226.

15. Jarl Fossum, "The New *Religionsgeschichtliche Schule:* The Quest for Jewish Christology," in SBLSP 1991, ed. E. Lovering (Atlanta: Scholars, 1991), 638-46.

16. In the preface to the second edition of *One God, One Lord* (1998), vii-xxii, I mentioned a number of such studies, especially those that appeared subsequent to (and often in interaction with) the first edition. Fossum's paper was given at a consultation that led to the formation of a program unit in the Society of Biblical Literature devoted to the historical context

these scholars are from academic institutions in a number of countries (e.g., the USA, Great Britain, Germany, Israel), whereas the original *Schule* was basically a group of colleagues in the faculty of theology at the University of Göttingen. Moreover, the Göttingen scholars all shared a very similar theological position, the liberal Protestantism at the turn to the twentieth century (about which, more below), whereas the scholars identified with the current research are by no means of one religious persuasion (e.g., they come from Jewish as well as various Christian traditions).[17] If, therefore, we can speak of a new history-of-religions "school," it could be only in a much looser sense of the term, in this case connoting a group of contemporaries with a shared interest in historical investigation of early devotion to Jesus in the context of the Roman-era religious environment, and a shared conviction that the Jewish religious matrix of the Christian movement is more crucial than was recognized in the older *religionsgeschichtliche Schule*.

Still, I think there is reason to describe this more recent body of work as constituting a "new history-of-religions" effort that can be linked with and likened to the classic efforts of the Göttingen circle. The work in question (as is true of nearly all historical investigation of early Christianity in the years since the original *Schule*) is of course all heavily indebted to the prodigious contributions of the various scholars associated with the *religionsgeschichtliche Schule*, even if scholars involved in today's effort would object in various ways to that earlier body of work. In several publications I have lodged criticisms of a num-

---

and analysis of Christ-devotion that met from 1991 to 1997 and was the venue for a number of scholars (including particularly younger and emergent scholars) to present their research. Fossum, Alan Segal, Carey Newman, Donald Juel, and I collaboratively drafted the proposals that led to this program unit. In 1998 the University of St. Andrews hosted the International Conference on the Historical Origins of the Worship of Jesus, which brought together scholars from several countries who have contributed to the question. See Carey C. Newman, James R. Davila, and Gladys S. Lewis, eds., *The Jewish Roots of Christological Monotheism: Papers from the St. Andrews Conference on the Historical Origins of the Worship of Jesus,* JSJSup 63 (Leiden: Brill, 1999).

17. E.g., among those linked with the current renewal of research are Martin Hengel, Richard Bauckham, Alan Segal, Jarl Fossum, Donald Juel, Karl-Wilhelm Niebuhr, Carey Newman, Loren Stuckenbruck, as well as others, among whom, I am pleased to note, are a younger generation of scholars, such as Charles Gieschen and Darrell Hannah. In my own work, Hengel's contributions have been valuable, particularly his influential studies of the intersection of Jewish and Hellenistic cultures (esp. *Judaism and Hellenism: Studies in the Encounter in Palestine during the Early Hellenistic Period,* 2 vols. [Philadelphia: Fortress; London: SCM Press, 1974]) and his several writings on early christological matters (esp. *The Son of God* [1976; German ed., 1975; rev. ed., 1977]; and see now *Studies in Early Christology* [Edinburgh: T. & T. Clark, 1995]). As well, studies by Bauckham and Segal were crucial in shaping questions in the early stages of my own work on this topic.

ber of characteristics of work of the *religionsgeschichtliche Schule* (especially Bousset's), along with appreciative appraisals of some other features.[18] In order to clarify the relationship between this book and the older work, I will summarize observations I have offered in these previous publications. My aim is not simply to carp about the work of others, especially learned scholars long dead, but to indicate why this book is called for and the reasons why I hope it marks an advance and might thus be worth the attention of readers.

For the study of devotion to Jesus in the first two centuries, the book that gathers up and reflects all that was best and all that was wrongheaded in the *religionsgeschichtliche Schule* is Wilhelm Bousset's landmark study, *Kyrios Christos,* which originally appeared in 1913.[19] It made a major impact when it appeared, drew a number of vigorous and critical responses, generated some impressive counterproposals, and has clearly been the single most influential work in twentieth-century study of the subject.[20] After a revised edition in 1921, there were several further editions to supply the continuing demand for the book. As further indication of its persistent importance and the wider interest in the book, there was an English translation in 1970. *Kyrios Christos* will not appear on the trade best-seller lists. But for a full-scale scholarly monograph, it is a success story that is hard to beat. As I stated in a 1996 article, "Bousset's *Kyrios Christos* has influenced the agenda of historical investigation of belief in Christ in the formative period of Christianity as has no other work."[21]

18. E.g., L. W. Hurtado, "New Testament Christology: A Critique of Bousset's Influence," *TS* 40 (1979): 306-17 (German version: "Forschungen zur neutestamentlichen Christologie seit Bousset: Forschungsrichtungen und bedeutende Beiträge," *TB* 11 [1980]: 158-71); Hurtado, "New Testament Christology: Retrospect and Prospect," *Semeia* 30 (1984): 15-27; and "Christ-Devotion in the First Two Centuries."

19. Wilhelm Bousset, *Kyrios Christos: Geschichte des Christusglaubens von den Anfängen des Christentums bis Irenaeus* (Göttingen: Vandenhoeck & Ruprecht, 1913; rev. ed. 1921); ET: *Kyrios Christos: A History of the Belief in Christ from the Beginnings of Christianity to Irenaeus,* trans. J. E. Steely (Nashville: Abingdon, 1970), from the 1965 German edition. Unless otherwise indicated, I cite the English translation.

20. I draw here upon paragraphs of "Christ-Devotion," 17-19. The important early critiques were by Paul Wernle, "Jesus und Paulus: Antitheses zu Bousset's Kyrios Christos," *ZTK* 25 (1915): 1-92, and Paul Alhaus, "Unser Herr Jesus: Eine neutestamentliche Untersuchung. Zur Auseinandersetzung mit W. Bousset," *NKZ* 26 (1915): 439-57. Bousset replied to these critiques in *Jesus der Herr, Nachträge und Auseinandersetzungen zu Kyrios Christos,* FRLANT 8 (Göttingen: Vandenhoeck & Ruprecht, 1916). An early account of the debate is by Geerhardus Vos, "The Kyrios Christos Controversy," *PTR* 15 (1917): 21-89. Major responses in English were by A. E. J. Rawlinson, *The New Testament Doctrine of the Christ: The Bampton Lectures for 1926* (London: Longmans, Green, 1926), and J. G. Machen, *The Origin of Paul's Religion* (1925; reprint, Grand Rapids: Eerdmans, 1965).

21. Hurtado, "Christ-Devotion," 18. Among the many helpful analyses of the history of

Given the wide acquaintance with *Kyrios Christos,* and its continuing availability, a summary of the argument of the book will suffice here. Two points are central in Bousset's discussion: (1) The emergence of the "Christ cult," the treatment of Jesus as a divine figure, especially in liturgical actions and settings, is absolutely crucial for all subsequent developments in Christology in the early centuries; and (2) this Christ cult, though early, was a second-stage development and, most importantly, does not go back to the earliest circles of Jesus' followers in Palestine. These Palestinian Jewish Christians (the "primitive community") developed a view of the risen Jesus as "the son of man" (which Bousset along with many others supposed was a well-known title for a widely expected apocalyptic figure who would act as God's agent in the eschatological vindication of the righteous). At a secondary stage of development (but still very early), in the "Hellenistic Gentile" communities there arose a new and influential view of Jesus as divine *Kyrios* (Lord), a view influenced by pagan analogies of divine heroes and cult deities. It was into this latter stage and version of the Christian movement that Paul was converted, and in his letters we see the beliefs of this Hellenistic Gentile Christianity presupposed and developed. The divinization of Jesus is developed further in the Johannine writings, and in second-century figures such as Ignatius, Justin, and Irenaeus we are offered a still more thoroughly Hellenized version of the Christ cult, which constitutes the emergence of classical Christianity at considerable religious distance from the faith of the primitive community. In a later section of this introduction I offer some criticisms of *Kyrios Christos* to indicate why it is not a satisfactory account of things and why I offer this fresh analysis. Nothing of the criticism I and others have offered, however, can detract from the impact of *Kyrios Christos* upon scholarly study of early devotion to Christ.

In combined depth and scope, erudition, and influence, nothing equivalent has appeared in the nearly ninety years now since it was first published. Serious studies of the last several decades have been both more narrowly focused and often are still heavily indebted to *Kyrios Christos.* Cullmann's magisterial study of New Testament christological titles took issue with Bousset impressively on some key historical-critical matters, but is limited to the New Testament material.[22] Cullmann also seems to have anticipated, and perhaps helped to generate, the scholarly focus on christological titles such as "Christ," "Lord," "Son of God," and, the title that most vexed and fascinated scholars, "son of

scholarship, note esp. Horst Balz, *Methodische Probleme der neutestamentlichen Christologie,* WMANT 25 (Neukirchen-Vluyn: Neukirchener Verlag, 1967), and the other literature cited in my essay "New Testament Christology: A Critique of Bousset's Influence," 306 n. 1.

22. Oscar Cullmann, *Die Christologie des Neuen Testament* (Tübingen: Mohr [Siebeck], 1957; ET, Philadelphia: Westminster, 1959; rev. ed., 1963).

man."[23] But (with Cullmann as a notable exception) nearly all these scholars accepted the basic framework for the development of Christ-devotion given in *Kyrios Christos* (discrete, unilinear stages of development).[24] Perhaps the most widely known study from English-speaking scholars in the 1960s, by Reginald Fuller, was basically a distillation of the results of these studies of christological titles, and it adopted (with minor modifications) the developmental scheme of discrete stages of first-century Christianity promulgated in *Kyrios Christos*.[25]

In more recent years there has been a spate of books on the Christology reflected in the New Testament, but none are the equivalent weight study to Bousset's classic. A number are simply introductory expositions of the christological themes of the individual New Testament writers/writings, with very limited treatment of the larger historical questions of how and why early Christ-devotion developed and was expressed.[26] There are some more in-depth discussions of particular issues, such as J. D. G. Dunn's sizable and controversial book on the origins of the idea of the incarnation of Christ.[27] Petr Pokorny fo-

---

23. Major studies include H. E. Tödt, *Der Menschensohn in der synoptischen Überlieferung* (Gütersloh: Gerd Mohn, 1959; ET, London: SCM Press, 1965); Werner Kramer, *Christos, Kyrios, Gottessohn* (Zürich: Zwingli-Verlag, 1963; ET, London: SCM Press, 1966); Ferdinand Hahn, *Christologische Hoheitstitel, Ihre Geschichte im frühen Christentum* (Göttingen: Vandenhoeck & Ruprecht, 1963; ET, New York: World Publishing, 1969). The journal literature is too extensive to list here, but numerous publications are cited in Hurtado, "New Testament Christology: A Critique of Bousset's Influence" and "Christ-Devotion in the First Two Centuries." Studies of historical background and meaning of the "Son of Man" expression continued into more recent years. Among influential studies note Geza Vermes' appendix on the use of the Aramaic expressions in Matthew Black, *An Aramaic Approach to the Gospels and Acts*, 3rd ed. (Oxford: Clarendon, 1967), 310-30; P. M. Casey, *Son of Man: The Interpretation and Influence of Daniel 7* (London: SPCK, 1979); Barnabas Lindars, *Jesus Son of Man* (London: SPCK, 1983); D. R. A. Hare, *The Son of Man Tradition* (Minneapolis: Fortress, 1990). More recently, however, note the challenge to some earlier opinion on the Aramaic evidence by Paul Owen and David Shepherd, "Speaking Up for Qumran, Dalman and the Son of Man: Was *Bar Enasha* a Common Term for 'Man' in the Time of Jesus?" *JSNT* 81 (2001): 81-122.

24. Hahn (*The Titles of Jesus in Christology*, 12) modified Bousset's two-stage scheme (Palestinian-Jewish, Hellenistic-Gentile) by inserting a "Hellenistic-Jewish" stage in between. Bousset's scheme is usually thought to have been adopted from W. Heitmüller, "Zum Problem Paulus und Jesus," *ZNW* 13 (1912): 320-37.

25. Reginald H. Fuller, *The Foundations of New Testament Christology* (New York: Charles Scribner's Sons, 1965).

26. E.g., Marinus de Jonge, *Christology in Context: The Earliest Christian Response to Jesus* (Philadelphia: Westminster, 1988); Earl Richard, *Jesus: One and Many: The Christological Concept of New Testament Authors* (Wilmington, Del.: Michael Glazier, 1988); Frank J. Matera, *New Testament Christology* (Louisville: Westminster John Knox, 1999).

27. J. D. G. Dunn, *Christology in the Making* (Philadelphia: Westminster, 1980; 2nd ed., London: SCM Press, 1989).

cused on very early christological formulae in the New Testament and argued that the various christological ideas reflected in them are not remnants of independent Christologies but signal efforts to articulate convictions shared among various Christian groups.[28] Paula Fredriksen's 1988 book sketched for general readers the beliefs about Jesus in the New Testament writings.[29]

As illustration of the continuing influence of the scheme of development laid out in *Kyrios Christos*, we may cite Burton Mack.[30] Like Bousset, Mack distinguishes sharply the Christ cult (in which Jesus is treated as a divine figure) from an allegedly earlier stage of the Christian movement in Galilee and Judea, attributing this Christ cult to Hellenizing circles in Antioch. Also, with Bousset he evaluates the Christ-cult as a regrettable shift from what he calls the "Jesus people" of Jewish Palestine, for whom (commendably in Mack's view) Jesus was by no means Messiah, Lord, or recipient of devotion, but simply a Cynic-like sage, an inspiring exponent of clever sayings and a carefree lifestyle.

Mack's particular rendition of an original Jesus movement as a noncommunitarian, noneschatological collection of individuals with only a shared, low-key appreciation of Jesus as a stimulating teacher of aphorisms is somewhat different from the more eschatologically oriented "primitive community" postulated in *Kyrios Christos*.[31] I will offer my own appraisal of what we can say about the earliest followers of Jesus in later chapters of this book. For now it is sufficient to note that his explanation of the rise of Christ-devotion, his sharp distinction of it from his Palestinian Jewish Jesus people, and his negative and theologically driven appraisal of the Christ cult are all essentially rephrasings of Bousset.[32]

One of the few recent studies to attempt a fresh historical explanation of

---

28. Petr Pokorny, *Die Entstehung der Christologie* (Berlin: Evangelische Verlagsanstalt, 1985); ET, *The Genesis of Christology* (Edinburgh: T. & T. Clark, 1987).

29. Paula Fredriksen, *From Jesus to Christ: The Origins of the New Testament Images of Jesus* (New Haven: Yale University Press, 1988), esp. 158.

30. His main study is *A Myth of Innocence: Mark and Christian Origins* (Philadelphia: Fortress, 1988). See my critical discussion in "The Gospel of Mark: Evolutionary or Revolutionary Document?" *JSNT* 40 (1990): 15-32 (reprinted in *The Synoptic Gospels*, ed. C. A. Evans and S. E. Porter, "The Biblical Seminar 31" [Sheffield: Sheffield Academic Press, 1995], 196-211). More recently Mack has focused on theses about the Q sayings collection: *The Lost Gospel: The Book of Q and Christian Origins* (San Francisco: Harper Collins; Shaftsbury: Element, 1993).

31. But Mack does project a shift from an originally noneschatological ethos to a more eschatologically oriented stage within the history of his "Jesus people" (e.g., *The Lost Gospel*, 105-70).

32. But Mack's disapproval of the Christ cult is much more stridently expressed, and he attributes much more to it, including twentieth-century American imperialism (e.g., *A Myth of Innocence*, 353-76)!

how and why Christ-devotion developed is by Maurice Casey.[33] Like Bousset, Casey claims that a significant departure from earlier christological convictions took place, involving a divinization of Jesus. But in Casey's scheme this departure really happened later than Bousset thought, not in the Christian circles of Antioch in the early decades of the Christian movement but in the closing decades of the first century and among Johannine Christians heavily influenced by what Casey calls "Gentile self-identification." This social/mental condition (crucial in Casey's scheme) resulted from a combination of a critical mass of Gentile converts and the expulsion of Johannine Jewish Christians from the larger Jewish community.[34] The vigor of Casey's discussion makes the book engaging, but, for reasons I have given elsewhere, it does not convince.[35] In part, this is because he fails to see the significance of the Christian devotional/worship practices, which are evident decades earlier than the supposed christological revolution that he attributes to the Gospel of John. In other respects too his scheme is insufficiently responsive to the evidence.[36]

Thus, in spite of the continuing appearance of the sorts of studies I have mentioned, *Kyrios Christos* remains unrivaled in weight, scope, and influence.[37] Bousset was a very erudite scholar, and his breadth of knowledge is enviable. In *Kyrios Christos* he built upon his many more specialized studies and those of his colleagues in the *religionsgeschichtliche Schule,* setting Christ-devotion within his picture of the wider religious environment of the Roman world. Moreover, the combination of in-depth discussion and chronological scope of the book is daunting, covering developments in Christ-devotion from the beginnings of Christianity down to the great church leader of the late second century, Irenaeus of Lyons. There are, of course, a few scholars who have contributed

33. Maurice Casey, *From Jewish Prophet to Gentile God: The Origins and Development of New Testament Christology* (Cambridge: James Clarke; Louisville: Westminster John Knox, 1991). See also now his essay, "Monotheism, Worship and Christological Developments in the Pauline Churches," in *The Jewish Roots of Christological Monotheism,* 214-33.

34. Casey, *From Jewish Prophet,* e.g., 37-38.

35. I have offered criticisms in "Christ-Devotion," 27-28. For more lengthy critique, see J. D. G. Dunn, "The Making of Christology — Evolution or Unfolding?" in *Jesus of Nazareth: Lord and Christ. Essays on the Historical Jesus and New Testament Christology,* ed. J. B. Green and Max Turner (Grand Rapids: Eerdmans, 1994), 437-52.

36. See, e.g., L. W. Hurtado, "Pre–70 c.e. Jewish Opposition to Christ-Devotion," *JTS* 50 (1999): 35-58.

37. Although not nearly so influential (indeed, unjustifiably little known today), Jules Lebreton, *Histoire du dogme de la trinité: des origines au concile de Nicée,* 2 vols. (Paris: Gabriel Beauchesne, 1910, 1928), is certainly an in-depth treatment that remains valuable, particularly because Lebreton included discussion of the religious practice of early Christianity, thus ranging much wider than the title of the work implies.

studies of early Christian faith that have covered even broader time periods. But they do not engage the thorny questions of historical origins and earliest developments in the same depth as did Bousset.[38]

But, in addition to erudition and impressive scope, like all good history writing, *Kyrios Christos* offered a cohesive "story" and an explanatory theory or model for the developments recounted in the story. The point of departure and the focus of that story is what Bousset called the "Christ cult," the reverence of Christ as a divine figure manifested both in beliefs about him and, even more importantly, in the devotional practices of early Christians, their worship.[39] The crucial thesis that is also the basis of that story line is that this Christ cult does not go back to the original or "primitive" Christian groups of Jewish Palestine but appeared subsequently, in "Hellenistic communities" of Christians in Antioch, Damascus, and Tarsus, places where Christians were more susceptible to the pagan religious environment.[40] The whole story told in *Kyrios Christos* is the continuing development of the Christ cult through subsequent and still further influences from the larger Hellenistic culture. In short, as I have already stated, the development of Christ-devotion and the model of the historical process behind it is a progressive syncretism or Hellenization of an earlier, purer (and, to Bousset, more congenial) form of Christianity.

38. Aloys Grillmeier, *Christ in Christian Tradition*, vol. 1, *From the Apostolic Age to Chalcedon (451)*, trans. J. Bowden, 2nd rev. ed. (London: Mowbray & Co.; Atlanta: John Knox, 1975), devotes a scant thirty pages to the first century, and is entirely concerned with doctrinal issues. Jean Daniélou's magisterial volumes on early Christianity are topically organized and mainly concerned with questions about how Christian faith appropriated and interacted with Jewish and "Hellenistic" culture: *The Theology of Jewish Christianity*, trans. and ed. J. A. Baker (London: Darton, Longman and Todd, 1964); *Gospel Message and Hellenistic Culture*, trans. and ed. J. A. Baker (London: Darton, Longman and Todd, 1973). Martin Werner attempted (unsuccessfully, to judge by scholarly responses) to explain the whole of the early centuries of christological development as a reaction to the failure of the original Christian apocalyptic expectation of a soon return of Christ (*Die Entstehung des christlichen Dogmas* [Tübingen: Katsmann-Verlag; Bern: Verlag Paul Haupt, 1941; 2nd ed., 1954]; ET, *The Formation of Christian Dogma* [New York: Harper and Brothers, 1957; reprint, Boston: Beacon Press, 1965]). Werner was also unpersuasive in his claim that in the earliest Christology the exalted Christ was seen as a high angel (cf. *Formation of Christian Dogma*, 120-30).

39. Bousset, *Kyrios Christos*, 11.

40. "The great and decisive turning point of Christianity is marked by its transition to Gentile-Christian territory in its very earliest beginnings" (Bousset, *Kyrios Christos*, 12). See his description of the Gentile Christian primitive community on 119-52.

This Study

Kyrios Christos is still so influential in the field, and in several respects has remained so superior to anything else written to this point, that it will be sufficient to position this book in relationship to it. To do this I must indicate briefly both the shortcomings in *Kyrios Christos* that require this fresh treatment of the subject and also the more positive ways in which my work is shaped by Bousset's.

From as far back as 1979 I have lodged criticisms of *Kyrios Christos* as an account of early devotion to Christ and have called for a fresh, equivalent study. It would be a bit tedious to write here a detailed itemization of points of my disagreement with *Kyrios Christos,* and so I hope that a summary of some major matters will be sufficient. I draw here upon several previous publications in which I have engaged Bousset's classic work.[41]

1. Bousset's portrayal of an early "son of man" Christology, in which Jesus was identified simply as a heavenly redeemer figure of the future allegedly well known by this title in pre-Christian Jewish tradition, though asserted by numerous other scholars as well, has increasingly been recognized as dubious over the last thirty years or so.[42] There is no evidence for a supposed pre-Christian use of the expression "the son of man" as a title in Jewish sources.[43] Nor is there any evidence that the expression was used confessionally in earliest Christianity. Though there remains some disagreement among scholars as to how best to account for the expression and its meaning(s) in the Gospels, "son of man" does not represent the christological confession of a "primitive community."[44]

---

41. See, e.g., Hurtado, "New Testament Christology: A Critique of Bousset's Influence"; "New Testament Christology: Retrospect and Prospect," esp. 19-23; "Christ-Devotion in the First Two Centuries."

42. The recent study by Hare, *The Son of Man Tradition,* both fully interacts with previous scholarship and presents cogent and well-argued conclusions.

43. Note, e.g., Hare, 21: "No scholar can fairly claim on the basis of the extant evidence that 'the Son of man' had become a widespread, universally recognized title for a supernatural figure who was expected to function as God's deputy in the last judgment." Hare's review of the evidence (9-21) is representative of a growing body of scholarly judgment.

44. "The very fact that the phrase [the Son of man] was rigidly restricted to sayings attributed to Jesus and, conversely, absent from all New Testament statements about his significance suggests that, like Paul and John of Patmos, the Palestinian Christians did not find the phrase useful for talking about the meaning of Jesus for faith" (Hare, 243). Note also Hare, 257: "[I]f the earliest Christology issued from this identification, it is inexplicable why no relic of the alleged confessional use of 'the Son of Man' has been preserved in the resurrection narratives, the archaizing speeches of Acts, pre-Pauline formulas, or the Apocalypse. Here the argument from silence must be given its due." The entirety of Hare's discussion of the "pregospel tradition," 213-56, is well worth reading.

Its primary function in the Gospels is as *a self-designation by Jesus,* not an expression used to refer to him honorifically by others. Moreover, Jesus' use of the term in the Gospel narratives does not there trigger any objection or controversy, unlike the other honorific terms such as "Messiah/Christ," "Son of David," and "Son of God."[45]

To be sure, it is highly likely that the earliest circles of Jesus' followers expected him to return in eschatological glory to consummate God's redemptive purposes (as we shall see later in this book), and passages in the Gospels indicate that the scene in Daniel 7:13-14 where God gives dominion and vindication to "one like a son of man" was interpreted as a prophecy of Jesus' eschatological victory (e.g., Mark 14:62-64; Matt. 25:31). But there is no indication that "the son of man" was used by early Christians as a confessional title that expressed this expectation. Instead, they preferred other christological terms. For example, in what is usually taken as a very early confessional fragment, 1 Thessalonians 1:10, Jesus is referred to as God's "Son," whom believers await from heaven to deliver them from eschatological wrath.

Nor, contra Bousset, is there any basis for restricting the earliest estimation of Jesus' significance simplistically to a future redemptive role. Instead, the data indicate a much richer and wider role of Jesus in the religious beliefs and practice of the earliest circles of Christians to which we have any historical access, whether the "primitive Palestinian" groups or those in diaspora locations.

2. Bousset's characterization of the christological views of his "Hellenistic" Christians and of Paul has also been shown to be badly off base. If "son of man" represented for Bousset the earliest confession of Palestinian Jewish Christians, the confession of Jesus as "Lord" *(Kyrios)* represented the "Hellenization" of Christian faith in Gentile Christian circles (into which Paul was allegedly converted).[46] But in the ensuing investigation Bousset has been shown wrong here as well.

Contra Bousset, the *Kyrios* title does not represent some major terminological or christological innovation among Gentile Christians who supposedly appropriated the title from pagan cults. Instead, the term goes back to the devo-

---

45. In Mark 14:61-64, the high priest's cry of "blasphemy" seems to be in response to Jesus' affirmative response to the question whether he is "the Messiah, the Son of the Blessed One" (v. 61). The term "Son of Man" in v. 62 seems to function both as a self-designation and as part of the allusion to the scene in Dan. 7:13-14 where a humanlike figure receives divine vindication. There is no hint that the use of the term here is to be taken as Jesus' offense.

46. Bousset's chapter entitled "The Gentile Primitive Christian Community" (*Kyrios Christos,* 119-52) is wholly a discussion of the *Kyrios* title. I draw here on paragraphs of my article "New Testament Christology: A Critique of Bousset's Influence," 312-16.

tional life of Jewish Christian circles.[47] It is clear that *Kyrios* was used by Greek-speaking Jews for the Hebrew tetragrammaton *(Yahweh)* when reading aloud the biblical texts, and so it had long been indigenized as part of the religious vocabulary available to Greek-speaking Christian Jews.[48] It is also clear that acclaiming and invoking Jesus as "Lord" was done in Aramaic-speaking Christian circles as well as in Greek-speaking ones, as indicated by the invocation formula, *maranatha*, preserved by Paul in 1 Corinthians 16:22. This Aramaic formula was so familiar already by the date of this epistle that no translation of it was required for his Greek-speaking Gentile Christian readers in Corinth.[49] The formulaic acclamation of Jesus as *Kyrios* reflected in several Pauline passages (Rom. 10:9-10; 1 Cor. 12:3; Phil. 2:9-11) and taken there as unexceptionally characteristic of Christian practice has to be seen in light of these things.

We should also notice that references to Jesus as "Lord" in Pauline epistles frequently involve allusions to Old Testament passages (e.g., Phil. 2:9-11; 1 Cor. 8:5-6) and appropriation of biblical phrasing (e.g., Rom. 10:9-13). This confirms that the early use of the title in Christian circles derives from Jewish religious vocabulary and not, as Bousset claimed, from its use in mystery cults or emperor veneration. I will say more about the meaning of this acclamation later in this book. My object here is merely to point out that Bousset's presentation of matters is not tenable.

Likewise, Bousset's view of the derivation and meaning of the theme of Jesus' divine sonship in Paul has to be rejected.[50] Bousset correctly noted that Jesus' divine sonship was important in Paul's religious views. But he also claimed that this represented the key category by which Paul communicated Jesus' divine status to his Gentile converts and justified for them the worship of Jesus. In Bousset's view, the meaning of the references to Jesus' divine sonship

---

47. See esp. J. A. Fitzmyer, *A Wandering Aramean: Collected Aramaic Essays*, SBLMS 25 (Missoula: Scholars, 1979), chap. 5, "The Semitic Background of the New Testament *Kyrios*-Title" (115-42).

48. See, e.g., J. R. Royse, "Philo, Kyrios, and the Tetragrammaton," *Studia Philonica Annual* 3 (1991): 167-83; A. Pietersma, "Kyrios or Tetragram: A Renewed Quest for the Original Septuagint," in *Studies in Honour of John W. Wevers on His Sixty-Fifth Birthday*, ed. Albert Pietersma and Claude Cox (Mississauga, Ontario: Benben Publishers, 1984), 85-101.

49. See my discussion of this passage and citation of other scholarly literature in *One God, One Lord*, 106-7, 131-32 n. 11, 164 n. 43. Esp. see Joseph A. Fitzmyer, "New Testament Kyrios and Maranatha and Their Aramaic Background," in *To Advance the Gospel: New Testament Studies* (New York: Crossroad, 1981), 218-35.

50. For more full discussion of the theme of Jesus' divine sonship in Paul, see later in this book, and also Hurtado, "Son of God," in *DPL*, 900-906; Hurtado, "Jesus' Divine Sonship in Paul's Epistle to the Romans," in *Romans and the People of God*, ed. Sven K. Soderlund and N. T. Wright (Grand Rapids: Eerdmans, 1999), 217-33.

was taken directly from the pagan religious environment where sons of the gods were themselves venerated as divine beings. Paul had thus appropriated a religious category from the pagan religious setting of his converts that would promote cultic reverence of Jesus in terms they could readily appreciate.[51] In effect, Bousset portrayed divine sonship as a clever marketing device used by Paul.

There is no dispute that divine sonship was a category in the pagan religious environment of the Roman era, and that those referred to as sons of the gods were treated as divine. But a careful analysis of the theme in Paul's epistles shows that *his* attribution of divine sonship to Jesus derives its meaning from *biblical and Jewish traditions,* in which divine sonship did not necessarily connote divinity. In these traditions divine sonship language was applied to the divinely chosen king, the devout, righteous individual, and to Israel collectively, particularly in the Second Temple period; in these cases divine sonship connoted *special favor and relationship with God.*[52]

Paul's references to Jesus' divine sonship all involve primarily connotations of God's direct involvement in Jesus, Jesus' special status with God, and Jesus' consequent honor and authority. The biblical and Jewish associations of the language of divine sonship in Paul are further indicated by the fact that references to Jesus as God's Son are heavily concentrated in Romans and Galatians, the two epistles in which Paul makes the most detailed presentation of his message in connection with the Old Testament and Jewish traditions.[53]

Moreover, the major christological title Paul used in formulas and contexts reflecting worship was not "Son of God" (which in fact appears only four times in letters attributed to Paul, and is clearly not a standardized expression), but *Kyrios.*[54] In short, contra Bousset, the theme of Jesus' divine sonship does not function in Paul (and, we must presume, in the form of Christian devotion into which he was converted) primarily to connote Jesus' divinity, and does not

---

51. Bousset, *Kyrios Christos,* esp. 91-98, 206-10. Bousset's influence on this question is illustrated in Rudolf Bultmann, *Theology of the New Testament,* 2 vols. (New York: Charles Scribner's Sons, 1951, 1955), 1:128-29; H. J. Schoeps, *Paul: The Theology of the Apostle in the Light of Jewish Religious History* (Philadelphia: Westminster, 1961), 149-59.

52. For the Jewish background, see, e.g., Gerhard Delling, "Die Bezeichnung 'Söhne Gottes' in der jüdischen Literatur der hellenistisch-römischen Zeit," in *God's Christ and His People: Studies in Honour of Nils Alstrup Dahl,* ed. J. Jervell and W. A. Meeks (Oslo: Universitetsforlaget, 1977), 18-28.

53. This was noted by Hengel, *The Son of God,* 7.

54. "Son of God" translates a variety of Greek phrasings in the Pauline corpus and appears only in Rom. 1:4 *(tou . . . huiou theou),* 2 Cor. 1:19 *(ho tou theou . . . huios),* Gal. 2:20 *(tou huiou tou theou),* and Eph. 4:13 *(tou huiou tou theou).* On the meanings and functions of *Kyrios* in Paul, see Hurtado, "Lord," in *DPL,* 560-69.

thus seem at all derived from the pagan religious realm in which divine sonship language functions precisely to connote the divine status of human figures.

To summarize up to this point: Bousset has been shown to be seriously wrong both in his portrayal of his "primitive" Jewish Christian community and in his characterization of key features of the devotion of Paul and the Christian groups he represents. These alone are major reasons to set aside *Kyrios Christos* as an account of the development of Christ-devotion. The extent of the problems with Bousset's characterization of early devotion to Jesus is such that one wonders how such an erudite scholar could have made such mistakes, and the answer, I suggest, has to do with the approach and assumptions that Bousset brought to his analysis. As I have stated already, Bousset sought to make the story of early Christ-devotion a simple tale of Hellenization, more specifically, the progressive paganization of a supposedly pure, primitive Christian faith. The prior conviction that this had to be the way things went seems to have prevented him from seeing what now seems so obvious. It is clear that his portrayal of the "primitive" community was both simplistic and inaccurate, and that his characterization of Paul and the supposed "Gentile Christianity" was also badly wrong. His sharp distinctions between the beliefs of Jewish Christians and Gentile Christians in the first few decades of the first century were artificial and without foundation, and by all indications the cultic veneration of Jesus began both incredibly early and among groups made up largely of, and dominated by, Jewish Christians with profound loyalty to a monotheistic religious stance. ✱

3. Bousset operated with a distinction between "Palestinian" and "Hellenistic" that, though widely accepted then and in many subsequent studies, has been shown to be simplistic.[55] The sequential layering of early Christian development in neat strata of "Palestinian Jewish," "Hellenistic Gentile," and "Pauline" was crucial in *Kyrios Christos;* but, even when supplemented with the "Hellenistic Jewish" stratum added in later scholarship, the scheme is highly questionable.

It does not adequately allow for the clear interplay of influences characteristic of the Hellenistic and Roman periods. Jews had encountered Hellenistic language and culture for three hundred years by the time of Jesus. Though Jewish responses to Greek culture varied considerably, all forms of Jewish culture of the Roman period were "Hellenized" in varying degrees and ways, whether located in Roman Judea or in the diaspora.[56]

---

55. Hurtado, "New Testament Christology: A Critique of Bousset's Influence," 308-9, and the literature cited there.

56. Martin Hengel has been particularly influential in making this point in several publications, esp. *Judaism and Hellenism.* See also the discussion and literature cited by I. H. Marshall, "Palestinian and Hellenistic Christianity: Some Critical Comments," *NTS* 19 (1972-73):

If it is now recognized as wrong to speak of a "Palestinian Jewish" setting free from Hellenistic influences, we should also realize that it is inaccurate to speak of a purely "Hellenistic Gentile community" prior to Paul. Paul established churches largely composed of Gentile converts, of course. But well into the decades of Paul's ministry and beyond, Christian groups, including the Pauline communities, continued to be led and shaped to a significant degree by Christian Jews, among whom Paul must certainly be counted! Furthermore, there is a scant twenty years between the death of Jesus and the earliest of Paul's extant letters, and these letters reflect an already well developed pattern of devotion to Jesus, key features of which likely even predate Paul's own conversion and probably helped to provoke his own prior efforts to stamp out the Jewish Christian movement.[57]

So both Bousset's theory or model of development (pagan influences) and his framework of early Christian development (discrete unilinear layers/stages) are to be rejected, along with the key features of his portrayal of Christ-devotion that I have criticized in the preceding paragraphs here. However impressive the influence of *Kyrios Christos* on subsequent scholarship, and in spite of the undeniable erudition Bousset brought to his work, we are long overdue for a more accurate discussion of equivalent scope. This is what I attempt to provide in this book. Having illustrated major problems with *Kyrios Christos,* I also want now to indicate more positive features that I have sought here to emulate.

1. This book has a similar chronological scope, reaching from the beginnings of what became Christianity down toward the late second century. I intend no theological statement thereby for or against the traditional Christian view of the New Testament canon. For my purposes here, the writings of the New Testament are invaluable historical sources, and the collection includes our only extant first-century Christian writings. The first-century period is, of course, of special interest, and the earlier in this period, the more intriguing things are in some ways. But I contend that extending the chronological sweep well into the second century is important in giving us a better historical perspective for this earliest period.

271-87. On the use of Greek in Palestine, see esp. A. W. Argyle, "Greek among the Jews of Palestine in New Testament Times," *NTS* 20 (1973-74): 87-90; S. Lieberman, *Greek in Jewish Palestine* (New York: Feldheim, 1965 [1942]); J. N. Sevenster, *Do You Know Greek? How Much Greek Could the First Jewish Christians Have Known?* NovTSup 19 (Leiden: Brill, 1968); J. A. Fitzmyer, "The Languages of Palestine in the First Century A.D.," in *A Wandering Aramean,* 29-56.

57. On the chronological issue, see Martin Hengel, "Christologie und neutestamentliche Chronologie," in *Neues Testament und Geschichte,* ed. H. Baltensweiler and B. Reicke (Zürich: Theologischer Verlag, 1972), 43-67 (ET in Hengel, *Between Jesus and Paul,* 30-47).

Moreover, it allows us to see better the possible effects upon Christ-devotion as the Christian movement became dominantly made up of Gentiles, and as Christians sought to articulate their faith and piety in categories drawn more than before from the Greek intellectual traditions. In the second century we begin to see a "Christianity" that is a new religion with exponents and critics who distinguished it sharply from Judaism and the larger religious "cafeteria" of the Roman period; there is also a greater body of evidence extant from this period that indicates interesting diversities in Christian faith. Like the better-known second-century Christian witnesses, such as Justin Martyr, these other forms of Christian faith as well may have roots or (to change the metaphor) tributaries feeding them in the first century. In short, there is clear historical continuity as well as development in the first two centuries, and so it makes sense to have this chronologically larger field of vision.

2. As indicated earlier, I aim to consider in this book the breadth of phenomena accessible to us that constitute and reflect the central role and significance of Jesus in the religious thought and practice of the Christian movement in these first two centuries. In this breadth of phenomena to be studied, this book has another deliberate similarity to *Kyrios Christos*. I agree with scholars such as Bousset, Adolf Deissmann, Johannes Weiss, and others of the early decades of the twentieth century that the christological beliefs of early Christians are best seen, and more profoundly understood as well, in the context of their piety and the patterns of their religious devotion.

3. This is a historical and developmental analysis in which my concerns will be to understand probable sequences and relationships of the various forms of Christ-devotion. I will pay attention to chronology, geographical location (where known), and any other indications that allow us to place forms of devotion to Jesus in relation to one another. We should, however, avoid any assumption of an inevitable and unilinear development, and allow for the greater likelihood of more complex patterns and unpredictable phenomena involving, for example, multilinear "trajectories," parallel or regressive developments, and even patterns that may be closer to an explosion than any orderly progression.

4. In another affirmation of the broad aims of the *religionsgeschichtliche Schule,* I attempt to take due account of the historical setting and context of early Christian devotion, both the Jewish matrix out of which the Christian movement grew and the larger historical and religious environment of the Roman period. Obviously, to keep to our focus it will be necessary to be selective and to deal with those features of the historical context that can plausibly be posited as particularly relevant for understanding Christ-devotion in its various forms.

5. Finally, similar to *Kyrios Christos,* one of the important contributions

offered in this study is a proposed theory or model of the historical forces and factors that drove and shaped Christ-devotion in these crucial early centuries. Historical understanding of a phenomenon or period involves more than simply recounting what happened. It also includes asking why things happened and how. Over the last decade or more I have devoted a great deal of effort to identifying the key factors and the particular contributions of each to the process of development and diversification in Christ-devotion. In this book I wish to lay out in detail the fruit of my continuing efforts to grasp the reasons for the particular ways devotion to Christ exhibited itself. To this I turn in the following chapter.

CHAPTER ONE

Forces and Factors

The real challenge in historical understanding is to figure out not only what happened, but also how it happened and why. The accurate logging and description of the sources and all relevant data is crucial, of course, and is itself a fully worthy and demanding historical task. But the difficult intellectual tasks are to identify the forces and factors that prompted and shaped people and events, and to understand how these forces and factors operated. Probably every scholar who has examined any aspect of early Christ-devotion has had some notion of these things, but, to judge by their publications, few seem to have made these *how* and *why* questions much of a conscious or explicit focus. As I stated in the introduction, a good many scholars have simply subscribed to the syncretism theory of the *religionsgeschichtliche Schule* and have fitted their readings of the historical sources into this scheme. Of those who have explicitly attempted to offer a theory of their own (e.g., Casey, discussed below), none seems to me to have done adequate justice to the range of relevant data and the particularities of early Christ-devotion, and none seems to have drawn adequately upon what we can learn from other relevant disciplines about the rise and development of new religious movements.

When we are dealing with something as remarkable and historically significant as early Christ-devotion, it is all the more crucial to try to grasp the factors involved.[1] The more unusual something is, however, the more difficult it is to explain, especially because modern historical understanding is so unavoid-

---

1. There is no denying the historical significance of the emergence of Christ-devotion, as it led to Jesus becoming perhaps the best-known figure in human history. In *One God, One Lord: Early Christian Devotion and Ancient Jewish Monotheism* (Philadelphia: Fortress, 1988; 2nd ed., Edinburgh: T. & T. Clark, 1998), I demonstrated that it was unusual and cannot be fitted easily within a pattern of analogous developments of the time.

ably dependent upon analogy. Unlike those who conduct research in the experimental sciences, when doing historical research we cannot repeat historical events in laboratories under controlled conditions to observe recurring features that permit us to formulate theories. Instead we have to look for other historical (and contemporary) phenomena that might be fully or even partially analogous, and then see if we can identify common factors that might also have been efficacious in the particular historical people and events that we are trying to understand.

In this process accurate observation and comparison are crucial, lest we pose as analogies phenomena that are not, or that are analogous only at such a high level of generalization that they do not actually provide us with the explanatory factors that we seek. Inaccurate observations and misguided comparisons produce theories that attribute too much significance to this or that and overlook other vital factors. Although historical theories cannot be as easily verified or falsified as can theories in experimental science, some historical theories can be shown to be better than others. Any theory that can be shown to rest upon an oversimplified or distorted view of what is being explained, or overlooks an important factor, or simply gets wrong the interaction of relevant historical factors is justifiably to be rejected or seriously modified.

In this chapter I present a theory of the historical factors and forces that "drove" and shaped Christ-devotion in the first two centuries. This theory both arises from and shapes the historical analysis given in subsequent chapters. Over the past decade or more, in previous publications I have sketched ideas that are discussed here more fully and, I hope, developed more adequately. I think developing a theory adequate to the subject of inquiry is important, and I am a bit puzzled that so few scholars have seriously pursued the matter.[2] Historical theories not only offer explanations of why and how things happened, they also contribute to our perception of what happened and the significance of the event(s) in question. That is another reason why it is good to strive for adequacy and accuracy in building our theories. I offer the following theory to

---

2. In their jointly authored book, *Trajectories through Early Christianity* (Philadelphia: Fortress, 1971), James M. Robinson and Helmut Koester offered several studies that basically urge the view that early Christianity developed along several different paths, and they rightly proposed that Christian sources of the first two centuries or so, whether canonical or noncanonical, should all be taken account of in developing a picture of historical developments. With these basic points I agree. They do not, however, develop a general model or theory of how and why the developments happened as they did. William Horbury (*Jewish Messianism and the Cult of Christ* [London: SCM Press, 1998]) proposes that honorific language of Jewish messianism accounts for Christ-devotion, but his proposal does not seem to me to take adequate account of the phenomena involved in Christ-devotion.

28

help us understand better how and why Christ-devotion emerged and developed in the particular ways it did, to grasp more fully what Christ-devotion was, and thereby to see more profoundly how remarkable it was.

Two brief points before we proceed with a discussion of specifics. First, this theory involves several factors. Whatever the adequacy of the set of factors I will discuss, the basic thrust of the theory is that we have to think in terms of *multiple* factors and not a simple explanation such as the syncretistic model of the *religionsgeschichtliche Schule*. Maybe further factors in addition to those I propose here should be considered, but certainly not fewer factors! Second, I want to emphasize the *interaction* of these factors. Each factor had its own contribution, as I hope to show; but I contend that the particulars of early Christ-devotion are best accounted for by positing a dynamic (and varying) combination of the forces and factors I shall now attempt to specify.[3]

Jewish Monotheism

What became "Christianity" began as a movement within the Jewish religious tradition of the Roman period, and the chief characteristic of Jewish religion in this period was its defiantly monotheistic stance.[4] I contend that any consideration of early Christ-devotion must set it in the context of this central feature of the religious matrix out of which the Christian movement sprang. I also contend that Jewish monotheism had a powerful role in shaping Christ-devotion, particularly in the Christian groups that we know about in the New Testament and the later groups that were formative of what became familiar, "orthodox" Christianity.

As has become clearer in recent decades of scholarly study, the religion of ancient Israel had not always manifested the monotheistic emphasis that was so familiar a feature of Jewish religious teaching and practice by the Roman era.[5]

3. I have emphasized these points in previous publications. It is, therefore, disappointing to encounter criticism that is in fact directed against a distortion of my position, and does not really engage it. E.g., Timo Eskola, *Messiah and the Throne*, WUNT 2/142 (Tübingen: Mohr Siebeck, 2001), 9-10, 322-28, wrongly attributes to me the claim that "divine agency" explains the emergence of early Christian beliefs about Jesus. In fact, however, as in the following discussion, I have consistently invoked the *interaction* of *several* factors (e.g. *One God, One Lord*, 114-24), and I have indicated clearly that the ancient Jewish traditions I call "divine agency," though important, were *not* by themselves sufficient to explain the emergence or distinctive character of devotion to Jesus.

4. I draw here upon my essay "First-Century Jewish Monotheism," *JSNT*, no. 71 (1998): 3-26, and the scholarly literature cited there, and *One God, One Lord*, esp. 17-39.

5. See, e.g., Bernhard Lang, ed., *Der einzige Gott: Die Geburt des biblischen Monotheismus*

Although the Hebrew Scriptures present Israel as summoned from the first to an exclusive worship of *Yahweh,* and as condemned for worshiping other deities, the earliest and clearest expressions of a genuinely monotheistic belief (that is, a denial of the efficacy or reality of any other deity) are found in Isaiah 43–48, in a section of the book that is widely seen among scholars as coming from the period of the Babylonian exile (sixth century B.C.E.).[6] This suggests that it may have been precisely in the forcible encounter with the many gods of other nations and peoples, indeed, an encounter on the "home turf" of these gods in lands of Israelite/Judean exile, that the rather pugnaciously monotheistic claims that came to characterize religious Jews were explicitly formulated.

In the continuing experience of devout Jews in the religious environment of the ancient Near East in the Persian period and thereafter, an exclusivist monotheism became so fully identified with Jewish piety that by the Roman period failure to maintain such a stance was perhaps the greatest sin possible for a Jew. It is likely that the religious crisis generated in the second century B.C.E. by the attempt of Antiochus IV to impose a programmatic religious and cultural assimilation of the Jews made devoutly traditionalist Jews thereafter even more sensitive to any challenge to the exclusivity of the God of Israel.[7] The more flexible readiness of non-Jewish religion to accommodate many deities (and also human objects of cultic devotion such as rulers) was portrayed by devout Jews as utter stupidity and the worst of many corrupt features of Gentiles.[8]

This exclusivist religious posture is all the more striking when we consider how, in a good many other matters, many (perhaps most) Jews showed a readiness to accommodate themselves (though in varying ways and degrees) to other features of Hellenistic culture. Language, dress, dining practices, intellectual categories and themes, sports, and many other things were widely adopted, but there could be no negotiating away the monotheistic posture of Jewish religion. As Lester Grabbe put it, "For the vast majority, this was the final barrier that could not be crossed; we know from antiquity of only a handful of exam-

(Munich: Köselverlag, 1981); Lang, *Monotheism and the Prophetic Minority* (Sheffield: Almond Press, 1983); Saul M. Olyan, *Asherah and the Cult of Yahweh in Israel,* SBLMS 34 (Atlanta: Scholars, 1988); Mark S. Smith, *The Early History of God: Yahweh and the Other Deities in Ancient Israel* (San Francisco: Harper and Row, 1990).

6. E.g., Richard J. Clifford, "Isaiah, Book of (Second Isaiah)," in *ABD,* 3:490-501; R. N. Whybray, *The Second Isaiah* (Sheffield: JSOT Press, 1983).

7. See the detailed and sensitively nuanced discussion in Martin Hengel, *Judaism and Hellenism: Studies in the Encounter in Palestine during the Early Hellenistic Period,* 2 vols. (London: SCM Press, 1974), 1:255-309.

8. Note this emphasis even in the urbane and sophisticated diaspora Jew, Philo of Alexandria (e.g., *Decal.* 52-81). The same stance is expressed also in other Jewish texts of the Hellenistic and Roman period, e.g., Wisd. of Sol. 13–16.

ples of Jews who abandoned their Judaism."[9] Grabbe's wording nicely conveys my point: to engage in the worship of other deities was to abandon Judaism. For devout Jews, the core requirement of Judaism was the exclusive worship of Israel's God.[10]

For assessing the historical significance of the devotion given to Jesus in early Christian circles, with Jesus represented variously as unique agent of God "the Father," it is still more important to note that the Jewish resistance to worshiping any figure but the one God of Israel was manifested not only against the deities of other peoples and traditions but also with reference to figures that we might term "divine agents" of the God of Israel. Even the angelic figures that formed part of God's vast heavenly entourage and that feature so prominently in some Jewish writings of the Greek and Roman periods, and also the great human heroes in the Bible (e.g., Moses) or of postbiblical history (e.g., the Maccabean heroes), were not treated as rightful recipients of cultic worship in any known Jewish circles of the time.

This withholding of cultic worship from these highly revered "agents" of God (whether angelic or human) is important for two reasons. First, it shows that the ancient Jewish concern about the uniqueness of God was a genuinely exclusivist "monotheism" and not simply a negative attitude toward the deities of foreigners. The refusal to give worship to any other extended to members of the "home team" too. Secondly, it means that the accommodation of Christ as a recipient of cultic devotion in the devotional practice of early Christian groups was a most unusual and significant step that cannot be easily accounted for on the basis of any tendencies in Roman-era Jewish religion. In short, the incorporation of Christ into the devotional pattern of early Christian groups has no real analogy in the Jewish tradition of the period. The firmly monotheistic commitment of the religious matrix of earliest Christianity both makes Christ-devotion an intriguing phenomenon and, as we shall see, was an important factor in shaping its development.

A large part of my book *One God, One Lord: Early Christian Devotion and Ancient Jewish Monotheism* was given over to demonstrating these things, and

---

9. Lester L. Grabbe, *Judaism from Cyrus to Hadrian*, vol. 1, *The Persian and Greek Periods* (Minneapolis: Fortress, 1992), 170.

10. Because the word "worship" and its Greek and Hebrew equivalents can connote a variety of degrees and forms of reverence, I wish to make it clear that by "worship" here I mean the sort of reverence that was reserved by ancient devout Jews for God alone and was intended by them to indicate God's uniqueness. I use the term to designate "cultic" worship, especially devotion offered in a specifically worship (liturgical) setting and expressive of the thanksgiving, praise, communion, and petition that directly represent, manifest, and reinforce the relationship of the worshipers with the deity.

having followed the reviews and continuing investigation since its initial publication in 1988, it seems to me that the basic case made there stands.[11] Scholarly responsibility requires that I give reasons for this judgment and take account of the very lively debate of relevant matters that has characterized the last decade or so.

Was Jewish Religion Really Monotheistic?

The monotheistic stance of Roman-era Judaism has received a good deal of discussion in recent scholarship, some scholars actually questioning whether Jewish religion of the time really was monotheistic and others emphatic that it was.[12] But in my judgment there have been some confusion, inaccuracy, and insufficient attention to proper method on both sides of the argument. I wish, therefore, to try to clarify matters before we proceed further.[13]

In a provocatively titled essay Peter Hayman questioned whether it was really appropriate to attribute "monotheism" to Jewish religion until late in the medieval period.[14] Hayman claimed that ancient Judaism retained a "dualistic pattern" from the ancient Canaanite background and that "functionally Jews believed in the existence of two gods," though he provides scant evidence of this.[15] Instead, Hayman invokes five things in support of his proposal that monotheism is not properly to be attributed to ancient Jewish religion: (1) absence of a clear doctrine of creation ex nihilo until well into the Middle Ages; (2) references to the possibility of mystical unity with God and to ideas of metamorphosis of human beings (e.g., Enoch) into heavenly/angelic figures; (3) the prominence of angels in ancient Jewish texts, along with prohibitions against worshiping them; (4) evidence of Jewish practice of magic involving the invocation of a variety of heavenly figures (usually named angels) along with God as sources of power; and (5) the alleged survival of a divine consort of *Yahweh* in postexilic Jewish references to Wisdom and Logos. These phenomena certainly indicate a fascinating complexity in ancient Jewish religion, but they do not make Hayman's case for a ditheistic pattern in Roman-era Jewish

---

11. Hurtado, *One God, One Lord,* 17-92. I have responded to contrary suggestions in the preface to the second edition (x-xiii) and in "First-Century Jewish Monotheism," esp. 18-22.

12. See the literature cited in Hurtado, "First-Century Jewish Monotheism," 4-5 nn. 2, 5.

13. I draw here upon portions of an earlier essay of mine, "What Do We Mean by 'First-Century Jewish Monotheism'?" in SBLSP 32, ed. Eugene H. Lovering (1993), 348-68, esp. 348-56.

14. Peter Hayman, "Monotheism — a Misused Word in Jewish Studies?" *JJS* 42 (1991): 1-15.

15. Hayman, 14.

religion. Before justifying this judgment, I want to refer to another scholar who has posed a distinguishable but somewhat similar line of argument.

In her book *The Great Angel,* Margaret Barker contends that the early Christian cultic reverence of Christ represented an adaptation of an alleged theology of two deities *(Elyon/Elohim* and *Yahweh)* from preexilic Israelite religion that somehow survived in Jewish circles of the Roman period, in spite of the monotheistic reforming efforts of Deuteronomists in the postexilic centuries.[16] In her view, this more ancient ditheistic pattern found new expression in early Christian circles, with Jesus being understood as *Yahweh* and God as *Elyon/Elohim.* Her aim seems to be to make early Christ-devotion an understandable (and, in her logic, historically and religiously valid) phenomenon by giving it this putatively venerable pedigree. She rightly identifies the crucial question as "how it could have been possible for monotheistic Jews to have *worshipped* Jesus,"[17] but she answers it with a simplistic set of alternatives, a false dilemma.

The only alternatives she considers are that the worship of Jesus is either a later intrusion from the pagan world or simply Christian relabeling of authentic Jewish religious traditions. It seems not to occur to her to consider whether there might be any other possibility. To be sure, religious traditions can be maintained, and can undergo significant change through syncretistic encounter with other traditions and cultural forces. But also, in some circumstances adherents of a religious tradition can develop reconfigurations or variant forms of the tradition (sometimes creative and significant ones). This is what I argue happened in the emergence and development of Christ-devotion in early Christianity: the reconfiguring of Jewish monotheistic practice and thought to accommodate Jesus with God as rightful recipient of worship under the impact of a set of factors and forces which I lay out in this chapter.

There are other problems as well with Barker's argument on a number of points, especially her handling of a number of relevant texts, but the larger sub-

---

16. Margaret Barker, *The Great Angel: A Study of Israel's Second God* (London: SPCK, 1992). In a more recent essay, Barker proposes that the worship of Jesus is to be explained by alleged traditions of the real apotheosis of divine kings and priests in ancient Israel, who were worshiped by Israelites as human embodiments of the God of Israel. It is not entirely clear how her various explanations fit together. See Barker, "The High Priest and the Worship of Jesus," in *The Jewish Roots of Christological Monotheism: Papers from the St. Andrews Conference on the Historical Origins of the Worship of Jesus,* ed. C. C. Newman, J. R. Davila, and G. S. Lewis, JSJSup 63 (Leiden: Brill, 1999), 93-111. Moreover, examination of the evidence she proffers often makes it difficult to accept her claims. One example: Barker cites one line from *Somn.* 2.189 as showing that Philo knew and accepted the divinity of the high priest, whereas the context makes it clear that Philo specifically demurs from any such idea ("Is he then a god? I will not say so . . .").

17. Barker, *The Great Angel,* 1.

stantial problem I focus on here pertains to both Barker's and Hayman's claims about ditheistic tendencies in Roman-era Jewish religion.[18] Neither is able to show an actual *devotional pattern* involving public and corporate worship offered to any figure other than the God of Israel in the extant sources that derive from and reflect the worship practices of Jewish groups of the period. This is really rather crucial. Whatever might have been going on in preexilic Israelite religion, it is evidence of *Roman-era* Jewish practice that is relevant. Moreover, the issue is Roman-era Jewish worship *practice:* how and to whom Jews prayed, offered sacrifice, and otherwise gave what they intended as worship of a divine figure. For this, we have in fact a good deal of evidence that devout Jews were quite scrupulous in restricting full worship to the God of Israel alone.

The closest we come to the possibility of anything contrary is in the prohibitions against worship of angels that we find in rabbinic texts and in a couple pseudepigraphical writings (which we will note again later in this chapter).[19] But the most that can be made of these data is that they may reflect criticism of those Jews who dabbled in magical practices (including the invocation of angels) in their private lives. None of the texts in question gives evidence of public, corporate cultic devotion given to figures other than the God of Israel among Jews who identified themselves with their ancestral religious tradition.[20] There is, for example, no evidence of an "angel cultus," that is, worship offered to angels as part of the devotional pattern of any known Jewish group of the time. As Stuckenbruck showed in his very detailed study of the evidence, the "venerative language" used by ancient Jews about angels and even the occasional appeals to angels for assistance (often along with God) did not amount to cultic worship of angels; and the incorporation of angels into their view of God's sovereignty was apparently seen by devout Jews as compatible with their monotheistic commitment.[21] The prohibitions in the rabbinic texts may indicate, however, that historical developments in ancient Judaism in the second century C.E. and later (e.g., rabbinic concerns to consolidate and unify Judaism under their teachings, perhaps partly in reaction against what they regarded as dangerous sectarian developments such as Jewish Christianity) involved rab-

---

18. I have expressed some specific criticisms of *The Great Angel* in a brief review in *Theology* 96 (1993): 319-20.

19. I have discussed the data in *One God, One Lord*, 28-35.

20. See the discussions of the magical data by C. E. Arnold, *The Colossian Syncretism: The Interface between Christianity and Folk Belief at Colossae*, WUNT 2/77 (Tübingen: Mohr-Siebeck, 1995), 8-102, esp. 59-60, 82-83.

21. Loren Stuckenbruck, *Angel Veneration and Christology*, WUNT 2/70 (Tübingen: J. C. B. Mohr [Paul Siebeck], 1995), 200-203. The expression "venerative language" is used by Stuckenbruck to designate the honorific ways angels are referred to in ancient Jewish sources.

binic authorities taking a more negative view of the way angels had figured in Jewish religious thought and practice in the previous period.[22]

There are of course indications of what may have been syncretistic experiments involving Jews here and there in the Hellenistic and Roman periods, as Morton Smith and Martin Hengel have noted.[23] But these seem to have been ad hoc, localized, none of them reflecting or leading to a religious movement within Judaism or a new rival religious movement stemming from Judaism that affirmed cultic veneration of figures other than the one God. Bickerman was likely correct (and is followed by Hengel) in attributing a large role to assimilationist Jews among Judean elite circles in promoting the disastrous Hellenization of Judaism supported by Antiochus IV that apparently involved an identification of the God of Israel with Zeus and Dionysus.[24] But it is all the more important to note that this effort failed largely because it could not obtain sufficient *popular* support among the masses of Jews in Judea who rallied instead behind the Hasidim and the Maccabees.

Both in profession and in public religious practice, devout Jews of the Roman era were clearly monotheistic. In fact, it appears that the monotheistic stance was more firm and characteristic in the Hellenistic and Roman era than in any previous period. The weakening or undermining of a supposedly pure Old Testament monotheism in the Judaism of the period of Christian origins alleged by some previous scholars such as Bousset is directly the opposite of the actual historical movement in Judaism of the time toward a more emphatic monotheism.[25] Ancient Jews certainly saw the heavens as full of angels and made ample space for the involvement of various figures from God's heavenly entourage in the operation of God's sovereignty over the world and God's redemptive purposes.[26] But in the expression of their religious beliefs, they showed a concern to preserve God's uniqueness, and even more significantly in their cultic worship they maintained

---

22. On early rabbinic concerns about Jewish sectarian forces, see, e.g., Shaye J. D. Cohen, "The Significance of Yavneh: Pharisees, Rabbis, and the End of Jewish Sectarianism," *HUCA* 55 (1984): 27-53. On Jewish views of angels during the period in question, see now Michael Mach, *Entwicklungsstudien des jüdischen Engelglaubens in vorrabbinischer Zeit*, TSAJ 34 (Tübingen: Mohr Siebeck, 1992).

23. Morton Smith, *Palestinian Parties and Politics That Shaped the Old Testament* (1971; reprint, London: SCM Press, 1987), esp. chap. 4; Hengel, *Judaism and Hellenism*, 1:261-67.

24. Elias Bickerman, *From Ezra to the Last of the Maccabees* (New York: Schocken Books, 1962), 93-111; Hengel, *Judaism and Hellenism*, 1:267-303.

25. Cf. W. Bousset, *Die Religion des Judentums im späthellenistischen Zeitalter,* ed. H. Gressmann, 3rd ed. (Tübingen: J. C. B. Mohr, 1926). See my critique of Bousset's characterization of Judaism in *One God, One Lord,* 22-27.

26. Hans Bietenhard, *Die himmlische Welt im Urchristentum und Spätjudentum* (Tübingen: J. C. B. Mohr, 1951).

an exclusivity. Other scholars have documented amply the evidence of Jewish monotheistic commitment, and I have cited and drawn upon these studies in an earlier discussion of the topic.[27] As I concluded in that essay, two major themes or concerns come through in the *monotheistic rhetoric* of ancient Jews: (1) God's universal sovereignty as creator and ruler over all, even over the evil forces that oppose God; and (2) God's uniqueness, expressed by contrasting God with the other deities of the religious environment, but also expressed in contrasts or distinctions between God and God's own heavenly retinue, the angels.[28]

Furthermore, as already emphasized, in their religious/cultic *practice* as well, devout Jews of the Roman period exhibited a monotheistic commitment.[29] In fact, in this outward and tangible sphere of worship practices we have still more obvious and crucial indications of this commitment. It is possible to misinterpret the honorific descriptions of principal angels and other exalted figures in ancient Jewish texts (a possibility exhibited in some scholars' readings of these texts!), particularly if we treat these references out of the context of the religious practice of those who wrote the texts. Thus, for example, it is possible to mistake Philo's reference to the Logos as "the second god" (*ton deuteron theon,* in *Quaest. Gen.* 2.62) as evidence of a ditheistic outlook unless we take account of the larger context of these statements and Philo's emphatic affirmation that worship is to be restricted to the one God of Israel alone (e.g., *Decal.* 65).[30] In terms of how devout Jews of the Roman period thought, we would know if another figure were being treated as a deity and were really functioning in ways that compare and compete with the one God if we had evidence of cultic worship being offered to the figure. As I wrote in a 1998 article,

> Jews were quite willing to imagine beings who bear the divine name within them and can be referred to by one or more of God's titles . . . beings so endowed with divine attributes as to make it difficult to distinguish them descriptively from God, beings who are the very direct personal extensions of God's powers and sovereignty. About this, there is clear evidence. This clothing of servants of God with God's attributes and even his name will perhaps seem to us "theologically very confusing" if we go looking for a

27. Hurtado, "First-Century Jewish Monotheism," 9-14. Among these studies, the unpublished D.Phil. thesis of Paul A. Rainbow is particularly valuable as a mine of evidence ("Monotheism and Christology in 1 Corinthians 8:4-6" [D.Phil. thesis, Oxford, 1987]).

28. Hurtado, "First-Century Jewish Monotheism," 12-14.

29. For further discussion and evidence, see Hurtado, "First-Century Jewish Monotheism," 14-22, and *One God, One Lord,* esp. 22-39.

30. On the Logos and other "personified divine attributes," see my discussion in *One God, One Lord,* 41-50.

"strict monotheism" of relatively modern distinctions of "ontological status" between God and these figures, and expect such distinctions to be expressed in terms of "attributes and functions." . . . The evidence . . . shows
that <u>it is in fact in the area of worship that we find "the decisive criterion"</u>
<u>by which Jews maintained the uniqueness of God over against both idols</u>
<u>and God's own deputies.</u> I may also add that the characteristic willingness
of Graeco-Roman Jews to endure the opprobrium of non-Jews over their
refusal to worship the other deities, even to the point of martyrdom, seems
to me to reflect a fairly "strict monotheism" expressed in fairly powerful
measures.[31]

Very recently, Crispin Fletcher-Louis has offered a direct challenge to my
position, contending that there are several texts that reflect a readiness of ancient Jews to worship other figures alongside God.[32] Because he has marshaled
the putative evidence for this view and expresses it so strongly, it will be useful
to examine it critically. I do not find his case persuasive, and courtesy requires
that I should indicate why.

Acceding to the evidence that the worship of angels was not a feature of
Roman-era Jewish religion, Fletcher-Louis contends that there is "considerable
evidence" that the tradition did allow for the worship of "a particular righteous
humanity which in one way or another had become divine or angelomor-
phic."[33] The key evidence he offers is five texts where he contends "in one way
or another a human figure . . . is worshipped" by devout Jews, and he claims
that this was accommodated "within a genuinely Jewish monotheism."[34] There

---

31. Hurtado, "First-Century Jewish Monotheism," 21-22. The words within quote marks
here are lifted from Andrew Chester, "Jewish Messianic Expectations and Mediatorial Figures
and Pauline Christology," in *Paulus und das antike Judentum*, ed. M. Hengel and U. Heckel,
WUNT 58 (Tübingen: J. C. B. Mohr [Paul Siebeck], 1991), 17-89, esp. 64-65, whose otherwise
helpful essay shows here an inadequate appreciation of these points.

32. Crispin H. T. Fletcher-Louis, "The Worship of Divine Humanity as God's Image and
the Worship of Jesus," in *The Jewish Roots of Christological Monotheism*, 112-28. Fletcher-Louis
here refines and focuses his argument from his book *Luke-Acts: Angels, Christology, and
Soteriology*, WUNT 2/94 (Tübingen: Mohr Siebeck, 1997). Margaret Barker makes somewhat
similar claims in "The High Priest and the Worship of Jesus."

33. Fletcher-Louis, "Worship of Divine Humanity," 112.

34. Fletcher-Louis, "Worship of Divine Humanity," 112-13. The five texts (discussed by
Fletcher-Louis, 113-20) are (1) the "Son of Man" figure in *1 Enoch* 48:5 and 62:6-9; (2) God's or-
der that the angels should reverence Adam in the *Life of Adam and Eve* 12-16; (3) a description of
Jerusalem temple activities ascribed to Hecataeus of Abdera (quoted in Diodorus Siculus,
Bibliotheca historica 40.3.3-8); (4) Josephus's account of Alexander the Great encountering the
Jewish high priest (*Ant.* 11.331-35); (5) the paean of praise to Israel's heroes and the high priest
Simon in Sir. 44:1–50:21.

are basically two problems with his case that make it unpersuasive, one conceptual and the other practical.

The conceptual problem is reflected in the looseness of his phrase "in one way or another." Fletcher-Louis seems to lump together a range of reverential gestures as all indicating "worship" of various figures as divine beings. In the ancient world of these texts, however, reverence was expected for, and rather freely given to, any superior person or being, whether human or heavenly; and obeisance was given to any victor in battle and by subject peoples to those who subdued them. Moreover, all these cases involve basically the same gesture, a bowing or prostration; and the same terms were used for the reverence (e.g., in Greek, *proskynein*), whether given to a god or to any one of an assortment of one's social superiors.[35] But the specific connotation of the prostration or other gestures depended entirely on what kind of honor the person offering the reverence intended to attribute to the figure receiving the gesture. Jews scrupulous about reserving worship for "the true and living God" refused to bow down to the images of Gentile gods, but nevertheless showed reverence and obeisance for other figures, e.g., for rulers and those in high office, for parents, and for anyone from whom they badly needed a favor or mercy. So we really cannot take every example of bowing and obeisance as "worship" in the "hard" sense of reverencing a figure as a deity.[36]

This brings me to the practical problem in Fletcher-Louis's argument: none of the texts he uses really seems to be an example of "worship" in this sense of the word. Let us examine the texts on which his case rests, commencing with passages in *1 Enoch* where we are given dream-visions of a future triumph of a Son of Man/Elect One. Read in their contexts, the references in *1 Enoch* 48:5, 62:1-9 to the obeisance given by all the inhabitants of the earth and by the mighty kings and rulers to the Son of Man/Elect One simply envision the eschatological acknowledgment of this figure as God's appointed one who will gather the elect and subdue the haughty kings and nations who have not acknowledged the true God and who have oppressed the Jewish righteous. As

---

35. For more detailed discussion of this, see L. Hurtado, "The Binitarian Shape of Early Christian Worship," in *The Jewish Roots of Christological Monotheism*, 187-91 (187-213). The most complete analysis is still Johannes Horst, *Proskynein: Zur Anbetung im Urchristentum nach ihrer religionsgeschichtlichen Eigenart*, NTF 3/2 (Gütersloh: C. Bertelsmann Verlag, 1932).

36. As indicated earlier, in this book I use the term "worship" to mean the actions of reverence intended by the person(s) offering it to express specifically religious devotion of the sort given to a deity in the culture(s) or tradition(s) most directly relevant to earliest Christianity. That is, I use the term to designate "cultic" worship, especially devotion offered in a liturgical setting and intended to represent, manifest, and reinforce the relationship of the devotee(s) to a deity.

Matthew Black noted in his commentary on *1 Enoch,* these passages seem intended to show the fulfillment of divine promises in Isaiah of the vindication of Israel and the Servant of the Lord and the acknowledgment of this vindication to be given by foreigners and former oppressors (Isa. 45:14; 49:7, 23; 60:14).[37] There is no reason given in these Isaiah passages (in the most emphatically monotheistic section of the Hebrew Scriptures) or in *1 Enoch* to take the prophesied reverential actions as "worship" of any of these figures as a divine being.[38] We have a Christian appropriation of the same promises in Revelation 3:9, where the Philadelphian Christians are promised that their religious opponents will come and give obeisance *(proskynēsousin)* at their feet.

The scene in the Latin tradition of the *Life of Adam and Eve* 12-16, where God orders the angels to reverence the newly created Adam, is likewise not at all a Jewish precedent for the worship of a second figure alongside God, as I have shown before.[39] Even if for purposes of discussion we ignore the very real questions about the date and provenance of this passage and treat it as reflecting a pre-Christian Jewish tradition, we have only a literary scene set in the mythic past where heavenly beings are told to reverence Adam as God's image.[40] As

37. Matthew Black, *The Book of Enoch or 1 Enoch: A New English Edition with Commentary and Textual Notes,* SVTP 7 (Leiden: Brill, 1985), 210 (note on 48:5).

38. Fletcher-Louis's supporting reasons for seeing worship of the Son of Man/Elect One in these passages ("Worship of Divine Humanity," 114) simply fail on close examination. The allusion in *1 Enoch* 46:1 is in fact not to Ezek. 1:26 and God, but instead to Dan. 7:13-14, where "one like a human being" comes with God and is given dominion. There is no reason, thus, to take the Son of Man of *1 Enoch* as "the anthropomorphic form of God." The Son of Man sits on "the throne of his glory" in *1 Enoch* 51:3; 62:2, 5; 69:29, but this is quite obviously a throne on earth, where he can be given obeisance. Also, I cannot see the basis for the assertion that in *1 Enoch* 69:13-29 the Son of Man is shown "in possession of God's Name," or how this has any relevance to the obeisance given him in 48:5 (where it is the Son of Man's own name that is revealed, not God's). Contrary to Fletcher-Louis's somewhat misleading statement, it is not a "prior assumption" that prevents scholarly acceptance of worship of the Son of Man as a divine being in *1 Enoch* (114); it is the lack of clear evidence in support of this view.

39. Hurtado, *One God, One Lord,* 2nd ed. (Edinburgh: T. & T. Clark, 1998), x-xi. Cf. Fletcher-Louis, "Worship of Divine Humanity," 114-15. Fletcher-Louis cites Steenburg's article on this text, but mischaracterizes his claims. Steenburg did not contend that the text was a true precedent for Jewish worship of a second figure. He suggested only that the passage may indicate that the *idea* that it might be appropriate to worship God's image was entertained among ancient Jews, and that, as Jesus became identified as God's *eikōn,* this might help account for him being a recipient of worship. David Steenburg, "The Worship of Adam and Christ as the Image of God," *JSNT* 39 (1990): 95-109.

40. See, e.g., the summary of critical issues about the textual and tradition history of the Adam and Eve materials by M. D. Johnson, "The Life of Adam and Eve," in *OTP,* 2:249-52. The scene does not appear in the Greek textual tradition, on which see Daniel A. Bertrand, *La vie grecque d'Adam et Ève* (Paris: Librairie Adrien Maisonneuve, 1987). For discussion of all the

Fletcher-Louis acknowledges, "there is no straightforward correlation with any form of contemporary Jewish praxis";[41] but this is precisely what we need in order to have a real precedent for the worship of Jesus. What is at issue is whether devout Jews in the Roman period actually worshiped as a divine being any figure in addition to their God, not what imaginative scenes they might pen for etiological or laudatory purposes.[42]

The early Christian phenomenon for which we seek historical explanation and any possible precedent is not merely this or that imaginative scene of some eschatological acknowledgment of Jesus, but a full *pattern of religious behavior* practiced in early Christian groups, featuring Jesus, and made up of specific devotional actions which I have itemized and discussed at some length in previous publications.[43] Philippians 2:6-11 pictures such an eschatological acknowledgment of Jesus. But what makes this passage so remarkable is that it also reflects the sort of regular, corporate devotion that featured Jesus and that characterized the religious practice of Christian circles already within the first decades of the Christian movement.

The report of Jewish temple worship attributed to Hecataeus of Abdera which says that in the temple ceremony the Jewish people bowed down to reverence the high priest, and Josephus's story of Alexander the Great bowing down before the high priest, who went out to plead with him not to sack Jerusalem, hardly bear the weight Fletcher-Louis puts upon them.[44] Josephus certainly portrays Alexander astutely showing reverence for the appointed priest of the god of a conquered people to whom he wished to present himself positively. Reverencing the gods of conquered peoples in the hope of being seen by

---

versional evidence, see Michael E. Stone, *A History of the Literature of Adam and Eve*, SBLEJL 3 (Atlanta: Scholars, 1992). The various versions are set out with English translations in Gary A. Anderson and Michael E. Stone, *A Synopsis of the Books of Adam and Eve*, 2nd rev. ed., SBLEJL 17 (Atlanta: Scholars, 1999). In 15:3 (Latin), Satan's words are a clear allusion to Isa. 14:13-14, and Corrine Patton has pointed also to the possible hint of the tradition in Wisd. of Sol. 2:23-24 ("Adam as the Image of God: An Exploration of the Fall of Satan in the *Life of Adam and Eve*," in SBLSP 33 [1994], 294-300, esp. 296), noting that the scene in *Life of Adam and Eve* could be a haggadic narrative prompted by the passage in Wisdom of Solomon. It is interesting to note also the recurring references to this tradition in the Quran (2:34; 7:11; 15:29-31; 17:61; 18:50; 20:116; 38:71-76).

41. Fletcher-Louis, "Worship of Divine Humanity," 113.

42. In the case of the vignette in Latin *Life of Adam and Eve* 12-16, for example, it is fairly clear that we have an etiological tale explaining the origin of Satan's evil disposition toward humanity.

43. I discuss six specific ritual actions in *One God, One Lord*, 100-114, elaborated in "Binitarian Shape," esp. 192-211.

44. Cf. Fletcher-Louis, "Worship of Divine Humanity," 115.

them as a decent sort of fellow, even claiming to be the divinely appointed guardian of the gods, is commonly attested behavior of the astute conquerors of the ancient Near East. But, as Josephus makes very clear, devout Jews regarded Alexander's prostration before the high priest as reverence for the God of the Jews. Contra Fletcher-Louis's assertion, the high priest himself is certainly not presented in the account as if regarded or reverenced as divine in himself or ex officio.

It is also hard to see the basis for Fletcher-Louis's assertions about the account of Jewish temple worship attributed to Hecataeus of Abdera in Diodorus's *Bibliotheca historica*. To be sure, the Jewish crowds are pictured as showing reverence to the high priest as the expositor of God's commandments, reverence fully fitting for a person holding such a revered office; and the setting of this action in the courts of the Jerusalem temple "excludes any purely secular understanding of their genuflection."[45] It is a religious ceremony taking place in a religious site, and the high priest is given proper reverence there because that is where he exercises his religious role on behalf of the people. But this does not give us reason to see this reverence as indicating that the high priest was worshiped as a divine being.[46]

Finally, there is the panegyric on Simon II in Sirach 50:1-21 that concludes the long section of "praises of famous men" that begins in 44:1. The lavish description of Simon in his priestly robes in 50:5-11 is an impressive series of similes. But Fletcher-Louis's claim that the passage portrays Simon as "the embodiment of *the* Glory of God" (emphasis his) on the basis of the rainbow simile in 50:7 (perhaps adapted from Ezek. 1:28), seems rather extravagant.[47] Clearly, the placing of this panegyric to the deceased Simon as the final section of a rhapsody on famous ancestors has the effect of linking him with great figures of the Bible through whom God led and blessed Israel. Simon is obviously lauded, but neither "at the literary level" nor in actual temple practice do we have any basis for Fletcher-Louis's attempt to portray Simon as worshiped as a divine being.[48] In 50:17 the people bow to worship God, and in 50:21 they prostrate themselves

---

45. Fletcher-Louis, "Worship of Divine Humanity," 115. It is in fact hard to guess what a "purely secular understanding" would mean for the ancient Jewish setting.

46. Philo describes the high priest as acting on behalf of the Jews, the whole human race, and the whole of the natural order (*Spec. leg.* 1.97), but not as some sort of embodiment of divinity. In *m. Tamid* 7.1-4 there is another lengthy description of the priests' actions in the temple service of daily sacrifice, and it mentions frequent prostrations by the Jewish crowds at various points when the temple trumpets were sounded in the ceremony (esp. 7.3).

47. Cf. Fletcher-Louis, "Worship of Divine Humanity," 116.

48. Fletcher-Louis, "Worship of Divine Humanity," 117-19. Cf. Patrick W. Skehan and Alexander A. Di Lella, *The Wisdom of Ben Sira*, AB 39 (New York: Doubleday, 1987), 546-55.

again to receive God's blessing. To be sure, the high priest pronounces this blessing, at which point the people bow. But nothing in ancient Jewish sources indicates that such actions were understood by Roman-era Jews as signifying that the high priest was himself worshiped as a divine figure, and it thus seems rather excessive to read such connotations into a text like this.

Fletcher-Louis repeatedly refers to those who disagree with his assertions as bound by an *assumption* that Jewish monotheism could not accommodate the worship of figures other than God.[49] If among early Jewish Christians Jesus was reverenced in ways that amount to a genuinely "binitarian" devotional pattern, there is in principle no reason to assume that in other circles of devout Jews something similar could not have developed. I contend, however, that the extant evidence does not show any true parallel or precedent in Roman-era Jewish religious practice, and I have attempted to show here that my view of the matter is not an assumption but comes as a *conclusion* to a close examination of the evidence.

The Nature of Jewish Monotheism

Other scholars have also emphasized the monotheistic nature of Roman-era Judaism, but here too some comments are in order. In particular, some scholars refer to Jewish monotheism in fairly simple terms as a fixed creedal constraint against attributing any real divinity to figures other than the one God, thus constituting mainly a doctrinal commitment. For these scholars, this constraint means it would have been impossible for Jewish Christians to have developed a view of Christ that amounted to attributing divinity to him. In short, these scholars invoke their portrayal of Jewish monotheism as a basis for determining in advance what could or could not have happened christologically among Christians with allegiance to the monotheistic stance of the Jewish tradition.

Anthony Harvey's 1982 study is an example of this.[50] In Harvey's view, it was not until Ignatius of Antioch that we have the "first unambiguous instances" of Jesus being described as divine. It would have been impossible for this to happen among Jewish Christian circles. "It was not until the new religion had spread well beyond the confines of its parent Judaism that it became

---

49. E.g., Fletcher-Louis, "Worship of Divine Humanity," 112, 113, 119-20 ("the rigidly held assumption that Jewish monotheism, by its very nature, excludes the worship of the human being concerned"). Barker too characterizes those who disagree with her as holding "assumptions" ("High Priest," 94).

50. A. E. Harvey, *Jesus and the Constraints of History* (Philadelphia: Westminster, 1982), esp. the chapter "The Constraint of Monotheism."

possible to break the constraint and describe Jesus as divine."[51] Both his description of ancient Jewish monotheism and his understanding of the sort of reverence of Christ reflected in the New Testament are subject to challenge, but I restrict my comments to the former matter here.

Two things in particular are important to note. First, his references to Jewish monotheism solely as a "constraint" give the impression of a rather rigid doctrinal commitment that could not easily be "broken" (to use his image). He (along with other scholars mentioned below) does not consider the possibility of a religious commitment such as monotheism being adapted and reformulated by adherents of a tradition so as to take account of their own religious experiences or other developments. Second, like a good many other scholars, Harvey portrays Jewish monotheism (and early Christian developments too) in terms of doctrines and concepts, giving insufficient attention to the cultic/liturgical practices and scruples involved. But these are the matters emphasized in ancient Jewish tradition as the key boundary markers that distinguished the one God from other heavenly/divine beings and that set apart valid devotion from its idolatrous counterfeits.

In Maurice Casey's Cadbury lectures we have another study of the development of New Testament Christology that employs an understanding of Jewish monotheism similar to Harvey's.[52] Casey too invokes Jewish monotheism to argue that it was impossible for Jesus to have been regarded as divine so long as Christianity was dominated by a Jewish religious outlook. In Casey's view, however, the restraint was effectively (and lamentably) overcome a bit earlier than posited by Harvey, within the Johannine community after 70 C.E., when the community became dominated by the attitudes of the increasing numbers of Gentile converts. Under the influence of this Gentile mentality, in the Johannine community "Jesus was hailed as God," a second deity alongside the God of the Bible.[53] Ignoring for the moment Casey's oversimplified characterization of Johannine Christology and his equally dubious effort at a sociological explanation of the development of early Christology, I restrict myself here to his handling of Jewish monotheism.[54]

---

51. Harvey, 157.

52. P. M. Casey, *From Jewish Prophet to Gentile God: The Origins and Development of New Testament Christology* (Louisville: Westminster John Knox; Cambridge: James Clarke, 1991). See now Casey's essay, "Monotheism, Worship and Christological Developments in the Pauline Churches," in *The Jewish Roots of Christological Monotheism*, 214-33.

53. Casey, *From Jewish Prophet*, 36. See also, e.g., 138, 144, 156.

54. For a critique of Casey's views, see J. D. G. Dunn, "The Making of Christology — Evolution or Unfolding?" in *Jesus of Nazareth: Lord and Christ. Essays on the Historical Jesus and New Testament Christology*, ed. Joel B. Green and Max Turner (Grand Rapids: Eerdmans;

As does Harvey, Casey makes his view of Jewish monotheism the crucial premise that allows him then to determine in advance the possible limits of early Christian reverence for Jesus in groups made up largely of Jews. Like Harvey, Casey portrays Jewish monotheism as a fixed restraint that could only either be in force (among Jews) or broken (among Gentiles), and he is then able to insist in case after case that pre-Johannine New Testament passages that might appear to reflect a reverence for Jesus as divine cannot in fact be taken that way. As in Harvey, there is scant consideration of the possibility of new adaptations of a religious tradition from within by adherents of the tradition. Likewise with Harvey, Casey sees the restraining force of Jewish monotheism as manifested primarily in a conceptual/doctrinal distinction of God from other figures, that is, in the language used to describe and distinguish God and other figures such as high angels.[55] But I am not persuaded that these rhetorical distinctions were quite as firm as Casey and Harvey claim.[56] Moreover, like Harvey, Casey seems not to have appreciated fully the importance of cultic practice in understanding ancient Jewish monotheism and early Christ-devotion.[57]

In several publications over a number of years, J. D. G. Dunn also has in-

---

Carlisle: Paternoster, 1994), 437-52. I do not imply here that sociological factors are not relevant, only that Casey's explanation has major unacknowledged problems. He assumes that Gentile Christians were automatically less likely to be concerned about monotheistic commitment, an error he could have avoided by taking account of the literature of second-century Gentile Christians, who often seem more concerned about asserting monotheism than Christology (e.g., Joseph Lortz, "Das Christentum als Monotheismus in den Apologien des zweiten Jahrhunderts," in *Beiträge zur Geschichte des christlichen Altertums und der byzantinischen Literatur: Festgabe Albert Ehrhard*, ed. A. M. Koeniger [Bonn and Leipzig: Kurt Schroeder, 1922], 301-27). His claim that a Gentile-dominated new religious movement would have had to deify its identification figure (in this case, Jesus) in order to provide sufficient cohesiveness for itself is refuted by the example of Islam, which felt no need to deify its central figure, yet quickly acquired a quite impressive cohesion!

55. Casey, *From Jewish Prophet*, 85.

56. See my discussion of various types of divine agent figures as portrayed in ancient Jewish sources in *One God, One Lord*, 41-92.

57. In his recent essay "Monotheism, Worship and Christological Developments in the Pauline Churches," however, Casey seems to have taken more notice of this matter, acceding that "Pauline Christians worshipped God differently from non-Christian Jews and that Jesus was central to these occasions" (e.g., 229). He also grants that "in Pauline Christology we have a significant change in Jewish monotheism" (231) and "a serious development of monotheism which goes beyond anything found in non-Christian Judaism" (233). On the other hand, Casey insists that there is sparse evidence that Jesus was worshiped in the Pauline churches (222), but his discussion of the evidence (222-29) is incomplete, and focuses on small linguistic matters, failing to take account of the larger significance of the actions themselves as constituting an early and major reshaping of devotional practice, both among Jewish and Gentile Christian circles.

voked Jewish monotheism as crucial in his efforts to analyze early Christian reverence for Jesus. In a 1982 essay Dunn posed two questions. (1) Was pre-Christian Jewish monotheism "threatened" by beliefs about "heavenly redeemer figures and intermediary beings"? (2) Did earliest Christology constitute a threat to or departure from Jewish monotheism?[58] He answered both questions in the negative. Later in this book I examine in detail early Christ-devotion and its relation to Jewish monotheism; at this point I focus on the way Dunn dealt with the first question.

Although Dunn contends that the ancient Jewish interest in redeemer/intermediary figures was not a significant threat to the monotheistic stance of Jewish tradition, he seems to allow for some development and change in Jewish tradition of the Greco-Roman period, implying a bit more than Harvey or Casey that Jewish monotheism was able to stretch and bend somewhat without breaking.[59] Drawing upon Alan Segal's study of references to "two powers" heresies in rabbinic texts, Dunn has suggested that "strains" on, and dangers to, Jewish monotheism appeared in the late first and early second centuries.[60] He has proposed, for example, that the "high" Christology of the Epistle to the Hebrews, the Gospel of John, and Revelation (all commonly thought to have been written in this period) may be Christian versions of a larger number of speculations about divine figures in contemporary Jewish (and Jewish-related) groups, speculations that distended or were seen as threatening monotheism by some devout Jews.[61]

But in his discussion of Paul and these later New Testament writings, Dunn, like Harvey and Casey, still basically works with only two possibilities: monotheism could either have remained intact or been broken. Commendably he pictures developments stretching or even distending Jewish monotheism, but he too seems not to consider the possibility of significant reformulations and new adaptations of a religious commitment by adherents of a religious tradition.

---

58. J. D. G. Dunn, "Was Christianity a Monotheistic Faith from the Beginning?" *SJT* 35 (1982): 303-36. The questions are posed on 307. There have been subtle shifts and developments in Dunn's views since this essay, but on his major contentions he has remained firm. See Dunn, *Christology in the Making* (London: SCM Press; Philadelphia: Westminster, 1980); "Foreword to the Second Edition," in *Christology in the Making*, 2nd ed. (London: SCM Press, 1989); *The Parting of the Ways between Christianity and Judaism and Their Significance for the Character of Christianity* (London: SCM Press, 1991), esp. chaps. 9–11; and most recently, *The Theology of Paul the Apostle* (Edinburgh: T. & T. Clark; Grand Rapids: Eerdmans, 1998), esp. 28-38, 244-65.

59. E.g., Dunn, "Was Christianity?" 321-22; cf. "Foreword," xxiv, xxviii-xxix.

60. Alan F. Segal, *Two Powers in Heaven: Early Rabbinic Reports about Christianity and Gnosticism*, SJLA 25 (Leiden: Brill, 1977).

61. Cf. Dunn, "Was Christianity?" 322; "Foreword," xxvii-xxix; *Parting*, 223-25, 228.

In his earlier portrayals of Jewish monotheism and the significance of intermediary figures, Dunn dwelt entirely on the honorific descriptions of these figures and the ways they were conceived by Jews. That is, like most scholars, he focused on the verbal expressions of beliefs about God and other figures and neglected the data of devotional practice. More recently, however, he has shown greater recognition of the importance of cultic practices (worship) in understanding both Jewish monotheism and early Christian developments.[62] Nevertheless, in my view he still does not grant fully the significance of the Christ-oriented cultic practices that he agrees characterized Christian worship in the earliest decades. It seems very important to Dunn to attribute a mental monotheistic "reserve" to Paul that was "soon lost to sight" in Johannine Christianity. There are certainly distinctions between Paul and the Johannine writings in their christological rhetoric, but it seems to me that Dunn has underestimated the place of Christ in Paul's religion and overestimated the difference between Paul and the Johannine community, because Dunn has not sufficiently appreciated the import of the devotional pattern that is already attested in Paul's writings.[63]

Among recent studies of the relevance of Jewish monotheism for early Christ-devotion, one of the most important is an essay by Richard Bauckham in which he drew attention to the motif of angelic refusal of worship in Jewish and Christian writings.[64] Bauckham showed that in a number of writings that feature a glorious angel appearing to a human seer, we can see a monotheistic concern to maintain a distinction between God and such heavenly representatives and that this concern manifests itself in scruples about worship. In several

62. Cf. Dunn, *Parting*, 219-20, where he takes the "clear and uninhibited worship of the Lamb" in Rev. 5 to indicate a significant departure from typical monotheistic "inhibitions," showing (along with the theophanic portrayal of Christ in the visions of Revelation) that "the constraints of monotheism previously observed were being challenged." On 204-6 Dunn grants my emphasis that the cultic veneration of Jesus was the decisive Christian innovation in Jewish monotheistic tradition, but he questions whether it developed as early and as quickly as I have maintained (cf. Hurtado, *One God, One Lord*, 93-124). Most recently, in *Theology of Paul*, 257-60, Dunn holds to this view. But in his critique of Casey he affirms my emphasis that the early origins of cultic devotion to Christ ("The Making of Christology," 451-52) signal a major development in monotheistic tradition.

63. Cf. Dunn, *Theology of Paul*, 260.

64. Richard Bauckham, "The Worship of Jesus in Apocalyptic Christianity," *NTS* 27 (1981): 322-41. I gratefully acknowledge the stimulation that this essay gave to my own research and thinking early in the work that led to my book *One God, One Lord*. An expanded version appears in Bauckham, *The Climax of Prophecy: Studies on the Book of Revelation* (Edinburgh: T. & T. Clark, 1993), 118-49, and I cite this version of the essay in the following discussion. See also Bauckham, "Jesus, Worship Of," in *ABD*, 3:812-19. On the motif of angelic refusal of worship, see also Stuckenbruck, *Angel Veneration*, 75-102.

passages in these writings, when the human seer mistakes the glorious angel for God and starts to offer worship, the angel forbids this and directs the human to worship God alone.[65] Bauckham showed that this refusal motif is found also in Christian writings (e.g., Rev. 19:10; 22:8-9) and cogently argued that this makes the cultic reverence given to the Lamb in other passages of Revelation (esp. 5:6-14) all the more striking evidence of the exalted place of Christ in this writing and in the Christian traditions it reflects.

I think he is correct, both in his analysis of this motif of angelic refusal of worship as an important manifestation of Jewish (and early Christian) monotheism and in his argument about what the early Christian references to the worship of Christ indicate.[66] Bauckham's essay was influential in shaping the questions I pursued in *One God, One Lord,* where I demonstrated in some detail that in Second Temple Jewish tradition there was an impressive interest in various figures pictured as God's principal agent, and that the crucial line distinguishing these figures from God was in worship. God was to be worshiped, and worship was to be withheld from any of these figures. I contend that this was the decisive and clearest expression of what we call Jewish "monotheism." In the essay on first-century Jewish monotheism referred to above, I provided further substantiation of this.

To underscore two important points: Jewish monotheism of the Roman period (1) accommodated beliefs and very honorific rhetoric about various principal-agent figures such as high angels and exalted humans like Moses, and (2) drew a sharp line between any such figure and the one God in the area of

---

65. Bauckham cites Tob. 12:16-22; *Apocalypse of Zephaniah* 6.11-15; *Joseph and Aseneth* 15.11-12; *Apocalypse of Paul* (Coptic Version); *Apocryphal Gospel of Matthew* 3.3; *Ladder of Jacob* 3.3-5; *3 Enoch* 16.1-5; *Cairo Genizah Hekhalot* A/2, 13-18; and compares these with passages in Revelation (19:10; 22:8-9) and *Ascension of Isaiah* (Ethiopic 7.21-22; cf. Greek Legend 2.21-22).

66. In more recent publications Bauckham seems to back away a bit from his earlier emphasis on worship as the crucial criterion and manifestation of Jewish monotheism, and on the worship of Christ as the crucial indicator of Christ's significance in early Christian groups, preferring to characterize both Jewish monotheism and early Christ-devotion mainly in conceptual/doctrinal terms (cf. now Bauckham, *God Crucified: Monotheism and Christology in the New Testament* [Carlisle: Paternoster, 1998], 13-16, esp. 14 n. 20; and his essay, "The Throne of God and the Worship of Jesus," in *The Jewish Roots of Christological Monotheism,* 43-69). Both Jewish monotheism and Christ-devotion obviously involved beliefs about God's uniqueness and about Christ's significance. But I remain persuaded that the key way that Jews and Christians distinguished God and Christ from other honorific figures was in giving and withholding worship. Contra Bauckham's claims, the representation of Christ as participating in God's sovereignty (e.g., sitting on/sharing God's throne) is not unique, and Bauckham's attempts to deny the analogies in ancient Jewish texts (e.g., Moses' enthronement in *The Exagoge of Ezekiel*) are not persuasive. Likewise, in Rev. 3:21, Laodicean Christians are promised a seat with Christ on his throne, which he shares with God!

cultic practice, reserving cultic worship for the one God. Both features are significant in appreciating the Christ-devotion we see in early Christianity.

Monotheism in the New Testament

I contend that the exclusivist monotheism of ancient Judaism is the crucial religious context in which to view early Christ-devotion, and that this monotheistic concern helped powerfully to shape that Christ-devotion, especially in those Christian circles concerned to maintain a fidelity to the biblical tradition of the one God. We do not have to assume that this monotheistic stance was taken over into early Christian circles, however. For the sources show conclusively that it was a characteristic and powerful factor in the religious devotion of Christians from the earliest years onward, among Gentile as well as Jewish adherents of the young religious movement. Indeed, this hardly requires substantiation for anyone acquainted with the New Testament and the great majority of extant early Christian writings. A couple well-known illustrations will suffice.

In 1 Corinthians 8 and 10 Paul engages at some length unavoidable questions for Christians living in Roman cities, questions about their participation in pagan religious activities; and his directions are to shun these activities entirely. He refers to the pagan religious ceremonies as *eidōlothyta* (8:1, 4), "offerings to idols," reflecting the scornful attitude toward the pagan deities characteristic of his Jewish background. Over against what Paul calls derisively the many "so-called gods in heaven or on earth" of the religious environment, he poses the "one God, the Father, from whom are all things and for whom we exist, and one Lord, Jesus Christ" (8:5-6). In 10:14-22 Paul again demands that his converts completely avoid participation in the "worship of idols" *(eidōlolatria)*, insisting that participation in the Christian sacred meal ("the cup of the Lord . . . the table of the Lord") is incompatible with joining in the religious festivities devoted to these other deities, whom he here calls "demons" (10:20-21). Though Paul freely states a willingness to adapt himself on a number of matters "to those [Gentiles] outside the law" (9:21), he maintains a totally negative stance toward worship of anything or anyone other than the one God of Israel and the one *Kyrios* Jesus Christ.[67]

Paul's easy inclusion of devotion to Christ within his emphatically mono-

---

67. Similarly, note how in 1 Thess. 1:9-10 Paul contrasts the preconversion religious life of his converts with their Christian orientation: "you turned to God from the idols to serve the true and living God, and to await his Son from heaven."

theistic posture nicely illustrates the intriguing nature of early Christ-devotion. For Paul, and for many other Jewish and Gentile Christians of the time it appears, devotion to Christ was compatible with a vigorously monotheistic faith and practice. Here and elsewhere (e.g., Rom. 1:18-25), Paul has only contempt for the other recipients of cultic reverence in the Roman religious environment. How to understand and account for the reverence for Christ reflected in Paul and other early Christian sources will occupy us in the rest of this book, but 𝒳 there is no denying the exclusivist monotheism attested in Paul and characteristic also of many other early Christian writings, whether from Jewish or Gentile Christian hands.

For another illustration of this exclusivist monotheistic stance in early Christian writings, I point to the New Testament book of Revelation. In Paul we have a Christian Jew writing in the first few decades of the Christian movement. In Revelation we have another Christian Jew commonly thought today to have written toward the end of the first century, and both these points are important.[68] Revelation shows both the continuing influence of Christian Jews outside Palestine late in the first century and also how among such Christians monotheism continued to be the emphatic context within which they offered devotion to Christ.

The author accuses the churches of Pergamum and Thyatira of accommodating some who encourage others to "eat food sacrificed to idols" (2:14-15, 20). It is difficult to be sure of what precise behavior is in view here, but this pejorative wording indicates clearly that the author thinks it compromises in some way the monotheistic exclusiveness he regards as obligatory for Christians. Running throughout the book is a contrast between the worship of God (e.g., 4–5; 7:9-12; 11:15-19; 14:6-7) and the improper worship of idols (e.g., 9:20-21) and of the Beast (e.g., 13:5-8, 11-12; 14:9-11). Moreover, as Bauckham noted, in two passages John is forbidden to worship even the glorious angel who as divine emissary brings the revelations of the book (19:10; 22:8-9).[69] These things all indicate a complete contempt for the larger religious life of the Roman world and a strong (indeed, one could say fierce) fidelity to the tradition of exclusivist

---

68. Most scholars date Revelation toward the end of the reign of Domitian (ca. 95), though some scholars in the past and today have proposed a date in the time of Nero. Although the early church tradition of the author as John Zebedee is today widely rejected, the otherwise unknown John of Revelation is commonly taken to have been a Christian Jew, and a rather conservative one at that. See standard introductions such as W. G. Kümmel, *Introduction to the New Testament*, ed. and trans. H. C. Kee, rev. ed. (Nashville: Abingdon, 1975), 466-72; and Helmut Koester, *Introduction to the New Testament*, 2 vols. (Philadelphia: Fortress, 1982), 2:248-57.

69. Bauckham, "The Worship of Jesus in Apocalyptic Christianity"; see also Stuckenbruck, *Angel Veneration*, esp. 75-102.

monotheism that extends to a prohibition against the worship of heavenly representatives of God.

The scene in Revelation 5 where the Lamb is pictured receiving with God the idealized worship of heaven, is all the more remarkable in the light of this, and surely indicates an amazingly exalted status of Christ in the religious belief and practice advocated by the author. In fact, as I have demonstrated in *One God, One Lord,* we have no analogous accommodation of a second figure along with God as recipient of such devotion in the Jewish tradition of the time, making it very difficult to fit this inclusion of Christ as recipient of devotion into any known devotional pattern attested among Jewish groups of the Roman period. It is important to note the specific nature of the devotional pattern reflected in these Christian texts. There are two key components: (1) a strong affirmation of exclusivist monotheism in belief and practice, along with (2) an inclusion of Christ along with God as rightful recipient of cultic devotion.

The Effects of Monotheism on Christ-Devotion

This unusual "binitarian" devotional pattern certainly requires further analysis and adequate explanation, and the present chapter is intended to present the main lines of the explanation that I find most adequate. Essential to any such explanation and analysis is the recognition that the devotional commitment and pattern illustrated in Paul and Revelation (and found also in many other Christian writings from the period we are studying in this book) are shaped by the exclusivist monotheism inherited from the Jewish tradition. The Christ-devotion we see in these Christian writings is certainly a novel development. It is equally clearly presented as a religious stance that seeks to be faithful to the concern for the one God, and therefore it must be seen in historical terms as a distinctive variant form of monotheism.[70]

70. In previous publications I have referred to a Christian "mutation" in Jewish monotheism, without in any way intending the term pejoratively. Nevertheless, some have objected to the term "mutation," contending that it is unavoidably pejorative in connotation, at least in popular usage. So I have also used the term "variant" in this book, adapting it from the field of textual criticism where it refers to variant readings that appear in the transmission of a text. All readings (other than nonsense readings, demonstrable scribal errors, and minor orthographic differences), including what one might judge to be the original reading, are variant readings, each of which tells us something important about how the text was transmitted and, in most cases, how it was read and used meaningfully by various groups. See, e.g., E. J. Epp, "Toward the Clarification of the Term 'Textual Variant,'" in E. J. Epp and G. D. Fee, *Studies in the Theory and Method of New Testament Textual Criticism,* SD 45 (Grand Rapids: Eerdmans, 1993), 47-61, esp. 60.

Thus, for the purpose of developing an adequate theory of the formation and development of Christ-devotion, we have to make Jewish monotheism a central factor. It was certainly central in the Jewish religious matrix of earliest Christianity, and it was clearly affirmed with equal force in the sorts of early Christian sources we have sampled here.[71] But it is necessary here to consider further how exclusivist monotheism might have shaped Christ-devotion. Given that we have no other example of the sort of binitarian form of exclusivist monotheism that we see reflected in these Christian sources, Jewish monotheism by itself is not an adequate explanation for Christ-devotion, and other factors will have to be explored as well. But we must also take seriously the likely force of the exclusivist monotheism affirmed in the Christian sources.

Inasmuch as exclusivist monotheism is manifested essentially as a sharp discrimination between legitimate and illegitimate recipients of worship, and more specifically in a refusal to offer worship to any figure other than the one God, it is appropriate for scholars to refer to the constraining effect of monotheism. It is certainly correct to say that Jewish monotheism would have worked against the deification of Jesus along the lines of the apotheosis of figures that we know of elsewhere in the religious environment of the Roman period.[72] In light of the constraining effect of exclusivist monotheism, it is in fact initially difficult to imagine how the sort of Christ-devotion that we see reflected in the early Christian sources could have emerged and flourished so early and so fully among people who professed a fidelity to the monotheistic tradition. But, however it emerged and however it is to be understood, the Jesus-devotion of early Christians is not an example of simple apotheosis. Jesus did not become for them an additional god. It is very productive heuristically to take seriously their monotheistic orientation, which helps us avoid simplistic characterizations of Jesus-devotion and also alerts us to the need to develop a theory adequate to account for this remarkable phenomenon.

Granted, the exclusivist monotheism of Roman-era Judaism characteristically operated as a constraint against anything fully comparable to the Jesus-devotion we are examining in this book. So, are we to think of this constraint only as maintained or as "broken" in early Christian circles, as some scholars mentioned above have formulated the question? In light of the continuing monotheistic professions and evident scruples in these Christian circles, I pro-

71. As we will see later in this book, there appear to be forms of early Christianity that show little or no monotheistic concern, especially at least some examples of what are called "gnostic" Christians with their elaborate mythologies of multiple divinities.

72. See, e.g., Erich Berneker, "Apotheosis," in *Der Kleine Pauly Lexikon der Antike*, ed. Konrat Ziegler and Walther Sontheimer, 5 vols. (Munich: Deutsche Taschenbuch Verlag, 1979), 1:458-59. For an illustration of Jewish attitudes about apotheosis, see Philo, *Embassy to Gaius* 118.

pose that we also consider as a third possibility whether their Jesus-devotion constitutes an apparently distinctive and variant form of exclusivist monotheism, and that we inquire then how monotheism helped shape this devotional stance. Later in this chapter I will say more about how such a variant form of a tradition can arise, and I will defend further the view that the Jesus-devotion evident already in the New Testament constitutes such a development. To anticipate that discussion, my point is that the constraining effect of monotheism may not have prevented this variant form from emerging, though it may have contributed significantly to the particular form that it took.

In this light, monotheism has to be reckoned as one of the important forces or factors that, together with other factors to be sure, helps account for the why and how of Jesus-devotion, particularly in the formative period and among those Christian circles that sought to maintain an authentic relation with the tradition of biblical monotheism. The Jesus-devotion attested in the New Testament writings, for example, operates in such a context. That is, Jesus is not reverenced as another deity of any independent origin or significance; instead, his divine significance is characteristically expressed in terms of his relationship to the one God. The cultic reverence given him is likewise characteristically offered and justified with reference to the actions of the one God. The New Testament claim is that it is the one God who has exalted Jesus to an exceptional position of reverence and given him a "name" of divine significance (*Kyrios,* e.g., Phil. 2:9-11). It is God who now requires that Jesus be reverenced as the divine *Kyrios,* and one reverences Jesus "to the glory of God the Father" (Phil. 2:11). Indeed, in the polemical rhetoric of the Johannine writings, to fail to give such reverence to Jesus ("the Son") is to fail to give proper reverence to God ("the Father," e.g., John 5:23; 1 John 2:22-23; 5:9-12).

In other words, the vigorous Jesus-devotion promoted in New Testament writings and, as we shall see, perpetuated and developed also in Christian circles of the second century does not amount to a separate cultus offered to Jesus as a new second god. Instead, there are a fairly consistent linkage and subordination of Jesus to God "the Father" in these circles, evident even in the Christian texts from the later decades of the first century that are commonly regarded as reflecting a very "high" Christology, such as the Gospel of John and Revelation.[73] This is why I have referred to this Jesus-devotion as a "binitarian"

---

73. As is well known, the Gospel of John combines an exalted view of Christ with a clear subordinationist emphasis. See, e.g., Paul N. Anderson, *The Christology of the Fourth Gospel* (Valley Forge, Pa.: Trinity Press International, 1996), appendices on 266-67; C. K. Barrett, "'The Father Is Greater Than I'. John 14:28: Subordinationist Christology in the New Testament," in his *Essays on John* (London: SPCK, 1982), 19-36; W. G. Loader, *The Christology of the Fourth Gospel: Structure and Issues,* 2nd rev. ed., BBET 23 (Frankfurt am Main: Peter Lang, 1992).

form of monotheism: there are two distinguishable figures (God and Jesus), but they are posited in a relation to each other that seems intended to avoid a ditheism of two gods, and the devotional practice shows a similar concern"(e.g., prayer characteristically offered *to* God *through/in the name of* Jesus). In my judgment this Jesus-devotion amounts to a treatment of him as recipient of worship at a surprisingly early point in the first century, and is certainly a programmatic inclusion of a second figure unparalleled in the monotheistic tradition of the time.[74] But the worship of Jesus clearly shows a recognizably monotheistic concern shaping it. This Jesus-devotion (indeed, the christological rhetoric of the New Testament generally) involves an adaptation of the principal-agent traditions that I have shown to be a feature of ancient Jewish monotheism.[75] Jesus functions as God's principal agent, Jesus' revelatory and redemptive actions consistently portrayed as done on God's authority, as expressions of God's will, and as serving God's purposes and glory. The accommodation of Jesus as recipient of cultic worship with God is unparalleled and signals a major development in monotheistic cultic practice and belief. But this variant form of monotheism appeared among circles who insisted that they maintained faithfulness to the monotheistic stance of the Jewish tradition. Any theory of the origins and development of Jesus-devotion must, therefore, grant a significant role to this monotheistic concern.

Jesus

Exclusivist monotheism is the crucial religious context in which to view Christ-devotion in early Christianity, and was a major force shaping what Christ-devotion looked like, but monotheism hardly explains why devotion to Jesus emerged. What was the impetus? There are really two questions involved. (1) Why was there such a focus on, and thematizing of, this particular figure, Jesus? (2) Why did Christ-devotion assume the proportions it did in early Christianity, i.e., amounting to a new binitarian devotional pattern unprecedented in Jewish monotheism? I address the second question in the next two sections of this chapter. It is the first question that we take up at this point, and this involves invoking another force/factor in my theory. I propose that the only reasonable factor that accounts for the central place of the figure of *Jesus* in early

---

74. For discussion of the indications that Christ-devotion (a) appeared and generated sharp opposition very early, and (b) amounts to a genuinely binitarian devotional pattern, see Hurtado, "Pre–70 C.E. Jewish Opposition to Christ-Devotion," *JTS* 50 (1999): 35-58, and "The Binitarian Shape of Early Christian Worship."

75. Hurtado, *One God, One Lord*, esp. 17-39.

Christianity is the impact of Jesus' ministry and its consequences, especially for his followers.

As is well known to any specialist in the origins of Christianity (and indeed, in light of the impressive recent promotional efforts of some authors and publishers, to many general readers as well), the last couple decades have witnessed a veritable flood of scholarly studies of Jesus as a historical figure.[76] It is in fact now difficult even for professional scholars in the New Testament and Christian origins to keep fully current on all the latest books on Jesus and the varied views and approaches they offer. Moreover, predictably, the differences among some scholars writing on the historical Jesus are such as to tempt one toward discouragement as to what specific conclusions one can entertain with any confidence about his message and purposes. But my aim here is considerably more modest, and more feasible, than a detailed portrait of Jesus, and all that is essential to claim will, I believe, command fairly wide assent.

The current scholarly studies of the historical Jesus tend to focus on Jesus' own aims, intentions, concerns, emphases, and characteristic actions. If the scholarly objective is to understand Jesus in historical terms, this is all very appropriate in principle (however difficult it has proven in practice to secure wide

---

76. In 1994 I wrote a survey of "historical Jesus" studies that had appeared in the preceding decade, and by the time it was published in 1997 further significant books had appeared! L. W. Hurtado, "A Taxonomy of Recent Historical-Jesus Work," in *Whose Historical Jesus?* ed. W. E. Arnal and Michel Desjardins, ESCJ 7 (Waterloo, Ontario: Wilfrid Laurier University Press, 1997), 272-95. The works I discussed there were E. P. Sanders, *Jesus and Judaism* (London: SCM Press, 1985); three Jesus books by Geza Vermes, *Jesus the Jew* (New York: Macmillan, 1973), *Jesus and the World of Judaism* (Philadelphia: Fortress, 1983), and *The Religion of Jesus the Jew* (Minneapolis: Fortress, 1993); Ben Witherington III, *The Christology of Jesus* (Minneapolis: Fortress, 1990); the first of a multivolume set by John P. Meier, *A Marginal Jew,* vol. 1, *Rethinking the Historical Jesus* (New York: Doubleday, 1991); Marcus Borg, *Jesus: A New Vision* (San Francisco: Harper and Row, 1987); Richard Horsley, *Jesus and the Spiral of Violence: Popular Jewish Resistance in Roman Palestine* (San Francisco: Harper and Row, 1987); Sean Freyne, *Galilee, Jesus, and the Gospels: Literary Approaches and Historical Investigations* (Philadelphia: Fortress, 1988); and John Dominic Crossan, *The Historical Jesus: The Life of a Mediterranean Jewish Peasant* (San Francisco: Harper San Francisco, 1991). Further studies particularly worth noting that appeared after my essay are the second volume from John P. Meier, *A Marginal Jew,* vol. 2, *Mentor, Message, and Miracles* (New York: Doubleday, 1994); Craig A. Evans, *Jesus and His Contemporaries: Comparative Studies,* AGJU 25 (Leiden: Brill, 1995); N. T. Wright, *Jesus and the Victory of God* (Minneapolis: Fortress, 1996); Marius Reiser, *Jesus and Judgment* (Minneapolis: Fortress, 1997; German ed., 1990); and Dale C. Allison, *Jesus of Nazareth: Millenarian Prophet* (Minneapolis: Fortress, 1998). I ignore here books advocating views without any scholarly basis — though they more often appear on the shelves of the bookstore chains! — in which, for example, Jesus is portrayed as having learned mystical teachings from Druids at Glastonbury or from extraterrestrial aliens.

agreement for any particular scholarly proposal). But for a theory of the origin and development of Christ-devotion in Christian circles of the first two centuries, I contend that it is not necessary to make a specific case about what might have been Jesus' own aims or purposes. Neither is it necessary to defend a specific proposal as to the contents of Jesus' own message, in particular what specific claims he may have made for himself. It is quite sufficient to take adequate account of the *results*, the effects of his career, as a contributing factor in the place he occupied in early Christian religious belief and practice. This is the focus here.

However one prefers to characterize Jesus' public persona and how he was perceived by contemporaries (e.g., prophet, messianic claimant, exorcist/healer, holy man/Hasid, shaman, magician, teacher/rabbi, sage, peasant spinner of tales, clever wordsmith, revolutionary, establishment critic, friend of social outcasts, a liberal Jew ahead of his time), and whatever one posits as Jesus' message and intention (e.g., to found a new religion/religious movement, to reform Judaism, to call for national repentance of Israel, to announce God's eschatological kingdom, to promote the overthrow of Roman colonialism in Jewish Palestine, to encourage new patterns of social interaction, to articulate a more carefree lifestyle), it is clear that he quickly became a figure of some notoriety and controversy.[77] He had followers, including some who seem to have been quite closely attached and keenly devoted to him and closely involved in his activities; he also had his critics, and at some point generated deadly serious opposition from some powerful people. That is, whatever may have been Jesus' intentions (often difficult to establish with certainty for historical figures, even when we have their own statements on the subject!), the *effect* of his public activity was very much to polarize a good many of his contemporaries over the question of how to regard him, whether to take a negative or positive stance about him. It is, I think, a reasonable inference that there was likely something in Jesus' own actions and statements that generated, or at least contributed to, this polarization. But for the present investigation the point is that, already in Jesus' own lifetime, people were strongly polarized over what to make of him.

There may have been a range or diversity of positive and negative stances among Jesus' contemporaries, and there were certainly rather strongly positive and negative views toward either end of a possible spectrum. It appears that some followers left their normal occupations, and their familial ties too, and formed a small band inspired by and drawn to him. These followers were com-

---

77. Those acquainted with historical Jesus literature will recognize both that the options I list here allude to various scholarly characterizations of Jesus in recent scholarship, and that I have given only an illustrative sampling of the varying characterizations available!

mitted to his teachings and what they understood to be his aims. This means, unavoidably, that they were also committed to his own personal validity. It was Jesus' message to which they responded, and he was thus the impetus and basis for their commitment. By far, most scholars who have given attention to the subject have concluded that his followers likely saw Jesus in one or another way in terms and categories prominent in their Jewish Palestinian setting, a setting heavily characterized by religious issues and concerns, though for a few scholars the putative influence of Hellenistic philosophical traditions figures importantly.[78] The varying estimates of Jesus given in some Gospel passages (e.g., Mark 6:14-16) are widely thought to be a generally authentic, though perhaps also only a selected, set of opinions held about him: a prophet, perhaps even a herald of eschatological events (Elijah), someone to be likened (as a troublemaker?) to John the Baptizer. A plausible case has been made that there was an even wider variety of views that included at one end a hope that Jesus was a messianic figure and at the other end the conviction that he was a bad example and perhaps even a false teacher, magician, and arrogantly dangerous agitator.

Nils Dahl wrote a classic essay arguing cogently that the early Christian claim/confession of Jesus' messianic significance is best explained by Jesus' crucifixion as a royal-messianic pretender.[79] Moreover, as Dahl suggested, the charge against Jesus did not require Jesus' own messianic claim, but can in principle be accounted for as occasioned by messianic claims/hopes of Jesus' followers and/or the settled conviction of the authorities that his activities provided the basis for such a charge. That is, on this view, whatever Jesus' claims about himself in his teachings, the governing authorities found their own good reasons to crucify him, and these reasons likely had to do with fears that he was being taken by his followers as a messianic figure.[80] The Gospel narratives certainly make the royal-messianic charge the basis of his execution (e.g., Mark 15:1-26; Luke 23:1, 32-38; Matt. 27:11-14, 20-23, 37; John 18:33-37; 19:12), and the attempts of Matthew and Luke to play down the political side of things do noth-

78. I allude here to proposals about possible similarities of Jesus to Cynics, on which see, e.g., H. D. Betz, "Jesus and the Cynics: Survey and Analysis of a Hypothesis," *JR* 74 (1994): 453-75.

79. Nils A. Dahl, "The Crucified Messiah," in his *Jesus the Christ: The Historical Origins of Christological Doctrine*, ed. D. H. Juel (Minneapolis: Fortress, 1991), 27-47. This essay first appeared in *Der historische Jesus und der kerygmatische Christus*, ed. H. Ristow and R. Mattiae (Berlin: Evangelische Verlagsanstalt, 1960), and then in Dahl, *The Crucified Messiah and Other Essays* (Minneapolis: Augsburg, 1974), 10-36.

80. Of course, one might well ask what Jesus said or did to contribute to messianic hopes among his followers and/or to excite such anxieties about his messianic pretensions among the authorities. But to explore such questions would require much more space than I can devote here.

ing to hide this. The Gospels agree in having Jesus crucified with others who were judged guilty of serious crimes.[81] Based on what we know of the Roman use of crucifixion as a form of capital punishment, Jesus' execution had to have been based on one or more charges of a very serious nature, perhaps involving a threat to public order, which would certainly correspond to a perceived royal-messianic claim, whether made by him or his followers.[82]

It is also likely that the Jerusalem temple authorities, who served at the pleasure of Rome, were involved in Jesus' execution.[83] Graham Stanton has shown that Jesus was probably held by some such contemporaries to be a false teacher/prophet, a religious deceiver, in terms of Deuteronomy 13 and 18.[84] That is, there is good reason to think that Jesus ran afoul of both Jewish and Roman authorities and was taken to be deeply offensive on both religious and political grounds. Certainly, death by execution indicates a seriously negative construal of one's behavior! And execution by crucifixion indicates a clear intent to humiliate and eliminate an offender by the strongest measure in Roman judicial usage.[85]

A few other scholars, however, have proposed that Jesus' execution was basically an overly hasty and misguided judicial bungle, and that we cannot thus infer much from it. That is, Jesus' execution does not indicate that he (intentionally or unintentionally) generated such opposition and anxiety that he had to be dealt with in this forcible manner. In the preface to one of his several books on Jesus, Geza Vermes asserts that there was no direct basis for Jesus' crucifixion in his words and deeds. Instead, "nervous authorities in charge of law and order" became unduly alarmed at Jesus' ill-timed "affray in the Temple" and mistakenly executed him as a messianic claimant. But it was a tragic error of perception on their part: "He died on the cross for having done the wrong thing (caused a commotion) in the wrong place (the Temple) at the wrong time (just before Passover). Here lies the real tragedy of Jesus the Jew."[86]

---

81. They are called "bandits" *(lēstas)*, which indicates some sort of violent crime. See, e.g., R. E. Brown, *The Death of the Messiah. From Gethsemane to the Grave: A Commentary on the Passion Narratives in the Four Gospels,* 2 vols. (New York: Doubleday, 1994), 1:283-84, 2:969-71.

82. Martin Hengel, *Crucifixion in the Ancient World and the Folly of the Message of the Cross* (Philadelphia: Fortress, 1977).

83. See the extensive discussion in Brown, 1:372-83.

84. G. N. Stanton, "Jesus of Nazareth: A Magician and a False Prophet Who Deceived God's People?" in *Jesus of Nazareth, Lord and Christ: Essays on the Historical Jesus and New Testament Christology,* ed. J. B. Green and M. Turner (Carlisle: Paternoster; Grand Rapids: Eerdmans, 1994), 164-80.

85. Hengel, *Crucifixion in the Ancient World and the Folly of the Message of the Cross.*

86. Vermes, *Religion of Jesus,* ix-x. The quote is from p. x. Though Vermes does not notice it, one might also say that on his view of events Jesus would have to be seen as seriously naive or stupid not to have foreseen that his "commotion" in the temple was scheduled so badly!

This is perhaps an attractive view for some (such as Vermes) who understandably wish to find ways to approach the historical figure of Jesus positively apart from theological claims in the New Testament and the harsh history of Christian-Jewish relations. But Vermes never gives a defense of his claim, and I think for most scholars of whatever religious persuasion, accepting his view requires a strong need to ignore probabilities. Miscarriages of justice are known, undeniably, even in jury-based trials in modern democracies. But Vermes' picture of things would make notorious examples of court stupidity like the Dreyfus affair or the Dred Scott case minor blips by comparison. They only led respectively to a prolonged national crisis in France and the American Civil War, whereas the crucifixion of Jesus led to the two thousand years of Christianity with all its positive and negative consequences! Though Roman justice could be rough, and a governor like Pilate may have cared little about judicial niceties for the colonials, it is on balance more likely that the religious and political authorities saw things in Jesus' behavior that in their eyes justified their action. It was not a lynching by a mob; it was state execution on serious charges.[87]

In his hefty and widely noticed 1991 volume *The Historical Jesus,* John Dominic Crossan portrays Jesus as proclaiming a "brokerless kingdom" of unmediated divine acceptance, who intended no special role or significance for himself.[88] Crossan devotes a number of pages to proposing how various features of the Gospel passion narratives arose and what kind of historicity might lie behind them.[89] But, curiously for such a lengthy book on the historical Jesus, he makes only the briefest suggestion about why Jesus was executed, what it was that made the authorities take such a venomous measure against him. After concluding that Jesus carried out some sort of action in the courts of the Jerusalem temple and uttered a saying about its "symbolic destruction," in a couple paragraphs Crossan simply asserts that, in "the confined and tinder-box atmosphere of the Temple at Passover, especially under Pilate," this "*could* easily have led to arrest and execution."[90] Beyond this subjunctive Crossan does not allow himself to go, as to the cause of Jesus' execution. But, as to the event itself, Crossan expresses himself more confidently in the indicative: "[T]here is not the slightest doubt about the *fact* of Jesus' crucifixion under Pontius Pilate."[91]

---

87. For a respected treatment of Roman judicial procedures with reference to Jesus' execution, see A. N. Sherwin-White, *Roman Society and Roman Law in the New Testament (The Sarum Lectures, 1960-61)* (Oxford: Oxford University Press, 1963; reprint, Grand Rapids: Baker, 1978).

88. Crossan, *The Historical Jesus,* e.g., 422, 423-24.

89. Crossan, *The Historical Jesus,* 354-94.

90. Crossan, *The Historical Jesus,* 360, emphasis his.

91. Crossan, *The Historical Jesus,* 375, emphasis his; and see also 372.

Personally, I find it a bit more difficult than Crossan allows in his extremely brief statement to understand how the authorities would have seen the sort of figure that Crossan portrays as posing so much a threat as to warrant crucifixion. Josephus's account of the actions taken against another Jesus, son of Ananias, who prophesied the temple's destruction, shows that those in charge of the temple did not take kindly to such actions. But, after being arrested and "severely chastised" by the temple authorities and "flayed to the bone with scourges" by the Roman governor, he was let go as a madman.[92] So, the outcome of the arrest of Jesus of Nazareth means that he must have been taken as a much more serious threat than the poor wretch described by Josephus, and that probably something more than a disturbance in the temple courts during a tense holy-day period was involved. But it is not necessary to my purpose here to argue the matter further. It is the impact and outcome of Jesus' activities, the impact upon followers and upon opponents, that is my emphasis for this discussion.

Given the outcome of Jesus' life, however, it is difficult to ignore the gigantic irony involved in Crossan's scenario. Though (per Crossan) Jesus supposedly saw and intended absolutely no special attention or significance for himself, he was singled out for execution by the means reserved for the most heinous of offenses against Roman order. On the other hand, all his followers, or, to follow Crossan again, Jesus' partners in "open commensality," were ignored by the authorities. Moreover, an astonishingly short time afterward these partners identified themselves with reference to him and proclaimed his uniquely authoritative significance for them in God's purposes. By common scholarly consent, scarcely more than a year after Jesus' execution (dated variously from 27 to 33 c.e.), the Jesus movement had attracted the ire of religious zealots such as Saul of Tarsus (whose subsequent conversion is widely reckoned by scholars to have happened within a couple years of Jesus' crucifixion). Furthermore, this Saul/Paul also claims that his conversion to the Jesus movement involved his capitulation to a very high view of Jesus ("God . . . [revealed] his Son to me," Gal. 1:14-16).[93] All this indicates that the groups Saul/Paul was seeking to discipline were already characterized by a fervent thematizing of the exalted significance of Jesus in their beliefs and religious practices.[94]

So, in view of the virtual preoccupation with Jesus' significance that characterized the Jesus movement from the earliest days (at least those circles to

---

92. Josephus, *Jewish War* 6.301-9.

93. On these chronological matters, see, e.g., Martin Hengel, *Between Jesus and Paul*, trans. John Bowden (London: SCM Press, 1983), 31; H. D. Betz, "Paul," in *ABD*, 5:191; Brown, *The Death of the Messiah*, 2:1350-78.

94. Hurtado, "Pre–70 c.e. Jewish Opposition," esp. 50-57.

which we have any direct reference in the surviving sources), if he intended no special role for himself in their religious life, Jesus would have to be seen as spectacularly unsuccessful in communicating his intentions to his followers. Or else he chose followers who felt particularly free (or compelled?) to ignore his message.

In any case, whether in keeping with his intention or not, people were polarized over Jesus.[95] His execution by the Roman governor, on charges preferred and supported by the Jerusalem religious authorities, both demonstrates this and explains why it was unavoidable for his followers as well as his opponents to take an explicit position on his significance. Very little choice was left beyond either consenting to the judgment of the authorities that Jesus was worthy of the harsh punishment meted out to him or reaffirming Jesus' validity and significance. Moreover, the latter unavoidably would have involved having to offer a rationale for Jesus' fate, and reasons for continuing to regard him in positive terms. There may well have been efforts along these lines, with various interpretations of Jesus' role and significance, but in all of them his own person was inescapably to the fore. So, even if we take a view of Jesus such as that promoted by Vermes (Jesus as a Palestinian Jewish holy man who got caught up in a judicial process by mistake) or by Crossan (Jesus as a peasant advocate of broad social generosity whose references to a symbolic destruction of the temple were wrongly interpreted as a threat by the authorities), it makes little difference to the point I am making here. It is possible that the impact of Jesus may have gone far beyond, or been different from, his own intentions, in generating an intensity of opposition and of discipleship. In my view, however, it is more plausible to think that Jesus' actions had something to do with their outcome.

In any case, it is the *impact* of Jesus, the *results* or outcome of his activities, that we have to consider in explaining why the devotional life of early Christian groups is so heavily concerned with him. Jesus became an issue, the key issue for his followers, from his execution onward, and probably even before that. We should not, thus, be surprised to find that their religious discourse and activities featured much reference to him.

Burton Mack has claimed, however, that in the very early years after Jesus' execution there were followers of Jesus who had little interest in questions about Jesus' significance.[96] Mack alleges that his earliest followers in Roman

---

95. Paula Fredriksen, *Jesus of Nazareth, King of the Jews: A Jewish Life and the Emergence of Christianity* (New York: Knopf, 2000), proposes that Jesus did not himself make a messianic claim, but nevertheless was seen as a messianic figure by Jerusalem crowds. Therefore the authorities executed Jesus to nip these notions in the bud.

96. Burton Mack, *The Lost Gospel: The Book of Q and Christian Origins* (San Francisco: Harper Collins, 1993).

Palestine were simply individuals with shared interests in "sane and simple living" who collected aphorisms, attributing them to Jesus but without any interest in either thematizing him or forming any religious movement within or apart from the Judaism of the time.[97] Why they should have attributed sayings to Jesus in particular is not, so far as I can tell, ever really explained by Mack, though it seems to be a fairly crucial historical question. Actually, there are a troubling number of important historical questions in Mack's proposal, for which he shows surprisingly little interest. But it is not my purpose here to assess fully Mack's claims. In a subsequent chapter of this book I will discuss more extensively what we can say about followers of Jesus in Roman Judea/Palestine in the early years after his execution. Here, two points will suffice.

First, the only basis for the sort of early Jesus-followers that Mack asserts is his conjectures about a supposed sayings Gospel, the contents and nature of which Mack conjures up out of the body of sayings attributed to Jesus commonly thought to have come from a sayings collection that scholars refer to as Q.[98] In a later chapter I discuss Q more extensively. At this point I make only a few points directly relevant to Mack's claims.

There are at present a number of proposals about what kind of literary history this Q material may have gone through before it was adapted and incorporated by the authors of the Gospels of Matthew and Luke; and there are likewise various views as to what kind of information about early groups of Jesus followers we can derive with confidence from any of these hypotheses.[99] In the early Christian sources of the first century, there are no confirmatory references to the particular kinds of circles of Jesus followers that Mack portrays. The eloquent absence of corroborating evidence is illustrated in Paul's letters. Given that Paul shows knowledge of Jewish Christian as well as Gentile Christian groups, both in Palestine and the diaspora (e.g., Gal. 1:18–2:14; 1 Cor. 15:3-7; 1 Thess. 2:14; 2 Cor. 11:16-23; Rom. 15:22-32), and that he felt free to criticize

---

97. Mack, *The Lost Gospel*, esp. 4-5, 9, 105-30.

98. As admitted by Mack, *The Lost Gospel*, 3.

99. For an excellent, balanced assessment of major issues in current studies of Q, see C. M. Tuckett, *Q and the History of Early Christianity: Studies on Q* (Edinburgh: T. & T. Clark; Peabody, Mass.: Hendrickson, 1996). On the literary history of Q, see esp. 41-82. In the current debate about supposed strata or stages of Q, John Kloppenborg's *The Formation of Q: Trajectories in Ancient Wisdom Collections* (Philadelphia: Fortress, 1987) is particularly influential. This is one of the few scholarly publications that Mack cites, but he fails to convey Kloppenborg's emphasis that the *literary* history of Q does *not* amount to or necessarily correspond to a *tradition history* of the Jesus tradition. That is, early and authentic Jesus tradition might have been added to the Q collection subsequent to its initial composition. Mack, on the other hand, collapses the distinction between stages of composition and tradition history without explanation.

those with whom he differed, his silence about anything like the groups Mack describes cannot be dismissed. If there were such Jesus followers for whom Jesus was relatively insignificant except as a figure to whom to attribute aphorisms, we would expect Paul to mention them in unsparing terms, unless they were so nearly invisible as to fail to come to anyone's attention then.

Likewise, if, as Mack alleges, an original "Q Gospel" was modified to serve different religious emphases and aims, we might expect to find some indication of this in the supposedly adapted form of the material. For example, in the *Gospel of Thomas,* there are indications of Christians seeking to distinguish themselves and their beliefs from other (previous) Christians and their beliefs by reformulating sayings of Jesus.[100] But, to my knowledge, neither Mack nor others who offer a redaction history of the Q material have shown any evidence of later redactors refuting and correcting the religious views from earlier stages of the sayings material. Neither "Matthew" nor "Luke," for example, exhibits a clear effort to refashion the sayings of Jesus over against the religious views of those from whom they obtained them. Moreover, neither Matthew nor Luke shows knowledge of followers of Jesus for whom he is merely a quotable spinner of aphorisms. So, though Mack presents his case with enthusiasm, one has to take it heavily on faith; and in critical historical work, this is hardly supposed to be the way cases win acceptance.

On the other hand, we do have direct evidence of how Jesus' sayings were used by a number of Christian circles, and none of these circles corresponds to the sort of group that Mack posits. All three Synoptic Gospels have significant bodies of Jesus' sayings, and they incorporate them readily enough within narratives of Jesus' ministry, death, and resurrection that reflect more familiar early Christian beliefs about him. The Synoptic authors seem unaware of any major transition in beliefs or usage supposedly involved in what they do with this sayings material. Earlier still, Paul makes use of Jesus sayings-traditions also. Though it is not clear how much Jesus sayings-tradition Paul knew, he uses what he knew to help shape Christian behavior (e.g., 1 Cor. 7:10-11).[101] So our earliest direct evidence consistently indicates the use of Jesus' sayings as authoritative teachings to shape behavior within the context of more familiar forms of Christianity, and with no indication that this usage of the Jesus tradition is a departure from any previous usage of it.

Even if we entertain the possibility of Mack's proposed circles of Jesus fol-

---

100. John W. Marshall, "The *Gospel of Thomas* and the Cynic Jesus," in *Whose Historical Jesus?* 37-60.

101. See, e.g., David L. Dungan, *The Sayings of Jesus in the Churches of Paul* (Philadelphia: Fortress, 1971).

lowers, they would have to be seen as a very short-lived variant form of the Jesus movement that had little or no impact on subsequent religious history. By Mack's own account, within a short time their sayings collection was reworked so heavily that their own emphases were replaced with others, and Mack's Jesus followers and their concerns lay unknown until rediscovered by him and the few other recent scholars whose work he finds congenial.[102] If among the various early groups of Jesus followers there were some such as Mack describes, then in historical terms they would be an interesting curiosity but are not very important for understanding anything else. Indeed, the more aberrant Mack makes them, the less significant they become for historical purposes. If we use a biological analogy, they would represent unsuccessful life-forms or dysfunctional mutations, so peculiar as to be unrepresentative of the species, unable to sustain themselves without significant further transformation, and not very influential in shaping the forms that come after them. In terms of intellectual or technological analogies, Mack's Jesus followers would resemble the sort of unsuccessful concept or invention that was tried out but found to fail, or was surpassed in favor of more convincing or satisfying ideas, or more efficient or reliable inventions.

In a later chapter I will return to the question of what we can say about the earliest known groups and their views of Jesus. As I have already indicated, however, from Paul's letters, and other sources too, we know of a certain diversity, including some Christians whom Paul scathingly describes as "false brothers" who sought to oppose his Gentile mission (Gal. 2:4). In principle it is not impossible that this diversity may also have included the sort of Jesus followers that Mack writes of so enthusiastically. But given that Mack criticizes scholars who assume a single point of origin and a unilinear development of the Jesus/Christian movements, it is strange that he refers to his putative Q Gospel circles as the "first" and "earliest" followers of Jesus, as if all other kinds of Jesus movements came later in some kind of unilinear scheme. If there were such "Jesus people" (to use one of Mack's terms for them), they were one comparatively short-lived type among others that survived and adapted better. There is no particular reason to see them as having any priority in telling us what Jesus' other followers or opponents made of him.

So I reiterate my main point stated at the outset of this section. If we wish to account for why there is the focus on the specific figure of Jesus in the early

---

102. Had not Matthew and Luke "incorporated sizable portions" of Q, "the sayings gospel of the first followers of Jesus would have disappeared without a trace in the transitions taking place. We never would have known about the Jesus movements that flourished prior to the Christian church." Mack, *The Lost Gospel*, 3.

Christian sources, the best way forward is to note that the immediate and dominant outcome of Jesus' career was a sharply divided set of views about him, with some so negative as to justify his crucifixion and some so positive as to form the basis of one or more new religious movements of dedicated followers. In the earliest stages to which we have any access and onward, the devotional life of the followers of Jesus was marked by a high importance given to him. The specific nature of that importance, the claims that they made about him, arose from several factors, and in my view cannot be attributed solely to Jesus' teaching and activities. But the most likely explanation of why the question of Jesus' legitimacy and authority featured so prominently in early Christian circles is this polarization of views about Jesus that we have looked at here, a polarization over Jesus that is evident already during his own ministry and that remained (and probably escalated) as a result of his execution. This polarizing effect or outcome of Jesus' ministry is thus a second force/factor to include in an adequate theory of the origin and formation of Christ-devotion. I proceed now to the second question mentioned at the beginning of this section: Why did Christ-devotion assume the proportions it did in early Christianity, i.e., amounting to a new binitarian devotional pattern unprecedented in Jewish monotheism?

Religious Experience

Earlier in this chapter I proposed that Christ-devotion quickly amounted to what may be regarded as an unparalleled innovation, a "mutation" or new variant form of exclusivist monotheism in which a second figure (Jesus) was programmatically included with God in the devotional pattern of Christian groups. Outside the Jewish-Christian circles in which this binitarian pattern arose, the characteristic force of exclusivist monotheism seems to have prevented any other figure being treated as rightful recipient of cultic devotion, just as this monotheistic constraint served in early Christian circles to work against any additional figures other than God and Jesus being accorded such reverence. So, how should we account for such a novel development? The outcome of Jesus' career was a deeply polarizing force that accounts for the thematizing of him and his general prominence among his followers. But this particularizing focus on Jesus would hardly be expected to amount to the binitarian devotional pattern we see so quickly in evidence. Something more is required, something sufficient to have generated such a significant and apparently novel development, especially given the concerns about God's uniqueness and the apparent lack of precedent for this development in Roman-era Jewish tradition.

I propose that the most plausible factor for this is the effect of powerful

religious experiences in early Christian circles, experiences that struck the recipients (and other participants in these circles as well) as having revelatory validity and force sufficient to demand such a significant reconfiguring of monotheistic practice. It is not necessary for my theory, however, that we grant the
religious *validity* of these (or any other) experiences. All that is necessary is for
us to recognize two things: (1) the demonstrable *efficacy* of such experiences in
generating significant innovations in various religious traditions, and (2) the
likelihood that this efficacy is to be granted in the case of early Christianity as
well. As I have sought to provide a persuasive case for these matters elsewhere, I
shall restrict myself here to a summary presentation.[103]

For various reasons the religious experiences described in the early Christian sources have not always been done justice in scholarly studies. From its in-
ception, scholarly study of the New Testament has mainly had theological concerns, mining the New Testament for what it has to say that would inform,
support, or challenge Christian beliefs. This is the case, whether the scholars in
question were sympathetic or antithetic to conventional Christian beliefs. Naturally, therefore, the scholarly traditions, the issues, the apparatus of scholarship, the questions and approaches were all focused heavily on the religious
thought of the New Testament and other early Christian texts, and comparatively less attention was given to the nature and importance of the religious *experiences* attested. Those scholars who were more positively disposed to Christian faith were also inclined to focus on doctrines; those more negatively/
critically disposed were usually uncomfortable with the whole idea of religious
experience.

Gunkel's classic work on the Spirit in Paul is commonly regarded today as
a watershed publication, and in the decades after its appearance numerous other
studies focused on early Christian religious experience.[104] In more recent years a
few other scholars have made useful contributions, among which Dunn's study,
Jesus and the Spirit, is particularly worth noting.[105] Nevertheless, scholars still

---

103. L. W. Hurtado, "Religious Experience and Religious Innovation in the New Testament," *JR* 80 (2000): 183-205.

104. Hermann Gunkel, *Die Wirkungen des heiligen Geistes nach der populären Anschauung
der apostolischen Zeit und der Lehre des Apostels Paulus* (Göttingen: Vandenhoeck & Ruprecht,
1888). The continuing significance of this study is reflected in its translation into English in 1979
(*The Influence of the Holy Spirit: The Popular View of the Apostolic Age and the Teaching of the
Apostle Paul,* trans. R. A. Harrisville and P. A. Quanbeck [Philadelphia: Fortress]). Subsequent
scholars who have contributed to the topic include Adolf Deissmann, P. Gardner, H. B. Swete,
and H. W. Robinson from the early part of the twentieth century (publications cited in Hurtado,
"Religious Experience and Religious Innovation in the New Testament").

105. J. D. G. Dunn, *Jesus and the Spirit: A Study of the Religious and Charismatic Experience of Jesus and the First Christians as Reflected in the New Testament* (London: SCM Press; Phil-

tend to ignore or give little importance to religious experiences in describing and understanding early Christianity. The more conventional historical investigations have tended to focus on questions about the origins of the written sources, the beliefs and events reflected in them, and the circumstances that evoked the writings. Even in more recent studies of the social and cultural characteristics of early churches there is a tendency to focus on other aspects and questions, such as the economic levels of early Christians, the roles exercised by women, or the organizational structures, or rituals.[106] Luke Johnson has complained about this neglect in a very recent book, in which he advocates a phenomenological approach involving comparisons with religious experiences of other times and places to develop a sense of how they likely functioned.[107]

Beyond an adequate appreciation of the general importance of religious experiences in early Christian circles, however, I contend that we need to allow specifically for the *causative* significance of revelatory experiences in the religious innovations that took place in these circles. That is, I hold that an adequate historical understanding of early Christianity requires us to give significant attention to the religious experiences that obviously formed such a major part of the early Christian ethos. Having made this point in previous publications, I know also that some scholars are reluctant to grant it.[108] It is worth noting, therefore, that I am not alone in my view.

Dunn, for example, has warned about "discounting the *creative force of religious experience*" (emphasis his), citing Paul as an important case study. Granting that Paul drew upon his Jewish and Greek backgrounds for much of his language and concepts, Dunn insisted that we also have to grant "the creative power of his own religious experience — a furnace which melted many concepts in its fires and poured them forth into new moulds. . . . Nothing should be allowed to obscure that fact."[109] Philip Almond acknowledged the

---

adelphia: Westminster, 1975). Note also G. D. Fee, *God's Empowering Presence: The Holy Spirit in the Letters of Paul* (Peabody, Mass.: Hendrickson, 1994).

106. For example, the justly praised study by W. A. Meeks, *The First Urban Christians: The Social World of the Apostle Paul* (New Haven: Yale University Press, 1983), has no significant treatment of the religious experiences that characterized early Christian groups. See also the survey of scholarship by Bengt Holmberg, *Sociology and the New Testament: An Appraisal* (Minneapolis: Fortress, 1990).

107. Luke T. Johnson, *Religious Experience in Earliest Christianity: A Missing Dimension in New Testament Studies* (Minneapolis: Fortress, 1998).

108. Hurtado, *One God, One Lord,* esp. 117-22, and my interaction with critics of this view in "Christ-Devotion in the First Two Centuries: Reflections and a Proposal," *TJT* 12, no. 1 (1996): 17-33, esp. 25-26. See also my essay "Religious Experience and Religious Innovation in the New Testament."

109. Dunn, *Jesus and the Spirit,* 3-4, quote on 4. We might also note Hermann Gunkel's

connection between the nature of one's religious experience and "the context that informs it," but he also emphasized that in our analysis of religious developments we must allow for "those experiences which go beyond or are at odds with the received context."[110] He pointed specifically to powerful religious experiences that "may lead to the creative transformation of a religious tradition" and that are "capable of generating new interpretations of the tradition."[111] Similar points have been made by Carl Raschke, who described revelation experiences as involving "the transposition of certain meaning systems," that is, the reformulation or reconfiguring of religious convictions.[112]

Among social scientists, though the tendency has been to regard religious experiences as derivative phenomena, the (dysfunctional) outcomes of stressful social circumstances and the manifestation of psychopathology, there are scholars who question this approach.[113] Characteristically, social science approaches assume one or another form of "deprivation theory," whether the deprivation be regarded as social and cultural conditions or individual (psychological) conditions of stress, sexual frustration, etc. Thus religious experiences are taken as "false consciousness," and dysfunctional responses to life. Powerful, "revelatory" experiences are taken quite often as "hallucinatory" and delusional, and therefore of not much significance in themselves.[114] But some scholars have questioned this rather negative view of religious experiences and have offered resources for

---

comments against attempts of his day to make Paul's religious thought simply a borrowing from other sources: "The theology of the great apostle is the expression of his experience, not of his reading" (*Influence*, 100).

110. Philip C. Almond, *Mystical Experience and Religious Doctrine: An Investigation of the Study of Mysticism in World Religions* (Berlin: Mouton, 1982), 166-67.

111. Almond, 168.

112. Carl Raschke, "Revelation and Conversion: A Semantic Appraisal," *ATR* 60 (1978): 420-36, quote from 424.

113. The social science literature on religious experience is too vast to attempt more here than a citation of a few illustrative and heuristically useful studies. The pioneering classic was of course William James, *The Varieties of Religious Experience* (New York: Mentor Books, 1962 [1902]). Among more recent work, see, e.g., W. H. Clark, H. N. Malony, J. Daane, and A. R. Tippett, *Religious Experience: Its Nature and Function in the Human Psyche* (Springfield, Ill.: C. C. Thomas, 1973); Rodney Stark, "A Taxonomy of Religious Experience," *JSSR* 5 (1965): 97-116. For a critique of the negative view of religion and religious experiences often found in social-scientific circles, see Rodney Stark, "Normal Revelations: A Rational Model of 'Mystical' Experiences," in *Religion and the Social Order*, vol. 1, *New Developments in Theory and Research*, ed. David G. Bromley (Greenwich, Conn.: JAI Press, 1991), 239-51.

114. The classic statement of "relative deprivation theory" is by David Aberle, "A Note on Relative Deprivation Theory as Applied to Millenarian and Other Cult Movements," in *Reader in Comparative Religion: An Anthropological Approach*, ed. W. A. Lessa and E. A. Vogt, 3rd ed. (New York: Harper and Row, 1972), 527-31.

understanding that some such experiences seem to serve as the occasion for the emergence of sometimes significant innovations in religious traditions. That is, such powerful religious experiences can themselves contribute significantly, sometimes crucially, to religious innovations, and are not limited to serving merely as "legitimizing devices" for previously formed beliefs and practices.

In a now classic essay, in which he offered a model of the processes involved in the emergence of major religious innovations such as new sects, Anthony Wallace referred to "mazeway reformulation," involving the restructuring of elements such as religious beliefs, which in the history of religions often happens in the mind of a prophet figure abruptly and dramatically as "a moment of insight." He also noted that "the religious vision experience per se is not psychopathological but rather the reverse, being a synthesizing and often therapeutic process."[115]

More recently, Rodney Stark also has recognized the capacity of "revelational" religious experiences to "contradict and challenge prevailing theological 'truths.'"[116] He also noted the efficacy of such experiences to produce in the recipient a sense of personal divine commission, and to generate messages taken as directed to a wide public, "such as in the case of new theologies, eschatological prophecies, or commissions to launch social reforms."[117] In another study Stark focused specifically on religious experiences of "revelation," positing as "the most fundamental question confronting the social scientific study of religion: How does new religious culture arise?"[118] Stark expressed dissatisfaction with his own earlier attempts to account for the emergence of new religious movements, because he had not allowed for "normal people" (by which Stark meant mentally healthy people) to have "revelations sufficiently profound to serve as the basis of new religions."[119] Noting that reports of this kind of revelatory experience are comparatively infrequent in comparison to lower-intensity religious experiences, Stark proposed that "unusually creative individuals" might have such "profound revelations" and attribute them to divine action, though he also granted the possibility that revelations actually occur and that

---

115. A. F. C. Wallace, "Revitalization Movements," *American Anthropologist* 58 (1956): 264-81, these citations from 270.

116. Stark, "Taxonomy of Religious Experience," 108.

117. Stark, "Taxonomy of Religious Experience," 110-11.

118. Stark, "Normal Revelations," 239.

119. Stark, "Normal Revelations," 240-41. Cf. W. W. Meissner, *The Cultic Origins of Christianity: The Dynamics of Religious Development* (Collegeville, Minn.: Liturgical Press, 2000), whose attempt to portray the emergence of religious innovation and innovators in psychological categories is beset with his use of terms such as "paranoid," and his heavy dependence upon analyses of leaders such as Hitler.

there is "an active supernatural realm closed to scientific exploration."[120] Stark was obviously trying to develop a theoretical model that allowed for the efficacy of such experiences and did not require a prior acceptance of a divine agency behind them.

The important points for my purposes are (1) that Stark defends the idea that certain powerful religious experiences themselves can produce significant innovations in religious traditions, and (2) that such experiences, though shaped by social and cultural contexts, are not merely confirmations of religious ideas otherwise generated and are also not necessarily merely manifestations of psychopathology. Moreover, I agree with Stark that revelatory experiences are more likely to happen to "persons of deep religious concerns who perceive shortcomings in the conventional faith(s)," that persons are more likely to perceive shortcomings in conventional faith(s) during times of increased social crisis, that during such periods there is a greater likelihood of people being willing to accept claims of revelations, and that it is crucial to the success of the revelation that some others accept it as such.[121]

So, just as it is a mistake to dismiss all claims of revelatory experiences as psychopathology, it is also a mistake to ignore such experiences in accounting for religious innovations. This is recognized by scholars working on religious innovations in other cultures as well, such as Mark Mullins, Byron Earhart, and others.[122] As Earhart noted, "The innovative decision of the founder cannot be completely subsumed by either social factors or the influence of prior religious factors,"[123] and in a good many cases the "innovative decision" of founder and reformer figures is attributed by them to experiences of revelation.

In most cases we are dealing with innovations within a religious tradition. Werner Stark referred to the "minor founder" figure as "a charismatic individual who gives birth to a new religious movement" in an attempt to address religious needs felt by members of an established tradition, "while at the same time conceptualising the movement as an extension, elaboration, or fulfilment

120. Stark, "Normal Revelations," 243-44, 241.

121. Stark, "Normal Revelations," 244-46.

122. Mark R. Mullins, "Christianity as a New Religion: Charisma, Minor Founders, and Indigenous Movements," in *Religion and Society in Modern Japan*, ed. Mark R. Mullins, Shimazono Susumu, and Paul Swanson (Berkeley: Asian Humanities Press, 1993), 257-72; H. Byron Earhart, *Gedatsu-kai and Religion in Contemporary Japan: Returning to the Center* (Bloomington and Indianapolis: Indiana University Press, 1989); Earhart, "Toward a Theory of the Formation of the Japanese New Religions: A Case Study of Gedatsu-Kai," *HR* 20 (1981): 175-97; and Marilyn Robinson Waldman and Robert M. Baum, "Innovation as Renovation: The 'Prophet' as an Agent of Change," in *Innovation in Religious Traditions*, ed. M. A. Williams, C. Cox, and M. S. Jaffee (Berlin and New York: Mouton de Gruyter, 1992), 241-84.

123. Earhart, *Gedatsu-kai,* 236.

of an existing religious tradition."[124] Of course, characteristically those who have sought reformations or innovations within their own religious traditions, and could thus be thought of as "minor founder" figures, can be rejected by the parent tradition, which can result in new religious traditions forming out of efforts at reformation or innovation. This is likely the best way to understand what happened in early Christianity.

To summarize matters to this point, I contend that it is either ideological bias or insufficiently examined assumptions that prevent some scholars from taking seriously the view that revelatory religious experiences can directly contribute to religious innovations. I have pointed here to religious scholars and social scientists who support my contention, based on their study of historical examples and more recent and contemporary religious developments. In light of this I submit that in developing a theory to account for the religious innovation constituted by early Christ-devotion, it is thoroughly reasonable in principle to posit a significant causative role to revelatory religious experiences. Moreover, in the case of early Christianity, such a view is supported by the evidence.

Revelatory Experiences in the New Testament

In later chapters where we look in detail at the Jesus-devotion reflected in various early Christian sources, I shall more extensively analyze evidence that shows the effects of religious experiences. At this point I hope it will be sufficient to give initial indication that we have a basis in the relevant sources for making revelatory experiences of early Christians one important factor in my theory of the forces that drove and shaped the innovation constituted in Jesus-devotion.[125]

In what follows, my focus is on the effects of revelatory experiences in early Christian circles after Jesus' crucifixion. Some readers might well agree that Jesus may have had such experiences, that they may have had a significant role in shaping his own sense of himself and his mission, and that in a certain sense Jesus could be thought of as a "founder figure" whose own revelatory experiences helped to generate a significant religious innovation. In my view this is a perfectly reasonable line of inquiry and argumentation, and I could also

---

124. Werner Stark, *The Sociology of Religion: A Study of Christendom*, vol. 4 (New York: Fordham University Press, 1970), 265. Anthony Blasi has used this "minor founder" category to describe the apostle Paul in *Making Charisma: The Social Construction of Paul's Public Image* (New Brunswick, N.J.: Transaction Books, 1991), esp. 14-15.

125. Also in the essay referred to earlier (Hurtado, "Religious Experience and Religious Innovation in the New Testament"), I have more fully discussed evidence indicating a significant role of revelatory religious experience in the New Testament.

point to scholarly studies that support various versions of such a proposal.[126] But there are two reasons for not taking up this question here. First, there is a practical one. It would require a great deal more space here, in an already large book, to deal with this question adequately and with a chance of persuading anybody of what I might have to say. Second, the early Christian sources all indicate that "after Jesus' execution there was a significant reformulation of the faith of his followers and a new and powerful sense of revelation," these things connected to religious experiences that were perceived by recipients to have a new quality and frequency in their lives. So in this study I shall focus on the religious experiences that are attributed to early circles of Christians subsequent to Jesus' ministry and its traumatic outcome.

In 1 Corinthians 15:1-11, in a letter written scarcely twenty years into the Christian movement, the apostle Paul recites as a "sacred tradition" the claims that Jesus died redemptively for sins and that he was "raised on the third day in accordance with the scriptures" (v. 4). There follows a series of resurrection appearances to various figures, and it is commonly recognized that these are listed here as the basis for the traditional conviction that Jesus was resurrected. There is no reference to an empty tomb, but it would exceed the warrants of the passage to say that Paul knew of no tradition about the tomb. Whether he did or did not know of such reports, however, it is clear that in the tradition that he learned and circulated among his churches the resurrection appearances were the crucial bases for the faith that God had raised Jesus from death. Moreover, the reports of such experiences are attributed to figures who take us back to the earliest known circles of the Christian movement (e.g., Cephas, James, the Twelve, all of whom are well-known figures connected with the Jerusalem church).

These appearances must have been such as to contribute significantly to the specific convictions drawn from them.[127] The earliest indications are that

---

126. In my view the most useful study is Dunn, *Jesus and the Spirit*, esp. 11-92. From another standpoint, there is also Stevan L. Davies, *Jesus the Healer: Possession, Trance, and the Origins of Christianity* (New York: Continuum, 1995). From another perspective still, there is Margaret Barker, *The Risen Lord: The Jesus of History as the Christ of Faith* (Edinburgh: T. & T. Clark; Valley Forge, Pa.: Trinity Press International, 1996).

127. The term "appearances" here, and the term "visions" which I use later in this discussion, refer to visual experiences which the recipients described as specially given to them by God and, as such, distinguishable from everyday and public visual experiences understood as resulting from encounter with objects and events that are freely visible to anyone on site at the time. To refer to these experiences of early Christians as "hallucinations" would indicate a negative philosophical/theological judgment about them, for which a specific defense would be required, just as much as would be expected for an acceptance of their claim to have been special acts of God. As indicated already, my focus here is on the historical effects/efficacy of such experiences in earliest Christianity, and I leave the philosophical/theological question for another occasion.

these convictions were the following: (1) that God had released Jesus from death, so that it really is Jesus, not merely his memory or influence, who lives again; (2) that God has bestowed on Jesus uniquely a glorious new form of existence, immortal and eschatological bodily life; (3) that Jesus has also been exalted to a unique heavenly status, thus presiding by God's appointment over the redemptive program; and (4) that those who were given these special encounters with the risen Jesus were divinely commissioned to proclaim Jesus' exalted status and to summon people to recognize in his resurrection/exaltation the signal that the eschatological moment of redemption has arrived. The experiences, therefore, likely involved an encounter with a figure recognized as Jesus but also exhibiting features that convinced the recipients that he had been clothed with divinelike glory and given a unique heavenly status.

These convictions constituted an innovation in religious belief in the historical setting in which they first were expressed. The earliest traditions attribute the innovation to powerful experiences taken by the recipients as appearances of the risen Christ. We have no historical basis for attributing the innovative convictions to some other source, and we have surveyed scholarly bases for accepting that such experiences can generate novel religious convictions. Whether one chooses to consider these particular experiences as hallucinatory, projections of mental processes of the recipients, or the acts of God, there is every reason to see them as the ignition points for the christological convictions linked to them.

I reiterate the observation that, in terms of the religious scruples of the ancient Jewish tradition, the most striking innovation in earliest Christian circles was to include Christ with God as recipient of cultic devotion. What could have prompted such a major innovation in the devotional scruples and practices that were inherited from the Jewish tradition? What might have moved Christian Jews to feel free to offer to Christ this unparalleled cultic devotion? In light of the characteristic reluctance of devout Jews to accord cultic reverence to any figure other than God, it seems likely that those very early circles who took the step of according Christ such reverence would have done so only if they felt *compelled by God.* That is, in these groups there must have been some who experienced what they took to be revelations sent by God that convinced them that obedience to God demanded of them this cultic reverence of Christ. We shall have to test this proposal in following chapters. My purpose here has been merely to give sufficient reason to take it seriously.

The experiential forms that such "revelations" may have taken were likely several, based on references in early Christian sources.

1. I have already referred to visions, especially visions of the resurrected/exalted Christ. Based on other traditions about such experiences (e.g., 2 Cor. 12:1-4;

Acts 7:54-56; Rev. 5:1-14), they seem to have included visions of (and/or ascents to) God's heaven, in which the glorified Christ was seen in an exalted position, and perhaps receiving heavenly cultus with God. It would appear that corporate worship was a frequent setting for such visions and "revelations" and other experiences understood as prompted by the Holy Spirit (e.g., 1 Cor. 14:26).

2. It is highly likely that inspired/spontaneous utterances in the form of prophetic oracles and also inspired songs were another important medium for religious innovation. Inspired songs were perhaps particularly important for the emergence of christological insights and claims, as Martin Hengel has argued.[128] Based on what appear to most scholars to be remnants of earliest Christian hymns in the New Testament (e.g., Phil. 2:6-11), they were heavily concerned with celebrating and lauding Christ.[129] These were not the products of trained poets but arose out of the religious exaltation of Christians, were likely taken as having the force of prophetic oracles, and again seem to have been particularly associated with the worship setting (1 Cor. 14:26; Col. 3:16).

3. What might be termed "charismatic exegesis" of biblical (Old Testament) texts was still another important medium for new insights.[130] The New Testament preserves the results of these experiences in the sometimes astonishing appropriation of biblical passages to express Christ-devotion.[131] For example, the utterly remarkable allusion to Isaiah 45:23 in Philippians 2:10-11 involves finding a reference to Christ as *Kyrios* as well as God in what is perhaps the most stridently monotheistic passage in the Old Testament![132] The christo-

---

128. Martin Hengel, *Studies in Early Christology* (Edinburgh: T. & T. Clark, 1995), 227-91.

129. Reinhard Deichgräber, *Gotteshymnus und Christushymnus in der frühen Christenheit: Untersuchungen zu Form, Sprache und Stil der frühchristlichen Hymnen*, SUNT 5 (Göttingen: Vandenhoeck & Ruprecht, 1967).

130. David E. Aune, "Charismatic Exegesis in Early Judaism and Early Christianity," in *The Pseudepigrapha and Early Biblical Interpretation*, ed. James H. Charlesworth and Craig A. Evans, JSPSup 14 (Sheffield: Sheffield Academic Press, 1993), 126-50; Aune, *Prophecy in Early Christianity and the Ancient Mediterranean World* (Grand Rapids: Eerdmans, 1983), 339-46. In the latter discussion, Aune rightly observes that "charismatic" exegesis was "indeed widely practiced" (345), and that "the phenomenon of prophecy (direct revelation) was an integral part of early Christian religious experience" (345-46). But, curiously in my view, he assumes that because early Christians believed that "divine revelation was directly available through inspired persons, charismatic exegesis did not and probably could not occupy the central place that it did in the Qumran community" (346). The inference simply does not follow, and it does not take adequate account of what can be observed down the centuries in "charismatic" movements in Christian, Jewish, and Muslim traditions, that prophetic inspiration and revealed insights often focus on scriptural texts.

131. See, e.g., David Capes, *Old Testament Yahweh Texts in Paul's Christology*, WUNT 2/47 (Tübingen: J. C. B. Mohr [Paul Siebeck], 1992).

132. On the allusion to/use of Isa. 45:23 here, see esp. Takeshi Nagata, "Philippians 2:5-11:

logical interpretation of Isaiah 6:1 in John 12:41 is another striking case. References in the New Testament to experiences of inspired insights into biblical texts (e.g., 2 Cor. 3:12-16; Luke 24:27, 31-32, 44-47), and comparative phenomena in the history of religions, should make us seriously consider experiences of inspired interpretations of biblical texts as key occasions for christological developments. These experiences were likely in the context of group worship, which included prayer for and expectations of divine revelations, and other phenomena that raised questions that drove devout believers to their Scriptures searching for new insights and answers.

So, if we seek a factor to account for the striking innovation constituted by the incorporation of Christ into a binitarian devotional pattern, that is, if we seek an answer to the question of why Christ-devotion assumed the proportions it did and so quickly, I propose that we have to allow for the generative role of revelatory religious experiences. This is the third factor in the theory that I offer. I turn now to the final factor.

The Religious Environment

The fourth force or factor in my theory is the effects upon early Christ-devotion of encounters with the Roman-era religious environment. This includes, of course, both Jewish and pagan components, and in part I have already addressed this in the discussion above about monotheism. Second Temple Judaism was certainly the central component in the religious environment of the earliest Christian circles, and the monotheistic concern was a central feature of Judaism. If we accord Jewish monotheism a major role in shaping Christ-devotion in early Christian circles, this surely demonstrates the influence of the religious environment.

To mention the influence of the religious environment of earliest Christianity will seem so obvious to most scholars as to be a rather banal matter. Assuming that it requires little argument to invoke the religious environment as a significant factor, I shall not take up a great deal of space here in defense of my doing so. At least since the classic study by Edwin Hatch, scholars have taken seriously various influences of the Greek background and Roman religious setting of early Christianity.[133] How could there be any group or individuals not

A Case Study in the Contextual Shaping of Early Christology" (Ph.D. diss., Princeton Theological Seminary, 1981), 279-337.

133. Edwin Hatch, *The Influence of Greek Ideas and Usages upon the Christian Church: The Hibbert Lectures, 1888*, ed. A. M. Fairbairn (London: Williams and Norgate, 1907).

shaped in various ways by the cultural setting in which they live? How could any group such as the early Christian circles, concerned to communicate with and recruit from their contemporaries, not deliberately seek to make their efforts meaningful in terms appropriate to the setting? So, of course, in these senses at least, early Christians were shaped, and shaped themselves, by influences of their environment. To refer to Jesus as *Christos* (Messiah) reflects a claim directed to Jewish hopes of the time for God's messianic mercy. Virtually all the christological rhetoric of early Christians was appropriated from their environment, although in a great many cases the meanings were significantly altered.[134]

Likewise, although attempts to make early Christian rituals entirely derivative from pagan practices have been shown to be simplistic, there are undeniable historical connections. For example, early Christian baptism was adapted from Jewish phenomena such as the repentance rite advocated by John the Baptizer; and in a religious environment where sacred meals were a common feature, it is not surprising that early Christians, too, made a sacred common meal a central feature of their practice. To cite another matter, in a subsequent chapter on the books about Jesus written in early Christianity, I shall discuss the question of whether the canonical Gospels were influenced by and can be likened to biographical literature of the Roman era.

In addition, however, there are other ways the early Christian encounters with and existence in the Roman-era religious environment were influential. I mention here two things in particular. First, it is clear that in their efforts to commend their religious views and practices, the early Christians sought to differentiate their message from others of the time. That is, they took account of their religious environment much more consciously and critically than they would have had they seen their message and devotional pattern as simply one of many acceptable versions of religiosity of their cultural setting. This means that the Roman-era religious environment was influential, but not only, perhaps not primarily, in terms of the simple or direct appropriation of ideas and practices. In their efforts to articulate and justify their distinctives in message and practice in the Roman-era religious setting, and in their reactions against features of the religious environment, their religious rhetoric and religious practices were also shaped. For example, I contend that the rising frequency in the christological use of divine sonship language that we see in the Christian writings of the late first century and thereafter may very well reflect a reaction against the contemporaneous in-

---

134. See the programmatic essay by N. A. Dahl, "Sources of Christological Language," in his *Jesus the Christ*, 113-36.

crease in the use of the same rhetoric in the emperor cult under the Flavians and thereafter.[135]

Second, it is also clear that the early Christian movement suffered opposition and criticism, initially from other sectors of the Jewish matrix and then in the pagan religious and political arenas as well. The Jewish opposition and critique came immediately, at least from the Jerusalem authorities who colluded with Pilate in bringing Jesus up on the charges that led to his execution. In fact, of course, the execution of Jesus itself meant that opposition to any positive thematizing of him was there even before what is usually regarded as the birth of the Christian movement! As already argued earlier in the section entitled "Jesus," this condemnation of Jesus would have put tremendous pressure on his followers either to capitulate or to reinforce and defend any positive claims about him.[136]

In an earlier publication I gathered evidence of continuing Jewish opposition to Christ-devotion particularly in the first century, supplementing the study by Claudia Setzer, which surveys more broadly the period down to circa 150 C.E.[137] Paul's preconversion opposition to Jewish Christians was of course a very early and, by his own testimony, very vigorous example (e.g., Gal. 1:13).[138] This Jewish opposition obviously involved polemics against Jesus and any attempt to make him religiously significant by his followers. It is likely that at least some Jews regarded Jesus as deserving, or under, a divine curse for his false teaching.[139] That is, the opposition to the early Jesus movement was heavily concerned with denial and refutation of its message, practices, and claims for Jesus.

This being so, such Jewish opposition and critique must be seen, together with the early Christian interaction with the pagan religious scene, as constituting another major force driving and shaping early Christ-devotion. The dynamics involved in such polemical encounters have been characterized classically by Berger and Luckmann as the maintenance of a "symbolic universe" by a

---

135. I have proposed this in an earlier publication: "Christ-Devotion in the First Two Centuries," 24-25, with citations of other relevant literature in nn. 34-35 on pp. 31-32. See also my analysis of divine sonship language in Paul: "Son of God," in *DPL*, 900-906.

136. This is one of several reasons why recent claims that there were very early circles of Jesus' followers who took no interest in thematizing him or his execution are implausible and require considerably more supporting evidence than has thus far been furnished.

137. Hurtado, "Pre–70 C.E. Jewish Opposition to Christ-Devotion"; Claudia Setzer, *Jewish Responses to Early Christians: History and Polemics, 30-150 C.E.* (Minneapolis: Fortress, 1994); and see also G. N. Stanton, "Aspects of Early Christian-Jewish Polemic and Apologetics," *NTS* 31 (1985): 377-92.

138. Hurtado, "Pre–70 C.E. Jewish Opposition," 50-54.

139. E.g., Hurtado, "Pre–70 C.E. Jewish Opposition," 56-57.

group over against challenges from other groups or from dissidents ("heretics") within the group. They note that the need to defend a religious or political view against opposition can in fact contribute significantly to the further conceptualization of the view by its defenders/advocates.[140] Here again, my proposal about a significant force/factor in the origin and development of Christ-devotion has support in social scientific studies.

I cite an example of these dynamics from the New Testament. It is widely accepted that Paul's assertions of Jesus' superiority over Torah were, in a significant measure, in opposition to those Christian Jews who either demanded circumcision and Torah observance of Gentile converts (e.g., the "false brethren" of Gal. 2:4-5) or in Paul's eyes behaved in such a way as to give implicit support for such demands (e.g., the behavior of Cephas and Barnabas as described in Gal. 2:11-14). That is, Paul's conceptualizing and verbal expressions of Christ's significance were in this case shaped in a polemical encounter with his religious environment, though in this example it was the immediate Christian sector of that environment. To cite another instance, it is also likely that Paul's treatment of Christ as "becoming a curse for us" in Galatians 3:10-14 was shaped in reaction to Jewish charges that Jesus was accursed (charges which Paul himself had likely pressed upon Christian Jews in his own preconversion days of opposition to them).[141] Here again, Paul's conceptualization of Christ's significance probably reflects the effects of opposition from the religious environment of the earliest Christian circles.

Still other examples can be given, but I trust these will suffice for the present purpose, which is to contend that the (often adversarial) encounter with their religious environment was a major factor driving and shaping the Christ-devotion of early Christian circles. As such, this factor must be included in an adequate theory.

Summary

In answer to the demand that a fully adequate historical analysis of early Christ-devotion should include a clearly formulated and explicitly stated theory of the forces/factors that drove and shaped it, I have laid out such a theory at some length in this chapter. Having discussed them individually, I simply re-

---

140. Peter L. Berger and Thomas Luckmann, *The Social Construction of Reality* (Garden City, N.Y.: Doubleday, 1966), esp. 99.

141. E.g., Dieter Sänger, "'Verflucht ist jeder, der am Holze hängt' (Gal. 3,13b): Zur Rezeption einer frühen antichristlichen Polemik," *ZNW* 85 (1994): 279-85.

state here the four major forces/factors that constitute this theory: (1) Jewish exclusivist monotheism, as the most important context and a powerful shaping force that accounts particularly for the characteristically "binitarian" nature of Christ-devotion; (2) the impact of Jesus, particularly the polarizing effects of his career, which at one extreme involved outright condemnation of him, this in turn contributing heavily to the very positive thematizing of him from the earliest known circles of the Jesus movement onward; (3) revelatory religious experiences, which communicated to circles of the Jesus movement the conviction that Jesus had been given heavenly glory and that it was God's will for him to be given extraordinary reverence in their devotional life; and (4) the encounter with the larger religious environment, particularly the dynamics of countering Jewish polemics and of differentiating and justifying Christian devotion over against the dominant pagan practice.

Although I have proposed something of the individual effects of these forces, I emphasize again that they are to be seen as having operated in a dynamic interaction in early Christian circles. Thus, for example, although the revelatory experiences appear to have prompted an extraordinarily exalted place for Jesus in the devotional life of very early Christians, the inherited commitment to monotheism, obvious in what became the characteristic forms of early Christianity, helped shape this devotion in what I have termed a "binitarian" direction rather than toward an apotheosis of Jesus as a new deity in his own right after the pagan pattern. The resulting devotional pattern was an unparalleled innovation, and in view of the clearly expressed monotheistic self-understanding of these early Christians, their inclusion of Christ as recipient of cultic devotion can be taken as constituting a new variant form of exclusivist monotheism.

With this explicit discussion of a theory intended to indicate my answer to the *how* and *why* questions, I turn now to a historical analysis of the Christ-devotion reflected in Christian evidence of the first two centuries.

CHAPTER TWO

Early Pauline Christianity

Where to Begin?

In any study of earliest Christ-devotion the letters of Paul certainly must loom large, for these invaluable writings reflect an intense religious devotion to Jesus at a remarkably early point in the emergence of the Christian movement. But some readers will perhaps wonder why I commence here with a chapter on Paul, and then turn to an analysis of early Jewish Christianity in Roman Judea (Palestine). In strict chronological order there were, of course, Christians before the apostle Paul, as we learn from Paul himself. In his letter to Rome, for example, Paul sends greetings to Andronicus and Junia, two members of the Roman church who were fellow Jews and who "were in Christ before me" (Rom. 16:7), and in his letter to the Galatians Paul refers to "those who were apostles before me" in the Jerusalem church (Gal. 1:17).[1] By all accounts the first groups in the emergent Christian movement were made up of Jewish adherents

---

1. The variant reading *Ioulian*, though attested early (P46), is now widely thought to be a later corruption of an original *Iounian*, who is often thought by commentators to be linked with Andronicus as sister or wife. Paul's reference to them as *syngeneis* could connote their being his relatives or members of the same nationality, as in Rom. 9:3 where Paul refers to the Jewish people as "my kindred according to the flesh" (see, e.g., MM, 595). There is also a variation among manuscripts in Rom. 16:15, where *Ioulian* is likely original and *Iounian* a later variant. Commentators offer various suggestions about how these two pre-Paul Christians came to be in the Roman church. Their names may indicate that they were diaspora Jews who came into contact with the Christian gospel during a pilgrimage to Jerusalem for one of the Jewish festivals (e.g., Passover); or conversely they could be Palestinian Jewish Christians who moved to Rome for some reason. All of the figures named by Paul in Rom. 16 are likely leaders and respected figures among Roman Christians. On Rom. 16 as an authentic part of Paul's letter to Rome, see esp. Harry Gamble, Jr., *The Textual History of the Letter to the Romans*, SD 42 (Grand Rapids: Eerdmans, 1977).

in Jerusalem and elsewhere in Roman Judea (Palestine). Once again, among the relevant evidence (indeed, the earliest evidence we have) are references by Paul to Christian groups in "Judea" as far back as his own conversion in the early 30s (Gal. 1:22-23; 1 Thess. 2:14).[2] It might at first seem more logical, therefore, to commence with an analysis of these "pre-Pauline" Jewish Christian groups. But there are several reasons for my choosing to commence with Paul.

A practical (and considerable) problem is that we have no undisputed source that stems directly from any of these very early circles of "pre-Pauline" Jewish Christians. For example, the New Testament writings that claim to be written by leading figures associated with the Jerusalem church (Peter, James, Jude) are all widely (but not universally) regarded by scholars as pseudonymous and written in the late first or early second century.[3] In some recent scholarship the sayings material thought to come from a collection commonly designated Q is proffered as reflecting circles of Jesus' followers in Palestine in the early decades of the first century. But Q survives only in the Gospels of Matthew and Luke, which are commonly dated approximately 75-90 C.E., and this sayings material thus went through a process of transmission and adaptation for several decades before being incorporated (and adapted further) by the authors of these two Gospels into their narratives of Jesus' ministry. Moreover, any claim about how to use the Q material to infer the features of the groups in which it was first collected and circulated requires an elaborate and highly hypothetical procedure (a matter to which I return in chap. 4). So I have chosen to start with a body of evidence whose provenance, contents, and historical usefulness are much more widely agreed upon.

2. "Judea" in the narrow sense was the area south of Samaria and north of the Negev, and associated with the tribe of Judah; but the Roman province of "Judea" at various points included virtually the whole of what came to be referred to as "Palestine" after Hadrian. Scholars differ over whether Paul used the term in the more narrow sense or in the wider sense of the Roman province. Cf. the variation in the reference of the term in Luke-Acts (Martin Hengel, "The Geography of Palestine in Acts," in *The Book of Acts in Its Palestinian Setting*, ed. Richard Bauckham [Grand Rapids: Eerdmans; Carlisle: Paternoster, 1995], 27-78, esp. 32-33). On the area and its Roman-era history, see M. Stern, "The Province of Judaea," in *The Jewish People in the First Century: Historical Geography, Political History, Social, Cultural, and Religious Life and Institutions*, ed. S. Safrai and M. Stern, CRINT 1/1 (Philadelphia: Fortress, 1974), 1:308-76.

3. To be sure, there are dissenting voices in support of the authenticity of 1 Peter (e.g., E. G. Selwyn, *The First Epistle of St. Peter* [London: Macmillan, 1964]) and the Epistle of Jude (R. J. Bauckham, *Jude, 2 Peter*, WBC [Waco, Tex.: Word, 1983]; Bauckham, *Jude and the Relatives of Jesus in the Early Church* [Edinburgh: T. & T. Clark, 1990]), and others who propose connections of the Epistle of James to the Jerusalem leader James the Just (e.g., P. H. Davids, *The Epistle of James*, NIGTC [Grand Rapids: Eerdmans, 1982]). I find some of the arguments impressive, but I choose to proceed here on the basis of views of the sources more commonly shared.

In the next chapter I shall offer my own description of what kind(s) of devotion to the figure of Jesus may have characterized Jewish Christian circles of the first two decades or so of the Christian movement. As that chapter, and any genuinely scholarly study of the matter, will show, relevant evidence has to be recovered out of Christian sources from later decades and other situations in the first century, prominent among which are Paul's letters and other New Testament writings such as the Gospels and Acts. Also, scholars disagree about what in these later sources may in fact reflect the beliefs and practices of Jewish Christian groups in Palestine and adjacent areas from the 30s, 40s, and 50s, and about the best critical procedures to follow in developing and checking hypotheses about these groups.

Another reason for starting with Paul is that the earliest extant Christian writings are his epistles, the undisputed ones commonly dated approximately 50-60 C.E. Pauline Christianity is thus the earliest sector of the Christian movement to which we have direct access through firsthand sources. Paul certainly had contacts with Jewish Christians and sought to maintain links and foster mutual acceptance between his (dominantly Gentile) churches and the Christian circles in Judea/Palestine, his efforts most tangibly demonstrated in the collection for Jerusalem from his churches, a project with which he concerned himself over several years.[4] One of the key questions, therefore, is how to identify and use specific material in Paul's letters that may have originated earlier from Jewish Christian groups, including Jewish Christian groups in Roman Judea.[5] A related question is how much the Christ-devotion generally reflected in Paul's letters also represents or is different from that of contemporary non-Pauline circles and of Christian groups of the two decades or so prior to when he probably wrote his extant epistles. How much was the Paul of the 50s distinctive, and how much does he reflect of wider and earlier circles of Christians? To deal with these questions adequately we must first take full account of the Christ-devotion attested in Paul's letters.

So, though one could commence by developing and defending a hypothe-

---

4. Paul refers to the collection effort several times, most extensively in 1 Cor. 16:1-4, 2 Cor. 8–9, Gal. 2:10, Rom. 15:25-33. See, e.g., Scot McKnight, "Collection for the Saints," in *DPL*, 143-47 (and bibliography).

5. The classic English-language study of this question, far too little known today, is A. M. Hunter, *Paul and His Predecessors,* rev. ed. (London: SCM Press; Philadelphia: Westminster, 1961). In the first edition of this work, in 1940, Hunter was right to claim himself "something of a pioneer" (116). In the appendix of the revised edition (116-50) he updates his 1940 discussion, and it is interesting to observe where his own mind changed on matters. He was right to observe that the work of the twenty years subsequent to his first edition "materially strengthened my original thesis" (117).

sis as to the faith and piety of "Palestinian" Jewish Christian circles, I have chosen instead to start our analysis with Paul. That is, we commence with a study of the indisputably earliest extant Christian sources (Paul's letters), and see what they tell us about the earliest Christ-devotion to which we have direct access, the devotion that is indeed already well developed and presupposed in the Pauline letters. We can then try to see what hints and glimpses we can obtain about what was going on in other kinds of Christian groups and what might have come earlier and/or alongside Paul. This procedure allows us to develop and test hypotheses about non- and pre-Pauline groups with information that we can date and place with greater confidence.

This contrasts with the sequence of the discussion in Bousset's *Kyrios Christos,* to cite an influential example. But I trust that any scholar who reads Bousset's first chapter, "The Palestinian Primitive Community," will readily see that its premises are all highly questionable, and will acknowledge also what I have written here about the unavoidably hypothetical character of any statement one might make today about Palestinian Jewish Christianity.[6]

My decision contrasts even more with the approach taken more recently by J. D. Crossan in his book *The Birth of Christianity,* and it may be useful to interact with Crossan on this matter.[7] Early on Crossan indicates that he intends to "bracket" out and programmatically omit Paul, and to focus on Christianity of the 30s and 40s.[8] It is, of course, a perfectly valid scholarly choice for Crossan to restrict the time frame of his discussion to these early decades, but there are at least two problems with omitting Paul from the story of this period.

First is the problem already mentioned of not having any direct source from Jewish Christian groups from these earliest decades on which to build a discussion. Crossan's book illustrates this problem vividly. He speaks of going back earlier than Paul, but in developing his views of Christian groups of the 30s and 40s he depends upon, and hypothesizes from and about, material from sources that are in fact much later than Paul. For example, Crossan draws upon the canonical Gospels (ca. 70-90 C.E.); other Gospels that are at least as late, and likely later *(Gospel of Peter, Gospel of Thomas);* and also the *Didache,* an interesting early Christian document that may have a complicated and lengthy tradition history but reached its present form sometime between 100 and 150. In fact, of the sources that may be relevant to the 30s and 40s, the earliest by far are Paul's letters. So, given that Paul's letters are the most proximate sources for

---

6. On problems in Bousset's classic work, see, e.g., Hurtado, "New Testament Christology: A Critique of Bousset's Influence," *TS* 40 (1979): 306-17.

7. John Dominic Crossan, *The Birth of Christianity* (New York: Harper Collins, 1998).

8. Crossan, *The Birth of Christianity,* xxvii, and also 15.

Christianity of the first decades, and given that he is the only named figure of that period from whom we have direct sources, does it really make sense to bracket him out and programmatically omit a proper discussion of him?

There is also a second, related problem in bracketing out Paul. The fact is that Paul was not simply a Christian figure of the 50s (the approximate years to which his extant letters happen to be dated); the Christian Paul takes us back much earlier. Crossan considers Paul part of the "growth" of Christianity, not its "birth." But Paul's conversion is most likely to be dated within a couple years (at most) of Jesus' execution, that is, within what in terms of social history must be regarded as the "birth" of the Christian movement.

In fact, of course, Paul's acquaintance with Palestinian Jewish Christians and their faith goes back even earlier than his participation in the Christian movement. Prior to his conversion, as a zealous Pharisee, he had become sufficiently acquainted with the beliefs and practices of Jewish Christians to determine that they were so dangerous as to justify his firm efforts to "destroy" the Christian groups and the ideas they promoted (as he testifies in Gal. 1:13-14; 1 Cor. 15:9; and Phil. 3:6).[9]

Furthermore, according to autobiographical statements in his letters, following his conversion Paul was active in Christian circles in Arabia, Damascus, and then "the regions of Syria and Cilicia"; and in the first few years he became personally acquainted with Cephas (Peter) and James the Just, leaders of the Jerusalem church (e.g., Gal. 1:13-24; 2 Cor. 11:32-33).[10] The Paul who wrote the letters that we date in the 50s had been for some time prior a very widely and well-connected participant in the Christian movement, acquainted with Jewish Christians of Judean/Palestinian provenance all through the 30s and 40s as well as with Gentile congregations of the 50s (the main period of his Gentile mission). We can put locations of Pauline activity on the map of the Roman world with confidence (e.g., Jerusalem, Damascus, Antioch, Thessalonica, Philippi, Corinth), and we have names of people involved with him (e.g., Barnabas, Timothy, Silvanus, Titus, and a rather impressive list of others that we could put together from Paul's letters).[11]

---

9. Martin Hengel, *The Pre-Christian Paul* (London: SCM Press; Philadelphia: Trinity Press International, 1991), esp. 63-86; Martin Hengel and Anna Maria Schwemer, *Paul between Damascus and Antioch: The Unknown Years* (Louisville: Westminster John Knox, 1997); Rainer Riesner, *Paul's Early Period: Chronology, Mission Strategy, Theology* (Grand Rapids: Eerdmans; Carlisle: Paternoster, 1998).

10. On Paul's rhetorical purposes in using autobiographical material, see George Lyons, *Pauline Autobiography: Toward a New Understanding*, SBLDS 73 (Atlanta: Scholars, 1985).

11. Thirty-five Christian men and women are named in Rom. 16 alone, and we are given quite interesting details for many of them. Such references permit a limited prosopographical

In other words, in any thorough discussion of Jewish Christians of these early decades, it is not only appropriate to take full account of Paul and the rich evidence in his letters, <u>it is a failure of method not to do so</u>. Among the Christians of these years, Paul is one of the few we know by name; and, I repeat for emphasis, he is the only one from whom we actually have writings of undisputed authenticity. Paul's persecution of Jewish Christians, his conversion and subsequent participation in Christian circles, and the full pattern of faith and piety that he professes to have shared with Jewish Christians from the beginning (e.g., 1 Cor. 15:11) are all key data for any adequate account of the Christian movement in the first two decades. In fact, as the best-known convert of the very first couple of years of the Christian movement, Paul is a top priority figure if we want to understand what kind of Christianity it was that provoked his opposition and then to which he converted.

Actually, in spite of Crossan's stated procedure of skipping over Paul to go back to the 30s and 40s, he does give a cursory treatment of Paul that is basically intended to justify bracketing him out from the rest of the book.[12] But the rationale proffered does not reflect sound historical reasoning. I mention a couple of matters by way of illustration.

As the first of his "four factors" for leaving Paul out, Crossan opines that Paul was not as important or influential in the first century as he became theologically in later centuries. But whatever the validity of Crossan's judgment here, the extent of Paul's personal influence upon the theology of first-century Christianity is an irrelevant issue. Paul is important for historical analysis of the earliest Christian decades mainly because of his personal participation in Christian circles in these early years, his acquaintance with Christian traditions from the earliest years of Christianity, and the reflections in his letters of the beliefs and practices of Christian circles of the 50s and previous decades.

The "most basic" reason offered by Crossan for excluding Paul is the notion that, unlike John the Baptist, Jesus, and James, Paul had been influenced by Platonic dualism.[13] Now in my judgment this is a dubiously adequate charac-

---

analysis such as done by Edwin Judge, "The Early Christians as a Scholastic Community," *JRH* 1 (1961): 4-15, 125-37. Note also Bengt Holmberg's discussion of Paul's coworkers in *Paul and Power* (Philadelphia: Fortress, 1978), 57-67, and Wayne Meeks's justly praised study of the social characteristics of Pauline churches, *The First Urban Christians: The Social World of the Apostle Paul* (New Haven: Yale University Press, 1983).

12. Crossan, *The Birth of Christianity*, xxi-xxvii.

13. Crossan, *The Birth of Christianity*, xxi. In a response to N. T. Wright's review article, Crossan ("Blessed Plot: A Reply to N. T. Wright's Review of *The Birth of Christianity*," *SJT* 53 [2000]: 92-112) admits that "Paul is representative of Pauline Christianity but he is also reflec-

terization of Paul.[14] But even if for the sake of argument we accept Crossan's claim that Paul reflects a "moderate Platonic dualism," this too is irrelevant as a reason for omitting him from a portrait of Jewish Christians of the first two decades of the Christian movement.[15] Paul is in fact crucial for understanding what was going on in Jewish Christian circles of these early years, for the reasons that I have already stated.

Crossan concludes these few pages on Paul with an aphorism: "Start with Paul and you will see Jesus incorrectly."[16] In the same spirit, I will give an aphorism in reply: Fail to take adequate account of Paul and you will describe "the birth of Christianity" incorrectly. In a scholarly study of earliest Christianity, even one restricted to the 30s and 40s, the choice not to take adequate account of Paul is a serious error for which there is simply no basis in historical method. Surely if we want to know what Christianity was like in the very earliest years, it is necessary to give careful attention to the most famous Christian convert of that same period.

I summarize my reasons for placing an analysis of Paul at this early point in my discussion of devotion to Jesus in earliest Christianity. (1) Pauline Christianity is the earliest form of the Christian movement to which we have direct access from undisputed firsthand sources. (2) Paul's letters, which are addressed to Christian circles already established and operative in the 50s, also incorporate and reflect emergent Christian traditions of belief and religious practice from still earlier years. (3) Paul's own associations with Christian circles, which include important Jewish Christian figures such as Peter, James the brother of Jesus, Barnabas, and others, go back to his conversion, which is to be dated approximately 32-34, and so his acquaintance with beliefs and practices of Christian circles is both wide and extremely early. (4) Several of Paul's letters reflect disagreements between him and other Christians, in particular some Jewish Christians with different views of the terms for full acceptance of Gentile converts, making Paul's writings our earliest and most unambiguous evidence that

---

tive of Jerusalem Christianity" (98), and denies that Paul's alleged Hellenism was the reason for bracketing out Paul (100), citing his statement (*The Birth of Christianity*, xxvii) that he did so merely "to concentrate on a Christianity that had to be born before [Paul] could notice its existence and persecute its presence." But the quoted phrasing comes at the end of an eight-page discussion of Paul's alleged "dualism and inconsistency," after which he writes, "In this book, *therefore* [emphasis mine], I bracket Paul. . . ."

14. Among the discussions of Paul's thought that I find more instructive and adequate is T. L. Donaldson, *Paul and the Gentiles: Remapping the Apostle's Convictional World* (Minneapolis: Fortress, 1997).

15. Crossan, *The Birth of Christianity*, xxv.

16. Crossan, *The Birth of Christianity*, xxvii.

there was a certain diversity of beliefs and groups in the earliest decades of Christianity, and also our best indication of the nature of this diversity and whatever commonality linked the groups. (5) The Christ-devotion attested in Paul's letters amounts to a notable development in the history of religions, especially when set in the context of the Jewish religious tradition and the larger Roman-era religious environment, and his letters exhibit this development as having already taken place at a remarkably early point in the young Christian movement. (6) Finally, the place of Christ in the Pauline letters also anticipates, represents, and likely helped to promote the christological beliefs and devotional practices that came to be widely characteristic in Christian groups after Paul.

Key Personal Factors

This chapter focuses mainly on what Paul's letters tell us of the beliefs and devotional practices of early Christian groups, both the churches he founded and other Christian circles. Although I will note some points where Paul's own beliefs and devotional life are evident, I am not primarily concerned here with emphasizing Paul's particular views or his own contribution to the theological beliefs of other and later Christians. This chapter does not offer a "theology/Christology of Paul"; instead it is mainly a study of Paul's letters as historical sources for Christ-devotion of the first few decades.[17] Nevertheless, before we look at what Paul's letters tell us specifically about the place of Jesus in the religious life and beliefs of early Christianity, it is well to take account of a few important factors that conditioned Paul and everything that we find in these texts.[18] Part of the historical value of Paul's epistles lies precisely in their reflecting the historical events that shaped both the author and his original readers in the various churches to which the letters were sent. Even though, with most scholars, I hold that Paul's letters embody a good deal of Christian tradition that was earlier than his letters and was shared by Christian groups wider than his own churches, the letters are best read with some account taken of the man who wrote them. I propose that for understanding and appreciating the Christ-

17. For a somewhat similar focus, see Peter Stuhlmacher, "Das Christusbild der Paulus-Schule — eine Skizze," in *Jews and Christians, the Parting of the Ways, A.D. 70 to 135*, ed. J. D. G. Dunn, WUNT 66 (Tübingen: Mohr-Siebeck, 1992), 159-75. I dissent, however, from Stuhlmacher's view that a central feature of Paul's Christian message was criticism of Torah (cf. 170-72).

18. I expand here points I make in another publication: "Paul's Christology," in *The Cambridge Companion to Paul*, ed. J. D. G. Dunn (Cambridge: Cambridge University Press, 2003).

devotion affirmed in his letters, it is necessary to reckon with three major personal factors in particular.

Paul's Jewishness

In chronological terms, and in terms of its pervasive relevance, the first factor to take very seriously is Paul's Jewish religious background and its continuing effect in his Christian beliefs and life. Of course, in the time of Paul the overwhelming majority of Christian adherents, and nearly all the earliest Christian leaders, were Jewish. But precisely because Paul is remembered mainly for his efforts to win believers among Gentiles, it is important to recognize that the formative religious tradition for him was Judaism of the Roman period.[19]

The profound continuing impact of his Jewish religious background is evident in the many ways that Paul's Christian beliefs and efforts carry forward features of Jewish religion. For several decades now important studies have shown that Paul continued to be deeply shaped by his Jewishness in such things as his conceptions, attitudes, and modes of thought.[20] It is clear that even in his role as apostle to the Gentiles Paul's motives and conceptions were heavily indebted to biblical and Jewish categories.[21] For example, he likened his apostolic appointment to a prophetic calling (Gal. 1:15, echoing Isa. 49:1), and he seems to have seen his mission to the Gentiles in terms of passages in Isaiah about the nations coming to worship the God of Israel (e.g., Rom. 15:21, quoting Isa. 52:15).

19. I do not consider Hyam Maccoby's claim (*The Mythmaker: Paul and the Invention of Christianity* [New York: Harper and Row, 1986]) that Paul was not a Jew but the Gentile "inventor" of Christianity and the father of anti-Semitism as justifying refutation here, for other scholars have adequately shown the faults in Maccoby's argument (e.g., J. Louis Martyn, *Theological Issues in the Letters of Paul* [Edinburgh: T. & T. Clark, 1997], 70-76).

20. From earlier influential studies such as W. D. Davies, *Paul and Rabbinic Judaism* (New York: Harper and Row, 1948), to more recent studies such as E. P. Sanders, *Paul and Palestinian Judaism* (Philadelphia: Fortress, 1977), the impact of Paul's Jewish religious background on his thought and activity as apostle has been abundantly demonstrated.

21. Among earlier studies, Johannes Munck's *Paul and the Salvation of Mankind* (London: SCM Press, 1959; German original, 1954) remains important. Among more recent studies, see, e.g., Karl-Wilhelm Niebuhr, *Heidenapostel aus Israel: Die jüdische Identität des Paulus nach ihrer Darstellung in seinen Briefen*, WUNT 62 (Tübingen: Mohr [Siebeck], 1992); Karl Olav Sandnes, *Paul — One of the Prophets?* WUNT 2/43 (Tübingen: Mohr [Siebeck], 1991); and now Donaldson, *Paul and the Gentiles:* "Paul conceives of himself as apostle not to an undifferentiated mass of humanity in general, but to the *Gentiles* in particular; such a self-conception betrays an underlying view of reality in which the distinction between Jew and non-Jew is fundamental" (182).

In his letters Paul continues to identify himself as a Jew (e.g., Rom. 9:1-5; Gal. 2:15) and to think of humanity as composed of Jews and Gentiles (e.g., Rom. 1:16; 9:24; 1 Cor. 1:22-25; 10:32), a recognizably Jewish view of the world. Perhaps the most gripping indication of Paul's continuing commitment to his Jewishness was his readiness to undergo repeated synagogue floggings, which could be given only to a Jew who submitted to the punishment, and which he describes as inflicted for unspecified charges arising from his apostolic activities (2 Cor. 11:24). Paul held together fiercely two things that most of Christianity subsequently came to regard as incompatible: (1) he affirmed the continuing ethnic identity of Jews and the continuing special significance of "Israel" (by which Paul always refers to a group made up of Jews); and (2) he affirmed the necessity for all peoples to obey the gospel and, through faith in Jesus, to receive God's eschatological salvation.[22]

On the one hand, Paul seems to have had no problem with fellow Jews, including particularly Jewish Christians, maintaining their particular identity, especially as manifested in observance of the Torah, so long as it was not used as a basis for rejecting Gentile Christians.[23] We have to remember always that Paul's delimitation of the significance of the Jewish law (e.g., in Gal. 3:1–5:15; Rom. 3:9–4:24) was entirely in defense of Gentile conversion on the basis of faith in Christ, over against those who wished to make circumcision and Torah observance a requirement for all. On the other hand, it is also clear that, as a result of his "conversion" from persecutor to proponent of the Christian move-

22. The claim that Paul saw Jesus as relevant *only* for Gentiles is not persuasive. Cf. Lloyd Gaston, *Paul and the Torah* (Vancouver: University of British Columbia Press, 1987). On Paul's use of "Israel," see now the excellent discussion by W. S. Campbell, "Israel," in *DPL*, 441-46, which is rightly influenced by Peter Richardson, *Israel in the Apostolic Church*, SNTSMS 10 (Cambridge: Cambridge University Press, 1969). Donaldson (*Paul and the Gentiles*, esp. 215-48) describes Paul as thinking of his Gentile converts as redefined proselytes through faith in Christ, and thus as made part of an "Israel" whose core was made up of Jewish believers. Contrary to Crossan's claim (*The Birth of Christianity*, xxv), if Paul had had a son, he would almost certainly have circumcised him. The tradition in Acts (16:1-3) of Paul having Timothy circumcised (whom Paul could refer to religiously as his "child," e.g., 1 Cor. 4:17) suggests that the author of Acts would answer similarly!

23. This is, of course, easier to state as a principle than it was for Jewish Christians to carry out in practical circumstances, as noted by E. P. Sanders, *Paul, the Law, and the Jewish People* (Philadelphia: Fortress, 1983), 177-78. Especially in the demand that Jewish Christians have full table fellowship with Gentile believers, it would have been necessary for them to share food under Torah-observant conditions. But my point is that Paul did not demand that Jewish believers renounce observance of Torah. Instead, Torah observance was problematic in Paul's eyes only if it was used as a basis for refusing (a) to put faith in Jesus (e.g., by Jews who rejected the gospel) and (b) to accept Gentile believers as fully enfranchised into salvation through their faith in Christ.

ment, Paul held that faith in Jesus now defined the circle of those whom God accepted, and that Torah observance was no longer the essential basis for a relationship with God and for being included among those to whom the blessings of Abraham were promised. In this sense Christ is the "end of the law" (Rom. 10:4): Christ, and not Torah, is the effectual means to "righteousness" (i.e., being "put right" with reference to God) for anyone who trusts in him ("to everyone who trusts/believes").[24]

Nevertheless, even when Paul advocates what looks like an innovation in belief or practice, he characteristically does so by explicit reference to Jewish religious tradition. Thus, for example, he refers to his Gentile converts in Thessalonica as having "turned to God from idols, to serve a living and true God" (1 Thess. 1:9), reflecting a decidedly Jewish view of religious matters! To cite another, even more striking example, in contending over against some other Jewish Christians that his Gentile converts were free from the requirements involved in the full observance of Torah, Paul insists that whether Jew or Greek, slave or free, male or female, "you are all one in Christ Jesus," and as such "are Abraham's offspring, heirs according to promise" (Gal. 3:28-29). That is, even in affirming the admission of Gentiles into full Christian fellowship as Gentiles without having to undergo a proselyte conversion to the Jewish law, Paul does not ridicule or reject the Jewish idea of a promise made to Abraham or the meaningfulness of being his heirs. Though he certainly redefines what is required for Gentiles to be included in the benefits of this promise (faith in Christ rather than Torah observance), it is clear that the very Jewish categories of Abrahamic promise, covenant, the purposes of God giving the Torah, and other matters as well, all continued to be of vital meaning and importance for Paul. As Terence Donaldson has argued, under the impact of powerful religious experiences that struck Paul as revelations, he manifests a "reconfiguration" of

---

24. In Rom. 10:1-13 Paul contrasts the stance of "unbelieving" Israel (zealously seeking to establish their own righteousness through Torah observance, but thereby ignoring the righteousness of God, 10:1-3) with those (among Jews and Gentiles, 10:12) who instead confess Jesus as the risen Lord (10:9-10) and so are saved (10:13). In 10:5-8 Paul contrasts the righteousness that comes from Torah observance (and, thus, can be attempted only by those to whom the Torah was given) with the righteousness that is given through the preaching of the gospel ("the word of faith which we preach," 10:8b). This righteousness is readily available to all, Jew and Gentile (10:12), and is accessed through faith, involving confessing "with your mouth" and believing "in your heart" (10:8-10), which, ironically, Paul presents as corresponding to Deut. 30:10-14. It is clear that in Paul the Greek noun *dikaiosynē* and its verbal cognates (from *dikaioō*) have to do with a positive relationship and standing with God. The English word "righteousness" hardly connotes this effectively. See the exhaustive study of the matter by Richard Kingsley Moore, "Right with God: Paul and His English Translators" (Ph.D. diss., University of Queensland, 1978).

convictions and categories, nearly all of which derive from his Jewish religious background.[25]

Of course, Paul was an intelligent and widely traveled man of his time, and so he reflects the broad dissemination of ideas and categories (e.g., rhetorical conventions) that were part of the general intellectual and cultural environment of his day, some of which had derived from Greek philosophical traditions. But in Paul these traditions appear in a very diluted form, and he seems to have absorbed them simply by being a participant in the Roman period.[26] Paul can hardly be said to have had formal study in, or serious familiarity with, Greek philosophy. Any serious comparison between Paul and another devout Jew of the period who does show a certain formal acquaintance with Greek philosophy, Philo of Alexandria, will easily show how much more characteristically and programmatically there is in Philo a familiarity with and usage of Greek philosophical traditions. By comparison, Paul seems to have acquired a much more elementary and secondhand acquaintance, such as one might have picked up by stopping to listen to the many wandering speakers in Roman-era cities, and, as likely, such as had widely become absorbed into even the most devout and particularistic forms of Judaism of the Roman era.[27] We could speak of various features of originally Greek culture that by the first century had seeped into the cultural "groundwater" and were taken up, in diluted form, by Jews as simply part of their own culture.[28] This was possible wherever Jews judged that elements of Greek culture did not pose a conflict or challenge to their religious beliefs and practices. In this Paul was no different from many other devout Jews of his time. Hengel proposes that as a student of Jewish tradition in Jerusalem, Paul would have "basic knowledge of a Jewish-Greek rhetoric aimed at synagogue preaching which was essentially different from the literary style of the Greek schools."[29] It would, however, be mislead-

---

25. Donaldson, *Paul and the Gentiles,* esp. 293-307.

26. Note the judicious conclusions of R. Dean Anderson, Jr., *Ancient Rhetorical Theory and Paul* (Kampen: Kok Pharos, 1996), esp. 249-57.

27. Above all, Martin Hengel, *Judaism and Hellenism: Studies in the Encounter in Palestine during the Early Hellenistic Period,* 2 vols. (London: SCM Press, 1974); and Hengel, *The "Hellenization" of Judaea in the First Century after Christ* (London: SCM Press, 1989); Saul Lieberman, *Hellenism in Jewish Palestine: Studies in the Literary Transmission, Beliefs, and Manners of Palestine in the I Century B.C.E.–IV Century C.E.,* 2nd ed., Texts and Studies of JTSA 18 (1950; reprint, New York: Jewish Theological Seminary, 1962).

28. For example, Moshe Weinfeld argues that the very particularist Qumran group shows organizational patterns like those of the wider Greco-Roman era guilds, collegia, and related voluntary associations (*Organizational Pattern and the Penal Code of the Qumran Sect: A Comparison with Guilds and Religious Associations of the Hellenistic-Roman Period,* NTOA 2 [Göttingen: Vandenhoeck & Ruprecht, 1986]).

29. Hengel, *The Pre-Christian Paul,* 54-62, quote from 61.

ing, and would exceed the evidence considerably, to characterize Paul as, for example, in any significant degree a Platonizing thinker.[30]

For appreciating the Christ-devotion affirmed and reflected in Paul's letters, it is particularly important to take account of the monotheistic emphasis of the Jewish tradition that shaped him. In terms of beliefs and practical consequences for Jews living in the Roman period, especially (but by no means exclusively) in the diaspora, nothing was more central and more indicative of Jewish tradition than its monotheism.[31] Jewish insistence on the uniqueness of the God of Israel and the exclusive validity of worship offered to their God made them unique (and in the eyes of some, notorious) among the ethnic groups of the Roman Empire. Their religious exclusivity provoked significant questions and difficulties as well, for virtually all aspects of Roman-era life were linked to the gods and were charged with a certain religious character.

Two features of Jewish monotheism are especially important for appreciating the historical significance of the devotion to Christ that is reflected in Paul's letters. First, in addition to refusing to accept and worship any of the other deities of the Roman religious environment, conscientious Jews also maintained a distinction between the God of Israel and any of the exalted figures who could be seen as prominent in God's entourage, such as principal angels or revered human figures like Moses or Enoch. This distinction was most clearly maintained in discouraging the worship of these figures; and devout Jews insisted that worship was to be given to God alone. In light of this attitude, the level of reverence for Christ reflected in Paul's letters is historically remarkable, and will require some explanation.

Second, the Jewish monotheistic stance forbade apotheosis, the divinization of human figures, and thus clashed with a major theme in pagan religion of the time.[32] Philo's quip about Gaius Caligula's claim to divinity aptly

---

30. Contra Crossan, *The Birth of Christianity,* xx-xxvii; and Daniel Boyarin, *A Radical Jew: Paul and the Politics of Identity* (Berkeley: University of California Press, 1994). Boyarin mistakenly attributes the dualistic language and motifs in Paul to Platonic influence (e.g., 59-64), apparently not realizing that Paul simply reflects (and adapts in the light of his Christian beliefs) the dualistic categories that characterized ancient Jewish apocalyptic traditions. Cf. Martyn, *Theological Issues,* 111-23. Likewise, Paul's varied uses of the term for "flesh" *(sarx)* reflect recognizably biblical and Jewish traditions, not Platonism (not even a "moderate" version); see, e.g., R. J. Erickson, "Flesh," in *DPL,* 303-6. Crossan's neologism, "sarcophobic," is utterly misleading (*The Birth of Christianity,* xxiii).

31. I refer readers back to my discussion of monotheism in the preceding chapter.

32. E.g., Erich Berneker, "Apotheosis," in *Der Kleine Pauly Lexikon der Antike,* ed. Konrat Ziegler and Walther Sontheimer, 5 vols. (Munich: Deutscher Taschenbuch Verlag, 1979), 1:458-59 (with bibliography); E. R. Bevan, "Deification (Greek and Roman)," *Encyclopaedia of Religion and Ethics,* ed. James Hastings (Edinburgh: T. & T. Clark, 1911), 4:525-33; Stephan Lösch, *Deitas*

illustrates Jewish attitudes, and is all the more important in coming from a diaspora Jew who in some other respects shows a cosmopolitan attitude: "Sooner could God change into a man than a man into God" (*Embassy to Gaius* 118). This rejection of apotheosis as ridiculous and blasphemous seems in fact to have been characteristic of devout Jews of the Roman period, and this in turn makes highly implausible any explanation of the Christ-devotion attested in, and affirmed by, Paul as resulting from the prevalence of the notion of apotheosis in the Roman era. Though Jewish writings of the time show that principal angels and revered human figures such as Moses or Enoch could be pictured in a highly exalted status, and described in terms that can be compared with divinization, the refusal to accord any such figure cultic worship shows that we are not dealing here with a genuine apotheosis.[33] In light of the allergic sensitivity of devout Jews of the time about claims of apotheosis, any scholar who wishes to propose the relevance of this category for explaining the Christ-

---

Jesu und Antike Apotheose (Rottenburg: Bader'sche Verlagsbuchhandlung, 1933). Lösch shows very well that the New Testament writings are consistently opposed to pagan notions of apotheosis and that this makes it difficult to attribute much influence of such ideas upon earliest Christian views of Jesus. But his own solution to the question of how Jesus came to be viewed as divine (Jesus taught such a view of himself and the Jerusalem church echoed it) strikes me as simplistic. L. J. Kreitzer, "The Apotheosis of the Roman Emperor," in *Striking New Images: Roman Imperial Coinage of the New Testament World*, JSNTSup 134 (Sheffield: Sheffield Academic Press, 1996), 69-98, offers a very valuable discussion with illustrations from coins and other visual artifacts of the Roman era. However, his brief suggestion that some Christians may have "found that the incarnational basis of their faith was readily synthesized with the prevailing religious system of the Romans, which included the apotheosis of the Emperor" (97) is both unsupported and does not explain how the cultic reverence of Jesus could have begun (as it obviously did) *among circles of Jewish believers and others governed by Jewish monotheistic scruples,* for whom the whole idea of apotheosis was abhorrent. Bruce Winter, "The Imperial Cult," in *The Book of Acts in Its Graeco-Roman Setting*, ed. D. W. J. Gill and C. Gempf (Carlisle: Paternoster; Grand Rapids: Eerdmans, 1994), 93-103, shows from more recently available evidence that the imperial cult developed *in the eastern provinces* much earlier than has previously been thought by some scholars.

33. E.g., L. W. Hurtado, *One God, One Lord: Early Christian Devotion and Ancient Jewish Monotheism* (Philadelphia: Fortress, 1988; 2nd ed., Edinburgh: T. & T. Clark, 1998), 51-69. Cf. J. J. Collins, "A Throne in the Heavens: Apotheosis in Pre-Christian Judaism," in *Death, Ecstasy, and Other Worldly Journeys*, ed. J. J. Collins and M. A. Fishbane (Albany: State University of New York Press, 1995), 43-58. Collins surveys references to heavenly ascent and exaltation in canonical texts (Exod. 24:9-10; Dan. 7:13-14; 12:3) and Jewish extracanonical writings (1 Enoch 13–15; 3 Enoch; Exagoge of Ezekiel; and 4Q491: frag. 11, col. 1, ll. 10-18). As Collins notes, the scenes function to claim an authorization/authority for the figures given such exaltation, but there is no cultus devoted to these figures. Cf. also Morton Smith, "Ascent to the Heavens and Deification in 4QM^a," in *Archaeology and History in the Dead Sea Scrolls*, ed. L. H. Schiffman (Sheffield: Sheffield Academic Press, 1990), 181-88.

devotion of the first couple decades of the Christian movement is obliged to provide a cogent description of the specific process by which Christian Jews could have adopted this repellent category without realizing it.[34]

As a zealot for the religious integrity of Judaism and "the traditions of [his] ancestors" in his pre-Christian religious life (Gal. 1:14), Paul was devoted above all to the uniqueness of the God of Israel; and he continues to exhibit a firm monotheistic stance in his Christian letters. This is evident, for example, in his critique of pagan religion in Romans 1:18-32 (which reflects the sort of Jewish attitudes also seen in texts such as Wisd. of Sol. 12–15), and also in 1 Corinthians 8–10, where he replies to various questions from the Corinthian Christians about social activities that could involve reverence for the various deities of the Roman period. So we must remember that for Paul, as for other Jewish Christians, and also for the Gentile converts they sought to make obedient to the one God of the biblical/Jewish tradition, devotion to Christ is expressed in the context of a firmly monotheistic stance.

Paul the Convert

Paul's monotheistic stance unites him with other Christian believers of his time, but two other factors distinguish him from anyone else we know of in the early decades. The first is Paul's dramatic turnabout from dedicated opposition against the early Christian movement to enthusiastic affirmation and promotion of Christian beliefs.[35] There were likely other Jews who moved from initial unbelief to acceptance of the gospel, but we know of none who moved from the sort of vigorous effort aimed against the Christian movement that Paul professes to have been his. Paul refers to his efforts to destroy "the church of God" (Gal. 1:13; Phil. 3:6; 1 Cor. 15:9), and characterizes his preconversion motivation as "zeal" for Jewish religion (Phil. 3:6; Gal. 1:14), a term that in ancient Jewish

34. Thus Adela Yarbro Collins's proposal ("The Worship of Jesus and the Imperial Cult," in *The Jewish Roots of Christological Monotheism: Papers from the St. Andrews Conference on the Historical Origins of the Worship of Jesus*, ed. C. C. Newman, J. R. Davila, and G. S. Lewis, JSJSup 63 [Leiden: Brill, 1999], 234-57) that non-Jewish ideas about divine heroes and divinized humans were adapted in the first decade or so among Jewish Christians, not consciously but "unreflectively," seems to me implausible. It is entirely possible that Phil. 2:6-11 *could* have been read by Gentile converts in the light of ideas of heroes and apotheosis, but this does not give us either the explanation for the origin of the ideas in the passage or the historical explanation of how it became acceptable to accord such reverence to Christ in the circles of Christian Jews, where this devotional practice first began.

35. L. W. Hurtado, "Convert, Apostate or Apostle to the Nations? The 'Conversion' of Paul in Recent Scholarship," *SR* 22 (1993): 273-84.

tradition was associated with the biblical account of Phinehas (Num. 25:5-13), who is praised for his violent action against a fellow Israelite caught in a flagrant and public offense. The terms Paul uses in Galatians 1:13 *(diōkō, portheō)* connote a determined, even violent set of actions that take in more than mere verbal refutation.

It is necessary to appreciate the nature of Paul's zealous preconversion stance in order to grasp the significance of the change in his religious convictions. Study of the Phinehas-zeal tradition in ancient Jewish sources has provided us with valuable help in catching the force of Paul's allusion in his references to his religious "zeal."[36] The offenses mentioned in ancient Jewish sources as justifying (even demanding) "zeal" of the type associated with Phinehas were serious: idolatry, perjury, sorcery and poisoning, and false prophecy.[37] Against fellow Jews publicly committing such offenses, the devout Jew was authorized to take vigorous action, which could even involve the death of the offender. The rationale seems to have been that the religious integrity of the Jewish people, the collective Jewish responsibility to exhibit faithfulness to the God of Israel, was at stake. If, as seems likely from his references to his own preconversion actions, Paul saw himself as carrying out this sort of firm disciplinary effort, then he was responding to something he found deeply offensive, even dangerous, in the beliefs and practices of the unfortunate Jewish Christians on the receiving end of his zeal. Consequently Paul's shift from this attitude to an enthusiastic participation in the Christian movement is remarkable, and must have involved profound changes in his religious views.

It is likely that Paul's letters preserve indications of his preconversion views of Jesus and the beliefs of Christian circles that he opposed. For example, Galatians 3:13 refers to Jesus having become "a curse for us [*hyper hēmōn katara*], for it is written, 'Cursed [*epikataratos*] is everyone who is hanged upon a tree.'" This may be an adaptation of Paul's preconversion view of Jesus as a false teacher whose crucifixion reflected his being cursed by God.[38] Also, in 2 Corinthians 3:7–4:6, references to the veiled minds of non-Christian Jews, to the illumination that comes "when one turns to the Lord," and to the spiritual blindness of those who cannot see "the glory of God in the face of Jesus Christ"

---

36. Torrey Seland, *Establishment Violence in Philo and Luke: A Study of Non-Conformity to the Torah and Jewish Vigilante Reactions* (Leiden: Brill, 1995). See also T. L. Donaldson, "Zealot and Convert: The Origin of Paul's Christ-Torah Antithesis," *CBQ* 51 (1989): 655-82.

37. Seland, esp. 37-42 and 103-81, which gives detailed exposition of Philo, *Spec. leg.* 1.54-57; 1.315-18; 2.252-54.

38. E.g., Hans Dieter Betz, *Galatians,* Hermeneia (Philadelphia: Fortress, 1979), 152 n. 136; Dieter Sänger, "'Verflucht ist jeder, der am Holze hängt' (Gal. 3,13b): Zur Rezeption einer frühen antichristlichen Polemik," *ZNW* 85 (1994): 279-85.

are likely informed by Paul's memory of his own preconversion attitudes and his sense of having undergone a revelatory change of view.[39]

The appropriateness of referring to Paul as a "convert" and to his change in religious commitment as a "conversion" has rightly been questioned on the basis of the incompatibility of Paul's experience with characteristic examples of famous converts.[40] Paul did not move from neutrality, and was not a rebellious or irreligious "sinner" (as in the classic mold of an Augustine) who found a cathartic resolution to his doubts or wayward tendencies; nor does he seem to have been (like Luther) frustrated in his previous religious life. On the basis of his references to his preconversion life (e.g., Phil. 3:6), it appears that Paul had what Stendahl memorably referred to as a "robust conscience."[41] Paul certainly underwent a major redirection of his religious energies, but he himself characteristically refers to his experience more in terms of a prophetic calling than a conversion. Yet, as Alan Segal has proposed, given that Paul's change of religious direction was so serious (180 degrees!), and for Paul so wrenching, the term "conversion" may be used.[42]

As a convert, especially having moved from opposition against the Christian movement to being an adherent, Paul had to undertake a rather thorough reformulation of his religious views, indeed his whole religious "self." As anyone acquainted with political or religious converts (or even with smokers who become nonsmokers!) will know, a radical shift in commitment often involves a more enthusiastic and also a more thoroughly thought-out appropriation of the views to which one converts than may be characteristic of those whose acceptance of the position came less traumatically.

This is part of the reason why we sense in Paul's letters that we are dealing with both an enthusiast and a "thinker," or at least with someone who has given a good deal of consideration to his religious views; and it makes Paul's letters all the more valuable as historical sources. In them we have affirmations of Christian beliefs and practices that are accompanied by, or give indications of, a rationale for them. Having worked out his understanding of his Christian beliefs in various Christian communities of the very earliest years of Chris-

---

39. Carey C. Newman, *Paul's Glory-Christology: Tradition and Rhetoric*, NovTSup 69 (Leiden: Brill, 1992).

40. See the discussion of the scholarly literature in Hurtado, "Convert, Apostate or Apostle?" 274-76.

41. Krister Stendahl, "The Apostle Paul and the Introspective Conscience of the West," *HTR* 56 (1963): 199-215, reprinted in Stendahl, *Paul among Jews and Gentiles* (Philadelphia: Fortress, 1976), 78-96, which I use here. The phrase quoted is from p. 80, and see also 89-91.

42. Alan F. Segal, *Paul the Convert: The Apostolate and Apostasy of Saul the Pharisee* (New Haven: Yale University Press, 1990), esp. 5-7.

tianity, he gives us at least a glimpse of the sorts of reflections going on in such groups.

Moreover, it is reasonable to think that the basic christological views that he embraced and espouses in his epistles reflect the beliefs he had previously found objectionable and had opposed so vigorously.[43] In fact, in a number of places Paul recites traditional formulations that likely illustrate the beliefs of those he persecuted, beliefs he then accepted as a convert (e.g., Rom. 4:24-25; 1 Cor. 15:1-7; 1 Thess. 1:10).

The Gentile Mission

Another distinctive feature of Paul, and the third key factor to bear in mind in considering Paul's letters, is his mission to the Gentiles. Paul refers to himself as given a special responsibility to win adherents to the gospel among the Gentiles (Rom. 1:5; 11:13; 15:17-20), and compares this special apostolate to Gentiles with that of Peter to Jews ("the circumcision"; Gal. 2:7-8). Moreover, he even makes this mission the divine purpose in his own conversion to Christian faith (Gal. 1:15-16), picturing himself as chosen by God before birth for this task!

It is not clear, however, how soon after the "revelation" that secured his assent to Christian faith Paul became convinced of his special calling, and how quickly he began his efforts to secure the obedience of Gentiles to the gospel. Galatians 1:15-16 does not actually say more than that this mission was the divine *purpose* in Paul's conversion; the passage asserts no specific chronological connection. In his account in Galatians 1–2, Paul explicitly mentions a message and activity already directed specifically at Gentiles in 2:1-2, in his description of a visit to Jerusalem "after fourteen years." If this time span is reckoned from his conversion, this would take us back at least as early as the mid-40s. Probably, however, we should think of Paul as having come to see himself as called to evangelize Gentiles a number of years earlier still.[44]

---

43. L. M. Hurtado, "Pre–70 C.E. Jewish Opposition to Christ-Devotion," *JTS* 50 (1999): 50-57.

44. For judicious discussion of the question, see Riesner, 235-63, who proposes that it was during Paul's stay in Jerusalem, three years after his conversion, that he may have come to the conviction that he was specially called to the Gentiles. Cf. the implausible argument by Nicholas Taylor that Paul's sense of apostolic authority came only after his residence in Antioch (*Paul, Antioch, and Jerusalem: A Study in Relationships and Authority in Earliest Christianity*, JSNTSup 66 [Sheffield: Sheffield Academic Press, 1992]). Oddly, Taylor treats Paul's firsthand statements with skepticism but builds his own view in dependence upon the later and secondhand narratives of Acts!

But whether he came to this conviction immediately after his conversion or within a few or several years thereafter, by all indications he understood the terms of Gentile conversion as requiring obedience to the gospel but not proselyte conversion to the Torah. Over against some other Jewish Christians, Paul insisted that faith in Christ was sufficient basis for the full inclusion of Gentiles as partakers in God's salvation, fellow members of the *ekklēsia,* and fellow heirs of Abraham (e.g., Gal. 2:1-5, 11-18; Rom. 4:13-17), and he insisted that Holy Spirit–empowered obedience to Christ was the defining content of their ethical obligation (e.g., Gal. 5:6, 13-26).

Paul's conflicts over this matter show that his views were not obviously compelling to all others, especially among Jewish Christians. In light of his own preconversion zeal for Torah observance, Paul himself must have required some very efficacious basis for shifting to the view that Jesus superseded Torah as the key divine overture; and he must have needed to satisfy himself that he could integrate such a high view of Jesus into a (howbeit reformulated) continuing commitment to the God of Israel who had given the Torah through Moses.

So, whether his conviction that Gentiles were to be enfranchised on the basis of faith in Christ came to him as a "revelation," or (as some scholars suggest) he formed this conviction through pondering implications of Jesus' redemptive death, either way Paul's mission to the Gentiles likely shaped the emphases in his Christology.[45] Paul includes the belief that "Christ died for our sins" among the traditions that he received and among the beliefs common to him and the other Jewish Christian leaders he refers to in 1 Corinthians 15:1-11. But Paul's mission required him to develop the rich implications of Christ's redemptive death that he presents in passages such as Galatians 3:1-29 and Romans 3:9-31. In these passages Paul seems to be presenting his own reflections rather than simply reciting christological tradition. Particularly in his views of how Christ is to be understood in relation to the Torah, it is likely that Paul's Christology shows the effects of his special mission to the Gentiles.

Nevertheless, given Paul's concern to maintain links with, and acceptance of his mission in, the Jerusalem church, and given also his need to present arguments for his own views with premises that could command the assent of those with whom he disagreed, we should be careful about attributing too much originality and distinctiveness to him. Though he drew practical inferences that were apparently not shared by all, specifically as to Gentile Christian obligations and the proper Jewish Christian attitude toward Gentile converts, it is not at all clear that in other respects the beliefs about Christ and the devotional

---

45. E.g., Donaldson (*Paul and the Gentiles,* esp. 293-307) proposes that Paul's Gentile mission was essentially an inference from his Christology.

practices reflected in his letters constitute a major departure from prior Christian tradition.

Christological Language and Themes

We turn now to specific beliefs about Jesus and the devotional pattern evidenced in Paul's letters. At the risk of a slightly artificial distinction, I discuss first the beliefs about Jesus, and in a later part of this chapter I turn to the ways Jesus features in the devotional life that Paul attests. In addressing Pauline christological ideas, we are traversing frequently explored territory, some discussions of which take up much more space than I can give to the matter here.[46] It is not my purpose to treat comprehensively all aspects of Paul's Christology. Instead I concentrate on major features that show how Jesus functions in Pauline Christianity as a divine figure and recipient of devotion. I am not primarily concerned here with a discussion of Paul as a theologian, but rather with the beliefs about Jesus that were broadly characteristic of Pauline churches.

Interestingly, nowhere in Paul's letters does he give us anything like a systematic or comprehensive presentation of his christological beliefs. In fact, other than the passages where he found it necessary to explicate the implications of these beliefs for the admission of Gentiles (e.g., Gal. 3:10–4:7), or where he sought to promote behavior shaped by beliefs about Christ, Paul characteristically seems to *presuppose* acquaintance with the christological convictions that he affirms, and most often he expresses them in brief, somewhat formulaic terms. So it is necessary for anyone who discusses Pauline christological beliefs to supply some sort of organization of them. In the following discussion I focus on the key honorific terms and themes that constitute the ways Paul expresses Christian beliefs about Jesus. In each case, my major aim will be to clarify important matters and correct the misunderstandings that have made their way into some scholarly studies.

Jesus as "Christ"

By far, the honorific term most frequently applied to Jesus in Paul's letters is *Christos* (some 270 uses in the seven undisputed Pauline epistles, more than

---

46. E.g., J. D. G. Dunn, *The Theology of Paul the Apostle* (Edinburgh: T. & T. Clark; Grand Rapids: Eerdmans, 1998), 163-315 (with copious bibliographies); and, among somewhat older studies, Werner Kramer, *Christ, Lord, Son of God*, SBT 50 (London: SCM Press, 1966).

half the 531 uses in the New Testament).[47] As is well known among scholars, the use of *Christos* as a title derives entirely from Jewish usage as the Greek translation for the Hebrew term *mashiach* ("anointed [one]," "Messiah"; e.g., *Pss. Sol.* 17–18).[48] Most frequently Paul uses *Christos* on its own to refer to Jesus (about 150 times; e.g., 1 Cor. 15:3; Rom. 10:4); but he also uses the term in varying combinations with others: "Christ Jesus," "Jesus Christ," "Jesus Christ our Lord," and "Our/the Lord Jesus Christ" (examples of all appear in Rom. 1:1-7).

On the one hand, in Paul's letters the term "Christ" has clearly become so closely associated with Jesus that it functions almost like an alternate name for him. It is at least clear that "Christ," even when used on its own, always refers to Jesus. In Paul's letters we see no need to make the claim that Jesus is Christ/Messiah, which can only suggest that in the Christian tradition and circles lying behind these writings there is hardly any question for his readers as to who is being referred to when Paul uses the simple *Christos*. That is, the identification of Jesus as the Messiah/Christ has become so firm and routinized that the title itself is a sufficient way to designate him. This routine association is reflected in the way Paul can even use the expressions "in Christ" and "in Christ Jesus" to refer to the Christian fellowship (e.g., 1 Cor. 4:15; Rom. 12:5; 16:3, 7, 9, 10). These references show that the circle of Christian fellowship can be thought of as defined by and linked closely to Jesus in his significance as *Christos*.[49] Also, of course, when used with the name "Jesus" (Gk. *Iēsous*), *Christos* would have had another function for ancient readers of the Jewish Scriptures in Greek that is lost to readers of the Christian Bible in modern translations. "Jesus Christ" and "Christ Jesus" served to distinguish this *Iēsous* from his biblical namesake, the hero of the book that bears his name and the great successor of Moses, whose name is today usually transliterated from the Hebrew form, "Joshua" (Heb. *Yehoshua;* Gk. *Iēsous*).

On the other hand, the varying position of the term in the fuller expressions is one of several indications that for Paul and others who used these

---

47. The figures are based on the data in the *Computer-Konkordanz zum Novum Testamentum Graece,* ed. Institut für Neutestamentliche Textforschung (Berlin: De Gruyter, 1985), which is based on the twenty-sixth edition of the Nestle-Aland Greek New Testament. Important studies of Paul's use of *Christos* include Hengel, "'Christos' in Paul," in his *Between Jesus and Paul,* trans. John Bowden (London: SCM Press, 1983), 65-77; N. A. Dahl, "The Messiahship of Jesus in Paul," in *Jesus the Christ: The Historical Origins of Christological Doctrine,* ed. D. H. Juel (Minneapolis: Fortress, 1991), 15-25, in addition to Kramer, 19-64, 131-50.

48. E.g., W. Grundmann et al., "χρίω, χριστός, etc.," in *TDNT,* 9:493-580.

49. In other cases, Paul uses "in Christ" to convey more of a relation to or a kind of "mystical" participation of believers somehow in Jesus. See now the discussion in Dunn, *Theology of Paul,* 390-401.

terms, *Christos* had not simply been reduced to a name (e.g., Jesus' cognomen) but instead retained something of its function as a title. Paul's use of the term with the definite article — "the Christ" *(ho Christos)* — in Romans 9:3, and again in 9:5 in a list of things that pertain to, and derive from, the Jewish people (his "brothers, kin by race," 9:3), without further explanation shows that he expected his Gentile readers to recognize the title and to have some acquaintance with Jewish traditions connected with it.[50] So, in Pauline circles, it remained the case that to refer to Jesus as "Christ" (with or without the definite article) was to assert his significance as the divinely approved figure who acts as the eschatological agent of God.[51] For example, as the first to be raised from death to eschatological glory, Christ is the "first fruit" of the promised resurrection of the elect (1 Cor. 15:20-23). The royal-messianic connotation of *Christos* seems to be retained in Paul's reference to Jesus being enthroned by God's appointment to secure God's complete supremacy (15:23-28).

There is no basis for thinking that Paul's Gentile converts were incapable of appreciating the royal-messianic significance of the term *Christos,* and that thus it functioned merely as another name for Jesus. One has only to note, for example, that in the canonical Gospels, written some twenty to thirty years later than Paul's letters and addressed to circles of Christians that were either largely Gentiles (Mark and Luke) or at least included significant numbers of them (Matthew and John), the title "the Christ" *(ho Christos)* remains a very prominent feature of their christological claims, and the royal-messianic meaning remains very much to the fore.[52] The prominent and meaningful place of the messianic claim among Gentile Christians that was registered in these writings several decades later than Paul easily refutes the notion that first-century Gentile Christians found it difficult to apprehend the sense of *Christos.*

As Werner Kramer noted several decades ago, it is also significant that *Christos* is particularly used in sentences that refer to Jesus' death and resurrection (e.g., Rom. 5:6; 14:9, 15; 1 Cor. 5:7; 8:11; 15:20; Gal. 2:21; 3:13).[53] In these expressions, which in a number of cases are thought to be Paul's use of traditional

---

50. This could be accounted for if at least some of Paul's Gentile converts had been "God-fearing" adherents of Jewish synagogues. To judge from Paul's letters, it appears also that he simply presented his message in categories that derived from Jewish tradition and Scriptures, and expected his readers to cope!

51. Amid the variations in messianic expectation in ancient Jewish texts, "messiah" always indicates an eschatological figure. See now J. J. Collins, *The Scepter and the Star: The Messiahs of the Dead Sea Scrolls and Other Ancient Literature* (New York: Doubleday, 1995); W. Horbury, *Jewish Messianism and the Cult of Christ* (London: SCM Press, 1998).

52. L. W. Hurtado, "Christ," in *DJG*, 106-17.

53. Kramer, 26-28.

faith formulations from earlier Christian circles, the term *Christos* functions to
assert the messianic significance of Jesus' death and resurrection (it is as
Christos that Jesus died "for us" and rose again); and at the same time these
statements declare the innovative early Christian claim that the work of
Christos/Messiah involves his redemptive death and resurrection. In short,
Paul's use of *Christos* shows how early the term had become a conventional fea-
ture of the claims asserted in early Christian belief. It also shows how much
Christian understanding of the work and nature of the Messiah was shaped by
Jesus' execution, and by the conviction that he had been resurrected by God.

As noted above, the prevalence of *Christos* in Paul's christological expressions can be accounted for only by positing the messianic claim as a feature of
Christian proclamation for a considerable period earlier than his letters. Probably we have to take the claim back to the earliest circles, those whom Saul/Paul
the zealous Pharisee sought to gag and destroy. Their proclaiming this dis-
graced false teacher as Messiah would certainly help account for the outrage
that seems to have prompted Saul's efforts (though I think their offense went
even farther, in reverencing their Christ in ways that seemed to Saul to compromise the uniqueness of God, as I will indicate in the next chapter).

The traditional designation of Jesus as Christ/Messiah is explicitly what
Paul asserts in 1 Corinthians 15:1-11. In this block of material, which is commonly recognized as coming from the Jerusalem church, the kernel of the condensed expression of faith is that *Christ* "died for our sins according to the
scriptures, and was buried, and was raised on the third day according to the
scriptures" (15:3-4).[54] That is, both the messianic claim and the messianic interpretation of his death and resurrection are specified as stemming from this tradition and as among the beliefs shared by Paul and the other figures connected
with Jerusalem (15:11).

Jesus' Divine Sonship

At the other extreme in comparative frequency of usage in Paul is the category
of divine sonship.[55] There are only fifteen references to Jesus as God's "Son" in
the seven undisputed Pauline letters (and only two more in the remaining Pau-

---

54. E.g., Hans Conzelmann, *1 Corinthians,* Hermeneia (Philadelphia: Fortress, 1975), 248-
62; G. D. Fee, *The First Epistle to the Corinthians,* NICNT (Grand Rapids: Eerdmans, 1987), 717-
37.

55. I draw here upon my earlier studies: "Son of God," in *DPL,* 900-906; and "Jesus' Divine Sonship in Paul's Epistle to the Romans," in *Romans and the People of God,* ed. Sven K.
Soderlund and N. T. Wright (Grand Rapids: Eerdmans, 1999), 217-33.

line epistles). Moreover, in these references the actual title "Son of God" is neither fixed nor frequently used, appearing only three times (four if we include Eph. 4:13) and in varying Greek phrasing (*tou horisthentos huiou theou,* Rom. 1:4; *ho tou theou huios,* 2 Cor. 1:19; *tou huiou tou theou,* Gal. 2:20). Focusing on this infrequency of reference to Jesus' divine sonship, Kramer mistakenly concluded that the theme was simply a remnant of "pre-Pauline" tradition and no longer an important christological category for Paul.[56] Kramer was right that Jesus' divine sonship was a feature of "pre-Pauline" tradition, but he erred in thinking it was not important in Paul or his churches.

Instead, Bousset was surely correct in seeing Jesus' divine sonship as central in Paul's beliefs. But Bousset seriously erred both in claiming that Paul adopted the category from the pagan religious environment where sons of gods were supposedly a common category of divine beings, and in asserting that Jesus' divine sonship functioned as the means by which Paul communicated Jesus' divine status to his Gentile converts and justified to them the worship of Jesus.[57] Unfortunately, however, Bousset's view was repeated in writings of other very influential scholars such as Bultmann and Schoeps.[58]

But, as Nock and Hengel have shown, it is hard to demonstrate the relevance of pagan references to divine sonship.[59] There are references to the human race as offspring of Zeus or other high gods, but this hardly relates to the way Paul attaches special significance to Jesus as God's unique Son. Great figures such as Alexander the Great might be portrayed as a son of a deity, but this was essentially an honorific gesture in recognition of some quality such as wisdom or military prowess, and with the intention of presenting the figure as an exceptionally impressive human being. In fact, the phrase "son of god" was not common in Greco-Roman paganism. The deities of the so-called mystery cults, to which early history-of-religions scholars attached such importance for early Christianity, were not referred to as "son of god." The title does seem to have been promoted in the Roman emperor cult, but any influence of emperor devo-

56. Kramer, 183-94, esp. 189.

57. W. Bousset, *Kyrios Christos: Geschichte des Christusglaubens von den Anfangen des Christentums bis Irenaeus* (Göttingen: Vandenhoeck & Ruprecht, 1913; rev. ed., 1921); ET (from the 4th German ed., 1965), *Kyrios Christos: A History of the Belief in Christ from the Beginnings of Christianity to Irenaeus,* trans. J. E. Steely (Nashville: Abingdon, 1970), 91-98, 206-10.

58. R. Bultmann, *Theology of the New Testament,* 2 vols. (New York: Charles Scribner's Sons, 1951, 1955), 1:128-29; H. J. Schoeps, *Paul: The Theology of the Apostle in the Light of Jewish Religious History* (Philadelphia: Westminster, 1961), 149-59.

59. A. D. Nock, "'Son of God' in Pauline and Hellenistic Thought," in *Essays on Religion and the Ancient World,* ed. Z. Stewart, 2 vols. (Oxford: Clarendon, 1972), 2:928-39; M. Hengel, *The Son of God: The Origin of Christology and the History of Jewish-Hellenistic Religion,* trans. John Bowden (Philadelphia: Fortress; London: SCM Press, 1976), 21-41.

tion upon early Christianity was probably much later than Paul and likely was considered blasphemous and rejected rather than considered something to be appropriated.[60] The judgment of that master of the Roman period, A. D. Nock, still holds concerning the Pauline attribution of divine sonship to Jesus: "[T]he attempts which have been made to explain it from the larger Hellenistic world fail."[61]

Divine sonship was, however, a familiar category in the biblical and Jewish tradition that shaped the religious vocabulary of early-first-century Christian circles. In what appears to be an archaic use of the expression in the Hebrew Scriptures, the heavenly hosts are referred to as "sons of God" (e.g., Gen. 6:2-4; Deut. 32:8; Job 1:6; 2:1; Pss. 29:1; 89:6). Though in a number of cases the Greek Old Testament translates the phrase "angel(s) of God" (e.g., Deut. 32:8), this is not done consistently (e.g., Deut. 32:43), meaning that Greek-speaking Jews too would have known this use of "sons of God." The more influential uses of the language of divine sonship, however, are in references to the Davidic king (2 Sam. 7:14; Pss. 2:7; 89:26-27), and still more frequently to righteous individuals (e.g., Wisd. of Sol. 2:18; 5:5; Sir. 4:10; *Pss. Sol.* 13.9; 18.4) and Israel collectively (e.g., Exod. 4:22; Deut. 14:1; Isa. 1:2; Jer. 3:22; Hos. 1:10; 11:1; Wisd. of Sol. 12:21; 16:10, 26; 18:4, 13) as son(s) and "firstborn" of God.

In view of recently published texts from Qumran, it now seems more likely than earlier thought by some scholars that divine sonship was also part of the royal-messianic rhetoric of pre-Christian Judaism, and that biblical passages originally referring to Davidic kings were read as messianic texts.[62] In this messianic usage, divine sonship did not function to connote divinity, but it certainly indicated a special status and relationship to God. The same is true for the uses of divine sonship language in reference to righteous individuals and groups and Israel collectively. So the category of divine sonship lay close to hand in the Jewish matrix of earliest Christianity, and can even be said to have been more prominent there than in the pagan religious environment.

Moreover, if we make an inductive analysis of Paul's references to Jesus as

---

60. See, e.g., Dominique Cuss, *Imperial Cult and Honorary Terms in the New Testament,* Paradosis 23 (Fribourg: University of Fribourg, 1974).

61. A. D. Nock, *Early Christianity and Its Hellenistic Background* (New York: Harper and Row, 1964), 45.

62. 4Q174 (4QFlorilegium) contains a commentary on 2 Sam. 7:14 and applies the passage to the royal Messiah. Another fragmentary text, 4Q246, refers to a ruler who will be acclaimed as "son of God" and "son of the Most High." On the use of divine sonship language in Jewish messianism, see, e.g., J. J. Collins, *Scepter and the Star,* 154-72. Note also the discussion of messianism reflected in the LXX Psalter by Joachim Schaper, *The Eschatology of the Greek Psalter,* WUNT 2/71 (Tübingen: Mohr-Siebeck, 1995), esp. 138-44.

God's Son, it becomes clear (1) that the background lies in biblical and Jewish traditions, and (2) that in Paul's usage Jesus' divine sonship does not function as a way of expressing his divinity or of justifying worship of him, but instead primarily expresses Jesus' unique standing and intimate favor with God, and God's direct involvement in Jesus' redemptive work. To be sure, in the beliefs and devotional practice reflected in Paul's letters the glorified Christ holds a status that connotes a participation in divinity. But, contra Bousset and Bultmann, in Paul the christological category of sonship was not the principal way of expressing this.

Bousset's claims about the provenance and purpose of Paul's references to Jesus' divine sonship are immediately rendered dubious if we note where Paul does and does not employ the category. Eleven of the fifteen references in his undisputed epistles are in Romans (seven uses) and Galatians (four uses), the two letters where Paul makes sustained efforts to present, and obtain approval for, his gospel in categories adapted from the Jewish tradition. By contrast, in 1 Corinthians 8–10, where Paul explicitly compares Christian worship with the worship of the many deities of the Roman world, we have no reference to Jesus' divine sonship. Yet this is just the sort of passage where we should expect to find Paul using a divine sonship claim to promote reverence for Jesus, if Bousset's view were correct.

A survey of the individual references to divine sonship in Paul's letters yields specific conclusions about how the category functions. In several passages Jesus' divine sonship primarily connotes his royal status and role. This is evident in Romans 1:3-4, where Jesus is referred to as the "seed [*sperma*] of David" raised up from death by God, alluding to God's promise to David to "raise up your seed [*sperma*]" in 2 Samuel 7:12. Also, Jesus' appointment as God's Son here echoes the divine promise in 2 Samuel 7:14, "I will be a father to him, and he will be to me a son," and Psalm 2:7, where the enthroned Davidic king is proclaimed as God's Son.[63]

In 1 Thessalonians 1:10 as well, Jesus' divine sonship is mentioned in connection with his resurrection and his eschatological role as divinely appointed deliverer from God's wrath. The combination of strong eschatological flavor and the contrast between "the living and true God" and "idols" indicate a provenance shaped by Jewish religious views, and the reference to Jesus as "Son" here likely designates him as God's messianic agent. We encounter the same sphere of meaning also in 1 Corinthians 15:24-28, where Christ's rule as "Son" is

---

63. Paul's reference to his mission to secure "obedience of faith among all the nations" (Rom. 1:5) may allude to God's promise to the royal Son in Ps. 2:8 to give "the nations as your inheritance."

described with allusions to Psalms 110:1 and 8:7(6), and as entirely at God's appointment and directed toward God's eschatological supremacy.[64]

To be sure, the scope and basis of Jesus' sonship are distinguishable from that of the Davidic kings and Jewish messianic figures. There is no precedent for the idea that the Messiah was to be appointed through a resurrection from a shameful death; and the transcendent nature and cosmic scope of Jesus' sonship are approached perhaps only in references to "the Elect One" of *1 Enoch* 37–71. But in all these Pauline passages we have motifs, imagery, and terms from Jewish royal-messianic traditions adapted to express boldly beliefs about Jesus' exalted place in God's purposes.

In three other passages Paul refers to Jesus as the Son who was given over by God, or gave himself over, to redemptive death. Here it is likely that divine sonship expresses Jesus' intimate place in God's plan and God's direct involvement in Jesus' redemptive work. In Romans 8:32 there is the striking statement that God "did not withhold his own Son but gave him over for us." The Greek verb translated "gave over" here *(paradidōmi)* appears in another reference to "Jesus our Lord" in 4:24-25, who was "given over for our trespasses," and is the same verb Paul uses to describe divine judgment upon sinful humanity in 1:24-28. There is another reference to God having acted redemptively in the death of Jesus in 5:6-10, where Paul designates him both as "Christ" (vv. 6, 8) and God's Son (v. 10). These references show a certain flexibility in christological titles in references to Jesus' redemptive death. But in 5:10, and even more clearly in 8:32, the references to Jesus as God's Son are intended to underscore the significance of the one given over, and to present Jesus' death as God's redemptive act. In the latter passage the description of God as not withholding his own Son is likely an allusion to Genesis 22:12, 16, where Abraham is commended for not withholding his own son, thus likening God's offering up of Jesus to Abraham's offering of Isaac.[65]

The third reference is in Galatians 2:20, where Paul proclaims his life of faith in "the Son of God who loved me and gave himself up [*paradidōmi*] for me."[66] Seven other times in the context (2:15-21) Paul refers to "Jesus Christ"

---

64. The reference to "the kingdom of the Son of his [God's] love" in Col. 1:13 likewise alludes to Jesus in royal-messianic role. L. J. Kreitzer, "Kingdom of God/Christ," in *DPL*, 524-26.

65. In Rom. 8:32, "did not withhold" translates *ouk epheisato*, the same verb used in the LXX of Gen. 22:12, 16.

66. The variant "God and Christ," though supported by some important Greek witnesses, probably resulted from an accident in copying. See B. M. Metzger et al., *A Textual Commentary on the Greek New Testament* (London and New York: United Bible Societies, 1971), 593. Cf. B. D. Ehrman, *The Orthodox Corruption of Scripture: The Effect of Early Christological Controversies on the Text of the New Testament* (Oxford: Oxford University Press, 1993), 86-87, who

and "Christ," but the use of "Son of God" in this verse emphasizes the stature and divine favor of the one whose love and self-sacrifice are praised. Here too, however, God is implicitly involved, as is confirmed in the following statement (2:21) where Paul refers to "the grace of God" in connection with Jesus' death.

⌐It is important to note that the Pauline references to Jesus as divine Son consistently use the Greek definite article, thus connoting Jesus' unique status as "the" Son and distinguishing him from any others referred to as sons of God(s) in Jewish or pagan sources of the time (e.g., angels, the righteous, great men, or wonder-workers). But in several passages Paul either explicitly or implicitly refers to the enfranchisement of the redeemed into a filial relationship with God that is based on and patterned after Jesus' sonship. Galatians 4:5 states that God sent his Son "that we might receive sonship [*huiothesia*]," and 4:6-7 refers to believers as God's sons and heirs who have received "the Spirit of his Son" and who join the Son in calling upon God as "Abba, Father."[67]

In Romans 8 as well, Paul connects the filial status of believers with Jesus' divine sonship.[68] After referring to God's sending of "his own Son" (*ton heautou huion*) in verse 3, and the bestowal of the Spirit (vv. 5-13), Paul characterizes believers as adopted "sons of God" (v. 14) and "God's children" (v. 16) who now call to God as "Abba, Father" through "the Spirit of sonship/adoption [*huiothesias*]" (v. 15) and are "fellow heirs with Christ" (v. 17). In verses 18-27 Paul states both present and future consequences of this divine adoption of believers, which include their revelation as God's sons (v. 19), their glorious freedom as children of God (v. 21), and "the redemption of our bodies," which must mean resurrection/transformation into immortal life (v. 23). Then come verses 28-30, a highly theocentric passage which proclaims God's love toward the elect who have been "predestined to be conformed to the image of his Son, in order that he might be the firstborn among many sons." Clearly Jesus' status as God's unique Son is not exclusionary; instead he is the redemptively inclusive prototype and basis for all others who are brought into filial relationship with God.

Other references echo this idea. 1 Corinthians 1:9 describes believers as

---

agrees that "the Son of God" is the original reading but proposes that the variants may have been theologically motivated.

67. Gal. 3:27-28 makes it clear that female and male believers are included on equal terms as "sons" and "heirs."

68. It has been claimed by some that Rom. 8:3 and Gal. 4:4 are evidence of an early christological "formula" expressing the sending of God's Son. I have no particular stake in the question, but personally I do not see much to support this claim. There is nothing formulaic in the two passages, which use different phrases for Jesus ("his own Son," "his Son"), and even different verbs for the sending (*pempō* in Rom. 8:3; *exapostellō* in Gal. 4:4).

called by God into the "fellowship/participation [*koinōnia*] of his Son," which means that their status is both dependent upon the Son and also partakes in his filial status. There is probably another allusion in 2 Corinthians 1:19-20, which declares God's redemptive "yes" as communicated in the preaching of God's Son, in whom all God's promises are assured and through whom believers gratefully say "amen" back to God.

Scholars commonly see in Romans 1:3-4 and 1 Thessalonians 1:10 Paul's use of traditional confessional formulations that stem from years earlier than these letters. As with Paul's references to Jesus as "Christ," the divine sonship category takes us back much earlier than the date of the Pauline epistles, and likely back to Jewish Christian circles of the earliest years. Bultmann granted this, but contended that in Paul Jesus' divine sonship assumed a different meaning, one more shaped by pagan notions of sons of gods; but I can see no basis for this view.[69] Instead, in the references we have examined here, Jesus' divine sonship continues to show the influences of Jewish traditions. It connotes Jesus' special relationship to and favor with God, his royal-messianic status, his unique significance in God's plan, and God's close involvement in Jesus' appearance. Jesus' status as God's "Son" does not particularly function in Paul's epistles to indicate Jesus' own divinity (for which *Kyrios* much more clearly serves, as we note in the following section of this chapter). Ironically, it is even possible that Paul's desire to avoid among his converts the sort of misunderstanding of Jesus' sonship that Bultmann fell into, that is, likening him to divine heroes and demigods, may help account for the infrequency of Paul's references to Jesus as God's "Son."

But, although Jesus' divine sonship does not appear as frequently as some other christological categories, and the "Son of God" title in particular is neither a prominent feature nor a fixed expression in Paul's christological rhetoric, the concentration of references in Romans and Galatians shows that Paul found the category useful in conveying Jesus' significance in terms of Jewish and biblical traditions. Moreover, several passages indicate that referring to Jesus' divine sonship was particularly meaningful for Paul personally. Note that he describes the cognitive content of the divine disclosure that turned him from opponent into dedicated proponent of the Christian gospel as God's revelation of "his Son to/in me [*en emoi*]" (Gal. 1:16). Moreover, Paul can characterize his proclamation as presenting "God's Son, Jesus Christ" (2 Cor. 1:19), and he can portray his own devotional stance as living "by faith in the Son of God who loved me and gave himself for me" (Gal. 2:20).

If, as is likely, in his preconversion opposition Paul rejected early Jewish

69. Bultmann, *Theology*, 1:128-29.

Christian claims that Jesus was God's unique Son, and then, by force of divine "revelation," was brought in his innermost being to the conviction that it was all true, this would help explain the importance that Jesus' divine sonship seems to have had in Paul's postconversion religious life. I suggest that for Paul Jesus' divine sonship expressed the total opposite of what he had thought of Jesus prior to his conversion. Whereas previously the zealous Pharisee had regarded Jesus as a miserable false teacher who justly had suffered an accursed death, Paul came to see Jesus as sent by God and as having a uniquely favored status and relationship to God; and for Paul the biblical category "Son" was a profoundly expressive way of registering this radically changed view of Jesus.

Jesus as Lord

The remaining key christological title, used about 180 times in the undisputed Pauline letters, is *Kyrios* (Lord).[70] Here too the obvious questions are about the derivation of the practice of applying *Kyrios* to Jesus, and the meanings and contexts of doing so as indicated in Paul's letters.

In Roman-era Greek, *kyrios* was used to refer to and address someone in a variety of socially superior positions. For example, the owner of a slave was the slave's *kyrios* ("master," e.g., Eph. 6:5, 9). More generally *kyrios* was used in polite address, roughly the equivalent to "sir" in English (and "my lord" in more courtly speech). This basic notion that anyone referred to as *kyrios* holds a superior status and a certain power or authority is there in all uses of the term.

As Paul's derisive reference to the "many so-called gods" and "many lords" of the Roman era indicates (1 Cor. 8:5), *kyrios* was also a familiar part of the religious vocabulary of the time, as a reverential epithet given to deities (e.g., the Lord Serapis). It also came to be used for the Roman emperor, more so in the eastern provinces where traditions of divine kingship were strong and cultic devotion to the living emperor (and not only the deceased ones) was more acceptable than in the West.[71] This pagan religious usage certainly illustrates the wider linguistic context within which early Christian use of *kyrios* is to be seen, and it shows that pagans could easily have understood the term as connoting reverence for Jesus as divine. But the antipathy of devout Jews to-

70. I draw upon my much more extensive discussion in Hurtado, "Lord," in *DPL*, 560-69. In addition to the bibliography listed there, see now also Neil Richardson, *Paul's Language about God*, JSNTSup 99 (Sheffield: Sheffield Academic Press, 1994).

71. Duncan Fishwick, *The Imperial Cult in the Latin West* (Leiden: Brill, 1987); S. R. F. Price, *Rituals and Power: The Roman Imperial Cult in Asia Minor* (Cambridge: Cambridge University Press, 1984).

ward virtually any aspect of pagan religion makes it unlikely that pagan usage of *kyrios* was the impetus or the provenance that directly shaped the christological use of the term in Paul's letters and among his congregations. To understand where the christological use of *kyrios* comes from and how the term functioned in Christian circles of the first few decades, we have to look elsewhere.

Most recent studies of these questions conclude that the key semantic background lies in Jewish tradition, and that the christological designation of Jesus as "Lord" goes back into the very earliest circles of Jewish Christians.[72] Two features of the Jewish tradition of the time are particularly relevant: (1) the religious use of translation equivalents to *kyrios* in Hebrew and Aramaic in reference to God, and (2) the use of *kyrios* itself in the religious vocabulary of Greek-speaking Jews.

By the first century, among devout Jews there had developed a widely observed avoidance of pronouncing the Hebrew name of God *(Yahweh)*, and various substitutes were used, even in reading the scriptural passages where the divine name appears. The most frequent Hebrew substitute was *adonay*. As illustrated in Qumran texts, the Aramaic term *maryah* (definite form of *marêh*) was used similarly, and both mean "Lord." Among Greek-speaking Jews it is likely that *kyrios* was favored as a substitute for the divine name.[73] This is reflected in the New Testament writings, which likewise prefer *kyrios* in citing biblical passages where God's name appears in Hebrew. That is, by all indications, in Jewish circles of the first century *kyrios* and its Semitic-language equivalents for "lord" were used to refer to the God of the Bible; and in their determinative/emphatic forms ("the Lord") these terms functioned as substitutes for the divine name.

So, in addition to the generally honorific sense of *kyrios* (e.g., "sir," "mas-

---

72. See, e.g., W. Foerster and G. Quell, "κύριος," in *TDNT*, 3:1039-98; J. A. Fitzmyer, "The Semitic Background of the New Testament Kyrios Title," in his *A Wandering Aramean: Collected Aramaic Essays*, SBLMS 25 (Missoula: Scholars, 1979), 115-43.

73. See Fitzmyer, "The Semitic Background of the New Testament Kyrios Title," for the Qumran Aramaic evidence. We know that *Yahweh* was written in Hebrew characters in extant Jewish Greek biblical manuscripts of the pre-Christian period, but by all indications Jews used a substitute term in reading aloud and in oral references to God. Josephus, writing in Greek toward the end of the first century, preferred *despotēs* in place of God's name, but he may have wanted to avoid using *kyrios* on account of it having become one of the titles of the Roman emperors under whose sponsorship he worked. Philo (early first century) prefers *kyrios;* see also J. R. Royse, "Philo, Kyrios, and the Tetragrammaton," *Studia Philonica Annual* 3 (1991): 167-83; A. Pietersma, "Kyrios or Tetragram: A Renewed Quest for the Original Septuagint," in *Studies in Honour of John W. Wevers on His Sixty-Fifth Birthday*, ed. Albert Pietersma and Claude Cox (Mississauga, Ontario: Benben Publishers, 1984), 85-101.

ter") and the application of the term to divine figures in the wider religious environment, there is also the more specific use in the religious vocabulary of Greek-speaking Jews of the first century as a reverential way of referring to God, parallel to the way *adonay* and *marêh* were used in Hebrew and Aramaic. Given the Jewish religious background and religious scruples of Paul and influential Christians of the first decades, this Jewish religious use of *kyrios* and the Semitic equivalents is the far more directly important linguistic provenance for the christological use of *kyrios* evidenced in Paul's letters.

In fact, the connections between Jewish use of "Lord" and the christological use of *kyrios* in Pauline Christianity are mediated through the prior practice of referring to Jesus as "Lord" in Greek-speaking and also Aramaic-speaking Jewish Christian circles in the earliest years of the Christian movement. This is confirmed by a crucial piece of evidence I referred to earlier, the transliterated Aramaic devotional formula Paul uses in 1 Corinthians 16:22 that is probably vocalized *marana tha,* "Our Lord, Come!" The expression certainly comes from circles of Aramaic-speaking Jewish Christians, where it was a feature of their worship practice, an invocation addressed to the glorified Jesus appealing either for his presence in the worship setting or for his eschatological appearance.[74] Paul's use of *marana tha,* without translation or explanation in this epistle written to a Greek-speaking congregation composed mainly of Gentile Christians, indicates that he counts on his readers being already acquainted with it. The likely reason is that he himself had introduced the expression to the Corinthians earlier as a verbal link to the devotional practices of their Aramaic-speaking, Jewish Christian coreligionists. This in turn means that the practice of invoking Jesus as "our Lord" must already have been sufficiently routinized in Aramaic-speaking circles by the time Paul taught the phrase to the Corinthians, that it carried a certain cachet of tradition and could serve to unite believers across linguistic and cultural lines in a shared devotional practice.[75]

We know from Romans 8:15 and Galatians 4:6 that Paul similarly taught

---

74. See, e.g., Fee, *Corinthians,* 838-39, and the literature cited there. Often overlooked but still valuable is the discussion in Franz J. Dölger, *Sol Salutis: Gebet und Gesang im christlichen Altertum mit besonderer Rücksicht auf die Ostung in Gebet und Liturgie,* 3rd ed., LQF 16/17 (1925; reprint, Münster: Aschendorffsche Verlagsbuchhandlung, 1972), 198-206.

75. Fitzmyer judged that *marana tha* here "gives evidence of a veneration of Jesus by early Jewish Christians as 'Lord,' as a figure associated with Yahweh of the Old Testament, even as one on the same level with him, without saying explicitly that he is divine" ("New Testament Kyrios and Maranatha and Their Aramaic Background," in *To Advance the Gospel: New Testament Studies* (New York: Crossroads, 1981), 229). I would only reiterate the point that for ancient Jews to have given corporate liturgical reverence to Jesus in this way would have involved an unprecedented and momentous innovation in traditional Jewish liturgical practice.

his Gentile converts to use another Aramaic devotional term, *Abba* (Father), as a specially meaningful Christian way of addressing God in prayer. It is very interesting that Paul passed on to his Greek-speaking converts these two Aramaic *X* prayer-expressions used by Jewish Christians to address both God and Jesus, which, taken together, reflect a "binitarian" devotional pattern originating among Aramaic-speaking Jewish Christians in Judea/Palestine and then promoted among Greek-speaking Pauline churches.[76]

The point I want to emphasize is not only that the christological use of *kyrios* in Pauline Christianity had translation equivalents in Aramaic-speaking Jewish Christian circles of earlier decades, but also that the religious meaning and functions of the application of *kyrios* to Jesus in Pauline circles were shaped by this earlier practice of appealing to the risen Jesus as "Lord" *as a feature of the devotional life of Aramaic-speaking circles*. That is, there was *a shared religiousness*, and not merely an inherited vocabulary. We have no basis for thinking that the designation of Jesus as "Lord" in Pauline Christianity represents some major development in meaning distinguishable from the reverential use of *maryah* for Jesus earlier in Aramaic-speaking circles of Jewish Christians in Palestine. Instead we have indications that Paul sought to align the christological terms and devotional practices of his converts with those of earlier circles of Jewish Christians.[77]

Let us now look more closely at the uses of the *Kyrios* title in Paul's letters. We look first at the referents to whom the title is applied. In the seven undisputed Pauline epistles there are just over 200 occurrences of *Kyrios*, in about 180 of which Paul applies the term to Jesus (the proportion is about the same if we include the uses in the disputed Pauline letters). Clearly, *Kyrios* characteristically functions in Paul's letters as a christological term. But that makes it all the more important to note that Paul also refers to God as *Kyrios*. The certain passages where Paul does this are citations of the Old Testament, and *Kyrios* is there the translation/substitute for *Yahweh*: Romans 4:8 (Ps. 32:1-2), Romans

---

76. Cf. Bousset's desperate proposal that *maranatha* was an Aramaic translation of an originally Greek invocation of Jesus (*Kyrios Christos*, 129), and B. L. Mack (*A Myth of Innocence: Mark and Christian Origins* [Philadelphia: Fortress, 1988], 100-102), who sharply distinguishes Palestinian "Jesus movements" from "the Christ cult" and attributes the latter to "the Hellenistic community" in "northern Syria." Among other things, Mack ignores the absence of any evidence in Paul for the supposed influence of these Syrian Christian circles. Instead, Paul frequently promotes links with and imitation of Jewish believers in Judea/Palestine (e.g., 1 Thess. 2:14-16; 1 Cor. 15:1-11; 2 Cor. 8–9; Rom. 15:25-33). I focus on these circles in the next chapter.

77. There is further indication of the routinized christological use of "Lord" among Jewish Christian circles of the earliest years in Paul's references to "the brothers of the Lord" (1 Cor. 9:5, *hoi adelphoi tou kyriou*) and to James, "the brother of the Lord" (Gal. 1:19, *ton adelphon tou kyriou*). In both cases Paul seems to be deliberately referring to these figures in formulaic expressions by which they were honorifically designated in their own circles.

9:28-29 (Isa. 28:22; 1:9), Romans 10:16 (Isa. 53:1), Romans 11:34 (Isa. 40:13), Romans 15:11 (Ps. 117:1), 1 Corinthians 3:20 (Ps. 94:11), 2 Corinthians 6:17-18 (Isa. 52:11; 2 Sam. 7:14). Even clearer as evidence that *Kyrios* was a part of Paul's own vocabulary for God are the several other citations of the Old Testament where Paul supplies an explicit reference to God as *Kyrios* for which there is no direct equivalent in the Old Testament passages: Romans 11:3 (1 Kings 19:10), Romans 12:19 (Deut. 32:35), 1 Corinthians 14:21 (Isa. 28:11). All these passages show that in Paul's inherited religious vocabulary the term *Kyrios* could serve to designate God, and functioned as a Greek substitute for God's name.

So it is remarkable that, in other citations of Old Testament passages which originally have to do with God, Paul applies the passages to Jesus, making him the *Kyrios*: Romans 10:13 (Joel 2:32), 1 Corinthians 1:31 (Jer. 9:23-24), 1 Corinthians 10:26 (Ps. 24:1), 2 Corinthians 10:17 (Jer. 9:23-24). In two other places it is more difficult to be certain whether it is God or Jesus to whom Paul applies the Old Testament citations: Romans 14:11 (Isa. 45:23) and 1 Corinthians 2:16 (Isa. 40:13).[78] There are also a number of cases where Paul alludes to Old Testament passages that mention *Yahweh* as the *Kyrios* and Paul clearly makes Jesus the referent: 1 Corinthians 10:21 (Mal. 1:7, 12), 1 Corinthians 10:22 (Deut. 32:21), 2 Corinthians 3:16 (Exod. 34:34), 1 Thessalonians 3:13 (Zech. 14:5), 1 Thessalonians 4:6 (Ps. 94:2).[79] But the most striking example of this is surely Philippians 2:10-11, which appropriates Isaiah 45:23-25 (originally proclaiming a universal submission to God) to portray the eschatological acclamation of Jesus as *Kyrios* "to the glory of God the Father."

These applications of Old Testament *Kyrios* passages to Jesus connote and presuppose the conviction that in some profound way he is directly and uniquely associated with God. For example, in Philippians 2:9-11 Jesus' status is bestowed by God, who has exalted Jesus and given him "the name above every name." The creative understanding of Isaiah 45:23 in these verses as predicting a universal acknowledgment of Jesus as *Kyrios* shows that being given this title must be the Greek equivalent of bearing the Old Testament name of God. We must note that Philippians 2:6-11 is widely thought to be Paul's adaptation of a christological hymn that likely originated much earlier than the epistle in which it is preserved, and that Paul shows no need to explain or justify its christological content.[80] Once again, this means that Paul here is no christological innovator, at least as far as the contents of this passage and the

---

78. D. B. Capes, *Old Testament Yahweh Texts in Paul's Christology*, WUNT 2/47 (Tübingen: J. C. B. Mohr [Paul Siebeck], 1992), argues that these are also applied to Jesus.

79. Also 2 Thess. 1:7-8 (Isa. 66:15); 2 Thess. 1:9 (Isa. 2:10, 19, 21); 2 Thess. 1:12 (Isa. 66:5).

80. One of the best studies is T. Nagata, "Philippians 2:5-11: A Case Study in the Contextual Shaping of Early Christology" (Ph.D. diss., Princeton Theological Seminary, 1981).

devotional practice it reflects are concerned. Instead the passage gives us valuable historical evidence of devotion to Jesus that was so familiar that Paul could use this fascinating christological recitation as a basis for making his real point here, which is to call for appropriate Christian ethical behavior.[81]

In 2 Corinthians 3:15-18 Paul's statement that "when one turns to the Lord the veil is lifted" (v. 16) applies to Christ, the phrasing adapted from Exodus 34:34 (where God is clearly the *Kyrios* before whom Moses takes off his veil). Paul goes on to link Christ with the divine Spirit (vv. 17-18), and refers to him as the agent of transforming glory (*doxa* = Heb. *kavōd*, one of the most important attributes of God in the Old Testament, borne here by Christ) and as the divine image (*eikōn*, 4:4) proclaimed as the *Kyrios* (4:5), in whose face the glory of God shines forth (4:6).[82]

Additional important evidence that Paul's references to Jesus as the *Kyrios* involve a direct association of him with God is found in the several passages where Paul appropriates the Old Testament theme of "the day of the Lord [*Yahweh*]" to refer to the eschatological victory of Christ (e.g., 1 Thess. 5:2; 1 Cor. 5:5; 2 Thess. 2:2), even modifying the phrase to identify Jesus explicitly as the *Kyrios* (1 Cor. 1:8; 2 Cor. 1:14). Larry Kreitzer focused on the close association of Christ with God reflected in Paul's use of *Kyrios* to designate Christ acting in the role of God in these passages, and Kreitzer rightly described a "conceptual overlap between God and Christ" in Paul.[83]

In another set of Pauline passages we have *Kyrios* applied to Jesus in expressions that are commonly recognized as having originated as acclamations of Jesus in early Christian worship. 1 Corinthians 12:3 refers to the acclamation formula *Kyrios Iēsous* ("Lord Jesus," or "Jesus is Lord") as prompted by the Holy Spirit. Romans 10:9-10 is another reference to this early liturgical acclamation of Jesus as "Lord," here connected to faith in his resurrection, which shows that Jesus' resurrection continued to be regarded as the historic basis and demonstration of his exaltation (as reflected also in Rom. 1:3-4). In Philippians 2:9-11 we have a slightly fuller acclamation, *Kyrios Iēsous Christos* ("Jesus Christ is Lord," or "Lord Jesus Christ"). Though the passage projects this universal acclamation as the divine purpose for the future, the phrase also echoes early Chris-

---

81. L. W. Hurtado, "Jesus as Lordly Example in Philippians 2:5-11," in *From Jesus to Paul: Studies in Honour of Francis Wright Beare,* ed. P. Richardson and J. C. Hurd (Waterloo, Ontario: Wilfrid Laurier University Press, 1984), 113-26. More generally, see S. E. Fowl, *The Story of Christ in the Ethics of Paul: An Analysis of the Function of the Hymnic Material in the Pauline Corpus,* JSNTSup 36 (Sheffield: JSOT Press, 1990).

82. Newman, *Paul's Glory-Christology.*

83. Larry J. Kreitzer, *Jesus and God in Paul's Eschatology,* JSNTSup 19 (Sheffield: JSOT Press, 1987), 116. See also Neil Richardson, *Paul's Language about God.*

tian devotional practice. As already indicated, <u>Philippians 2:6-11 is commonly</u>
✱ <u>understood as derived from early Christian worship</u>; the acclamation of Jesus
in early Christian worship settings was intended as an anticipation of this universal recognition of him as *Kyrios.*

We should also note 1 Corinthians 8:5-6, where there is another indication of the liturgical acclamation of Jesus as *Kyrios,* and the close association of
him with God in devotional practice. Here, in explicit contrast to the worship
practices of the polytheistic environment, Paul affirms a two-part exclusivistic
confession of "one God [*heis Theos*] the Father" and "one Lord [*heis Kyrios*] Jesus Christ" (the latter phrase resembling the longer, sonorous wording of the
acclamation in Phil. 2:11). In this astonishingly bold association of Jesus with
God, Paul adapts wording from the traditional Jewish confession of God's
uniqueness, known as the Shema, from Deuteronomy 6:4, "Hear, O Israel: The
Lord our God is *one Lord" (Kyrios heis estin* [LXX], translating Heb. *Yahweh
'echad).* This adaptation of the Shema may be Paul's own creative formulation
here, but, as we have seen, the acclamation of Jesus as "Lord" obviously had
long been a traditional feature of Christian devotional practice in Pauline
Christianity and in other Christian circles as well, in both Greek and Aramaic.

In addition to the types of uses of *Kyrios* already mentioned, there are
about 170 cases where the term is applied to Jesus in several somewhat formulaic expressions. In sociolinguistic perspective these are routinizations in the religious discourse of early Christians, which shows how thoroughly familiar it
was to use *Kyrios* as a christological title. In about 65 cases *Kyrios* is used with
other christological terms: "Jesus Christ our Lord" (e.g., Rom. 1:4; 5:21), "Our
Lord Jesus Christ" (e.g., Rom. 5:1, 11; 16:20; Gal. 6:18), "the Lord Jesus Christ"
(e.g., 2 Cor. 13:13), and "the Lord Jesus" (e.g., Rom. 14:14; 1 Cor. 11:23). In many
cases these constructions appear in the openings and closings of Paul's letters,
where scholars have identified Paul's use of greeting and benediction formulas
from early Christian worship settings.[84] These phrases are thus evidence of the
devotional expressions characteristic of Christian worship in which Jesus was
routinely referred to as "Lord."

The most frequently found use of *Kyrios* in Paul (about 100 times in the
undisputed letters) is the absolute use (with the definite article) to designate Jesus simply as "the Lord" (*ho Kyrios;* e.g., Rom. 14:6, 8; 16:2, 8, 11, 12, 13; 1 Cor. 3:5;
4:4-5). <u>In these cases it is clear that for Paul and his intended readers, "the Lord"</u>
<u>is sufficient and no further identifying words are needed</u>. As noted earlier, this
absolute use of *Kyrios* had its precedents and equivalents in Hebrew *(Adonay)*

---

84. See, e.g., D. E. Aune, *The New Testament in Its Literary Environment* (Philadelphia:
Westminster, 1987), 192-94.

and Aramaic *(Maryah)* references to God, and in Aramaic-speaking Jewish Christian practice where *Maryah* was also applied to Jesus. This indicates that Paul must have inherited this christological use of "the Lord" from his Christian predecessors, and these include Aramaic-speaking as well as Greek-speaking believers.[85]

There are three main kinds of contexts and statements in which *Kyrios* is applied to Jesus. One frequent kind of context is where Jesus' authoritative status for believers is the focus. Kramer noted that in Paul's letters Jesus is referred to as *Kyrios* "most frequently in statements about the practical conduct of the Church or of the individual."[86] As their *Kyrios,* Jesus claimed the obedience of believers and defined for them the sphere of their ethical endeavor. A few examples of Pauline passages will illustrate this.

In a larger section on how believers are to treat one another, Romans 14:1-12 urges believers who differ over foods and special days to respect one another as servants who are answerable to their Lord (v. 4). Paul portrays positively believers on both sides of these issues as acting "unto [NRSV, 'in honor of'] the Lord [*kyriō*]" and in thankfulness to God, both those who abstain and those who eat, both those who observe certain days and those who do not (vv. 5-6). Indeed, their living and dying are to be wholly "to/for the Lord [*tō kyriō*]" (vv. 7-8), and in the context this Lord is clearly Christ who "died and came to life anew [*ezēsen*] so that he could be Lord [*kyrieusē*] of the dead and the living" (v. 9).[87]

In 1 Corinthians 6:12–7:40 Paul deals with several questions about sexual behavior, often referring to Jesus as the *Kyrios.* Having been resurrected by God (6:14), "the Lord" is now the one to whom the bodies of Christians belong (6:13)

---

85. For reasons evident from my discussion here, Kramer's assertions that the acclamation of Jesus as "Lord" could have originated only in a "Hellenistic" context are unreliable and ill founded (cf., e.g., Kramer, 99-107).

86. Kramer, 169.

87. Consequently, in Paul's citation of Isa. 45:23 in Rom. 14:11, I propose that Jesus is probably to be taken as the *Kyrios* to whom every knee is to bow in a life of obedience, thereby also giving praise *(exomologēsetai)* to God. Phil. 2:9-11 shows that Isa. 45:23 was read in very early Christian circles as referring to Jesus and God. Such an interpretation of Isa. 45:23 would also explain why Paul modifies the text here to make explicit reference to the *Kyrios* as well as God. Cf., e.g., J. D. G. Dunn, *Romans 9–16,* WBC 38B (Waco, Tex.: Word, 1988), 810, who contends that *Kyrios* in 14:11 refers to God. To be sure, in some of Paul's Old Testament citations the *Kyrios* is God, but Dunn exaggerates things in claiming that this is Paul's "usual practice." As I have noted, in about ten citations *Kyrios* clearly designates God, and in another ten or so citations and clear allusions it designates Jesus. Paul's easy linkage of Jesus and God is illustrated in the context, where he uses the same verb *(proselabeto)* in referring to God as having "welcomed" believers (14:3) and to Jesus as having "welcomed" them "for the glory of God" (15:7).

and to whom they are joined in spirit also (6:17). In answering questions about marriage and singleness, Paul cites a saying of "the Lord" as a command (7:10-11), as he does elsewhere in this epistle (9:14; 14:37), and he distinguishes between these sayings of the Lord and his own advice (7:12, 25). Moreover, as in other passages, so here "the Lord" is the realm of Christian life: believers are called "in the Lord" (7:22), the unmarried are encouraged to devote themselves "to the Lord" (7:32-35), and the widow may remarry only "in the Lord" (7:39, i.e., within the Christian fellowship).

The same idea is reflected in Romans 16:2-20, where Paul repeatedly refers to believers as being "in the Lord [*en Kyriō*]" as well as "in Christ [*en Christō*]," meaning that they share in Christian fellowship and service (vv. 2, 8, 11-13). By contrast he mentions certain troublesome individuals who "do not serve our Lord Christ" (v. 18). Elsewhere Paul uses the phrase "the work of the Lord" to designate the activity of promoting the gospel (1 Cor. 15:58; 16:10). Paul portrays his own personal movements in his ministry as dependent upon the will of "the Lord" (1 Cor. 4:19; 16:7). In 1 Thessalonians 1:6 the believers are praised for being "imitators of us and of the Lord" in their obedience to the gospel amidst affliction; later in this epistle Paul exhorts the Thessalonians to observe ethical instructions that he gave them on the authority of "the Lord Jesus" (4:1-2), who will judge their behavior (4:6).

A second frequent kind of context where Jesus is referred to as the *Kyrios* is in eschatological passages. I have already mentioned the way the Old Testament idea of "the day of the Lord" is applied to the eschatological return of Jesus. In other passages as well where Paul refers to Jesus' future appearance and victory, he designates him as *Kyrios*. For example, in 1 Corinthians 4:1-5 Jesus is "the Lord" who at his coming will judge Paul and other believers, and in Philippians 4:5 the phrase "the Lord is near" reflects the expectation of Jesus' eschatological return that was shared by Paul and his converts. In these passages the designation of Jesus as *Kyrios* connotes much more than simply "master." As indicated also in the christological interpretation of the Old Testament theme of "the day of the Lord," the returning Jesus was thought of with attributes and functions that likened him to God. This association of Jesus with God in eschatological hopes has parallels in ancient Jewish references to principal agents of God's eschatological victory, such as the "Elect One" of *1 Enoch* 37–71. It is, however, rather stunning for early Christian circles to have placed in such a role a near contemporary who had suffered a disgraceful death and had fallen under the judgment of religious and political authorities.

The third kind of context is in statements that stem from and reflect the worship setting. Recall the earlier observation about the acclamation formulas commonly found in Paul's letters in which Jesus is confessed and invoked liturgically as the *Kyrios*, and also the liturgical greetings and benedictions referring to Jesus as *Kyrios* which Paul adapted to serve as letter openings and closings. We can illustrate this connection of the *Kyrios* title with worship contexts with a couple of representative passages.

In 1 Corinthians 11:17-33 Paul issues directions over proper celebration of the Christian sacred meal, which he refers to as "the Lord's supper" (*kyriakon deipnon*, 11:20), just as he refers to "the Lord's cup" and "the Lord's table" in distinguishing this meal from the cult meals of the pagan gods (11:27; 10:21). Throughout 11:17-33 Jesus is consistently designated *Kyrios* (11:23, 26, 27, 32). In the reference to "the Lord's death" in 11:26, where we might expect Paul to use *Christos*, the use of *Kyrios* probably stems from the statement having to do with Jesus' eschatological return and its use here in the setting of worship.

To cite another passage, in 1 Corinthians 5:1-5 Paul instructs the Corinthian congregation to carry out disciplinary action against a member guilty of "sexual immorality" (*porneia*). This is not the sort of action familiar in the experience of most Christians today, and it likely was not a frequent liturgical action in the first century either. But the action is clearly to be taken in the setting of the gathered church, where Jesus is characteristically affirmed as *Kyrios*. We should probably take "in the name of the Lord Jesus" as describing their assembly (alluding to the liturgical practice of invoking Jesus as *Kyrios*), and perhaps also as the spiritual power they are to invoke in handing the offender "over to Satan for the destruction of his flesh" (v. 5). Moreover, once again, in this passage concerned with a liturgical gathering, we have a reference to Jesus' eschatological return, "the day of the Lord."

There are thus three main types of Pauline contexts in which Jesus is characteristically referred to as *Kyrios:* (1) In hortatory statements and passages Jesus is the Lord/Master whose teaching and example are authoritative for believers. (2) In references to eschatological expectations, Jesus is designated the Lord who will come again as agent of God. (3) In formulae and passages reflecting actions of the worship setting, *Kyrios* designates the unequaled status given to Jesus by God and is the characteristic title given to Jesus in the worship practices of early Christian circles.

We can identify particular nuances in referring to Jesus as *Kyrios* in each type of context, but these connotations were likely all linked in the religious thought and life of the Pauline Christians and among those earlier Christians with whose beliefs and practices Paul sought to align his converts. We have noted how references to Jesus as the coming Lord appear in worship contexts where *Kyrios* also designates Jesus as recipient of corporate devotion. The overly sharp distinctions in meaning and in chronology between references to Jesus as eschatological Lord and as Lord of the gathered congregation (e.g.,

Bousset, Bultmann) are, thus, artificial and unrealistic. Instead we have to think of an exciting, dynamic, and rather complex "development" (explosion would be nearer the mark) of convictions about Jesus in the earliest months and years of what became the Christian movement. These earliest believers were less interested than some modern scholars in precise distinctions of nuance and in keeping their convictions in tidy compartments and carefully attached to discrete vocabulary. The various nuances of calling Jesus "Lord" were all connected in the semantics of earliest Christian circles, though one or another nuance may be more to the fore in different contexts (e.g., *Kyrios* as "master" to be obeyed in hortatory contexts, or as divine recipient of devotion in worship contexts).

We have to think in terms of a similar interconnection of connotations and convictions for all the christological titles we have looked at here. Certainly "Christ," "Lord," and "Son" each has its own connotation, and each seems to be used somewhat more characteristically in particular kinds of contexts in Paul's letters, as we have noted. But we should not impute modern analytical concerns to the religious life of early Christian believers. The easy way Paul varies his designations of Jesus, combines titles (e.g., as "Jesus Christ our Lord," "the Lord Jesus," "the Lord Jesus Christ"), and uses more than one title in the same passage (e.g., "Christ" and "Son" in Gal. 2:17-21; "Lord" and "Christ" in Rom. 14:5-9) shows the rich interplay of meanings operating in the religious life of believers in these early decades.

Preexistence

In recent years some scholars have questioned whether Paul's letters attest a belief in Jesus' "preexistence," that is, that Jesus had some sort of heavenly state/status prior to his historical, earthly life.[88] It is clear that belief in Jesus' preexistence did arise at some point, and it is commonly thought to be registered in New Testament writings of the latter decades of the first century (especially in John 1:1-18). But there are questions about how early this view of Jesus arose, how to account for the belief historically, and what Jesus' preexistence meant for early Christians.[89] There are also theological-philosophical questions about whether the preexistence of Christ can still be credible and meaningful

88. E.g., Jerome Murphy-O'Connor, "Christological Anthropology in Phil., II, 6-11," *RevB* 83 (1976): 25-50; and J. D. G. Dunn, *Christology in the Making* (London: SCM Press; Philadelphia: Westminster, 1980; 2nd ed., 1989).

89. In addition to Dunn, *Christology in the Making*, see also Jürgen Habermann, *Präexistenzaussagen im Neuen Testament* (Frankfurt am Main: Peter Lange, 1990).

today, and if so, what the significance would be; but these latter really lie beyond the scope of my discussion here.[90] In this chapter my concern is what Paul's letters tell us about the Christ-devotion that characterized Pauline Christianity, and perhaps other and earlier circles as well.

Though scholarly majorities can sometimes be wrong, we should note that the overwhelming majority of scholars in the field agree that there are at least a few passages in Paul's undisputed letters that reflect and presuppose the idea of Jesus' preexistence. Philippians 2:6-11 (esp. vv. 6-8) is usually considered the most explicit attestation, with shorter and more allusive references often seen in several other Pauline statements, among which 1 Corinthians 8:6 is prominent on account of an apparent link of Christ with creation ("one Lord Jesus Christ, through whom all things [are] and through whom we [are]"). Other references include 1 Corinthians 15:47 (Jesus is the "man from heaven"), 2 Corinthians 8:9 (Jesus "became poor so that through his poverty you might become rich"), Galatians 4:4 (God sent forth his Son to be "born of a woman"), Romans 8:3 (God sent his Son "in the likeness of sinful flesh"), and 1 Corinthians 10:4 (the "spiritual rock" that accompanied Israel in the wilderness was Christ).[91] But if some kind of preexistence is reflected in at least some of these references, can we say more precisely what this idea entails? Before we proceed to this question, however, we had best examine how secure the majority opinion is.

Prominently among those who take a dissenting view, James Dunn has argued that there is no idea of Christ's personal preexistence and incarnation in Paul's letters (in Dunn's discussion this includes Colossians, in which 1:15-20 is crucial on this question), and that all the Pauline letters attest is some kind of association between Christ and the Jewish concept of God's wisdom. That is, Dunn contends, in Pauline Christianity Christ may have been seen as the human expression or embodiment of God's attribute of wisdom, which in Jewish sources is often portrayed in personified form.[92] Because Dunn has dissented from, or attempted to qualify, more widely held views of these passages, he has

---

90. See now Karl-Josef Kuschel, *Before All Time? The Dispute over Christ's Origin* (New York: Crossroad, 1992). The collection of essays on the subject edited by John Hick (*The Myth of God Incarnate* [London: SCM Press, 1977]) generated controversy in English-speaking circles by questioning the meaning and logical validity of the belief and by claiming its origins in early Christian appropriation of pagan myths. See, e.g., Michael Goulder, ed., *Incarnation and Myth: The Debate Continued* (London: SCM Press; Grand Rapids: Eerdmans, 1979).

91. But Kuschel (298) sees a clear Pauline reference to Jesus' preexistence only in Phil. 2:6-11, which "stands 'in isolation' in the whole of Pauline theology."

92. Dunn, *Christology in the Making*, esp. 113-28, 176-96; and his more recent discussion in *Theology of Paul*, 266-93.

probed the topic at some length. In the interests of an economic treatment of the matter here, therefore, I shall engage the topic by way of interaction with him.[93] Even with a concern for a concise discussion, however, it will take a few pages to address the main issues involved in understanding what the several short passages in Paul tell us about Christ's preexistence.

First, Dunn is obviously correct to point out that there is metaphorical language in these references, and that metaphors should not be read woodenly. A prime example is the reference in 2 Corinthians 8:9 to Christ having graciously "impoverished" himself for the redemptive "enrichment" of believers. The reason for this particular set of metaphors lies in the context, which is not a christological treatise but an extended appeal for the Corinthians to participate generously in the Pauline financial collection for the Jerusalem church (the whole of 2 Cor. 8–9). Paul's reference to Christ's generosity is clearly intended to make it the supreme example for the practical generosity that Paul urges from the Corinthian believers.

✱ But in every intelligent use of metaphor the imagery represents a reality. ✱ So in this case we have to ask what constituted Christ's self-impoverishment and how it produced the "enrichment" of believers. Granted, Jesus' self-abasement here is referred to holistically, and in light of the repeated affirmation of the redemptive significance of Jesus' death in Paul's letters, it is reasonable to see Jesus' death as the apex of Jesus' generosity (though the nadir of abasement for him). Moreover, in Paul's letters it is surely Jesus' death and resurrection that constitute the decisive action on which the redemption of believers rests. But Dunn dubiously claims that 2 Corinthians 8:9 is *only* a "one-stage act of abasement" and that this can *only* be Jesus' death. The redemptive action of Christ is recounted by means of a single metaphor, self-impoverishment, but this is hardly a basis for restricting the reference to a single act, Jesus' death. Nothing in the passage demands this, and (contra Dunn) nothing in Paul's other references to the "grace" of Christ requires this either.[94] What Pauline Christians might have seen as being involved in Christ's self-impoverishment remains an open question.

To help address this question, we have to see what else Paul's letters tell us about views on Christ's self-abasement current in his churches. The most im-

---

93. I point readers to my earlier discussion, Hurtado, "Pre-existence," in *DPL*, 743-46 (with further bibliography).

94. Dunn's claim that Paul's other references to the "grace" of Christ *always* refer to his death and resurrection is flatly incorrect, as can be verified by use of a Greek concordance. In fact, Paul's most frequent references to the "grace" of Christ are in the grace benedictions of his epistles, where he simply invokes Christ's favor upon believers (e.g., Rom. 16:20; 1 Cor. 16:23; 2 Cor. 13:13; 1 Thess. 5:28; Gal. 6:18; Phil. 4:23; Philem. 25).

portant (and most contested) passage is Philippians 2:6-11.[95] In particular, how are we to understand verses 6-8, which refer to Christ being "in the form of God" and having been able to demur from exploiting for his own advantage "being equal with God"? Most scholars take these verses to reflect a belief in the personal preexistence and incarnation of Christ.[96] But Dunn contends that they allude to the Genesis accounts of the creation and disobedience of Adam, and that the Philippians passage simply contrasts the self-sacrifice of the human Jesus with the hubris of Adam in reaching for divinity. That is, Philippians 2:6-8 refers solely to the actions of the earthly Jesus, and no preincarnate state is in view.[97] Because Philippians 2:6-11 is recognized as a key passage for assessing the Pauline view of Christ, and the key passage on whether Pauline Christianity held an idea of Christ's preexistence, we should take some time to examine these verses.

It is true that, when they are suggested by scholars, we can see contrasts between Jesus' self-humbling in verses 6-8 of this passage and the serpent's claim that if they eat of the forbidden tree Adam (and Eve) will be "like gods" (LXX: *hōs theoi*) in Genesis 3:1-7. But Dunn's claim that Philippians 2:6-8 is a clear and direct allusion to the Genesis account and is thus intended to be read simply as "Adam Christology" greatly exceeds the warrants of the passage.[98] To cite a crucial matter, with a good many others Dunn asserts that *en morphē theou* (in the form of God) in 2:6 is simply a variant way of saying "image of God" *(eikōn theou)*, basing his assertion entirely on the partial overlap of the lexical range of meanings of the two words *morphē* (form, outward appearance, shape) and *eikōn* (image, likeness, form, appearance).[99] But, as modern linguistics has demonstrated, words acquire their specific meanings and denotations when used in phrases and sentences with other words. So the question is not

95. Dunn seems to have thought so as well, for he devotes nearly twice as many pages to this passage as to any of the others he addresses in his discussion of preexistence in *Theology of Paul*, 266-93 (discussion of Phil. 2:6-11 on 281-88). See also my other discussions of this passage: "Philippians 2:6-11," in *Prayer from Alexander to Constantine: A Critical Anthology*, ed. Mark Kiley (London: Routledge, 1997), 235-39; and "Jesus as Lordly Example in Philippians 2:5-11." Among recent commentaries, see esp. Gordon D. Fee, *Paul's Letter to the Philippians*, NICNT (Grand Rapids: Eerdmans, 1995), 191-229, and G. F. Hawthorne, *Philippians*, WBC (Waco, Tex.: Word, 1983), 71-96.

96. E.g., Habermann, 91-157.

97. Dunn proposes, however, that the passage "set in motion the thought of Christ's preexistence" and that the idea of the preexistent Christ making "an Adamic choice . . . in effect to become man" was "the almost inevitable corollary" (*Theology of Paul*, 288).

98. Indeed, it seems to me that in general Dunn attributes far too much to a supposed "Adam Christology" in Paul's letters.

99. E.g., BAGD, s.v. *eikōn* (222), *morphē* (528).

whether the general meanings of *morphē* and *eikōn* have resemblances, but whether the specific expression *en morphē theou* is actually used interchangeably with *eikōn theou* in Greek texts.[100]

The answer is clearly negative. In the Genesis passages *eikōn theou* is used to express the status and significance of the human creature (Gen. 1:26-27; 5:1; 9:6), and when subsequent writers wish to make allusions to this idea, they consistently use the *eikōn theou* phrase (Wisd. of Sol. 2:23; 7:26; Sir. 17:3; and as Paul himself does in 1 Cor. 11:7; cf. also Col. 3:10). Moreover, New Testament writers consistently use *eikōn* in statements that seem to make explicit christological appropriations of this theme (2 Cor. 4:4; Col. 1:15), and in other passages as well where the allusion/appropriation is less direct but still likely (1 Cor. 15:49; 2 Cor. 3:18). By contrast, *morphē theou* is never used elsewhere in any allusion to Adam. In fact, *morphē theou* is not used at all in the Greek Old Testament, nor, to my knowledge, in any other pre-Pauline Greek writing.

So the alleged use of *en morphē theou* as an allusion to Adam in Philippians 2:6 would be a singular phenomenon, and a particularly inept one as well. For allusions to work one must use, or at least adapt, at least a word or two from the alluded-to text so that readers can catch the allusion.[101] In Philippians 2:6-8, other than "God," there is not a single word from the Greek of the Genesis 1:26-27 description of God's creation of the human in "the image of God" or from the Genesis 3 temptation story.[102]

The phrase "being equal with God" *(to einai isa theō)* is never used elsewhere in any identifiable allusion to Adam. It is used, however, in several texts, and always negatively to describe the hubris of human efforts to become or be seen as divine: e.g., a Jewish accusation against Jesus in John 5:18; the dying lament of Antiochus over his own hubris in 2 Maccabees 9:12; and Philo's scornful reference to human vanity in *Legum allegoriae* 1.49.[103]

In Philippians 2:6, however, "being equal with God" seems to be presented

---

100. See also David Steenburg, "The Case against the Synonymity of *Morphē* and *Eikōn*," *JSNT* 34 (1988): 77-86, who shows that the two words are not simply interchangeable. My argument, however, makes use of modern linguistics principles to focus on the two Greek constructions, *en morphē theou* and *eikōn theou*. On semantics, see, e.g., John Lyons, *Language and Linguistics: An Introduction* (Cambridge: Cambridge University Press, 1981), 136-78; Moisés Silva, *Biblical Words and Their Meaning* (Grand Rapids: Zondervan, 1983).

101. See, e.g., Richard B. Hays, *Echoes of Scripture in the Letters of Paul* (New Haven: Yale University Press, 1989), 29-32.

102. Among the eight Old Testament allusions in Philippians identified by E. E. Ellis (*Paul's Use of the Old Testament* [1957; reprint, Grand Rapids: Baker, 1981], 154), there are none to Genesis.

103. Note also Philo, *Somn.* 2.130-31; *Decal.* 61; and see my discussion of John 5:18 and related references later in chap. 6.

as something already held by Christ or really within Christ's grasp, for he is pictured as refusing to exploit this status for selfish advantage.[104] It appears also that "being equal with God" is here equivalent or linked to "being in the form of God," the latter presented as the basis or condition for Christ being able to make a choice about not taking personal advantage of "being equal with God."[105]

Furthermore, given that 2:8 explicitly refers to the earthly Jesus' self-abasement and obedience to death on the cross, it would be somewhat redundant if 2:6-7 were simply recounting the same action. I suggest that the more plausible way to read 2:6-8 is as a narrative sequence, with Jesus' earthly obedience in 2:8 as the apex of a set of actions of selflessness that are then answered by God's exaltation of Jesus (2:9-11). All this means, as astonishing as it may be ~~see~~ that the idea developed so early, that Philippians 2:6-7 should be read as de- ~~p. 112~~ scribing the action of the "preincarnate" or "preexistent" Christ.

This raises the likelihood that Paul's Corinthian readers also would have been expected to think of Jesus' self-impoverishment in 2 Corinthians 8:9 as involving the range of actions that seem to be referred to in Philippians 2:6-8, which includes the selfless readiness of the preexistent Jesus to give himself over to costly obedience. To be sure, 2 Corinthians 8:9 is a *reminder* to readers of Jesus' generosity and self-impoverishment from some prior position of advantage ("you know the grace of our Lord Jesus Christ, that, being rich, for your sakes he impoverished himself"); so Paul does not explain what he expects his first readers to know already. But, with other scholars, I contend that various references in Paul's letters indicate that among the ideas he expected his converts to be acquainted with and to appreciate was the belief that Jesus had really come from God, and that the story of Jesus' own involvement in redemption extended back beyond his earthly existence and his crucially redemptive death and resurrection.

In another tantalizingly brief passage, 1 Corinthians 8:6, Jesus is explicitly identified as the one "through whom (are) all things and we through him." That is, Jesus here is linked with God, and the repetition of the prepositional phrases using "through" *(dia)* makes emphatic his role as agent in creation as well as redemption. As Conzelmann stated, "His preexistence is accordingly presupposed."[106] Exactly. Jesus' preexistence is logically presupposed in the ref-

---

104. On the phrase *oux harpagmon hēgēsato,* see esp. Roy W. Hoover, "The Harpagmos Enigma: A Philological Solution," *HTR* 64 (1971): 95-119.

105. The structure of the Greek of Phil. 2:6 indicates this. *Hos en morphē theou hyparchōn* is an adverbial clause giving the circumstance for the action of the main clause, *oux harpagmon hēgēsato to einai isa theō* [he did not regard being equal with God as an opportunity to be exploited].

106. Conzelmann, 145; Fee, *Corinthians,* 373-76.

erence to his agency in creation. But Paul's brief statement of this also seems to presuppose that the idea was already known to his readers, thus requiring no elaboration from him here. We would be very grateful if Paul had elaborated the idea of Jesus' preexistence, but this sort of passing reference to it is in fact very important for historical purposes. It indicates that the idea had already become disseminated among his churches so early that by the time he wrote his epistles he could take it for granted as known.

Scholars have sometimes asserted that the background of this idea lies in Greek philosophical traditions, noting that the prepositional phrases in 1 Corinthians 8:6 resemble language developed in Stoic pantheism.[107] But, though the Greek phrasing of this passage has parallels in Greek philosophical traditions, in fact the background and the logic of the statement in 1 Corinthians 8:6 and the other Pauline passages where Jesus' preexistence is alluded to lie in Jewish tradition, especially Jewish apocalyptic notions. The idea of Jesus' agency in creation and redemption is not driven by speculative interests, and does not respond to philosophical questions about how a transcendent deity could create the material world. Instead, the logic proceeds from profound convictions about the sovereignty of the one God reflected in Jewish apocalyptic tradition, which posit that all of history is subject to God, to whose predetermined purposes all things correspond.[108] Thus, in spite of the vagaries and evils of history, God's redemptive purpose is supreme and will triumph in eschatological glory. This eschatological triumph corresponds to and fulfills God's creation purpose, and so eschatological entities can be referred to as preexistent in various ways.[109]

In the Pauline references we have noted here, and in other New Testament references as well (e.g., Col. 1:16-17; Heb. 1:2; John 1:1-3), it is clear that attributing preexistence to Jesus proceeds from the conviction that he is the eschatological agent of redemption. Convinced as early believers were that Jesus has been sent from God, and that final salvation is to be realized through Jesus, it was, in

107. E.g., Conzelmann, 144 (references to philosophical writings in n. 44). For fuller discussion of the Greek phrasing in pagan sources, see Erik Peterson, *Heis Theos: epigraphische, formgeschichtliche und religionsgeschichtliche Untersuchungen*, FRLANT, n.s., 24 (Göttingen: Vandenhoeck & Ruprecht, 1926).

108. Nils A. Dahl, "Christ, Creation and the Church," in *The Background of the New Testament and Its Eschatology: Studies in Honour of C. H. Dodd*, ed. W. D. Davies and D. Daube (Cambridge: Cambridge University Press, 1954), 422-43. See also R. G. Hamerton-Kelly, "The Idea of Pre-Existence in Early Judaism: A Study in the Background of New Testament Theology" (Th.D. diss.; Union Theological Seminary, New York, 1966); Hurtado, "Pre-existence," 743-44.

109. As Dahl noted, "The distinction between 'real' and 'ideal' pre-existence is often fluid, and so is also the distinction between existence from the foundation of the world, pre-creational or eternal existence" ("Christ," 429).

the logic of Jewish apocalyptic, only a small and very natural step to hold that he was also in some way "there" with and in God from before the creation of the world.[110]

In fact, in the conviction that Jesus was clothed with the very glory of God and was to be reverenced in unprecedented ways as the *Kyrios*, early Christians seem to have gone beyond the notions about eschatological figures found in Jewish apocalyptic texts (such as the idea that the Elect One/Son of Man was "named," "chosen and hidden" before God "before the world was created, and for ever," *1 Enoch* 48.1-3).[111] Paul's formulaic statement in 1 Corinthians 8:6 indicates that already at that early point in the Christian movement believers were attributing to Christ not only preexistence or foreordination, but also an active role as divine agent in creation. Scholars commonly (and cogently) suggest that this reflects an appropriation of biblical/Jewish traditions about God's Wisdom pictured as God's companion in creation (Prov. 8:22-31; Sir. 24:9; Wisd. of Sol. 7:22; 8:4; 9:9).[112]

This is a suitable point at which to underscore certain key results of this discussion of Jesus' preexistence. First, there is good reason to see condensed references to the idea in Paul's undisputed letters, which means that it appeared astonishingly early in the Christian movement. Second, the condensed nature of the references indicates that Paul was not introducing the idea but presumed acquaintance with it already among his converts, which takes us back even earlier than the letters themselves.[113] Third, these references include reflections of the idea that Christ was actively involved as divine agent in creation. Fourth, the traditions and resources reflected in the belief in Christ's preexistence are biblical and Jewish, apocalyptic/eschatological traditions in which final things are seen as primal things, and traditions about God's Wisdom participating in creation. Thus the idea of Christ's preexistence is not to be attributed to "Hellenistic" influences and is probably not to be presumed as

110. On the early origin of the idea of Christ's preexistence and its connection with eschatological ideas, see also Hengel, *The Son of God*, 66-76.

111. Cf. also *T. Mos.* 1.14 (Moses "prepared from the beginning of the world, to be the mediator of [God's] covenant"), and 4 Ezra 12:32 (the Messiah is kept by God "until the end of days"), and 13:25-26 (the messianic man from the sea is "he whom the Most High has been keeping for many ages").

112. Hermann von Lips, *Weisheitliche Traditionen im Neuen Testament*, WMANT 64 (Neukirchen-Vluyn: Neukirchener Verlag, 1990), esp. 290-317.

113. Kuschel (303-8) mistakenly takes the lack of any elaboration of the idea of Christ's preexistence in Paul as indicating that the idea played little or no role in his religious views. But Paul had no need to expound Christ's preexistence, and could refer to the idea in the sort of condensed statements that we note here because he presumed an acquaintance with the idea through his previous missionary teaching in the churches to which he writes.

requiring supposed Hellenistic Christian circles for its provenance, but more likely arose in Jewish Christian circles that held Jewish eschatological categories as important.

One final point: in these Pauline statements it is the historic figure Jesus who is referred to as preexistent. It is difficult for us to imagine how this is to be reconciled with the equally strong early Christian awareness that Jesus was a real human figure of relatively recent time. Dunn proposes, for example, that 1 Corinthians 8:6 does not mean that Jesus was personally preexistent "as such," but only "that preexistent Wisdom was now to be recognized in and as Christ." In Dunn's view, "It is the preexistence of divine Wisdom" that is referred to here, not the personal preexistence of Christ.[114] The problem with this is that it is not what the Pauline passage says. Granted, in the passages where Jesus is described as agent in creation, it is likely that Jewish Wisdom traditions are drawn upon and adapted. But in some way that escapes easy philosophical categories, these passages directly attribute to Jesus personally a preexistence and a central role in creation. These claims resist philosophical categories because they do not arise from speculative interests. Instead they were prompted by profound religious convictions about the transcendent significance, unique status, and role of Jesus Christ, who was sent forth from God for the redemption of the world. In my view, we should understand these attributions of preexistence to Jesus as the expression of profound theological/christological convictions that we risk making banal if we attempt to fit them into what may seem to us more reasonable categories.

The preexistence passages reflect two key christological convictions: (1) Jesus' origins and meaning lie in God, above and before creation and human history, making his appearance an event of transcendent significance (e.g., Phil. 2:6-8; 2 Cor. 8:9); and (2) Jesus' agency in creation corresponds to his central role in redemption (1 Cor. 8:6), expressing his unique significance and the unity of divine purpose in creation and redemption. The Pauline references to Jesus' preexistence not only presuppose acquaintance with these affirmations, they also use them as a basis for making appeals for Christian behavior (humility and concern for others in Phil. 2:1-18; generosity in 2 Cor. 8:8-15).

Jesus' Redemptive Death and Resurrection

There is no dispute that in Paul's letters Jesus' death and resurrection hold powerful redemptive significance, and there are numerous and extensive scholarly

---

114. Dunn, *Theology of Paul*, 274.

discussions of the relevant Pauline texts and ideas.[115] Our concern here, however, is not primarily with Paul as a "theologian" and how he personally may have developed his ideas, but rather with the sorts of beliefs that were embraced broadly in the Pauline congregations. So it will be sufficient to summarize beliefs about the redemptive effects of Jesus' death and resurrection reflected in Paul's letters, and to focus on their religious function in Pauline Christianity and the degree to which they may represent an innovation or the appropriation of beliefs from earlier Christian circles.

Several specific observations about Paul's references to the redemptive effects of Jesus' death and resurrection are in order. First, in a goodly number of places Paul simply refers to these matters in brief, formulaic statements, without further explanation, which indicates that Paul presumed an acquaintance with them among the churches. In fact, in some cases Paul's references to Christ's redemptive death/resurrection are tucked into statements that really have some other focus. In 1 Thessalonians 5:10, for example, Paul refers to "our Lord Jesus Christ, who died for us" in a statement about God's eschatological salvation, and in the larger context of an exhortation for ethical preparedness for this coming event (5:1-11). In the midst of another hortatory passage, Romans 14:1–15:13, there is a brief reference to Christ having died and risen to be Lord of the living and the dead (14:9), and an appeal to show regard for fellow Christians as those "for whom [*hyper hou*] Christ died" (14:15). A similar sentiment appears in 1 Corinthians 8:11, in a passage urging Christians to shape their behavior with regard for "the brother for whom [*di' hon*] Christ died." In 1 Corinthians 6:12-20, where Paul urges believers to avoid fornication, there is an allusion to Christ's redemptive death (v. 20) with the reminder to believers: "You were bought with a price; therefore glorify God in your body." There is also the short reference to Jesus as "our paschal lamb" in 1 Corinthians 5:7-8, which requires and presupposes an acquaintance with passages such as Deuteronomy 16:1-8 and with this paschal interpretation of Jesus' death. Here, too, we have a passing reference to Jesus' death set in a context all about Christian behavior.

Earlier in 1 Corinthians (1:18-25), Paul famously contrasts "the message of the cross" with human wisdom, characterizing his message as "Christ crucified" (1:23); and in 2:2 there is his epigram-like statement, "I decided to know nothing among you except Jesus Christ, and him crucified." Both statements seem to presuppose that the intended readers share with Paul an understanding of the significance of Christ's crucifixion. This is confirmed by two other passages in 1 Corinthians where Paul explicitly reiterates teachings and traditions previ-

---

115. E.g., Dunn, *Theology of Paul*, 207-65.

ously delivered to the Corinthian believers, and in which the redemptive meaning of Jesus' death and resurrection is stated.

The first of these is 11:23-26, where Paul reminds the Corinthians of the tradition about Jesus' last supper, which includes words of Jesus about the bread representing "my body which is for you [*to hyper hymōn*]" and the cup representing "the new covenant in my blood." Both of these formulaic and compressed phrases refer to Jesus' death as redemptive. Thus Paul reminds the Corinthians that in their eucharistic meal they "proclaim the Lord's death until he comes" (v. 26).

In another rehearsal of a relevant tradition previously conveyed to the Corinthians (15:1-8), there is the statement that "Christ died for our sins [*hyper tōn hamartiōn hēmōn*] according to the scriptures," and that after burial "he was raised on the third day according to the scriptures" (vv. 3-4). This tradition presents Jesus' death and resurrection as fulfillment of divine purposes, and briefly but explicitly indicates the redemptive meaning of Jesus' death ("for our sins").

This introduces my second observation. Paul not only presumes an acquaintance with the redemptive meaning of Jesus' death and resurrection among his converts on the basis of his prior teaching of them, he also attributes this view of Jesus' death and resurrection to previous circles of Christians. In fact, in 1 Corinthians 15:1-11 Paul explicitly claims an agreement in such a view of Jesus' death and resurrection among all the previous Christians he names here (v. 11), which includes the Jewish Christian leadership of the Jerusalem believers (Cephas, James, and the Twelve).

Scholars commonly see the very compressed and formulaic wording of Romans 4:25 as yet another example where Paul uses a traditional statement about Jesus' death and resurrection: "[Jesus] who was given over [to death] for our trespasses and raised [from death by resurrection] for our justification" (that translations have to insert something like the words I have put into brackets reflects the very compressed and formulaic nature of the expression).[116] I agree with Cranfield that this formulation alludes to, and seems to draw upon, ideas and wording from Isaiah 52:13–53:12, which repeatedly refers to God's "servant" (LXX: *pais*) undergoing suffering for the sins of others, and on their behalf (Isa. 53:4-6, 11-12).[117]

---

116. Kramer (30-32, 119) cites a number of scholars who see Rom. 4:25 as "pre-Pauline." His rejection of this view rests upon unsupported and unpersuasive claims about an intricate tradition history of early Christian statements about Jesus as "given over" *(paradidonai)*.

117. C. E. B. Cranfield, *The Epistle to the Romans: Volume 1, Romans 1–8*, ICC (Edinburgh: T. & T. Clark, 1975), 251-52. Important verbal links to the LXX of Isa. 52:13–53:12 include the use of the verb *paradidonai* ("hand over," used three times in Isa. 53:6, 12), and the repetition of the preposition *dia* ("on account of/for," used three times in Isa. 53:5, 12).

This is fully compatible with the additional suggestion that this statement in Romans 4:25 likely goes back to circles of believers much earlier than the Pauline mission, people who naturally turned to the Old Testament Scriptures for an understanding of God's purposes, and who were sufficiently familiar with relevant biblical passages that this kind of allusive formulation was adequate. It is certainly worth noting that Paul presumes a familiarity with the idea that Christ's death and resurrection are redemptive among the Roman Christians to whom this epistle is addressed, circles he had no role in founding, and that had been established at a very early point by other Jewish Christians who "were in Christ before I was" (such as Andronicus and Junia, Rom. 16:7). The compressed reference to Jesus' death, resurrection, exaltation at God's right hand, and intercession for the elect in Romans 8:34 can be understood only as alluding to a whole body of christological teaching that Paul presumes was already well known among his readers.

In some other passages Paul appears to offer his own statements about Jesus' redemptive death and resurrection, though these are informed and shaped by the sort of traditional material we have noted here. For example, in a couple of passages Paul uses the Greek term *paradidonai* (to give/hand over), which probably stems from the sort of traditional formulation we see in Romans 4:25. In Galatians 2:20 he refers to Jesus as "the Son of God who loved me and gave himself [*paradontos*] for me [*hyper emou*]," and in Romans 8:32 Paul writes that God "did not spare his own Son but gave him up [*paredōken*] for us all [*hyper hēmōn pantōn*]."[118]

In still other passages Paul expresses more extensively the meaning of the death and resurrection of Jesus; in these we probably have Paul's own phrasing, though obviously he reflects these traditional convictions about Christ's redemptive death. Note his statement in 2 Corinthians 5:14-15 about being urged on in his mission by Christ's love, for Christ "died for all [*hyper pantōn*], so that those who live might live no longer for themselves but to/for him who died and was raised for them [*hyper autōn*]." The immediate context (5:11-21) is about Paul's aims in his ministry, and just a few verses later he characterizes God as the one who "for our sake [*hyper hēmōn*] made him [Christ] to be sin who knew no sin, so that in him we might become the righteousness of God." The phrasing "made him to be sin" is Paul's arresting way of referring to Christ's death for the sins of others.[119] In Romans 8:3 Paul uses another expression, re-

---

118. Note Eph. 5:2 ("Christ loved us and gave himself up for us"). If, as is widely thought, Ephesians is pseudepigraphical, the author echoes here Gal. 2:20. Kramer's view of the relation of Eph. 5:2, Rom. 8:32, and Gal. 2:20 as earlier formulations from which Rom. 4:25 developed stands all likelihood on its head (Kramer, 31).

119. Richard H. Bell, "Sacrifice and Christology in Paul," *JTS* 53 (2002): 1-27.

ferring to God's sending of his own Son "in the likeness of sinful flesh, and for sin [*peri hamartias*]," the latter phrase certainly alluding to Christ's redemptive death.

It is worth noting that the more extensive Pauline passages about Christ's death, which have received so much attention in scholarship and in subsequent Christian tradition, are in fact found in two epistles: Galatians (esp. 2:15-21; 3:10-29; 4:4-6) and Romans (esp. 3:21-26; 5:6-11; 6:1-11). In the one, Paul is desperately concerned to persuade Gentile Christians in Galatia to retain their trust in Christ as the sufficient basis for their redemption, over against those who advocated circumcision and observance of Torah as additional necessary conditions for Gentiles to be received as fully converted. In the epistle to Rome Paul presents himself and his ministry to Roman Christians (who likewise seem to be mainly Gentiles; e.g., 1:5-6; 11:13-14), in the hope that they will accept him and perhaps even cooperate with him in his future mission plans (esp. 15:22-33). In both letters Paul explicates and defends the validity of his mission to Gentiles, and his message that all believers are redeemed through Christ, and so Gentiles are not required to supplement their conversion by observance of Torah.

Paul's emphasis on the adequacy of redemption through Christ was directed most acutely to those concerned with the question of how Gentile Christians could fit into the biblical picture of Israel, the Sinai covenant, and Torah, among whom, obviously, Jewish Christians, and the Gentile believers influenced by them, were prominent. The need to justify the inclusion of Gentiles apart from proselyte conversion through Torah was serious. This accounts for the space devoted in these particular letters to expounding the redemptive significance of Jesus' death and resurrection, and it also helps account for what Paul says.[120]

Among those Gentile Christians for whom the biblical (Old Testament) "story" of Israel and Torah were authoritative categories for understanding God and themselves, the question of how Gentiles could be included in the elect without converting to Torah observance was understandably meaningful, and even urgent (e.g., the Galatian Gentile Christians whom Paul so vigorously sought to reassure and correct). It is clear that Paul taught his converts that Jesus' death and resurrection were "for our sins." Paul thereby communicated to

---

120. When concerns about Gentile converts were lost (or at least became less pressing) in subsequent Christian tradition (largely because Jewish Christians became so few and irrelevant), this crucial context of Paul's emphasis upon the redemptive meaning of Jesus' death and resurrection was likewise lost to Christian theological reflection. Consequently, Christian theology has characteristically ignored the questions that prompted Paul's discussion of Jesus' death and resurrection, and has treated Pauline passages as if they were written for the questions of subsequent Christian tradition.

them an interpretation of these events that went back to the Jerusalem church. In the Jerusalem tradition, however, the redemptive interpretation of Jesus' death likely functioned primarily as a rationale for why he suffered the ignominious fate of crucifixion. That is, "for our sins" was initially a christological apologia that answered the question of how Jesus' death formed part of God's purpose with the claim that it was a fulfillment of God's plan as predicted in Scripture.[121]

But Paul's own particular articulation of the implications of the traditional claim that Jesus' death and resurrection were "for our sins" was concerned more with providing a different apologia or rationale, one that gave a basis for the salvation of sinful Gentiles apart from Torah. The letters in which he explicates the meaning of Christ's death at any length were prompted by situations in which he especially needed to provide such a rationale. Perhaps, however, Paul had to develop these basic implications for himself, as a Torah-observant Jew who was then called to conduct a mission to Gentiles that did not require their conversion to Torah. In any case, where he did not see the need to justify further the status of his Gentile converts, that is, where their legitimacy was not called into question or a source of anxiety, he did not elaborate on the implications of Jesus' death and resurrection as he did in the epistles to the Galatians and the Romans. Thus, for example, we find no extensive treatment of these matters in the epistles to the Thessalonians, the Corinthians, and the Philippians.[122]

Right from the opening of the letter to the Galatians (1:4), Paul refers to the redemptive effects of Jesus' death and resurrection, anticipating the comparatively more extensive discussions that come later in the epistle. It is interesting that in 2:15-21, where Paul writes about his dispute with Cephas/Peter in Antioch, the issue between them is not whether Jesus' death is redemptive but whether Gentile Christians can be treated as full partners in Christian fellowship without their full observance of Torah. Paul protests to Cephas/Peter that,

---

121. I contend that this is the original function of the reference to Jesus' death as "for our sins" in the old tradition that Paul cites in 1 Cor. 15:3. Echoes of this early apologetic interpretation of Jesus' death are preserved in Luke-Acts (whose author, of course, emphatically claims to have drawn upon earlier traditions and sources in Luke 1:1-4). See, e.g., Luke 24:25-27, 44-47; Acts 2:22-36; 3:17; 4:27-28. Though these narratives, speeches, and prayers are composed by "Luke," they appear to incorporate very traditional affirmations that stem from Jewish Christian circles.

122. The warning about "the circumcision [party/promoters]" in Phil. 3:2-3 seems a more general warning and not occasioned by any specific threat in Philippi (e.g., Fee, *Letter to the Philippians*, 289-90), and the same seems to be the case in 1 Cor. 7:18-20, where Paul's reference to circumcision illustrates a general principle to "remain in the condition in which you were called."

by not relying solely on Torah ("the works of the law") but by instead trusting in Christ, Jewish Christians such as he and Cephas have shown that Torah observance is not a sufficient basis for being "justified," and that trust in Christ is necessary and sufficient (esp. 2:16).

But if Gentile Christians were to be expected to supplement their faith in Christ with "works of the law," that would imply that Christ is inadequate, and would have the effect of making Torah the essential basis of redemption and Christian fellowship. Thereby Cephas and Paul themselves would be shown to be transgressors in going beyond Torah to trust in Christ, 2:17-18, and it would mean that "Christ died for nothing" (2:21). In short, the basic conviction that Christ's death was redemptive is presented here as shared by Jewish Christians, and Paul's own contribution is to develop an argument from this shared conviction in support of the inclusion of Gentile believers.

Likewise, Paul's reference to Jesus' death in 3:13 as redeeming believers from the "curse of the law" (which threatens all who fail to observe all the commandments of Torah, 3:10) shows how "in Christ Jesus the blessing of Abraham might come to the Gentiles" (3:14). The larger context (3:1–4:7) is entirely concerned with giving a theological rationale to his Galatian Gentile converts for why they should not feel the need to supplement their faith in Christ by Torah observance, but instead should regard themselves as made fully children of God through Christ (e.g., 4:6).[123]

Paul's references to the meaning of Christ's death and resurrection in Romans are all shaped heavily by the same basic issue, though this epistle is absent the sort of heated desperation that drives Paul's discussion in Galatians. The discussion in Romans is occasioned by Paul's desire to make sure the Roman Christians have a direct acquaintance with his message and its rationale so that they can "be mutually encouraged by each other's faith" (1:12), and so they may endorse his ministry (15:24) and support him against opponents ("unbelievers in Judea") in his hope of having his mission accepted also in Jerusalem (15:30-32).

The first of the key Romans passages is 3:21-26, which sets forth Christ's death as the manifestation of God's righteousness "apart from the law" (v. 21), making it possible for "all who believe" to be "justified" and redeemed (vv. 22-24). Paul here refers to Jesus as put forth by God to be an atoning sacrifice "in his blood," to be received by faith (v. 25), so that God now "justifies the one who has faith in Jesus" (v. 26) "apart from the works of the law" (v. 28). The intricacy

---

123. It may well be that those Christian Jews who advocated circumcision and Torah observance by Gentile Christians were proceeding in the light of such passages as Isa. 56:3-8, which promises divine acceptance of Gentiles who "hold fast my covenant."

of the wording (and the thought!) arises from Paul's wish to show that Jesus' redemptive death provides the rationale for Jews and Gentiles alike to receive God's saving mercy (v. 30).[124] The Torah is thereby shown not to be the basis of redemption, and so it cannot be made obligatory for Gentile Christians.

In Romans 5:6-11 Paul presents Christ as dying "for the ungodly" (5:6), "sinners" (5:8), "enemies of God," who are now reconciled to God "through the death of his Son" (5:10-11). These verses are part of a larger section of the epistle (5:1-21) that follows logically ("therefore," 5:1) from the discourse in Romans 3–4. This preceding material emphasizes that redemption is offered to all, "adherents of the law" and Gentiles also on the basis of faith in Christ (4:13-16), whose death and resurrection make this possible (4:24-25). The whole of Romans 1–5 articulates the message of redemption through faith in Christ in relation to biblical and Jewish categories and with a special concern to affirm Christ as the defining basis of redemption for all, both Jewish and Gentile believers.

So Paul's own innovation or contribution was not to coin the idea that Jesus' death and resurrection were redemptive, nor to make this idea central to early Christian beliefs. The tradition that Paul cites explicitly shows that this idea had long been a key feature of circles of believers that appear to take us back to the Jerusalem church. But in Jewish Christian usage, the view of Jesus' death as redemptive had served mainly christological concerns, giving a rationale for the death of God's Messiah. Paul's innovation lay in contending that this traditional view of Christ's death and resurrection also gave a rationale for the programmatic salvation of Gentiles without their observance of Torah, an aim which he believed himself called to obtain through his Gentile mission.

Jesus as Example

In light of the emphasis on Jesus' redemptive death and resurrection that we find in some of Paul's letters, it is also worth noting that Jesus functions as in-

---

124. In this passage (and only here in the New Testament!) Jesus is referred to as put forward by God as a *hilastērion,* a term used twenty-one out of twenty-seven times in the LXX (and also in the only other New Testament use of the term, Heb. 9:5) to refer to the "mercy seat" (Heb. *kapporet*), the lid of the ark of the covenant where atonement is made for Israel. For discussion of how to translate the term in Rom. 3:25, see, e.g., Cranfield, 1:214-18. On the history-of-religions background to the reference to Christ's atoning death here, see, e.g., J. W. van Henten, "The Tradition-Historical Background of Romans 3.25: A Search for Pagan and Jewish Parallels," in *From Jesus to John: Essays on Jesus and New Testament Christology in Honour of Marinus De Jonge,* ed. Martinus C. De Boer, JSNTSup 84 (Sheffield: JSOT Press, 1993), 101-28.

spiring example for believers.[125] To be sure, this Jesus is also the *Kyrios* who is accorded worship and whose words are now authoritative for believers (e.g., 1 Cor. 7:10; 9:14; 1 Thess. 4:15).[126] But it is also part of the spirituality and beliefs that Paul promotes in his letters for believers to regard Jesus' actions of self-abasement (Phil. 2:5-11), redemptive generosity (2 Cor. 8:9), and service for the sake of others (Rom. 15:7-9) as authoritative examples for their own attitudes and behavior. Paul commends his Thessalonian converts for becoming "imitators of us and of the Lord" (1 Thess. 1:6), for thereby they became, in turn, an example for other believers (1:7).

What Paul calls for is not, however, a simple imitation arising from human efforts of contemplation and practice. Instead these references fit within a larger notion of believers being transformed inwardly by divine power (God's Spirit; 2 Cor. 3:18). Thereby they are enabled to embody Jesus' death and life in their own lives (e.g., 2 Cor. 4:7-12). Jesus is the "firstborn Son," to whose image believers are destined to be conformed (Rom. 8:29). In his own intensely emotive profession of religious aims in Philippians 3:7-16 (which he commends to his converts for imitation, v. 15), Paul aspires to a knowledge of the risen Christ that also involves "the sharing of his sufferings by becoming like him in his death, if somehow I may attain the resurrection from the dead" (vv. 10-11).

Clearly, in Pauline Christianity Jesus is the basis of redemption. But to a very real extent Jesus also functions as the inspiring model of the ethical qualities that are to characterize the present life of the redeemed and of the eschatological outcome of their redemption as well.

Binitarian Worship

The christological material we have surveyed here reflects an impressive, indeed extraordinary, place given to Jesus in Pauline Christianity. As Kreitzer and Richardson have shown, in Pauline Christianity we see a remarkable "overlap" in functions between God and Jesus, and also in the honorific rhetoric used to refer to them both.[127] This is all the more phenomenal when we note that Paul's letters show that this was already rather well developed by the 50s, and could be

125. David Stanley, "Imitation in Paul's Letters: Its Significance for His Relationship to Jesus and to His Own Christian Foundations," in *From Jesus to Paul*, 127-41. As Stanley shows, Paul links imitation of himself and imitation of Christ.

126. D. L. Dungan, *The Sayings of Jesus in the Churches of Paul* (Philadelphia: Fortress, 1971).

127. Kreitzer, *Jesus and God in Paul's Eschatology*; Neil Richardson, *Paul's Language about God*.

taken for granted by Paul. Indeed, there is hardly any indication in Paul's letters that he knew of any controversy or serious variance about this exalted place of Jesus among the various other Christian circles with which he was acquainted. In historical terms we may refer to a veritable "big bang," an explosively rapid and impressively substantial christological development in the earliest stage of the Christian movement. As Martin Hengel pointed out in an essay that should be required reading for any student or scholar investigating these matters, "The time between the death of Jesus and the fully developed christology which we find in the earliest Christian documents, the letters of Paul is so short that the development which takes place within it can only be called amazing."[128] Though Christians struggled over the next few centuries to articulate in varying ways more completely a view of the relationship of God and Christ, the Pauline letters indicate that at an astonishingly early point basic convictions about Jesus that amount to treating him as divine had become widely shared in various Christian circles.

But the data that we have examined thus far are not by any means the whole story. In my view it is still more remarkable that at an equally early point in the emergent Christian movement we find what I have described as a "binitarian pattern" of devotion and worship, in which Christ is treated as recipient of devotion with God and in ways that can be likened only to the worship of a deity. David Aune has expressed a similar view: "Perhaps the single most important historical development within the early church was the rise of the cultic worship of the exalted Jesus within the primitive Palestinian church."[129] I have analyzed the matter in detail in previous publications, and so here shall limit the discussion to reviewing and underscoring major points.[130]

Early Origins

The first point to emphasize is that this pattern of devotion appeared in Christian circles astonishingly early. As was true of the christological beliefs we sur-

---

128. Hengel, "Christology and New Testament Chronology," in *Between Jesus and Paul* (London: SCM, 1983), 31.

129. David E. Aune, *The Cultic Setting of Realized Eschatology in Early Christianity*, NovTSup 28 (Leiden: Brill, 1972), 5. See also the valuable discussion by Richard Bauckham, "Jesus, Worship Of," in *ABD*, 3:812-19.

130. Hurtado, *One God, One Lord*, 93-124; Hurtado, "The Binitarian Shape of Early Christian Worship," in *The Jewish Roots of Christological Monotheism*, 187-213; Hurtado, *At the Origins of Christian Worship: The Context and Character of Earliest Christian Devotion* (Carlisle: Paternoster, 1999; Grand Rapids: Eerdmans, 2000), 63-97.

veyed, the binitarian devotional pattern began so early that no trace is left of any stages of development; it is also taken for granted as uncontroversial among Christian circles in the Pauline letters, which, again, are our earliest extant Christian writings. In all of Paul's letters cultic devotion to Christ is presupposed as already characteristic of the Pauline congregations, which means it must be traced back at least to the 40s. Indeed, important data such as the *marana tha* formula discussed earlier, and the lack of indication that the devotional life of the Pauline churches constitutes any major innovation in previous Christian practice, combine to make it necessary to attribute the origins of the cultic reverence of Christ to Aramaic-speaking and Greek-speaking circles, and to the first years of the Christian movement (the 30s).

As I noted earlier, Paul was not reticent about mentioning differences between himself and other Christians, and was not shy about condemning those who differed on major matters. He lambastes "false brethren" in Galatians 2:4, the "hypocrisy" of Cephas in Galatians 2:13, the Judaizing "dogs" and "evil workers" in Philippians 3:2, and "false apostles, deceitful workers" who are Satan's ministers in 2 Corinthians 11:13. But neither in these references nor elsewhere in Paul's letters do we have indication of Christians who refuse to reverence Christ in ways that Paul approves. His sharp criticism in all these references is directed at those who were reluctant to accept the Torah-free Gentile mission (especially in Galatians, and Philippians) and some others who interfered in his churches and made various claims about their superiority (in 2 Cor. 10–12).[131] Given this, the absence of any conflict over cultic reverence of Christ is a rather eloquent silence. It is thus practically an unavoidable conclusion that there was a veritable explosion in devotional innovation as well as in christological beliefs in the very few earliest years (perhaps even the earliest months) that quickly became pervasive.

In the next chapter I will consider more extensively what we can say about the forms of Christianity that operated prior to and alongside Pauline Christianity. I confine myself here to the basic point that we cannot attribute the origins of the cultic worship of Jesus to Pauline Christianity. Instead, Pauline Christians took over and perpetuated from previous circles of Christians a devotional pat-

---

131. Paul's reference in 2 Cor. 11:4 to "another Jesus [*allon Iēsoun*]," "a different spirit [*pneuma heteron*]," and "a different gospel [*euangelion heteron*]" must be taken as mutually defining, and clearly have to do with efforts by unnamed people who question Paul's authority and teach a message that leads astray from "the simplicity and purity which is [due] to Christ" (cf. Paul's aim to obtain obedience to Christ, 10:8-9). Certainly nothing in Paul's strenuous rhetoric of refutation in 2 Corinthians suggests that these Christian opponents were circulating a view of Jesus that denied his divine status. Cf. Paul's description of *non-Christians* as unable to see the glory of Jesus (2 Cor. 3:12–4:6). See, e.g., C. K. Barrett, *The Second Epistle to the Corinthians* (London: Adam and Charles Black, 1973), 273-77.

tern in which Jesus functioned with God as subject matter and recipient of worship. Whatever other kinds of Christianity there may have been at the time, and whether or not all Christian circles were characterized by this "binitarian" devotional pattern, it is clear that Pauline Christianity was not idiosyncratic in reverencing the exalted Christ in the ways reflected in Paul's letters.

Worship

It is an important and legitimate question, however, whether the devotion to Christ reflected in Paul's letters really amounts to "worship" in the sense of reverence directed to a deity.[132] I am in full agreement on the importance of this question, and fully aware of the flexibility and potential vagueness of the term "worship" (which can cover a wide range of reverence beyond "cultic" worship such as one gives a deity). In several publications over a decade or more, therefore, I have insisted that we have to consider the specific devotional actions attested in Paul's letters.[133] Before we look briefly at these phenomena here, I want to underscore several important points.

First, I contend that the phenomena of Jesus-devotion reflected in Paul's letters are to be assessed collectively, and amount to a constellation or *pattern* of devotional practice, a programmatic treatment of Jesus as recipient of cultic devotion. It is this cluster of devotional phenomena that constitutes the striking development. We may be able to propose examples here or there in Jewish texts where some figure other than God is appealed to for help in what looks like a prayer, for example, or where something like a hymn or paean celebrates some figure (e.g., the paean in honor of "famous men" in Sir. 44–50); but these hardly constitute a *pattern* of devotional actions that could be regarded as cultic worship of such figures.

Second, the specific devotional phenomena in view were all connected

---

132. Dunn (e.g., *Theology of Paul*, 257-60) and P. M. Casey, "Monotheism, Worship and Christological Development in the Pauline Churches," in *The Jewish Roots of Christological Monotheism*, 214-33. Both insist that the reverence given to Jesus in Pauline Christianity did not amount to "worship" in the proper sense of the word, for Paul was a monotheist and thus simply could not have been involved in a "breach" of Jewish monotheistic practice and theology, and there would be evidence of Jewish objections in Paul's letters had his veneration of Christ been seen to be worship. They both also claim that the earliest evidence of Jewish views of Jesus-devotion as violating God's uniqueness comes with the Gospel of John, and must therefore be placed decades later than Paul. I refer readers to my discussion of these claims in the previous chapter.

133. In particular, see my attempt to clarify terms in "Binitarian Shape," 187-91 (which also appears in Hurtado, *At the Origins*, 65-69).

with, and were constituent actions of, the *corporate liturgical gatherings* of early Christian groups, and this further indicates that the phenomena should be understood as constituting "worship." We are not talking about acts of private piety, much less secretive activities such as seem to have been involved in the practice of "magic." The question before us is what *public, open, corporate* devotional practices characterized Pauline Christianity.

Third, when this constellation of devotional actions is set in the general first-century religious context, it is properly understood as constituting the cultic worship of Jesus. Certainly, as we shall see in the next section, there is not a separate cultus to Jesus as another deity, after the pattern of Roman paganism. Instead Jesus is characteristically reverenced by early Christians as part of their worship of the one God of the biblical tradition. Nevertheless, the devotional actions we shall examine shortly seem to have their closest analogies in the kinds of devotion given to divinities in the Roman religious environment, to the God of Israel in Jewish circles, and to the various deities reverenced in non-Jewish groups.

Fourth, this Jesus-devotion amounts to a striking *innovation* for which we simply have no precedent or analogy in the patterns of cultic practices and scruples of Jewish religious circles of the first century. As far as Roman-era Jewish religious practice is concerned, these devotional actions look like the sort of reverence reserved for the one God of Israel. Just as importantly, they represent the sort of reverence characteristically denied to any other figure, including God's own agents (such as principal angels or exalted patriarchs).[134] Thus, for this reason, too, these devotional actions are best taken as "worship" in the specific sense of the reverence that devout monotheists otherwise reserved for God. Let us look now at the specifics of the six types of phenomena in question.[135]

Prayer

The first category of devotional action is Christian prayer practice. As several studies have demonstrated, in Paul's letters, and most other early Christian writings as well, prayer is most characteristically offered to God "the Father" (e.g., Acts 4:24-30).[136] In Pauline Christianity we derive conclusions about

---

134. See esp. Hurtado, *One God, One Lord*, 17-92.

135. I draw here upon my previous discussions in *One God, One Lord*, 100-114, and "Binitarian Shape," 192-211 (= *At the Origins*, 70-94).

136. Major studies include Adalbert Hamman, *La prière I. Le Nouveau Testament* (Tournai: Desclée, 1959); Joseph Jungmann, *The Place of Christ in Liturgical Prayer*, 2nd rev. ed. (London and Dublin: Geoffrey Chapman, 1965).

prayer practice mainly from Paul's descriptions of his own prayers, and from what we can term "prayer-wish" passages which read very much like prayers.

In the openings of his letters (with the notable exception of Galatians), Paul usually refers to his prayers of thanks to God for the recipients (1 Thess. 1:2-3; 1 Cor. 1:4-5; Phil. 1:3-5; Rom. 1:8). There is a slight variation on this in 2 Corinthians 1:3-4, where Paul gives a *berakah* ("blessing," the Greek phrase here is *eulogētos ho theos*), a traditional form of praise prayer in Jewish practice. Note, however, that here God is specifically identified as "the God and Father of our Lord Jesus Christ" (phrasing echoed also in Col. 1:3; Eph. 1:3; cf. 1:17, "the God of our Lord Jesus Christ, the Father of Glory").[137] We should also note Paul's reference to giving thanks to God "through Jesus Christ" in Romans 1:8. Whether this last phrase alludes to actual prayer formulations that named Jesus as the one through whom prayer was made or merely indicates the religious viewpoint that Christian prayer was always offered "through" (as a result of) Jesus' redemptive work, it signifies the significant place of Christ in the prayers of Paul and his converts.

This is reinforced in Pauline prayer-wish passages, which most likely reflect actual prayer practices, and in which God and Jesus were addressed and invoked together (1 Thess. 3:11-13; 2 Thess. 2:16-17; 3:5). In 1 Thessalonians 3:11-13 Jesus ("the Lord") is specified in the prayer-wish that he will bring believers successfully to God in his eschatological appearance "with all his holy ones" (vv. 12-13). Further indication of the close connection between Jesus and God in prayer practice is given in the characteristic "grace and peace" greetings in Pauline letter openings, which invoke God and Christ together, and the equally characteristic "grace benedictions," which conclude Paul's letters and feature Jesus even more emphatically (e.g., Rom. 16:20; 1 Cor. 16:23). Both the salutations and the benedictions are commonly thought to represent Paul's use of early Christian liturgical formulas in epistles that were intended to be read out as part of the liturgical gathering of the groups to which they were sent.[138] This shows that already in the 50s, it was common (and uncontroversial among believers) to link Jesus with God as the source of the blessings invoked in Christian worship gatherings.

---

137. Several important Greek manuscripts (P45, ℵ*, B*, and others) omit *kai patēr* (and Father) from Eph. 1:3. This may be a scribal harmonization of this verse to Eph. 1:17; or conversely the phrase could have been added by scribes familiar with the fuller expression securely in 2 Cor. 1:3 and Col. 1:3.

138. Paul Schubert, *Form and Function of the Pauline Thanksgivings* (Berlin: Töpelmann, 1939); Peter T. O'Brien, *Introductory Thanksgivings in the Letters of Paul*, NovTSup 49 (Leiden: Brill, 1977); John L. White, "New Testament Epistolary Literature in the Framework of Ancient Epistolography," in *ANRW*, 2.25/2:1730-56.

There is also explicit indication of direct, personal prayer to Jesus in 2 Corinthians 12:8-9, where Paul refers to his repeated appeals to "the Lord" to remove some affliction. Paul's easy recounting of his prayer actions here suggests that he knew his readers to be familiar with direct prayer-appeals to Jesus as a communally accepted feature of Christian devotional practice.[139] In other early Christian writings as well, we have evidence of prayer to Jesus (e.g., Stephen's dying appeal in Acts 7:59-60). In fact, in apocryphal Christian literature prayer to Jesus is much more common than in the canonical writings and in other texts that reflect the liturgical practices promoted in developing orthodox Christianity.[140]

Overall, we get the impression of a remarkably well established pattern of prayer in which Jesus features very prominently, either as recipient or as unique agent through whom prayer is offered. Moreover, there is simply no analogy in Roman-era Jewish groups for the characteristic linking of Jesus with God in the prayer practice reflected in Paul's letters.[141]

Invocation and Confession of Jesus

Jesus was also addressed and invoked in other ritual actions of corporate worship, and these practices also go back to the earliest decades of the Christian movement. The previously mentioned fragment of Aramaic liturgical invoca-

---

139. Bauckham has complained that "The NT evidence for personal prayer to Jesus has sometimes been underestimated" ("Jesus, Worship Of," 813). On the Pauline evidence, Hamman is crucial (245-337), especially his discussion of the recipient of prayers in Paul's letters (264-80). More generally, see A. Klawek, *Das Gebet zu Jesus. Seine Berechtigung und Übung nach den Schriften des Neuen Testaments: Eine biblisch-theologische Studie*, NTAbh 6/5 (Münster: Aschendorffschen Verlagsbuchhandlung, 1921).

140. Jungmann, 165-68. This may indicate that in "popular" Christian piety, as distinguished from more tutored and "official" practice in the corporate worship setting, direct prayer to Jesus figured more prominently than is explicitly evidenced in the New Testament.

141. Daniel K. Falk, "Jewish Prayer Literature and the Jerusalem Church in Acts," in *The Book of Acts in Its Palestinian Setting*, 267-301; Falk, *Daily, Sabbath, and Festival Prayers in the Dead Sea Scrolls*, STDJ (Leiden: Brill, 1998); Esther G. Chazon, "Hymns and Prayers in the Dead Sea Scrolls," in *The Dead Sea Scrolls after Fifty Years: A Comprehensive Assessment*, ed. Peter Flint (Leiden: Brill, 1998), 244-70; Agneta Enermalm-Ogawa, *Un langage de prière juif en grec: Le temoinage des deux premiers livres des Maccabées*, ConBNT 17 (Uppsala: Almquist and Wiksell, 1987); Norman B. Johnson, *Prayer in the Apocrypha and Pseudepigrapha: A Study of the Jewish Concept of God*, SBLMS 2 (Philadelphia: SBL, 1948); Stefan Reif, *Judaism and Hebrew Prayer* (Cambridge: Cambridge University Press, 1993). For the wider religious environment, see Wolfgang Fenske, *Und wenn ihr betet . . . (Mt 6,5): Gebete in der zwischenmenschlichen Kommunikation der Antike als Ausdruck der Frömmigkeit*, SUNT 21 (Göttingen: Vandenhoeck & Ruprecht, 1997).

tion preserved in 1 Corinthians 16:22, *marana tha,* takes pride of place for the provenance of these practices.[142] Scholars tend to understand the formula as an imperative/appeal addressed to Jesus, "Our Lord, come!" that arose in the worship gatherings of Aramaic-speaking Christians and by the date of 1 Corinthians had become such a familiar liturgical expression (even among Greek-speaking Gentile believers!) that no introduction or translation was required.[143]

Whether the expression is an appeal to Jesus "the Lord" to be present at the worship gathering or for him to come eschatologically, it is evidence that the invocation of Jesus was a widely known feature of early Christian worship that clearly began among Aramaic-speaking believers, and already by the 50s had become well known among Pauline Christians too.[144] That Pauline Christians were not merely taught to invoke Jesus but were given this Aramaic invocation formula as well reflects a concern to promote a shared liturgical practice between Paul's Gentile churches and their Aramaic-speaking, Jewish Christian coreligionists and predecessors in the faith.

Once again we have here an unparalleled feature of earliest Christian worship. Such a corporate cultic appeal to Jesus simply has no analogy as a regular feature of any other known group connected to the Jewish religious tradition of the time, and it, too, indicates an incorporation of Jesus into the corporate, public devotional life of early Christians in a way that is otherwise reserved

---

142. See my discussion in *One God, One Lord,* 106-7; Conzelmann, 300-301; Fitzmyer, "New Testament Kyrios and Maranatha and Their Aramaic Background"; Hans Georg Kuhn, "μαραναθά," in *TDNT,* 4:471-72; and C. J. Davis, *The Name and Way of the Lord,* JSNTSup 129 (Sheffield: Sheffield Academic Press, 1996), 136-39, whose conclusions seem a bit weaker than the evidence warrants.

143. The formula also appears untranslated in *Did.* 10.6 as part of the eucharistic prayer prescribed there. This is further indication of how widely disseminated the formula and its liturgical usage were, even among Greek-speaking Christians in the early period. See, e.g., Kurt Niederwimmer, *The Didache,* Hermeneia (Minneapolis: Fortress, 1998), 163-64. I return to the *Didache* in chap. 10.

144. The eschatological appeal to Christ in Rev. 22:20, "Come Lord Jesus!" is often thought to be a Greek adaptation of the *marana tha* formula. Conzelmann (310) regards it still "an open question" whether Jesus is invited to the worship setting or is appealed to eschatologically, whereas Fee finds the eschatological sense "most likely" (*Corinthians,* 838-39). Siegfried Schulz's ("Maranatha und Kyrios Jesus," *ZNW* 53 [1962]: 125-44) distinction between invoking Jesus as "Lord" in this Aramaic formula and cultic acclamations in Greek-speaking Christian groups is refuted by more recently published evidence that the Aramaic term *maryah* could (contra Schulz) be used as a divine title (Fitzmyer, "The Semitic Background of the New Testament Kyrios Title") and by the fact that the *marana tha* formula was itself a *cultic acclamation,* addressed to Jesus as part of the worship of the Aramaic-speaking believers among whom the practice arose.

for God. Even if the appeal was for Jesus to come eschatologically, this places him in the role more typically attributed to God in Jewish expectation (e.g., *1 Enoch* 1.9).[145] In any case, as a feature of the liturgical practice of Christian groups, this appeal to Jesus is also an unparalleled modification of otherwise-known monotheistic practice.

Other ritual actions are also directed toward Jesus by name. Among important references, Romans 10:9-13 is particularly worth noting. Paul here commends the act of "confessing" *(homologeō)* with the mouth that "Jesus is Lord" *(Kyrion Iēsoun),* which is to be accompanied by heartfelt belief that God has raised Jesus from death; Paul portrays these acts as having salvific consequences (vv. 9-10). That the confession is a ritual act in the context of worship is indicated by Paul's adaptation of Joel 2:32 (LXX 3:5) to describe the action.[146] To "call upon the Lord" is a frequent biblical expression for worship of *Yahweh,* and it usually involved sacrifice in the sacred precincts of a sanctuary/temple.[147] In Romans 10:9-13, however, it is clear that Paul refers to ritual acclamation/invocation of *Jesus* in the setting of Christian worship, and that he does so by deliberately using this biblical phrase for worshiping God. Thereby is the ritual acclamation/invocation of Jesus likened to (or included within) the worship of God.

Other well-known references to this ritual acclamation of Jesus are in 1 Corinthians 12:3 and Philippians 2:10-11. The former reference is in the midst of a larger context in which Paul takes up various questions about Christian worship (1 Cor. 11:2–14:40), and the formula "Jesus is Lord" *(Kyrios Iēsous)* here is the ritual acclamation that is prompted by the Holy Spirit.[148] Likewise, the universal acclamation of Jesus as Lord in Philippians 2:10-11 *(Kyrios Iēsous Christos)* is commonly understood as an eschatological projection of the actual worship practice of Christian groups (corresponding to the early Christian view of their worship gatherings as anticipating eschatological realities).[149] It

---

145. M. Black, "The Maranatha Invocation and Jude 14, 15 (*1 Enoch* 1:9)," in *Christ and Spirit in the New Testament,* ed. B. Lindars and S. S. Smalley (Cambridge: Cambridge University Press, 1973), 189-96.

146. V. H. Neufeld, *The Earliest Christian Confessions,* NTTS 5 (Grand Rapids: Eerdmans, 1963), 42-68, is correct to see links of "confession" of Jesus with situations of trial, conflict, and persecution, but he errs in ignoring the evidence that the act was equally (initially?) a ritual of early Christian worship.

147. On the biblical background of the phrase and action, and study of all New Testament references, see now Davis, 103-40; K. L. Schmidt, "ἐπικαλέω," in *TDNT,* 3:496-500.

148. With a number of other scholars, I see the contrasting action of cursing Jesus *(Anathema Iēsous)* as an allusion to the views of real non-Christian opponents, probably including hostile Jews. See Hurtado, "Pre–70 C.E. Jewish Opposition to Christ-Devotion."

149. See esp. Aune, *The Cultic Setting of Realized Eschatology in Early Christianity.*

bears noting that in all these references Jesus' own name is explicitly pronounced in the cultic acclamation, thus identifying him by name as the Lord whom the gathered circles reverence and affirming that this Lord is the specific historical person, Jesus, and not some mythical figure or abstraction. This ritual use of Jesus' name to define and constitute the worship circle is probably what is referred to in Matthew 18:20, where Jesus is pictured as promising to be present "where two or three are gathered in my name."

Though "to call upon" Jesus was probably initially the specific ritual (collective) confession/acknowledgment of his exaltation as "Lord," the phrase quickly came to connote the broader devotional praxis of treating Jesus as recipient of liturgical worship through invocation, prayer, and praise. In 1 Corinthians 1:2 Paul refers to Christians everywhere *(en panti topō)* as "all those who call upon the name of our Lord Jesus Christ," which both explicitly indicates the christological appropriation of the biblical phrase and also makes this cultic reverence of Jesus the universal description of Christian believers. This use of the phrase as a way of designating Christians appears also in other New Testament writings (e.g., Acts 9:14, 21; 22:16; 2 Tim. 2:22). But, as with the *marana tha* formula, the appropriation of the biblical expression to describe and understand the ritual reverence of Jesus probably goes back well before Paul's Gentile mission.

Moreover, once again there is simply no parallel for this in any other group of the period in the Jewish tradition. For example, note the emphasis on the name of God in the "Similitudes" section of *1 Enoch*. There we find numerous references to denying (45.1; 46.7) and glorifying/blessing/extolling (46.6; 48.6; 61.9, 11-12; 63.7) God's name, and the elect are made victorious through God's name (50.2-3). In the early Christian groups whose worship life is mirrored and presupposed in the Pauline letters, the name of Jesus plays a comparable role.[150]

Baptism in Jesus' Name

The characteristic rite through which people became members of early Christian groups was "baptism," a ritual immersion that included the invocation of Jesus' name (e.g., Acts 2:38; 8:16; 10:48).[151] The practice is indirectly reflected in

---

150. Adelheid Ruck-Schröder, *Der Name Gottes und der Name Jesu: Eine neutestamentliche Studie*, WMANT 80 (Neukirchen-Vluyn: Neukirchener-Verlag, 1999); Wilhelm Heitmüller, *"Im Namen Jesu": Eine sprach-und-religionsgeschichtliche Untersuchung zum Neuen Testament, speziell zur altchristlichen Taufe*, FRLANT 1/2 (Göttingen: Vandenhoeck & Ruprecht, 1903).

151. Heitmüller, *"Im Namen Jesu"*; Lars Hartman, *"Into the Name of the Lord Jesus": Baptism in the Early Church* (Edinburgh: T. & T. Clark, 1997).

Paul's reminder to the Corinthians that they had certainly not been baptized into his name (1 Cor. 1:15), and in his reference to them as "washed," "sanctified," and "justified in the name [*en tō onomati*] of the Lord Jesus Christ and in the Spirit of our God" (6:11). The ritual invocation of Jesus in baptism helps explain why Paul describes those baptized as having "put on Christ" (Gal. 3:27) and having been "buried with him [Christ] into his death" through the rite (Rom. 6:4). As Hartman has argued, the reference to baptism as done "in/into the name of Jesus" meant to represent Jesus as "the fundamental reference of the rite."[152]

X Suppositions about direct influence of pagan cults upon earliest Christian practice and thought have been shown to be simplistic and unfounded.[153] Nevertheless, there are certain phenomenological similarities between the significance and role of Jesus in early Christian baptism and the place of the deities of pagan mysteries. As in the pagan initiation rites, so in the baptismal practice reflected in Paul's letters, initiates were assured of the power of the figure into whose rites they entered, Christian initiates coming under the power of Jesus as the God-appointed *Kyrios*. Yet Hartman persuasively argues that baptism "in the name of Jesus" emerged in Palestinian Jewish Christian circles, and that here, too, lies the historical origin of believers ritually identifying themselves by reference to Jesus' name. This is both remarkable and unparalleled in the context of Jewish tradition of the Roman period.[154]

The "Lord's Supper"

It is not necessary here to take up questions about various meal forms and the possible evolution of sacred-meal practices and formulas in early Christian groups.[155] As Klauck has noted, the early Christian celebrations of their sacred

---

152. L. Hartman, "Baptism," in *ABD*, 1:583-94 (citation from 586); Hartman, *"Into the Name of the Lord Jesus."*

153. A. J. M. Wedderburn, *Baptism and Resurrection: Studies in Pauline Theology against Its Graeco-Roman Background*, WUNT 44 (Tübingen: Mohr [Siebeck], 1987); Nock, *Early Christianity*, e.g., 132: "Any idea that what we call the Christian sacraments were in their origin indebted to pagan mysteries or even to the metaphorical concepts based upon them shatters on the rock of linguistic evidence."

154. In his reference to "our ancestors" being "baptized into Moses," as in his reference to the Israelites in the wilderness consuming "spiritual" food and drink (1 Cor. 10:1-5), Paul retroactively applies the cultic rituals and language of Christian circles back into the biblical narratives in question (see, e.g., Fee, *Corinthians*, 443-48; G. R. Beasley-Murray, *Baptism in the New Testament* [Grand Rapids: Eerdmans, 1962], 181-85). There is no evidence that conversion to or between Jewish groups (e.g., Qumran) involved a ritual invocation of Moses or any figure other than God.

155. Jerome Kodell, *The Eucharist in the New Testament* (Wilmington, Del.: Michael Gla-

meals "experienced a rapid and stormy development which tended to go in various directions in the first few decades after Easter."[156] Nevertheless, it is commonly accepted that a sacred meal that signified the religious fellowship of participants was a characteristic feature of Christian circles from the earliest years onward.[157] As with so many other things, the earliest references to a Christian sacred meal are in Paul's letters.

Responding to reports of improper behavior at the sacred meal, in 1 Corinthians 11:17-34 Paul reiterates a tradition that he had himself learned "from the Lord," by which he probably means that the tradition came to him via predecessors in Christian faith. In 10:14-22 he compares and contrasts the Christian sacred meal with the cult meals of pagan deities. My main interests here have to do with the connection of the Christian meal with the exalted Jesus.

The first thing to note is that the meal is obviously a "cultic" occasion that formed a key part of the devotional/liturgical life of early Christian groups. Christians ate these common meals to express their fellowship with one another and also with direct reference to Jesus. Paul refers to the meal as the "Lord's supper" (*kyriakon deipnon*, 1 Cor. 11:20), which clearly associates the meal with Jesus as the *Kyrios* of the Christian group.[158] In 1 Corinthians 11:27 and 10:21, he refers to "the cup of the Lord" and "the table of the Lord," which reflect the same explicit association. In the tradition that Paul recites in 11:23-26, he associates the bread and wine of the meal directly with Jesus' redemptive death, which is constitutive of "the new covenant"; Paul also characterizes the continuing cult-meal practice as a proclamation of the death of "the Lord" until his eschatological return.

Paul's discussion of questions about Christian participation in the cult

---

zier, 1988), 22-37, gives an overview of recent scholarship and issues, as does I. H. Marshall, *Last Supper and Lord's Supper* (Grand Rapids: Eerdmans, 1980), and H.-J. Klauck, "Lord's Supper," in *ABD*, 4:362-72.

156. Klauck, "Lord's Supper," 367. But Klauck finds somewhat simplistic Hans Lietzmann's theory of two quite distinguishable forms (*Mass and Lord's Supper: A Study in the History of the Liturgy* [Leiden: Brill, 1979]).

157. John Koenig has recently argued that the early Christian "eucharist meals" were connected to missionary efforts, defining and fueling efforts to promote "outreach ministries" (*The Feast of the World's Redemption: Eucharistic Origins and Christian Mission* [Harrisburg, Pa.: Trinity Press International, 2000]).

158. *Kyriakos* is used outside Christian circles in the Roman period with reference to Roman imperial matters and items, as shown many years ago by Adolf Deissmann (*Bible Studies* [Edinburgh: T. & T. Clark, 1901], 217-19; Deissmann, *Light from the Ancient East* [1927; reprint, Grand Rapids: Baker, 1965], 257-60). I cannot engage here Deissmann's intriguing thesis that the term was deliberately taken over in Christian circles as expressive of a political stance critical of the claims of the Roman emperor. Cf. Werner Foerster, "κυριακός," in *TDNT*, 3:1095-96.

meals of the pagan gods (1 Cor. 10:14-22) directly poses as exclusive alternatives these feasts and the Lord's supper. Here he refers to the cup and bread as a "participation" *(koinōnia)* in the blood and body of Christ (v. 16), and he draws a direct comparison between the Christian meal and the eating of sacrificial food in the Jerusalem temple (v. 18). He also warns here about "provoking the Lord to jealousy" (v. 22), biblical phrasing that originally referred to God, appropriated here to refer to Jesus as the *Kyrios* whose divine power is to be taken seriously. This is reflected also in 11:29-32, where Paul warns about the serious consequences of being judged by "the Lord" (Jesus) for inappropriate behavior at the Christian sacred meal.

Clearly the Lord's supper is here the Christian cult meal where the Lord Jesus plays a role that is explicitly likened to that of the deities of the pagan cults and, even more astonishingly, to the role of God![159] This is not merely a memorial feast for a dead hero. Jesus is perceived as the living and powerful *Kyrios* who owns the meal and presides at it, and with whom believers have fellowship as with a god.

There is no analogy for such a cultic role for any figure other than God in Jewish religious circles of the Roman era. For example, none of the figures so prominent in the eschatological expectations of the Qumran sect functioned equivalently in their common meals.[160] Yet Paul's explicit disdain for the polytheism of the Roman religious environment, and his use of biblical analogies and categories in expounding the significance of the Lord's supper, combine to make it clear that the exalted thematizing of Jesus reflected in the meal was not intended as a departure from the monotheistic tradition of Jewish worship. Moreover, Paul's recitation of early tradition in 1 Corinthians 11:23-26 indicates that the cultic significance of Jesus in the meal was not a Pauline innovation, but stemmed from earlier Christian circles.

Hymns

Scholars commonly recognize that hymns formed a characteristic feature of early Christian worship, and have shown great interest in finding and studying

---

159. H.-J. Klauck, "Presence in the Lord's Supper: 1 Corinthians 11:23-26 in the Context of Hellenistic Religious History," in *One Loaf, One Cup: Ecumenical Studies of 1 Cor 11 and Other Eucharistic Texts*, ed. B. F. Meyer (Macon, Ga.: Mercer University Press, 1993), 57-74; Klauck, *Herrenmahl und hellenistischer Kult*, NTAbh 15 (Münster: Aschendorffsche Verlagsbuchhandlung, 1982).

160. K. G. Kuhn, "The Lord's Supper and the Communal Meal at Qumran," in *The Scrolls and the New Testament*, ed. Krister Stendahl (London: SCM Press, 1958; reprint, New York: Crossroad, 1992), 65-93, esp. 77-78; Hurtado, *One God, One Lord*, 111-12.

hymns in the New Testament and other early Christian texts.[161] Paul refers to the *psalmos* as one of the features of the worship gathering (1 Cor. 14:26), which likely refers to a song of praise;[162] and there are other references to "psalms, hymns and spiritual songs" (*psalmois, hymnois, ōdais pneumatikais;* Col. 3:16-17; Eph. 5:18-20), compositions that were apparently sung or chanted collectively (cf. also Acts 16:25; James 5:13).[163] A number of New Testament passages are widely thought to incorporate hymnic material from the worship of first-century Christian circles (e.g., Phil. 2:6-11; Col. 1:15-20; John 1:1-18; Eph. 5:14; 1 Tim. 3:16), among which the Pauline passages are the earliest. Scholars have mainly been concerned with their contents and formal characteristics, and whether any might have originated in Aramaic.[164] My emphasis here, however,

---

161. E.g., Gunter Kennel, *Frühchristliche Hymnen? Gattungskritische Studien zur Frage nach den Liedern der frühen Christenheit,* WMANT 71 (Neukirchen-Vluyn: Neukirchener Verlag, 1995); Jack T. Sanders, *The New Testament Christological Hymns: Their Historical Religious Background,* SNTSMS 15 (Cambridge: Cambridge University Press, 1971); Reinhard Deichgräber, *Gotteshymnus und Christushymnus in der frühen Christenheit: Untersuchungen zu Form, Sprache und Stil der frühchristlichen Hymnen,* SUNT 5 (Göttingen: Vandenhoeck & Ruprecht, 1967); Gottfried Schille, *Frühchristliche Hymnen* (Berlin: Evangelische Verlagsanstalt, 1965); Klaus Wengst, *Christologische Formeln und Lieder des Urchristentums,* SNT 7 (Gütersloh: Gerd Mohn, 1972). Martin Hengel has emphasized the importance of hymns in earliest christological developments: "Hymns and Christology," in his *Between Jesus and Paul,* 78-96; Hengel, "The Song about Christ in Earliest Worship," in his *Studies in Early Christology* (Edinburgh: T. & T. Clark, 1995), 227-91. See also R. P. Martin, "Some Reflections on New Testament Hymns," in *Christ the Lord: Studies Presented to Donald Guthrie,* ed. H. H. Rowdon (Leicester: InterVarsity, 1982), 37-49. Joseph Kroll, *Die christliche Hymnodik bis zu Klemens von Alexandreia* (Königsberg: Hartungsche Buchdruckerei, 1921), surveys references beyond the New Testament. For the wider religious background, see Michael Lattke, *Hymnus: Materialien zu einer Geschichte der antiken Hymnologie,* NTOA 19 (Göttingen: Vandenhoeck & Ruprecht; Fribourg: Editions universitaires, 1991); Johannes Quasten, *Musik und Gesang in den Kulten der heidnischen Antike und christlichen Frühzeit,* 2nd ed. (Münster: Aschendorffsche Verlagsbuchhandlung, 1973 [1930]); K. E. Grözinger, *Musik und Gesang in der Theologie der frühen jüdischen Literatur* (Tübingen: Mohr [Siebeck], 1982).

162. BAGD, s.v. ψάλλω, ψαλμός, 891.

163. I think it unlikely that "psalms, hymns and spiritual songs" are to be taken as sharply distinguishable types of liturgical singing in Col. 3:16-17 and Eph. 5:18-20. But it may well be that "spiritual songs" refers specifically to spontaneous songs taken as inspired (like prophecy) by the Spirit. "Psalms" and "hymns" could well include the singing of biblical psalms, which, early on, were interpreted christologically.

164. The voluminous scholarship on Phil. 2:6-11 illustrates scholarly preoccupation with these questions. See Ralph P. Martin, *Carmen Christi: Philippians 2:5-11 in Recent Interpretation and in the Setting of Early Christian Worship* (Cambridge: Cambridge University Press, 1967; rev. ed., Grand Rapids: Eerdmans, 1983). See, e.g., the recent essay collection, Ralph P. Martin and Brian J. Dodd, eds., *Where Christology Began: Essays on Philippians 2* (Louisville: Westminster John Knox, 1998).

is on the singing of christological songs/hymns as a feature of the corporate devotional *practice* of early Christians.[165]

The first thing to note is how much this hymnic material in the Pauline letters and other early Christian writings is focused on the celebration of *Jesus, his significance and work*.[166] If, for example, Philippians 2:6-11 is (or reflects) an early Christian hymn, it illustrates this focus on Jesus, lauding his prehistorical status "in the form of God" and his breathtaking self-abnegation even to the point of crucifixion, and then proclaiming God's exaltation of Jesus to an equal status that entitles him to universal reverence.[167] Thus it is likely that singing/chanting (the singing was probably unaccompanied) in honor of Jesus was a very characteristic feature of early Christian worship. Much later, to be sure, the report of the Roman administrator Pliny about Christian gatherings, in a letter to the emperor Trajan (111-12 C.E.), refers to antiphonal singing "to Christ as to a god" *(carmenque Christo quasi deo)* as a chief feature of the worship of Christians.[168] The Pauline letters hint strongly that Christian circles of the early decades of the first century practiced something similar.

In addition to the passages that scholars often point to as hymnic material, we should also recognize that a great part of earliest Christian "hymnody" involved the chanting of biblical psalms, which were interpreted christologically.[169] The well-known importance of, and frequency of reference to,

165. See also Leonard Thompson, "Hymns in Early Christian Worship," *ATR* 55 (1973): 458-72.

166. Deichgräber (60-61, 207-8) notes that far more of this hymnic material is concerned with Jesus than with God.

167. Fee (*Letter to the Philippians*, 191-97) questions whether the passage really is a hymn, although he grants its "poetic and exalted nature" (193). In judgments about the question, we should avoid narrow notions of what features "poetry" or "hymn" should represent. It is most likely that the Psalms (which do not involve syllabic rhythm or word rhymes, and have lines of varying length) served as the most important models of what liturgical praise should sound like, and the melodic practices were more likely closer to chanting, with simple melodic patterns.

168. Pliny, *Epistles* 10.96.7. See A. N. Sherwin-White, *The Letters of Pliny: A Historical and Social Commentary* (Oxford: Clarendon, 1966), 691-710. Tertullian (*Apology* 2.6) and Eusebius (*HE* 3.33.1) understood Pliny's statement as referring to hymns sung about and to Christ.

169. "Next to Isaiah the psalter was not only — from the beginning — the most important Old Testament prophetic text, which was interpreted as statements about the person and work of Christ, but it was also *the hymnbook* of the Church. . . . The first songs of the early Christian congregation were the 'messianicly' interpreted psalms of the old covenant" (Hengel, "Song about Christ," 260). See also H. O. Old, "The Psalms of Praise in the Worship of the New Testament Church," *Int* 39 (1985): 20-33; and now the very valuable study by Margaret Daly-Denton, "Singing Hymns to Christ as to a God (cf. Pliny *Ep.* X, 96)," in *The Jewish Roots of Christological Monotheism*, 277-92.

148

Psalm 110 and other psalms in the New Testament is to be accounted for through prior widespread and frequent usage in Christian worship.[170] Under the impact of the religious "illumination" that came through the gospel and their religious experiences, early Christians chanted biblical psalms as features of their Christ-devotion. It is difficult to tell whether the "psalm" that Paul describes as a feature of worship in 1 Corinthians 14:26 refers to this practice or to fresh compositions emerging in Christian circles and likely shaped by biblical psalms, analogous to the psalmlike compositions that emerged among the Qumran sect (1QH, and the extracanonical psalms in scrolls such as 11QPs).[171] Perhaps no strict distinction was made as to the function of either kind of composition in worship, for in both cases the inspiration of the Spirit was believed to be the impetus, whether in revealing the christological meaning of biblical psalms or in inspiring new hymnic praise.

This undeniable christological focus in hymnody is another distinctive feature of Christian worship in comparison with known Jewish groups of the period.[172] Granted, the biblical psalms include praises of the king (e.g., Pss. 2; 42; 110), which were intended to be sung in Jewish worship settings. Also, among the extracanonical writings are compositions that concerned a messianic figure (e.g., *Pss. Sol.* 17–18), and these may have been used liturgically in the circles where these writings originated. But the emphasis on Jesus in early Christian worship songs is unprecedented, and constitutes at the least a significant degree of difference from the liturgical practices and pattern characteristic of Jewish groups of the period.

170. See, e.g., Donald Juel, *Messianic Exegesis: Christological Interpretation of the Old Testament in Early Christianity* (Philadelphia: Fortress, 1988); D. M. Hay, *Glory at the Right Hand: Psalm 110 in Early Christianity,* SBLMS 18 (Nashville: Abingdon, 1973). But these and other valuable studies of the use of the Old Testament do not usually sufficiently recognize the worship setting as the place where biblical texts first were seen as meaningful christologically. See my comments in "Binitarian Shape," 205-7.

171. James M. Robinson, "Die Hodajot-Formel in Gebet und Hymnus des Frühchristentums," in *Apophoreta: Festschrift für E. Haenchen zu seinem siebzigsten Geburtstag am 10 Dezember 1964,* ed. W. Eltester and F. H. Kettler (Berlin: A. Töpelmann, 1964), 194-235. Maurya P. Horgan and Paul J. Kobelski, "The *Hodayot* (1QH) and New Testament Poetry," in *To Touch the Text: Biblical and Related Studies in Honor of Joseph A. Fitzmyer, S.J.,* ed. Maurya P. Horgan and Paul J. Kobelski (New York: Crossroad, 1989), 179-93, show similarities between the Qumran hymns and the Magnificat (Luke 1:47-55) and the Benedictus (Luke 1:68-79).

172. David Flusser, "Psalms, Hymns and Prayers," in *Jewish Writings of the Second Temple Period,* ed. M. E. Stone (Assen: Van Gorcum; Philadelphia: Fortress, 1984), 551-77; James H. Charlesworth, "A Prolegomenon to a New Study of the Jewish Background of the Hymns and Prayers in the New Testament," *JJS* 33 (1982): 265-85; Charlesworth, "Jewish Hymns, Odes, and Prayers (ca. 167 B.C.E.–135 C.E.)," in *Early Judaism and Its Modern Interpreters,* ed. Robert A. Kraft and G. W. E. Nickelsburg (Atlanta: Scholars, 1986), 411-36.

Prophecy

Speaking forth prophetic oracles believed to have come to the speaker by inspiration was another feature of first-century Christian worship gatherings.[173] Paul lists prophecy as one of the common phenomena attributed to the Spirit in Christian worship (1 Cor. 12:10; Rom. 12:6; reflected also in Eph. 4:11); and in an extended comparison of prophecy and tongue speaking in the public worship setting (1 Cor. 14), he indicates that he considered prophecy especially valuable (see esp. vv. 1-5, 24-25, 31). As with the Old Testament phenomenon, the essential character of early Christian prophecy was the claim to be speaking under direct divine inspiration.

The characteristic connection of prophecy with early Christian worship gatherings makes it relevant to this survey, and even more so because the prophetic oracles were at least sometimes presented as inspired by the ascended Jesus. In 1 Corinthians 12:4-11 Paul gives a sampling of the charismatic phenomena of early Christian worship, which includes several types of inspired/ prophetic speech ("a word of wisdom," "a word of knowledge," "prophecy," 12:8-11), and it is interesting that he attributes them all to "the same Spirit," "the same Lord [Jesus]," and "the same God" (12:4-6). That is, it appears that Christian prophecy was understood as prompted by and in service to the *Kyrios* Jesus.

In his study of early Christian prophecy, Aune identified nineteen New Testament prophetic oracles in which Jesus is either the speaker or is identified as the source and authority of the prophetic speech, and he found another nine examples of prophetic oracles of Jesus in the early Christian hymn collection known as the *Odes of Solomon*.[174] In his list are several instances from Paul's letters; for example, in 2 Corinthians 12:9 Paul cites a prophetic word of Jesus given to him personally, and it is widely thought that in 1 Thessalonians 4:15-17 Paul cites an oracle of the risen Jesus. In comparison with other passages where he cites (or notes the lack of) an authoritative saying attributed to the earthly Jesus that Paul uses to order Christian behavior (e.g., 1 Cor. 7:10-12, 25), the teaching in 1 Thessalonians 4:15-17 is introduced with the biblical prophetic formula as "a word of the Lord" *(en logō Kyriou)*.[175] The "Lord" here is clearly Je-

---

173. M. E. Boring, "Prophecy (Early Christian)," in *ABD*, 5:495-502; David Hill, *New Testament Prophecy* (Atlanta: John Knox, 1979); and esp. D. E. Aune, *Prophecy in Early Christianity and the Ancient Mediterranean World* (Grand Rapids: Eerdmans, 1983).

174. Aune, *Prophecy*, 328-29. The NT texts include the seven oracles to churches in Rev. 2–3, plus Rev. 16:15; 22:12-15, 16, 20; 2 Cor. 12:9; Acts 18:9-10; 23:11; 1 Thess. 4:2, 15-17; 1 Cor. 14:37-38; 2 Thess. 3:6, 12.

175. On the various suggestions about this passage, see, e.g., Ernest Best, *A Commentary*

sus. Thus Paul here uses the sacred biblical formula for introducing prophetic oracles to refer to a saying of the exalted Jesus, probably delivered initially through a Christian prophet.

Given the negative stance of biblical tradition against prophecy in the name of any other deity (e.g., Deut. 13:1-5), and the lack of any parallels of prophetic oracles delivered in first-century Jewish group worship in the name of any figure other than God, this attribution of prophecy to the exalted Jesus is simply extraordinary. Oracles of the risen Jesus were apparently a fully acceptable mode of early Christian prophecy, with the risen Christ understood to function in a role like that of God. The association of such prophetic oracles with the early Christian worship setting provides us another important and remarkable way in which the risen Christ functioned in the corporate devotional life of early Christians.

"Binitarian"

As I have repeatedly noted, the phenomena we have been considering do not have parallels in any other known group with ties to the Jewish tradition of the time, and they amount to a programmatic inclusion of Jesus in the devotional life of the Christian groups reflected in Paul's letters. Jesus is reverenced in a constellation of actions that resemble the ways a god is reverenced in the Roman-era religious scene. Yet it is equally clear that this is different from the polytheistic pattern. This is also not ditheism. Jesus is not reverenced as another, second god. Just as Jesus is regularly defined with reference to the one God in Pauline christological statements, so Jesus is consistently reverenced with reference to God in the devotional actions of Pauline Christians.

Jesus does not receive his own cultus, with his own occasions or holy days. The "Lord's Supper," for example, is so named with reference to Jesus, of course; but he is the Lord of the supper by God's appointment and affirmation. Pauline Christians acclaim Jesus as *Kyrios* "to the glory of God the Father." Their worship is certainly shaped by the inclusion of Jesus, but is characteristically offered to God through Jesus. There are two distinguishable figures, God and Jesus, but in Paul's letters there is an evident concern to understand the reverence given to Jesus as an extension of the worship of God. This concern to define and reverence Jesus with reference to the one God is what I mean by the term "binitarian." Here we see the powerful effect of Jewish monotheism, combining with a strong im-

---

on the First and Second Epistles to the Thessalonians (London: A. and C. Black; New York: Harper and Row, 1972), 189-93.

petus to reverence Jesus in unprecedented ways, in the innovative and vigorous devotional pattern advocated and reflected in Paul's letters. I think we can properly refer to <u>the cultic worship of Jesus in Pauline Christianity</u>, but it is offered in obedience to the one God, and God "the Father" is given primacy.

One of the clearest bodies of evidence testifying to this devotional stance is comprised of several devotional expressions called "doxologies" that appear in Paul's letters (and in other New Testament writings as well).[176] This rhetorical form derives from Jewish liturgical practice (e.g., 4 Macc. 18:24), and involves ascribing "glory" (Gk. *doxa*) to God, sometimes with other attributes as well.[177] As remains true in subsequent Christian practice, the Pauline doxologies are characteristically directed to God "the Father" (Rom. 11:36; Gal. 1:5; Phil. 4:20 among the uncontested Pauline letters).[178] In all these contexts, however, God's work in/through Jesus is the *occasion* and *content* of the praise expressed in the doxology. This close involvement of Jesus in the praise of God is explicitly reflected in 2 Corinthians 1:20, which states that *through Jesus Christ* believers say "'Amen' to the glory of God."[179]

Doxologies are also directed specifically to Jesus, but they appear in writings widely thought to have been composed comparatively later than the uncontested Pauline letters (e.g., 2 Tim. 4:18; 2 Pet. 3:18; Rev. 1:5-6), and so the devotional use of doxologies directed to Jesus may have been a development of the late first century and thereafter. But even in these cases the larger context of the writings makes it clear that the reverence given to Jesus is set firmly within a monotheistic stance.[180] That is, the basic pattern evident in Paul's letters re-

176. These obviously liturgical expressions have received surprisingly little scholarly attention in discussions of the place of Jesus in the devotional thought and practice reflected in the New Testament. One of the few commendable exceptions is Arthur W. Wainwright, *The Trinity in the New Testament* (London: SPCK, 1962), 93-97, which focuses on those that seem to be directed to Jesus. See also the brief but pithy analysis by Carey C. Newman, "Glory," in *DLNTD*, 395-96 (395-400); and also J. L. Wu, "Liturgical Elements," in *DPL*, 557-60; Wu, in *DLNTD*, 659-65; P. T. O'Brien, "Benediction, Blessing, Doxology, Thanksgiving," in *DPL*, 68-71.

177. The frequency and connotation of the Greek work *doxa* (glory) as an attribute of God in the New Testament reflect the influence of Greek-speaking <u>Jewish usage of the term as a translation equivalent for the Hebrew word</u> *kavōd*. See, e.g., Harold Hegermann, "δόξα," in *EDNT*, 1:344-48. Indicative of the variations possible, the doxology in 1 Pet. 5:11 ascribes "power" *(kratos)* solely to God. Cf. Rom 9:5, where a related form of praise ascribes "blessing" to "the God who is over all," a kind of devotional speech also derived from Jewish practice (the *berakah*, in which the worshiper[s] "bless" God). See, e.g., H. Patsch, "εὐλογέω," in *EDNT*, 2:79-80.

178. See also 1 Tim 1:17, and the disputed ending of Romans (16:27).

179. Similarly, Eph. 3:21; and in other writings usually dated in the late first century: 1 Pet. 4:11; Jude 25.

180. I note the doxologies in Christian texts of the late first and second centuries in the final chapter.

mains dominant in the Christian writings and devotional practice that represent the emergent "proto-orthodox" faith in the late first and early second centuries.

Summary

Although this has been a lengthy chapter, I have in fact attempted to describe the place of Jesus in the religious thought and devotional practice of Pauline Christianity with a balanced concern for economy of space as well as adequacy of treatment. Consequently we have not considered everything by any means, and I am sure some readers have wished for further reference to this or that matter of Pauline Christology. Remember, however, that my concern has not been primarily with Paul himself and the full complexity of his christological thought, but with the beliefs and practices reflected in his letters, and that likely characterized Pauline congregations by the mid–first century. But I believe we have more than enough to conclude that the Pauline letters show an impressively full and amazingly early pattern of belief and religious practice in which Jesus figures very prominently.

As noted at various points in this chapter, this pattern of devotion and belief seems in fact to be presupposed as already in place by the time Paul wrote his epistles to various churches. That is, between the execution of Jesus and the date of these epistles, a scant twenty years, all that we have surveyed here appeared and became characteristic beliefs and practices, at least among Pauline Christians and those to whom they looked as their predecessors in faith. Already in the earliest extant Christian writings we have this historically noteworthy devotional pattern. It did not appear through some slow evolution or in easily definable stages. The obvious next questions include whether and in what ways the Christ-devotion characteristic of Pauline Christianity was novel or unique, and how much it was shared with other circles of Christians. In particular, what characterized the Jewish Christian circles, including those in Palestine, that were earlier than the Pauline churches? To these questions we turn in the next chapter.

CHAPTER THREE

Judean Jewish Christianity

As we have seen, the Pauline letters show a well-developed pattern of Christ-devotion involving remarkable beliefs and devotional practices that was already conventionalized and apparently uncontroversial among his churches at an impressively early date. This presents us with an important historical question (indeed, some might say it is the key historical question about first-century Christianity): How and why did this pattern of devotion to Jesus emerge so early and so fully? In particular, what relation was there between the Christ-devotion of the Pauline churches and the beliefs and practices of the Jewish Christian predecessors of Paul's converts in Roman Judea? Does the Pauline Christ-devotion represent a major innovation in or departure from the religious views and practices of these earlier Christian circles (or at least some of them), or is there considerable continuity? Further, what kind of significant diversity might there have been in the Christ-devotion of Christian circles in Roman Judea?[1] These are the questions to which we turn in this chapter.

Although there are additional reasons for the universally agreed-upon view that there were such earlier Christian circles, in fact our earliest and most

---

1. I use the geographical term "Judea" here to refer to the area that later was designated "Palestine" by the Romans, which takes in the biblical areas of Judea and Galilee. Paul seems to use "Judea" to mean the larger entity (i.e., the Roman province), and this is a common first-century use of the term. I refer to the groups in question as "Christianity" or "Christian" simply because they are historically attached to the religion that came to carry this name, without necessarily prejudging their particular forms of beliefs about Jesus or their religious practices. Some scholars distinguish putative "Jesus movements" in Palestine (or specifically Galilee) from the "Christian" groups more directly reflected in the New Testament. But this terminological distinction in fact is more driven by certain polemical and theological concerns than by historical understanding, and rests upon claims that I do not find particularly persuasive, as I will explain in this chapter.

secure historical sources, the letters of Paul, provide us with the strongest basis. Moreover, we know that early Christian groups were not uniform in their beliefs and practices; we know this, too, with equal certainty because, among other reasons, once again Paul unhesitatingly says so in his extant letters. But what can we specifically attribute to early Jewish Christian circles, especially regarding their devotion to Jesus, and on what bases?[2]

We noted at the outset of the previous chapter that the big problem with saying very much about what kinds of other Christian circles there were earlier than, and contemporary with, Paul's Gentile mission is what sources to use and what to make of them. There are several categories of source material to assess. There are writings that claim to come from leading figures in Jewish Christian circles of Roman Judea, including several New Testament writings (the epistles of James, Peter, and Jude). But the authorship, dates, and original provenance of these writings are all disputed among scholars, which makes it difficult to build a persuasive case that depends very much on this material. Narratives in Acts (esp. chaps. 1–12) purport to tell us about people and events in Jerusalem and elsewhere in Roman Judea, but here again there is much dispute about how much of these narratives is authentic historical evidence about the early years of Jewish Christianity. A number of scholars say the Q sayings source derives from early circles of Jewish followers of Jesus, but how to mine this material properly for information about these groups is also much disputed. The *Didache*, a second-century composite writing probably put together across several decades, contains traditions thought to come from Jewish Christian circles, but we cannot be sure of their date(s) or provenance(s). Finally, there is the information in Paul's letters. In an effort to build upon sources that claim the greatest amount of scholarly agreement as to date, authorship, and provenance, we shall again commence with the Pauline material, and then add to this through a critical appraisal of the other categories of evidence.

Pauline Evidence

It is worth noting that Paul's letters give us an impressive body of information about Jewish Christian circles in Roman Judea, and that he had ample opportunities to know about their religious beliefs and practices. Moreover, Paul gives the impression that he thought it important to promote a sense of linkage between his congregations and these circles. This all makes it plausible that the

---

2. Richard N. Longenecker, *The Christology of Early Jewish Christianity,* SBT 17 (London: SCM Press, 1970), is a valuable discussion too little dealt with in subsequent scholarship.

Christ-devotion reflected in Paul's letters has some real continuity with, and indebtedness to, the religious stance of these Jewish Christians.

Paul's Acquaintance with Judean Christianity

Let us first take stock of the knowledge of, and appreciation for, Judean Christian circles conveyed in Paul's letters. In Galatians 1:22-23 Paul says "the churches of Judea in Christ" noted that after his conversion he proclaimed "the faith he once tried to destroy." This suggests that Paul thought his present Christian beliefs and devotional practice corresponded to those of the Jewish Christians in Judea that he had previously opposed. In 1 Thessalonians 2:14-16 Paul encourages the Thessalonian believers to think of themselves as linked particularly with "the churches of God which are in Judea in Christ Jesus" in suffering persecution for their faith.[3] It is interesting that he mentions Judean churches here, for both culturally and geographically he could have pointed to much closer churches as allies and models for the Thessalonians. "Why did Paul pick on the relatively remote Judean churches and not on some community which he had himself evangelized?"[4] In both cases "Judea" probably means the whole of what is later known as Roman "Palestine," and Paul specifically invokes these believers as fully coreligionists with his converts.

In fact, from Paul's letters we can gather an interesting catalogue of information about Judean Christianity, which suggests that Paul was reasonably well informed about this stream of the early Christian movement. As illustration of this, his autobiographical account in Galatians 1–2 indicates that he was particularly concerned to keep in good relations with the Jerusalem Christian leaders (2:2), and he names here the key figures of that day: Cephas (Peter), James (whom Paul identifies as "the Lord's brother," 1:19), and John (probably John Zebedee of the Gospels).[5] It is from Paul that we learn that these three were regarded as leaders (*tōn dokountōn einai ti*, 2:6), and were apparently also referred

---

3. Contra B. A. Pearson ("1 Thessalonians 2:13-16: A Deutero-Pauline Interpolation," *HTR* 64 [1971]: 79-94), 1 Thess. 2:13-16 is not a later interpolation. See, e.g., Ingo Broer, "'Antisemitismus' und Judenpolemik im Neuen Testament: Ein Beitrag zum besseren Verständnis von 1 Thess. 2.14-16," *Biblische Notizen* 29 (1983): 59-91; Karl P. Donfried, "1 Thessalonians 2:13-16 as a Test Case," *Int* 38 (1984): 242-53; Carol H. Schlueter, *Filling Up the Measure: Polemical Hyperbole in 1 Thessalonians 2:14-16*, JSNTSup 98 (Sheffield: JSOT Press, 1994).

4. Ernest Best, *A Commentary on the First and Second Epistles to the Thessalonians* (New York and London: Harper and Row, 1972), 112.

5. J. D. G. Dunn, "The Relationship between Paul and Jerusalem according to Galatians 1 and 2," *NTS* 28 (1982): 461-78.

to as "pillars" (*styloi*, 2:9), which probably alludes to a view of the Jerusalem church as a sacred community, perhaps as a spiritual temple like the Qumran sect.[6] In this same account of a visit to Jerusalem to discuss his Gentile mission, Paul indicates that the Jerusalem church incorporated sharply different views about the terms for the inclusion of Gentiles. He describes those in Jerusalem who opposed his view as "false brethren" (2:3-5), and he claims that the "pillars" of the Jerusalem church did not question the legitimacy of his mission and its terms (2:6-10). I will say more about Paul's references to such major differences among believers a bit later.

In the Christian tradition about the gospel that Paul cites in 1 Corinthians 15:3-7, we again hear of Cephas and James, and have here our earliest mention of a particular group called "the Twelve" (v. 5), later referred to also in the canonical Gospels and in Acts (e.g., Mark 14:10; Acts 6:2). Both in 1 Corinthians 15:7 and in Galatians 1:19 Paul also refers to "apostles," a group of unspecified number that apparently has some special role or significance in the Jerusalem church. In 1 Corinthians 9:3-6 Paul compares his choices to work manually for his own support and to refrain from marriage with the practices and marital status of Cephas and "the other apostles and the brothers of the Lord," which he here professes to know. These all must be Jewish Christian figures, and the allusive nature of the argument here suggests that Paul expected the Corinthians to know more specifically who they are and their special status.[7] Otherwise Paul's argument would carry no force. The "brothers of the Lord," for example, are invoked but nowhere identified in Paul's letters. That Paul cites (and does not further identify) Barnabas as following a practice like his own in these matters indicates that he expects the Corinthians to know this Jewish Christian figure too, and to appreciate the force of his example. The same presumptions are reflected also in the reference to Barnabas in Galatians 2:13. As Jervell contended, there is thus good reason to think that Paul conveyed to his churches traditions about the Jerusalem church, and that he encouraged his converts to think of themselves as linked with Judean Christians in a common faith.[8]

---

6. C. K. Barrett, "Paul and the 'Pillar' Apostles," in *Studia Paulina (Festschrift J. De Zwaan)*, ed. J. N. Sevenster and W. C. van Unnik (Haarlem: Bohn, 1953), 1-19; cf. R. Aus, "Three Pillars and Three Patriarchs: A Proposal concerning Gal 2:9," *ZNW* 70 (1979): 252-61; Bertil Gärtner, *The Temple and the Community in Qumran and the New Testament*, SNTSMS 1 (Cambridge: Cambridge University Press, 1965).

7. On "the brothers of the Lord" and their special status in Judean Christian circles, see esp. Richard Bauckham, *Jude and the Relatives of Jesus in the Early Church* (Edinburgh: T. & T. Clark, 1990), 5-37, 125-33.

8. Jacob Jervell, *Luke and the People of God* (Minneapolis: Augsburg, 1972), 19-39, esp. 32-36.

The Jerusalem Offering

The most impressive indication that ties with the Jerusalem church were profoundly important to Paul is of course the offering for Jerusalem from his churches to which he devoted considerable energy over a number of years.[9] No account of the relationship of Pauline Christianity and its Judean predecessors is adequate that fails to take this project seriously.[10] In addition to his other references to the project (Gal. 2:10; 1 Cor. 16:1-4), there is his lengthy and highly charged appeal to the Corinthians to contribute liberally (2 Cor. 8–9), his characterization in Romans of his final trip to Jerusalem as mainly concerned with delivery of the offering (Rom. 15:25-27), and the anxiety he expresses about the success of the offering (15:28-33). These all combine to indicate that the offering was hugely important to Paul.

In an article published some time ago, I proposed that those Judaizing Christians who challenged Paul's authority in Galatia may have presented his effort to prepare a collection for Jerusalem as an obligatory tax laid on him by the Jerusalem leaders; they urged this as evidence that he was not a true apostle with authentic status.[11] This would help explain the rather defensive tone of Galatians 2:6-10 with its denial that the Jerusalem leaders laid any obligations on Paul, and the emphasis that the idea of an offering for Jerusalem only confirmed something he had already intended to do (2:10). If my proposal is correct that the collection was being used against him, Paul's refusal to back away from it shows how much the project meant to him. This was not some merely token effort, and Paul clearly sought to deliver an impressively large offering with participation from all his churches.

The reason for Paul's effort is that he intended the offering to express and promote a shared religious stance and experience, and mutual acceptance as well, between Judean and Gentile Christian believers. In Romans 15:27 Paul

---

9. See Bengt Holmberg's excellent discussion in *Paul and Power* (Philadelphia: Fortress, 1978), 35-43; Scot McKnight, "Collection for the Saints," in *DPL*, 143-47, and his bibliography; and more recently still J. D. G. Dunn, *The Theology of Paul the Apostle* (Grand Rapids: Eerdmans, 1998), 706-11. But Dunn's reluctance to see the Jerusalem collection referred to in Gal. 2:10 (706 n. 170) is not persuasive.

10. Crossan's discussion (*The Birth of Christianity* [New York: Harper Collins, 1998], 473-76) of the collection completely fails to take account of its relevance for assessing Paul's intended relationship of his churches and their piety with Judean Christianity.

11. L. W. Hurtado, "The Jerusalem Collection and the Book of Galatians," *JSNT* 5 (1979): 46-62. Cf. A. J. M. Wedderburn, "Paul's Collection: Chronology and History," *NTS* 48 (2002): 95-110, who rejects my proposal (esp. 96 n. 3). But his objections all strike me as reflecting a failure to understand and engage my argument. His own view of Gal. 2:10 seems to me driven overmuch by fear that it works against his effort to date Galatians early.

refers to his Gentile converts as having come to share in the same "spiritual blessings" *(pneumatikois autōn)* as Judean believers. In 2 Corinthians 9:13-15 he tells the Corinthian Christians that through their participation in the offering, they glorify God and show their "obedience to the confession of the gospel of Christ," and he predicts that the Judean believers in turn will be moved to reciprocate by relating to his Gentile converts as full partners in the grace of God. Craig Hill has succinctly characterized the Pauline evidence as follows: "Paul assumed that the Jerusalem Christians were Christians, that there was a unity and a consistency to the gospel both they and he preached (Rom. 15:27; Gal. 2:7-10)."[12]

Paul's aims for such mutual recognition, and his view of Judean and Gentile believers as fully coreligionists, work against the claims by some scholars that Pauline Christianity represents a sharp departure from the religiousness of Judean "Jesus movements," and in particular, that there were major christological differences between the latter and the "Christ cult" that we see reflected in Paul's letters. If there were such major differences as is sometimes alleged, Paul's view of the relationship of Judean and Gentile Christians would have been either insincere or completely unfounded. But both the knowledge of Judean Christianity alluded to in Paul's letters and his passionate concern that the faith and practice of his converts be associated with that of their Jewish Christian predecessors make it unlikely that he was misinformed about Judean believers; and his continuing efforts to maintain good relations with Judean believers (especially shown in the Jerusalem collection) make it unlikely that he was insincere.

As Dunn has noted, Paul's frequent reference to the Jerusalem church simply as "the saints" (1 Cor. 16:1; 2 Cor. 8:4; 9:1, 12; Rom. 15:25, 31; cf. "the poor among the saints who are in Jerusalem," Rom. 15:26) "clearly implies that the Jerusalem church held a central place among all the churches."[13] This is confirmed by Paul's geographical description of his mission as "from Jerusalem and as far around as Illyricum," which reflects "how natural it was for Paul to regard Jerusalem as the source of the word of God, and to take this, somewhat unhistorically, as the starting point of his own apostolic work."[14]

---

12. Craig C. Hill, *Hellenists and Hebrews: Reappraising Division within the Earliest Church* (Minneapolis: Fortress, 1992), 174. I recommend the whole of Hill's discussion of the Jerusalem offering, 173-78.

13. Dunn, *Theology of Paul,* 708.

14. Holmberg, 50.

Differences

Yet there were sharp differences among Christians of the early decades. We briefly noted in the preceding chapter that Paul was not reluctant to indicate differences between himself and other Christians, and he portrays some of them in very stark terms. But the issues seem to have been mainly about the terms of conversion of Gentile Christians and about Paul's apostolic legitimacy and authority.[15] Because the validity of Paul's view of Gentile conversion was unavoidably connected with his claim to apostolic authority and a direct commission from God, any challenge about the adequacy of his message required also questioning his legitimacy and independent authority.

Many, perhaps most, Jewish Christians seem generally to have found no incompatibility between putting faith in Jesus as Messiah and glorified Lord and continuing their traditional observance of Torah, which they still regarded as the commandments of God. Some Jewish Christians (the "circumcision party") demanded that Gentile believers, in addition to putting faith in Jesus, also take up full observance of Torah. Otherwise they had not made a full conversion to the God of Israel. In short, these Jewish Christians saw Gentiles who were baptized in Jesus' name as having made a good, decisive step in the right direction, but they should complete their conversion by also committing themselves to observance of Torah.

That is, these Jewish Christians apparently continued to take the same view of Gentiles as did many diaspora Jews in the Roman period.[16] "God-fearing" Gentiles who showed an interest in the God of Israel and abstained from idolatry were often welcomed by diaspora synagogues. These Gentiles were regarded by Jews as an outer circle of adherents, their interest in Judaism appreciated and their benefactions welcomed. But they could be treated as full members of the Jewish people only if they made a proper conversion that involved a commitment to observance of Torah (e.g., Sabbath, food laws, and for males, circumcision).[17]

---

15. See, e.g., the useful discussion in Holmberg, 43-56.

16. Scot McKnight, *A Light among the Gentiles* (Minneapolis: Fortress, 1991), shows that diaspora Judaism of the time was open to Gentile inquirers but did not pursue a "mission" to convert Gentiles. Likewise, Martin Goodman, *Mission and Conversion: Proselytizing in the Religious History of the Roman Empire* (Oxford: Clarendon, 1994). Cf. James Carleton Paget, "Jewish Proselytism at the Time of Christian Origins: Chimera or Reality?" *JSNT* 62 (1996): 65-103 (who contends that some diaspora Jews did make efforts to encourage Gentile conversion; but this does not amount to a Jewish "mission" to the Gentiles).

17. See, e.g., Paul F. Stuehrenberg, "Proselyte," in *ABD*, 5:503-5; S. J. D. Cohen, "Crossing the Boundary and Becoming a Jew," *HTR* 82 (1989): 13-33, itemizes seven categories of Gentile "sympathizers," but he affirms that, for Gentiles to join the Jewish community and be treated by

Participation in their fellowship meals was an important means by which early Christians indicated acceptance of one another as members of the redeemed. We shall get nowhere in understanding a number of New Testament texts unless we recognize the enormous significance that first-century Christians attributed to their fellowship meals. If a group of Christians wished to signal their strongest disapproval of an erring believer, they could exclude the person from sharing in their meal fellowship. For example, Paul ordered the Corinthian Christians to expel the Christian man who was having a sexual relationship with "his father's wife," and refuse to admit him to their fellowship meals (1 Cor. 5:9-13).

But it did not require something as sensational as having sex with one's stepmother to raise the question of whether to refuse that person Christian meal fellowship. Those Jewish Christians who thought Gentile believers in Jesus were obliged to observe the Torah as part of their conversion deemed it inappropriate to share a Christian fellowship meal with those who had not made such a commitment, even if they had confessed faith in Jesus and had been baptized.[18] Such an attitude is reflected in Acts 11:1-3, where "the circumcision party" *(hoi ek peritomēs)* object to Peter's meal fellowship with Cornelius and his household *(synephages autois)*.[19] In the narrative Cornelius is described as "a devout man"

Jews as full members (e.g., allowed to participate as members in Jewish sacred meals), they had to practice Jewish laws, and males had to undergo circumcision (e.g., 26-27).

18. Space does not permit me here to deal with the issues fully. But it is necessary to emphasize a few matters in the face of some disoriented scholarly discussion. First, although some Jews refused any meal with Gentiles under any circumstances, for many, probably most religious Jews in the Hellenistic-Roman period, eating ordinary meals with Gentiles was not an insuperable problem; any claims by scholars to the contrary are simply misinformed. In principle, so long as the food on the table fell within what was permitted for Jews to eat under Torah (e.g., no pork), and so long as eating did not implicate a Jew in participating in a feast in honor of a god (e.g., no libation of wine or consecration of meat to a god), there was no major problem. Second, Jewish Christians' objections to eating with Gentile Christians in Acts (11:1-18) and Galatians (2:11-21) were not about what food was served, but about having meal fellowship with Gentiles whom they regarded as incompletely converted. This issue was not "purity laws," but the requirements for treating Gentiles as fully converted to the God of Israel. For fuller discussion of relevant issues and texts, including critical appraisal of other recent studies, see now Markus Bockmuehl, *Jewish Law in Gentile Churches: Halakhah and the Beginning of Christian Public Ethics* (Edinburgh: T. & T. Clark, 2000), 49-83 (esp. 56-61, 71-75); and Peter J. Tomson, *Paul and the Jewish Law: Halakha in the Letters of the Apostle to the Gentiles,* CRINT 3/1 (Assen: Van Gorcum; Philadelphia: Fortress, 1990), 222-58. In a book with other fine features, John Painter's discussion of the Antioch episode and the attendant issues, unfortunately, illustrates the misunderstanding operative in many references to these matters: *Just James: The Brother of Jesus in History and Tradition* (Columbia: University of South Carolina Press, 1991), 67-73.

19. Whatever the historicity of the events in the narrative, the attitude attributed to "the

who "feared God" (10:1-2); nevertheless, in the view of these rigorist Jewish Christians, he was still an uncircumcised Gentile, some way short of being eligible to be treated as having fully converted to the God of Israel.

Other Jewish Christians inclined to be more flexible in accepting Gentile believers could be swayed by such concerns, as illustrated by Paul's account of the incident in Antioch (Gal. 2:11-14). Though having initially participated in Christian fellowship meals with uncircumcised Gentile believers, Cephas, Barnabas, and other Jewish Christians in Antioch ceased doing so when certain people arrived "from James." Paul accuses Cephas and the others of acting out of fear of "the circumcision party" (*tous ek peritomēs*, 2:12). What he probably means is that they feared that those Jewish Christians who insisted that Torah observance was obligatory for all believers would condemn their meal fellowship with Gentile Christians as amounting to condoning the Gentiles in their failure to observe Torah fully.

For their part, "the circumcision party" may have been concerned that making Torah observance optional for Gentile Christians could well weaken the continued commitment of Jewish believers to Torah observance, especially in diaspora cities where Jews needed always to maintain resolve in observing their distinguishing commandments. The men from James, and perhaps those subsequently who advocated circumcision among the Galatian Christians, may also have been anxious that full fellowship with Gentile believers without requiring them to observe Torah would bring repercussions against the Jerusalem Christians from rigorist, nationalistic Jews in Judea.[20] Whatever their motivation, they advocated a view very different from Paul's as to what Gentile Christians had to do to become full partners with traditionalist Jewish Christians.

This was clearly a crucial matter for Paul, and he used strong terms to characterize those he saw as seeking to require Gentile Christians to take up Torah observance, in effect to become Jewish, as a condition of their full acceptance by Jewish Christians as coreligionists. In Jerusalem there were some Paul described as "false brethren" (Gal. 2:4), because they did not treat Gentile Christians as full partners "in Christ" and did not recognize their "freedom" from full Torah observance. Paul complains that those who demand that Gentiles come fully under observance of Torah proclaim "a different gospel" and "confuse" and "pervert the gospel of Christ" (1:6-7). An exasperated Paul

circumcision party" reflects the view of some Jewish Christians of the early centuries. About a century later than the Antioch episode, Justin distinguished between those Jewish Christians who practice Torah but do not require Gentile Christians to do so, and other Jewish Christians who demand full Torah observance of Gentile believers (*Dial.* 47 [ANF, 2:218]).

20. E.g., Bockmuehl, 73-75; Robert Jewett, "The Agitators and the Galatian Congregation," *NTS* 17 (1971): 198-212.

even wished that those who advocate Gentile circumcision would castrate themselves (5:12)!

In his reference to the incident in Antioch, Paul specifically accuses Cephas (Peter) and Barnabas of insincerity (*hypokrisis,* 2:13) in withdrawing from meal fellowship with Gentile believers. Because he saw this behavior as unfaithful to "the truth of the gospel," Paul states that he openly withstood Cephas in particular (2:11, 14), accusing him of a serious failure to live out the social-ecclesial consequences of the message that he professed to believe. From Paul's standpoint, by ceasing to have fellowship meals with Gentile believers, Cephas and the others were making Torah observance the basis of Christian fellowship, and were thereby treating the Gentiles' faith in Jesus as an inadequate and incomplete conversion. These Jewish believers probably had no intention to relativize the significance of Jesus vis-à-vis the Torah. More likely they were simply assuming that Torah continued to represent what God required of all who fully wished to serve him. Paul insisted, however, that to "compel the Gentiles to live like Jews [*Ioudaïzein*]" was to fail to see adequately the profound implications of Jesus' crucifixion, and to "nullify the grace of God" (2:19-21).

Similarly, in 2 Corinthians 10:12–12:13 Paul lays down a sustained barrage against unnamed fellow Christian Jews, implying that they proclaimed "another Jesus" and "a different gospel" from what he taught in Corinth (11:4). They appear to have visited Corinth making much of their Jewishness and their Christian ministry (and/or that of the Jerusalem leaders; 11:22-23), challenging Paul's teaching and comparing Paul unfavorably with the (Jerusalem?) apostles. These latter might be those whom Paul twice characterizes ironically as "superapostles" (*tōn hyperlian apostolōn;* 11:5-6; 12:11-12), insisting that he is not inferior to them in Christian knowledge and God-given signs of apostleship. But Paul refers to those who visited Corinth and caused this dissension much more harshly as "false apostles, deceitful workers," even implying that they are servants of Satan (11:13-15).[21]

Part of Paul's outrage is probably due to these people violating his sphere of responsibility. In Paul's description of his conference with the Jerusalem leaders in Galatians 2:1-10, he claims he had an agreement with them, giving him full rights to pursue his Gentile mission on his God-appointed terms (esp. 2:7-9). That is, Paul seems to have thought that he had obtained recognition from Jerusalem of his apostolic rights to Gentile "territory." Consequently he

---

21. Craig Hill argues that the Jewish Christian opponents who came to Corinth were not "Judaizing representatives of the Jerusalem church," and that "superapostles" and "false apostles" were both labels for this same group of interlopers (*Hellenists and Hebrews,* 158-73). Cf., however, P. W. Barnett, "Opposition in Corinth," *JSNT* 22 (1984): 3-17.

regarded as intrusive those who came to Galatia and urged Paul's Gentile converts to complete their conversion by subscribing to the full Torah obligations of the Sinai covenant, challenging Paul's authority to have taught otherwise. Likewise, Paul's hostility toward the Jewish Christians who visited Corinth is in response to their questioning his apostolic authority, and to what he regards as an interference in his rightful field of mission (esp. 2 Cor. 11:12-18).[22]

I have discussed these conflicts between Paul and other Jewish Christians to emphasize two points. First, Paul did not hesitate to disagree with other Christians, including Judean-based Jewish Christians. Second, among the disagreements with other Jewish Christians registered in Paul's letters, there is a conspicuous lack of evidence of specifically christological matters, for example about the person of Jesus, his status, or the reverence due him. In making these points, I echo a judgment by Helmut Koester:

> What Paul preached was never the subject of the controversy between Paul's Gentile mission and the church in Jerusalem. Jesus' death and resurrection was the event upon which their common proclamation was based. . . . Looking back to the death of Jesus, they celebrated their common meals in anticipation of his return in glory (1 Cor. 11:23-26). What was debated was the admission of Gentiles into the community of the New Israel as well as the celebration of a common meal in which both circumcised Jews and uncircumcised Gentiles could participate together.[23]

A Conspicuous Silence

Indeed, the silence about any significant differences over Christ-devotion is conspicuous and pervasive, and it deserves further comment. The absence of any defense of Christ-devotion in Paul's letters is noteworthy because Paul was rather keen on major theological points, and as I have demonstrated, not at all reluctant to defend his theological concerns when they were questioned. But not only does Paul not indicate any conflict over specifically christological matters from his standpoint, we also have no indication of problems from the side

---

22. On this passage, see, e.g., C. K. Barrett, *The Second Epistle to the Corinthians* (London: Adam and Charles Black, 1973), 262-69. It is not so clear that the Jewish Christians who came to Corinth were advocating the same message that Paul opposes in Galatians about circumcision and Torah observance. At least there is nothing in 2 Corinthians like the theological argument over this question in Galatians.

23. Helmut Koester, *Ancient Christian Gospels: Their History and Development* (Philadelphia: Trinity Press International, 1990), 51-52.

of Judean Christians. We have no hint that the Judaizing advocates who caused problems for Paul in Galatia made any issue of the pattern of devotion to Jesus that they encountered in the Galatian churches. Surely, had they done so, Paul would have responded as vigorously as he does in his Galatian epistle on the questions of circumcision and his own apostolic legitimacy. The "different gospel" that Paul alleges (Gal. 1:6) clearly has to do with the terms of Gentile conversion, not a contrary view of Jesus, as the argument of Galatians makes clear.

Likewise, we have no reason to think the self-proclaimed devotees of the Judean leaders who visited Corinth were perturbed by the christological beliefs and devotional practices of the Corinthian believers. Had they raised objection on these matters, Paul surely would have made clear in no uncertain terms what he thought of it! To judge by the argument that precedes and follows Paul's reference to "another Jesus," "a different spirit . . . or a different gospel" in 2 Corinthians 11:4, these terms are all directed against visitors to Corinth who denigrated Paul as weak and unimpressive (10:1-11; 12:11-12; 13:1-4) and emphasized manifestations of spiritual power (e.g., in miracles) as authenticating signs of their own authority.[24] Paul shows no need to reiterate and defend either beliefs in Jesus' exalted status or the characteristic cultic reverence given to him that we surveyed in the previous chapter.[25]

To judge by Paul's comments in 1 Corinthians, the "divisions" (*schismata*, 1:10) and "quarrels" (*erides*, 1:11) in Corinth had to do with such things as elitist tendencies among some believers who imagined that they had a superior knowledge that justified disdain for those whom they judged less "spiritual," a "hyper-realized" eschatology (e.g., 4:8-13), a misguided approval of improper sexual relations (e.g., 5:1-8), and a readiness to go to court against fellow believers (6:1-6). These differences may also have been involved in the behavior in the common sacred meal that Paul criticizes (11:17-22), and in the prizing of showy charismatic manifestations without sufficient concern for mutual edification (1 Cor. 12–14). But in none of this do we see any indication of an issue over reverence for Christ.

To be sure, arguments from silence have to be treated critically. Silences

---

24. Barrett, *Second Epistle*, 243-340, is a careful treatment of 2 Cor. 10–13, and interacts judiciously with other scholars.

25. It is, I trust, not necessary anymore to refute Bultmann's long-discredited view of 2 Cor. 5:16-17 (taken up also by H. J. Schoeps) as contrasting knowledge of the "historical Jesus" with a heavenly Christ. The immediate context (5:11-21) should always have made it quite clear that Paul is contrasting here the sort of view of Jesus that he himself held prior to his conversion with the view of Jesus that now motivates him to proclaim reconciliation through Jesus' death and resurrection. There is, thus, no hint here of an alternate "Christology" held by some other party of Christians. On the passage and the issues, see, e.g., Barrett, *Second Epistle*, 170-72.

are significant only where we have reason to expect something else, and I submit that in these cases we have very good reason to expect Paul to have responded to any serious challenges to the Christ-devotion he advocated in his churches. The lack of any such response can only mean that there were no challenges to the exalted status of Jesus asserted in Paul's gospel or to the devotional practices by which Jesus was reverenced in Paul's churches.

We can hardly think that those who presented themselves in Corinth as emissaries of Jerusalem, were shaped by the Jewish tradition of exclusivist monotheism, and also had no hesitation about questioning quite directly Paul's authority would have been reluctant to object to cultic reverence of Jesus if they judged it inappropriate. The Judaizers, who seem to have been quite ready to tell Paul's Galatian converts that Paul's gospel was faulty and their conversion incomplete, would surely have not hesitated to correct christological beliefs and devotional practices they found questionable. Yet there is no hint of any such matter being an issue.

I emphasize this because it does not fit with the assertions that Pauline Christianity represented some major departure in belief and practice from Jewish Christian circles in Judea. In principle, it is fully possible to imagine considerable variation in earliest Christian beliefs, including significant differences in beliefs about Jesus. But scholarly imagination should be answerable to the historical evidence, and proposals should be subject to corroboration and refutation by relevant data. There obviously were differences in beliefs between Paul and some other Jewish Christians, about such things as Torah observance and even his apostolic legitimacy. But I submit that we have no basis in Paul's letters for thinking that these differences extended to major points about Christ-devotion. So far as we can tell from Paul's letters, there was never any conflict or complaint from Jerusalem leaders, or from those Jewish Christians who made it their aim to correct features of Pauline Christianity, about the Christ-devotion that was practiced in Pauline congregations. The most natural inference is that the pattern of devotional practices was not very different from that followed in the Judean circles with which Paul had these contacts. In a later section of this chapter I turn to the question of whether other sources indicate Judean circles that might have had a very different Christology and devotional pattern.

Judean Christian Traditions in Paul's Letters

There is, of course, much more to go on than this eloquent silence in mining Paul's letters for information about the Christ-devotion of Judean Christianity.

In the previous chapter we noted passages where Paul explicitly cites traditions that are commonly accepted by scholars as having derived from Christian circles prior to his Gentile churches. In my previous reference to these traditions, my main concern was simply to indicate that Paul acknowledged roots and connections with prior Christian circles. I return to the topic here to note more precisely whether these traditions go back specifically to Jewish Christian groups, including those in Roman Judea, and what they tell us about the Jesus-oriented beliefs and practices of such groups.

Pride of place probably goes to 1 Corinthians 15:1-7, which is a compressed series of affirmations that "Christ died for our sins according to the scriptures, and that he was buried and that he rose on the third day according to the scriptures," and that Christ then appeared to a number of figures who function as witnesses to his resurrection: Cephas, "the twelve," over five hundred others at one time, James, and "all the apostles." The largest amount of space in this tradition is given to this list of witnesses to the risen Christ, and this fits with Paul's main concern in 1 Corinthians 15 to reaffirm and clarify the hope of the resurrection of believers, the assurance of which, according to Paul, rests upon the reality of Christ's own resurrection (esp. 15:12-19, 49).

Paul does not explicitly locate the source of this body of tradition, other than to say that, just as the Corinthians had received it from him, so, still earlier, he himself had received it (15:1-3). The probable reason he does not give a specific provenance for the tradition is in 15:11, where he emphasizes that this tradition represents the message proclaimed both by him and these other figures. That is, Paul's aim here is to present the beliefs in question as nonnegotiable and unquestioned among all the authoritative figures listed, which provides a basis for his reaffirmation of a real resurrection of Jesus and of believers in the rest of 1 Corinthians 15.

It is widely accepted, however, that the tradition that Paul recites in 15:1-7 must go back to the Jerusalem church.[26] The use of the term *Christos* (the Greek

26. See, e.g., Hans Conzelmann, *1 Corinthians*, Hermeneia (Philadelphia: Fortress, 1975), 251-54; Koester, 51; Arland J. Hultgren, *The Rise of Normative Christianity* (Minneapolis: Fortress, 1994), 27 (and note the list of other scholars he cites, 124 n. 15). Cf. Bousset's assertion that 1 Cor. 15:1-7 derives "first of all" from "the Gentile Christian community in Antioch" and is "only indirectly" from the Jerusalem community (*Kyrios Christos: Geschichte des Christusglaubens von den Anfangen des Christentums bis Irenaeus* [Göttingen: Vandenhoeck & Ruprecht, 1913; rev. ed., 1921]; ET [from the 4th German ed., 1965], *Kyrios Christos: A History of the Belief in Christ from the Beginnings of Christianity to Irenaeus,* trans. J. E. Steely [Nashville: Abingdon, 1970], 120). This assertion of the supposed importance of Antioch for Pauline Christology and cultic practice has received a justifiably sharp critique from Martin Hengel and Anna Maria Schwemer, *Paul between Damascus and Antioch: The Unknown Years,* trans. John Bowden (London: SCM Press, 1997), esp. 286-91. On 1 Cor. 15:1-8 in particular, see 290-91.

term had no special meaning outside of Jewish and then Christian usage), the repeated reference to the "scriptures" (the Old Testament), the unexplained reference to resurrection (the meaning of the Greek word for "raised" here presupposes an acquaintance with Jewish notions of resurrection), and the list of figures who are not further identified all combine to show that this is "in-group" community tradition. It was obviously formulated initially in a setting where these terms were familiar, and where the Scriptures and these figures were revered. As we have already noted, Paul elsewhere identifies Cephas and James as leaders in the Jerusalem church (e.g., Gal. 2:6-9). All other references to "the twelve," though from sources somewhat later than Paul's letters (the canonical Gospels and Acts), also associate them with Jerusalem.

Whether Paul obtained this tradition directly from Cephas and James in his personal contacts with them (which include a fifteen-day residence with Cephas in Jerusalem mentioned in Gal. 1:18) or indirectly through others, the tradition likely stems from Jerusalem, and Paul claims that it represents beliefs about Jesus affirmed by Judean circles as well as by him.[27] Likewise, it matters little whether 1 Corinthians 15:3-7 is a translation from Aramaic, was formulated by Greek-speaking Jewish Christians, or is Paul's own condensed statement of the key relevant beliefs and traditions that he claims are affirmed by the Jerusalem leaders.[28] What matters is the content of this tradition.

27. As H. D. Betz notes, Paul's reference to his fifteen-day Jerusalem visit with Cephas and James in Gal. 1:18-20 is part of a larger argument for the independent validity of his apostleship (*Galatians,* Hermeneia [Philadelphia: Fortress, 1979], 76). But this makes Paul's statement in Gal. 1:18 that this first trip to Jerusalem after his conversion was specifically to see *(historēsai)* Cephas all the more interesting. Paul clearly saw no conflict between his claim that his apostolic calling came directly from a revelatory experience of Christ and obtaining a firsthand knowledge of the Jerusalem leaders and their key traditions. C. H. Dodd's widely quoted quip about the two weeks that Paul resided with Cephas in Jerusalem remains apposite: "[W]e may presume they did not spend all the time talking about the weather" (*The Apostolic Preaching and Its Developments* [New York: Harper and Row, 1964], 16). On the connotation of the Greek verb *historēsai,* see, e.g., W. D. Davies, *The Setting of the Sermon on the Mount* (Cambridge: Cambridge University Press, 1966), 453-55; MM, 308.

28. Thus the question of how easily 1 Cor. 15:3-7 can be retro-translated into Aramaic is a red herring. There was no requirement for Paul and Greek-speaking believers to develop a wooden translation of any Aramaic traditions, just so modern scholars could satisfy themselves on this point! Moreover, by all indications, the Jerusalem church (as is true of much of Roman Judea) was bilingual, with Greek and Aramaic used from the outset (e.g., Acts 6:1-6), so it is quite likely for the Jerusalem tradition to have been expressed from the first both in Aramaic and Greek formulations, without one having been translated from the other. On the mutual presence of Greek and Semitic linguistic and cultural influences, see, e.g., Martin Hengel, *The "Hellenization" of Judaea in the First Century after Christ* (London: SCM Press; Philadelphia: Trinity Press International, 1989).

The reference to Jesus simply as "Christ" in 1 Corinthians 15:3 reflects the messianic claim that originated among Jewish Christian circles, and it invokes an eschatological scheme or point of view. But the novel nature of the claim expressed in the confession is the focus on the death and resurrection of Christ/Messiah as redemptive ("for our sins," 15:3), and as fulfilling Scripture/the divine purpose ("according to the scriptures," 15:3, 4). As I argued in the preceding chapter, the presentation of Jesus' death as "for our sins" and "according to the scriptures" likely had a strong apologetic intention in the Judean circles where these claims were first expressed. That is, these claims explained why Messiah/Christ has suffered death and been resurrected. Judean Christian circles in Acts consistently interpret Jesus' death and resurrection in very similar terms (e.g., 2:23-36, 38-39; 3:18-26; 4:24-28): as a messianic death that was part of God's plan. That a messianic claim was characteristic of the very first stage of Christian proclamation in Judean circles is also consistent with the routinized use of "Christ" for Jesus that is so frequently attested in Paul's epistles.

The reference here to Jesus' burial (1 Cor. 15:4) functions to indicate a real death, and to assert, thus, a real resurrection, not merely a postmortem apparition but a new and momentous eschatological event. The resurrection is attested by witnesses who saw the *risen Christ* (15:5-7), not the resurrection event itself. But both the reference to Jesus' burial and the larger context of this chapter make it clear that what Paul is anxious to reaffirm as the tradition is that Jesus has been raised from death to glorious eschatological bodily existence (15:42-49), and that his resurrection is the unique pattern for, and proof of, the future resurrection of believers.[29] In short, the tradition that Paul cites in 1 Co-

---

29. Crossan's discussion of this early tradition of resurrection vision (Crossan, xiv-xx) is a bit misleading. That "the vision of a dead person" was "neither totally abnormal nor completely unique" (xix) is correct but irrelevant, as is his statement, "That the dead could return and interact with the living was a commonplace of the Greco-Roman world" (xvi). The claim reflected in 1 Cor. 15:3-11 is not that people have had visions of the dead Jesus such as the vision of Hector in *Aeneid* (bk. 2), nor that Jesus has been resuscitated as in the miracles stories of the Gospels and Acts (e.g., Mark 5:21-23, 35-43; Luke 7:11-17; Acts 9:36-43). Instead, the claim is that chosen figures have been made special witnesses to the resurrection of Jesus, which involves a completely new form of *bodily* existence. Whether fictional or not, the story of the misunderstanding and ridicule from Athenians at Paul's reference to resurrection in Acts 17:16-34 illustrates the attitude of many pagans to this new and strange sort of claim. Gregory J. Riley, *Resurrection Reconsidered: Thomas and John in Controversy* (Minneapolis: Fortress, 1995), gives a generally helpful survey of pagan and Jewish attitudes toward death and possible afterlife (7-68), but he implies incorrectly that Paul's reference to "a spiritual body" (1 Cor. 15:44) meant something close to pagan notions of "nonphysical, postmortem survival." In fact, however, the contrast in 1 Cor. 15:35-58 between the "physical" (*psychikos*) body patterned after "the man of dust" (vv. 47-49, terms from the Genesis story of Adam as made from the earth as a "living soul,"

rinthians 15:3-7 makes Jesus' death and resurrection crucial messianic/eschato-
logical events of unique redemptive efficacy that also signal Jesus' paradigmatic
meaning for believers.

This emphasis on the redemptive significance of Jesus' death and resurrection is reflected in another Pauline passage that we have previously noted,
and that is also commonly thought to be a traditional formulation, Romans
4:24-25 ("handed over to death for our trespasses, and raised for our justification"). In still other Pauline passages widely regarded as traditional, Jesus' resurrection is particularly prominent. Romans 1:3-4 is generally accepted as a
piece of tradition that likely goes back to Jewish Christian circles; here Jesus'
royal Davidic lineage is affirmed and his resurrection is referred to as the event
through which he has been declared to be "Son of God in power." We can also
note again 1 Thessalonians 1:10, one more instance of the citation of creedal tradition likely from Jewish Christian provenance. Here Jesus' divine sonship and
his work of eschatological redemption are linked with God raising him from
death.

In other words, there is a web of Pauline references and allusions to traditional material that focuses on Jesus' death and resurrection. In the traditional
material, however, there appears to be a greater emphasis on Jesus' resurrection,
and the specific redemptive effects of Jesus' death are not underscored as much
as Paul did in his own elaborations of the gospel for his converts.[30]

In another passage in 1 Corinthians (11:23-26) that we noted in the preceding chapter, Paul relates yet another comparatively extensive piece of tradition. This passage, too, presents Jesus' death as redemptive ("my body which is
[given] for you," v. 24; "the new covenant in my blood," v. 25). The material has
an obviously liturgical tone, however; so the question is from what previous
circles of believers do this tradition and liturgical practice derive. Specifically,
does this tradition also come from Judean circles such as the Jerusalem church?
Or (as is sometimes asserted) are we to invoke other circles of "Hellenistic"

---

psychēn zōsan, cited in v. 45) and the "spiritual" *(pneumatikos)* resurrection body (v. 44) in no
way means that the latter is likened to the notion of a disembodied soul. The contrast is between
an Adamic body that is subject to mortality and an eschatological body that is glorious and im-
perishable (esp. vv. 42-44). "Spiritual" here can only mean empowered by the Spirit, as Paul
consistently uses the term in this epistle. For a careful discussion, see G. D. Fee, *The First Epistle
to the Corinthians,* NICNT (Grand Rapids: Eerdmans, 1987), 775-809.

30. On this matter, see, e.g., Joel B. Green, *The Death of Jesus,* WUNT 2/33 (Tübingen:
Mohr [Siebeck], 1988), esp. 321-23. Kenneth Grayston has demonstrated the variety of ways in
which Jesus' death is treated in the various New Testament writings (*Dying, We Live: A New Enquiry into the Death of Christ in the New Testament* [London: Darton, Longman and Todd,
1990]); and see also Arland J. Hultgren, *Christ and His Benefits: Christology and Redemption in
the New Testament* (Philadelphia: Fortress, 1987).

Christians as the matrix of the "Christ cult" (in the technical sense of a devotional/liturgical practice in which Jesus functions as a recipient of worship/devotion)? The *wording* is of course likely to reflect and derive from Greek-speaking circles of believers, among which Antioch (but also Jerusalem!) is of course to be included as a possible provenance. But our concern here is more with the *cultic practice itself,* a sacred meal in which Jesus is honored in a corporate liturgical action.

In approaching this question we should note that one of Paul's repeated emphases in 1 Corinthians is that sectarian attitudes have no place, and that he and other leaders such as Cephas (associated with Jerusalem) and Apollos (whom Paul refers to as building upon his work among the Gentiles in 3:5-9 and as coming to Corinth in 16:12, also associated with diaspora settings in Acts 18:24) are involved in a common religious effort (e.g., 1 Cor. 1:10-15; 3:5-23; 4:1-7). We have noted that this emphasis on a common tradition of core beliefs and christological claims is expressed in 15:1-7. It is worth remembering, too, that in 16:1-4 Paul explicitly reminds the Corinthians of his offering for Jerusalem, and that at the end of this epistle he gives the Aramaic invocation, *maranatha* (which I will discuss further shortly), its Semitic and traditional cachet likely intentional. All this indicates Paul's concern to oppose certain unacceptable innovations in Corinth by reasserting traditional beliefs and practices that link Jewish and Gentile circles of the Christian movement. I suggest that it would have ill served this concern to cite beliefs and liturgical practices that were not supported by such important circles as the Jerusalem church, and that were innovations characteristic of only some other sectors of the early Christian movement.[31]

Indeed, in the opening sentences of 1 Corinthians Paul addresses the recipients as those who "together with all those who in every place call on the name of our Lord Jesus Christ" (1:2), which explicitly makes the liturgical practice that was familiar to the Corinthians (to "call upon the name" of Jesus) also generally characteristic of believers irrespective of location ("in every place"). We have noted that Jewish Christian critics of Paul who claimed links with Jerusalem went into Pauline churches such as Corinth with critical intent. Paul would thus have been rather foolish to claim something not embraced by Judean believers as universally shared liturgical practice. Had he done so, it would have laid him open to attack. To reiterate a point made earlier: surely

---

31. As Hengel and Schwemer have noted, especially in Romans it is most likely that Paul invoked traditions that he knew the Roman Christians would recognize as connected with Jerusalem. To put it mildly, in Romans, especially, there was nothing to gain in citing traditions that would have been disavowed by Jerusalem!

Judean Jewish Christians, shaped by the well-attested Jewish concern about avoiding the worship of any figure other than the one God, could not have countenanced the cultic reverence of Jesus practiced in Corinth and characteristic of Pauline Christianity if it were not also a part of their own corporate devotional life. Yet, to judge by the issues that Paul is constrained to engage in the Corinthian correspondence, there was no objection on this matter. The more reasonable conclusion, therefore, is that there was no objection because this cultic reverence of Jesus was in fact a shared devotional pattern among Judean and Pauline circles.

As reinforcement of this judgment, I return to that particularly striking piece of evidence that Jesus was invoked in the cultic setting of Aramaic-speaking believers, the appeal to Jesus cited by Paul in 1 Corinthians 16:22, *maranatha*.[32] Though a small artifact of early devotional practice, its importance and meaning justify more extensive discussion. First, this expression obviously derives from the cultic life of Aramaic-speaking Christians, and is likely a prayer/invocation-formula. This is consistent with its appearance at the end of this epistle, for Paul characteristically used liturgical expressions in the opening and closing of his epistles. Furthermore, the same expression appears also in our earliest extant collection of Christian worship material, the *Didache*, as part of a prayer to be offered at the end of the Eucharist meal (10.6). Also, an equivalent Greek expression appears in Revelation 22:20 ("Come, Lord Jesus"), where it, too, is obviously a prayer-appeal.

Secondly, this cultic appeal is addressed to the exalted Jesus.[33] The *maranatha* expression is thus clearly evidence of corporate cultic devotion to Jesus in the Aramaic circles where the expression first emerged. More important than philological arguments over the connotation of the Aramaic term *mar* (lord) and whether it was used as a divine title (it was) is the fact that the expression represents the cultic invocation of Jesus. For this shows that he was a recipient of devotion in the worship gathering of Aramaic-speaking believers in the earliest decades of the Christian movement.[34]

---

32. Oscar Cullmann's discussion of *maranatha* and the cultic life of Palestinian Jewish Christian circles in *The Christology of the New Testament*, rev. ed. (Philadelphia: Westminster, 1963; German ed., 1957), 203-15, remains essential reading on the subject.

33. Bousset's varying and desperate attempts to avoid the plain force of the *maranatha* expression (followed also by Bultmann) are discussed by Cullmann, *Christology*, 213-14.

34. On the uses of *mar*, see now J. A. Fitzmyer, "The Semitic Background of the New Testament Kyrios Title," in his *A Wandering Aramean: Collected Aramaic Essays*, SBLMS 25 (Missoula: Scholars, 1979), esp. 123-25. There is also an infrequently noticed reference to the term as a title of royal acclamation in Philo, *Flaccus* 36-39, where Alexandrians mock Agrippa in a parody.

The only serious question about the *maranatha* expression is its geographical provenance: Does it come from Judean circles such as the Jerusalem church, or (as has sometimes been asserted) did it emerge in an allegedly very different kind of Christianity, in places such as Antioch or from otherwise unknown groups in "northern Syria"?[35] I have two points to make in answer to this question.

First, the circles to which Paul points his Gentile converts and to which he strives to link his congregations are specifically Judean Jewish Christian circles, and it is Jerusalem that Paul registers more than once as having a historic primacy, as we have noted already (e.g., Judean believers cited in 1 Thess. 2:14-16; the importance of agreement with Jerusalem leaders in Gal. 2:1-10; the spiritual indebtedness of Gentile Christians to Jerusalem Christians in Rom. 15:25-27; the importance of a generous expression of solidarity with Jerusalem Christians in 2 Cor. 8–9; his geographical characterization of the spread of the gospel from Jerusalem in Rom. 15:19). By contrast, Antioch and any other congregations supposed by some scholars to have had formative influence on "the Christ cult" are never specifically cited in Paul's epistles as coreligionists with whom he particularly promotes solidarity, as models for his converts, or as centers to which he grants any special importance or spiritual indebtedness. In short, we have no basis for thinking that Paul regarded Christian circles in Antioch and Syria as having any special significance for patterns of devotion and beliefs. Instead, all indications are that Paul promoted tangible links and a sense of shared religious endeavor between his congregations and Judean Christian circles in particular. So it seems more likely for Paul to have taught his congregations the Aramaic liturgical expressions that he mentions in his epistles (*maranatha,* and also *Abba* in Gal. 4:6; Rom. 8:15) because they came from the Judean circles with which he sought to foster a sense of spiritual linkage among his churches.

Secondly, if "the Christ cult" were the significant departure from the beliefs and practice of the "Palestinian primitive community" as portrayed by Bousset, and/or the Judean "Jesus people" portrayed more recently by Mack, we should expect to find evidence of objections from Judean believers. The silence that I have already noted on this matter is telling.

For these reasons, therefore, as uncomfortable as it will be to certain cherished opinions, the more likely answer to the question about the original prove-

---

35. Bousset (e.g., 119-38) argued for "Hellenistic communities in Antioch, Damascus, and Tarsus" as the matrix of the worship of Jesus, and in his latest view on the subject proposed that *maranatha* was an Aramaic translation of a liturgical expression that originated in Greek! Burton Mack takes essentially the same unlikely view of the origin of "the Christ cult" in *A Myth of Innocence: Mark and Christian Origins* (Philadelphia: Fortress, 1988), 98-102. On this question, see now esp. Hengel and Schwemer, 279-91.

nance of this Aramaic liturgical expression, *maranatha,* and the more likely matrix for the cultic devotion to Jesus that the expression reflects, is Judean Christianity, and the Jerusalem church in particular. Admittedly, this means that in an astonishingly short period of time this significantly innovative cultic pattern emerged, and among circles made up of people whose religious tradition did not dispose them to such cultic reverence of figures other than the one God. Later in this chapter we shall consider what might have prompted this notable development; my point here is that the evidence requires us to place it as tonishingly early. I defer to later in this chapter the question whether there were other circles of Judean followers of Jesus among whom this cultic devotion to Jesus was not practiced. My point here is that the Christ-devotion promoted by Paul seems to have had its origins in at least some circles of Judean Christianity that included Jerusalem.

This conclusion is reinforced by other references to Judean Christian devotional practice in other sources. We shall take up this material more fully in the next section, but I select one illustration here. In the Acts material, for example, Judean circles are described as baptizing adherents "in the name of Jesus" (e.g., 2:38) and believers are referred to as "all those who invoke your [Jesus'] name" (9:14). Both expressions refer to invoking Jesus' name in cultic actions. Moreover, ritual use of Jesus' name is an important feature of other religious practices attributed to Judean Christians, such as healing and exorcism (e.g., 3:6; 4:29-30).

In summary, the Pauline evidence that points toward the devotional life of Judean Christianity constitutes the following: (1) Paul freely cites traditional formulas of belief and traditions of religious practice from Jewish Christian circles as fully appropriate for, and reflective of, the practice of his own congregations; (2) these traditions specifically affirm a broad commonality in beliefs about Jesus as Christ/Messiah, about his death and resurrection as redemptive, and about the eschatological context in which his significance is understood; and (3) these traditions include religious practices in which Jesus functions as recipient of cultic devotion, practices that seem to have been a part of the devotional life of Judean Christian circles as well as the Pauline congregations.

One final and very important further indication of the religious beliefs and practices of "pre-Pauline" Jewish Christians has already been mentioned, but is worth highlighting again here. Prior to his conversion experience, Paul saw Jewish Christian beliefs and practices as so improper and dangerous as to call for urgent and forceful action to destroy the young religious movement. He said his own conversion specifically involved a "revelation" of Jesus' significance that produced a radical change in him, from opponent to devotee (e.g., Gal. 1:12; 2 Cor. 5:16). So far as we can tell, immediately after this experience he espoused the remarkable "high" christological claims and "binitarian" devotional practice that we noted in the previous chapter. The only things he refers to as novel and unique about his own Christian religious stance are the convictions that he is personally called to obtain "the obedience of the Gentiles" to the gospel, and that Gentiles are not to be required to take up Jewish observance of Torah as a condition of their salvation and their full acceptance by Jewish believers.

I submit that the most reasonable inference from these things is this: what drew the intense ire of the preconversion Paul against Jewish Christians was not (as has often been alleged, though with scarcely any basis) their supposed laxity of Torah observance or an unseemly association with Gentiles; instead it was the Christ-devotion that is basically reflected in what he embraced and advocated after his conversion. The religious zeal of Saul the Pharisee against Jewish Christians is best accounted for as provoked by what he regarded as their undue reverence of Jesus. They acclaimed a false teacher as Messiah, and may even have seemed to Paul to have compromised Jewish responsibilities to observe the uniqueness of the one God in their devotional practice.

This indication that christological claims and devotional practices were key points of conflict is also consistent with references to Jewish opposition to the Judean Christian movement in other sources. For example, the famous account of the stoning of Stephen (Acts 7:54-60) looks very much like an instance of the Phinehas-type action against serious infractions of Torah.[36] Stephen is initially accused of "blasphemous words against Moses and God" by men "secretly instigated" to say this (6:11). He is brought before the Jewish council where "false witnesses" also allege that he spoke against the temple and the Torah (6:13-14). But, though his long speech about Jewish disobedience leads to bitter anger (7:54), the actual "vigilante" action of killing him is presented as the direct reaction to his oracular christological statement about seeing Jesus exalted to heavenly glory "at the right hand of God" (7:55-58). Whatever the relation of the Stephen narrative to actual events, the point stands that the account presents a christological claim as engendering mortal opposition. Likewise, in the Acts accounts of the actions of Jewish authorities against other figures in the Jerusalem church (e.g., 4:1-22; 5:27-42), the emphasis is upon objections to their christological assertions, and related practices (note the repeated prohibitions against teaching, healing, and exorcism in Jesus' name).

---

36. T. Seland, *Establishment Violence in Philo and Luke: A Study of Non-Conformity to the Torah and Jewish Vigilante Reactions* (Leiden: Brill, 1995).

Judean Christ-Devotion in Acts

This makes it appropriate to look a bit further at what Acts tells us about the place of Jesus in the beliefs and practices of Judean circles. But the requisite prior question is what kind of general credibility to grant the references to Judean Christianity in Acts, a complicated matter that I deal with briefly here, depending heavily on the work of others.[37] Scholars today are broadly receptive to the claim of the author of Luke-Acts (Luke 1:1-4) that he had access to traditions, and possibly written sources also, about the characters and events that he narrates. But, especially in Acts, it is difficult to know what they were precisely.[38] Moreover, following the literary conventions of his day, the author drew upon traditions and sources, but the narratives and the speeches in particular are fully his own compositions.[39] That is, we have to be very careful about reading the narratives without taking account of the author's own literary purposes, and <u>we should not take the speeches as records of what was said by the characters to whom they are attributed</u>. Fortunately, for my purpose here the important matters are the comparatively more readily assessable christological terms and other indications of the devotion to Jesus attributed by the author to Judean Christians. My concern is not to determine what kinds of sources the author of Acts used, but rather to note that he preserved and used

---

37. The scholarly literature on the historical-critical assessment of Acts is immense. For general analyses see, e.g., W. Ward Gasque, *A History of the Criticism of the Acts of the Apostles* (Grand Rapids: Eerdmans; Tübingen: J. C. B. Mohr [Paul Siebeck], 1975); Ernst Haenchen, *The Acts of the Apostles* (Philadelphia: Westminster, 1971; German 14th ed., 1965), esp. 14-49; C. K. Barrett, *Luke the Historian in Recent Study* (Philadelphia: Fortress, 1970); I. H. Marshall, *Luke: Historian and Theologian* (Grand Rapids: Zondervan, 1970). On the specific question about using Acts as a source for Judean Christianity, see, e.g., Jacob Jervell, "The Problem of Traditions in Acts," in his *Luke and the People of God,* 19-39; Gerd Lüdemann, *Early Christianity according to the Traditions in Acts: A Commentary* (London: SCM Press, 1989; German ed., 1987); Richard Bauckham, ed., *The Book of Acts in Its Palestinian Setting* (Carlisle: Paternoster; Grand Rapids: Eerdmans, 1995); J. A. Fitzmyer, "Jewish Christianity in Acts in the Light of the Qumran Scrolls," in *Essays on the Semitic Background of the New Testament* (Missoula: Scholars, 1974), 271-304.

38. Lüdemann *(Early Christianity according to the Traditions in Acts),* for example, was dubious about identifying sources, but concluded that Acts incorporates a considerable amount of very early traditions. Marshall, a more conservative scholar in the field, admits, "We are, therefore, left almost completely in the dark with regard to the sources of Acts. Consequently, it is impossible to characterize Luke's use of them in any detail, beyond noting that he will have written them all up in his own style. Other methods of investigation must be brought into play" (Marshall, *Luke: Historian and Theologian,* 68).

39. E.g., David Aune, *The New Testament in Its Literary Environment* (Philadelphia: Westminster, 1987), 77-157; Marion L. Soards, *The Speeches in Acts: Their Content, Context, and Concerns* (Louisville: Westminster John Knox, 1994).

very early traditions (however he came to have them). At the risk of a somewhat artificial distinction, we shall first look at items of christological belief and then at the devotional practices attributed to Judean Christians in Acts.

Christological Categories

As for the christological terms and categories attributed to Judean Christians in Acts, we have material in speeches put on the lips of Jerusalem-based Christian leaders (2:14-40; 3:11-26; 4:8-12; 5:27-32; 7:51-53; 10:34-43), a prayer of Jerusalem Christians in 4:24-30, the account of Philip expounding Isaiah to the Ethiopian eunuch in 8:30-35, and a few other references to the beliefs and message of these circles (5:40-42; 8:12; 9:20-22).[40]

A number of the christological terms and themes are familiar to us from what is likely traditional material in Paul's epistles. Jesus' resurrection is underscored as the key divine action to which witness is to be given (e.g., 2:22, 24-32; 3:15; 4:10, 33; 5:30-32). God's raising of Jesus from death also involves his designation for the key role as eschatological redeemer, and his exaltation to heavenly status and divine designation as "Lord," Messiah, "Leader and Savior" (2:33-36; 3:20-21; 5:31), the one through whom salvation comes (4:10-12). These passages can be compared with Pauline references that are thought to incorporate traditional confessional statements that Jesus was "declared/designated [*horisthentos*] Son of God" (Rom. 1:4) and "exalted" *(hyperypsōsen)* by God as Lord (Phil. 2:9-11).

The royal-messianic and eschatological emphases (involving the repeated use of *Christos*) come out in these and other references in Acts (e.g., 5:42; 8:22), along with the theme that Israel is a special object of God's salvific intention (e.g., 2:38-39; 3:26; 5:31). It is certainly very difficult to account for the use of *Christos* as such a regular appellative for Jesus in Paul's letters unless the messianic claim characterized Christian proclamation so early that by the 50s it had already become a stock feature of christological vocabulary, even among Gentile Christian congregations. This is consistent with the Acts representation of a strongly messianic interpretation of Jesus in earliest Judean Christianity.

Moreover, the emphasis on redemption specifically for Israel sounds credible in light of Paul's indication that the Jerusalem church was particularly concerned with a mission to Jews. In his description of the conference with the Jeru-

40. Still worth consulting (though not always persuasive) on this material is Henry J. Cadbury, "The Titles of Jesus in Acts," in *The Beginnings of Christianity*, ed. F. J. Foakes Jackson and Kirsopp Lake, 5 vols. (London: Macmillan, 1920-33), 5:354-75.

salem leaders in Galatians 2:1-10, Paul says that they recognized that the mission to Gentiles was his own special responsibility (*tēn charin tēn dotheisan moi,* 2:9), whereas Peter "had been entrusted with the gospel for the circumcised [*to euangelion tēs akrobystias*]" (2:7). In fact, the reference to Peter here seems intended to represent the view of the whole Jerusalem church as to its own mission and aim: to take the gospel to Jews, and thus to help secure the eschatological redemption of Israel. The Acts representation of the preaching of the Jerusalem church is fully consistent with this. Indeed, the deliberate decision of Galilean followers of Jesus to relocate in Jerusalem indicates a desire to bear witness to Israel in the sacred and venerable city of royal and temple traditions.

"Lord"

Still more prominent and striking than the references to Jesus' messianic status, however, are the attributions to him of the title "Lord" *(Kyrios)* in the Acts descriptions of the Jerusalem believers. In fact, there is a clear emphasis on Jesus as "Lord" that associates him in astonishing ways with God. The first unambiguous use of the title comes early, in 1:21, when Jerusalem believers seek a successor to Judas Iscariot as a witness to "the Lord Jesus." But it is really in Peter's Pentecost speech that the author commences his emphasis on this title and its significance, through a series of three biblical citations.

Acts 2:17-21 cites Joel (2:28-32; Heb. 3:1-5), making the "day of the Lord" (Acts 2:20) Jesus' eschatological appearance in glory, and making the reference to the cultic act of calling upon "the name of the Lord" (2:21) cultic reverence of the exalted Jesus.[41] Likewise, in Acts 2:25 the phrase "David says concerning him," which introduces the quotation of Psalm 16 (LXX Ps. 15), seems intended to specify that the *Kyrios* here is Jesus (who is also of course the "Holy One" whom God will not abandon in death in Acts 2:26-28). In the climactic biblical citation in this series, the quotation of Psalm 110:1 (LXX 109:1) in Acts 2:34-35,

---

41. In Acts 2:17 the likely original reading is "And it shall be in the last days, God says," which means the author deliberately modified the opening line of the quotation to make clear the attribution of the oracle to *God (ho theos).* This seems intended to distinguish God from the *Kyrios* referred to in the quotation — Jesus. On the textual variants here, see, e.g., Bruce M. Metzger et al., *A Textual Commentary on the Greek New Testament* (London and New York: United Bible Societies, 1971), 296. In Acts the author much more frequently uses *Kyrios* in reference to Jesus, and where he wishes to make a clear reference to God uses *theos* (e.g., 2:22, 30, 36), or other expressions such as "the Lord our God" (e.g., *Kyrios ho theos,* 2:39; 3:22). Note especially 20:21 ("repentence toward God and faith in our Lord Jesus") and 28:31 ("preaching the kingdom of God and teaching the things concerning the Lord Jesus Christ"). In prayer God is addressed as *Despota* ("Lord/Master," Acts 4:24; Luke 2:29), whereas Jesus is addressed as *Kyrie* (e.g., Acts 7:59).

both God and Jesus are referred to as *Kyrios* ("the Lord said to my Lord"). These three biblical citations provide the warrants for, and the full significance of, the climactic claim made in Acts 2:36, "therefore, let the entire house of Israel know with certainty that God has made him both Lord and Christ."

Given that throughout Acts *Kyrios* is a frequent christological title (indeed, applied far more frequently to Jesus than to God), of course the title reflects the author's own religious vocabulary. But this in itself does not necessarily mean that the author thereby misrepresents the faith of these Judean circles in characterizing them as reverencing Jesus as their "Lord." In fact, as we have seen in our analysis of Pauline evidence, the representation of Jesus as *Kyrios* in Luke-Acts reflects a christological category that had long and widely been a part of the religious belief and practice of Christians. Among both Gentiles and Jewish Christians, both in Greek-speaking and Aramaic-speaking settings, and most likely among Judean Christians as well as believers in diaspora locations, the reference to Jesus as "Lord" was common.

Furthermore, the most likely explanation for this widespread and early use of "Lord" as a christological appellative, both in Aramaic and Greek, is that it must have emerged in a bilingual circle of believers sufficiently early and sufficiently influential for other and subsequent believers to have followed their devotional practice. First-century Jerusalem was a thoroughly bilingual city, and the Jerusalem church was fully a bilingual group, with both *Hellēnistai* (Greek-speaking) and *Hebraioi* (Aramaic-speaking) adherents.[42]

In light of the unrivaled significance attached to Jerusalem and the church in that city in the early years of the Christian movement, both in Jewish Christian circles and the Pauline congregations as well, the Jerusalem church is easily the most likely candidate for exercising such influence. Although some scholars have been reluctant to assent to this conclusion, no adequate reason has been given for this reluctance. Jerusalem is a considerably more likely candidate for such influence in christological belief and devotional practice than the other congregations proffered, such as Antioch, which, by contrast, is given no particular status among Pauline churches.

Of course, references to Jesus as "Lord," in Greek or Aramaic, could carry a range of specific connotations, from a polite expression of deference at one extreme to a divine title at the other. In keeping with respectful conventions of

---

42. These terms are used in Acts 6:1 and 9:29, and refer to the two primary languages of Jews residing in Jerusalem. See, e.g., J. Wanke, "Ἑλληνιστής," in *EDNT*, 1:436. Thus Paul's insistence that he too was a *Hebraios* (Phil. 3:5; 2 Cor. 11:22) must mean that he claimed a linguistic facility in Aramaic (and Hebrew?). Timothy Lim contends that Paul was conversant in Greek and Aramaic, and could probably also read his Scriptures in Hebrew: *Holy Scripture in the Qumran Commentaries and Pauline Letters* (Oxford: Clarendon, 1997), esp. 161-64.

the time, Jesus' disciples likely addressed him as "Master" (and most likely in Aramaic).[43] That is, the *usage* of the term likely has its origin in the circle of Je-sus' followers and in the period of his ministry. But what happened among the "Jesus movement" after Jesus' crucifixion was a marked (and quite rapid) escalation in the *connotation* of the term as applied to Jesus, this rapid escalation driven by experiences of the "risen" Jesus exalted by God into eschatological and heavenly glory. At the very least, the "Lord/Master" Jesus had become a heavenly figure whose lordship took on a transcendent dimension. Referring to him as "Lord" thus reflected the belief in his exaltation to this enhanced status at God's "right hand."

But the Acts material suggests that things quickly went even much further. In the biblical quotations cited in Acts 2, as I have already pointed out, the exalted Jesus is identified as (or associated with) the "Lord" in places in the biblical texts where God (Heb. *Yahweh*) was the original referent (vv. 20-21, 25).[44] It is surely remarkable enough to identify "the great and notable day of the Lord" as the future coming of Jesus (2:20, citing Joel 2:31 [3:4 Heb.]), for in the Old Testament "the day of the Lord" consistently refers to a time of God's own special action of deliverance or judgment.[45] As Kreitzer has shown, this bold conception is attested as a conventionalized Christian understanding of the phrase already in Paul's letters; so it must have appeared very early indeed.[46]

It is, however, an absolutely more stunning move still for early Christians to have taken the biblical expression that means the cultic worship of God, to "call upon the name of the Lord [*Yahweh*]," as referring also to cultic acclamation/invocation of Jesus (Acts 2:21, citing Joel 2:32 [3:5 Heb.]). There can be no doubt that this phrase was adopted to refer to the specific invocation of the

---

43. In Aramaic, forms of *mar*: e.g., *mari* (my lord/master).

44. I express some uncertainty here because the texts exhibit some ambiguity in this matter. On the one hand Jesus is linked with, and identified as, the *Kyrios*, but on the other hand God can be referred to as the *Kyrios* by the same authors (e.g., 2:39; 3:22, "the Lord our God"; 4:26, "the Lord and . . . his Christ"; 4:29, "Lord [*Kyrie*], look at their threats"; cf. 4:24, "Sovereign Lord [*Despota*]"). It is also clear that the author of Acts, along with all other Christians whose faith is reflected in the New Testament writings, thought of God and Jesus as distinguishable and yet also as linked/associated in astonishingly direct and close ways. This is, of course, especially apparent in the functions of God that are shared by Jesus. In the discussion of Pauline Christianity, I noted that already in Paul's letters there is this association of Jesus with biblical texts that refer to *Yahweh*.

45. See, e.g., references and discussion in Richard H. Hiers, "Day of the Lord," in *ABD*, 2:82-83.

46. L. J. Kreitzer, *Jesus and God in Paul's Eschatology*, JSNTSup 19 (Sheffield: JSOT Press, 1987). Lüdemann concludes that the christological use of the Joel passage and Ps. 110 (LXX 109) began "at a very early stage," well before the Pauline letters (Lüdemann, *Early Christianity*, 48-49).

name of Jesus, both in corporate worship and in the wider devotional pattern of Christian believers (e.g., baptism, exorcism, healing), as the subsequent chapters of Acts show. Moreover, this appropriation of the biblical phrase to designate and justify the cultic invocation of Jesus also happened amazingly early. We have previously noted that this practice, too, is already conventionalized and uncontroversial (among Christian believers) in Paul's letters.

These radical steps, reading biblical references to "the Lord" as to the exalted Jesus, and even liturgically "translating" biblical references to "calling upon the Lord" by the action of cultic invocation of Jesus, are crucial. They certainly indicate that "Lord" applied to Jesus quickly acquired a connotation considerably higher than "master/sir." In fact, "Lord" clearly functions in these cases as a divine title. But could this really have happened as early as the Acts narratives of Judean Christianity claim, in the earliest years of the Jerusalem church? I contend that none of the alternative proposals is as compelling as this option.

As an illustration of the attempts to explain matters by other routes, let us consider George Howard's contention that this identification/association of Jesus with *Yahweh* originated at a secondary stage of the Christian movement and among Gentile Christians.[47] Pointing to the extant pre-Christian Greek biblical manuscripts in which *Yahweh* is not translated but retained in Hebrew characters, Howard plausibly contended that the practice of rendering *Yahweh* as *Kyrios* evident in the (later) Greek biblical manuscripts from Christian provenance was a Christian scribal development. But, more dubiously, he further contended that this Christian scribal practice introduced an ambiguity into biblical passages that first made it possible to read them as references to Jesus.

Howard granted that from earliest days Christians called Jesus "Lord" in Greek-speaking and Aramaic-speaking circles. But he argued that this did not carry the connotation *Kyrios* came to have until Christian copies of the biblical writings began to use the same term to represent *Yahweh*. This, he further argued, could have happened only among Gentile Christians, who were unable to read Hebrew, and were thus unable to distinguish where in the Old Testament *Kyrios* represented the Hebrew name of God from where it was only a title of

---

47. George Howard, "The Tetragram and the New Testament," *JBL* 96 (1977): 63-68. But cf. Albert Pietersma's argument that the representation of the tetragrammaton in Hebrew characters in Jewish Greek biblical manuscripts was Roman-era scribal archaizing, that the original practice had been to write *Kyrios,* and that in any case it never affected the way the texts were actually read by Greek-speaking Jews: "Kyrios or Tetragram: A Renewed Quest for the Original Septuagint," in *Studies in Honour of John W. Wevers on His Sixty-Fifth Birthday,* ed. Albert Pietersma and Claude Cox (Mississauga, Ontario: Benben Publishers, 1984), 85-101. One Greek biblical manuscript from Qumran represents the tetragrammaton as *IAŌ.*

respect. To cite an important example, in Psalm 110:1 (LXX 109:1) the Hebrew says, "*Yahweh* says to my lord [*'adoni*]," whereas the Christian LXX manuscripts have "The Lord [*ho Kyrios*] said to my lord [*tō kyriō mou*]." In pre-Christian Greek manuscripts of the Psalms, the phrase would have been written, "*Yahweh* said to my lord [*tō kyriō mou*]," and it would have been quite clear that *kyrios* here was not used for God but referred to a figure distinguishable from God.

But Howard's argument does not stand up well under critical analysis. First, though it is true that *Yahweh* is not characteristically *written* as *Kyrios* in extant pre-Christian Greek biblical manuscripts, solid evidence indicates that *when biblical passages were read (out) in early Greek-speaking Jewish circles, the word* Kyrios *was characteristically used for* Yahweh,[48] That is, among Greek-speaking Jewish readers, *Kyrios* was the *spoken* way of referring to God, just as it appears that *Adonay* was widely used as a reverential oral substitute for *Yahweh* by Hebrew-speaking readers of the Bible.[49]

More seriously still, Howard failed to take account of the very early date by which the cultic invocation of Jesus as "Lord" had become a conventional and uncontroversial practice among Christians, both in Greek-speaking and Aramaic-speaking circles. As I have emphasized before, the chronology is crucial. Remember that Paul's letters show that addressing/invoking Jesus as "Lord" was a commonplace Christian worship practice well before 50 C.E., and that it likely began in Aramaic-speaking circles. Christian copies of biblical writings in Greek prepared by and for Gentile believers are unlikely to have been very common this early. In any case, at such an early point the putative exegetical confusion of Gentiles is most unlikely to have had the crucial and momentous effect that Howard alleges. In the first couple of Christian decades, Jewish Christians were dominant in leadership and influence, and the dominant religious practice and beliefs of Christian circles were all attributable to them.

Moreover, in the light of traditional Jewish concerns about the worship of figures other than God, the cultic practice of invoking Jesus as "Lord" was a revolutionary step; its widespread acceptance by Jewish Christians such as Paul

---

48. James R. Royse, "Philo, Kyrios, and the Tetragrammaton," *Studia Philonica Annual* 3 (1991): 167-83. *Kyrios* is also used to refer to God in other writings from early Greek-speaking Jewish circles, such as Wisdom of Solomon (about twenty-six times, e.g., 1:1, 7, 9).

49. For early evidence of Jewish scribal treatment of the divine name, see Patrick W. Skehan, "The Divine Name at Qumran, in the Masada Scroll, and in the Septuagint," *BIOSCS* 13 (1980): 14-44; M. Delcor, "Des diverses manières d'écrire le tétragramme sacré dans les anciens documents hébraïques," *RHR* 147 (1955): 145-73; Jonathan P. Siegel, "The Employment of Paleo-Hebrew Characters for the Divine Names at Qumran in the Light of Tannaitic Sources," *HUCA* 42 (1971): 159-72.

and his Jewish Christian coreligionists, as well as among Gentile believers, cannot be attributed merely to a Gentile Christian scribal practice of writing *Yahweh* as *Kyrios*. Actually, it is much more likely that the Christian scribal practice of writing *Kyrios* for *Yahweh* in Greek biblical manuscripts reflects the *prior* Christian interpretation of key biblical passages that mention *Yahweh* as referring to Jesus, and also the (likewise prior) Christian cultic practice of "calling upon the name" of Jesus as "Lord" that seems to go back so early.

However, some scholars hesitate to agree that the cultic invocation of Jesus as "the Lord," and the interpretation of biblical references to the *Kyrios* as referring to Jesus, likely have their origin in the Jerusalem church and in the earliest years of the Christian movement. But, though asserting that these steps were taken at such an early stage may seem bold, it is necessary to have the courage to submit to what the historical evidence seems to require.

Circumstances and Dynamics

We may, however, well ask a couple of further questions. Did the cultic invocation of Jesus, "calling upon the name" of Jesus, arise from interpreting biblical passages as referring to this practice? If so, what could have prompted (driven?) Jewish Christians to understand these biblical passages as referring to Jesus "the Lord" and as justifying the rather radical liturgical innovation involved in the cultic acclamation/invocation of Jesus? I take the time to sketch here my proposal for the historical circumstances and dynamics involved. My proposal is based both upon the data in our historical sources and upon analogies of innovations in beliefs and practices in religious movements across history.[50]

According to the earliest traditions, very soon in the "post-Easter" setting Jewish followers of Jesus had experiences of "seeing" Jesus as uniquely resurrected to eschatological existence and heavenly glory. Of course, these Jewish believers brought to their experiences an acquaintance with their scriptures, and a confidence that these sacred writings contained God's redemptive purposes and could help them make full sense of their religious experiences. In a dynamic interaction between devout, prayerful searching for, and pondering over, scriptural texts and continuing powerful religious experiences, they came to understand certain biblical passages in an innovative way as prefiguring and portraying God's vindication of Jesus. These "charismatic" insights into biblical passages in turn shaped their understanding of their experiences, reinforced their confidence in the validity of these experiences, stimulated their openness

---

50. See, e.g., my references in "Religious Experience and Religious Innovation in the New Testament," *JR* 80 (2000): 183-205.

to further experiences of Jesus' exalted status, and helped shape these subsequent experiences.[51]

I propose that in this lively process, and apparently very quickly, through their "revelatory" experiences and their searching of Scriptures they even came to the startling conviction that God required them to assent to his exaltation of Jesus in cultic action. Thereby they inaugurated a novel pattern of devotion in which Jesus was incorporated into their devotional practice in ways otherwise reserved for reverencing God in the Jewish tradition of their day. In their devotion to Jesus, however, they always saw themselves as obeying God, and saw their reverence of Jesus as an expression and extension of their reverence for God. So, since they knew experientially that God had exalted Jesus to unique glory, and that Jesus was duly to be reverenced in cultic devotion, they saw "calling upon (the name of) the Lord" as properly including specifically calling upon (the name of) Jesus.

But whatever we may imagine that the process involved, it is clear that the exalted view of Jesus reflected in associating him with the *Kyrios* of biblical texts, and the cultic veneration of Jesus illustrated in "calling upon" him/his name, appeared very early, and quickly became powerfully influential among various circles of the young religious movement. My main point here is that we have good reasons for taking seriously the Acts representation of the early Judean circles as characterized by this exalted view of Jesus and this devotional practice. Let us now look at some other features of the christological beliefs attributed to Jerusalem Christians in Acts.

Jesus' Redemptive Death

There is also repeated emphasis that Jesus' death was in accordance with the divine plan disclosed in Israel's Scriptures (Acts 2:23, 30-31; 3:18; 4:28), a theme found in the Lukan postresurrection narratives as well (Luke 24:25-27, 44-49). The story of Philip and the Ethiopian eunuch gives Isaiah 53:7-8 as one of the scriptural passages that predict Jesus' suffering. The rejection of Jesus and the role of Israel's leaders in his execution are treated as blameworthy actions that resulted from a failure to recognize God's purpose (both in Peter's speech in Acts 3:17 and later in Paul's speech in the Antioch synagogue, 13:27).[52] In 3:20-21

---

51. D. Aune, "Charismatic Exegesis in Early Judaism and Early Christianity," in *The Pseudepigrapha and Early Biblical Interpretation,* ed. James H. Charlesworth and Craig A. Evans, JSPSup 14 (Sheffield: Sheffield Academic Press, 1993), 126-50; Aune, *Prophecy in Early Christianity and the Ancient Mediterranean World* (Grand Rapids: Eerdmans, 1983), 339-46.

52. The very interesting "ignorance motif" in Acts passages (3:17; 13:27), and the "anti-Judaic" tendency in Codex Bezae and the "Western text" of Acts exhibited in the omission of

Peter appeals to Israel to repent of its rejection of Jesus, and to recognize him as the divinely "fore-appointed" *(prokecheirismenon)* Messiah, who is now in heaven until "the times of restoration of all things" predicted in the scriptural prophets.[53]

In Acts the Judean Christians certainly proclaim forgiveness of sins through Jesus (2:38; 3:19; 10:43; and cf. 13:38-39), an offer now made possible through his death and resurrection. Indeed, the emphasis that Jesus' death was a necessity in God's redemptive plan appears also in the representation of Paul's proclamation (e.g., 17:2-3), and this emphasis posits an obvious connection between his death and redemption. But in Luke-Acts generally (not only in the representation of Judean Christianity), the author emphasizes the theme of divine necessity and fulfillment of Scripture. He does not tend to favor the kinds of statements about Jesus' death that are typical in Paul's letters: e.g., that Christ died "for us/our trespasses/our sins," or references to Jesus' death as a sacrifice or an expiation for sins (but cf. 20:28).[54]

Did this lack of emphasis on Jesus' atoning death also characterize Jerusalem Christians? Though the author of Luke-Acts must be given some credit in shaping the representation of early Judean proclamation, I think his characterization deserves to be taken seriously. I propose that, on other grounds as well, it is reasonable to suppose that the particular *emphasis* upon Jesus' death as atoning for sins that we find developed in Paul may not have been made in the early Jewish Christian setting. In discussing Paul in the previous chapter, I suggested that he may have placed greater emphasis on Jesus' atoning death to explain (to his converts and to others who opposed the terms of his mission) how sinful Gentiles could be accepted fully by God. I also proposed that for Jewish Christian circles, and also in their proclamation to fellow Jews, the idea that Messiah's death was a necessary redemptive event functioned more as an apologetic explanation for Jesus' crucifixion.

---

these phrases, have been discussed by E. J. Epp, *The Theological Tendency of Codex Bezae Cantabrigiensis,* SNTSMS 3 (Cambridge: Cambridge University Press, 1966), 41-64.

53. Note the use of the same verb, *procheirizein* (to appoint [in advance]), in Acts 22:14 and 26:16, where it refers to Paul as destined by God for the Gentile mission. The term, thus, is likely attributable to the author, though the idea of divine election of Jesus as Messiah must stem from Jewish Christian tradition.

54. See, e.g., the recent discussion of Jesus' death in Luke-Acts by J. A. Fitzmyer, *The Gospel according to Luke I–IX* (Garden City, N.Y.: Doubleday, 1981), 22-23, 219-23, and for the theme of divine necessity in Luke, 179-80; also John T. Carroll and Joel B. Green, *The Death of Jesus in Early Christianity* (Peabody, Mass.: Hendrickson, 1995), 60-81. It is interesting that the reference to the church having been "obtained through the blood of his own (Son)" (*dia tou haimatos tou idiou* is probably the right reading among the variants) in Acts 20:28 is part of a speech put on the lips of Paul.

The early Jewish believers obviously considered Israel in need of redemption, and announced that Jesus' death and resurrection provided an extraordinary opportunity for forgiveness of sins to make that redemption possible, as is attested in the Acts material. I propose that the formulaic expressions in Paul about Christ/Messiah's death "for our sins/us" (e.g., Rom. 4:24-25; 1 Cor. 15:3) are probably traditional "pre-Pauline" expressions that originated in Judean Christian circles but received particular emphasis and new application in Paul's teaching and his defense of his Gentile converts. On the basis of his study of the origins of the Gospel *narratives* of Jesus' death, Joel Green concluded along lines that seem broadly similar to my proposals about the ways Jesus' death was referred to in the very earliest Christian circles: "Apparently, for earliest Christianity, the highest priority was on proving that Jesus' death was no surprise to God and constituted no contradiction of the christological claims that had been and were being advanced. The idea that Jesus died 'for us' evidently constituted one very early and important means of making this point clear."[55]

In assessing how Jesus' death was seen in early Jewish Christian circles, we also have to take account of interesting references to Jesus having been "hanged on a tree." This expression appears in Peter's speeches to the Sanhedrin (Acts 5:30) and to the household of Cornelius (10:39), and is clearly an allusion to Deuteronomy 21:22-23, which says criminals "hanged on a tree" are under God's curse.[56] Another, slightly less direct allusion appears in Paul's speech to the synagogue in Pisidian Antioch, which says the Jewish leaders in Jerusalem took Jesus down from "the tree" (Acts 13:29) after colluding in his crucifixion.

Outside of Acts, the only other references to Jesus' death on a "tree" are in Galatians 3:13, another explicit citation of Deuteronomy 21:23, and 1 Peter 2:24, which says Jesus "himself bore our sins in his body on the tree," phrasing that seems to be influenced also by Isaiah 53:4, 12, though "the tree" probably also alludes to the Deuteronomy passage. As we have noted already, Paul certainly had direct acquaintance with Jewish Christian circles both in Judea and the diaspora, and 1 Peter clearly presents a very Jewish Christian face to its (Gentile) readers.[57]

---

55. Green, *The Death of Jesus*, 323, and 320-23 for confirmations and corrections of Martin Hengel, *The Atonement: The Origins of the Doctrine in the New Testament* (Philadelphia: Fortress; London: SCM Press, 1981).

56. There is now evidence that Deut. 21:22-23 was also applied to crucifixion by the Qumran community: J. A. Fitzmyer, "Crucifixion in Ancient Palestine, Qumran Literature, and the New Testament," *CBQ* 40 (1978): 493-513.

57. Even if, as many scholars believe, 1 Peter presents a contrived face of the Jewish Christian Peter, the author shows knowledge of a range of early Christian traditions that include Judean Jewish Christian material. See, e.g., John H. Elliott, "Peter, First Epistle Of," in *ABD*, 5:269-78, esp. 271-72.

In short, this christological allusion to Deuteronomy 21:22-23 is both very early (as shown by the date of Galatians) and seems to be particularly associated with Jewish Christian circles. There is good reason to take seriously the Acts attribution of this motif to Judean Christianity in framing a view of their christological expressions.

Moreover, the clear allusion to the divinely cursed death described in Deuteronomy 21:22-23, in the Acts references to Jesus having been "hanged on a tree," can only mean that Jesus' death is taken as redemptive. It is quite possible (I would say likely) that the reference to Deuteronomy 21:22-23 was first made by hostile Jews, who sought to discredit Jesus and the early Jewish Christian circles who proclaimed him as Messiah. But obviously, early Christians could have used the Deuteronomy passage to interpret Jesus' death only if they understood him to have suffered the divine curse on behalf of others, and not simply as a punishment for his own sins. Consequently, in these Acts narratives of Judean Christian proclamation, the references to Jesus' death "on a tree" presuppose the interpretation of Jesus' death as redemptive, and not only as an eschatological necessity and fulfillment of biblical prophecy.

Arland Hultgren proposed cogently that in the initial convictions about Jesus in earliest Christian circles, "the cross and resurrection together were considered the redemptive event." Hultgren offers a very plausible model of the factors that generated this conviction, involving (1) the collective impact upon them of Jesus' words and actions (e.g., proclamation of the kingdom of God, summoning disciples, performing miracles, declaring forgiveness of sins), (2) Jesus' crucifixion as a messianic pretender, (3) the disciples' postcrucifixion experiences of Jesus "in majestic power and glory," and (4) continuing experiences of the Holy Spirit among them, which they understood as mediated to them by the risen Jesus. Under the impact of these continuing experiences of the Spirit, at a very early secondary stage of reflection "the death of Jesus came to be considered an atoning death." Yet, as he rightly notes, even when the cross and resurrection were distinguished, "there was never a separate concentration on either to the exclusion of the other."[58]

Other Primitive Epithets

We also find christological terms and categories in this Acts material that are not so common elsewhere. *Archēgos* (leader, founder, author) appears in the New Testament solely as a christological title, and only in Acts 3:15 ("Author/ leader of life") and 5:31 ("Leader and Savior"), and in Hebrews 2:10 ("*archēgos*

---

58. Hultgren, *Christ and His Benefits*, 32.

[pioneer/leader] of salvation)" and 12:2 ("pioneer [*archēgon*] and perfecter of our faith)." Though the Greek term has meanings of "hero," "founder/origina-tor," and "captain" in non-Christian writings, the LXX use of the word is proba-bly responsible for its christological appropriation in early Christian circles.[59] Müller is probably correct that, in the New Testament usage of the term, Jesus is referred to as "the eschatological *leader* of the new people of God," the biblical theme of Israel being led (by God) out of Egypt here "transposed into christo-logical-titular usage."[60] The appearance of the title only in Acts and Hebrews (another writing commonly thought to draw upon Jewish Christian tradi-tions), and its absence in the christological expressions more characteristic of Gentile Christian circles, combine to make it highly likely that the christo-logical use of the Greek word began early, among Greek-speaking Jewish Chris-tians in a bilingual setting such as Jerusalem.[61]

Another term used as a title or christological epithet, "the Righteous/Just One" *(ho dikaios)*, appears in Acts only in sayings attributed to Jewish Chris-tians.[62] In Acts 3:14 Peter accuses his fellow Jews of rejecting "the Holy and Righteous One [*ton hagion kai dikaion*]," and in 7:52 Stephen similarly con-demns Israel for persecuting prophets and killing "those who foretold the com-ing of the Righteous One." The final application of the title to Jesus comes in 22:14, where Paul is pictured telling how the Jewish Christian, Ananias, told him that God had chosen him "to see the Righteous One and to hear his own voice" (referring to Paul's Damascus road encounter with the risen Jesus as narrated in 9:3-9).

The term may also be used as a christological title in a few other New Tes-tament texts that have connections with Jewish Christian usage (1 Pet. 3:18; 1 John 2:1; cf. 2:29; 3:7). As well, several scholars have argued that "the righteous one" of Romans 1:17 who "shall live through/out of faith(fulness)" is a reference

---

59. Cf. G. Delling, "Ἀρχηγός," in *TDNT,* 1:487-88; Paul-Gerhard Müller, ΧΡΙΣΤΟΣ ΑΡΧΗΓΟΣ. *Der religionsgeschichtliche und theologische Hintergrund einer neutestamentlichen Christusprädikation* (Frankfurt and Bern: Peter Lang, 1973); Müller, "Ἀρχηγός," in *EDNT,* 1:163-64 (and bibliographical references listed there).

60. Müller, "Ἀρχηγός," 1:163.

61. See also Harold W. Attridge, *The Epistle to the Hebrews,* Hermeneia (Philadelphia: Fortress, 1989), 87-88, on the use of the term in Hebrews.

62. In these Acts references the adjective *dikaios* has the definite article, is used in "abso-lute" form as a substantive, and clearly functions as a title. The term is also applied to Jesus in other New Testament references, but not so obviously as a title (1 Pet. 3:18; 1 John 2:1, 29; 3:7). Though some see "the righteous one" in James 5:6 as a reference to Jesus, most do not agree. Cf., e.g., Sophie Laws, *A Commentary on the Epistle of James* (London: Adam and Charles Black, 1980), 204-6; Luke T. Johnson, *The Letter of James,* AB 37A (Garden City, N.Y.: Doubleday, 1995), 304; Longenecker, 47.

to Jesus and the revelatory and redemptive efficacy of his faithfulness to God.[63] In this view Paul here preserves a very primitive Jewish Christian appropriation of "the Righteous One" as a messianic title for Jesus, and an early christological exegesis of Habakkuk 2:4.[64]

It is a reasonable suggestion that the use of the term as an epithet for Jesus comes from biblical passages read christologically in early Jewish Christian circles, such as Isaiah 53:11 and Habakkuk 2:4.[65] In support of the likelihood that this title is an authentic item of early Jewish Christian christological vocabulary are passages in the "Similitudes" (or "Parables") of *1 Enoch* where the term is applied to an eschatological figure (38.2, "the Righteous One"; cf. 53.6, "the Righteous and Elect One").[66] Moreover, in Wisdom of Solomon 2:12-18 "the righteous one" is also called "servant of the Lord [*paida Kyriou*]" and "son of God [*huios theou*]." These passages at least show that the expression "the righteous one" was an honorific epithet in Jewish religious usage of the time; and *1 Enoch* shows that the term could be used as a title for a messianic figure.

Still another christological term that appears only rarely outside the Acts references to Judean Christianity is *pais* (which can refer to a "servant" or a "boy/child").[67] It is clear that in these christological uses we should understand

---

63. Recently, Richard B. Hays, "'The Righteous One' as Eschatological Deliverer: A Case Study in Paul's Apocalyptic Hermeneutics," in *Apocalyptic and the New Testament: Essays in Honor of J. Louis Martyn*, ed. Joel Marcus and Marion L. Soards, JSNTSup 24 (Sheffield: Sheffield Academic Press, 1989), 191-215. Earlier exponents include C. H. Dodd, *According to the Scriptures* (London: James Nisbet, 1952; reprint, London: Collins/Fontana, 1965), 49-51; A. T. Hanson, *Studies in Paul's Technique and Theology* (London: SPCK; Grand Rapids: Eerdmans, 1974), 39-51.

64. That is, the traditional Christian understanding of "the righteous/just one" in Rom. 1:17 as a generic reference to believers is completely set aside.

65. The MT (Hebrew) of Isa. 53:11 says "my righteous servant [*tsadik 'avdi*] will justify many, and he will bear their iniquities," whereas the LXX says the "righteous one serving well will justify many [*dikaiōsai dikaion eu douleuonta pollois*], and will himself bear [*anoisei*] their sins." The wording of Hab. 2:4 likewise varies among extant Greek and Hebrew witnesses, but any of the variants easily permits a messianic/christological interpretation. See, e.g., D.-A. Koch, "Der Text von Hab 2:4b in der Septuaginta und im Neuen Testament," *ZNW* 76 (1985): 68-85.

66. See Matthew Black, *The Book of Enoch or 1 Enoch: A New English Edition with Commentary and Textual Notes*, SVTP 7 (Leiden: Brill, 1985), 195.

67. *Pais* is used twenty-four times in the NT, but mainly in its ordinary sense referring to a child. It is used with special religious meaning only in Matt. 12:18 (citing Isa. 42:1 in reference to Jesus), and in Luke-Acts with reference to Israel (Luke 1:54), David (Luke 1:69; Acts 4:25), and Jesus (Acts 3:13, 26; 4:27, 30). Cf. Cadbury, "Titles," 364-70; Jacques Ménard, "*Pais Theou* as Messianic Title in the Book of Acts," *CBQ* 19 (1957): 83-92; J.-A. Bühner, "παῖς," in *EDNT*, 3:5-6; Joachim Jeremias, "παῖς θεοῦ," in *TDNT*, 5:677-717; O. Michel, "παῖς θεοῦ," in *NIDNTT*, 3:607-13; Cullmann, *Christology*, 73-79. Unfortunately, scholarship has been primarily occupied with the

the meaning as "servant (of God)," a strong basis for this understanding being the use of the term in Matthew 12:18, in a quotation from Isaiah 42:1-4 that is applied to Jesus ("Here is my servant [*ho pais mou*] whom I have chosen").[68]

But the only cases in the New Testament where people directly refer to Jesus as God's *pais* (i.e., not in biblical quotations) are in Acts. Twice in his speech to fellow Jews in the temple area Peter calls Jesus God's *pais*, whom God has "glorified" over against Israel's denial and participation in his death (3:13), and whom God has "raised up" to provide Israel with eschatological blessing as they "turn from [their] evils" (3:26). In this same speech Peter refers to Jesus as Messiah (*Christos*, 3:18) and as the "prophet like me" predicted by Moses (3:22). So the clear impression is that *pais*, like *Christos* and "prophet," is another honorific appellative claimed for Jesus. The remaining two cases are in the prayer of the Jerusalem believers in 4:24-30. Here Jesus is God's "holy servant" against whom Israel colluded in his execution (v. 27); and the believers pray that God will perform "signs and wonders" through the name of his "holy servant" (v. 30), and will embolden the believers ("your servants [*doulois!*]," v. 29) "to speak your word."

When we take into account the other uses of this Greek term in Luke-Acts, I contend that it becomes clear that these applications of *pais* to Jesus carry a specifically Israel-oriented and royal-messianic connotation.[69] The Lukan nativity account has two other relevant occurrences, both in passages that celebrate eschatological blessings in Israel, which in the narrative are connected to the birth of Jesus. The psalmlike speech of Mary in Luke 1:46-55 proclaims God's remembrance of his mercy for "his servant Israel," and Zechariah's "prophecy" in Luke 1:67-79 announces that God has raised up a savior "in the house of his servant David" (v. 69). Similarly, in the prayer in Acts 4:24-30, David is again specifically referred to as God's "servant [*pais*]" (v. 25). These uses are all influenced by, and probably allude to, biblical references to Israel and David as God's servant (Heb. *'ebed*).[70] Moreover, the royal-messianic connota-

---

question of whether *pais* reflects the "suffering" servant passages/idea in Isaiah, and thus has not adequately considered other matters.

68. In Isa. 42:1, as in the overwhelming majority of the uses of *pais* in the LXX, it translates the Hebrew term *'ebed* (servant). Of the 870 occurrences of *'ebed* in the Hebrew Bible, the LXX translators mainly used *pais* (340 times) and *doulos* ("slave," 327 times). For full counts of Greek terms used, see Michel, 3:609.

69. In all the other uses of *pais* in the New Testament beyond those discussed here, the term carries the ordinary meanings, referring either to children (e.g., Acts 20:12; Jesus as child in Luke 2:43) or to servants of a king or master (e.g., Matt. 8:6; 14:2).

70. Emphasis on Israel as God's chosen servant (*pais* as translation for Hebrew *'ebed*): e.g., Isa. 41:8-9; 42:1; 43:10; 44:1, 2, 21; 45:4; and somewhat ambiguously in 49:5-6; 50:10; 52:13 (cf. use of *doulos* in 48:20; 49:3). David as God's *pais* in Pss. 18:1; 69:17 (LXX 68:18); 86:16 (LXX 85:16);

tion of *pais* in Acts 4:25-26 is specifically supported by the quotation here of Psalm 2:1, the hostility against God's "holy servant" Jesus presented as a fulfillment of the psalm's reference to opposition "against the Lord and against his Messiah [*Christos*]."

This messianic connotation and the use of the term in prayer that is characteristic of Acts are both retained in the few occurrences of *pais* as a christological appellative in early Christian writings outside the New Testament. In fact, outside of quotations of the LXX and a very few other cases, the only places where *pais* is used as an appellative for Jesus are in prayers and liturgically shaped material in a few Christian writings of the late first and early second centuries.[71] There are several applications of the term to Jesus in the lengthy liturgical prayer toward the end of *1 Clement* ("his beloved servant Jesus Christ," 59.2, 3; "you are the only God and Jesus Christ is your servant," 59.4), and in a prayer and a doxology in *Martyrdom of Polycarp* ("your beloved and blessed servant," 14.1; "beloved servant," 14.3; "his servant, the unique Son Jesus Christ" [*tou paidos autou, tou monogenous Iēsou Christou*], 20.2).

Additional instances are in the *Didache*, in the prayers prescribed for Eucharist. Note that here, as in Luke-Acts, *pais* is applied both to David and to Jesus (9.2, 3; 10.2-3), in liturgical passages that have a strongly Jewish Christian flavor and are thought by some scholars to be among the earliest material in this composite writing.[72] The prayer over the eucharistic cup gives thanks to God "for the holy vine of David your servant, which you have made known to us through Jesus, your servant" (9.2); the prayer over the broken bread thanks God for "the life and knowledge which you have made known to us through Jesus, your servant" (9.3). In the prayer prescribed to follow the meal, thanks are given to God "for your holy name which you have caused to dwell in our

---

and as God's *doulos* in 78:70 (LXX 77:70); 89:3, 20 (LXX 88:4, 21); 132:10 (LXX 131:10); 144:10 (LXX 143:10). Though *pais* was clearly the preferred term (over *doulos*) as appellative for David and Jesus among early Greek-speaking Jewish Christians (but cf. Phil. 2:7!), in a bilingual setting such as the Jerusalem church, believers would have been aware that in all these passages *pais* and *doulos* translated the same Hebrew word for "servant" (*'ebed*). Note the preference for *pais* also in *Psalms of Solomon* in references to Israel as God's servant (12.6; 17.21).

71. Citations of LXX passages: e.g., *Barn.* 6.1, citing Isa. 50:8-9; and *Barn.* 9.2, citing Ps. 33:13. There are also three christological uses of *pais* in *The Epistle to Diognetus* in discursive statements (8.9, 11; 9.1) which, however, look as if they may be shaped by liturgical use of the term. Cf. the preference for "Son" (*huios*) elsewhere in *Diognetus* (e.g., 9.2, 4).

72. E.g., Johannes Betz, "The Eucharist in the Didache," in *The Didache in Modern Research*, ed. Jonathan A. Draper (Leiden: Brill, 1996), 244-75. For a recent review of scholarship on the *Didache*, see Draper's essay in the same volume: "The Didache in Modern Research: An Overview" (1-42). Cf. the preference in the *Didache* for *teknon* (child) for believers in the wisdom-instructional material (e.g., 3.1, 4, 5, 6; 4.1).

hearts, and for the knowledge and faith and immortality which you have made known to us through Jesus your servant" (10.2), and for "spiritual food and drink and eternal life through your servant" (10.3). When these prayers were composed cannot be decided with certainty, but they seem to be Christian adaptations of Jewish prayer expressions, and they also employ archaic-looking Christian vocabulary such as the *pais* appellative. It is a reasonable scholarly guess that they may derive from very early Jewish Christian circles and their eucharistic practices.

So, in light of the pattern of christological usage of *pais*, i.e., almost entirely in citations of the LXX, in texts and traditions that seem to have come from a Jewish Christian ethos, and in prayers and liturgical materials (which by their nature tend to be more conservative of traditional vocabulary), we probably have here an authentic item of the christological vocabulary of very early Jewish Christian circles. The use of this term in these Acts narratives of Judean Jewish Christian faith and piety must be taken, therefore, as another example of the author presenting authentic aspects of these circles. It is a fair observation that these Acts narratives are deliberately archaized and that the author must have done this because it fitted his literary purposes. But it is an equally fair conclusion that in his archaizing representation of Judean Christianity he was able to employ authentic traditions that reflect their faith and practice.[73]

As still another example of this, I come back to the speech attributed to Peter in Acts 3:12-26, specifically 3:22-24, where Jesus is described as the eschatological prophet. Here the prediction in Deuteronomy 18:15-18 that God will "raise up" *(anastēsei)* a prophet like Moses, and the demand that Israel obey this figure, are both applied to Jesus, whom God "raised up" *(anastēsas,* 3:26, referring to Jesus' resurrection?) for Israel's salvation.[74] The same Deuteronomy passage is cited in the speech of Stephen in Acts 7:37, where we must take it as again applied to Jesus; but this Deuteronomy text is not invoked elsewhere in the New Testament.[75] The Gospels tell us that some of Jesus' contemporaries took him

---

73. Lüdemann (*Early Christianity,* 54) concludes that the christological use of *pais* is very early, and that the whole of Acts 3:12-26 "is to be termed a primitive Christian conversion tradition which had its context in a Jewish-Christian community the faith of which was strongly orientated on the future."

74. Deut. 18:18-19 is also included in the biblical texts cited in the Qumran writing 4Q Testim (4Q175), which some have contended was a collection of messianic texts, e.g., J. M. Allegro, "Further Messianic References in Qumran Literature," *JBL* 75 (1956): 174-87.

75. There are, however, possible allusions to Deut. 18:15-18 and the idea of an eschatological prophet (like Moses) in a few other New Testament passages, e.g., John 1:21 (where John the Baptist is asked if he is "*the* prophet") and perhaps John 5:46 (where Jesus claims that Moses "wrote about me").

for a prophet (e.g., Mark 6:15), and in Luke 13:31-33 Jesus is pictured as implicitly claiming to be a prophet. As we shall note in the next chapter, in the Q material the association of Jesus and his followers with the biblical prophets is a salient theme; and in 1 Thessalonians 2:15 Paul links the Jewish hand in the death of Jesus with the tradition of Israel slaying the prophets sent to her, a point also made in Stephen's speech (Acts 7:51-53). But neither the category of prophet nor Moses' prediction of another prophet like him found much favor in the christological themes that came to be most widely used in the first century and thereafter. So once again it is likely that the references to Deuteronomy 18:15-18, and the presentation of Jesus as the (final?) eschatological prophet predicted by Moses in the Acts description of Judean Christianity, represent another case of the author of Acts showing knowledge of very early christological tradition.[76]

In summary, the Acts portrayal of Judean Christianity incorporates a number of christological terms and categories that have strong warrants as authentic traditions of the earliest years of the Judean Christian movement. Some of the christological categories and terms (e.g., *pais*, eschatological prophet like Moses, Messiah especially sent to redeem Israel) appear to have become archaic already by the time of the writing of Acts. There is also a strong eschatological, Davidic-messianic, and Israel-oriented tone in the christological claims made by Judean Christians, all of which fits the mission to fellow Jews that seems to have characterized these circles.

Devotional Practice

As with Pauline Christianity, so too with Judean Christian circles it is necessary to take account of their devotional *practices* if we wish to understand adequately the place of Jesus in their religious life and thought. The general picture of the piety of Judean Christians in Acts is a combination of recognizably Jewish religious practice with some of the novel features that characterize Christian devotion.

---

76. See also, e.g., Longenecker, *Christology,* 32-38, who notes the frequently observed parallels and contrasts between Moses and Jesus in the Gospel of Matthew (esp. the Sermon on the Mount, chaps. 5–7) and the Gospel of John (e.g., 1:17; 5:39-47), and the "true prophet" emphasis in the material in the *Pseudo-Clementines* known as the *"Kerygmata Petrou."* But this "true prophet" theme is quite different from the eschatological prophet-like-Moses theme in the Acts passages, and the *Kerygmata Petrou* material is much later. See, e.g., Johannes Irmscher and Georg Strecker, "The Pseudo-Clementines," in *New Testament Apocrypha,* ed. Wilhelm Schneemelcher, trans. R. Mcl. Wilson, rev. ed. (Louisville: Westminster John Knox, 1991-92; German ed., 1989), 2:483-541, esp. 531-41.

The Temple and the Jerusalem Church

The most obvious aspect of Jewish piety in the Acts narratives of the Jerusalem believers is the place of the temple in their religious behavior.[77] The Jerusalem Christians are pictured as regularly meeting in the temple (Luke 24:53; Acts 2:46; 5:12), observing the daily times of temple prayer (3:1), and using the temple as a venue for teaching and proclaiming their message about Jesus (3:11-26; 5:20-21, 42). Indeed, in the Acts account of Paul's final visit to Jerusalem, he assents to James's proposal that he enter the temple to offer a sacrifice as part of a rite of purification (21:17-26). The author of Acts clearly had no problem with Jewish Christians (including Paul!) treating the temple as a sacred site and an appropriate venue for expressing piety.

Of course, the Jerusalem temple plays a significant role overall in Luke-Acts, from the nativity narratives onward, and the author refers to it far more often than any other New Testament author.[78] Although Luke 21:5-6 gives a version of the tradition of Jesus' prediction of the temple's destruction, in the main the author shows a concern to associate Jesus and his followers positively with the temple. However, it also seems perfectly plausible historically for Jewish believers to have regarded the temple as sacred and an especially suitable place of prayer. Furthermore, as I have noted previously, the choice of Jerusalem by Galilean followers of Jesus as the key initial venue for the proclamation of the christological claims that emerged so quickly after his crucifixion can only mean that they regarded the city as especially important; a key reason for the importance of Jerusalem was its temple.[79]

Some scholars who assume that Jesus condemned the Jerusalem temple outright and taught that he himself "would somehow replace the temple" find it puzzling that Jerusalem believers continued to treat the temple as sacred and valid.[80] The narratives of Jesus "cleansing" the temple found in all four canonical Gospels (Matt. 21:12-13; Mark 11:15-17; Luke 19:45-46; John 2:13-22) are widely regarded as based on an actual incident. But any indictment of the temple by Jesus need not have indicated a total rejection of the legitimacy of the temple as

---

77. D. K. Falk, "Jewish Prayer Literature and the Jerusalem Church in Acts," in *The Book of Acts in Its Palestinian Setting*, esp. 268-76.

78. Luke-Acts has thirty-nine of the seventy-one uses of *hieron* in the Greek NT, and another four uses of *naos* (of the forty-five total uses in the NT).

79. For a convenient selection of references to the Jerusalem temple in Greek- and Roman-era Jewish sources, see C. T. R. Hayward, *The Jewish Temple: A Non-Biblical Sourcebook* (London and New York: Routledge, 1996).

80. E.g., David Peterson, "The Worship of the New Community," in *Witness to the Gospel: The Theology of Acts*, ed. I. Howard Marshall and David Peterson (Grand Rapids and Cambridge: Eerdmans, 1998), 375-76.

such; his action could well have been motivated by something else, such as perceived sins of the priestly leadership then in charge.[81] He could even have been
laying a claim to royal/messianic authority to cleanse the temple to make it fit
for eschatological redemption. In fact, if Jesus warned of a divine judgment to
fall upon Jerusalem and the temple, this would most likely have been based on a
view that the city and the temple had a special place and responsibility in God's
will.

cf, wr18t JJG

The place of the temple in the religious behavior of Jerusalem Christians
should not be so puzzling, and it is not a case of what some might regard as re-
sidual or vestigial Judaism. The Jerusalem church was not there because the believers did not yet have a better conception of their Christian faith, or because
the city was simply a convenient place to find accommodation. The choice of
Galilean followers of Jesus of Nazareth to relocate in Jerusalem and to make the
city the geographical base of their religious life and witness appears to have
been made very promptly and deliberately after they were convinced Jesus had
been resurrected and exalted by God to heavenly glory. The obvious reasons
have to do with the ancestral significance of Jerusalem as the royal and temple
city, the traditional Jewish site of king, worship, and pilgrimage.

The Galilean followers of Jesus (e.g., Cephas, John and James Zebedee,
James the brother of Jesus) took pains to form themselves as a group in *Jerusalem,* which can only mean that they saw themselves as witnesses to the nation
and sought to position themselves in its ancestral capital and worship center.
This is also fully compatible with the royal-messianic emphasis that was a feature of their interpretation of Jesus. They proclaimed Jesus as Israel's Messiah,
the divinely appointed heir of David and the one through whom Israel could
now hope to obtain forgiveness of her sins and redemption (e.g., Acts 2:36, 39;
4:18-21). It is therefore also perfectly understandable that the Jerusalem church
made a special point of the temple as a place for giving their witness to Jesus.
The place of the temple in the canonical Gospels preserves the notion from the
early Judean Christian circles that, as Messiah, Jesus has a rightful claim over
it.[82] Moreover, there appears to have been an association of king/messiah and
temple in ancient Jewish traditions (reflecting the common link of king and

---

81. Craig A. Evans, *Jesus and His Contemporaries: Comparative Studies,* AGJU 25 (Leiden:
Brill, 1995), 319-80, sets Jesus' temple action in the context of other ancient Jewish evidence of
temple criticism.

82. Particularly notable among the Gospel traditions are the scenes where Jesus
"cleanses" the temple, clearly making a claim with respect to it (as reflected, e.g., in the demand
of the temple priests in Mark 11:27-33 to know Jesus' authority for his actions), the teaching
and controversies in the temple (e.g., Mark 12), and the prediction of its destruction (e.g.,
Mark 13).

temple in the ancient Near East generally), and this provides the historical background and context for the Jerusalem Christian stance.[83]

For the Jerusalem believers, the temple was thoroughly a component-feature of their faith and piety *as followers of Jesus.* Seeing themselves as followers and witnesses to the divinely appointed Messiah, their presence in the Jerusalem temple was for them not only appropriate but, so they likely felt, obligatory. Moreover, even if Jesus did warn of a future divine judgment to fall upon Jerusalem and its temple, his followers probably believed that, until God carried out this action, the city and its temple retained their traditional significance. Also, if Jesus was critical of the priestly administration of the temple, it is likely that the Jerusalem church would have taken a similar view (and the continuing, vehement opposition of the temple leaders against Jesus and against leaders of the Jerusalem church is consistent with this).[84]

But a view of the temple leadership as sinful or invalid would not necessarily have meant that the temple itself was now an invalid institution or that its religious significance was removed. Instead, to reiterate the point for emphasis, for the early Jerusalem church the temple was a completely appropriate place to express both their continuing commitment to the God of Israel and their convictions and responsibilities as witnesses to Jesus' exalted status and high significance.

Jesus' Name

The principal novel feature of the piety of Jerusalem Christianity in Acts is the direct expression of devotion to Jesus. I mentioned the cultic practice of "calling upon the name" of Jesus/the Lord in the preceding chapter, but it is sufficiently important to return to the matter. As previously noted, the phrase "to call upon the name of the Lord" is derived directly from the Old Testament usage, where it functions as a technical expression designating prayer and sacrifice offered specifically to *Yahweh* (e.g., Gen. 4:26; 13:4).[85] In the early Christian

---

83. Donald Juel, *Messiah and Temple,* SBLDS 31 (Missoula: Scholars, 1977), 169-209; Donna R. Runnalls, "The King as Temple Builder: A Messianic Typology," in *Spirit within Structure (Festschrift for George Johnston),* ed. E. J. Furcha (Allison Park, Pa.: Pickwick, 1983), 15-37.

84. In addition to high priestly collusion in the execution of Jesus, Acts refers to priest-led opposition to Jerusalem Christian leaders: e.g., 5:17-42 (and note the contrast in the narrative between the priests and the Pharisee Gamaliel); 6:8–8:1 (Stephen); 9:1-2 (Saul obtains letters from the Jerusalem high priest in support of his efforts to combat Jewish Christians); 22:30; 23:12-15; 24:1 (priestly opposition to Paul). Note also Josephus's report of the execution of James (the brother of Jesus), which he describes as contrived by the high priest Ananus (*Ant.* 20.197-203).

85. E.g., K. L. Schmidt, "ἐπικαλέω," in *TDNT,* 3:496-500. The verb *epikaleō* is also used for

sources, however, this biblical phrase also refers to cultic invocation and acclamation of Jesus, especially in the corporate worship setting.

The crucial line from Joel cited in the Acts account of Peter's speech (Acts 2:21), "Everyone who calls upon the name of the Lord shall be saved," is also cited years earlier by Paul in Romans 10:13, in a context (Rom. 10:9-13) that indicates that Paul means the biblical phrase to refer to the ritual act of "confessing [*homologeō*]" the Lord *Jesus* (10:9). We also noted earlier that in 1 Corinthians 1:2 Paul refers to believers universally as "those who call upon the name of our Lord Jesus Christ." He probably also alludes to this cultic practice in 1 Corinthians 12:3 (which refers to the saying "Jesus is Lord [*Kyrios Iēsous*]" in a larger context concerned with worship), and again in Philippians 2:11 (the statement "every tongue shall confess [*exomologēsētai*], 'Jesus Christ is Lord [*Kyrios Iēsous Christos*],'" projecting a universal acclamation of Jesus in phrasing drawn from Christian worship practice).

In Acts, therefore, the references to "calling upon" (the name of) Jesus reflect what we have good reason to see as a cultic practice that goes back to very early moments of the Christian movement. Twice in Acts, Saul/Paul is said to have opposed those who "called upon" Jesus' name (9:14, "all those who call upon your name"; 9:21, "those who call upon this name"). The Damascus Jewish Christian Ananias is pictured encouraging Paul to be baptized and to "call upon his [Jesus'] name" (22:16). The familiarity of "calling upon" Jesus among early Christians is further reflected in the Acts account of Stephen. Here a shortened expression appears in Greek, the verb form used without explicit object: Stephen "called upon and said [*epikaloumenon kai legonta*], 'Lord Jesus, receive my spirit'" (7:59).

The following points are important to underscore in considering further what "calling upon" Jesus represented. First, this Christian cultic action involved the explicit invocation/acclamation of Jesus, using his name and characteristically referring to him as "Lord," in Greek-speaking and (as the *maranatha* formula indicates) Aramaic-speaking Christian circles. That is, "Jesus" functioned as "the name of the Lord," which one pronounced aloud as a key part of the cultic act that was seen by believers as now the proper liturgical expression of the biblical phrase, to "call upon the name of the Lord." This ritual use of Jesus' name reflects an explicit identification of Jesus as an appropriate recipient of such cultic devotion; it also shows that the name "Jesus" itself

---

calling or summoning someone, which can include a god or spirit (see magical examples in MM, 239). But the full expression, "to call upon the name (of the Lord/God)," is particularly common in the Old Testament, and the NT usage is obviously influenced by this traditional usage and meaning.

was reverenced and functioned in the devotional life of these believers. There is further indication of this in the other ritual uses of Jesus' name, which I shall discuss shortly.

Second, the practice is very early. For reasons I have already given, we must place its origins in Jewish Christian circles, and these must include Judean circles such as the Jerusalem church. To repeat one crucial reason from earlier in this discussion, for such a major cultic innovation to have so quickly become widespread, conventionalized, and uncontroversial among various Christian groups, it must necessarily have originated among one or more sufficiently influential, respected, and very early circles of believers.

It is completely incredible to think that the cultic acclamation of Jesus was a Pauline innovation. Only slightly less improbable are the claims of some scholars who have struggled to manufacture other circles to which to assign responsibility for the cultic reverence of Jesus (e.g., Bousset's pre-Pauline "Hellenistic Gentile" churches, or Mack's anonymous "Christ cult" circles somewhere in Syria), or have simply credited the origins vaguely to "Hellenistic" influences in diaspora locations. Such unlikely claims represent an apparent effort to avoid the uncomfortable conclusion that the cultic veneration of Jesus in fact had its origins in Judean Christian groups.

Third, in history-of-religions terms, the cultic acclamation/invocation of Jesus is a remarkable innovation. It represents the inclusion of Jesus with God as recipient of public, corporate cultic reverence. That is, we are dealing here with an innovation precisely in the area of religious behavior that was most sensitive in Roman-era Jewish tradition about protecting the uniqueness of the one God. In earlier research (summarized in chap. 1) I demonstrated both the readiness of ancient Jews to attribute to various "divine agent" figures very exalted status, roles, and powers, and also the characteristically firm refusal by these same Jews to treat any such figure as a legitimate recipient of cultic veneration. In the historical context of this strongly held religious concern, therefore, the readiness of Christian Jews in the very first years of the Christian movement to extend cultic reverence to Jesus is astonishing.

It is also unprecedented. As a public, corporate ritual action by which Christian circles openly registered their religious stance, the cultic veneration of Jesus is, for example, completely different from the contemporary invocation of angels reflected in Jewish "magical" material.[86] The latter are private practices, often secretive, never formally affirmed by any religious group, and never characteristic of public Jewish liturgy. Whatever we may speculate about the

---

86. Clinton E. Arnold, *The Colossian Syncretism: The Interface between Christianity and Folk Belief at Colossae*, WUNT 2/77 (Tübingen: Mohr, 1995), esp. 8-102.

possible indirect relevance of the "venerative language" used for angels, and the magical invocation of them and other divine-agent figures, the sort of open, corporate cultic reverence of Jesus represented in the liturgical practice of "calling upon" him/his name constitutes a major new step in the religious behavior of those Christian Jews among whom it has its origins. The cultic reverence of Jesus was also momentous for the subsequent developments in Christian tradition, and for this reason too must be seen as profoundly important historically.

In the Acts narratives about Judean Christianity, this "calling upon" the name of Jesus also forms part of a wider pattern of devotional practice in which Jesus was central. In particular, other ritual practices are mentioned that feature use of Jesus' name: baptism, healing, and exorcism.[87] There is, thus, a cluster of phenomena in which Jesus' name itself is treated as powerful and efficacious in various ways; this emphasis upon Jesus' name also seems to have been very particularly a feature of Jewish Christian devotional practice and christological thought.[88] The early origin of the role of Jesus' name in devotional practice is reflected in the widespread references in early Christian sources to various actions done in connection with it.[89]

Jesus' Name in Baptism

Scholars have tended to focus on the use of Jesus' name in baptism (perhaps because they were more comfortable with this more familiar rite, and also perhaps because baptism acquired/retained a more central theological significance

---

87. Silva New, "The Name, Baptism, and the Laying on of Hands," in *The Beginnings of Christianity*, ed. F. J. Foakes Jackson and Kirsopp Lake (1933; reprint, Grand Rapids: Baker, 1966), 5:121-40. In Acts, baptism is "in/to the name of Jesus" (2:38; 8:16; 10:48; 19:5), Christians speak "in [*epi*] the name of Jesus" (4:17-18; 5:28, 40), miracles happen "through" Jesus' name (*dia* 4:30; *epi* 3:16; *en* 4:7), and believers suffer persecution "for (the sake of)" Jesus' name (*hyper* 5:41; 9:16; 21:13).

88. Indeed, the emphasis on Jesus' name continued to characterize subsequent forms of Christianity that were influenced by, or appropriated features of, early Jewish Christian thought and practice. J. Daniélou, *The Theology of Jewish Christianity*, trans. and ed. J. A. Baker (London: Darton, Longman and Todd, 1964), 147-63.

89. In addition to references to healing and exorcism using Jesus' name in other early Christian texts (e.g., Mark 9:38; Matt. 7:22; James 5:14), note, e.g., Paul's directions about expelling the incestuous man in the Corinthian church "in the name of the Lord Jesus" (1 Cor. 5:3-5), which seems to be roughly synonymous in the context to doing so "with the power of our Lord Jesus." In the Gospel of John, commonly thought to reflect Jewish Christian traditions, there is a strong emphasis on the efficacy of Jesus' name, e.g., in prayer, 14:13-14, 15:16, 16:23-24, and as the object of saving faith (e.g., 1:12-13; 20:31). See now the comprehensive discussion of references to the name of Jesus in the NT by Adelheid Ruck-Schröder, *Der Name Gottes und der Name Jesu: Eine neutestamentliche Studie*, WMANT 80 (Neukirchen-Vluyn: Neukirchener-Verlag, 1999).

in Christian tradition).[90] It is not necessary here to go into great detail concerning the history of this discussion. In the Acts narratives baptism is "in the name of (the Lord) Jesus (Christ)," and the various Greek prepositions used in the references *(epi, eis, en)* suggest that the expressions originated in Semitic-speaking circles and were variously expressed in Greek.[91] We should not, therefore, make too much of the variation in prepositions, as they all indicate that the rite is done with primary reference to Jesus.[92]

It is also quite clear that in all cases we are to think of a ritual act of entrance into the circle of believers that involved the cultic invocation of Jesus' name as a component action which was seen as both marking the rite and as giving it special efficacy.[93] Thus Paul's statement in 1 Corinthians 6:11, "but you were washed, you were sanctified, you were put right in the name of the Lord

---

90. Among older studies, the classic is Wilhelm Heitmüller, *"Im Namen Jesu": Eine sprach-und-religionsgeschichtliche Untersuchung zum Neuen Testament, speziell zur altchristlichen Taufe*, FRLANT 1/2 (Göttingen: Vandenhoeck & Ruprecht, 1903). Among recent studies, see esp. Lars Hartman, *"Into the Name of the Lord Jesus": Baptism in the Early Church* (Edinburgh: T. & T. Clark, 1997); Hartman, "Baptism," in *ABD*, 1:583-94.

91. E.g., baptism *epi* the name of Jesus (Acts 2:38), *eis* (8:16; 19:5; cf. 1 Cor. 1:13, 15), and *en* (10:48; cf. 1 Cor. 6:11). In the Hebrew Scriptures the most common expressions are *l*ᵉ*shem*, "for (the sake of) [God's] name" (e.g., 2 Sam. 7:13; 1 Kings 8:41; Ps. 23:3), and *b*ᵉ*shem*, "by/in the name of" (e.g., Deut. 6:13; 10:8; 1 Sam. 17:45). For fuller discussion of the philological issues, see Hans Bietenhard, "ὄνομα," in *TDNT*, 5:242-81, esp. 252-53, 258-68. "A review of the prepositional combinations in the NT shows wide Semitic influence" (271). See also Lars Hartman, "'Into the Name of Jesus,'" *NTS* 20 (1974): 432-40.

92. The Greek expressions *epi tō onomati* and *en tō onomati* are reasonably common in the LXX, and so may reflect the influence of "biblical" Greek. Hartman contends that the expression *eis tō onoma*, however, "is both unbiblical and a bit strange as compared to normal Gk" ("Baptism," 1:586), and he cogently argues that it represents a translation of a Hebrew expression *(l*ᵉ*shem)* and the Aramaic equivalent *(l*ᵉ*shum)*. He also notes that in rabbinic texts one finds *b*ᵉ*shem* "with no recognizable difference in meaning," and so it is quite possible that both *eis* and *en* were used from the earliest days of Christian baptism.

93. This is particularly clear in the story in Acts 19:1-7. In response to Paul's question about what kind of baptism they had undergone, certain "disciples" reply, "into John's baptism" *(eis to Iōannou baptisma)*. Accepting Paul's proclamation of Jesus as the one John foretold, they are then baptized "into [*eis*] the name of the Lord Jesus" and receive the Holy Spirit with the further ritual action of Paul laying his hands upon them. Matters are less obvious in the preceding pericope (18:24-28). Here Apollos "taught accurately the things concerning Jesus," although "he knew only John's baptism." That Priscilla and Aquila felt it necessary to "expound to him more accurately the Way (of God)" suggests that Apollos is implicitly presented here (howbeit in very carefully respectful terms) as not quite fully a Christian convert. Out of deference for Apollos, the author may have omitted mentioning that the "more accurate" teaching given by Priscilla and Aquila involved also a Christian baptism "in Jesus' name," like that given to the other Ephesian disciples of John (so, e.g., Hartman, "Baptism," 1:585).

Jesus Christ [*en tō onomati tou Kyriou Iēsou Christou*] and in the Spirit of our God," in all likelihood refers to the ritual use of Jesus' name in baptism. With some other scholars, I also see the reference to "the beautiful name that is invoked upon you" in James 2:7 as another allusion to the ritual use of Jesus' name in baptism.[94]

The emphatic prominence of Jesus' name in this central and public cultic action makes the early Christian rite of baptism a remarkable development. Although John the Baptist demanded a baptism of repentance, this did not involve the ritual use of his own name; neither did Jewish proselyte baptism (which may have begun in the first century) involve invoking the name of any "divine agent" figure.[95]

The close connection between Jesus' name and person in early Christian ritual practice and belief is reflected in Paul's reference to believers being baptized "into [*eis*] Christ" (Gal. 3:27) and into "Christ Jesus" and "his death" (Rom. 6:3). In my view, Hartman has shown persuasively that the conceptual and linguistic background of the Greek expressions in question is Semitic, and that, based on analogous Semitic expressions, "baptizing 'into the name of Jesus' (etc.) meant that one saw Jesus as the fundamental reference of the rite."[96] More specifically, baptism in Jesus' name presupposed and expressed the belief "that he was of decisive importance to the person baptized . . . the one who meant salvation in the approaching judgment . . . [the] portal figure into the eschaton."[97]

Thus baptism was seen as linking one closely to Jesus and to the redemptive benefits believed to be provided through him, although the precise way in which this was understood or interpreted likely varied among various Christian circles. So Paul may well have thematized the baptism of his Gentile converts in distinctive ways (as, e.g., in his response to Corinthian factionalism in 1 Cor. 12:12-31, where he portrays believers as "all baptized into one body" made up of

94. So Laws, 105; Johnson, 226; Peter H. Davids, *The Epistle of James,* NIGTC (Grand Rapids: Eerdmans; Exeter: Paternoster, 1982), 113-14. Cf. Ruck-Schröder, 233-35.

95. Paul's reference to the Israelites who went through the Red Sea as "baptized into Moses in the cloud and the sea" (1 Cor. 10:1-2) is, as the context (10:1-13) shows, part of his Christianized interpretation of the wilderness events. Moses certainly was regarded by devout Jews as special, the great teacher of Israel appointed by God. But there is no indication that either the exodus or proselyte baptism was ever referred to or understood as bringing people into some special relationship with Moses such as is asserted in the NT about believers who undergo Christian baptism. On 1 Cor. 10:1-2, see, e.g., Fee, 443-46.

96. Hartman, "Baptism," 1:586.

97. Lars Hartman, "Early Baptism — Early Christology," in *The Future of Christology: Essays in Honor of Leander E. Keck,* ed. Abraham J. Malberbe and Wayne A. Meeks (Minneapolis: Fortress, 1993), 191-201, quote from 196.

various "members"). But the cultic practice of baptizing, importantly including the specific ritual use of Jesus' name, seems to have been so widely practiced that we know nothing of any problem with it, or objection taken to it, in any kind of Christian circle of the earliest decades.

For several reasons we are able to locate the probable provenance of the rite. First, the Christian practice of baptism represents an adaptation from John the Baptist, a Jewish religious figure associated with Galilee, which makes an origin among Christian circles in Roman Judea most reasonable. Secondly, this provenance is also fully consistent with the indications of Semitic linguistic influence in the Greek expressions translated "in the name" of Jesus. That is, "Semitized" Greek most readily is accounted for as the Greek used by people in close cultural and geographical proximity to speakers of Semitic languages; and Roman Judea is demonstrably such a setting. Thirdly, as with other features of the devotional practice of first-century Christianity, the widespread acceptance of baptism in Christian circles as the defining initiation rite, and involving the ritual use of Jesus' name as a constituent feature, is best accounted for by positing its origin among early, respected and influential circles of believers, among whom the Jerusalem church held unrivaled status.

Jesus' Name in Healing and Exorcism

If the use of Jesus' name in baptism is something of an innovation, its use in healing and exorcism has more clear analogies. Names of deities and other powerful figures such as angels were characteristically used in the "magical" practices of the day, among which efforts to heal and exorcise were common.[98] We have evidence of this among pagans and Jews. For the latter, for example, Josephus makes passing reference to a Jewish exorcist named Eleazar, whose technique included the use of Solomon's name (*Ant.* 8.46-49).[99] The ready appropriation of names perceived to be efficacious is characteristic of magical practice as reflected in the story in Acts 19:11-20, where Jewish exorcists, im-

---

98. In addition to Arnold's discussion of appeals to and invocation of angels (Arnold, esp. 11-102), see Heitmüller, 128-265. On what constitutes "magic" and what it means/meant to refer to practices by this term, see esp. Alan F. Segal, "Hellenistic Magic: Some Questions of Definition," in *Studies in Gnosticism and Hellenistic Religions*, ed. R. Van Den Broek and M. J. Vermaseren (Leiden: Brill, 1981), 349-75; David E. Aune, "Magic in Early Christianity," in *ANRW*, 2.23/2:1507-57; Fritz Graf, *Magic in the Ancient World*, trans. Franklin Philip (Cambridge: Harvard University Press, 1997).

99. The pseudepigraphical *Testament of Solomon*, though probably from Christian hands and from the Byzantine period, reflects ancient traditions about Solomon's expertise as exorcist and the use of powerful names to effect cures.

pressed with the "unusual miracles" worked through Paul, attempt to use the name of Jesus to cure demoniacs.[100]

There are, however, two distinguishing features of the Christian practice referred to in Acts and other early Christian writings. First, the more typical practice of Roman-period "magic" (in pagan, Jewish, and Christian examples) usually involved the use of a number of powerful names to effect miracles, but in the publicly affirmed and corporately practiced devotional pattern of Christian circles, Jesus' name was invoked as uniquely efficacious. This emphasis on the particular, indeed unique, efficacy of Jesus and his name has its only analogy in the ancient Jewish view of the one God and the efficacy of his name *(YHWH)* in the public profession and practice of devotion, which of course accords with the Jewish "monotheistic" concern to maintain the uniqueness of the one God.[101]

I propose that the early Christian use of Jesus' name represents a novel adaptation of this Jewish "monotheistic" concern and religious practice. Early Christians saw Jesus as the *uniquely* significant agent of the one God, and in their piety they extended the exclusivity of the one God to take in God's uniquely important representative, while stoutly refusing to extend this exclusivity to any other figures. Likewise, in their public and corporate religious practice they extended the traditional Jewish concern about God's exclusivity to Jesus, treating him as singularly efficacious in ritual power as the supremely significant agent of the one God. Both the "privileging" of Jesus

100. Their action implicitly indicates that the use of Jesus' name by Paul in the "unusual miracles" (Acts 19:11), along the lines of such narratives as 16:16-18, where Paul uses Jesus' name to cure a demoniac slave girl, could be seen as like the wider use of powerful names in magic. The author of Acts clearly presents Jesus' name as powerful in some of the things attempted in magic, but at the same time he wants to differentiate the Christian phenomena from magic. Thus his story of the inability of the exorcists of Acts 19:11-20 emphasizes that it was their own lack of relationship to Jesus that was their undoing, not any lack in the power of Jesus' name. Moreover, he claims that "the name of the Lord Jesus was praised" as a result, and that a number of people involved in magic dramatically renounced the practice (19:18-20).

101. Note, e.g., the Qumran texts dealing with combating demons (4Q510 [4QShir[a]], 4Q511 [4QShir[b]], 11Q11 [11QapPs[a]]. Though the texts are fragmentary, it is clear that the name of *YHWH* is the efficacious power invoked. See esp. 11Q11, col. 4, ll. 1-10, which refers to *YHWH* sending a powerful angel to evict Satan/Belial [?] from the earth and to cast him into "the great abyss"; and col. 5, l. 4, which refers to "[an incanta] in the name of *YHW[H]*." See Florentino García Martínez and Eibert J. C. Tigchelaar, *The Dead Sea Scrolls: Study Edition*, 2 vols. (Leiden: Brill; Grand Rapids: Eerdmans, 1997), 2:1202-3. I emphasize the valid distinction again between secret, private "magical" practices in which Jews may have engaged and the public, corporately affirmed devotional practices of devout Jews. The Christian phenomena we are analyzing here find their proper analogies in the latter, in the light of which we are able to see their innovative features.

over any other figure in their beliefs and religious practices and the character-istic definition of Jesus with reference to the one God show recognizable, in-deed identifying, influences of the Jewish "monotheistic" tradition. Of course, it is equally easy to recognize why devout Jews who did not share such a high view of Jesus found this "extension" of monotheistic practice unac-ceptable and even blasphemous.

Secondly, as with the other Christian devotional practices involving the use of Jesus' name, use in healing and exorcism was part of the *publicly affirmed and corporately shared* devotional practice of Christian circles. That is, the so-cial function and religious significance of these phenomena are distinguishable from what is characteristically referred to by scholars as "magic." There were, to be sure, Jewish exorcists and magicians, and these people likely invoked the names of God, angels, and perhaps other deities as well. But such practices were never accorded the status or public religious function in the Jewish tradition that these Christian practices enjoyed in early Christian circles. That is, they never were represented as the communally practiced and formally affirmed ex-pressions of Jewish piety and devotion. Consequently the use of Jesus' name in healing and exorcism is properly included as a relevant feature of the devo-tional practice of early Christianity that illustrates the very exalted and impor-tant place of Jesus in their beliefs and religious life.

If we ask whether such practices and their christological implications can reliably be attributed to Judean Christian circles, as claimed in the Acts narra-tives, I contend that the answer is affirmative. Given the rather widespread in-terest in miraculous healing and exorcism in the Roman era, among the Jewish as well as pagan populace, and in Palestinian/Judean as well as diaspora loca-tions (e.g., the Qumran exorcistic texts cited above), there is nothing improba-ble in the Acts references to such phenomena as features of the religious prac-tices of Judean Christianity. It also tallies with the strong traditions about Jesus' own involvement in healing and exorcism to find indications that his followers of the earliest years in Roman Judea engaged in similar practices.[102] Moreover, the use of Jesus' name in these practices is consistent with other evidence that a high reverence of Jesus and the invocation of Jesus' name featured prominently in their religious life. Finally, all this is also consistent with the indications pre-viously given that the exalted place of Jesus in the religious thought and life of Pauline Christianity largely represents a devotional pattern inherited by Paul from "those who were in Christ before [him]," and that these included circles of Judean Jewish Christians such as the Jerusalem church.

102. See, e.g., Graham H. Twelftree, *Jesus the Exorcist: A Contribution to the Study of the Historical Jesus*, WUNT 2/54 (Tübingen: J. C. B. Mohr [Siebeck], 1993).

So, in summary of the devotional practice and the christological categories that can be attributed to early Judean circles of the Christian movement,
based on traditions in Acts, we can say that they were both recognizably Jewish
(e.g., in such things as participation in the Jerusalem temple, and the strongly
Israel-oriented proclamation and eschatological-messianic tone of their message and claims) and identifiably "Christian." The latter, of course, is most obviously revealed in the prominence accorded Jesus in their religious beliefs and
practices. Furthermore, we can say that the information given in the Acts narratives is broadly consistent with the traditions incorporated in Paul's letters; I
have noted the good reasons we have to think that these traditions take us back
to Judean circles.

But was this all generally characteristic of Judean Christian circles, or
were there notable differences in religious views and devotional practice in
Judean Christianity, perhaps even in the Jerusalem church itself? We noted
above the differences among early Christians described in Galatians 2:1-10,
where Paul distinguishes between "false brothers," who pushed for observance
of the Torah as a requirement of Gentile believers, and the Jerusalem church
leaders (James, Cephas, and John), who held a more tolerant or moderate view
and accepted (at least in principle) Paul's Gentile mission on his terms. A somewhat similar difference in views on Gentile conversion is indicated in the Acts
15 account of an assembly in Jerusalem to debate the matter. The author there
refers to advocates of Gentile Torah observance as belonging to "the sect of the
Pharisees" (Acts 15:5), and likewise portrays the Jerusalem leadership as standing for a more moderate position (15:6-11, Peter; 15:13-21, James; 15:22-29, "the
apostles and the elders").

These differences between early Christians concern the terms of Gentile
conversion, a serious matter to be sure, very much shaping the future complex-
ion of the early Christian movement. But there is no indication that this issue
involved any major difference about how Jesus was regarded and reverenced. So
far as we can tell, the various sides mentioned in these references shared in re-
vering Jesus as Messiah and Lord, and shared too in the sorts of rituals of devotion that we have reviewed here.

Hellenists and Hebrews

Another indication of some kind of diversity in early Judean Christianity is
given in the Acts references to "Hellenist" believers in Jerusalem. These seem to
be Jews from the diaspora whose primary (or only) language was Greek, and
who had resettled in Jerusalem. The "Hebrew" believers such as Peter, John,

James Zebedee, and James the brother of Jesus came from Palestine/Judea, and their primary language was Aramaic.[103] A good many scholars have attributed much more than cultural and linguistic differences to these two groups in the Jerusalem church, but I am not inclined to assent to these assertions.[104] Because I dissent from views held by a number of important scholars, it is appropriate to give some reasons for my view.

Hellenists as "Proto-Paulinists"

Perhaps no contemporary scholar has made more of the Jerusalem Hellenists' supposedly distinctive religious views than has Martin Hengel, and so it will be convenient to examine the question by testing his case. Hengel has specifically claimed that the Hellenists differed theologically from the "Hebrew" believers: they said that Jesus made redundant both the Jerusalem temple and the Torah. Indeed, Hengel says that the Hellenist wing of the Jerusalem church was crucially influential in other ways, including formulating confessional traditions such as those conveyed by Paul in 1 Corinthians 15:3-7 and Romans 1:3-4, and even more importantly, constituting "the real bridge between Jesus and Paul," as those who "prepared the way for Paul's preaching of freedom by [their] criticism of the ritual law and the cult."[105] My suspicion about these claims of the great

103. The most compelling discussion of the meaning of the terms "Hellenists" and "Hebrews" in Acts, which also takes account of the history of scholarly debate, is Martin Hengel, *Between Jesus and Paul*, trans. John Bowden (London: SCM Press, 1983), esp. 1-11; German original in the essay "Zwischen Jesus und Paulus," *ZTK* 72 (1975): 151-206. As will become clear in the following paragraphs, however, I do not find persuasive Hengel's characterization of the theological distinctives of the Hellenists. Cf. also the recent review of issues by Heikki Räisänen, "Die 'Hellenisten' der Urgemeinde," in *ANRW*, 2.26/2:1468-1514.

104. See, e.g., what Thomas W. Martin describes as "the consensus of recent scholarship" ("Hellenists," in *ABD*, 3:135-36): "Thus it is now thought that it was this community of Christian Hellenists who accelerated the transferral of the Jesus tradition from Aramaic into Greek, who helped bring Christian theology fully into the realm of Greek thought freed from Aramaic pre-acculturation, who were instrumental in moving Christianity from its Palestinian setting into the urban culture of the larger Empire, who first saw the implication of Jesus' resurrection for a Law-free Gospel for the gentiles (and the Jews), and who were the bridge between Jesus and Paul" (136). As the following discussion will show, I find this much overblown and without a foundation in the evidence. Cf. C. C. Hill, "Hellenists, Hellenistic and Hellenistic-Jewish Christianity," in *DLNTD*, 462-69. For a full critical analysis of scholarship on the Hellenists, see now Todd C. Penner, "In Praise of Christian Origins: Stephen and the Hellenists in Lukan Apologetic Historiography" (Ph.D. diss., Emory University, 2000), esp. 13-113.

105. Hengel, *Between Jesus and Paul*, esp. 25-29, quotes from 29. More recently, a basically similar view is presented by Wolfgang Krauss, *Zwischen Jerusalem und Antiochia: Die "Hellen-*

Tübingen scholar arises in part because, contrary to his usual practice, he provides so little evidence in specific support of his claims. Instead we have largely a string of assertions loosely based on the Stephen narrative of Acts 6:1–7:60.

Noting that the author of Acts likely composed Stephen's speech in 7:1-53, Hengel first contends that therefore we can not safely characterize the theology of the Hellenists from the speech (which, as a matter of fact, does not clearly reflect a view of the Torah and temple as redundant). Then, however, disregarding the Lukan characterization of the charges in Acts 6:13-14 as leveled by "false witnesses," Hengel curiously treats these accusations (Acts 6:13-14) as reliable evidence that Stephen and the Hellenists did actually proclaim a message that involved criticism of the Torah and the temple.[106] Hengel even proposes that Luke has "toned down" this evidence by "the insertion of the speech," interrupting the supposedly original connection between the accusations and Stephen's execution.[107] That is, the basis for Hengel's attribution of a radical criticism of Torah and temple to the Jerusalem Hellenists is the Lukan reference in Acts 6:13-14 to the claims of "false witnesses," which Hengel has to take (against the author of Acts) as in fact not false at all but truly representative of the Hellenists' theology.

We may ask, therefore, why Hengel makes so much of these Hellenists, and the answer appears to be largely tied to his perception of the theological usefulness (or necessity) of doing so. Essentially, Hengel wants to posit a historical link between what he takes to be the message of Paul and Jesus, this continuity giving *theological* validity to Paul. Portraying Paul's message as a "criticism of the ritual law and the cult," Hengel also attributes a similar teaching to Jesus.[108] The behavior attributed in Acts, to the Jerusalem believers who are shown continuing in observance of Torah and in frequenting the temple, suggests, however, two other alternatives, neither of which seems very comfortable to Hengel. Either Jesus may not have taught (at least very clearly) the sorts of things Hengel attributes to him, or there is no obvious continuity in teaching between Jesus and Paul. But by attributing a theology critical of Torah and temple to the Hellenist wing of the Jerusalem church, the problem of continuity is solved for Hengel.[109]

---

isten," *Paulus, und die Aufnahme der Heiden in das endzeitliche Gottesvolk,* SBS 179 (Stuttgart: Verlag Katholisches Bibelwerk, 1999).

106. Hengel, *Between Jesus and Paul,* 19-21.

107. Hengel, *Between Jesus and Paul,* 23. Into what did Luke "insert" the speech? If there was a pre-Lukan narrative of Stephen and the views of the Hellenists, how does Hengel know that it was congenial to his own views?

108. Hengel, *Between Jesus and Paul,* 25.

109. "We owe the real bridge between Jesus and Paul to those almost unknown Jewish-

In my view, however, the problem Hengel seeks to solve is basically of his own making. Although theological issues are not my focus here, it does not seem to me as necessary as Hengel and some other scholars think to make the theological validity of Paul's message (however one characterizes it) rest upon continuity with some equivalent teaching of Jesus.[110]

Another unnecessary part of the problem in my view is Hengel's characterization of Paul's message. I regard it as a misconstrual that shows the telltale signs of the influence of traditional Lutheran theological categories of law *versus* gospel. But I do not think that the central feature of Paul's gospel was criticism of Torah and temple. In the preceding chapter I indicated that I understand Paul's relativizing of Torah as wholly prompted because (and when) he needed to oppose efforts to make Torah observance (and thus, circumcision for males) a condition for the full acceptance of Gentile Christians as fellow believers by "Judaizing" Christians.[111] That is, what appear to be sharp criticisms of Torah are in context really directed against the efforts of Judaizers, and his emphasis on freedom from Torah for his converts is to be seen as a corollary of his Gentile mission.

Of course, the efforts of the Judaizers were in reaction to Paul's prior proclamation of God's acceptance of Gentiles through faith in Christ without their having to become Torah proselytes. But Paul's apparent critique of Torah was, in turn, a response to the Judaizers' demand that Gentiles had to observe

---

Christian 'Hellenists' of the group around Stephen and the first Greek-speaking community in Jerusalem which they founded; this was the first to translate the Jesus tradition into Greek and at the same time prepared the way for Paul's preaching of freedom by its criticism of the ritual law and the cult" (Hengel, *Between Jesus and Paul*, 29).

110. It should be at least interesting for this question, if not instructive, that for his part Paul apparently felt no need to ground the validity of his message by asserting continuity with Jesus' teaching. Instead, as Gal. 1:11-12, Rom. 15:14-21 illustrate, Paul claimed that his message and mission came by divine revelation and that the validity of his gospel rested also upon the evidence of God working through it in the operations of the Spirit (e.g., Gal. 3:2-5; 2 Cor. 12:11-12), and upon the conformity of his own style of ministry to the pattern laid down in Jesus' humble obedience to the point of crucifixion (e.g., Paul's "boasting" in his apostolic sufferings in 2 Cor. 11). To be sure, Paul can cite Jesus' sayings as authoritative for Christian conduct. But Paul bases his mission and message to Gentiles in a divine commission and revelation.

111. It is significant that Paul's discussions of Torah appear only in those epistles that either combat the immediate efforts of Judaizers (Galatians) or treat more general questions about how Gentile believers and Jewish believers are to see each other, and how Torah and Christ can both be seen as valid revelations from God (Romans, esp. 1–8). Paul's warning about advocates of circumcision and the autobiographical passage that follows in Phil. 3:2-11 seem to be prompted by a general concern about Judaizers, and a desire to offer his converts models of piety (the latter reflected also in the narrative of Jesus in 2:1-11). Elsewhere in Paul's letters there is little reference to Torah.

Torah as a condition for salvation. As to any alleged Pauline criticism of the Jerusalem temple, there is simply nothing explicit in Paul's letters as supporting evidence.[112] Consequently, since Paul's comments about Torah were occasioned by specific circumstances of his Gentile mission and are not really the core of his teaching, and since there is scant basis for attributing to Paul an antitemple theology, there is no need to find some proto-Pauline group with an anti-Torah and antitemple theology to give a historical source or theological grounding for the sort of Pauline teaching that Hengel asserts.

There are also historical difficulties in Hengel's view of the Hellenists. He contends that, through a combination of their more cosmopolitan background and a Spirit-inspired "enthusiasm," Greek-speaking Jerusalem Christians were better able than the "Hebrews" of the Jerusalem church to comprehend and articulate meaningfully Jesus' message, which also was "critical of the Torah."[113] The historical irony (indeed, improbability) of this is scarcely troubling in Hengel's scheme. Those with the most extended direct contact with Jesus' own teaching and actions, fellow Aramaic-speaking Galileans such as Peter, the Zebedee brothers, and Jesus' brother James, were not able to understand properly Jesus' message and aims. But Greek-speaking Jews who had relocated in Roman Judea and became early converts of the Jerusalem church, but likely had no direct historical acquaintance with Jesus, were uniquely able to catch the truth of the matter. I have enormous appreciation for Hengel's many contributions to scholarship, and I sincerely do not intend to belittle him here. But in the interests of clear thinking on this issue, I have judged it necessary to lay bare the weakness in his representation of the Hellenists.

112. Paul's references to believers individually and collectively as God's "temple" or sanctuary (*naos*, 1 Cor. 3:16-17; 6:19; 2 Cor. 6:16; cf. Eph. 2:21) do not automatically signal a rejection of the Jerusalem temple and its worship system. In fact, Paul refers to the temple and the service of its priests approvingly (or at least with no criticism) in 1 Cor. 9:13-14, as an analogy for the right of "those who proclaim the gospel" to be financially supported. Furthermore, if 2 Thessalonians be taken as genuinely from Paul (which I am inclined toward), the reference in 2:4 to the "lawless one" taking a seat "in the temple of God" implies a positive view of the status of the Jerusalem temple (the definite article makes it likely the referent here).

113. Hengel, *Between Jesus and Paul,* 23-25. The Aramaic-speaking believers, however, were more obtuse because of their cultural background: "Palestinian Judaism had a particular fixation on the law and the temple" (25). See also Hengel, *Judaism and Hellenism: Studies in the Encounter in Palestine during the Early Hellenistic Period,* 2 vols. (London: SCM Press, 1974), 1:313-14.

Hellenists as Jewish Christians

Thus far, however, I have only given reasons to suspect Hengel's portrait of the unique theological significance of the Hellenist believers. A more substantial basis for rejecting the various claims of Hengel and other scholars that there were significant theological divisions between Hebrew and Hellenist Jerusalem Christians has been provided by Craig Hill.[114] Because Hill's study is so thorough and persuasive, I shall merely summarize his key results here, and refer readers to it for more extensive treatment of matters. Hill examines carefully the bases offered for positing major differences between Hebrew and Hellenist wings of the Jerusalem church, and shows that they rest upon rather sandy foundations.

One of the main reasons for thinking Hellenist believers espoused a more radical theology is the frequent claim that only (or particularly) the Hellenist Christians in Jerusalem were persecuted for their religious views by Jewish authorities, and that the Hebrew Christians were basically spared. But Hill cogently demolishes this claim, showing that "the Hebrews are, if anything, the more persecuted by these same Jewish leaders" who are pictured as opposing Stephen and the Hellenists.[115] To illustrate this point, if in Acts the Jerusalem Hellenist believers have their martyr, Stephen, so do the Jerusalem Hebrews, in James Zebedee (12:1-2). Also, if we itemize the instances of Jewish opposition/persecution in the Acts narratives of the Jerusalem church, the leaders of the Hebrew Christians are more frequently on the receiving end (e.g., Peter and John in 4:1-22; "the apostles" in 5:17-41; Peter again in 12:3-19).

Moreover, the persecution that erupts after Stephen's death is directed broadly against "the church in Jerusalem," not simply against Hellenist Christians; and it resulted in the flight of "all except the apostles" throughout Judea and Samaria (8:1). The reference to the apostles refusing to be scattered is probably to be taken as the author attributing courage and dedication to them, and certainly does not indicate that the Hebrew believers generally were spared persecution. Later in Acts some of the religious refugees from the persecution in Jerusalem even traveled "as far as Phoenicia, Cyprus, and Antioch" (11:19-20). Together with the previous reference to others who resettled in "Judea and Samaria," this suggests that those who fled the persecution included both "He-

---

114. Hill, *Hellenists and Hebrews*. See p. 15 n. 68 for further references to Hengel's published statements on the Hellenists. Hill acknowledges that other scholars had questioned the frequent attributions of major theological distinctives to the Hellenists, but also rightly notes that his study is the most thorough discussion (16-17). Among previous discussions, see esp. Johannes Munck, *Paul and the Salvation of Mankind* (Richmond: John Knox, 1959), 218-28.

115. Hill, *Hellenists and Hebrews*, 19-40, citation from 36.

brews," whose background was in Roman Judea and so fled to places outside Jerusalem there, and "Hellenists," whose background and contacts perhaps made departure to diaspora locations more practical.

The further report (11:19-20) that those who fled the persecution "spoke the word to no one except Jews," and that it was "men from Cyprus and Cyrene" who began to proclaim Jesus to "Greeks," is difficult to harmonize with the notion that the refugees were solely "Hellenists," with a supposedly cosmopolitan theology of freedom from Jewish particularities.[116] Instead, the passage suggests that the bulk of the refugees were Jewish believers with a strong sense of mission to fellow Jews, and that *some* among those from a diaspora background began to communicate their faith to non-Jews as well.

In any case, it is more likely that the Gentiles to whom Jewish believers communicated their faith were "God-fearers," who frequented synagogues and had some knowledge of, and interest in, Jewish religious ideas. Though the author of Acts may have seen in this proclamation to these particular Gentiles a prefiguring of the programmatic inclusion of Gentiles that he portrays later in his narrative (Acts 13–28), Acts 11:20 is hardly indication of a "Gentile mission" by the "Hellenists." There is also here no basis for attributing to them a distinctive theology that transcended Jewish particularities of Torah. That in Antioch Gentiles were spoken to about Jesus does not mean that those Jewish Christians who did so ceased to identify themselves as Jewish and departed from Jewish practices.[117]

Furthermore, Hill examines in detail the claims about the supposedly distinctive theology of Stephen and the Hellenists, and analyzes closely the Acts narratives about the Jerusalem church, James and the "Hebrew" believers, and the "Hellenists," as well as Pauline references to Jewish believers in Jerusalem and Antioch. He concludes that assertions that the Hellenists held a distinctive ideology have no adequate basis. "We have no genuine reason to suppose that Stephen was a radical critic of the law or the temple. Inasmuch as his views on these matters were the subject of controversy, we have instead good cause to believe that they were shared by other Christians, Hebrews and Hellenists alike, who suffered for the sake of their faith."[118]

---

116. There is a frequently noted textual variation in Acts 11:20. Some witnesses read "they spoke also to the *Hellēnistas*" ("Hellenists," "Greek-speaking persons"), but other witnesses have *Hellēnas* (Greeks) as those addressed. There are grounds for preferring either variant, and it is difficult to choose between them. See the discussion in Metzger et al., 386-89; C. K. Barrett, *The Acts of the Apostles,* ICC (Edinburgh: T. & T. Clark, 1994), 1:550-51. In any case, the contrast with *Ioudaioi* ("Judeans," "Jews") in 11:19 means that, whatever Greek term one prefers, it refers to "Greek-speaking persons" who were also most likely Gentiles.

117. See also Hill, *Hellenists and Hebrews,* 103-7, 137-40.

118. Hill, *Hellenists and Hebrews,* 101. Note also Hill's observation that the same priestly

Hill also rightly complains that the widely echoed compartmentalization of Jerusalem Christianity into two different ideologies called "Hebrew" and "Hellenist" not only rides roughshod over the evidence but, in addition, often reflects "an unfair stereotyping of non-Pauline Jewish Christianity as backward, severe, and legalistic."[119] This is another aspect of the theologically driven nature of much of the scholarly characterization of these groups, with Pauline theology (and indeed, often a debatable characterization of it as anti-Torah) being treated as the apex of the gospel, and anything other being seen as inferior.

Still more directly relevant to my focus is Hill's conclusion that the stereotyped portrayals of "Hebrews" and "Hellenists," which attribute to the one group a more "conservative" view of Torah observance and to the other a kind of proto-Pauline transcending of Torah and temple, miss the mark as to what was central for all Jewish Christians. Then, as subsequently, Jews often differed over what it meant to be Jewish in terms of observance of Torah. We should expect that early Jewish Christians differed among themselves on this matter as well. But whatever their linguistic background, and whatever their particular views on Jewish identity, the key distinguishing feature of Jewish Christians, and what mainly prompted opposition from other Jews, was the combination of their reverence for Jesus and their fierce commitment to define themselves with reference to him. "Classifications of Jewish Christians as liberal and conservative are, therefore, inherently misleading. A Jewish Christian's attitude toward the law or toward the Gentiles was a function of a larger <u>attempt to understand what faith in Christ meant within the context of Judaism</u>. That was the central question, and it is only because we live at such a distance from it that its importance is missed."[120]

Though Hill does not mention it specifically, the strong likelihood that Judean Christianity practiced baptism in Jesus' name as a rite of initiation and group identity is clear indication that, whether "Hebrews" or "Hellenists," they defined themselves as Jews in a significantly revised way. For them it was no longer sufficient simply to be Jewish and to observe Torah; it was necessary also to recognize Jesus' divinely vindicated significance, and through him to be positioned for eschatological salvation.

Whatever one thinks of the idea that the Hellenist believers of Jerusalem

---

figures were likely involved in the executions of Jesus, Stephen, and James, the latter two being "the reputed champions of the Hellenists and of the Hebrews," and that this too goes against notions that the Hellenists were selectively persecuted (190-91). I also again refer here to Paul's statement in 1 Thess. 2:14-16, which implies that the persecution of Jewish Christians in Judea was not selectively directed toward a "Hellenist" wing.

119. Hill, *Hellenists and Hebrews*, 194.
120. Hill, *Hellenists and Hebrews*, 195.

had developed a distinctively radical view of Torah and temple, however, for my purposes here the key question is whether they dissented from the sorts of christological categories and devotional practice that came to expression initially among Judean circles of the early Christian movement. The answer: there is no evidence that the Hellenists as a group had a distinctive Christology, or that they collectively rejected the sort of reverential practices studied in this chapter. But, even if one prefers to think of the Hellenists as some sort of proto-Pauline group that was critical of "the ritual law" and the Jerusalem temple, this does not in itself provide any basis for thinking that they also developed a significantly different view of Jesus or a distinctive pattern of devotional practice. Within the limits of our evidence (secondhand reports in Acts and traditions in Paul's letters), it appears that the "Hebrews" and the "Hellenists" in Jerusalem made similar christological statements and engaged in similar devotional practices.[121]

Summary

"Judean" Christianity as I define it here, comprising circles of followers of Jesus located in Roman Judea/Palestine in the first few decades, is visible to us only indirectly through echoes of their faith and practice, especially those preserved in Paul's letters and represented in Acts. Our main concern here has been with Judean Christian beliefs about Jesus and how they expressed their devotion to him in religious practices. With due recognition of the limits of the evidence available to us, we can say that Judean Christianity accorded a central place to Jesus in faith and practice.

Jesus was interpreted very much in biblical categories. He is David's rightful heir, the royal-messianic redeemer sent from God. In the proclamation of Judean Christians, Israel is especially addressed with an urgent appeal to recognize Jesus' messianic status, and to orient itself to the eschatological promises that have been fulfilled, and will be fulfilled further, through him.

But Jesus had a place in the belief and piety of Judean Christian circles that goes beyond any other comparable figure, including other ancient Jewish

---

121. Todd Penner ("Christian Origins," esp. 572-84) argued recently that Acts reflects rather well the ancient conventions of history writing, according to which *historia* does not represent or address the concerns of moderns about "what really happened." Thus scholars have been misguided in attempts to separate out and "re-create" the historical realities behind the Acts accounts. Penner contends that we do not have the basis for saying anything much about what the "Hellenists" might have been, and certainly no basis for the elaborate portrayals of a supposedly distinctive "Hellenist" theology.

notions of messiahs. By the divine action registered in raising Jesus from death into eschatological and glorious life, he has been declared to be God's "Son" and "holy servant." Indicative of Jesus' exalted status, his name has been made powerfully efficacious. Healing and other miracles can be worked through faith in his name. Indeed, it is now requisite to "call upon" him/his name, and this appears to have become the distinguishing feature of cultic practice at an astonishingly early point in Judean circles (so early that we cannot see clearly a time when the practice was not operative among them).

I have restricted my discussion here to traditions in Paul that may stem from Judean circles, and to the representations of the Jerusalem church in Acts. These are probably most widely regarded as the data with the strongest claims to being evidence of the beliefs and religious practice of Judean believers. But we should note that the kinds of christological beliefs and devotional stances evidenced in these two bodies of material are also reflected in other sources that may have some bearing on Judean Christianity. For example, the reference to Jesus as their "Lord" among Judean Christians is consistent with the christological vocabulary favored in texts that claim to come from leaders of Judean circles, especially the epistles of James and Jude.[122] Likewise, the "functional overlap" of Jesus and God, especially in eschatological expectations and in devotional practices, is reflected in these epistles and (as we shall see in the next chapter) in the Synoptic sayings source Q.[123] If these texts were written in the names of these figures by their admirers, they would be either Judean Christian circles or perhaps others who associated themselves with Judean Christians and may well have had access to their christological traditions.

The most important points to make here are these, by way of summary: The high place of Jesus in the beliefs and religious practice of Judean Christianity that comes across in this evidence confirms how astonishingly early and quickly an impressive devotion to Jesus appeared. This in turn helps explain why and how it all seems to have been so conventionalized and uncontroversial already by the time of the Pauline mission to the Gentiles in the 50s. As Bengt Holmberg notes, when Paul visited Jerusalem three years after his conversion

---

122. See, e.g., Davids, 39-41. *Kyrios* is applied to Jesus eleven times in James, and is the author's favorite christological term. On Jude's Christology, see esp. Bauckham, *Jude*, 281-314, who shows that the emphasis in Jude is on Jesus' lordship. See also the judicious discussion of the possible provenance and significance of the Epistle of James by Todd C. Penner, *The Epistle of James and Eschatology: Re-reading an Ancient Christian Letter*, JSNTSup 121 (Sheffield: Sheffield Academic Press, 1996), esp. 257-81.

123. Penner, *Epistle of James*, 266-68, refers to "a common pattern of early Christian thought into which James would fit comfortably" (267), involving strong connections of Jesus with God reflected in James, Jude, and Q also.

(or perhaps about five years after Jesus' execution), "he there encountered a religious group which had reached a fairly high degree of development in doctrinal tradition, teaching, cultic practice, common life and internal organization."[124] To be sure, there were differences and important developments, especially represented in Paul's convictions about the programmatic conversion of Gentiles without requiring them to observe Torah. But a veritable explosion of devotion to Jesus took place so early, and was so widespread by the time of his Gentile mission, that in the main christological beliefs and devotional practices that he advocated, Paul was not an innovator but a transmitter of tradition.

In short, the most influential and momentous developments in devotion to Jesus took place in early circles of Judean believers. To their convictions and the fundamental pattern of their piety all subsequent forms of Christianity are debtors.

---

124. Holmberg, *Paul and Power*, 180. He further comments that "it would not be an exaggeration to say that by the time Paul visited Cephas in Jerusalem the church had become institutionalized and had taken on its fundamental, first-generation pattern. Of course doctrine, cult and organization did continue to develop during the period up to the death of the first generation (c. A.D. 60-70), but the fundamental pattern remained the same" (181).

CHAPTER FOUR

Q and Early Devotion to Jesus

Over the last couple decades a number of scholars have proposed that a collection of Jesus' sayings, commonly thought to have been used by the authors of Matthew and Luke and usually referred to today as Q, represents a very early type of first-century followers of Jesus (often placed in Galilee), who held a view of him very different from those more familiar in the New Testament writings. The textual basis for this claim is the widely accepted view of what Q did and did not contain.[1] It is commonly agreed upon that Q was mainly a sayings collection (comprising some 225 to 250 or so verses, or a Greek text of about 3,500 to over 4,000 words).[2] Scholars also agree, in particular, that Q contained no narrative of Jesus' crucifixion, no saying where Jesus directly predicts his death, and no explicit references to Jesus' death as an atoning event or to his resurrection.[3]

---

1. The great majority of New Testament scholars accept the hypothesis that a sayings collection used by the authors of Matthew and Luke best accounts for the large body of sayings material shared by these two Evangelists. I intend no disrespect for those who dissent from this position, but I cannot engage here their objections and alternative views.

2. In his valuable tool, *Q Parallels: Synopsis, Critical Notes, and Concordance*, FFNT (Sonoma, Calif: Polebridge Press, 1988), 209, John S. Kloppenborg gives the following statistics on Q material: 4,464 Matthean Q words; 4,652 Lukan Q words, with 2,400 verbatim agreements. The proposed reconstruction of the Greek text of Q from the International Q Project amounts to 3,519 words (with "a total vocabulary of some 760 words"): James M. Robinson, Paul Hoffmann, and John S. Kloppenborg, eds., *The Critical Edition of Q* (Minneapolis: Fortress; Leuven: Peeters, 2000), 563.

3. The basic contents and their general arrangement in Q are widely agreed upon. The Q material is *mainly* sayings of Jesus, but it also includes sayings set within *chriae* (short narratives in which a saying of Jesus is climactic), and other narratizing elements such as the material on John the Baptist (Q/Luke 3:3, 7-9, 16-17), Jesus' baptism (Q/Luke 3:21-22), and the healing story

The scholars who advocate the view that Q is the key artifact of a distinctive strand of the early Jesus movement contend that these particular followers of Jesus had a distinctive view of him. They revered Jesus as teacher and key herald of the kingdom of God, but christological claims were not their central concern, and Jesus' death and resurrection were not interpreted as redemptive. For the scholars who take this approach, it is *essential* to regard Q as functioning among its originally intended readers as a self-standing presentation of Jesus that adequately represents the extent of their beliefs about him, at least at the point at which Q was composed. These scholars often urge that Q be referred to, thus, as a "sayings *Gospel*" (as distinguished from a sayings *collection*), and they present what Q does and does not contain as very significant for reconstructing the beliefs of the circles from which Q came.

Accepting the hypothesis that Q was a sayings source/collection used by the authors of Matthew and Luke, and also accepting that scholars have been able to propose the likely contents and arrangement of Q with some persuasiveness, I agree that understanding what Q tells us about early Christianity is important. It is particularly important here to deal with questions about what Q tells us about the ways that early Christians thought of Jesus. Doing so gets complicated, however, as a number of inferential steps and contentious issues are involved in the current discussion; there are also several interesting differences among those scholars who espouse this basic approach to Q. But my discussion of matters in this chapter has been made considerably easier by several recent studies devoted to Q, particularly noteworthy among them a recently published volume from John Kloppenborg Verbin.[4] In this valuable study, he

in Q/Luke 7:1-10. In Robinson, Hoffmann, and Kloppenborg, the following verses are included in Q (Luke's chapter and verse numbers are used, with a proposed restoration of original sequences of material in Q; square brackets indicate uncertainty by the editors as to original wording of verses enclosed): 3:2-3, 7-9, 16b-17, [21-22]; 4:1-4, 9-12, 5-8, 13, 16; 6:20-23, 27-29, 30-32, 34-49; 7:1, 3, 6-10, 18-19, 22-28, [29-30], 31-35; 9:57-60; 10:2-16, 21-24; 11:2b-4, 9-15, 17-20, [21-22], 23-26, ?27-28?, 16, 29-35, 39a, 42, 39b, 41, 43-44, 46b, 52, 47-48, 49-51; 12:2-12, 33-34, 22b-31, 39-40, 42-46, [49], 51, 53, [54-56], 58-59; 13:18-21, 24-27, 29, 28, [30], 34-35; 14:[11], 16-18, ?19-20?, 21, 23, 26-27; 17:33; 14:34-35; 16:13, 16-18; 17:1-2; 15:4-5a, 7, [8-10]; 17:3-4, 6, [20-21], 23-24, 37, 26-27, ?28-29?, 30, 34-35; 19:12-24, 26; 22:28, 30. Cf., e.g., the list of Q contents given by John S. Kloppenborg Verbin, *Excavating Q: The History and Setting of the Sayings Gospel* (Minneapolis: Fortress; Edinburgh: T. & T. Clark, 2000), 100 (fig. 16).

4. Kloppenborg Verbin, *Excavating Q*. The literature on Q is now abundant, as is indicated by the sixty-page bibliography in his book. (Having previously published as John S. Kloppenborg, with this book he added the name Verbin. Because he became known as Kloppenborg, I shall use that throughout.) Among other important studies of major issues, see esp. Arland D. Jacobson, *The First Gospel: An Introduction to Q* (Sonoma, Calif.: Polebridge Press, 1992); Christopher M. Tuckett, *Q and the History of Early Christianity: Studies on Q* (Edinburgh: T. & T. Clark; Peabody, Mass.: Hendrickson, 1996).

provides a wide-ranging discussion of the whole history of research on Q, commendably interacts with other scholars on all the issues, and offers his own nuanced view of Q as a "sayings Gospel" that is evidence of a very early and distinctive form of Christianity. I judge his discussion on all counts to be easily superior to anything else by scholars who advocate similar views. In what follows, therefore, I shall make this book the point of departure and the major dialogue partner in dealing with Q.

Untenable Options

Kloppenborg assists discussion by persuasively showing that some proposals about the kind of early Jesus movement that Q represents are not tenable. To cite an important example, Helmut Koester claimed that the "catalyst" that led to the formation of the early collection of Jesus' sayings was "the view that the kingdom is uniquely present in Jesus' eschatological preaching and that eternal wisdom about man's true self is disclosed in his words"; Koester further claimed that this view had an obviously "gnostic proclivity."[5] As Kloppenborg rightly notes, however, "Little in Q falls under the rubric of anthropological revelations," and instead Q simply shows an "elongation of the standard sapiential view" of the revered sage as exemplary of "the divine ethos" in his knowledge, teaching, and conduct.[6]

Even in what Kloppenborg regards as the earliest stage or layer of the Q collection (Q¹), he notes that the distinctive feature is "the degree to which the speaker's [Jesus'] own person comes into focus as a privileged exponent of that divine ethos, which Q calls 'the kingdom of God.'"[7] That is, from its putative

---

5. Helmut Koester, "One Jesus and Four Primitive Gospels," in James M. Robinson and Helmut Koester, *Trajectories through Early Christianity* (Philadelphia: Fortress, 1971), 158-204, esp. 186. For further critical engagement with Koester's claims, see also Tuckett, Q, 65-69, 241-43, 343-45.

6. Kloppenborg, *Excavating Q*, 394.

7. Kloppenborg, *Excavating Q*, 394. In his highly influential study, *The Formation of Q: Trajectories in Ancient Wisdom Collections* (Philadelphia: Fortress, 1987), Kloppenborg defends at length the view that Q underwent three editorial stages. His proposed first stage/layer, Q¹, was made up of six "wisdom speeches" and belonged to the genre of "instruction." Subsequently this material was expanded by the addition of further sayings, many of them *chriae* (i.e., sayings set within simple narratives), and other sayings expressing a "critical and polemical stance" toward Israel, thus producing Q². The final stage, Q³, involved the inclusion of the temptation narrative, adding thereby an explicitly "biographical dimension" to Q (p. 317). There are in fact several different proposals that Q underwent two or more editorial stages, but in recent years Kloppenborg's has probably attracted the most attention, and has been more often invoked by

first stage and onward, <u>Q reflects a view of Jesus as the especially authoritative</u> <u>vehicle of God's revelatory and salvific purposes</u>: "[I]n both strata of Q Jesus is represented as intimately associated with the reign of God and not merely as its messenger."[8] Moreover, Kloppenborg insists that, although "Q contains elements that *might have developed* toward a completely contemporizing, non-eschatological presentation of Jesus and his message . . . the way the Jesus tradition was deployed in the *Gospel of Thomas*," there is nothing about the early sayings tradition that made this inevitable or more likely than any other appropriation of it.[9] "Although one of the *possible* transformations of sayings genres was in the direction of Gnosticism, that was not the only possibility, and Q shows no signs at all of moving in that direction."[10]

In fact, he correctly notes that Q actually shows a clear "proclivity" toward narrative presentations of Jesus, such as those in the canonical Gospels. The narrative of Jesus' temptation placed early in Q (Q 4:1-13) particularly shows a tendency toward a biographical-type presentation, and at least a basic notion of chronological sequence. This means it is unwise to use the allegedly gnosticizing appropriation of Jesus' sayings in the *Gospel of Thomas* as a basis for understanding the motives and religious ethos of those Christians of the early decades of the first century who made the collections of Jesus' sayings such as represented in Q.[11]

---

other scholars who try to use Q to postulate the history of a distinctive kind of early Christianity. <u>It is, however, more damaging to the credibility of the enterprise of "reconstructing" Q's</u> <u>redactional history than is sometimes recognized that the attempts to do so yield very different</u> <u>results.</u> For a critical review of this endeavor, see now Alan Kirk, *The Composition of the Sayings Source: Genre, Synchrony, and Wisdom Redaction in Q*, NovTSup 91 (Leiden: Brill, 1998), esp. 1-86. <u>Kirk provides a strong case that Q was composed as a single literary act.</u> Tuckett, too, has proposed that Q represents a single-stage composition that incorporated smaller collections of Jesus tradition (41-82, 96-100). David Catchpole, *The Quest for Q* (Edinburgh: T. & T. Clark, 1993), contends that the author of Mark used Q, and preserves important bits of Q not otherwise recognized (esp. 60-78). Criticism of theories of redactional stages of Q is also offered by Jens Schröter, *Erinnerung an Jesu Worte: Studien zur Rezeption der Logienüberlieferung in Markus, Q, und Thomas*, WMANT 76 (Neukirchen-Vluyn: Neukirchener Verlag, 1997).

8. Kloppenborg, *Excavating Q*, 395.

9. Kloppenborg, *Excavating Q*, 388. Unless otherwise indicated, here and in the following quotations the italics are his.

10. Kloppenborg, *Excavating Q*, 396.

11. Thus, e.g., the argument of Stephen J. Patterson, *The Gospel of Thomas and Jesus* (Sonoma, Calif.: Polebridge Press, 1993), on this point esp. 102-10, must be judged as unpersuasive. I return to the *Gospel of Thomas* in a later chapter. Here it is worth noting some key differences between Q and *Thomas* that make attempts to link them by some "trajectory" questionable. Only 46 of the 114 sayings in *Thomas* have parallels in Q (per Helmut Koester, *Ancient Christian Gospels: Their History and Development* [London: SCM Press; Philadelphia: Trinity

Furthermore, Kloppenborg shows that there is nothing about sayings collections as a genre that necessarily indicates a concern with "eternal wisdom" established on common experience or verified by appeal to any authority other than Jesus himself. Throughout Q it is clear that the "wisdom" advocated consists precisely in reacting positively to Jesus' words and actions as disclosures of divine truth and as exemplary for the readers. Jesus' sayings are not debatable, but instead definitive; "faithful adherence to Jesus' words is a fundamental criterion for Q (Q 6:46-49) and Q is careful to establish that Jesus' words via the disciples have the authority of divine speech (10:16)."[12]

In addition, though he believes "apocalyptic" notes such as the sayings about the coming of the son of man entered the Q material in his secondary stage (Q²), Kloppenborg grants that even in his earliest layer of Q there is an "eschatological" outlook: "While lacking most of the apocalyptic elements of Mark or 2 Thessalonians or the Apocalypse — detailed previews, timetables, and elaborated scenarios of judgment and reward — Q clearly undergirds its ethical appeals by invoking the impermanence of the present and the hope of a divinely established future."[13] So it is incorrect to think of the "Q people" simply circulating aphorisms of timeless value among themselves, and experimenting with a countercultural lifestyle, without much in the way of recognizably religious motivations.[14] "To characterize Q as 'sapiential' is not, therefore, to imply a depiction of Jesus as a teacher of this-worldly, prudential wisdom, or still less to imply an intellectual world that was hermetically sealed against eschatology, prophetic traditions, and the epic traditions of Israel."[15]

In his critique of these other views of Q, Kloppenborg seems to me persuasive. I now summarize his view of the place and interpretation of Jesus in Q, after which I offer some criticisms and my own analysis.

Press International, 1990], 87). Unlike Q, *Thomas* has no perceptible rationale for its arrangement of sayings. E.g., Allen Callahan is able to propose some catchword linkages of small groups of sayings in *Thomas,* but scarcely any organizing principle or reason for the "'odd sequence' that constitutes the sayings": "'No Rhyme or Reason': The Hidden Logia of the Gospel of Thomas," *HTR* 90 (1997): 411-26. (I thank Dale Allison for this reference.) Also, *Thomas* clearly expresses a dissenting Christian stance over against other forms of Christianity, whereas there is no hint of this sort of polemic in Q.

12. Kloppenborg, *Excavating Q,* 142.
13. Kloppenborg, *Excavating Q,* 387.
14. Cf. Burton Mack, *The Lost Gospel: The Book of Q and Christian Origins* (San Francisco: Harper Collins, 1993).
15. Kloppenborg, *Excavating Q,* 388.

Kloppenborg's View of Q's Christology

Because of the care with which he develops his own views about the proper characterization of Q and the circles in which it arose, I propose to test their warrants.[16] Toward that end, I give first a summary of his views about the religious character of the people Q represents, with special concern for the place of Jesus in their thought and life. Afterward I shall indicate some historical problems in the sort of position Kloppenborg supports, and then offer my own analysis of the view of Jesus reflected in Q.

For Kloppenborg the key things about Q are these: (1) Q focuses more on Jesus' sayings than his deeds; (2) Q refers to the future advent of the son of man but not to his "vicarious death or a resurrection"; and (3) Q reflects and extols "a social marginality," that is, a radical obedience that involves a readiness to part with possessions and to subordinate family relationships for the sake of the kingdom of God.[17] Essentially these three observations reflect the main contents of Q and are thus not in themselves terribly controversial. The issues begin with how to proceed to a description of the history of earliest Christianity. Kloppenborg presents questions about the import of Q for reconstructing early Christianity as unavoidable "entailments" of "holding that the [two-document hypothesis, involving Q as the key source of the sayings material shared by Matthew and Luke], best accounts for the origin of the Synoptics" (x). I agree that the questions he raises are reasonable consequences of the Q hypothesis, but, as will become clear in what follows, in spite of his careful efforts, I find some of his answers unpersuasive. This includes his attempt to locate the composition of Q among Galilean circles of Jesus' followers, and his proposals about their socioeconomic status and ethos.[18] But, as the focus of this book is on the kinds

---

16. I note that James M. Robinson, in a comment appearing on the back cover, proclaims Kloppenborg's book "the most thorough, wide-reaching, and convincing analysis of Q" and "required reading for anyone wanting to discuss Q."

17. Kloppenborg, *Excavating Q*, 1. The parenthetical numbers in the following text refer to pages in this work.

18. I simply note that I do not find the assumption persuasive that references to Bethsaida and Chorazin are evidence of the provenance of Q. These sites are retained in Luke and Matthew, but obviously do not indicate the provenance of these writings. So why should they indicate the provenance of Q? Nor do I find persuasive the assumption that we can determine the socioeconomic circumstances of original readers from references in Q material to the socioeconomic characteristics of characters mentioned. As Richard Bauckham has complained about similar approaches to the Gospels, scholars often treat a Gospel writing as "transparently revelatory of the community for which it was written" because their interpretative aim of reconstructing this community requires it, and not because there is otherwise good reason for taking this approach ("For Whom Were the Gospels Written?" in *The Gospels for All*

of christological beliefs and devotion offered to Jesus in early Christian circles, I shall not engage those other issues here.

As a fundamental emphasis, he contends, "To posit Q amounts to positing 'differentness' at the very beginning of the Jesus movement" (1). Acknowledging that "Q exhibits greater commonalities with other 'theologies' of the early Jesus movement" than is often supposed, he insists nevertheless that "at the same time, Q's 'differentness' is substantial" (363). More specifically, he posits circles in which Jesus' death was not interpreted as redemptive, and his vindication was not conceived in terms of resurrection.[19]

He grants, however, that in spite of the absence of a narrative of Jesus' death, there are clear indications of "reflections on Jesus' death" in the Q material (369). To cite one important reference, Q 14:27 indicates that discipleship was seen as "inextricably connected with the willingness to undergo the same shameful death as Jesus," and that "Jesus' fate was an integral part of [Jesus'] identity and activity." Kloppenborg also proposes that "it does not require too much imagination to suppose that Q 6:22-23 has in view Jesus' fate and, like 14:27, associates the disciples' fates with that of their teacher" (370). But he emphasizes that, though Jesus' death has identifiable significance in Q, this does not amount to a view of Jesus' death as "salvific," by which term he seems to mean (atoning) "for sins." "Again it is necessary to insist that at issue is not whether Q knows of Jesus' death and includes sayings that comment on it at least indirectly. The various references to persecution and opposition (6:22-23; 11:49-51; 13:34-35), and the explicit use of 'cross' (14:27) were most likely read with Jesus' death in mind. The issue is whether a *soteriological function* was assigned to that death" (371).

Rejecting as untenable the notion that Q shows indifference to Jesus' death, Kloppenborg contends instead that "Q is well aware of the death of Jesus" and that it is interpreted by a discernible "framework." Q appropriates "the Deuteronomistic understanding of the prophets" (as rejected and, in later traditions, even killed) to present Jesus' death as "an instance of the 'typical' — perhaps climactic — prophetic death." Also, Q uses "the elements of the wisdom tale," which include persecution, rejection, suffering, death, and vindication, but does not apply them to Jesus' fate exclusively but "*generally* to the Q people and to the sages and prophets who preceded them" (371-73, quotes from 373).

But Kloppenborg insists that in answer to the question of whether Q re-

---

Christians: Rethinking the Gospel Audiences, ed. Richard Bauckham [Grand Rapids: Eerdmans, 1998], 26).

19. Kloppenborg's most extended discussion of this is in chap. 8, "Making Difference," esp. 363-79.

flects knowledge of a "passion account or a salvific interpretation of Jesus' death, the answer must be, no." The reason for his confidence about the limits of the knowledge of the redactors of Q is that at the "numerous points" where Q might have referred to Jesus' death as redemptive, *"it consistently fails to do so"* (374). I shall say more a bit later about the adequacy of his argument, but I offer two observations at this point.

First, although he denies that conclusions he favors about Q's treatment of Jesus' death are based on "elaborate arguments from silence," his handling of the aforementioned question repeatedly seems to me just that (cf. 371). Arguments from silence are valid to the extent that the silence can be shown to be sufficiently conspicuous to justify the inference one urges, and I shall indicate later that I do not think he has done this. Secondly, it is unhelpful that he did not indicate specifically the "numerous points" where Q's failure is allegedly so significant. They are not so readily obvious to me as he appears to think.[20]

Kloppenborg also contends that Q reflects a notably different view of Jesus' vindication. Whereas the notion that is likely more familiar to readers of the New Testament is that God raised Jesus from death by resurrection, Kloppenborg maintains that Q indicates other conceptions. He grants that "the textual evidence is slender" (376), and that "there is practically nothing to go on when discussing Q's view of the 'resurrection' of Jesus" (378). In his view there are only Q 13:35, where Jesus says, "I tell you, you will not see me again until you say, 'Blessed is he who comes in the name of the Lord,'" and "the general conviction that Q must have imagined some sort of vindication of its hero." He takes 13:35 as plausibly reflecting a view that Jesus was vindicated by ascending to heaven (patterned after traditions of the heavenly ascent of such figures as Elijah and Enoch). Together with references in Q to Jesus' future return as the son of man (e.g., 12:8-10, 40; 17:23-24), we have, therefore, what Kloppenborg describes as "a death-assumption-judgment scenario, not the death-resurrection pattern that was to become common in Christian thinking after Paul" (378-79). "The conclusion to be drawn is not that Q was oblivious to the issues of the death and vindication of Jesus but that Q's approach to these issues is *significantly different* from those of Paul (and his immediate predecessors) and the Markan and post-Markan gospels" (379). Later in this chapter I shall indicate why on historical grounds I do not judge his views on these matters satisfactory.

---

20. Kloppenborg contends, e.g., that it is significant that Jesus' death is not recited or plotted "as a specific station" in the "narrative world" of Q (*Excavating Q*, 372-73), and that in Q there is a different "framework" by which to view Jesus' death. I agree that this is significant, but he does not provide adequate warrants for the specific inferences that he draws from these data.

The third issue important for my purposes that Kloppenborg also addresses is the place or role of Christology in Q.[21] Complaining that German scholars have focused almost exclusively on "the identification of Jesus as the coming Son of Man," Kloppenborg insists that "the center of Q's theology is not Christology but the reign of God" (391). He contends that, at all putative stages of Q's redaction, christological statements are subordinated to "defending the ethos of the Q group and threatening those who are seen as opponents" (392). This does not mean that in Q Jesus is simply a messenger. "A necessary connection between the person of Jesus and the message" is present in Q, "if only incipiently." Citing passages in his Q¹ stage (9:57-60; 10:2-16), he argues that these diverse materials yield "a Christocentric conclusion" that "the specific lifestyle, therapeutic practice, and kingdom message of *Jesus*" (emphasis his) define the activities of the "workers" called here to proclaim the kingdom of God. Likewise, in Q 6:20-49, he concludes, "it is clear that Jesus himself is represented as a necessary link in the communication of the ethos of the kingdom that is elaborated" (393).

But Kloppenborg observes that the particular relationship between Jesus and his message in Q¹ is not exhibited in explicit christological claims involving "Jesus' self-consciousness as a bringer of salvation" and in the use of "christological epithets." Instead, in Q Jesus is held up for emulation. Kloppenborg allows that in his proposed "main redaction," Q², "the central role of Jesus in the soteriological equation emerges more clearly" (e.g., 12:8-9), that "one's stance toward Jesus is a criterion in the judgment," and that "an exclusive mediation of saving knowledge is assigned to Jesus" (citing 10:22) (394).[22] In all his proposed strata of Q, we have an "intensified soteriology," and Jesus is presented as "intimately associated with the reign of God and not merely as its messenger." But Kloppenborg sees the "focus" of Q as "less on christological characterization than on the message of the kingdom and its defense," a focus that did not require "explicit christological developments" (though these "would come later") (395). In what follows I first indicate problems that I see in the sorts of views espoused by Kloppenborg, and then offer my own characterization of the view of Jesus reflected in Q.

---

21. The key portion in Kloppenborg's book is 388-95, "The Theological 'Center' of Q."

22. I think it more accurate to say that Q 12:8-9 makes one's "stance toward Jesus" *the* "criterion in the judgment." Cf. Kloppenborg, *Excavating Q*, 375: "Q affirms that . . . Jesus is the exclusive conduit of the knowledge of God among humans (Q 10:21-22)."

Historical Plausibility

For several reasons that have to do with historical plausibility, I find the sorts of views I have summarized here difficult to accept, even Kloppenborg's more subtly articulated versions.[23] He and advocates of similar views require us to accept that Q reflects a discrete form of early belief about Jesus; that Q sufficiently represents the state and extent of beliefs about Jesus among the people who composed the document, at least at the point when they did so; and that we can make far-reaching conclusions on the basis of what is and is not found in Q. Kloppenborg repeatedly refers to the *theological* consequences of this approach, but I wish to focus here on the *historical* problems involved in what he and advocates of similar views suppose and assert, problems I think are considerable.[24]

Let us begin by noting what is agreed upon. On the basis of conventional approaches to reconstructing the likely textual contents and arrangement of Q, scholars widely agree that it did not contain the features whose absence figures so crucially (and so often) in proposals that Q was a "gospel" of a distinctive "Q people." There appears to have been no narrative of Jesus' crucifixion, no sayings in which Jesus directly predicts his death (though clearly in Q/Luke 14:27 Jesus may be presented as anticipating his own crucifixion), and no passage where Jesus' death is explicitly referred to as "salvific" (if the standard used is a passage such as Mark 10:45). But the question is what we are to make of this.

From traditions incorporated into Paul's letters that I have previously cited (e.g., 1 Cor. 5:7; 15:1-11; Rom. 4:24-25; 1 Thess. 1:9-10), we certainly know

23. See also Arland Hultgren's judicious comments in *The Rise of Normative Christianity* (Minneapolis: Fortress, 1994), 31-41; also Dale C. Allison, *The Jesus Tradition in Q* (Harrisburg, Pa.: Trinity Press International, 1996), 43-45.

24. It is curious to me that Kloppenborg so repeatedly focuses on the *theological* issues and consequences. From numerous references to the matter in *Excavating Q*, note, e.g., 374 (on the alleged lack of knowledge of salvific interpretations of Jesus' death in Q) and 398 (on whether to refer to Q as a "gospel"). Granted, he does show that some critics of his approach to Q (such as James Dunn, John Galvin, and Brevard Childs) show keen concern about the theological consequences of Q (357-59, 366-69). Further, he is justified in noting that theological concerns often masquerade as historical arguments (among advocates of various points of view on Q). But not all forms of theological thinking require one to have such anxieties about the consequences of *historical* and *exegetical* judgments as to the contents and function(s) of Q in the early first century. For my part, I consider both theological and historical issues about Christian origins to be so important in their own right that we should try to deal with each kind of issue on its own terms and with as little anxiety as possible about the possible consequences of the one for the other. This is not the place to attempt any further discussion of theory in the matter. I simply offer the historical analysis here as an attempt to demonstrate what I advocate, leaving it for others to judge the integrity of my effort and the cogency of my results.

that "salvific construals" of Jesus' death (e.g., "for us/our sins," as "Passover lamb," etc.), and beliefs that Jesus had been resurrected and exalted to heavenly status and would return in glory, were widely circulating among followers of Jesus all through the early decades of the Christian movement. This is the same period when Q is widely thought to have been produced and used, prior to being used as a source by the authors of the Gospels of Matthew and Luke. As we have already noted, with wide scholarly support these beliefs can be attributed to Jewish and Gentile Christians alike, to Pauline congregations and to predecessors of Paul in diaspora settings such as Damascus and Antioch, and also to Judean circles such as the Jerusalem church. If, thus, Q rather adequately reflects the sum of christological beliefs of a group of Jesus' followers in the early decades of the Christian movement, how would a supposed Q people have remained immune to these other beliefs and construals of Jesus?[25] After all, travel and communication were well developed in the Roman world:

> people traveled on business as merchants, traders, and bankers, on pilgrimage to religious festivals, in search of health and healing at the healing shrines and spas, to consult the oracles which flourished in this period, to attend the pan-Hellenic games and the various lesser versions of these all over the empire, as soldiers in the legions, as government personnel of many kids, and even on vacation and as sightseers. . . . It was certainly not only the wealthy who traveled. Quite ordinary people traveled to healing shrines, religious festivals, and games. Slaves and servants frequently accompanied their masters on journeys. . . . Travel was usually by foot and so was cheap. Therefore people quite typical of the members of the early Christian churches regularly traveled. Those who did not, if they lived in the cities, would constantly be meeting people passing through or arriving from elsewhere. . . . So the context in which the early Christian movement developed was not conducive to parochialism; quite the opposite.[26]

The various circles of the early Christian movement made particularly impressive efforts to "network" with one another (whether for sharing faith and encouragement, appeals for help, criticism and debate, or denunciation) through letter writing, visits of leaders/representatives, and probably a lot of contacts

25. Similar objections have been raised by others, e.g., Hultgren, *Normative Christianity,* 38; Marinus de Jonge, *Christology in Context: The Earliest Christian Response to Jesus* (Philadelphia: Westminster, 1988), 83-84; G. N. Stanton, "On the Christology of Q," in *Christ and Spirit in the New Testament,* ed. S. S. Smalley and B. Lindars (Cambridge: Cambridge University Press, 1973), 27-42, esp. 42.

26. Bauckham, "For Whom," 32. See also Lionel Casson, *Travel in the Ancient World* (London: Allen and Unwin, 1974).

made in the course of other activities such as Christian merchants conducting their business.[27] So, under what specific circumstances would those who framed Q not have been exposed to the beliefs of other followers of Jesus, the sorts of beliefs whose putative absence in Q is supposedly so crucial? Those who composed Q were obviously not dwelling in isolated mountain redoubts in Syria.

Let me make the point clearly. It can be claimed that particular Christians did not know particular *texts*. Perhaps, e.g., Ignatius of Antioch did not know the Gospel of Mark or John. But the sort of view that I am questioning involves claiming that a "Q people" successfully remained ignorant and/or uninterested in key *ideas* and *beliefs* that we know were circulating widely, acquaintance with which did not require access to particular writings. I am not mounting here a counterargument from silence. I simply contend that there are very good reasons for demanding that those who portray Q people as unaware of certain "salvific construals" of Jesus provide plausible explanations of *how* this is likely, in light of what else we know about early Christian groups, their beliefs, and the communication and travel of their first-century setting.

Even if, following Kloppenborg's preferences, we locate Q people in Galilee, and we take the initially intended readership of Q as "persons living at or near a subsistence level," this still places them in a region with close and established social and trading contacts in that district of Roman Judea. They would also have had contacts with centers elsewhere, such as Jerusalem, which in turn were conduits of information from still wider circles of Christians.[28]

27. Bauckham, "For Whom," 33-38; Abraham Malherbe, *Social Aspects of Early Christianity* (Baton Rouge: Louisiana State University Press, 1977), 62-70; Harry Y. Gamble, *Books and Readers in the Early Church: A History of Early Christian Texts* (New Haven: Yale University Press, 1995), 82-143; Michael B. Thompson, "The Holy Internet: Communication between Churches in the First Christian Generation," in *The Gospels for All Christians*, 49-70; Eldon Jay Epp, "New Testament Papyrus Manuscripts and Letter Carrying in Greco-Roman Times," in *The Future of Early Christianity: Essays in Honor of Helmut Koester*, ed. Birger A. Pearson (Minneapolis: Fortress, 1991), 35-56. John Barclay, *Jews in the Mediterranean Diaspora: From Alexander to Trajan (323 BCE–117 CE)* (Edinburgh: T. & T. Clark, 1996), 418-24, discusses Jewish travel. The "networking" ethos of early Christian circles is reflected in the adaptation of the letter form as a literary vehicle for extended teaching (e.g., Romans and Hebrews among New Testament examples), and for delivery of apocalyptic material (esp. Revelation). The popularity of pseudepigraphical letters (e.g., James, 1 Peter, 2 Peter) further testifies to the strongly communicative nature of early Christianity (i.e., pseudepigraphical letters presuppose the popularity of letters as a well-known means of communication among early Christians).

28. See James F. Strange, "First-Century Galilee from Archaeology and from the Texts," in SBLSP 33, ed. E. H. Lovering, Jr. (Atlanta: Scholars, 1994), 81-90, esp. 81-85 for revisions of earlier notions of Galilee as an isolated area in the light of recent archaeological work. Jonathan L. Reed's more extensive discussion is along similar lines: *Archaeology and the Galilean Jesus: A Reexamination of the Evidence* (Harrisburg, Pa.: Trinity Press International, 2000).

Moreover, Kloppenborg shows that Q appears to have been composed by people with some level of scribal training (though the sayings they incorporated into the collection may have been transmitted previously by less learned people and in oral mode).[29] Those with scribal training, even if only village scribes, obviously had some level of readiness to communicate, exchanging information and acquiring news from others. Also, as seems now increasingly agreed upon, Q was likely composed in Greek (not Aramaic, as is often assumed in earlier scholarship), which means that it stemmed from people with some interest in using the lingua franca of the first-century Roman world as the medium in which to disseminate this collection of Jesus' sayings. This suggests a document composed by people with a horizon wide enough to exchange religious ideas with other followers of Jesus, and with a readiness to do so.

In fact, the most cogent suggestion for a likely provenance of Q may be the "Hellenists," Jewish Christians whose primary language was Greek.[30] According to Acts, the Hellenists emerged in the Jerusalem church in the very earliest years of the young religious movement. They would have had rather good access, thus, to those with firsthand knowledge of Jesus' sayings. The thematic similarities between Q and the speech attributed to Stephen in Acts are certainly interesting, especially the "Deuteronomistic" tradition of the suffering prophets (7:51-53), which also has a significant place in Q. It is also plausible that Greek-speaking diaspora Jews were entirely capable of preparing the sort of Greek text that scholars increasingly recognize Q to have been. Their diaspora background would certainly have given them a broad horizon, and an appreciation of the importance of an arranged edition of teachings of Jesus in support of Christian proclamation. Perhaps Q was initially prepared to serve the proclamation of the gospel in the Jewish diaspora, but then quickly acquired a still wider circulation among Christian circles of various types. In any case, the likely language and literary character of Q reflect a concern to speak to a wide readership; and it does not seem to come from a sectarian circle.

Kloppenborg recognizes the need to account historically for the contents of Q. He grants that Q's "silence" about the redemptive significance of Jesus' crucifixion cannot credibly have resulted from its composers "consciously re-

---

29. Kloppenborg, *Excavating Q*, 200-201. He also notes, however: "There is not much evidence in Q to sustain the supposition that the Q people were primarily peasants (i.e., agriculturalists)" (208). Kirk (*Composition*, 399) judges those responsible for Q to be of a somewhat higher level than the village scribes proposed by Kloppenborg.

30. This suggestion was sketched by R. A. Piper, *Wisdom in the Q-Tradition: The Aphoristic Teaching of Jesus*, SNTSMS 61 (Cambridge: Cambridge University Press, 1989), 184-92. See also Martin Hengel, *Studies in Early Christology* (Edinburgh: T. & T. Clark, 1995), 76.

jecting [salvific] construals of Jesus' death."[31] Though he does not mention it, a factor supporting this judgment is the absence in Q of any polemic against any other Christian group or kind of Christian faith. This is unlike the Gospel of Thomas, for example, which clearly shows that its framers knew and rejected other versions of Christian teaching.[32] So, Kloppenborg opines, "the only plausible solution" for why we have no passion narrative and other redemptive interpretations of Jesus' death is that "Q simply does not know them." But he apparently recognizes that it is also not credible to imagine these Q people as somehow remaining ignorant, while all about them interpretations of Jesus' death as redemptive, and belief in Jesus' resurrection as well, were circulating among followers of Jesus.[33] So he proposes that "Q appears to represent an early treatment of Jesus' death," earlier than the passion-narrative traditions reflected in Mark and "perhaps at least as early as Paul's view of Jesus' death."

It should be clear, however, that this proposal is hardly more credible than the other options that he rightly rejects. The basic problems here are an inadequate regard for chronology and other relevant data, and insufficient attention to the difficulties entailed in his and other proposals of a supposedly distinctive Q people whose christological traditions are only those found in Q.[34] We do not have to wait till the years "after Paul" to find references to Jesus' resurrection "common in Christian thinking."[35]

To repeat an earlier emphasis: the interpretations of Jesus' death attested

31. In this paragraph I interact with, and cite several phrases from, Kloppenborg, Excavating Q, 374.

32. See John W. Marshall, "The Gospel of Thomas and the Cynic Jesus," in Whose Historical Jesus? ed. William E. Arnal and Michel Desjardins (Waterloo, Ontario: Wilfrid Laurier University Press, 1997), 37-60.

33. By "all about them" I mean a variety of places such as Antioch, Damascus, Jerusalem, and others. Once again, the consistent evidence from Paul (e.g., 1 Cor. 15:1-7; Gal. 2:1-10) is that the christological beliefs of Jerusalem are basically those that he preaches.

34. Jacobson states that those who composed Q must have been "a relatively isolated community" (italics his), "not a community which corresponds very well with any group that we know of in early Christianity." Given the rapid developments in early Christian beliefs, however, he notes that "it is hard to imagine a community remaining for so long immune to these developments unless it was both early and isolated." But, as with other such proposals, he attempts no explanation of how such isolation was achieved. He accounts for Q being known to the authors of Matthew and Luke by proposing that they both "may have been in the area of Antioch and thus not far distant from the Q group." But was this distance traversable in only one direction, or was it equally possible for Q people to receive influences as well as provide them? See Jacobson, 260.

35. And what does "after Paul" mean specifically? After his conversion, his Gentile mission, his influence came to be felt, or his death? The vagueness of the claim does not assist us in testing it.

in Paul's letters, by all accounts, derive from his "predecessors," including Judean circles such as the Jerusalem church. Moreover, as also previously noted, Paul's acquaintance with Jewish Christian beliefs began in the very first few years (ca. 30-35 C.E.). The only meaningful period of Christian development "before" Paul is at most the very first few months or perhaps years.[36] But Paul's introduction to Jewish Christian beliefs must even be dated prior to his conversion, for his opposition could have been directed only against a prior Jewish Christian phenomenon.

Furthermore, Paul claims that the traditions such as he repeats in 1 Corinthians 15:3-7 represent not only his own prior missionary message but also the proclamation of Judean leaders (15:11). Scholars may dispute the validity of Paul's claim, of course. But we must also note that those to whom he attributed these traditions (e.g., Peter/Cephas and James) were still very much active and able to speak for themselves. He was not at as much liberty to make specious attributions and claims about the origins of Christian traditions as we modern scholars!

To his credit, Kloppenborg rejects the idea that Q comes from circles that somehow sustained an isolation from christological developments over any significant period. But that leaves precious little time for Q people to have been ignorant of the christological traditions that Paul took up at his conversion and then passed on to his own converts. It is certainly reasonable to ask whether there were Christian circles for which Jesus' resurrection, for example, was not part of their beliefs, but it goes against all indications to treat belief in Jesus' resurrection as becoming common among Christian circles only "after Paul." It is certainly interesting that in Q Jesus' vindication is not explicitly represented as his resurrection, but it seems to me dubious to assert that this indicates some supposedly primitive stage of Christian belief that had not yet adopted resurrection imagery.

There is another problem in the sort of proposal that Kloppenborg makes. Depending on when Q was initially composed (whether a Q¹ or essentially the whole document, so far as we can reconstruct it), likely sometime from the 30s to the 60s, it must have been transmitted thereafter for a time ranging from a few years to a few decades, being copied by hand and subject to alteration with every copy. Precisely if Q is taken as a reliable mirror of the be-

36. Neither in Kloppenborg's studies nor in the publications of others who make similar claims about Q can I find any extended treatment of these chronological issues or such evidence as the traditions in Paul's letters that appear to come from his predecessors and he claims were widely shared. For example, I can find only two passing references to 1 Cor. 15:1-11 in *Excavating Q*, neither addressing the force of the passage for critical reconstruction of earliest Christian beliefs.

liefs of those who composed it, then the later we posit its composition, the more difficult to explain the "silence" about christological beliefs that were common currency in Christian circles from a very early point onward. Kloppenborg's resort to positing a very early date for Q ("the only plausible solution") is his effort to respond to this difficulty. Presumably he means his Q¹, for he proposes the 50s or early 60s for his Q² redaction, and a date just after 70 for the "final form" of Q.[37]

But on the same assumption that Q functioned as a mirror of the beliefs of those who used the document, the earlier we posit its composition, the more difficult it is to explain how and why it *remained* free of these beliefs as it circulated and was copied. This difficulty is even greater if with Kloppenborg we posit a redaction history in which Q was readily expanded with further sayings material and religious ideas. If, for example, as he claims, in this revision process an apocalyptic theme and a clearer emphasis on Jesus' significance were added, why were "salvific construals" of Jesus' death not included as well? If the form(s) of Q used by Matthew and Luke sometime after 70 still did not include a passion narrative, passion predictions, and references to Jesus' resurrection, and yet, by then, Q had been circulating among Christians who had such traditions and beliefs, this question becomes especially forceful.

I am not claiming some "retrospective harmony."[38] I simply observe that the evidence indicates that early Christian groups were able to accommodate a variety in christological emphases and rhetorical genres in their repertoire of beliefs, teachings, and proclamations. My point is not that there are no observable differences in beliefs and emphases in the extant evidence of early Christianity. Instead, I want to emphasize precisely that early Christian groups were evidently able to generate and accommodate varieties of beliefs and themes, and that our ability to see distinctions does not amount to sufficient proof that they correspond to different groups or different "stages" of early Christianity.

Perhaps part of the solution to these problems lies in questioning the as-

---

37. *Excavating Q,* 87. I say "presumably" because Kloppenborg does not specify a possible dating of Q¹. Cf., e.g., Tuckett, *Q,* 101, who doubts Kloppenborg's theory of several redactions, and places a single-stage composition of Q sometime from 40 to 70.

38. "Retrospective harmony" is Kloppenborg's accusation in a note to me on an earlier draft of the preceding paragraph. In turn, I suggest that he and a regrettable number of other scholars work with two simplistic alternatives: either a "diversity" which must correspond to socially differentiated groups of Christians or a refusal to recognize the evident diversity of beliefs and emphases in New Testament texts. This is simply a false dilemma. Individual Christian groups, even individual Christians, then and subsequently, were quite able to generate and accommodate various diversities of beliefs.

sumption that Q reflects fully the christological traditions and beliefs of those who composed the collection of Jesus' sayings. To his credit, Kloppenborg states, "Q does not offer a complete catalogue of the Q group's beliefs."[39] Moreover, he explicitly agrees with Marinus de Jonge's point that those among whom Q circulated almost certainly knew traditions and beliefs about Jesus in addition to those reflected in Q.[40] Yet, curiously, he repeatedly states that Q's alleged "silence" as to beliefs about Jesus' redemptive death and his resurrection is the crucial indication of a group of Jesus' followers at a point in their development when such beliefs could not yet have been held among them.[41]

It is difficult for me to avoid seeing this as a contradiction. I propose that it would be more reasonable to approach the question of what Q tells us about early Christianity without the prior assumption that its contents and "silence" must map the extent of the beliefs (and concerns) of the people who composed it. I propose that, in fact, we have good reasons for thinking otherwise.[42]

An Inductive Approach

Let us attempt an inductive approach to understanding the contents and probable functions of Q. The place to begin is where there is the greatest comparative scholarly agreement. All who entertain the hypothesis of Q grant that it was used independently by the authors of Matthew and Luke as a Greek text. It is also widely assumed that, between them, these authors probably preserved all or nearly all of Q.[43]

It follows that, for both authors to have chosen to incorporate Q so fully, Q must have circulated among various Christian circles, for years or even a few decades, and was readily available. Also, Q must have been sufficiently well regarded (or represented traditions that were sufficiently well regarded) in various circles that both authors independently judged it appropriate and rhetorically useful to make a rather full appropriation of Q in their narrative portraits of Jesus. As Gerald Downing has argued, in the first-century Mediterranean world, in order to hope for success, authors were likely to produce texts that intended readers would see as congenial with ideas and traditions with which

39. Kloppenborg, *Excavating Q,* 371; also 176.
40. Kloppenborg, *Excavating Q,* 374-75, citing de Jonge, 83-84.
41. Kloppenborg, *Excavating Q,* e.g., 374-79.
42. To be fair, it is probably Kloppenborg's readiness to accommodate valid points from other perspectives that helps account for the complexity, and what appear to be contradictions, in his discussion at some points. A more simplistic thinker would not have such problems!
43. See, e.g., Tuckett, *Q,* 92-96; Kloppenborg, *Excavating Q,* 91-101.

they were already acquainted.[44] This suggests that the sayings traditions from Q that were apparently so richly employed in Matthew and Luke represented the sorts of traditions that were likely generally known and appreciated already among the intended readers.

This wide distribution and appreciation of Q are consistent with it having been composed in Greek, the principal transethnic language of the time. That is, it fits the actual reception history of Q better to suppose that it may have been prepared from the first for a wide readership, and may not (ever?) have been a document produced for one particular type or circle of the early Christian movement. Instead, those who composed Q may well have had rather more "catholic" intentions and outlook, for this certainly accords with what became of the document.[45]

If, however, Q originated as the expression of a distinctive kind of early Christianity, as the *Community Rule,* the *Damascus Document,* and the *Pesharim* (commentaries) represent a distinctive Jewish group of the Roman era, it is obvious that, unlike these Qumran texts, Q rather quickly obtained a much wider usage and a much richer reception history.[46] The independent choices by the Evangelists "Matthew" and "Luke" to incorporate Q so fully into their narrative Gospels surely suggest that Q was known at least by the intended readerships for whom these two authors wrote. Thereafter, as a result of the obviously wide reception of the Gospels of Matthew and Luke, Q has been bequeathed to all subsequent Christianity. Of course, scholars are free to speculate about the original function(s) of Q. But I contend that we must have good reasons to posit a function and provenance of Q very much different from what is suggested by the apparently wide circulation and usage of Q that is logically entailed by the hypothesis of the Synoptic sayings source.[47]

I contend further that the contents of Q align it with the beliefs, themes, and interests reflected in other Christian texts of the first century. Certainly there are noteworthy things about Q. It is basically a sayings collection, a genre for which we have no other first-century example in the extant Christian texts. That observation is not intended to work against the plausibility of Q, but in-

---

44. F. Gerald Downing, "Word-Processing in the Ancient World: The Social Production and Performance of Q," *JSNT* 64 (1996): 29-48.

45. Bauckham, "For Whom," 42-43, notes evidence that by the late first century, in at least some Christian circles, there were people with particular responsibility to send out copies of writings to other churches (citing *Herm. Vis.* 2.4.3).

46. For introductions to the Qumran texts, see, e.g., Geza Vermes, *The Complete Dead Sea Scrolls in English* (London: Penguin Books, 1997).

47. Allison (*Jesus Tradition in Q,* 44-45) makes a similar point. Bauckham, "For Whom," 9-48, contends that the canonical Gospels were originally intended for wide circulation as well.

stead to highlight its potential significance. Moreover, the previously noted characteristics of Q are frequently invoked in current discussion: no narrative account of Jesus' crucifixion, no direct predictions of his death, no explicit treatment of his death as an atonement or redemptive event, and no direct reference to his resurrection. In Q Jesus' death is linked with the tradition of the rejection of the biblical prophets, and with the opposition to be suffered by his followers. In the one Q passage where Kloppenborg finds a direct reference to Jesus' vindication (Q/Luke 13:35), he sees "a death-assumption-judgment scenario, not the death-resurrection pattern that was to become common."[48] So, is there a distinctive early Christian group for whom the genre, contents, and emphases of Q indicate who they were and what they did, or did not, believe and practice? To deal with this question requires me to make two main points.

Is Q Peculiar?

The first point is that Q is not nearly as peculiar as some scholars make it.[49] By "peculiar" I mean so different that its contents show a far greater degree of distinctiveness in first-century Christianity than is otherwise indicated by the New Testament writings. I trust that some illustrations will suffice to make my point. For example, Q shows a regard for Jesus' sayings as authoritative for believers, but this is, of course, hardly an indication of some particular kind of Christianity. Paul, too, cites sayings of Jesus as authoritative teaching for his churches (e.g., 1 Cor. 7:10-11; 9:14); he even indicates when he has no suitable command of Jesus and has to offer his own opinion instead (7:25). We must presume, therefore, that Paul either had learned a body of Jesus' sayings or, quite possibly, even had a written collection himself. David Dungan concluded that Paul and his readers probably knew a much larger body of Jesus' sayings than those explicitly cited in Paul's letters.[50] Dale Allison has recently discussed indications that Paul had "possible or probable contact" with sayings of Jesus that are also attested in Q.[51] Moreover, the wholesale incorporation of Q into Matthew and

---

48. Kloppenborg, *Excavating Q,* 378-79.

49. Kloppenborg grants (*Excavating Q,* 363) that "Q exhibits greater commonalities with other 'theologies' of the early Jesus movement than detractors sometime suppose." Yet this statement appears in a chapter titled "Making Difference," in which his main point seems to be that a proper appreciation of Q requires a view of early Christianity involving a much greater diversity than would otherwise be known (e.g., 408).

50. David Dungan, *The Sayings of Jesus in the Churches of Paul* (Philadelphia: Fortress, 1971), esp. 146-50.

51. Allison, *Jesus Tradition in Q,* 54-60. See also Allison, "The Pauline Epistles and the

Luke confirms a wide interest in and appreciation of the kind of material that Q contained, and this likely well before, and prompting, the inclusion of Q into these two Gospels. This all works against the notion that Q represents some kind of distinctive circle(s) of followers of Jesus with little in common with other circles.

It might be objected, however, that this misses the issue. Those who strongly assert that Q represents a distinctive kind of Christian belief will perhaps grant that Jesus' sayings were revered and used in various Christian circles. But they insist that Q is distinctive because the other circles (such as Pauline churches) "did not take Jesus' words as foundational for a theological schema."[52] But the objection actually *presupposes* precisely what needs to be *demonstrated*: that in Q we have a "theological schema" formed solely on the basis of Jesus' sayings. What we do have in Q is a particular kind of first-century Christian *text*. Whether, however, Q represents and requires a *distinctive* "theological schema" depends on whether this kind of text and christological expression is to some degree *incompatible* and *incommensurate* with the christological expressions and Jesus traditions attested in other first-century Christian texts. That has not been shown.

It is also dubious to make strong contrasts between the "death-resurrection" christological schema reflected, e.g., in Paul and the canonical Gospels and the "death-ascent/assumption-future judgment" pattern reflected in Q. In fact, several christological schemas are reflected in various New Testament writings, and they all seem to have emerged and circulated alongside one another in Christian circles. I cite some Pauline texts that are commonly thought to appropriate traditional christological formulations.

In 1 Thessalonians 1:9-10 Paul points to Jesus' future salvific appearance from heaven, the realm to which Jesus ascended by God raising him from the dead. Jesus' death is obviously presumed in this formulation, but no salvific significance is explicitly attributed to it here. So the explicit schema is one of resurrection-assumption-return.

In what is thought to be another Pauline appropriation of another traditional formulation, Romans 1:3-4, we have a birth-resurrection schema: descended from David, declared/appointed the Son of God by resurrection. His death is again implicit, but there is no explicit significance attributed to it, though we know Paul could emphasize the salvific importance of Jesus' cruci-

---

Synoptic Gospels: The Pattern of the Parallels," *NTS* 28 (1982): 1-32; Michael Thompson, *Clothed with Christ: The Example and Teaching of Jesus in Romans 12:1–15:13*, JSNTSup 59 (Sheffield: JSOT Press, 1991).

52. I cite phrasing from Kloppenborg's criticisms of an earlier draft of these pages.

fixion when he wanted to. Jesus' future return is not mentioned here either, although we presume that it figured prominently in the beliefs of those from whom this formulation stems, just as it did for Paul. In other passages the death-resurrection schema for which Paul is so famous is certainly found, for example, in Romans 4:24-25 and 1 Corinthians 15:3-7, and in both passages the redemptive significance of these events is explicitly stated.

However, in perhaps the most frequently studied christological passage in Paul's letters, Philippians 2:6-11, we have what might be described as a "humiliation-obedience-exaltation-acclamation" schema. Jesus' crucifixion is explicitly mentioned as the extremity of his obedience, but no salvific significance is cited. It is striking that there is also no reference to Jesus' resurrection here, yet Paul clearly did not find the passage deficient for shaping the attitudes of the Philippian believers. In other references in the same epistle, however, Paul uses a death-resurrection schema (3:10-11) and a resurrection-assumption-return schema (3:20-21).

I could multiply further examples of the variety of christological expressions found in New Testament writings. The lengthy christological exposition in the Epistle to the Hebrews is dominated throughout by a (redemptive) death-assumption/exaltation emphasis, with only a passing reference to Jesus' future return (9:28); the author refers to Jesus' resurrection only in the sonorous, liturgical-sounding doxology in 13:20-21. Obviously this writer believed in Jesus' resurrection and future return, but for the purposes of this exposition concentrates almost entirely on Jesus' redemptive death and heavenly status (in this case, as high priest in the heavenly sanctuary). The main point here is that the death-ascension schema of Q is neither incompatible with the other christological schemas nor unique to Q.

Q is also not unique either in focusing on Jesus' death as exemplary for disciples or in collectively associating the sufferings of followers with Jesus' sufferings. Kloppenborg contrasts Q with Mark on these matters, but this seems to me misjudged. As is well known, for example, Mark 8:34-38 parallels very closely the thrust of Q 14:26-27 and 12:8-9, which shows that the theme of Jesus' fate as the criterion of discipleship was by no means exclusive to Q. Furthermore, although Mark 10:45 and 14:22-24 obviously present a redemptive view of Jesus' death, in fact the dominant christological emphasis in Mark makes Jesus the perfect model for disciples to follow.[53] That is, in Mark Jesus is not only the

---

53. L. W. Hurtado, "Following Jesus in the Gospel of Mark — and Beyond," in *Patterns of Discipleship in the New Testament*, ed. Richard N. Longenecker (Grand Rapids: Eerdmans, 1996), 9-29. The Markan collective emphasis is even reflected in Mark's greater use of plural verbs to refer to movements of Jesus and his disciples, as shown many years ago by C. H. Turner, "Marcan Usage: Notes, Critical and Exegetical, on the Second Gospel," *JTS* 26 (1925): 225-31.

basis of redemption but also, and much more emphatically, the pattern of discipleship. As Philip Davis has proposed, the author's concern to make this story of Jesus instructive for discipleship even accounts for the shape and extent of the Markan "story" of Jesus — baptism, mission, opposition, death, and divine vindication — which is the narrative "shape" of the life of discipleship for the first readers.[54]

Though Paul attributes unique redemptive significance to Jesus' death, he also links the sufferings of Jesus and those endured by Christians as a result of their faith. I take Paul as the author of Colossians, who refers to sufferings experienced while conducting his Gentile mission as "completing what is lacking in Christ's afflictions for the sake of his body, that is, the church" (1:24). In another vivid reference in Galatians 6:17, Paul describes himself carrying "the marks of Jesus [*ta stigmata tou Iēsou*] branded on my body," probably referring to the scars he received from sufferings endured in his ministry.[55] A similar notion is reflected in 2 Corinthians 4:7-12, where he refers to his mission sufferings as "always carrying in the body the death of Jesus, so that the life of Jesus may also be made visible in our bodies" (v. 10).

Remember too that Paul likens the opposition endured by Gentile believers in Thessalonica to the sufferings experienced by Judean Christians, and also links the opposition meted out in Judea with Jewish rejection of "both the Lord Jesus and the prophets" (1 Thess. 2:14-16). This is the "Deuteronomistic" theme identified also in Q, where opposition to Jesus and his disciples is likened to the opposition experienced by the biblical prophets (e.g., Q 6:22-23; 11:49-51; 13:34-35). This is also the basic thrust of the speech of Stephen in Acts 7:1-53 (esp. vv. 51-53). Indeed, Mark, too, is acquainted with this theme in the parable of 12:1-12, which plays a crucial role in the Markan account of Jesus' final days in Jerusalem.[56]

True, this Deuteronomistic theme has more prominence in Q than in these other writings, and thus Q perhaps shows that the theme played more of a

---

54. Philip Davis, "Christology, Discipleship, and Self-Understanding in the Gospel of Mark," in *Self-Definition and Self-Discovery in Early Christianity: A Study in Shifting Horizons, Essays in Appreciation of Ben F. Meyer from His Former Students*, ed. D. J. Hawkin and Tom Robinson, Studies in Bible and Early Christianity 26 (Lewiston, N.Y.: Edwin Mellen Press, 1990), 101-19, esp. 109.

55. So, e.g., H. D. Betz, *Galatians*, Hermeneia (Philadelphia: Fortress, 1979), 324-25. Paul gives a well-known list of his apostolic sufferings in 2 Cor. 11:23-29, which includes, e.g., floggings and a stoning.

56. Kloppenborg notes references to the Deuteronomistic motif in 1 Thess. 2:14-16 and Mark 12:1-12 (*Excavating Q*, 82-84, 210), but he does not consider adequately their relevance for his emphasis on the distinctive nature of Q.

role in early Christian proclamation than might otherwise be thought. But, although Q confirms the range in the repertoire of first-century christological expression, its Deuteronomistic emphasis has clear connections in other New Testament texts.

In short, every major christological motif or theme in Q (emphasis on Jesus' teachings, a death-assumption/exaltation scheme, his death linked with sufferings of his followers and the rejection of the prophets) is found in other New Testament writings also. The picture, thus, is one of considerable overlap in christological themes between those behind Q and other Christian circles. Perhaps this is why the really crucial argument used by proponents of a distinctive "Q people" is not what is in Q, but what is not in Q. The repeatedly invoked claim is that the lack of certain material — predictions of Jesus' death, a passion narrative, redemptive construal of Jesus' death, and explicit references to his resurrection — must mean that those who composed Q either had no knowledge of such things or no concern with them. I have indicated that the rich variety of christological expressions, formulas, and schemas attested in early Christian groups makes it dubious to demand that a text such as Q be categorized by some christological checklist. Reference to Jesus' death as redemptive, for example, was hardly a shibboleth in early Christian circles. So why should we treat it that way in modern historical study of ancient Christian texts? In the next section I indicate further why I do not regard the argument from Q's "silence" persuasive.

The Argument from Silence

In attempting historical work, it is almost impossible to avoid considering arguments from silence. In most historical subjects, especially those from the distant past, we scarcely ever have all the evidence to hand that we would like or need. We have to make do with what survives, and attempt to make the most reasonable use of it. Historical work often involves comparing inferences from the fragments of some past person, event, or period to determine the most likely inference. Readers will remember, for example, that I drew attention to the lack of indication in Paul's letters that the christological beliefs and devotional practices characteristic in his churches were a matter of controversy with Christians from other venues, especially Judean circles. But an argument from silence is only as strong as the alleged "silence" can be shown to be conspicuous and difficult to account for except on the explanation one offers. That is, we have to show (as in the famous Sherlock Holmes story) that a dog that should have barked did not. If a cat does not bark, that is nothing remarkable.

So, are the things absent from Q to be taken as indicative of the limits of beliefs of its redactors, as is repeatedly claimed by those who propose that Q represents a distinctive kind of early circle of Christians? I contend that this particular argument from silence is not very strong.[57] Let us begin by considering the undisputed absence of a narrative of Jesus' crucifixion. Q 14:27 shows, rather unsurprisingly, that those who composed Q knew that Jesus had been crucified. More notably, the demand that disciples bear their own crosses and thereby "come after me" can only mean that readers, too, are expected to know some report of Jesus' crucifixion, although the event is not related in Q itself. That is, Q presumes here acquaintance with tradition about Jesus beyond what it relates. This unrelated tradition is, however, obviously quite crucial in Q, for Jesus' crucifixion is made the criterion of discipleship in 14:27.[58] This immediately shows that Q was not intended to communicate all the Jesus tradition known and meaningful for redactors and readers.[59] For example, Q also presumes accounts of Jesus' healing and exorcistic activities beyond what the one miracles story and the one exorcism in Q recount.[60] Q 7:31-35 also presumes knowledge of traditions about Jesus' associations with sinners. The thrice-repeated challenge of the devil ("if you are the Son of God") in Q 4:1-12 seems to presume acquaintance with this claim (or perhaps with a story of Jesus' baptism where God acclaims Jesus as his Son). We should thus be cautious about using the putative limits of the text of Q to determine what was or was not known by and meaningful for those among whom Q was composed.[61]

57. See a somewhat similar discussion by Allison, *Jesus Tradition in Q*, 43-46.

58. There is a version of this saying in *Gospel of Thomas* (saying 55), with a variant form also in saying 101. But in *Thomas* bearing one's cross looks like a metaphor for having to live in the world, whereas Q (14:26; cf. 17:33) and Mark (8:34) call for preparedness for real martyrdom patterned after Jesus' execution. See, e.g., Kloppenborg, *The Formation of Q*, 230-31; Richard Valantasis, *The Gospel of Thomas* (London: Routledge, 1997), 132-33, 181-82.

59. A similar point is made by Marco Frenschkowski, "Welche biographischen Kenntnisse von Jesus setzt die Logienquelle voraus? Beobachtungen zur Gattung von Q im Kontext antiker Spruchsammlungen," in *From Quest to Q, Festschrift James M. Robinson*, ed. Jon Ma. Asgeirsson, Kristin De Troyer, and Marvin W. Meyer (Leuven: Peeters, 2000), 3-42.

60. The only healing story (Q 7:1-10) concerns the centurion's slave in Capernaum. The only exorcism is Q 11:14, which introduces the controversy story about whether Jesus is in league with Beelzebub or is the agent of God. Yet the agreement of Matthew and Luke that the delegation from John the Baptist was prompted by reports of Jesus' miracles indicates that this detail is likely from Q. Jesus' response (Q 7:22) certainly alludes to a wider range of miracles than Q recounts, as does the saying in Q 10:13 about miracles done in Chorazin and Bethsaida.

61. On the one hand, Kloppenborg himself states as much (e.g., *Excavating Q*, 176, 371). Yet elsewhere in the book he repeatedly insists that the contours (and silence) of Q indicate rather directly the shape of the beliefs of those who composed it (and their ignorance of or lack of interest in other beliefs and schemas).

The redactors of Q chose to provide an organized collection of Jesus' teachings, not a narrative of his ministry (though I contend that a narrative outlook or scheme is presupposed in Q). Accordingly, there is no narrative of his execution, no "passion account." This is definitely interesting for historical purposes, indicating that, for those acquainted with who Jesus was and what happened to him, a collection of his teachings was deemed appropriate and desirable, and that the "instructional genre" was one of the forms of early Christian literature.[62] We do not know if other collections circulated, but if there was one, it is more likely there were others. The collection we call Q, however, seems to have been particularly popular and successful, if we are correct in concluding that Matthew and Luke used basically this same sayings source. But by itself, the choice of the composer(s) of Q to prepare an organized sayings collection, and not to narrate Jesus' death, means little more than the obvious: as a sayings collection, Q has no extended narrative of *anything*, including Jesus' death. It was apparently the author of Mark who first combined a significant body of sayings tradition (including sayings clusters topically arranged, e.g., Mark 4:1-34) with a full-scale narrative of Jesus' ministry, although in Luke and Matthew this is done still more programmatically. Both Q and Mark are, thus, notable in the literary history of first-century Christianity, and those who composed these works had distinguishable intentions and emphases. But I see no reason for thinking that the authors of either work would have regarded the other as holding radically different christological views, so why should we?[63]

Given that the redactors of Q chose to provide an instructional text that presumes acquaintance with a story of Jesus' crucifixion (e.g., Q 14:27), it is not surprising that they did not provide explicit predictions of Jesus' death. Predictions of events make more literary sense in narratives that then show the fulfillment of the prediction. In Mark, for example, where three explicit predictions of Jesus' death feature prominently, they all appear in a repeated literary pattern of prediction, followed by misunderstanding by the disciples, followed then by Jesus correcting them and teaching on discipleship that links with his own fate. Moreover, the three predictions are all "plotted" in the chapters where Jesus and the disciples are "on the way" to Jerusalem, where the predictions will receive

---

62. It is also widely thought among scholars that there were written collections of Jesus' miracles, perhaps written collections of controversy stories, and also one or more written "passion" narratives, all of which may have been drawn upon by the author of Mark and the other Gospels. See, e.g., Koester, *Ancient Christian Gospels*, 286-89.

63. "Radically different" is my attempt to reflect the claims of some (e.g., Mack) that Q represents a form of the first-century "Jesus movement" that cannot have been connected with other known forms of first-century Christianity. Kloppenborg does not use the term and does not appear to go quite this far.

their grisly fulfillment.[64] As I have already noted, in the "implicit narrative" of Q, with Jesus pictured teaching his disciples during his Galilean ministry, 14:27 is in fact an indirect prediction of Jesus' fate. In Q, as in Mark, reference to Jesus' death indicates his heroic readiness to face his own fate, and so functions in connection with the call to follow him as a disciple (Q 14:26-27; 17:33).

As to Q's lack of explicit reference to Jesus' death as redemptive, I have already noted that this hardly makes Q unique, and that various interpretations of Jesus' death circulated and were employed for varying rhetorical and thematic purposes in Christian circles. In this instructional text intended primarily to call for obedience to Jesus, and aiming to "position" that obedience by its eschatological significance and outcome, the composer(s) chose to focus on Jesus' death as inspiring example. But this choice hardly indicates an ignorance of, or lack of interest in, other construals of Jesus' death.

In principle, we cannot be absolutely sure on the basis of Q alone whether its composer(s) knew various interpretations of Jesus' death and *for the purposes of this particular text* simply chose to treat it the way they did, or were ignorant of any other construal of Jesus' death. For reasons already given, the first option seems to me more likely. It is also theoretically possible that they consciously rejected salvific interpretations of Jesus' death. But were this the case, we would expect some indication of differences over the matter with other Christian circles.

Neither does Q have a narrative of Jesus' resurrection or explicit reference to Jesus' vindication by resurrection. Instead, in Q hostility against Jesus on earth is contrasted with the divine approval with which he came, and also with the divine validation he will be shown openly in his future return and which, implicitly, is already bestowed on him in heaven. Moreover, readers of Q are urged to involve themselves in continuing Jesus' message and ministry, in the expectation that they too will experience hostility and can expect divine vindication for their allegiance to Jesus (e.g., Q 12:8-10; 22:28, 30). But those who are hostile to Jesus and his followers now will regret it later (e.g., 6:46-49; 10:8-16; 13:28-30). In short, the focus in Q is on facing the costs of following Jesus, with confidence that those who do so will share the divine vindication given to him. It is very interesting that Jesus' vindication and theirs are not explicitly portrayed as a resurrection. However, I propose that it is quite likely that the expectation of resurrection is implicit in Q, which means that vindication by resurrection was not an unknown or unfavored category.

For example, in the exhortation in Q 12:4-12 not to fear those who can kill

---

64. Mark 8:31-38; 9:30-50; 10:32-45. These chapters make up the well-known central section of Mark (8:27–10:52), which is especially focused on discipleship. I discuss the Gospels further as literary expressions of devotion to Jesus in the following chapter.

but have no further power over Jesus' followers, it is rather obviously God who has power to cast folk into Gehenna (12:5), but who also will not forget those who fearlessly confess Jesus (12:6-12). The contrast with those who can kill makes it entirely likely that God's remembrance involves giving life back to those who have been slain. It is correct to observe that Q does not make explicit reference to resurrection as the specific mode by which Jesus has been vindicated, and does not emphasize that Jesus' followers can expect their own postmortem vindication in the form of a resurrection. But did the authors of Q not think at all about resurrection? Or did they simply wish to emphasize that God would provide eschatological and postmortem vindication, and were less concerned to state explicitly the mode by which he would do so? The answers to these questions are finally a matter of exegetical and historical judgment.[65] All things considered, I tend to think the latter much more likely.

If Q was composed sometime between 40 and 70, and circulated widely thereafter before being incorporated into Matthew and Luke, then by the latter events there were certainly lots of Christians who believed that Jesus had been resurrected and that they could hope for the same reward. It is thus difficult to imagine that Q's redactors were ignorant of these notions. If they *rejected* them in favor of some other view of the divine vindication of Jesus and his followers, it is strange that they did not indicate this (as is done in the *Gospel of Thomas*, e.g., 51). If Q was transmitted among Christian circles for whom resurrection was an important category, as seems to have been the case, and yet these circles added to Q no explicit references to resurrection, this suggests that they saw no reason for concern about Q on this point. That is, they too must have been comfortable with Q's construal of Jesus' vindication, and they likely presumed that it implicitly reflected belief that Jesus was raised from death and that they would be vindicated likewise.

In short, the absence of these christological themes (or at least the lack of explicit reference to them) in Q hardly seems to constitute adequate evidence of serious differences in belief and of a distinctive kind of early Christianity. There certainly were serious (i.e., conflictual) differences in first-century Christianity, as indicated in a number of New Testament texts (e.g., Gal. 2:4; Phil. 3:2; 1 John 2:18-25; Jude 4, 8-16; Rev. 2:2, 14-16, 20-23)! So I am not urging some notion of early Christianity as all "sweetness and light," and romantic harmony. The question before us is specifically what to make of Q. I contend that Q's alleged "silence" is not terribly conspicuous, and does not require the theory of a distinctive form of Christianity behind Q to explain it.

---

65. Again, I emphasize that it is a *historical* judgment, and that theological concerns should really not get in the way.

All things considered, Q seems to fit reasonably well within the rich diversity of early Christian beliefs and emphases, and overlaps considerably with some specific traditions attested elsewhere in the New Testament. This does not involve some model of a homogenized "mainstream" into which Q is to be fitted. Q, along with a number of other texts, suggests that first-century Christianity was comprised of various groups, with varying complexions of constituents and emphases. Furthermore, often (perhaps characteristically) within each group was a variety or repertoire of christological beliefs, emphases, and modes of expression. The particular repertoire may have varied somewhat from group to group, and within a given group likely varied across the decades of the first century too. Therefore, we should avoid simplistic notions that "diversity" in first-century Christianity necessarily means multiple groups of relatively monochrome character in beliefs, rhetoric, and the kinds of texts they produced. There were divisive differences. But, perhaps much more characteristically, there were various groups of varying polychrome character engaging in a lively interchange with one another.

Devotion to Jesus in Q

My differences with some scholars over what specifically to make of Q must not obscure my agreement that Q is a very important body of evidence about early devotion to Jesus. As stated already, I accept that Q is a reasonably well established hypothesis for helping to explain the relationships of the Synoptic Gospels, and that the scholarly effort to reconstruct the contents and literary shape of Q has been largely persuasive. Moreover, I agree that Q was probably composed in Greek, and that it was not an unorganized grab bag of Jesus tradition but had a literary design. Consequently, I consider it essential to take Q seriously in mapping the expressions of devotion to Jesus that emerged in the earliest decades of the Christian movement. In the final section of this chapter, therefore, I summarize the view of Jesus reflected in Q.[66]

---

66. Important studies focused on this topic include the following: G. N. Stanton, "On the Christology of Q"; Athanasius Polag, *Die Christologie der Logienquelle*, WMANT 45 (Neukirchen-Vluyn: Neukirchener Verlag, 1977); Polag, "The Theological Center of the Sayings Source," in *The Gospel and the Gospels*, ed. Peter Stuhlmacher (Grand Rapids: Eerdmans, 1991), 97-105; de Jonge, 71-90; Tuckett, *Q*, 209-82.

Centrality of Jesus

I must contend immediately that Q presents *a clear and sustained emphasis on the importance of Jesus*. I am unable, therefore, to consent to the notion that the focus in Q is not so much on Jesus, but more on the kingdom of God. To draw such a distinction misses an important point in Q, for Q emphasizes repeatedly that recognition of the significance of Jesus is the key condition for recognizing the eschatological presence of the kingdom of God now, and for the hope of future participation in it.[67] In other words, in Q the key claim is that in Jesus the kingdom of God came to decisive eschatological expression, and the key emphasis about the kingdom of God is that one receives and enters it only through recognizing Jesus as its decisive vehicle. The decision about *Jesus' validity* is the central question, for on it hangs the chance of one's participation in the kingdom of God.

The likely shape and contents of Q bear out this point. In Q the sole authoritative teacher is Jesus. Unlike, for example, the Mishnaic tractate *Pirke Aboth,* Q was not a collection of sayings of a line of respected sages/teachers. Furthermore, what Jesus proclaims and teaches is not an accumulated body of wisdom established over time and based on acute observations about everyday life, such as we have, for example, in the book of Proverbs. Q was a shaped literary expression devoted to Jesus, and expressive of his impact and continuing importance for those who composed it and fellow followers of Jesus for whom they composed it. At every point in Q, readers must decide whether to assent to what is said, and at every point, either explicitly or implicitly, that assent depends upon a judgment about Jesus.

A look at the framing portions of Q will demonstrate this. Q commences with the herald of Jesus' appearance (3:3, 7-9, 16-17), John the Baptist, summoning Israel to repentance, and announcing a "more powerful one" who comes after him with the momentous purpose of sorting out the "wheat" and the

---

67. Unfortunately, it is not easy to reconcile Kloppenborg's statements on this matter. On the one hand, he states that in Q 11:31-32, "at issue is not the recognition of the person of Jesus but rather grasping the significance of the time as the dawning of God's kingdom" (*Excavating Q,* 124), and in "The Theological 'Center' of Q" (388-95), he states, "The center of Q's theology is not Christology but the reign of God" (391). Though he sees his Q² redaction as introducing further christological statements, he refers to them as "embedded in a broader strategy of defending the ethos of the Q group and threatening those who are seen as opponents" (392). Yet he also grants that in Q, "Jesus is the exclusive conduit of the knowledge of God among humans (Q 10:21-22)," that "Jesus himself is represented as a necessary link in the communication of the ethos of the kingdom that is elaborated in 6:20b-45" (393), and that "Q leaves little doubt that the message of the kingdom, itself definitive, is connected to the person of Jesus" (396).

"chaff"; in Q this coming authoritative figure is clearly Jesus, as 7:19-23 makes plain. Q ends (22:28-30) with Jesus claiming that God has conferred on him a kingdom, and Jesus promises to those who have stood with him (which, obviously, readers are to see as inclusive of them) a royal reward and rich vindication for their service. At the beginning of Q Jesus is heralded, and at the end he stands vindicated and promising vindication for those who follow him. In between these key framing passages, the whole of Q makes Jesus central.

Q's Narrative World and Jesus

Though Q is to be seen as fitting into the broad "instructional genre" of the ancient world, a specific narrative "world" is presumed in Q, to which the text often makes allusion. Clearly the biblical (Old Testament) "story" in particular is presumed and invoked at numerous points.[68] We have references to Abel, Noah, Abraham, Lot, Isaac, Jacob, Jonah, Solomon, Zechariah, the prophets, and the twelve tribes of Israel.[69] There are citations of, and undeniable allusions to, biblical writings: e.g., Deuteronomy, Psalms, Exodus, Malachi, and Isaiah at the least.[70]

Moreover, there is an implicit narrative in Q itself, and it is wholly concerned with Jesus. Jesus is heralded by John, and an eschatological role is posited for him. Jesus then appears in the text, probably in a baptismal/acclamation scene, and then is tested/tempted by the devil to prove his validity. Then follows a body of material in which Jesus is further identified as the promised one (Q

---

68. See now Dale C. Allison, *The Intertextual Jesus: Scripture in Q* (Harrisburg, Pa.: Trinity Press International, 2000). On 182-84 he gives a handy table of biblical passages cited, quoted, or alluded to in Q, pointing to clear references to passages in Genesis, Exodus, Leviticus, Deuteronomy, 1-2 Kings, Isaiah, Jeremiah, Ezekiel, Jonah, Micah, Malachi, Psalms, Proverbs, Daniel, and 2 Chronicles. "Q's favorite manner of reference is to draw key words, phrases, themes, or images from well-known texts. Enough is borrowed so that the borrowing can be recognized: Q wants to be found out" (187). Note also the earlier list and discussion of biblical references in Q by Edward P. Meadors, "The Orthodoxy of the 'Q' Sayings of Jesus," *TB* 43 (1992): 233-57, esp. 249-55.

69. Noted by Kloppenborg, *Excavating Q,* 203 (Q references given there), who, however, puts this all down to his Q² redaction. But I do not find his proposal of discrete historical stages of the redaction of Q persuasive. In any case, as he grants, it is unlikely that this supposed redaction could have invoked, de novo and without introduction, the biblical "narrative world." Readers were clearly presumed to have an appreciative acquaintance with biblical stories and characters.

70. Deut. 8:3 (Q 4:4); 6:13 (Q 4:8); 6:16 (Q 4:12); Pss. 91:11-12 (Q 4:10-11); 6:9(8) (Q 13:27); 104:12/LXX 103:12 (Q 13:18-21); Mal. 3:1/Exod. 23:20 (Q 7:27); Isa. 35:5-6/26:19/29:18/61:1 (Q 7:22).

6:20-49; 7:1-10, 18-35), and exhibits his own mission of teaching and miracles. Afterward Jesus gives instructions to his followers for joining in his mission (e.g., 9:57-60; 10:2-16, 21-22). There follows material concerned with controversies and opposition to his and their efforts (e.g., 10:23-24; 11:2-13, 14-23, 24-26, 29-35, 39-52), and encouragement to be bold (e.g., 12:4-12) and to have faith in God's provision (e.g., 12:22-31). Then, after further material that includes warnings about rejecting him, including a clear reference to his own death (14:27), and encouragement to his followers about the future significance of their efforts, Q finishes up with a number of sayings pointing toward a future vindication/judgment (e.g., 17:20-24, 26-30, 34-35; 19:12-13, 15-26), and a dominical promise in 22:28-30 of an eschatological consummation of God's kingdom.

What we have, thus, is a text that presumes a narrative of Jesus that proceeds from an announcement of his appearance, through his introduction and activities, the formation of a following, opposition to him that includes his death by crucifixion, his postmortem vindication and continuing authority for the intended readers, and the promise of a future triumphant manifestation. I submit that those who composed Q fully expected readers to bring this "story," which we might term the "enabling narrative," to their reading of this text. That is, Q reflects an underlying "narrative substructure" concerned with Jesus as the special and authoritative figure presented as heralded, active, rejected, and vindicated.[71]

In numerous specific ways as well, Q presents Jesus as crucial. In 6:20-23, for example, those who see the kingdom of God (6:20) and are promised eschatological rewards (6:21, 23a), are those who suffer *"on account of the Son of Man"* (6:22), and *thereby* they can associate the hostility shown to them with that shown to the biblical prophets (6:23b). The famous statements in 6:46-49 demand that Jesus' followers genuinely reverence him as their master *(Kyrie)* by obeying what he commands, and then present readers with stark choices between establishing one's life on his teachings and failing to do so, with dramatically contrasting consequences (security or disaster) depending on one's choice. In 7:18-19, 22-28 the messengers from John the Baptist echo John's announcement about one who is to come after him (7:18-19) in their question to Jesus. Jesus' positive reply uses phrasing from Isaiah to present his miracles as eschatological blessings (Q 7:22), and the climactically placed beatitude in 7:23 makes one's judgment about Jesus the crucial issue.[72] In this context Jesus' vali-

---

71. I borrow the term "narrative substructure" from Richard B. Hays, *The Faith of Jesus Christ: An Investigation of the Narrative Substructure of Galatians 3:1–4:11*, SBLDS 56 (Chico, Calif.: Scholars, 1983), who showed that Paul's argument in Galatians presupposes and alludes to a narrative message about Jesus.

72. Jesus' reference to his miracles in Q 7:22 alludes to several passages in Isaiah (esp. 35:5-6; 26:19; 29:18; 61:1), which seems intended to make a broad claim that in him all these eschatolog-

dation of John (7:24-28) as the eschatological herald foretold in Scripture (7:27), confirms Jesus as the one whose way John was sent to prepare.[73] Thus, for all John's eschatological importance, Jesus is emphatically his superior in Q.[74] In 10:2-16 Jesus authorizes his disciples to announce the kingdom of God and directs how they are to do so, warning also that the response of people to their message will be decisive (esp. 10:12-15). The maxim in 10:16 indicates that his followers speak on Jesus' authority, and that Jesus in turn bears the most direct representative relationship to God. In 11:29-32 the son of man (Jesus) is explicitly the sign that must be recognized (11:30). Thus his ministry is the "something greater" *(pleion)* than the wisdom of Solomon and the proclamation of Jonah, and failure to respond properly will incur condemnation from those who did respond favorably to these biblical personages.[75]

Jesus the Polarizing Issue

Repeatedly Jesus is presented as the polarizing issue, and the decision about his validity is the key question upon which all else depends. In Q 11:14-23, for example, the only two options are either that Jesus is in league with Beelzebul or that his exorcisms signal the advent of the kingdom of God. The climactic statement (11:23) sharpens matters to a razor's edge, where there is no room given for neutrality: if you are not with Jesus, you are against him; to fail to "gather" with him is to oppose him (to "scatter").[76] As mentioned above, 6:20-23 portrays the

---

ical hopes are coming to fulfillment. In Isa. 35 and in the Qumran text (4Q521, the "Messianic Apocalypse"), the miracles are the works of God. In this light the explicit attribution of these works to Jesus in Q 7:21-23 portrays Jesus acting in a capacity associated with God. (I am grateful to Kloppenborg for reminding me of 4Q521, although he did not draw quite the same inference.)

73. Q/Luke 7:27 seems to be a verbal adaptation of Mal. 3:1 influenced by Exod. 23:20.

74. In Q/Luke 7:35 the children of wisdom are Jesus' followers, not (as often asserted) John and Jesus. See now Kirk, 376-77, who cogently proposes that the mention of the "children" of 7:35 forms a literary frame that echoes back to the children of 3:8.

75. Cf. Kloppenborg, *Excavating Q*, 204: "what is at issue is the recognition in Jesus and his activities of 'something greater than Jonah or Solomon'"; but on 124: "At issue is not the recognition of the person of Jesus but rather grasping the significance of the time as the dawning of God's kingdom."

76. The logic and rhetorical force of Q 11:17-20 is sometimes missed, especially the reference to Jewish exorcists in v. 19. They illustrate the basic point made in vv. 17-18 that it is silly to think that exorcism can be so easily attributed to Satan attacking himself. The force of 11:20 hangs on the premise that Jesus' exorcisms are distinguished from those of other exorcists by being linked to his proclamation of the advent of the kingdom of God. Consequently, if it is by God's power that he casts out demons, then in his exorcising the kingdom of God really "has come upon you." On the structure of Q 11:14-23, see now Kirk, *Composition*, 183-92.

suffering that Jesus' followers received "on account of the Son of Man." Though they certainly are promised the kingdom of God (e.g., 6:20), and are comforted through associating their persecution with the sufferings of the prophets (6:23), the specific cause of their trouble is their allegiance to Jesus. In 12:2-12 Jesus' followers are urged to confess him fearlessly and are warned about denying him, for their future status before God depends on their stance toward Jesus (esp. 12:8-9).[77]

The most explicit reference to the polarizing effect of Jesus, however, is in 12:49, 51-53, where Jesus claims to come to cast fire upon the earth and to create division that even runs through the closest of natural kin. In this context the insight called for in 12:54-56 is specifically the recognition that in Jesus the kingdom of God makes its crucial appearance. Moreover, this is the explanatory context of the rather urgent imagery of 12:57-59. In the context of Q, Jesus is quite transparently the master in 13:24-30 who will determine whether people participate in the consummation of the kingdom of God, as 13:26 obviously alludes to Jesus' own activities.

The authority of Jesus is patently a corollary theme of all that we have noted thus far. This is especially explicit in 6:46-49, which, as previously observed, demands that Jesus' followers genuinely treat him as their authoritative master (esp. v. 46). The episode in 9:57-60 is another rather important instance. In addition to people coming here offering themselves to be his followers, and Jesus making himself the pattern to which they must conform (explicitly in 9:58 and implicitly in 9:62), it is even more notable that Jesus is pictured as *summoning* followers (9:59-60). As Hengel has shown, the tradition of Jesus calling followers is unusual in Jewish or pagan teacher-pupil practice, and has its closest analogy in the divine call of prophets.[78] As in other passages, of course those called by Jesus are sent to proclaim the kingdom of God (9:60), but the basis and authority for their doing so comes from Jesus' call.

The association of Jesus with the actions and authority of God is reflected also in the opening of the passage that follows in both Luke and Q (10:2-16). In

---

77. When they are brought before Jewish and pagan authorities, Jesus' followers are promised the Holy Spirit to enable their witness (12:11-12), which in the context means that the Holy Spirit functions in support of confessing Jesus faithfully. As Kirk has proposed (*Composition*, 210-12), Q/Luke 12:8-9 calls for faithful confession by Jesus' followers, whereas 12:10 means that outsiders (such as the authorities before whom witness is given) will be judged for rejecting the Spirit-prompted witness called for here.

78. Martin Hengel, *The Charismatic Leader and His Followers*, trans. J. C. G. Greig (Edinburgh: T. & T. Clark, 1981). But Hengel may exaggerate things somewhat in apologetic zeal. In comments on an earlier version of this chapter, Kloppenborg points to the stories of Socrates and Xenophon as instances of Greek teachers inviting people to become students.

Q 10:2 Jesus directs his followers to petition "the Lord of the harvest" to put forth *(ekbalē)* workers. In the very next moment (10:3) he himself officially sends out *(apostellō)* followers and authoritatively directs the manner of their mission. It is difficult to avoid the conclusion that Jesus himself is the Lord of the harvest, for in 10:2-3 he is shown exercising this very function.[79] Moreover, in 11:2-4 Jesus directs the prayer practice/form of his followers, and in 11:9-13 his words provide the basis for his followers approaching God with confidence. In 11:39-44 Jesus' woes against the Pharisees imply that he is the superior authority for interpreting what proper behavior should be.

Another important expression of Jesus' authority is in 13:34-35, the lament over Jerusalem. Whatever the tradition-historical origins of these verses, in the context of Q the otherwise unidentified "I" who speaks here is most readily taken as Jesus.[80] If this is correct, then Jesus is pictured in a rather astonishingly grand role here, with authority to gather Jerusalem's children (13:34b), their refusal of his overtures leaving them with only their abandoned "house" (likely the temple), and the summons to recognize in Jesus "the one who comes in the name of the Lord." Indeed, Kirk contends that the passage reflects the conviction that in Jesus "the presence, revelation, and blessing of God, has come" to dwell among his followers, and that "for Q Jesus constitutes the new axis between earth and heaven."[81]

If, as is thought likely, 19:12-13, 15-26 originally followed immediately after 17:23-35, then the parable of the nobleman who goes away to obtain a kingdom and returns to settle accounts with his servants is most naturally taken as a reference to Jesus. In Q, thus, Jesus is clearly the unique mediator of the kingdom on whose authority his followers further his proclamation of it, and he will also return with decisive consequences for all.

Christological Terms

The christological categories used in Q are somewhat like those of the Synoptic Gospels generally. The most frequent expression that is often taken as a title is

79. Kloppenborg (*Excavating Q*, 393) refers to "the algebra of association" in Q passages such as 10:2-12 that yields "a Christocentric conclusion" that associates Jesus closely with God's actions.

80. Whether 13:34-35 followed 13:28-30 in Q or, as Kirk has proposed, formed the concluding lines of a discourse composed of 10:23-24; 11:2-13, 14-26, 29-35, 39-52; 13:34-35 (Kirk, *Composition*, 309-36) makes no difference to the point I am making here. Allison argues that 11:49-51 was followed by 13:34-35, and that these verses alluded to 2 Chron. 24:17-25 (*The Intertextual Jesus*, 149-52).

81. Kirk, *Composition*, 313-14.

"the son of man."[82] But, as recent studies have shown, the expression was not an established title in pre-Christian Jewish texts.[83] Furthermore, in Q, as in the Gospels overall, "the son of man" is Jesus' characteristic way of referring to himself, but never functions as either a claim disputed by others or a confession affirmed by followers. In the Jesus tradition "son of man" is clearly what we may call a technical expression with special usage, but it does not function as a confessional title. Essentially it functions as Jesus' characteristic and distinctive self-referential expression. Thus, for example, the reference to suffering that is endured "on account of the Son of Man" in Q 6:22 does not mean that Jesus' followers were persecuted for proclaiming him as "the son of man," but rather that they suffer on account of their allegiance to and confession of Jesus. As "the son of man," Jesus is presented both in presently humble circumstances (e.g., 9:58) and in future vindication (e.g., 12:8-9, 40; 17:24-30). But I repeat: the term never functions as a claim made or disputed in Q, or any other New Testament text for that matter. So, in what christological/confessional categories does Q indicate that Jesus' followers express their faith in him?

Most obviously, Jesus is referred to as the "lord" *(Kyrios)* of his followers (e.g., 6:46). This certainly connotes his supremely authoritative status as the master of his followers, and indicates that they identify themselves with reference to him. In considering whether in Q this title also has something of the more transcendent connotation reflected in other New Testament texts, we should note again the passages where Jesus seems to be linked directly with God's actions. Among important texts, we have already noted Q 7:27, where John the Baptist is the messenger prophesied in Malachi 3:1, the one sent to prepare the way of God ("the Lord [*Yahweh*] whom you seek will suddenly come to his temple"). If, as I think likely, the alteration of the wording of Malachi 3:1 in Q 7:27 (the messenger sent "ahead of *you*" and "to prepare *your* way," instead of "to prepare the way before *me*") was deliberate, the most probable meaning is that Jesus functions here in the eschatological capacity that Malachi attributes to God. Moreover, the question from John in Q 7:19 ("Are you the one who comes [*ho erchomenos*]?") echoes John's own oracle in Q 3:16-17 about a mighty figure to come after him ("The one who is mightier than I comes [*erchetai*]") with awesome status and authority. The mighty one who comes will "baptize in/with the Holy Spirit and with fire," and will have authority ("his winnowing fan") to determine who are the "wheat" and the "chaff," assigning to each group

---

82. See, e.g., Tuckett, *Q,* 239-82.

83. In the next chapter I return to the thorny issues and questions surrounding the expression "the Son of Man," so I reserve further consideration of the matter and references to scholarly literature till then.

its fate. It should be obvious that assigning such a role to Jesus at the very least amounts to him serving as direct agent of God, executing the eschatologically decisive functions. The closest analogy is perhaps the "Elect One" of the "Similitudes" in 1 Enoch (37–71).[84]

Further, if my analysis of Q 13:34-35 is correct, then here as well Jesus functions in a divinelike role as the figure who summons Jerusalem to himself and pronounces her fate for rejecting him. In light of these passages, I think it unwise to conclude too quickly that for the composers of Q the Kyrios Jesus was merely their authoritative teacher. The evidence we have surveyed here is rather more consistent with the conclusion that Q in fact reflects a highly exalted view of Jesus, that compares quite closely with other indications of "high Christology" in the early Christian decades.

The title "Christ" is not found in Q, but then neither is it found very frequently in the sayings material in the Synoptic Gospels.[85] For example, although Jesus' messianic status is obviously important for the author of Mark, the term "Christ" does not appear until Mark 8:29 in the words of Peter. Afterward in Mark, "Christ" appears in sayings of Jesus for which there is no Q version at all (12:35; 13:21). In order to make the absence of the term "Christ" in Q a signal of a rejection of it by the composer(s), we would need to have Q versions of sayings without the title paralleling versions in the Gospels with the title. We do not have this.[86]

Furthermore, the lack of the term "Christ" in Q has to be seen alongside the Q references to Jesus noted already, where he is the one who comes to bring God's eschatological blessings. Like the "Elect One" of 1 Enoch, Jesus in Q is not directly referred to as "Christ/Messiah."[87] Instead, both figures are more characteristically described in other (still more exalted?) terms as direct representatives of God.[88]

Another christological category reflected in Q and consistent with this

---

84. Cf. Tuckett, Q, 214-18, whose reading of the connotations of Kyrios as a term for Jesus seems to me somewhat tone-deaf.

85. Possibly in Mark 9:41 (but note the textual variation), and cf. the form in Matt. 10:42 which does not use "Christ." Jesus poses a question about "Christ" in Mark 12:35/Matt. 22:42/ Luke 20:41, and in Mark 13:21/Matt. 24:23 he warns about false messianic claims. Of course, the climactic Markan reference is in 14:61-62, where Jesus answers positively to the high priest's question, "Are you the Christ, the Son of the Blessed?"

86. To his credit, Kloppenborg does not claim that the absence of "Christ" in Q signals a rejection of it.

87. Granted, in 1 Enoch 48.10 and 52.4 the "Messiah" is probably the "Elect One." But the "Messiah" is not a favorite term for this figure.

88. Note also Edward P. Meadors, "The 'Messianic' Implications of the Q Material," JBL 118 (1999): 253-77.

conclusion is divine sonship. Most explicit, of course, is the temptation narrative (Q 4:1-13), where the devil twice taunts Jesus about the claim that he is Son of God (4:3, 9).[89] The taunt logically requires the prior claim that Jesus is in fact the Son of God, and this is one major reason for including a scene of Jesus' baptism and divine acclamation as God's Son as likely a part of Q.[90] We noted earlier that the category of divine sonship has a diverse background in Jewish tradition (angels, e.g., Gen. 6:2-4; Ps. 29:1; the Davidic king, e.g., Ps. 2:7; Israel as a whole, e.g., Deut. 14:1; Hos. 1:10; righteous/wise individual, e.g., Wisd. of Sol. 2:18; *Pss. Sol.* 13.9). But in the larger context of Q, it should be obvious that Jesus is singled out specially, not merely made one of a class, and that in his case divine sonship connotes a unique relationship with God.

More specifically, Q 3:21-22 forms part of what is now termed "the Inaugural Discourse" in Q, a large unit that includes 3:7-9, 16-17, 21-22; 4:1-13; 6:20b-49; 7:1-10, 18-35. In this material Jesus is endowed with God's Spirit for his unique mission as direct envoy and agent of God.[91] The theme of divine sonship that emerges in the baptismal scene (3:21-22) is then implicitly reaffirmed and clarified in the temptation account in 4:1-13. The devil's taunts about Jesus' divine sonship are expressed in Greek phrasing that does not challenge the claim. Instead, the devil is presented as attempting to get Jesus to act upon his divine sonship in inappropriate ways (4:3, 9), and Jesus is portrayed as defeating the devil by a steadfast loyalty to God that shows the truth of his divine sonship.

Jesus' sonship is then directly echoed and expounded later in Q, in the striking christological declaration in 10:21-22. In this passage the Spirit-inspired Jesus himself rejoices in the revelation of things "hidden from the wise and learned," and now brought forth uniquely through him as "the Son," to whom all things have been given and who has a privileged, intimate relationship with God. Recognition that Jesus is "the Son" of God is itself a revelation of God to Jesus' followers, and only Jesus can reveal "who the Father is" (v. 22). This passage is emphatically christological and confirms both that Jesus' divine sonship is an important theme in Q and that it connotes a transcendent status.[92]

---

89. Scholarly opinion has divided over whether the original order of the three temptations in Q is represented by the Matthean or Lukan order; see Kloppenborg, *Q Parallels*, 20. The International Q Project edition prefers the Matthean order, so the proposed arrangement is Q 4:1-4, 9-12, 5-8, 13 (Robinson, Hoffmann, Kloppenborg, 22-41).

90. In Robinson, Hoffmann, Kloppenborg, 18-21, Q 3:21-22 is included but marked off to indicate disagreement among the editors as to whether it was in Q. There is no doubt, however, that the scene involves God's acclamation of Jesus as his Son.

91. See now Kirk's extended discussion of this discourse (*Composition*, 365-97).

92. For a similar view of the passage, see John S. Kloppenborg, "Wisdom Christology in Q," *LTP* 34 (1978): 129-47.

I trust that this consideration of how Jesus is presented in Q will show why I consider it incorrect to think that Q reflects a "low" Christology, a view of Jesus merely as inspiring sage, for example.[93] Instead, Q reflects a very high view of Jesus' role, powers, and person. He is directly associated with God in crucial eschatological functions, and he has unquestioned authority in the lives of his followers. He is uniquely endowed with God's Spirit, and in his powerful activities that include healing, exorcism, and other remarkable miracles, as well as in his proclamation, God's kingdom comes to eschatological expression. Through him, his followers are privileged to participate in declaring and demonstrating God's kingdom, and he is paradigmatic for all their activities. They suffer opposition precisely for his sake, and on his account; he promises them a spectacular vindication that will involve sharing his kingdom.

The alleged "silence" of Q, I contend, has much more to do with the genre and purposes of its composer(s), and is far less an indication of their ignorance or the limits of their beliefs. Q is a remarkably important (even if hypothetical) text. The collecting and use of Jesus' sayings led to the production of this significant literary product that appears to have been widely circulated and appreciated in the first century. Then, through its incorporation into the Gospels of Matthew and Luke, it was bequeathed to all subsequent Christian tradition, serving to provide centuries of believers with some of their most familiar and treasured traditions of the teachings of their Master and Lord.[94]

Religious Life in Q

Because in this book I am focusing more broadly on the role of Jesus in the religious life and thought of his followers, and not only on their "Christologies," their beliefs, it is also worth noting the kind of religious life or piety affirmed in Q. Overall, the tone of the Q material is one of great religious vigor and intensity. We must, of course, be cautious about taking the religious aspirations expressed in texts as direct reflections of the actual religious attainments of their

---

93. "Inspiring sage" and "low" Christology are characterizations of Q by scholars such as Mack. Kloppenborg, however, agrees that this is not an accurate view of the Christology of Q.

94. Kloppenborg refers to the incorporation of Q by Matthew and Luke in terms that could be taken as pejorative. E.g., "Q provides an instrument by which to measure how much the intracanonical Gospels have covered their own tracks" (*Excavating Q*, 2). I see no indication that the authors of Matthew and Luke were trying to hide anything about early Christianity, or trying to correct, suppress, or subvert any distinctive expression of Christian belief in their generous and full-scale appropriation of Q. In private communication, Kloppenborg assures me that no pejorative connotation was intended.

authors and intended readers. If, as I contend, Q is not to be taken as a direct re-flection of the social, geographical, and economic provenance of its intended readers, neither can we use it simplistically to describe their religious life.[95] But, as an instructional text that seems intended to encourage and help shape disci-pleship to Jesus, Q gives us valuable evidence of the ideals and aspirations pro-moted for, and among, the first-century followers who wrote it and were in-tended to use it.

Q presents Jesus' followers entering into his mission of proclaiming the kingdom of God (Q 10:2-16), and so being authorized by him to declare with official force the approach/presence of God's kingdom just as he did (10:9-11). Moreover, just as Jesus worked miracles, such as healings and exorcisms, so he also commissions them to exhibit the miraculous power of the kingdom of God in similar miracles (10:9). 17:5-6 colorfully encourages them to have great faith in God's power to work wonders.

The prayer Jesus is portrayed teaching his followers in 11:2-4 reflects the complete trust in God for provision of their needs that Jesus exhibits and de-mands of them. Note how the specific petition for "daily bread" (v. 3) corre-sponds to the directions to those engaged in itinerant proclamation to depend upon the provision that will be provided by those to whom they speak (10:4-7). Of course, as 10:7b indicates, those who take up such a mission have a right to expect to have their needs met (as is also reflected in Paul's allusion to Jesus' saying in 1 Cor. 9:14), and failure to respond properly to Jesus' followers can bring dire consequences from God (Q 10:10-12). Whether Q 11:13 promises Je-sus' followers the Holy Spirit (per Luke) or "good things" (per Matthew), the whole of 11:5-13 encourages a bold confidence in God's readiness to answer

---

95. The geographical and socioeconomic character of the Christians for whom Q was initially written is not a crucial matter in this book, so I shall not devote much space to the ques-tion. But another reason is my judgment that attempts to propose a provenance for Q are far too speculative (i.e., they do not adequately show how to eliminate alternatives in favor of one provenance), and involve confusing the likely provenance of *sayings* with the provenance of Q *as a textual production*. I do not dispute that sayings in Q seem to reflect a setting that can be fit-ted into first-century Galilee, for example; that is likely because that was Jesus' setting, and the sayings either go back to him or were crafted in imitation of the traditional mode of his speech. But it is a mistake to think that this tells us that *the Q document* itself comes from circles of Jesus' followers in Galilean villages. Maybe it did. But this cannot be established by the approach that Kloppenborg describes (esp. *Excavating Q*, 171-75) and takes as his working assumption (214-61). With appreciation for the learning exhibited in his discussion of Galilee, his promotion of a Galilean provenance for Q seems to me misguided. Cf. now also Reed, 170-96, who also pro-poses a Galilean provenance for Q. But Reed's argument seems to depend heavily on his as-sumption that "Q lacks a literary design with a concomitant narrative world" (181), which I re-gard as fallacious.

prayers generously. This confidence in God is the basis for the call in 12:22-34 not to be preoccupied about acquisition of possessions or even daily needs.

Jesus' followers are also to be courageous and forthright in dealing with opposition. Even when called before authorities, they are to count on the inspiration of the Holy Spirit in giving an account for themselves (12:11-12). This further indicates a lively "charismatic" religious outlook, in which the Spirit's empowerment and operation is sought, expected, and tangibly experienced. In addition, of course, Jesus' followers are to know that their faithfulness under duress will be richly rewarded in the eschatological consummation (e.g., 22:28-30).

Indeed, this eschatological outlook is pervasive in Q. The kingdom of God which Jesus and his followers announce and manifest in mighty works is not some timeless principle or inward condition to achieve by dint of cognitive or disciplinary effort. It is the action of God that breaks in upon normal life of the present, and will be so radical in its future manifestation that all else pales into insignificance in comparison.

There is also a strong concern for the quality of communal life in 17:1-4, which makes large demands for offenders against their fellow believers in Jesus to repent, and requires those offended to forgive generously. The fact that in Q Jesus consistently addresses readers in the second-person plural further reflects the communal ethos. Moreover, 13:24-30 both subverts any presumption about participation in God's kingdom and also envisions a great breadth of those who are to make up the redeemed. This likely reflects the perception of Jesus' followers that is espoused in Q: they are a diverse body of universal scope who are called to make up a new eschatological collective.

Summary

If, contrary to some scholars, Q is not the product of a distinctive, otherwise unknown circle of Jesus' followers with a form of faith significantly different from what is offered in other evidence of the first century. Q is, however, for other good reasons, an important body of material. In the main it probably includes a number of authentic sayings of Jesus (howbeit translated and likely adapted in the process of transmission), and it represents the most substantial body of sayings of Jesus that can make a plausible claim to authenticity. But if scholarly efforts to identify and reconstruct the contents and arrangement of Q are basically as successful as I take them to be, in Q we also have a unique textual product of the early decades of Christianity (or at least uniquely extant).

If Q was composed by Hellenist believers such as the Jerusalem circles linked with Stephen in Acts, this would account satisfactorily for how it came to embody such a sizable collection of Jesus tradition with good claims to authenticity. It would also help account for Q being composed in Greek with some literary skill, and thereafter quickly acquiring the wide circulation that it enjoyed.

Q is apparently a carefully designed text, not a grab bag of Jesus tradition.[96] It has plausible thematic concerns and shows a noticeable level of scribal competence in its arrangement (unlike, e.g., the *Gospel of Thomas*). It probably does not reflect fully the beliefs of those who composed and used it. But Q does give us a valuable picture of one of the several ways in which early Christians expressed their faith and sought to promote discipleship to Jesus. As noted above, Q was also a very successful literary product. It does not represent some Christian backwater, but generally reflects the sort of devotion to Jesus that is consistent with the other evidence we have looked at thus far in this book. This probably explains why Q was so well received and so fully appropriated by the authors of the Gospels of Matthew and Luke.

In fact, the "narrative substructure" of Q, and the central place of Jesus in it, combine to make the appropriation/preservation of Q in Matthew and Luke more readily understandable. We can even see in Q one of the key literary steps that may have contributed to making the full-scale narrative Gospels seem to their authors an obvious and appropriate expression of devotion to Jesus.

---

96. "Grab bag" is the term for Q used by John P. Meier, *A Marginal Jew: Rethinking the Historical Jesus*, vol. 2, *Mentor, Message, and Miracles* (New York: Doubleday, 1994), 180-81, 271.

CHAPTER FIVE

Jesus Books

Perhaps the four best-known writings in the New Testament, and certainly the most influential literary portraits of Jesus across the history of Christianity, are the four canonical Gospels. Though the contents of all New Testament writings are heavily shaped by beliefs about Jesus and the consequences of faith in him for personal and collective life, each canonical Gospel is entirely concerned with presenting a narrative account of Jesus. Thus, among the New Testament writings, these four are "Jesus books" in a particular sense and represent a distinctive kind of early Christian literary work.[1]

I offer the expression "Jesus books" for writings that are more characteristically referred to as "Gospels." Among scholars, the term "gospel" has been disputed in recent decades.[2] There is no agreement on when the term first began to be applied to writings, though most think that it probably became a label sometime in the second century. The familiar titles of the four canonical Gospels (e.g., "The Gospel according to Matthew") were attached at some point after these writings began to circulate among early Christian groups, but there is disagreement as to exactly when.[3] Moreover, scholars do not agree on what the term

---

1. As I shall note later in this chapter, the canonical Gospels are best seen as an identifiably Christian adaptation of and contribution to the Roman-era literary genre of *bios* writings. But in comparison with other known first-century Christian writings, the Gospels are a distinctive genre.

2. Helmut Koester, *Ancient Christian Gospels: Their History and Development* (Philadelphia: Trinity Press International, 1990), is the most wide-ranging and detailed discussion, though his views on a number of issues are very debatable.

3. Martin Hengel, *The Four Gospels and the One Gospel of Jesus Christ* (London: SCM Press; Harrisburg, Pa.: Trinity Press International, 2000), vigorously asserts positions on a number of related issues.

"gospel" means, as to the literary character of a writing, or on the kinds of writings to which it should apply properly (largely because scholars use different criteria). As we noted in the preceding chapter, some have insisted recently that Q should be thought of, and referred to, as a Gospel, and not merely a sayings collection or source. Certainly, as I shall note shortly, in the early Christian centuries the term came to be applied to writings that exhibit a variety of literary types and contents. So my term "Jesus books" is intended to take in all the earliest Christian writings whose contents are concerned with a representation of Jesus, whatever the remaining differences among them in content or literary character.

Though there are various contrary proposals supported by a few, most scholars regard the four canonical Gospels as the earliest narrative portraits of Jesus; they are commonly thought to have been written between roughly 65 and 100. The overwhelmingly dominant view is that the Gospel of Mark was the pioneering work, the earliest extant attempt to give a connected narrative account of Jesus' ministry, and that it probably appeared sometime between 65 and 72. Mark then quickly obtained a wide circulation, and was both the influential basic literary model and a principal source used by the authors of the Gospels of Matthew and Luke, which are generally dated sometime during the decade or so after Mark appeared. Most scholars date the Gospel of John later still; unlike Matthew and Luke, John is not usually judged today to exhibit a direct literary dependence on Mark. But it is possible that, in some more indirect and general way, John as well may have been influenced and shaped by the example of Mark.

Whether one calls Q a "gospel" or (as I judge it) a "sayings collection," if we are correct in thinking that there was such a document, and that scholars have basically reconstructed its contents and probable arrangement, Q was certainly all about Jesus. It was thus a first-century "Jesus book" earlier than the canonical Gospels of Matthew and Luke, at the least. Because of the intense interest in Q in recent scholarship, in the preceding chapter I considered what to make of it with reference to early devotion to Jesus. In the present chapter, however, we shall examine those Jesus books that remain extant (whereas Q is an inferred entity), with special concern for those that had continuing influence and elicited sustained interest in Christian circles of the first few centuries. Of course, this means that the canonical Gospels come in for prime attention.

But there were also a number of other early Christian writings that are today referred to as extracanonical or apocryphal "gospels."[4] At least in their ex-

---

4. Wilhelm Schneemelcher, ed., *New Testament Apocrypha*, vol. 1, *Gospels and Related Writings*, ed. and trans. R. McL. Wilson, rev. ed. (Louisville: Westminster John Knox; Cambridge: James Clarke, 1991), gives introductions and English translations. For a concise survey of the evidence, see Richard J. Bauckham, "Gospels (Apocryphal)," in *DJG*, 286-91.

tant form, ⌐the earliest of these (e.g., *Gospel of Thomas, Gospel of Peter, Protevangelium of James, Infancy Gospel of Thomas*) are most commonly χ thought to date from a few to several decades after the four canonical Gospels.⌐ Moreover, although there are obvious differences in content and literary character among the four canonical Gospels, the extracanonical gospels add much greater diversity to the kinds of "Jesus books" produced in early Christian circles. In chapter 7 I discuss these writings more extensively. A few illustrations will suffice at this point.

Probably the most widely known extracanonical Jesus book today is the *Gospel of Thomas,* a collection of 114 sayings attributed to Jesus.[5] A few sayings have very short narrative settings, and they illustrate a literary form variously referred to as "apothegm," "pronouncement story," or *chreia,* but there is no overall narrative "story line" connecting the sayings, and scholars have not even been able to identify any overall organizational scheme.[6] As we will see in chapter 7, a number of contentious issues are connected with this fascinating writing. For now, the uncontroversial thing to note is that the *Gospel of Thomas* is the prime example of a Jesus book that is essentially a sayings collection, a writing very different in form as well as contents from the narrative Gospels familiar to readers of the New Testament.⌐

There are still other kinds of books about Jesus. These include "nativity" or "infancy" gospels, which were wholly concerned with elaborating stories of Jesus' birth and early childhood, among which the *Protevangelium of James* and the *Infancy Gospel of Thomas* are two prime and early specimens.[7] These also are undoubtedly later than the canonical Gospels, but they are interesting evidence of how early Christian imagination was exercised by the nearly complete silence about Jesus' childhood in the canonical Jesus books. In addition, the fragmentary *Gospel of Peter* probably shows that Christians in the second century continued to produce books about Jesus patterned after, and drawing upon, what became the canonical Jesus books.

5. The Coptic text that forms part of the Nag Hammadi manuscripts has "The Gospel according to Thomas" at the end of the tractate, but the original title of the work was probably something such as "The Hidden Sayings of the Living Jesus," taken (as was customary in antiquity) from the opening words: "These are the hidden sayings which the living Jesus spoke and Judas Thomas wrote down." The extant Greek fragments of an earlier version of this text do not cover the ending, and so we cannot be sure what title it may have had in its late second-century/early third-century Greek form.

6. On the "pronouncement story" form, see, e.g., James L. Bailey and Lyle D. Vander Broek, *Literary Forms in the New Testament: A Handbook* (Louisville: Westminster John Knox, 1992), 114-22.

7. Ronald F. Hock, *The Infancy Gospels of James and Thomas,* Scholars Bible 2 (Santa Rosa, Calif.: Polebridge Press, 1995).

Of all the ancient Christian writings, however, there is no question that the canonical Gospels are the most influential Jesus books, from the period of their composition and onward through subsequent history, which makes them the most significant in historical terms. This, plus the dominant scholarly view (which I share) that they are the earliest extant Jesus books, are the key reasons why I devote greater space to them. That is, the canonical Gospels probably give us the earliest and most important examples of the literary presentation or "rendition" of Jesus. In what follows, I first take note of the literary characteristics shared by the canonical Gospels, after which I set them in their literary "environment" to see better what kind of writings they comprise. Then I focus on the portraits of Jesus presented in each of the three "Synoptic Gospels." For a variety of reasons, I reserve extended discussion of the Gospel of John for the next chapter.

Shared Features of the Canonical Gospels

To assess the canonical Gospels as expressions of devotion to Jesus, it is necessary to take account of their literary characteristics.[8] The most obvious common feature is their basic literary nature as connected narratives of Jesus' activities. The sequences of their respective connected narratives vary, in some cases quite markedly, but each portrayal of Jesus presents a narrative framework and an overall "plot" or "story line," and each author "plots" each particular saying and incident within this sequential narrative.

In light of the differences among them, it is all the more interesting that they all have a recognizably similar narrative framework for Jesus' activities that commences with John the Baptist, then ushers Jesus on stage, followed by a sequential presentation of Jesus' deeds, which include calling disciples, miracles, teaching, controversy, and opposition. They all culminate in a trip to Jerusalem, with an extended narrative of events there that is focused on final words to disciples, his arrest, hearings before religious and civil authorities, his state execution, and his resurrection and a postresurrection affirmation of his disciples.[9]

---

8. Among the surprisingly few publications concerned with the literary character of the Gospels, see William A. Beardslee, *Literary Criticism of the New Testament* (Philadelphia: Fortress, 1970), 14-29; Frank Kermode, "Introduction to the New Testament," in *The Literary Guide to the Bible,* ed. Robert Alter and Frank Kermode (Cambridge: Harvard University Press, Belknap Press, 1987), esp. 375-83; David E. Aune, *The New Testament in Its Literary Environment* (Philadelphia: Westminster, 1987), 46-63; Edgar V. McKnight, "Literary Criticism," in *DJG*, 473-81.

9. In the Gospel of Mark, the original ending of which I take to be 16:8, the affirmation of the disciples is of course in the words of the "young man" in 16:6-7, which include a reiteration of Jesus' promise to meet his wayward followers again in Galilee.

Without downplaying the variations in their accounts, we can say that they all present interesting "renditions" of a basically similar story. In other words, there are clear family resemblances that link them, and among these is their common character as narratives with a recognizable kinship in the general contours of their accounts.

The differences among the canonical Gospels include emphases, selection, and order of incidents. There are variations in the ways the same incidents are described, and in the forms of the same sayings, the kinds of material favored, and the specific literary aims and plan of each author. Sometimes these differences are quite striking, as in the well-known difference between John and the other canonical Gospels over the placement of the "temple-cleansing" incident, which in John appears early (2:13-22) but in the others is in their accounts of Jesus' fateful final trip to Jerusalem. Both their many specific differences and their general similarity are important, and neither should be glibly played off against the other if we wish to do justice to these early Jesus books. I shall return to the major distinguishing features of each of the four canonical Gospels later. For now, I emphasize what they have in common, prominent among which is their literary nature as connected narratives of Jesus' activity.

Secondly, in all the canonical Gospels, Jesus is paradigmatic and uniquely authoritative in his teachings and actions. In the "narrative world" of the four Gospels, God is of course the ultimate authority and "reliable voice," whose endorsement of Jesus is either explicitly related (e.g., in the Synoptic scenes of Jesus' baptism and transfiguration where God proclaims Jesus his Son) or claimed.[10] But among the earthly characters in the Gospels, Jesus is the unrivaled hero. His voice is always reliable; he is never mistaken, and the readers are never given reason to doubt him. His teachings are completely authoritative and superior to all other authorities. He is also presented as completely sympathetic to those with the values espoused in the writings, with references to his compassion, his regard for the vulnerable (e.g., women, lepers, children), and his criticism of religious ostentation and hypocrisy. His opponents are clearly and always wrong, and are characterized as spiritually obtuse at best, and at worst, as hypocrites and morally corrupt.

Jesus is also the key issue. Though he preaches a message of God's kingdom as present and/or approaching, the Gospel narratives emphasize that everything else turns upon what characters in the narratives make of Jesus. He is the polarizing force. The characters in the story must recognize the presence of God's kingdom in Jesus' proclamation and deeds. Jesus' actions are the key matters of complaint by opponents, and the judgments of all have to do with

---

10. See Larry W. Hurtado, "God," in *DJG*, 270-76, and other works listed there.

whether he is to be treated as the valid vehicle of God's purposes or as an erring teacher and dangerous example, and perhaps even something worse. He is nearly always "on stage" and the central character in every scene, and he is at the center of the controversy that swirls through these four narrative accounts from their beginnings to their turbulent climaxes in his arrest, trial, and execution. Even afterward, in the crucial postcrucifixion scenes, the news of his divine vindication by resurrection and his authoritative summons to his disciples (whether delivered through an angel, as in Mark, or personally in post-resurrection appearances as in the other canonical Gospels) make him the key subject and character.

Jesus' disciples, however, have an ambiguous quality. On the one hand, they are chosen by Jesus specifically to become key participants in his mission, and are deputized to preach and work miracles themselves in his name. Yet on the other hand, they are also distinguished from and vastly inferior to Jesus. Though the individual Gospel authors vary in the severity of their portrayal of the failures and shortcomings of the disciples, Mark being the most severe, they all make the disciples utterly beholden to Jesus; he alone is presented as consistently faithful and exemplary.

All four canonical accounts also agree in basic honorific terms (christological titles) by which to identify Jesus and express his significance; these include the key christological titles attested elsewhere in New Testament writings. In all four accounts the Greek term *Christos* is used overwhelmingly as a title, "the Christ"; all four affirm that Jesus is now to be recognized as the legitimate bearer of this title, though they all indicate that Jesus redefines the work of the Christ/Messiah.[11] Likewise, all four affirm that Jesus is Son of God. Indeed, they all treat Jesus' divine sonship as a crucial claim and category, although this is more frequently and programmatically so in John. They also all reflect the reverential use of *Kyrios* (Lord), especially Luke, although *Kyrios* does not function as a confessional title as much in the Gospels as in other New Testament writings.

In all four Gospels "son of man" is Jesus' most characteristic way of referring to himself, but this term does not function as a confessional title. Because of the massive controversy over the meaning and function of this expression, I will discuss it more thoroughly later in this chapter. At this point, it will suffice to indicate that "son of man" appears frequently in the Gospels, but only on the lips of Jesus, and does not appear elsewhere in the New Testament as a confessional

---

11. Larry W. Hurtado, "Christ," in *DJG*, 106-17. This contrasts with Paul's usage, in which "Christ" functions characteristically almost like a name for Jesus, and only occasionally as a clear title (e.g., Rom. 9:5).

claim or expression of his significance. It will be necessary to give an adequate account of these facts, which I offer in my discussion of the Gospel of Mark.

A third characteristic of all four canonical Gospels, one much more important than seems to be recognized by some scholars, is how fully they site their accounts of Jesus in a specific historical, cultural, and geographical setting. Each writer locates Jesus in early-first-century Roman Judea (Palestine), and each rendition of Jesus' activities is rich in "local color." Incidents tend to be placed in specific locations, and frequent readers of the Gospels will become mentally acquainted with a goodly number of sites in and near Roman Judea. Prominent examples include the "Sea" (Lake) of Galilee (or Tiberias), Capernaum, Nazareth, Bethsaida, Caesarea Philippi, the Decapolis, Samaria, Jericho, Bethlehem, the Jordan River, Tyre and Sidon, and Jerusalem. During incidents set in Jerusalem, specific features of the temple and the precincts of the Roman governor are referred to (especially in John),[12] as are nearby villages such as Bethany and Emmaus.[13]

There are lots of references to the religious and cultural setting. We learn of Jewish groups of the day: Sadducees, Pharisees, Herodians (not referred to in any other sources), temple priests and their leaders, and Jewish scribes. Various specific questions surface about observance of Jewish religious law, with reference to such matters as legitimate activities on the Sabbath, food laws, divorce and remarriage, skin diseases, swearing oaths, tithing, and still other questions such as taxation. There are references to Jewish religious festivals, such as Passover; we learn of issues of belief such as the resurrection of the dead. We get information on the governing authorities and structures: e.g., Herod the Great (in Matthew's nativity account), Herod Antipas (ruler of Galilee during Jesus' adult years), the high priest Caiaphas, and the Roman governor Pontius Pilate. We also learn of local occupations such as fishing, farming (including details of sowing and harvesting), tax gathering, and shepherding.

The use of Semitic words and expressions in these Greek texts is another very interesting category of narrative "local color." The incidence varies among the Gospels, with Mark using them most frequently.[14] More familiar examples

---

12. In the temple, Solomon's portico (John 10:23); the receptacle for temple offerings (Mark 12:41/Luke 21:1); Pilate's headquarters (the praetorium, John 18:28); the place of Pilate's sentencing of Jesus (Gabbatha, John 19:13).

13. Rainer Riesner, "Archeology and Geography," in *DJG*, 33-46, gives a handy overview of geographical references in the Gospels.

14. Michael O. Wise, "Languages of Palestine," in *DJG*, 434-44, refers to some thirty instances where the canonical Gospels use Semitic loanwords "in the context of reporting Jesus' interaction with his contemporaries" (441), judging most of the instances to involve Aramaic (442). Later in this chapter I return to Mark's particular fondness for Semitic expressions.

include the exclamation "Hosanna" during Jesus' final entry into Jerusalem (Mark 11:9-10/Matt. 21:9/John 12:13); Jesus' references to Gehenna, the place of perdition (e.g., Mark 9:43-47; Matt. 10:28; 23:15, 33; Luke 12:5); the respectful terms "Rabbi" and "Rabbouni";[15] and Jesus' words on the cross reported in varying forms by Mark (15:34) and Matthew (27:46).[16]

The narratives are also studded with individuals given specific identities. There are named figures such as Jesus' twelve disciples and Jairus, Lazarus, Bartimaeus, Nicodemus, Barabbas, Caiaphas, and Pontius Pilate. But even un-named figures are identified specifically and memorably, such as the woman with the blood flow, the clever Syrophoenician woman with a daughter in need, the Gerasene man with a legion of demons, the woman who was "forgiven much" and lavished her gratitude upon Jesus in a dining scene, the man with a demoniac son who confessed belief and his need of help in believing, and the scribe who was "not far from the kingdom."

In short, this all amounts to a shared programmatic effort to locate Jesus in a specific historical, geographical, and cultural setting. It represents an insis-tence that the Jesus whom the writers and intended readers of these Gospels reverenced (who include Gentile and Jewish believers in various locations in the Roman world), and were to see as linked with God's purposes in a unique way, is quite definitely *Jesus of Nazareth*. He is not some timeless symbol, not a mythical figure of a "once upon a time," but instead very specifically a Jew whose life and activities are geographically and chronologically located in a particular place and period of Jewish history in Roman Judea.

Readers of the canonical Gospels may become so accustomed to these things that they have to pause to note the sheer abundance of local color. More-over, a surprising number of the details that I have mentioned here seem au-thentic.[17] That is, the canonical Gospels provide us with an impressive body of information about the geography and sociocultural features of Roman Judea (Palestine) in the early decades of the first century. Of course, this does not au-tomatically mean that all the incidents the Gospel writers narrate actually hap-pened (or happened just the way they are related in the Gospels), or that all the figures who appear in the Gospels are real, historical individuals. But it does mean that the Gospel writers have striven to locate Jesus in a specific historical

---

15. Hayim Lapin, "Rabbi," in *ABD*, 5:600-602.

16. On the variations in wording (the Markan version more likely Aramaic, whereas Mat-thew's version seems to be Hebrew), see Raymond E. Brown, *The Death of the Messiah. From Gethsemane to the Grave: A Commentary on the Passion Narratives in the Four Gospels*, 2 vols. (New York: Doubleday, 1994), 2:1051-56.

17. See, e.g., C. H. Dodd, *Historical Tradition in the Fourth Gospel* (Cambridge: Cam-bridge University Press, 1963).

and cultural context, and that in doing so they have apparently drawn upon some often-reliable information about that setting.

We can appreciate the abundance and important literary role of historical and cultural "location" in the canonical Gospels if we turn briefly to the extracanonical "Jesus books." Among these, perhaps the writing with the best claims to being taken seriously as an early compilation of Jesus tradition is the *Gospel of Thomas.*[18] It contains a few named characters such as Simon Peter (sayings 13 and 114), Matthew and Thomas (13), Mary (probably Mary Magdalene, 21 and 114), and Salome (61), but far more often we simply have a collective reference to "his disciples." There are a couple references to Adam and John the Baptist (46 and 85), a couple more to Pharisees (39 and 102), and one to a Samaritan (60). But, though many of the sayings have short narrative introductions, there is scarcely any indication of a geographical, chronological, or cultural setting. From *Thomas* we would not even know that Jesus was Jewish and 𝗫 that his activities were in Roman Judea! In saying 28 Jesus speaks vaguely of having appeared "in the midst of the world and in flesh," but more precisely when and where is not related.

By contrast, in what is probably the closest analogous saying in the canonical Gospels, John 1:10-12, Jesus is referred to as having been "in the world," having come "to his own" (*eis ta idia,* his own heritage of people and place), and having been rejected by "his own people" (*hoi idioi,* here obviously the Jewish people of his time and setting). Certainly the rest of the Gospel of John makes emphatic the specific geographical, cultural, and religious setting of Jesus' ministry. Even though John (analogously to *Thomas*) reflects a cosmic view of Jesus' significance and origins, the book exhibits clear concern to locate the specific historical setting of Jesus' appearance.

In short, the comparative lack of concern in the *Gospel of Thomas* to locate Jesus historically makes the wealth of historical setting in the canonical Gospels much more noticeable, and it shows that in the earliest centuries this explicit historical siting of Jesus was not the only way a Jesus book could be written. Indeed, it must have been a conscious and thematic concern of the authors of all the canonical Gospels to present for faith a Jesus who is a historical figure with a real and particular setting.

In addition, all the canonical Gospels emphasize an explicit, larger "narrative world" or story line into which they place their stories of Jesus. This narrative horizon extends both backward to include the story line of the Scriptures

---

18. Richard Valantasis, *The Gospel of Thomas* (London: Routledge, 1997), gives an accessible introduction and commentary, though some of his views on *Thomas* (e.g., an alleged first-century origin) are highly debatable.

of Israel (Tanach/Old Testament) and forward chronologically to the eschatological triumph of God's purposes. It runs from the creation of all things by God through the stories of Israel's ancestors such as Abraham, and on through the drama of Israel, from Moses through the kings and the prophets, and functions in all the Gospels most fundamentally to provide the meaning-context in which to see the appearance of Jesus. All the canonical Gospels refer frequently back to the biblical writings and the personages, events, and religious ideas in them as the crucial matrix of meaning in which to see Jesus' significance. Whether by explicit quotation and the accompanying claim of fulfillment of prophecy (e.g., Mark 1:2-3, or the so-called "formula" quotations of Matthew, e.g., 1:22; 2:6, 17), by general claims of collective fulfillment of the Scriptures in Jesus (e.g., Luke 24:25-27, 44-47; John 5:39), or by articulation of Jesus and his message in connection with Old Testament material (e.g., Jesus and the Torah in Matt. 5:17-48; the Sabbath questions in Mark 2:23-28 or John 5:9-18; divorce in Mark 10:2-12/Matt. 19:1-12; comparisons of Jesus and the wilderness manna in John 6:29-34), the canonical Gospels rather consistently present Jesus' significance by reference to the texts, personages, events, and themes of the Old Testament Scriptures.

If the biblical sweep of the horizon "backward" in time gives the meaning-context of Jesus, the eschatological sweep of the horizon "forward" holds out the hope in which following Jesus is to be ventured, and the divine purpose that Jesus serves. In this eschatological theme as well, all four Gospels agree, although they register this hope in somewhat varying ways. Whatever the validity of the contention by some scholars that Jesus and/or the earliest circles of his followers were not particularly concerned with eschatological hopes (and I do not think these contentions are persuasive), it is undeniable that all the Gospels present Jesus in eschatological perspective, and under the strong influence of the view that there is to be a decisive future victory of God's purposes over all evil and all that opposes God's saving design.[19]

In fact, this eschatological hope even colors the canonical Gospels' presentation of Jesus' historical activity. He both announces the coming "kingdom of God" as a future event and also manifests it by way of anticipation in his own actions such as his exorcisms, healings, and welcome of sinners (e.g., Luke 11:20/Matt. 12:28). That is, Jesus is himself an eschatological "event" and figure. Eschatological hopes find in him specific confirmation, and in his historical activity their partial and initial fulfillment. This gives the story of Jesus a keen

---

19. On whether Jesus himself held eschatological ideas, see, e.g., Dale C. Allison, *Jesus of Nazareth: Millenarian Prophet* (Minneapolis: Fortress, 1998); Bart D. Ehrman, *Jesus: Apocalyptic Prophet of the New Millennium* (New York: Oxford University Press, 1999).

edge of excitement and drama. <u>He is not simply a powerful wonder-worker, an impressive teacher and debater, and/or a heroic leader of his followers</u>; he is the special vehicle of the purposes of God, which involve (ultimately) the transformation of the world, the judgment of evil, and the vindication of those who ally themselves with God's purposes.

In each Gospel this larger "narrative world" of biblical story and promise and eschatological expectation, which could be thought of as "mythic," and is cosmic in dimension and function, is linked with the "real" or finite historical setting of Roman-era Judea/Palestine.[20] This is done most formally in Luke's several chronological references to historical figures, by which he embeds his story of Jesus in specific times and places of human history (note especially "in the days of Herod the King of Judea," Luke 1:5; the alleged decree of Caesar Augustus in the administration of Quirinius in Luke 2:1; and the multiple chronological locators in Luke 3:1-2). But in all four Gospels there is an intersection of a grand narrative of God's promises and purposes with people, places, and actions that make up what is more customarily thought of as comprising "history."

The dramatic quality of the Gospel narratives is also evident at every point. For example, Jesus works miracles, curing with the mere power of his command demoniacs and those afflicted with various illnesses. He even commands the wind and sea, and he likewise raises the dead by powerful word alone (e.g., Mark 5:35-43; John 11:38-44). His curse can wither a fig tree. He feeds multitudes by miraculously multiplying loaves and fish. <u>Clearly the miracle-working power of Jesus was a crucial aspect of beliefs about him for all the circles of Christians for whom the four canonical Gospels were written.</u>

The tensions in the controversy stories (e.g., Mark 2:1–3:6; 3:20-30; 11:27–12:37) further contribute to the dramatic tone of the narrative. He generates stern criticism; his teaching involves conflict with religious teachers and authorities, with him accused of promoting dangerous errors of behavior and he in turn treating these criticisms as obstinate blindness to the will of God. The level of disputation is intense, and his enemies attempt to use deceit and trickery to entrap him. They even conspire to arrest him, and eventually some of his opponents collude with the Roman authority in having him executed. This mortal opposition, which readers are expected to know about prior to reading the Gospels, gives to them from their opening scenes a note of ominous inevitability.

Much more could be said about the literary characteristics of the canoni-

20. To refer here to the biblical narrative world as "mythic" in function does not necessarily involve a judgment about the historicity of particular figures and events, but instead has to do with the way the biblical narrative world serves the Gospel writers as the meaningful framework for their beliefs and understanding of God, Jesus, and the divine plan of redemption.

cal Gospels, but these comments are sufficient to illustrate that they are genuinely literary works with very serious religious emphases and aims. Scholars
commonly conclude that the Gospels' authors drew richly upon traditions
about Jesus that had probably circulated in Christian circles for decades orally,
and also likely in earlier kinds of writings (e.g., written sayings collections such
as Q). Moreover, as I shall note again later in this chapter, the canonical Gospels
are heavily conditioned and shaped by the basic pattern of proclamation that
characterized known Christian circles from the earliest decades of the young
religious movement, the sort of traditional pattern of proclamation that Paul
recites in 1 Corinthians 15:1-7 as characteristic of both his proclamation and
that of the Jerusalem-based leaders. This is, of course, most patently clear in the
huge place given to Jesus' "passion" (his arrest, trials, and crucifixion) and resurrection.[21] But at the same time, the Gospels are significant literary efforts in
their own right, and their appearance constitutes a notable development in the
literary history of first-century Christianity. They comprise a particular kind of
dedicated literary expression of devotion to Jesus, and as Richard Burridge has
contended, their literary genre is itself a significant christological statement
that deserves attention.[22] I shall return to this last matter later, but first let us
take greater note of the kinds of writings the canonical Gospels comprise.

The Literary Genre of the Canonical Gospels

In his very valuable study of the literary context of the New Testament writings,
David Aune stated that the genre (literary type) of a writing "consists of the interrelated elements of form, content, and function."[23] Literary genres are not
timeless categories, but instead reflect the tastes and conventions of particular
times and cultures. The nature and significance of the literary genre of the canonical Gospels become clearer when we set these writings in their ancient literary "environment" or context.[24] There are three concentric circles of that
context: (1) the Christian literary output of the first century and shortly there-

21. R. E. Brown, *The Death of the Messiah,* is now probably the most extensive discussion
of the "passion narratives" of the canonical Gospels and the traditions they incorporated.

22. Richard A. Burridge, "Gospel Genre, Christological Controversy and the Absence of
Rabbinic Biography: Some Implications of the Biographical Hypothesis," in *Christology, Con-
troversy, and Community: New Testament Essays in Honour of David R. Catchpole,* ed. David G.
Horrell and Christopher M. Tuckett (Leiden: Brill, 2000), 137-56.

23. Aune, *The New Testament,* 24.

24. In addition to the other scholars cited in the following paragraphs, see my earlier discussion, "Gospel (Genre)," in *DJG,* 276-82.

after, (2) the ancient Jewish literary context in the Greco-Roman and Roman periods, and (3) the larger Greco-Roman and Roman-era literary context. We can draw some significant conclusions from each circle.

The Gospels and Early Christian Literature

As we have noted, the canonical Gospels are probably the first such literary efforts in first-century Christianity. The author of Luke-Acts, however, refers to "many others" who had written accounts of "the things that have been fulfilled among us" (Luke 1:1).[25] Most scholars think this author had at hand the Gospel of Mark in particular, but whatever other writings he was referring to, they were either considered superseded by or (as is thought to be the case with Q) incorporated into the canonical Gospels' accounts of Jesus. Indeed, a "successful" incorporation of earlier accounts and traditions into the canonical Gospels may well have made most Christians think the earlier accounts had been both adequately preserved and also superseded.[26]

So there were likely writings about Jesus prior to the canonical Gospels, especially written collections of Jesus' sayings/teachings, and perhaps other | * kinds of writings such as collections of stories of Jesus' miracles and one or more narratives of Jesus' "passion." Q in particular, as we noted in the preceding chapter, appears to be a reasonably well ordered collection of Jesus' sayings that suggests the involvement of Christians who had at least modest scribal/editorial skill. The probable arrangement of material in Q reflects an implicit narrative or narrative substructure that has an interesting congruence with the basic narrative of the canonical Gospels: announcement/herald of Jesus, Jesus' appearance and probably his certification/identification by God, a testing/temptation, instructional material by Jesus (including the idea that Jesus' death is the index of discipleship), commissioning of disciples, promises and warn-

25. Luke 1:1 refers to "many" who "attempted [*epecheirēsan*] to compile an account [*anataxasthai diēgēsin*] of the things that have been fulfilled among us," probably meaning accounts pertaining to Jesus. To some degree Luke 1:1-4 is a stylized literary preface, and so we cannot be sure how far to press what the author says. See, e.g., I. H. Marshall, *The Gospel of Luke: A Commentary on the Greek Text*, NIGTC (Grand Rapids: Eerdmans, 1978), 39-44. I refer to the anonymous author as "he" largely because historical circumstances of the Roman period make it most likely that the author was a male. See also p. 280 below.

26. E.g., Marion L. Soards, "The Question of a PreMarcan Passion Narrative," in R. E. Brown, *The Death of the Messiah*, 2:1492-1524, reviews evidence and scholarly opinion and concludes that Mark likely used a prior narrative of Jesus' arrest, arraignment, and execution, but that Mark has so skillfully woven his sources into his own account of Jesus that we cannot with much confidence reconstruct it in detail.

ings of eschatological vindication and judgment (including a promise that Jesus' disciples will receive eschatological reward for their faithfulness). Therefore, as Kloppenborg also has noted, we can say that Q reflects an inherently narrative tendency and quality.[27] So, although the narrative Gospels represent a notable further development in literary genre, they are also congruent with the implicit narrative that seems to supply the logic to the arrangement of material in Q.

From Paul's summary of early Christian proclamation in 1 Corinthians 15:1-11 we get a narrative message focused on Jesus' death and resurrection, and from other Pauline passages such as Romans 15:8 we get allusions to (probably oral) accounts of Jesus that portray him as sent to/among his own Jewish people in fulfillment of divine promises to Israel's ancestors in the biblical writings. This all corresponds very broadly to the contents and shape of the canonical Gospels, which all place Jesus clearly as sent to Israel and make his death and resurrection the culminating events of their accounts.

That is, the canonical Gospels seem to have a direct relationship to at least some influential patterns of proclamation and teaching that circulated among various Christian groups of the first century. As to their general contents, they are literary expressions of a lot of Jesus tradition that was disseminated orally, and likely also in various written forms, before and for some time after they were written. The Gospel of Mark appears to have been an innovation, as the first known effort to provide a literary portrait of Jesus from the beginning of his ministry through his death and resurrection. We can call Mark a significant new development in literary genre. But, as with nearly all innovations, so with this pioneering effort, the author drew upon, and made his own contribution to, a prior and larger body of tradition and Christian activity, including previous writings about Jesus. The canonical Gospels are thus not really revolutionary, but instead constitute a significant evolutionary development, innovative more as landmarks in the literary history of early Christianity than as revolutionary theological statements.[28]

They represent, in varying ways and at a relatively "popular" level to be sure, the "literaturization" of prior oral discourse and written expressions about Jesus.[29] These prior traditions included stories of particular deeds and sayings (e.g., miracle stories and brief narratives of pithy sayings), narrative ref-

27. John S. Kloppenborg, *The Formation of Q: Trajectories in Ancient Wisdom Collections* (Philadelphia: Fortress, 1987), 262; John S. Kloppenborg Verbin, *Excavating Q: The History and Setting of the Sayings Gospel* (Minneapolis: Fortress, 2000), 372-73.

28. L. W. Hurtado, "The Gospel of Mark: Evolutionary or Revolutionary Document?" *JSNT* 40 (1990): 15-32.

29. I adapt a term from Aune, *The New Testament*, 65.

erences to Jesus' death and resurrection, and representations of him in connection with the story of biblical Israel and the eschatological hopes held by many devout Jews of the early Roman period. That is, both in specific contents and in their general nature as narratives, the canonical Gospels show the influence of prior Jesus traditions. But in the comparative fullness of their presentation of Jesus, each Gospel comprising a sequential narrative of Jesus from the beginning of his ministry through his resurrection, and in their other aspects as *literary* works (e.g., authorial purposes and employment of literary design), the canonical Gospels are unquestionably a notable development.

Along with their shared literary characteristics mentioned earlier, each Gospel is also a distinctive literary work. Even though the Synoptic Gospels are commonly thought to reflect direct literary relationships (i.e., Mark as the key source used by Matthew and Luke), each of them also has its own character and emphases. This is evident both in the overall nature of each Gospel and also in specific units of material. One has only to read parallel passages carefully where two or more canonical Gospels relate what are obviously variant versions of the same story or saying to see this (cf., e.g., Mark 6:45-52/Matt. 14:22-32 or Mark 10:2-12/Matt. 19:3-12). This individuality is also illustrated in passages where two or more authors made similar choices about what to include. For example, the authors of Matthew and Luke both decided to include a genealogy (Matt. 1:1-17; Luke 3:23-38), but each genealogy is differently configured, differently placed in the narrative sequence of the Gospel, and designed to support a distinguishable christological point. We cannot attribute all of the differences that characterize each of the Gospels merely to the effects of transmission of Jesus tradition prior to the writing of these books. Clearly we are dealing in each case with *authors* as well as with shared traditions appropriated by each.

But these Gospels were literary works in the service of serious religious purposes. The authors wrote for other Christian readers and clearly aimed to have their works deemed useful to fellow religionists. That the authors did not attach their names to what they wrote probably indicates that the Gospels were offered in service of the faith they shared with their intended readers, and that they did not write to obtain a name for themselves or to promote themselves as authors. Even if they wanted to (and there is no good reason to think they did), they were not able to operate with the degree of authorial freedom that we associate with modern creative fiction, or with some modern notions of scholarly "creativity" in which one can write something quite deliberately at odds with what everyone else thinks and still aim for success in sales and notoriety, if not in persuading others of one's views. The canonical Gospels simply cannot be accounted for as to content, reasons for their composition, and their intended use except in light of the larger religious ethos and activities of the early Christian movement.

As to form, they are sequential narratives of Jesus' activities that have broad resemblance to biographical writings. As to contents, they incorporate early Christian traditions about Jesus, each author choosing which material to include, its arrangement/ordering, the "rendition" (i.e., the interpretive adaptation) of each unit of material, and the larger themes and emphases. The intended function of each canonical Gospel appears to have been to serve, support, and contribute toward shaping early Christian proclamation, teaching, worship, group solidarity, behavior, and apologetics. David Aune proposed that the Gospels were intended "to awaken or strengthen faith" and to convey and reinforce "the paradigmatic function of Jesus" for Christian behavior.[30] In the combination of their overall narrative form as sequentially arranged accounts of Jesus, the greater diversity of their contents in comparison with the kinds of writings about Jesus that likely preceded them, and to some degree, in their ambitious functions, the canonical Gospels constituted a new kind of Christian writing, a literary genre of considerable historical significance and subsequent influence.

The Gospels and Jewish Literature

The historical significance of the canonical Gospels is further indicated when compared with Jewish writings of the Roman period. Several scholars have drawn attention to the lack of anything directly comparable to the Gospels among rabbinic Jewish writings, and all have judged that this signals something very important that distinguishes early Christianity and rabbinic Judaism from each other.[31] Philip Alexander, for example, noted that the rabbinic corpus includes an abundance of stories and sayings of rabbinic sages, fully sufficient for connected accounts of such figures as Hillel, Shammai, or others. Yet, as he went on to emphasize, "there are no Rabbinic parallels to the Gospels as such," and he declared this "by far the most important single conclusion to emerge" from his investigation, describing it as "a profound enigma."[32]

30. Aune, *The New Testament*, 59-60.
31. Philip Alexander, "Rabbinic Biography and the Biography of Jesus: A Survey of the Evidence," in *Synoptic Studies: The Ampleforth Conferences of 1982 and 1983*, ed. C. M. Tuckett, JSNTSup 7 (Sheffield: JSOT Press, 1984), 19-50 (esp. 40-41); Jacob Neusner, *Why No Gospels in Talmudic Judaism?* BJS 135 (Atlanta: Scholars, 1988); Burridge, "Gospel Genre, Christological Controversy and the Absence of Rabbinic Biography."
32. Philip Alexander, 40.

In several works Jacob Neusner made similar observations about the lack of writings like the Gospels among rabbinic texts.[33] He helpfully makes direct comparisons between the Gospels and two rabbinic writings, *Pirke Aboth* (a tractate in the Mishnah, initially codified sometime after 200 C.E.) and *The Fathers according to Rabbi Nathan* (an amplification of *Pirke Aboth*).[34] A couple points will suffice here.

Pirke Aboth gives sayings of a number of revered sages, whereas in the Gospels Jesus is the sole authoritative figure. Although the rabbinic traditions about revered sages also include stories about their behavior, there is no connected narrative about any of them. These sages functioned genuinely as inspirational and exemplary figures, certainly; but for none of them is there any writing like the canonical Gospels.

More recently Richard Burridge has underscored this, in pointing to the significance of the Gospels as biographical-type writings devoted to Jesus. Burridge correctly proposes that the Gospel writers' decisions to write biographical-type accounts of Jesus had "important christological implications."[35] That is, as Philip Alexander also noted, the appearance of such writings in the early decades of the Christian movement obviously indicates "the central position that Jesus held in early Christianity," a position for which there was simply no equivalent in rabbinic Judaism.[36] In Burridge's view, the composition of the canonical Gospels, which he properly fits within the genre of ancient biographical writings (a matter to which I return in the next section), represented "an enormous christological and theological claim."[37]

I am less confident, however, with his passing observation that the rabbinic material, sayings and anecdotes about revered sages, is more like Q or the *Gospel of Thomas* than the canonical Gospels. This is of course correct, but only on a very general level of comparison. Q and *Thomas* are collections of sayings and anecdotal stories, not the sequential, biographical-type narratives found in

---

33. Neusner, *Why No Gospels?* esp. 33-47, 72. See also Neusner, *In Search of Talmudic Biography: The Problem of the Attributed Saying*, BJS 70 (Chico, Calif.: Scholars, 1984); Neusner, *Are There Really Tannaitic Parallels to the Gospels?* SFSHJ 80 (Atlanta: Scholars, 1993). Note similar observations also by A. Goshen Gottstein, "Jesus and Hillel: Are Comparisons Possible?" in *Hillel and Jesus*, ed. J. H. Charlesworth and L. L. Johns (Minneapolis: Fortress, 1997), 31-55, esp. 34-35.

34. H. L. Strack and G. Stemberger, *Introduction to the Talmud and Midrash*, trans. Markus Bockmuehl (Minneapolis: Fortress, 1992), 119-66 (on the Mishnah); R. Travers Herford, *The Ethics of the Talmud: Sayings of the Fathers* (New York: Schocken Books, 1962 [1945]), is a sympathetic commentary on *Pirke Aboth*.

35. Burridge, "Gospel Genre," 153.

36. Philip Alexander, 41.

37. Burridge, "Gospel Genre," 155.

the canonical Gospels.[38] But the differences between the relevant rabbinic texts on the one hand and Q and *Thomas* on the other are perhaps more significant than this very general similarity.

Unlike the rabbinic texts but like the canonical Gospels, both Q and *Thomas* are entirely about Jesus, who in both texts is the sole authoritative teacher. Moreover, as we noted in the preceding chapter, there are profound differences between the literary nature of Q and *Thomas*, the latter being a sayings collection with no obvious organizational scheme whereas Q seems to exhibit literary and rhetorical patterns at both the level of its component discourses and at the macrolevel of its overall organization. Indeed, the general structure of material in Q seems to reflect what I have referred to as an implicit narrative or a narrative substructure. Consequently, comparisons of rabbinic texts such as *Pirke Aboth* with the *Gospel of Thomas*, and even more so with Q, have only limited validity and usefulness. Even in these two early Christian texts we have a preoccupation with the person and significance of Jesus for which there is no equivalence in the rabbinic material.

But unquestionably, the narrative Gospels mark a further and very notable step in the literary expression of devotion to Jesus in first-century Christianity. How do we account historically for their appearance, when we reckon with the lack of rabbinic parallels to them and their innovative nature in comparison to the early Christian writings of the decades preceding their composition? They are an innovation in Christian writing. But are they therefore unique, or are they analogous to anything in the wider literary "environment" of their time?

The absence of rabbinic biographies does not mean the absence of Jewish biographical writings in the Roman period. In particular we have three extended biographical writings by Philo of Alexandria (ca. 20 B.C.E.–50 C.E.), on the biblical characters Abraham, Joseph, and Moses.[39] Philo presents these figures as living embodiments of God's law (the Torah given through Moses), in keeping with the Greek notion of biography as the presentation of characters who are exemplary of the qualities prized by those for whom one writes. We can also note the autobiographical account by Flavius Josephus (late first century C.E.), which reflects the same sort of purpose and understanding of biography. Only in this case, in what moderns will likely see as amusing self-promotion, Josephus presents himself as exemplary![40]

38. Burridge, "Gospel Genre," 151.

39. Text and translation in F. H. Colson, trans., *Philo with an English Translation*, LCL (Cambridge: Harvard University Press; London: William Heinemann, 1966), 6:2-593.

40. Text and translation, H. St. J. Thackery, *Josephus*, LCL (Cambridge: Harvard University Press; London: William Heinemann, 1966 [1926]), 1:2-159.

On the one hand these Jewish *bios* writings illustrate the influence of the larger literary environment. They help make it plausible to consider whether and how this literary environment helps us appreciate better the nature of the canonical Gospels. That is, the Gospel authors might have consciously and deliberately shaped their accounts in the light of their literary environment, and/ or they might have been unconsciously influenced and disposed by their literary and cultural environment to write the sorts of accounts they chose.

On the other hand, the Jewish *bios* writings clearly illustrate how the canonical Gospels do not fit perfectly within the conventions of Greek and Roman biography. These Jewish texts adopt the ancient notion that biography presents characters as exemplary of values and traits that are previously known and prized, and also in principle attainable, by the intended readers. The Gospels, by contrast, clearly present Jesus as unique; they reflect a powerful devotion to Jesus in particular that characterized early Christian groups. To be sure, the Jesus of the Gospels is also in some measure paradigmatic for his followers, but even in this he is not simply a paragon of general virtues such as courage, honesty, and wisdom. In all four accounts Jesus is presented as the unique envoy of God who announces and brings the kingdom of God in his own person and actions in an unparalleled way.

Furthermore, the lives of Abraham, Joseph, and Moses by Philo do not reflect a proclamation of these figures or a pattern of devotion focused on them. The Gospels, by contrast, clearly reflect the focus on Jesus that characterized all known varieties of early Christianity in their proclamation, their formation of behavior, and their sense of group identity. So the relevance of the larger Roman-era literary environment will have to be seen in connection with the particular purposes and ethos of early Christianity if we wish to take an adequate measure of the Gospels.

Nevertheless, it is worthwhile to consider now the larger cultural and literary context of the Gospels. Whatever the nature and degrees of their distinctiveness collectively and individually, it is reasonable to ask whether they may also have been shaped by this context. Because they are important literary artifacts of early Christian devotion to Jesus, it is appropriate to try to set them in their historical and literary environment.

The Roman-Era Literary Environment

Although for some time in the twentieth century the dominant view among New Testament scholars was that the canonical Gospels represented a novel and unique kind of writing without valid comparisons among Roman-era literature, in more recent years a growing number of scholars have concluded other-wise. It is increasingly clear that the Gospels can be validly compared with a broad and diverse genre of writings that are referred to as ancient biography, or *bios* writings.[41]

χ

In the last few decades a number of scholars have made important contri-butions to this discussion, including Charles Talbert, Philip Shuler, David Aune, Robert Guelich, Albrecht Dihle, and most recently, Richard Burridge.[42] This is a complex matter, however, and one gets the impression that scholars are sometimes talking past each other. Some emphasize the similarities of the Gos-pels and ancient *bios* literature (especially in some features of form and con-tents), and others emphasize the ways the Gospels differ and cannot be thought of simply as biographies of Jesus.[43] The best approach to the question is proba-bly to avoid oversimplification and to allow for a certain complexity.

To be sure, the Gospels have distinguishing features that reflect the par-ticular beliefs and orientation of early Christians, and signal their specific in-tended functions in early Christian circles. They cannot be accounted for solely on the basis of features analogous to Greek and Roman *bios* literature. Obvi-ously, the authors did not aspire simply to contribute literary biographies of Je-sus to the larger world of Roman-era literature. This is reflected in the authors

41. The scholar generally credited with shaping the view dominant for several decades that the canonical Gospels were a unique kind of writing is Karl Ludwig Schmidt, "Die Stellung der Evangelien in der allgemeinen Literaturgeschichte," in *Eucharisterion: Studien zur Religion und Literatur des Alten und Neuen Testaments. Hermann Gunkel zum 60. Geburtstag,* ed. Hans Schmidt (Göttingen: Vandenhoeck & Ruprecht, 1923), 50-134. A few years earlier Clyde Weber Votaw argued that the Gospels were to be likened to ancient biographies: *The Gospels and Con-temporary Biographies in the Greco-Roman World* (Philadelphia: Fortress, 1970), reprint of arti-cles from *AJT* 19 (1915): 45-73, 217-49. Votaw's basic view has been reaffirmed in most studies of the question in the last couple decades.

42. C. H. Talbert, *What Is a Gospel? The Genre of the Canonical Gospels* (Philadelphia: Fortress, 1977); Talbert, "Biographies of Philosophers and Rulers as Instruments of Religious Propaganda in Mediterranean Antiquity" in *ANRW,* 2.16/2:1619-57; P. L. Shuler, *A Genre for the Gospels: The Biographical Character of Matthew* (Philadelphia: Fortress, 1982); David E. Aune, "The Problem of the Genre of the Gospels: A Critique of C. H. Talbert's *What Is a Gospel?*" in *Gospel Perspectives 2,* ed. R. T. France and D. Wenham (Sheffield: JSOT, 1981), 9-60; Aune, *The New Testament in Its Literary Environment;* Robert A. Guelich, "The Gospel Genre," in *The Gos-pel and the Gospels,* ed. Peter Stuhlmacher (Grand Rapids: Eerdmans, 1991), 173-208; Albrecht Dihle, "The Gospels and Greek Biography," in *The Gospel and the Gospels,* 361-86; Richard A. Burridge, *What Are the Gospels? A Comparison with Graeco-Roman Biography,* SNTSMS 70 (Cambridge: Cambridge University Press, 1992).

43. E.g., John P. Meier, "Matthew, Gospel Of," in *ABD,* 4:622-41, rejects comparisons with Roman-era biography, insisting that the Gospel authors "created a new literary genre that is best labelled simply 'gospel'" (623).

not thinking it important to attach their names to their accounts. Moreover, I repeat that for them Jesus was not simply a great man who exemplified traits of character to be emulated. Instead, all four sought to promote the Christian view of Jesus as a uniquely significant figure, the singular vehicle of God's redemptive purposes. These authors saw their writings as part of the larger early Christian activities of proclamation, consolidation of converts, defense of faith, and formation of group identity. These wider and prior activities are the immediate context and the particular impetus of the canonical Gospels.[44]

But to associate a writing with this or that literary genre does not mean that it is the same in all respects as other examples of that genre. As previously noted, judgments about genre involve the contents, form, and intended function of a writing, and almost every genre has many examples that exhibit distinguishing features and interesting variations on general patterns, especially in form and contents. Furthermore, literary genres range from more narrowly defined examples (e.g., the modern paper in the experimental sciences) to broader and more loosely composed ones, and ancient biography was a rather broad classification. Also, literary genres can develop in particular directions over time, and in response to changing cultural factors. So, in considering whether and how the Gospels are like ancient *bios* literature, we should allow for differences as well as similarities, and assess the relative weight of each.

Alongside the differences, however, the Gospels do have a number of formal similarities to various examples of *bios* writings of the Greco-Roman era, as Burridge, for example, has shown.[45] Further, the Gospels and these non-Christian *bios* writings are all roughly contemporaneous. This makes it reasonable to consider the similarities in developing a view of what the Gospels were in their own setting, and why they took the form they did. The question is whether the ancient *bios* literature helps us understand any better what kinds of writings the Gospels are.

In practical terms "genre" refers to the features of a writing that set up certain expectations in readers and that dispose them to treat a given writing in a particular way. Thus, for example, we know to suspend disbelief in reading stories in the modern genre of science fiction, whereas we should demand to

---

44. Dihle ("The Gospels and Greek Biography") sensitively identifies the philosophical and political presuppositions behind ancient Greek biography and the Roman adaptation of the genre, and also notes how the Gospels reflect yet another standpoint.

45. Burridge, *What Are the Gospels?* It is interesting to note, e.g., G. N. Stanton's shift in view in response to Burridge's work. Cf. Stanton's earlier view in *Jesus of Nazareth in New Testament Preaching*, SNTSMS 27 (Cambridge: Cambridge University Press, 1974) and *The Gospels and Jesus* (Oxford: Oxford University Press, 1989), esp. 14-33, with his more recent expression in *A Gospel for a New People: Studies in Matthew* (Edinburgh: T. & T. Clark, 1992), 59-66.

know the experimental demonstration behind the results of a scientific paper. We know we are to react differently to the report of a violent murder in the newspaper than to the account of such a crime in a murder mystery novel. The practical question about the Gospels is whether they exhibit features from the wider literary practice of the time that appear to have been intended to dispose readers to respond to these writings in particular ways, or at least would have had such an effect upon readers.

In assessing the relevance of the larger literary environment of the first century, we have to make some distinctions among the four canonical Gospels. It may well be that the different authors related differently to their literary environment. The author of Luke-Acts shows some acquaintance with literary conventions and techniques of his day, and consciously employs them in his account of Jesus and the early church. The frequently noted prefaces to Luke (1:1-4) and Acts (1:1-2) in particular are clear evidence of this; other features in Luke-Acts also show an author working in light of the reading tastes and literary practices of the first century.[46] The genealogies in Matthew and Luke are another feature that gives each writing a more obvious biographical-like shape. They clearly did not get this feature from Mark, and neither genealogy seems to have been derived from the other. Instead, the two genealogies appear to have been composed independently of each other, either by the authors of Matthew and Luke or in the traditions upon which each drew. That both authors independently chose to include a genealogy of Jesus suggests that each of them consciously sought to augment thereby the Gospel pattern in Mark with fuller biographical material. With some justification David Aune has said the Gospels of Matthew and Luke, in particular, represent a "literaturization" of the Jesus tradition, which included taking Mark's account of Jesus (which has a more "popular" style) in a more recognizably biographical direction.[47]

46. Scholars disagree, however, as to which Roman-era genre gives us most appropriate comparisons for Acts. See, e.g., Loveday C. A. Alexander, *The Preface to Luke's Gospel: Literary Convention and Social Context in Luke 1.1-4 and Acts 1.1*, SNTSMS 78 (Cambridge: Cambridge University Press, 1993), who suggests comparisons with ancient technical treatises. Richard Pervo, *Profit with Delight* (Philadelphia: Fortress, 1987), contends that Acts has certain Roman-era "novelistic" features that were likely intended to make the account arresting and stimulating for readers. Cf. the following chapters in Bruce W. Winter and Andrew D. Clarke, eds., *The Book of Acts in Its Ancient Literary Setting*, The Book of Acts in Its First-Century Setting 1 (Grand Rapids: Eerdmans; Carlisle: Paternoster, 1993): Darryl W. Palmer, "Acts and the Ancient Historical Monograph," 1-29; L. C. A. Alexander, "Acts and Ancient Intellectual Biography," 31-63; and I. Howard Marshall, "Acts and the 'Former Treatise,'" 163-82.

47. Aune, *The New Testament*, 65-66. Aune identifies several features that suggest that "the Lukan and Matthean use and modification of Mark, together with other traditions, was a self-conscious literary enterprise" (66).

Does the ancient category of *bios* writing help us understand any better why the author of the Gospel of Mark wrote the account that he left us?[48] As already indicated, Mark, with all the canonical Gospels, shows a recognizable relationship to the sort of early Christian account of Jesus summarized by Paul in 1 Corinthians 15:1-7 as characteristic of various Christian groups. That is, the narrative character of the Gospels seems to derive at least in part from the narrative nature of at least much of early Christian proclamation, in which Jesus' death and resurrection were central. Further, as the Q material shows, a good deal of the wider tradition about Jesus took the form of anecdotes of his actions and sayings; yet Q appears itself to presuppose and reflect a narrative mode of discourse about Jesus. But Mark is not simply a string of anecdotes stuck onto an account of Jesus' death. Instead the author of Mark seems to have attempted in his own way to give an ordered *story* of Jesus.

In addition to rather elementary devices such as groupings by catchword (e.g., the "salt" sayings in Mark 9:49-50) and by kind of material (e.g., parables in 4:1-34; controversy stories in 2:1-28 and 12:13-37), there are also larger and more sophisticated patterns and arrangements of material (e.g., the three cycles of passion prediction–disciples' misunderstanding–clarification of discipleship in 8:31–10:45). Therefore the Gospel of Mark, too, constitutes (although in a more modest way) a "literaturization" of tradition about Jesus. That is, Mark is a *written* rendition of Jesus from the beginning of his activities through his death and resurrection, with the material in between ordered in rough sequence and in purposeful manner.

Granted, Mark shows far less than Luke and Matthew do the influence or imitation of more formal literary practices and conventions. Nevertheless, the literary and cultural environment, in which *bios* writings had become a feature, may well have disposed the author of Mark toward preparing an account of Jesus that in a certain sense presents him in heroic terms. In other words, it seems reasonable that the larger cultural and literary environment provided all the authors of the canonical Gospels, including Mark, with a broad concept and category for use in their aim to write books about Jesus. This concept comprised the "life" of a figure given in the form of a sequential narrative, and this may have made a written presentation of Jesus in narrative form seem to the authors both an appropriate and attractive step to take.

As Richard Burridge has proposed, the choice to write books about Jesus in the *bios* shape likely seemed to the Gospel authors an effective way to focus attention on the person of Jesus as "a unique individual revealing God

---

48. Cf. Joel Marcus, *Mark 1–8: A New Translation with Introduction and Commentary*, AB (New York: Doubleday, 2000), 64-69.

in his deeds and words, life, death and resurrection."[49] For making this kind of christological emphasis, the basic *bios* form excelled other and prior modes of Jesus tradition, such as collections of miracles, anecdotes, and teachings, and rehearsals of the death-resurrection proclamation as well. In the canonical Gospels these various types of discourses about Jesus were assembled in larger, continuous, biographical-type narratives, each Gospel providing a memorable and cohesive portrait and rendition of Jesus. The beliefs that moved them and that they sought to promote, involving claims about Jesus' unique significance, differed radically from the philosophical bases of ancient Greek biography. This required the authors to write accounts of Jesus that went beyond the customary aims of the genre, and the Gospels constitute a distinctive kind (or subgenre) of *bios* literature. But the flexibility of the *bios* genre was such that the authors apparently saw it as a literary form they could successfully adapt in their individual ways to serve the profound, christologically driven, and ecclesiologically oriented concerns that moved them to write.

If so, then a confluence of factors shape the Gospels as particular expressions of devotion to Jesus. In addition to the religious experiences of the authors and of those who shaped the Christian religious ethos of which the authors were a part, there is also the effect of the larger cultural environment. Such a confluence of factors is not unusual in the history of religions, and this particular confluence seems perfectly plausible.

Yet we also have to remember that written accounts of Jesus with this quasi-*bios* character were not written immediately in early Christianity, and also that other kinds of "Jesus books" appeared both before and after the narrative Gospels of the New Testament. These other kinds of writings about Jesus, previous ones such as Q and subsequent ones such as *Gospel of Thomas* and other extracanonical writings, were also produced by people living in the same broad period of the Roman era. So obviously the general literary environment does not by itself explain the appearance of the narrative Gospels. Factors particular to all these authors, their circumstances, beliefs, concerns, and religious outlook, were influential as well. In the next section I consider individual Jesus books, what may have prompted their authors, and what each represents as an expression about Jesus.

49. Burridge, "Gospel Genre," 156.

The Synoptic Renditions of Jesus

Each of the "Jesus books" of early Christianity presents Jesus from a given standpoint, with particular emphases, and for particular purposes.[50] To use a musical metaphor, in each book we have a "rendition" of Jesus. To stay with the musical imagery: the differences among the various renditions in the Jesus books of the first two centuries range from interesting variations on a recognizably common "score," or at least a common basic "melody line," all the way to what seem to be performances of a very different composition altogether. Even among the examples examined in this and later chapters, the four canonical Gospels and a few of the earliest extracanonical writings about Jesus, we can see this range of variations.

In what follows it will not be possible to discuss in detail all the questions about the religious beliefs of the individual writers.[51] Whole volumes have been written (and continue to be written!) on the Christology of individual Gospels, and there is an oceanic amount of journal literature on a plethora of related questions. In this book my primary aims are to analyze the larger historical developments in devotion to Jesus across the better part of the first two centuries. So the main tasks in the following discussion will be to characterize the distinguishing features of each one and to set each in the larger context of the devotion to Jesus attested for the time frame we are considering here. The latter task will involve addressing questions about how and why the individual books may have been composed.

Mark

If we assume the dominant scholarly view that the Gospel of Mark was the first sequentially arranged narrative account of Jesus, and that Mark was then used as principal source by the authors of Matthew and Luke, Mark is particularly important in historical terms. Mark powerfully influenced and/or rather successfully anticipated what became a popularly received shape for books about Jesus, and how Jesus was subsequently "rehearsed" in Christian tradition. An-

---

50. In addition to the plenitude of studies of individual writings, see also the study of the four canonical Gospels by Rudolf Schnackenburg, *Jesus in the Gospels: A Biblical Christology*, trans. O. C. Dean, Jr. (Louisville: Westminster John Knox, 1995).

51. The authors of the four canonical Gospels do not identify themselves, and the traditional authorship is today rightly disputed or treated with caution. In what follows, where I refer to the authors by their traditional names, e.g., "Mark," I do so only for the sake of convenience and intend no claim about authorship.

other way to think of the "Synoptic" Gospels (Matthew, Mark, and Luke) is to see them as having a basic "Markan" shape and character, which means as literary renditions of Jesus in a narrative mode and with an obviously similar story line. Indeed, for all its distinctives, even the Gospel of John has some basic similarities to the Synoptic renditions, whether this is due to Markan inspiration/influence or to coincidence. As the earliest such account of Jesus, therefore, the Gospel of Mark justifiably receives our attention first.

In my earlier discussion of the basic literary features shared by the canonical Gospels, I summarized the basic "plot" or story line reflected in them all. In Mark we have not only the earliest but also the most compact presentation of this basic story.[52] I use the word "compact" because Mark is not merely shorter overall, it is also a comparatively simpler account that moves much more directly from beginning through to end.[53] I illustrate this with something easily confirmed: although Mark frequently refers to teaching as one of Jesus' main activities, Mark has considerably less sayings material than Matthew and Luke and devotes proportionately less space to Jesus' sayings.[54] There are a few blocks of teaching material (parables in 4:1-32; teaching on what defiles in 7:1-23; the eschatological discourse in 13:3-37), but otherwise the narrative moves along without the major "interruption" of discourses such as those that are so prominent in Matthew. For the most part, Jesus' teachings are given in narrative episodes, such as the controversy stories in 2:1–3:6 or the numerous scenes with disciples in 8:27–10:45. Readers experience an account much more dominated by narrative action, which comes at a faster pace than in the other canonical Gospels.

As is also well known, Mark's account focuses on Jesus' adult life and activity, commencing with his baptism in response to John the Baptist and running on through to his execution and the announcement of his resurrection. During the narrative we are given some personal background, that he comes from Nazareth (1:9), and something of his family (3:20-21, 31-35; 6:1-6), but unlike Matthew and Luke, Mark gives no account of Jesus' birth and no family genealogy. Nor, as is now commonly accepted by scholars, did Mark give any narrative of the appearances of the risen Jesus. Instead the story ends with the announcement of Jesus' resurrection and the women followers of Jesus being

---

52. David M. Rhoads and Donald Mitchie, *Mark as Story: An Introduction to the Narrative of a Gospel* (Philadelphia: Fortress, 1982).

53. Often, however, Mark's account of individual incidents is longer, more wordy, than the parallel in Matthew and/or Luke. At the level of individual incidents, thus, Mark may reflect a closer proximity to features of oral storytelling.

54. See, e.g., Robert P. Meye, *Jesus and the Twelve: Discipleship and Revelation in Mark's Gospel* (Grand Rapids: Eerdmans, 1968), 30-87.

charged to convey Jesus' summons to Peter and the other disciples to encounter him in Galilee (16:1-8).[55] I shall say more about a probable reason for the shape and limits of the Markan story line later. But for now, let us observe some of the features of Mark's story of Jesus.

This relative simplicity of Mark's story line makes it easier to see the author's emphases, and provokes some interesting observations. The main point is that this simple story line is the vehicle of a rather carefully nuanced and impressive presentation of Jesus.[56] The Jesus of Mark is an active and vigorous figure; the limitation of the story line to his adult activity reinforces this impression. The focus on narrative action is furthered through the geographical movements frequently mentioned in the text (e.g., back and forth across Lake Galilee, movement about in Galilee and elsewhere, and a final journey to Jerusalem). There is also a strong sense of drama, bafflement, and conflict. From his initial appearance in the narrative onward, Jesus acts with divine approbation (1:11), yet already in the healing story in 2:1-12 opponents accuse him of blasphemy (v. 7), and in the first scene of public activity and thereafter the crowds of ordinary people scarcely know what to think of him (e.g., 1:27-28). Much earlier than in the other Synoptic Gospels, Mark sounds the conflictual and ominous note of a conspiracy to destroy Jesus (3:6), the shadow of Jesus' cross thus falling across the entire account thereafter.

Several allied themes combine further to make the Markan Jesus a figure of power and transcendent significance.[57] Some scenes do seem "epiphanic," with Jesus pictured in actions deliberately likened to God's. The two sea-miracle stories are important examples.[58] In one story (4:35-41), after being awakened by the disciples, Jesus dramatically orders the wind and sea to be still. The disciples' awe-filled question in verse 41, "Who then is this, that even the wind and the sea obey him?" underscores the scope of power displayed, and functions rhetorically to hint at the right answer, that Jesus has shown godlike

---

55. Contrary to many scholars, I do not understand Mark 16:8 as portraying the women disciples as disobeying the instruction of the "young man" at the tomb. On the Greek phrasing of 16:8, see David R. Catchpole, "The Fearful Silence of the Women at the Tomb: A Study in Markan Theology," *Journal of Theology for Southern Africa* 18 (1977): 3-10.

56. Among the vast scholarly literature on the Markan presentation of Jesus, see, e.g., Jack Dean Kingsbury, *The Christology of Mark's Gospel* (Philadelphia: Fortress, 1983); Philip G. Davis, "Mark's Christological Paradox," *JSNT* 35 (1989): 3-18; and the recent review of scholarly studies by Jacob Chacko Naluparayil, "Jesus of the Gospel of Mark: Present State of Research," *CRBS* 8 (2000): 191-226.

57. For an insightful sketch of Mark's combined emphasis on Jesus as human and also participating in divine attributes and functions, see Davis, "Mark's Christological Paradox."

58. See now the discussion by Marcus, *Mark 1–8*, 332-40 (on 4:35-41) and 421-35 (on 6:45-52).

superiority over the elements. In the other sea miracle Jesus walks across the stormy waves to the disciples who are struggling with rowing in their boat; again the sea and wind become calm at his command, all this producing understandable amazement in his disciples (6:51). The reference to their inability to perceive the truth about Jesus that is revealed in the scene (6:52) is obviously intended to provoke readers to draw the proper christological conclusion. Jesus' actions here, which include a numinous self-identification, "I am he" (*egō eimi*, 6:50), echo biblical references to God's own use of the same formula and his power over the sea.[59] Marcus has observed that although Mark does not explicitly claim divinity for Jesus, "he comes very close to doing so here," and Marcus rightly judges that "the overwhelming impact made by our narrative is an impression of Jesus' divinity."[60]

The two feeding accounts (6:30-44; 8:1-9) are likewise epiphanic stories with numerous allusions to Old Testament passages about God's miraculous provision, especially passages relating to Passover and to Moses and Israel in the wilderness. We cannot explore here the details of either passage. But, as Marcus stated about the feeding of the four thousand in 8:1-9, in fact each feeding account is "for those with eyes to see, a 'secret epiphany'" revealing Jesus as the special vehicle of God's eschatological power.[61] The Markan scene where Jesus presses his disciples unsuccessfully about the meaning of the number of baskets of fragments gathered after each feeding (8:17-21) indicates that the feeding accounts disclose important truth about Jesus. The earlier reference to the disciples' failure to perceive the meaning of the first feeding miracle (6:52) confirms that the author points readers to the feeding miracles as especially important disclosures of Jesus' significance.

There are also the frequently noted summary statements in Mark which focus on Jesus as both teacher and miracle worker (e.g., 1:34, 39; 3:11-12).[62] Jesus' power over demons is a particular emphasis among his miracles.[63] In the first Markan scene of Jesus' ministry (1:21-28), he teaches and delivers a demoniac,

---

59. God's power over the sea: e.g., Job 9:8; Pss. 77:19; 107:23-32; Isa. 43:16. "I am" as divine self-identification: e.g., Isa. 43:11, 25; Exod. 3:13-14.

60. Marcus, *Mark 1–8*, 432.

61. Marcus, *Mark 1–8*, 497. For the allusions to Old Testament passages and a reasoned treatment of both feeding accounts overall, see 404-21 (on 6:30-44), 482-97 (on 8:1-9).

62. Timothy Dwyer, "The Motif of Wonder in the Gospel of Mark," *JSNT* 57 (1995): 49-59, argues that the bewildered response of the crowds to Jesus' miracles is not presented negatively. Against proposals that the miraculous element in Mark is simply a pandering to popular notions of "divine men," see, e.g., Barry Blackburn, *Theios Anēr and the Markan Miracle Traditions: A Critique of the* Theios Anēr *Concept as an Interpretative Background of the Miracle Traditions Used by Mark*, WUNT 2/40 (Tübingen: J. C. B. Mohr [Paul Siebeck], 1991).

63. James M. Robinson, *The Problem of History in Mark* (London: SCM Press, 1968).

and the longest and most detailed miracle story is about the demoniac afflicted with a legion of demons (5:1-20). Exorcism figures prominently in the summary statements mentioned already, and Mark describes Jesus appointing the Twelve to preach, giving to them authority to cast out demons as well (3:14-15; cf. Matt. 10:1; Luke 9:1). The Markan Jesus himself makes it clear that his exorcisms are not merely feats of power; instead they vividly demonstrate the binding of "the strong man," Satan, and the "plundering" of his "household" (3:23-27). Consequently Jesus warns those who dismiss his miracles as sorcery that they are in danger of blasphemy against the Holy Spirit, the divine power at work in him (3:28-30).

This concern to disassociate Jesus' miracles from magic and sorcery may at least in part account for the way Mark handles Semitic expressions on the lips of Jesus. There are in fact more Semitic loanwords in Mark overall than in the other canonical Gospels, and they appear particularly in accounts of miracles and other numinous scenes *("Abba"* in Jesus' prayer in Gethsemane, and his utterance on the cross, *"Eloi, Eloi, lema sabachthani").*[64] This might at first appear similar to the use of incomprehensible, foreign terms characteristic of Greco-Roman era magic. Indeed, the use of real or phony Semitic terms and names seems to have been thought especially potent.[65] But the Semitic expressions used in the Markan miracle stories are consistently translated, which is the decisive difference from all known magical texts, and also clear indication that the aim is precisely to disassociate them from magical practices.[66]

In the Markan scenes of exorcism the recognition of Jesus by demons dramatically shows his superiority, and in their acclamations they testify to his transcendent status: "the Holy One of God" (1:24), "the Son of God" (3:11), "Son of the Most High God" (5:7), all echoing God's own affirmation of Jesus' filial status (1:11; 9:7). One of the several Markan uses of irony is that the demons, those powers that Jesus comes to destroy, recognize Jesus' transcendent status. The human characters, however, in one way or another miss the truth.

---

64. In addition to the transliterated Semitic words/expressions that Mark shares with the other Gospels (mentioned earlier in this chapter), a number of others appear only in Mark, for which the text gives a translation equivalent: *Korban* ("offering/gift" [*dōron*], 7:11), *Boanerges* ("sons of thunder," 3:17), *Abba* ("father," 14:36), *talitha koum* ("little girl [*korasion*], arise," 5:41), and *ephphatha* ("be opened," 7:34). R. E. Brown refers to Mark's "tendency" to give transliterated Aramaic (whereas, e.g., the preference in Matthew is for transliterated Hebrew): *Death of the Messiah,* 2:1052 and n. 62.

65. Campbell Bonner, *Studies in Magical Amulets, Chiefly Graeco-Egyptian* (Ann Arbor: University of Michigan Press; London: Oxford University Press, 1950), 186-95.

66. In all the canonical Gospels, the only Semitic loanwords for which there is no translation are *Amen* and the *Hosanna* of the crowds in Jesus' final entry into Jerusalem (Mark 11:9-10/Matt. 21:9/John 12:13).

The religious authorities consistently mislabel him (e.g., as a blasphemer, 2:7; 14:63-64; or a sorcerer, 3:22), and the crowds and Jesus' own disciples scarcely know what to make of him (e.g., 1:27-28; 2:12; 4:41; cf. 8:27-28).[67]

Indeed, the question of Jesus' true significance and identity pulses through the whole of Mark. In a pivotal scene Jesus himself puts the question of his status directly to his disciples (8:27-30), alluding back to an earlier passage where various inadequate responses to him are listed (6:14-16). The various opinions of him by the people (John the Baptist, Elijah, one of the prophets), and even the messianic acclamation expressed by Peter in 8:29, all fall far short of understanding who he really is and what he must do. The author uses the obtuseness of crowds and disciples to underscore for readers the truth missed by the characters in the narrative.[68] Thus, for example, the questions about what to make of Jesus from those who witness the exorcism in the synagogue (1:27), and from the disciples after the storm stilling (4:41), are clearly intended to provoke in the readers a knowing smile. From the opening words in 1:1, Mark affirms that Jesus is "Christ," and then in 1:11 and several episodes thereafter attributes to Jesus divine sonship. But Mark emphasizes that it is Jesus himself who gives the christological titles and categories their proper meaning.[69]

In Mark the full truth is emphatically paradoxical. The Jesus who is the divine Son and David's lord (12:35-37), and who will be given glorious vindication by God (14:62), is also "the son of man" who came "to serve, and to give his life a ransom for many" (10:45). In another important irony, the Markan crucifixion narrative makes the mockeries of Jesus' opponents speak the truth of his person and work. Readers are to understand that Jesus really is the king of the

---

67. Jerry Camery-Hoggatt, *Irony in Mark's Gospel: Text and Subtext*, SNTSMS 72 (Cambridge: Cambridge University Press, 1992).

68. John R. Donahue, "Jesus as the Parable of God in the Gospel of Mark," *Int* 32 (1978): 369-86, notes some thirty-four references in Mark to "surprise, wonder, awe, and fear," and points out that "these reactions embrace all the major aspects of Jesus' ministry" (380-81). On Mark's presentation of the disciples, see, e.g., David J. Hawkin, "The Incomprehension of the Disciples in the Marcan Redaction," *JBL* 91 (1972): 491-500; Robert C. Tannehill, "The Disciples in Mark: The Function of a Narrative Role," *JR* 57 (1977): 386-405.

69. Adela Yarbro Collins, "Mark and His Readers: The Son of God among Greeks and Romans," *HTR* 93 (2000): 85-100, helpfully provides background on the usage of divine sonship language in Jewish tradition and pagan culture of the first century. But curiously, she does not consider whether Mark presents readers with a basis for reinterpreting such language in the light of the story of Jesus he conveys. That is, the intended readers of Mark were likely Christians, whether from Jewish or Gentile background; so their understanding of such language would also likely have been shaped by their Christian associations and usage, and not merely by their respective pre-Christian cultural backgrounds.

Jews and Israel (15:18, 26), and that, <u>in truth, to save others "he cannot save him-</u> ✗
<u>self</u>" (15:31-32). In fact, <u>only through and after Jesus' obedient death can the</u>
<u>truth of his person be perceived clearly and then correctly proclaimed.</u> Thus the
centurion's statement in 15:39, "Truly, this man was God's Son," spoken as he
sees Jesus' death, is also probably intended to portray him as inadvertently
pointing to the truth that Jesus really is God's Son.[70] <u>The only human figure</u>
(demoniacs do not qualify!) <u>allowed in Mark to refer to Jesus' divine sonship</u>
<u>does so in light of Jesus' crucifixion, and ironically, the figure in question is in</u>
<u>charge of carrying out the execution.</u>[71]

The revelatory importance of Jesus' crucifixion also explains the secrecy
motif in Mark.[72] For example, although the demonic acclamation of Jesus as
God's Son is verbally correct, Jesus consistently silences the demons (1:25, 34;
3:11-12) because his divine sonship cannot be understood properly apart from
the insight given through his obedient death. Similarly, following the transfiguration scene and God's affirmation of Jesus as divine Son, Jesus orders the three
disciples not to speak of the matter until after his resurrection (9:9), which obviously presupposes his death. Likewise, Jesus forbids the disciples to speak of
him as Messiah (8:30) because, in his divinely mandated sufferings which he refers to repeatedly in the following chapters (8:31; 9:31; 10:32-34), he must first **L**
(re)define and reveal what messiahship really means.

I emphasize that <u>Mark describes the *redefinition* of royal messiahship in</u>
<u>Jesus</u>, not a rejection of the Messiah category altogether. Any notion that Mark
advocates a "Son of Man Christology" over against views of Jesus as Messiah
and Son of God has no basis. Likewise, it is incorrect to think that he plays off
against each other the traditions he relates about Jesus' miraculous works and
the theme of Jesus' suffering.[73] Surely, any such notion is immediately implau-

---

70. As Earl S. Johnson has noted, the imperfect-tense verb in 15:39 (*ēn*, "he was") shows
that the centurion does not directly mouth the confession of the intended readers, for whom Jesus now *is* God's Son ("Is Mark 15:39 the Key to Mark's Christology?" *JSNT* 31 [1987]: 3-22, esp. 7-
8).

71. Whether the centurion's statement in Mark 15:39 is to be taken as a full declaration of
the christological insight advocated in Mark or as an imperfect and ironic "pagan" expression
("this one was a son of god"), early Christian readers/audiences of Mark were likely expected to
see the centurion's statement as anticipating their own acclamations of Jesus. For an argument
that the centurion's statement functions as the christological climax of Mark, see, e.g., Davis,
"Mark's Christological Paradox."

72. Among the voluminous literature on this topic, see, e.g., J. D. G. Dunn, "The Messianic Secret in Mark," *TB* 21 (1970): 92-117, who critiques William Wrede, *Das Messiasgeheimnis
in den Evangelien* (1901); ET, *The Messianic Secret* (Cambridge: James Clark, 1971).

73. See Kingsbury's cogent critique of various theories of "corrective Christology" in
Mark: *Christology of Mark's Gospel*, 25-45.

sible because of the amount of space Mark devotes to accounts of Jesus' miracles, which the author obviously thought an important feature of his portrayal of Jesus! Instead, the Markan account makes the point that the Jesus who surrenders to his divinely ordained destiny of redemptive suffering is also the divinely empowered figure who heals the sick, delivers demoniacs, stills the wind and waves, and even raises the dead (5:35-43). Mark does not sentimentalize weakness and suffering over against some supposed "divine man" Christology; instead the author enables Jesus' miraculous power and obedient suffering to illuminate each other. Thus, in Mark, Jesus' miracles are not mere wonders, but must be seen in the light of the redemptive purposes more fully disclosed in his death; at the same time, the miracles indicate the divinely empowered and authoritative status of the suffering Jesus.[74]

The Son of Man

In attempting to characterize Mark's presentation of Jesus, we also have to take account of the repeated use of the expression "the son of man," which in fact appears numerous times in all four canonical Gospels.[75] At the risk of attempting the impossible, I shall endeavor to deal with this thorny matter adequately for my main concern of analyzing the ways early Christians expressed their beliefs in and devotion to Jesus, and as briefly as possible. So I am not here primarily concerned with questions about whether Jesus used some equivalent Aramaic expression and what it meant for him to do so. These "historical Jesus" questions have in fact fueled most other inquiries about "the son of man" expression (and have not led to any consensus, despite the strenuous assertions of particular advocates of this or that view). I will address questions about what kind of expression Jesus might have used (e.g., in Aramaic) only insofar as they

74. Marcus, *Mark 1–8*, 75-79, gives a balanced discussion along similar lines.

75. The scholarly publications on the expression are so numerous that it is practical here to cite only selected studies. Among recent publications, Douglas R. A. Hare, *The Son of Man Tradition* (Minneapolis: Fortress, 1990), is a particularly thorough discussion. For a history of scholarship on the expression, see now Delbert Burkett, *The Son of Man Debate: A History and Evaluation*, SNTSMS 107 (Cambridge: Cambridge University Press, 1999). In his review of Burkett's book, Dale C. Allison (*JBL* 119 [2000]: 766-68) likely expressed the doubts of many that "the guild will ever again be able to approach a consensus on the meaning of 'Son of Man' in the canonical Gospels or whether Jesus ever used the expression and, if so, to what end" (768). Most often the expression is capitalized, but this would be appropriate only if it were clearly a fixed honorific title, which is precisely a prior question to be addressed. Consequently I lowercase the phrase in this discussion. Cf. also the review of issues and scholarship by Otto Michel and I. H. Marshall, "Son," in *NIDNTT*, 3:613-34. Gustaf Dalman, *The Words of Jesus*, trans. D. M. Kay (Edinburgh: T. & T. Clark, 1902), 234-67, remains an important analysis of the linguistic data.

assist us in understanding how and why early Christians read the expression so consistently in the canonical accounts of his ministry.[76]

First, let us quickly note the basic data concerning the use of the expression in the New Testament. The precise expression "the son of man" appears some 81 times altogether in the four canonical Gospels (14 times in Mark, 30 in Matthew, 25 in Luke, and 12 in John).[77] It is important to underscore that in all these cases the Greek form of the expression includes the definite article in a stereotyped and formulaic construction, *ho huios tou anthrōpou*.[78]

Furthermore, this particular set of words, with the definite article, is a rather novel and unusual expression in Greek. Prior to the canonical Gospels we have no instance of this expression in the entirety of extant Greek literature of the ancient world.[79] There are related expressions in the Greek Old Testament (the singular form without the definite article, "a son of man," and the plural forms, "[the] sons of men," used more often with the article but less frequently without the article), but there is no instance of the singular form with

76. Hare, 21-27, somewhat similarly advocated starting with the empirical Greek data of the canonical Gospels, leaving the question of what kind of Aramaic expression Jesus might have used to a subsequent stage of investigation.

77. For an overview of the use of the expression in each canonical Gospel, see I. H. Marshall, "Son of Man," in *DJG*, 775-81, but I dissent from some of his conclusions about the origins and function of the phrase.

78. The statement in John 5:27 that God has given "the/his Son" authority to execute judgment *hoti huios anthrōpou estin* should probably be translated "because he is a son of man," meaning "because he is (also) a human being/a man." So also Ragnar Leivestad, "Exit the Apocalyptic Son of Man," *NTS* 18 (1971-72): 252; Hare, 255. This reference does not fit the otherwise consistent pattern, either in form or in syntactical function. (But cf. C. F. D. Moule, *An Idiom Book of New Testament Greek* [Cambridge: Cambridge University Press, 1963], 116, who notes that the absence of the definite articles in this case may be accounted for by the *huios anthrōpou* coming before the verb in the sentence.) In any case, contra numerous commentators, in this verse we do not have a reference to the supposed title of an apocalyptic figure; cf., e.g., C. K. Barrett, *The Gospel according to St. John*, 2nd ed. (London: SPCK; Philadelphia: Westminster, 1978), 262-63. Such an "exegesis" simply presupposes precisely what must first be demonstrated, and has not been demonstrated: i.e., that "(the) son of man" was an established title in pre-Christian Jewish tradition.

79. I could find no trace of this particular expression prior to the Gospels, using the *Thesaurus Linguae Graecae* to search several hundred years of ancient Greek literature. Moreover, outside the LXX, one instance in Philo (*Vit. Mos.* 1.283), and early Christian writings, there is no usage of "(a) son of man" (i.e., without the definite article), and no instance of the plural "sons of men" with or without the article. As C. F. D. Moule pointed out, however, although the expression is novel, the grammar (noun with definite article followed by genitive noun and corresponding definite article) is fully acceptable Greek: "Neglected Features in the Problem of 'the Son of Man,'" in *Neues Testament und Kirche*, ed. Joachim Gnilka (Freiburg: Herder, 1974), 413-28, esp. 420. On the use/nonuse of the Greek definite article in such phrases, see, e.g., BDF §259.

the definite article.[80] In this the Greek Old Testament reflects the pattern of the underlying Hebrew and Aramaic passages, in which we find no instance of the equivalent of "the son of man" (with the Hebrew definite article, or the Aramaic emphatic form). I shall say more about the likely significance of the peculiar and consistent use of the definite article in the Gospels' expression a bit later.

It is also striking that in all four Gospels, "the son of man" is used only by Jesus (except for John 12:34, where the Jewish crowd asks Jesus what he means by the expression). In linguistics the term that refers to this kind of distinctive pattern of speech of an individual is "idiolect," and we may say that "the son of man" in the Gospels is a characteristic feature of Jesus' idiolect or distinctive "voice" (manner of speaking).[81] Moreover, whatever may be speculated about

80. The indefinite form, "son of man" (without article), appears about ten times in the LXX (e.g., Pss. 8:4; 79:15 [Heb. 80:15]), and another ninety-one times or so in Ezekiel in the vocative form "O son of man" *(huie anthrōpou)*. The plural form without the article is used about eleven times (e.g., Ps. 4:2), and with the article about twenty-six times (e.g., Ps. 10:5 [Heb 11:4]). Philo has "the sons of men" only twice *(Conf. ling.* 11 and 142), each time in a biblical quotation. The Hebrew construction most common for the singular is *ben 'adam* ("a son of man," ninety-three quasi-vocative uses in Ezekiel, plus another fourteen uses elsewhere), with *ben 'enosh* used once in Ps. 144:3 (LXX 143:3). Behind the Greek plural most commonly is *b^eney 'adam*, and occasionally *b^eney 'ish* (e.g., Pss. 4:2; and 62:9 [LXX 61:9]), where these two Hebrew constructions are used synonymously. In Aramaic portions of Daniel, "son of man" translates *bar 'enash* (e.g., 7:13), and the plural form is *b^eney 'enasha'* (2:38). See J. A. Fitzmyer, "The New Testament Title 'Son of Man' Philologically Considered," in *A Wandering Aramean: Collected Aramaic Essays*, SBLMS 25 (Missoula: Scholars, 1979), 143-60, esp. 146. Fitzmyer discusses the apparent addition of the definite article in a manuscript of the Qumran text 1QS11:20, producing *ben ha-'adam*, the sole ancient example of this precise Hebrew construction.

81. Another of the features of Jesus' "idiolect" in the Gospels is the expression "Truly, I say" *(Amēn, legō)*, used some 49 times in the Synoptics (Matthew, 30; Mark, 13; Luke, 6; and cf. Luke's several uses of "truly" [*alēthōs*], 9:27; 12:44; 21:3; and *ep' alētheias*, 4:25). John consistently prefers the variant form "Truly, truly, I say" *(Amēn, amēn legō*, 25 times). As with "the son of man," this formulaic and nonresponsive use of "amen" is not attested outside the Gospels, where in frequency and fixity it is a distinctive speech-formula of Jesus. See, e.g., H.-W. Kuhn, "αμην," in *EDNT*, 1:70; Hans Bietenhard, "Amen," in *NIDNTT*, 1:97-99; cf. Bruce Chilton, "Amen," in *ABD*, 1:184-86 (and the references cited there). Joachim Jeremias drew attention to some distinctive features of Jesus' "voice" in the Gospels in *The Prayers of Jesus*, SBTss 6 (London: SCM Press, 1967), 108-15, including a treatment of the "amen" expressions (112-15). Curiously, however, he did not include reference to "the son of man" construction. For the linguistics use of "idiolect," see, e.g., John Lyons, *Language and Linguistics: An Introduction* (Cambridge: Cambridge University Press, 1981), 26-27. It is a continuing curiosity that biblical scholars, whose work involves precise judgments about words, are only occasionally acquainted with the valuable insights and categories of modern linguistics. See a similar observation by Lincoln D. Hurst, "The Neglected Role of Semantics in the Search for the Aramaic Words of Jesus," *JSNT* 28 (1986): 63-80, and Eugene A. Nida, "Implications of Contemporary Linguistics for

any prior meaning of the expression, in the Gospels "the son of man" always functions as Jesus' self-designation, indeed his most characteristic form of self-reference. In fact, where it appears, "the son of man" essentially functions as a semantic equivalent for the emphatic first-person pronoun ("I/me/my"). As Leivestad observed in an important article, we can substitute the appropriate first-person pronoun for "the son of man" in the sentences with no difficulty.[82]

Additionally, the expression appears only once in the rest of the New Testament (Acts 7:56), and is never used as a confessional title for Jesus.[83] That is, the phrase *never* functions *itself* to express an honorific claim made about Jesus. Even within the Gospels no one ever addresses Jesus as "the son of man," proclaims him to be such, or contests his own use of the expression; and it never functions with the several other appellations bandied about as possible categories for Jesus, such as "a prophet/one of the prophets," John the Baptizer, Messiah, Son of God/the Blessed (e.g., Mark 6:14-15; 8:27-29; 14:62; Matt. 26:63; and cf. also the various appellatives directed to John the Baptizer in John 1:25).[84] So

---

Biblical Scholarship," *JBL* 91 (1972): 73-89. On determining meanings, see, e.g., Ruth M. Kempson, *Semantic Theory,* Cambridge Textbooks in Linguistics (Cambridge: Cambridge University Press, 1977).

82. Leivestad, "Exit the Apocalyptic," esp. 256. Leivestad properly saw John 5:27 as an exception, because "a son of man" here is not the otherwise consistent phrasing; but in my judgment he erred in seeing John 9:35 as another exception. In my view, in the latter reference, as in all the other eighty in the Gospels, readers are intended to take "the son of man" as synonymous for Jesus. Delbert Burkett, "The Nontitular Son of Man: A History and Critique," *NTS* 40 (1994): 504-21, objects that "the son of man" is not used in "mundane" statements but "only with reference to his coming and ministry" (506). But this is hardly persuasive. How many "mundane" statements of Jesus are there in the Gospels with which to make comparison! Moreover, granted that "the son of man" functions in sentences about Jesus' work and fate, it remains the case that in these sentences the expression clearly functions as a self-referential formula, and that the variation between *egō* and *huios tou anthrōpou* in manifestly parallel versions of the same sayings demonstrates a certain interchangeable usage in the Jesus tradition.

83. The variation between the first-person pronoun and "the son of man" in parallel sayings in the canonical Gospels is clear indication that in the Jesus tradition of that time these two forms of Jesus' self-reference were taken as somewhat interchangeable (e.g., Luke 6:22/Matt. 5:11; Matt. 16:13/Luke 9:18/Mark 8:27; Luke 12:8-9/Matt. 10:32-33/Mark 8:38). The usage in Acts 7:56 is not an exception. Stephen's claim here to see "the son of man" at God's right hand seems to be the author's device to link Stephen's vision with Jesus' prediction of his heavenly vindication in Luke 22:69 (which, unlike the Synoptic parallel accounts, does not refer to Jesus' opponents seeing the son of man). Heb. 2:6 cites Ps. 8:5(4), "a son of man" (*huios anthrōpou,* without the definite article), and in Rev. 1:13 and 14:14 the references to "one like a son of man" are simply echoes of the phrasing of Dan. 7:13, referring to a figure in a vision as having a humanlike appearance. In none of these latter three cases do we have the actual expression "the son of man," and in none is "son of man" a confessional title.

84. The charge of blasphemy in Mark 14:61-64 is in response to Jesus' affirmative reply to

it is a fundamental problem to account for the very frequent and quite specific application of the term in the Gospels, as well as the scarcity of the expression otherwise in the New Testament and in any pre-Christian text.

In the history of investigation of the Gospels material, scholars commonly identify several categories of sayings in which Jesus uses the phrase. Basically these are simply the broad types of sentences in which the expression is found. For example, among the Markan references are cases where "the son of man" is attributed authority in contested matters (to forgive sins, 2:10; lord of the Sabbath, 2:28), and other references predicting his rejection, suffering, and vindication (8:31; 9:31; 10:33-34) or his future appearance in eschatological glory (8:38; 13:26). Also, in 10:45 "the son of man" gives his life "as a ransom for many," and in 14:21 he faces what is "written of him" (in the Scriptures), a fate that includes betrayal (14:41). In passages commonly thought to be Q material, "the son of man" warns followers that they follow one who is homeless (Matt. 8:20/Luke 9:58), and in another saying that both links and contrasts him with John the Baptizer, "the son of man" is accused of being a glutton and drunkard, and an associate of public sinners (Matt. 11:19/Luke 7:34). As well, both Matthew and Luke use the phrase in ways peculiar to each of them. Matthew has additional references to the future actions of "the son of man" executing divine redemption and/or judgment (Matt. 13:41; 25:31; and cf. 19:28 with Luke 18:28-30). Luke's additional uses largely fall into the same pattern, though we may also note his distinctive reference to "the son of man" coming "to seek and to save the lost" (Luke 19:10).

The Johannine use of the expression is formally the same as in the Synoptics. What is different in John is the content of the statements in which it functions. For example, there are Johannine statements about "the son of man" descending or being lifted up/glorified (3:13-14; 8:28; 12:23, 34; 13:31), about believing in him (9:35), about angels descending/ascending on him (1:51), and about eating his flesh and drinking his blood (6:53). These are all identifiably Johannine themes. But as in the Synoptics, so also in John, "the son of man" is essentially a synonym for "I," and does not itself represent a claim to some established title. This is most easily seen in 6:30-58, in the alternation between

---

the high priest's question, which is whether he claims to be "the Messiah, the Son of the Blessed." Jesus' claim that "the son of man" will appear in glorious vindication, "coming with the clouds of heaven," fits the larger pattern of his use of this expression for self-references, and no supposed titular use of the expression is needed to explain its function here. On "blasphemy" in the Jewish setting of the time, see now Darrell L. Bock, *Blasphemy and Exaltation in Judaism and the Final Examination of Jesus: A Philological-Historical Study of the Key Jewish Themes Impacting Mark 14:61-64*, WUNT 2/106 (Tübingen: Mohr-Siebeck, 1998; reprint, Grand Rapids: Baker, 2000).

sayings using "I/my" and parallel sentences using "the son of man" (e.g., vv. 35, 48, "I am the bread of life"; cf. v. 51, "my flesh"; v. 52, "his [son of man's] flesh"; v. 53, "the flesh/blood of the son of man"; vv. 54-56, "my flesh/my blood").

But, though scholars have argued incessantly about which (and how many) types of sayings, and which specific examples in each type, might be "authentic" (i.e., representations of actual sayings of Jesus), this is not my concern here. The focus of this discussion is to understand what the expression indicates about earliest Christian views of Jesus. This sets it apart from the overwhelming number of other studies of the expression. It is of course a valid question as to the possible relationship between Jesus' own speech habits and the kinds of expressions attributed to him in the Gospels. I shall say something about this shortly, but only insofar as we are concerned to account historically for the fixed form and widespread usage of "the son of man" in the Gospel renditions of Jesus.

In the voluminous and complex body of scholarly publication on this expression, I suggest there are three basic viewpoints on how to account for it. A position represented frequently (perhaps even dominantly) in older scholarship held that the expression appeared in the canonical Gospels because it was an established title used in pre-Christian Jewish tradition to designate a heavenly figure expected to appear in eschatological triumph as the agent of God.[85] On this view the uses in the Gospels were to be understood as reflecting the supposed claim that Jesus is (or is to become) "the son of man," and thus will one day appear from heaven as a figure identified in Jewish tradition to execute God's eschatological purposes. Bousset, for example, was absolutely sure that this claim constituted the core of the earliest Christology of "the Palestinian primitive community," the Jewish Christian circles in Roman Judea.[86] Usually it was a corollary of this position that, though Jesus might have spoken of the coming of "the son of man," he could not have referred to himself by this title. Instead the title came to be applied to him in the very early "post-Easter" circumstances of

---

85. Those who took this view usually distinguished Jewish expectations of a heavenly "son of man" from expectations of a Davidic Messiah. A classic presentation of this view is Sigmund Mowinckel, *He That Cometh*, trans. G. W. Anderson (New York and Nashville: Abingdon, 1954). This basic viewpoint was also advocated by Heinz-Edward Tödt, *The Son of Man in the Synoptic Tradition* (London: SCM Press, 1965; German, Gütersloh: Gerd Mohn, 1959), and a number of other scholars, mainly prior to the 1970s, such as R. H. Fuller, *The Foundations of New Testament Christology* (New York: Charles Scribner's Sons, 1965).

86. Wilhelm Bousset, *Kyrios Christos: Geschichte des Christusglaubens von den Anfangen des Christentums bis Irenaeus* (Göttingen: Vandenhoeck & Ruprecht, 1913; rev. ed., 1921); ET (from the 4th German ed., 1965), *Kyrios Christos: A History of the Belief in Christ from the Beginnings of Christianity to Irenaeus*, trans. J. E. Steely (Nashville: Abingdon, 1970), 35-56.

the Christian movement, as his followers identified him as this heavenly "son of man" supposedly familiar in Jewish eschatological expectation.[87]

Though once very widely and confidently held, for a number of years now it has been clear that this viewpoint is not tenable, at least not without substantial modification.[88] Crucially, there is in fact no evidence that the expression was a fixed title in pre-Christian Jewish tradition. Daniel 7:13-14 does not refer to a titled "the son of man" but to a figure described as appearing "like a son of man" (i.e., looking like a human), who receives glory and universal dominion. This passage seems to have figured in Jewish eschatological expectations, but the humanlike figure is never referred to as "the son of man" in any subsequent Jewish sources.[89] Neither of the two writings frequently cited in the past as the key evidence is unambiguously pre-Christian, and in any case, in neither do we find an expression that actually corresponds directly to "the son of man."[90] There were expectations of this or that figure to come from heaven

87. Hare *(The Son of Man Tradition)* refers to this as "the dominant view of critical scholarship for the past half-century," and devotes his study to showing that the premise (an established Jewish expectation of "the son of man") is without merit. On the other hand, Joachim Jeremias basically accepted that "the son of man" was a pre-Christian apocalyptic title, but believed Jesus originated the claim that he was this figure: *New Testament Theology: The Proclamation of Jesus,* trans. John Bowden (New York: Charles Scribner's Sons, 1971), 257-76. On the allergic reaction of many scholars to apocalyptic categories, see Klaus Koch, *The Rediscovery of Apocalyptic,* SBTss 22 (London: SCM Press, 1972), esp. 57-97, "The Agonized Attempt to Save Jesus from Apocalyptic."

88. As far back as 1979 I cited scholarly studies that demonstrated the fallacies in this viewpoint. See my article, "New Testament Christology: A Critique of Bousset's Influence," *TS* 40 (1979): 306-17, esp. 309-12. Leivestad's article, "Exit the Apocalyptic Son of Man," is particularly important. For a fuller statement of his views, see "Der apokalyptische Menschensohn ein theologisches Phantom," *ASTI* 6 (1968): 49-105.

89. Maurice Casey, *Son of Man: The Interpretation and Influence of Daniel 7* (London: SPCK, 1979).

90. As to the "Parables/Similitudes" of *1 Enoch* (chaps. 37–71), this portion of this composite writing is now widely thought to have been composed in the first century C.E. and *may* reflect some earlier traditions. See, e.g., C. L. Mearns, "Dating the Similitudes of Enoch," *NTS* 25 (1979): 360-69. In any case, several different Ethiopic expressions in this material are commonly translated "son of man," which suggests that the Ethiopic translators did not find fixed phrasing in the text they translated and saw no reason to use a fixed expression themselves. Cf. Matthew Black, *The Book of Enoch or 1 Enoch: A New English Edition with Commentary and Textual Notes,* SVTP 7 (Leiden: Brill, 1985), 206-7, who helpfully gives the three Ethiopic expressions in question but then strangely asserts that they all "clearly go back to an original" fixed form in Hebrew *(ben ha-'adam),* Aramaic *(bar '[e]nasha'),* or Greek *(ho huios tou anthrōpou),* that is, titular expressions which all mean "the son of man." As to the "man from the sea" in 4 Ezra 13, here again we have a text of uncertain provenance (ca. 100 C.E.?), and with phrasing that is neither fixed nor the same as the formulaic expression in the Gospels, *"ille homo," "ille vir"* (cf. 4 Ezra 13:3, "a

and act as God's eschatological agent, but there is no evidence that any such figure was ever referred to as "the son of man."[91]

Furthermore, and even more crucial for the present discussion, there is also no evidence for the idea that "the son of man" was a confessional title in first-century Christian circles or that it represented some specific christological claim *in itself*. The expression occasionally may be used to allude to Daniel 7:13-14 (as may be the case in Mark 14:62). But in these instances the expression functions as a *literary device*, not an established title, and the claim registered is that Jesus is the figure of that passage. By contrast, the rife usage of "Christ *(Christos)*" in Christian sources, from Paul's letters onward, is the indelible mark of the messianic claim as a prominent feature of earliest Christian proclamation. To cite another contrasting example noted in a previous chapter, we have what appear to be vestigial traces of a very early use of "servant" (Gk. *pais;* Heb. *'ebed*) as a christological title in Acts (4:27, 30) and in later sources (e.g., *1 Clem.* 59.4; *Did.* 9.2). But in the New Testament there is no trace of "the son of man" used as a title in early Christian proclamation, confession, or liturgy.[92] It is also worth noting that outside the canonical Gospels, the early Christian writers who refer to Jesus as "son of man" seem completely unaware of any association with Daniel 7 or Jewish apocalyptic figures. So far as they use the expression at all, it simply connotes Jesus as a genuinely human figure (e.g., Ign. *Eph.* 20.2; *Barn.* 12.10).[93]

---

man come up out of the heart of the sea"; and 13:5, "the man who came up out of the sea"). See, e.g., B. M. Metzger's introduction and translation in *OTP*, 1:519-59.

91. Thus, e.g., John J. Collins, "The Son of Man in First-Century Judaism," *NTS* 38 (1992): 448-66, argues that there was an expectation of a figure influenced by the humanlike figure in Dan. 7:13, but he acknowledges that there is no evidence for the use of "the Son of Man" as a title for such a figure. See also now Collins, *The Scepter and the Star: The Messiahs of the Dead Sea Scrolls and Other Ancient Literature* (New York: Doubleday, 1995), 173-94.

92. See Leivestad, "Exit the Apocalyptic," 248-53. The uses of "the son of man" as a quasi title in Christian writings of the second century and later are not relevant for the expression in the canonical Gospels or in first-century Christian circles. From Ignatius onward, "son of man" designates Jesus as genuinely human, and is often paired with "Son of God" to express his divinity (e.g., Ign. *Eph.* 20.2). See Hare's survey of Christian tradition (Hare, 29-45). For a study of the gnostic use of the expression, where it carries the sense of "the Son of (the heavenly) Anthropos," see Frederick H. Borsch, *The Son of Man in Myth and History* (London: SCM Press, 1967).

93. Noted by Randall Buth, "A More Complete Semitic Background for Bar-Enasha, 'Son of Man,'" in *Studies in Scripture in Early Judaism and Christianity,* ed. Craig A. Evans and James A. Sanders (Sheffield: Sheffield Academic Press, 1998), 176-89, esp. 179. Buth's own proposal, that Jesus taught in Hebrew and used the Aramaic expression *bar 'enasha'* to allude to Dan. 7:13-14, seems improbable to me. It is neither necessary nor persuasive to see allusions to Dan. 7 in any more than one or two sayings in which "the son of man" expression appears in the Gospels.

Granting that "son of man" was not a title in Jewish tradition, other scholars contend that the expression nevertheless functions as an important *title* in the Gospels, and they hold that it was coined, either by Jesus or in early Christian circles in the post-Jesus period, as a novel device consistently intended to point back specifically to the "one like a son of man" in the visionary scene in Daniel 7:13. That is, in *all its uses* the expression was intended to make an implicit or explicit claim that Jesus is (or decisively represents) the vindicated humanlike figure of that passage. C. F. D. Moule, for example, maintained that Jesus himself had seen in Daniel 7:13-14 a picture of his own destiny, which was to involve his own suffering and vindication. Moule further proposed that Jesus coined and used an Aramaic expression that must have been the equivalent of "the son of man," and that, though somewhat ambiguous, this expression was nevertheless intended to allude to the figure in the visionary scene in Daniel 7.[94] By contrast, Norman Perrin proposed that all Gospel occurrences of "the son of man" derived from the Christian exegesis of Old Testament passages in the early years after Jesus, among which Daniel 7:13 was particularly crucial.[95]

Either position is possible in principle. But it is a problem for either that there is little evidence in first-century Christian sources that Daniel 7:13-14 played the crucial role that is alleged for it. To be sure, there are likely allusions to the passage in Jesus' reply to the priest's question in Mark 14:62 (parallel in Matt. 26:64), the saying in Mark 13:26 (parallels Matt. 24:30/Luke 21:27), and also in Revelation 1:7, 13. But these are all comparatively late New Testament texts, and provide nothing like the many and early indications of the influence of other, and much more obviously influential, biblical passages such as Psalm 110.[96] Moreover, though Revelation echoes wording from Daniel 7:13 (Rev. 1:7), the author uses the full phrase "*one like a* son of man" to describe the glorious Jesus of the vision recounted here (1:13), and not the supposed title "the son of man." It is curious (and, I think, fatal for this viewpoint) that this early Christian writer (otherwise so acquainted with Christian traditions) seems unaware that "the son of man" expression supposedly had been developed precisely to refer to Daniel 7:13-14!

Also, if the Gospel expression "the son of man" was shaped by, and intended to allude to, Old Testament passages, we should not assume that Daniel

---

94. Moule, "Neglected Features," 413-28. Cf. Hare's more tentative treatment of this as a possibility (277-80).

95. Norman Perrin, "Mark 14:62: The End Product of a Christian Pesher Tradition?" *NTS* 12 (1965-66): 150-55.

96. David M. Hay, *Glory at the Right Hand: Psalm 110 in Early Christianity,* SBLMS 18 (Nashville: Abingdon, 1973); Martin Hengel, *Studies in Early Christology* (Edinburgh: T. & T. Clark, 1995), 119-226.

7:13 was so obviously central among them as modern scholars sometimes contend.[97] We have, for example, better and earlier indications that Psalm 8 was widely influential in Christian circles as a christological passage (e.g., 1 Cor. 15:27; Eph. 1:22; Heb. 2:6; Matt. 21:16); and this psalm also refers to "a son of man" to whom all things are made subject. Likewise in Jesus' response to the high priest (Mark 14:62/Matt. 26:64/Luke 22:69), the biblical allusions are likely multiple. The mention of "the son of man" at God's "right hand" is usually (and probably rightly) taken as alluding also to Psalm 110:1, but Psalm 80:17 (LXX 79:18) is relevant, too, as the Old Testament passage where we have a chosen "man of/at your right hand" *(andra dexias sou)* who is also referred to in the next line as that "son of man whom you have strengthened for yourself."[98]

③ A third viewpoint that has gained considerable allegiance in the last few decades holds that the Greek expression "the son of man" derives from one or more related Aramaic expressions, none of which was used as a title for the figure of Daniel 7:13; instead these expressions were simply idiomatic ways of re- ⌐ ferring to human beings.[99] The Aramaic expressions most commonly thought to account best for the Greek phrase *ho huios tou anthrōpou* are *bar 'enasha'*, which is the singular "definite" form for "(the) son of man," and/or *bar 'enosh*, the "absolute" or "indefinite" singular form ("[a] son of man").[100]

Scholars associated with this basic viewpoint differ as to the precise range of connotations of the Aramaic phrases in question. Vermes contends that one or more of the Aramaic expressions could be used to make a deliberate self-reference. Bauckham proposes that, although the Aramaic for "(a) son of man" *(bar 'enash*, the "absolute" form) mainly designated a person as a human being, the expression was also capable of being used with a certain particularizing connotation, alluding to Daniel 7:13. Casey, however, insists that both the defi-

---

97. I leave out of account here the more than ninety uses of "son of man" as God's form of address to Ezekiel in the Old Testament book by his name.

98. For other suggestions about the possible influence of Ps. 80 (LXX 79), see, e.g., C. H. Dodd, *According to the Scriptures* (London: James Nisbet, 1952; reprint, London: Collins/Fontana, 1965), 101-2, 113-14; Donald Juel, *Messianic Exegesis: Christological Interpretation of the Old Testament in Early Christianity* (Philadelphia: Fortress, 1988), 168, and see 165-70 for his proposals about "the son of man" expression and christological exegesis of Old Testament passages.

99. Geza Vermes is usually given credit for providing the initial impetus for the recent popularity of this viewpoint in an appendix to Matthew Black, *An Aramaic Approach to the Gospels and Acts,* 3rd ed. (Oxford: Clarendon, 1967), 310-30.

100. The "definite" form of Aramaic nouns (with a final *aleph*) at least originally had a function roughly similar to a definite article in other languages. Of course, the singular ("absolute") and plural Aramaic expressions are the direct equivalents of Hebrew expressions in the Old Testament referring to individuals (usually, *ben 'adam*, e.g., Ps. 8:4) and to humans collectively (usually *b^ene 'adam*; occasionally *b^ene 'ish*; cf., e.g., Pss. 21:10; 4:2).

nite and the absolute forms of the Aramaic expression were frequently used, and without much distinction in connotation simply referred to human beings in a generic sense, whereas Lindars claims that in some cases "son of man" could be used by a person to link himself with people in similar circumstances, thus meaning "someone/anyone in my situation."[101]

This debate is relevant for my discussion here in that one of my concerns is to ask about the likely historical cause(s) behind the fixed and widely attested Greek expression *ho huios tou anthrōpou*. Those who think that the Aramaic expressions allowed a speaker to make a particularizing, self-referential statement tend to see the Greek construction, with its undeniably particularizing force, arising from and reflecting in one way or another Jesus' own Aramaic speech practice. These scholars think that Jesus made statements that connoted, whether directly or ambiguously, something particularly true for or about himself, and so they take *ho huios tou anthrōpou* as a reasonably good attempt to convey this connotation in a Greek formulation, "whose definiteness would clearly suggest that, namelike, it was intended to point to a single individual."[102]

On the other hand, those scholars who insist that the relevant Aramaic expressions referred to someone only in generic/generalizing terms (as a member of humanity or some group) tend to see the Greek *ho huios tou anthrōpou* as rather more particularizing than was warranted by anything in Jesus' own/authentic speech practice. Casey, perhaps the most emphatic exponent of this position, has insisted that *ho huios tou anthrōpou* results from a combination of linguistic "interference" and deliberate (religiously motivated) translation-adaptation of Jesus' Aramaic expression in Greek-speaking Christian circles.[103] That is, in Casey's view the articular Greek construction *ho huios tou anthrōpou* in part represents an honest attempt of early bilingual Christians to translate

101. Cf. Vermes in Matthew Black, *An Aramaic Approach to the Gospels and Acts;* Vermes, *Jesus and the World of Judaism* (Philadelphia: Fortress, 1984), 89-99; Barnabas Lindars, *Jesus Son of Man* (London: SPCK, 1983); Maurice Casey's numerous publications on the subject, e.g., "General, Generic and Indefinite: The Use of the Term 'Son of Man' in Aramaic Sources and in the Teaching of Jesus," *JSNT* 29 (1987): 21-56; "Method in Our Madness, and Madness in Their Methods: Some Approaches to the Son of Man Problem in Recent Scholarship," *JSNT* 42 (1991): 17-43; and most recently, *Aramaic Sources of Mark's Gospel*, SNTSMS 102 (Cambridge: Cambridge University Press, 1998), esp. 111-21; and Richard Bauckham, "The Son of Man: 'A Man in My Position' or 'Someone'?" *JSNT* 23 (1985): 23-33. I have used gendered language above, "a man/himself," because the only examples of the Aramaic expressions that I know of clearly refer to males.

102. E.g., Hare, 241-56, quote from 255.

103. See, e.g., Casey's discussion in *Aramaic Sources*, 119-20, and 255, where he refers to *ho huios tou anthrōpou* as "the most controversial and misunderstood term in the whole of the New Testament."

Jesus' Aramaic expressions, but they introduced, perhaps inadvertently, a more specific and restrictive self-reference into Jesus' sayings in the process, which then became regularized as a way of expressing Jesus' particular significance in early Christian faith.[104] He sees the fixed and frequent usage of the Greek expression by the authors of the canonical Gospels as their efforts to provide their Christian readers with "another Christological title" intended clearly to refer to Jesus.[105]

In a major article, Paul Owen and David Shepherd recently provided a detailed study of the relevant Aramaic expressions in extant texts from the time of Jesus, and their results are directly relevant.[106] With previous scholars they observe that Vermes and subsequent scholars such as Casey have tended to rest their views heavily on Aramaic texts from periods considerably outside Jesus' time, and on evidence from Aramaic dialects other than that of first-century Roman Judea/Palestine.[107] This was initially unavoidable, given the previous paucity of readily available Aramaic texts from Jesus' time. It is, however, a bit like using modern American English to propose the meanings of words and expressions in Elizabethan English texts.[108] But in the last few decades the continuing publication of texts from Qumran has significantly expanded the database for establishing features of Aramaic of Jesus' time and locale. In a survey of a number of relevant Qumran Aramaic texts, Owen and Shepherd present some

---

104. Casey consistently refers to *bar '(e)nash(a)'*, lumping together both the definite and absolute forms of the Aramaic for "son of man," claiming they were used indifferently and interchangeably in first century c.e. Judean/Palestinian circles. As I shall note shortly, however, this claim now appears debatable.

105. Casey, *Aramaic Sources*, 117-18, 119-20, 255-56.

106. Paul Owen and David Shepherd, "Speaking Up for Qumran, Dalman and the Son of Man: Was *Bar Enasha* a Common Term for 'Man' in the Time of Jesus?" *JSNT* 81 (2001): 81-122. The chronologically relevant Aramaic texts are all from Qumran, and have come to light only in recent decades. The influential study by Vermes was based on the *Genesis Apocryphon* text from Qumran, and Jewish writings from a few centuries later, i.e., the Jewish Targums and rabbinic writings. Lindars and Casey have largely adopted Vermes' evidence in building their own views of the matter as well.

107. Owen and Shepherd, esp. 81-96. It is, for example, very curious that in Casey's most recent discussion of the matter (*Aramaic Sources*, 111-21), though he lists several Aramaic texts from Qumran as crucially important (111), of the twelve Aramaic passages that he then builds his case on, all but one (1QapGen 21:13) are from a few to several centuries later or earlier than Jesus' time (112-18).

108. Indeed, as someone who has lived and worked on both sides of the Atlantic, both north and south of the Canadian and U.S. border, and both north and south of the river Tweed, I can attest from vivid experience that there are significant differences in expressions used and even in the meanings of the same words among the several dialects of the English language spoken contemporaneously in these locales!

significant findings, the broad effect of which is to place in strong doubt the claim that the Aramaic equivalents to "son of man" were simply the ordinary ways of referring to human beings generically, and were not capable of connoting any strong particularizing reference to himself in Jesus' sayings.

First, there seems to be scant basis for the claim that in the Aramaic dialect of Jesus' provenance, the semantic distinction between the "definite" and "absolute" forms of nouns had eroded away, which means it is dubious to assert that bar 'enash and bar 'enasha' likely had undifferentiated meanings and were used somewhat interchangeably.[109] Second, in fact the Aramaic "definite" singular expression, bar 'enasha', is "only clearly attested in Eastern Aramaic materials that derive from a period several centuries removed from the historical Jesus," and does not appear in the Aramaic texts of Jesus' provenance.[110] Granted, we have only a few examples to work with, and the absence of any instance of the singular "definite" form should probably not be taken to mean that it was not used at all or could not be used. But the extant evidence suggests strongly that the definite form was not in *common* usage and was not used *interchangeably* with the absolute form. Thirdly, Owen and Shepherd show that it is also dubious to claim that the Aramaic equivalents of "son of man," in either the definite or the absolute singular form, were the characteristic ways of referring to human individuals.[111] There were other Aramaic terms available and more commonly used in the extant texts of the relevant time for this (e.g., 'enash, and gebar). All of this amounts to the cogent judgment that the relevant Aramaic evidence "does not provide solid linguistic grounds for the solution to the Son of Man problem offered by Vermes, Lindars and Casey."[112]

109. Owen and Shepherd, 96-104.

110. Owen and Shepherd, 104-20, quotation from 105. They cite (107) three uses of the "absolute" singular construction, bar 'enosh/"(a) son of man" (11QtgJob [11Q10] 9.9; 26.3; 1QapGenar 21.13); four uses of the plural "emphatic," bᵉne 'enasha'/"the sons of men" (11QtgJob [11Q10] 13.9; 13.2; 4QEnastᵇar [4Q209] 23.9; 1QapGen 6.8-9); and one use of the plural "absolute" form, bᵉne 'enosh/"sons of men" (1QapGen 19.15). See also the citations of forms used in the Aramaic fragments of 1 Enoch in J. T. Milik, ed., The Books of Enoch: Aramaic Fragments of Qumran Cave 4 (Oxford: Clarendon, 1976), 371, s.v. בר, which likewise includes no example of the singular "definite" form bar 'enasha'.

111. E.g., Owen and Shepherd (111-12) present a table comparing expressions used in the Qumran Aramaic translation of Job and in significantly later Aramaic versions of Job, showing that, of the sixteen extant places where humans are referred to individually or collectively, the Qumran text uses the singular form bar 'enash twice (in both cases rendering directly the Hebrew ben 'adam) and the plural bᵉne 'enasha' once, the more frequently used term for "a man" being gebar (six uses). By comparison, in the Job Targum, from significantly later, at these same sixteen points there are eight uses of bar nash and one use of bar nasha.

112. Owen and Shepherd, 121.

This does not settle the question of what expression(s) Jesus might have used in Aramaic that may have contributed to the rather unusual Greek construction translated "the son of man"; and fortunately, it is not necessary for my present purpose to attempt to do so here.[113] The relevant Aramaic evidence extant does not, however, forbid positing, with some confidence, one important proposal. Jesus' own speech practice could easily have included an Aramaic expression capable of being used in statements with a particularizing *connotation*, this connotation then being conveyed in the rather novel Greek expression *ho huios tou anthrōpou.*[114] That is, in at least partial answer to the historical question as to what led to the construction and widespread use of this unusual Greek expression, it seems entirely plausible that Jesus' own speech practice was a major factor.

Let us return now from the Aramaic evidence to the more readily accessible and agreed-upon Greek data relevant to the background and meaning/function of the Gospel expression "the son of man." I begin by reiterating a point made earlier: <u>the expression is unprecedented in Greek</u>, and apparently novel in construction. Not only does *ho huios tou anthrōpou* not occur prior to the Gospels in extant literature composed in Greek, it is also not found once among the scores of times the translators of the Greek Old Testament rendered the Semitic expressions for "(a) son of man." Nor do we find any use of it in the extant Greek portions of *1 Enoch* translated from the Aramaic.[115] Casey's assertion that it was initially just the sort of irregular expression that might result in translation from one language to another would be considerably more plausible if we had other examples where the same translation move happened; but we have not a one.[116] I think it far more likely, thus, that *ho huios tou anthrōpou*

---

113. Nor, I must confess, can I personally claim sufficient expertise in the niceties of the various Aramaic dialects and the full body of Aramaic evidence to attempt an authoritative solution.

114. I leave for further debate whether Jesus' speech practice involved his own use of an unusual expression such as *bar 'enasha'*, or the more attested "absolute" form *(bar 'enash)* but used in statements that connoted a particularizing force, or some other construction (cf. Delbert Burkett, *The Son of Man in the Gospel of John*, JSNTSup 56 [Sheffield: Sheffield Academic Press, 1991], who proposes *bar gabra*, an improbable option in my view). It is in the nature of human languages that competent speakers/writers can adapt idiomatic expressions either in form or connotation. See, e.g., Lyons, 22-23. An understanding of "speech act semantics" and linguistic "pragmatics" involves taking account of all that speakers of languages use to convey their meanings. See, e.g., Kempson, 50-74.

115. Milik, *The Books of Enoch.* For the text of the extant Greek portions of *1 Enoch*, see, e.g., R. H. Charles, *The Book of Enoch or 1 Enoch* (Oxford: Clarendon, 1912), app. 1, pp. 273-305.

116. Though Casey invokes in general terms studies of bilingual speakers and studies of translation from Hebrew to Greek in the LXX, he does not provide direct evidence of the partic-

was deliberately constructed from the first by, and in, bilingual circles of Jesus' followers to serve as his distinctive self-referential expression in conveying his sayings in Greek. As already indicated, it seems to me that the most plausible reason they did this was that in the early traditions of Jesus' Aramaic speech practice available to them, he made statements that connoted a special significance attached to him and to his actions.

The remaining and "foregrounded" question here, however, is more particularly what was meant by this prominent feature of the "renditions" of Jesus in the canonical Gospels. As a first observation, I propose that original readers/hearers of *ho huios tou anthrōpou* would have recognized that it was not an ordinary idiom in Greek, but was similar to expressions in the Greek Old Testament (the singular form "[a] son of man," *huios anthrōpou,* and the plural form "[the] sons of men," [*hoi*] *huioi* [*tōn*] *anthrōpōn*). So they would likely have seen it as having a certain scriptural ring to it, the expression sounding like what we might call "Bible Greek" to them. In short, those who read and heard the Gospels in Greek would not have seen the linguistic context of "the son of man" as some supposedly prior usage as the title of a known eschatological figure, but instead as the use of similar expressions in the Greek Old Testament. Yet the definite article would have connoted a distinctively emphatic force to the construction — "*the* son of man." As Nigel Turner wrote about the Greek definite article, "it particularizes an individual member of a group or class."[117] That is, the semantic force of the expression was almost certainly to posit Jesus (the obviously consistent referent in all Gospel passages) as somehow a human figure of particular significance.

The function of the expression is further indicated in the fact that Jesus is not only the sole referent of its eighty-one uses in the Gospels, he is also the only one who uses it. "The son of man" is Jesus' own special way of referring to himself. As already stated, along with "Truly, I say to you," it is a salient feature of Jesus' "idiolect," his own way of speaking, in the Gospels. This would have made both expressions sacred features of early Christians' traditions of their

---

ular sort of translation "interference" that he crucially alleges for the construction of *ho hyios tou anthrōpou.* That is, he does not offer supporting evidence that ancient Greek translators of Semitic texts tended to construct articular forms of indefinite Semitic expressions as a result of language "interference" (i.e., nonidiomatic use of articles in Greek without basis in the sense of the Semitic expression being translated). Cf. Casey, *Aramaic Sources,* 93-106.

117. MHT, 3:165. On the force and functions of the Greek definite article, see the entire discussion, 165-84; Moule, *Idiom Book,* 106-17; BDF, 131-45, esp. 135 (§259). "The function of the article is to point out (it was in origin a demonstrative), to determine, to 'set apart from others,' to identify as *this* or *these* and not simply 'such.'" Maximilian Zerwick, *Biblical Greek,* English ed. adapted by Joseph Smith (Rome: Pontifical Institute Press, 1963), 53 (§165).

"Master/Lord"; this in turn explains why and how the expression so obviously became formulaic and so widely transmitted. For "the son of man" to be used so heavily by all three Synoptic authors and also by the author of the Gospel of John surely indicates that this feature of the Jesus tradition endeared itself early and widely to a broad swath of Christians.[118]

I repeat for emphasis: in an important sense of the word, "the son of ✳ man" is not a *title*. That is, it does not designate an office or figure previously established and identified by this expression in the speech patterns of pre-Christian Jewish circles/traditions. Nevertheless, in the canonical Gospels the expression is obviously a fixed, formulaic construction with a specific, indeed exclusive, reference.[119] It functioned, thus, more in the way a name functions, to identify and distinguish a person, in this case Jesus.

However, as I indicated above, unlike proper names (at least in some languages such as modern European ones), "the son of man" also had a semantic meaning, referring to Jesus as "the" particular human being/figure. That is, the expression did not attribute to Jesus an established office or claim, but rather referred to him emphatically as human descendant. Also, "the son of man" clearly functioned to some degree interchangeably with the first-person pronoun in the handing on of Jesus' sayings. This is why we do not find the expression except on the lips of Jesus. Out of reverence for what they understood to be Jesus' own speech practice in referring to himself, early Christians both preserved "the son of man" expression and also hesitated to use it as their own statements about him, except when they represented the "voice" of Jesus (i.e., in transmitting, and perhaps even coining, sayings of Jesus).

This expression, "the son of man," is thus an important historic feature of Christian devotion to Jesus in the first century. The semantic force of the

---

118. The expression "the son of man" appears also (but considerably less frequently) in some of the Coptic Nag Hammadi extracanonical Christian texts, *Ap. Jas.* 3.14, 17-18; *Treat. Res.* 44.23, 30-31; 46.14-15; *Gos. Thom.* 86; *Gos. Phil.* 63.29-30, which further illustrates its widespread appropriation in very diverse early Christian circles. But in at least some cases the expression designates a heavenly figure, illustrating the very different conceptual world of some of these writings. In addition to Borsch, see also Majella Franzmann, *Jesus in the Nag Hammadi Writings* (Edinburgh: T. & T. Clark, 1996), esp. 97-98. The meaning of the Coptic expression in *Gos. Thom.* 86 is disputed. Some claim that it is not here the formulaic expression from the canonical Gospels, and simply means "a human being" (e.g., Helmut Koester, "One Jesus and Four Primitive Gospels," *HTR* 61 [1968]: 203-47, esp. 215; Valantasis, 166-67); others see the expression as a case of the self-designation formula (e.g., Franzmann, 97 n. 1).

119. These are the features that seem to lead Burkett to insist that "the son of man" is a title "in the bulk of its [Gospel] occurrences" ("Nontitular Son of Man," 520). But a speech formula is not the same thing as a "title," at least not in the sense of the recognized label of an established office or otherwise/previously-known figure.

expression is an emphatic reference to Jesus as human being, *the* human being/descendant. Also, the concern to "echo" and preserve what they saw as Jesus' own speech patterns in these expressions shows a profound reverence for Jesus. Incidentally, along with the "Amen, I say to you" formula, the wide and fixed use of "the son of man" indicates a strikingly early instance of "conventionalization" in practice across a number of first-century Christian circles represented by Mark, Matthew, Luke (plus the probable Q source behind Matthew and Luke), and even John. We should also note that the apparent emphasis in the expression on the particularity of Jesus as human figure has a striking coherence with the nature of the canonical Gospels as accounts of Jesus, which quite deliberately set him within the chronological, geographical, ethnic/cultural, and political particularities of early-first-century Roman Judea/Palestine.

One final observation about "the son of man" expression is necessary. In the "discourse world" of the canonical Gospels, this emphatic way of referring to Jesus as human functions along with the clear assertion of Jesus' transcendent significance, even his "intrinsic divinity."[120] This latter emphasis is what seems to be included in the presentation of Jesus as God's "Son," which features prominently in all four canonical accounts.[121] Surely, early readers of these accounts could not have avoided the pairing of these two related and contrasting ways of referring to Jesus in filial terms: as "the son of man" and God's "Son."[122] The one designates Jesus operating in the human/historical sphere, and the other discloses the higher significance of who this human figure really is. This dynamic relationship of these two filial categories seems to be operative in Mark and in all the other canonical Gospels as well.

Further Markan Emphases

We return now to other features of the "rendition" of Jesus in the Gospel of Mark. It is important to note that Mark links his story of Jesus with a larger "narrative world" of scriptural (Old Testament) prophecy and personages, and

---

120. I borrow the term "intrinsic divinity" from Davis, "Mark's Christological Paradox," 13.

121. See, e.g., D. R. Bauer, "Son of God," in *DJG*, 769-75, esp. 772-75; Joachim Bieneck, *Sohn Gottes als Christusbezeichnung der Synoptiker* (Zürich: Zwingli-Verlag, 1951).

122. However, whereas references to Jesus' human participation employ the fixed, formulaic expression "the son of man," the references to Jesus' divine sonship involve several related expressions. For example, the Markan expressions are "my beloved Son" (1:11; 9:7; cf. 12:6); "the Son of God" (3:11); "Son of God Most High" (5:7); "the Son" (13:32); "the Son of the Blessed One" (14:61).

also with the early Christian proclamation of the gospel in the circles for which he wrote.[123] Let us note first the importance laid upon the connection with the biblical material. The Markan use of Old Testament Scripture has been studied superbly by Joel Marcus, and I shall therefore limit my own comments here to some basic points.[124]

Perhaps the most illuminating Markan reference to the Old Testament is the first one in the narrative. Immediately after what I take to be the author's intended title for the Gospel (1:1), an explicit quotation is attributed to Isaiah (actually a composite quotation of Isa. 40:3; Mal. 3:1; Exod. 23:20), which functions to introduce the entirety of the Markan account of Jesus: "Behold, I send my messenger before your face who will prepare your way. A voice crying out in the wilderness, 'Prepare the way of the Lord; make straight his paths.'" The form of the quotation here has God sending a messenger (subsequently identified as John the Baptizer) ahead of another who is obviously Jesus ("before your face," "your way"). Indeed, as Marcus has shown, Mark then presents the subsequent account of Jesus as "the way of the Lord."[125] Thereby Mark both links Jesus' appearance and activity with the scriptures of Israel and also makes a profound statement about Jesus, associating him closely with God (who is "the Lord" originally referred to in Isa. 40:3 and Mal. 3:1).

In addition to several other explicit quotations of the Old Testament, a number of citations are also incorporated into the text but not explicitly introduced as such, and also a goodly number of allusions.[126] These all combine to

---

123. For an analysis of the readers for whom Mark was composed, see Paul L. Danove, *The End of Mark's Story: A Methodological Study*, Biblical Interpretation Series 3 (Leiden: Brill, 1993), 167-202. Danove shows that the intended readership/audience "has a very positive valuation of Jesus, John, and the (eleven) disciples and previous familiarity with much of the content of the stories relating the ministry of Jesus and with the Septuagint, especially those passages used to interpret the significance of Jesus" (187).

124. Joel Marcus, *The Way of the Lord: Christological Exegesis of the Old Testament in the Gospel of Mark* (Louisville: Westminster John Knox, 1992). Cf. Hugh Anderson, "The Old Testament in Mark's Gospel," in *The Use of the Old Testament in the New and Other Essays: Studies in Honor of W. Stinespring*, ed. J. Efird (Durham, N.C.: Duke University Press, 1972), 280-306; Siegfried Schulz, "Markus und das Alte Testament," *ZTK* 58 (1961): 184-97; Howard Clark Kee, "The Function of Scriptural Quotations and Allusions in Mark 11-16," in *Jesus und Paulus: Festschrift für Werner Georg Kümmel*, ed. E. E. Ellis and E. Grässer (Göttingen: Vandenhoeck & Ruprecht, 1975), 165-88.

125. Marcus, *Way of the Lord*, 37-41. Mark uses the term "way" (*hodos*) exclusively in references to Jesus' disciples (2:23; 8:27; 9:33; 10:52), who follow Jesus in his "way." References in Acts suggest that "the way" also functioned as an in-group term of self-reference in some circles of the early Christian movement (Acts 9:2; 19:9, 23; 22:4; 24:14, 22).

126. Explicit citations: 1:2-3 (Isa. 40:3; Mal. 3:1; Exod. 23:20); 7:6 (Isa. 29:13); 10:7 (Gen. 2:24); 10:19 (from Exod. 20:12-16; Deut. 5:16-20); 11:17 (Isa. 56:7; but "den of thieves" in Mark

constitute an account of Jesus that is heavily shaped by the Old Testament, and prepared for readers who regard the Old Testament as Scripture. That is, the text of Mark seems to presuppose readers for whom the Old Testament functions very importantly in shaping and expressing their "life world" of religious vocabulary, symbols, and fundamental beliefs. The unintroduced quotations suggest intended readers who could recognize the quotations readily enough without an explicit marker.

Indeed, the allusions suggest a still more impressive familiarity with the specific Greek wording of the Old Testament writings in question by readers with a keen appreciation of the effect of the allusions in associating Jesus' activities with scriptural passages. For example, the allusions to Isaiah 35:5-6 in the account of the healing of the deaf and mute man in Mark 7:31-37 present Jesus' healing miracles in terms of Isaiah's prophecy of marvelous blessings to be bestowed by God.[127] Thus, although formally a miracle story, the healing of this deaf and mute man is implicitly rehearsed as fulfillment of Scripture and as part of the eschatological drama that is Jesus' ministry. That Mark so often can rely on this sort of *implicit* linkage of Jesus with the Old Testament indicates that this story of Jesus very much presupposes and adverts to a good deal of prior interpretative reflection and discourse about Jesus in Christian circles of the time.

In addition to linking Jesus to the world of biblical narrative and prophecy, Mark also makes a very emphatic connection between Jesus and those called to follow him.[128] That is, the Markan story of Jesus elicits others to "enter" the story, to follow Jesus in his "way," and to further his ministry in their own lives. Mark's use of "gospel" *(euangelion)* illustrates this. The initial use of the term is in the programmatic introductory statement in 1:14-15, which presents Jesus preaching "the gospel of God." Subsequently in Mark the term represents the mission of his followers. In 8:35 and 10:29 his followers are those

---

11:17b is probably an allusion to Jer. 7:11). Unintroduced quotations include 4:12 (Isa. 6:9-10); 8:18 (Jer. 5:21); 11:9 (Ps. 118:26); 12:26 (Exod. 3:6, 15); 13:24-25 (Isa. 13:10); 14:62 (Dan. 7:13); 15:34 (Ps. 22:1). Allusion to the Old Testament is particularly frequent in the Markan narrative of Jesus' suffering, death, and resurrection, on which see now Marcus, *Way of the Lord,* 153-58. Note also 14:49, which makes no readily identifiable reference to any specific biblical passage and instead more generally claims that the events narrated (Jesus' arrest, trial, execution) are fulfillment of "the scriptures."

127. The term *mogilalon* (mute) in the description of the man in Mark 7:32 appears only here in the New Testament, and only in Isa. 35:6 in the Greek Old Testament. The reference in Mark 7:37 to people marveling about Jesus' miracles is another easily recognized allusion to Isa. 35:5-6.

128. Larry W. Hurtado, "Following Jesus in the Gospel of Mark — and Beyond," in *Patterns of Discipleship in the New Testament,* ed. Richard N. Longenecker (Grand Rapids: Eerdmans, 1996), 9-29.

who may lose their lives, possessions, and relationships on account of Jesus and "the gospel," that is, through their involvement in an activity patterned after Jesus' mission. Note also 13:10, which refers to "the gospel" being proclaimed "to all nations," and 14:9, which likewise refers to "the gospel" preached "in the whole world." Both statements clearly anticipate the proclamation of the early Christian movement in the years after Jesus' death in terms that link it to Jesus' own proclamation.

The most extended evidence of this is in the eschatological discourse in 13:3-37. The passage explicitly looks beyond the immediate time of Jesus and the Twelve to a proclamation to all nations (v. 10) that must be undertaken in a continuing period of general distress (vv. 5-8) and persecution directed specifically against Jesus' followers (vv. 9-13). The repeated concern is that followers should not be deceived by false messianic and prophetic claimants and should not think that the distresses signal an immediate end (vv. 5-8, 13b, 21-23). Jesus assures followers that there will be a glorious consummation (vv. 24-27), but only at some point *after* the suffering painted so vividly; and he explicitly warns that neither they *nor he* knows when (vv. 32-36). The concluding exhortation makes plain that a wider circle is addressed: "What I say to you [those mentioned in v. 3] I say to all [readers here addressed directly in second-person form]: Keep awake."

This intended connection between Jesus' ministry and the subsequent mission of his followers is a further reason for taking the opening words in 1:1, "The beginning [*archē*] of the gospel of Jesus Christ," to refer to the whole of the following account of Jesus, and not merely the introductory material in 1:1-15.[129] Jesus' own activity is in Mark the *archē*, the origin and foundation of the gospel, and thereby the authoritative pattern for his followers called to proclaim the gospel in his train.[130]

---

129. With many other scholars, I take 1:1 as the superscription/title for the whole of Mark. See, e.g., M. Eugene Boring, "Mark 1:1-15 and the Beginning of the Gospel," *Semeia* 52 (1990): 43-81; but cf. Robert A. Guelich, "'The Beginning of the Gospel' — Mark 1:1-15," *BR* 27 (1982): 5-15. Marcus proposes that the phrase "introduces both the prologue (1:1-13 or 1:1-15) and the Gospel as a whole" (*Mark 1–8*, 143 and also 145-46). In the debate about how to read Mark 1:1, it is infrequently noted that the author of Luke-Acts appears to have taken it as referring to the whole of the story of Jesus, as is suggested by his own wording at a couple of crucial points. The reference in Luke 1:2 to "those who from the beginning [*ap' archēs*] were/became eyewitnesses and servants of the word," must refer to the disciples who accompanied Jesus through his ministry. In Acts 1:1-2 the author refers to his previous volume as an account of "all that Jesus began [*ērxato*] to do and teach," the cognate verb perhaps reflecting Mark's use of *archē*, with Acts as the sequel to the beginning of the gospel in Jesus. I also now consent to the view that "son of God" (*huios theou*) was likely not original to Mark 1:1, but was probably a reverential addition that became popularly received. See esp. Peter M. Head, "A Text-Critical Study of Mark 1:1," *NTS* 37 (1991): 621-29.

130. The Greek term *archē* had a rich body of connotations beyond mere chronological

The human "realism" of Mark's presentation of Jesus noted by John Donahue also furthers a connection between Jesus and intended readers.[131] Donahue points to "a series of strong emotions," including pity (1:41), violent displeasure (1:43), anger (3:5), indignation (10:14), groanings and deep sighs (1:41; 8:12), surprise at disbelief (6:6), and love (10:21), noting also that Matthew and Luke omit them all in their retelling of the same incidents. Donahue also mentions as relevant the places in Mark where Jesus is portrayed as not knowing something: who touched him (5:31-32), what the disciples were discussing (9:33), and the eschatological "day or hour" (13:32), all of which likewise are altered in the retelling by Matthew and Luke. Mark's greater "realism" is probably deliberate, and not merely a vivid style of storytelling. His Jesus successfully proceeds through his mission to his divinely ordained fate exhibiting emotions and the limitations of knowledge that help make him an inspiring example for readers.

The Markan emphasis on Jesus as example explains the treatment of the Twelve, which has been so misconstrued by some scholars.[132] As many have observed, Mark presents the Twelve in a noticeably more negative manner than any other Gospel.[133] But it is simplistic to take this as merely an attack on them (and thereby on some group in early Christianity with which they are supposedly to be associated). Instead their failures serve as vivid warnings to readers that following Jesus is a difficult and dangerous venture.[134] These failures include not only dullness (e.g., 4:13, 41; 8:14-16) but also desertion (14:50) and even apostasy (14:66-72).[135] But both in Jesus' prediction (14:28) and in the

---

"beginning": e.g., origin, authority, first cause, source, foundation. BAGD, 111-12, s.v. Note its use as an epithet for Christ in Col. 1:18.

131. Donahue, 379.

132. Most famously, Theodore J. Weeden, "The Heresy That Necessitated Mark's Gospel," *ZNW* 59 (1968): 145-58; Weeden, *Mark — Traditions in Conflict* (Philadelphia: Fortress, 1971).

133. Among numerous studies, see, e.g., Tannehill, "The Disciples in Mark"; Elizabeth S. Malbon, "Disciples/Crowds/Whoever: Markan Characters and Readers," *NovT* 18 (1986): 104-30; Günter Schmahl, *Die Zwölf im Markusevangelium. Eine redaktionsgeschichtliche Untersuchung,* TTS 30 (Trier: Paulinus Verlag, 1974); Ernest Best, *Disciples and Discipleship: Studies in the Gospel according to Mark* (Edinburgh: T. & T. Clark, 1986).

134. E.g., Elizabeth Struthers Malbon, "Fallible Followers: Women and Men in the Gospel of Mark," *Semeia* 28 (1983): 29-48, reprinted with several others of her essays on Mark in *In the Company of Jesus: Characters in Mark's Gospel* (Louisville: Westminster John Knox, 2000), 41-69.

135. The verbs used in Mark's account of Peter's "interrogation" by a serving girl, "deny" (*arneisthai*) and "curse" (*anathematizein*), portray Peter's actions in the terminology of apostasy. On the other hand, Jesus' behavior in his interrogation/trial (14:55-65) follows exactly his own instruction to his followers, to say nothing in self-defense and to use their interrogations as opportunities to give witness to the gospel. Mark intends the interleaved accounts of Jesus and Peter in 14:55-72 to give readers positive and negative models of behavior under interrogation on account of their faith and proclamation.

postresurrection announcement that confirms its validity (16:7), their restoration is posited, their failures overcome by Jesus' own contrasting faithfulness and authoritative summons.

In fact, this concern to make Jesus both the basis of redemption (10:45; 14:22-24) and the pattern for his followers probably gives the best explanation for the overall shape and limits of the Markan account, for what Mark does and does not include in it.[136] We have in Mark a story of Jesus that is shaped just like the life of disciples. In the words of Philip Davis, the Markan story line is "a blueprint for the Christian life": it begins with a baptism and then issues in mission, opposition, and persecution involving death, and ends with divine vindication by resurrection.[137]

Whether Mark knew of any miraculous birth tradition we cannot say. But if he did, he had good reason for not including one in a story of Jesus shaped to serve as a paradigm for his readers. As Christians, their life too began with their baptism, and Mark emphasizes that they too are called to follow Jesus in proclaiming the gospel and with a readiness to undergo persecution, trusting that if they lose their life for the sake of Jesus and the gospel, they shall receive eschatological vindication (e.g., 8:34-38). Likewise, no resurrection appearance was necessary or even appropriate. For readers who are to live with trust in God for their own vindication, it was sufficient to affirm that God has raised Jesus, the paradigmatic figure for their own lives and hopes (16:5-6).[138]

These observations about Mark's emphases also go a long way toward answering the question of why the book was written. It was clearly intended to encourage readers to follow Jesus, which includes following him in proclamation of the gospel, for which his own ministry is the *archē*, the origin and foundation. As we have already noted, there are narrative tendencies and an implicit narrative (or narrative substructure) in the earliest extant summaries of Christian proclamation (e.g., 1 Cor. 15:1-7) and also in Q, and these forces also likely contributed to the basic idea of a narrative account of Jesus. But all this is still too imprecise to answer the more specific question of why the author wrote this kind of work when he did. Why did the author apparently feel moved to write

---

136. I owe the following suggestion to Philip G. Davis, "Christology, Discipleship, and Self-Understanding in the Gospel of Mark," in *Self-Definition and Self-Discovery in Early Christianity: A Study in Shifting Horizons,* ed. David Hawkin and Tom Robinson, Studies in Bible and Early Christianity 26 (Lewiston, N.Y.: Edwin Mellen Press, 1990), 101-19.

137. Davis, "Christology," 109.

138. Of course, the empty tomb and the announcement by the "youth" in 16:5-6 are to be read in the light of Jesus' prophecies of his resurrection (8:31; 9:9, 31; 10:34; 14:28). For the intended Christian readers of Mark, the ending was not nearly so doubtful in meaning as it has often been made by modern scholars.

this particular "rendition" of Jesus sometime around 70, thereby anticipating and perhaps also precipitating several subsequent accounts with recognizable similarities?

The concerns underscored in Mark may give us important clues. There is exhortation to resolute discipleship, and warning about the consequences of failure (8:34-38). As already noted, Mark 13 is probably the most transparent address to readers, and thus gives us the clearest hints of their situation. The main concerns here are that followers may be deceived by false claims (vv. 5-6, 21-23), may be caught up in misguided calculations of the nearness of the end (vv. 7-8, 14-20), may be overcome by threats of opposition (vv. 9-13), or may become lethargic at the delay in the consummation (vv. 32-37).

We should also note that the central section (8:27–10:45) has a thrice-repeated pattern of predictions of Jesus' sufferings followed by teaching on discipleship (8:31-38; 9:30-41; 10:32-45), which clearly has the effect of making Jesus' own fate the index and pattern for the attitudes and commitment of his followers. This conveys a concern that those who claim to be followers should really make Jesus the informing paradigm for their life.

It is a reasonable supposition that the traumatic events connected and contemporaneous with the Jewish revolt against Rome in 66-72 are reflected in Mark 13 especially, and that the author saw in these distresses particular dangers to the believers for whom he wrote. The years of the Jewish revolt were indeed tumultuous. For example, in the midst of this war (in 68), Nero was assassinated and three different emperors (Galba, Otho, Vitellius) came to power and fell in the space of a year, before Vespasian's more successful installation in 69. Some might have thought the empire was in danger of falling apart; some Christians might have seen these events as presaging the apocalyptic end.[139] Moreover, although Christians were persecuted locally from the 30s onward, the reign of Nero in the 60s was marked by particularly violent actions against Christians in Rome.[140] These included the martyrdom of Peter and Paul.[141] Whether, as I think more likely, Mark was composed in Rome, or (as some

---

139. Marcus (Mark 1–8, 28-39) relates the distresses listed in Mark 13 to historical reports of the time. I demur, however, from his preference for a Syrian provenance for Mark.

140. Tacitus (Annals 15.44) describes "vast numbers" of Christians convicted under Nero and given over to various hideous forms of death including crucifixion. Also 1 Clem. 5–6 highlights, as "champions who lived nearest to our time," the executions of Peter and Paul along with "a vast multitude of the elect" who suffered various torments.

141. Daniel W. O'Connor, Peter in Rome: The Literary, Liturgical, and Archaeological Evidence (New York: Columbia University Press, 1969); Harry W. Tarja, The Martyrdom of St. Paul: Historical and Judicial Context, Traditions, and Legends, WUNT 2/67 (Tübingen: Mohr, 1994), and the review by R. A. Bauman, JBL 116 (1997): 751-53.

other scholars prefer) in some other place such as Syria, the sufferings of the Roman Christians, along with the war in Roman Judea, would have been matters of great import to the author and other believers.[142]

In the midst, or the aftermath, of such events, it may well have seemed particularly timely to warn believers about being led astray by false prophets and false hopes, and to emphasize that followers of Jesus must not be discouraged from proclaiming their message and must prepare themselves for whatever sacrifice may be required of them. The particular shape of Mark's Gospel, a sequential rendition of Jesus' own ministry, may have emerged in the author's mind as the most suitable way to summon believers to follow Jesus and to provide them with a pattern for their efforts. As I proposed above, the emergence of *bios* writings in the Greco-Roman period also may have influenced the author (even if indirectly and unconsciously) toward seeing a written sequential narrative of Jesus as a useful innovation.

Presuming readers who are baptized and participate in the Eucharist as a sacred meal (the latter practice directly reflected in 14:22-25), the author calls them to be prepared for the full consequences of their profession and ritual practice. Thus in the Markan account of the request for special positions in Jesus' "glory" (10:35-40), after their glibly confident claim that they are able to drink Jesus' "cup" and undergo his "baptism," James and John are told ominously that they will indeed experience what these two principal rituals of early Christianity really involve.[143] Allied to this, Mark also summons readers to ap-

---

142. It is a mistake to assume that the reference to the Jewish War and attendant sufferings in Mark 13 must indicate a provenance in or near Roman Judea. The Jewish revolt was a major war of rebellion, followed closely all over the empire; it would certainly have been a matter of great concern to the Jewish population of Rome and to those such as first-century Roman Christians who also took interest in such developments. I also find very plausible the suggestion of G. W. H. Lampe that the Markan account of Peter's denials (14:66-72) may have been written in the aftermath of the Neronian persecution and the apostasy of some Christians during it (as described by Tacitus, *Annals*, 15.44.2-5). The threefold denial fits Roman judicial practice (as reflected in Pliny the Younger's reference to interrogations of Christians, *Epistles* 10.97), and Mark uses the terminology of apostasy to describe Peter's denials (*arneō, anathematizō*, both used absolutely without object). Lampe proposed that the account of Peter's apostasy together with the word of his restoration (16:7) may have been intended to support the view that apostates in the Neronian crisis could also be restored. G. W. H. Lampe, "Church Discipline and the Interpretation of the Epistles to the Corinthians," in *Christian History and Interpretation: Studies Presented to John Knox*, ed. W. R. Farmer, C. F. D. Moule, and R. R. Niebuhr (Cambridge: Cambridge University Press, 1967), 337-61, esp. 357-58.

143. Cf. Matt. 20:20-28, which refers only to drinking Jesus' "cup," which seems to be simply the use of a biblical metaphor to refer to Jesus' coming fate. But the Markan reference to Jesus' baptism and cup is almost certainly a deliberate allusion to the principal rituals of early Christianity. Luke does not have the incident.

prehend adequately the significance of Jesus. Readers were likely expected to see the two feeding accounts as anticipations of their own eucharistic meals, and thus to view the references to the perceptual failures of the disciples as warnings to them also to probe the christological truths and behavioral requirements conveyed in their own sacred meal practice. These two concerns, for insight into Jesus' significance and for commitment to discipleship shaped by Jesus' own example, go a long way toward accounting for the contents and character-istics of this pioneering narrative.

Moreover, contrary to the varying proposals of some scholars, canonical Mark most likely represents basically what the original author wrote. Of course, any writing frequently copied by hand will likely incur both accidental and de-liberate changes. But claims that an earlier and significantly different writing (e.g., "Secret Mark" or a "proto-Mark") was used by the authors of Matthew and Luke have justifiably been judged unpersuasive by most scholars.[144]

The more recent and intricate theory, from Helmut Koester, I judge no more persuasive than previous ones. He posits an "original Mark" that lacked 6:45–8:26 and was used by Luke, and then an augmented Mark including 6:45–8:26 that was used by Matthew and also formed the basis for "Secret Mark" (an esoteric version produced early in the second century). This Secret Mark then was edited further in a still more esoteric direction by a group like the Carpocratian heretics condemned by Clement of Alexandria ("Carpocratian Mark"), and this was followed by another edited form of Secret Mark which was the canonical Mark that we know subsequently in copies of the New Testa-ment.[145] But Sellew has shown that Koester's claim that Luke used a form of Mark lacking 6:45–8:26 is implausible.[146] Furthermore, as a good many other

---

144. E.g., J. Pairman Brown, "An Early Revision of the Gospel of Mark," *JBL* 78 (1956): 215-27; Olaf Linton, "Evidences of a Second-Century Revised Edition of St. Mark's Gospel," *NTS* 14 (1968): 321-55; and earlier Emil Wendling, *Ur-Marcus: Versuch einer Wiederherstellung der ältesten Mitteilungen über das Leben Jesu* (Tübingen: Mohr-Siebeck, 1905). These claims rest on dubious inferences from minor stylistic agreements of Matthew and Luke against Mark, which are all more readily explained as the sort of coincidental changes that writers seeking a more el-evated style would make to the text of Mark. Essentially the same sorts of changes were made in the text of Mark itself by some copyists. See, e.g., L. W. Hurtado, *Text-Critical Methodology and the Pre-Caesarean Text: Codex W in the Gospel of Mark*, SD 43 (Grand Rapids: Eerdmans, 1981), 67-84, esp. 82-83, and literature cited there.

145. Koester, *Ancient Christian Gospels*, 273-303; his theory is presented in an earlier form in "History and Development of Mark's Gospel: From Mark to Secret Mark and 'Canonical' Mark," in *Colloquy on New Testament Studies: A Time for Reappraisal and Fresh Approaches*, ed. Bruce C. Corley (Macon, Ga.: Mercer University Press, 1983), 35-57. Cf., e.g., Marcus, *Mark 1–8*, 47-51, and other literature cited by him.

146. See Philip Sellew, "Secret Mark and the History of Canonical Mark," in *The Future of*

scholars have concluded, it is inadvisable to rest too much on Secret Mark.[147] The alleged letter of Clement that quotes it might be a forgery from more recent centuries. If the letter is genuine, the Secret Mark to which it refers may be at most an ancient but secondary edition of Mark produced in the second century by some group seeking to promote its own esoteric interests.[148]

To be sure, the Gospel of Mark has an interesting textual history, and from an early point scribes felt the text needed "improving" in various ways. Of course, the most notable place where such improvements were attempted was in the ending, with four different endings attested in extant manuscripts.[149] Moreover, scribes often made many smaller stylistic changes to bring the rather unsophisticated Markan Greek slightly closer to literary Greek expression. Scribes also often made many small harmonizations of Mark to the more familiar wording of the other Gospels, particularly Matthew (which from a very early point became the favorite Gospel of most Christians). But both the number and the antiquity of extant manuscripts enable us to detect these efforts. This textual evidence also allows us to say with reasonable confidence that our estimates of what kind of writing Mark originally represented, and why it was originally composed, must (and can) be based on critical editions of canonical Mark, not on some putative writing such as Secret Mark.[150]

Likewise, we can say with reasonable confidence that it was essentially what we know as canonical Mark (and probably with an ending at 16:8) that was emulated and drawn upon by the authors of Matthew and Luke-Acts. We turn

---

Early Christianity: Essays in Honor of Helmut Koester, ed. Birger A. Pearson (Minneapolis: Fortress, 1991), 242-57, esp. 247-52. Sellew also showed that the wording of Mark 14:51 ("a certain youth") argues against Koester's claim that in some previous form of Mark there was a preceding reference to the youth such as found in the text of "Secret Mark" (251-53). Sellew's own proposal for salvaging Koester's theory seems to me less plausible than the conclusion that canonical Mark was essentially original Mark.

147. I return to "Secret Mark" in chap. 7.

148. So also, e.g., Marcus, *Mark 1-8,* 47-51.

149. For a review of the textual data, see Bruce M. Metzger et al., *A Textual Commentary on the Greek New Testament* (London and New York: United Bible Societies, 1971), 122-28. On the "long ending" of Mark (16:9-20), see now James A. Kelhoffer, *Miracle and Mission: The Authentication of Missionaries and Their Message in the Longer Ending of Mark,* WUNT 2/112 (Tübingen: Mohr-Siebeck, 2000).

150. See, e.g., L. W. Hurtado, "Beyond the Interlude? Developments and Directions in New Testament Textual Criticism," in *Studies in the Early Text of the Gospels and Acts,* ed. D. G. K. Taylor (Birmingham: University of Birmingham Press, 1999), 26-48, esp. 40-43, in criticism of the claims of Helmut Koester, e.g., that all extant New Testament manuscripts reflect "substantial revisions of the original texts," in his essay, "The Text of the Synoptic Gospels in the Second Century," in *Gospel Traditions in the Second Century: Origins, Recensions, Text, and Transmission,* ed. William L. Petersen (Notre Dame, Ind., and London: University of Notre Dame Press, 1989), 19-37.

now to these two other important Jesus books. In the interests of space, I shall restrict the discussion to those matters that differentiate Matthew and Luke-Acts from Mark, especially regarding their portraits or "renditions" of Jesus.

Matthew

On the one hand, along with the Gospel of Luke (and perhaps even more plainly than Luke), the Gospel of Matthew is a vivid demonstration of the circulation and influence of the Gospel of Mark. Matthew incorporates some 90 percent of Mark (whereas Luke incorporates about 55 to 60 percent), and, as is true also of Luke, Matthew follows a story line that has a recognizably Markan core. On the other hand, Matthew is obviously the product of somebody who thought something more than (and somewhat different from) Mark was needed. That Matthew incorporates so much of Mark likely means that the author heavily admired and approved of the basic contents and shape of Mark, and expected his intended readers to have a similar attitude. Yet, equally obviously, the author felt Mark was not fully adequate. Perhaps he even felt Mark needed correction in some matters. The same attitude was probably shared by the author of Luke-Acts as well. Each of these authors who used Mark as a source and example ("Matthew" and "Luke" the obvious examples) simply sought to write an account of Jesus that most adequately addressed the perceived needs of his intended readers.[151] We cannot, however, linger long over all the questions involved in the composition of Matthew and the many observations that have been made about this important text.[152] I am primarily concerned with the Matthean "rendition" of Jesus, and how it compares with that given in Mark.[153]

---

151. Oscar Cullmann expressed a similar view: "The Plurality of the Gospels as a Theological Problem in Antiquity," in *The Early Church*, ed. A. J. B. Higgins (London: SCM Press, 1956), 43-44.

152. Among important studies of Matthew, Stanton, *A Gospel for a New People*; Anthony J. Saldarini, *Matthew's Christian-Jewish Community*, Chicago Studies in the History of Judaism (Chicago: University of Chicago Press, 1994); J. Andrew Overman, *Matthew's Gospel and Formative Judaism* (Minneapolis: Fortress, 1990); Ulrich Luz, *The Theology of the Gospel of Matthew* (Cambridge: Cambridge University Press, 1995). Among recent commentaries, Craig S. Keener, *A Commentary on the Gospel of Matthew* (Grand Rapids: Eerdmans, 1999), is a voluminous and richly documented discussion.

153. For studies of Matthew's christological emphases, see Ulrich Luz, "Eine thetische Skizze der matthäischen Christologie," in *Anfänge der Christologie*, ed. Cillers Breytenbach and Henning Paulsen (Göttingen: Vandenhoeck & Ruprecht, 1991), 221-36; D. J. Verseput, "The Role and Meaning of the 'Son of God' Title in Matthew's Gospel," *NTS* 33 (1987): 532-56; Jack D. Kingsbury, *Matthew: Structure, Christology, Kingdom* (Philadelphia: Fortress, 1975); Kingsbury, "The

So, perhaps the most direct way to proceed is to take note of the major ways in which Matthew differs from Mark in this matter.

The most obvious general observation is that the Gospel of Matthew is a considerably larger account, nearly 60 percent larger than Mark.[154] To be sure, Matthew often modifies material taken from Mark in an interesting way, but foremost, in comparison with Mark, Matthew represents a markedly augmented account of Jesus. Clearly the author had things to say about Jesus that Mark did not convey, or did not convey adequately, and to a considerable degree these things are presented in readily identified bodies of material. Matthew presents an augmented story line, with significant new material at the beginning and end of Mark's story. Matthew also provides a large body of teaching/sayings material, which he groups in five easily recognized discourses.

The first major augmentation of Mark is the nativity account (Matt. 1–2). Like the author of Luke-Acts, the author of Matthew precedes and enlarges his Markan-shaped story of Jesus' ministry with an account of Jesus' birth, including a genealogy, although it appears that neither the two birth accounts nor the genealogies in Matthew and Luke have any direct literary relationship to each other. Each account of Jesus' birth, however, is a significant expression of the

---

Figure of Jesus in Matthew's Story: A Literary-Critical Probe," *JSNT* 21 (1984): 3-36; and esp. Schnackenburg, *Jesus in the Gospels*, 74-130.

154. In a printed edition of the Greek New Testament (without any critical apparatus) on my shelves, Mark takes up thirty-nine pages, and Matthew sixty-three. At sixty-six pages, Luke is actually the longest canonical Gospel, and John occupies fifty-nine pages. In the Nestle-Aland Greek text, which includes an apparatus of variants and supporting witnesses (*Novum Testamentum Graece*, 27th ed. [Stuttgart: Deutsche Bibelgesellschaft, 1993]), the amount of space taken up by the textual apparatus in Mark distorts somewhat the comparative size of the texts of the Gospels. Robert Morgenthaler, *Statistik des neutestamentlichen Wortschatzes* (Zürich: Gotthelf-Verlag, 1958), gives the following word counts: Luke, 19,428; Matthew, 18,305; John, 15,416; Mark, 11,242.

155. Among recent studies, see esp. Raymond E. Brown, *The Birth of the Messiah* (Garden City, N.Y.: Doubleday, 1977); and on Matthew, Brian Nolan, *The Royal Son of God: The Christology of Matthew 1–2 in the Setting of the Gospel* (Göttingen: Vandenhoeck & Ruprecht, 1979). Among older studies, J. Gresham Machen, *The Virgin Birth of Christ* (New York: Harper and Row, 1930; 2nd ed., 1932; reprint, Grand Rapids: Baker, 1965), which, though dated and openly apologetic in intent, remains a useful analysis of ancient sources and related issues aired at the time of the book; Martin Dibelius, *Jungfrauensohn und Krippenkind: Untersuchungen zur Geburtsgeschichte Jesu im Lukas-Evangelium*, Sitzungsberichte der Heidelberger Akademie der Wissenschaften (Heidelberg: Carl Winters Universitätsbuchhandlung, 1932), is a classic study with special reference to the Lukan birth story arguing for "Hellenistic" influences; and Vincent Taylor, *The Historical Evidence for the Virgin Birth* (Oxford: Clarendon, 1920), remains a model of careful and reasonable analysis. Most recently, Ben Witherington III provides a good review of major issues connected with the birth narratives and a valuable bibliography in "Birth of Je-

author's view of Jesus, and both accounts present Jesus' birth as resulting directly from divine initiative.[155] Before we go further in surveying Matthew's rendition of Jesus, let us explore the origins and earliest meaning of this idea of Jesus as miraculously conceived.

Jesus' Conception and Birth

In a historical approach to the origins and meaning of the idea that Jesus was miraculously conceived by special action of the Holy Spirit, we can begin by noting that the earliest explicit references to this notion are in these nativity accounts of Matthew (1:18-25) and Luke (1:26-35). In fact, among New Testament writings, the idea is explicit *only* in these two passages. The first questions, therefore, are the probable date and provenance of the belief.

As scholars such as Raymond Brown have cogently shown, in light of the considerable differences between the Matthean and Lukan nativity narratives, it is most unlikely that either narrative derives from the other, or that there was a common source-narrative.[156] Actually, other than the central characters (Jesus, Mary, and Joseph), the most striking common features of the two accounts are the motif of an angelic announcement of Jesus' conception, the attribution of his conception to the Holy Spirit, and the emphasis that he is son of David, although the scenes where these features are expressed are clearly independent of each other (Matt. 1:18-21; Luke 1:26-35). I think it is difficult to imagine these common features as coincidental agreements, especially the joint testimony to Jesus' conception through the Holy Spirit (Matt. 1:18, 20; Luke 1:35). Instead it is highly likely that the basic idea of Jesus' miraculous/virginal conception was earlier than either account.[157]

If the two nativity *narratives* are the products of the two Gospel authors themselves, then the origin of the *idea* must be at least a few years earlier. We have to allow time for the idea to have circulated widely enough to become known independently to both authors and to have been seen as something their respective intended readers would be likely to react to favorably, and perhaps even recognize as reflecting familiar traditions. I suggest that this would require us to take the idea back at least a decade earlier than the composition of the

---

sus," in *DJG*, 60-74. But he does not mention the wide-ranging study by Thomas Boslooper, *The Virgin Birth* (Philadelphia: Westminster, 1962).

156. R. E. Brown, *Birth of the Messiah*, esp. 32-37 (on the question of the historicity of the narratives, and showing their differences) and 160-63 (on the historical provenance of the idea of Jesus' miraculous conception). In this paragraph I depend largely upon Brown's analysis and make a few inferences of my own.

157. I agree here with R. E. Brown's judgment (*Birth of the Messiah*, 247 n. 41).

these two Gospels, to approximately 65-75, depending on one's preferred dates for Matthew and Luke, and perhaps even somewhat earlier. If, as has sometimes been suggested, the Matthean and/or Lukan birth narratives represent the adaptations of previous narratives (or bodies of narrative material) about Jesus' birth, then the idea that Jesus was miraculously conceived could be quite a bit earlier than Matthew and Luke.[158]

In attempting to determine how early the idea might be, it is also necessary to note a few other passages in other first-century Christian writings. We may begin with the curious reference in Mark 6:3 to Jesus as "the carpenter, the son of Mary."[159] With Marcus, I judge it likely that this matronymic reference to Jesus by those pictured in the scene as offended by him, is to be taken as their "slur against his legitimacy."[160] It is certainly interesting that all the parallel statements in Matthew 13:55, Luke 4:22, and John 6:42 refer to Jesus as the son of Joseph, probably reflecting their reverential efforts to avoid the sort of expression found here (especially likely for Matthew and Luke, who used Mark as their principal source).

At least three possibilities might account for the expression in Mark. Marcus suggests that Mark 6:3 reflects first-century Jewish slurs against Jesus experienced by early Christians, and which formed part of what became a widespread disdainful response to the early Christian proclamation among Jews. Marcus thinks this aspersion corresponds also to "the tendency in later

---

158. See, e.g., R. E. Brown's proposals about the nature of a pre-Matthean nativity narrative (*Birth of the Messiah*, 104-21), which he proposes may have been patterned after traditions about Moses' birth. In his discussion of pre-Lukan nativity traditions and sources (239-50), he suggests that these reflected "a tendency to compare the conception of Jesus to the conception of OT salvific figures . . . and the idea of a virginal conception" (247).

159. Gk. *ho tektōn, ho huios tēs Marias*. The chief alternative reading at Mark 6:3, *tou tektonos huios kai tēs Marias*, though supported by P45 (editor's reconstruction) and a number of other witnesses, is almost certainly a (very early!) scribal harmonization of the Markan passage to the more familiar parallel in Matt. 13:55 (cf. Luke 4:22, "the son of Joseph [*huios estin Iōsēph houtos*]; John 6:42, "Jesus the son of Joseph" [*Iēsous ho huios Iōsēph*]); and it may also reflect early Christian embarrassment over the description of Jesus as a carpenter (e.g., Origen's reply to the mockery of Celsus on this matter, *Contra Celsum* 6.34, 36; but cf. Justin, *Dial.* 88.8, who refers to Jesus having worked as a carpenter). For further discussion of the text-critical issue, see, e.g., Metzger, *A Textual Commentary*, 88-89; but cf. Vincent Taylor, *The Gospel according to St. Mark*, 2nd ed. (London: Macmillan, 1966), 300.

160. Marcus, *Mark 1–8*, 374-75. Cf. R. E. Brown, *Birth of the Messiah*, 537-41, who sees in Mark 6:3 "no firm support for a Jewish charge of illegitimacy." Also Harvey K. MacArthur, "Son of Mary," *NovT* 15 (1973): 38-58; and Tal Ilan, "'Man Born of Woman . . .' (Job 14:1), the Phenomenon of Men Bearing Metronymes at the Time of Jesus," *NovT* 34 (1992): 23-45, both offer cases where Jewish men could be referred to as sons of their mothers. But the examples are all where the mother's lineage is regarded as superior to the father's, or in amulets, neither of which seems relevant to Mark 6:3.

Jewish traditions to portray Jesus as a bastard."[161] Echoing a suggestion made earlier by Stauffer, he calls the assertion of Jesus' virginal conception "the church's eventual response" to this slur.[162] That is, the slur could have come first, simply as a feature of Jewish polemics against early Christian christological assertions; the claim that Jesus had been miraculously conceived through the power of God's Spirit could then have been an early Christian response intended not only to refute the slur but to assert in very strong terms that Jesus' birth was unique and holy.

An interesting variation on this proposal has been offered recently by Jane Schaberg and defended by Gerd Lüdemann. They contend that Mark 6:3 preserves knowledge (originating among the folk of Jesus' home village) that Jesus was actually illegitimate.[163] In their view, because reference to Jesus as illegitimate then came to be a feature of Jewish polemics against the Christian message, Christians responded with the claim that Jesus was virginally conceived.

In my view, however, this is not a persuasive proposal for at least two reasons. First, it involves reading Mark 6:3 somewhat naively, as if it preserves some local gossip from Nazareth, and as if the author had the capacity or interest to do so. Surely all critical study of the Jesus tradition recognizes that the material in the Gospels is there because it was meaningful in some way to the intended readers. Consequently reports such as Mark 6:3 can hardly be taken as the author wishing to preserve for antiquarian reasons actual conversations of the inhabitants of Nazareth in Jesus' time. Second, if the charge that Jesus was illegitimate had been circulating from the outset of the Christian movement, it is surprising not to have any more direct hint of it in the earliest references to Jewish opposition prior to the Synoptic Gospels (e.g., Paul). By contrast, for ex-

161. Marcus (*Mark 1–8*, 375) cites references to later Jewish charges that Jesus was a bastard in Origen, *Contra Celsum* 1.28-32, 39, 69, and in *b. Sanh.* 67a, to which we could add a few other Talmudic references (e.g., *b. Sanh.* 106a, and the Jewish text known as *The Toledoth Jesu*). For discussion of references to Jesus' birth in Jewish sources, see R. Travers Herford, *Christianity in Talmud and Midrash* (1903; reprint, Clifton, N.J.: Reference Book Publishers, 1966), 35-45; Morris Goldstein, *Jesus in the Jewish Tradition* (New York: Macmillan, 1950), esp. 147-66 (on the *Toledoth Jesu*); and Johann Maier, *Jesus von Nazareth in der talmudischen Überlieferung* (Darmstadt: Wissenschaftliche Buchgesellschaft, 1978).

162. Marcus, *Mark 1–8*, 375; Ethelbert Stauffer, "Jeschu ben Mirjam: Kontrovergeschichtliche Anmerkungen zu Mk 6:3," in *Neotestamentica et Semitica: Studies in Honour of Matthew Black*, ed. E. Earle Ellis and Max Wilcox (Edinburgh: T. & T. Clark, 1969), 119-28.

163. Jane Schaberg, *The Illegitimacy of Jesus: A Feminist Theological Interpretation of the Infancy Narratives* (New York: Crossroad, 1990; reprint, Sheffield: Sheffield Academic Press, 1995), 160-64; Gerd Lüdemann, *Virgin Birth? The Real Story of Mary and Her Son Jesus* (London: SCM Press, 1998; German original, 1997), 49-55.

ample, Paul does probably allude to the Jewish view of Jesus' crucifixion as the death of a malefactor cursed by God (esp. Gal. 3:13-14, also implied in his reference to the preaching of Jesus' crucifixion as "a stumbling block to Jews" in 1 Cor. 1:22-23). But in mentioning Jesus' birth (e.g., Gal. 4:4-5), Paul gives no hint that it was the subject of Jewish slander.[164]

I find a third option considerably more plausible in accounting for Mark 6:3. In this approach the verse reflects a slur against Jesus that by the time of Mark's Gospel had already begun circulating as a Jewish polemical response to what were regarded as outrageous christological claims by Jesus' followers; it could be a response perhaps specifically directed against a claim that Jesus had been miraculously conceived. That is, I think it more likely that the slur alluded to in Mark 6:3 appeared in reply to prior Christian assertions about Jesus' birth. It is reasonably well accepted that elsewhere Mark employs irony, for example in the taunts of people in the crucifixion account, where the mockery actually says the truth.[165] So it is worth considering whether the crowd's hostile reference to Jesus as "son of Mary" is another example of what we see elsewhere in Mark: a derogatory comment that unwittingly says what readers can recognize as truth. Indeed, perhaps the intended readers were expected to know the claim that he really is "son of Mary" and not the offspring of his father, Joseph, because he was conceived by divine miracle.

To help assess these options, I offer a couple further observations. First, the *later* Jewish traditions about Jesus' illegitimacy are all commonly thought to be disdainful Jewish responses to prior Christian assertions that Jesus was virginally conceived.[166] This being the case then, it seems likely true also for the sort of *earlier* slur that may be alluded to in Mark 6:3.

Second, although it is possible that first-century Christians responded to a prior Jewish slander about Jesus' birth by counterasserting that he had been miraculously/virginally conceived, such a Christian response does seem to me just a bit "over the top," and even almost predictably counterproductive. That is, it is the sort of counterassertion that would hardly quell a slur against Jesus' birth, and would instead almost invite further scurrilous comments ("Vir-

---

164. The phrasing in Gal. 4:4, "born of a woman [*genomenon ek gynaikos*]," does not itself seem to carry a slur, as illustrated in similar phrasing in other texts such as Job 14:1.

165. E.g., the taunt about Jesus building the temple in three days (Mark 15:29), and the mockery of him as "Messiah, the King of Israel" who "saved others, but cannot save himself" (15:31-32).

166. This is the sort of view taken, e.g., by Herford. See also the earlier discussion by Heinrich Laible, "Jesus Christ in the Talmud," in Gustav Dalman, *Jesus Christ in the Talmud, Midrash, Zohar, and the Liturgy of the Synagogue* (Cambridge: Deighton, Bell, 1893; reprint, New York: Arno, 1973), 1-98.

ginally conceived, indeed!"). I suspect that if the Jewish slur had come first, it is more probable that the Christian response would have been simply to assert vigorously Jesus' full legitimacy, and perhaps even to claim that his family was of noble descent (i.e., the line of David, which is of course a part of what is claimed in both of the canonical nativity accounts). To claim a miraculous conception with no identifiable father does not appear terribly wise if early Christians simply wanted to refute successfully the slur that Jesus was illegitimate.

So I think it more likely that the claim that Jesus was miraculously conceived circulated originally, not as a reply to slurs about Jesus' birth, but as a "doxological" statement intended to assert Jesus' significance. More specifically, it was a way of referring to Jesus as truly and uniquely come from God, from his earthly origins in the womb onward.[167] I shall say a bit more later about the likely original meaning and function of asserting Jesus' virginal conception. My point here is that, once the assertion was circulating, it is quite easy to understand how religious polemics would have generated the sort of counterclaim that seems to be alluded to in Mark 6:3, and that went to the opposite extreme of casting aspersions on his legitimacy.

Consequently, if Mark 6:3 does allude to Jewish slurs about Jesus' conception that were circulating by the time Mark wrote, then I judge it likely that still earlier the prior claim that Jesus was miraculously conceived (perhaps even the specific claim of virginal conception) was circulating widely enough to generate such aspersions. Moreover, the slur on Jesus' birth had to have been around long enough that Mark could expect his Christian readers to recognize it in Mark 6:3. On this reasoning we might posit that a claim about Jesus' miraculous conception was circulating as much as a decade or more earlier than Mark.

But if the idea that Jesus was miraculously conceived was known by the time Mark wrote, why did he not directly refer to it in his account of Jesus? Doubtless the absence of any explicit reference to the idea that Jesus was miraculously conceived is the major reason some scholars would dissent from the suggestions I offered in the preceding paragraph. I grant that Mark's silence about Jesus' birth has at least some initial force.[168] But for at least two reasons I do not regard this particular silence to be as telling as some have concluded.

167. I refer here only to the motives and meaning for early Christians in the *circulation* of the claim. As to the historical basis for any claim about Jesus' conception, it is obvious that only Jesus' mother would have any direct knowledge, and neither Gospel nativity account makes any explicit claim to be based on the testimony of Mary or of Joseph.

168. On the Markan silence about Jesus' conception and birth, see, e.g., Taylor, *Historical Evidence*, 8-12.

First, there is good reason to doubt that the silence of New Testament writers is such a good indication of the limits of their knowledge of early Christian beliefs. I cite an example. Along with the other Synoptic Gospels, Mark makes no direct reference to Jesus' "preexistence" either.[169] Yet, on the basis of the Pauline letters, most scholars agree that this idea was circulating at least from the 50s of the first century onward. Moreover, most scholars grant that Mark's Gospel probably reflects Christian circles acquainted with the sorts of beliefs that we see attested in Paul's letters. Of course, this does not prove that Mark was acquainted with the idea of Jesus' preexistence. But it is more difficult to imagine that he did not know of the idea than to consider that he probably did know of it and chose not to make direct reference to it. Also, given that they appeared at least several years later than Mark, it would seem still more difficult to imagine that neither Matthew nor Luke had ever heard of the idea. My point is simply that it would be dubious to take the silence about Jesus' preexistence in Mark, Matthew, and Luke to indicate that the authors could not have known of the idea.

Second, Mark's concern to present Jesus as the role model and example for the lives of the intended Christian readers may specifically account for the silence about Jesus' miraculous conception, indeed the absence of a birth narrative altogether. As I noted earlier, the contours and limits of Mark's story of Jesus seem deliberately drawn to follow the typical shape of the Christian life of Mark's intended readers, from baptism, on through mission and opposition, to vindication by resurrection. It is not easy to see how reference to Jesus' miraculous conception fits or advances this emphasis, for it hardly was something that Mark's readers could be urged to emulate. Again, this obviously does not constitute evidence that Mark was acquainted with the claim that Jesus' conception was miraculous. But we do have a plausible reason for Mark not including an account of Jesus' miraculous conception other than ignorance of this idea. Of course, I have not offered proof that Mark and his intended readers were acquainted with a claim about Jesus' miraculous conception, and some scholars may well hesitate to think that they were. But I hope to have shown that, contrary to the assumptions of some, it is not implausible that Mark and his readers were acquainted with this claim.

A couple other passages are usually considered as possibly alluding to the claim, so I shall briefly consider them now. The earliest is Paul's reference to Jesus as "born of a woman [*genomenos ek gynaikos*], born under the Law" in Galatians 4:4. But this seems to be simply a two-part statement expressing in

---

169. But note Davis's observations that the Markan account of Jesus' baptism may well presuppose the idea of his preexistence ("Mark's Christological Paradox," 12-13).

recognizable idioms that Jesus appeared in human history and specifically as a Jew.[170] I find no basis for seeing here an allusion to the idea that he was conceived without a human father.

On the other hand, the statement put on the lips of the hostile Jewish crowd in John 8:41 ("We [hēmeis] were not born of fornication") does have an emphatic tone that some see as implying a contrast with Jesus, and perhaps alluding to a charge that his birth was of dubious legitimacy. But, given that in the immediately preceding exchange Jesus has challenged their claim to be proper children of Abraham, the crowd's emphatic reply is perhaps not so strange. Moreover, John uses emphatic pronouns at other points in the passage (e.g., 8:48-49) where there is no indication that they represent anything more than vigorous speech.[171]

Nevertheless, it is curious that the Jewish crowd not only denies birth from fornication but also claims, "We have one father, God himself." If John expected his readers to know the idea that Jesus was conceived directly by divine empowerment, he could have intended the crowd's claim here to be taken as an ironic counterclaim that actually hints at the truth of Jesus' own conception. Certainly, given the comparatively late date commonly assigned to the Gospel of John (80s or even 90s in its canonical form), and the likelihood that the idea of Jesus' conception was already circulating by about 70 or earlier, it is quite possible in principle that the Johannine readership knew this claim. If this view is entertained, then the two Johannine references to Jesus as "son of Joseph" (1:45; 6:42) may be intended to function as a "public" designation of Jesus, link-

---

170. For the phrasing "born of a woman," note the similar expression in Job 14:1. The use of *genomenos* for birth in Gal. 4:4 is paralleled in Paul's reference to Jesus as "born [*genomenou*] of the seed of David" in Rom. 1:3, and in the reference to Jesus being "born [*genomenos*] in human likeness" in Phil. 2:7. I agree with Betz that the phrase "born under the Law" derives from Jewish usage and originally carried no negative connotation, but I dissent from the commonly held view that in Paul's usage here the expression has acquired a negative sense (cf., e.g., H. D. Betz, *Galatians*, Hermeneia [Philadelphia: Fortress, 1979], 207). Elsewhere Paul says he had no problem with Jews being "under the Law," and when among them exhibited his own Jewishness (e.g., 1 Cor. 9:20), so long as this did not involve either the rejection of Gentile believers or the imposition of Torah observance upon them. In Galatians Paul clearly urges his Gentile converts not to aspire to be "under the Law"; but that is because for them that would amount to trying to supplement their salvation through Christ with Torah observance, implying that Christ was insufficient for them. He also appears to picture humanity ("we") as kept "under the Law," which served as a child minder (*paidagōgos*, "disciplinarian" NRSV) until Christ appeared (Gal. 3:23-24) and made possible faith in his redemptive work as the new requisite response that brings salvation. For Paul, that Jesus was born "under the Law" surely implies nothing more than what he affirms in Rom. 15:8, that Jesus came as a Jew.

171. E.g., in John 8:49, the emphatic "I [egō] do not have a demon" seems to be simply a firm denial of the crowd's allegation about Jesus in the preceding verse.

ing him to an earthly father, and thereby falling short of Jesus' higher identity and origins.[172]

In any case, the idea of Jesus' miraculous conception was circulating in at least some Christian circles circa 65, and perhaps even earlier. So what was the provenance of the idea, and what was its meaning or "function"? If by the 50s Christians were already ascribing "preexistence" to Jesus, thus representing him with cosmic significance "before" all things and above all things (e.g., 1 Cor. 8:4-6), what additional intention and significance did they want to convey (subsequently?) by ascribing his earthly conception and birth to God's own direct action? Perhaps the best places to turn to address this question are the two nativity narratives in which the idea is first explicitly presented in extant Christian literature.[173]

Three quick points, I trust, can be made without controversy because they represent widely agreed-upon observations among scholars. First, each narrative is placed prominently as the *initial unit* of the Gospel in which it appears, a very good indication of the importance of the nativity stories for the authors of Matthew and Luke. Second, both Gospels are very concerned to present Jesus in relation to the story of biblical Israel and hopes for its prophetic and redemptive future. Although both Matthew and Luke-Acts open their stories of Jesus out into a mission to all nations (e.g., Matt. 28:18-20; Luke 24:44-49), both authors claim that Jesus and the message about him are the fulfillment of the story of Israel. Third, both nativity accounts are themselves thoroughly crafted to present Jesus' *birth* in connection with the biblical story of Israel. In what follows I hope to show in some further detail the importance of this last point for discerning the probable provenance and original import of the idea of Jesus' miraculous conception.

The early placement of the genealogy in Matthew (1:1-17) shows that it is an important component of the larger narrative of Jesus' birth, and by various features the author indicates that the genealogy expresses Jesus' link with Israel,

---

172. This is a clearer possibility in John 6:42, the statement of the (somewhat hostile) crowd. Philip's reference to Jesus in 1:45 as Joseph's son and from Nazareth may, however, likewise reflect what is in John an inadequate estimate of Jesus' origins and meaning.

173. For contrasting views to what follows, see recently Lüdemann, *Virgin Birth?* and Schaberg, *The Illegitimacy of Jesus,* both of whom portray the idea of Jesus' miraculous conception as a patriarchal reaction to the accusation that Jesus was born illegitimately (an accusation that was in their view true). In my view the particular theological objectives of each author (for Schaberg, a version of feminist thought; for Lüdemann, his own private war with traditional Christian beliefs) so occupy the center of their attention that neither is able to give adequate consideration to the historical question of where and why the claim that Jesus was miraculously conceived arose.

and particularly with the royal house of David.[174] The reference to Jesus as son of David has very old roots in early Christian proclamation (reflected in an already traditional formulation in Rom. 1:3-4), and is certainly one of the christological claims that Matthew found also in Mark (e.g., Mark 10:47-48; 12:35-37). But from the opening words in 1:1 onward, Jesus' Davidic sonship is much more frequently echoed in Matthew (e.g., 9:27; 12:23; 15:22; 20:30; 21:9, 14-16), and plays a more prominent role in Matthew's presentation of Jesus.

Another important feature of the Matthean nativity account is the citation of biblical passages as fulfilled in the events narrated (1:22-23; 2:5-6, 15, 17-18, 23). In addition to these explicit citations, there are probable allusions to other biblical passages, such as the star (Num. 24:17) and the foreign Magi and their gifts (Isa. 60:1-3, 6). Obviously by these references to the Old Testament the author links his account of Jesus' birth with the biblical story of Israel. He makes the events in his nativity account both eschatological fulfillments of biblical prophecy and also signs and anticipations of the later recognition of Jesus' significance and accomplishments (e.g., the explanation of the name Jesus in 1:21; the reference to a shepherd for Israel in 2:6, which anticipates the descriptions of Jesus ministering to the "lost sheep" of Israel, e.g., in 9:36; 10:6; 15:24). That is, whatever very general resemblance could be seen between this account of Jesus' birth and contemporary accounts (pagan or Jewish) of the births of great men, heroes, and demigods, these explicit citations function to bring the story firmly within the sphere of biblical imagery and themes, presenting Jesus' birth as an eschatological event that brings the biblical story to fulfillment.[175]

In fact, throughout the Gospel of Matthew there is a repeated and frequent reference to the Old Testament as the predictive material of which Jesus is fulfillment.[176] Yet, as in a number of other matters, in this emphasis Matthew essentially has extended and elaborated an affirmation that is already made in

174. E.g., in Matt. 1:1 Jesus is "son of David and son of Abraham." The genealogy commences with Abraham (1:2), and 1:17 makes the history of Israel the framework for the genealogy, with Abraham, David (specified as "the king" in 1:6), and "the Christ/Messiah" (identified in 1:16 as Jesus) as the three key figures in that history. The number fourteen is commonly thought to allude to the numerical value of the Hebrew name of David: $D = 4$; $w = 6$; $d = 4$. See esp. Marshall D. Johnson, *The Purpose of the Biblical Genealogies*, SNTSMS 8 (Cambridge: Cambridge University Press, 1969).

175. "No other section of the Gospels is so clearly linked to [Old Testament] prophecy as is Matthew 1–2." Witherington, "Birth of Jesus," 63.

176. Schnackenburg (*Jesus in the Gospels*, 344 n. 78) counted some seventy-two quotations and allusions to the Old Testament that are identified in the Nestle-Aland Greek New Testament, compared to about thirty-five in Mark. Major studies include Krister Stendahl, *The School of St. Matthew and Its Use of the Old Testament* (Philadelphia: Fortress, 1968); Robert H. Gundry, *The Use of the Old Testament in St. Matthew's Gospel*, NovTSup 18 (Leiden: Brill, 1967).

Mark, which opens (1:2-3) with a citation of "Isaiah the prophet" to introduce and frame the ensuing story of Jesus.

The Lukan nativity account shows a similar concern and emphasis, even though the author uses different techniques in presenting them.[177] One major difference is the space given to the birth of John the Baptizer (Luke 1:5-25, 57-80), which the author weaves into this account of Jesus. But whatever the provenance of the material about John, in this Lukan context it assists in making Jesus' own birth a crucial part of God's eschatological visitation of Israel (especially evident in Zechariah's prophecy in 1:67-79). Whereas Matthew uses explicit citations of the Old Testament to link Jesus with the biblical story and heritage, Luke achieves the same purpose by placing a number of speeches on the lips of memorable characters in his narrative of Jesus' birth. As is well known to students of Luke, the very "Semitized" Greek of Luke 1–2, and the thoroughly Judaic tone and content of these speeches in particular, have led some scholars to propose that the Lukan narrative here may represent pre-Lukan sources and the speeches may derive from pre-Christian circles of devout Jews.[178] But whether Luke 1–2 embodies pre-Lukan or even pre-Christian sources/material or is substantially the author's own effort to produce a deliberately Judaic and biblical-like narrative of Jesus' birth, my point here is that the very tone and cadences of the Lukan nativity account clearly function to present Jesus' birth in the closest connection with biblical Israel and the messianic hopes that the author sees confirmed in Jesus.

Luke's genealogy of Jesus has a universal dimension (running from Jesus all the way back to Adam) and, unlike Matthew's, is placed outside the nativity narrative after the account of Jesus' baptism (3:23-38).[179] Nevertheless, it also undeniably traces Jesus' ancestry back through names connected with the story of Israel in the Old Testament. That is, both the Matthean and the Lukan genealogies represent distinguishable, independent efforts forming part of a larger strategy to link Jesus' birth with the "narrative world" of the Old Testament.

As briefly noted earlier, both nativity accounts explain Jesus' conception explicitly by reference to the power of the "Holy Spirit" (Matt. 1:18, 20; Luke

---

177. I consider Luke's birth narrative here along with Matthew's. In a later section of this chapter, I discuss other features of Luke's rendition of Jesus.

178. E.g., see R. E. Brown, *Birth of the Messiah*, 239-50 (on possible sources behind Luke 1–2) and 346-66, 377-92 (on the Lukan "canticles").

179. Note that, whereas Matthew's genealogy has a numerical "shape" alluding to its royal Davidic tone (the three groups of fourteen generations alluding to the numerical value of David's name in Hebrew), the seventy-seven generations (or eleven groups of seven) in the Lukan genealogy may reflect a play on the numbers seventy and seven, both of which had some associations with the Gentile nations in ancient Jewish traditions.

1:35). This obviously makes use of another biblical category, the Spirit associated in the Old Testament particularly with creation (Gen. 1:2) and prophetic inspiration (e.g., Num. 11:24-30; Joel 2:28-29 [3:1-2 MT]). This means that even at the point in the accounts of a miraculous (virginal) conception that is unparalleled among the biblical stories of the conceptions of figures such as Isaac, Samson, and Samuel (which are divinely aided conceptions involving human fathers), both authors give us deliberately biblical language and imagery. Likewise, in both nativity narratives the nature of Jesus' conception is conveyed in appropriations of the biblical "genre scene" of an angelic annunciation (to Joseph in Matt. 1:20; to Mary in Luke 1:26-30), patterned after Old Testament annunciations of the miraculous births of Isaac (Gen. 18:9-15) and Samson (Judg. 13:2-7). Moreover, as Brown has shown, Matthew in particular also reflects appropriation of extracanonical Jewish traditions about the birth of Moses.[180]

In sum, both nativity narratives are thoroughly suffused with biblical and Judaic tradition and are composed in the idioms of that tradition. The same is true of what appears to be the common prior tradition of Jesus' miraculous conception upon which both narratives depend. All this means that the most likely provenance for the idea that Jesus was conceived miraculously by God's Spirit is in circles of Jewish Christians and/or mixed Gentile and Jewish Christian circles that preferred to articulate their faith in Jesus in the idioms and conceptual categories of Jewish tradition. It is, thus, highly unlikely that the idea of Jesus' miraculous conception resulted from the influx of Gentile Christians who produced the claim by drawing upon various myths of divinely impregnated women who give birth to heroes and kings.[181]

The earliest observable function or meaning of the claim that Jesus was miraculously conceived was also strongly concerned with the biblical and Judaic heritage. In the Matthean and Lukan nativity narratives, Jesus is born as the Messiah (Matt. 1:18), the savior of "his people" (Matt. 1:21; cf. Luke 1:68-69), the "son of the Most High" and inheritor of the throne of David destined to reign over the "house of Jacob" (Luke 1:32-33; Matt. 2:1-6). Indeed, the specifically Davidic connection of Jesus is one of the features shared by both narratives (e.g., Matt. 1:1; Luke 1:32). That is, in both birth narratives, and in the common tradition upon which they depend as well, Jesus' unique conception functions as a way of asserting his significance as the true royal heir of David and the fulfillment of royal-messianic hopes. Certainly the birth narratives in-

---

180. R. E. Brown, *Birth of the Messiah*, 111-16.

181. Though varying in some issues, numerous scholars have reached a broadly similar conclusion: e.g., Adolf von Harnack, *History of Dogma*, trans. Neil Buchanan (reprint, New York: Dover Publications, 1961 [from 3rd German ed., 1900]), 100 n. 1; Taylor, *Historical Evidence*, 124-27; R. E. Brown, *Birth of the Messiah*, passim.

tend this fulfillment to also foreshadow the salvation of the Gentiles (e.g., Luke 2:32), but they present Jesus' birth primarily with reference to traditions that deal with the redemption of Israel.

The new feature in comparison with biblical stories of miraculous conceptions, conception without a human father, appears to function as "trumping" all the biblical precedents, and it expresses the aim of presenting Jesus' birth as the most momentous of all. In the Old Testament stories God enables infertile women to give birth, thereby addressing their concerns and those of their husbands for progeny. In some births, especially those of Isaac, Jacob, and Samson, God's purposes for the child are also specifically mentioned. The Lukan story of the conception of John the Baptizer fits these biblical analogies exactly: a conception granted to a barren couple, and a child with a divinely ordained purpose.

But in Jesus' case the emphasis is entirely on God's initiative and purposes. Mary is not an infertile married woman anxious about her status or her husband's view of her, and the angelic visit is not in response to any prior appeal either from her or from others concerned that she should conceive. Instead, Jesus' conception happens entirely by God's own power, completely at God's initiative, and solely with reference to God's redemptive purposes.

"Virginal conception" is a handy label used to refer to this, but in both birth narratives the focus is on Jesus' conception being unaided by a human father, not on Mary's sexual history or any ascetic portrayal of her.[182] The emphasis upon the Holy Spirit as the effective power in Jesus' conception (which, again, is in the core tradition behind both narratives) surely has the effect of attributing it to God, in terms drawn deliberately from biblical tradition; it may also be intended to distinguish Jesus' conception from the pagan stories of heroes, which almost always involve a sexual liaison between a god and a human woman.[183] In any case, there is not a hint in either nativity narrative of any aim to present Jesus' birth in competition or comparison with the pagan stories

---

182. E.g., in Matt. 1:18-21 the concern is to stress that Mary's pregnancy is not the result of any ordinary act of procreation, and 1:25 even reserves coital relations between Joseph and Mary till after Jesus' birth. Likewise, in Luke 1:34-35 the emphasis is that Mary will be enabled to conceive even though she is not in a sexual relationship with a man ("I do not have sexual knowledge of a man" [*andra ou ginōskō*], v. 34b). The term "virgin" (*parthenos*) in fact appears only once in each nativity account (Matt. 1:23; Luke 1:27), and the narratives reflect no particular prizing of virginity in itself.

183. It must be noted that in the pagan stories there is scarcely any emphasis upon the virginal status of the human woman. Indeed, in some forms of these stories the woman is married. For summaries of stories of such divine births in various religious traditions, see, e.g., Boslooper, 135-86.

(unless the emphasis upon the Holy Spirit was intended to draw an implicit distinction from the pagan stories). This, too, works against the theory that the original function of the claim that Jesus was miraculously born was to present Jesus in competition with the pagan heroes.

Consequently I must dissent from Boslooper's characterization of the birth narratives as "Christian stories in a primarily Hellenistic mode of thought cast into a Jewish setting and designed to make a universal appeal."[184] Both narratives of Jesus' virginal conception are certainly "Christian stories," but the mode of thought as well as the setting reflect biblical categories and traditions, and this suggests that the intended "appeal" is to people who appreciate these concerns and traditions. The narratives are profoundly christological statements and sophisticated compositions that require readers with serious competence in biblical and Jewish traditions to appreciate anything specific in them. They were written out of an ethos immersed in these traditions, and were intended to express the claim that these traditions find their fulfillment in the appearance of Jesus.

There is, however, no indication that claims about Jesus' miraculous birth formed a part of early Christian proclamation, least of all the proclamation to pagan audiences. The idea was not intended primarily to impress or attract the general public. I underscore the observation that the accounts in Matthew and Luke are both obviously intended for *Christian* circles, indeed, for readers acquainted with and appreciative of the very Judaic and biblical terms in which they are written.

Subsequently the function of asserting Jesus' miraculous conception and birth shifted, as is already evident in Ignatius of Antioch, for whom Jesus' birth was an important expression of the physical reality of the incarnate Jesus over against the teaching that Jesus only seemed to be human and only appeared to suffer death (Ign. *Eph.* 7.7; 18.2; 19.1; Ign. *Magn.* 11; Ign. *Trall.* 9.1-2; Ign. *Smyrn.* 1.1-2).[185] Under the impact of the battles with "heresies" of the second century, the groups of what we may call "proto-orthodox" Christians affirmed Jesus' miraculous conception and birth as an important confessional marker.[186]

Having considered at some length the provenance and function of the Matthean and Lukan birth narratives, and the idea of Jesus' miraculous conception that these narratives reflect, we now turn to other features of the Gospel of Matthew, with a view to seeing further how the author provides his own "rendition" of Jesus.

184. Boslooper, 228.
185. I return to Ignatius in chap. 10.
186. I discuss what I mean by the term "proto-orthodox" in chap. 8.

Matthew's Postresurrection Narrative

At the conclusion of Matthew, and corresponding to the nativity account in some interesting ways, is a sizable postresurrection narrative (28:1-20). Whereas Mark appears to have been content to conclude with the empty tomb (Mark 16:8), the announcement of the "youth" that Jesus has risen from the dead, and his command to the women to convey this news to the other disciples and to summon them to see Jesus again in Galilee, in Matthew things are much more elaborate. The mysterious "youth" is explicitly identified as "an angel of the Lord," who descends from heaven in a dramatic show of power (28:2-4) that frightens the guards at the tomb in 27:62-66. Matthew also has Jesus reinforce the command to the women (28:9-10), and makes it clear that they intended to do as they were told (28:8), which removes any lingering doubt or ambiguity about them from the reference to their fear in Mark 16:8. Then, after the story of the Jewish "elders" bribing the guards to lie about the disappearance of Jesus' body (28:11-15), the concluding scene is the formal commissioning of the eleven disciples in 28:16-20.

This final scene in Matthew is obviously crucial, but among the various observations that could be made about this passage, I focus on the way it presents Jesus.[187] Three features stand out. First, the risen Jesus who speaks here claims to have been given cosmic authority in 28:18. On the one hand, the universal dimensions of his statement ("all authority in heaven and on earth") reflect an august, divinelike status. On the other hand, that Jesus is given this authority (by God, as hinted by the "divine passive" verb here) means that his status derives from, and is linked with, God, and that Jesus is neither hubristic nor a rival to God.

Second, Jesus orders the eleven disciples to initiate a mission to make disciples of "all nations." Matthew's first readers were intended to see here the authorization for the proclamation of the gospel to all peoples, an activity of which they themselves were results, and to which they too were called to be involved. That is, Matthew here connects his story of Jesus with the continuing life and efforts of the Christian circles after Jesus. As we shall note later, Luke-Acts makes this connection still more explicit in a programmatic literary representation of Jesus as the first part of a larger story in which the activities of Jesus' followers in the decades after his execution and resurrection form the second part. But just as Mark clearly anticipates the post-Jesus Christian mission (especially in Mark 13), so Matthew's whole account of Jesus is implicitly set within the ongoing story of the proclamation of the gospel.

---

187. Benjamin J. Hubbard, *The Matthean Redaction of a Primitive Apostolic Commissioning: An Exegesis of Matthew 28:16-20*, SBLDS 19 (Missoula: Scholars, 1974).

The third feature of this passage is Jesus' continuing authority and efficacy in the worldwide mission that he commands. Those converted are to be
baptized and taught "to obey everything that I have commanded you" (28:19-
20), which looks back to the considerable body of teaching/sayings material
that Matthew introduced into his expanded version of Mark and arranged in
the form of discourses. Clearly Matthew wanted his account of Jesus' teachings
to be treated as a resource for the continued dissemination of Jesus' words as
authoritative for believers. In addition, Jesus' promise of perpetual presence
with his followers (28:20b) indicates that he is not simply their authoritative
teacher but also a living and powerful force with divine attributes. "I am with
you always" also recalls the uniquely Matthean reference to Jesus as "Emmanuel" and the explanation of the name as "God with us" in 1:23, these two phrases
likely intentional echoes of each other and forming a literary *inclusio,* a device
that brackets the whole of the Matthean story of Jesus. Certainly the promise of
continued presence "till the close of the age" demands that Jesus be regarded as
having divine power, and this fits with the many other indications that Matthew thoroughly affirms a transcendent view of Jesus' status like that projected
also in Mark.

Matthew's Discourses

In between the bracketing accounts of the nativity and the postresurrection
narrative, Matthew's other most prominent additions to the Markan material
and structure are the five commonly recognized discourses, which present substantial amounts of Jesus' authoritative teaching on a number of subjects (5:1–
7:28; 10:1–11:1; 13:1-53; 18:1–19:1; 23:1–26:1). Each ends with a statement indicating
that Jesus has "finished" *(etelesen)* giving a body of teaching *(tous logous,* 7:28
and 19:1), mission instructions *(diatassōn,* 11:1), or parables *(parabolas,* 13:53);
26:1 serves to conclude both the final discourse and the whole series of discourses ("when Jesus had finished *all* these sayings," *pantas tous logous toutous*).
The five discourses amount to 380 verses, about 35 percent of Matthew, and a
body of material roughly 60 percent the size of Mark.[188] It was obviously a major aim of the author to present Jesus as the authoritative teacher for readers. Of
course, Matthew found the emphasis on Jesus as a teacher already there in
Mark, which frequently mentions teaching as a component activity in Jesus'
ministry, but it was Matthew's contribution to supply a substantially larger

---

188. There are 1,071 verses of material in Matthew and 666 verses in Mark 1:1–16:8. Some
of the material in the five Matthean discourses has parallels in Mark (e.g., Matt. 24/Mark 13;
Matt. 13/Mark 4). But the structural prominence given to discourses is peculiar to Matthew.

body of material to give more ample indication of Jesus' teaching. Likewise, it is even possible that the idea of providing blocks of Jesus' teaching in the form of such discourses may have been suggested by the discourse-like blocks of teaching material in Mark (parables in Mark 4:1-34; eschatological discourse in 13:1-37). But Matthew clearly made discourses a much more prominent feature of his account of Jesus, and the particular idea of a fivefold discourse arrangement is the author's own literary choice.[189]

The most well-known block of material is the first of these discourses, the "Sermon on the Mount" in 5:1-7:29.[190] Here we have a programmatic presentation of Jesus as authoritative teacher on a variety of related topics. Some of the material is paralleled in the "Sermon on the Plain" in Luke (6:20-7:1), but Matthew both provides a much larger collection of sayings material and also favors a mountain location, both here and in other important scenes in his story.[191] The "Beatitudes," which open the discourse in 5:1-12, pronounce blessings upon those who exhibit the proper stance toward God, and form an introduction to the whole discourse. Then 5:17-48 is focused on Jesus' purposes and teachings in relation to the Torah. Thereafter are teachings on almsgiving, prayer, and fasting (6:1-18; important features of piety in Jewish tradition), followed by exhortations on directing one's life entirely toward God with confidence in God's provision (6:19-34) and further exhortations on several other matters (7:1-20). The discourse ends with an emphasis upon Jesus' authoritative status and the consequences of either accepting or disregarding his teachings (7:21-29).

189. As the commentaries indicate, scholars debate whether the five discourses are intended to allude to the five books of Moses, implicitly presenting Jesus' teaching as a new Torah (or new authoritative interpretation thereof), or whether the arrangement simply reflects an ancient fondness for five-book arrangements of material (e.g., the canonical Psalter). In part, opinions on the meaning of the fivefold discourse arrangement are connected with whether readers grant Moses typology as one of Matthew's larger emphases. See, e.g., Dale C. Allison, *The New Moses: A Matthean Typology* (Minneapolis: Fortress, 1993).

190. Among the voluminous publications on this discourse is the recent and hefty study by Hans Dieter Betz, *The Sermon on the Mount*, Hermeneia (Minneapolis: Fortress, 1995). I cannot comment here on Betz's theory of the history of this material, which I do not find particularly persuasive. Cf. Robert H. Gundry, "H. D. Betz's Commentary on the Sermon on the Mount," *CR* 10 (1997): 39-58. Cf. also Stanton, *A Gospel*, 285-306.

191. Terence L. Donaldson, *Jesus on the Mountain: A Study in Matthean Theology,* JSNTSup 8 (Sheffield: JSOT Press, 1985). Donaldson suggests that Matthew fashioned the location for the sermon "on the basis of Mark's account of the mountain-top commissioning of the Twelve" (194, also 107-8). Mountains form the backdrop to Matthean scenes in the temptation narrative (4:8-11, the climactic temptation in Matthew), the initial discourse (5:1), the feeding account (15:29), the transfiguration scene (17:1, the mountain setting also in Mark 9:2), the discourse about the temple and the future (24:3, also in Mark 13:3), and the final commissioning (28:16).

The material relating Jesus' authority to the Torah in 5:17-48 has received particularly close attention, and has generated predictably varying conclusions as to whether Jesus is presented here as replacing Torah with his teaching or reinforcing and validating Torah through his interpretation of it. In the context of the sermon, the "commandments" of 5:19 that are to be rigorously observed must be the sorts of rulings from Jesus that we have in 5:21-48, the fulfillment of which amounts to the righteousness that "exceeds that of the scribes and Pharisees" (5:20) and illustrates what it means to "be perfect . . . as your heavenly Father is perfect" (5:48). Moreover, it is clear in 5:21-48 that Jesus' stipulations on obedience to God are given indisputable authority and are set over against the entirety of other interpretations (note especially the repeated formula, "you have heard it said . . . but I say"). Jesus' commands here even surpass those of the Torah as defining righteousness (e.g., 5:21-26).[192] The apodictic way that Jesus here specifies right behavior, and the repeatedly emphatic "I" with which he speaks in the entirety of the Sermon on the Mount, combine to make the teaching given in the discourse a profound statement of Jesus' authority and unique significance for the author and intended readers.

Jesus is the one by whom they are to understand what God requires, and obedience to Jesus' teaching fully constitutes the righteous response to God that is superior to any other. The concluding units of the sermon (commonly thought to be Q material) transparently indicate this. Those seeking entry to the kingdom of heaven in the future will acclaim him as "Lord," and will prophesy and work miracles of healing in his name; but he will admit only those who have also done the will of God (as defined in his teachings), and will dismiss those who have not demonstrated such obedience (7:21-23). The parable of the houses built either upon rock or upon sand makes it clear that doing God's will means hearing Jesus' teachings and acting upon them (7:24-27), which also will constitute the difference between future disaster or salvation.

The second Matthean discourse (10:1–11:1, although 9:35-38 is an introduction to it) gives directions to the twelve disciples as they are sent out to proclaim the approach of the kingdom of heaven to "the lost sheep of the house of Israel" (10:6). Matthew here combines material that appears in various places in Mark. The sending scene parallels Mark 6:7-13, but Matthew also embeds the names of the disciples (paralleled in Mark 3:13-19); and he relocates here sayings from the Markan discourse on the future (compare Matt. 10:17-22 with Mark

---

192. As Stanton notes, the "antitheses" of Matt. 5:21-48 present Jesus' commandments as superseding the demands of Torah, yet Matthew probably does not intend these contrasting statements to constitute a contradiction of Torah but rather as setting forth the "greater righteousness" that Jesus rightly demands (*A Gospel*, 301-2).

13:9-13). The net effect of this editorial work is to make the sending of the twelve disciples a more transparent anticipation of the wider post-Jesus mission to all nations. Here, as in all the discourses in Matthew, readers are to recognize that "the risen Lord is speaking through the earthly Jesus."[193] Curiously, although the author explicitly situates this discourse in Jesus' past (the references to "Samaritans" and the "towns of Israel"), the warning about being dragged before "governors and kings . . . as a testimony to them and the Gentiles" (10:18) opens out the horizon to the post-Jesus mission, as do the promise of the prophetic inspiration of the Spirit (10:20) and the exhortation to endure to "the end" (10:22). Quite obviously, this discourse is not merely a reminiscence about Jesus and the twelve disciples in their own setting, but functions also to inspire and give encouragement to the intended readers of Matthew by merging the horizon of their own mission with that of Jesus and his Galilean disciples. The particularity of the situation of Jesus and his original disciples is respected and explicitly reflected, but the author also invites readers to see that Galilean mission as inspirational and in some ways paradigmatic for their own.

The third Matthean discourse (13:1-53) is made up of parables. Of course, both the precedent of such a discourse and some of the parables in it were presented to the author in Mark 4:1-34, but Matthew has his own emphases. We recognize again here the Matthean use of explicit quotations of the Old Testament Scriptures to emphasize that Jesus is to be seen as the fulfillment of them (13:14-15 citing Isa. 6:9-10, and 13:35 citing Ps. 78:2). Also, Matthew includes several parables not found in the Markan discourse. Among these, the parable of the good seed and weeds (13:24-30) and its interpretation (13:36-43) combine to emphasize the eschatological triumph of the Son of Man as vindicator of his elect ("the righteous") and judge of "all evildoers" (13:41-43).

But, here and elsewhere, Matthew departs from Mark's characterization of Jesus' disciples as obtuse. For example, in this discourse Matthew omits Jesus' complaint about the disciples' inability to perceive what he is saying (cf. Mark 4:13; Matt. 13:10-13). Instead he has Jesus proclaim how blessed the disciples are in what is set before them (13:16-17), and has them answer affirmatively to Jesus' question whether they have understood all that has been presented (13:51-52). As I noted earlier, in Mark the repeated failures of the disciples support his emphasis on Jesus as the only true and positive pattern of discipleship for readers, and the fallible disciples are contrasting examples intended to warn readers to take the demands of following Jesus seriously. But whereas Mark presents Jesus as the pattern *for* disciples and readers, Matthew presents Jesus more as the au-

---

193. Frank J. Matera, *New Testament Christology* (Louisville: Westminster John Knox, 1999), 33 (I use here wording from his comments on the Sermon on the Mount).

thoritative master *of* and *over* the disciples and readers. And so in Matthew the twelve disciples function much more as figures with whom readers can identify themselves positively.

The discourse in 18:1–19:1 is concerned entirely with the internal relations of the Christian circles for whom Matthew wrote. Jesus here commands humility (18:1-5) and concern for the spiritual welfare of others as well as one's own (18:6-9). Jesus warns against disdain for the "little ones," those fellow believers who may seem insignificant but are dear to God (18:10-14). He sets forth directions on how offenses are to be handled among his followers (18:15-20), and notably here we have one of the two distinctive Matthean uses of *ekklēsia* ("church," 18:17; 16:18), which makes it transparent that this teaching is to be applied in the circles of the intended Christian readers.[194] The discourse concludes with a strong emphasis on the forgiveness that Jesus' followers owe to one another, as those who have themselves been forgiven and who continue to depend upon God's mercy toward them (18:21-35).

The final of the five Matthean discourses comprises chapters 23–25, and has a strong emphasis on future judgment. Although in 23:1-39 Jesus pronounces woes upon the scribes and Pharisees for various alleged hypocrisies and failures, the opening words (23:1-2) picture disciples among those addressed, making the woes also warnings instructive for Christian readers. In this sweeping condemnation of Jewish scribes and Pharisees, their climactic offense is the rejection of, and violence against, those "prophets, sages, and scribes" sent to declare God's messages (23:29-36), including those sent to "this generation" (v. 36). In addition to Jesus' authoritative stance reflected in the woes, his lament over Jerusalem in 23:37-39 even more clearly reflects a view of him acting in capacities that are divine. Moreover, Jesus here gives his followers (including, of course, the intended readers of Matthew) the proper viewpoint in confronting and assessing opposition, especially opposition from Jewish religious authorities who claim to have Moses' authority in their actions (23:2). Rejection of the gospel is hereby aligned with the rejection that Jesus experienced, and is set within the frame of a future appearance of Jesus in triumph (23:39).

There follows the Matthean version of the directions and warnings about future distresses for Jesus' followers in 24:1-51, which are given in reply to the questions of his disciples triggered by his prophecy of the destruction of the Jerusalem temple. Matthew's concluding exhortation in 24:45-51 appears to be Q material inserted here. In the context of the preceding verses in 24:36-44, it is

---

194. It is interesting to compare the directions given in Matt. 18:15-17 with the Qumran text, CD 9.1-8, which has somewhat similar directions about avoiding offenses and handling them when incurred.

clear that Jesus is the master whose return will bring reward for followers who are faithful, and dire consequences for followers who live carelessly.

The last section of this fifth discourse comprises three extensive parables, all of which have a strong eschatological tone of warning. In the Matthean context here, the parables of the ten bridesmaids (25:1-13) and the servants entrusted with funds (25:14-30) appear to be warnings to Jesus' followers to "keep awake" and to be a "good and trustworthy slave," these parables extending the emphasis of 24:45-51. The third parable, however, which contrasts those who show proper hospitality and benevolence for Jesus' "brothers" with those who do not, has a worldwide scope ("all the nations" are gathered before the enthroned son of man, 25:31-32); it probably concerns the responses given to those who proclaim the gospel message in the post-Jesus situation of Matthew's readers. Of course, given the emphasis in early Christian circles on hospitality and concern for the needs of fellow believers, Jesus' followers could also be included among those warned here.

In all of this final discourse, Jesus continues to speak in a majestic, powerful, and completely authoritative stature. Though later in the Matthean narrative Jesus will face a violent and humiliating death at the hands of his enemies, the material in Matthew 23–25 anticipates his subsequently glorious and powerful place in the future consummation of God's plan. As Frank Matera put it, "Although Matthew emphasizes that Jesus is the crucified Messiah, he shows the church that the crucified one is its exalted Lord."[195] Of course, the "high" view of Jesus here is fully consonant with the exalted place he has throughout Matthew, and it obviously reflects the view of him cherished among the intended readers of Matthew.

Other Features of Matthew's Presentation of Jesus

This high view of Jesus is also reflected in Matthew's fondness for scenes where people give reverence to Jesus. Much more frequently than the other Gospel authors, Matthew uses the Greek word *proskynein* to describe the reverence that people offer Jesus.[196] The verb designates a reverential posture that one adopts toward a social superior when pleading for mercy or seeking a favor (e.g., Matt. 18:26), but also it can mean the worship one gives to a god (e.g., 4:9-10). The

---

195. Matera, 27.

196. Matthew uses *proskynein* thirteen times; in Mark it is used only to describe the reverence given by the Gerasene demoniac (5:6) and the mock reverence given to Jesus as "king of the Jews" by the Roman soldiers (15:19). In Luke the term appears in the temptation narrative (4:7-8), where Satan solicits worship from Jesus, and otherwise only in 24:52, where it probably carries the connotation of the worship given to the risen Jesus by his followers.

Magi come to reverence Jesus, and Herod falsely professes a readiness to do so (2:2, 8, 11). Those who seek a miracle (8:2; 9:18; 15:25) and the mother of the Zebedee brothers, who requests a special place for them in Jesus' future kingdom (20:20), make this reverential gesture (all of which uses of *proskynein* have no parallel in the other Synoptic Gospels). In these cases the gesture is perfectly plausible in the cultural context of the events narrated, but it is also likely that the intended readers would have seen the reverence as an unwitting anticipation of post-Jesus Christian circles.

In at least three Matthean scenes, the gesture still more obviously connotes reverence that readers are to see as reflecting their own worship practice, in which Jesus is recipient along with God. In the concluding sentence of the Matthean version of the story of Jesus walking on the waves (14:22-33; cf. Mark 6:45-52), the disciples reverence and acclaim Jesus, saying, "Truly you are the Son of God" (v. 33). This is a striking modification of the Markan version, which ends with the disciples amazed but not perceptive of what has been revealed (6:52). Finally, twice in the postresurrection narratives Jesus' followers give this reverence to the risen Jesus: the women hurrying from the tomb (Matt. 28:9), and in the climactic scene, where Jesus meets his followers and commissions them in august tones (28:17). In all three scenes Jesus' transcendent status and power are indicated, and it seems undeniable that the intended readers were to take the scenes as paradigmatic anticipations of the reverence for Jesus that they offered in their worship gatherings.

Another indication of the high view of Jesus reflected in Matthew is given in the honorific titles applied to Jesus. Although Matthew employs a number of terms for Jesus, it is widely agreed that "Son of God" and other expressions of Jesus' divine sonship ("my/his Son," 2:15; 3:17; 17:5; 21:37; "the Son," 11:27; 21:38; 24:36; 28:19) are central to all that the author wishes to affirm.[197] In this, Matthew expresses a conviction similar to Mark's (and probably also affirmed in Q, as we have noted). But in Matthew Jesus' divine sonship is more prominently featured, and it is not so much the christological secret that it is in Mark.

For example, in the more extended temptation narrative in 4:1-11 (likely taken from Q), Jesus' divine sonship is explicitly mentioned twice (vv. 3, 6) and is probably implicit in the third temptation too (vv. 8-10). Also, as noted already, in the Matthean version of the story of Jesus walking on the water, the

---

197. See esp. Kingsbury, *Matthew* (40-83 on Son of God, 84-127 on other titles), who is acknowledged as influential in showing the centrality of the divine sonship emphasis in Matthew. On p. 84 Kingsbury lists the other christological terms in two categories. Other "major" terms are "Messiah," "Son of David," "Kyrios," and "Son of Man"; "minor christological terms" are "Jesus" (esp. Matt. 1:21), "Son of Abraham," "the Coming One," "Shepherd," "prophet," "rabbi-teacher," "Servant," and "Emmanuel."

disciples acclaim him as "the Son of God" (14:33; cf. Mark 6:52). In the Matthean scene where Jesus asks his disciples who they say he is, Matthew adds "the Son of the living God" to the messianic affirmation in the Markan parallel (16:16; cf. Mark 8:29). As well, in the crucifixion narrative Matthew adds that bystanders twice taunted Jesus as "Son of God" (27:40, 43; cf. Mark 15:29, 32). In two other key passages Matthew has Jesus refer to himself as "the Son" and to God as "my/the Father": one relates Jesus' celebration of God's gracious revelation and his own intimate relationship with God in 11:25-27, which is Q material (cf. Luke 10:21-22); the other is the "great commission," crucially placed as the ending of Matthew (28:16-20), which includes Jesus' command to baptize "in the name of the Father and of *the Son* and of the Holy Spirit" (28:19).

In addition to this strong affirmation of Jesus' divine sonship (referred to over twenty times), Matthew expresses other christological convictions characteristic of New Testament writings. Jesus' messianic status is clearly important, and *Christos* is a major Matthean christological title. Matthew's sixteen references to Jesus as the "Christ/Messiah" double the frequency of the title in Mark (cf. twelve uses in Luke and nineteen in John), and show a comparatively more frequent connection of Jesus as *Christos* with Israel, especially in the nativity account (1:1, 16-18; 2:4). Nevertheless, for Matthew, as for all the New Testament writers, it is Jesus who defines the meaning of "Christ/Messiah," not finally Jewish expectations. Thus Jesus the Christ is also "Son of God," with a transcendent connotation clearly included; and his rejection and execution form part of his messianic mission.[198]

Also, as in the other canonical Gospels, "the son of man" is one of Jesus' characteristic self-referential terms. But, also in keeping with the other Gospels, it never expresses anyone's belief about Jesus, or is contested, and so is not really a confessional title like the others. Matthew is however especially concerned to assert Jesus as rightfully the "son of David," expanding the three Markan references to the title to nine (1:1; 9:27; 12:23; 15:22; 20:30-31 [twice]; 21:9, 15; 22:42-45).[199] Of course, this accords with the many other indications in Matthew of a concern to present Jesus very much in terms of the Jewish tradition of the first century. But, as Stanton has noted, Matthew's use of "son of David" seems to reflect a Jewish hostility to the claim, a hostility that the intended readers are expected to recognize in their own experience.[200]

198. I adapt here some lines from my study of the use of the term *christos* in all four canonical Gospels: "Christ," in *DJG*, 106-17, here esp. 112.

199. J. D. Kingsbury, "The Title 'Son of David' in Matthew's Gospel," *JBL* 95 (1976): 591-602; Christoph Burger, *Jesus als Davidssohn*, FRLANT 98 (Göttingen: Vandenhoeck & Ruprecht, 1970), 72-106.

200. Stanton, *A Gospel*, 180-85.

It is not difficult to see why Matthew became the favorite Gospel rendition of Jesus in many early Christian circles.[201] Matthew gave his readers an august Jesus who delivered authoritative teachings, fulfilled biblical prophecy, demonstrated his power in miracles, received divine vindication in his resurrection, then commissioned his followers to pursue a worldwide mission and also assured them of his continuing, powerful presence as they did so. That the author made a rather full appropriation of Mark does not reduce the significance of his own literary contribution to the devotion that Christians have offered to Jesus from the late first century to the present day.

Luke

As I have already made several references to the presentation of Jesus in the Gospel of Luke, in what follows I shall restrict the discussion to a few other salient matters that distinguish this important writing.[202] The most obvious distinguishing feature is that the Gospel of Luke was the first volume of a major two-volume literary work that links a narrative of the activities of the churches to a story of Jesus. Mark clearly anticipates, and gives directions for, following Jesus subsequent to the time covered in the story line that ends at Mark 16:8, and this involved a proclamation to "all nations" and consequent opposition (esp. Mark 13). Matthew has Jesus directly commission this activity in a final scene that points toward the post-Jesus period (esp. Matt. 28:16-20). Luke-Acts, however, is one explicitly linked narrative of the story of Jesus and the religious movement that came after him. This major work thereby constitutes a notable literary innovation. We know of no other account such as the book of Acts in the first century and for some time thereafter, and we have no other literary work like Luke-Acts that combines a full-scale account of Jesus with a narrative of early Christianity. Moreover, the sheer size of this two-book work is impressive among other first-century Christian literature, amounting to about one-quarter of the New Testament.[203]

---

201. This has been fully documented for the earliest period by Edouard Massoux, *The Influence of the Gospel of Saint Matthew on Christian Literature before Saint Irenaeus*, ed. Arthur J. Bellinzoni, trans. Norman J. Belval and Suzanne Hecht, 2 vols. (Macon, Ga.: Mercer University Press, 1990).

202. For a more extensive discussion, see, e.g., Schnackenburg, *Jesus in the Gospels*, 131-218.

203. E.g., in the twenty-seventh edition of the Nestle-Aland Greek text of the New Testament, Luke and Acts together amount to 184 pages of a total 680 pages, about 27 percent. I do not know that scholars have adequately asked about what the writing of such sizable texts may suggest about the economic situation of the authors. Obviously the composition of Luke-Acts

Yet it is quite possible that the basic idea of attaching an account of the early churches to a Gospel was suggested to the author by the Gospel of Mark. As Joel Marcus observed, "Mark is more the biography of a movement, or at least that movement's beginnings *(archē)*, than it is the biography of an individual, and the narrative points toward the continuation of that movement after Jesus' death, both through explicit prophecies (e.g., chapter 13) and through the way in which Jesus and his followers and opponents constantly become symbols for groups in the Markan present."[204] So, with the Markan story of Jesus before him, an account designated by its author as the "beginning of the gospel of Jesus Christ," the author of Luke-Acts took the further step of conceiving his own dramatic narrative with its larger, distinctive two-volume shape.

The Lukan rendition of Jesus also reflects, more obviously and perhaps more frequently than the other canonical Gospels, an acquaintance with literary conventions of the Roman era, and an apparent effort to make this account of Jesus meaningful for readers with an appreciation of literary technique. The most obvious, and most frequently cited, illustration of the author's literary concerns is the preface in Luke 1:1-4. It is not possible here to discuss the particulars of this sentence, very skillfully constructed by an author who aimed to show a certain literary artistry.[205] However, unlike most modern authors (and many ancient ones as well), this writer employed his evident literary skill not to promote his own reputation, but in the service of the religious faith to which he subscribed (Luke 1:4).[206]

For our purposes, it is important that this author saw a full-scale narrative of Jesus as the obvious and indispensable foundation volume for a literary work that effectively presents and advocates "the Christian story."[207] Moreover, of course, even in Acts the author makes Jesus central to the continuation of the

---

required both considerable literary skill (which demands the opportunity to have acquired it) and the time to carry out such a literary effort (which was normally done by people with the time that only adequate economic circumstances could provide).

204. Marcus, *Mark 1–8*, 66.

205. One of the best discussions of this passage remains that by Henry J. Cadbury, "Commentary on the Preface of Luke," in *The Beginnings of Christianity*, ed. J. J. Foakes Jackson and Kirsopp Lake (London: Macmillan, 1922-33), 2:489-510, which includes copious parallels from Roman-era literature. Cadbury says Heb. 1:1-2 vies with the preface to Luke "for the honour of being the most carefully constructed period in the New Testament" (492), and points to the "rhetorical balance and periodic construction" as "the work of an artist" (490). Also worth noting is Cadbury's survey of Greek and Jewish traditions of writing history (7-29). More recently, see Loveday C. A. Alexander, *The Preface to Luke's Gospel*.

206. He gives the name of an intended reader (Theophilus), but did not include his own.

207. The quoted words are from Cadbury, 510, paraphrasing "the things about which you have been instructed" (Luke 1:4).

account of Christian mission in the first three decades after Jesus. The transitional preface to Acts (1:1-2) explicitly points back to the preceding account of Jesus as the context and foundation for what follows. In the subsequent narrative Jesus is everywhere the substance of the message proclaimed (e.g., 1:22; 2:29-36; 10:36-43), the one in whose name believers are opposed and persecuted (e.g., 4:17-18; 5:40-42) and the sick and demonized are delivered (e.g., 3:11-16), and the one in whose future return the divine consummation of redemptive purposes will be achieved (e.g., 3:17-22; 17:30-31).

As we noted earlier, Luke and Matthew offer extended versions of the Markan story line, with a birth narrative at the opening and departure/farewell scenes added at the closing, giving the story of Jesus a more recognizably *bios* shape. The various Lukan chronological references represent another (more distinctive) literary device that was intended specifically to link the story of Jesus with figures and events of world history ("the days of King Herod," 1:5; references to Caesar Augustus and Quirinius, 2:1-2; references to Tiberius, Pilate, Herod [Antipas], Philip, Lysanias, Annas and Caiaphas, 3:1-2).

At the same time, Luke emphatically places Jesus in a story of salvation that connects with Israel and the Old Testament. Earlier we noted how the "speeches" of the Lukan nativity account present Jesus' birth firmly in the context of Israel's hopes for redemption. In the rest of the Lukan story of Jesus also, the whole "story world" and major conceptual categories derive from the Old Testament and Jewish postbiblical traditions. For example, Luke 16:16, which has figured prominently in modern scholarly characterizations of the author as "a theologian of the history of salvation," refers to the sweep of history in periods comprised of "the law and the prophets," followed by "the gospel of the kingdom of God." That is, we have a time of promise and expectation, followed by the time of fulfillment and salvation, which the author presents in two stages comprised of Jesus and the subsequent Spirit-empowered work of the churches.[208]

The Lukan presentation of Jesus in relation to Israel and the Old Testament is patently reflected in the prominence of Jerusalem and its temple throughout Luke-Acts. The nativity narrative opens with a scene set in the Jerusalem temple (Luke 1:5-23), and at various subsequent points in these early chapters the author connects Jesus with the sacred city and its shrine in vi-

---

208. As Schnackenburg notes (*Jesus in the Gospels*, 133), Hans Conzelmann's influential study of Luke's conception of salvation history does not give an adequate representation of matters (*Die Mitte der Zeit: Studien zur Theologie des Lukas*, 4th ed. [Tübingen: Mohr, 1962]). Cf. the other literature cited by Schnackenburg (348 n. 7), and also John T. Carroll, *Response to the End of History: Eschatology and Situation in Luke-Acts*, SBLDS 92 (Atlanta: Scholars, 1986). I thank Paul Owen for alerting me to Carroll's study.

gnettes that are unique to Luke (especially the extensive account of the presentation of Jesus in the temple in 2:22-38 and the story of the boy Jesus in dialogue with Jewish teachers in the temple in 2:41-51).

Perhaps the most distinctive structural feature of Luke's account is the so-called travel narrative, all the material in 9:51–19:44 placed within a narrative movement of Jesus toward Jerusalem. This has the intended effect of casting the shadow of Jesus' final time in Jerusalem directly over this huge body of material, and it portrays Jesus directly in connection with Jerusalem and what it represents.

Bracketing the Jerusalem/temple references of the nativity narrative, the final words of Jesus in 24:46-49 portend a worldwide proclamation "beginning from Jerusalem"; Jesus commands the disciples to remain in the city "until you have been clothed with power from on high" to perform this mission. This Jerusalem-centered emphasis characterizes Acts as much as Luke, as illustrated in Jesus' mission statement in Acts 1:8, which calls for a Spirit-empowered proclamation that ripples from Jerusalem outward "to the ends of the earth."

For the author of Luke-Acts, it is obviously crucial that Jesus and the early Christian movement are seen as answering the hopes of Israel, and as fulfilling the biblical prophecies of God's redemptive faithfulness. The risen Jesus repeatedly refers to himself (authoritatively!) as "the Messiah/Christ" whose sufferings and vindication were predicted in the Old Testament Scriptures (Luke 24:25-27, 45-46); in these postresurrection scenes it is obviously a crucial christological claim that Jesus' death and resurrection have this scriptural validation.

At the same time, Luke-Acts asserts in the strongest terms the universal significance of Jesus. I noted earlier that the Lukan genealogy presents Jesus as descended from Adam, not only from Abraham and the line of Israel. The distinctive second mission charge in Luke 10:1-12, to the seventy (or seventy-two) disciples (cf. the mission of the Twelve in 9:1-6), is commonly thought to prefigure the post-Jesus proclamation of the gospel to all nations.[209] In the final directions of Jesus given in Luke 24:46-49, which command the disciples to remain in Jerusalem for empowerment, they are explicitly told that the proclamation of forgiveness of sins in his name is to go to all nations. Clearly it is an important Lukan emphasis that Jesus is the Messiah of *Israel*, and precisely

---

209. See, e.g., I. H. Marshall, *Commentary on Luke* (Grand Rapids: Eerdmans, 1978), 415. On the variation in Greek manuscripts between "seventy" and "seventy-two" disciples, see, e.g., Metzger, *A Textual Commentary*, 150-51. In Jewish tradition both numbers were associated with the Gentile nations (e.g., seventy-two nations listed in the LXX of Gen. 10, but seventy nations in the Hebrew; or the seventy "weeks of years" in Dan. 9:24-27 during which Israel is dominated by Gentile powers).

as such also brings *universal* redemption. As Schnackenburg proposed, the distinctively frequent use of the title "Savior" *(Sōter)* in Luke-Acts (Luke 1:47; 2:11; Acts 5:31; 13:23) probably represents the author's choice of a term that "has connections with both Jewish tradition and Hellenistic conceptions"; this term further illustrates a concern to assert Jesus' significance both in biblical and universal dimensions.[210]

There is in Luke another, somewhat similar dual emphasis on Jesus as human hero and also divine Lord. For example, 4:1 describes Jesus as "full of the Holy Spirit"; and in the programmatic scene in 4:16-30, Jesus explicitly identifies himself as the Spirit-anointed figure spoken of in Isaiah 61:1-2 (a theme echoed in Acts 10:38). Thereby Jesus serves as role model for believers, who are promised the Spirit as empowerment for their own life and service (e.g., Luke 24:49; Acts 1:8). In other ways as well, the Lukan Jesus is a genuinely human figure (e.g., the distinctive reference to Jesus' cognitive, social, and religious development in 2:51-52) and a model of piety.[211] The frequent references to Jesus at prayer are additional illustrations of this emphasis (3:21; 5:16; 6:12; 9:18, 28-29; 11:1; 22:32; 23:34, 46), and the author must have intended these scenes to be exemplary for his readers. The distinctive prominence of women in Luke's account may at least in part be yet another feature of the author's emphasis on Jesus' humanity, picturing him thereby in company that is more representative of real life.[212]

In the Lukan account of Jesus' trial before Pilate, and the subsequent crucifixion, the distinctively strong emphasis on Jesus' innocence combines with other features to present Jesus' execution as a heroic submission to an unjust fate. Repeatedly Pilate affirms Jesus' innocence (23:4, 14-15, 22), citing the same judgment by Herod. The uniquely Lukan conversation among Jesus and the two criminals crucified with him makes the same point (23:39-43), and Jesus' assurance that the penitent criminal will join him in paradise (v. 43) reflects the

---

210. Schnackenburg, *Jesus in the Gospels,* 145-48, quotation from 147.

211. See, e.g., Schnackenburg, *Jesus in the Gospels,* 181-86, 210-18.

212. Passages unique to Luke featuring women include the reference to the widow of Zarephath (4:25-26), the widow of Nain (7:11-17), the sinful woman of 7:36-50, named women followers in 8:1-3, Mary and Martha (10:38-42), the healing of the crippled woman in 13:10-17, the woman and the lost coin (15:8-10), the woman and the unjust judge (18:1-5). Of course, this greater salience of women in Luke (and in Acts) may also represent the author's concern to reflect the participation of women in early Christian communities. For fuller discussion, see, e.g., Schnackenburg, *Jesus in the Gospels,* 198-209; but cf. Allen Black, "Women in the Gospel of Luke," in *Essays on Women in Earliest Christianity,* vol. 1, ed. Carroll D. Osborn (Joplin, Mo.: College Press Publishing Co., 1993), 445-68, who argues that the stories of Jesus' ministry to women function as part of the author's emphasis that biblical promises of the restoration of God's people are being fulfilled (e.g., Joel 2:28-30).

confidence of a righteous man (in fact a royal figure who will "come into [his] kingdom," v. 42).[213] The Lukan version of the centurion's statement, "Certainly this man was righteous/innocent [*dikaios*]," gives climactic reaffirmation of this Lukan emphasis (23:47). In the interchange with the weeping women of Jerusalem in 23:27-31, Jesus is a confident figure, able to give prophetic warning of the fate awaiting the city. This heroic posture is also reflected in the final utterance of the Lukan Jesus, as he confidently entrusts himself to God, whereas Mark and Matthew place on Jesus' lips the lament of Psalm 22:1.

Yet, along with this portrait of the heroic man, Luke also projects a very high view of Jesus' transcendent significance. For example, much more frequently than in other canonical Gospels Luke refers to the earthly Jesus as "the Lord" (e.g., 7:13, 19; 10:1, 39, 41; 12:42; 13:15; 17:5-6; 18:6; 19:8; 22:61; 24:3, 34), thereby (in deliberate anachronism?) using the key term of early Christian liturgical devotion.[214] The reverence that the disciples give the risen Jesus in the final verses of Luke (24:52, "they worshipped [*proskynēsantes*] him") is certainly intended by the author as the full reverence given to a figure of divine status/ significance, this action anticipating the cultic reverence of Jesus familiar to the author and his intended readers.

Another indication of Jesus' high significance is in the distinctively Lukan scenes of Jesus' postresurrectional ascension into heaven (Luke 24:50-53; Acts 1:9-11). These scenes have been shown to echo Old Testament and postbiblical Jewish traditions of ascents (or "raptures") of worthies such as Enoch, Elijah, and Moses, and may also have reminded a Roman-era readership of stories of ascensions in Greco-Roman traditions.[215] The author of Luke-Acts fully professes that Jesus' resurrection involved his heavenly exaltation, and the Lukan ascension accounts do not constitute an alternative version of Jesus' exaltation.

---

213. On the term "paradise" and ancient Jewish notions about it, see, e.g., Marshall, *Commentary on Luke*, 872-73.

214. Ben Witherington III, "Lord," in *DJG*, 484-92, esp. 488-91, who notes that there are 210 uses of the term *Kyrios* in Luke-Acts (not all of them, however, with reference to Jesus), of a total of 717 uses in the New Testament. See also Ignace de La Potterie, "Le titre Kyrios appliqué à Jésus dans l'Évangile de Luc," in *Mélanges biblique en hommage au R. P. Béda Rigaux*, ed. Albert Descamps and R. P. André Halleux (Gembloux: Duculot, 1970), 117-46.

215. Alan F. Segal, "Heavenly Ascent in Hellenistic Judaism, Early Christianity and Their Environment," in *ANRW*, 2.23/2:1333-94, surveys various traditions. Major studies of the Lukan ascension scenes and the probable traditions behind them include Gerhard Lohfink, *Die Himmelfahrt Jesu: Untersuchungen zu den Himmelfahrts-und Erhöhungstexten bei Lukas*, SANT 26 (Munich: Kösel, 1971); and Mikeal C. Parsons, *The Departure of Jesus in Luke-Acts*, JSNTSup 21 (Sheffield: Sheffield Academic Press, 1987). But the most impressive and persuasive study is A. W. Zwiep, *The Ascension of the Messiah in Lukan Christology*, NovTSup 87 (Leiden: Brill, 1997).

Instead, as Zwiep has shown, the narratives of Jesus' ascension in Luke-Acts serve the author's emphasis on the panorama of the divine program of salvation ("salvation history"), marking the transition from the period of Jesus' own activity to the activity of the churches.[216] Moreover, references in Acts connect Jesus' ascension with his future return (1:11; 3:20-21), these two events marking the period of proclamation as itself an eschatological time. Of course, the ascension also vividly refers to Jesus as presiding in heavenly status over the unfolding story of the churches conveyed in Acts.

It is obvious that the author of Luke-Acts provided fellow believers of the late first century with a memorable and influential literary rendition of Jesus. Though dependent on Mark (incorporating some 60 percent of Mark into his own account), "Luke" writes an innovative account of Jesus that shows literary craftsmanship, profound religious commitment, and specific "pastoral" concerns and emphases. Though reflective of the techniques of Roman-era historical writing, and showing an interest and ability in conveying something of the atmosphere of the places and events that it describes, Luke-Acts is by no means an antiquarian account. Luke is an endearing rendition of Jesus to which the author adds the first narrative of the spread of the movement for which Jesus was the defining expression of God's purposes.

Summary

Sometime around 70 C.E. at the latest, Christians began writing full-scale narrative accounts of Jesus, which quickly became widely read and influential for all subsequent centuries of Christian history. These "Jesus books" promoted and reflected the intense devotion to Jesus that characterized the circles of Christians for whom the authors wrote. Each is a notable literary "rendition" of Jesus in its own right, with particular emphases, and was probably intended to address what the author regarded as pressing needs of the intended readers. There were, of course, numerous other books about Jesus as well in the period of "earliest Christianity" that we are studying in this book. But along with the Gospel of John, the three that I have focused on in this lengthy chapter were easily the most influential. To judge by their widespread usage, they also must have been

---

216. I depend here on Zwiep, esp. 194-99. "Luke sharply distinguishes the resurrection-exaltation from the ascension and never presents Jesus' ἀνάλημψις *(Entrückung)* [rapture] as the occasion of his *exaltatio ad dexteram Dei* [exaltation to God's right hand] (as Mk 16:19 does!). The post-resurrection appearances recorded in Luke-Acts are all manifestations of the already exalted Lord from heaven; the ascension rounds off the last one" (197). See similar views by K. Giles, "Ascension," in *DJG*, 46-50.

the most widely representative of Christian beliefs about Jesus, and of how traditions about him were treasured and used to guide the behavior of those who called upon him as their Lord.

In the next chapter I turn to the remaining canonical Jesus book, the Gospel of John, and the other writings associated with it that exhibit the distinctive expression of devotion to Jesus that we call "Johannine Christianity."

CHAPTER SIX

Crises and Christology
in Johannine Christianity

The Gospel of John (GJohn) is without doubt one of the most important and most influential "Jesus books" ever composed. Particularly in the christological disputes of the early centuries, it was unexcelled as the favorite arsenal of textual ammunition (often by both sides of the disputes!).[1] Moreover, as one of the four canonical accounts, GJohn is of course historically linked with the Synoptic Gospels, but unlike them, it is more directly associated with certain other writings in the New Testament, especially the three epistles of John. GJohn and these other "Johannine" writings are commonly thought by scholars to have come from the same (or closely related) circles of first-century Christian believers; they were all probably composed in their present form within a decade or so of one another.[2] Also, most scholars hold that GJohn does not demonstrate a direct literary relationship with any of the other three canonical Gospels, but rather, reflects a discrete stream of Jesus tradition (a matter to which I

1. See esp. Maurice Wiles, *The Spiritual Gospel: The Interpretation of the Fourth Gospel in the Early Church* (Cambridge: Cambridge University Press, 1960); T. E. Pollard, *Johannine Christology and the Early Church*, SNTSMS 13 (Cambridge: Cambridge University Press, 1970). On the usage and influence of John, see the classic work by F.-M. Braun, *Jean le théologien et son Évangile dans l'église ancienne*, Ebib (Paris: J. Gabalda, 1959); and René Kieffer, "Les premiers indices d'une réception de L'Évangile de saint Jean," in *The Four Gospels 1992: Festschrift Frans Neirynck*, ed. F. Van Segbroeck, C. M. Tuckett, G. Van Belle, and J. Verheyden (Leuven: Leuven University Press/Peeters, 1992), 3:2225-38.

2. Although early Christian tradition also ascribed the book of Revelation to the "John" (Zebedee) to whom the Gospel and epistles of John were attributed, most scholars today doubt that Revelation comes from the same author, and perhaps not even from the same circles of Christian believers, as the Gospel of John and the Johannine epistles. I discuss the presentation of Jesus in Revelation in chap. 10.

return shortly). Furthermore, with the other Johannine writings, GJohn constitutes a quasi-independent witness to the place of Jesus in what appears to many
scholars to have been a discrete strand of early Christianity.[3] So in this chapter
we focus on these Johannine writings and the particular devotion to Jesus that
they manifest.

Scholars also widely agree that all these "Johannine" writings have a
strongly polemical tone, and that they probably reflect at least two major historical crises that powerfully affected the Christian circles in which, and for
which, they were originally composed. I say more about these crises and their
probable effects later in this chapter. This polemical tone certainly characterizes
the strong assertions about Jesus in these writings, and this is probably the result of these crises, which involved controversies about Jesus.[4] This does not
mean that the beliefs about Jesus in the Johannine writings were *simply* the
product of these post-Jesus controversies. But it is not reductionistic to allow
that the Johannine Christians probably sharpened and refined their views of Jesus in response to opposition and controversy. A good deal of scholarly effort
has been spent on attempting to reconstruct the history of the Johannine believers by whom and for whom these writings were prepared and the nature of
these controversies, and in the following discussion I shall draw upon this work
in relating the Johannine affirmations about Jesus to their probable historical
circumstances.

The religious controversies reflected in the Johannine writings probably
help considerably to explain in particular why the assertions about Jesus' transcendent significance are so much more explicit and emphatic than in some
other New Testament texts. For example, the differences between the christo-

---

3. The scholarly literature on the Johannine writings and the circle(s) from which they
came is so enormous that it is preposterous to cite anything here other than a few of the relatively recent major publications that address broader historical issues, e.g., Raymond E. Brown,
The Community of the Beloved Disciple (New York: Paulist, 1979); John Ashton, *Understanding
the Fourth Gospel* (Oxford: Oxford University Press, 1991); John Painter, *The Quest for the Messiah: The History, Literature, and Theology of the Johannine Community*, 2nd ed. (Edinburgh:
T. & T. Clark; Nashville: Abingdon, 1993; 1st ed., 1991); Martin Hengel, *The Johannine Question*
(London: SCM Press, 1989). For recent surveys of issues pertaining to the Johannine writings,
see Robert Kysar, "John, Epistles Of," in *ABD*, 3:900-912; and Kysar, "John, Gospel Of," in *ABD*,
3:912-31. Robert Kysar, *The Fourth Evangelist and His Gospel: An Examination of Contemporary
Scholarship* (Minneapolis: Augsburg, 1975), remains a valuable, though already now dated, resource. Cf. now the helpful analysis of scholarship by P. Anderson, *The Christology of the Fourth
Gospel*, WUNT 2/78 (Tübingen: Mohr-Siebeck, 1996), 1-69.
4. "The Christology of this Gospel was not spun out of whole cloth but developed in the
bosom of a community that underwent several changes." F. J. Matera, *New Testament Christology* (Louisville: Westminster John Knox, 1999), 216.

logical rhetoric of GJohn and the other canonical Gospels are quite striking. Scholars debate the extent to which the *substance* of Johannine beliefs about Jesus is different from the convictions reflected in the other Gospels, but it is undeniable that the *expression* of Johannine beliefs and the rendition of Jesus in GJohn are distinctive at least in vocabulary, emphases, and cadences.

Also, despite the arguments of scholars over many other matters in the Johannine writings, all agree that these texts focus on issues of belief in and about Jesus. A bit more precisely, we may say that in GJohn the emphasis is on the necessity of *believing in* Jesus, and this is stated over against an unwillingness to acknowledge him as Messiah and Son of God that is attributed to *Jewish outsiders* to the Johannine "community" of faith. In the *epistles,* however, especially in 1 John and 2 John, the emphasis is on *proper beliefs about* Jesus, over against the teachings of certain *other Christians.* The Johannine writings collectively testify to the centrality of belief in/about Jesus in constituting Johannine Christians as a discrete religious group in the religious environment of their time. As well, beliefs about Jesus were central in subsequent struggles among Johannine Christians over their continuing identity, directions of development, and religious integrity.

I repeat that it would, however, be simplistic to make the emphasis on Jesus merely the product of the controversies that afflicted the Johannine believers. I remind readers that the model I sketched in chapter 1 involves the *interaction* of *several* forces/factors, among which the encounter with the religious environment (which can include opposition) is only one, albeit important, phenomenon.

To be sure, controversy often has the effect of sharpening and intensifying the efforts of groups to assert and define their core commitments. As a religious group defends its beliefs and practices against the ridicule and refutation of outsiders, the group often clarifies for itself what is central and nonnegotiable, thereby making more emphatic the "boundary markers" that identify the group, the sorts of distinguishing marks and clear expressions of group identification that are essential for the survival and growth of any group. Also, as a group deals with internal disagreements in beliefs and practices, there are efforts (on all sides of controverted matters) to articulate those beliefs and practices more clearly over against unacceptable versions of them ("heresies," in the sense that the term came to acquire in early Christianity). Thereby, those involved in such disputes often produce more explicit statements of their beliefs and more precise articulations of their core practices.[5] In fact, in some cases it

---

5. A classic analysis of these processes was given by Peter L. Berger and Thomas Luckmann, *The Social Construction of Reality* (Garden City, N.Y.: Doubleday, 1966), who observed,

appears that such polemics can actually promote further developments in doctrinal formulation.

But it is clear that the controversies and crises that marked the Johannine circles were largely the product of their *prior* emphasis on, and strong assertions about, Jesus.[6] For example, most scholars believe Johannine Christianity began as, and among, certain circles of Jewish Christians who initially continued to conduct themselves as part of the larger Jewish community where they were living. Then at some point prior to the composition of GJohn they were expelled from, or at least severely marginalized by, the authorities of that Jewish community.[7] Whatever effects this action had upon the articulation of the beliefs of Johannine Christians thereafter, the most likely *cause* of this hostility was that their claims about, and reverence of, Jesus became intolerable to those other Jews who took action against them.[8]

"Historically, the problem of heresy has often been the first impetus for the systematic theoretical conceptualization of symbolic universes" (their term for the worldviews of religious groups). Citing the example of early Christian doctrinal development through the controversies with heresies, they noted that "new theoretical implications within the tradition itself appear in the course of this process [maintenance against challenges], and the tradition itself is pushed beyond its original form in new conceptualizations" (99).

6. Wayne A. Meeks, "The Man from Heaven in Johannine Sectarianism," *JBL* 91 (1972): 44-72, referred to a "dialectical" relationship between the strong christological claims of Johannine Christians that led to their expulsion from their Jewish community, this expulsion, in turn, helping to generate "explanation" of it, expressed in the beliefs reflected in GJohn (esp. 68-72). Meeks suggested that an intensified "sectarian" (separatist) mentality among Johannine Christians was one result. Without engaging that suggestion, I simply propose that the intensification and elaboration of beliefs in Jesus that we find in GJohn were also fairly likely at least partly shaped in this crisis.

7. As I trust is clear in the wording I use here, in referring to Johannine Jewish Christians expelled from a "Jewish community," I mean some local Jewish community where the Johannine Christians (commonly thought now to have been a particular group) were located at the time. There was, of course, no monolithic "Jewish community" of the late first century, and no structure in place to effect/enforce an expulsion globally.

8. There are three references to believers in Jesus being expelled from the synagogue: John 9:22, 12:42, and 16:2. In all of them, devotion to Jesus is the issue. The work that perhaps more than any other (at least in English-speaking scholarship) emphasized as a crucially traumatic event in the history of the Johannine believers their expulsion from the Jewish community is J. Louis Martyn, *History and Theology in the Fourth Gospel,* 2nd ed. (Nashville: Abingdon, 1979; original ed., 1968). Scholars continue to debate Martyn's contention that the expulsion of Johannine Jewish Christians was related to the use of the *Birkhat ha-Minim* ("curse of/upon the heretics/schismatics"), which forms part of the "Eighteen Benedictions," the synagogue prayer that became regularized at some point in the early centuries c.e. Cf., e.g., Reuven Kimelman, "The *Birkat Ha-Minim* and the Lack of Evidence for an Anti-Christian Prayer in Late Antiquity," in *Jewish and Christian Self-Definition,* vol. 2, ed. E. P. Sanders, A. I. Baumgarten, and

In Johannine Christianity, after all, we are dealing with one version of a religious movement for which beliefs about Jesus seem always to have been the defining issue. Johannine Christians were not alone in experiencing opposition to their devotion to Jesus.[9] But this opposition was one important factor that shaped the expression of devotion to Jesus in GJohn. Later in this chapter I return to the relationship between the claims of Johannine Christians and the hostility that these claims generated.

Jesus in the Gospel of John

Although we are some way short of a consensus among scholars on the historical sequence in which the Johannine writings were probably composed, I discuss first the presentation of Jesus in GJohn.[10] To be sure, most scholars are persuaded that the present form of GJohn is the later (or latest) of two (or more) literary stages or editions, and it is quite possible that this final canonical form was produced a bit later than some or all of the Johannine epistles.[11] But there is also wide agreement that GJohn embodies traditions, and probably a

---

A. Mendelson (Philadelphia: Fortress, 1981), 226-44; Shaye J. D. Cohen, "The Significance of Yavneh: Pharisees, Rabbis, and the End of Jewish Sectarianism," *HUCA* 55 (1984): 27-53; and William Horbury, "The Benediction of the *Minim* and Early Jewish-Christian Controversy," *JTS* 33 (1982): 19-61. Whatever the relevance of the *Birkhat ha-Minim*, GJohn testifies to expulsion of believers in Jesus from the larger Jewish community, and it makes devotion to Jesus the defining issue in the expulsion. For wider evidence of early Jewish responses to Jewish Christian claims, see Hurtado, "Pre–70 C.E. Jewish Opposition to Christ-Devotion," *JTS* 50 (1999): 35-58; and Claudia J. Setzer, *Jewish Responses to Early Christians: History and Polemics, 30-150 C.E.* (Minneapolis: Fortress, 1994).

9. Hurtado, "Pre–70 C.E. Jewish Opposition to Christ-Devotion."

10. For a survey of different views on the sequence of the Johannine writings, see Raymond E. Brown, *The Epistles of John*, AB (Garden City, N.Y.: Doubleday, 1982), 30-35. Among valuable studies of Jesus in John, David L. Mealand, "The Christology of the Fourth Gospel," *SJT* 31 (1978): 449-67, is a concise and insightful survey. Also notable is W. E. Sproston, "'Is Not This Jesus, the Son of Joseph . . . ?' (John 6.42): Johannine Christology as a Challenge to Faith," *JSNT* 24 (1985): 77-97. Among more extensive recent discussions, see, e.g., R. Schnackenburg, *Jesus in the Gospels: A Biblical Christology*, trans. O. C. Dean, Jr. (Louisville: Westminster John Knox, 1995), 219-94; Matera, 215-42; Painter, esp. 137-435; Ashton, 199-382; W. Loader, *The Christology of the Fourth Gospel: Structure and Issues*, 2nd rev. ed., BBET 23 (Frankfurt am Main: Peter Lang, 1992); P. Anderson, *The Christology of the Fourth Gospel*.

11. E.g., Brown proposed that "the body of the Gospel [of John]" was written sometime near 90, and that the "final redaction," producing the form that became canonical, should be dated shortly after 100 (*The Epistles of John*, 32; Brown, *Community*, 22-23). He dated 1 John and 2 John near 100, and 3 John between 100 and 110 (*The Epistles of John*, 101).

body of written material as well, that represent the core beliefs of the Johannine Christians from a time earlier than the composition of the epistles. Consequently, we can take GJohn as our best access to the traditions that identified Johannine believers prior to the internal controversies that appear to be reflected in the Johannine epistles.

All the same, parts of GJohn probably reflect religious developments and events from relatively late in the history of the circles of believers represented in this Gospel account. At the very least, John 21, for example, is commonly seen as an epilogue that was added to an earlier form of the Gospel that ended at 20:31.[12] Although all the Jesus books incorporate and adapt traditions about Jesus that circulated for some time both orally and in written form, each of the Synoptic Gospels is commonly thought to have been composed by an *author* and at a particular time and place. But in addition to drawing upon a body of Jesus tradition, GJohn also seems to represent a literary process that may have involved several successive authors/editors and "editions" across perhaps a couple decades. In what follows, however, I am most concerned with the final text of GJohn as we know it in its canonical form, as an artifact of devotion to Jesus that was probably produced among a particular circle of Christians in the final decades of the first century.

Some Literary Observations

Before we look at Johannine christological themes and emphases, however, I want to refer to some general literary features of GJohn. Once again the reason for this is that "Jesus books" such as GJohn are literary expressions of devotion to Jesus. In the preceding chapter we noted some features shared by all four canonical Gospels; here I focus briefly on some things that distinguish GJohn's literary rendition of Jesus. These are well known among scholars, and my aim is

---

12. As Kysar noted, "It is generally recognized that some revision-redaction of the gospel did take place, regardless of how one views the process of composition," and he judged that chap. 21 of GJohn is "almost universally acknowledged as a later addition to the gospel which ended [in its prior form] at 20:31" ("John, Gospel Of," 3:922). But cf. now Willem S. Vorster, "The Growth and Making of John 21," in *The Four Gospels 1992*, 3:2207-21. Theo K. Heckel, *Vom Evangelium des Markus zum viergestaltigen Evangelium*, WUNT 120 (Tübingen: Mohr-Siebeck, 1999), contends that GJohn 21 was composed to make John the basis of a fourfold Gospel collection, and a somewhat similar view is advanced by David Trobisch, *Die Endredaktion des Neuen Testaments. Eine Untersuchung zur Entstehung der christlichen Bibel* (Freiburg: Universitätsverlag Freiburg; Göttingen: Vandenhoeck & Ruprecht, 1996); ET, *The First Edition of the New Testament* (New York: Oxford University Press, 2000).

to explore briefly what historical inferences we can draw from the kind of writing we have in GJohn.[13]

Perhaps the most basic observation is that GJohn is strikingly different in contents, vocabulary, narrative sequence, geographical focus, and major themes, and yet it also has some undeniable general similarities to the other canonical Gospels.[14] In GJohn there are no parables, exorcisms, tax collectors, or Sadducees. There is no temptation account, no transfiguration story, none of the material in the Sermon on the Mount, no institution of the Lord's Supper. But among the unique material in GJohn are the following: dialogue scenes with Nicodemus and the Samaritan woman, the controversies with the crowds, the predicative "I am" sayings, the foot-washing scene, the "Paraclete" material in John 14–16, Jesus' prayer in John 17, Jesus' conversation with Pilate, and distinctive scenes where the risen Jesus encounters his disciples (including Mary Magdalene as well as the males). GJohn also frequently uses a number of terms that have scarcely any prominence in other Gospels: "truth," "witness," "world," "abide," "love," "believe," "light and darkness," "(eternal) life," the "Father," and the "Son." The Synoptics relate Jesus' "miracles" *(dynameis)*, but GJohn recounts Jesus' "signs" *(sēmeia)*.[15] Whereas the Synoptics narrate only one fateful visit to Jerusalem, GJohn presents Jesus ministering a good deal in Jerusalem and the surrounding area. Whereas the Synoptics relate the famous "temple cleansing" incident among the events of the final days in Jerusalem, GJohn's account is placed very early in Jesus' ministry (2:13-22). In the Synoptics Jesus eats a Passover meal on the night before his death, but in GJohn he dies on the day the lambs are slain in preparation for the Passover meal. This illustrative list of distinctives should suffice to make the point.

If we employ the criteria that scholars commonly use to identify evidence of some kind of direct literary dependence among the Synoptic Gospels (e.g., strong similarities of wording, contents, narrative order, etc.), we have to conclude that there is not a good basis for positing any equivalent literary connection between any of them and GJohn. Therefore, probably most (but by no means all) scholars nowadays hold that the author(s) of GJohn (at least at the earliest stage of the process that led to our present text) either did not know of, and refer to, any of the Synoptic Gospels or, at the least, did not

13. Note the similar descriptions of the structure and literary features of John in, e.g., Kysar, "John, Gospel Of," 3:913-17; M. M. Thompson, "John, Gospel Of," in *DJG*, 368-83, esp. 373-76.

14. I adapt here the helpful summary of Johannine distinctives given by Thompson, "John, Gospel Of," 374-75. Kysar, "John, Gospel Of," 3:920, gives a similar summary.

15. On the Johannine theme of Jesus' "signs," see, e.g., Rudolf Schnackenburg, *The Gospel according to St. John,* 3 vols. (New York: Seabury Press, 1980-82), 1:515-28.

use them as sources in the way the authors of Matthew and Luke used Mark (and Q).[16]

This means it is dubious to assume that GJohn was written directly to refute or correct the Synoptic accounts. It is also dubious to imagine that GJohn was produced as a commentary or elucidation of them. If either were the case, we should expect to find direct references to them. Thus, so far as most of us can judge, GJohn is an independent account of Jesus, written at least primarily to present this particular rendition of him for its own sake and basically to advance the beliefs in Jesus that the text favors.

Each Gospel should really be treated as the product of a competent author able to judge, use, reject, and modify whatever was in any available written sources and in the larger body of accessible tradition about Jesus. For example, even if Matthew is directly dependent on Mark as inspiration and source, it nevertheless represents a witness to early devotion to Jesus in its own right. But GJohn seems to be a rather more fully independent effort to present a narrative account of Jesus and his religious significance.

All the same, as I pointed out in the preceding chapter, GJohn exhibits broad similarity to the kind of account given in the Synoptics. At the most basic level GJohn, too, is a *narrative* Gospel account. Moreover, GJohn also is fundamentally a narrative of a Galilean Jesus who gathers disciples, performs miracles (though, granted, the Johannine miracle stories are largely different), and clashes with Pharisees and the Jerusalem priesthood. In GJohn, as in the Synoptics, a "passion narrative" occupies a disproportionate amount of narrative space, relating as crucial events in the story line Jesus' fateful visit to Jerusalem during which he is arrested, arraigned and executed, and then resurrected.

For the purposes of my discussion, the apparent independence of GJohn combines with its general similarity to the Synoptics to amount to an important finding. If the originating author of GJohn did write without reference to the Synoptic Gospels (and perhaps even without knowledge of them), this means the general idea of producing a narrative account of Jesus with a story line broadly similar to that of the Synoptics occurred independently to that author. That is, if it is correct to see GJohn and the Synoptics as varying expressions of a basically shared genre of a narrative account of Jesus' ministry, then the originat-

---

16. Cf., e.g., Kysar, "John, Gospel Of," who refers to "a widespread view" that GJohn does not reflect use of the Synoptics (3:920), but then judges that until a more decisive case is made one way or the other, "the issue remains at a stalemate" (3:921). For a fuller discussion and review of scholarship, see D. Moody Smith, *John among the Gospels: The Relationship in Twentieth-Century Research* (Minneapolis: Fortress, 1992). Smith contends that neither the assumption that the authors of GJohn did nor the assumption that he did not use any of the Synoptics is today safe (189).

ing impulses of this genre are broader and earlier than any of the particular expressions of it in the extant narrative Gospels. Probably the best inference would be that GJohn attests a rather wide distribution and appreciation of a preliterary narrative mode and tendency in the Jesus tradition that, along with variations in the specifics of expression, also had a very general similarity.

I want to emphasize this point. To the degree that GJohn really is an independent narrative account of Jesus, the predilection for such an account has to be considered impressively wide and strong in early Christianity. Negatively, this means we cannot simply attribute the origins of the idea of a narrative rendition of Jesus to the author of Mark alone. Positively, the best explanation for what appears to have been an immediately very successful reception of the narrative renditions of Jesus that we know as canonical Gospels is by seeing them as written expressions of a mode of discourse about Jesus readily recognized and appreciated across a wide number of early Christian circles of the late first century.

In assessing the relationship of GJohn to the Synoptics, however, we should remember that GJohn probably acquired its present form in two or more stages and across a number of years. Accordingly we should probably distinguish between what knowledge of the Synoptics was likely in earlier and later editorial stages. Personally I find it somewhat more difficult to imagine that those responsible for the final, present form of GJohn, sometime between 90 to 110 (to cite the time span most commonly favored by scholars), were still ignorant of any of the Synoptic Gospels. After all, Mark in particular had probably been circulating fairly widely (as is reflected in it being used as a source independently by the authors of Matthew and Luke) since around 70 (or perhaps a bit earlier). But if an originating narrative core or body of GJohn was written as early as the 70s or just a bit later, it becomes more plausible to imagine that its author was not familiar with Mark.[17]

In any case, to my mind the important matter is not whether the author of GJohn knew of any of the Synoptics; the important observation is that, much more fully than Matthew and Luke, GJohn confirms the popularity of the basic narrative Gospel form of the "Jesus book" in the late first century. At the very least, GJohn is an "independent" narrative Gospel, in that it is scarcely indebted to any other known account for its contents, vocabulary, emphases, and narrative arrangement. So let us now consider specifics of the Jesus of GJohn.

17. It is neither essential nor possible here to engage fully the thorny question of the editorial process and timescale involved in the production of GJohn. See, e.g., the influential discussion by Raymond E. Brown, *The Gospel according to John*, 2 vols. (Garden City, N.Y.: Doubleday, 1966, 1970), 1:xxxiv-xxxix (on the editorial process/history) and lxxx-lxxxvi (on the dates). Brown proposes a "first edition" of John which he dates "somewhere between 70 and 85 (a dating which is very much a guess)" (lxxxvi).

Messiah and Son of God

As I noted earlier, John 20:30-31 is commonly regarded by scholars as the climactic conclusion to the earlier form of this Jesus book, to which chapter 21 was added as a kind of epilogue (perhaps along with other, smaller additions elsewhere in John). John 20:30-31 is certainly the most explicit statement of purpose anywhere in GJohn, and also it probably captures the heart of the religious concerns of all who may have been involved in composing this Gospel, from the earliest on through all its subsequent editorial stages: "These things are written that you may believe that Jesus is the Messiah, the Son of God, and that believing you might have life in his name." This statement likely represents the core faith commitment of those who formed the Johannine circles from the earliest moments of their existence as an identifiable group. So it is appropriate to make this statement our entry point in the following discussion of Johannine beliefs about Jesus.

The first thing to note is that the two christological titles in the statement, "Messiah" and "Son of God," reflect a provenance in Jewish and biblical traditions, and probably also the historical origins of Johannine Christianity in Jewish Christian circles of the early first century. In our analysis of the evidence for Judean/Palestinian Jewish Christianity in Paul and Acts, we noted that the messianic claim was in all likelihood part of the distinguishing beliefs and proclamation of followers of Jesus from the first years onward. In fact, the messianic claim likely has its roots in the hopes and beliefs about Jesus that were circulating among his followers during his own lifetime, and then became a basis for his arraignment and execution by the Roman authorities as a royal pretender.

Whereas in the Synoptic Gospels Jesus' messianic status is affirmed but presented in restricted settings, and is treated as a covert claim (especially in Mark) that is mooted only among Jesus' disciples and at Jesus' arraignment before the temple authorities, in GJohn the messianic issue is openly and publicly aired and debated (4:29; 7:26-27, 41; 12:34). There is, however, a "messianic secret" of sorts in GJohn, as well as in Mark. The Markan messianic secret is the claim *that* Jesus is Messiah, which cannot be disclosed properly until Jesus' death and resurrection (e.g., Mark 8:30; 9:9). By contrast, in GJohn Jesus' messianic claim is more openly mooted by characters in the narrative, but the secret known to readers and unperceived (or imperfectly perceived) by characters in the story is who this Messiah *really* is (the preexistent, divine Son), and from *whence* he really comes (God), as reflected in, e.g., John 7:25-29; 8:12-20, 25. This transcendent dimension to Jesus (including, e.g., his "preexistence") is what GJohn emphasizes (I return to this emphasis later in this chapter). In fact, from the opening lines onward, GJohn overtly makes the messianic claim central.

Whatever else this Gospel asserts about Jesus, he is certainly also presented as the proper fulfillment of Israel's hopes for eschatological redemption.

The messianic category is first made prominent in 1:19-28, where John the Baptizer answers negatively the question of whether he is the Messiah (esp. v. 20), and thereafter endorses Jesus as "the Lamb of God who takes away the sin of the world" (1:29) and "the Son of God" (1:34). That these latter two designations are to be taken as complementary ways of referring to Jesus as Messiah is indicated in 1:35-42, where the Baptizer's second reference to Jesus as "Lamb of God" (1:36) is followed and rephrased by Andrew's statement, "We have found the Messiah" (1:41).

In the following verses of John 1, other disciples refer to Jesus as "him about whom Moses in the law and also the prophets wrote" (1:45), and as "the Son of God . . . the King of Israel" (1:49, echoed in the cry of the Jerusalem crowd in 12:13). The cumulative effect of all these honorific designations is to present Jesus positively in terms of the biblical story of Israel and traditional Jewish hopes for a messianic Savior.[18] Indeed, GJohn is the only New Testament writing that uses *Messias,* the Greek transliteration of the Hebrew word *Mashiach* ("Messiah" in 1:41 and 4:29). This deliberate use of linguistic "color" probably reflects a desire to assert Jesus' significance with unambiguous reference to Jewish messianic hopes.[19] In light of the constellation of honorific terms for Jesus in John 1, we can take it that reference to Jesus under any one of these terms thereafter is intended to invoke for the readers the connotations of them all.

In subsequent passages in GJohn the messianic claim surfaces explicitly, again and again. In the extended dialogue scene involving Jesus and the Samaritan woman, after she initially recognizes that Jesus is a prophet (4:19), Jesus identifies himself as Messiah (4:26). The woman then summons her Samaritan compatriots and excitedly moots the possibility of Jesus' messianic status.[20] The Samaritans' subsequent acclamation that Jesus is "the savior of the world"

---

18. Over against the misguided notions of a dismaying number of scholars that the honorific titles applied to Jesus in the New Testament represent discrete "Christologies," it is necessary to emphasize that in the religious "logic" of the New Testament text the honorific designations of Jesus are characteristically intended to be taken as functioning cumulatively to express Jesus' significance. Note Hengel's emphasis that ancient people did not use such designations analytically to make sharp differentiations, but rather in a "multiplicity of approximations" (*The Son of God: The Origin of Christology and the History of Jewish-Hellenistic Religion,* trans. John Bowden [Philadelphia: Fortress; London: SCM Press, 1976], 57-58).

19. And 1:41 specifies that *Messias* is translated *Christos* ("Christ" or "Anointed"), which makes explicit the connection with the confessional title affirmed for Jesus in 20:31.

20. On the Greek phrasing *mēti houtos estin ho Christos,* see BDF §427(2): "that must be the Messiah at last, perhaps this is the Messiah."

is, in this context, likely intended as another synonymous and complementary phrase that both affirms and explicates the messianic designation. Later, in 7:25-31 and again in 7:40-44, the Jewish crowd seethes with the question of whether Jesus is in fact the Christ/Messiah, and the readers are expected to smile knowingly at their quandary. In the story of the healing of the blind man, the confession of Jesus' messianic status is referred to as a basis for expulsion from the synagogue (9:22) by the Jewish authorities. The controversial air continues in 10:24, where the authorities demand that Jesus answer plainly whether he claims to be Messiah, and Jesus' answer both affirms that claim and trumps it with words about his relationship to God that bring the charge of blasphemy (10:25-39). In this episode, once again, Jesus' messianic status and divine sonship are linked (esp. 10:36).

The story of the raising of Lazarus features Martha's acclamation of Jesus as "the Christ/Messiah, the Son of God," which anticipates and models the confession presented later in 20:31 as the summative aim of the text. To be sure, GJohn affirms more about Jesus than his messianic status. Or perhaps we should say that GJohn defines the meaning of Jesus' messianic status with additional affirmations of his significance (e.g., as divine "Son"). But the additional claims it makes for Jesus are never at the expense of insisting that he is also the Messiah of God, the true and proper fulfillment of biblical prophecy and hope, the one in whom Israel should find the climactic expression of God's faithfulness and redemptive purpose.

Certainly GJohn reflects a circle of Jesus' followers that takes in a transethnic diversity, including Samaritans (4:5-42) and Greeks (12:20-24), who represent the "other sheep" to be included in Jesus' fold (10:11-18). Scholars commonly, and properly, see in these passages deliberately placed reflections of the transethnic vision of the Johannine Christians, and probably also the actual mixed composition of their circles. But the continuing Johannine emphasis on Jesus' messianic status and his rightful claim as king of Israel (1:49; 12:12-13) shows that, though the Johannine door was wide open to all who would believe in Jesus, that door led into a form of Christianity that continued to express itself in relation to biblical traditions and the hopes of historic Israel.

As we note shortly, the Johannine believers attributed to Jesus a status in their religious life and thought that exceeds anything we know of by way of analogy in the impressive Jewish traditions about messiahs or other agents of God of that or subsequent periods. To be sure, these Jewish traditions included the notion that an angelic or even a human figure could be exalted to a heavenly status that could even be pictured as an enthronement. As I have shown in a previous book, there are a variety of Jewish traditions about this or that figure functioning as what we may call God's "principal agent," such a figure being described in ways that look like divinization (e.g., clothed with divinelike attributes, endowed with a name that connotes divinelike status, and even referred to as a "god").[21] The very exalted way in which Jesus is referred to in GJohn likely shows early Christian appropriation of such traditions, and in my view the intensification of them, in the effort to express devotion to Jesus. Indeed, from the earliest layers of extant Christian historical evidence, it appears that the devotion given to Jesus quickly involved a distinctive innovation and intensification, especially marked in the way Jesus functioned as a recipient of worship in early Christian circles, something for which we have no clear analogy in contemporary Jewish circles and traditions.[22]

But it is dubious to ascribe the elevated place of Jesus in Johannine Christianity to supposed influence from Gentile converts.[23] It should be clear that the sort of intense devotion to Jesus reflected in GJohn is not some subsequent stage of the religiousness of the circles that made up this important strand of early Christianity. A keen devotion to Jesus, and high claims for him, characterize all stages of the tradition incorporated in GJohn. It should also be clear that converts to these circles, from whatever demographic quarter of the Roman world, were reoriented into a fervent religious ethos, and into the use of vocabulary and conceptual categories that derived from, and were intended to speak to, the biblical/Jewish traditions of the time. Granted, the present form of GJohn likely reflects a situation sometime subsequent to the expulsion of Johannine believers from their synagogue(s), and at that point the event was still a painful memory. Nevertheless, the presentation of christological assertions in GJohn in sharply polemical encounters with Jewish crowds (especially in John 6 and 8) likely indicates a continuing strong concern to address the larger Jewish community in spite of the breach; it also suggests that there were still active skirmish lines of religious controversy, attempts by each side at per-

---

21. Hurtado, *One God, One Lord: Early Christian Devotion and Ancient Jewish Monotheism* (Philadelphia: Fortress, 1988; 2nd ed., Edinburgh: T. & T. Clark, 1998), esp. chaps. 1–5. See also now John J. Collins, *The Scepter and the Star: The Messiahs of the Dead Sea Scrolls and Other Ancient Literature* (New York: Doubleday, 1995), 136-94.

22. Hurtado, *One God, One Lord*, esp. chap. 6.

23. I have in mind in particular Maurice Casey's allegation of an ill-defined "Gentile mentality" as the factor that caused the elevated Christology of GJohn. Aside from insufficiently explicating what this term really means, he distorts Johannine Christology in portraying the Johannine Jesus as a second deity. The strongly subordinationist emphasis in GJohn is precisely intended to counter any such misunderstanding of the assertion of Jesus' divine status. Cf. Casey, *From Jewish Prophet to Gentile God: The Origins and Development of New Testament Christology* (Louisville: Westminster John Knox; Cambridge: James Clarke, 1991), 36. See also, e.g., 138, 144, 156.

suasion, and mutual denunciation between Johannine believers and Jewish religious authorities.

Let us look again at the statement of purpose and confessional aim in John 20:31. Here and elsewhere in GJohn, the messianic claim is wedded to an assertion of Jesus' divine sonship. Of course, this category also has roots in biblical traditions. Of particular relevance was the notion that the Davidic king is "Son" of God (e.g., Ps. 2:7). These royal traditions are echoed and appropriated for Jesus in GJohn, as part of the Johannine medley of messianic expressions.[24]

For example, there is an explicit linkage of divine sonship and royal categories in Nathanael's acclamation, "You are the Son of God! You are the King of Israel!" (1:49). In 6:15 is the curious reference to Jesus avoiding efforts to "take him by force to make him king," following the miraculous feeding of the five thousand (6:1-14). This reference must be intended to present Jesus as having excited rather traditional messianic expectations about himself. There is another combination of divine sonship and royal categories in the Johannine account of Jesus before Pilate. Along with the question of whether Jesus claims to be "King of the Jews" (e.g., 18:33-38; 19:12), and the mocking references to him as such (18:39; 19:3, 14-15, 19-22), the temple authorities also accuse Jesus of claiming to be "the Son of God" (19:7), which may here be an allegation of a royal claim.

But in GJohn, asserting Jesus' messiahship and divine sonship means much more than the claim that he is Israel's rightful king. The Johannine assertions that Jesus is "Christ" and "the Son (of God)" connote the belief that Jesus is in some intrinsic way also divine and of heavenly origin. As we noted in the preceding chapter, Jesus' divine sonship is also an important christological category in the other canonical Gospels. Moreover, in all four Gospels it is clear that Jesus' divine sonship includes a transcendent significance and quality (e.g., the Markan scenes of demonic recognition, and the epiphanic sea miracles). But in GJohn this transcendent significance and status is thematized much more explicitly, more frequently, and more prominently.

One of the striking differences in GJohn is the frequency with which Jesus

---

24. The only explicit reference to Davidic tradition in John is in 7:42. Just as readers know that Jesus comes from God/heaven, and therefore in 7:27 are to view as invalid the claim of the Jerusalemites to know Jesus' origin, so also in 7:41-42 readers are probably expected to know the tradition that Jesus was born in Bethlehem, and are to see the Jewish crowd as confused and mistaken in their hesitation to accept Jesus' royal messianic status. See, e.g., Brown, *Gospel according to John*, 1:330. Margaret Daly-Denton has recently shown that the Johannine use of the Psalter reflects the appropriation of Davidic tradition for christological purposes (*David in the Fourth Gospel: The Johannine Reception of the Psalms*, AGJU 47 [Leiden: Brill, 2000]).

refers to himself as God's Son, both to disciples and to the larger public. In the Synoptics Jesus' only overt reference to himself as God's Son is in the scene where he responds to the high priest's question (Mark 14:62-64/Matt. 26:63-64/ Luke 22:70). Jesus' only other self-referential uses of divine sonship language are in two statements to his disciples: the jubilant passage in Matthew 11:25-27 and Luke 10:21-22 about the intimate mutual knowledge of "the Son" and "the Father," and Jesus' statement that even the Son does not know the day and hour determined by "the Father" for the consummation of all things (Mark 13:32/ Matt. 24:36). In the parable of the wicked vineyard tenants (Mark 12:1-12/Matt. 21:33-46/Luke 20:9-19), the owner's son is unquestionably Jesus. But in GJohn divine sonship is a recurring and much more prominent category of self-characterization.

There may be some ambiguity in John 3:16-17, 35-36 as to whether it is Jesus or the author who refers to God's "Son" and "unique Son [*monogenēs huios*]," but not in other passages where Jesus speaks variously to disciples and the wider public. As God's Son, Jesus is obedient to God (e.g., 5:19, and see 5:30), and also intimately associated with "the Father," who loves "the Son" (5:20), has given him power to raise the dead and judge all (5:21, 25-27; 17:2), now expects all people to honor the Son just as they honor God (5:22-23), and also demands belief in the Son as the basis for eternal life (6:40). God seeks to glorify the Son (11:4; cf. 17:1, 3, 22), and the Son seeks to glorify "the Father" (14:13; 17:4). Uniquely in GJohn, Jesus' self-reference as God's Son in public debate produces the charge of blasphemy (10:31-36), whereas in the Synoptics the blasphemy charge erupts only in the trial narrative, at his hearing before the Jewish authorities (e.g., Mark 14:62-64). Moreover, uniquely in GJohn Jesus' public claim to be God's Son is also cited specifically as the cause of his arrest and condemnation to Pilate (19:7). In fact, Jesus' use of divine sonship language to refer to himself is so characteristic in GJohn that readers are probably supposed to see this christological category in other Johannine passages as well, where Jesus refers to God as "the Father" and simply uses the first-person pronoun for himself (e.g., 14:2, 10-11, 28, 31).

Furthermore, GJohn presents Jesus' divine sonship as unique, an emphasis especially evident in the Johannine use of *monogenēs* ("only/unique," 1:14; 3:16, 18). Whereas those who believe in Jesus are given "authority to become children [*tekna*] of God" (1:12), Jesus alone is "*the* Son [*ho huios*]" to whom God has given authority over all people, to give eternal life to the elect, and who uniquely shared in divine glory "before the world was made" (17:1-5). This uniqueness is also reflected in the requirement that the Son be honored just as the Father is honored (*timaō*; 5:23). This obviously connotes general reverence and obedience, but it also likely alludes to the cultic practice of

Johannine believers in which Jesus was liturgically reverenced along with "the Father."[25]

Preexistence

Jesus' transcendent status and origins are directly indicated in the Johannine emphasis on Jesus' preexistence, which meets readers in the opening lines of the famous "prologue" in 1:1-18 and resurfaces repeatedly thereafter. Just as we noted in the earlier discussion of Pauline references, so also in these Johannine statements the reason for attributing to Jesus this premundane chronological priority and activity is to postulate his radical preeminence. Moreover, in all New Testament references to the idea of Jesus' preexistence, the premise is not philosophical or mystical speculations; instead, they express the conviction that Jesus is the eschatological savior truly sent forth from God.[26] Given the connection in ancient Jewish and Christian apocalyptic between final (eschatological) things and primal things that I have pointed to already, it was for many early Christians an obvious conviction that, as the final figure who uniquely bears and accomplishes God's eschatological plan, Jesus held a premundane significance and status.

The importance of the idea of Jesus' preexistence in GJohn is signaled by its position as the first claim in the opening verses of this account of him. As Frank Matera observed, although it may have been composed and added toward the later stages of the redactional process that produced the canonical form of GJohn, the prominent position of this passage now "controls how readers understand the narrative, and they must interpret this narrative in light of the prologue."[27] Furthermore, the Pauline evidence shows that, whatever the date and provenance of John 1:1-18, the idea of Jesus' preexistence was circulat-

25. I say more about the devotional practice of Johannine Christians, especially the experience of the divine Spirit among them, later in this chapter.

26. As, for example, Hans Weder observed about the Johannine "Logos hymn" (John 1:1-18): it "does not originate in the religious speculation . . . (for example) concerning just how a connection between God and world might be conceived." Instead, the impetus for this passage was "how one might appropriately understand the experience with Jesus of Nazareth" ("The Hermeneutics of Christology in the Johannine Writings," in *Exploring the Gospel of John: In Honor of D. Moody Smith*, ed. R. Alan Culpepper and C. Clifton Black [Louisville: Westminster John Knox, 1996], 325-45, citing 329). Weder rightly says the "we have received" in 1:16 directly reflects the religious experiences in question. See further his incisive observations about the similarity, and distinction, between Wisdom theology and the aim and import of the Johannine appropriation of it in the prologue (332). See also Schnackenburg, *St. John*, 1:494-506.

27. Matera, 217.

ing among adherents within the first decades of the Christian movement. Moreover, the belief is reflected in a number of other passages in GJohn that can hardly all be attributed to late stages in its redaction, or to late phases of the religious development of Johannine circles. Instead, we can properly take the assertion of Jesus' preexistence as characteristic of Johannine circles for some time prior to the date of the present form of GJohn. The Johannine prologue is a remarkable passage that has justifiably received enormous scholarly attention. But the religious conviction expressed in the passage about Jesus as somehow preexistent is hardly unique to it.[28]

The use of the terms *ho Logos* ("the Word," 1:1-2, 14) and *to Phōs* ("the Light," 1:4-5, 7-9) should not be taken to imply that for the author the preexistent figure is anyone other than he whose earthly story GJohn goes on to relate. As Sproston observed, "Thus John presents the man Jesus of Nazareth as one who, before the incarnation, was a divine being existing with God from eternity and as one who [in the Johannine narrative at various points] 'remembers events which occurred in his pre-existent state.'"[29] Obviously, the "light" to which the Baptizer bore witness (1:6-8) can only be Jesus, as the succeeding narrative goes on to relate in 1:19-34. Likewise, the manifestation of "the true Light" in the world and among "his own people" in 1:9-10 must refer to the historical appearance of Jesus. Also, it can only be Jesus' name in which people believe and through which they were made children of God in 1:12-13. Most vividly, 1:14 expresses the historical and bodily manifestation of the Word and Light as this historical figure, Jesus.[30] Then, as part of the climactic movement of the pro-

---

28. Among the voluminous scholarly literature on the prologue, C. H. Dodd, *The Interpretation of the Fourth Gospel* (Cambridge: Cambridge University Press, 1965), 263-85, remains valuable (though I am not persuaded by some of his exegetical judgments), but unfortunately Dodd failed to take adequate account of Jewish divine-name tradition and angelology in assessing the conceptual background of the passage. See also J. Habermann, *Präexistenzaussagen im Neuen Testament* (Frankfurt am Main: Peter Lange, 1990), 317-414; Painter, 137-62; Eldon Jay Epp, "Wisdom, Torah, Word: The Johannine Prologue and the Purpose of the Fourth Gospel," in *Current Issues in Biblical and Patristic Interpretation: Studies in Honor of M. C. Tenney*, ed. G. F. Hawthorne (Grand Rapids: Eerdmans, 1971), 128-46; Schnackenburg, *St. John*, 1:481-93; Craig A. Evans, *Word and Glory: On the Exegetical and Theological Background of John's Prologue*, JSNTSup 89 (Sheffield: JSOT Press, 1993).

29. Sproston, 78, quoting a phrase from A. T. Hanson, *Grace and Truth* (London: SPCK, 1975), 72. Examples of the Johannine Jesus remembering preexistent events include 8:14, 58; 17:5.

30. One has only to follow the sequence of thought in the passage to see that there is full continuity of the Logos and Jesus. The Word is the Light (1:1-5). John the Baptizer bore witness to this Light (1:7-8), and this Light came into the world and came to his own people (1:9-11). Divine sonship is given to those who believe in his *name* (1:12), which is then explicitly presented in 1:17.

logue, in 1:17-18 the author explicitly names "Jesus Christ," expressly claiming his unsurpassable revelatory significance.

It is widely thought that the use of the term "Logos" in 1:1-18 was influenced by, and was intended to allude to, biblical and Jewish traditions about God's Word and Wisdom, sometimes pictured as the uniquely intimate and efficacious agent of divine purposes.[31] It is important to note that God's "Word" and "Wisdom" are sometimes linked in Jewish tradition of the time. Of various references, perhaps the parallel-structure statement in Wisdom of Solomon 9:1-2 is a particularly good example of this: "O God . . . who has made all things by your word [en logō sou], and by your wisdom [tē sophia sou] has formed humankind."

In an important study, however, Fossum has shown persuasively that the prologue and, indeed, Johannine Christology more broadly also seem to draw heavily upon biblical and postbiblical Jewish traditions about the name of God and the angel of the Lord.[32] Certainly, across the rest of GJohn Jesus is much more explicitly linked with God's name than with wisdom, as I show later in this discussion.

About the historical background and associations of the Johannine prologue, however, I want to underscore two points. First, if the aim is to understand what those who composed GJohn were intending, whatever associations about the term "Logos" one could pull from Greek philosophical traditions are not terribly relevant. The narrative world and conceptual categories of GJohn are thoroughly dependent upon (albeit adaptations of) biblical traditions, and the whole aim and issue in GJohn is to assert Jesus' significance for, and in the light of, *these* traditions. There is no evidence that the author of GJohn had direct acquaintance with Greek philosophy. In any case, whatever Greek philosophical origins or influences may have been behind the use of "Logos" in GJohn were mediated, and thoroughly adapted, by the Jewish tradition on which the author drew. For by the time GJohn was written, devout Jews (and

31. See, e.g., Epp, "Wisdom, Torah, Word"; and Martin Scott, *Sophia and the Johannine Jesus*, JSNTSup 71 (Sheffield: Sheffield Academic Press, 1992), 94-115. Key passages illustrating the linking of God's Word or Wisdom and creation include Ps. 33:4-9 (esp. v. 6, "By the word of the Lord the heavens were made"); and wisdom passages such as Prov. 8:22-31; Wisd. of Sol. 7:22–8:1; 9:1-2; Sir. 24:1-12. Note also the likely allusion to Wisd. of Sol. 7:25 in Heb. 1:3. For fuller discussion of early Christian appropriation of Wisdom tradition, see now H. von Lips, *Weisheitliche Traditionen im Neuen Testament*, WMANT 64 (Neukirchen-Vluyn: Neukirchener Verlag, 1990), esp. 241-64, 308-17, on Wisdom tradition in John.

32. Jarl E. Fossum, "In the Beginning Was the Name: Onomanology as the Key to Johannine Christology," in his *The Image of the Invisible God: Essays on the Influence of Jewish Mysticism on Early Christology*, NTOA 30 (Göttingen: Vandenhoeck & Ruprecht, 1995), 109-33.

not simply apostates or those restless with their own tradition) had interacted with, and for more than three hundred years had creatively appropriated, Greek terms and categories, both in Judea/Palestine and in the diaspora.[33]

My second point is that whatever "background" we speak of, we should avoid simplistic notions of "influence." Healthy religious movements use and redefine terms and categories they inherit from their "parent" traditions, as any scholarly observer of new religious movements can attest. But this appropriation is for the purpose of expressing and commending the *convictions of the new movement.* The impetus comes from these convictions, and these convictions are prompted and shaped primarily by the religious experiences and ethos of the movement. This is certainly the case in the use of terms and categories in the Johannine prologue.

As C. H. Dodd observed in his magisterial study of GJohn, in at least two particular and central affirmations the Johannine prologue goes beyond what was previously affirmed in the Word, Wisdom, or divine name traditions: (1) the statement in 1:1 that "the Word was God," and (2) the audacious claim that "the Word became flesh" in 1:14.[34] The closest that we can get to the latter statement is in the references to divine Wisdom residing among humankind and making friends of them (e.g., Wisd. of Sol. 7:27; Sir. 24:8-12), and to "the book of the covenant . . . the law that Moses commanded" as the particular expression of Wisdom (Sir. 24:23). But this is undeniably still a good deal short of the direct "incarnation" of the Logos as this particular man, Jesus, in John 1:14.

Likewise, the stark statement in John 1:1, "the Word was God," takes us noticeably beyond Wisdom tradition. Wisdom is closely associated with God's works in passages such as Wisdom of Solomon 10:1–11:1, there directly linked with the history of God's saving and revelatory actions in the Old Testament narratives. Also, Wisdom can be referred to as "a breath [*atmis*] of the power of God," "an emanation [*aporroia*]" of God's glory, "a reflection [*apaugasma*] of eternal light," "a spotless mirror [*esoptron akēlidōton*] of God's working, and an image [*eikōn*] of God's goodness" (Wisd. of Sol. 7:25-26). But, as Dodd observed, the evidence indicates that in this Jewish Wisdom tradition, a statement such as "Wisdom was God" was apparently "unthinkable."[35]

Now let us look more closely at the preexistence claim expressed here. As is characteristic of most preexistence references in other New Testament writings, the Johannine prologue links Jesus specifically with the moment of cre-

---

33. I refer again to my discussion in chap. 1, and to the scholarly studies cited there.

34. Dodd, *Interpretation,* 275. See the list of Wisdom parallels on 274-75, and parallels with Philo's Logos references on 276-77. I was reminded of Dodd's observations by Fossum, "Beginning," 109.

35. Dodd, *Interpretation,* 275 n. 1.

ation (John 1:1-3; also Heb. 1:2; Col. 1:15-16; 1 Cor. 8:6). By attributing this central role in creation ("all things came to be/were made [*egeneto*] through him," 1:3) to the one through whom redemption comes as well, the text reflects the belief in a direct link between redemption and creation; the statement also affirms Jesus' cosmic significance across the whole sweep of divine purposes. The simplicity of the New Testament preexistence passages sets them apart from the more elaborate presentations in some later (apocryphal) Christian texts, in which one or more premundane divine emanations or figures are postulated under various names, and in complicated accounts of origins. To cite another crucial difference, in these later ("gnostic") accounts a strict distinction is often made between creation (presented as an unfortunate event, and due to an inferior or evil deity) and redemption (often portrayed as mainly a revelatory event/process in which the elect are [re]awakened to their true identity).[36]

Granted, there is a complexity in the Johannine references to "the world," some of them with negative overtones and others with very positive connotations. For example, on the one hand Jesus says that neither he nor his disciples are "of this world" (8:23; 15:19; 17:16; cf. 18:36), and that "the world" hates them and is a place of hostility to the truth (15:18; 16:33; 17:14). Also, Jesus refers to Satan as "the ruler of this world" (12:31; 14:30; 16:11), claims victory over the world (16:33), and prays for his disciples but not for the world (17:9). On the other hand, God loves the world (3:16), and Jesus comes as its Savior (1:29; 3:17; 4:42; 12:47), gives his life for the world (6:33, 51), is the light of the world (8:12; 9:5), and sends his disciples into the world just as he was sent to bring the world to knowledge and belief (17:18-23). Clearly, in GJohn the created order is in darkness, ignorance, and sin, but equally clearly (and unlike the later "gnostic" beliefs), the world was created by the one God and remains both the theater and the object of redemptive purpose.

Other references in GJohn show that belief in Jesus' cosmic priority and heavenly origins was highly meaningful for the believers whose devotion to him is mirrored in this Gospel. In various passages where he refers to himself in the characteristic Gospel idiolect expression as "the son of man," Jesus claims to have descended from heaven (John 3:13; 6:62); he makes the same claim in the disputation with the crowd in John 6 where he identifies himself as "the bread of life" (see esp. vv. 35, 38, 41-42, 48-51, 58). In the bitter dispute with Jewish antagonists in John 8, Jesus claims variously to have come "from above" (v. 23) and from God (v. 42), and he declares what he has seen "in the Father's presence" (v. 38). Using wording that hints directly at his premundane, heavenly status, Jesus specifically claims, "Before Abraham was, *I am*" (8:58). In the crucially

---

36. I discuss some early examples of these other renditions of Jesus in subsequent chapters.

important prayer of John 17, Jesus' appeal for divine vindication may be intended to hark back to the preexistent and heavenly status ascribed to him in the prologue: "So now, Father, glorify me in your presence with the glory that I had in your presence [*para soi*] before the world existed" (v. 5). This last reference also seems to approximate the phrasing in 1:1-2, that "the Logos was with [*pros*] God [*ton theon*]" (echoed also in 1 John 2:1, "with the Father [*pros ton patera*]").[37]

It is, however, the final clause of John 1:1, already noted above as an unparalleled expression, that has probably provoked the most intense puzzlement: "and the Word was God [*kai theos ēn ho logos*]." As Brown noted, in the literary structure of GJohn, this phrase is "almost certainly" meant to anticipate and correspond to Thomas's acclamation in 20:28, "My Lord and my God [*ho theos mou*]." The statement in 1:1 also likely represents the Johannine corrective to the charge made against Jesus later in GJohn that he made himself God (or "a god" [*poieis seauton theon*], 10:33).[38] That is, Jesus was not wrong to claim divine status, and he did not attempt to appropriate it for himself; it was his by rights from the beginning.

But more exactly, what does the statement "the Word was God" mean? Two senses of the phrase, possible in principle if the words are read in isolation, are excluded in the context of GJohn: Jesus neither is a second deity, nor is he to be taken simply as fully comprising "God." In GJohn Jesus is distinguished from "the Father," and yet GJohn also clearly affirms Jesus' divinity and his unique association with "the Father." To grasp more precisely the intended sense of the phrase "the Word was God" in 1:1, it will be necessary to set the phrase in the context of other features of the Johannine rendition of Jesus and his relationship to God.

---

37. Cf. 1 John 1:2, "this eternal life which was with the Father [*pros ton patera*] and was manifested to us."

38. Brown, *Gospel according to John*, 1:5. The absence of the article with *theos* in the final phrase in 1:1 is often accounted for by the Greek grammatical practice that predicate nouns preceding the verb in a sentence do not usually have a definite article. See, e.g., BDF §273, and a fuller discussion in C. F. D. Moule, *An Idiom Book of New Testament Greek* (Cambridge: Cambridge University Press, 1963), 114-16. The variant reading *ton theon* in 10:33 is supported by the original scribal hand of P66, but is unlikely to be the original reading of John here. On the influence of various christological concerns in textual variants here, see B. D. Ehrman, *The Orthodox Corruption of Scripture: The Effect of Early Christological Controversies on the Text of the New Testament* (Oxford: Oxford University Press, 1993), 84, 114 n. 185.

"I Am"

Among the other important features of the Johannine presentation of Jesus is a recurrent form of expression that functions to indicate vividly his transcendent significance, "I am [*Egō eimi*]," used in a variety of statements.[39] In particular, there are in GJohn a number sentences in which "I am" is itself the stated claim, and other sentences in which "I am" is followed by predicates that express Jesus' significance.

In the preceding discussion of preexistence I cited John 8:58, one of several instances where Jesus applies the expression "I am" in this absolute form (i.e., without a predicate) to himself. The immediate outraged response of the crowd — they prepare to stone him (8:59) — indicates the enormity of what the expression connotes in the narrative: it is either (as the crowd judges) blasphemy or truly expresses an astonishing claim. Other Johannine instances of this absolute form confirm that it functions as an important christological expression. Note the following examples: "Unless you believe that *I am,* you will surely die in your sins" (8:24); "When you lift up the son of man, then you will realize that *I am*" (8:28); "When this [what Jesus has foretold] happens, then you will believe that *I am*" (13:19).

Clearly, in all these cases "I am" itself expresses a vital christological claim that can be perceived, and either believed or rejected, with momentous consequences. Yet, equally, to perceive the claim requires some special knowledge of the significance of this "I am" formulation, for it is as strange-sounding and mysterious in Greek as it is in literal translation. As Jarl Fossum put it, "In Greek, the phrase 'I am' without a predicate is meaningless. Thus, there must be some esoterical significance of the use of *egō eimi* in these [Johannine] passages."[40]

---

39. See Brown, *Gospel according to John*, 1:533-38, and Schnackenburg, *St. John*, 2:79-89, for analysis and background of the expression, and for citation of other important publications. Also Dodd, *Interpretation*, 93-96; Philip B. Harner, *The "I Am" of the Fourth Gospel: A Study in Johannine Usage and Thought* (Philadelphia: Fortress, 1970); and more recently, David Mark Ball, *"I Am" in John's Gospel: Literary Function, Background, and Theological Implications,* JSNTSup 124 (Sheffield: Sheffield Academic Press, 1996); and Catrin H. Williams, *I Am He,* WUNT 2/113 (Tübingen: Mohr-Siebeck, 2000).

40. Fossum, "Beginnings," 127. Of course, as Catrin Williams has noted, *egō eimi* can be used where a predicate appears in a preceding statement (e.g., 2 Sam. 2:20; John 9:9), and in other cases *egō eimi* is an expression of self-identification. That is, the expression does not always carry an esoteric or numinous significance. However, there are instances in the Gospels where the expression probably has both an ordinary meaning and a hint of Jesus' transcendent significance (e.g., Mark 6:50; 14:62; John 4:25-26; 18:1-14). See Catrin H. Williams, "'I Am' or 'I Am He'? Self-Declaratory Pronouncements in the Fourth Gospel and Rabbinic Tradition," in *Je-*

It is commonly recognized by scholars that the expression was often intended to have a strongly numinous connotation. Indeed, this use of "I am" is probably influenced by, and alludes to, Old Testament passages where God uses the same sort of self-referential language, particularly passages in Isaiah (e.g., LXX Isa. 43:10, 25; 45:18 for uses of *Egō eimi*).[41] In fact, in the Old Testament passages the Greek expression, and the Hebrew expressions it translates, appear to function almost like the name of God. So in the story of Jesus walking on the water in John 6:16-20, Jesus' use of the expression (v. 20) both identifies him (in the sense of "It is I") and also probably signals readers that this is an epiphanic scene (the same seems to be the case in the Synoptic versions of this story too, in Mark 6:50/Matt. 14:27). This latter connotation is also suggested dramatically in John 18:5-6, where the soldiers sent to arrest Jesus fall to the ground when he utters the expression. A few examples of this sonorous expression appear in the Synoptic Gospels, and they are also clearly intended to have a connotation beyond mere self-identification.[42]

Most importantly, in light of the biblical passages to which the obvious allusions are directed, this absolute use of "I am" in the Gospels amounts to nothing less than designating Jesus with the same special referential formula that is used in the Greek Old Testament for God's own self-declaration. That is,

---

sus in Johannine Tradition, ed. Robert T. Fortna and Tom Thatcher (Louisville, London, and Leiden: Westminster John Knox, 2001), 343-52.

41. The Hebrew expression most often translated into Greek as *ego eimi* is *'anī hū'* ("I am He," Isa. 41:4; 43:10; 46:4), and in one case *'anī Yhwh* ("I am Yahweh," e.g., Isa. 45:18). Other relevant biblical expressions are "I am Yahweh/the Lord" (often with further identifying phrasing; e.g., Exod. 20:2; Ezek. 33:29; 36:36; 37:6, 13; 39:28; Isa. 44:6, 24). "I am [+ predicate]" statements abound especially in religious texts of the ancient world, but the absolute form, *Egō eimi*, does not occur in classical Greek literature; it is in fact very difficult to posit any assured uses of the expression in sources prior to (or not influenced by) the New Testament writings *except for the uses in the Greek Old Testament* such as those cited here (and others, e.g., Deut. 32:39). See, esp. Heinrich Zimmermann, "Das absolute Ἐγώ εἰμι als die neutestamentliche Offenbarungsformel," *BZ* 4 (1960): 54-69, 266-76; Eduard Schweizer, *Egō Eimi. Die religionsgeschichtliche Herkunft und theologische Bedeutung der johanneischen Bildreden, zugleich ein Beitrag zur Quellenfrage des vierten Evangeliums,* 2nd ed., FRLANT 56 (Göttingen: Vandenhoeck & Ruprecht, 1965 [1939]); G. Braumann and H.-G. Link, "I Am," in *NIDNTT,* 2:278-83; Ball, 24-45.

42. In addition to the Synoptic parallels of the sea miracle cited above, note also the following uses of the absolute "I am" expression. Jesus' prediction that people will come falsely claiming *"Egō eimi"* (Mark 13:6/Luke 21:8) may be patterned after the christological use of this expression, but cf. the form of the saying in Matt. 24:5, "I am (the) Christ." In Mark 14:62 Jesus uses the expression in replying to the high priest's question about whether he claims to be Christ and Son of God; but cf. Luke 22:70, "You say that I am," and Matt. 26:64, "You say so." Cf. also Luke 24:39, where the risen Jesus urges disciples to see from his bodily reality that "it is I myself" *(ego eimi autos).*

the "I am" expression as used in GJohn reflects the belief that Jesus is in some direct way *associated with God*. I shall say more on this later in this chapter, but the basic point here is that this appropriation of the "I am" expression reflects a daring christological conviction, and itself constitutes a breathtaking devotional move. In the Isaiah uses to which direct allusion is made in GJohn, "I am" expresses the *uniqueness* of the God of Israel. The application of this self-designation formula to Jesus can indicate only that those who did this associated him with God "the Father" so closely that he can rightly share in its self-referential usage.[43]

In addition to a more frequent use of this absolute "I am" form, GJohn also has a number of other striking and unique statements of Jesus in which the "I am" is combined with a predicate, the sentence making an exclusive christological claim. There are several related statements in the debate with the Jewish crowd in John 6, after the bread miracle: "I am the bread of life [*ho artos tēs zōēs*]" (vv. 35, 48); "I am the bread that came down from heaven" (v. 41); and "I am the living bread [*ho artos ho zōn*] which came down from heaven" (v. 51). In the context, the force of these statements is to express Jesus' redemptive significance through comparison and contrast with the biblical story of manna provided to Israel by God ("bread from heaven," Ps. 78:24, cited in John 6:31). Thus Jesus comes from heaven, and is the true life-giving provision from God ("the true bread from heaven," 6:32), for which the Old Testament manna is only an inferior comparison.

Jesus also claims to be "the light of the world" (8:12; 9:5), which echoes and affirms the statements in the prologue that he is "the light of all people" (*to phōs tōn anthrōpōn*, 1:4) and "the true light that illumines all people" (1:9).[44] In 10:7, 9 Jesus says, "I am the gate of/for the sheep" and "I am the gate"; in the same context he also twice claims to be "the good shepherd" (10:11, 14) who lays down his life for his sheep and knows his own as they know him. To Martha Jesus claims, "I am the resurrection and the life" (11:25), and to Thomas he makes the strong exclusivist statement, "I am the way, the truth and the life; no one comes to the Father but by me" (14:6). Finally, in 15:1-5 Jesus claims, "I am the true vine, and my Father is the vine-grower," and then "I am the vine, and you are the branches."

These "I am" statements (both the absolute forms and the predicate forms) combine to form an impressive constellation of christological claims, each of them attributing to Jesus a unique and utterly superior status and sig-

43. See, e.g., Ball, 190-91.
44. I return to Johannine references to Jesus as "light" below in discussing "Jesus as/and the Glory of God."

nificance. The consistent use of the definite article in the predicative statements expresses Jesus' exclusivity: e.g., "*the* way, *the* truth, *the* life." The repeated use of the adjective "true" posits Jesus' superiority to any other claimant. Thus, as "the *true* light" (1:9; cf. 1 John 2:8), Jesus is superior to the revelation given through Moses (John 1:16-18); as "the *true* bread that came down from heaven" (6:32), Jesus supersedes the manna given by Moses; and as "the *true* vine" (15:1), Jesus redefines the elect as those who abide in him, an allusive contrast to Old Testament references to Israel as God's sacred vine (e.g., Isa. 5:1-7).[45]

Furthermore, especially in the absolute "I am" statements but also in some of the predicative statements, Jesus speaks in the manner of God, and claims to be authorized to exercise the powers and prerogatives of God. To cite one transparent example, the statement in John 11:25, "I am the resurrection and the life," corresponds to statements in 5:21-29 that the Father who has power to raise the dead has granted the Son resurrection power as well (vv. 21, 26, 28), and has authorized the Son to execute "all judgment" (vv. 22, 27).[46] In the coming resurrection "the dead will hear the voice of the Son of God, and those who hear will live" (v. 25). Consequently, obeying Jesus' word is the determining factor as to whether one comes into eschatological life or judgment (v. 24). Still further, it is God's will that "all may honor the Son just as they honor the Father"; indeed, to refuse to honor the Son is to dishonor the Father (v. 23). As I have indicated already, the term for "honor" used here can refer to worship-honor given to a deity,[47] so worship is obviously what is intended in verse 23.

The Son and the Father

Another distinctive and crucial christological theme in GJohn is the emphasis on the intimate association of "the Son" and "the Father." In the controversy over his healing a paralytic on the Sabbath (5:2-47), Jesus claims that the miracles he performs are the works of God (v. 17), that God has sent him to do these deeds (v. 36), and that they thus form God's testimony about Jesus' validity as sent and empowered by God (v. 36). God has "set his seal" upon Jesus (6:27), signifying his authority to act on God's behalf. Other statements as well emphasize the Father's love for, and authorization of, the Son (3:35; 5:20; 15:9). The Son

45. Note the use of "true" as an attribute of God in John 17:3 ("the only true God") and 7:28 ("the one who sent me is true, whom you do not know").

46. Catrin Williams has suggested to me that Deut. 32:39 may have influenced John 5:21, 26, 28.

47. J. Schneider, "τιμή, τιμάω," in *TDNT*, 8:169-80.

and the Father also share a unique and intimate knowledge of each other (1:18; 6:46; 10:15).

But the Johannine expressions of the unity of the Son and the Father seem to suggest something still more profound than a unity of purpose and affection. The most concise expression is probably in John 10:30, "The Father and I are one." Granted, the use of the neuter form for "one" *(hen esmen)* points away from taking "the Father" and "the Son" to be interchangeable labels for the same figure; the author of GJohn appears to have no intent to replace God with Jesus, or to confuse the two. John 10:38 claims a mutual "indwelling" of Jesus and the Father: "The Father is in me and I am in the Father"; in 14:10-11 Jesus twice appeals for belief that "I am in the Father and the Father is in me." But note also that in 14:20 a similar expression is followed by a parallel statement affirming an indwelling of Jesus and his disciples: "I am in my Father, and you in me and I in you." Likewise, in 17:21-23 Jesus prays to the Father for his disciples, "may they be one just as we are one [*hen kathōs hēmeis hen*], I in them and you in me." This directly makes Jesus' unity with the Father the standard for the unity of the disciples, and makes the Father's indwelling of Jesus the pattern for his indwelling of them.

There are other expressions of the unity of Jesus with God in statements that in various ways link seeing Jesus with seeing God. For example, in response to Philip's request to be shown the Father, Jesus says, "Whoever has seen me has seen the Father" (14:9). By itself, such a statement might be taken to refer to Jesus as the special envoy of God. But other Johannine passages point to a much more daring notion, as we shall see in the following section.

Jesus as/and the Glory of God

One of the recurrent themes in GJohn is divine "glory"; it is attributed both to God and to Jesus. One of the most extraordinary references is in 12:37-43. After describing the unbelief of Jesus' contemporaries in 12:37-38 as fulfillment of the words of Isaiah 53:1, the author (in 12:39-40) cites Isaiah 6:10 as further explanation of this unbelief. Then we are told in 12:41 that Isaiah "saw his glory and spoke about him."[48] In the immediate context, the antecedent of "his" and "him" has to be Jesus. For example, in 12:37 there is the complaint about this

---

48. The variant reading here, that Isaiah saw "the glory of God [*tēn doxan tou theou*]," is supported by a few Greek manuscripts of comparatively later date (Codex Koridethi and Family 13), but is probably a scribal change prompted by the perceived difficulty in making Isaiah's vision of "the Lord" a vision of the preincarnate Son.

unbelief, in spite of Jesus' many signs. It may not be unambiguously clear whether it is God or Jesus whom the author intends as the "Lord" *(Kyrie)* addressed in the quotation of Isaiah 53:1 in John 12:38, but Jesus is surely the "arm of the Lord" of the Isaiah passage who is now revealed, though not properly recognized. Thus 12:41 seems to claim baldly that *Jesus* was the glorious figure seen in the prophetic vision described in Isaiah 6:1-5![49] GJohn is not alone in this stunning understanding of Isaiah's vision, but it is the earliest explicit reference to the idea that Isaiah saw the glorious/glorified Jesus.[50]

But it would be mistaken to think that here or elsewhere, GJohn (or, for that matter, any other New Testament writing) simply collapses the distinction between Jesus and God "the Father" and flatly identifies Jesus *as Yahweh* of the Old Testament.[51] In fact, as we shall see a bit later, GJohn distinguishes "the Father" and "the Son" just as consistently as it affirms an unprecedented linkage of them and attributes to Jesus/the Son an astonishing participation in divine attributes and status. What, then, are we to make of John 12:41?

The clue is probably in the reference here to "his glory." The term "glory" *(doxa)* and the cognate verb, "glorify" *(doxazein)*, are both used with particular frequency in GJohn; divine glory is clearly a major theme.[52] In this, as in so many other matters, GJohn demonstrates a keen aim to communicate in terms and motifs drawn from the biblical tradition.[53] In the Old Testament, refer-

---

49. On this passage in John, see Anthony Tyrrell Hanson, *Jesus Christ in the Old Testament* (London: SPCK, 1965), 104-8. Hanson discusses an array of passages in Paul's letters, Hebrews, Acts, John, and other New Testament writings that reflect a similar readiness to identify Jesus with the "Lord" in certain (but not all) Old Testament passages.

50. Darrell D. Hannah, "Isaiah's Vision in the *Ascension of Isaiah* and the Early Church," *JTS* 50 (1999): 80-101, analyzes early Christian references to Isaiah's vision. Hannah proposes two early Christian traditions. In one, Jesus is the figure on the throne, as in John 12:41. In another set of texts, however, the figure on the throne is taken as God the Father, and the two seraphim are interpreted as the Son and the Spirit, these texts reflecting an early trinitarian interpretation of Isaiah, which Hannah proposes may have been an early "corrective" interpretation intended to promote a more "orthodox" Christology.

51. See, e.g., Hanson's sensitive summary discussion in *Jesus Christ,* 161-78.

52. "Glory" *(doxa)* appears nineteen times in John, "glorify" *(doxazō)* twenty-three times, more frequently than in any other New Testament writing. Some cases (John 5:41, 44; 7:18; 12:43a) may reflect ordinary Greek usage (e.g., "opinion," "reputation," and so "honor," "distinction"). But in other important instances in John "glory" and "glorify" reflect the special meaning the terms acquired from being used to translate the Hebrew *kavōd* in the Old Testament. As Dodd noted (*Interpretation,* 206), God's *kavōd* is "the manifestation of God's being, nature and presence, in a manner accessible to human experience," and *doxa* "does not bear this meaning anywhere except where Jewish influence is probable." On "glory" in GJohn, see the whole of Dodd's discussion in *Interpretation,* 201-8.

53. E.g., Günter Reim, *Studien zum Alttestamentlichen Hintergrund des Johannes-*

ences to God's "glory" denote "the luminous manifestation of his person, his glorious revelation of himself."[54] Thus God's "glory" is characteristically a *visual* phenomenon, and is often referred to as appearing, shown, revealed, and seen (e.g., Exod. 16:7, 10; 33:18; Deut. 5:24; Isa. 40:5; 60:1). It is also important to note that God's glory is referred to in connection with his saving actions, both those of the past (e.g., Exod. 14:17-18; Ps. 96:3) and those expected in the future, when God will rescue and restore Israel (Isa. 60:1-2; Ezek. 39:21-22) and even convert the nations (Ps. 96:3-9; Zech. 2:5-11 [Heb. 2:9-15]). In a wide-ranging and sensitive study that includes analysis of references to God's "glory" in the Old Testament and ancient Jewish and Christian writings, Carey Newman has shown that, already in the earliest layers of extant evidence (Paul), early Christians drew upon this "glory-tradition" as an important christological category.[55] So the Johannine christological appropriation of "glory/glorify" has a rich background, both in pre-Christian tradition and in earlier Christian practice as well.

The importance of the theme of "glory" is signaled early in GJohn, in 1:14, a statement intended to help frame the entirety of the following account of Jesus: "We beheld his [the incarnate Logos/Jesus] glory, glory as the uniquely begotten one/son [*monogenous*] from the Father, full of grace and truth." That is, the account of Jesus that follows in GJohn is to be read as the manifestation of the glory of the divine Son, as numerous subsequent references confirm.[56] We see it confirmed in 2:11, where the text tells us that the wine miracle narrated in 2:1-10 is the first of Jesus' signs in which he "manifested his glory." There is further confirmation in what is probably the final (seventh) sign narrated in John

---

evangeliums, SNTSMS 22 (Cambridge: Cambridge University Press, 1974); M. J. J. Menken, *Old Testament Quotations in the Fourth Gospel,* CBET 15 (Kampen: Kok Pharos, 1996); F.-M. Braun, *Jean le théologien: Les grandes traditions d'Israël et l'accord des écritures selon le quatrième évangile* (Paris: J. Gabalda, 1964); Johannes Beutler, "The Use of 'Scripture' in the Gospel of John," in *Exploring the Gospel of John,* 147-62; Andreas Obermann, *Die christologische Erfüllung der Schrift im Johannesevangelium,* WUNT 2/83 (Tübingen: Mohr-Siebeck, 1996); Daly-Denton, *David in the Fourth Gospel.*

54. S. Aalen, "Glory," in *NIDNTT,* 2:44-48, citing 45. In this paragraph I draw upon Aalen's concise discussion. See also G. Kittel and G. von Rad, "Δόξα," in *TDNT,* 2:233-55.

55. C. Newman, *Paul's Glory-Christology: Tradition and Rhetoric,* NovTSup 69 (Leiden: Brill, 1992). Newman focuses on Paul's association of "glory" and Jesus, a matter I referred to in chap. 2.

56. On the Johannine theme of the "glorifying" of the Son, see, e.g., Loader, *Christology,* 107-21, and cf. Margaret Pamment, "The Meaning of *Doxa* in the Fourth Gospel," *ZNW* 74 (1983): 12-16, who reduces the glorification of Jesus to his crucifixion and loving self-sacrifice. But I think that Loader has the better of it in contending that in GJohn the glorification of Jesus is not simply his suffering, but *through* his suffering to a heavenly status with God.

1–11, the story of the raising of Lazarus (11:1-44). Having learned that Lazarus is deathly ill, Jesus says this illness is "for the glory of God, that the Son of God might be glorified through it" (v. 4). Then, in verse 40, Jesus promises Martha that if she believes, she "will see the glory of God," which we are evidently to recognize in the raising of Lazarus that follows.

Other Johannine passages draw a contrast between human glory and glory from/of God (5:44; 12:43), and Jesus disdains seeking his own glory in favor of the glory that comes from God (7:18; 8:50, 54). In GJohn the Son glorifies God and God glorifies the Son (both in Jesus' earthly activities, 8:54, and in his death and resurrection, 12:23; 17:1, 5); several passages contain the direct statement that the glorification of the one involves the glorification of the other. 13:31-32 says that in the events then in motion that will culminate in Jesus' death and resurrection, "the son of man is glorified [by God], and God is glorified in him"; Jesus promises that when his disciples pray in his name, he will respond "so that the Father may be glorified in the Son" (14:13). In the prayer to the Father in 17:22, Jesus says that he gave his disciples "the glory which you gave to me," which is probably to be taken as characterizing Jesus' ministry as essentially a manifestation of God's glory.

In the Johannine scenes of Jesus' ministry, the unbelieving opponents do not perceive the glorious significance of his works, as reflected in the summarizing statement in 12:37-38 mentioned earlier: "Although he had performed so many signs in their presence, they did not believe in him." Even Jesus' disciples had to await his glorification in his resurrection before they perceived fully (e.g., 2:22; 12:16). But 1:14-18 tells the readers what they are to see in the account of Jesus that follows. Jesus is the incarnate divine Word, Light, and Son, whose glory is manifested (and to be perceived) in the events narrated in the Gospel of John. These events comprise his miraculous signs, and all other aspects of his activity, including his teaching and even his death, through which his glorification is culminated in being given heavenly glory with God (17:5).[57]

Jesus' prayer in John 17 is clearly intended to be read as offered on behalf of all his disciples, and so readers should probably take the petition in verse 24, "that they may see my glory which you [the Father] have given me because you loved me before the foundation of the world," as inclusive of them as well. This is confirmed by the statement in 16:13 that "the Spirit of truth" who comes after Jesus' death will glorify Jesus and declare to Jesus' followers what he receives from Jesus. As 16:15 explains, "all that the Father has" belongs to Jesus, and all this is what the Spirit will declare to Jesus' followers, glorifying Jesus to them by revealing to them powerfully that Jesus bears the glory of God. This revelation

57. Cf. Schnackenburg, *St. John*, 2:398-410.

of Jesus' glory by the Spirit likely involved revelatory and prophetic experiences, in which newly perceived truths about Jesus were apprehended as disclosures given by God. As I shall show more fully later in this chapter, these revelatory experiences were likely focused on (or at least heavily included) christological insights into biblical texts, "finding" Jesus in the Scriptures of Israel with the aid of the Spirit.

This Johannine theme of divine glory is almost certainly derived and adapted specifically from passages in Isaiah 40–66, a body of material that was richly mined in earliest Christian circles as a resource for christological reflection.[58] Particularly Isaiah 40–55, "Deutero-Isaiah," was heavily used. In his study of the Old Testament background of GJohn, Günter Reim states, "No other Old Testament writing stamped the theology of John as strongly as did Deutero-Isaiah, and no other New Testament author was as strongly influenced by Deutero-Isaiah as was John."[59]

Therefore it is important to note that throughout Isaiah 40–66 in particular, "glory" is frequently used in statements about a future manifestation of God that will involve redemption for Israel and even the illumination of Gentile nations.[60] For example, note the statement in Isaiah 40:5 that "the glory of the Lord shall be revealed, and all people shall see it." We know from the Johannine application of Isaiah 40:3 to John the Baptizer in John 1:23 that the author considered this chapter of Isaiah predictive of the events that he narrates.[61] Note also Isaiah 60:1, which links "light" and "the glory of the Lord," two terms and categories that are frequent and linked also in GJohn (e.g., the close association of "light" and "glory" in the Johannine prologue, 1:4-5, 14).[62]

58. Franklin W. Young, "A Study of the Relation of Isaiah to the Fourth Gospel," *ZNW* 46 (1955): 215-33; and Donald Juel, *Messianic Exegesis: Christological Interpretation of the Old Testament in Early Christianity* (Philadelphia: Fortress, 1988), 119-33. But Juel's discussion is almost entirely restricted to the association of Jesus and the "Servant" of Isa. 40–55, and does not take up the several other important christological uses of this material. Richard Bauckham's discussion of the use of Isa. 40–55 is suggestive of a thoroughgoing early Christian usage: *God Crucified: Monotheism and Christology in the New Testament* (Carlisle: Paternoster, 1998), 47-77.

59. Reim, 183 (translation mine). See 162-83 for Reim's discussion of the Johannine use of Isaiah. On 162-63 Reim lists Johannine citations and allusions to Isaiah. Of the seven Isaiah citations that Reim identifies, five are from Isa. 40–66, and four are from Isa. 40–55. Of the twenty-two "obvious" allusions to Isaiah, nineteen are from Isa. 40–55.

60. L. H. Brockington, "The Greek Translator of Isaiah and His Interest in ΔΟΞΑ," *VT* 1 (1951): 23-32.

61. The Qumran community also saw Isa. 40 as an important passage, and indeed saw 40:3 as predictive of themselves (1QS 8:14). So it appears that passages in "Second Isaiah" were very much the center of attention in Jewish circles of the first century.

62. Indeed, I propose that John 1:5 may be shaped by Isa. 60:1-3, which also presents the

Brockington showed that the Greek translator of Isaiah seems to have had a special fondness for the word *doxa,* which the translator "associated, directly or indirectly, with God's redemptive work."[63] As Brockington put it, in Isaiah *doxa* serves as an appropriate special term "to use in relation to the appearance of God in theophany."[64] In fact, both the Greek and the Hebrew texts of Isaiah 40–66 present the future manifestation of God's "glory" as a favorite way of portraying God's eschatological triumph.[65]

This Johannine appropriation of "glory" from Isaiah fits with the christological adaptation of the "I am" expression that is also used so prominently in Isaiah, providing (along with other terms and motifs used in GJohn) further indication of how GJohn reflects a vigorous mining of passages in Isaiah in particular for resources to understand and declare Jesus' significance. Like the appropriation of the "I am" formula, this Johannine use of the Isaiah "glory/glorification" motif signals an intimate association of Jesus with God that is unparalleled in any known Jewish traditions of the time. This is also clearly indicated in the mind-boggling Johannine statement in 12:41 that Isaiah 6:1-5 was a vision of Jesus. For the author(s) of GJohn, Jesus was the "Lord" (*ton Kyrion;* *Adonay* in the Hebrew) seated in glory in Isaiah 6:1.[66] Whether the author of John meant to say that Isaiah saw the glory of the preexistent Son or had a prophetic vision of the heavenly glory that was given to Jesus at/after his resurrection (and as John 17:5 indicates, the author thought in terms of both stages of Jesus' glory), either way it was a completely novel assertion in Jewish tradition. As I have stated already, however, GJohn does not replace the God of the Old Testament with Jesus. Instead, there is this amazing linkage and extension to Jesus of Old Testament ways of referring to God.

This interesting development, which, I repeat, involves preserving a commitment to the uniqueness of the biblical God, together with an unprecedented treatment of Jesus in terms otherwise reserved for God, is apparent in the Johannine statements that "the Father" *glorifies* Jesus, and *gives* him glory. That is, Jesus' glorious status is consistently described with reference to God "the Father." Even in a passage such as John 17:5, where Jesus is pictured referring to his

---

coming redemption as light and glory appearing in "thick darkness," in turn a possible allusion to the creation account (Gen. 1:2), thereby making the redemption like a new creation.

63. Brockington, 26. See also p. 30, where he cites instances where the LXX translator introduces *doxa* and combines references to "glory" and "salvation": e.g., Isa. 12:2; 40:5.

64. Brockington, 31.

65. See, e.g., Newman's discussion of Old Testament prophetic references to God's "glory" (*Paul's Glory — Christology,* 53-75), among which passages in Isaiah are prominent.

66. See, e.g., C. K. Barrett, *The Gospel according to St. John,* 2nd ed. (Philadelphia: Westminster, 1978), 432; Schnackenburg, *St. John,* 2:416-17.

own premundane glory in heaven, it is a glory that he had with God ("with you," *para soi*).

Nevertheless, the Johannine treatment of Jesus amounts to him being the one in whom God's glory is manifested, the unique human embodiment of God's glory on earth. This is why the Johannine Jesus can say, in reply to Philip's request to be shown the Father, "Whoever has seen me has seen the Father" (14:9). In GJohn Jesus not only is associated with the glory of God, he *is* the glory of God *manifest*.[67]

But how could early Christians such as the author of GJohn have made this astonishing appropriation of material from passages generally regarded as expressing emphatically the uniqueness of *Yahweh*, the God of Israel? In particular, how could they associate so directly the "glory" of God with Jesus (e.g., 11:4, 40)? How could they go so far as to claim that "the Father" gave heavenly glory to Jesus (17:5, 24) and glorified Jesus (e.g., 7:39; 12:16; 13:31-32; 14:13), when statements in these same Isaianic passages expressly say that God's glory is uniquely his? Twice, in Isaiah 42:8 and again in 48:11, *Yahweh* states, "I will give my glory to no other." It is difficult to think that the author of GJohn somehow missed these emphatic statements. Even if he had missed or chosen to ignore them, we can be sure that the Jewish critics of Johannine christological claims, who are commonly seen as reflected in the objections voiced to Jesus' claims in GJohn, would have pointed to these statements in Isaiah.

I propose, therefore, that the Johannine references to God giving glory to Jesus may in fact be deliberate allusions to these Isaiah passages which state that God does not give his glory to another, and that the Johannine statements reflect a creative and distinctive early Christian reading of these Isaiah statements and the larger body of material in Isaiah 40–66. Specifically, I suggest that behind (i.e., even earlier than) GJohn there was a Christian pattern of reading Isaiah 40–55 in particular that involved seeing two *divine* figures, the Lord God and another figure to whom God was understood to have given unique status that included sharing in God's glory. It is widely thought that GJohn and other early Christian texts evidence an interpretation of the "servant" of Isaiah 40–55 as (fulfilled in) Jesus.[68] I contend, however, that Isaiah was read much more creatively and daringly still. I propose that the servant and other features of the Isaiah passages were combined to refer to Jesus in such a way that they confirmed early Christian views of him sharing in divine status and worthy of worship, and that this reading of Isaiah facilitated the first-century Christian effort

---

67. So also, e.g., Sproston, 79.

68. Again, Juel, *Messianic Exegesis*, 119-33, and Bauckham, *God Crucified*, 47-69, are recent examples.

to articulate those views in biblical vocabulary and conceptual categories. To present the full warrants for my proposal would require a more substantial treatment of the matter than I can provide here. But in what follows I will focus on one other important theme in GJohn, the divine name, to show that references to God's name in Isaiah were also taken christologically, and that this proposed early Christian reading of Isaiah explains how GJohn could present Jesus as given and sharing the glory of God.

Jesus as/and the Name of God

References to God's name and to the name of Jesus constitute a major theme in GJohn, and they include distinctive expressions that indicate a close association of Jesus and God's name.[69] In the prayer of John 17, in particular, there are several interesting references. Jesus says that he "manifested your [God's] name to those whom you gave to me" (v. 6), and in verse 26 he affirms, "I made known to them your name and I will make it known." In other statements in the same prayer, Jesus appeals to God to keep the disciples "in your name which you have given me" (v. 11), and says, "While I was with them, I myself kept them in your name which you have given to me" (v. 12). In Johannine passages elsewhere, Jesus claims, "I have come in the name of my Father" (5:43), and refers to his deeds as done "in my Father's name" (10:25). This note is echoed in the cry of the crowd in the Jerusalem entry: "Blessed is he who comes in the name of the Lord" (12:13); in response to Jesus' appeal, "Father, glorify your name," the voice of God replies, "I have glorified it, and I will glorify it again" (12:28).

These references amount to a significant interest in the divine name; they also include some curious expressions that suggest important convictions about Jesus. On the one hand, GJohn reflects acquaintance with ancient biblical and Jewish traditions about the name of God. On the other hand, these

---

69. Franz Georg Untergassmair, *Im Namen Jesu — Der Namensbegriff im Johannesevangelium: eine exegetisch-religionsgeschichtliche Studie zu den johanneischen Namenaussagen* (Stuttgart: Katholisches Bibelwerk, 1974); Adelheid Ruck-Schröder, *Der Name Gottes und der Name Jesu: Eine neutestamentliche Studie,* WMANT 80 (Neukirchen-Vluyn: Neukirchener-Verlag, 1999), 210-12; Fossum, "In the Beginning Was the Name." Fossum emphasizes Johannine appropriation of Jewish divine-name tradition. Untergassmair's major conclusion is that GJohn contains a unique name-revelation theology which finds no ready parallel in Jewish or pagan circles. He reviews the *Gospel of Truth,* the *Odes of Solomon,* and of course Jewish texts. In his view the whole revelation of the name (through Jesus) is a unique Johannine contribution. Among earlier studies, Dodd, *Interpretation,* 93-96, remains particularly worthy of attention. Jean Daniélou, *The Theology of Jewish Christianity,* trans. and ed. J. A. Baker (London: Darton, Longman and Todd, 1964), 147-63, surveys the wider references to Jesus as the name of God in early Christian sources.

Johannine statements reflect some notable appropriation of that tradition, in order to make claims about *Jesus*.

For example, in what way could Jesus "manifest" and "make known" God's name to fellow Jews, in whose religious tradition the divine name had long been revered and was very familiar? It seems clear that these Johannine expressions must have a sense that is much more profound and subtle than Jesus telling his disciples what God's name was. Also, given the enormous concern in ancient Jewish tradition about the sanctity of God's name, how are we to take these references to God giving his name to Jesus? To draw attention to yet another curious matter, does the statement that God has glorified and will glorify his name in John 12:28 have something to do with the statement just a few verses earlier that "the hour has come for the Son of Man to be glorified"?

Both the number and the nature of the Johannine references to God's name confirm that the author is appropriating and creatively adapting biblical and Jewish divine-name tradition to express what he considers an important christological conviction. But before we attempt to describe more exactly what this conviction was, I want to give a brief overview of the divine-name tradition that these Johannine statements presuppose.

In the Old Testament God's name is presented as itself a revelation, and in various strands of Old Testament material the divine name is an important way of making statements about God's activity, presence, character, and being.[70] In the crucial scene in Exodus 3:13-16, we have the revelation of God's name (*Yahweh*) to Moses, along with a wordplay of sorts on it (based on the Hebrew verb *hayah*), in a Hebrew phrase that is often translated "I am who I am" (*'ehyeh 'asher 'ehyeh*).[71] Although the biblical deity is referred to by various other titles and epithets as well (e.g., "the Holy One," "God [*El; Elohim*]," "Lord [*Adonay*]," "God Almighty [*El Shaddai*]"), von Rad acutely notes that in bibli-

---

70. Gerhard von Rad, *Old Testament Theology*, 2 vols. (New York: Harper and Row, 1962), 1:179-87, discusses the religious meaning and function of the divine name in biblical material. Among numerous studies of the tetragrammaton, G. H. Parke-Taylor, *Yahweh: The Divine Name in the Bible* (Waterloo, Ontario: Wilfrid Laurier University Press, 1975), surveys well the biblical material and wider ancient Near Eastern evidence about divine names, with references to numerous other scholarly studies. Perhaps the classic study is Oskar Grether, *Name und Wort Gottes im Alten Testament*, BZAW 64 (Giessen: Alfred Töpelmann, 1934). E. E. Urbach discusses references in Jewish sources to the liturgical and magical uses of the divine name: *The Sages: Their Concepts and Beliefs*, trans. Israel Abrahams, 2 vols. (Jerusalem: Magnes Press, 1979), 1:124-34 (notes on pp. 733-40).

71. As von Rad observes, however, the sense of the wordplay on the Hebrew verb *hayah* in Exod. 3:14 "is to be understood in the sense of 'being present,' 'being there,' and therefore precisely not in the sense of absolute, but of relative and efficacious, being — I will be there (for you)" (*Old Testament Theology*, 1:180).

cal writings and subsequent Jewish tradition *Yahweh* was treated as the unique and particular *name* of God, the other terms (many of which came from very old traditions) not regarded as full equivalents.[72]

More specifically, since *Yahweh* was regarded as God's unique name, it was seen as participating directly in God's holiness, and "indeed it was, so to speak, a double of his being," with special associations with the temple and the approach to God that was particularized and especially efficacious there.[73] As I noted earlier, in discussing references in Paul's letters and also in Acts to "calling upon" the name of Jesus/the Lord, the biblical expression "to call upon the name of the LORD [Heb. *qara' beshem Yahweh*]" originally designated approaching God in sacrifice and invoking him by the use of this name (e.g., Gen. 12:7-8; Ps. 116:4, 17). Indeed, it is worthwhile to note von Rad's judgment that in the biblical tradition the divine name "takes the place which in other cults was occupied by the cultic image."[74] That is, in a number of texts it is the presence of the divine name which sanctifies and legitimates the temple site as the valid location for sacrifice. As Martin Rose puts it, "The legitimacy of the entire cultic service (the word and the sacrifice) depends on the legitimization of the name of God."[75]

Particularly in Deuteronomy we encounter statements about the divine name that illustrate this. God puts his name *(Yahweh)* upon a particular place to make it the uniquely appropriate site for sacrificial worship (e.g., Deut. 12:4-7, 21), and there God's name will "dwell" (e.g., 12:11; 14:23; 16:2, 6, 11; 26:2).[76] The Psalms, too, refer to the Jerusalem sanctuary as "the dwelling-place [Gk. *to skēnōma*; Heb. *mishkan*] of your [God's] name" (Ps. 74[LXX73]:7), and in Jere-

---

72. Von Rad, *Old Testament Theology*, 1:185. This is in contrast with other ancient religious traditions in which the gods are often explicitly said to have many names. Von Rad also proposes that variation in the ways God is referred to in biblical texts seems often deliberate and context-sensitive. Thus, e.g., Ps. 104 is addressed to *Yahweh* as creator and sustainer of all (1:1), but animals, such as the "young lions" of v. 21, are said to seek their food from *"El,"* probably reflecting the view that Israel alone was given the privilege of addressing the one God as *Yahweh* (186). See also Martin Rose, "Names of God in the OT," in *ABD*, 4:1001-11, esp. 1004-9. The importance of the name *Yahweh* in the Old Testament is signaled by the overwhelmingly larger number of uses of it than any other epithet: 6,823, plus another 50 uses of the shortened form, *Yah* (as in the phrase, *"hallelu-yah"*), and another 150 cases where a shortened form (*yô*, or *yehô* at the beginning, *yah* or *yahu* at the end) is part of the name of a biblical character, e.g., Joshua (*Yehoshua*).

73. Von Rad, *Old Testament Theology*, 1:183.

74. Von Rad, *Old Testament Theology*, 1:183.

75. Rose, 1003.

76. In the LXX of Deuteronomy, the chosen site is consistently referred to as the place "where his name may be invoked" *(epiklēthēnai to onoma autou ekei)*.

383

miah 7:12 Shiloh is similarly characterized ("where I made my name to dwell [kateskēnōsa] at first"). In other psalms the Jerusalem sanctuary is also referred to as "the house where you [God] reside, the dwelling place [Heb. *mishkan;* Gk. *topon skēnōmatos*] of your glory" (Ps. 26[LXX25]:8), and God's own "dwelling place" (78[LXX 77]:60; 91[LXX 90]:10; cf. "dwelling places" in 84[LXX 83]:1). Similar expressions in other texts make the presence of God's name an interchangeable way of referring to the presence of God, especially the presence of God that is associated with the sanctuary.[77]

In light of the frequency of reference to God's name as "dwelling" upon the earth among Israel, Fossum is surely correct to contend that this tradition about the divine name should be seen as a likely background of the statement in John 1:14 that the Word "dwelt [eskēnōsen] among us."[78] Indeed, given that Wisdom is never referred to in GJohn, whereas the divine name is a very salient theme, perhaps divine-name tradition is considerably more important overall than Wisdom tradition for the Christology of GJohn.

We should also note the references to the divine name in Isaiah 40–66, given the other indications of the importance of these chapters for the christological vocabulary and themes of GJohn. In Isaiah 52:5-6 God complains that his name is blasphemed and promises a future time ("in that day") when "my people will know my name," and will know "that it is I [Heb. *'ani 'hū;* Gk. *egō eimi*] who speak." In the context, this future knowledge of God's name is part of the eschatological blessings that will come from the Lord's return to Zion to comfort his people (55:1-9). That is, this eschatological knowledge of the *name* of the Lord is linked with, and perhaps an alternate expression for, the manifestation of the *glory* of the Lord (e.g., 40:5; 60:1; 66:18). A couple statements in the Greek text of Isaiah refer to God's name and do not correspond directly to what we know as the Hebrew text. For example, in the passage about the servant of the Lord (42:1-9), the LXX of 42:4 predicts that "the nations will hope in his name" (whereas the Hebrew says the nations will "wait/hope for his teaching [*toratī*]"). In 42:10 the Greek has "sing a new song to the Lord," and exhorts readers to "glorify his name" (whereas for the latter phrase the Hebrew simply calls for praises to God from all creation). As Franklin Young observed several decades ago, the terminology of these passages of Greek Isaiah makes it obvious that "the revelation of the name of God is to be

77. For example, cf. the LXX of Ezek. 43:7 ("my name will dwell [*kataskēnōsei*]") with the MT ("I will dwell there"); cf. 2 Sam. 7:5 ("a house for me") and 7:13 ("a house for my name"). See also Ezra 6:12 and Neh. 1:9 (LXX 2 Esd. 6:12; 11:9); *Pss. Sol.* 7.6. In Jer. 7:12 Shiloh is referred to as "the place where I caused my name to dwell at first."

78. Fossum, "Beginning," 121-25. Cf. the divine direction to personified Wisdom in Sir. 24:8: "Make your dwelling [*kataskēnōson*] in Jacob, and in Israel receive your inheritance."

a decisive factor in His day of salvation. . . . In reality, the revelation of the name will be the revelation of God himself."[79]

In light of these Isaiah references, when we consider the several Johannine references to the divine name, we can see the background that is presupposed and adapted in GJohn to make important claims about Jesus. GJohn draws upon this rich, close, almost interchangeable association of God and God's name to express a uniquely intimate relationship between Jesus and the Father. Indeed, for the author of GJohn, for whom the biblical traditions provided the authoritative store of vocabulary, images, and themes by which to express the significance of Jesus, this divine-name tradition constituted the most profound way to portray the relationship of the "Son" to the "Father." To speak of Jesus as invested with the divine name, as coming with and in the name of God, as given the name, and as manifesting God's name in his own words and actions, was to portray Jesus as bearing and exhibiting God in the most direct way possible in the conceptual categories available in the biblical tradition, and within the limits of the monotheistic commitment of that tradition.

In the next century or two after GJohn, Christians began appropriating and adapting terms and conceptual categories from the Greek philosophical traditions (e.g., "being" [*ousia*], "essence" [*hypostasis;* Lat. *substantia*]). But it is perhaps not excessive to suggest that the Johannine use of divine-name tradition is in its own terms an equivalently radical and direct claim about the linkage of Jesus to God.

To think of Jesus being given the divine name (John 17:11-12) is fully consonant with, and also explains, other features of Johannine Christology. Obviously he is thus able to make the divine name known (17:6, 26) in his own actions, which he performs in the name of the Father (10:25), and in his words as well, which are also the works of the Father who "abides" *(menōn)* in him (14:10; see also 12:49-50). Moreover, of course, the idea that Jesus has been given the divine name accounts for the Johannine Jesus' frequent use of the divine self-referential formula *egō eimi* (I am), which is virtually a synonym for God's name, both in Isaiah and probably in GJohn. Furthermore, the statements in John 14:9-10, "whoever has seen me has seen the Father" and "I am in the Father and the Father is in me," are likely to be taken as reflecting and cohering with the idea that Jesus has been given the divine name, and in some direct sense embodies it on earth.[80]

---

79. Young, 222-24, citing 223.

80. Although the text is not cited explicitly in GJohn, Exod. 23:20-21 may lie somewhere in the background, for it refers to God placing his name within a figure to whom Israel was to give attentive submission. This text was particularly provocative for various speculations about

Still further, I propose that the contextually proximate references to Jesus' glorification (12:16) and to God glorifying "the son of man" (12:23) and God's own name (12:28), are probably to be taken as synonymous. In GJohn this "son of man" bears, manifests, and in some profoundly unique sense *is* the divine name in earthly expression, and so the coming glorification of Jesus is also the glorification of God's name.[81] Consequently, readers of GJohn are also probably to understand in the shout of the crowd in 12:13, "Blessed is he who comes in the name of the Lord" (citing Ps. 118[LXX 117]:26), a meaning more radical than the ordinary connotation. In GJohn Jesus comes not simply as one approved by God, but "in the name of the Lord," which has a sense unforeseen and unparalleled: Jesus is personally bestowed with the divine name.

The idea that Jesus has been given the divine *name*, and bears and manifests it in his own words and deeds, may also help account for the related idea that he has been given a share in the *glory* of God. We noted earlier that the name and glory of God are related and prominent themes in Isaiah 40–66, the eschatological action of God being portrayed there as the manifestation of God's glory and the making known of God's name, the one being roughly equivalent in effect to the other. I propose that, through the identification of Jesus as the historical manifestation of the divine name, early Christians such as the author of GJohn were able to find scriptural warrant for describing him as sharing in, and manifesting, the glory of God. The text of GJohn does not explicate the thinking behind the christological assertions that it promotes and reflects, but a Christian text from a few decades later may preserve an important bit of the rationale behind the Johannine association of Jesus with the glory and name of God.

The Dialogue with Trypho, by Justin Martyr, is the oldest extant Christian text that is wholly devoted to a presentation of Christian faith over against Jewish objections. Although probably written sometime in the middle of the second century, the *Dialogue* is widely thought to incorporate disputations that Justin may have had with Jews in the aftermath of the Bar Kokhba war (132-35).[82] Moreover, it is also widely accepted that a good deal of Justin's argument

---

"divine agent" figures, as shown by Alan F. Segal, *Two Powers in Heaven: Early Rabbinic Reports about Christianity and Gnosticism,* SJLA 25 (Leiden: Brill, 1977), 169-72. Justin's explicit reference to Exod. 23:20-21 most likely echoes a Christian use of the text that goes back much earlier (*Dial.* 75).

81. "Christ, who has received the name of God from God himself (17:11), and now reveals this name to the community of believers (17:6), is in a certain sense himself this (divine) name" (Ruck-Schröder, 211, translation mine).

82. See, e.g., Johannes Quasten, *Patrology,* vol. 1, *The Beginnings of Patristic Literature* (Westminster, Md.: Christian Classics, 1986 [1950]), 202-3.

in the *Dialogue* reflects traditional early Christian thought that had been around for some time, a good deal of which likely came from Jewish Christian circles.[83]

I draw attention to a particular passage where Justin's Jewish interlocutor, Trypho, cites the statement in Isaiah 42:8, "My glory I will not give to another," to refute Justin's view that Jesus shares in God's glory and is rightly worthy of worship (*Dial.* 65.1). Justin's response is to claim that the Isaiah passage in fact asserts that God *did* give his glory "to his Christ alone" (*ho theos tō christō autou monō tēn doxan didōsin; Dial.* 65.3), and in support of this he quotes the surrounding statements (Isa. 42:5-13). For Justin the immediately adjacent statements in 42:6-7 are crucial, where God speaks to another figure whom God called and gave as "a covenant to the people [Heb. *berith 'am;* Gk. *diathēkēn genous*], a light [*phōs*] to the nations." Justin clearly reads the following words of Isaiah 42:8, "this is my name," as a further reference to this same figure (i.e., as "this [one] is my name"), and he takes the statement "My glory I give to no other [*heterō*]" to mean that God *does* rightly give his glory to *this* "light/name" figure, but not to any *other!*[84] Justin's summary statement to his Jewish partners in dialogue is worth quoting: "Have you perceived, O friends, that God says that he will give glory to this one [*toutō*], whom he established for a light of the nations, and to no other, and not, as Trypho said, as though God kept his glory to himself?" (*Dial.* 65.7).

Although this is our earliest explicit evidence of this reading of Isaiah 42:8, I think it a safe bet that Christians did not have to wait until the mid-second century to have this text thrown at them by Jewish opponents of their veneration of Jesus. Given that Johannine Jewish Christians were thrown out of their synagogues and regarded as blasphemous by Jewish opponents on account of their reverence of Jesus, it is almost impossible to imagine that they did not have to come to terms with Isaiah 42:8 (and its echo in 48:11).[85] In fact, I propose that the Johannine references to God giving glory to Jesus (e.g., John

---

83. Oskar Skarsaune, *The Proof from Prophecy: A Study in Justin Martyr's Proof-Text Tradition: Text-Type, Provenance, Theological Profile*, NovTSup 66 (Leiden: Brill, 1987), refers to "the considerable influence exerted by Judaeo-Christians" reflected in Justin's exegetical material (432). I return to Justin for fuller discussion in chap. 10.

84. The Greek phrasing in Isa. 42:8, *touto mou estin to onoma*, permits Justin's interpretation, for the neuter pronoun, *touto* (this), corresponds both to the neuter noun *onoma* (name), and to the neuter noun *phōs* (light). Cf., e.g., D. Moody Smith, *John: Abingdon New Testament Commentaries* (Nashville: Abingdon, 1999), 243 (I thank Catrin Williams for this reference).

85. It is, I trust, not necessary to defend the view that passages such as John 10:31-33, though set in the time of Jesus, more directly reflect the accusations hurled against Johannine Christians from Jewish opponents.

17:5, 24) intentionally allude to the sort of early Christian reading of Isaiah 42:8 that Justin explicitly attests in the *Dialogue*. That is, GJohn expresses the direct claim that God *has* given glory to Jesus, *because* he is the "light" promised in Isaiah 42:6 (John 1:4-9; 12:35-36) and the "name" pointed to in Isaiah 42:8.

I hasten to add that I am not suggesting for a moment that these daring convictions about Jesus were produced simply through pondering texts such as Isaiah in some speculative exercise in early Christian circles. The fundamental christological convictions of these circles initially arose from, and were sustained for some time by, powerful religious experiences in which Jesus was "seen" in such a manner as to convey the notion that he had been given a glorious status and form. In the light of such experiences, devout Christians (in the first instances, Jewish Christians) went to their Scriptures, searching for resources with which to make proper sense of, and to reflect upon, these experiences. Moreover, they searched their Scriptures in corporate settings of prayer and worship, in which further "revelations" were sought and expected; it is likely that these further revelations often took the form of "inspired" insights into scriptural passages such as Isaiah 40–66.[86]

Indeed, among the scriptural resources most closely explored, and found most productive for early Christian reflection, this part of Isaiah seems to have featured prominently. Here early circles of believers found what we may call "a pattern of duality" involving God and a second figure, who is variously referred to as God's "servant," the "light," the "arm (of the Lord)" (e.g., Isa. 53:1, cited in John 12:38), and God's "name," with whom God shared his glory.

I want to make a further point about the influence of Isaiah in early christological reflection. The sort of reading of Isaiah that, in my view, is reflected and presupposed in GJohn seems to have been not only pre-Johannine but in fact *very* early indeed. A reference that seems to me to make this an almost inescapable conclusion is the clear allusion to Isaiah in a well-known passage in Paul's letter to the Philippians (2:9-11), a reference that we noted in chapter 1. To repeat briefly from that discussion, the use of Isaiah 45:23 in Philippians 2:9-11 seems to indicate an interpretation of the Isaiah passage as itself predicting the acclamation of Jesus as Lord "to the glory of God the Father."

---

86. I remind my readers of Paul's characterization of early Christian worship in 1 Cor. 14:26 as including phenomena such as "a hymn, a teaching, a revelation, a tongue or an interpretation," which terms seem to refer to "charismatic" phenomena, "manifestations" of the Spirit (1 Cor. 12:4-6). Likewise, it is commonly accepted among scholars that the Lukan scenes where the risen Jesus opens his disciples' eyes to the christological import of the Scriptures (Luke 24:25-27, 44-47) were expected to be credible to intended readers because they reflected the sorts of inspired christological "exegesis" experiences that were a familiar feature in early Christian circles.

That is, in this interpretation *two* figures were seen in Isaiah 45:23-25, God and another figure the Philippians passage identifies as Jesus. This latter figure chose to accept a servant role as agent of God (Phil. 2:6-8), was subsequently given "the (divine) name above every name" *(Kyrios)*, and will share in the universal acclamation described there "to the glory of God the Father." As with the use of Isaiah material in GJohn, so here in Philippians as well, the christological reading of Isaiah is not explicated or presented as if it needed defense; *it is presupposed*, and so merely alluded to in making the larger point of Philippians 2:5-11, which is to promote behavior that is motivated and shaped by Jesus' own "Lordly example."[87]

We should think in terms of a fervent mining of material from Isaiah, especially 40–66, in the service of a radical christological interpretation of these chapters that was under way with explosive rapidity in circles of Jewish Christians, and within the first few years (at the most) of the Christian movement. The indication of a creative christological use of Isaiah already by the time Philippians was composed means there was plenty of time for a rather thorough christological interpretation of Isaiah material to have become known and presupposed by the author of GJohn. In this reading of Isaiah, Jesus is seen as the unique and personal expression/embodiment of the divine glory, the divine name, the "arm of the Lord" (John 12:38, citing Isa. 53:1), and the servant of the Lord, through whom redemption comes to Israel, the nations are offered religious enfranchisement, and the eschatological glory of God is manifested.

The Name of Jesus

This kind of close association of Jesus with the glory and name of God in turn helps to explain another notable Johannine emphasis: the significance and efficacy of Jesus' own name.[88] It is as if, through the intimate relationship of Jesus with "the Father," Jesus' own name is irradiated with divine significance and potency. Those who saw Jesus as given God's name and glory (John 17:11-12), and exalted by God to unique heavenly status as "Lord," regarded Jesus' own name as itself powerful; consequently, Jesus' name was used ritually.

As we noted previously, the use of Jesus' own name in healings, exorcisms, baptisms, and corporate liturgical invocations seems to go back to the earliest

---

87. L. H. Hurtado, "Jesus as Lordly Example in Philippians 2:5-11," in *From Jesus to Paul: Studies in Honour of Francis Wright Beare*, ed. P. Richardson and J. C. Hurd (Waterloo, Ontario: Wilfrid Laurier University Press, 1984), 113-26.

88. See recently Ruck-Schröder, 203-19.

observable Christian circles. It is taken for granted in the earliest extant evidence of Christian devotion reflecting both Pauline churches and Jewish Christian settings. In GJohn, therefore, it should not be surprising that Jesus' name is thematized as powerful, and is promoted as a conventional feature of the devotional practices of Johannine believers. But the extent of emphasis on Jesus' name in GJohn justifies taking note of it here.

There is a repeated insistence that belief must be directed specifically to Jesus/Jesus' name. All who believe in/on Jesus' name *(eis to onoma autou)* are given authority to become *(genesthai)* children of God (John 1:12). In John 3:18, believing in Jesus and believing "in the name of the unique Son of God" are synonymous; such belief makes all the difference for divine judgment (cf., e.g., 6:40). The same sort of equation seems to be reflected in 2:23, referring to those who saw his signs and "believed in his name." And of course, the climactic purpose statement in 20:31 calls for belief in Jesus as Messiah and Son of God, offering "life *in his name*" to all who so believe.

This repeated assertion of the significance of Jesus and his name does not, however, reduce the significance of "the Father" in GJohn. Instead, belief in Jesus is the will of the Father (6:40), just as it is the Father's intention "that all may honor the Son just as they honor the Father" (5:22-23). The close duality of Jesus and God is reflected everywhere in GJohn, as in the statement that eternal life comes through knowing "the only true God, and Jesus Christ" who has been sent by God (17:3). To repeat an observation made earlier, Jesus' significance is always expressed with reference to God "the Father" in GJohn. At the same time, GJohn insists that proper obedience to, and reverence of, God now requires that Jesus be explicitly included with God as recipient of faith and devotion. This means that "the Father" is now defined with reference to Jesus, through whom in a uniquely full and authoritative measure the Father is revealed.

In the distinctive body of teaching in John 14–16, there is an emphasis on the efficacy of invoking Jesus' name in prayer. The promise that the Spirit will be sent to Jesus' disciples after his departure explicitly makes the teaching here applicable to the life of Christian circles in the post-Jesus period. Repeatedly Jesus' followers are told to make their petitions in Jesus' name *(en tō onomati mou;* 14:13-14; 15:16; 16:23-24, 26). In 14:13-14 Jesus himself promises to respond to petitions offered in his name, whereas in 15:16 and 16:23-27 "the Father" will answer them. These statements call for the actual invocation of Jesus' name as a feature of the prayer practice advocated here. Although there is some textual uncertainty in 14:13-14, the dominant impression is that prayer is to be directed to "the Father."[89] But the explicit use of Jesus' name in prayer marks off those

89. The textual variants in John 14:13-14 and 15:16 show scribes reflecting the influence of

who recognize Jesus as sent from God; it also signifies that, as divinely sent and authorized, Jesus' very name is now efficacious.

Of course this is not some "magical" conception, as if merely pronouncing the syllables of Jesus' name had automatic efficacy. The context makes it clear that the efficacy of the petitions rests on Jesus' disciples believing Jesus was sent from God and is one with the Father (14:11-12), loving Jesus and keeping his commandments (14:15, 21, 23-24), and remaining in close relationship with Jesus (15:1-10).[90] But it is also undeniable that these Johannine passages do attribute a powerful efficacy to Jesus' name when used by those who are faithful believers in Jesus.

Additionally, these passages show Jesus' name being explicitly invoked *as a feature of the prayer practice promoted and observed in Johannine circles*. That is, in these references we have a glimpse of the actual devotional customs advocated and followed by Johannine Christians. This ritual use of Jesus' name has no known parallel in Jewish tradition of the time, and it amounts to "Jesus" being treated in devotional practice as itself carrying and representing divine efficacy and significance. Given that ancient Jewish tradition widely regarded God's name as uniquely sacred, this practice of invoking Jesus' name in prayer is momentous; Jewish opponents would likely have seen it as an unwarranted and dangerous innovation. The references to Christians being hated *because of Jesus' name* (Mark 13:13; Matt. 10:22; Luke 21:12) likely reflect the outraged response of those outside the Christian circles to their astonishing readiness to treat Jesus' name as worthy of such devotion.

But the Johannine emphasis on Jesus' name seems only to thematize a conviction and devotional practice involving Jesus' name that is attested already in Paul's letters (e.g., 1 Cor. 1:10). The other canonical Gospels confirm how widespread the practice was of treating Jesus' name as efficacious in exorcisms and healings (Mark 9:38-39; Matt. 7:22; Luke 10:17). In fact, in earlier chapters we noted that "calling upon" Jesus ritually, in worship and baptism

---

devotional practices, and also perhaps occasionally seeking to harmonize the directions given in John 14–16 about prayer. E.g., 14:14, which promises that Jesus will answer petitions, is omitted in some witnesses (X, fam 1, 565, and some Latin and Syriac witnesses), probably to avoid a conflict with 15:16 and 16:23-27, which promises that the Father will respond. The variation in 14:14 between "if you ask/ask me" may have arisen from scribes similarly deleting an offending "me" (the view favored by most commentators), but it is also just possible that the "me" was inserted and became the more popular reading because it reflected the early Christian practice of offering prayer to Jesus as well as to "the Father."

90. Emphasized, e.g., by Schnackenburg, *St. John*, 3:73. The humorous scene in Acts 19:11-20, where (non-Christian) exorcists attempt to use Jesus' name magically, has the serious intention of disassociating the early Christian practice from magic, while at the same time claiming that Christian practice was much more efficacious.

as well, is attested in the earliest extant layers of evidence of Christian devotional practice.

The early origin of ritual use of Jesus' name in Jewish Christian circles raises the intriguing question of whether the suggestive etymology of the Semitic form of the name may have been a factor. "Jesus" (Gk. *Iēsous*) derives from the Hebrew name *Yeshua,* a shortened form of *Yehoshua* (the name given to the trusty aide of Moses). The name is a compound from the Hebrew verb meaning "to deliver/save" *(yasha')* and a shortened form of the divine name *Yahweh.*[91] Hence, etymologically "Jesus" means something like "God *(Yahweh)* saves"; Matthew 1:21 confirms that in some early Christian circles with strong Jewish Christian influences this etymology was known and seen as highly meaningful.

So, did the earliest circles in which Jesus' name was ritually invoked perceive this "theophoric" quality? If so, did this quality confirm for them that Jesus himself was the expression of God's name and presence, and did it also help promote the ritual invocation of "Jesus" and its use in prayer? We do not have an adequate basis for an indisputable answer one way or the other. But I suspect that the Semitic etymology of the name Jesus was meaningful and influential at an early stage. This is certainly consistent with the Johannine emphasis on the religious significance and devotional efficacy of Jesus' name.

In any case, GJohn associates Jesus with the glory and name of God, and presents Jesus as the uniquely direct expression of God's purposes, so that to encounter Jesus amounts to an encounter with God. Moreover, the Jesus of GJohn demonstrates a full self-awareness of his premundane glory and heavenly origins, and he explicitly summons people to faith in him as the heaven-sent redeemer. All this amounts to a distinctively Johannine portrait of Jesus in which his divine significance is programmatically presented. I turn now to other aspects of the Johannine Jesus that are often believed difficult to reconcile with this emphasis on Jesus' divinity.

Subordination and Distinction

The apparent "tensions" in the Johannine presentation of Jesus are well known in scholarly circles.[92] One feature of GJohn that has caused considerable schol-

91. The first use of the name is in Num. 13:16, where Moses changes the name of "Hoshea the son of Nun" to "Joshua," who then becomes the earliest of several figures who bear the same name. George W. Ramsey, Stanley E. Porter, and William Scott Green, "Joshua," in *ABD,* 3:999-1002.

92. See now, P. Anderson, esp. 1-32, for a helpful analysis of the various elements in the Johannine rendition of Jesus that have been seen as "tensions."

arly puzzlement is that Jesus is presented in extraordinarily exalted terms and yet also is distinguished from, and subordinate to, "the Father." Likewise, the Johannine Jesus has both divine and human properties and characteristics. Some scholars have proposed that insufficiently digested sources and/or successive (and somewhat clumsily conducted) redactions account for the complexity in Johannine Christology. The key basis for any theory that GJohn is a patchwork of various sources or a stratigraphic record of shifting Christologies is the judgment that GJohn's various christological emphases are irreconcilable. But in a recent study of unity and diversity in the Johannine presentation of Jesus, Paul Anderson has acutely and persuasively shown that such judgments reflect inaccurate readings of GJohn.[93]

Anderson rightly contends that the Johannine emphases on Jesus as both one with and subordinate to "the Father" fit together as "a reflection of the *evangelist's agency christology*" (emphasis his). That is, Jesus is to be honored and regarded in the same way that "the Father" is honored and regarded, precisely because Jesus represents the Father so fully. Jesus' own authority rests on his authenticity as uniquely adequate spokesman for God, uttering only what "the Father" has given him to say (e.g., John 5:19-20; 6:38; 14:10). "In John, subordinationist and egalitarian christological motifs are both central component parts to John's pervasive *agency christology*," and are "two sides of the same coin."[94] Superseding Moses and the law of God, Jesus is the uniquely full revelation of God (1:18). "The Son" is to be revered by people, and is exalted and glorified by "the Father" precisely as the one who manifests in unique manner the Father's name and will (17:4-5).

Any notion that Jesus' subordination to the Father represents some supposedly early stage of Johannine Christology that was superseded later by a "high" view of Jesus as sharing fully in the glory of God is rendered implausible by the repeated assertion of Jesus' subordination in material that likely comes from *various* stages of the redaction of GJohn. Thus, to cite a body of material widely thought to represent a mature stage of Johannine thought, Jesus' prayer for his disciples in John 17, we find repeated references to Jesus' premundane and future heavenly glory with God bound together with clear expressions of Jesus' subordination to the Father.[95] For example, eternal life involves knowledge of "the only true God, and Jesus Christ whom you have sent" (v. 3), an assertion of Jesus' essential significance and also his role as unique agent of God.

93. P. Anderson, *The Christology of the Fourth Gospel.* Anderson focuses on John 6 and considers alleged tensions involving present and future eschatology, determinism and free will, and Jesus as both one with and subordinate to the Father.

94. P. Anderson, 260-61.

95. On the genre and origins of John 17, see, e.g., Schnackenburg, *St. John*, 3:197-202.

Jesus and the Father are one (v. 22b). Yet Jesus possesses and bestows the glory given to him by the Father (v. 22a), and Jesus prays that the world may believe that God has sent him (vv. 21, 23). Jesus' desires for the disciples include their seeing his divine glory, and yet this glory is given to him in love by God (v. 24).

In spite of the Johannine distinctives in vocabulary and motifs, this consistent reference to Jesus in relation to God attests to a profound agreement in christological perspective with the rest of the New Testament. Furthermore, this "subordinationist" emphasis, this presentation of Jesus as unique agent of God, also shows the pervasive influence of the biblical/Jewish tradition with its strong monotheistic concern. John 10:33 probably reflects accusations of ditheism from the Jewish community that were hurled against Johannine Christians. Certainly the stress on Jesus being sent from God, speaking what God has revealed, exercising authority delegated to him by God, manifesting God's name and glory, revealing God, and being glorified by God attests a firm resolve to assert Jesus' divine significance; yet at the same time, this is done within a fervently held (though distinctively reshaped) monotheistic faith. In GJohn, as Anderson concluded, the assertion of Jesus' divine significance and also his "subordination" to the Father are not in tension; instead, each assertion is vital to the validity and particular meaning of the other.

Another frequently perceived tension in GJohn involves the relationship between Jesus' divinity and humanity. In an influential study of GJohn's Christology, Ernst Käsemann contended that GJohn is "naïvely docetic," meaning that it presents Jesus as so thoroughly divine that his human nature is merely a decorative trapping.[96] Against those for whom John 1:14 reflects a genuinely incarnational view of Jesus, Käsemann contended that Jesus' divine glory remains so dominant in the Johannine presentation of his earthly life that GJohn comes close to denying Jesus' true humanity.

I find Käsemann's characterization of GJohn one-sided and methodologically flawed. He sets up his own definition of what "true humanity" must involve and how it ought to be portrayed, and then faults GJohn for failing to observe these (somewhat anachronistic) demands. To be sure, the Johannine Jesus is emphatically divine in significance, and heavenly in true origins and destination. Moreover, the Johannine Jesus operates with an awareness of his heavenly origins and divine significance that we moderns will find difficult to harmonize with our notions of "normal" human psychology. But in its own terms, GJohn affirms a genuinely human Jesus. Indeed, I contend that Jesus' humanity is an *essential* feature of the Johannine rendition of him. I am grateful to be able to

---

96. Ernst Käsemann, *The Testament of Jesus: A Study of the Gospel of John in the Light of Chapter 17*, trans. Gerhard Krodel (Philadelphia: Fortress, 1968).

point to a fine study by Marianne Meye Thompson that treats the question more fully, making it sufficient here for me to provide a summary of her discussion and a sample of the relevant evidence.[97]

Thompson discusses four key features of Jesus' humanity in GJohn persuasively and at chapter length: Jesus' origins, his incarnation and "flesh," his "signs," and his death. It is, of course, an important Johannine theme that Jesus' true origins are in God and that his ultimate provenance is premundane and heavenly. Consequently in GJohn the references to Jesus' earthly origins by characters in the narrative can signal their failure to perceive the full truth of his person and significance (e.g., Nathanael's disdainful remark about Nazareth in 1:46; the crowd's claim to know his origins in Galilee in 7:27, 41-44, and to know his family in 6:42). Yet GJohn does not deny Jesus' historical and earthly origins. Indeed, GJohn can refer to Jesus' biological family in rather matter-of-fact terms, as in the story of the wine miracle in Cana (2:1, 12). Granted, in 7:2-9 Jesus' brothers are clearly presented as not believing in him (7:5), which seems to vividly illustrate the Johannine statement in 1:11 that Jesus came to "his own *(ta idia)* and they did not receive him." But this hardly seems different from the critical distinction that Jesus is pictured making between his biological family and "whoever does the will of God" in Mark 3:31-35.

In GJohn, to define Jesus simply with reference to his earthly family and origins is to fall far short of an adequate perception of him. But GJohn consistently posits the importance of a real historical particularity to Jesus and to all the characters and events of the narrative. As is true of the other canonical renditions of Jesus, so too in GJohn we meet a whole cast of characters who (even if some of them be literary creations) are given specific location in time, place, and culture (e.g., John the Baptist, Nicodemus, the Samaritan woman, Caiaphas and the council, Pilate, and others). Indeed, scholars have noted how much curiously specific historical tradition GJohn seems to include.[98] Whatever one makes of the accuracy of the particulars of that tradition, my point here is that GJohn shares a concern to embed Jesus fully within a specific geographical, cultural, religious, political, chronological, and ethnic setting. The Johannine rendition of Jesus is no atemporal meditation by a "talking head." Instead, the Johannine Jesus is undeniably a Jew who affirms the validity of the historic revelation to which his nation bears witness (John 4:22), and precisely

---

97. Marianne Meye Thompson, *The Humanity of Jesus in the Fourth Gospel* (Philadelphia: Fortress, 1988). Also important here is Sproston, who rightly emphasizes that the purpose in GJohn is precisely to underscore the paradox of a Jesus who is "fully human and yet fully identified with the divine pre-existent Logos" (Sproston, 80).

98. The classic study is still C. H. Dodd, *Historical Tradition in the Fourth Gospel* (Cambridge: Cambridge University Press, 1963).

in keeping with this conviction, he claims to be sent from this true God. That is, in the Johannine view of Jesus, his specific historical connections and real humanity are in fact essential to the claim of his divine significance. In the programmatic affirmation in John 1:14, for example, both parts are vital: Jesus really and fully is the divine, premundane Logos, and this divine figure really did "become flesh," taking on a specific human existence, family, and name.

Perhaps the main reason that Jesus' "flesh" is essential is Jesus' redemptive death, which is also probably the key demonstration of the reality of the "incarnation" of the divine Son. The key passage is of course John 6:51-58. Here the true bread of life is Jesus' flesh that he will give for the world (v. 51). In deliberately provocative phrasing, the passage requires followers to eat Jesus' flesh and drink his blood as the basis and condition for receiving eternal life and resurrection "on the last day" (vv. 53-54). The passage clearly looks ahead to Jesus' coming execution, making his real physical death (registered in the references to his "flesh" and "blood") the basis of redemption and life. The distinctive reference to the piercing of Jesus' side, and the solemn affirmation of the reality of the effects of the wound (19:34-35), show that the divine significance of the Johannine Jesus does not eclipse the reality of his humanity. Likewise, the distinctive Johannine episode where the risen Jesus appears to Thomas (20:24-29) emphasizes the bodily reality of the resurrected Jesus, and connects his resurrection state with his crucified body (the marks of the wounds).

To be sure, the Johannine Jesus does not fit easily with a modern understanding of "normal" human psychology. For example, his awareness of his premundane existence, his knowledge of who would believe and who would betray him (6:64), and his self-possessed awareness of his approaching ordeal (13:1) all give the Johannine Jesus an almost preternatural aura when judged by normal human experience. But the Johannine concern was not to minimize Jesus' humanity, and the author shows no embarrassment or hesitation in affirming the reality of Jesus' human nature. The Johannine Jesus is pictured in heroic terms, but he is not a modern hero with all the self-doubts and foibles requisite for "authenticity" today. But neither is he a god walking about in disguise. In GJohn Jesus' humanity is essential, and is presented as the specific embodiment and historical manifestation of divine glory, a manifestation that involved a real life and death, and a real resurrection of this particular human who bears divine glory.

Jesus and the Spirit

In accounting for the exalted way in which Jesus is presented in GJohn, we must reckon with the emphasis on Jesus as endowed with the Spirit. Early on in the narrative Jesus is presented as the one especially marked with God's Spirit. In 1:29-34, where the Johannine testimony of John the Baptizer is related, Jesus is twice referred to as the one upon whom the Spirit descended and remained (1:32-33). In consequence of this, Jesus is recognized as the one who will himself "baptize in the Holy Spirit," and as "the Son of God" (1:33-34). Another distinctive Johannine reference to Jesus as uniquely Spirit-endowed is in 3:31-36, which says that God gives the Spirit to him "without measure" (3:34). That is, "God gives the Spirit in unlimited fullness to this last envoy, who speaks the word of God as no one has done before."[99] Surely this notion that Jesus was exceptionally endowed with the Spirit goes a long way toward explaining why the Johannine Jesus seems to operate with preternatural knowledge of people, with such serene confidence in where his story is going, and with such heroic ability to fulfill his mission.

Furthermore, given this unlimited fullness of the Spirit, Jesus is not only able to perform the powerful "signs" that structure most of John 1–11; after his resurrection he is himself also able to bestow the Spirit upon others. The Synoptic traditions have parallels to the statement that Jesus will baptize in the Spirit (Mark 1:8/Matt. 3:11/Luke 3:16). But there are additional and distinctive Johannine references to Jesus giving the Spirit, which suggest that this is a particularly important idea in GJohn. Jesus' promise of "rivers of living water" to those who believe in him (7:37-39) is explicitly decoded in the text as predicting the postresurrectional gift of the Spirit. Note the tight connection between Jesus and the Spirit here. Belief in Jesus is the condition for being given the Spirit, and Jesus' glorification (through death and resurrection) is the prerequisite for the Spirit to be made available to believers. Again, in 15:26, Jesus promises to send to his followers "the Spirit of truth," identified in the same verse as the Spirit who "proceeds from the Father."

Finally, in the obviously paradigmatic scene in 20:19-23, the risen Jesus literally infuses his disciples with "the Holy Spirit," an action that seems intended to fulfill the earlier references that Jesus will himself bestow the Spirit after he has been glorified. Note that in this passage Jesus' imparting of the Spirit is linked to deputizing his disciples with a mission likened to his own (v. 21), and to authorizing them to "forgive the sins of any," in the confidence that their action has divine validation (v. 23). The scene also seems intended to portray the fulfillment of the statements about the coming of the Spirit-Advocate in John 14–16. This account of Jesus' bestowal of the Spirit expresses a major claim about the significance and efficacy of the Christian community (who seem to

---

99. Schnackenburg, *St. John,* 1:386 (see 386-87 for his full discussion). So also, e.g., Barrett, *St. John,* 226-27.

be represented in the gathered disciples). It also presents Jesus acting in God-like capacity, dramatically conveying the Spirit with (and as?) his own breath (v. 22a)!

This latter phenomenon is yet another remarkable indication of the high view of Jesus embraced in GJohn. As Max Turner has argued, to portray Jesus as dispensing the Spirit of God is both without parallel in Jewish traditions of other redemptive agents and in fact attributes to Jesus a role otherwise uniquely God's in biblical/Jewish tradition.[100]

Of course, in positing a special connection of the Spirit and Jesus, GJohn reflects a conviction attested much earlier in Christian sources. In Galatians Paul refers to "the Spirit of [God's] Son" sent into the hearts of believers, which enables them to address God as "Abba, Father" (Gal. 4:6). The synonymous references in Romans 8:9-11 to "the Spirit of God," "the Spirit of Christ," and "the Spirit of him who raised Jesus" eloquently indicate how profoundly Paul associated Jesus with God's Spirit. In the Synoptic Gospels Jesus' followers are promised the prompting of the Holy Spirit when they are arraigned on account of their faith in Jesus (Mark 13:11; Matt. 10:20; Luke 12:12), so that they may give a proper testimony about him.[101]

But John 14–16 is the most sustained treatment of the relationship of the Spirit and Jesus in any Christian writing of the first century, and this material has distinctive features. In particular, uniquely here the Spirit is referred to as the "advocate" (*paraklētos*; 14:16, 26; 15:26; 16:7); it is clear that the advocacy of the Spirit concerns Jesus. Note that the text says the Spirit was given by the Father on Jesus' request (14:16), and sent by the Father in Jesus' name (14:26). Yet other statements in these chapters refer to Jesus himself sending the Spirit (15:26; 16:7).[102] This duality in the way the sending of the Spirit is portrayed seems to be deliberate, another indication of the Johannine emphasis on Jesus as sharing in divine attributes.

The work of the Spirit-Advocate still more emphatically focuses on Jesus. The Spirit "will teach you all things, and remind you of all the things which I have said to you" (14:26), the "all things" being synonymous here with what Jesus has said. This "reminding" by the Spirit seems to be a pet Johannine term

---

100. Max Turner, "The Spirit of Christ and 'Divine' Christology," in *Jesus of Nazareth: Lord and Christ: Essays on the Historical Jesus and New Testament Christology*, ed. Joel B. Green and Max Turner (Grand Rapids: Eerdmans; Carlisle: Paternoster, 1994), 413-36.

101. Note that this promise of the Spirit's aid in speaking about Jesus is found both in Mark and in Q (Luke 12:12/Matt. 10:20), which confirms how widespread the idea was.

102. The words in 16:7, "but if I depart I will send him to you," are missing in P66, probably through scribal accident ("homoioteleuton") caused by the similarity of the final words of the preceding sentence *(pros hymas)*.

for what amounts to an insightful appreciation of Jesus and his sayings, such as is illustrated in 2:19-22, where after Jesus' resurrection the disciples "remembered" his words about raising the temple in three days (2:22). But it appears that their remembrance actually involved an *interpretation* of the saying as having to do with Jesus' body being raised, this insightful "remembrance" accompanied by greater faith in Jesus' words. In 12:16 we have another postresurrection "remembering" that involves a greater understanding of events and their scriptural meaning than was apparent to Jesus' disciples in the preresurrection period.

The other terms used to describe the work of the promised Spirit-Advocate confirm that it is heavily focused on producing in Jesus' followers deeper insights into Jesus' own significance, and fuller apprehension of his teachings. In 15:26 the Spirit will "testify" concerning Jesus to his followers. GJohn uses the terms "testify/bear witness" and "testimony/witness" to refer to disclosing and affirming Jesus' status and significance (e.g., the Baptist in 1:6-8, 19, 34), and so the Spirit's testimony clearly means bringing to the disciples an enhanced sense of Jesus' importance.

This is elaborated in 16:7-15, which describes the mission of the Spirit toward "the world" (vv. 7-11) and among Jesus' followers (vv. 12-15). The Spirit will "prove the world wrong" with respect to unbelief about Jesus (v. 9) and the failure to perceive the significance and effects of his appearance (vv. 10-11). As for his followers, Jesus explicitly distinguishes between what he was able to convey to them then (v. 12) and the fuller disclosure that the Spirit will give. The Spirit "will guide you along in all the truth" (*hodēgēsei hymas en tē alētheia pasē*, v. 13), which seems to be synonymous with glorifying Jesus (v. 14) and declaring to them Jesus' high status and significance ("what is mine," vv. 14-15).[103] The statement in 16:15, "all that the Father has is mine," explains "what is mine" and indicates that what the Spirit declares about Jesus is vast indeed! In sum, both toward the world and among Jesus' followers, the Spirit is portrayed here as affirming Jesus' exalted status, leading his followers in particular into the depths of the truth of his person and his words.

We may say, therefore, that as Jesus serves as spokesman and agent of the Father, so these references to the Spirit in John 14-16 portray the Spirit as advocate, spokesman, and agent of Jesus. This amounts to a radical and momentous interpretation of the nature and function of the Spirit of God in comparison with pre-Christian Jewish traditions. Yet the basic idea that the divine Spirit is

---

103. The variant in 16:13, "into [*eis*] all truth," supported by some textual witnesses, has hardly much difference in meaning. See, e.g., Barrett, *St. John*, 489; Brown, *Gospel according to John*, 1:707.

directly linked with Jesus, and that reception of the Spirit conveys something of Jesus, is reflected much earlier in Paul (Rom. 8:9-11; Gal. 4:6-7), who refers to the divine Spirit and also the Spirit of Christ, through whom "Christ is in you" (Rom. 8:10) and Christ's own sonship is extended to believers. But it is right to see in John 14–16 a distinctively extended focus on, and development of, this idea. That the Spirit who advocates, glorifies, and declares Jesus' high significance is sent by the Father shows how fully in GJohn the glory of Jesus is presented as manifesting and serving the purposes of God.

The Spirit and Johannine Christianity

These references to the Spirit also show us one of the powerful factors that account for GJohn and its distinctive rendition of Jesus. The circles of those whose religious life and beliefs are reflected in this writing were sure that they had been given both the divine Spirit through their faith in Jesus and profound insights into Jesus' person and work through the operation of the Spirit among them.

GJohn does not give much detail about how exactly the Spirit was thought to operate among believers. But on the basis of other indications of the phenomena characteristic of first-century Christian circles, I propose that insights were experienced and received as prophetic revelations, the sorts of "charismatic" experiences of revealed "knowledge" and "wisdom" to which Paul's epistles (e.g., 1 Cor. 12:4-11) and other early Christian texts refer. This strongly charismatic tone seems to me to be reflected also in John 14:12-14, which promises that after Jesus has departed to the Father his followers will be enabled to do the sorts of mighty deeds Jesus performed, and that, then, "anything you ask in my name I will do." Clearly the scope of expectation for miraculous powers was considerable![104]

104. Cf. April D. DeConick, *Voices of the Mystics: Early Christian Discourse in the Gospels of John and Thomas and Other Ancient Christian Literature,* JSNTSup 157 (Sheffield: Sheffield Academic Press, 2001), esp. 68-85. Though I applaud her emphasis that an ethos of real religious experiences (and not merely rhetorical/literary conventions) is reflected in GJohn, I am not persuaded by her notion that GJohn expresses a "Johannine polemic against vision mysticism" and that a "Thomasine" group was the object of this polemic. I agree, however, that John 14–16 authorizes a vigorous "charismatic" ethos of revelational experiences. Moreover, I think that the contrast between those who have seen Jesus and those who believe without seeing him (esp. in 20:24-29) is intended to assure readers of two things: (1) Jesus' historical life was the visible manifestation of God's glory (e.g., 1:14-18), and yet (2) those who did not see him then are called to trust the witness given by those who did, which GJohn conveys in written form (20:30-31), and are given Jesus' blessing for doing so (20:29b). On the possible connections of GJohn and "Thomasine" Christianity, see my discussion of the *Gospel of Thomas* in the next chapter.

Moreover, we should probably posit as the characteristic setting and occasion for the "revelations" of Jesus' glory the gatherings of believers for worship. In an insufficiently noticed study, David Aune showed that for ancient Jewish and Christian circles corporate worship was the characteristic setting in which eschatological realities were experienced, and that from this worship setting came the expressions of "realized eschatology" in which future and heavenly realities are referred to as already present.[105]

In Johannine Christianity the eschatological glory of Jesus and the assurance of the eschatological blessings that he confers (e.g., eternal life) were made real and present in the worship gathering. It is significant that, in all the statements that promise the Spirit's revelatory work in John 14–16, the "you" to whom the Spirit will disclose Jesus is plural. The examples given in GJohn of insights received by Jesus' followers subsequent to his earthly life concern sayings of Jesus (2:22) and also scriptural passages perceived as referring to Jesus (2:17; 12:16). So we may rightly suppose that collective, prayerful pondering of the Jesus tradition and their Scriptures in the expectation that the Spirit would grant them flashes of prophetic insight formed a characteristic feature of the devotional life of Johannine Christians. Indeed, this sort of religious "microculture" of intense expectation of prophetic-type revelation seems to have been characteristic more widely in the early Christian movement.[106]

The experience of new insights into the glories of Jesus in Johannine Christianity probably goes a long way toward accounting for the particular kind of rendition of Jesus that we have in GJohn. Famously, in GJohn Jesus expresses the christological insights of the Johannine believers, insights that they consider to be freshly given to them by the Spirit after Jesus' earthly life. All the same, of course, they considered these post-Jesus insights to be simply revelations as to who Jesus really was all along.

I propose that those responsible for GJohn were well aware that much of what they attributed to Jesus in the preresurrection period actually represented the christological perspective and insight of the postresurrection period. Several distinctive statements in GJohn have Jesus distinguishing explicitly between what he was able to teach his disciples during his historical ministry and the deeper truth that the Spirit would be able to communicate to them about him and on his behalf after his glorification (14:25; 16:12-13, 25). But those responsible for GJohn thought it fully appropriate to use the christological insights that had

---

105. David E. Aune, *The Cultic Setting of Realized Eschatology in Early Christianity*, NovTSup 28 (Leiden: Brill, 1972).

106. David E. Aune, *Prophecy in Early Christianity and the Ancient Mediterranean World* (Grand Rapids: Eerdmans, 1983).

been experienced in the postresurrection period to assert explicitly the heavenly origins and transcendent significance of Jesus. To reiterate an important point, although this insight came to believers after the period of Jesus' activity, it was for them an insight into what had always been true of Jesus. Though such an understanding is portrayed as not recognized at all by Jesus' opponents, and perceived only in limited measure by his disciples during his ministry (e.g., 2:11), the glory of God was manifest in Jesus' historical appearance.

The programmatic statement in John 1:14, "We beheld his glory, glory as of the unique Son from the Father," refers thus to a process of perception that extended through Jesus' ministry, and beyond it in the post-Jesus glorification and disclosure of Jesus given by the Spirit. GJohn reflects the fundamental conviction, however, that this process simply made evident the significance of the historical figure of Jesus. In GJohn this conviction is put to explicit literary expression in a distinctive rendition of Jesus that draws heavily upon the experience of the Spirit's glorification of Jesus among Johannine believers.

Christology and Controversy

Another important factor that helped shape GJohn is Jewish opposition to the devotion to Jesus that was advocated and practiced by Johannine believers. As I noted early in this chapter, scholars commonly recognize in GJohn indications of sharp opposition that seems to have led to a traumatic expulsion of Johannine Jewish Christians from the larger Jewish community at some point prior to the composition of GJohn.[107] It is also commonly thought that GJohn reflects the real accusations of Jewish opponents against the christological claims and devotional practices of Johannine Jewish Christians. Indeed, in GJohn the opposition to Jesus is focused very much on explicitly christological issues. Clearly GJohn presents these issues as the crucial differences between the Johannine followers of Jesus and their religious opponents in the wider Jewish community. I think this judgment was likely shared by the non-Johannine Jews, and that the major reason why they expelled the Johannine Jewish believers was that their devotion to Jesus became intolerable for them.

---

107. The term consistently used in John is *aposynagōgos*, which probably means something like "expelled from the community." In the first century, the Greek term *synagōgē* was still often used to designate the Jewish community, though the term subsequently came to be used exclusively as the standard designation of the buildings used by Jews for gatherings to read Scripture and say collective prayers. The term *proseuchē* (prayer house) seems to have been the earlier term for these buildings. See, e.g., Eric M. Meyers, "Synagogue," in *ABD*, 6:251-60, esp. 252-53 on the terminology.

In the Synoptics, too, the crucial issue behind everything else is really what to make of Jesus, but in GJohn the controversies are much more transparently stated in terms of the christological claims characteristic of the post-resurrection period, and the outraged responses that these claims elicited from Jewish opponents. The Synoptic Gospels portray conflicts between Jesus and his contemporaries over a number of matters. For example, Mark 2:1–3:6 recounts clashes over Jesus' forgiveness of sins (2:1-12), Jesus' association with "sinners" (2:13-17), fasting (2:18-22), and Sabbath (2:23–3:6). Mark 7:1-23 offers an extended treatment of traditions about kosher food. As I have said, in all such episodes the real underlying issue is the authority of Jesus.

But the only such issue about Torah observance in GJohn is Sabbath keeping, and the christological question is actually much more explicit. Note how in the account of Jesus healing the paralytic man in John 5:1-18, the Sabbath issue is linked to, and quickly subsumed under, the charge that Jesus made himself "equal to God."[108] Also, in the lengthy narrative about the healing of the blind man in 9:1-38, the Sabbath issue functions simply as an avenue for addressing the real question — whether Jesus is a "sinner" (v. 24) or perhaps a "prophet" (v. 17). In fact, his unprecedented power to open blind eyes shows that he is sent from God (v. 33) and worthy of belief (v. 35) and reverence (v. 38).[109]

In numerous other passages in GJohn, the issue is simply and solely Jesus, the alternatives stark, and the stakes ultimate. Set against each other in the bitter controversy running through 8:31-59 are the Jewish charges that Jesus is demonic (vv. 48, 52) and Jesus' astonishing claims that he is able to confer freedom and life to those who keep his words (vv. 31, 51), that he is especially sent from God (v. 42), and even that he precedes Abraham (v. 58). Echoing the charge we already noted in 5:18 that Jesus makes himself equal to God, Jewish opponents in 10:31-33 make moves to stone Jesus for blasphemously making himself "a god" (*theos*, 10:33).[110] As Martyn observed, we should understand the Jewish opposition to Jesus in 5:16-18 as reflecting hostile steps taken against Jewish Christians, because they were perceived to be worshiping Jesus as "a second god."[111]

---

108. Note the similar expression in 2 Macc. 9:12, where it refers to the delusional arrogance of the pagan Antiochus Epiphanes.

109. Note also John 3:25-30. Although the passage opens with a reference to a discussion about purification (*peri katharismou*, v. 25), the subject quickly shifts to Jesus' messianic status and superiority to John the Baptist.

110. The more likely reading in 10:33 is *theos* without the definite article (cf. *"ton theon"* in the original hand of P66). Probably, therefore, the charge is that Jesus makes himself a rival to the one true God.

111. Martyn, *History*, 72, 81. Also now Wayne A. Meeks, "Equal to God," in *The Conversa-*

In fact, in all these passages we are probably to take the Jewish accusations as distortions of what the intended readers of GJohn are expected to hold as true. This is most obvious for the charge that Jesus "has a demon." But likewise, the charges that Jesus makes himself equal to God, and makes himself a god, seem to be hostile versions of Johannine claims. These charges correspond to the Johannine claims that Jesus shares in divine powers and attributes such as raising the dead, that Jesus does the very works of God, that God gives Jesus divine glory, that Jesus comes from heaven, and that he and God are "one."

A similar outraged and hostile response to Johannine christological claims is reflected in the complaint of the Jewish leaders to Pilate in 19:7 that Jesus "claimed to be the Son of God," and therefore deserves death under biblical law. There is, of course, a still more transparent reflection of Jewish opposition to Jewish Christians in the Johannine references, previously noted, to Jesus' followers being put out of the Jewish community for confessing Jesus as Messiah (9:22; 12:42). In both cases, however, the Jewish objections are expressed in terms of the actual christological claims of Johannine believers, who really do hail Jesus as Messiah and Son of God (e.g., 20:31).

Furthermore, when we take account of what these christological terms meant in Johannine Christianity, the extremely negative Jewish response portrayed in GJohn is quite plausible, and must reflect the kind of treatment of their claims experienced by Johannine believers. In GJohn, to confess Jesus as "the Son (of God)" and "Messiah/Christ" clearly includes claiming that he is of heavenly origin and participates in divine glory and attributes in ways that exceed any analogies among other Jewish ideas about divine-agent figures. That is, the Jewish cries of "blasphemy," and the expulsion of Johannine Jewish believers from the Jewish community, were not provoked simply by these honorific terms themselves and what they might have meant in Jewish usage, but rather by what these Jewish Christian believers meant by them.[112]

We also see in GJohn a vigorous response to Jewish rejection of these

---

tion Continues: Studies in Paul and John in Honor of J. Louis Martyn, ed. Robert T. Fortna and Beverly R. Gaventa (Nashville: Abingdon, 1990), 309-21.

112. It is quite beside the point (and anachronistic as well) to limit the meaning of the term "blasphemy" to the very technical/legal definition in the Mishnah (*m. Sanh.* 7.5), which restricts the crime to pronouncing the divine name *(Yahweh)*. As Darrell Bock has shown, in ancient Jewish texts "blasphemy" can connote a much wider assortment of acts that are seen to show arrogance and disrespect toward God: *Blasphemy and Exaltation in Judaism and the Final Examination of Jesus: A Philological-Historical Study of the Key Jewish Themes Impacting Mark 14:61-64,* WUNT 2/106 (Tübingen: J. C. B. Mohr [Siebeck], 1998), esp. 110-12. Note, e.g., that Philo includes as blasphemy comparing oneself to God (*Somn.* 2.130-31; *Decal.* 61; and cf. *Leg. alleg.* 1.49).

christological claims. The assertions about Jesus' significance in GJohn are particularly strident, even belligerent, which must reflect the frustration of the Johannine Christians over having their devotion to Jesus rejected as blasphemous by large segments of the Jewish community. John 1:11 is programmatic for the account of Jesus that follows in GJohn, and is probably also indicative of the situation of Johannine Christians. Jesus came to his own people and they rejected him, just as Johannine Christians were rejected by the larger Jewish community.

This very adversarial tone is found in other Johannine passages as well. For example, 1:18 claims that the uniquely divine Jesus *(monogenēs theos)* has special intimacy with God, and has manifested God in unique fullness. Similarly 3:13 proclaims that the Son alone has ascended into heaven, with a unique ability to speak about God; 6:46 claims that Jesus alone has seen the Father. 3:18 and 36 assert that belief in Jesus guarantees divine approval but unbelief brings judgment and the wrath of God. There is a correspondingly exclusivist tone in 5:22-23, which insists that the only way to honor God is to honor Jesus. In 5:45-46 the Jews are told that Moses (the great intercessor for Israel in Jewish tradition) is now their accuser because they refused to recognize Jesus. In the bitter exchanges of 8:12-59, the Johannine Jesus seems intent on infuriating his Jewish interlocutors with such tactics as the argument in verses 31-47 that they will indicate whether they are truly children of Abraham and really hear God *only* if they receive Jesus as God's ultimate spokesman.

The polemical nature of all these passages surely indicates that they reflect counterresponses to Jewish rejection of the christological claims of Johannine believers. That is, the christological issues between these believers and the Jewish community are brought directly into this narrative rendition of Jesus. This gives to these Johannine passages their sharp edge. There is no negotiation, no compromise offered, no middle ground. Belief in Jesus is not an option but an absolute obligation; a refusal to recognize him as Messiah and Son of God (with all that Johannine Christianity meant in these terms) constitutes rank disobedience to God, over against which no other claim (e.g., to be children of Abraham) is sufficient or valid.

As I have already stated, disputation can cause participants to reflect further on their convictions, leading to intensification, refinements, and noticeable developments in the way convictions are expressed and even in their substance. Consequently it is appropriate to ask if the sharp disputation reflected in GJohn may have contributed in some way to the substance of Johannine christological convictions, as well as to the emphases and tone with which they were expressed. The problem is that we do not have a sufficient amount of evidence to track diachronically Johannine christological convictions, especially for the period prior to GJohn (i.e., prior to approximately 80-100).[113] GJohn probably provides our earliest glimpses of the beliefs of Johannine Christianity, and before its composition the disputation between Johannine believers and the Jewish community had already led to their expulsion. Moreover, that expulsion seems to have been in response to Johannine believers persisting in christological assertions that were deemed blasphemous. So, whatever heightening of christological claims may have been produced through disputation and the expulsion of Johannine believers, these events were in fact generated by the prior devotion to Jesus advocated by these Johannine believers.

Furthermore, there is evidence that well before the composition of GJohn, and in circles beyond Johannine Christianity, at least some devout Jews saw the devotion to Jesus advocated by some Jewish Christians as blasphemous, dangerous to Jewish religious integrity, and incompatible with Jewish commitment to the uniqueness of God.[114] For example, the Synoptic Gospels also show Jewish authorities accusing Jesus of blasphemy, and these accounts likewise are commonly seen as reflecting issues between Jesus' first-century followers and the Jewish community: Jesus' forgiveness of sins (Mark 2:7; Matt. 9:3; Luke 5:21) and his claims for himself in the arraignment scene before the Jewish authorities (Mark 14:64; Matt. 26:65). In both cases the Jewish opponents see Jesus as transgressing the bounds of proper respect for God's uniqueness. In the Markan and Matthean scenes of the Jewish arraignment, the same basic christological claims that are controversial in GJohn (messiahship and divine sonship) are highlighted as blasphemous.[115] Indeed, there is a reasonable body of evidence that from the earliest years of the young Christian movement the christological assertions and associated devotional practices of Jewish Christians were taken by some zealous Jews (such as Saul of Tarsus) as an infringement upon the uniqueness of God, the most serious offense against the Torah possible.[116]

113. In saying this, I indicate considerable caution about such elaborate attempts to offer a history of Johannine Christianity as in Brown's *Community of the Beloved Disciple.* To his credit, Brown fully acknowledged the highly speculative nature of his proposal, expressing satisfaction if even 60 percent of his "detective work" was found persuasive to others (see esp. p. 7). Because we have relevant texts such as the Johannine epistles, I am more convinced by his proposals about the latter stages of Johannine Christianity (i.e., subsequent to GJohn) than the earlier ones, for which we have nothing other than scholarly guesswork.

114. In the following comments I condense a fuller discussion of evidence in Hurtado, "Pre–70 C.E. Jewish Opposition to Christ-Devotion."

115. On the blasphemy charge in the Synoptic trial narratives, see Raymond E. Brown, *The Death of the Messiah. From Gethsemane to the Grave: A Commentary on the Passion Narratives in the Four Gospels,* 2 vols. (New York: Doubleday, 1994), 1:520-27.

116. I refer readers back to my discussion in chap. 2.

Consequently, although I freely grant that the christological assertions of GJohn likely show the marks of controversy with Jewish opponents, I find it far easier to detect these marks in the antagonistic tone and emphases of these claims than in their substance. For example, the distinctively Johannine use of *monogenēs* (unique/only) as a christological term (1:14, 18; 3:16, 18; and also 1 John 4:9) more emphatically expresses Jesus' uniqueness, but the basic claim that Jesus is God's unique Son is hardly a Johannine innovation (e.g., Rom. 8:29). Likewise, to rehearse another example noted previously, though the Johannine emphasis on Jesus' heavenly origins is unarguably distinctive, most scholars see the idea of Jesus' preexistence reflected already in Paul's letters.

In short, we should certainly note that GJohn shows the effects of controversy. This controversy was mainly prompted by and concerned with the devotion to Jesus practiced and advocated by Johannine Jewish Christians. Moreover, it likely involved a hardening of attitudes and a sharpening of assertions, on both sides. In consequence of post–70 C.E. concerns by Jewish authorities to deal with what they regarded as various dangerous sectarian forces in the Jewish community, of which Jewish Christians represented one important example, the refusal of Johannine Jewish Christians to compromise in their devotion to Jesus led to them being expelled.[117] In response, Johannine Christians characterized the Jewish community as turning its back on God's Messiah, refusing the light of God, disregarding what they claimed was the clear meaning of Jewish Scriptures, and dishonoring God in their refusal to honor God's Son.

In summary, the clash with their Jewish opponents likely led Johannine Christians to emphasize Jesus' divine status and attributes, his heavenly origins, and his exclusive significance over against all other figures and religious claims in Jewish tradition. The clash may also have been one factor that disposed Johannine Christians to cultivate religious experiences in which the Spirit-Advocate could reveal to them the glories of Jesus. Because of these revelatory experiences, they were likely emboldened in their faith and were prompted further to emphasize his divinity over against detractors. These responses to the external threat of Jewish opposition may also help us to understand some of the circumstances that contributed to the subsequent christological controversy in Johannine Christianity reflected in 1 John. To this internal crisis, we turn in the following pages.

---

117. Cohen, "The Significance of Yavneh."

The Christological Crisis in Johannine Christianity

From the two little writings traditionally referred to as 1 John and 2 John, commonly seen among scholars as coming from the same early Christian circles as are reflected in GJohn, it is clear that a serious internal crisis broke out among these believers at some point subsequent to the expulsion of Johannine Jewish Christians from the Jewish community.[118] Scholars dispute the specifics of this crisis, but on two main points they widely agree.[119] First, this was an internal crisis in which the key issue was Christology, what to make of Jesus, although "perfectionist" claims (i.e., claims about being sinless and a special relationship with God) seem to have been involved as well. The author of 1 John clearly portrays serious differences over right belief about Jesus, contrasting his point of view with that of a group of people who apparently had been part of the Johannine circle(s); and he directly challenges their claims about their own special spirituality and ethical propriety as well.

Secondly, this dispute over beliefs quickly led to social consequences, a painful schism in the Johannine community. Let us look more closely at what we can glean about this crisis from the Johannine epistles.[120]

Characterization of the Opponents

The key passage is 1 John 2:18-27. Here, labeling them "antichrists" (that is, manifestations of the expected eschatological opposition to the truth of God expressed in Jesus, v. 18), the author refers to unnamed people who had been members of the Johannine group but then had abandoned their association with this group (v. 19). The references in this passage to lies (v. 21), liars (v. 22), and "those who would deceive you" (*planōntōn hymas*, v. 26) are probably also to those who left the Johannine circle(s). There are similar references in 2 John

---

118. The other Johannine epistle, 3 John, does not offer evidence of this crisis, and is not so concerned with christological issues. So it may have been written in a different situation in the Johannine churches. In any case, it is not so important for the present discussion.

119. Among many studies of the Johannine epistles and the crisis reflected in 1 John, I have found the following particularly helpful: Brown, *The Epistles of John*, esp. 47-115; Brown, *Community*, esp. 93-144; Georg Strecker, *The Johannine Epistles*, Hermeneia (Minneapolis: Fortress, 1996); Painter, *Quest*, esp. 437-64.

120. In the following discussion I shall treat 1 John and 2 John as coming from the same author, a position taken also by Brown, *The Epistles of John*, 14-19. It makes little difference, however, whether one takes this view or postulates different authors. Both epistles are most widely seen as reflecting the same crisis in Johannine Christianity.

7 to "deceivers" who have gone out "into the world" and are "the antichrist."[121] That is, those attacked in these statements promoted a religious viewpoint that so differed from the previous beliefs of Johannine Christianity that the author regarded them as an unacceptable innovation. Those who promoted these innovations appear to have severed their previous fellowship with the other Johannine Christians who did not accept their ideas.

The only hint in 1 John 2:18-27 as to what these people may have asserted is in verses 22-23, which darkly refer to "the one who denies that Jesus is the Christ" and contrast denying and confessing "the Son." Other references in 1 John and 2 John may provide further hints about the issues at stake and the viewpoint of those who left the Johannine group, and I shall turn to them shortly, but they only confirm the impression given by 1 John 2:22-23 that the issue concerned serious differences with how Jesus was interpreted.

Over against the beliefs and claims of these "secessionists" (to use one of several labels for them found in modern scholarly discussions of 1 John), the author makes two points, which may further assist us to sketch the nature of the crisis.[122] First, he assures the intended readers that they have "an anointing from the Holy One" (i.e., a spiritual endowment from God and/or "the Son"), and that all of them know the truth well enough to recognize error for themselves (vv. 20-21, 27).[123] This may well be intended to counteract a claim of the secessionists that their innovative views came through Spirit revelation.

Secondly, I take the exhortation in 1 John 4:1-3 to "test the spirits" in order to distinguish the Spirit that comes from God, and the warning that many false prophets are active, as further indications that those who left the Johannine

121. The Greek terms for "deceive" *(planan)* and "deceiver" *(planos)* here appear to have the special connotation they acquired in the Greek Old Testament, where they are used particularly to refer to being led astray from the true God of Israel.

122. Painter notes terms used by scholars, including "secessionists," "adversaries," "deceivers," "propagandists," "schismatics," and "heretics," and tends himself to refer to those who departed as the "opponents" of the author of 1 John (Painter, *Quest*, 437).

123. I take "anointing" *(chrisma)* here to be a figurative term, referring to the gift of the Spirit to believers. The three appearances of the word *chrisma* in 1 John (2:20, 27) are the only cases in the entire New Testament. Painter (*Quest*, 444-45) believes this indicates that the term was part of the vocabulary of the secessionists, and he endorses the proposal that the term reflects their pagan background. But the idea of "anointing" as a religious category obviously does not derive from Greek culture but from biblical traditions and Semitic practices; cf. 2 Cor. 1:21, where Paul refers to God establishing and anointing believers, which shows that the idea of being "anointed" by God had long been a part of Christian tradition. Indeed, as "the Christ," Jesus was for early Christians the archetypal anointed one (e.g., Acts 10:38). On the term, see esp. Brown, *The Epistles of John*, 342-47; Strecker, 64-66. The "Holy One" of 1 John 2:20, from whom the anointing came, could be God or Jesus, whereas in 2:27 most commentators take the statement that the believers have an anointing "from him" to have Jesus as the referent. See Brown, *Epistles*, 347-48.

group claimed inspiration of the Spirit as their authority, and declared their new beliefs with the conviction of prophetic revelation.[124]

In the discussion of John 14–16 earlier in this chapter, we noted that Johannine Christianity was characterized by a strong appreciation for revelations believed to come from the Spirit and probably received through experiences of prophetlike inspiration.[125] This interest in revelations of the Spirit helps provide a plausible ethos and religious context in which the sorts of prophetic claims to new truths that seem to have been at the heart of the secessionist crisis could quite readily have emerged. Johannine Christianity was a religious setting in which the Spirit was expected to inspire new insights, leading believers into "all truth," beyond the things the earthly Jesus had said (14:25-26; 16:12-15).

What was problematic about the "secessionists," therefore, was not a claim to Spirit revelation involving further and newer insights, including insights into the glory and significance of "the Son." In principle, this kind of experience seems to have been much prized in Johannine Christianity. Instead, the problems were with the *contents* of the particular claims of the secessionists, and with their behavior, especially toward fellow believers. For the author(s) of the Johannine epistles, and probably for those addressed in them, the secessionists advocated an unacceptable innovation in what they affirmed and denied about Jesus. So our author urges the readers to have confidence in their own inspiration and ability to distinguish true and erroneous ideas, to stand firm in "the truth" (beliefs) that they already know, and not to let themselves be intimidated or "led astray" by the spiritual claims of these secessionists (2:20-21, 24-25).

In accounting for this crisis in Johannine Christianity, I do not think that scholars have sufficiently allowed for the innovative effects of religious experience, especially in a religious group that cultivated and prized such experiences. For example, some scholars have proposed that the crisis was caused by the influx of Gentiles who brought with them ideas from pagan mystery religions or gnosticizing tendencies.[126] Granted, we have insufficient information to ex-

---

124. So also, e.g., Painter, *Quest*, 443.

125. Of course, the evidence of other first-century Christian writings is that Johannine Christianity was by no means exceptional in cultivating and prizing revelatory experiences of the Spirit. For this and other reasons as well, I find unpersuasive Judith Lieu's curious reluctance to recognize in 1 John the indications that claims about such experiences of the Spirit almost certainly were involved in the secessionist crisis in Johannine Christianity. Cf. Lieu, *The Theology of the Johannine Epistles* (Cambridge: Cambridge University Press, 1991), 45-49.

126. E.g., John Bogart, *Orthodox and Heretical Perfectionism*, SBLDS 33 (Missoula: Scholars, 1977), 4, 135, proposes that "outside gnostic influence *perverted* [Johannine perfectionist tradition] and produced a rival type, against which the author of 1 John reacted," though Bo-

clude any such influence, and I have no particular concern to do so. It certainly seems that Johannine Christianity of the late first century included Gentile converts as well as Jewish believers, and all converts to any cause bring with them something of their cultural background. My point is that one major factor involved in the specific innovation in belief that is attacked in 1 John and 2 John (however we portray the innovation) was the effect of religious experiences of inspiration.

Of course, recipients of such experiences are also shaped by their previous religious, cultural, and intellectual influences. But the crucial question is what might have encouraged the secessionists to develop their innovative views and present them with such conviction, and the best answer is the religious "microculture" of Johannine Christianity with its strong appreciation for Spirit revelations. The author of 1 John seems to concede that the secessionists may have received spiritual inspiration (e.g., 4:1-3), but he judges their inspiration to have come from spiritual forces other than God! I contend that whatever one thinks of the religious validity of the views of the author or his opponents, a proper historical grasp of the church situation addressed in the Johannine epistles requires recognizing that it involved a fervent cultivation of religious experiences that recipients believed imparted new insights and truths.

Another aspect of this passage that helps us see what particular kind of belief(s) the secessionists might have promoted is the author's emphasis that the readers should reject the blandishments of the secessionists and remain true to the formative and foundational christological teaching of the Johannine community. Thus the author urges his readers to let the teaching that they heard "from the beginning [*ap' archēs*]" (v. 24) remain authoritative among them *(en hymin menetō)*. He assures them that their own divine anointing remains in effect *(menei)* among them, and he urges them also to remain "in" that anointing *(menete en autō)*. By this last expression he probably means that they are to continue to affirm what their own earlier endowment of the Spirit had attested and had led them to affirm in the foundational stage of their faith in Jesus.

Other references to the importance of "the beginning," in the opening words of 1 John (1:1) and several times thereafter (2:24; 3:11), and in 2 John 5-6 as well, confirm that both writings stress Johannine christological tradition over against newer teaching of the secessionists, which both epistles repudiate as

---

gart also grants that the secessionists probably saw themselves as true interpreters of Johannine tradition. Although Painter rightly sees the secessionists' claims as likely springing from what they held to be revelatory experiences of the Spirit, at some points he attributes the schism to Gentile converts who "did not understand the Johannine tradition" and were "influenced by the thought and language of the mystery religions" (Painter, *Quest*, 463; cf., e.g., 457).

conflicting with that tradition. Indeed, the whole of 1 John 1:1-4 emphasizes that what this author joins in testifying to and maintaining is "that which was from the beginning," "the life" which was tangibly manifested and experienced in Jesus (1:2), on the basis of which the Johannine fellowship includes God and his Son Jesus Christ (1:3).[127]

In 2:7 the author declares that his exhortation in 2:3-6 to remain true to traditional teachings of belief and behavior does not constitute a new commandment but is rather a commandment that his readers had "from the beginning," which is "the word which you (previously) heard." Then, however, in an obvious rhetorical device, he refers to his exhortation as a "new commandment," perhaps alluding to the Johannine tradition of Jesus' "new commandment" to love one another (John 13:34).[128] Similar phrasing, and with the same intent, appears in 2 John 5-6, likewise emphasizing that the command to love one another is not new but "from the beginning."

That is, the authoritative teaching that the author advocates is "new" in the sense that it came from Jesus, but, as a command from Jesus, it comes "from the beginning" (of the Christian tradition) and does not spring from the sort of claim that the secessionists seem to have been making about having a special, new truth that justified their refusal to continue fellowship with those who did not submit to their teaching.

Probably the most transparent accusation that the secessionists departed from traditional teaching is in 2 John 7-11. In the context of the warning about "deceivers" who do not confess "Jesus Christ come [*erchomenon*] in the flesh" (v. 7), and from whom the readers are to guard themselves (v. 8), verse 9 refers to "everyone who goes on ahead [*ho proagōn*] and does not remain in the teaching of Christ." This must surely indicate that the author believed that the "deceivers" asserted a religious viewpoint that was a major departure from the tradition. The term *proagein* (to go ahead) is not a pejorative term in other uses in the New Testament and elsewhere, and here in 2 John 9, therefore, it may be the author's sarcastic reflection of how the "deceivers" see themselves, as radical progressives offering a major improvement in Christian teaching.[129] In this

127. As Brown concluded, the neuter pronoun in 1:1, 3 ("that which," *ho*) "refers to the whole career of Jesus, . . . *the person, the words and the works*" (emphasis his), which made up the body of sacred tradition which the author of 1 John cites as authoritative here (*The Epistles of John*, 154).

128. See the discussion of 1 John 2:7-8 in Brown, *The Epistles of John*, 264-67.

129. Brown translates v. 9 as "Anyone who is so 'progressive' that he does not remain rooted in the teaching of Christ" (*The Epistles of John*, 673-74), and Brown correctly notes that the variant *parabainōn* (to overstep, transgress), found in some manuscripts in place of *proagōn*, shows scribal preferences for a more clearly pejorative term.

context "the teaching of Christ" in which readers are urged to remain must be (or at least must be focused on) key beliefs about Jesus, in particular, beliefs about the reality and/or redemptive significance of Jesus as the human figure who is also the divine Son.

Other statements confirm a christological focus in the dispute.[130] Yet 1 John and 2 John show no interest in giving free publicity to the specific views of the secessionists; instead they are characterized negatively in formulaic terms. So it is difficult to be very sure about what *specific* beliefs the secessionists advocated. I shall offer a cautious characterization of their christological views shortly, but first I give an inventory of the relevant references in 1 John and 2 John.

We can begin with the reference noted already in 1 John 2:22-23 to anyone who "denies that Jesus is the Christ," and thus "denies the Father and the Son." There is a similar note in 5:1, which commends as "born of God" "everyone who believes that Jesus is the Christ," and which is probably intended as a contrast to the teaching of the secessionists. Perhaps a bit more specifically, 2 John 7 warns against those who "do not confess Jesus Christ come/coming [*erchomenon*] in the flesh," and 1 John 4:1-3 contrasts every "spirit" (spirit inspiration) that "confesses that Jesus Christ has come [*elēlythota*] in (the) flesh" with any other spirit that "does not confess Jesus." In other references the author emphasizes confessing and believing "that Jesus is the Son of God" (1 John 4:15; 5:5), contrasts believing "in the Son of God" with failing to believe God's testimony concerning his Son (5:10), assures readers that "the person who has the Son has life" (5:12), and praises those who "believe in the name of the Son of God" (5:13). In 5:20 the author advocates as the correct faith stance the conviction that "the Son of God has come [*hēkei*] and has given us understanding to know the truth . . . which is in his Son Jesus Christ."

As this list of references shows, in 1 John and 2 John the christological affirmations and the characterizations of those opposed are very formulaic. There are probably two reasons for this. First, as noted already, the author likely had no desire to give expression to views he considered erroneous, and so, instead, he characterizes the opponents from the standpoint of the key christological beliefs against which he judges their views. Second, because he considers their key christological error a departure from traditional teaching, he uses very formulaic and traditional confessional language both in his condemnations of the opponents and in his positive statements of right belief. Be-

---

130. Brown provides a chart of references to the views of the secessionists in 1 John and 2 John (*The Epistles of John*, 762-63), but it is curiously incomplete, failing to list several references that I cite here.

fore we try to characterize the actual christological views of the secessionists, let us quickly note another (associated?) matter that seems to have been at issue.

In addition to their christological views, the secessionists seem also to have made strong claims about their own spiritual status, which the author of 1 John refutes.[131] I agree with the widely accepted view that 1 John reflects the spiritual claims of the secessionists in a number of formulaic statements, which I shall now quickly review. In 1 John 1:6-10 there is a series of three conditional statements, each one posing a possible claim ("If we say . . .") that is then shown to be erroneous because it violates an essential condition of its validity. In the first such statement (1:6-7), any claim to having fellowship *(koinōnia)* with God made while "walking in darkness" constitutes a lie; the author contrasts this with walking "in the light" and in "fellowship with one another," the redemptive death of "Jesus his Son" cleansing those in this fellowship from all sin.

The second statement (1:8-9) contrasts the self-deceptive claim to be sinless ("we have no sin") with confession of sins and the consequent forgiveness and cleansing that "he who is faithful and just" will provide.[132] This leads to the third of these statements (1:10), which basically looks like a variant expression of the previous claim: "If we say that we have not sinned, we make him [God?] a liar, and his word is not in us."

On the assumption that we have reflections of the secessionists in these three statements, we begin to get a picture of people claiming an especially close relationship with God that involves an immunity from sinning, and possibly even a certain divinelike freedom from the whole question of sin.

1 John 2:3-11 contains another series of three formulaic statements which likewise probably are intended by the author as reflections of the spiritual claims of the secessionists. These three statements all begin with the words "Whoever says/claims" *(ho legōn)* and focus on claims that are falsified by ethical failures described in progressively more specific ways through the statements. Thus in 2:4-5, whoever claims to have come to know God *(egnōka auton)* but does not observe God's commandments is a liar, for only in the one who keeps God's word has the love of God been perfected. A similar statement follows in 2:6, that whoever says "I abide in him [God]" ought to exhibit behavior patterned after Jesus' practice.[133] Finally, in 2:9-11 the third statement is that

---

131. See esp. Bogart, *Orthodox and Heretical Perfectionism,* and Painter's proposals as to the boasts of the secessionists (*Quest,* 441-59). Brown (*The Epistles of John,* 762-63) gives a chart of relevant references in 1 John.

132. God is probably the one referred to, although Jesus, too, is characterized as "just" in 1 John (2:1, 29; 3:7). See, e.g., Brown, *The Epistles of John,* 209-10.

133. Literally, "he ought to walk just as that one [*ekeinos*] walked" (2:6), which I take here to be Jesus. So also, e.g., Brown, *The Epistles of John,* 261; Strecker, 43-46.

"Whoever claims to be in the light and hates his brother is still in darkness," whereas "Whoever loves his brother abides in the light and in him there is no cause for stumbling [*skandalon*]."

In these three "whoever says/claims" statements we move from the general obligation to obey God's commandments (2:4-5), on through the somewhat more specific requirement to follow Jesus' own example (2:6), to the still more explicit necessity of showing love for fellow believers (2:9-11). That is, the alleged ethical shortcoming of those reflected in these statements appears to be focused specifically in failing to show proper care for fellow religionists.

This leads us to the remaining accusation made against those whose christological views and spiritual claims the author of 1 John rejects: they have broken fellowship with the Johannine believers to whom he writes. Near the beginning of this discussion of the crisis reflected in the Johannine epistles, we noted the reference in 2:18-19 to those who "went out from us," and who thereby revealed themselves to be not really "of us" but instead so many "antichrists." Read in the light of this schism, a number of other passages take on a greater specificity of reference. For example, the statement about loving or hating a fellow believer ("brother") in 2:10-11 likely has its specific meaning in this rending of the Johannine fellowship. To "love" or "hate" one's fellow believer in this context means to recognize or disavow a "brother," and to maintain or disdain one's fraternal obligations. Likewise, the exhortation in 3:11-18 includes the reminder that mutual love is a command "from the beginning" (i.e., it has the force of foundational tradition; 3:11), and the reference to sharing worldly goods *(ton bion tou kosmou)* with fellow believers (3:17) makes it clear that the "love" called for involves the practical demands of committed relationships ("let us not love only in words but also in deeds and truly"; 3:18).

That is, the emphasis in 1 John on loving fellow believers as the indication that one is truly born of God, and as a reflection of God's own love (esp. 4:7-21), is fueled by the author's profound disappointment and outrage over those who have broken with his readers. It is their action which represents what he condemns as the hatred of fellow believers; the love for which he so passionately calls is the continuing acceptance of one's fraternal obligations to fellow believers.

If, then, we combine the evidence surveyed here, the following picture emerges. A group arose in the Johannine circle(s) who based their novel christological assertions on professed revelatory experiences of the Spirit. They may well have agreed with the author that their new insights amounted to a notably different stance from what the author continued to see as binding tradition, but if so, they likely thought their own revelations validly superseded all previous understanding of Jesus and his significance.

These people also appear to have claimed a special relationship with God that distinguished them from other Johannine Christians; that is, they claimed that their christological views and their own spiritual status were superior. In short, they were religious elitists, and likely sought to have their claims about a superior understanding and spirituality accepted by other Johannine believers. The most likely explanation for the departure of the "secessionists" is that the other Johannine Christians were reluctant to accept their claims. So, convinced of their own elitist claims, they took this reluctance to indicate a spiritual darkness and an unworthiness that justified their departure from the fellowship of the other Johannine believers.

The Christological Issue

For the purposes of this book, it is important to address more precisely what the christological issue was, and in particular, what christological stance was taken by the secessionists. A great number of scholars have posed the question, and have offered a rich variety of specific answers, but it is neither necessary nor wise here to review them all in detail.[134] The main reason for the multiplicity of proposals, and the main difficulty in proposing a persuasively specific view of what the secessionists advocated, is the limited evidence available. As we have seen, several statements in 1 John and 2 John are commonly (and in my view validly) taken as referring to the secessionists, but they are all very brief and employ very formulaic language. Moreover, we need to ask how transparently these statements convey the specific beliefs of the secessionists.

In political and religious controversies, exaggeration and other distortions of opponents are characteristic. The main aim in such polemics is to condemn one's opponents as erroneous, their error characteristically stated in terms convenient to the critic condemning them. Furthermore, in disputations involving multiple opponents, the important thing each participant often wants to stress is that all other options are erroneous or inferior to his or her viewpoint. Consequently there is often a tendency to portray all opponents as having in common some fundamental error and/or as sharing in some fundamentally wrong aim. I suggest that we have to allow for such polemical tendencies in assessing the relevant passages in 1 John and 2 John.

This has not always been sufficiently recognized. To cite a recent example, Paul Anderson takes the references to denying that Jesus is the Christ and the Son of God, and to denying the Son (1 John 2:22-23; 5:1, 5), as indication that

---

134. See, e.g., the review in Brown, *The Epistles of John,* 47-68.

those condemned in these statements were "obviously" Jewish believers who seceded from the Johannine circle to rejoin the Jewish *synagōgē*. He also takes the references to confessing that Jesus has come in the flesh (4:1-3; 2 John 7) as directed against *another* seceding group that was "obviously docetising" and probably made up of "Gentiles who forfeited Christian fellowship to escape Roman persecution."[135] But Anderson's confidence seems to me ill suited for the kind of polemical material in 1 John and 2 John.

The most popular scholarly view is that these passages all refer to one group of secessionists who were docetists, or at least whose christological stance can be described by views attributed to docetists in early patristic sources.[136] Those who support this view take the emphasis on Jesus having come in the flesh as a relatively transparent indication of what the secessionists denied, and as the key evidence in the light of which the more general references to denying that Jesus is the Christ and Son of God are to be understood. But even if this identification is widely asserted, I hesitate to subscribe to it without some qualifications.

The first problem is that it is not very clear what we gain by referring to the Johannine secessionists as docetists or docetizing. The label (from the Greek verb *dokein*, which can mean "to think, believe, suppose" and also "to seem, to have the appearance [of something]") is used pejoratively in several Christian writings of the second and third centuries to describe beliefs that are rejected, but the descriptions of the beliefs of those to whom the authors apply the term vary considerably.[137] Ignatius of Antioch (ca. 110-117) is usually cited as making the earliest references to people who said Jesus only appeared to suffer death (*to dokein peponthenai*; Ign. *Trall.* 10; Ign. *Smyrn.* 2; cf. 4.2). But we know little more about their beliefs than this statement, and not whether they were the same as those condemned in 1 John and 2 John.[138]

Noting that the various ancient patristic references "furnish nothing akin to an official or agreed definition," and that "the proper application of the term *Docetism* is a matter of dispute among patristic scholars," David Wright proposed that the common element was an inability to affirm "inseparable lifelong

---

135. P. Anderson, 122 n. 12.

136. E.g., Strecker, 69-76.

137. See, e.g., David F. Wright, "Docetism," in *DLNTD*, 306-9, for a good overview of issues. Michael Slusser, "Docetism: A Historical Definition," *SecCent* 1 (1981): 163-72, surveys references and proposes that, because the early patristic sources lump together a variety of teachings under the label, "only a broad definition is appropriate" (172). See also Norbert Brox, "'Doketismus' — eine Problemanzeige," *ZKG* 95 (1984): 301-14.

138. Note Brown's differentiation of those condemned by Ignatius and those opposed in 1 John and 2 John (*The Epistles of John*, 58-59).

identity between the heavenly or divine One (often distinguished as Christ) and the human Jesus."[139]

The references from the late second and third centuries describe some docetists as teaching that Jesus was born and lived naturally, but was indwelt by the divine Christ temporarily (e.g., from baptism till crucifixion). Others are said to have taught that the Jesus of the Gospel narratives was a mere semblance of a human, a phantomlike figure, or an optical illusion. Still others are portrayed as representing Jesus' humanity as somehow not normal, with different qualities and substance, so that he was not subject to real suffering and death. So if we call the secessionists docetic(s), this does not particularly help us to specify what they actually taught.

Nor does it help to invoke other terms such as "gnostic" and "gnosticizing." Though frequently used by scholars, these terms cover an even wider diversity of teachings. In fact, Michael Williams has cogently argued that the terms are so imprecise in what they designate that they should probably cease to be used in historical descriptions of early Christianity![140]

The Johannine secessionists probably asserted special, likely revelatory, knowledge about God and salvation, but so did most other Christians of the early centuries. As with the term "docetic," referring to them as "gnostic" pretends to distinguish and specify much more than the term warrants.

A further reason for caution in specifying what they asserted or denied about Jesus is that even the references in 1 John 4:1-3 and 2 John 7 to denying that Jesus has come "in the flesh" are polemical statements, and may thus caricature as much as convey what the secessionists actually taught. Granted, there was obviously some significant difference in beliefs between the secessionists and the author(s) of 1 John and 2 John. This difference likely focused on the figure of Jesus, and *from the standpoint of the author(s)*, the secessionists failed to hold adequately the reality or redemptive significance of Jesus' human life and death.

Proposing that the secessionists developed their view of Jesus as a distinctive interpretation of traditions represented in the Gospel of John, Raymond Brown suggested that they may have granted the reality of Jesus' humanity "but refused to acknowledge that his being in the flesh was essential to the picture of Jesus *as the Christ*, the Son of God."[141] More specifically, Brown took the insistence in 1 John 5:6 that Jesus came "not in water only, but in water and in blood" to imply that the secessionists had a "lack of interest in the death of Jesus"; he

139. Wright, "Docetism," 306.

140. Michael Allen Williams, *Rethinking "Gnosticism": An Argument for Dismantling a Dubious Category* (Princeton: Princeton University Press, 1996).

141. Brown, *The Epistles of John*, 76.

proposed that they could have interpreted elements of the representation of Jesus in the Gospel of John as justifying their view. In particular, Brown pointed to the august representation of Jesus in the Johannine account of his arrest, trial, and crucifixion as perhaps having led the secessionists to de-emphasize the salvific meaning of Jesus' death and to interpret his life and death simply as the continuing revelation of the divine glory that crucially began to appear through his baptism by John the Baptizer.[142]

I find it plausible that the secessionists drew upon Johannine traditions, and even considered themselves the valid interpreters of those traditions. Nevertheless, it is clear that the author(s) of 1 John and 2 John thought that they not only abandoned the ties of fellowship with other Johannine believers but also departed from traditional christological convictions. That is, the secessionists seemed to assert something novel and distinguishable from the views of other Johannine believers. Furthermore, their apparently volitional secession suggests that they, as well, thought that they had gone far beyond the level of understanding of those they abandoned. These things in turn make it likely that there really was something novel in their beliefs, novel at least in comparison with previous Johannine views.

But it is more difficult than some scholars seem to realize to be sure what *specifically* the secessionists asserted. To illustrate the difficulty, in the next two subsections I briefly offer two possible scenarios of the circumstances and nature of their christological stance, each of them capable of being covered by the somewhat opaque references to the secessionists' views in 1 John and 2 John.

Jesus as Heavenly Visitor

In the first scenario, we will take the Johannine secessionists to hold the sort of christological view commonly attributed to them by scholars. That is, in one way or another they emphasized Jesus' divine nature at the expense of a real human existence. As historical background for such a view of Jesus, scholars most often propose the influence of Greek philosophy and/or pagan religious tradition; the secessionists thus become Gentiles whose religious and conceptual background made a real incarnation of a divine being impossible to imagine. I wish to propose, however, that they also could have been influenced by Jewish tradition in formulating the sort of christological view we are considering here. Thus they could as easily have been Jewish Christians as Gentiles.

We have noted already that Johannine believers emphasized Jesus' divine

142. Brown, *The Epistles of John*, 78-79.

significance and heavenly origins, over against the allegations of their Jewish opponents that their reverencing of and claims for Jesus were inappropriate and even blasphemous. In short, devotion to Jesus by Johannine Jewish Christians led to sharp polemics with Jewish opponents; in these polemical exchanges Johannine believers further sharpened their emphases on Jesus' divine glory and provenance.

This, however, may well have underscored a serious conceptual problem for some Johannine Christians. How could a heavenly/divine being have lived a genuinely human existence such as was referred to in the Jesus tradition that nourished Johannine believers as well as other Christian circles? As J. G. Davies showed decades ago, this was a problem that was felt in Jewish as well as in pagan tradition.[143]

Jewish emphasis on God's transcendence discouraged the thought of God taking human existence or even being subject to ordinary sensory apprehension. For example, Philo insisted that humans can apprehend the invisible true God "solely by the understanding," all visual manifestations of God being "shadows" that point the mind to God's true transcendence (*Abr.* 119-23). We may also take the declaration in John 1:18 that "no one has ever seen God" as a further reflection of the concern to maintain God's transcendence and inaccessibility to ordinary apprehension.

Still more relevant for our scenario is the way Jewish sources portray the earthly appearances of angels in human form: they bear a human form in appearance only and not in reality. For example, Philo described the three men who dined with Abraham at Mamre (Gen. 18:1-15) as angels "transformed from their spiritual and soul-like nature into human shape [*eis anthrōpomorphon idean*]" (*Abr.* 113), and he wrote that "though they neither ate nor drank they gave the appearance [*phantasian*] of both eating and drinking" (118). Josephus took an identical view of the incident, referring to Abraham's visitors as angels who "gave him to believe [*hoi de doxan autō pareschon*] that they did eat" (*Ant.* 1.197).

The account of the angel Raphael in the book of Tobit indicates further the wide currency in Jewish tradition of the view that heavenly beings only appear to be human in their earthly manifestations.[144] After feigning (sometimes

---

143. J. G. Davies, "The Origins of Docetism," in *Studia Patristica, Vol. VI,* ed. F. L. Cross, TU 81 (Berlin: Akademie-Verlag, 1962), 13-34, esp. 15. In the following discussion, I develop evidence cited by Davies.

144. Copies of Tobit in Hebrew and Aramaic discovered among Qumran manuscripts have now led most scholars to view it as likely composed in one or the other Semitic language (ca. 225-175 B.C.E.), and then translated into Greek, enjoying a wide readership initially in Jewish and then Christian circles. See, e.g., Carey A. Moore, "Tobit, Book Of," in *ABD,* 6:585-94.

humorously) to be human all through the story, Raphael finally declares his true identity and nature in 12:6-22, specifically stating, "I did not really eat or drink anything, but what you saw was a vision [*horasin hymeis etheōreite*]" (v. 19).

With such notions in their background, and troubled by how to conceive of Jesus as divine and yet also manifested in human form, some Johannine Christians might well have developed a christological stance that emphasized Jesus' divine status, and interpreted his earthly form as something less than real human existence. Or at the least, their treatment of his human form may have been judged insufficiently crucial and real by the standards of the author(s) of 1 John and 2 John. In sum, in this scenario some sort of stance along these lines can be accounted for as an appropriation of Jewish angelophany tradition.

The secessionists may have viewed this understanding of Jesus' human appearance as a revelatory insight, which they then advocated as an inspired solution to a serious christological problem.[145] Against such a view of Jesus, the opening emphasis in 1 John (1:1-4) on the fully tangible nature of the revelation witnessed to in the tradition ("from the beginning") makes perfect sense. Likewise, the repeated references to Jesus' real death and its efficacy (1:7; 2:2; 4:10; 5:6-9) can be seen as directed against a view of Jesus as only appearing to be human.

The secessionists could have been (or included) Jewish Christians, or they could have been Gentile believers whose conceptual categories were shaped by Jewish angelophany tradition. The point is that we do not have to restrict ourselves to invoking "mystery religions" or some other restrictively pagan religious influence to account for such a christological stance. I do not say that the evidence forbids them, only that the scenario I sketch here is fully plausible without requiring them. Actually, given the Jewish Christian background of Johannine Christianity, and given also that most early Christian circles regarded pagan religion with serious disdain, it is perhaps more plausible that any docetic tendencies among Johannine believers reflected the influence of Jewish angelological traditions.

Jesus as Mystical Exemplar

To illustrate why I hesitate to endorse one scenario confidently to the exclusion of all others, I offer another which I think also has good plausibility. This one involves a significantly different christological stance. In this scenario the focus

145. See Brox's somewhat similar proposal (e.g., 314).

of the secessionists was on radical claims about their own special and direct relationship to God, which perhaps amounted to a mystical participation in divine things that connoted a spiritual status and nature superior to what they attributed to other believers. Their christological stance may have involved a correlative emphasis on Jesus as an exemplary (but not unique) "son" of God, who basically illustrated and perhaps revealed in his earthly appearance a heavenly provenance and spiritual status that the secessionists believed that they shared with him. Jesus may have exemplified and declared the special intimacy with God that the secessionists believed they had come to share, but they may have believed that their own status and nature were effectually conveyed or revealed to them individually through mystical experiences of enlightenment.

Thus, in this scenario the statements in 1 John that are thought to reflect the spiritual claims of the secessionists are the crucial evidence. However, claims to "have fellowship" with God (1:6), to "have come to know" God (2:4), to "abide" in God (2:6), to be "in the light" (2:9), and so forth are not by themselves treated as inappropriate by the author. In fact, they sound a lot like the sort of religious rhetoric that was probably familiar in Johannine Christianity. In 1 John, for example, the author makes very similar claims for himself and his intended readers (e.g., 1:3; 2:12-14, 21, 28; 3:9).

But, as expressed by the secessionists, the claims were problematic to the author for one or both of two reasons. First, the secessionists' assertions about their spiritual status may have seemed (and may have been intended as) exclusivist and elitist. That is, they may have claimed to know God, abide in God, and walk in divine light in a sense not shared by those outside their charmed inner circle. Secondly, and perhaps as a consequence of such elitist convictions, the secessionists appear to have felt free to treat those fellow believers who demurred at their spiritual claims and correlative revisionist view of Jesus as no longer worthy of their fellowship and fraternal obligation.

Also, the secessionists may have had little use for the messianic emphasis of GJohn. Moreover, believing themselves to have a special spiritual status and nature that were revealed or conveyed in mystical experiences, they may have seen no particular reason for taking Jesus' death as redemptive. This could be what the author meant in saying they denied that Jesus is "the Christ" (2:22), and why he makes this confession the crucial indication of being begotten of God (5:1). Likewise, it could account for his emphasis on the redemptive efficacy of Jesus' death that we noted under the previous scenario. If the secessionists saw Jesus' divine sonship as merely illustrative of their own (quasi-divine?) status, the author could well have taken this as a denial of the uniqueness of Jesus as "*the* Son (of God)" (*ho huios*, 2:23). Also, it would explain why he so frequently affirmed *Jesus'* particular divine sonship (3:23; 4:15; 5:10, 13), the uniqueness of Jesus' sonship reflected in his consistent use of the definite article.[146]

In 1 John 3:1-3 the author affirms that he and his readers have been given the designation of children of God (*tekna theou*, echoing John 1:12-13). But he emphasizes in 3:2 that their filial status is derivative from, and patterned after, Jesus, and that the full understanding and appropriation of this status will come only in the eschatological manifestation of Jesus. This may well be intended as a direct correction of a secessionist claim that they possess a fully realized divine sonship, perhaps a claim devoid of any eschatological reservation, and perhaps also failing to match the author's emphasis on Jesus' special status.

The religious stance of the secessionists in this scenario is not purely imaginative, but has certain similarities to the stance reflected, for example, in the *Gospel of Thomas* (a text I discuss in the next chapter). This text fairly clearly reflects a significant reinterpretation of traditional Christian categories (e.g., *logion* 51), and a dismissive attitude toward Christians who do not share the views it espouses (e.g., *logia* 13, 62).[147] The scenario I have sketched does not, however, require a direct relationship between the secessionists and those whose views are represented in the *Gospel of Thomas*. But for the purpose of hypothesizing about what the secessionists might have taught, the *Gospel of Thomas* shows that the scenario is by no means implausible.

Historical Results

If, then, as I have proposed, we cannot confidently identify the christological stance of the secessionists with this or that later heretical group to the exclusion of other possibilities, what can we conclude about the crisis reflected in 1 John and 2 John? First, it involved views of Jesus that were sufficiently different that each side in the struggle seems to have considered its opponent's views as stark alternatives. This means that the sharp divisions in belief among Christian groups that are more explicitly described in later sources had an antecedent in the internal crisis that wracked Johannine Christianity toward the end of the first century. Whether, however, the Johannine secessionist group was the direct ancestor of any later heterodox group is another matter on which I do not think we can justifiably make confident assertions.

146. Note 1:3 *(tou huiou autou)*; 2:22-23 *(ton huion)*; 3:8; 4:15; 5:5 *(ho huios tou theou)*; 5:13 *(tou huiou tou theou)*; and the emphasis in 3:23 on "the *name* of his Son [*tou huiou autou*] Jesus Christ."

147. See, e.g., Richard Valantasis, *The Gospel of Thomas* (London: Routledge, 1997), esp. 6-12.

Second, it is interesting to note that the resulting schism appears to have been caused when certain people voluntarily seceded from the circle of Johannine fellowship. It is important to note that apparently they were not evicted. Instead, they seem to have believed that they had been given a new and superior insight, whatever that insight actually comprised; and they may have concluded that the refusal of other Johannine believers to accede to their insight justified severing ties of Christian fellowship with them. In addition to asserting an innovative view of Jesus (and possibly as a corollary to their view of Jesus), the secessionists also may have claimed that they possessed (or had been given) a fellowship with God that was superior to that enjoyed by other Johannine Christians, and that their higher spiritual status justified (and perhaps in their view required) severing ties. Whatever the specifics may have been, it seems they were sufficiently persuaded of the superior validity of their inspiration that they removed themselves from the circle of Johannine Christianity, refusing to submit to its traditions and also to suffer any challenge to their own views.

It would not by any means be the only time in the history of Christianity that a particular group so cherished its own religious experiences and views that it could tolerate no hesitation from other Christians to submit to them! But the Johannine secession is the first fairly clear example of this sort of thing in an identifiable Christian circle in the extant sources of first-century Christianity, and the secessionists may have been the first such full schismatic party. To be sure, there had been previous controversies and even severe denunciations among Christians. As we noted in chapter 2, Paul's letters include scathing references to "false brethren," "false apostles," "dogs," all of whom seem to have been people who laid down requirements for Gentile converts that Paul found unacceptable. Also, in 1 Corinthians (esp. 1:11-17; 3:5-23) Paul speaks against the dissensions that have been reported to him, which may have included lawsuits (6:1-8), and certainly manifested themselves in divisive behavior at the Lord's Supper (11:17-34). But in their apparent decision to secede fully from the remaining Johannine believers, the secessionists may have the dubious honor of setting what became an unfortunate precedent.

Whatever the secessionists' particular christological stance, it apparently involved something that the author of 1 John and 2 John deemed at odds with the tradition of Johannine Christianity. The core matter at stake for the author was probably the unique significance of Jesus. If the secessionists presented Jesus' earthly appearance along the lines of Jewish angelophany traditions, Jesus thus became one of a class of earthly manifestations of heavenly beings. Even if he was seen as the latest/last, greatest, and most significant example, by no means would he have been categorically different. Indeed, part of the probable allure of understanding Jesus in terms of angelophany traditions was that it solved the conundrum of his earthly appearance by an established/known conceptual category that was adapted from the Jewish matrix of Johannine Christianity. If, on the other hand, the secessionists taught that Jesus' divine sonship was simply illustrative and exemplary of the divine sonship equally shared by (or accessible to) all believers who affirmed their new insight, Jesus was also made one of a class and was scarcely unique.

The author of 1 John makes a three-pronged critique of the claims of the secessionists. First, he emphasizes the reality and redemptive significance of Jesus' human existence, particularly his real and redemptive death, and he accuses the secessionists of failing to affirm this (e.g., 1:7–2:2; 3:5, 16). Second, and allied with this, he affirms the uniqueness of Jesus and accuses the secessionists of denying it (e.g., 3:23). Third, he insists that spirituality claims are to be matched with, and exhibited in, fulfillment of obligations to fellow believers (e.g., "Let us love one another," 4:7-8). Indeed, judged by the frequency of the theme and the emphatic way the author treats it, 1 John gives the clear impression that this last matter most clearly shows that the secessionists' claims are invalid.

Crises and Jesus-Devotion

As we have seen here, the Johannine writings reflect the tensions and drama of serious religious crises in the late first century. First, there was a crisis between Johannine Jewish Christians and their Jewish opponents in GJohn, both sides apparently in agreement that the central issue was what to make of Jesus. Then came a crisis *within* Johannine Christianity, a clash between the point of view advocated by the author(s) of 1 John and 2 John and a group who seceded from Johannine Christianity and professed a view of Jesus that was likely innovative in some manner. This innovative belief had probably emerged among the group through what they took to be revelatory experiences.

In the struggle with the Jewish community, Johannine Christians further underscored Jesus' divine status and heavenly origins. In the subsequent internal struggle, the issue may well have involved the reality and/or redemptive significance of his human existence. In both these controversies, Johannine Christians not only battled to defend their beliefs about Jesus, they also further sharpened and shaped the articulation of their beliefs. We might suppose that their beliefs even underwent in some ways substantial developments as well. In any case, the results were historic and highly influential for practically all known forms of subsequent Christian belief about Jesus. It was particularly the rendition of Jesus in GJohn that memorably presented him as unquestionably divine and yet also as a human figure of real history. Brought together with particular clarity in this rendition are the factors that made unavoidable what were perhaps the principal intellectual problems for Christianity across the subsequent several centuries: How could Jesus be truly divine if there was only one God, and in what way could he have been human if he was truly divine?

But the Johannine writings show that, from the beginning, these were also practical problems with profound social implications. The conflict with the larger Jewish community reflected in GJohn illustrates with special force what appears to have been the characteristic social consequences of such belief in Jesus for Jews: from fellow Jews, initially, vehement objection, denunciation, and even serious disciplinary measures, and then ostracism. In their own internal crisis reflected in 1 John and 2 John, Johannine Christians seem to have anticipated the radical diversity and schisms in early Christianity that are more overtly attested in sources of the next couple of centuries. Along with these later writings, the Johannine texts show that Christian views of Jesus were the central issue distinguishing some believers from others; they also show that serious divergence in beliefs about Jesus could have major consequences for Christian fellowship. In the following chapters I turn to the radical diversity in views of Jesus that is richly witnessed in the decades after the likely date of the Johannine writings; I also take account of the contemporaneous manifestations of "proto-orthodox" devotion to Jesus.

CHAPTER SEVEN

Other Early Jesus Books

Any adequate diachronic analysis of "earliest" Christianity must extend well into the second century at least, and must take account of extracanonical books about Jesus in addition to the more well known canonical ones. In this chapter I give attention to the many extracanonical "gospels" that were probably composed at various points in the second century, and that in any case certainly circulated then. In the following chapters I discuss additional phenomena and the broader dynamics of devotion to Jesus, and I characterize the second century in terms of "radical diversity" and the emergence of what we may call "proto-orthodox" expressions of Christianity.

Jesus Books

Although it is increasingly recognized among scholars that the four accounts of Jesus that became canonical were widely disseminated and appreciated from at least the early decades of the second century, other writings devoted to Jesus also circulated and were appreciated in Christian circles of that time and later.[1]

---

1. For a recent, concise taxonomy of extracanonical Jesus books, see Stephen J. Patterson, "Gospels, Apocryphal," in *ABD*, 2:1079-81, with bibliography of editions and key major studies. Ron Cameron, ed., *The Other Gospels: Non-Canonical Gospel Texts* (Guildford, Surrey: Lutterworth, 1983), is an enthusiastic introductory handbook, though a number of his specific claims are debatable. See also Stephen Gero, "Apocryphal Gospels: A Survey of Textual and Literary Problems," in *ANRW*, 2.25/5 (1988): 3969-96. Among older standard works, Johannes Quasten, *Patrology*, 4 vols. (Westminster, Md.: Christian Classics, 1950-86), 1:106-28, remains a valuable, concise treatment of extracanonical gospels. Two standard works on early Christian extracanonical writings are Wilhelm Schneemelcher, ed., *New Testament Apocrypha*,

The reference in Luke 1:1 to "many" others who had given "an account of the events that have been fulfilled among us," is commonly taken to refer to prior first-century writings about Jesus; the statements in John 20:30 and 21:25 also probably reflect awareness of such books.[2] However, no such Jesus book written prior to the canonical Gospels survives.[3] For some time after the composition of the canonical Gospels as well, Christians continued to produce and circulate other writings about Jesus. In the following pages I review the evidence for these books, with particular concern for their views of Jesus.

Rumors

As every scholar concerned with early Christianity laments, we have only the titles of some accounts of Jesus mentioned, or at most a few brief quotations said to be from them, in other Christian writings (e.g., *Gospel of the Nazoraeans, Gospel of the Hebrews, Gospel of the Ebionites,* and *Gospel of the Egyptians,* referred to in the writings of figures such as Irenaeus, Clement of Alexandria, Origen, Eusebius, Epiphanius, Jerome, and later writers). The references to these Jesus books amount to a very small body of data, and they also suggest that the patristic writers were confused about how many such works there were and what literary character they had. So it is almost impossible to say with confidence what were their general contents, or even how much to depend on these secondhand characterizations of them.[4] William Petersen well described the in-

---

2 vols. (Louisville: Westminster John Knox; Cambridge: James Clarke, 1991-92), hereafter *NTA;* and J. K. Elliott, ed., *The Apocryphal New Testament: A Collection of Apocryphal Christian Literature in an English Translation* (New York: Oxford University Press, 1993). Among contemporary scholars, Helmut Koester has produced the most wide-ranging studies of early Jesus books: esp. *Ancient Christian Gospels: Their History and Development* (Philadelphia: Trinity Press International, 1990), and "Überlieferung und Geschichte der frühchristlichen Evangelienliteratur," in *ANRW,* 2.25.2:1463-1542.

2. Of course, if, as is widely believed, the author of Luke used Mark and at least one collection of sayings (Q), these would be prominent examples of the prior writings referred to in Luke 1:1. I suspect also that the phrasing of John 20:30-31, on the aim of "*this* book," and the reference in 21:25 to Jesus having done "many *other* things" which would require many other books to contain them allude to other accounts of Jesus.

3. I anticipate here my conclusions about various hypotheses, such as those built on "Secret Mark" and the "Cross Gospel" which I set forth more explicitly below.

4. For a list of patristic references to these now-lost writings about Jesus, along with critical introductions, see *NTA,* 1:134-78, 209-15, and the following articles on individual writings in *ABD:* Ron Cameron, "Hebrews, Gospel of The," 3:105-6; William Petersen, "Ebionites, Gospel of The," 2:261-62, and "Nazoraeans, Gospel of The," 4:1051-52. Dieter Lührmann and Egbert Schlarb, *Fragmente apokryph gewordener Evangelien in griechischer und lateinischer Sprache*

vestigation of these texts as "the most enigmatic and irritating problem in the NT Apocrypha: enigmatic because all are now lost, and irritating because our knowledge of these early (pre–170 c.e.) gospels comes only indirectly via the [church] Fathers' cryptic and inconsistent remarks."[5]

In a recent book-length analysis of the evidence for the extracanonical gospels associated with Jewish Christian circles, A. F. J. Klijn concludes that there were three such writings: (1) A *Gospel according to the Hebrews,* composed in Greek in the second century in Egypt and known to Clement of Alexandria, Origen, and still later, Jerome; (2) a *Gospel of the Nazoraeans* (or "Nazaraeans"), known from Jerome, the Latin translation of Origen's *Commentary on Matthew,* and Eusebius; and (3) a *Gospel of the Ebionites,* known only through citations in Epiphanius. Klijn also lists all the references to these lost Jesus books in the patristic sources, indicating the degree of confidence he thinks we can place in them.[6] Though there is broad support for Klijn's basic views, predictably other scholars take issue with his judgments on some particulars. This, however, reflects the difficulty in obtaining agreement when the extant evidence is so scanty.[7] There were certainly such writings about Jesus. But although scholars desire to push as far as learned speculation will allow, little more than very general impressions can be offered about the specifics of the contents of these apocryphal accounts.

Their mere existence, however, is an important indication that there were a number of such books about Jesus in the first few centuries of the Christian movement. I contend that the production of such writings obviously expresses devotion to Jesus, whatever the specifics affirmed about him, and that reference to the production and circulation of such writings must be an important feature of any characterization of devotion to Jesus in earliest Christianity. Beyond this basic observation, I can only summarize broadly shared views about the better known of these lost writings with particular reference to their views of Jesus.[8]

The *Gospel of the Nazoraeans* is the name given by scholars to a writing de-

---

(Marburg: Elwert, 2000), provide original-language texts, German translations, and notes in one handy volume.

5. Petersen, "Nazoraeans," 4:1051.

6. A. F. J. Klijn, *Jewish-Christian Gospel Tradition,* VCSup 17 (Leiden: Brill, 1992). A previous publication provides citations of these gospels in early Christian writers: A. F. J. Klijn and G. J. Reinink, *Patristic Evidence for Jewish-Christian Sects,* NovTSup 36 (Leiden: Brill, 1973).

7. Citing several proposals as to how many extracanonical Jewish Christian gospels there were and what they contained, Petersen states, "Given our present state of knowledge, it is difficult to say which, if any, theory is correct" ("Nazoraeans," 4:1052).

8. Origen and later Jerome also refer to a "Gospel according to the Twelve" or "according to the Apostles," which may be another name for one of the extracanonical gospels, or may be still another unknown gospel.

scribed in early patristic writings as circulating among Jewish Christians, possibly in Syria, and thought by many scholars to have been closely related to the Gospel of Matthew in contents and overall shape.[9] But the snippets attributed to this writing in patristic sources suggest that it was likely a secondary narrative about Jesus, influenced by, and incorporating material from, Matthew and Luke, along with other bits of legendary/novelistic embroidery. It was probably either composed in Aramaic (or perhaps Hebrew) or translated from Greek. Also, the general impression from the quotations is that this account reflects Jewish Christian believers of relatively "proto-orthodox" stance, and that it was not intended originally to serve or reflect recognizably "heterodox" views.[10]

The *Gospel of the Ebionites* is likewise a modern scholarly title given to a work that Epiphanius (ca. 315-403) several times says was used among certain Jewish Christians who are sometimes called "Ebionites."[11] The alleged quotations in Epiphanius indicate that this too was apparently a Synoptic-like gospel written in Greek. It may have begun, as does the Gospel of Mark, with the appearance of John the Baptizer; it seems to have drawn heavily upon the Synoptic Gospels.[12] Indeed, scholars refer to it as a harmonization of canonical Gospels, with some additional novelistic material included, a form of Christian literature perhaps particularly popular in the second century, for which there are varied examples, Tatian's *Diatessaron* (to which I return in chap. 9) being obviously the best-known one.[13] Once again, the quotations said to be from the *Gospel of the Ebionites* do not themselves indicate any blatantly heterodox standpoint, although it is quite possible that the alleged absence of a nativity account in the writing may reflect a denial of Jesus' virginal conception, a stance attributed to Ebionites by Irenaeus and Tertullian.[14] But as for a fuller

---

9. Petersen points out that the name *Gospel of the Nazoraeans [or Nazaraeans]* actually does not appear until references in medieval sources ("Nazoraeans," 4:1052), although earlier sources refer to a gospel read among Jewish Christians called "Nazoraeans." See also Stephen Goranson, "Nazarenes," in *ABD*, 4:1049-50, for a concise review of data and issues about these Jewish Christians. In chap. 9 I say a bit more about Jewish Christianity of the second century.

10. For English translations of the patristic and medieval references, see *NTA*, 1:160-64, and Cameron, *The Other Gospels*, 97-102.

11. E.g., Epiphanius, *Pan.* 30.13.1. The seven snippets of the Ebionite gospel in Epiphanius are the only direct references to this work. They are listed in *NTA*, 1:169-70; Cameron, *The Other Gospels*, 103-6. See also Petersen, "Ebionites"; and George Howard, "The Gospel of the Ebionites," in *ANRW*, 2.25/5 (1988): 4034-53.

12. Epiphanius, *Pan.* 30.13.6.

13. E.g., the *Gospel of the Ebionites* is characterized in *NTA*, 1:168, as a "gospel harmony." Petersen comments, "The harmonized form of the *Gospel of the Ebionites* is noteworthy," and he points to references to several analogous writings of the second century ("Ebionites," 2:262).

14. Irenaeus, *Adv. haer.* 3.21.1; 5.1.3; cf. 1.26.2; 3.11.7; Tertullian, *Haer.* 33. Curiously, Irenae-

statement of what "Ebionites" might in fact have believed, almost everything depends on how one views the various secondhand characterizations of them in patristic sources (which are usually hostile, and often seem confused). The quotations of what scholars refer to as the *Gospel of the Ebionites* tell us very little.

The *Gospel of the Hebrews,* however, was actually used by the ancient patristic sources. The *Stichometry of Nicephorus* (a ninth-century catalogue of canonical and noncanonical Christian writings) lists it as one of several disputed works, and represents it as about nine-tenths the size of the Gospel of Mark.[15] But once again, what actually survives of this Jesus book is only a handful of quotations by patristic authors (Clement of Alexandria, Origen, Jerome, and a discourse ascribed to Cyril of Jerusalem).[16] Cameron has aptly characterized these quotations as indicating "a syncretistic, Jewish-Christian document."[17] Jesus is referred to as "Christ," "the Lord," and "the Savior," and is a preexistent figure born as a human through Mary. In the scene of his baptism, "the whole fount of the Holy Spirit" descends upon him, and the Spirit (whom Jesus refers to as "my mother, the Holy Spirit" in another of the quotations) there acclaims him as "my first-begotten Son who reigns for ever."[18] Another peculiar feature appears in one of the quotations given by Jerome, which describes the risen Lord's appearance to James, his brother, an incident not related in any of the other early canonical or extracanonical gospels, this account probably reflecting (and inspired by?) the very early tradition given by Paul (1 Cor. 15:7).[19] The *Gospel of the Hebrews* was written in Greek and is thought to have originated among Egyptian Christians, perhaps in the early second century. But it does not show

---

us claims that the Ebionites used only the Gospel of Matthew! Ebionites are mentioned also by Hippolytus, Origen, Eusebius, and Epiphanius, but the references seem confused and must be treated with great caution. For basics, see, e.g., Stephen Goranson, "Ebionites," in *ABD,* 2:260-61; F. Stanley Jones, "Ebionites," in *EEC,* 1:357-58; and esp. David F. Wright, "Ebionites," in *DLNTD,* 313-17.

15. The *Stichometry* lists works in canonical *(ekklēsiazontai),* disputed *(antilegomena),* and apocryphal categories, and gives their size by *stichoi* (regular line lengths of fifteen syllables or about thirty-five letters). The *Gospel of the Hebrews* is there said to have comprised 2,200 *stichoi,* and the Gospel of Mark 2,500. See *NTA,* 1:41-42.

16. See *NTA,* 1:172-78; the seven patristic quotations are listed on 177-78; and Cameron, "Hebrews"; Cameron, *The Other Gospels,* 83-86; and A. F. J. Klijn, "Das Hebräer- und das Nazoräerevangelium," in *ANRW,* 2.25/5 (1988): 3997-4033.

17. Cameron, "Hebrews," 3:105.

18. Jerome (*Commentary on Isaiah* on Isa. 11:2) gives a quote from "the gospel written in the Hebrew speech, which the Nazaraeans read," narrating the Spirit's descent upon Jesus. In a quotation in Origen (*Commentary on John* 2.12), Jesus refers to the Spirit as his mother. Texts in *NTA,* 1:177.

19. Jerome, *Vir. illus.* 2; *NTA,* 1:178.

the more direct use of the canonical Gospels that seems to be exhibited in the *Gospel of the Nazoraeans* and the *Gospel of the Ebionites;* the quoted extracts suggest circles with a greater interest in speculative and mythological themes.

There is also a *Gospel of the Egyptians* that is known to us through several references in Clement of Alexandria (ca. 160-215).[20] From these references it appears that this writing espoused a strongly ascetic stance, particularly toward sexual relations and procreation. Also, it is interesting that in several of Clement's quotations of the text, Jesus (consistently referred to as "the Lord") is pictured in short dialogue scenes responding to questions put to him by followers (most often by a "Salome").[21]

This justifiably has led some scholars to propose that the *Gospel of the Egyptians* may have been an early example of the "revelation dialogue" genre, a form of writing in which Jesus teaches in response to questions put by disciples. I shall say a bit more about this genre of Jesus book toward the end of this chapter. As Pheme Perkins proposed, although the dialogue form was used by proto-orthodox believers, it was perhaps particularly favored by Christians who sought to promote esoteric teachings involving views different from those (more traditional beliefs) that characterized circles of what became the "great church."[22] This esoteric tendency certainly is evident in most examples of this genre, those found among the Nag Hammadi Coptic texts. If, as is widely thought by scholars, the *Gospel of the Egyptians* was written in the second century in Egypt, this means that the strongly ascetic ideas espoused in it were finding favor there already at that point. This text also shows that, despite the differences it reflects over matters of belief, those behind it agree with other

20. *NTA,* 1:209-15; cf. Cameron, *The Other Gospels,* 49-52. This writing must be distinguished from the fourth-century Coptic text of the same name found among the Nag Hammadi cache of writings. On the latter, see, e.g., Frederik Wisse, "Egyptians, Gospel Of," in *ABD,* 2:413-14; and the introduction and English translation of the Coptic text by Alexander Böhlig and Frederik Wisse in *NHLE,* 208-19.

21. This "Salome" must be the figure named in Mark 15:40 and 16:1 as a witness of Jesus' death and one of the women who find the empty tomb and are given news of Jesus' resurrection. On the references in canonical and early extracanonical sources, see esp. Richard J. Bauckham, "Salome the Sister of Jesus, Salome the Disciple of Jesus, and the Secret Gospel of Mark," *NovT* 33 (1991): 245-75.

22. Pheme Perkins, *The Gnostic Dialogue: The Early Church and the Crisis of Gnosticism* (New York: Paulist, 1980). See also *NTA,* 1:228-31, and the discussions and translations of eight specific examples that follow (232-84), all but two of which are "gnostic" texts from Nag Hammadi. The other two examples given are the "Freer Logion" (a short dialogue scene that follows Mark 16:14 in the Freer Gospels [Codex W]) and the *Epistle of the Apostles* (probably written mid–second century, a postresurrection dialogue in which Jesus affirms basically orthodox teachings). On this interesting text, see also Julian V. Hills, *Tradition and Composition in the "Epistula Apostolorum,"* HDR 24 (Minneapolis: Fortress, 1990).

Christians of the time in expressing their devotion to Jesus in literary form by portraying him as teaching their favored religious views.

Secret Mark

It is still more difficult to be sure what to make of the so-called secret Mark, a supposedly esoteric version of the Gospel of Mark mentioned and excerpted in a putative letter of Clement of Alexandria replying to an otherwise unknown Theodorus. The letter actually refers to three versions of Mark: (1) the familiar canonical version; (2) an expanded version prepared subsequently to the canonical Mark and reserved for those "initiated into the great mysteries," this expanded version referred to positively in the letter as the "secret" Mark; and (3) a third version which the letter claims was used by a group called the Carpocratians and which contained heretical ideas. Neither of the latter two versions nor the letter itself was otherwise known until the text of Clement's letter was put before scholars by Morton Smith in 1973.[23] In fact, despite the efforts of several scholars to obtain access to the artifact itself, to this day all we have are photographs and Smith's descriptions.[24]

Under these circumstances, many scholars believe there are good reasons for remaining open about all the relevant issues.[25] Is this letter of Clement genuine, or is it an ancient pseudepigraph or subsequent hoax?[26] If it is genuine, this

23. Morton Smith, *Clement of Alexandria and a Secret Gospel of Mark* (Cambridge: Harvard University Press, 1973). Smith also published a more sensationalized treatment of the text for popular consumption: *The Secret Gospel: The Discovery and Interpretation of the Secret Gospel according to Mark* (New York: Harper and Row, 1973).

24. Smith says that in a visit to the Mar Saba Monastery in Judea in 1958 he found the letter written in Greek on blank pages at the back of an edition of the letters of Ignatius of Antioch printed in 1646. In a recent article Charles Hedrick reviews matters and presents previously unpublished color photographs of the letter: "Secret Mark: New Photographs, New Witnesses," *Fourth R* 13, no. 5 (September-October 2000): 3-16. In an account to appear in *JECS* in spring 2003, which he kindly sent to me, Guy Stroumsa relates a trip to the Mar Saba monastery to see the artifact in the spring of 1976, noting that he may now be the sole living Western scholar to have seen the putative letter of Clement.

25. E.g., Joel Marcus, *Mark 1–8: A New Translation with Introduction and Commentary*, AB (New York: Doubleday, 2000), 47-51, and I remind readers of my earlier comments on Secret Mark in chap. 5.

26. Though Clement is reported to have written many letters, no other survives. The judgment that this is a fake has been offered by Quentin Quesnell, "The Mar Saba Clementine: A Question of Evidence," *CBQ* 37 (1975): 48-67; Charles E. Murgia, "Secret Mark: Real or Fake?" in *Longer Mark: Forgery, Interpolation, or Old Tradition? Colloquy 18 of the Center for Hermeneutical Studies in Hellenistic and Modern Culture*, ed. Wilhelm Wuellner (Berkeley: Cen-

copy is well over 1,400 years later than its original composition. So how was this letter transmitted without being known or referred to prior to Smith's discovery of it in 1958? And how is it that this is the only letter of Clement to have survived? Nevertheless, reluctant to allege deception and understandably eager to make the most of any scrap of possible further evidence about early Christianity, most scholars seem willing to give the letter the benefit of the doubt, and entertain the hypothesis that Smith's photographs may show a seventeenth-century copy of a real letter of Clement.[27]

If, then, it is a real letter of Clement, how accurate is what it says about the editorial history of the Gospel of Mark? Many are also ready to grant the possibility that there were different versions of Mark that may have included the sort of expansion described in the letter. We certainly know that from the second century onward the Gospel circulated with different endings. So it is in principle possible that there were other substantial variations that amounted to distinguishable "editions" of Mark. Moreover, there are rough analogies. The book of Acts, for example, circulated in two editions, the "Western text" being about one-tenth larger than the "Alexandrian text," the additional material generally picturesque and novelistic expansions of incidents related more simply in the Alexandrian text.[28]

The putative quotation of a "secret" version of Mark in the letter of Clement relates additional material said to be placed between 10:34 and 10:35 of the canonical text. This additional material is an account of Jesus coming to Bethany, where a certain woman begs him to revive her dead brother. Jesus does so, and "after six days" he commissions the young man and proceeds to teach him "the mysteries of the kingdom of God." There is a basic resonance of this story with the raising of Lazarus in John 11, and the phrasing echoes a number of other passages in Mark and John as well.[29] If, as Clement's letter claims, this

---

ter for Hermeneutical Studies, 1975), 35-40; and now A. H. Criddle, "On the Mar Saba Letter Attributed to Clement of Alexandria," *JECS* 3 (1995): 215-20, gives fresh reason to suspect that the letter is pseudepigraphical.

27. See, e.g., the cautious appraisal by Bruce M. Metzger, *The Canon of the New Testament: Its Origin, Development, and Significance* (Oxford: Clarendon, 1987), 132-33, and John Dominic Crossan, *Four Other Gospels: Shadows on the Contours of Canon* (Minneapolis: Winston, 1985), 91-110, esp. 103. Smith produced his own review of scholarly judgments on the issues: "Clement of Alexandria and the Secret Mark: The Score at the End of the First Decade," *HTR* 75 (1982): 449-61. See also Saul Levin, "The Early History of Christianity in the Light of the 'Secret Gospel' of Mark," in *ANRW*, 2.25/6 (1988): 4270-92. The text is now often referred to as *The Letter to Theodorus*.

28. E. J. Epp, "Western Text," in *ABD*, 6:909-12; Bruce M. Metzger et al., *A Textual Commentary on the Greek New Testament* (London and New York: United Bible Societies, 1971), 259-72.

29. See the list of allusions in *NTA*, 1:109, and the commentary on the allusions in F. F. Bruce, *The "Secret" Gospel of Mark* (London: Athlone, 1974), 11-13.

quotation comes from an actual secondary edition of Mark, it seems to have been basically an effort at amplification and embellishment that reflected rather recognizable Christian interests and piety. It also demonstrates rather impressive acquaintance with the canonical Gospels. As Raymond Brown says, "in vocabulary, style, and content almost every line of [secret Mark] resembles canonical Gospel material."[30]

As to the nature of the Christian piety it reflects, the episode from secret Mark quoted in the letter seems to indicate an interest in an initiatory baptismal rite and its significance, which could in fact have been the main focus for this expansion of canonical Mark.[31] Indeed, Thomas Talley offers an intriguing suggestion that annual liturgical practice in early Egyptian Christian circles (of a proto-orthodox character) accounts quite satisfactorily for the expansion.[32] It is also plausible that some heterodox circle in Alexandria, such as the Carpocratians mentioned in the letter, may well have produced a writing that was, or could be taken to be, their own version of Mark and that included references to more esoteric ideas and practices that they favored.[33]

But it is much more difficult on scholarly grounds to accept the rather more sweeping claims and intricate proposals urged by some enthusiasts of secret Mark. In particular, the contentions that secret Mark is earlier and canonical Mark is a secondary revision of it seem based on improbable judgments of

---

30. Raymond E. Brown, "The Relation of 'The Secret Gospel of Mark' to the Fourth Gospel," *CBQ* 36 (1974): 476-77 (466-85). Brown's chart on 471-74 shows the resemblances line by line. "In any hypothesis a remarkable knowledge of individual Gospel style(s) has to be attributed to the author of [secret Mark]" (480).

31. The scene where the young man comes to Jesus clad in a linen garment is widely seen as a baptismal scene. See Philip Sellew, "Secret Mark and the History of Canonical Mark," in *The Future of Early Christianity: Essays in Honor of Helmut Koester,* ed. Birger A. Pearson (Minneapolis: Fortress, 1991), 256-57. As will be apparent, however, I do not follow Sellew in assenting to Koester's proposal of an "original" Mark from which both canonical Mark and "secret" Mark were derived.

32. Thomas Talley, "Liturgical Time in the Ancient Church: The State of Research," *Studia Liturgica* 14 (1982): 34-51, esp. 44-47. Talley points to indications that pre-Nicene Egyptian Christians followed a course of readings from Mark that began in January with an observance of Jesus' own baptism and ran on through to an observance of Jesus' death and resurrection. He proposes that the material in "secret" Mark was "inserted into chapter 10 in close conjunction with the conferral of baptism in the sixth week [of the course of readings], and the celebration of the entry into Jerusalem with chapter 11 of Mark on the following Sunday" (45-46).

33. The Carpocratians are a group described by Irenaeus, *Adv. haer.* 1.25, as claiming esoteric truth and advocating libertine behavior. He also mentions that they produced writings claiming that they had special access to secret teachings delivered by Jesus privately to his disciples (1.25.5). We know little more about them. See, e.g., Kurt Rudolph, *Gnosis: The Nature and History of Gnosticism* (San Francisco: Harper and Row, 1983), 209, 256-57.

the data and a disregard of other indications of the harmonistic and expansionary tendencies in Christian handling of gospel texts in the second century.[34] Secret Mark employs phrasing with uncanny resemblances to the canonical Gospels to narrate an incident that looks suspiciously like a novelistic expansion of the Markan narrative. The expansion was likely prompted by the unexplained "young man" in canonical Mark and yet was also inspired and shaped by the story of the raising of Lazarus in John.[35]

To entertain the claim that secret Mark is earlier than canonical Mark would also require us in fact to disregard what the *Letter to Theodorus* says (our *only* basis for thinking there might have been a secret Mark!) about the relationship of canonical Mark to other versions. We have to ignore what most scholars see as clear evidence that canonical Mark is a reasonably organized narrative that requires no previous version to account for anything in it, and ignore indications that secret Mark is more readily explained as derivative from canonical Mark.[36] In sum, the picture of Jesus in canonical Mark does not demand either secret Mark or the Carpocratian version to account for it, whereas both of the latter are much more plausible in light of other evidence of how the

---

34. Helmut Koester has put forth perhaps the most fully articulated and widely known proposal involving a five-stage redactional history of Mark in which canonical Mark is derived from secret Mark, which in turn was derived from hypothetical earlier forms that go back to "original" Mark: "History and Development of Mark's Gospel: From Mark to Secret Mark and 'Canonical' Mark," in *Colloquy on New Testament Studies: A Time for Reappraisal and Fresh Approaches,* ed. Bruce C. Corley (Macon, Ga.: Mercer University Press, 1983), 35-57, and his fuller discussion in *Ancient Christian Gospels,* 273-303. Cf. also Crossan, *Four Other Gospels,* esp. 106-10.

35. For a similar judgment, see, e.g., R. E. Brown, "The Relation," esp. 474-85.

36. Though Sellew judged Koester's proposal "correct in its basic insights," nevertheless he too faulted Koester's characterization of original Mark ("Secret Mark," esp. 250-53). Bauckham has also shown that the treatment of Salome in secret Mark is more likely explained as adapted from the references to her in canonical Mark (Bauckham, "Salome," esp. 268-75). Likewise, the account of the "young man" in secret Mark is much more easily seen as an attempt to explain the undefined figure in Mark 14:51-52 who flees the scene of Jesus' arrest. The Markan young men here and in 16:5 bracket the account of Jesus' arrest, death, and resurrection, and the "linen garment" *(sindona)* anticipates Jesus' burial cloth (15:46). But it is easy to see the story in secret Mark as an attempt at once to explain this figure and to link him with the Johannine Lazarus. The proposal that the figure in canonical Mark is a remnant of the story in secret Mark reflects a strange ignorance of the well-demonstrated fact that ancient scribes tended to resolve narrative difficulties, not create them. The text-critical principle that the reading that accounts better for the other variants is to be preferred seems obviously to point to the abrupt reference in canonical Mark as prior to the filled-out account in secret Mark. As Bruce noted decades ago, the material said to come from secret Mark in Clement's letter is "largely a pastiche of phrases from Mark ('contaminated' by Matthean parallels), coupled with some Johannine material" (esp. from John 11:17-44). Bruce, "Secret," 11.

canonical Gospels were handled in the second century and of the kinds of developments in beliefs that characterized that period.[37]

Fragments

We also have small, fragmentary portions surviving directly from now-lost writings about Jesus that we cannot even identify by name, and whose larger contents remain a mystery (the texts known simply as P.Oxy. 840, P.Oxy. 1224, P.Cairensis 10,735, the "Fayyum Fragment," P.Egerton 2, "the Strasbourg Coptic Papyrus," and the Akhmîm and other fragments of the *Gospel of Peter*).[38] Furthermore, it is very difficult to tell how early any of these writings may have been composed. The fragments are themselves datable only approximately, through paleographic and codicological expertise, and in any case are likely only copies of the original compositions, which may be significantly older still. A few more comments about these fragmentary texts will suffice for our present purposes.

For the most part, scholarly study of these fragments has been heavily occupied with trying to determine whether they come from writings that were in some way dependent upon the canonical Gospels, or instead represent independent literary works that drew directly upon the varied traditions about Jesus that circulated in the earliest Christian centuries. I cannot enter fully the now complex scholarly discussion of these matters. Instead I want to focus on these texts as illustrative of the rich diversity of writings about Jesus produced

---

37. I have to say that I am puzzled at the confident construction of elaborate redactional theories for Mark that involve secret Mark. For example, Koester has been extremely skeptical about our ability to say much about the text of any of the canonical Gospels because our earliest extensive manuscripts are from ca. 200 and later: "The Text of the Synoptic Gospels in the Second Century," in *Gospel Traditions in the Second Century: Origins, Recensions, Text, and Transmission,* ed. William L. Petersen (Notre Dame, Ind., and London: University of Notre Dame Press, 1989), 19-37 (cf. my criticism in "Beyond the Interlude? Developments and Directions in New Testament Textual Criticism," in *Studies in the Early Text of the Gospels and Acts,* ed. D. G. K. Taylor [Birmingham: University of Birmingham Press, 1999], 26-48). Yet Koester curiously makes so much rest on one seventeenth-century copy of an otherwise unknown and uncorroborated letter (that, if genuine, was in any case composed no earlier than 200!).

38. For concise introductions to several, see Harry Y. Gamble, "Egerton Papyrus 2," in *ABD,* 2:317-18; "Fayyum Fragment," in *ABD,* 2:778-79; and S. Kent Brown, "Sayings of Jesus, Oxyrhynchus," in *ABD,* 5:999-1001. For fuller discussion with English translation of the contents of all these fragmentary writings, see *NTA,* 1:92-105, 216-27. Again, Joseph van Haelst, *Catalogue des papyrus littéraires juifs et chrétiens* (Paris: Publications de la Sorbonne, 1976), provides concise paleographical and codicological descriptions.

in the period we are considering here. However, I offer some general observations about the production of such writings.

On the one hand, in light of the evidence of a varied and rich body of tradition/lore about Jesus in the first couple centuries or so, it is perfectly plausible in principle to propose that Christians then were capable of producing books about Jesus without direct dependence upon, or the direct influence of, the Gospels we know as Matthew, Mark, Luke, and John. On the other hand, given the early and impressive circulation and usage of these four familiar Jesus books, it is also perfectly plausible to think that Christians wishing to write their own books about Jesus may well have been stimulated and influenced by them.

Of course, this does not necessarily mean that authors of other books about Jesus had copies of the canonical Gospels open before them as they wrote. In fact, it is likely that the influence of the Gospels was exercised more broadly through the frequent public reading of them in worship gatherings of Christians (referred to famously by Justin, *1 Apol.* 67.3; cf. 66.3), their phrasing, cadences, and contents thereby becoming familiar to many Christians who may never have read them as we are accustomed to reading books. In addition, as we shall see later in this chapter, scholars have shown that within the first few decades of the second century texts circulated in which material (especially sayings of Jesus) from the canonical Gospels was harmonistically combined for didactic purposes. These harmonization texts were a further way for the contents and phrasing of the canonical Gospels to influence other writings. As Frans Neirynck observed, "'Harmonization' is a general characteristic of the extracanonical gospel literature in the second century."[39] The combination of phrasing and motifs from the Synoptics and John that is such a feature of a number of extracanonical Jesus books (e.g., P.Egerton 2, P.Oxy. 840), and also seems to characterize the "long ending" of Mark, may in general reflect the ways Christians through the centuries have tended to blend together the stories and phrasing of the four canonical Gospels into a composite reverential image and "recollection" of Jesus.

Granted, the evidence of each extracanonical text has to be considered in its own right, and it is best to build up inductively our generalizations of how such texts were likely written. But it is wise to consider any particular text in the light of the other analogous texts as well before making final judgments about what kinds of relationships there may be to other accounts of Jesus, particularly the four very influential accounts that came to constitute the canonical rendi-

---

39. Frans Neirynck, "The Apocryphal Gospels and the Gospel of Mark," in *The New Testament in Early Christianity*, ed. Jean-Marie Sevrin (Leuven: Leuven University Press, 1989), 169 (123-75).

tions of him. In my view the cumulative weight of the evidence points toward the conclusion that in the second and third centuries Christians frequently produced writings about Jesus that show the influence of the canonical Gospels (whether direct or mediated through other sources). These subsequent writings also both drew upon and contributed to the wider body of written and oral lore about Jesus circulating in the early centuries.

But what might have been the motives of the authors of these writings? If they knew of the canonical Gospels, were they perhaps intending to displace them with their own accounts of Jesus? Or did they hope that their books might acquire a similar circulation and standing in the churches? Or did they simply wish to write for Christian edification, not necessarily aiming to have their works accepted for liturgical usage but instead hoping to add their own accounts to the stock of material about him circulating among Christians?

The fragmentary nature of these writings makes it difficult to say with confidence which motives and aspirations might have moved the authors. I would only caution us against assuming too quickly that the production of a Jesus book in the ancient church was intended necessarily to rival others, or even to obtain some sort of authoritative status. As we shall note later, Jesus books do appear to have been produced with such aims. But I suspect that for some authors, perhaps more typically, the aims were benign, for edification and inspiration, their Jesus books written with a "doxological" motive. That is, their aspirations were not that different from many subsequent Christians who have added to the store of hymns, sermons, and even books about Jesus without intending to dislodge other and previous expressions of devotion to him.

The amount of extant material in these fragmentary texts upon which to form a judgment about the larger writings from which they come is woefully small. But it seems to me that none of the texts indicates an adversarial attitude toward other accounts, and none reflects a form of Christian faith that was consciously at odds with the piety and beliefs that we familiarly associate with proto-orthodox circles of the early centuries.

For example, in P.Oxyrhynchus 840 (Haelst, 585), a single leaf from a miniature parchment codex usually dated to the fourth or fifth century, we apparently have the conclusion of a statement of Jesus to his disciples, followed by an interesting vignette relating an encounter between Jesus and "a Pharisaic chief priest" that is set in the court of the Jerusalem temple and concerns whether Jesus and his disciples are entitled to enter the temple precincts without a ceremonial washing.[40] In another single-leaf portion of an unknown writing, P.Cairensis 10,735

---

40. One of my Ph.D. students, Michael J. Kruger, is producing a study of P.Oxy. 840 as his thesis. He has already persuaded me that there is scant basis for the frequently repeated view

(Haelst, 588, sixth-seventh century), we have bits of scenes having to do with the birth of Jesus and the flight to Egypt. The so-called Fayyum Fragment (Haelst, 589, third century) contains lines relating a single scene very close to that portrayed in Mark 14:27-30.[41] As for the "Strasbourg Coptic Papyrus," only two fragmentary leaves of a fifth- or sixth-century manuscript survive, containing bits of a prayer and sayings of Jesus in what looks like a pastiche of phrasing resembling lines from various New Testament writings (e.g., John, Matthew, 1 Corinthians). P.Oxyrhynchus 1224 (Haelst, 587, fourth century) comprises six fragmentary pages of a papyrus book, only two of which provide enough text to permit us to read it. One page has a bit of a controversy story resembling the one in Mark 2:15-19; the other has a saying that looks like a pastiche of sayings paralleled in Matthew 5:44 (Luke 6:27-28) and Mark 9:40 (Luke 9:50).

The Egerton Manuscript

The portion of an "unknown gospel" that has received the most attention from scholars, however, is P.Egerton 2 (Haelst, 586); there is also a bit more of this writing preserved.[42] For both of these reasons, I shall give somewhat more extended attention to this fragmentary text. First published in 1935 were portions of three leaves of a papyrus codex initially dated to the middle of the second century. But more recently the discovery of an additional fragment of the same manuscript containing about five more lines of the text has led paleographical opinion to move the probable date to around 200 or perhaps a bit later.[43] This

---

that it was written to serve as an amulet: "P.Oxy. 840: Amulet or Miniature Codex?" *JTS* 53 (2002): 81-94.

41. This appears to be a small portion of a scroll, not a codex, which is very interesting in view of the overwhelming preference for the codex in early Christian circles, especially for writings treated as Scripture. Whatever the larger writing was from which this is a fragment, this copy at least was likely prepared for private use, and not for use in liturgical reading.

42. The major recent study is the unpublished Ph.D. thesis by Jon B. Daniels, "The Egerton Gospel: Its Place in Early Christianity" (Ph.D. diss., Claremont Graduate School, Claremont, Calif., 1989).

43. The Egerton fragments were initially published by H. Idris Bell and T. C. Skeat, *Fragments of an Unknown Gospel and Other Early Christian Papyri* (London: British Museum, 1935). The additional fragment, P.Köln 255, was published by Michael Gronewald, "Unbekanntes Evangelium oder Evangelienharmonie (Fragment aus dem 'Evangelium Egerton')," in *Kölner Papyri (P.Köln), Vol. VI* (Cologne: Rheinisch-Westfälischen Akademischer Wissenschaften unter Universität Köln, 1987), 136-45. This revised dating of the Egerton manuscript has not always been noted, even in some scholarly references that appeared well after the publication of the Köln fragment: e.g., Gamble, "Egerton Papyrus 2." Also, of course, a number of discussions

means that the composition of the writing, of which P.Egerton 2 gives us a fragmentary copy, can be placed any time prior to the end of the second century. To my mind, the conflated language (echoing phrasing from the Synoptic Gospels and John) and the contents (resembling scenes and motifs in the canonical accounts) make a composition sometime in the second century much more plausible than an earlier date.[44]

The extant lines contain portions of a controversy between Jesus and Jewish leaders (containing wording resembling passages in John, e.g., 5:39, 45-46; 9:29), the healing of a leper (lines echoing Mark 1:40-44/Matt. 8:2-4/Luke 5:12-14), another controversy scene about paying tribute tax (phrasing resembling John 3:2; 5:14; 10:25; Mark 12:13-17/Matt. 22:15-18/Luke 20:20-23; 6:46; Mark 7:6-7/Matt. 15:7-8), and a saying that leads into an apparent miracle story at the river Jordan for which we have no canonical parallel. As with the other fragmentary texts that I have referred to here, nothing in P.Egerton suggests a heterodox stance or an intention to compete with other accounts. Instead we have fragments of what appears to have been a narrative rendition of Jesus that was prepared for the edification of fellow believers by some now-unknown Christian of the second century, and likely someone of fairly proto-orthodox faith.

Gospel of Peter

A more extensive portion of another early Jesus book, the *Gospel of Peter,* is preserved in the "Akhmîm Fragment" (P.Cairensis 10,759; Haelst, 598). The text occupies part of a small parchment book of thirty-three leaves written in Greek

---

of the extracanonical gospels that are of relatively recent vintage but prior to the publication of the Köln fragment and the consequent later dating of the Egerton manuscript are now shown to be in need of revision: e.g., Crossan, *Four Other Gospels,* 72-75. It is now incorrect to say that Egerton must have been composed no later than the mid–second century.

44. Cf. Koester, *Ancient Christian Gospels,* 205-16; Cameron, *The Other Gospels,* 72-75. Koester's proposal (207) that the combination of Synoptic and Johannine language in the Egerton text may attest a period earlier than the canonical Gospels when "pre-Johannine and pre-synoptic characteristics of language still existed side by side" seems to me implausible. The conflated language and motifs in the Egerton text are more obviously accounted for under the influence of John and the Synoptics (*influence,* not necessarily direct literary dependence), and also reflect the harmonistic tendencies otherwise associated with the second century. The Markan "long ending" is only one example among others. With sincere appreciation for Koester's efforts to encourage serious attention to extracanonical gospels, I am bound to regard his analysis of the Egerton text as veering into special pleading. Cf. David F. Wright, "Apocryphal Gospels: The 'Unknown Gospel' (Pap. Egerton 2) and the *Gospel of Peter*," in *The Jesus Tradition Outside the Gospels,* ed. David Wenham (Sheffield: JSOT Press, 1985), 207-32, esp. 210-21.

and dated paleographically to sometime in the seventh to ninth centuries.[45] The extant fragments contain a narrative of Jesus' trial, execution, burial, resurrection, the discovery of his empty tomb by Mary Magdalene and other women disciples, and Peter's first-person account of his subsequent departure with Andrew and Levi "to the sea." Unfortunately the text breaks off abruptly here, though what probably ensued was an account of an appearance of the risen Jesus to the disciples by Lake Galilee. It is reasonable to assume that the complete *Gospel of Peter* originally comprised a full narrative of Jesus' ministry.

Although two fragments from circa 200+ have been identified more recently among the Oxyrhynchus material (P.Oxy. 2949), confirming that the *Gospel of Peter* was composed sometime before the close of the second century, they contain only eighteen very incomplete lines and scarcely add much to the extant text.[46] These earlier fragments do, however, differ textually from the readings of the Akhmîm manuscript, indicating that the text of the *Gospel of Peter* underwent changes (the full extent of which we cannot know) while being transmitted across the several centuries that separate the Akhmîmic and Oxyrhynchus fragments. This means that it is dangerous to make too much rest upon the details of the wording of the Akhmîmic text in theories about the *Gospel of Peter* in the second century.[47]

---

45. The book was discovered in the 1886-87 season of excavations of Christian graves near Akhmîm in Egypt, and it contains portions of the *Gospel of Peter, 1 Enoch*, and the *Apocalypse of Peter*. In addition, a single leaf of the Greek text of the *Acts of John* is pasted onto the inside back cover. See, e.g., H. B. Swete, *The Akhmîm Fragment of the Apocryphal Gospel of St. Peter* (London: Macmillan, 1893), for full description, analysis, transcription, and English translation. An updated introduction and translation is in *NTA*, 1:216-27. The essential work for scholarly study, however, is M. G. Mara, *Évangile de Pierre: Introduction, Text critique, traduction, commentaire et index*, SC 201 (Paris: Éditions du Cerf, 1973).

46. R. A. Coles in *The Oxyrhynchus Papyri, Vol. 41*, ed. G. M. Browne et al. (London: Egypt Exploration Society, 1972), 15-16; Dieter Lührmann, "POx 2949: EvPet 3-5 in einer Handschrift des 2/3 Jahrhunderts," *ZNW* 72 (1981): 216-26; and Lührmann, "Das neue Fragment des P Egerton 2 (P Köln 255)," in *The Four Gospels 1992: Festschrift for Frans Neirynck*, ed. F. Van Segbroeck, C. M. Tuckett, G. Van Belle, and J. Verheyden, 4 vols. (Leuven: Leuven University Press/Peeters, 1992), 3:2239-55. It bears noting that this fragment probably comes from a roll, not a codex (Haelst, 592). Still more recently, Lührmann has cautiously proposed the identification of another Oxyrhynchus fragment as possibly from *Gospel of Peter*: "POx4009: Ein neues Fragment des Petrusevangeliums?" *NovT* 35 (1993): 390-410; cf. Dieter Lührmann and P. J. Parsons, "P.Oxy. LX 4009," in *The Oxyrhynchus Papyri, Vol. 60*, ed. R. A. Coles et al. (London: Egypt Exploration Society for the British Academy, 1994), 1-5. This is a leaf of a codex, perhaps a miniature one. For review of the issues and these publications, see now S. R. Pickering, "Transmission of Gospel Materials in the Second Century: Evidence of a New Fragment from Oxyrhynchus," *New Testament Textual Research Update* 2 (1994): 105-10.

47. See the analysis of textual variants in Wright, "Apocryphal Gospels," 221-27.

A *Gospel of Peter* is mentioned in a number of early Christian sources, though no quotation is preserved in them.[48] The most important reference appears in Eusebius's *Ecclesiastical History* (6.12.2-6; composed and frequently revised ca. 300-320). Citing a writing by Serapion (bishop in Antioch, 199-211), Eusebius says that Serapion found that Christians in the little town of Rhossus (which was within his episcopal jurisdiction) enjoyed reading from a gospel that they attributed to Peter. After initially permitting them to continue using this writing, Serapion subsequently was alerted that it was being used to support unorthodox teaching. Thereupon he studied the text more carefully, and discovered that "most of it was in accordance with the true teaching of the Savior, but some things were added," which Serapion highlighted for correction.

Unfortunately, however, the only hint as to what bothered Serapion is the reference to the ideas of "docetics" being somehow involved in the church controversy. But as we noted earlier, in early Christian sources the terms "docetics" (or "docetists") and "docetism" are not uniform in what they connote. Moreover, Serapion does not actually say that the *Gospel of Peter* was itself heretical, only that some statements in it were being used to support ideas he considered to be tending toward heresy. As we shall see, scholars are increasingly questioning the earlier labeling of the *Gospel of Peter* as "docetic" and as representing some heretical point of view.

I underscore four features of this interesting document of early Christian faith. First, the extant material exhibits Greek phrasing with clear resemblances to the canonical Gospels, yet this text seems to be the author's own effort to write a narrative of the events.[49] In this there are obvious similarities to the

---

48. Origen, *Commentary on Matthew* 10.17, refers to some who thought the brothers of Jesus were from a prior marriage of Joseph (as in *PJ* 9.2) on the basis of a so-called *Gospel of Peter,* but Origen then says, "or the book of James," which makes ascertaining whether Origen actually was acquainted with our *Gospel of Peter* difficult. Eusebius (*HE* 3.3.2; 3.25.6) twice includes the *Gospel of Peter* among books not recognized as authoritative in the churches, but does not comment on its contents. The Decretum Gelasianum (sixth century) lists a gospel under the name of Peter among apocryphal writings (see *NTA*, 1:38).

49. See the detailed lists of distinctive material, and the material and phrasing shared with one or more of the canonical Gospels, in Swete, *Akmîm Fragment,* xiii-xx. Swete judges that the eighteen items not found in the canonical accounts nevertheless all "rest upon the basis of a story which is in the main identical with that of the canonical Gospels" (xv). Cf. Jürgen Denker, *Die theologiegeschichtliche Stellung des Petrusevangeliums,* Europäische Hochschulschriften 23/36 (Bern: Herbert Lang; Frankfurt: Peter Lange, 1975), 31-57. But Denker's judgment that the *Gospel of Peter* shows no knowledge of the canonical Gospels rests upon the arbitrary criterion that the text makes no direct citation of them (56-57), and he seems to have had a rather wooden view of how ancient authors could work. As Schneemelcher remarked about Denker's position, "the verbal agreements between the *GosPet* and the canonical Gospels are too numerous to allow us to uphold so sharp a rejection of their knowledge and use" (*NTA,* 1:219).

Egerton text, which I take as another example of a gospel-like writing that shows a creative combination of phrasing and traditions from (and inspired by) the canonical Gospels and the wider stock of material about Jesus that circulated then.[50] That is, the *Gospel of Peter* is properly regarded as composed in the second century, and as reflecting the avid interest of that period in numerous accounts of Jesus.[51]

Second, the narrative shows a strong anti-Jewish tone reflective of the sharp Jewish and Christian exchanges attested in other second-century writings.[52] Whereas the canonical Gospels present the Jewish religious authorities as complicit in Jesus' death, the *Gospel of Peter* makes them and the Jewish people entirely responsible; Pilate is pictured as merely responding to their demands at all points.[53] This shift of the entire responsibility for Jesus' execution to Jewish figures is more consistent with a second-century date of composition.

Third, a good deal of narrative color has been added, such as the earthquake when the Jews drew out the nails from the dead Jesus (6.21), the sealing of the tomb with "seven seals" (8.33), the visit of Jewish crowds to see the sealed tomb (9.34), and the dialogue of the women disciples on their way to the tomb

50. Cf. David F. Wright, "Papyrus Egerton 2 (the Unknown Gospel) — Part of the *Gospel of Peter?*" *SecCent* 5 (1985-86): 129-50, whose detailed comparison led him to suggest tentatively that the two manuscripts might be portions of the same composition.

51. I reiterate, however, that this originating composition was not exactly the same as the extant text in the Akhmîm fragment. I am not persuaded by Crossan's attempt to postulate a "cross gospel" source behind both the *Gospel of Peter* and the canonical accounts of Jesus' trial and execution. Cf. John Dominic Crossan, *The Cross That Spoke: The Origins of the Passion Narrative* (San Francisco: Harper and Row, 1988); Raymond E. Brown, "The *Gospel of Peter* and Canonical Gospel Priority," *NTS* 33 (1987): 321-43; Raymond E. Brown, "Appendix I: *The Gospel of Peter* — a Noncanonical Passion Narrative," in his *The Death of the Messiah. From Gethsemane to the Grave: A Commentary on the Passion Narratives in the Four Gospels,* 2 vols. (New York: Doubleday, 1994), 2:1317-49. But see now Crossan's latest contribution: "The *Gospel of Peter* and the Canonical Gospels," *Forum,* n.s., 1 (1998): 7-51.

52. On the anti-Jewish tone, see also Alan Kirk, "The Johannine Jesus in the *Gospel of Peter:* A Social Memory Approach," in *Jesus in Johannine Tradition,* ed. Robert T. Fortna and Tom Thatcher (Louisville, London, and Leiden: Westminster John Knox, 2001), 313-22; Kirk, "Examining Priorities: Another Look at the *Gospel of Peter's* Relationship to the New Testament Gospels," *NTS* 40 (1994): 572-95. The increasingly negative treatment of Jews in second-century Christianity and thereafter is classically described by Marcel Simon, *Verus Israel* (Paris: Editions E. de Boccard, 1964; ET, Oxford: Oxford University Press, 1986; reprint, London: Littman Library of Jewish Civilization, 1996). See now Stephen G. Wilson, *Related Strangers: Jews and Christians, 70-170 C.E.* (Minneapolis: Fortress, 1995).

53. E.g., Herod orders Jesus' crucifixion (1.1) and delivers Jesus to "the people" (*tō laō,* 2.5), who carry out Jesus' execution, bringing upon their heads "the full measure of their sins" (5.17), and then, after drawing out the nails from Jesus' dead body (6.21), they first rejoice (6.23) but then lament their killing him (7.25).

(12.52-54). However, the greatest narrative expansion is in the account of Jesus'
resurrection (9.35–11.45), which includes the opening of the heavens, the descent
of two bright, towering angelic figures, who accompany the still more glorious
and towering Jesus from the tomb, followed by a cross, a voice from heaven and
an answering voice from the cross, and then another opening of the heavens and
the descent of a third heavenly figure, who enters the tomb (later to be encountered by the women disciples). Clearly the author sought to provide readers with
a dramatic, and even spectacular, account. He had precedent for the more won-
drous events in the canonical traditions of the rending of the temple veil at Jesus'
death (Mark 15:38) and of the accompanying earthquake and appearance of
many dead people in Jerusalem (Matt. 27:52-54). But the *Gospel of Peter* carries
this dramatic interest still further. Indeed, the "filling in" of narrative color and
dramatic detail seems best understood as both encouraged by the canonical narratives of Jesus' death and resurrection and also as intentional expansion of their
comparatively more restrained accounts of these momentous events.

Finally, and the most important point for our analysis here, Jesus is presented consistently in a very elevated status. He is always referred to as "the
Lord" (never as "Jesus"), and the author also affirms him to be "the Son of
God" and "King of Israel." A "young man" from heaven in angelic attire at the
empty tomb proclaims Jesus' resurrection and ascent "back to from where he
was sent," which probably alludes to a belief in Jesus' preexistence and descent
to human existence.

Although some earlier scholars tended to attribute the *Gospel of Peter* to
"docetists," more recent studies have persuasively shown this to be inaccurate.[54]
For example, Peter Head has shown that the *Gospel of Peter* "cannot simply be
labelled gnostic or docetic," and that features previously thought to support either characterization are better regarded simply as "indicative of the popular
nature of the document."[55]

The statement that as he was crucified Jesus "held his peace, as if he felt
no pain" (4.9-10), often taken previously as the chief indication of a docetic
stance, is correctly seen simply as portraying Jesus acting nobly and coura-
geously in his sufferings.[56] As both Head and Denker conclude, the form of Je-

---

54. Among important studies of the Christology of the writing, cf. Denker, esp. 93-125
(the Christology of the *Gospel of Peter* is not docetic but could have encouraged docetic views,
esp. 113); J. W. McCant, "The *Gospel of Peter*: Docetism Reconsidered," *NTS* 30 (1984): 258-73
(who challenged the earlier widespread view); and now P. M. Head, "On the Christology of the
Gospel of Peter," *VC* 46 (1992): 209-24 (who also strongly denies any docetic intent). A concur-
ring judgment is given in *NTA*, 1:220-21.

55. Head, "Gospel of Peter," 218.

56. Head ("Gospel of Peter," 212) refers to this statement as "for many scholars the linch-

sus' dying cry on the cross, "O my Power, O Power [*hē dynamis mou, hē dynamis*], you have abandoned me" (5.19), is best taken as a reverential form of prayer, the word "power" attested in other texts as a circumlocution for God.[57] The reference to drawing nails from Jesus' body (6.21), and the burial of his body and the subsequently empty tomb (6.23-24; 13.56), certainly seem to reflect a realistic enough view of Jesus' death. That is, the religious stance of the *Gospel of Peter* fits plausibly within the circles that were part of emergent "orthodox/catholic" Christianity.

In his detailed study of the Christology of the writing, Jürgen Denker rightly notes that Jesus' resurrection receives the most space in the extant fragment; he shows that this material is particularly redolent of ideas that are also reflected in other Christian texts of the first two centuries. For example, the description of the descent of two mighty angels who accompany Jesus from the tomb, and a third angel who remains in the tomb to announce his resurrection to the women, looks like a more elaborate and colorful version of the scene in Matthew 28:2-10, itself a more vivid account than the rather austere and brief lines of Mark 16:1-8. As Denker observes, the query of the heavenly voice as to whether Jesus has "preached to them that sleep" and the positive reply "from the cross" in *Gospel of Peter* 10.41-42 reflect a tradition that in death Jesus had preached to the righteous dead, the Old Testament worthies, who are thereby incorporated into the elect with Christian believers.[58] Although the picture of the cross following Jesus out of the tomb will perhaps seem surreal or even humorous to modern readers, Denker rightly characterizes the scene as conveying the early Christian view of the cross of Jesus as "the sign of the power of the risen Lord."[59]

In short, nothing in the extant text of the *Gospel of Peter* indicates a connection with any heretical ideas or groups. Instead, it too was probably written originally by and for second-century believers in some circle that formed part of emergent "proto-orthodox" Christianity. They were, however, also believers with a taste for dramatic narrative, an anti-Jewish attitude (unfortunately, all too familiar for the time), and fairly unsophisticated but sincere views of Jesus'

---

pin for a theory of GP's docetism," but the Greek phrase (*autos de esiōpa hōs mēdena ponon echōn*, 4.10) does not in fact assert that Jesus suffered no pain, only that he did not show pain. Head (221 n. 20) points to similar statements in other early Christian writings that cannot be labeled "docetic," e.g., Origen, *Commentary on Matthew* 125 (on Matt. 27:27-29); Dionysius, *Commentary on Luke* 22.42-44.

57. Head, 214; Denker, 119. Other examples of "power" as a circumlocution for God include Matt. 26:64/Mark 14:62.

58. See Denker, 93-94, for discussion and references to the idea in other early Christian sources, among which 1 Pet. 3:18-20 may be our earliest reference.

59. Denker, 99.

transcendent nature. In fact, although the writing never seems to have won wide approval for public reading in the churches, we should regard the *Gospel of Peter* as a very valuable fragment of this "popular"-level Christianity.[60]

Infancy Gospels

Other books about Jesus also reflect similar popular-level religious tastes among early Christians, in particular the so-called Infancy Gospels. Essentially, these writings presuppose the canonical nativity accounts, and they seek to fill in the narrative spaces and resolve questions left by the comparatively sparser canonical references to Jesus' birth and childhood. Of these, the two that are widely thought today to be the earliest are the *Protevangelium of James* and the *Infancy Gospel of Thomas*.[61] These two are also the most influential, or at least the most representative of religious tastes and ideas that were widely shared at the time of their composition and in the following centuries.[62] Scholars do not agree on the date for either work, but most today lean toward sometime in the latter half of the second century. Each work presents us with a bundle of complicated issues which I cannot deal with here.[63] Instead, once again I focus on what they may add to our grasp of second-century interest in Jesus.

Protevangelium of James

Although both writings reflect an obvious early Christian interest in stories about Jesus and his family, and an appreciation of the marvelous and novelistic,

60. Kathleen E. Corley, "Women and the Crucifixion and Burial of Jesus," *Forum,* n.s., 1 (1998): 181-225, includes an analysis of the *Gospel of Peter,* concluding that it "should be considered a late novelistic account of the crucifixion and the empty tomb" (211).

61. *NTA,* 1:414-51, introduces the genre and provides an English translation of these two writings. More recently Ronald F. Hock, *The Infancy Gospels of James and Thomas,* Scholars Bible 2 (Santa Rosa, Calif.: Polebridge Press, 1995), gives full introductions, and a Greek text and annotated English translation of both, with copious bibliographical references as well. I cite these writings according to Hock's chapter and verse numbering scheme.

62. For example, as Quasten noted (*Patrology,* 1:121-22), although the *Protevangelium of James* was listed as heretical in the Decretum Gelasianum (perhaps sixth century), its influence upon Christian devotional practice, literature, and art "cannot be overestimated."

63. For example, both writings were obviously subject to considerable changes during their textual transmission, and it is difficult to obtain a consensus on what the earliest text of either might have included. Furthermore, even their original titles are disputed. I shall simply refer to them here as they are most commonly designated in scholarly studies today.

they are also very different from each other in contents and literary character. The bulk of the *Protevangelium of James* (hereafter *PJ*) actually concerns Jesus' mother, Mary, emphasizing her virginity. Indeed, the writing asserts her life-long virginity, even after her marriage to Joseph, who is portrayed as an elderly widower with no desire for sexual relations with her, and who marries her to protect her from the interests of other men. The "brothers" of Jesus mentioned in the New Testament are explained as Joseph's (grown) children from his first marriage. In fact, the title of the work in the earliest complete copy, the third- or fourth-century Bodmer V manuscript, reflects this focus on Mary: "Birth of Mary, Revelation of James."[64] Even in the account of Jesus' birth (in a cave en route to Bethlehem), the emphasis is on Mary miraculously remaining physically an intact virgin in spite of having given birth (*PJ* 19.18-19).

We see both the influence of the canonical nativity stories and the creativity of subsequent Christian piety in the account of Mary's miraculous birth to elderly and childless parents (Joachim and Anna). Resembling the Lukan account of the annunciation to Mary, there is a scene where Anna learns from an angel that she is to conceive and give birth to a child who "will be talked about in all the world" (*PJ* 4.1). After Mary's birth, her mother makes Mary's bedroom a sanctuary, and sees that she maintains a state of constant ritual purity.

At three years of age Mary goes to live in the Jerusalem temple, where she is fed daily by an angel. When she turns twelve (and so will commence menstruating), the priests become concerned that she should not remain in the temple precincts, and the elderly Joseph is miraculously designated the widower to be given charge to care for her (and maintain her virginal status). Indicative of this celibate status, she is included among seven virgins from the tribe of David chosen to weave a veil for the temple. While performing this task, she is herself confronted by the angel who announces that she will conceive "by means of [God's] word" the holy child who will be called "son of the Most High" (*PJ* 11.7).

As Hock has shown, *PJ* shows impressive literary creativity, with numerous explanatory and amplifying links to the canonical accounts.[65] *PJ* also draws heavily upon the Greek Old Testament in phrasing, in information about ancient Jewish life, and in narrative inspiration for a number of scenes and

---

64. The title *Protevangelium of James* was first applied to the work in the 1552 Latin translation by Guillaume Postel, prior to which the writing had been little known in the West for several centuries. On P.Bodmer V, see Haelst, 212-13, and for review of the manuscripts, Hock, 28-30. The James to whom this pseudonymous work is attributed is the figure referred to in the New Testament as one of Jesus' brothers.

65. The expanded account of the visit of the Magi and Herod's slaughter of infants in *PJ* 21–24 is a prime example.

themes (for example, readers are to see echoes of biblical stories of Abraham and Sarah in the account of the aged and childless parents of Mary). There are also numerous influences from New Testament writings and the wider literary environment of the Greco-Roman era.[66] In short, the author/editor was skilled in Greek composition and in the literary conventions of the time.[67]

The focus on Mary might at first make one question how this writing contributes to our understanding of devotion to Jesus. But the particular way she was honored indicates Christian values of the time of the composition and first circulation of the writing. In particular, the emphasis on Mary's continuing virginity clearly reflects the growing valorization of sexual renunciation in the late second century and thereafter.[68] Honoring Mary must have seemed to those who produced the writing an appropriate religious extension of, and inference from, their belief that Jesus was virginally conceived through the power of God, and that he is uniquely the Son of God (a belief clearly stated in the text). That is, *PJ* in fact presupposes a rather traditional early Christian faith stance, and the religious logic behind the writing likely was that Jesus' special status properly requires that the woman who miraculously bore him be thought of as having a special origin and significance as well. It was obviously a religious logic that many Christians then and subsequently found attractive.[69]

Infancy Gospel of Thomas

The writing nowadays most commonly referred to as the *Infancy Gospel of Thomas* (hereafter *IGos. Thom.*) is very different in content and literary character.[70] It is a collection of stories about the boyhood of Jesus set at five, six, eight, nine, and twelve years of age (21.1; 11.1; 12.4; 18.1; 19.1), with no overall narrative

---

66. Hock, 15-27.

67. I sidestep here questions about whether the work as we have it combines earlier sources. In any case, in all its portions it reflects an author or editor(s) with a certain literary ability.

68. See, e.g., Margaret A. Shatkin, "Virgins," in *EEC*, 2:1165-67; Peter Brown, *The Body and Society: Men, Women, and Sexual Renunciation in Early Christianity* (New York: Columbia University Press, 1988).

69. E.g., Eugene LaVerdiere, "Mary," in *EEC*, 2:733-36 (with bibliography of further references).

70. This writing too has borne a variety of titles, and the original title may have been "Boyhood Deeds [*Paidika*] of our Lord Jesus Christ." See Hock's review, 84-85. The title dominant today is intended to distinguish this writing from the Nag Hammadi text known as the *Gospel of Thomas*, which I discuss in the next section of this chapter.

thread or plot to the collection.[71] Scholars do not agree on the date of composition, with estimates ranging from the late second century to the sixth century; in fact, the complicated textual transmission of *IGos. Thom.* may make the idea of a single composition implausible. Instead, *IGos. Thom.* may more likely be the product of a continuing and very fluid agglutination of such material about the divine boy Jesus. But at least some of the material goes back to the second century, particularly the stories in 6.19-20, 14.3, where the child Jesus confounds a Jewish teacher over the mystical meaning of the letters of the alphabet. There are references to such a story in Irenaeus (*Adv. haer.* 1.13.1), and in the second-century writing called the *Epistula Apostolorum* (4).[72]

To put the most positive spin on it, the basic point in all the stories in *IGos. Thom.* is to show the child Jesus exercising miraculous power. Some incidents have a certain charming note, such as the story of Jesus miraculously lengthening a beam of wood for Joseph (13.1-4) or healing the foot of a young man who injured it while splitting wood (10.1-4). But several others are likely to cause modern readers to see what Hock describes as "a vindictive, arrogant, unruly child."[73] For example, at five years of age, when playing with other children on a Sabbath at making pools of water and molding clay birds, Jesus commands muddy water to become clear. But when Joseph reprimands him in response to someone complaining that he violated the Sabbath in his play, he impishly shows off by commanding the clay birds to come alive and fly away (2.1-7).[74] Still more disturbing are the incidents where, when slighted by other children, Jesus causes them to wither and die (3.1-4; 4.1-4), and he curses with blindness those who complain about him (5.1-2). In the extended story of a Jewish teacher instructing him (6.1–8.4), Jesus repeatedly and insolently humiliates him, haughtily proclaiming his own superior knowledge.

At several points the child Jesus openly declares his transcendent status and heavenly origins (6.5-7, 10; 8.2); several other times others wonder at him and pose the likelihood that he is no ordinary mortal but instead a divine child (7.4-5, 11; 17.4; 18.3). This is clearly the main premise and point of the compilation. In one sense, of course, this is a version of the familiar Christian belief that

---

71. Again, I cite *IGos. Thom.* according to the chapter and verse scheme in Hock, *The Infancy Gospels of James and Thomas.* See also Stephen Gero, "The *Infancy Gospel of Thomas:* A Study of the Textual and Literary Problems," *NovT* 13 (1971): 46-80.

72. Irenaeus links the story to a heretical group he calls "Marcosians." Gero ("*Infancy Gospel,*" 56 n. 1) contends that these references are not sufficient to date *IGos. Thom* in the second century, but Hock disagrees (92 n. 35). Cf. also Koester, *Ancient Christian Gospels,* 312.

73. Hock, 86.

74. The popularity and wide circulation of this story is indicated by the approving allusion to it in the Quran (5:110).

Jesus is divine. But in comparison to some other expressions of early Christian belief, *IGos. Thom.* represents a very naive or crude version (albeit quite frequent throughout Christian history) in which Jesus' divine status is taken to have meant that from his infancy he exercised miraculous powers and was fully self-conscious of his transcendent nature and origins. That is, in *IGos. Thom.* what appears to be a young boy is actually a divine being in thin disguise.

I think we must assume that *IGos. Thom.* represents a sincere (but very unsophisticated) religious inference that, as the Son of God from his birth onward, Jesus should (or can) be portrayed as already manifesting his divine powers, which include his knowledge of all that Christian faith came to claim about his transcendent status and origins. Of course, this also involves portraying him as not really subject to normal human limitations or development. But once again, we should probably hesitate to use the term "docetic," because, as noted earlier in probing Johannine Christianity, the term can refer to a spectrum of beliefs, and also because the religious inferences and impulses reflected in *IGos. Thom.* were probably not confined to identifiably heterodox circles of Christians. A good many Christians in the second century and thereafter (perhaps particularly those less sophisticated in their theology) may have found little in *IGos. Thom.* to which to object; they may, instead, have found its tales simply reflective of their religious sentiments.

But these religious sentiments were not only the simple reverence of Jesus as divine that issued in stories of him as a wonder-working child. There is also a more negative tone to a number of the stories that indicates a strongly anti-Jewish attitude. The intended readers were apparently expected to enjoy the boy Jesus' ridicule of Jewish teachers, his disdain for those (Jews) who fail to see who he really is, and even his vindictive and harmful actions against other (Jewish) children. In this there is a certain resemblance to the strongly anti-Jewish tone of other second-century writings such as the *Gospel of Peter,* which we noted earlier. In a time when some Christian leaders had moved beyond condemning Jewish unbelief in the gospel message, and were fully and permanently "disinheriting the Jews" (e.g., the *Epistle of Barnabas*), it should not be difficult to imagine that at least some Christians found the anti-Jewish strain in *IGos. Thom.* to their liking, and fully compatible with what they regarded as reverence for Jesus.[75]

---

75. The quoted phrase alludes to Jeffrey S. Siker, *Disinheriting the Jews: Abraham in Early Christian Controversy* (Louisville: John Knox, 1991).

Gospel of Thomas

Of all the forty-five distinguishable titles included in the cache of codices from the fourth century that were found at the Egyptian site of Nag Hammadi in 1945, the *Gospel of Thomas* (hereafter *Gos. Thom.*) has received the greatest scholarly interest (and the greatest popular notice as well). There are now several hundred books and articles devoted to the many questions provoked by this fascinating text.[76] But in spite of the impressive scholarly effort expended in the several decades since its discovery, the answers to many of these important questions remain under dispute.[77] I want to focus on what this writing contributes to our understanding of how Jesus was interpreted in Christian circles of the first two centuries, and on where we can place this sort of writing in the development of earliest Christianity.[78] Because of the importance appropriately attached to *Gos. Thom.* in scholarly discussion, my discussion of it will be more extensive than for the other extracanonical writings dealt with in this chapter.

One of the reasons *Gos. Thom.* is such an important text is that, unlike most of the other extracanonical books about Jesus that we have noted, it defi-

76. Surveys of this sea of scholarly literature are given by Francis T. Fallon and Ron Cameron, "The *Gospel of Thomas*: A *Forschungsbericht* and Analysis," in *ANRW*, 2.25/6 (1988): 4195-4251, who counted over 600 publications by 1985; and Gregory J. Riley, "The *Gospel of Thomas* in Recent Scholarship," *CRBS* 2 (1994): 227-52, who referred to a "greatly increased" number between 1985 and his survey. The thirteen Nag Hammadi codices contained fifty-two tractates, but there were two or more copies of a few, and the number of distinct titles is forty-five. On the find, see, e.g., James M. Robinson, introduction to *NHLE*, 1-26. Brief introductions and English translations of all forty-five writings appear in the same volume. For description of the contents and physical features of Codex II of the Nag Hammadi cache (which includes several other writings in addition to *Thomas*), see the introduction (by Bentley Layton, 1-18) and "The Binding of Codex II" (by Linda K. Ogden, 19-25) in Bentley Layton, ed., *Nag Hammadi Codex II.2-7, Together with XIII, 2*, British Library Or. 4926(1), and P.Oxy. 1, 654, 655: With Contributions by Many Scholars, Volume One*, NHS 20 (Leiden: Brill, 1989). This volume also contains the standard critical edition of the Coptic with English translation, and an appendix (by Harold Attridge) giving a new critical edition of the Oxyrhynchus Greek fragments.

77. And it is misleading when scholars have occasionally announced a "consensus" on such things as the date of the originating compilation or the relationship of *Gos. Thom.* to the canonical Gospels. There are clusters of opinion, and it is understandably tempting to ignore or disregard those who disagree with one's confidently held views. But scholarship ought not be a mere contest or game, and issues are not settled by the equivalent of shouting louder than others, or by simply ignoring those whose views are inconvenient.

78. Majella Franzmann, *Jesus in the Nag Hammadi Writings* (Edinburgh: T. & T. Clark, 1996), gives a valuable description and classification of references to Jesus in this body of fourth-century texts. Her study is more relevant for studies of the diversity and/or coherence with one another of the views espoused in the various Nag Hammadi texts as a collection of writings; she does not distinguish between earlier and later stages of the beliefs she catalogues.

nitely represents a very different, indeed a dissonant, portrait of Jesus. The religious stance it advocates is deliberately set over against the more familiar expressions of devotion to Jesus in the writings that became part of the New Testament and those extracanonical writings that reflect emergent "proto-orthodox" faith.

The early-third-century Greek fragments of three different copies of *Gos. Thom.* from Oxyrhynchus, identified as such after the Coptic text was discovered, show that *Gos. Thom.* goes back much earlier than the fourth-century Nag Hammadi manuscripts, at least as far back as the latter part of the second century.[79] On the other hand, these Greek fragments also show that the text was neither fixed, nor even very stable, in wording, arrangement, and perhaps also contents, in the period between the Oxyrhynchus and Nag Hammadi manuscripts.[80] It also seems wise, therefore, to allow for a similar fluidity between the earliest Greek fragments and whenever the compilation that we know as *Gos. Thom.* first appeared.

In fact, it may be inappropriate to think of a single act of composition. The *Gos. Thom.* that we see in the Nag Hammadi manuscript may be the product of multiple redactions, or perhaps even a process of agglutination like a rolling snowball. Indeed, the three Oxyrhynchus fragments could represent two or three different redactions of *Gos. Thom.* circulating at the same approximate period.[81] Although there was likely a single originating composition, it is difficult to be sure of what it comprised.[82]

---

79. These Greek fragments are P.Oxy. 1, 654, and 655 (i.e., fragments of three different manuscripts), which were among the first papyri from Oxyrhynchus to be published (in 1897 and 1904). See now Harold W. Attridge, "The Greek Fragments," in Layton, *Nag Hammadi Codex II.2-7*, 95-128, which includes a full bibliography of earlier publications.

80. Attridge ("The Greek Fragments") characterizes the differences as "substantial" (99), and he concludes that they are due to various causes such as loose translation from Greek to Coptic, copying mistakes (in Greek and/or Coptic), and also deliberate changes such as omission or expansion, and other variations that may reflect "deliberate editorial alteration" (101). The earlier study by J. A. Fitzmyer remains valuable, "The Oxyrhynchus Logoi of Jesus and the Coptic Gospel according to Thomas," in *Essays on the Semitic Background of the New Testament* (Missoula: Scholars, 1974), 355-433.

81. The content of the Greek fragments does not overlap, so we cannot know how they may have differed. See now April DeConick, "The Original *Gospel of Thomas*," *VC* 56 (2002): 167-99.

82. Given this situation, we should hesitate to use Coptic *Gos. Thom.* simplistically, as if it were a second- (or first!)-century text. It most definitely is not. I submit the following methodological principles. (1) Nag Hammadi *Gos. Thom.* is *direct* evidence *only* of the transmission and translation of *Gos. Thom.* in Coptic-speaking circles of the late third or fourth century. (2) The *direct* evidence about what *Gos. Thom.* may have been and contained in the second century is the contents of the extant Greek fragments, which, so far as possible, must be the prime focus of exegesis. (3) Where the extant Greek fragments do not have a parallel saying, we may invoke a

Whenever the originating compilation first appeared, however, the extant
Gos. Thom. (the Coptic version and the earlier Greek fragments) represents the
transmission of an early and very important Christian text. It is a very different
kind of Jesus book from the canonical Gospels and the extracanonical ones that
we have noted already. Allow me to make some further observations particularly relevant for this discussion.

A Jesus Book

It is important to note that, with the exception of the incipit (opening sentence,
and perhaps also saying 1), to which I give further attention shortly, *Gos. Thom.*
is essentially a compilation of 114 sayings (Gk. *logia*) attributed to Jesus. Some
are set in very short and simple dialogue scenes involving Jesus' disciples, sometimes named and sometimes referred to as a group. All of the teaching, however, is put in the mouth of Jesus, and he is the authoritative figure, the only reliable voice.[83]

Clearly, therefore, as is the case for the canonical and other extracanonical
writings that we have considered, *Gos. Thom.* is a "Jesus book" and not merely a
"wisdom" text such as the Old Testament book of Proverbs or the rabbinic tractate *Pirke Aboth.* It is not a collection of "sayings of the wise," but a compilation
of *Jesus'* sayings; he is not one of a line or group of teachers, but the only teacher
recognized in the compilation.[84] Moreover, these sayings claim to encode truth

---

saying in Coptic *Gos. Thom.* with caution, and insofar as the Greek fragments preserve other
relevant sayings testifying to the same theme, vocabulary, and emphases, which would suggest
that there might originally have been a saying in the Greek transmission stage(s) equivalent to
that found in Coptic *Gos. Thom.* But even so, we must always take account of the evidence of
any tendencies evident in the transmission process that might have altered a saying in comparison to its form in the Greek. Cf. Philip Sellew, "The *Gospel of Thomas:* Prospects for Future Research," in *The Nag Hammadi Library after Fifty Years: Proceedings of the 1995 Society of Biblical
Literature Commemoration,* ed. John D. Turner and Anne McGuire, NHMS 44 (Leiden: Brill,
1997), 327-46, who favors focusing on Coptic *Gos. Thom.* "for literary purposes" (337). Whatever
that might mean, I am concerned here with historical issues of how to use *Gos. Thom.* to further
our knowledge of second-century views of Jesus.

83. Valantasis is correct to note that *Gos. Thom.* also designates Judas Thomas as Jesus'
spiritual twin and thus as the special "lens through which the sayings of the living Jesus are
viewed," and that this involves an interesting "pattern of authority" involving Jesus and Thomas
as the guiding interpreter (*The Gospel of Thomas* [London: Routledge, 1997], 31-32). But of
course, in this pattern the Thomistic Jesus holds the primacy, for *Gos. Thom.* claims to represent
the sayings of *Jesus.*

84. Therefore, the formal association of *Thomas* and Q with these wisdom texts has to be
qualified. Cf. James M. Robinson, "LOGOI SOPHON: On the Gattung of Q," in *Trajectories*

of ultimate value. Their cryptic meaning promises (and discovery of their meaning conveys) a profound awakening to one's own true being and transcendent significance. What is on offer is not simply a way of life intended to bring success and tranquillity (unlike ancient philosophical traditions), or even to manifest righteousness and the fulfillment of God's will (unlike Jewish Wisdom tradition). Instead, *Gos. Thom.* touts conscious participation in life of a wholly different plane.

Literary Character

My second point is that, unlike most examples of Wisdom books, and unlike Q as well, the sayings of *Gos. Thom.* have no readily discernible thematic organization.[85] This is a particularly curious feature of the writing, and perhaps more significant than commonly recognized. It certainly limits considerably any generic link between *Gos. Thom.* and Q, and also raises a serious question about what kind of historical connection ("trajectory") there could be between the two.[86] A sayings collection overtly organized thematically with a structure that also reflects an inchoate narrative (or narrative substructure), such as Q seems to have been, is hardly in quite the same genre as a compilation that, whether by design or default, is lacking in observable structure.[87]

---

through Early Christianity, by James M. Robinson and Helmut Koester (Philadelphia: Fortress, 1971), 71-113.

85. Stevan L. Davies (*The "Gospel of Thomas" and Christian Wisdom* [New York: Seabury Press, 1983], 149-55) proposed that *Thomas* has a thematic structure of four "chapters" (*Logia* 2-37, 38-58, 59-91, and 92-113, with *Logion* 1 as part of the incipit and 114 as the conclusion to the compilation), in each of which there are recurring themes. But he also granted that none of these "chapters" preserves intact the supposedly original thematic structure, attributing this to the effects of the transmission of *Gos. Thom.* Assuming that "whoever put the document together must surely have done it in what he or she thought a proper and rational order," Davies nevertheless granted that it was hard to see any such order; he looked "forward to the time when someone unambiguously uncovers the secret to Thomas' order or, indeed, to the time when we can conclude that the sayings are essentially random, for that seemingly discouraging result would in fact be a negative conclusion of considerable interest and significance" (155).

86. See similar observations earlier by Bertil Gärtner, *The Theology of the Gospel according to Thomas* (London: Collins; New York: Harper and Brothers, 1961), 30-32. Cf. James M. Robinson, "On Bridging the Gulf from Q to the *Gospel of Thomas* (or Vice Versa)," in *Nag Hammadi Gnosticism and Early Christianity,* ed. Charles W. Hedrick and Robert Hodgen, Jr. (Peabody, Mass.: Hendrickson, 1986), 127-75. In a recent analysis of the matter, Sellew stated, "In the long run, however, *Thomas* comes off rather poorly, or at least ends up at the far end of the spectrum, when Robinson's comparison with . . . Q is driven home" ("The *Gospel of Thomas,*" 329).

87. Cf. Stephen J. Patterson, "The *Gospel of Thomas* and the Synoptic Tradition: A For-

Yet Koester is correct to insist that Coptic *Gos. Thom.* is not a simply random compilation of whatever was to hand when its contents were put together, and then, probably in several stages across a century or more, subsequently when additions were made.[88] Scholars have noted small clusters of sayings in *Gos. Thom.* that are connected loosely by topic, or in some cases only by catchwords.[89] Moreover, and more importantly, there are recurring religious ideas that amount to thematic emphases which have apparently guided the selection of material.[90] *Gos. Thom.* is eclectic, but certainly not without purpose or emphases.[91] It is the product of the *selection* of sayings and also the *shaping* of these sayings individually, both processes guided by the religious concerns of the compilers at each point in what was apparently a rolling sequence of editions.

However, some effort is required to discern these religious concerns

---

schungsbericht and Critique," *Forum* 8 (1992): 45-97 (esp. 81-82). Patterson acknowledges some differences between *Gos. Thom.* and Q, but claims that *Gos. Thom.* represents "a mediating link" between Q and the revelation-dialogue books such as *Thomas the Contender* (82). But the fact that *Gos. Thom.* is not as different from Q as is *Thomas the Contender* is hardly a basis for positing a line of development connecting all three, as if *Thomas the Contender* evolved from Q via *Gos. Thom.* Red-haired people did not evolve from brown-haired people, with reddish-brown-haired people serving as mediating links!

88. Helmut Koester, "Introduction," in Layton, *Nag Hammadi Codex II.2-7*, 40 (38-49). Also Bentley Layton, *The Gnostic Scriptures* (Garden City, N.Y.: Doubleday, 1987), 377, stresses that *Gos. Thom.* is "by no means a well-distributed sample" of the various types of sayings attributed to Jesus in the early tradition, but instead "concentrates on particular types that are appropriate to its message of salvation," especially sayings that "emphasize the presence of god's [*sic*] reign ('kingdom') within Jesus and each believer."

89. Allen Callahan, "'No Rhyme or Reason': The Hidden Logia of the *Gospel of Thomas*," *HTR* 90 (1997): 411-26. But the fact that these catchword connections depend upon the Coptic means that, unless the material survives in the Greek fragments, we should not assume that these clusters go back earlier than the redaction(s) translation reflected in the Nag Hammadi Coptic *Gos. Thom.* I cannot comment here on the very recent claims by Nicholas Perrin, *Thomas and Tatian: The Relationship between the Gospel of Thomas and the Diatessaron* (Atlanta: Society of Biblical Literature, 2002), other than to say that I do not find his claims persuasive.

90. For concise characterizations of the themes of *Gos. Thom.*, see, e.g., Gärtner, 71; Koester, "Introduction," 43-44. Cf. Stevan Davies, "The Christology and Protology of the *Gospel of Thomas*," *JBL* 111 (1992): 663-82, who tries (with very limited success, in my judgment) to represent *Gos. Thom.* as "a text of christianized Hellenistic Judaism" (682).

91. *Thomas* continues to acquire a growing body of commentaries and thematic studies, among which the following are particularly useful: Gärtner, *The Theology of the Gospel according to Thomas*; Davies, *The "Gospel of Thomas" and Christian Wisdom*; Jacques Menard, *L'Évangile selon Thomas*, NHS 5 (Leiden: Brill, 1975); Michael Fieger, *Das Thomasevangelium: Einleitung, Kommentar, und Systematik*, NTAbh 22 (Münster: Aschendorff Verlag, 1991); Stephen J. Patterson, *The "Gospel of Thomas" and Jesus* (Sonoma, Calif.: Polebridge Press, 1993); Valantasis, *The Gospel of Thomas*; and Risto Uro, ed., *Thomas at the Crossroads: Essays on the "Gospel of Thomas"* (Edinburgh: T. & T. Clark, 1998).

clearly. For another crucially important literary feature of *Gos. Thom.* is that it is an *esoteric* compilation, with the sayings deliberately cast in cryptic form. This amounts to another important distinction from the genre of Wisdom collections and sayings collections in general, and from Q in particular.[92] The crucial opening words, which are almost certainly to be taken as the earlier and actual title of the compilation, proclaim that what follow are "the secret sayings [Gk. *houtoi hoi logoi hoi apokryphoi*] which the living Jesus [*Iēsous ho zōn*] spoke."[93] The word translated "secret" (or "hidden/cryptic") sounds at the outset the esoteric note.[94] Thereafter the first two sayings (1-2) summon readers to persistent effort to perceive the true meaning of the sayings that follow; the text promises immortality exclusively to whoever can succeed in this.

But *Gos. Thom.* 2 captures more specifically the challenge to rational reflection that is intended in the riddling form of the sayings throughout the compilation. It advocates a quest for meaning that will disturb and astonish the seeker, and promises dominion "over the all" to the one who perseveres to enlightenment. That is, the reader is offered reorientation by way of profound disorientation. These opening lines indicate that the sayings that follow in *Gos. Thom.* "do not speak plainly, or directly, but in a hidden way, a mysterious way about things that are at once obvious and riddling. These secret sayings of the living Jesus, then, present difficult and perplexing material to a select group of people."[95]

I suggest that this riddling intent may in fact also explain why there is no discernible thematic or logical structure to *Gos. Thom.* (beyond the opening lines, which operate to set the tone for the compilation). Given the standpoint

---

92. The same point was made earlier by Jean-Marie Sevrin, "L'interprétation de l'*Évangile selon Thomas*, entre tradition et rédaction," in *The Nag Hammadi Library after Fifty Years*, 347-60 (esp. 349-52).

93. It is commonly thought that the colophon at the end of the Coptic text of *Gos. Thom.*, "the Gospel according to Thomas," was added at some point in the transmission of the work. This colophon must reflect the success of the term "gospel" as the label of a new literary genre, and so probably dates from the late second century or later.

94. Wherever possible, I cite the Greek phrasing, as representing a far earlier form of *Thomas* than the Coptic, in this case from P.Oxy. 654, l. 1, as restored by Attridge, "The Greek Fragments," 113. On the linguistic issues involved in study of the Coptic Nag Hammadi texts, see esp. Bentley Layton, "The Recovery of Gnosticism: The Philologist's Task in the Investigation of Nag Hammadi," *SecCent* 1 (1981): 85-99. Cf. similar notes of secrecy and special revelation given to a chosen figure, who then conveys it to other select people in, e.g., the incipit of the *Apocryphon of John*: "The teaching [of the] savior and [the revelation] of the mysteries, [which] are hidden in silence [and which] it (the savior) taught to John [its] disciple" (trans. from Layton, *The Gnostic Scriptures*, 28), and also 2.16-25; 31.28–32.5.

95. Valantasis, 31. See also Marvin W. Meyer, "The Beginning of the *Gospel of Thomas,*" *Semeia* 52 (1990): 161-73. Saying 5 also urges recognition of what is "hidden/veiled" *(to kekalummenon)*, and in saying 62 Jesus tells his "secrets" only to those who are "worthy."

in *Gos. Thom.* that proper insight does not come by normal rational reflection, but only through a quest that involves being troubled and bewildered, it may well be that the staccato listing of sayings with no discernible logical or thematic progression in them was deemed most appropriate.[96]

Secret Knowledge

Granted, the motif of secret religious knowledge is also found in a number of early Christian writings, including those that represent "mainstream" circles of earliest Christianity (e.g., Mark 4:10-12; 1 Cor. 2:1-16). But in these earlier Christian writings there is a crucial difference. Usually, the secret (Gk. *mystērion*) is an insight into God's redemptive plan. This insight, though once undisclosed or not perceived, is now articulated overtly in the gospel message, which can either be rejected (e.g., as foolishness) or subjectively received as the very word of God (e.g., 1 Cor. 1:18-25; 1 Thess. 2:13).[97] That is, the secret/mystery is missed by (or withheld from) unbelievers (e.g., 2 Cor. 4:3-6), thus differentiating them from the elect. But in *Gos. Thom.* the secret truth differentiates the elect *from other Christians.* That is, it functions in a sectarian manner.

Along with this esoteric tone go also a seriously revisionist interpretation of important categories and matters of Christian faith, and an elitist, disdainful stance toward Christians who do not share the understanding of these things that is encoded and presumed in *Gos. Thom.*[98] It is interesting that in several cases where *Gos. Thom.* presents a revisionist view of some matter, this is done by Jesus replying to and correcting an unnamed group of "disciples" who appear to mouth a more conventional Christian view, often asking questions that Jesus answers in a negative or cryptic manner (*Gos. Thom.* 6, 12, 18, 20, 22, 24, 37, 43, 51-53, 99, 113).[99]

---

96. After concluding this myself, I was pleased to discover a similar judgment reached previously by Sevrin, 352, 359-60. Note also that Wesley W. Isenberg has proposed a similar explanation for the eccentric structure of material in the *Gospel of Philip* (in *NHLE*, 139).

97. On the New Testament usage of the word and its background, see, e.g., H. Krämer, "μυστήριον," in *EDNT*, 2:446-49 (with ample further bibliography).

98. I am unable to see the basis for Koester's assertion that "*Gos. Thom.* does not separate those who possess the special lifegiving knowledge of Jesus' words from the rest of the Christian people" (introduction to the *Gospel of Thomas*, 44). True, there is no explicit reference to excommunication or secession in *Gos. Thom.* But the distinction between those who are "sons of the living father" and those who are utterly impoverished in *Gos. Thom.* 3 surely indicates at least an extremely elitist stance, and may hint that "in-group" and "out-group" practices accompanied this attitude. Likewise, *Gos. Thom.* 13 undeniably indicates a disdain for other Christians whose beliefs are parodied here.

99. The Greek word for "disciple" (*mathētēs*) is one of a number of Greek terms taken

458

For example, in *Gos. Thom.* 52 "his disciples" profess that twenty-four prophets who "spoke in Israel" all "spoke by/in you" (which must reflect the sort of view of the Old Testament writings that is affirmed, for example, in Luke 24:44; John 5:39; 1 Pet. 1:10-12). But Jesus rejects the disciples' statement, accusing them of having abandoned "the living one [a key designation of Jesus in *Gos. Thom.*] in your presence" and of speaking instead about "the dead." This fairly obviously represents a rejection of the widely shared early Christian view that Jesus' significance is to be understood in light of Old Testament texts; indeed, the saying may even challenge the idea that the Old Testament is to be treated as Scripture.[100]

Moreover, the disdain expressed here is not only toward the Old Testament but also against the view of Jesus projected in other Christian circles on the basis of Old Testament prophecy. Instead, the text advocates a view of Jesus that is disconnected from biblical prophecy and is disclosed only through penetrating the secrets of the sayings in *Gos. Thom.*[101]

Revisionist

Other instances of revisionist teachings abound in *Gos. Thom.* For example, in response to another question from the disciples in *Gos. Thom.* 22 about entering the kingdom (of God) "by being little ones [children]," Jesus replies with a riddling saying that seems intended to set aside the question as puerile. However, the disciples' query echoes a saying attributed to Jesus in the canonical Gospels (Mark 10:15/Matt. 18:3/Luke 18:17), and so the Jesus of *Gos. Thom.* here corrects or reinterprets that saying to issue the radical demand for "a complete ascetical recreation of human subjectivity in every dimension of its existence."[102]

In another instance, *Gos. Thom.* 3 rejects the futurist-eschatological outlook advocated by "those who lead you" (probably leaders of other Christian circles), and defines the divine kingdom as purely a present and subjectively

---

over as loanwords into the Coptic of *Gos. Thom.* (this one used nineteen times in plural, the singular three times).

100. Ménard characterizes *Gos. Thom.* 52 as "près de Marcion" (*L'Évangile selon Thomas*, 155). The "twenty-four prophets" must allude to Jewish reckoning of the Tanach (Hebrew Old Testament) as comprised of twenty-four books (e.g., 4 Ezra 14:44).

101. Similarly, Valantasis, 130.

102. "More than any other saying, Saying 22 most specifically constructs the new subjectivity promulgated by this Gospel" (Valantasis, 96). See also Ménard, 113-15, who sees here a demand to produce "an ontological, androgynous unity" (113). The dullness of the disciples' question compares with Nicodemus's dull response in John 3:3-5, but the phrasing also echoes the sort of saying of Jesus given in Mark 10:15. Cf. also *Gos. Thom.* 46, where Jesus says that whoever "becomes a child will become acquainted with the [divine] kingdom."

disclosed reality.[103] The true nature of the kingdom is grasped only "when you come to know yourselves" and realize that "it is you [and not those other Christians whose futurist view is satirized here] who are the sons of the living father." In a number of other sayings as well, this mysterious divine kingdom features prominently (e.g., 27, 49, 113, 114).[104] Anyone who does not share this special enlightenment remains in utter spiritual impoverishment.

Clearly this saying reflects an elitist stance over against other believers and their ecclesiastical leaders, whose faith bears an obvious resemblance to that affirmed in New Testament writings and that which characterized emergent proto-orthodox circles.[105] Other sayings, too, express this radically "realized" (or better, "atemporal") eschatology involving, for example, a reinterpretation of "the end" (*Gos. Thom.* 18) and the "new world" (51) as in fact fully here but not recognized.[106]

---

103. John W. Marshall, "The *Gospel of Thomas* and the Cynic Jesus," in *Whose Historical Jesus?* ed. William E. Arnal and Michel Desjardins (Waterloo, Ontario: Wilfrid Laurier University Press, 1997), 37-60, identifies a number of sayings whose rhetoric reflects an effort to replace a chronologically prior futurist eschatology with the radically "realized" view advocated in *Gos. Thom.*

104. The word usually translated "kingdom" appears twenty-four times in twenty different sayings in Coptic *Gos. Thom.*, indicating that it is a major topic. See the lists of Coptic vocabulary and frequencies prepared by Michael W. Grondin (www.geocities.com/Athens/9068/index.htm).

105. The radical reinterpretation of the divine "kingdom" here, and the disdainful representation of dissenters as impoverished, remind one of the spirituality sarcastically referred to by Paul in 1 Cor. 4:8-13. This similarity is not, however, sufficient evidence of a historical connection between those Paul confronted in the Corinthian church and whoever compiled *Gos. Thom.* There is, e.g., no indication that the Corinthians whom Paul corrects had any particular interest in collecting sayings of Jesus. Paul refers to a "Christ" party in Corinth (1 Cor. 1:12), but *Gos. Thom.* does not use this appellative for Jesus, an additional datum that works against the idea of a direct link. The apparently similar subjectivization of eschatology and spiritually triumphalist attitude do rightly show that the sort of stance taken in *Gos. Thom.* 3 has precedents, and possibly roots, well back in the first century. But Koester's effort to connect more directly the Corinthian enthusiasts and *Gos. Thom.* (*Ancient Christian Gospels*, 60-62) requires him to establish one debatable claim by invoking other claims that are themselves at least equally debatable. The dynamics of early Christianity quite likely produced instances of coincidental similarities of beliefs. Periodic rereading of Sandmel's warning about simplistic conclusions from alleged parallels should be prescribed for all of us involved in assessing such things: Samuel Sandmel, "Parallelomania," *JBL* 81 (1962): 1-13.

106. Cf. Patterson, *"Gospel of Thomas" and Jesus*, 208-14, who prefers to characterize *Gos. Thom.* as espousing an "actualized" eschatology. I agree that there is likely a connection between the belief that the divine kingdom is fully present for those who perceive it and the strong ascetic stance in *Gos. Thom.* But I am not persuaded that those for whom *Gos. Thom.* was compiled were practicing "wandering radicalism."

Elitist

Perhaps, however, the key passage that counterpoises the religious standpoint of *Gos. Thom.* over against other Christian ideas is saying 13, which concerns what to make of Jesus. Indeed, with the incipit and first two sayings, *Gos. Thom.* 13 is among the most crucial for the whole compilation.[107] More precisely, this saying focuses on the two interrelated questions of whose view of Jesus is correct and which emblematic Christian leaders represent the truth about him.

In this vignette that (deliberately?) reminds us of an important scene found in all the Synoptic Gospels (Mark 8:27-30/Matt. 16:13-20/Luke 9:18-21), Jesus invites his disciples to express his significance. Simon Peter likens him to "a righteous angel," and Matthew acclaims him as like "a wise philosopher." Then, addressing Jesus as "Master (or 'Teacher')," [108] Thomas declares his further inability to compare Jesus to any figure. Jesus immediately denies that he is Thomas's master/teacher, and after describing Thomas as "intoxicated from the bubbling spring" which Jesus has "measured out," he removes Thomas from the others and tells him three "words/sayings," which are not, however, conveyed in the text.[109] Thereafter, when Thomas returns to the disciples, they ask him what Jesus said to him, and he replies that if he related (even) one of the things that Jesus spoke to him they would stone him (Thomas), and in turn fire would come out of the stones and burn up these other disciples. Because of the importance of this vignette, we need to give it some extended attention.

Essentially *Gos. Thom.* 13 does two things. First, it conveys a negative view of other apostles and their confessions, these figures likely emblematic of other contemporary Christian circles and their christological confessions.[110] In the

---

107. See, e.g., Sevrin, *L'Évangile selon Thomas,* 351-52, 354. Thomas is mentioned only twice, in *Gos. Thom.* 1 and 13, these two sayings functioning to assert him as the emblematic figure for the collection.

108. The Coptic term translated "master/teacher" appears only in saying 13.

109. The Coptic term here translated "words/sayings" is also used in *Gos. Thom.* 1 to translate the Greek word *logoi,* and also appears in sayings 19, 38 (and as a verb in 52). "Words/ sayings" probably represents the compiler's preferred label for the contents and genre of *Gos. Thom.* What these three secret sayings were is a matter of continuing bafflement and/or disagreement among scholars. Cf., e.g., Ménard, 31-33, 99; Fieger, 66-71. There is another reference to three secret sayings given to Thomas in *Acts of Thomas* 47 (see NTA, 2:359).

110. Of course, neither "righteous angel" nor "wise philosopher" replicates the actual confessional language of any known circles associated with Simon Peter or Matthew. I suspect that we have here a deliberate caricature of more commonly attested christological categories, "angel" alluding to views of Jesus as a figure of heavenly origin and transcendent nature, "wise philosopher" to views of Jesus as authoritative teacher (of a nonesoteric sort), both of which are presented as puerile in saying 13.

corresponding Synoptic scenes, Jesus first asks what the general public are making of him; the options that the disciples report back from outsiders (that he is John the Baptizer, Elijah, or one of the prophets) are all clearly to be taken as considerably short of the mark. Then, when Jesus asks what the disciples have to say, Simon Peter acclaims him Messiah (which, allowing for the different nuances of the Synoptic writers, seems to be intended as formally a correct confession).[111] In *Gos. Thom.* 13, however, the distinction is drawn *within* the circle of disciples, with Peter and Matthew coming off unfavorably and Thomas pictured as the only valid role-model disciple.[112] In fact, I suspect that saying 13 is a *consciously polemical adaptation* of the Synoptic tradition for the purpose of placing Peter and Matthew in the unfavorable status given to outsiders in the Synoptic version.

Second, whereas the Synoptic scenes all reflect the familiar early Christian advocacy of Jesus' messianic status over against inadequate estimates from outside the circle of faith, *Gos. Thom.* 13 clearly represents an intramural effort to ridicule the christological beliefs of other Christian circles in favor of another religious outlook that is cryptically presented in *Gos. Thom.* This secret view of Jesus also accounts for the absence of the familiar christological titles in *Gos. Thom.* (e.g., Son of David, Christ, Lord, Son of God, Word, Savior).[113] In place of the sort of confession of faith expressed in these more familiar terms, *Gos. Thom.* points to (but does not overtly disclose!) a mysterious viewpoint that is not shared by other Christians, and cannot even be communicated openly to them! *Gos. Thom.* is plainly sectarian. The promise of immortality in *Gos. Thom.* 1 (which by its early position in the text clearly signals the standpoint of the whole compilation) is strictly reserved for initiates of an inner ring of mysterious insight, an insight that is not in fact conveyed overtly in the sayings that make up *Gos. Thom.* but must be acquired in some other way and brought by readers to this particular compilation.[114]

---

111. All three Synoptic accounts have Jesus' command to secrecy (Matt. 16:20/Mark 8:30/Luke 9:21), but all three Synoptic authors also make it clear that confession of Jesus as Messiah/Christ is central and, properly understood, a correct title (e.g., Mark 1:1).

112. See, e.g., Valantasis, 78: "The real subject of this narrative sequence does not revolve about Jesus' identity, but Thomas' authority as a spiritual guide and revealer."

113. See, e.g., Maurice Carrez, "Quelques aspects christologiques de l'Évangile de Thomas," in *The Four Gospels 1992*, 3:2263-76 (esp. 2263-67).

114. As Carrez observed, "There are therefore two categories: those who are initiated and those who are not" (Carrez, 3:2276, translation mine).

Jesus and "Thomistic" Christianity

Consequently, as one would expect of such a deliberately cryptic compilation, it is difficult (though not, I hope, altogether impossible) for us through normal reading and interpretative effort to determine what view of Jesus is encoded in *Gos. Thom.* Moreover, it is not even clear that promoting a particular view of Jesus is the sole or even, perhaps, the central concern. It is at least as much a concern in *Gos. Thom.* to advocate a particular kind of spirituality of self-discovery in which individuals ("the solitary one") perceive their transcendent origin and destiny in the divine realm. To gather more precisely what view of Jesus *Gos. Thom.* does reflect, we have to comb through the compilation of sayings, synthesizing hints given at various points. That is, we have to work hard for any understanding of what this coded compilation means!

In several other short dialogue scenes, the disciples ask Jesus direct questions about his significance; Jesus' replies are obviously crucial hints of the correct viewpoint to hold. In *Gos. Thom.* 43 they ask, "Who are you, that you should say these things to us?" All too predictably, however, Jesus' reply simply denigrates them in a coded manner. He accuses them of having become "like the Jews," either loving the tree and hating its fruit or loving the fruit and hating the tree. If Jesus is the "tree" and his sayings the "fruit," perhaps the reply points away from him to his sayings as the (sole?) key to grasping who and what he is.[115] Similarly in saying 91 the unidentified "they" are probably the disciples, who ask Jesus to tell them who he really is so that they may believe in him (which has rather suspicious echoes of Johannine passages such as John 8:25, but even more directly 20:31!). Jesus' reply is again critical of them; he rejects their question as indicating their failure to recognize "the one who is before you" and to know "how to read this moment" (cf. Luke 12:56). This reply both reflects an emphasis in *Gos. Thom.* on discerning the presence of divine realities rather than awaiting them in the future, and also seems implicitly to reject the whole idea of believing in Jesus and expressing it through a christological confession.[116] As Ménard stated, "What matters for Thomas are the Revealer's teachings, not the person of Christ or faith in him."[117]

In *Gos. Thom.* 24 the disciples ask Jesus to show them "the place where you are" so that they can seek it. His reply, which on the surface scarcely seems to address the question, directs attention instead to a "light within a man of

---

115. So, e.g., Fieger, 140; Valantasis, 119-20.

116. It is very interesting that this is the only use of the verb "believe" in Coptic *Gos. Thom.*, whereas believing in Jesus is so crucial in GJohn (e.g., 1:12; 2:11; 3:15-16; and esp. 20:30-31).

117. Ménard, 193, translation mine.

light" which enables one to "light up the whole world," and without which light one "is darkness." The probable intention is to direct attention away from a connection to Jesus, urging instead awareness of an inner light, a special religious subjectivity that illumines a person's "whole world." In saying 37 the disciples ask Jesus when he will "become revealed" to them and when they will see him (an allusion to the early Christian hope of Jesus' future appearance in glory). His cryptic reply about disrobing without shame and trampling one's garments underfoot "like little children" probably again refers to a certain inner enlightenment as the requisite condition for seeing "the son of the living one."[118] Here, too, the focus is on the spiritual attainment of individuals rather than on Jesus himself.

When, however, Salome asks Jesus who he is (*Gos. Thom.* 61), she gets a somewhat more direct answer. Jesus declares, "I am he who exists from the One who is equal," and says that he has been "given (some) of the things of my father."[119] As Dunderberg has proposed, behind the Coptic phrase translated "I am he who . . ." must lie an original Greek "I am" expression *(egō eimi ho ōn ek . . .)*, and Jesus' statement thus discloses his (divine) origin in phrasing that resonates with the well-known Johannine "I am" statements.[120] Yet, though the following lines of saying 61 are broken and difficult to decipher, Jesus appears to go on to include other individuals as well as himself in the (divine) "equality" that he shares. This hints at the claim that Jesus expresses more transparently in *Gos. Thom.* 108: "Whoever drinks from my mouth will become like me; I myself shall become that person, and the hidden things will be revealed to him."[121]

---

118. In reading an earlier draft of this chapter, my colleague Peter Hayman proposed that the disrobing image may reflect a baptism ritual practiced by those whose piety is reflected in *Gos. Thom.*, which may have been the setting in which this spiritual illumination was expected to be received.

119. The Coptic term which appears only here in *Gos. Thom.*, and is translated "the undivided" by Thomas Lambdin (in Layton, *Nag Hammadi Codex II.2-7*, 53-93), is perhaps better translated "the equal (one)." See now esp. Ismo Dunderberg, "*Thomas*' I-Sayings and the Gospel of John," in *Thomas at the Crossroads*, 33-64 (esp. 49-56). This judgment is reflected also in Fieger's translation of the phrase, "der aus dem Gleichen ist" (Fieger, 177), and in Ménard's French rendering, "Je suis celui qui provient de Celui qui est égal" (Ménard, 66). But cf. Layton, *The Gnostic Scriptures*, 391, "that which is integrated"; and Marvin Meyer, *The "Gospel of Thomas": Hidden Sayings of Jesus* (San Francisco: Harper San Francisco, 1992), "what is whole" (and see also his comment, 93-94).

120. Dunderberg, "*Thomas*' I-Sayings," 53.

121. I cite here Valantasis's translation (188). On the one hand, this saying expresses the profound unity of the revealer Jesus with those who perceive aright what is revealed. On the other hand, it also directly indicates that the enlightened share fully in the same status as Jesus.

In several other statements as well, Jesus makes direct claims for himself, using phrasing that echoes the "I am" or "I have come" formulations characteristic in John.[122] In *Gos. Thom.* 77 Jesus identifies himself as "the light which is above them all" (cf. "I am the light of the world," John 8:12; 9:5; "the light/true light," 1:5, 9), and as "the all," the one from whom "the all came forth" and to whom "the all extended."[123] The last two phrases are somewhat similar to a number of New Testament texts (particularly, 1 Cor. 8:5-6; Col. 1:16-17; Eph. 1:9-10; John 1:3).[124] But the relevant New Testament passages rather consistently make Jesus the *agent* of creation, the source of creation being God (the Father), whereas in saying 77 Jesus identifies himself fully as the source of "the all."[125]

On the other hand, this imposing self-declaration must be read in light of other sayings in *Gos. Thom.*, such as 108, which promises that the one who

122. For all these sayings, see the discussion by Dunderberg, "*Thomas*' I-Sayings and the Gospel of John." Dunderberg refers to these as "identification sayings" (43). As he observed, "Among the canonical gospels, such identification sayings occur only in John, and elsewhere in the New Testament only in Revelation" (44). I return to the relationship of *Gos. Thom.* and John later in this chapter.

123. "Extended" here translates a Coptic verb that has a catchword connection to the verb "split (open)" in the next line ("split a [piece of] wood"), a wordplay possible in Coptic but not in Greek. See Fieger, 214. Note also that the saying about the wood and stone (in Coptic *Gos. Thom.* 77) is part of saying 30 in P.Oxy. 1 (which I will discuss shortly). This probably confirms that the linkage of the cryptic reference to the wood and stone with Jesus' self-declaration as "light" and "all" in saying 77 does not go back earlier than the Coptic translation (i.e., late third or fourth century). Moreover, the Coptic form is reversed from the Greek (stone/wood), and it is in fact not so evident that the "pantheistic" connotation frequently seen in the Coptic saying was there in the Greek text. One peculiarity that has not received sufficient notice is that in the form of the saying in P.Oxy. 1 (ll. 27-30), both "stone" and "wood/tree" have the definite article *(ton lithon, to xylon)*, which may suggest some specific reference. In a number of early Christian texts, *to xylon* (the tree) refers to Jesus' cross (e.g., Acts 13:29; 1 Pet. 2:24; *Barn.* 11.6-9), which leads one to wonder if the Greek form of the saying involved some kind of cryptic reference to Jesus' cross. And did "the stone" likewise have a special connotation (e.g., Jesus' tomb; or the cornerstone of *Gos. Thom.* 66)? See J. Schneider, "ξύλον," in *TDNT*, 5:37-41; H.-W. Kuhn, "ξύλον," in *EDNT*, 2:487; G. Q. Reijners, *The Terminology of the Holy Cross in Early Christian Literature* (Nijmegen: Dekker & Van De Vegt, 1965), esp. 6-96. A number of possible meanings of the "stone/wood" saying in P.Oxy. 1 were given in Hugh G. Evelyn White, *The Sayings of Jesus from Oxyrhynchus* (Cambridge: Cambridge University Press, 1920), 35-40 (although he presumed a restoration of lines 23-25 that is rendered dubious now by Attridge).

124. But it is not clear whether "the all" (used three times in *Gos. Thom.* 77, plus once each in 2 and 67 with what looks like a similar nuance) connotes the same thing as "all things" *(panta/ta panta)* in John 1:3, 1 Cor. 8:5-6, Col. 1:16-17 (i.e., all creation). See, e.g., Dunderberg, "*Thomas*' I-Sayings," 59-60.

125. Whether the Greek preposition used be *en* (in/by) or *dia* (through), the sense is basically the same.

drinks from Jesus' mouth (i.e., imbibes fully Jesus' words) will become like him and Jesus will become that person. Similarly saying 2 promises that the one who discovers the meaning of these secret sayings will not only obtain immortality but will also "rule over the all." That is, it appears that the main function of the exalted claims for Jesus in *Gos. Thom.* 77 is to set forth the exalted status that is held out for those who come to enlightenment through grasping the secret truth in Jesus' sayings.

Gos. Thom. 16 features Jesus' declaration that he has not come to bring peace to the world (*kosmos,* a loanword here) but to cast fire, sword, and war upon the earth. There will be division in "a house," with "father" and "son" each against the other, "and they will stand solitary." Jesus' role here is clearly a polarizing one, and we are supposed to see this role exercised through the sayings and their cryptic but shocking meaning. (Remember, e.g., *Gos. Thom.* 13, where Thomas warns that the truths revealed to him by Jesus would be regarded as outrageous by ordinary Christians represented by Peter and Matthew.) The division here is not, as some have thought, merely a reference to household tensions.[126] I propose instead that it alludes to schisms among believers over matters of belief and spirituality.

Note that the "solitary one" (*monachos,* another Greek loanword taken over in Coptic *Gos. Thom.*) praised in saying 16 comes in for a benediction in 49, where, as a group, the "solitary" are also the "elect." They (alone) "find the kingdom" for they are "from it," and to it, thus, they "will return." That is, they (as distinguished from other Christians) are the *chosen ones;* only they know their divine origin and destiny. They are those who are told in *Gos. Thom.* 50 to declare their special status to those who ask them about their religious identity: "*We* are the *elect* [chosen ones] of the living Father."[127]

The extant Greek version of *Gos. Thom.* 30 seems to echo this emphasis

---

126. As noted by Risto Uro, other familial relationships mentioned in the parallel sayings in Matt. 10:34-35/Luke 12:51-53 (daughter/mother, daughter-in-law/mother-in-law, members of one's household) do not appear in *Gos. Thom.* 16: "Is *Thomas* an Encratite Gospel?" in *Thomas at the Crossroads,* 140-62 (esp. 143-44).

127. Note the use of the cognate verb ("to choose/select") in *Gos. Thom.* 23, where Jesus proclaims that he *chooses* "one out of a thousand, and two out of ten thousand, and they shall stand as a solitary one [*monachos*]," and saying 8, where the fisher *chose* the "fine large fish" and threw all the others back. The latter saying is clearly a revisionist (sub)version of the parallel in Matt. 13:47-50. In Matthew the parable portrays the eschatological sorting of elect and sinners, but in *Gos. Thom.* 8 a distinction is drawn between "one fine large" fish and the lesser fish, the former obviously corresponding to the "solitary" elect ones praised in *Gos. Thom.* and the smaller fish almost certainly the lesser souls who constitute what the compiler regards as pedestrian Christian circles. Clearly one of the strong threads in the fabric of the spirituality of *Gos. Thom.* is this claim to special status *over against other Christian believers.*

on the special spiritual affinity that Jesus has for the elect in distinction from other believers.[128] The first part of Greek *Gos. Thom.* 30 must be a deliberate subversion or rejection of the saying in Matthew 18:19-20.[129] That saying promises special efficacy to the prayer requests agreed upon by two, followed by Jesus' promise that "where two or three are gathered" in his name, he is there "in their midst." In Greek *Gos. Thom.* 30, however, Jesus says, "Where there are three, they are without God [*atheoi*]; and where there is only one, I say, I am with that one."

The apparent force of this saying amounts to a rejection of the notion that Jesus' divine presence is linked to the gathered communities of ordinary Christians. Instead, the saying restricts Jesus' true presence to individuals who share the special knowledge of those reflected in *Gos. Thom.* These are the individuals whose unique spiritual worthiness distinguishes and privileges them over against the mere Christians and their vain (indeed, godless!) gatherings.[130] It is difficult to avoid the conclusion that *Gos. Thom.* advocates real physical separation from such gatherings.

We cannot take the time and space here to probe all the possible hints of the view of Jesus implied in *Gos. Thom.*[131] But before concluding, I include a few more sayings that address obviously important matters. In Greek *Gos. Thom.* 28 Jesus says, "I took my place in the midst of the world [*en mesō kosmou*], and I appeared to them in flesh [*en sarkei ōphthēn autois*]." Thereupon, finding an unidentified "them" intoxicated and none of them thirsty, Jesus was "afflicted for the sons of men" over their blindness, and he expresses hope that "when they shake off their wine, then will they repent." It is naive, however, to take the reference to Jesus appearing "in flesh" as necessarily indicating a genuine incarnation. As Ménard suggests, to "appear" in "flesh" here may well connote "an apparent flesh," not real mortal existence.[132] In any case,

---

128. I comment here on the restored wording of saying 30 in P.Oxy. 1 as given in Attridge, "The Greek Fragments," 119-20, which revises and corrects the earlier restoration by Grenfell and Hunt. Coptic *Gos. Thom.* 30 may be a garbled version. In any case, it is irrelevant for the earlier stage of the transmission and sense of the saying.

129. See Valantasis, 43-44. He notes that the first part of Greek *Gos. Thom.* 30 appears to be "an inversion" of Matt. 18:19-20, "offering a severe critique of that Matthean theology" (43). I quote here Valantasis's translation.

130. As Valantasis (43-44) notes, though the emphasis on the "solitary" worthies in *Gos. Thom.* does not necessarily mean they did not constitute circles or groups, the "solitary" elect would have associated only with "others of similar disposition and knowledge."

131. Cf. also Davies, "The Christology and Protology of the *Gospel of Thomas*"; Carrez, "Quelques aspects christologiques de l'Évangile de Thomas"; Ménard, 31-36.

132. Ménard, *L'Évangile selon Thomas*, 122-23, also 34, citing the use of "flesh" in *Gos. Phil.* 23.26, *Treatise on the Resurrection*, and *Gospel of Truth*.

Jesus' mission is implicitly one of revelation, offering the drunken and blind human race sight and drink, not redemption from sin.[133]

The sole explicit reference to Jesus' cross is in *Gos. Thom.* 55. After demanding the disciples to "hate" father, mother, brothers, and sisters, Jesus calls each to "take up his cross in my way." The latter exhortation echoes Synoptic passages (Mark 8:34/Matt. 16:24/Luke 9:23). It is, however, the curious qualifying phrase "in my way" that is without parallel and that also probably hints at the coded meaning. This phrasing is echoed in *Gos. Thom.* 10, where Jesus demands followers to hate father and mother "as I do." In light of the rather negative view of the body, "flesh," and other features of normal mortal life in *Gos. Thom.*, it is probable that taking up one's cross means a readiness to negate the world. That is, Jesus' "cross" comprises his negation of, and deliverance from, the confines of the flesh and world.[134] One takes up one's cross after Jesus' example, therefore, by ascetic practices now, and consummates it eventually in death, which brings permanent freedom from the world.

Two more sayings add notably to the picture of Jesus. In *Gos. Thom.* 82 Jesus announces, "Whoever is near me is near the fire, and whoever is far from me is far from the kingdom." Yet, as we have noted, other sayings show that *Gos. Thom.* does not really promote a spirituality focused on one's relationship to the person of Jesus. Consequently, to be "near to" or "far from" Jesus must have to do with whether one grasps inwardly the secret truths he offers and enacts them in one's outward behavior (e.g., renunciation of the "world" in favor of the "kingdom" perceived as mysteriously present).

In another saying that echoes Synoptic tradition, Coptic *Gos. Thom.* 90, Jesus summons hearers to come to him, for his "yoke is easy [*chrēstos*, Greek loanword]" and his "lordship is mild," and they "will find repose [*anapasis*, Greek loanword]" for themselves. The parallel saying in Matthew 11:28-30 follows a declaration by Jesus of his plenipotentiary authority and his exclusive revelatory significance and role. But in the context of *Gos. Thom.*, this version of the saying probably hints only at the need to discover and embrace Jesus' pattern of spirituality as expressed cryptically in his sayings. Thereby one will find "repose," a word used several times in Coptic *Gos. Thom.* that probably encodes the spiritual illumination and consequent state that is touted in the compilation.[135]

---

133. Valantasis, 103, sees *Gos. Thom.* 28 most clearly presenting "the traditional gnostic redeemer mythology," and articulating "a classically gnostic theology."

134. Valantasis, 32, proposes that we are intended "to identify the 'cross' with the world . . . as a garment to be shaken off." Fieger, 167, sees the demand here as "a metaphor for the readiness to negate the world" (translation mine).

135. "Repose" (*anapasis*, from the Greek *anapausis*) also appears in *Gos. Thom.* 50, an important confessional saying; in 51, where its true meaning is hinted at over against the inferior

In a couple of interesting sayings Jesus declares that he can give secret knowledge. *Gos. Thom.* 17 offers for a circle of initiates (the "you" here is plural) what "no eye has seen, no ear has heard, and no hand has touched, and what has not occurred to the human mind." This saying looks somewhat like Paul's statement in 1 Corinthians 2:9, about the unimaginable and utterly unanticipated things that have now been revealed through the Spirit to all who have embraced the gospel (2:6-16). But in the context of *Gos. Thom.*, and particularly following here saying 16 with its declaration that Jesus has come to sow dissension between the "solitary" and those others (inferior Christians) who do not share their glorious new insights, saying 17 must be taken as a comment on the deep truths revealed uniquely to the chosen ones.[136] It seems to me that, if there is any historical relationship between *Gos. Thom.* 17 and 1 Corinthians 2:9, it is more plausible to see *Gos. Thom.* 17 as a revisionist "spin" on the traditional saying cited in an earlier form by Paul.[137] The revelations are confined to the "solitary" and inner elect in the revisionist saying, whereas Paul states that "the mystery of God" (1 Cor. 2:1) is now openly disclosed in the gospel to all who hear it, which can take in all believers.[138]

---

sense of the term as used by Jesus' disciples; and in 60, where Jesus advises his hearers to seek "a place for yourselves within repose." All these cases indicate a special "insider" connotation of the term. That the Greek term is taken over as a loanword into the Coptic suggests that it had acquired this special insider connotation among readers of Greek *Gos. Thom.* Cf. the metaphorical sense of "rest" as belief in the gospel *(katapausis)* in Hebrews (3:11–4:11).

136. "It is only the restricted and esoteric circle of initiates who are able to know the secret teachings of the Master." Ménard, 105.

137. The saying in 1 Cor. 2:9 has a rich tradition history. See Klaus Berger, "Zur Diskussion über die Herkunft von I Kor II.9," *NTS* 24 (1978): 270-83. Key texts include *1 Clem.* 34.8; *2 Clem.* 11.7; *Acts Thom.* 36; *Acts Pet.* 39; Hippolytus, *Ref.* 5.24.1; 26.16; 6.24.4; *Exc. Theod.* 10.5; *Dial. Sav.* 57. We have no way to know whether any version of Coptic *Gos. Thom.* 17 was included in the earlier Greek stages of the compilation. On the basis of comparison that we can make between extant Greek evidence and the Coptic text of *Gos. Thom.*, it is clear that significant redactional changes took place, and that these may well have included further additions to what was apparently a kind of "rolling-redaction" compilation. Given the wide distribution of versions of this saying in Christian texts of the early period, it is far more likely that at some point in the Greek transmission stage, or perhaps even later in the Coptic stage, a form of the saying cited by Paul was adapted and included as *Gos. Thom.* 17. It is bad judgment to take *Gos. Thom.* 17 as preserving somehow a form of the saying earlier than all the other (earlier!) witnesses to the saying.

138. Koester's characterization of the saying in Matt. 13:16-17/Luke 10:23-24 as "a somewhat altered form" of the saying in *Gos. Thom.* 17 is an unsupported assertion. The revisionist tone throughout *Gos. Thom.* makes it far more likely that it comprises a later form of saying than those found in the Q material. Koester's characterization of the enthusiasts whom Paul was correcting in 1 Corinthians rests upon too many unsupported or manifestly dubious claims. E.g., there is, in fact, no evidence that the Corinthians ridiculed in 1 Cor. 4:8-13 were using a say-

Likewise, if there is a relationship between *Gos. Thom.* 17 and 1 John 1:1-3 (and it is not, in fact, so obvious that there is), it seems to me far more likely that *Gos. Thom.* 17 was inspired by the Johannine text.[139] The key indicator that *Gos. Thom.* 17 is secondary is the reference to "what no hand has touched," which is not a feature of the earliest-attested incidence of the saying (1 Cor. 2:9). Moreover, it was hardly necessary to emphasize that revealed truths expressed in the form of secret sayings are nontactile, so this phrase in *Gos. Thom.* is better understood as reflecting a revisionist concern over against the sort of assertion reflected in 1 John 1:1-3.

By contrast, the emphasis in 1 John 1:1-3 on the visible, oral, and tactile nature of the revelation/revealer simply reflects a widely attested and long-standing theme in first-century Christian circles. For it had long been characteristic of Christian teaching to insist on the personal significance and historical reality of Jesus as the distinctive expression of God's redemptive intention.[140] In short, we do not need *Gos. Thom.* 17 to explain the affirmation in 1 John 1:1-3. Granted, however, the latter affirmation is almost certainly a reaction against what the author perceived to be a radical departure from this historic emphasis on Jesus' personal and physical significance, that is, a reaction against a dodgy view of Jesus. But that hardly means he was reacting against *Gos. Thom.* Instead, I suggest that at some point in the rolling redaction process that characterized the transmission of *Gos. Thom.*, the sort of saying attested also in 1 Corinthians 2:9 was refashioned to support the sort of view that was opposed in 1 John 1:1-3, with the resulting saying (17) reflecting the transcendentalist and esoteric stance that runs all through *Gos. Thom.*

It is important to emphasize that *Gos. Thom.* rejects the emphasis on the unique importance of the *human person* of Jesus that is promoted in numerous early Christian writings, presenting instead a picture of Jesus as the otherworldly mouthpiece of a body of esoteric teachings. Also, *Gos. Thom.* emphasizes that these teachings offer devotees an insight and a spiritual sta-

---

ings collection that they treated as "the revelation of hidden wisdom" (cf. Koester, *Ancient Christian Gospels*, 58-62).

139. Cf. Takashi Onuki, "Traditionsgeschichte von Thomasevangelium 17 und ihre christologische Relevanz," in *Anfänge der Christologie*, ed. Cilliers Breytenbach and H. Paulsen (Göttingen: Vandenhoeck & Ruprecht, 1991), 399-415, who proposed that 1 John 1:1-3 responds against the saying in *Gos. Thom.* 17. See now the cogent treatment of *Gos. Thom.* 17 and connections with other early Christian texts by Ismo Dunderberg, "John and Thomas in Conflict?" in *The Nag Hammadi Library after Fifty Years*, 361-80 (esp. 365-70).

140. E.g., the emphasis on witnesses who saw and heard Jesus, 2 Pet. 1:16-18; and on the tactile reality of his risen state, Luke 24:36-43 (echoed also in Ign. *Smyrn.* 3.1-3). Indeed, the whole genre of the narrative Jesus book indicates an emphasis on the importance of the historical reality/physicality of Jesus and the revelation that he brought.

tus far beyond what is available to other Christians through the ordinary (and inferior) channels of preaching and instruction. It is therefore quite plausible that at some point in the multistaged redactional process that led to Coptic *Gos. Thom.* someone fashioned *Gos. Thom.* 17 as an expression of this elitist claim.

In the remaining saying that we consider here, *Gos. Thom.* 62, Jesus offers his "mysteries" solely to those who are "worthy" of them.[141] Two component assertions are obvious. Jesus reveals divine mysteries/secrets, and he does so only to a select group of worthies. Once again we have confirmation that in *Gos. Thom.* it was at least as important to affirm the special nature of the inner circle of initiates as it was to say anything about Jesus.[142] This severe distinction between those worthy of divine mysteries and the unworthy is also surely encoded in the second part of saying 62, where individuals (the "you" is singular) are told not to let their "left" know what their "right" will do.[143]

Summary and Placement

Even this extended discussion of *Gos. Thom.* does not exhaust all that this difficult but important text has to tell us of the religious views of its compilers.[144] I

141. "Mysteries" translates *mystērion*, yet another Greek loanword, which appears in *Gos. Thom.* only in saying 62.

142. See, e.g., Ménard, 163; Fieger, 18-82. Cf. Valantasis (140-41), who thinks the restrictive tone of *Gos. Thom.* 62 "at odds with the rest of the sayings," which he says (curiously in my view) express "an expansive ideology" of engagement with the outside world. I am unable to reconcile this characterization of *Gos. Thom.* with the text of the Coptic or Greek versions! I propose that *Gos. Thom.* 62 may be a revisionist appropriation of the Synoptic saying (Mark 4:11; Matt. 13:11; Luke 8:10), once again shifting the distinction made between unbelievers and believers in the Synoptic form to a distinction between the select circle of worthy enlightened ones and other Christians who are unworthy of Jesus' secret truths.

143. Here yet again *Gos. Thom.* appropriates a saying paralleled in the Synoptic tradition (Matt. 6:3). As *Gos. Thom.* rejects almsgiving (saying 14, along with prayer and fasting, also 104, 6), the reference to "left" and "right" is reinterpreted to advocate a sectarian stance. The appropriation of the imagery in *Gos. Thom.* may have been inspired by its use in Matt. 25:31-46 in distinguishing the righteous from the unrighteous. There is another revisionist move in *Gos. Thom.* 27, which demands one to "fast as regards the world," apparently an image for the disdain of the *kosmos* that is a recurring note in sayings 21, 56, 80, 110, 111.

144. And of course, those views may well have shifted somewhat across the stages of transmission of *Gos. Thom.* and the history of its usage/reception. For example, the Pachomian monks whose Coptic manuscripts were discovered at Nag Hammadi probably valued *Gos. Thom.* mainly for its strong ascetic stance. Perhaps, also, they were intrigued by its esoteric tone, though they likely were not "gnostics" as the term is characteristically meant by scholars.

conclude my discussion by underscoring briefly key features of the view of Jesus that it reflects.

On the one hand, with many other Christian writings of the early centuries, *Gos. Thom.* certainly presupposes and affirms that Jesus is fully divine. *Gos. Thom.* 77 is one of the most explicit statements; the other sayings that we have examined here confirm this. Yet, in *Gos. Thom.* Jesus' divine nature does not finally make him unique in comparison to those who are "worthy" to receive the secret knowledge that they, too, come from the light and are the elect children of the divine Father (*Gos. Thom.* 50). A comparison with Paul's emphasis on believers' filial relationship with God is instructive. Paul says believers are enfranchised through Christ into a relationship with God that is patterned after the image of Christ, who is the "firstborn among many brothers" (Rom. 8:14-17, 29-30). The Gospel of John also thematizes the filial relationship of the elect to God. But GJohn equally clearly makes the filial status of the elect completely derivative from, and dependent upon, Jesus' unique divine sonship, and GJohn insists that this filial status with God is mediated through knowledge of, and faith in, Jesus as Christ and Son of God (e.g., 1:12-13; 17:3; 20:30-31).

But the elect of *Gos. Thom.* are represented as more radically and intrinsically divine in their own right. They have not had divine sonship conferred on them; instead, they have come to realize that they have always had divine origins (*Gos. Thom.* 50), just as Jesus does. Jesus' exalted status is by no means unique. Instead, his own direct participation in "the living Father" functions essentially to exemplify the equally divine privileges of the elect, and also to underscore the validity of the truth of these privileges that is encoded in his sayings compiled in *Gos. Thom.* As the mouthpiece of these sayings, Jesus could be said to trigger the self-discovery of the elect. But having come to this self-discovery, the elect are now to understand Jesus simply as a fellow child of the living Father.

Unlike the familiar canonical Gospels, and unlike a good many other extracanonical Jesus books as well, there is no connected narrative of Jesus in *Gos. Thom.* (although there are a few allusions to a story of Jesus, as in sayings 12, 22, 60, 79). There is, however, a grand narrative that is presupposed and alluded to at numerous points. But this narrative is not focused on the earthly actions of Jesus, other than his delivery of these secret sayings. Instead, beneath *Gos. Thom.* is a grand mythic narrative in which the elect, who come from the divine light and Father, somehow find themselves situated within the "world," where most people live in an ignorant stupor (saying 28). But, through decoding Jesus' secret sayings, the elect come to see their own true nature and status (saying 18), becoming thereby divine like Jesus, and having further special hidden things revealed to them (108). They then orient themselves to their higher origins and destiny, disdaining the world and its priorities (e.g., 27, 56, 101). Like Jesus, they apparently are to regard the final negation of the world and the body, represented by their death (55), as simply the consummation of their true spiritual nature.

In *Gos. Thom.* there is no mention of the elect as sinners who need redemption, and no reference to Jesus as redeemer. There is perhaps one direct allusion to his death *en passant* in saying 55 (unless we are intended to understand his "cross" here as symbolic of something else), but there is certainly no hint that Jesus' crucifixion has any redemptive efficacy. Nor is there any emphasis on Jesus' own resurrection. As to future hopes of Jesus' return, of bodily resurrection, of the appearance of the divine kingdom in an outward manner, these are all treated with disdain. The Jesus of *Gos. Thom.* is a talking head, whose whole significance and role consist in speaking the cryptic statements collected in this text.

It is little wonder, then, that the intended devotees of this representation of Jesus found so little basis for fellowship with those other Christians whose beliefs are more familiar to us. *Gos. Thom.* does truly advocate "another Jesus," though the deliberately cryptic nature of its contents may have impeded the efforts of ordinary Christians in the early years of its circulation to be sure as to just what *Gos. Thom.* in fact was saying![145]

Where and when should we place the originating composition that lies behind the extant Greek and Coptic manuscripts of *Gos. Thom.*? What setting and circumstances might most plausibly account for it? Given its revisionist tone, particularly the explicit disdain for all those other Christians and their leaders whom it regards as failing utterly to perceive the secret truth of the kingdom, and given also the reinterpretation of futurist eschatology, the rejection of belief in Jesus as salvific, and the apparently subversionist reformulation of traditions paralleled in the Synoptics, I think the literary origin of *Gos. Thom.* is best located sometime between 90 and 160.

I emphasize that my view of the probable time frame for the originating compilation does not rest upon any particular judgment about the direct *literary* relationship of *Gos. Thom.* and any of the canonical Gospels. Scholars have too often treated the date of *Gos. Thom.* as dependent on whether it is literarily dependent on the Synoptic Gospels or represents an independent compilation of Jesus tradition.[146] *Gos. Thom.* is clearly an important "independent" compilation, at the least because its contents and curious literary character reflect religious emphases clearly distinguishable from those that guided the composition

---

145. I use Paul's phrase "another Jesus" from 2 Cor. 11:4, but I do not mean to suggest that what Paul complains about in 2 Cor. 10–11 has any direct connection with, or even much in the way of direct similarity to, the view of Jesus advocated in *Gos. Thom.*

146. Cf. Patterson, "The *Gospel of Thomas* and the Synoptic Tradition."

of the more familiar Gospel accounts. Given the varied way in which Jesus tradition was transmitted in earliest Christianity, it is entirely possible in principle that whoever was responsible for the originating compilation of *Gos. Thom.* could have drawn on oral and written sources other than the canonical Gospels.

On the other hand, given the obviously wide circulation and positive reception accorded the canonical Gospels from their composition onward, it is also perfectly reasonable to hypothesize either some direct acquaintance with, and use of, them, or at least their indirect influence. It is also quite reasonable to postulate that the compiler(s) of *Gos. Thom.* drew upon a combination of sources that included one or more of the canonical Gospels as well as extra-canonical tradition, and that the success of the canonical Gospels helped prompt people with very different views to circulate Jesus books that reflected their own concerns and religious outlook.

But whatever the literary relationship of *Gos. Thom.* to the Synoptics, its pervasively revisionist tone shows that it represents reaction against *prior* expressions of early Christian faith. As we noted, *Gos. Thom.* also seems to revise and/or subvert prior versions of Jesus' sayings (e.g., *Gos. Thom.* 30) and narrative vignettes about Jesus (e.g., 13), this material often paralleled in the Synoptics. Whether the original compiler(s) of *Gos. Thom.* were, or were not, directly consulting the Synoptic Gospels is finally not determinative for dating the initial compilation. But I do maintain that the Synoptics often seem to reflect, quite adequately, the versions of Jesus traditions against which those responsible for *Gos. Thom.* were reacting. That means that *Gos. Thom.* probably represents a stage of development in earliest Christianity that was somewhat subsequent to the stage of the parallel material represented in the Synoptics.

Gospel of Thomas and Gospel of John

Several scholars have investigated a possible special relationship between *Gos. Thom.* and the Johannine literature. In particular, some (though for varying reasons) have proposed that GJohn might to some extent represent a direct reaction against a prior expression of the sorts of ideas advanced in *Gos. Thom.*[147]

---

147. Esp. Davies, *Christian Wisdom*, 112-16; Gregory J. Riley, *Resurrection Reconsidered: Thomas and John in Controversy* (Minneapolis: Fortress, 1995); April D. DeConick, *Voices of the Mystics: Early Christian Discourse in the Gospels of John and Thomas and Other Ancient Christian Literature*, JSNTSup 157 (Sheffield: Sheffield Academic Press, 2001), esp. 68-108; DeConick, "John Rivals Thomas: From Community Conflict to Gospel Narrative," in *Jesus in Johannine Tradition*, 303-12; and Onuki, "Traditionsgeschichte von Thomasevangelium 17 und ihre christologische Relevanz," who argues that 1 John represents a reaction against the beliefs of *Gos. Thom.*

Gregory Riley contends that GJohn reflects a dispute between Johannine Christians and those represented in *Gos. Thom.* (a "Thomistic" community), a dispute which prominently included differences over the nature of the resurrection of Jesus and the salvation of believers.[148] Riley proposes that the dispute is reflected in the treatment of Thomas in GJohn, which Riley takes to be a negative portrayal intended to discredit the patron saint of "Thomistic" believers. In Riley's view, the aim in GJohn was thereby to refute the religious stance of Thomistic Christians, specifically their view of Jesus' resurrection.

On the other hand, April DeConick proposes that the dispute had to do with a predilection of Thomas circles for mystical visions, which, she claims, the Johannine Christians saw as dangerous. So they emphasized believing in Jesus over against the Thomistic focus on visions. She, too, takes the Johannine references to Thomas as negative and polemical in intent, seeing them reflecting a conflict between Johannine and Thomas groups.[149]

It is not possible to examine fully all the issues and relevant evidence here; and in light of detailed and generally judicious discussions by Ismo Dunderberg, it is not necessary either.[150] Instead I shall simply sketch my reasons for regarding these proposals as unlikely. As my discussion of Johannine Christianity earlier indicates, the Johannine writings reflect conflicts over religious beliefs, conflicts with unbelievers (especially in GJohn) as well as sharp differences between believers (especially 1 John and 2 John). So, in principle, it is entirely possible that some other early Christian text such as *Gos. Thom.* could give us further evidence of the same intra-Christian conflict, and it is certainly an intriguing possibility to consider. But there are problems with both of these particular proposals.

The key question about any hypothesis is whether it satisfactorily accounts for something that is otherwise unexplained (or less adequately explained). On the proposals of Riley and DeConick, the more precise question is whether either is required to account for the relevant features of GJohn; I think the answer is negative. For example, contra Riley, we hardly require a polemical exchange with a Thomas circle to account for what GJohn says about Jesus' resurrection.[151]

---

148. Riley, *Resurrection Reconsidered*, esp. 78-126.

149. DeConick, *Voices of the Mystics*, esp. 68-85, where she examines three scenarios in John (14:3-7, 20-23; 20:24-29), each of which represents Thomas as "the false hero, a fool who misunderstands the path of salvation" (85). Curiously she does not discuss John 11:7-16, another pericope where Thomas is named and has a speaking part.

150. Dunderberg, "*Thomas*' I-Sayings and the Gospel of John"; Dunderberg, "John and Thomas in Conflict?"; and Dunderberg, "*Thomas* and the Beloved Disciple," in *Thomas at the Crossroads*, 65-88.

151. For another critique of Riley's book but from another perspective, see Ron Cameron,

To be sure, the Johannine writings emphasize Jesus' *bodily* resurrection, involving a vacated tomb and postresurrection existence in a bodily form. But this reflects an emphasis attested in a number of other early Christian texts from Paul onward.[152]

It is also not clear in fact that GJohn reflects a dispute about the nature of Jesus' resurrected body. Actually, the resurrection appearances in John 20:11-29 (including the Thomas vignette in 20:24-29) are all focused on the *identification* of Jesus and the declaration of his risen authority and status (e.g., he can commission his disciples and endow them with the Holy Spirit, 20:21-22). Furthermore, although GJohn emphasizes a bodily resurrection, it also portrays Jesus' resurrection body as not like anything we know in ordinary experience. In the Johannine appearance stories, Jesus' resurrection body has properties quite unlike ordinary mortal bodies. For example, John pictures the risen Jesus as able to materialize in a locked room (20:19, 26), and then, it seems, disappear just as easily. Also, 1 John 3:2-3 reflects a certain reserve in speculating just what is the nature of Jesus' resurrection body ("Beloved . . . it is not yet clearly manifested what we shall be"), maintaining simply that it is enough for believers to know that the form and nature of their eschatological existence will be "like him."[153] This all scarcely reflects a supposed aim of making some specific assertion about the nature of Jesus' resurrection body over against a rival view.

Likewise, contra DeConick, the emphasis in GJohn on believing in Jesus without having seen him does not require opposition against Christian vision-mysticism, specifically, to account for it. Over against unbelief and rejection of Jesus (represented especially in GJohn by Jewish authorities), GJohn emphasizes that Jesus' earthly ministry was the uniquely direct manifestation of God's glory. This emphasis in turn made it necessary for the author(s) of GJohn to stress the validity and virtue of the faith of those who were not eyewitnesses of this historic revelation (that is, the intended readers), whose faith is properly to be elicited through testimony such as is conveyed in GJohn. Note that there is a similar emphasis in 1 Peter 1:8-9, which confirms that the distinction between

---

"Ancient Myths and Modern Theories of the *Gospel of Thomas* and Christian Origins," *Method and Theory in the Study of Religion* 11 (1999): 236-57.

152. I take Paul's reference to Jesus' burial in 1 Cor. 15:4 as most likely requiring the consequent belief that his resurrection involved vacating the tomb. Even if that inference is not compelling to others, it is indisputable that Paul thought Jesus was resurrected in an eschatological body, and that the other canonical Gospels explicitly claim an empty tomb. So, on this matter GJohn shares a Christian tradition that does not require *Gos. Thom.* to account for it.

153. I take the third-person pronouns in 1 John 3:2-3 to refer to Jesus, although God the Father is technically the immediate antecedent in 3:1. Clearly the "he" who was "revealed to take away sins" in 3:5 has to be Jesus, and the antecedent of these pronouns must be "the Son" in 2:23-28.

seeing and believing is neither unique to GJohn nor likely the product of the sort of anti-Thomas polemic that DeConick proposes.

Also, to reiterate a point made previously, the bold and enthusiastic expectation presented in John 14–16 that the Spirit will give further revelations of Jesus indicates a lively ethos of religious experiences that could convey new insights. It is not clear how such an open attitude toward revelatory experiences is consistent with the opposition to visionary experiences that DeConick attributes to Johannine Christianity. Johannine Christians seem to have been very keen on revelations.

Furthermore, although vision mysticism may have been a feature of the religious life of those who produced *Gos. Thom.* (e.g., sayings 83-84), in fact, what the text thematizes and promotes as crucial is the interpretation of esoteric sayings (esp. the prologue and saying 1). That is, it is not so evident from *Gos. Thom.* that vision mysticism is the key phenomenon that specifically identified those whose religious life is reflected in this text. Instead, it seems to me that meditation on esoteric ideas was a favorite pastime.

A further important reason to doubt the proposals of Riley and DeConick is that neither has corroboration from 1 John or 2 John, the Johannine writings that in fact most directly reflect some sort of serious crisis and conflict in Johannine Christianity. As we saw in the preceding chapter of this study, there is no hint that the situation to which these two writings speak was a controversy over the nature of Jesus' risen body or over vision mysticism as opposed to faith.

On the other hand, the spiritual elitism and the revisionist attitude toward more traditional and familiar categories of earliest Christian belief in *Gos. Thom.* do seem to me to correspond well with what 1 John and 2 John appear to oppose. In my view it goes beyond our evidence to say that *Gos. Thom.* comes from the Johannine secessionists, or that it emerged directly in polemics with Johannine circles. But there are certainly interesting similarities in elements of the religious stances of the Johannine secessionists and *Gos. Thom.*

But the idea that GJohn opposes people who venerated Thomas seems to me dubious. Contra Riley and DeConick, Thomas is not so clearly singled out as a figure of disdain or derision in GJohn. The disciples collectively argue against Jesus going to Judea in 11:7-10; and so, however one takes Thomas's comment in 11:16 ("Let us also go, that we may die with him"), it is hardly any more negative than the reluctance of the group. Thomas's statement that the disciples do not know where Jesus is going, and so cannot know the way (14:5), is simply one of three comments in the context by named disciples that also include Philip's request to be shown the Father (14:8) and the query from "Judas (not Iscariot)" about how Jesus will reveal himself to the disciples but not to the world (14:22). It is difficult to see the basis for the claims of Riley and DeConick that Thomas is presented as any more blameworthy than these other named disciples (if in fact any are to be taken as blameworthy at all).

The crucial text is the famous episode in John 20:24-29. Note that Thomas's demand to see the nail marks and touch Jesus' wounds is in fact answered *positively* by Jesus' appearance and invitation to Thomas to do just what he demanded.[154] Furthermore, Thomas's confession in 20:28, "My Lord and my God," is both the high point of the postresurrection narrative and a perfect expression of the view of Jesus that GJohn approves. To be sure, in these resurrection-appearance accounts in John 20, the belief of Thomas *and the other disciples* who have seen Jesus is distinguished from the subsequent faith of "those who have not seen and yet have believed" (20:29). But this distinction does not amount to a flat negative-positive contrast.[155] Brendan Byrne has shown that the accounts of Jesus' three postresurrection appearances in John 20 (to Mary Magdalene, 20:11-18; the other disciples, 20:19-23; and Thomas, 20:24-29) form a threefold pattern that builds to Jesus' climactic statement in 20:29 in which he pronounces a blessing upon all who will believe later on the basis of the things written in GJohn (including these resurrection appearances).[156] Moreover, in the epilogue narrative of John 21, where Jesus appears again to a group of seven disciples, Thomas is listed among them, and in fact is named right after Simon Peter. So it is hard to see a valid basis for thinking that Thomas is treated any more negatively than the others.

Undeniably, Thomas figures much more prominently in GJohn than in any of the other canonical Gospels. But it is characteristic of GJohn to feature named disciples, and often with speaking parts given to them: e.g., Andrew (1:40-41; 6:8; 12:22), Philip (1:43-45; 6:7; 12:21; 14:8-9), Nathanael (1:45-51), Judas Iscariot (6:70-71; 13:2, 26-27; 18:2-3), Lazarus (11:1-57; 12:10-11), Martha (11:20-27), Mary (11:28-37; 12:3-8), the other Judas (14:22), Mary wife of Clopas (19:25), and Mary Magdalene (19:25; 20:1, 11-18). The featuring of Thomas in GJohn appears to fit into a larger literary pattern, and we do not really require a polemical exchange with a "Thomas community" to account for it. Or are we also to suppose that behind all these other characters lie Christian circles attached to

---

154. Obviously showing the influence of John 20:19-29, in the (late second/early third century) *Epistula Apostolorum* (11-12; see *NTA*, 1:255-56) Jesus invites Peter as well as Thomas to touch him, and Jesus directs Andrew to observe that his feet leave footprints, all this to show "that he had truly risen in the flesh." Clearly the proto-orthodox circle in which this writing arose did not regard the Thomas episode as a condemnation of him.

155. Were such a flat contrast intended, we should expect the author to signal this with one of the Greek contrasting conjunctions such as *alla* or perhaps *de*.

156. Brendan Byrne, "The Faith of the Beloved Disciple and the Community in John 20," *JSNT* 23 (1985): 83-97.

them, and that the representation of each figure in GJohn is intended to address some ecclesiastical issue?

In fact, Thomas comes off no worse than does Peter in John 21:15-23, which refers to Peter's discomfort over being repeatedly asked by Jesus whether he loved him. The passage then recounts Jesus' admonition to Peter to mind his own business, in response to Peter's query about the beloved disciple. Granted, it is a widely accepted view that the treatment of Peter in GJohn reflects a fraternal engagement of Johannine Christians with those who revered Peter. But if for the sake of argument we take Thomas as likewise representing some particular circle of believers, why should we then imagine that, unlike Peter and his admirers, Thomas and "Thomasines" are being singled out for disdain or refutation?

I repeat the judgment that we do not require *Gos. Thom.* or a polemic with what it represents to account for the themes and characters featured in GJohn. *Gos. Thom.* is an extremely interesting compilation in its own right, reflecting a type of early piety of some Christians who distinguished themselves from the other circles of early Christianity that affirmed proto-orthodox beliefs. *Gos. Thom.* illustrates vividly the radical diversity in the interpretation of Jesus that we shall see more of in chapter 9.

Revelation Dialogues

The emphasis in *Gos. Thom.* on Jesus delivering secret teaching to particular disciples, and the exclusivist, sectarian attitude toward the beliefs of other Christians, link it with several other Jesus books that are described by scholars as "revelation dialogues," a literary genre to which I briefly referred earlier in discussing the *Gospel of the Egyptians*. With the publication of the Nag Hammadi cache of writings, we now have several texts that are commonly seen as leading extant examples of this kind of Jesus book.[157] But the dismayingly wide range of scholarly views about their date and provenance makes it difficult to place these writings historically in the present discussion of earliest Christianity without objection. So, to avoid making this discussion unduly long, there is no choice but to proceed with what seems most plausible to me.

157. *NTA*, 1:228-353, gives introductions and translations of widely agreed-upon members of this genre: the *Book of Thomas (the Contender)*, *Apocryphon of James*, *Dialogue of the Savior*, *First Apocalypse of James*, *Second Apocalypse of James*, *Letter of Peter to Philip*, all these Nag Hammadi writings of a recognizably "heterodox" character (also translated in *NHLE*), along with a couple of examples of more "orthodox" texts where the risen Jesus gives instruction to disciples, the *Epistula Apostolorum*, and the Freer Logion. For further discussion, see also Koester, *Ancient Christian Gospels*, 173-200; and esp. Perkins, *The Gnostic Dialogue*, which I regard as the most persuasive treatment of these texts and the attendant issues.

Essentially the revelation dialogue genre claims to present a body of Jesus' teachings which consists of a series of sayings that can range in length from one sentence to a minidiscourse. These are characteristically represented as spoken by Jesus in response to queries and comments from disciples. There are sometimes topical connections of two or three sayings, but overall the text does not typically comprise a linear development of a line of reasoning, or even an obviously organized set of teachings, although one can detect major emphases being promoted. As noted earlier, there are certain resemblances to the textual nature and tone of *Gos. Thom.*, and in comparison to *Gos. Thom.* the revelation dialogues may represent a further (or collateral) literary development of a genre particularly suited for promoting a body of special teachings that could be attributed to Jesus.

For several reasons I conclude that, as a literary genre, revelation dialogues probably belong to the late second century and thereafter. Of course, the dialogue is an ancient rhetorical vehicle for presenting teaching, and dialogues appear as units of material in the Synoptic tradition (e.g., Mark 4:10-34; 7:17-23), and are especially favored in GJohn as the form in which Jesus' teachings are conveyed. The specific postresurrection dialogue as well, in which the risen Jesus gives further revelation to his disciples, is instanced in first-century texts (e.g., Acts 1:6-8). But the origin of the revelation dialogue *as a literary genre* appears to lie in the effort to make particularist and dissenting claims for renditions of Jesus, over against the traditions and their authorities that became enshrined in the New Testament writings in particular. To underscore this point, in the earlier stages of tradition represented in the canonical Gospels, the dialogue form was used either as a simple vehicle of teaching or, in the postresurrection dialogues, to authorize the beliefs about Jesus reflected in early Christian proclamation and devotion. But the revelation dialogue as a *literary genre* appears to have been developed specifically to assert polemically ideas and beliefs different from those favored in what became the "mainstream" tradition.

To cite one important example, the repeated effort to relativize the significance of the twelve disciples of Jesus in the *Apocryphon of James* seems to make most sense historically as a reaction against the force of "great church" claims and structures that were becoming more effectively dominant in the closing decades of the second century and later.[158]

---

158. The *Apocryphon of James* claims to be a secret book conveying Jesus' teaching not given to the Twelve (incipit; *NHLE*, 30). The reference to the Twelve writing their recollections of Jesus' teaching (2.9-15; *NHLE*, 30) likely alludes to "great church" use of the canonical Gospels as apostolic memoirs (e.g., Justin, *Dial.* 103.8; 105.5); and in 16.4-10 (*NHLE*, 37) the tradition of the Twelve going to various parts of the world in mission is critically revised to present their dispersion as intended to prevent them from having much influence! I differ, thus, from Dankwart Kirchner ("The Apocryphon of James," in *NTA*, 1:285-99 [esp. 287]; Kirchner, *Epistula Jacobi*

Consequently I place the probable time of composition of these writings just beyond, or perhaps toward the end of, the time frame of "earliest Christianity" that I am using (ca. 70-170).[159] It is possible, however, that the earliest use of this literary genre might be pushed back to the first half of the second century.[160] There were clearly radically divergent versions of Christianity from at least the late first century onward, as we have seen; these radical differences provide a plausible situation for the creation of a genre of Jesus books that was intended to serve polemical concerns. In any case, the religious impulses and beliefs that these writings defend were probably older than these writings themselves. So this adequately justifies giving some attention to them here.[161]

I begin my discussion of the contents of these writings by reiterating something already mentioned: the essential claim in these texts is that they convey advanced teaching from Jesus, which is often portrayed as given secretly to particular disciples (e.g., *Ap. Jas.* 1.1-25; *Thom. Cont.* 138.1-5; *Ap. John* 1.1-5). Characteristically these texts claim that these teachings also go far beyond the level of understanding reflected in ordinary Christian proclamation and instruction. The revelation dialogue as a literary genre seems, in fact, to have been particularly preferred among Christian circles who sought to claim superiority for their ideas over against what came to be traditional Christian beliefs.[162]

Indeed, it is arguable that the development of revelation dialogues as a kind of early Jesus book specifically represents efforts to counter and supersede the well-known narrative Gospels and their portrayal of Jesus. As a series of statements and minidiscourses of Jesus in reply to queries from disciples, the revelation dialogue genre facilitated very different portrayals, which dispense

---

Apocrypha: Die zweite Schrift aus Nag-Hammadi-Codex I, TU 136 [Berlin: Akademie-Verlag, 1989], 6), who assents rather uncritically to Ron Cameron's proposed dating of the text to the early second century (*Sayings Traditions in the "Apocryphon of James,"* HTS 34 [Philadelphia: Fortress Press, 1984]). Cf. Perkins, 145-56, who successfully shows the writing to represent "a sustained and vigorous attack on orthodox attempts to eradicate Gnosticism" (154), which points strongly to the late second century or later still as the likely time of composition.

159. E.g., Marvin W. Meyer, *The Letter of Peter to Philip: Text, Translation, and Commentary,* SBLDS 53 (Chico, Calif.: Scholars, 1981), places this revelation dialogue "around the end of the second century or into the third," and notes that it presupposes and seeks to reinterpret the more familiar traditions of proto-orthodox Christianity (194).

160. See esp. Koester's arguments for earlier dates of what he claims are the originating versions of *Dialogue of the Savior* and the *Apocryphon of James,* in *Ancient Christian Gospels,* 173-200.

161. See also Perkins, esp. 177-90.

162. The *Epistula Apostolorum,* which is probably best dated in the late second or early third century, is an orthodox appropriation of the revelation dialogue genre to oppose heterodox beliefs. Cf. C. Detlef G. Muller, *NTA,* 1:251; Hills, *Tradition and Composition in the "Epistula Apostolorum"*; M. Hornschuh, *Studien zur Epistula Apostolorum,* PTS 5 (Berlin: Walter de Gruyter, 1965).

with major features of the narrative Jesus books, such as Jesus' historical location in Roman Judea/Palestine, miracle stories, and the presentation of his significance in relation to Israel and the Old Testament. This genre readily facilitated the delivery of, and focus on, *ideas* attributed to Jesus. And the motif of special/secret instruction given to particular disciples (and withheld or imperfectly grasped by others) was readily appropriate for promoting ideas that were not embraced by those Christians who preferred the narrative Gospels. The specific content of the teachings given in the revelation dialogues varies somewhat from one writing to another, but broadly speaking it is a varying combination of reinterpretations/revisions of traditional Christian confessional categories, along with certain other beliefs and emphases more particular to those behind these writings.

In these texts Jesus' role is essentially that of revealer and exemplar, his teachings and actions offering the crucial redemptive insight into the true nature of things, including particularly the origin and destiny of the elect, and how they are to live. Jesus came from above, from the Father, and entered the world to bring illumination to the elect so that they could understand who they really are, and could set themselves to achieve their divine destiny.

Where these texts refer to Jesus' death, they most often interpret it as his own exemplary stripping off of his bodily existence; his "resurrection" is his liberated mode of existence thereafter, in which his own divine nature is fully exhibited, no longer hindered and obscured by a body. Jesus thus demonstrates for the elect how their own divine nature and destiny are to be fully realized, his death and consequent state also serving as encouragement to them that such a divine self-realization after death awaits them as well. This is, for example, how we are to understand the call in *Apocryphon of James* 5.32-35, "Remember my cross and my death, and you will live," and the following demand for belief in Jesus' cross as the essential basis for participating in the kingdom of God (6.1-5). Likewise, in the statement in *Apocryphon of James* 13, "I have placed myself under the curse, that you may be saved," the curse is bodily existence, which Jesus took on temporarily so that he could convey and demonstrate to the elect the nature of their own present plight and their real (and glorious) future. Although *1 Apocalypse of James* (131.15-21) denies that "the Lord" ever suffered, this likely means that the crucifixion merely affected the fleshly body that he took on temporarily, not his true, divine being.

As in *Gos. Thom.*, so in these revelation dialogues, Jesus has a crucial functional importance, but no final uniqueness as to his nature, or even his status. To be sure, he is the one whose descent from the realm of light was vital for the elect. But although they did not know it until they were reawakened through the revealer's descent and teaching, the elect of these writings now realize that in fact they share as fully as Jesus in the same heavenly and divine origin and nature. And they simply expect to follow Jesus to the same glory and divine self-realization that he experienced.

In their present situation of bodily existence, the elect are usually exhorted to live out their disdain for, and hope to escape from, the body and all it represents. That is, these texts tend to urge a strongly ascetic way of life, which often particularly focuses on renunciation of sexual relations (e.g., *Dial. Sav.* 90-93; *Ap. John* 24.26-31; *Soph. Jes. Chr.* 108). As to other features of the religious practice urged and reflected in the revelation dialogues, there are sometimes hints of prayer, praise/worship of God (and Jesus as well), and revelatory experiences such as mystical visions (*Ap. Jas.* 14.15-25). But the variations in these writings warn us that there may have been significant differences in beliefs and practices among the circles of those who composed them.

Although the revelation dialogues are almost entirely sayings, a master narrative is usually alluded to and presupposed. The Savior, Jesus, has come from above, taking a body as a temporary costume or disguise for his earthly appearance (e.g., *Ep. Pet. Phil.* 136.17-29; *Ap. Jas.* 8.35–9.9). His descent was to reawaken the elect to their own true origins (e.g., *1 Apoc. Jas.* 28.8-20), so that they might despise the flesh and orient themselves to their return to the highest divine level (e.g., "the Father"). In his death Jesus threw off the bond of flesh, and his consequent glorification and heavenly status gives the elect the inspiring example for their own future liberation. Through the revelation that the Savior has brought, the elect are equipped to handle the spiritual powers ("archons") who will seek to prevent them from achieving their divine destiny. For example, in *1 Apocalypse of James* 33-34 the elect are instructed, when challenged by these archons, to declare that they are "from the Pre-existent Father, and a son in the Pre-existent One," and are returning to the (divine/heavenly) place from which they have come. Thus equipped, the elect are assured that they will escape the attacks of the archons.[163]

Summary

The various writings that we have noted in this chapter undeniably illustrate the diversity and abundance of books about Jesus in the second century. In fact, the many Jesus books produced in the first two or three centuries constitute an

---

163. There is a resemblance to saying 50 of *Gos. Thom.*, and the unidentified "they" there who challenge the elect are probably likewise the spiritual powers who would seek to prevent the liberation of the elect.

unparalleled phenomenon, and surely indicate the central place of Jesus in the religious devotion of the early Christian movement.

As the preceding discussion has shown, there are interesting variations in these writings. Some appear to be intended as elaborations, adornments, and renditions of the traditions about Jesus in the canonical Gospels. There is no indication that these writings were composed to displace or compete with the canonical accounts. Instead they probably reflect the curiosity and piety of many ordinary believers, though perhaps those with a somewhat unsophisticated mentality, for whom the canonical Gospels were familiar and respected texts. Other writings, however, were more clearly intended as alternative, competitive renditions of Jesus, and they appear to have been produced by, and for, "heterodox" circles who distinguished their views from the more familiar beliefs that marked "proto-orthodox" Christianity.

To underscore some observations from the foregoing discussion, the major distinguishing features that mark off the heterodox Jesus books from the others are the following. First, there is the particularist and elitist claim that what is presented is a special, often secretive rendition of Jesus and his teachings. Those Christians who do not share the special knowledge of the elect of these Jesus books are apparently included among the "drunken" and ignorant, and are scarcely differentiated from non-Christians as to their destiny. In some cases there are direct polemical references to these other circles of Christians, and those they revered as leaders.

Second, the heterodox writings do not characteristically present Jesus with reference to the Old Testament and the narrative world of Israel and the God of these Scriptures (at least not positively). Jesus is not, for example, usually presented as fulfillment of biblical prophecy, or of typological events or characters of the Old Testament. Indeed, in some cases the heterodox Jesus books specifically deny any relevance or validity to the Scriptures of Israel for understanding Jesus (e.g., *Gos. Thom.* 52). Instead of the narrative world of the Old Testament, the master narrative recited or alluded to in the heterodox writings posits a precosmic drama of alienation of the elect from their divine origin. This involved their becoming bound in fleshly existence, which brought forgetfulness of their true transcendent selves. In this drama the human predicament is not sinfulness and disobedience to God's commands, but forgetfulness (or ignorance); the key redemptive aims are the lifting of the veil of forgetfulness of the elect, and ultimately, the escape from bodily existence and a return to divine origins.

Third, these writings do not articulate Jesus' divine status with reference to the one God of the exclusivist monotheism that Christianity inherited from Jewish tradition of the Greco-Roman period. Instead they present Jesus in the context of a sometimes elaborate and complex notion of the divine realm, with a *plēroma* (fullness) of multiple gradations of divinity. Consequently, in the Jesus books written with such an outlook, there is no indication that Jesus' divinity posed any problem that required much thought. It was his *humanity,* more specifically the question of his bodily existence, that seems to have been somewhat more difficult to accommodate.

It is not so terribly surprising that some circles of Christians found the Old Testament and the exclusivist monotheism of the Jewish tradition uncongenial or insufficiently meaningful, and explored other conceptual schemes that probably derived more from philosophical and mythological traditions of the wider Greco-Roman era. In subsequent times as well, certain religious figures have preferred similar schemes for expressing their religious beliefs (e.g., Swedenborg).[164] But as with these later instances as well, it appears that the more successful versions of Christianity were those that continued to articulate their faith through appropriation and adaptation of biblical traditions inherited from the Jewish matrix of the Christian movement.

We have not considered here all the writings that are sometimes referred to as "gospels," and whose origin might be placed sometime in the second century. In particular there is the *Gospel of Philip* and the *Gospel of Truth.* These writings, however, are different again in literary genre. I shall give some attention to them in chapter 9, as we look further at the radical diversity of second-century Christianity and the consolidation of proto-orthodox Christian faith and practice.

Based on the writings that we have surveyed here, it is clear that mutually incompatible views of Jesus circulated in the second century, and probably earlier still. In addition to the complaints by exponents of early orthodoxy, such as Irenaeus *(Against Heresies),* we now have texts that consciously present radically heterodox views of Jesus, and that probably reflect the sorts of beliefs against which Irenaeus and other spokesmen of proto-orthodox Christianity campaigned. In their claims to superior knowledge, and their disdain for the beliefs of those Christians who do not share their insights, these texts provide us opportunities to hear the other side of the conflict between emergent orthodox Christianity and various alternative versions of the faith.

---

164. "Swedenborg, Emanuel," in *Oxford Dictionary of the Christian Church,* ed. F. L. Cross and E. A. Livingstone, 3rd ed. (Oxford: Oxford University Press, 1997), 1563-64 (with bibliography).

CHAPTER EIGHT

The Second Century — Importance and Tributaries

The aim in this chapter and the two which follow is to continue our analysis of devotion to Jesus chronologically through the closing decades of what I am categorizing "earliest" Christianity, which takes us well into the second century.[1] In the next chapter we examine key expressions of the "radical diversity" of interpretations of Jesus, focusing on "Valentinianism" and "Marcionism." The final chapter is devoted to phenomena that exhibit what I mean by "proto-orthodox" devotion to Jesus. The time frame to which we give attention in this chapter and the next two (ca. 70-170) constitutes the key transitional period toward what became classical Christianity of subsequent centuries: a distinguishable religion made up largely of Gentiles, with bishops, canon, and creeds.[2] In particular I want to emphasize the significance of the second century as the time when dynamics that had been operative for decades earlier more fully came to expression.

Before we look at particulars in the following chapters, there are a few important matters to address by way of orientation. First, we take account briefly of the broader importance of this period. Then I explain how my approach in these chapters distinguishes my analysis from some other relevant studies; I also define what I mean by "radical diversity" and "proto-orthodoxy." Thereafter it is

---

1. I draw upon and expand here my earlier analysis of Christian texts from ca. 70-150: "Christology," in *DLNTD*, 170-84.

2. In his editorial introducing the launch of a journal devoted to the study of the second century, Everett Ferguson quickly sketched the importance of this period: "A New Journal," *SecCent* 1 (1981): 4. Note also introductory comments by Arland J. Hultgren and Steven A. Haggmark, *The Earliest Christian Heretics: Readings from Their Opponents* (Minneapolis: Fortress, 1996), 1-3.

important to examine some further important "tributaries" of the late first century, which, along with the phenomena we examined in previous chapters, fed into the rich, varied, and controverted Christianity of the second century.

Christianity in the Second Century

To help set the scene for our discussion of second-century devotion to Jesus, some brief characterization of key developments in Christianity of the period may be helpful. On the one hand the evidence of the time shows the continuing importance and influence of Christian beliefs and devotional practices that originated in the first century. Actually, of course, in both the probable date of their composition and the religious stance they affirm and reflect, there is considerable overlap between the later writings in the New Testament and a number of other early Christian writings that can be dated in the approximate period 70-170. But there were also further developments in the second century, both monumental in their own right and also influential for the subsequent centuries of struggles among different Christian viewpoints over what to believe about God and Jesus, struggles that led to the classical confessional statements of the fourth and fifth centuries.[3]

To cite one important transition, there was a demographic shift. Through the first several decades of the first century, what became "Christianity" can be described as a new religious movement emerging within the Jewish religious tradition of the time. From about the middle of the first century onward, Gentile converts formed an increasingly significant portion of the Christian movement. But in the initial few decades at least, the influential leaders of known Christian circles (especially those leaders with translocal influence) were mainly Jewish believers (e.g., Simon Peter, Paul, James of Jerusalem, John Zebedee, Barnabas, Silas/Silvanus, Prisca and Aquila). By the closing decades of the first century and on into the second, however, it appears that the leadership as well as the constituency of the movement became more and more dominantly made up of Gentile converts. This is probably one major reason adherents and outsiders alike began to perceive the movement more and more as a distinguishable religion in its own right.

As we have seen in previous chapters, devotion to Jesus was intense in the

---

3. See, e.g., R. P. C. Hanson, *The Search for the Christian Doctrine of God* (Edinburgh: T. & T. Clark, 1988); Aloys Grillmeier, *Christ in Christian Tradition*, vol. 1, *From the Apostolic Age to Chalcedon*, rev. and trans. John Bowden, 2nd ed. (London: Mowbray & Co.; Atlanta: John Knox, 1975). Robin Lane Fox gives a readable and widely praised account of Christianity from the second through the Constantinian period: *Pagans and Christians* (New York: Knopf, 1987).

earliest decades; the success Christians achieved in promoting their beliefs was impressive. Only a few years after Jesus' execution the young religious movement already had small groups of adherents in major urban centers of the Jewish diaspora outside Roman Judea, including Damascus, Antioch, and probably Rome too. But the second century was almost as dramatic in developments of various kinds. For example, at the beginning of the century Christianity was still a comparatively small (though diverse) movement that most sophisticated pagans probably were either largely ignorant of or disdained as a curious and silly superstition. Leaders of Jewish communities in diaspora cities where the movement had adherents probably thought it involved an annoying misconstrual of the Scriptures, and promoted an offensive and even blasphemous reverence of a justifiably condemned troublemaker and false teacher.[4]

Across the second century, however, members of the cultural elite of the Roman Empire began to register an increasing awareness of (and concerns about) Christianity. Initially this mainly involved passing references and disdainful swipes, such as the remarks in Tacitus (d. 120; *Annales* 15.44), Suetonius (d. ca. 140; *Nero* 16.2), Epictetus (d. ca. 135; *Enchiridion* 4.7.6), and Galen (d. 199). Pliny's famous letter to Trajan (ca. 113) and Trajan's cautious reply hint that political authorities were beginning to have concerns about the Christian movement, though they were still ill informed as to specifics.[5] By the end of the century, in spite of occasionally vicious (but localized) persecution, Christianity had become sufficiently visible to be ridiculed extensively in Lucian of

---

4. This is a fair characterization of the views attributed to the Jewish interlocutors of Justin Martyr in *The Dialogue with Trypho,* and it is widely thought that they rather authentically voice the sorts of Jewish objections that Christians such as Justin encountered. See, e.g., Demetrios C. Trakatellis, "Justin Martyr's Trypho," in *Christians among Jews and Gentiles,* ed. G. W. E. Nickelsburg and G. W. McCrae (Philadelphia: Fortress, 1986), 287-97. See also Claudia J. Setzer, *Jewish Responses to Early Christians: History and Polemics, 30-150 C.E.* (Minneapolis: Fortress, 1994).

5. Molly Whittaker, *Jews and Christians: Graeco-Roman Views* (Cambridge: Cambridge University Press, 1984), gives excerpts in English translation. For accessible discussions of the major pagan references of the second through the fourth centuries, including Pliny, Galen, Celsus, Porphyry, and Julian the Apostate, see Robert L. Wilken, *The Christians as the Romans Saw Them* (New Haven and London: Yale University Press, 1984); and Jeffrey W. Hargis, *Against the Christians: The Rise of Early Anti-Christian Polemic,* Patristic Studies 1 (New York: Peter Lang, 1999). P. R. Coleman-Norton's collection of, and commentary on, extant Roman legal documents referring to Christians, *Roman State and Christian Church: A Collection of Legal Documents to A.D. 535,* 3 vols. (London: SPCK, 1966), includes a discussion of Trajan's reply to Pliny's famous letter (1-5). Peter Guyot and Richard Klein, *Das frühe Christentum bis zum Ende der Verfolgungen,* 2 vols. (Darmstadt: Wissenschaftliche Buchgesellschaft, 1993-94), give original-language citations, German translations, and commentary on the encounter between pre-Constantinian Christianity and the Roman state and society.

Samosata's (d. ca. 200) witty farce, *On the Death of Peregrinus*, which suggests that this ambitious author thought his readers would have heard something about Christians and would enjoy a story told at their expense.

In this period Christians were also the subject of more serious literary attacks. Probably around 160 Cornelius Fronto, the celebrated orator who was also the tutor and intimate of Marcus Aurelius, composed an address against Christians that is referred to in ancient sources but is unfortunately now lost. A bit later Celsus launched an impressively well researched critique of Christianity, *True Doctrine,* perhaps the first full-scale philosophical engagement with Christian faith from the perspective of an educated pagan.[6] As Jeffrey Hargis noted, Celsus's effort to demolish Christianity shows how successful and threatening it had become in the eyes of many of the cultured elite of the empire, their anxiety prompted by the growing numbers of Christians and by the movement's aggressive efforts for recognition and respect:

> Celsus' literary reply to Christianity was a symptom of the progress his opponents had made over the previous hundred years. . . . By the time Celsus and the other polemicists began their attack, however, their enemy had become a force to be reckoned with. The Christianity of the late second century and following was characterized by increasing intellectual sophistication, self-conscious separation from its Jewish parent, and a growing sense of mission. Perhaps most threatening of all to their pagan respondents, Christian thinkers were beginning to assert ownership of the cultural and intellectual property of their pagan opponents.[7]

Particularly in the later decades of the second century, Christian literary output was a "flood . . . and reached proportions that amaze the modern reader" in "volume, variety, and vigor."[8] In his study of Athenagoras, a Chris-

---

6. Fronto's (ca. 100-166) anti-Christian address does not survive, but elements are thought to be reflected in the speeches of the character Caecilius in the Latin Christian apologetic work *Octavius,* by Minucius Felix (third century). Celsus's work is preserved in the refutation by Origen. Whittaker gives relevant excerpts from *Octavius* (Whittaker, 172-76), and from Origen's *Contra Celsum* (178-87). For the full text of the latter, see Henry Chadwick, trans., *Origen: "Contra Celsum"* (Cambridge: Cambridge University Press, 1953). Studies include R. Joseph Hoffmann, trans. and ed., *Celsus, On the True Doctrine: A Discourse against the Christians* (New York and Oxford: Oxford University Press, 1987); Hargis, 17-62; Wilken, 94-125. For brief summaries of the careers of the figures I refer to, see entries on them in *OCD.*

7. Hargis, 15. Though Celsus's *True Doctrine* is often dated by scholars ca. 170 (e.g., Wilken, 94), Hargis (20-24) argues for a date closer to 200.

8. Edgar J. Goodspeed, *A History of Early Christian Literature,* revised and enlarged by Robert M. Grant (Chicago: University of Chicago Press, 1966), 5.

tian apologist of the latter half of the second century, Barnard also noted the astonishing literary activity in late-second-century Christianity, especially by Christian writers seeking to defend and establish Christian faith over against polytheism through the use of argument, often adapting philosophical traditions to their purposes.[9]

In the consolidation of what became the Christian canon, second-century developments are remarkable, and also were decisive for subsequent times. In one important development, though the writings that make up the New Testament were probably all (or nearly all) composed by about 100 (or not long thereafter), the second century was the crucial period for their copying, collection, dissemination, and subsequent inclusion in the Christian canon.[10] The canonical Gospels, for example, were probably first linked and marked off as a fourfold collection in the early decades of the second century; a few decades later Irenaeus was able to refer to them as a closed body with wide acceptance.[11] Sometime between 140 and 150 the Christian teacher Marcion compiled the first closed canon of Christian Scriptures, which he confined solely to the Gospel of Luke and ten epistles of Paul. Those Christians who regarded Marcion's canon as too narrow, and his theology dubious, probably found it necessary to consider what then should be regarded as Scripture. Although Christians continued to consider the exact limits of what to include in the developing Christian canon during the next few centuries, by about 200 there was increasingly widespread agreement on most of what now makes up the New Testament.[12]

Furthermore, the earliest extant physical artifacts of Christianity are fragments of manuscripts from the second century, and the earliest manuscripts that substantially preserve the text of some New Testament writings are commonly dated toward the end of the second and/or early decades of the following century.[13] So, for the history of the text of the New Testament writings, the sec-

---

9. L. W. Barnard, *Athenagoras: A Study in Second Century Christian Apologetic* (Paris: Beauchesne, 1972), 11-12.

10. Standard, critical introductions of recent vintage covering dates, authorship, provenances, and other matters include Helmut Koester, *Introduction to the New Testament,* 2 vols. (Philadelphia: Fortress, 1982); Werner Georg Kümmel, *Introduction to the New Testament,* ed. and trans. H. C. Kee, rev. ed. (Nashville: Abingdon, 1975).

11. I return to the fourfold Gospels collection in chap. 10.

12. See, e.g., Hans von Campenhausen, *The Formation of the Christian Bible* (Philadelphia: Fortress, 1972); Lee Martin McDonald, *The Formation of the Christian Biblical Canon,* rev. ed. (Peabody, Mass.: Hendrickson, 1995); Harry Y. Gamble, *The New Testament Canon: Its Making and Meaning* (Philadelphia: Fortress, 1985).

13. Among earliest copies of writings that became part of the New Testament, P52, a fragment of the Gospel of John identified in 1936, is usually dated ca. 130; but cf. now A. Schmidt,

ond century is again crucial, even though the surviving evidence from that period is frustratingly fragmentary and limited.

I shall not prolong this discussion by invoking other influential developments that make the period so important, such as "mono-episcopacy" (a single bishop presiding over a church in a given location).[14] Instead, I now wish to lay out the approach we will take in this and the next two chapters.

Approach and Focus

I begin by comparing my approach with that taken in some other studies. To cite one major contributor, over the last few decades Eric Osborn has focused several valuable studies on the second century as the setting for the origins of the subsequent Christian intellectual tradition. He has shown that key figures in the latter half of the century, particularly Justin, Athenagoras, Irenaeus, Clement of Alexandria, and Tertullian, hammered out the basics of an influential understanding of God in the energetic disputation among various competing Christian views of their day, and in desperate argumentation with pagan religion and philosophy.[15] In a memorable epigram, Osborn expressed the

---

"Zwei Anmerkungen zu P.Ryl. III," *Archiv für Papyrusforschung* 35 (1989): 11-12, who proposes a date no earlier than 170. Fragmentary manuscripts of Matthew (P103, P104, and a newly identified portion of P77) dated to the late second or early third century have been published in recent volumes of *The Oxyrhynchus Papyri* (vols. 64-66, 1997-99). In the same volumes are several newly identified fragmentary papyri of the Gospel of John, dated a bit later (third century) by the editors. See also Peter M. Head, "Some Recently Published NT Papyri from Oxyrhynchus: An Overview and Preliminary Assessment," *TB* 51 (2000): 1-16. The earliest manuscripts that preserve more substantial portions of New Testament writings are P75 (from 175-200, large portions of Luke and John), P66 (ca. 200, much of John), P45 (from ca. 200-250, portions of all four canonical Gospels and Acts), and P46 (ca. 250, Pauline epistles). Among Christian papyri from the second and third centuries we also have copies (usually fragments) of a number of extracanonical writings, including *The Shepherd of Hermas*, the *Gospel of Peter*, and the *Gospel of Thomas*. For an overview and bibliography of key publications, see Edwin A. Judge, "Papyri," in *EEC*, 2:867-72. The standard reference work is Joseph van Haelst, *Catalogue des papyrus littéraires juifs et chrétiens* (Paris: Publications de la Sorbonne, 1976), which I cite by the number he assigns to manuscripts.

14. See, e.g., Everett Ferguson, "Bishop," in *EEC*, 1:182-85. Ignatius of Antioch is our first extant witness to this pattern of local church leadership, but "by the middle of the second century, the Ignatian type of church order, with a single bishop at the head of each Christian community, was generally observed" (151).

15. Eric Osborn, *The Beginning of Christian Philosophy* (Cambridge: Cambridge University Press, 1981), and especially *The Emergence of Christian Theology* (Cambridge: Cambridge University Press, 1993). These analyses rest upon detailed studies of individual second-century

fervency and importance of their intellectual efforts: "Fortunately for posterity, Christian apologists had to argue for their lives."[16] Although the following pages will show my indebtedness to Osborn and other historians of Christian thought, particularly on these key figures of the latter part of the second century, there are some differences between their studies and my approach.

The first difference is in chronological focus. Because scholars such as Osborn are primarily concerned with the second century as the initial stage of certain conceptual categories and doctrinal formulations that are important in *subsequent* centuries of creedal development and "patristic" Christianity, they tend to focus on the great figures of the later decades (whom they rightly see as seminal thinkers).[17] I approach the second century from the other chronological end, however; I seek to trace connections with, and further developments in, the *earlier* devotional phenomena of the first century discussed in previous chapters. That is, in this discussion the second century *concludes* "earliest" Christianity. Consequently, also, I concentrate more on the first several decades of the century than the later ones.

The second difference is in subject focus. Because my concern here is the broader category of "devotion" to Jesus and not simply the development of formal christological doctrines, I consider a wider set of phenomena that more fully represent how Jesus figured in the religious *beliefs* and *practices* of second-century Christians. Although I want to acknowledge the intellectual achievements and influence of individual Christian thinkers of the second century, I

---

figures: *The Philosophy of Clement of Alexandria,* TS, n.s., 3 (Cambridge: Cambridge University Press, 1957); *Justin Martyr,* BZHT 47 (Tübingen: J. C. B. Mohr [Paul Siebeck], 1973); and most recently, *Tertullian, First Theologian of the West* (Cambridge: Cambridge University Press, 1997). Among other important contributors, I mention also L. W. Barnard, whose numerous studies include the following: *Justin Martyr: His Life and Thought* (Cambridge: Cambridge University Press, 1967); *Athenagoras; Studies in the Apostolic Fathers and Their Background* (New York: Schocken Books; Oxford: Blackwell, 1966). R. M. Grant, *The Christ of the Second Century: Jesus after the Gospels* (Louisville: Westminster John Knox, 1990), gives an introductory survey of some christological issues of the period. Because it is much overlooked, I also mention Antonio Orbe, *Introduccion a la Teologia de los Siglos II y III,* 2 vols. (Rome: Editrice Pontificia Universita Gregoriana, 1987).

16. Osborn, *Emergence of Christian Theology,* 3.

17. Among other examples of historians of Christian doctrine for whom the first century is basically background and the second century is approached mainly with reference to subsequent developments are magisterial studies such as Grillmeier, *From the Apostolic Age to Chalcedon;* Jules Lebreton, *Histoire du dogme de la Trinité, des origines au concile de Nicée,* 2 vols. (1910; reprint, Paris: G. Beauchesne, 1928); ET of vol. 1, *History of the Dogma of the Trinity from Its Origins to the Council of Nicaea* (London: Burns, Oates, and Washbourne, 1939); Jean Daniélou, *Gospel Message and Hellenistic Culture,* trans. and ed. J. A. Baker (London: Darton, Longman, Todd; Philadelphia: Westminster, 1973).

focus on beliefs and practices that were more broadly characteristic of various circles of Christian believers of the time. To be sure, we shall pay some attention to key figures, such as Valentinus and Marcion in the following chapter, and Justin Martyr in the final chapter. But the main concern will be how such figures reflect and represent a religious stance shared with other believers of the time.

Definitions

I will characterize devotion to Jesus in the second century with two contrasting but also related dynamics: radical diversity and the emergence of "proto-orthodox" (or "proto-catholic") conventions in belief and practice. By "radical diversity" I mean differences in belief and/or practice that *second-century Christians themselves* considered significant enough to justify such things as denunciation of, and even separation from, those who refused to share their stances on the issues involved. Not all the diversity of the second century was this radical, but instances were common enough.

Of course, as several generations of New Testament scholars have emphasized, diversity marked the Christian movement in the first century as well.[18] Indeed, we noted in an earlier chapter that at least one first-century example of genuinely "radical" diversity is represented in the full-blown schism among Johannine Christians that seems to have prompted the author of 1 John to pen that intriguing missive. But second-century Christianity was more obviously, and more frequently, marked by a number of serious differences, including radically different views of how to regard Jesus. We look at key examples of this in the next chapter.

By "proto-orthodox" faith I mean early examples and stages of the sorts of beliefs and practices that, across the next couple centuries, succeeded in becoming characteristic of classical, "orthodox" Christianity, and came to be widely affirmed in Christian circles over against the alternatives.[19] With some

---

18. E.g., J. D. G. Dunn, *Unity and Diversity in the New Testament* (Philadelphia: Westminster, 1977). The work most often cited today as influencing the interest in emphasizing the diverse nature of early Christianity is Walter Bauer, *Rechtgläubigkeit und Ketzerei im ältesten Christentum* (Tübingen: Mohr-Siebeck, 1934); ET, *Orthodoxy and Heresy in Earliest Christianity* (Philadelphia: Fortress, 1971). See, e.g., Daniel J. Harrington, "The Reception of Walter Bauer's *Orthodoxy and Heresy in Earliest Christianity* during the Last Decade," *HTR* 73 (1980): 289-98; Michel Desjardins, "Bauer and Beyond: On Recent Scholarly Discussions of *Hairesis* in the Early Christian Era," *SecCent* 8 (1991): 65-82.

19. I borrow the term "proto-orthodox" from Bart D. Ehrman, *The Orthodox Corruption*

other scholars I maintain that we can already identify a number of features of what is later labeled "orthodox" (or "catholic") Christian faith and practice in the second century, particularly in the ways devotion to Jesus was expressed.[20] We examine these specifics more fully in the final chapter. But it will assist that analysis to give here a preliminary characterization of the key features of what I mean by proto-orthodox Christianity.

As we shall see, to a remarkable extent early-second-century proto-orthodox devotion to Jesus represents a concern to preserve, respect, promote, and develop what were by then becoming traditional expressions of belief and reverence, and that had originated in earlier years of the Christian movement. That is, proto-orthodox faith tended to affirm and develop devotional and confessional traditions such as those we studied in previous chapters. Arland Hultgren has shown that the roots of this appreciation of traditions of faith actually go back deeply and widely into first-century Christianity.[21] But the emphasis on tradition was also a key feature of emergent proto-orthodox faith in the second century.

Also, of course, proto-orthodox circles were concerned to distinguish what they considered valid from invalid articulations of belief in Jesus, and acceptable from unacceptable expressions of the faith in devotional practice and other behavior. But this concern, likewise, was neither unique to them nor novel in the second century. Those Christians with whom they had sharp differences over proper belief and practice seem often in turn to have regarded proto-orthodox faith as benighted, and they were sometimes equally insistent that their own version of faith was the only right one. Moreover, from Paul's controversies with Judaizing believers and on through denunciations of "false teachings" in a number of later New Testament writings (e.g., 1 Tim. 4:1-5; 2 Tim. 2:14–3:9; 2 Pet. 2:1-21; Jude 5-16), it is clear that a concern to distinguish valid from invalid expressions of faith was an unavoidable feature of the early Christian movement. (Of course, what was deemed "valid" depended on the viewpoint in a given controversy.)

But along with concern to distinguish what they considered valid from invalid expressions of faith, those we can associate with proto-orthodox faith

---

of Scripture: The Effect of Early Christological Controversies on the Text of the New Testament (Oxford: Oxford University Press, 1993).

20. As used by historians of the period, "orthodox" and "catholic" do not designate the later formal divisions of Christianity ("Orthodox," "Roman Catholic"), but instead distinguish the mainstream body of Christians from others whom they regarded as heretical and sectarian. I use the terms descriptively, and no theological judgment about the various Christian views is conveyed.

21. Arland J. Hultgren, *The Rise of Normative Christianity* (Minneapolis: Fortress, 1994).

also demonstrated an interesting readiness to accommodate a certain diversity, affirming a measure of variation in beliefs and practices (though there certainly were limits to what was acceptable diversity). One of the most obvious and important demonstrations of this is the proto-orthodox preference for the four-fold Gospel collection that eventually became a key part of the New Testament canon (a topic to which I return in the final chapter). It was particularly proto-orthodox circles that appear to have promoted this *collection* of four distinguishable accounts of Jesus, affirming all four as having a special significance. In this readiness to recognize a certain diversity, proto-orthodox circles were, thus, also what we may call "proto-catholic." That is, they were comparatively (though critically) inclusive of some variations, over against the rather more narrowly exclusivist claims that characterized at least some examples of what became labeled "heretical" versions of early Christianity.[22]

One further important feature of proto-orthodox circles was their affirmation of the Scriptures of the Jewish tradition as authoritative. Consequently their characteristic interpretation of Jesus was with reference to this body of Scriptures, setting him in a positive relationship to the God they found revealed therein. There was a crucial corollary of the acceptance of the Old Testament as Scripture, with profound consequences for the reverence given to Jesus and the way his divine status was interpreted in their own time and thereafter. Proto-orthodox Christians of the first and second centuries worked out their faith within a commitment to the exclusivist monotheism of the biblical tradition. That is, they had to express Jesus' divine status in such a way that they did not (at least in their own eyes) compromise the uniqueness of the one God of biblical tradition. Of course, this is also another expression of the high regard for traditional patterns of belief and practice that characterized these circles, and that distinguished them from some radically different second-century versions of Christianity.

First-Century Tributaries

Neither the radical diversity nor the emergent proto-orthodoxy of the second century can be understood in historical terms without taking account of first-century traditions in Christian beliefs and practices. All forms of second-century Christianity, proto-orthodox and others, represent varying (and sometimes radical) adaptations of these earlier Christian traditions. In previous chapters we examined some major bodies of evidence concerning how first-

22. See the similar judgment in Hultgren, *Rise*, 97-101.

century Christians believed in, and expressed their devotion to, Jesus; these beliefs and practices were certainly influential for second-century Christians. In
particular the early Pauline, the Synoptic, and the Johannine texts and traditions were demonstrably important, as has been shown by studies of the influence and use of these writings in second-century Christian texts.[23] But although they are the most influential for subsequent developments, still other
texts should be noted. In the following pages, therefore, we take some account
of other important first-century texts that further illustrate the heritage drawn
upon by second-century Christians. That is, we look chronologically "up-
stream" to survey additional tributaries that fed into the diverse pool of variant
interpretations of Jesus that characterized Christianity of the second century.

The Epistle to the Hebrews

One of the most notable expressions of belief in Jesus in earliest Christianity is
the writing known as the Epistle to the Hebrews.[24] Scholars remain largely ag-
nostic about the identity of the author, and there is no unanimity on the date,
provenance, or destination of this, "the most elegant and sophisticated, and perhaps the most enigmatic, text of first-century Christianity."[25] Sometime between 60 and 100 (and I am inclined toward a more narrow range of ca. 65-85),
someone with an impressive command of literary Greek and rhetorical techniques, a familiarity with the Old Testament and Christian traditions of the
time, and a profound concern for the continued Christian commitment of the

23. E.g., Maurice Wiles, *The Spiritual Gospel: The Interpretation of the Fourth Gospel in
the Early Church* (Cambridge: Cambridge University Press, 1960); Wiles, *The Divine Apostle:
The Interpretation of St. Paul's Epistles in the Early Church* (Cambridge: Cambridge University
Press, 1967); Edouard Massoux, *The Influence of the Gospel of Saint Matthew on Christian Literature before Saint Irenaeus*, ed. Arthur J. Bellinzoni, trans. Norman J. Belval and Suzanne Hecht, 2
vols. (Macon, Ga.: Mercer University Press, 1990).

24. W. L. Lane, "Hebrews," in *DLNTD*, 443-58, is a recent overview of introductory issues
on this text. See also Craig R. Koester, "The Epistle to the Hebrews in Recent Study," *CRBS* 2
(1994): 123-46. Recent major commentaries include Harold W. Attridge, *The Epistle to the Hebrews*, Hermeneia (Philadelphia: Fortress, 1989); and W. L. Lane, *Hebrews*, 2 vols., WBC (Dallas:
Word, 1991). Note also Matthias Rissi, *Die Theologie des Hebräerbriefs*, WUNT 41 (Tübingen:
Mohr [Siebeck], 1987), and Barnabas Lindars, *The Theology of the Letter to the Hebrews* (Cambridge: Cambridge University Press, 1991).

25. Attridge, *Hebrews*, 1. He further characterizes Hebrews as "a masterpiece of early
Christian rhetorical homiletics" (1). On the unsuccessful efforts to achieve consensus on the
conceptual background of Hebrews, see L. D. Hurst, *The Epistle to the Hebrews: Its Background
of Thought*, SNTSMS 65 (Cambridge: Cambridge University Press, 1990).

addressees produced this vigorous argument for the superiority of Jesus over angels, Moses, the Aaronic priesthood, and all that was involved in the covenant articulated in the Torah.[26] Whenever it was written, the demonstrable dependence of *1 Clement* upon Hebrews shows that impressively early it obtained an appreciative readership and wide ecclesiastical usage. The allusive use of Hebrews in *1 Clement* suggests that the author of the latter text, written from Rome and probably circa 95, expected his intended readers in the Corinthian church to also be acquainted with Hebrews by that date and to hold it in high regard.[27]

But, although Hebrews develops christological claims notably, in fact everything in this "word of exhortation" (13:22) is deployed to urge the intended readers to maintain steadfastly their Christian allegiance. That is, this text is not an exercise in doctrinal development for its own sake. Repeatedly the discussion moves from setting forth christological claims to underscoring their behavioral consequences for the intended readers, as can be seen in the use of various Greek terms (for stylistic effect) that are translated "therefore" (2:1; 3:1, 7; 4:1; 6:1; 10:19; 12:1). Furthermore, the christological ideas are developed mainly in concentrated bursts in Hebrews 1–9, whereas chapters 10–13, the part where the author's objectives for this text are most clearly expressed, are wholly sermonic exhortation.

We should also note that in the christological material the author probably develops traditional themes and motifs.[28] For example, in his epistle to the Romans, Paul refers to Jesus' death as a sacrificial action (3:24-25); later in Romans (8:34) the idea that the exalted Jesus intercedes before God in heaven for believers is mentioned briefly, as if Paul expects his readers to be familiar with this notion. In 1 John 2:1-2, as well, from a few decades later, and probably from another provenance, Jesus is referred to as the "advocate [*paraklētos*] with the Father," and as the "atoning sacrifice" for the sins of the elect and the whole world.[29]

---

26. The latest possible date for Hebrews is the composition of *1 Clement*, which alludes to Hebrews. Most date *1 Clement* ca. 95, but, as Attridge has suggested (*Hebrews*, 6-9), it could have been written anytime between 70 and 140. However, taking the more widely supported date for *1 Clement*, and in light of the reference in Hebrews to Timothy as still alive and able to travel (13:23), I judge a date sometime ca. 65-85 as more plausible than a later one. Cf., e.g., Lane, *Hebrews*, 1:lxii-lxvi.

27. See, e.g., Attridge's discussion of the use of Hebrews in *1 Clement* (*Hebrews*, 6-7). As Attridge judges, in *1 Clem.* 36.2-6, "it is impossible to assume anything but literary dependence" (6).

28. William R. G. Loader, *Sohn und Hoherpriester: Eine traditionsgeschichtliche Untersuchung zur Christologie des Hebräerbriefes*, WMANT 53 (Neukirchen: Neukirchener Verlag, 1981).

29. See Attridge, *Hebrews*, 97-103, for discussion of the Jewish and Christian antecedents of the theme of Jesus as heavenly priest.

Nevertheless, Hebrews presents an impressive and distinctive exposition of these sorts of traditional and exalted claims for Jesus. This is all done in terms and categories that derive largely from the Old Testament and Jewish traditions of the Greco-Roman era. Attridge refers to the "rich Jewish heritage" drawn upon in Hebrews, which seems to have included ideas about eschatological redeemers, speculation about heavenly realities, and other conceptual categories that likely derived from circles of Greek-speaking Jews who had also absorbed and adapted elements of Greek thought.[30]

In the elegantly constructed single sentence that constitutes the whole of Hebrews 1:1-4, the author begins by affirming that in Jesus God has superseded all the prior revelations to previous generations that are attested in the Old Testament Scriptures (vv. 1-2); the sentence concludes by asserting Jesus' exalted superiority over the entire entourage of God's angelic beings (v. 4). In between these affirmations, the passage appropriates Jewish Wisdom tradition to assert Jesus' glorious relationship to God (cf., e.g., Wisd. of Sol. 7:22–8:1), referring to Jesus as the agent through whom God made the world, as the "radiance" *(apaugasma)* of God's glory, as the direct "imprint" *(charaktēr)* of God's very being *(hypostasis)*, and as the one who upholds everything by his own powerful word. But in the reference to Jesus having made "purification" for sins (v. 3), and in the description of his subsequent heavenly exaltation to the "right hand" of God (the latter expression certainly reflecting early Christian use of Ps. 110:1), the medley of motifs widens to incorporate priestly and royal traditions of the Old Testament as well.

Then, in 1:5-14 a seven-link catena of biblical citations elaborates Jesus' superiority to the angels.[31] There is, however, no good reason here for suspecting a polemical intent, as if the readers were flirting with undue reverence to angels at the expense of their devotion to Jesus. Instead the argument in Hebrews 1 works more powerfully if writer and reader agree on a high, positive view of angels, the point being that Jesus is even superior to these heavenly beings.

This contrast continues into the next chapter, where additional biblical passages emphasize that Jesus' participation in human existence also makes him both superior to angels and a more fitting redeemer of those who share "flesh and blood" (2:14). Following the strong claims about Jesus' glorious role and transcendent status in Hebrews 1, the striking emphasis here is on his full participation in human nature (2:14, 17), including specifically sufferings and death (2:9) and the testing that these things involved (2:10, 18). Taken together, these equally emphatic expositions of Jesus' transcendent status and his fully

---

30. Cf. Attridge, *Hebrews*, 28-31; Lane, *Hebrews*, 1:ciii-cx.

31. The biblical passages drawn upon are mainly from the Psalms. Simon J. Kistemaker, *The Psalm Citations in the Epistle to the Hebrews* (Amsterdam: Van Soest, 1961).

human existence constitute an important early expression of a duality about Jesus. This is developed further in the "two-natures" conception that figures prominently in the Christology of orthodox Christianity in the second century and thereafter.

The fully human existence of the unique divine Son especially qualifies *him,* in contrast to the angels, to be a "merciful and faithful high priest" on behalf of mortals (2:17); this priestly theme then plays a major role in the rest of Hebrews. After asserting the superiority of Jesus over Moses, and warning readers that disobedience to the gospel carries more severe consequences than those that befell the Israelites who rebelled against Moses in the wilderness (3:1–4:13), the author launches into an argument that Jesus' priesthood surpasses the Aaronic order of the Old Testament (4:14–7:28). In this exposition Jesus' divine sonship resurfaces as an important attribute that makes him superior to the priestly line of Aaron, as well as to angels (5:5-10; 7:28).

Perhaps the most curious feature of this material is the description of Jesus' priesthood with reference to the mysterious Old Testament figure, Melchizedek. This link is first mentioned in 5:6-10, and is then elaborated in several succeeding passages (6:20; 7:1-17). These are, in fact, the only references to Melchizedek in the New Testament, although he appears in ancient Jewish tradition prior to Hebrews (Qumran texts) and in Christian tradition subsequently.[32] Drawing upon the only two Old Testament passages that mention this figure (Gen. 14:17-20; Ps. 110:4), Hebrews creatively develops arguments for the uniqueness and superiority of Jesus' priesthood.

Although the extended "midrashic" treatment of the Genesis reference to Melchizedek in Hebrews 7:1-10 has interesting features, the more influential passage in generating the author's linkage of Jesus with this figure was almost certainly Psalm 110. The frequent and widely distributed citations and allusions to this psalm in the New Testament indicate that it was one of the most important Old Testament passages drawn upon by first-century Christians in their efforts to understand and articulate Jesus' significance, and to defend their convictions about him, especially perhaps among Jews. These New Testament uses, however, including some in Hebrews (1:3, 13; 8:1; 10:12), clearly reflect the particular influ-

---

32. Fred L. Horton, Jr., *The Melchizedek Tradition: A Critical Examination of the Sources to the Fifth Century* A.D. *and in the Epistle to the Hebrews,* SNTSMS 30 (Cambridge: Cambridge University Press, 1976). Cf. Paul J. Kobelski, *Melchizedek and Melchiresa',* CBQMS 10 (Washington, D.C.: Catholic Biblical Association, 1981), who focuses on the Qumran texts and draws upon studies by J. A. Fitzmyer: "Further Light on Melchizedek from Qumran Cave 11" and "'Now This Melchizedek . . .' (Heb 7:1)," in *Essays on the Semitic Background of the New Testament* (Missoula: Scholars, 1974), 245-67 and 221-43. The latter essay by Fitzmyer is particularly valuable for exegesis of Heb. 7:1-17.

ence of the first verse of this psalm, where "the Lord" (Heb. *Yahweh*) invites another figure, "my lord" (Heb. *'adony*), to sit at his "right hand." Numerous New Testament passages indicate that this poetic description of a divinely authorized royal coronation was taken as descriptive of Jesus' heavenly exaltation.[33]

But Hebrews also distinctively appropriates another statement in Psalm 110 — verse 4. In this verse God declares the exalted figure of 110:1 to be installed also as "a priest forever according to the order of Melchizedek."[34] So we must suppose that the author (or those fellow believers upon whom he may have depended for this exegesis) took Psalm 110 as a whole to be referring to Jesus, and sought to emphasize the particular christological meaning of 110:4. Spurred by this verse, he then also delved into Genesis 14, the only other biblical reference to Melchizedek, producing a christological reading of these passages that is not attested in prior Christian texts.

Among the writings of the Qumran sect, however, the fragmentary text known as 11QMelchizedek shows that in at least this pre-Christian Jewish circle, Psalm 110:4 was also probably influential. This Qumran text refers to Melchizedek as a heavenly being, specifically identifying him as the *Elohim* of Psalm 82:1 (11QMelch 2.10); he is also probably the same figure known as the archangel Michael in other Jewish texts.[35]

There are at least two possibilities. Hebrews could reflect an early Christian adaptation of Qumran ideas about Melchizedek. Alternatively, the biblical references to Melchizedek may have generated a varied body of speculation about this figure in Jewish tradition, of which Hebrews and 11QMelchizedek happen to be the two key extant remnants, with no direct connection to each other.[36] As Kobelski has shown, the latter is more probable, in light of the several differences in the treatment of Melchizedek in these two texts.[37]

---

33. Identifiable quotations outside of Hebrews include 1 Cor. 15:25; Mark 12:36; Matt. 22:44; Luke 20:42; and Acts 2:34; and it is commonly recognized that all other references to Jesus as exalted to the "right hand" of God are likely influenced by Ps. 110:1 as well (e.g., Mark 14:62/Matt. 26:64/Luke 22:69; Rom. 8:34; Eph. 1:20; Col. 3:1). See esp. David M. Hay, *Glory at the Right Hand: Psalm 110 in Early Christianity*, SBLMS 18 (Nashville: Abingdon, 1973); William R. G. Loader, "Christ at the Right Hand — Ps. CX.1 in the New Testament," *NTS* 24 (1977): 199-217; and now Martin Hengel, "'Sit at My Right Hand!' The Enthronement of Christ at the Right Hand of God and Psalm 110:1," in *Studies in Early Christology* (Edinburgh: T. & T. Clark, 1995), 119-225.

34. Attridge, *Hebrews*, 145, notes that Ps. 110:4 is not cited elsewhere in early Christian writings and judges its use in Hebrews as "probably original."

35. I depend here particularly on Kobelski's discussion, 49-74.

36. The third possibility is that Hebrews and 11QMelch are in fact the only two texts of the period (ca. 100 B.C.E.–100 C.E.) that demonstrate interest in Melchizedek, and it is pure coincidence that both are extant. I do not find the odds for this scenario as good as for the other two.

37. Kobelski, 127-29.

So an interest in Melchizedek in Jewish tradition of the time, perhaps including a notion that he was a heavenly being, may have contributed in some way to the rather grand treatment of him in Hebrews 7:1-10, but we should not minimize the distinctiveness of the christological appropriation of the figure in Hebrews. The author's rather robust discussion of the relationship between Jesus and Melchizedek is clearly driven and shaped fundamentally by powerful convictions about Jesus. These were not simply the product of the mechanical appropriation of exegetical speculations in the Jewish tradition. As we noted earlier, the conviction that Jesus' death was redemptive, the portrayal of this redemptive significance in sacrificial/cultic terms, the belief that Jesus' resurrection exalted him to heavenly glory, and the confidence that in his heavenly status he somehow interceded for those who call upon him in faith can all be traced back to the earliest extant Christian texts. Moreover, these convictions were forged initially in powerful religious experiences, which from the outset likely involved also a fertile interaction of Scripture and "revelation." Hebrews is to be taken fundamentally as a reflection of such convictions and the fervent searching of the Old Testament for understanding of the remarkable things that early Christians believed God had done in Jesus.

The fundamental belief in Jesus' unique standing and redemptive work is presented in Hebrews in several interlocking affirmations. He is a superior "great high priest" (4:14–5:10; 7:1-28), permanently superseding the priestly scheme described in the Old Testament, and able "for all time to save those who approach God through him, since he always lives to make intercession for them" (7:25). As eternal priest, he is also "guarantee of a better covenant" (7:22), the "new covenant" that rests upon "better promises" and fulfills prophetic hopes (8:1-13). His priestly service is offered in the true sanctuary, in heaven itself (9:1-14), which is superior to the earthly sanctuary prescribed in the Old Testament. The priestly sacrifice that he offered was his very self (9:23-28), its efficacy such that it supersedes all the "shadows of the good things to come" that constitute the Old Testament sacrificial system (10:1-18).

On the basis of these christological claims, from 10:19 onward Hebrews essentially exhorts readers to persevere in their Christian commitment. After parading the examples of named and unnamed faithful figures of prior times (11:1-39) who are presented as a great "cloud of witnesses" (12:1), Hebrews directs readers' attention to Jesus as "the pioneer and perfecter of our faith," whose endurance of shameful death on the cross was succeeded by his exaltation at God's "right hand" (12:1-2). The readers are urged to take inspiration from Jesus for their own endurance of hostility and suffering (12:3-13). In a subsequent reference to Jesus' having suffered "outside the city gate," Hebrews urges readers to "go to him outside the camp and bear the abuse he endured"

(13:12-13), Jesus here again serving as the inspiring model for Christian perseverance.[38] These statements indicate that for this author Jesus is both the final basis of redemption and the ultimate model of fortitude in faith.

In the final chapter of Hebrews, there are passages that probably reflect liturgical ideas and practices. The exhortation in 13:15 to offer *through Jesus* continually "a sacrifice of praise to God" attests to the characteristic pattern of prayer and worship that we noted in earlier texts as well, and that came to be dominant in subsequent Christian devotion. In 13:20-21 is an extended closing benediction that concludes with a doxology, these forms of expression obviously shaped by the liturgical practices with which the author was familiar, and which he deliberately echoes here.

This passage is not at all an afterthought or perfunctory statement, for it also echoes the key christological themes of the preceding exposition, particularly in the reference to Jesus' death as "the blood of the eternal covenant." The image of Jesus as "the great shepherd of the sheep," though appearing here for the first time in Hebrews, has analogies in other first-century Christian texts (more directly in John 10:11-16; 1 Pet. 2:25; 5:4; and indirectly in Mark 6:34/Matt. 9:36; Mark 14:27/Matt. 26:31; Matt. 2:6; 18:12); the image of Jesus as shepherd later became a favorite in early Christian tradition, including the early visual representation of Jesus.[39]

The prayer expressed in Hebrews 13:20-21 is directed to God. But God is identified here as having raised Jesus from death, and is invoked as able to make the readers "complete in everything good" so that they may do God's will and please God "through Jesus Christ." That is, Jesus figures centrally as the agency through whom God works and through whom the prayer will find its answer.

The doxology in 13:21 is an especially intriguing statement, for it is not entirely clear to whom the "glory forever and ever" is ascribed.[40] "Jesus Christ" is the closest antecedent of the relative pronoun ("to whom") here, and doxologies are occasionally directed to Jesus, though they are comparatively rare and

38. The reference in 13:12 to Jesus' death "outside the gate" *(exō tēs pylēs epathen)* is likely an allusion to a narrative of Jesus' crucifixion, the allusive reference probably indicating that the author expected readers to be acquainted with the story. As Attridge (*Hebrews,* 398) notes, John 19:17-20 reflects a similar narrative tradition.

39. For further discussion of textual references, see Joachim Jeremias, "ποιμην," in *TDNT,* 6:485-502; for early visual references, see, e.g., Graydon F. Snyder, *Ante Pacem: Archaeological Evidence of Church Life before Constantine* (Macon, Ga.: Mercer University Press, 1985), 22-24.

40. Cf., e.g., Attridge, *Hebrews,* 407-8, who takes Jesus as the object (and so sees the doxology reflecting "the latest examples of the form in early Christian literature," citing 2 Pet. 3:18 and *Mart. Pol.* 22.3); and F. F. Bruce, *The Epistle to the Hebrews,* NICNT (Grand Rapids: Eerdmans, 1964), 412, who takes the doxology as directed to God, citing 13:15 as showing that "it is through Christ that glory is given to God."

are also in Christian texts deriving from the later decades of the first century and thereafter (e.g., 2 Pet. 3:18). Given that "God" is the one addressed in the benediction-prayer that this doxology concludes, however, it seems to me slightly more likely that God is the primary referent in Hebrews 13:21.[41]

In any case, it is clear that this author, as characteristic in early Christian texts, sees God as operating uniquely through Jesus. As well, he sees the worship that Christians direct to God as necessarily offered through Jesus (e.g., 13:15). Indeed, the ambiguity of the phrasing is itself indicative that Jesus was so closely linked with God in earliest Christian devotion that the glorification of God could not be done properly without reference to Jesus.

Later Pauline Texts

In our earlier discussion of Pauline Christianity we focused on the evidence of the Pauline letters whose authorship is uncontested, as to what these letters reflect of beliefs and devotional practices that had already become conventionalized by the 50s. Here we turn to the larger, traditional Pauline corpus in the New Testament to deal with other epistles, those thought by many or most scholars (depending on the particular epistle) to be pseudonymous. In particular we will consider Colossians, Ephesians, and the "Pastoral Epistles" (1 Timothy, 2 Timothy, Titus). Even those who defend their Pauline authorship date these epistles comparatively later than the uncontested ones. So without engaging the complexities of the debate about authorship here, we shall simply treat these writings as indicative of how devotional belief and practice developed in Pauline Christianity in the later first century and thereafter.

Colossians

We can begin with Colossians. Of the disputed Pauline epistles that we examine here, Colossians enjoys a comparatively stronger measure of support for Pauline authorship among scholars.[42] Furthermore, whether authentic or pseudonymous, it is generally thought to have been written prior to the epistle to the Ephesians (which many think was directly dependent on Colossians) and the

41. A conclusion also reached by Arthur W. Wainwright, *The Trinity in the New Testament* (London: SPCK, 1962), 94.

42. Cf., e.g., recent reviews of issues by Victor Paul Furnish, "Colossians, Epistle to The," in *ABD*, 1:1090-96; Peter T. O'Brien, "Colossians, Letter to The," in *DPL*, 147-53. For a recent case for pseudonymity, see Mark C. Kiley, *Colossians as Pseudepigraphy* (Sheffield: JSOT Press, 1986).

Pastoral Letters. So it is reasonable to commence with Colossians and move forward chronologically.[43]

More importantly for the present discussion, Colossians is also perhaps the most noteworthy expression of faith in Jesus among these later Pauline epistles. Indeed, the key religious theme throughout Colossians is the centrality and supremacy of Jesus. For example, early on the author assures readers that God has "rescued us from the power of darkness and transferred us into the kingdom of his beloved Son, in whom we have redemption, the forgiveness of sins" (1:13-14). Through his death on the cross, Jesus has "reconciled" those formerly "estranged and hostile in mind, doing evil deeds" (1:21-22). God's great "secret" *(mystērion)* that was long hidden and has now been revealed is "Christ in/among you [*en hymin*], the glorious hope" (1:26-27). Christ is the content of the gospel proclamation (1:28); in Christ himself are hidden "all the treasures of wisdom and knowledge" (2:2-3).

But the christological passage that justifiably has received by far the greatest amount of scholarly attention in Colossians is 1:15-20. On account of the self-contained nature of the passage, its compact phrasing, and its cadences (more evident in the Greek than in translations), 1:15-20 is widely thought to be a devotional poem or "hymn." The scholarly literature records various proposals, however, about its derivation. One popular view is that the passage originated as a "Christ hymn" first used in the worship setting of some Christian circle, the author of Colossians then appropriating it. Others prefer to take the passage as the product of the author of Colossians. Still others propose that it may be a Christian adaptation of an original paean about divine Wisdom whose provenance was in pre-Christian Jewish circles. Though it was backed by important figures of the past, the proposal that 1:15-20 may represent a Christianization of a hymn to a heavenly redeemer from pre-Christian "gnostic" circles has suffered a considerable decline in scholarly support in recent decades.[44]

Actually, however, whichever option one prefers for its origins, Colossians 1:15-20 has to be reckoned with fully in its own right and in its present form.

---

43. If written by Paul, Colossians is more plausibly dated ca. 57-61 (Colossae was destroyed by an earthquake in 61), the time span customarily associated with Paul's imprisonment in Caesarea and Rome. If pseudonymous (and probably posthumous), Colossians can be placed sometime ca. 65 to 90 (and probably toward the earlier end of this period). See, e.g., Furnish, "Colossians," 1:1094-95.

44. See, e.g., the bibliographical references and discussion in Eduard Lohse, *Colossians and Philemon*, Hermeneia (Philadelphia: Fortress, 1971), 41-46, and cf., e.g., N. T. Wright, *The Climax of the Covenant* (Edinburgh: T. & T. Clark, 1991), 99-119; J. T. Sanders, *The New Testament Christological Hymns: Their Historical Religious Background*, SNTSMS 15 (Cambridge: Cambridge University Press, 1971), 75-87.

This is a truly remarkable expression of the enormous significance attributed to Jesus by the author of Colossians, and probably those Christians for whom he wrote.

A recent study by Christian Stettler has provided a solid basis for all further discussion of Colossians 1:15-20, and in my view presents persuasive proposals on several key matters.[45] First, Stettler shows that the passage as we have it exhibits such unity and coherence that the theory that it is an adaptation of some supposedly pre-Christian paean to Wisdom or to a gnostic heavenly redeemer is neither necessary nor finally very plausible.[46] Instead it is likely that it either originated within the context of early Christian praise and worship, as a hymn celebrating Jesus, or was composed by the author of Colossians himself as a hymnlike expression of Christ's supremacy. In the latter case, of course, the author almost unavoidably would have been influenced by hymnic practices of the Christian circle(s) with which he was acquainted. So in either case the passage reflects, whether directly or indirectly, the hymnic praise of Christ that was a feature of the devotional life of at least some circles of first-century Christians.

In a close, line-by-line analysis, Stettler also shows that Colossians 1:15-20 expresses Jesus' significance in vocabulary and conceptual categories most likely derived from Greek-speaking Jewish circles. For example, the reference to Christ as the one in whom "all the fullness was pleased to *dwell*" adapts Old Testament/Jewish traditions of God's dwelling in, and filling, the temple of Zion.[47] The same applies to the similar statement in 2:9, that in Christ "all the fullness of deity dwells bodily." As for the term "fullness" (*plērōma*) itself, in none of its several uses in Colossians or Ephesians does it carry any of the technical connotation that it acquires in later gnostic texts/groups (e.g., in Valentinianism, where it refers to a scheme of divine emanations distinguishable from the high God). Instead, we probably have here a distinctive, early Christian adaptation of a Greek term whose prior religious usage had been mainly in biblical reference to the "fullness" of the world/earth and the sea (e.g., Pss. 24:1/LXX 23:1; 50:12/LXX 49:12; 96:11/LXX 95:11; 98:7/LXX 97:7).[48]

---

45. Christian Stettler, *Der Kolosserhymnus: Untersuchungen zu Form, traditionsgeschichtlichem Hintergrund und Aussage von Kol 1,15-20*, WUNT 2/131 (Tübingen: Mohr Siebeck, 2000).

46. C. Stettler, 75-103.

47. C. Stettler, 252-59.

48. See also Lohse, 56-58; Hans Hübner, "πληρωμα," in *EDNT*, 3:110-11. Indeed, in Colossians and Ephesians the term "fullness" is used with several referents: God's fullness in Christ (Col. 1:19; 2:9), God's fullness in believers (Eph. 3:19), the church as God's fullness (Eph. 1:23), "the fullness of Christ" as Christian maturity (Eph. 4:13), the "fullness of the times" (Eph. 1:10; also Gal. 4:4). The term "fullness" was clearly the subject of some semantic development in these two writings. No theory of some putative derivation from pre-Christian speculation is

The frequently touted proposals to "reconstruct" a supposedly original pre-Christian paean, for example by excising the reference to the church *(ekklēsia)* in 1:18 and the mention of Jesus' crucifixion in 1:20, are unpersuasive. They are all based on one or both of two fallacious prior assumptions: that a poetic composition in Greek should be expected to follow Greek poetic conventions (e.g., meter), and/or that the passage derives from a pre-Christian provenance. But positing a pre-Christian provenance involves making a premise of something that must first be demonstrated (and cannot be), hardly a scientific way to proceed.

The error in trying to "reconstruct" the hymn on the basis of Greek poetic meter is the assumption that classical Greek poetic conventions are relevant. Among many Greek-speaking Jews and Christians of the time, however, the Greek Old Testament was scripture and, thus, a strong influence on their vocabulary and discourse patterns, as is easily shown in the New Testament writings.[49] It is thus far more likely that their own efforts at liturgical praise were modeled after the examples in the Old Testament, especially in the Greek Psalter.[50] The principal stylistic feature of Colossians 1:15-20 is in fact the parallel structure that is also the primary poetic feature of the Psalms. The uneven length of lines does not conform to Greek poetic conventions of syllabic meter because this particular statement of hymnic praise was composed as what Stettler rightly characterizes as a "Christ-psalm," lauding Jesus in the cadences of the Psalter.[51]

As to its content, the passage lyrically proclaims Christ as the unique divine agent of creation and redemption. In the Greek, the repeated use of the third-person pronouns ("he/him") has the effect of making his centrality emphatic at every point. In 1:15-17 the focus is on Christ and creation. He is "the image of the invisible God, the firstborn of all creation," the one through whom

---

necessary. In living languages words frequently undergo such diversification and development as users of the language find the need to express their thoughts in new ways.

49. The special influence of the Greek Old Testament upon the vocabulary and semantics of the New Testament was demonstrated by a predecessor in my professorial chair, H. A. A. Kennedy, *Sources of New Testament Greek or the Influence of the Septuagint on the Vocabulary of the New Testament* (Edinburgh: T. & T. Clark, 1895), and has been verified by many subsequently.

50. In support of this, as is well recognized, the poetic compositions in the Lukan birth narrative are all clearly shaped by Greek Old Testament poetic cadences, as are the hymnic passages in Revelation.

51. C. Stettler proposes that Col. 1:15-20 represents a mixed-form composition that combines features of psalms and the *berakah* prayer-praise form (79-86), and he suggests that in a liturgical setting the hymn may have begun with "Blessed [be] Jesus Christ" *(Eulogētos Iēsous Christos)*, to which the relative pronoun of 1:15 was originally connected.

everything was created whether earthly or heavenly, visible or invisible, including all ranks of spiritual powers ("whether thrones, or dominions, or rulers, or powers"). The claim in the first line of 1:16 that all things were created "in" (en) Christ is reiterated in slightly varied form and extended at the end of this verse, where Christ is also the one "through" (dia) whom and "for" (eis) whom everything was made. Then, concluding the first portion with its emphasis on Christ's relationship to creation, 1:17 asserts his chronological priority "before all things" and his continuing significance as the one in whom all things have been "constituted" (synestēken).[52]

The second part of the passage, 1:18-20, presents the other major emphasis: that this same Christ is also preeminent in redemption. He is the "head of the body, which is his/the church," the "beginning" (archē), and the "firstborn from the dead" (corresponding to his "firstborn" status in/over creation in 1:15), so that in all things he might be preeminent (1:18). All (divine) "fullness" was pleased to dwell in him, so to reconcile all things through him, making peace through "the blood of his cross" (1:19-20).

Fundamentally the two claims, that Jesus is the pretemporal agent of creation and the preeminent agent of redemption set over all things, are attested earlier in the Pauline tradition (e.g., 1 Cor. 8:6; 15:27-28; Phil. 2:9-11), and also in other texts indicative of various late-first-century Christian devotion (e.g., Heb. 1:1-4; John 1:1-18). Moreover, the vocabulary of Colossians 1:15-20 exhibits both commonality with other first-century texts and also evident creativity. For example, referring to Christ as God's "image" has precedent in 2 Corinthians 4:4, and the term "firstborn" is likewise featured in earlier Pauline usage (Rom. 8:29) and other texts (Heb. 1:6; Rev. 1:5, the latter a closely parallel instance of "firstborn of the dead"). Yet drawing upon a traditional vocabulary of devotion to Jesus, the author of Colossians 1:15-20 produced a fresh and memorable declaration of Christ's glorious status. Those who first heard this celebration of Jesus probably recognized basically familiar convictions expressed freshly and eloquently.

With the other early Christian texts that are likely hymns (or that imitate hymnic style), Colossians 1:15-20 also illustrates the content of first-century Christian "psalms, hymns and spiritual songs" sung in heartfelt fervor to God (Col. 3:16; similarly Eph. 5:19). In addition to appropriating biblical psalms, which were christologically interpreted and chanted in their worship settings,

---

52. Lohse, 52, documents the use of this Greek verb in Platonic and Stoic traditions to express the unity of the cosmos, whereas in Greek-speaking Jewish sources the verb is used in expressing the belief that the cosmos is surely constituted by the one God. C. Stettler, however, provides a fuller and more nuanced discussion of the term (159-62).

some early Christians were moved by their intense religious experience to compose the sort of fresh psalmlike glorification of Jesus that is preserved in Colossians 1:15-20. In this they anticipated a continuing form of Christian devotional practice, and they creatively expressed major religious convictions that provoked and helped shape the doctrinal controversies and formulations of subsequent centuries.

As in Hebrews, however, so in Colossians, the christological statements are all in service to the author's hortatory concern. He wants his readers to have knowledge and "spiritual wisdom" to enable them to "lead lives worthy of the Lord, fully pleasing to him, and bearing fruit in every good work" (1:9-10). At the same time, the exhortations are all framed with reference to Jesus. The author urges readers who have "received Christ Jesus the Lord" to carry on living their lives "in him," being "rooted and built up in him" (2:6-7); he warns against being ensnared by "philosophy and empty deceit" that is not "according to Christ" (2:8), in whom dwells "the whole fullness of deity [*pan to plērōma tēs theotētos*] bodily" (2:9). In Christ, who is "the head of every ruler and authority [*pasēs archēs kai exousias*]," the readers themselves have been "fulfilled" *(peplērōmenoi)* (2:10). Consequently they are not to allow themselves to be condemned by others for not observing strict rules about foods or religious festivals (2:16). Likewise, they are not to be intimidated by anyone who promotes an undue interest in the heavenly "worship of angels," making claims based on visionary experiences that distract from Christ "from whom the whole body [of believers]" is to derive its nourishment with "a growth that is from God" (2:18-19).[53]

In other imagery the author characterizes the readers (Gentile converts) as having been "circumcised with a circumcision not done by human hands" *(acheiropoiētō)*, that involves "putting off the body of flesh in the circumcision of Christ" (2:11). Jesus' death here is the pattern of a radical new "circumcision" that is manifested in the readers exhibiting a behavioral distinction from their former Gentile state when they were "dead in trespasses and the uncircumcision of [their] flesh" (2:13).

In still more dramatic terms, Colossians describes believers as "buried with him [Jesus] in baptism," and "also raised with him through faith in the

---

53. I remain persuaded that the "worship of angels" phrase here refers to what the author regards as a distracting speculative interest in participation in the worship that angels perform, as influentially proposed by Fred O. Francis, "Humility and Angel Worship in Col. 2:18," in *Conflict at Colossae*, ed. F. O. Francis and Wayne Meeks (Missoula: Scholars, 1975), 176-81. See also Clinton E. Arnold, *The Colossian Syncretism: The Interface between Christianity and Folk Belief at Colossae*, WUNT 2/77 (Tübingen: Mohr-Siebeck, 1995), 8-102; Christopher Rowland, "Apocalyptic Visions and the Exaltation of Christ in the Letter to the Colossians," *JSNT* 19 (1983): 73-83; and now C. Stettler, 65-69.

power of God who raised him from the dead" (2:12). God made them alive with Christ *(synezōopoiēsen hymas syn autō)*, forgiving their "trespasses" and "erasing the record that stood against us with its legal demands, nailing it to the cross" (2:13-14). These striking claims issue in major behavioral corollaries. Having died with Christ to "the elemental spirits of the universe" *(stoicheiōn tou kosmou)*, the readers are not to submit to "regulations" that amount to mere "human commands and teachings," which concentrate on "self-imposed piety, humility, and severe treatment of the body" but are of no worth in checking fleshly self-indulgence (2:20-23).

Raised by God with Christ, they are to "seek the things that are above, where Christ is, seated at God's right hand," setting their "minds on these higher things" (3:1-2). They have died and their life is now "hidden with Christ in God" (3:3). When Christ is "revealed" *(phanerōthē)*, they too will be "revealed with him in glory" (3:4). Consequently they are to now "put to death" all the evil behavior that they once practiced and that falls under divine judgment (3:5-9). They are now newly "clothed," and are being "renewed" after the image of the Creator; they are to recognize that distinctions between peoples and social classes do not remain valid, for "Christ is all and in all" (3:11).

Without detracting in any way from the significance of the christological affirmations expressed in Colossians, however, the text is not in fact primarily an exercise in doctrinal development or speculative innovation.[54] Instead it mainly represents a practical concern to motivate and reinforce the behavior of the intended readers, both devotionally and in the wider scope of their lives, so that they should aim to "do everything in the name of the Lord Jesus, giving thanks to God the Father through him" (3:17; and similarly Eph. 5:20).

Ephesians

The obviously close literary relationship between the epistles to the Colossians and to the Ephesians is evident in the considerable similarity of contents. Whether someone else wrote Ephesians after, and in dependence on, Colossians (and so perhaps Ephesians may be thought of as our earliest "commentary" on Colossians) or the same author(s) wrote both epistles is a question that cannot detain us here.[55] Instead let us compare Ephesians' presentation of Jesus to that in Colossians.

54. Similarly, Fred O. Francis, "The Christological Argument of Colossians," in *God's Christ and His People: Studies in Honour of Nils Alstrup Dahl*, ed. Jacob Jervell and Wayne A. Meeks (Oslo: Universitets forlaget, 1977), 192-208.

55. E.g., Ernest Best, "Who Used Whom? The Relationship of Ephesians and Colossians," *NTS* 43 (1997): 72-96.

Although Ephesians does not stress Jesus' agency in creation as does Colossians, in several Ephesians passages there is a similar emphasis on his centrality in redemption, and a similarly cosmic scope in the portrayal of Jesus' role. In 1:3-14 the focus is on Jesus as the one in whom the elect were chosen for redemption "before the foundation of the world," and were destined for adoption as children of God (1:3-6). This redemption *(apolytrōsin)*, the forgiveness of "trespasses" *(paraptōmatōn)*, is now secured through Christ's death (1:7). This redemption is accompanied by God's conferral of "wisdom and insight" into "the secret" *(mystērion)* of his will, which God was pleased to "set forth in Christ" and which will encompass "all things" in heaven and on earth (1:9-10). The author prays that God may grant readers continuing revelation of his good purposes, so that they may know the future hope that awaits them, "the riches of his glorious inheritance," and "the immeasurable greatness of his power for us who believe." This divine power was paradigmatically demonstrated in God's raising Jesus from death and his exaltation to supremacy over every power and authority and "above every name that is named" in this age or in any time to come (1:18-21). As in Colossians, so also in Ephesians, believers are portrayed as "raised up" (resurrection) and seated with Christ in a heavenly status (2:4-6).

A distinctive feature of the treatment of Jesus' redemptive death in Ephesians is the emphasis on its efficacy in overcoming the estrangement of Gentiles from the one God, the "commonwealth of Israel," and the "covenants of promise" (2:11-12). In vivid imagery Ephesians proclaims that Christ is "our peace" who "in his flesh" has broken down the "dividing wall" between Jews and Gentiles, abolishing the law of commandments, so that he could create "one new humanity" *(anthrōpon)* in place of the Jew/Gentile division (2:14-15). Through his cross Jesus put to death the "hostility" and announced peace to those who were "afar off" (Gentiles) and those near (Jews), and through him both now have access to God (2:16-18). Now, in Jesus as the "chief cornerstone," this enlarged "household of God" is joined and grows together into "a holy temple in the Lord (Jesus)" (2:19-21).

In another distinctive passage, Ephesians describes a diversity of grace given to believers as gifts of the exalted Christ, and specifically refers to apostles, prophets, evangelists, and pastor-teachers as given to build up "the body of Christ" (4:7-12). The aim is unity of faith and a mature "knowledge of the Son of God" that corresponds to "the measure of the full stature of Christ" (4:12-13). Christ is the "head," and "the whole body" (the company of the redeemed) is connected and equipped for growth through him (4:15-16). That is, in this outlook Jesus stands as the divine source of spiritual blessings and also the goal toward which the redeemed are to orient their endeavor.

Like Colossians (3:18–4:1), Ephesians too has a section of exhortations directed to believers in various social positions, and in the same sequence: wives, husbands, children, fathers, slaves, and masters (5:21–6:9).[56] As well, in both epistles these exhortations consistently summon readers in all the named categories to live out their respective social roles with reference to "the Lord (Christ)." That is, the social structures involved are not totally negated, but "reverence for Christ conditions the entire set of relationships" addressed.[57] Ephesians gives the most elaborated (and most influential) instance of this type of exhortation, largely on account of the extended attention given to the responsibility of husbands toward their wives (5:25-33). In this material Christ's self-sacrificial love for the church and her complete welfare is presented as the criterion and example for the behavior of husbands (5:25-27, 29).

Whatever shortcomings moderns might feel able to detect (with the benefit of nearly two thousands years' further experience, and under stimuli simply not available in the late first century), these passages undeniably illustrate how the early Christian circles reflected in Ephesians, Colossians, and other related texts sought to shape their everyday social behavior out of devotion to Jesus. That is, "devotion" to Jesus clearly extended beyond christological beliefs and worship practice. On the basis of traditions about Jesus and his significance, by the latter decades of the first century Christians were also seeking to formulate and extend their own conventions of behavior across the major social roles of the Roman era.

The "Pastoral Letters"

The final body of texts that we look at here among those explicitly tied to later Pauline Christianity comprises 1 Timothy, 2 Timothy, and Titus, often referred to in scholarly circles as the "Pastoral Epistles."[58] Though there remain doughty

---

56. These two passages are the two fullest versions of a form of exhortation found with variations in several early Christian writings (1 Tim. 2:1-15; 5:1-2; 6:1-2, 17-19; Titus 2:1–3:8; 1 Pet. 2:13–3:7; 1 *Clem.* 1.3; 21.6-8; Ign. *Poly.* 4.1–5.2; Pol. *Phil.* 4.2–6.1; *Did.* 4.9-11; *Barn.* 19.5, 7). Often referred to in scholarly discussion as "household codes" or "station codes," these passages are also widely thought to show influence of the ethical/social values of the larger Roman era; but in fact no exact parallel has been found. We must also note that there are interesting variations among these passages, warning us to beware of overgeneralization about them. See, e.g., P. H. Towner, "Household Codes," in *DLNTD*, 513-20; Towner, "Households and Household Codes," in *DPL*, 417-19.

57. J. I. H. McDonald, *The Crucible of Christian Morality* (London: Routledge, 1998), 162-63.

58. The term "pastoral" as a label for these epistles derives from German scholarly studies of the eighteenth century. The epistles are so described because they show a concern to "shepherd" the church that is expressed in the literary-rhetorical form of the revered Paul giving advice to junior Christian leaders.

defenders of the claim that these texts were written by Paul, most scholars today take them as pseudonymously composed sometime in the late first or early second century. In this view the intention of the real author(s) was to bring Paul's authority and "voice" to bear upon issues in Pauline circles at some time after his martyrdom.[59]

The dominant concerns that prompted the penning of all three writings were to affirm traditional Christian beliefs over against teachings that are referred to as false and foolish, and to promote stable structures of leadership and behavior.[60] Accordingly, at several points there are easily recognizable recitations of traditional expressions of faith, and in these Jesus has a crucial place. But precisely because these writings were concerned to reaffirm traditional beliefs, and the author presumed familiarity with the creedal formulations and what they mean, they are recited with scarcely any explication. We therefore must unpack the nuances that were understood by the author and intended readers as best we can. Fortunately our task has been made easier by several recent studies.[61]

The first such creedal formulation is 1 Timothy 1:15, a brief "faithful saying" that "Christ Jesus came into the world to save sinners." The characterization of Jesus' redemptive purpose is unsurprising and has parallels in other early Christian texts.[62] The more intriguing question, of course, is what was implied by saying that Jesus had come "into the world." By itself, the phrase could allude to Jesus' preexistence and incarnation, or merely to his historical/earthly origin in the same manner as any other human being. On the other hand, the

---

59. See, e.g., Jerome D. Quinn, "Timothy and Titus, Epistles To," in *ABD*, 6:568 (560-71); cf. E. E. Ellis, "Pastoral Letters," in *DPL*, 658-66. On the phenomenon of pseudepigraphy, see David G. Meade, *Pseudonymity and Canon* (Grand Rapids: Eerdmans, 1987); J. D. G. Dunn, "Pseudepigraphy," in *DLNTD*, 977-84.

60. There are numerous warnings about dangerous teachings/teachers, though they are none too explicitly described: 1 Tim. 1:3-12, 19-20; 4:1-5, 7; 6:3-5, 20-21; 2 Tim. 2:14-18; 3:1-9; 4:3-5; Titus 1:13-16; 3:9-11. Among passages concerned with structures and behavior, note, e.g., 1 Tim. 2:1–3:13; 5:3-22; Titus 1:5-9; 2:3-10. On the stress in the Pastoral Epistles on tradition, see Andrew Y. Lau, *Manifest in Flesh: The Epiphany Christology of the Pastoral Epistles*, WUNT 2/86 (Tübingen: Mohr Siebeck, 1996), 18-39. The distinctive reference to Christian tradition as the *parathēkē* (deposit, trust) in the Pastorals is indicative of the concern to maintain established belief and practice (1 Tim. 6:20; 2 Tim. 1:12, 14).

61. Lau, *Manifest in Flesh*; Hanna Stettler, *Die Christologie der Pastoralbriefe*, WUNT 2/103 (Tübingen: Mohr Siebeck, 1998); Frances Young, *The Theology of the Pastoral Letters* (Cambridge: Cambridge University Press, 1994), esp. 59-68. Lau and Stettler both give abundant references to earlier scholarly literature.

62. As H. Stettler notes (53), Luke 19:10 is among the obvious parallels. I am not so confident as she, however, that such parallels count as evidence of the use of the Synoptic Gospels in the Pastoral Epistles.

closest parallels to this particular phrasing in Christian texts, Johannine references where Jesus is sent (John 3:17; 10:36; 1 John 4:9) or has come (John 9:39; 11:27; 16:28) "into the world," are in writings that clearly attest belief in Jesus' preexistence and incarnation. Moreover, and more directly germane to the Pastoral Epistles, other texts from the Pauline tradition seem to reflect essentially the same belief (1 Cor. 8:6; Phil. 2:6; Col. 1:15-17). It is most likely, therefore, that in these writings of late-first-century Pauline Christianity the reference to Jesus having come "into the world" presupposes the view of him having come from his preexistent state to appear in earthly mode.[63]

In 1 Timothy 2:5-6, a more complete creedal statement affirms one God, and "one mediator between God and humans [*anthrōpōn*], Christ Jesus, himself human [*anthrōpos*], who gave himself as a ransom [*antilytron*] for all." The "binitarian" structure of this formulation, an affirmation of Jesus along with God in a statement that obviously derives from Jewish exclusivist monotheism, has earlier precedents (e.g., 1 Cor. 8:6), and also anticipates later creedal formulations such as the Apostles' Creed. But the frequency of this linked affirmation of one God and Jesus in later Christian tradition should not blind us to its striking and daring nature in the religious environment of the first century. Yet, already by the time of the Pastorals, in Christian circles it had long been a conventionalized feature of the "deposit" of the faith.

The linked emphasis in this confession on Jesus' own humanity and the redemptive efficacy of his death is broadly similar to themes in other Christian texts of the same approximate period (e.g., Heb. 2:5-18). This underscoring of a genuinely human Jesus may well reflect a concern about other early Christian views in which Jesus' divine status was emphasized at the expense of his real humanity (e.g., as may have been true of the Johannine "secessionists" we noted in an earlier chapter).

Another confessional expression of equivalent length is concerned entirely with Jesus, 1 Timothy 3:16. As in other confessional or hymnic passages in first-century texts (e.g., Phil. 2:6-11; Col. 1:15-20; Heb. 1:1-4), Jesus is not named, but instead is identified with reference to a series of key actions that express his significance.

The structure of this confession is probably to be viewed as a threefold series of two-part statements, Jesus being the subject of each of the six verbs. Each of the three two-part statements refers to Jesus on the historical/mundane and the transcendent planes.[64] In the first statement, "manifested in flesh" is a sum-

---

63. Cf. Martin Dibelius and Hans Conzelmann, *The Pastoral Epistles*, Hermeneia (Philadelphia: Fortress, 1972), 29; Lau, 66-67; H. Stettler, 53.

64. There is a symmetrical alternation between actions on the two planes: l. 1: earthly

mary reference to Jesus' historical appearance and life, "flesh" emphasizing his human reality, including his death (as is obvious in the context of 1 Timothy). "Vindicated in (the) Spirit" must refer to his resurrection, which is thus portrayed as conveying divine validation of Jesus (and thus validation of the claims made for him).[65]

In the next line, "seen by angels" refers to the vindicated/resurrected Jesus having appeared in the heavenly realm, where his exalted status was witnessed by God's angels. "Preached among the nations" represents the earthly counterpart, Jesus' significance and redemptive efficacy proclaimed in the mundane sphere as well as recognized in heaven. In the final line Jesus continues as the subject of the verbs, "believed (on) in the world" referring to the positive results of the proclamation of him referred to in the previous line, and "taken up in glory" correspondingly celebrating Jesus' glorious reception and status in the heavenly plane.

Other references make it clear that the Pastorals draw upon further early tradition about Jesus' Davidic descent (2 Tim. 2:8) and his interrogation before Pontius Pilate (1 Tim. 6:13), the latter incident an inspiring example for the steadfastness to which the readers are summoned. Jesus' hearing before Pilate is attested elsewhere among first-century Christian sources only in the canonical Gospels. So, although presented by the author(s) as explicitly linked with Paul, the Pastoral Epistles represent the amalgamation and affirmation of several distinguishable bodies or streams of earlier Christian tradition.[66]

Two other features of the presentation of Jesus in the Pastoral Epistles are important to mention here. The first is the striking verbal overlap between Jesus and God. We might also think of this as a verbal enfranchisement of Jesus with language that is otherwise used with special reference to God. As a prime example of a term especially favored in the Pastoral Epistles, "Savior" is a title given to God (1 Tim. 1:1; 2:3; 4:10; Titus 1:3; 2:10; 3:4) and also to Jesus (2 Tim. 1:10; Titus 1:4; 2:13; 3:6), and to them alone. In some cases God and Jesus are both referred to as "Savior" in such close proximity that we must infer a delib-

---

("manifest")/transcendent ("vindicated"); l. 2: transcendent ("seen")/earthly ("preached"); l. 3: earthly ("believed")/transcendent ("taken up").

65. As Lau notes (100), "vindicated" *(edikaiōthē)* reflects its usage in the LXX, where the connotation is to declare someone righteous. Rom. 1:4 represents an obviously parallel idea that Jesus was declared to be (or installed as) Son of God "with power according to the Spirit of holiness by resurrection from the dead." Note also Rom. 8:9-11, where the divine Spirit is mentioned in connection with Jesus' resurrection and the future resurrection of believers.

66. In my view we cannot claim with confidence that the author(s) of the Pastoral Epistles knew our canonical Gospels (though that is not impossible, depending on how late one dates the Pastorals), only that the canonical Gospels and the Pastorals show knowledge of elements of the same body of Jesus tradition.

erate effort to link them through this appellative: e.g., Titus 2:11 (God) and 2:13 (Jesus), 3:4 (God) and 3:6 (Jesus). Both in the biblical/Jewish tradition and in the larger religious environment of the late first century as well, "Savior" was widely used as an epithet for divine beings, including the Roman emperor. Consequently the restricted application of the term to Jesus and God surely connotes a deliberate linkage of Jesus with divine attributes that would have been readily perceived by the intended readers.[67]

Another important instance of this verbal enfranchisement of Jesus also takes us to the remaining feature of the Pastorals that I wish to highlight here. The term *epiphaneia* (manifestation) and the cognate verb *epiphainein* (to manifest) are both obviously significant in these writings. Five of the six New Testament uses of *epiphaneia* (from which, of course, comes the English loan-word "epiphany") are in the Pastorals (1 Tim. 6:14; 2 Tim. 1:10; 4:1, 8; Titus 2:13; otherwise only 2 Thess. 2:8), as are two of the four uses of the verb *epiphainein* (Titus 2:11; 3:4; also Luke 1:79; Acts 27:20).

As with "Savior," these two terms also were familiar in the religious vocabulary of Greek-speaking people, whether Jews or pagans, in references to the appearances and/or beneficent actions of divinities.[68] The verb is used in Titus 2:11 and 3:4, referring to God's gracious and beneficial purposes having been manifested; in both contexts this involves Jesus. In 2:11-14 the previous manifestation *(epephanē)* of God's saving grace (2:11) can allude only to the historical appearance of Jesus himself. This manifestation leads believers to a godly and disciplined life in the present age while they await the future glorious "manifestation [*epiphaneian*] of the great God and our Savior Jesus Christ."[69] Titus 3:4-7 likewise refers to the goodness and kindness *(philanthrōpia)* of "God our Savior" having been manifested *(epephanē)*, thereby mercifully saving and spiritually renewing believers "through Jesus Christ our Savior." Here again, Jesus' historical appearance is said to have "epiphanic" significance and purpose. That is, Jesus "manifested" God's saving purpose, and thus he constituted the divine "epiphany."

---

67. On the uses of "savior" *(sōtēr)* in Jewish and pagan sources, see, e.g., Dibelius and Conzelmann, 100-103; K. H. Schelkle, "Σωτήρ," in *EDNT*, 3:325-27.

68. See now esp. Lau, 179-225.

69. Scholars remain divided over whether Titus 2:13 refers to God *and* Jesus or to Jesus *as* "the great God." Cf., e.g., Dibelius and Conzelmann, 143; Lau, 243-48; Murray J. Harris, *Jesus as God: The New Testament Use of "Theos" in Reference to Jesus* (Grand Rapids: Baker, 1992), 173-85. If, in spite of the grammatical arguments supporting the latter position I see God and Jesus distinguished here. Nevertheless, the statement refers to "manifestation" of "the great God" as involving the full participation of Jesus. Indeed, perhaps the statement expresses the notion that the future manifestation of Jesus *constitutes* the eschatological manifestation of the "great God" for whose redemptive purposes Jesus is the unique agent.

Notably, in all five occurrences of the noun "epiphany" in the Pastorals, it is applied to Jesus, mainly with reference to his future appearance as Savior and judge (1 Tim. 6:14; 2 Tim. 4:1, 8; Titus 2:13).[70] This undeniably is another instance of the enfranchisement of Jesus in the language of divinity, his eschatological appearance thus endowed with divine significance. In 2 Timothy 1:10, however, Jesus' historical earthly appearance is referred to with the same term, which must carry the same connotation. That is, as is connoted in certain uses of the verb, so in these uses of the noun form, Jesus' historical appearance, involving his redemptive death and resurrection, is portrayed as a divine "manifestation/epiphany."[71]

The additional important point I wish to highlight is that the rather frequent application of these terms, "savior" and "epiphany," to Jesus in the Pastoral Epistles also reflects an appropriation of language for him that increasingly had also come to be used in the cult of the Roman emperor.[72] Indeed, Frances Young claimed, "More than other New Testament texts the Pastorals evidence the language that so intriguingly parallels the 'ruler-cult.'" She may also have been correct to suggest that this represents "a deliberate placing of this Christ-cult against the Caesar-cult."[73] That is, Jesus is designated as the one true universal Savior, whose historical and future appearances are divine "epiphanies" of the one God. Such a claim can only have been seen as calling into question the validity of the equivalent claims of the Roman emperor cult, which was emphasized more in the late decades of the first century and thereafter, precisely when most scholars think that the Pastorals were composed.[74]

---

70. P.-G. Müller incorrectly characterized all six occurrences of *epiphaneia* in the New Testament as referring to the future ("second") coming of Jesus ("επιφανεια," in *EDNT*, 2:44 [44-45]).

71. The claim that Jesus "abolished death and brought life and immortality to light through the gospel" can refer only to the gospel proclamation of the efficacy of his death and resurrection.

72. See, e.g., discussion and instances of usage of "savior" and "epiphany" in Dibelius and Conzelmann, 100-104; Dominique Cuss, *Imperial Cult and Honorary Terms in the New Testament*, Paradosis 23 (Fribourg: University of Fribourg, 1974); and the list of epithets accorded emperors in inscriptions from various locations in Lily Ross Taylor, *The Divinity of the Roman Emperor* (Middletown, Conn.: American Philosophical Association, 1931; reprint, Chico, Calif.: Scholars, n.d.), 267-83. It is a disappointing lack in Lau's otherwise very useful investigation that he does not discuss the use of *epiphaneia* in the emperor cult. The classic discussion, often ignored today but unwisely so, is in Adolf Deissmann, *Light from the Ancient East*, trans. L. R. M. Strachan (1927; reprint, Grand Rapids: Baker, 1965), 349-78.

73. Young, 65. Cf., however, Hanna Stettler (139-49), who doubts that the use of "epiphany" language in the Pastoral Epistles represents any polemic against the Caesar cult.

74. E.g., Kenneth Scott, *The Imperial Cult under the Flavians* (Stuttgart: W. Kohlhammer, 1936; reprint, New York: Arno Press, 1975).

As Young further observed, in the Roman world of the late first century the expression of devotion to Jesus in this kind of language had the effect of articulating "the public character of the Christian claim," in the knowledge that such a testimony might well lead to confrontation with the authorities, Jesus himself cited in the Pastorals as having borne such a testimony (1 Tim. 6:12-16).[75] It should not be entirely surprising, therefore, that in the period we are considering, and especially as we move into the second century, Christians were increasingly the objects of hostile attention from Roman authorities.[76]

Confluent Evidence

To the texts we have considered we could add others commonly dated to the same approximate period, especially 1 Peter, 2 Peter, Jude, and Revelation. In these writings as well, there is a strong affirmation of traditional beliefs and devotional practices, and similar concerns about teachings/teachers that represent serious variations from these traditions. Likewise, in the traditions that these texts reaffirm, Jesus is revered as divine; they reflect the same sort of unique linkage with God that we noted as characteristic of first-century Christian evidence right back to the earliest uncontested Pauline letters. Furthermore, these writings (especially 1 Peter and Revelation) confirm that devotion to Jesus was increasingly leading to (or threatening) clashes with Roman authorities, and not simply social harassment from other members of the populace.

Therefore, given that these other writings largely provide further evidence of the basic points that I have already underscored about the tributaries that fed into second-century Christianity and its devotion to Jesus, it would almost be gratuitous to discuss them further here. In the final chapter, however, we will have occasion again to note these writings, as we take account of major kinds of phenomena that constitute the patterns of belief and practice of emergent "proto-orthodox" devotion to Jesus in the second century. But contemporaneous with proto-orthodox Christianity were other Christian circles and voices that represent the radical diversity of the second century. In the next chapter we take a careful look at two particularly important examples.

---

75. Young, 65-66.

76. There was however no official or empire-wide policy on how to handle Christians until the third century. Between ca. 70 and 170, hostile treatment by Roman officials seems to have been localized and spasmodic. See, e.g., the recent review of the matter by Paul J. Achtemeier, *1 Peter*, Hermeneia (Minneapolis: Fortress, 1996), 23-36.

CHAPTER NINE

Radical Diversity

The really innovative developments in the period under review here illustrate what I mean by "radical diversity," and they are associated with figures and movements that came to be regarded (in some cases, rather quickly) as heterodox or "heretical" by "proto-orthodox" Christians. The high regard for traditions of belief and practice in early proto-orthodox Christian circles meant that they were often more suspicious of religious innovations and speculative thought than other circles of Christians seem to have been. That is, those who opposed these developments regarded the beliefs and practices as too innovative, and insufficiently compatible with the traditions they revered. As we shall see, the advocates of these radical innovations seem to have agreed that there were major differences between their beliefs and those favored by proto-orthodox Christians. We should not necessarily imagine that all the differences in second-century Christianity were equally significant, or that they all correspond to clearly distinguishable groups. But in some cases it is a fair representation of matters as they were perceived at the time to refer to examples of "radical diversity." And where we can identify instances of radical diversity, they represent major innovations, and rival interpretations of belief and practice, over against the comparatively more traditional preferences that marked proto-orthodox circles.

To be sure, for any form of religious belief and practice to survive across time and cultures, it must adapt. The claims of proto-orthodox circles to preserve primal Christian traditions can easily be shown to be simplistic, or at least only partly indicative of what characterized them. Actually, we could say that proto-orthodox Christianity succeeded more than competing versions of the faith, and became the generally dominant form of Christian faith precisely by adapting successfully. Proto-orthodox circles drew upon revered traditions, to be sure, but they also engaged the issues, circumstances, and settings of the early centuries in their efforts to articulate and promote adherence to their vision of Christian faith. To succeed as it did, proto-orthodox Christianity had to advocate its beliefs and practices in ways that appealed to comparatively wider circles, and larger numbers of believers, than the alternatives did. In the earliest period, long before imperial coercion could be brought to bear in favor of this or that doctrinal position, there was a "free-market" religious economy in the Christian movement!

This characterization of the historical process differs from a view preferred by some scholars. In this other, somewhat romanticized picture, the dominance of "orthodoxy" is asserted to have been only a late and coercive imposition of one version of early Christianity that subverted an earlier and more innocent diversity.[1] Indeed, what became orthodoxy is alleged to have been initially a minority or secondary version in most of the major geographical areas of Christianity's early success. Those who take this view today often cite as the scholarly basis Walter Bauer's 1934 book, *Orthodoxy and Heresy in Earliest Christianity*, which unquestionably has had great influence, especially since its English translation in 1971.[2] Over the years, however, important studies have rather consistently found Bauer's thesis seriously incorrect. In particular, Thomas Robinson's detailed analysis of earliest Christianity in Asia Minor, and studies of Alexandrian Christianity by James McCue and Birger Pearson as well, concur that forms of Christianity that became designated "heretical" seem to have emerged characteristically in settings where *prior* versions of Christianity represented emergent proto-orthodox faith and practice.[3] Moreover, Bauer's claim that the

---

1. I use the term "romanticized" to characterize the passion with which some advocates urge the view. Richard Oster referred to the curious "apologetic zeal" of some scholars with reference to early Christian heterodoxy ("Christianity in Asia Minor," in *ABD*, 1:943 [938-54]).

2. Walter Bauer, *Rechtgläubigkeit und Ketzerei im ältesten Christentum* (Tübingen: Mohr-Siebeck, 1934); ET, *Orthodoxy and Heresy in Earliest Christianity* (Philadelphia: Fortress, 1971). Bauer's book was not initially very influential, but was promoted vigorously in the decades after World War 2, especially in the United States. Perhaps the key advocate has been Helmut Koester. See, e.g., Koester's autobiographical reflections, "Epilogue: Current Issues in New Testament Scholarship," in *The Future of Early Christianity: Essays in Honor of Helmut Koester*, ed. Birger A. Pearson (Minneapolis: Fortress, 1991), 467-76, esp. 470-71. Ehrman's reference to Bauer's book as "possibly the most significant book on early Christianity written in modern times" certainly indicates the passion of those taken with it (*The Orthodox Corruption of Scripture: The Effect of Early Christological Controversies on the Text of the New Testament* [Oxford: Oxford University Press, 1993], 7).

3. Thomas A. Robinson, *The Bauer Thesis Examined: The Geography of Heresy in the Early Christian Church* (Lewiston, N.Y.: Edwin Mellen Press, 1988); James McCue, "Orthodoxy and Heresy: Walter Bauer and the Valentinians," *VC* 33 (1970): 118-30; Birger A. Pearson, "Pre-Valentinian Gnosticism in Alexandria," in *The Future of Early Christianity*, 455-66; Pearson,

second-century Roman church was able to impose its own forms of belief and order translocally is not borne out.[4] In fact, about all that remains unrefuted of Bauer's argument is the observation, and a rather banal one at that, that earliest Christianity was characterized by diversity, including serious differences of belief. Those who laud Bauer's book, however, obviously prefer to proceed as if much more of his thesis is sustainable. Unfortunately, for this preference, Bauer's claims have not stood well the test of time and critical examination.

There was, after all, no real means of "top-down" coercive success for any version of Christianity over others until after Constantine, when imperial endorsement and power could be brought to bear. Second-century bishops were elected by Christians of the locale in which they were to serve. So, for example, if a bishop did not have (or could not win) sufficient support from the local Christians, he could hardly impose on them some version of faith contrary to the preferences of the majority. Thus, if any version of Christianity enjoyed success and became more prominent than others in the first three centuries (whether locally or translocally), it was largely the result of its superior ability to commend itself to sufficient numbers of adherents and supporters. To reiterate the point, the apparent success of what I am calling "proto-orthodox" Christianity was probably the result of teaching and behavior that were more readily comprehended and embraced by larger numbers of ordinary Christians of the time than were the alternatives.

But in comparison with proto-orthodox Christianity, there were certainly more striking examples of Christian religious innovation in the early period under review here. I hasten to add, however, that they were perhaps more striking or radical *in the immediate context of the Christian traditions of the time,* but when set in the larger context of the Roman cultural, religious, and philosophical environment, in some ways they may be seen as comparatively more assimilative and less "radical" than proto-orthodoxy. Michael Williams has cogently argued along these lines about certain early Christian innovations usually referred to as constituting "gnosticism." Indeed, Williams proposes that

---

"Christianity in Egypt," in *ABD*, 1:954-60, esp. 958-59. As for Syrian Christianity, Bauer's other key area in which supposedly heterodox faith was initially dominant, David Bundy's recent review of matters emphasizes how far from certain we can be about the first two centuries, "Christianity in Syria," in *ABD*, 1:970-79. See also Michel R. Desjardins, "Bauer and Beyond: On Recent Scholarly Discussions of *Hairesis* in the Early Christian Era," *SecCent* 8 (1991): 65-82, and for an earlier report, Daniel J. Harrington, "The Reception of Walter Bauer's *Orthodoxy and Heresy in Earliest Christianity* during the Last Decade," *HTR* 73 (1980): 289-98.

4. I also think Bauer's claim has a suspicious air of German Protestant theological polemics. This is rather transparent in his claim that "orthodoxy" was essentially the form of Christianity foisted upon the rest of Christians by the Roman church!

part of the reason these heterodox innovations were less successful (in numbers and long-term viability) was that they were not dissonant enough from religious and philosophical ideas of the general culture. As Rodney Stark has shown, to appeal to significant numbers of ordinary people, new religious movements have to avoid being either too dissonant and weird or too indistinguishable from the general culture.[5] To be either tends to work against success.

We know of a number of Christian figures and movements that can be characterized as radical innovations *within contemporary Christian traditions,* and there were probably others (perhaps a good many) that were still less successful, and consequently did not get preserved or even mentioned in the historical records. Even for those innovative figures whose names are preserved, our knowledge is often fragmentary and/or uncertain. Largely, of course, this is because they were less successful in winning sufficient numbers of adherents and in generating viable movements that were able to preserve and adapt themselves across changing generations.

Across the centuries the overwhelming number of new religious movements have not survived beyond the first few years of their initial appearance; this continues to be the case with the many new religious movements that crop up around the world. In other cases some variant versions of Christianity proved to be reasonably viable for longer periods of time, but they never obtained majority status and went into decline after a while. We can see something similar in religious movements of the modern period by contrasting for example the fortunes of Christian Science, which enjoyed some success but in recent decades has been dying out, with the continued success of Mormonism. Note please: I am not here venturing a judgment about whether this or that variant form of early or modern Christian belief and practice is "correct" or "incorrect," "valid" or "invalid" (which could only be a theological judgment, not a historical one). I am simply noting that some forms of Christianity were (and today are) more successful than others.[6]

For example, John the prophet-author of Revelation was very troubled

---

5. Michael Allen Williams, *Rethinking "Gnosticism": An Argument for Dismantling a Dubious Category* (Princeton: Princeton University Press, 1996), 96-115, also 236-41. He draws upon Rodney Stark's theorizing about what makes for successful new religious movements. See esp. Rodney Stark and William Sims Bainbridge, *The Future of Religion: Secularization, Revival, and Cult Formation* (Berkeley, Los Angeles, and London: University of California Press, 1985); Stark, "How New Religions Succeed: A Theoretical Model," in *The Future of New Religious Movements,* ed. David G. Bromley and Phillip E. Hammond (Macon, Ga.: Mercer University Press, 1987), 11-29; Stark, *The Rise of Christianity* (Princeton: Princeton University Press, 1996).

6. See the somewhat similar discussion of early Christian heterodox figures/movements as religious "innovations" in Michael Williams, 80-95.

about "Nicolaitans" who were active among the churches to which he wrote (Rev. 2:6, 15), but we have no secure knowledge of what Nicolaitans believed or even what the name signifies.[7] We could add other named figures, such as Menander, Simon, Carpocrates, Cerinthus, Cerdo, Basilides, and Saturninus (a.k.a. Satornilus), for whom, however, we have only brief and polemical characterizations in antiheretical writers considerably later than their reputed period of activity.[8] The antiheretical sources of the early centuries often linked them with "gnostics," but we have scarcely any corroboration of anything specific; in fact, the very negative way they are portrayed may or may not represent their actual teachings and behavior.

Of all the figures of the second century who are connected with major Christian heterodox innovations, perhaps the two most successful (in notoriety and success in generating professed followers) were Valentinus and Marcion. So I give further attention to these two teachers and the religious movements named after them, particularly about their views of Jesus.

Valentinus and Valentinianism

Valentinus (ca. 100-175) became a Christian in Alexandria, and is said to have moved to Rome sometime between 117 and 138, where he was active as a teacher in Christian circles until his subsequent departure for Cyprus circa 160, after which we lose all track of him. He was probably gifted intellectually, with a strong interest in speculative philosophical thought, and an impressive teacher.[9] But there are major differences among specialists in Valentinian Christianity about what, more exactly, to make of Valentinus himself, and how much he ac-

---

7. The other references to Nicolaitans in Irenaeus (*Adv. haer.* 1.26.3; 3.11.1), Hippolytus (*Ref.* 7.24), Eusebius (*HE* 3.29) are all obviously dependent on Revelation; the additional legendary material is minimal and scarcely reliable. See excerpts and brief discussion in Arland J. Hultgren and Steven A. Haggmark, *The Earliest Christian Heretics: Readings from Their Opponents* (Minneapolis: Fortress, 1996), 28-31; and the assessment by Duane F. Watson, "Nicolaitans," in *ABD*, 4:1106-7.

8. Again, brief introductions and relevant extracts from the antiheretical writers in Hultgren and Haggmark, 32-76. Kurt Rudolph, *Gnosis: The Nature and History of Gnosticism* (San Francisco: Harper and Row, 1983), 9-25, reviews these antiheretical sources for our knowledge of "gnosticism." Among recent studies of particular figures, see, e.g., Winrich A. Löhr, *Basilides und seine Schule: Eine Studie zur Theologie- und Kirchengeschichte des zweiten Jahrhunderts*, WUNT 83 (Tübingen: Mohr-Siebeck, 1995); Abraham P. Bos, "Basilides as an Aristotelianizing Gnostic," *VC* 54 (2000): 44-60.

9. See Bentley Layton, *The Gnostic Scriptures* (Garden City, N.Y.: Doubleday, 1987), 217-22, for a widely accepted view of the historical Valentinus.

tually shared of the ideas that came to be identified as "Valentinianism." Some respected scholars, such as Bentley Layton and Gilles Quispel, confidently posit a significant continuity between Valentinus and the teachings of those subsequent figures whom early antiheresy writers portrayed as his followers, such as Ptolemy, Theodotus, Marcus, and Heracleon.[10] In their view, Valentinus's teachings included the mythic scheme attributed to him by Irenaeus (which I sketch briefly below); subsequent "Valentinian" teachers elaborated and modified it variously. But other scholars, among whom Christoph Markschies has been particularly prominent in recent years, have raised questions about the basis for this approach; they dispute the common view of Valentinus as a gnostic and the source of the elaborate mythological schemes attributed to Valentinianism in the ancient antiheretical writers such as Irenaeus.[11]

Indeed, in his review of Markschies' 1992 study of the fragments of Valentinus preserved in writings of Clement of Alexandria and Hippolytus, Hans Dieter Betz referred to Valentinianism as "one of the most contested areas of study."[12] Not only is there a major difference of approach toward the "historical Valentinus" and how to use the various putative sources for his teaching, there are also differences over who and what made up Valentinianism, and over the nature of the "Valentinian schools" that are often referred to in scholarly discussion.[13] It is worth noting that the ancient figures commonly classified as Valentinians seem not to have called themselves by this or any other party name, except probably the epithet "spirituals" (pneumatikoi). As Layton has suggested, the term "Valentinian" was probably coined, sometime circa 160, as a pejorative epithet, and was used by proto-orthodox writers of the second cen-

10. E.g., Layton, *Gnostic Scriptures*, esp. 217-353; Gilles Quispel, "The Original Doctrine of Valentinus the Gnostic," *VC* 50 (1996): 327-52. A similar view is echoed, e.g., in Hultgren and Haggmark, 82-83.

11. Christoph Markschies, *Valentinus Gnosticus? Untersuchungen zur Valentinianischen Gnosis mit einem Kommentar zu den Fragmenten Valentinus*, WUNT 65 (Tübingen: Mohr-Siebeck, 1992); Markschies, "Das Problem des historischen Valentin — Neue Forschungen zu Valentinus Gnosticus," in *Studia Patristica, Volume 24*, ed. Elizabeth A. Livingstone (Leuven: Peeters, 1993), 382-89. Cf. Gilles Quispel, "Valentinus and the Gnostikoi," *VC* 50 (1996): 1-4; and Markschies' reply, "Nochmals: Valentinus und die Gnostikoi, Beobachtungen zu Irenaeus, Haer. I 30,15 und Tertullian, Val. 4.3," *VC* 51 (1997): 179-87. Similar questions were raised earlier by G. C. Stead, "In Search of Valentinus," in *The Rediscovery of Gnosticism*, vol. 1, *The School of Valentinus*, ed. Bentley Layton (Leiden: Brill, 1980), 75-102.

12. Hans Dieter Betz, in *JR* 75 (1995): 268 (268-69).

13. E.g., see Christoph Markschies, "Valentinian Gnosticism: Toward the Anatomy of a School," in *The Nag Hammadi Library after Fifty Years: Proceedings of the 1995 Society of Biblical Literature Commemoration*, ed. John D. Turner and Anne McGuire, NHMS 44 (Leiden: Brill, 1997), 401-38.

tury and thereafter who attacked the teachers/teachings in question.[14] Further-more, though some scholars confidently use the fourth-century texts from the Nag Hammadi collection, in particular the *Gospel of Truth* and the *Gospel of Philip*, as additional direct evidence for second-century Valentinianism (in-deed, some scholars even attribute the *Gospel of Truth* to Valentinus himself), others challenge the basis for doing so and urge great caution.[15] I consider key Nag Hammadi texts later in this discussion.

Fortunately, however, in this study our questions are not what to attribute to Valentinus himself, or how to chart the details of the history and develop-ment of the Valentinian schools that are widely thought to have succeeded him. Instead, the concern here is restricted to taking stock of the ideas about Jesus that were linked with Valentinianism. This enables us to sidestep these unre-solved controversies among specialists in Valentinian studies, and we can focus on matters that are comparatively more feasibly handled. Whatever Valentinus himself taught, scholars widely agree that the elaborate mythic schemes de-scribed by Irenaeus (our earliest source on Valentinian teachers and beliefs) re-ally correspond to teachings being promoted in some second-century Christian circles, and that at least some of these circles had a historical connection to Valentinus, and so can be referred to as "Valentinian."[16]

"Valentinianism" in Irenaeus

The mythic schemes described by Irenaeus are varied, and each of them is com-plex, with a large cast of divine beings (emanations, aeons, angels, etc.) and elaborate narratives. These myths seem to have been primarily concerned with accounting for the origins of things, the world, humanity at large, and espe-cially, of course, of the elect. For example, Irenaeus's summary of the teaching of Ptolemy (*Adv. haer.* 1.1-8) describes a divine *plērōma* (fullness) comprised of a primal octet of aeons, another eleven pairs of additional aeons (including one that is the higher "Wisdom") that proceeded from the primal octet, then a heavenly "upper" Christ, his consort (the Holy Spirit), Jesus (called "Savior" and distinguished from the upper "Christ"), and a company of angelic body-

---

14. Layton, *Gnostic Scriptures*, 270.

15. Cf., e.g., Quispel, "Original Doctrine," 333; Layton, *Gnostic Scriptures*, 220-21 (who la-bels the *Gospel of Truth* a "sermon" of Valentinus); Stead, 78. On the *Gospel of Philip*, see the measured characterization by Einar Thomassen, "How Valentinian is *The Gospel of Philip*?" in *The Nag Hammadi Library after Fifty Years*, 251-79.

16. Irenaeus's account of various Valentinian teachings/teachers appears in *Adv. haer.* 1.1-22.

guards of Jesus. In addition, below/outside the *plērōma* is a lower wisdom figure ("Achamoth"), from which came forth the "Demiurge" (the creator of the material world and the god of Israel and of ordinary Christians, as distinguished from the "spiritual" elect).[17] Humankind is divided into three types/classes: "spirituals" (*pneumatikoi*, the elect, "Valentinian" Christians who are predestined ultimately to be joined to the angels), "animates" or "soulish" people (*psychikoi*, ordinary Christians who must rely on faith and works for salvation of a lower order than what awaits Valentinians), and the "material ones" (*choïkoi*, the remainder of humans for whom no redemption at all is provided).

Irenaeus attributes a slightly less complex myth to Valentinus himself (1.11.1), although a number of divine aeons still help to constitute the divine fullness. In this version, however, "Christ" and the human figure Jesus are both produced *outside* the *plērōma*, along with the Demiurge (the Creator deity of the Old Testament).[18] If in spite of the challenges of some scholars Irenaeus's report of Valentinus's teachings is accurate, then the mythic orientation of Valentinianism was there from the outset. But whatever the origins of the elaborate mythic schemes, scholars commonly think that Irenaeus was reporting the sorts of ideas that were actually circulating at least by the later decades of the second century when he wrote his massive account of Christian heresies (ca. 170).

Whereas proto-orthodox believers held Jesus as unquestionably the central figure in their religious beliefs, the one mediator between humans and God, the key agent of creation and redemption, the unique divine Son and Word, and the very image of the one God, in these Valentinian mythic schemes we have to look carefully even to find Jesus in the crowd that makes up the *plērōma* of numerous divine beings! Moreover, the curious distinction between "Jesus" and the "Christ" obviously contrasts with the more familiar insistence in the writings favored in proto-orthodox circles that the human, historic Jesus is himself the divine Son and the paramount divine revelation.

---

17. It is commonly recognized that the name Achamoth is derived from *hochmah*, the Hebrew word for "wisdom." I suggest that the identification of the inferior wisdom figure with the personification of the wisdom from the Old Testament is one of several expressions of disdain for the Old Testament and its deity. The term "Demiurge" was used in Greek philosophical tradition, and also appropriated among Greek-speaking Jews to refer to their God as "creator" of the world. On the background of the negative connotation of the term in "gnostic" usage, see Jaap Mansfeld, "Bad World and Demiurge: A 'Gnostic' Motif from Parmenides and Empedocles to Lucretius and Philo," in *Studies in Gnosticism and Hellenistic Religions*, ed. R. Van Den Broek (Leiden: Brill, 1981), 261-314.

18. Cf. the layouts of the mythic schemes attributed to Valentinus and Ptolemy respectively in Layton, *Gnostic Scriptures*, 224, 272-73.

As is characteristic of other texts we considered earlier (e.g., *Gospel of Thomas* and the revelation dialogues), so also in these various mythic schemes the human predicament is essentially an ignorance of the truths conveyed in the mythic accounts, and a captivity in the world of sense and matter. Redemption of the elect is illumination through "knowledge" *(gnōsis)*, their (re)discovery of the true story of the origins of the cosmos and their own predestined status. Consequently the primary mission of Jesus is portrayed as teaching and demonstrating the illumined outlook and corresponding behavior to which the elect are summoned. Jesus' crucifixion is allegorized as purification from the physical world and bodily life (*Adv. haer.* 1.3.5), not the crucial redemptive action that secures forgiveness of sins. Indeed, the Valentinians seem to have engaged in their own programmatic allegorizing of a number of key terms in the religious vocabulary of early Christianity such as "resurrection." As well, in the effort to commend and defend their beliefs, they allegorized the writings that were coming to be revered as scripture in widening circles of the Christian movement, and that became part of the New Testament.[19]

Clearly these mythic schemes reflect a profound anxiety about the material world, and bodily existence specifically, as being incompatible with spirituality and the divine. Consequently, it is not surprising that the creation of the world is not attributed to the ultimate/high deity, but to another figure, the Demiurge, who is at best an inferior and ill-informed being (as in Valentinian schemes), and sometimes (in other heterodox texts) is still more negatively portrayed as an arrogant and stupid figure. Indeed, it is striking how often in these mythic accounts the exclusivist monotheistic claim of the God of Israel that appears in Isaiah, "I alone am God" (46:9; 43:10), is cited as the height of the hubris and stupidity of the Demiurge (e.g., *Adv. haer.* 1.5.4).[20]

This negative view of the material creation has obvious implications for the understanding of Jesus' historical nature. Scholars often portray the Valentinian tradition in terms of two main schools, a Western "Italic" group linked with Ptolemy and Heracleon, and an Eastern group that derived from

---

19. Layton, *Gnostic Scriptures*, 272-74. And see the discussion of the use of New Testament writings in the *Gospel of Truth* below.

20. Observed by Alistair H. B. Logan, *Gnostic Truth and Christian Heresy: A Study in the History of Gnosticism* (Edinburgh: T. & T. Clark, 1996), 2, and 23 n. 7 (which gives references to a number of Nag Hammadi texts). For discussion, see Nils A. Dahl, "The Arrogant Archon and the Lewd Sophia: Jewish Traditions in Gnostic Revolt," in *The Rediscovery of Gnosticism: Volume Two, Sethian Gnosticism*, ed. Bentley Layton (Leiden: Brill, 1981), 701-6 (689-712); George W. MacRae, "The Ego-Proclamation in Gnostic Sources," in *The Trial of Jesus: Cambridge Studies in Honour of C. F. D. Moule*, ed. Ernst Bammel, SBT 2/13 (London: SCM Press, 1970), 123-29.

Theodotus and Marcus. The Western branch is said to have taught that "the Savior" put on a body of "soulish" *(psychikos)* substance that was "constructed in an ineffable manner so as to have been visible, touchable and capable of suffering [*pathēton genesthai*]," but "he did not take on anything material [*hylikon*], they say, for the material is not receptive of salvation" (1.6.1). The Eastern Valentinians, however, apparently taught that the body of the Savior was entirely of "spiritual" *(pneumatikos)* essence, a still higher quality of nonmateriality than the category of "soulish" substance.

Valentinian Innovations

In neither school of thought is there any room for Jesus to have borne a normal physical body and, thus, to have had a fully mortal nature. For example, a curious fragment said to come from Valentinus portrays Jesus as having eaten and drunk in a special manner, so that no excretal waste was produced. Being divine, what he ate "was not corrupted, for he did not experience corruption."[21] This discomfort with a genuinely human/mortal Jesus seems to have characterized a number of variant circles of Christians, of course. We noted in chapter 6 that the Johannine "secessionists" may have taken such a stance, and also possibly the "docetists" refuted by Ignatius of Antioch in the early decades of the second century. The issue represents a major fault line in early Christianity between the emphases of emergent proto-orthodox Christianity and other circles that came to be labeled heterodox.

Any student of the ancient references to Valentinian Christianity is unavoidably struck by additional emphases that are echoed in other heterodox circles as well. To cite one particularly important matter alluded to already, there is obviously no concern with the exclusivist monotheism that is the framing religious outlook of New Testament writings and the proto-orthodox traditions. Indeed, in the writings of second-century proto-orthodox Christianity, the dominant concern seems to have been to defend monotheism.[22] Eric Osborn contends that the major theological effort of key second-century proto-orthodox thinkers was to work out a view of God that maintained a

21. Clement of Alexandria, *Strom.* 3.59.3; translated in Layton, *Gnostic Scriptures,* 239. Valentinus may have drawn upon Ps. 16:10 here, offering his own explication of the promise that the "holy one" will not "see corruption."

22. Joseph Lortz, "Das Christentum als Monotheismus in den Apologien des zweiten Jahrhunderts," in *Beiträge zur Geschichte des christlichen Altertums und der byzantinischen Literatur: Festgabe Albert Ehrhard,* ed. Albert Michael Koeniger (Bonn and Leipzig: Kurt Schroeder, 1922), 301-27.

monotheistic stance while also doing justice to the divinity of Jesus.[23] But Valentinianism and some other equivalently radical innovations in earliest Christianity can be differentiated from proto-orthodoxy in their curious lack of serious concern about this issue.

It is clear that the mythic schemes attributed to Valentinians and related heterodox circles; the abundance of divine beings, with various roles assigned to them; and even more significantly, the view of creation as the product of an inferior level of divinity (the "Demiurge" = Craftsman) represent a very different religious outlook. Although a single ultimate divine principle may be posited, as in at least some versions of Valentinian thought, this seems to function essentially for philosophical purposes, to answer an intellectual need for a single metaphysical premise. The ultimate divine principle often in fact has scarcely a major role in the mythic drama, and the complexity of gradations of divinity dominates the accounts. Even the comparatively simpler scheme presented in the *Letter to Flora* (commonly attributed to the second-century Valentinian teacher Ptolemy), which distinguishes between a "first principle" (the high deity of perfection and goodness from whom "the Savior" came), an intermediate deity of justice (the Old Testament deity who gave the Law through Moses), and an evil "adversary" of injustice, is a long way from the exclusivist monotheism favored in proto-orthodox circles.[24]

The complexity of the mythic schemes obviously indicates a speculative bent by those who developed and circulated them. It is commonly thought that the developed Valentinian body of teachings represents a combination of middle Platonist philosophical traditions (Philo of Alexandria showing an earlier Jewish appropriation of middle Platonist categories) and themes and motifs that stemmed from Jewish mystical tradition of the time. These two streams of traditions were used to produce a bold reinterpretation of Christian vocabulary and themes. That is, the mythic schemes probably reflect the interests and orientation of certain Christians who were given to particular kinds of imaginative and speculative efforts to portray divine realities.[25]

Valentinus and those linked with him seem to have been in their own way academically oriented, aiming to produce a learned interpretation of Christian faith and, notably, the Christian writings that were coming to be widely treated as Scriptures. Our earliest commentary on any New Testament writing is by a second-century Valentinian, Heracleon, on the Gospel of John. As mentioned

---

23. Eric Osborn, *The Emergence of Christian Theology* (Cambridge: Cambridge University Press, 1993).

24. For introduction and English translation, see Layton, *Gnostic Scriptures,* 306-15.

25. See, e.g., Mansfeld, "Bad World and Demiurge," for an exploration of Greek philosophical traditions for issues and categories taken up in "gnostic" forms of early Christianity.

already, the basic approach Valentinians used was to allegorize the Christian terms and texts. Of course, the New Testament writings reflect innovative Christian interpretations of the Old Testament Scriptures, shaped by convictions about Jesus as the prophesied Messiah and Savior. Valentinianism, however, involved an equally innovative reinterpretation of Christian traditions and texts.

But, with no desire to minimize the ingenuity of Valentinus or others responsible for the radical diversity of second-century Christianity, I must note that there appear to have been precedents, somewhat analogous ideas that circulated in Christian circles earlier. There is, for example, the reference to two Christian teachers, Hymenaeus and Philetus (2 Tim. 2:16-19), who are linked with "godless chatter" and are specifically accused of having "swerved from the truth by holding that the resurrection is past already." The teaching in question likely involved a radical allegorization or reinterpretation of "resurrection" as a transformation of one's spiritual status or outlook that is available in the present, and a denial of a future transformation and bodily revivification of believers. The Nag Hammadi text *Treatise on the Resurrection*, which may have been composed sometime in the late second century by a Christian with Valentinian tendencies, appears to articulate such a view explicitly.[26] But if 2 Timothy dates from sometime circa 70-100, it gives evidence of such a radical allegorization/reinterpretation of key topics of Christian belief well before Valentinus and Valentinianism.

Likewise, it is commonly accepted that Paul's critique of worldly wisdom and the divisive spirituality of some in the Corinthian church in the mid–first century (1 Cor. 1:10–4:20) may address a still earlier manifestation of elitist and innovative distinctions between classes of Christians that is somewhat similar to those that characterized the heterodox groups we are considering here. Unfortunately, the extant references to these first-century developments do not provide us with enough information to describe the specific beliefs with confidence. But the tendencies seem to have gone in a broadly similar direction to some innovations more fully described in second-century sources.

I emphasize again that these same Valentinian Christians who developed and favored the sort of elaborate mythic scheme that I have summarized here also tended to downplay the Old Testament and its narratives. The mildest attitude toward the Old Testament in Valentinian texts is expressed in the *Letter to Flora*, which portrays the Old Testament and its commandments as a mixed bag that derives from a deity inferior to the highest god. From there the attitudes to-

26. See the introduction and English translation by Malcolm L. Peel, "The Treatise on the Resurrection," in *NHLE*, 52-57.

ward the Old Testament and its deity in other texts only get more negative. In this at least, the Valentinians can be likened to other heterodox circles that scholars often refer to as "gnostics."[27] For Valentinians and these others, it is likely that their myths were intended to substitute for the function of the Old Testament narrative world of events, characters, and themes. That is, the mythic schemes provided a replacement narrative world in which the elect could "situate" themselves meaningfully. And in this rival narrative world the Old Testament and its deity, along with Israel, and run-of-the-mill Christians as well, were assigned a vastly inferior status and significance.[28]

Valentinian Piety

It is also reasonable to ask about the kind of piety practiced by those who favored these elaborate Valentinian myths with their multilayered scheme of divinities. In particular, what kind of devotion to Jesus may have figured in their religious life? Among the limited materials available to us from the circles of the Christians in question, brief fragments attributed to Valentinus himself include expressions that may hint at a piety that focuses on inward, perhaps mystical, encounter with the divine. One fragment refers to "One there is who is good" (an obvious allusion to Matt. 19:17), through whose "free act of speaking [*parrēsia*] is the manifestation of the Son" (probably reflecting the Johannine

27. Layton observed, "What *is* first and foremost in gnostic scripture is its doctrines and its interpretation of Old and New Testament books — especially its open hostility to the god of Israel and its views on resurrection, the reality of Jesus' incarnation and suffering, and the universality of Christian salvation. On these points the gap between gnostic religion and proto-orthodox Christianity was vast." He proposed that "Valentinus, though essentially a gnostic, tried to bridge this gap," and that "he and his followers consciously limited themselves to a proto-orthodox Christian canon," avoiding reference to heterodox texts in their writings (Layton, *Gnostic Scriptures*, xxii). More precisely, Valentinian writings fairly consistently show use of the New Testament canonical texts *only*, not Old Testament writings. And, on all the issues Layton mentioned, Valentinianism seems to me to represent a stance closer to what he calls "gnostic" than to proto-orthodoxy.

28. Cf. Birger A. Pearson, "Use, Authority and Exegesis of *Mikra* in Gnostic Literature," in *Mikra: Text, Translation, Reading, and Interpretation of the Hebrew Bible in Ancient Judaism and Early Chrsitianity,* ed. Martin Jan Mulder, CRINT (Assen: Van Gorcum; Philadelphia: Fortress, 1988), 635-52, who claims to find positive and negative attitudes toward the Old Testament in "gnostic" texts from Nag Hammadi. But his few "wholly positive" examples *(Exegesis of the Soul* and *Pistis Sophia)* are, as he notes, quite late and eclectic (and thus may show influence of "orthodox" as well as "gnostic" stances). Also, to use the term "gnostic" for such diversity only illustrates its dubious quality as a descriptor of anything in particular, as Michael Williams has complained *(Rethinking "Gnosticism").*

theme of Jesus as the manifestation of the Logos), and solely through this one, the Father, "a heart can become pure." When "the Father, who alone is good, visits the heart, he makes it holy and fills it with light"; thereby a person is called "blessed" and "will see God" (alluding to Matt. 5:8).[29]

This fragment obviously alludes to texts and themes shared with proto-orthodox circles. The claims that "the Son" is the manifestation and expression of the Father, that God alone can make the heart pure and fit to see God obviously echo themes shared with a wide number of early Christian texts. Furthermore, the focus on "the Father," with "the Son" functionally subordinated as the expression of the Father, fits the general pattern of religious thought registered in proto-orthodox texts as well, as we noted in earlier chapters of this book. But even if we examine all the eight or so statements widely thought to derive from Valentinus himself, we have precious little on which to proceed. We certainly cannot go very far in portraying with confidence Valentinus's own teaching about Jesus or the kind of devotional practice he followed.

The early antiheresy writers such as Irenaeus claim to give information on some of the religious practices of Valentinians and others. But their accounts are so thoroughly polemical that they are likely to be both selective in what they convey and also probably caricatures. Certainly the focus in Irenaeus's accounts is on the beliefs and mythic schemes of Valentinians; his description of their religious practices concentrates on what he vilifies as magical and dubious.

At one point (*Adv. haer.* 1.13.6) he relates a prayer petition that he attributes to disciples of Marcus, which is addressed to *Sigē* ("Silence," one of the primal dyad of highest divine figures in the scheme Irenaeus attributes to Valentinus). *Sigē*, a mother figure, is addressed as she who sits beside God "the Father" *(Ō paredre theou)*, and is implored to intercede on behalf of the devotees so that they be spared from the indictments of "the judge" *(ho kritēs)*. Upon hearing this petition, "the Mother" will render the devotee(s) invisible "so that they may escape the judge," and will conduct them into "the bridal chamber" *(nymphōna)* where they will join their consorts (*nymphioi*, "bridegrooms"). Obviously, in this sort of piety *Sigē* appears to play the sort of intercessory and salvific role attributed to the ascended Jesus in more familiar Christian texts of the earliest period. As I have indicated, however, it is difficult to say how broadly this prayer is representative of Valentinian piety.

---

29. The saying is preserved in Clement of Alexandria, *Strom.* 2.114.3-6 (ANF, 2:372), introduction and translation in Layton, *Gnostic Scriptures*, 244-45.

Nag Hammadi Texts

The cache of fourth-century Coptic texts discovered at the Egyptian site of Nag Hammadi added significantly to the pool of sources for the study of early Christianity. More particularly, there is wide (but not universal) agreement among relevant specialists that among the forty-five distinguishable works in the Nag Hammadi codices, several can be taken as Valentinian.[30] The following works are often so regarded: *Prayer of the Apostle Paul* (1,1), *Gospel of Truth* (1,3; 12,2), *Treatise on the Resurrection* (1,4), *Tripartite Tractate* (1,5), *Gospel of Philip* (2,3), *Interpretation of Knowledge* (11,1), and *A Valentinian Exposition* (11,2).[31]

Problems

There are, however, valid questions about how confidently we can use any of the Nag Hammadi texts as direct, primary evidence for Valentinianism in the second century, although these questions are not always registered adequately in scholarly discussion of the matter. So, before we can determine their use, it will be a responsible first step to take account of these questions. They have been described with admirable clarity and candor by Michel Desjardins.[32] I shall draw upon his discussion and underscore a couple of additional matters.

First, none of the Nag Hammadi texts actually claims to be Valentinian, or even refers to Valentinians. The widely shared view that certain Nag Hammadi texts can be treated as Valentinian rests upon the prior conviction that there are sufficient similarities of their vocabulary, themes, and teachings with the accounts of Valentinian teachers given by early Christian writers such as Irenaeus. But what amounts to *sufficient* similarities? For example, it is not entirely clear that the appropriation of an allegedly Valentinian mythic scheme (or certain components thereof, such as the *plērōma*) in a text necessarily means that the text itself is of Valentinian provenance.

30. Fifty-two tractates were identified in the remains of thirteen codices from Nag Hammadi. But for some there is more than one copy, leaving us forty-five distinguishable writings. Of these, six works were previously known, and several more are very fragmentary. James M. Robinson has summarized matters by stating that Nag Hammadi has provided us with "thirty fairly complete texts, and ten that are more fragmentary" (introduction to *NHLE*, 12).

31. I cite the English titles given to the works in question in *NHLE*. The parentheses after each work indicate the number assigned to the particular codex (or codices) in which each work was found, followed by the sequential position of the work in the codex. Thus, e.g., two copies of the *Gospel of Truth* were found, one the third work in codex 1, and the other, a very fragmentary copy, the second work in codex 12.

32. Michel R. Desjardins, *Sin in Valentinianism*, SBLDS 108 (Atlanta: Scholars, 1990), esp. 5-12.

In the fluid and varied world of early Christianity, it is quite likely that Christians of various orientations experimented with appropriating this or that feature of belief and practice without buying into the whole version of Christianity from which the belief or practice derived. Thus vocabulary and themes that may have originated from Valentinian discourse could easily have been appropriated by Christians who did not imagine themselves to be Valentinians. We have to allow for the strong possibility of considerable eclecticism in the religious vocabulary and conceptual categories of Christians in the early period. Some early Christians were concerned for tradition and conventionalization of beliefs and practices (e.g., Clement of Rome), but others seem to have been more eclectic (e.g., Clement of Alexandria), more ready to appropriate religious terminology and ideas that they perceived as interesting and useful, and less apprehensive as to its derivation.[33] Thus these Nag Hammadi texts could preserve some themes and motifs that may have originated in Valentinian circles without the texts themselves being wholly evidence of Valentinianism.

A second reason for treating the Nag Hammadi texts cautiously in reconstructing second-century Christianity is that they are all Coptic texts from the late fourth century. Here a problem resurfaces that I identified in the discussion of the *Gospel of Thomas* (chap. 7). That is, for all the texts in the Nag Hammadi collection, a significant period and transmission process likely separates the fourth-century manuscripts from whatever may have been their originating compositions. Aside from possible effects of translation into Coptic from Greek (or other source languages), we also have to allow for the sorts of more serious reshapings that ancient texts were subject to in copying. This is particularly relevant for texts that may have been transmitted across a couple of centuries or more. At least some Nag Hammadi writings derive from earlier compositions that may have originated in the second century, about 150 to 200 years earlier than the date of the Nag Hammadi manuscripts. The further back one postulates an originating composition behind a Nag Hammadi writing, however, the more opportunity for deliberate as well as accidental changes as the writing was copied and circulated.

In fact, where the extant evidence permits us to test matters, it suggests significant reshaping of the texts in the Nag Hammadi cache during textual transmission. For example, as we noted in the preceding chapter, there are interesting differences between the single Coptic copy of the *Gospel of Thomas*

33. See similar cautions expressed earlier by Frederik Wisse, "Prolegomena to the Study of the New Testament and Gnosis," in *The New Testament and Gnosis: Essays in Honour of Robert McL. Wilson*, ed. A. H. B. Logan and A. J. M. Wedderburn (Edinburgh: T. & T. Clark, 1983), 138-45.

from the fourth century and the three Oxyrhynchus Greek fragments from about 150 years earlier. Moreover, even contemporaneous copies of the same works in the Nag Hammadi collection exhibit notable differences, which suggests considerable textual fluidity in the transmission process. Perhaps the most striking example is in comparing the four Nag Hammadi copies of the *Apocryphon of John* (a work which reflects a mythological scheme somewhat similar to what Irenaeus attributes to certain gnostic teachers). These four copies represent three distinguishable Coptic translations of at least two distinguishable Greek recensions of the work.[34]

Furthermore, given the kinds of texts represented in the Nag Hammadi collection, and the apparent roles these writings played in the circles that read and copied them, we should not be surprised that they appear to have been transmitted with considerable freedom in reshaping their contents. Many of the Nag Hammadi texts are loosely connected chunks of material of varying sizes, and often compendia of sayings and short to medium-sized meditations on religious themes that are strung together without an obvious logical order. I propose that this kind of text more readily facilitates expansion by the insertion of further similar material, and even invites readers to add their own meditations and speculations as well. The compendia-like nature of the text also means that any expansions and insertions would be difficult to detect, as there is hardly any continuous flow of thought or action to interrupt.

Furthermore, there is no indication that any of the writings in question ever really functioned as "Scripture," either among the Christians who composed them or those who subsequently read and copied them.[35] It is particu-

34. Michael Waldstein and Frederik Wisse, *The "Apocryphon of John": Synopsis of Nag Hammadi Codices II,1; III,1; and IV,1 with BG 8502,2*, NHMS 33 (Leiden: Brill, 1995), esp. 1-8. They conclude that Irenaeus likely did not know the *Apocryphon of John* but, instead, "a Gnostic document which was the apparent source of the first part of the main revelation discourse in the book"; and they set the original composition of the *Apocryphon of John* itself "probably during the early part of the Third Century," with at least one major redaction thereafter (1). Brief introduction and English translation by Frederik Wisse in *NHLE*, 104-23. See also Karen L. King, "Approaching the Variants of the *Apocryphon of John*," in *The Nag Hammadi Library after Fifty Years*, 105-37, and in the same volume, Frederik Wisse, "After the *Synopsis*: Prospects and Problems in Establishing a Critical Text of the *Apocryphon of John* and in Defining Its Historical Location," 138-53; and Stephen Emmel, "Religious Tradition, Textual Transmission, and the Nag Hammadi Codices," 34-43.

35. Consequently, the title of Layton's useful compendium of "Gnostic Scriptures" is somewhat misleading. The texts in question are valuable historical sources for our study of Christian beliefs and practices in the first several centuries of the common era. But there is no evidence that they were used as "scriptures," in the sense of texts read out publicly as part of the corporate worship life of Christian groups or as authoritative texts for defining beliefs and practices. Layton notes as much himself, characterizing the works in his collection as "probably edi-

larly important to note that we have no evidence that these writings were read out publicly as regular components of the liturgical activities of Christian groups. By contrast, we know from second-century reports (e.g., Justin Martyr, *1 Apol.* 67) that readings from the Old Testament and from writings that later became part of the New Testament formed a regular part of the liturgical activities of a good many Christian gatherings. I contend that the frequent public reading of a writing gives its contents a kind of "public ownership." That is, those who hear a text read frequently can more readily tell when it has been modified than is the case with a writing that is not so used.

To be sure, the text-critical evidence for the New Testament writings shows that even texts that were beginning to be used as Scripture were not immune from notable textual variation, perhaps more so in the very early stages of their circulation (e.g., the long ending to Mark, the account of the adulterous woman which was inserted into the Gospels of John and Luke, and the so-called Western text form of Acts). But I suggest that it is *comparatively* more difficult to continue to make sizable changes when texts are treated as the public property of a group, particularly after they have been so used for a while.[36] The Nag Hammadi writings, however, seem to have functioned essentially as edifying discourses or religious tractates, and perhaps propagandistic presentations of speculative and innovative ideas.[37] Such writings could be modified more readily, and across a longer period of time, without people feeling that a familiar text that was "owned" by a group had been altered inappropriately.

For these reasons, therefore, out of concern for careful scholarly method, we should regard the Nag Hammadi manuscripts as *direct* evidence of this, and really only this: the state of the texts of the writings in question in certain late fourth-century, Coptic-speaking Christian circles in Egypt.[38] They may well also be *indirect* evidence of the text of these writings prior to the late fourth century, and likewise may incorporate themes and practices whose provenance

---

fying scripture, not canon" (Layton, xxiii). The scribal notes and marks on the Nag Hammadi manuscripts indicate that they were prepared by devout Christians (of whatever stripe) who regarded these texts as congenial to their own religious stance. But the texts probably functioned more for personal devotional usage and not as communally affirmed texts in worship. See, e.g., James Robinson, introduction to *NHLE*, 13-18.

36. Thus the sort of major variants in the New Testament writings that I mention here seem to have appeared very early in the transmission of them (probably second century in each case); we do not continue to see such major variations in their texts subsequently.

37. So also, e.g., Frederik Wisse, "The Use of Early Christian Literature as Evidence for Inner Diversity and Conflict," in *Nag Hammadi, Gnosticism, and Early Christianity*, ed. Charles W. Hedrick and Robert Hodgson, Jr. (Peabody, Mass.: Hendrickson, 1986), 188 (177-90).

38. As James Robinson observed, the Nag Hammadi cache may well be a consolidation of three or more earlier and smaller collections of writings (introduction to *NHLE*, 15-16).

is much earlier than these Coptic manuscripts. But if, for example, we wish to use the Nag Hammadi texts as evidence of second-century Christianity, we have to give a soundly based argument for doing so, and on a case by case basis with corroborating evidence.[39]

The Texts

Furthermore, the specific basis for treating the seven or so texts mentioned earlier as particularly Valentinian varies from somewhat plausible to precarious. It would, for example, be a wonderful scholarly boon if a text such as the *Prayer of the Apostle Paul* could be treated confidently as a source for early Valentinian religious devotion. It is a moving prayer addressed to God as "Redeemer," "my treasure house," "my fullness," and refers to Jesus as "the Son of Man," and also to "the Spirit, the Paraclete." The petitioner claims to have come forth from God, and appeals for "gifts" that include "healing for my body when I ask you through the Evangelist," redemption for "my eternal light soul and my spirit," and other blessings that exceed what angels, archons, or the human heart can imagine. But although Jesus is apparently the one referred to as "the First-born of the Pleroma," and the prayer includes a few other expressions that are thought to derive from gnostic circles, it would exceed the warrants of evidence and reason to treat this text as if it were a second-century Valentinian document. It is actually more likely to derive from those who put together the Nag Hammadi codices in the fourth century, and these Christians (Pachomian monks?) are more likely to have been ascetic monks than Valentinians.[40]

The so-called *Valentinian Exposition* is a curious mélange of terminology and themes that may well come from speculative Christian circles such as early Valentinians, together with short discussions of the meaning of baptism and a prayer to God to "anoint" the petitioners so that they can triumph over the power of the devil. The text also has what appear to be eucharistic prayers that include rather conventional-sounding Christian doxologies (e.g., "Glory be to

---

39. As an analogy, there is the late-fourth-century compilation of materials on church order and worship, the *Apostolic Constitutions*, which is widely thought to draw upon several earlier texts, including the *Didache*. But no one would take the *Apostolic Constitutions* as a source for second-century liturgical practices and church order. On this text, see, e.g., G. D. Dragas, "Apostolic Constitutions," in *EEC*, 1:92-93. See also the frank appraisal by Wisse, "After the *Synopsis*," 149-50.

40. The prayer was written on the front cover sheet of Codex I (the "Jung Codex"), probably by the scribe who copied final text in this codex, *Tripartite Tractate* (1,5). See, e.g., James Robinson's discussion of the possible connection of the Nag Hammadi manuscripts to monastic circles, introduction to *NHLE*, 17-22; and Wisse, "After the *Synopsis*," 147-48.

you through your Son and offspring Jesus Christ forever, Amen," XI 43, 36-37).[41] Do we have here direct evidence of second-century Valentinian devotional beliefs and practices, or is it not more likely that the writing represents a complex history of textual and religious developments across the approximately three centuries of Christianity that passed before this Coptic text was produced in its present form?

To cite another interesting but notoriously difficult text, *Gospel of Philip (Gos. Phil.)* presents us with a mélange of material without a readily perceptible organizational scheme.[42] There are recurring themes, such as the deeper significance of the names of Jesus (56.3-15; 62.7-17; 63.21-24), the reinterpretation of resurrection as something to be experienced during one's life (56.15-20; 56.26-57; 66.16-23; 73.1-8), and the necessity of putting on "light" for protection from the hostile "archons" (70.5-9; 76.22-27; 86.4-10). These particular themes certainly reflect an esoteric and mystical orientation, and they likely derive from much earlier Christian circles. But whatever the original provenance(s) of the various themes, or even the originating composition itself (from the late second or third century?), as a compilation of loosely linked sayings and meditations it readily would have permitted (and perhaps even encouraged) a rather free adaptation and a rolling agglutination of additional material as the writing was transmitted. In short, *Gos. Phil.* may well preserve some beliefs and practices that characterized Valentinian Christians, and perhaps other Christians as well, from various points diachronically down through the late fourth century.[43] The sacramental ideas and practices in particular are fascinating.[44] But it would be dubious to press this fourth-century text very far as particularly *direct* evidence of the devotional practice and beliefs of second-century circles of Valentinianism without second-century evidence as corroboration.[45]

41. Introduction and translation adapted from Elaine H. Pagels and John D. Turner, *NHLE*, 481-89.

42. "It cannot be contended that [the Gospel of] Philip is a single coherent text composed according to normal standards of writing." R. McL. Wilson, *The Gospel of Philip, Translated from the Coptic Text, with an Introduction and Commentary* (London: A. R. Mowbray, 1962), 9. Wesley W. Isenberg even proposed that the compiler of *Gos. Phil.* "purposely disjoined what were once whole paragraphs of thought and distributed the pieces in various places in this work" ("The Gospel of Philip," in *NHLE*, 139 [139-60]). See also Jacques-É. Ménard, *L'Évangile selon Philippe: Introduction, texte, traduction, commentaire* (Paris: Letouzey & Ané, 1967), who refers to the text as a "collection of sentences or a florilegium" (6, my translation).

43. E.g., Isenberg proposes that the Coptic translation may have been made from 250 to 300, from a Greek text that may have originated anytime from 150 to 250 (*NHLE*, 141).

44. Five sacraments are mentioned: baptism, a "chrism" (anointing), Eucharist, "redemption," and the "bride chamber." *Gos. Phil.* 67.27-30.

45. For recent studies, see, e.g., Martha L. Turner, "On the Coherence of the *Gospel ac-*

Gospel of Truth

Of the several possibly "Valentinian" texts from Nag Hammadi, perhaps the most intriguing in what it says about Jesus, and certainly the one for which the boldest historical claims have been made, is designated the *Gospel of Truth (Gos. Truth)*.[46] Helderman judged the *Gos. Truth* and the *Gospel of Thomas* the best known and most frequently studied writings of the Nag Hammadi collection, judged by the huge amount of scholarly attention given to these texts since their appearance.[47]

Irenaeus complained that "those who are from Valentinus" promoted "their own compositions," among which he took particular exception to "their relatively recent writing 'the Gospel of Truth'" (*Adv. haer.* 3.11.9 [ANF, 1:429]).[48] Many scholars accept the proposal that the Nag Hammadi text is a later Coptic version of the writing mentioned by Irenaeus; this is reflected in the title given to the Coptic text by scholars (which actually has no title in the manuscript).[49] In this view of the Nag Hammadi text now called *Gos. Truth,* it originated in Greek among Valentinian Christians, perhaps sometime circa 140-180.

But a good many scholars go farther. Layton, for example, is a prominent exponent of the view that the work is an actual sermon from Valentinus himself.[50] Others might quibble over what kind of label best describes its contents (e.g., sermon, meditation, "laudatory, hortatory address"), but its attribution to Valentinus is widely accepted.[51] This view rests upon positing significant stylis-

---

cording to Philip," in *The Nag Hammadi Library after Fifty Years,* 223-50, and in the same volume, contributions by Einar Thomassen, "How Valentinian is *The Gospel of Philip?*" 251-79; Elaine H. Pagels, "Ritual in the *Gospel of Philip,"* 280-91. Also, April D. DeConick, "The True Mysteries: Sacramentalism in the *Gospel of Philip,"* *VC* 55 (2001): 225-61.

46. Harold W. Attridge and George W. MacRae, "The Gospel of Truth," in *Nag Hammadi Codex I (The Jung Codex): Introductions, Texts, Translations, Indices,* ed. H. W. Attridge, NHS 22, 23 (Leiden: Brill, 1985), 1:55-117, 2:39-135. There are two copies of *Gos. Truth* in the Nag Hammadi codices, one in codex 1 and another in codex 12, but the latter is so fragmentary that virtually all observations on the writing deal with the copy in codex 1. The two copies represent distinguishable Coptic translations of two somewhat different Greek texts.

47. J. Helderman, "Das Evangelium Veritatis in der neueren Forschung," in *ANRW,* 2.25/5 (1988): 4054-55 (4054-4106).

48. Benoit Standaert, "'Evangelium Veritatis' et 'Veritatis Evangelium': La question du titre et les témoins patristiques," *VC* 30 (1976): 138-50.

49. Attridge and MacRae characterize the identification of the Nag Hammadi text with the writing mentioned by Irenaeus as "quite possible" (*NHLE,* 38).

50. Layton, *Gnostic Scriptures,* 221, 250-52. This view goes back to W. C. van Unnik, "'The Gospel of Truth' and the New Testament," in *The Jung Codex,* ed. F. L. Cross (London: A. R. Mowbray, 1955), 79-129.

51. E.g., Helderman (4101), who subscribed to this view and referred to it as the com-

tic resemblances to the fragments of Valentinus quoted by Clement of Alexandria, in light of "the alleged genius and eloquence of Valentinus and the lack of a likely candidate for authorship among later Valentinian writers," plus the absence of the sort of complex mythic scheme that is attributed to the alleged successors of Valentinus by Irenaeus.[52]

There are, however, other views on the provenance of this work, and reasons for remaining cautious about authorship, and about other matters as well.[53] For example, the absence of a recognizable Valentinian mythic scheme is hardly an adequate basis for concluding that *Gos. Truth* must have been composed so early that it preceded the development of such schemes. It is a fallacy to date texts by their putative simplicity or complexity of thought. Early Christian thought did not develop in lockstep or unilinear fashion; at any given point there were both those who preferred simplicity and others whose tastes ran to greater complexity.

Moreover, we have already noted that in these ancient centuries texts could readily be altered to make them relevant as they were transmitted. Consequently, why would Valentinians preserve *Gos. Truth* sacrosanct, leaving its alleged "primitive" features unaltered? And why would they then circulate an obsolete text inviolate for a few centuries, even after their religious beliefs had supposedly come to focus on the elaborate mythic schemes attributed to them by the later second century and thereafter? It is much more reasonable to assume that the fourth-century Coptic text of *Gos. Truth* reflects the effects of its transmission between the originating composition and the extant copy. That is, its contents are what they are because they were meaningful to religious needs and interests of those Christians who transmitted and translated the writing across perhaps two centuries, including some Coptic Christians of the fourth

---

monly accepted view *("communis opinio")*. "Laudatory, hortatory address" is the characterization by Karl P. Donfried, *The Setting of Second Clement in Early Christianity*, NovTSup 38 (Leiden: Brill, 1974), 101-2, who compares *Gos. Truth* to *2 Clement* as to literary type, although they represent quite different theological stances.

52. Layton, *Gnostic Scriptures*, 251. Layton depends in part on the comparison of *Gos. Truth* and fragments of Valentinus in Clement of Alexandria by Benoit Standaert, "L'Évangile de Vérité: critique et lecture," *NTS* 22 (1975-76): 243-75.

53. Cf. the introduction to *Gos. Truth* by Attridge and MacRae, in *NHLE*, 38-39, who judge the hypothesis of Valentinus's authorship as "a distinct possibility, although it cannot be definitively established" (38). For reviews of research, see Helderman, "Das Evangelium Veritatis in der neueren Forschung"; R. McL. Wilson, "Valentinianism and the *Gospel of Truth*," in *The Rediscovery of Gnosticism*, vol. 1, *The School of Valentinus*, ed. Bentley Layton (Leiden: Brill, 1980), 133-41, who questions the basis for the view that *Gos. Truth* is the same writing referred to by Irenaeus, the attribution of the work to Valentinus, and even its characterization as Valentinian.

century. So if the work does not correspond to what we might think of as matured Valentinian teaching, then either those Christians who shaped the text as we have it were not proper Valentinians or our ideas of what Valentinianism might have been may need correction.

Indeed, perhaps widely shared notions among scholars, about discrete and identifiable groups to which texts such as *Gos. Truth* can be directly tied, need to be rethought. It is fairly clear that there were Christian groups that sharply distinguished themselves from others. But there were also probably more interchange and adaptation of themes, vocabulary, and texts among various early Christian circles than are allowed for if we draw the map of second-century Christianity as a number of discrete groups with well-established boundaries. In dealing with texts such as *Gos. Truth,* we may need to consider various possibilities. For example, Robin Wilson wondered, "Is it possible that the *Gospel of Truth* derives from some unknown group, which has certain affinities with Valentinianism or has borrowed something from that school, without being directly connected with it? Or was it the work of some unknown Valentinian at a later stage than that known to Irenaeus, who sought to work out a closer rapprochement with Christianity?"[54] As we shall see, still other possibilities are mooted by scholars.

There is, however, no question that *Gos. Truth* contains fascinating expressions of early Christian belief, particularly in its statements about Jesus.[55] Moreover, whatever the authorship and provenance of the writing itself, there are reasonable grounds for thinking that at least some of its themes and motifs derive from much earlier than the fourth-century date of the manuscript. In particular, as has been demonstrated by other scholars, *Gos. Truth* seems largely to embody meditative developments of vocabulary and categories drawn from writings that became part of the New Testament.[56] Indeed, *Gos. Truth* may be taken readily as an effort to present a particular, revisionist interpretation of terms and categories of belief that were widely shared in various Christian circles, particularly terms and expressions that were part of the religious discourse of those Christians we may characterize as proto-orthodox.

This means, of course, that *Gos. Truth* is therefore indirectly (but clearly) a witness to the priority of traditions and texts that were preferred in proto-orthodox circles. That is, whenever and wherever the work originated, it pre-

---

54. Wilson, "Valentinianism," 137.

55. Sasagu Arai, *Die Christologie des Evangelium Veritatis: Eine religionsgeschichtliche Untersuchung* (Leiden: Brill, 1964), remains the only monograph-length study of the representation of Jesus in *Gos. Truth.*

56. See especially Jacqueline A. Williams, *Biblical Interpretation in the Gnostic "Gospel of Truth" from Nag Hammadi,* SBLDS 79 (Atlanta: Scholars, 1988).

supposes a familiarity with and high regard for the writings and traditions to which it makes such frequent allusion; these writings happen to be part of the New Testament collection.[57] In fact, several scholars have described *Gos. Truth* as an "exoteric" writing. That is, it may have been directed to Christians of more traditional, proto-orthodox stance, with the intention of promoting revisionist interpretations of the faith subtly through using the vocabulary of those being addressed.[58] So, while balancing concerns about using a late-fourth-century text to describe second-century Christian devotion over against the possibility that this text preserves some features of early Christian diversity, let us look at some key features of the way this writing presents Jesus.

The first emphasis to note is the recurring characterization of the human predicament in *Gos. Truth* as "ignorance" of "the Father" (e.g., 17.1, 10, 30; 19.10-14; 28.32-33), and the corresponding portrayal of salvation as knowing/knowledge (e.g., 18.4-10, 20-21; 22.26; 24.29-36; 27.20; 30.1-16, 24-26; 37.37-38). Ménard counted some sixty uses of the Coptic terms for knowing and knowledge in this modest-sized text.[59] The opening lines proclaim that "the gospel of truth is joy for those who have received from the Father of truth the grace of knowing him" (16.31-33).[60] Shortly thereafter the text refers to "the Savior," whose title reflects the work he is to perform "for the redemption of those who were ignorant of the Father" (16.38-39). That is, in *Gos. Truth* Jesus' redemptive work is emphatically *revelatory* and its effects primarily *noetic*. As Barrett observed, *Gos. Truth*

57. Jacqueline Williams noted (175-76) as "particularly striking" that the sources that can be identified as referred to in *Gos. Truth* were "texts that were to become part of the New Testament"; she observed that the author evidently expected readers to recognize the texts used and to understand that he was interpreting them. She classified putative references into "probable," "possible," and "dubious" (179-83); the "probable" sources referred to are in Genesis (creation narratives), Matthew, Johannine writings (including 1 John and Revelation as well as the Gospel of John), and Pauline epistles (including deutero-Paulines such as Ephesians). See also Craig A. Evans, Robert L. Webb, and Richard A. Wiebe, *Nag Hammadi Texts and the Bible: A Synopsis and Index*, NTTS 18 (Leiden and New York: Brill, 1993), which lists biblical citations and allusions throughout the Nag Hammadi corpus (for *Gos. Truth*, 19-41).

58. Jacques-É. Ménard, *L'Évangile de Vérité*, NHS 2 (Leiden: Brill, 1972), 1; Helderman, 4072-77; J.-C. Fredouille, *Tertullian. Contre les Valentiniens*, 2 vols., SC 280 (Paris: Éditions du Cerf, 1980-81), 1:34-39; and particularly Harold W. Attridge, "The *Gospel of Truth* as an Exoteric Text," in *Nag Hammadi, Gnosticism, and Early Christianity*, 239-56.

59. Ménard, *L'Évangile de Vérité*, 17. The English translation of *Gos. Truth* in *NHLE* takes up a mere eleven and a half pages; cf., e.g., nineteen pages for *Gos. Phil.*

60. My citations of *Gos. Truth* are from the English translation of the text by Attridge and MacRae in *NHLE*, 40-51, unless otherwise indicated; the numbers indicate the page and line(s) in the Nag Hammadi manuscript. Layton provides another English translation with annotations (*Gnostic Scriptures*, 253-64). I have also consulted Ménard's French translation and commentary in *L'Évangile de Vérité*.

"diagnoses the human situation which is the scene and occasion of the work of redemption in terms of ignorance rather than sin." In fact, as to sin in *Gos. Truth,* Barrett noted an "almost complete failure to treat the subject at all."[61] To be sure, the idea that the Christian gospel message offers knowledge of God and God's purposes that is not otherwise available is a commonplace in early Christian circles (e.g., Eph. 1:15-19; John 17:3; 2 Cor. 4:3-6; *1 Clem.* 36.1-2). But in *Gos. Truth* such special knowledge of divine things is touted almost to the total exclusion of any of the other ways of referring to redemption.

Moreover, in *Gos. Truth* the knowledge of "the Father" given to the elect crucially involves (and perhaps mainly constitutes) their knowledge of their own transcendent origin, significance, and destiny. That is, what is revealed is very much their own ontic continuity with "the Father," who seeks to restore the lack previously caused by their having fallen into ignorance and darkness (e.g., 34.34–35.30). In the favored texts of proto-orthodox circles as well, we have references to an elect who are distinguished from unbelievers and given special significance (e.g., John 17:6-19), and whose salvation is preordained before the world was made (e.g., Eph. 1:3-6). But it seems that in *Gos. Truth,* not merely the divine decision to redeem them but the elect themselves have a pretemporal cosmic origin and nature. The redeeming knowledge touted in *Gos. Truth* enables the elect individual to know "where he comes from and where he is going" (e.g., 22.10-20; 30.5-15), and that the elect themselves "are the truth," that "the Father is within them and they are in the Father, being perfect" (42.26-29). Furthermore, although it is not so blatantly stated as in some other texts, the clear implication is that the elect of *Gos. Truth* are not coextensive with the full number of Christians, but instead constitute an elite inner circle.[62]

As a further expression of this emphasis on Jesus as revealer, in *Gos. Truth* "the Savior" is also the "Word" (16.34), the expression of "the hidden mystery, Jesus, the Christ" (18.15-16), who "enlightened those who were in darkness" and showed them "a way," which is "the truth which he taught them" (18.17-21). This

---

61. C. K. Barrett, "The Theological Vocabulary of the Fourth Gospel and the *Gospel of Truth,*" in *Current Issues in New Testament Interpretation: Essays in Honor of Otto A. Piper,* ed. William Klassen and Graydon F. Snyder (New York: Harper and Row, 1962), 214, 212 (210-23). The Coptic word for "sin" appears only twice, in 32.35-39 and 35.25-29.

62. E.g., in 42.1-10 the elect are distinguished from those who imagine God to be "small" and "harsh" and "wrathful," which is probably a polemical characterization of (proto-orthodox) Christians who identify the true God with the God of the Old Testament. Ménard, *L'Évangile de Vérité,* 188, noted that these epithets make allusion to the God of the Old Testament, and rightly observed that Marcion was by no means alone in finding irreconcilable tensions between what such Christians perceived as a stern, brutal, and cruel Old Testament deity and the God of goodness and love with whom they linked themselves and Jesus. See, e.g., Irenaeus, *Adv. haer.* 3.12.12.

Word reveals the Father's thought, and was "first to come forth" according to the Father's will (37.5-19). The Word reveals that the Father knows the origin and end of the elect, and this end is "receiving knowledge about the one who is hidden, and this is the Father," from whom their beginning came and "to whom all will return who have come forth from him" (37.35–38.5). The echoes of the Gospel of John are obvious.

But perhaps the most striking presentation of the role of Jesus as revelation of God in *Gos. Truth* is in the extended meditation on the idea that he has and is God's "name" (38.7–41.14). "Now the name of the Father is the Son," to whom the Father gave "his [own] name which belonged to him" (38.7-12; also 39.24-26). The true name of the Father is not spoken, but "it is apparent through a Son" (38.22-24). The Son "did not receive the [divine] name on loan as others do," but instead he is "the proper name," and he has the power to disclose it (40.5-20) to others. It pleased the Father that "his name which is loved should be his Son, and he gave the name to him," so that the Son "spoke about his secret things, knowing that the Father is a being without evil" (40.24-30).

On the one hand, this meditation on Jesus as the Father's "name" presupposes and develops a basic conviction attested in other early Christian texts that Jesus uniquely bore and manifested the name of God. In chapter 6 we noted the important place of this theme particularly in the Gospel of John.[63] Philippians 2:9-11 and Hebrews 1:4 are additional evidence of the early appropriation of the idea that God gave to Jesus a name that represents an incomparable, divine status. In *Gos. Truth,* as in these other early Christian texts, the uniquely close association of Jesus with the name of God obviously connotes a high view of Jesus and, probably, a correspondingly intense devotion to him.

On the other hand, in the context of *Gos. Truth* the emphasis on Jesus as the manifestation of the name of the Father functions as part of a subtly promoted intra-Christian polemic. In texts such as John, Philippians, and Hebrews, the association of Jesus with God's name supports the claim of Jesus' validity and his surpassing significance in comparison with other figures such as angels and Old Testament patriarchs (yet without invalidating them altogether). But in *Gos. Truth* the emphasis on Jesus as uniquely manifesting the proper name of "the Father" serves a concern to distinguish this true deity of

---

63. See "Jesus as/and the Name of God" in chap. 6; Jean Daniélou, *The Theology of Jewish Christianity,* trans. and ed. J. A. Baker (London: Darton, Longman and Todd, 1964), 147-63, cites a number of early Christian texts that demonstrate the designation of Jesus as being, bearing, and manifesting the name of God; e.g., *1 Clem.* 58.1; 60.4; *Herm. Vis.* 3, 3.5; *Herm. Sim.* 9, 14.5; *Excerpta ex Theodoto* 86.2. See also Arai, 62-72. Cf. also the curious references to the cryptic significance of the names "Jesus" and "Christ" in *Gos. Phil.* 56.4-15, and "Jesus," "Christ," and "Nazarene" in 62.8-17.

"sweetness" from the inferior notions of a "small" and cruel God held in those Christian circles for whom the Old Testament was Scripture (42.4-9).[64]

In a couple other passages *Gos. Truth* refers to Jesus as "the living book" (19.34–20.15; 22.38–23.18). Here again is an appropriation of an image attested in earlier Christian tradition. In 19.34–20.15, it seems particularly likely that Revelation 5:1-5 is presupposed in the reference to a "book" that "remains for the one who will take it to be slain" (cf. Rev. 5:1-5). Jesus, "the merciful, the faithful one," patiently accepted his sufferings "until he took that book, since he knows that his death is life for many" (*Gos. Truth* 20.10-15). Whereas in Revelation 5:1-10 the book (scroll) that the "Lamb" alone is worthy to open seems to represent the redemptive plan of God for the world, in *Gos. Truth* the book represents the "incomprehensibility" of the Father (20.1-4), the manifestation of which in Jesus brought the possibility of the "salvation" that is promoted in this text. This salvation consists in the knowledge given to the elect concerning the true identity of the Father and their own true nature (20.6-10).

We also have here one of several references to Jesus' death in *Gos. Truth*, and these merit further attention. The statement that Jesus' death is "life for many" in 20.13-14 certainly seems to echo traditional early Christian phrasing, perhaps particularly Matthew 20:28/Mark 10:45.[65] In *Gos. Truth*, however, Jesus' death does not provide a ransom for sins. Instead it vividly portrays the futility and unimportance of the flesh, and the secret of the transcendent destiny to which the elect can now aspire in consequence of Jesus' own pathfinding action.

In the following lines we are told that Jesus "put on that book" and was "nailed to a tree," thereby publishing "the edict of the Father on the cross" (*Gos. Truth* 20.24-27).[66] It is widely recognized that these lines probably draw upon Colossians 2:14. As is usually the case when elements of early Christian tradition are used in *Gos. Truth*, however, there is here a clever revision of the imagery.[67] Colossians 2:14-15 pictures God nailing to Jesus' cross the indictment of sins that stood against the elect, and refers to Jesus as thereby stripping the hostile cosmic powers (or stripping himself of them) through his death. In *Gos. Truth* 20.25-34, however, the divine "book" or "edict" (Jesus) conveys the knowledge of the hidden Father, which is literally posted on Jesus' cross. In his

---

64. One of the interesting (and distinguishing) features of *Gos. Truth* is the use of the terms for "sweet" and "sweetness" to characterize the true Father (e.g., 33.33; 41.3; 42.7-8), and Jesus as well in the memorable phrase, "Jesus of the infinite sweetness" (24.8-9).

65. See Jacqueline Williams, 46-48; Ménard, *L'Évangile de Vérité*, 97.

66. The only use of the term "cross" (Gk. *stauros*, taken over into the Coptic as a loanword) in *Gos. Truth* is in 20.27. In 18.24 and 20.25 the term "tree" (or "wood") is used.

67. See, e.g., Jacqueline Williams, 50-54.

death Jesus "stripped himself of the perishable rags" (bodily/fleshly existence) and "put on imperishability, which no one can possibly take away from him" (20.30-34). Thereby he became the inspiring model of the ephemeral nature of the material world and the transcendence of the true origins of "the living who are inscribed in the book of the living" (21.3-5).

There is a prior mention of Jesus' death in *Gos. Truth* 18.24-25. This passage refers to a persecution of Jesus by "Error" (the personification of the power of ignorance of God) which led to Jesus being nailed to a "tree."[68] Thereby Jesus became "a fruit of knowledge of the Father," the eating of which by the elect conveys to them discovery of the Father within them, and of themselves within the Father (18.27-31). Here Jesus' crucifixion appears to be interpreted by alluding to the Genesis tree of the knowledge of good and evil (Gen. 2:17). In contrast to the tragic effects of eating the fruit of the forbidden tree in the Genesis story, *Gos. Truth* proclaims that "Christ became a fruit of the Father's knowledge in his death and so brought discovery that some people belong to the Father."[69]

Just as Jesus' death is innovatively interpreted in *Gos. Truth,* so is his earthly, bodily existence. On the one hand *Gos. Truth* affirms that the divine Word "became a bodily form" (26.5-8), producing thereby great consternation for "Error" and the forces of the material world (26.10-29). In another passage (31.5-8) the Son is said to have come forth "in a fleshly form/likeness." As Jacqueline Williams proposed, this phrase is probably indebted to Romans 8:3, where Paul refers to God having sent forth "his own Son in the likeness [*homoiōmati*] of sinful flesh."[70] Ménard argued, however, that the term "flesh" here reflects the notion attributed to some Valentinians that Jesus' flesh was in fact a unique, "psychic" body, and not material substance of the ordinary kind; this certainly fits the disdain toward the material world reflected in *Gos. Truth.*[71]

But whatever the nature of the "fleshly form" of Jesus referred to in 31.5-8, throughout *Gos. Truth* Jesus' bodily existence is merely a temporary measure that had two functions. It had the effect of preventing those who were not the elect ("the material ones") from recognizing him as the divine Son/Word (31.1-6), and yet it also permitted him to appear in the world of sense and matter in order to reawaken the elect to their forgotten nature. In his death, however, Je-

68. "Error" (Gk. *planē*) in *Gos. Truth* is a personification of the hostile ignorance of the Father that afflicts the world of matter. See, e.g., 17.10–18.10.

69. Jacqueline Williams, 28-29. Similarly, C. I. K. Story, *The Nature of Truth in "The Gospel of Truth" and in the Writings of Justin Martyr,* NovTSup 25 (Leiden: Brill, 1970), 125.

70. Jacqueline Williams, 115-17.

71. Ménard, *L'Évangile de Vérité,* 144-46.

sus "stripped off the perishable rags" (20.28-33) of bodily existence, and instead of a bodily resurrection he underwent and exemplifies the *deliverance from bodily existence* that the elect aspire to experience as well.[72] If therefore *Gos. Truth* affirms some sort of "incarnation" of the divine Word/Son, then we must also say that both the nature and the significance of this incarnation are starkly different from the beliefs that were preferred in proto-orthodox circles.

It may be anachronistic to associate *Gos. Truth* itself with the schism addressed in 1 John. But the evident appropriation and variant interpretation of terms and concepts particularly shared with (and probably derived from) GJohn suggest the possibility of a historical connection between *Gos. Truth* and Johannine Christianity.[73] In particular, *Gos. Truth* may well reflect some influence of the sorts of beliefs about Jesus' bodily existence and death that characterized the opponents condemned in 1 John. However, whatever the historical connection between *Gos. Truth* and the Johannine community, I suspect strongly that the author of 1 John would have regarded the view of Jesus' "flesh" and his death in *Gos. Truth* as meriting the condemnations that he issued against the secessionists who left the Johannine circle in the late first century.[74]

Granted, *Gos. Truth* may well also reflect a further development of other earlier traditions.[75] For example, Paul distinguished the nature of the resurrection body in which Jesus arose, and which believers also are to inherit, from the mortal body. Declaring that "flesh and blood cannot inherit the kingdom of God," he projected an eschatological transformation in which the elect, whether alive or dead, will be given a newly immortal, glorious, powerful, and "spiritual" body (1 Cor. 15:35-57) patterned after Jesus' own resurrected state (15:49; likewise Phil. 3:20-21). However, Paul's discussion of the nature of the resurrection body in 1 Corinthians was intended to assert the reality of the

---

72. *Gos. Truth* 20.32-34 is the one reference to Jesus' postcrucifixion glorification, which is not described as a bodily resurrection. See, e.g., Story, 132.

73. Jacqueline Williams observed that "The gospel of John has profoundly influenced GTr," but that the Johannine theological motifs are "developed beyond their use in John" (187).

74. Cf. Story, 20, who took the reference to Jesus' "fleshly form" in *Gos. Truth* as evidence that it does not reflect the views of those condemned in 1 John. But, as I have previously argued, the accusation in 1 John that the secessionists denied that Jesus "has come in the flesh" (4:1-3) reflects the author's polemical judgment about the teaching of the secessionists, not a simple quotation of their teaching. The secessionists could well have referred to Jesus' "flesh," but if so, their interpretation of it was unsatisfactory to the author of 1 John, and he judged it to be, to all intents and purposes, a denial of Jesus' real fleshly existence.

75. Cf. James M. Robinson, "Jesus — from Easter to Valentinus (or to the Apostles' Creed)," *JBL* 101 (1982): 5-37; William L. Craig, "From Easter to Valentinus and the Apostles' Creed Once More: A Critical Examination of James Robinson's Proposed Resurrection Appearance Trajectories," *JSNT* 52 (1993): 19-39.

bodily resurrection of Jesus, and the future bodily resurrection of believers, in answer to objections and/or a radical redefinition of resurrection that seemed to him to amount to a denial of it (15:12-14, 35-36).[76]

But *Gos. Truth* does not share Paul's concern to assert real continuity between mortal bodily existence and resurrected existence in an immortal body. Instead it seems to reflect an outlook similar to that in *Gos. Thom.* For example, both texts present Jesus' earthly bodily existence as merely a temporary form that he took to enable him to serve as revealer to the elect who needed to be awakened from their slumber of forgetfulness. His death constituted his own escape from bodily existence and his return to divine transcendence, thereby providing the elect with the pattern of their own return to their transcendent origins. Likewise, in both texts the Old Testament is set aside as having scriptural force. But whereas *Gos. Thom.* displays more openly a disdain for the beliefs of those Christians outside the charmed circle of the elect, *Gos. Truth* is carefully phrased to present the author's stance more subtly and winsomely, in terms and tones that ordinary Christians might not find so readily off-putting. Of course, the similarities between the two do not mean necessarily that both texts came from the same circles, or even from the same time. Instead, these writings could be independent productions indicative of various circles of Christians with somewhat overlapping objections to proto-orthodox beliefs.

As for what is commonly thought to represent Valentinianism, the elaborate mythic schemes attributed to Valentinian teachers by Irenaeus clearly represent a religious outlook that is categorically different from the one in the texts favored by proto-orthodox circles. *Gos. Truth* itself reflects a standpoint that is distinguished from what was (or became) characteristic of mainstream Christianity. Although expressed in a guarded manner, the dissident stance behind *Gos. Truth* is apparent to careful readers. Insofar as *Gos. Truth* may preserve elements of second-century circles, perhaps (though not so clearly as some assert) Valentinians of some sort, it confirms that the crucial dividing line between them and contemporary proto-orthodox circles was whether to identify Jesus with the God of the Old Testament, the creator of the world. That is, beliefs about Jesus were heavily determined by how various Christian circles understood the God from whom Jesus was believed to have come. Actually, as we shall see in what follows, a sharp distinction between the deity with whom Jesus was associated and the deity referred to in the Old Testament was made by various dissident Christians.

---

76. See, e.g., the extended discussion of chap. 15 in Gordon D. Fee, *The First Epistle to the Corinthians*, NICNT (Grand Rapids: Eerdmans, 1987), 713-809.

Marcion

The other principal named figure who vividly exemplifies radical diversity in the first several decades of the second century is Marcion. The unavoidable problem in saying anything about Marcion with confidence, however, is that no writing of his survives. We are entirely dependent upon hostile references to him and his teachings in the writings of several antiheretical figures of the early centuries: Justin, Hippolytus, Irenaeus, and especially Tertullian's five-book refutation.[77] Nevertheless, certain biographical matters are widely treated as authentic by scholars.[78]

He was born in the Roman province of Pontus (on the Turkish coast of the Black Sea) sometime toward the end of the first century, and he probably went to Rome in the early second century (ca. 130). There he quickly became highly visible through his efforts to promote his own views of proper Christian beliefs. These were sufficiently controversial that he was expelled from the Roman church in 144. But absolutely sure of himself over against all criticism, he then started his own rival churches, first in Rome and then quickly in various other sites as well. So his teachings obviously held an attraction for a good many Christians of that time. Writing shortly after 150, Justin complained (perhaps with hyperbole) about the spread of Marcion's teachings among "many of every nation" (*1 Apol.* 26.5; 58.1). Whereas at least some other dissident Christians, such as the author of *Gos. Truth,* appear to have attempted to circulate their views from within proto-orthodox circles, Marcion set up his own

77. Hultgren and Haggmark, 101-15, give excerpted references to Marcion in early Christian writers. For a detailed analysis, see David Wayne Deakle, "The Fathers against Marcionism: A Study of the Methods and Motives in the Developing Patristic Anti-Marcionite Polemic" (Ph.D. diss., Saint Louis University, 1991). Tertullian's work *Against Marcion,* written in Latin ca. 207, gives the fullest account of Marcion's teachings, and is most heavily drawn upon by modern scholars. For text and English translation, see Ernest Evans, ed. and trans., *Tertullian Adversus Marcionem,* 2 vols. (Oxford: Clarendon, 1972).

78. See, e.g., Hendrik F. Stander, "Marcion," in *EEC*, 2:715-17; Barbara Aland, "Marcion — Marcionites — Marcionism," in *EECh*, 1:523-24; Johannes Quasten, *Patrology,* 4 vols. (Westminster, Md.: Christian Classics, 1950-86), 1:268-72. Cf. the very different views by R. Joseph Hoffmann, *Marcion: On the Restitution of Christianity, an Essay on the Development of Radical Paulinist Theology in the Second Century* (Chico, Calif.: Scholars, 1984); and Hoffmann, "How Then Know This Troublous Teacher? Further Reflections on Marcion and His Church," *SecCent* 6 (1987-88): 173-91; and the critical review of Hoffmann by Gerhard May, "Ein neues Marcionbild?" *TRu* 51 (1986): 404-13, and May's summary judgment that Hoffmann's case was "full of improbabilities and methodological errors" ("Marcion in Contemporary Views: Results and Open Questions," *SecCent* 6 [1987-88]: 131 [129-51]). Peter Head likewise found Hoffmann's argument unpersuasive: "The Foreign God and the Sudden Christ: Theology and Christology in Marcion's Gospel Redaction," *TB* 44, no. 2 (1993): 309-10 n. 7 (307-21).

churches, with ecclesiastical structures (bishops, priests, and deacons) intended to rival mainstream Christianity.

Marcion's main presentation of his teaching was in a work entitled *Antitheses,* which is now lost, though substantial extracts of it are preserved in the anti-Marcionite writings of the early church, especially in Tertullian's five-volume critique. In *Antitheses* Marcion lined up passages from the Old Testament with statements in the New Testament writings that he revered (which we note shortly), to show contradictions and incompatibilities. These supported the conclusions that the Old Testament could not be treated as Scripture by Christians, and, the single most important assertion for Marcion, that there was a complete distinction between the Old Testament deity and the "greater" God whom Jesus came to reveal and who was otherwise and previously unknown.[79]

In the New Testament writings and the tradition followed by proto-orthodox Christianity, Jesus is presented as the highest and fullest revelation of the true God, who is the deity also revealed in the Old Testament. According to this view of Jesus, he fulfilled but also superseded the prior and valid revelations of God that are witnessed to in the Old Testament (e.g., Rom. 3:21-22; Heb. 1:1-2). But somewhat similarly to other dissident Christians such as those behind *Gos. Truth* and *Gos. Thom.,* and the various circles often referred to as "gnostics," Marcion took a very different view. He insisted that the Old Testament witnessed accurately to the activity of an inferior deity who was the creator of the world, but not the highest God whom Jesus came to disclose.

However, although some other heterodox Christians portrayed this world creator (Demiurge) as morally evil, Marcion taught that this figure was merely inferior to the true God. Further, Marcion portrayed this inferior deity as the god of the Jews, on whose behalf the biblical prophets had spoken and from whom a Messiah was prophesied, who was not, however, to be identified as Je-

---

79. See Justin, *1 Apol.* 26.5; 58.1; Irenaeus, *Adv. haer.* 1.27.1-4. Still the best-known and most influential treatment of Marcion is Adolf von Harnack's classic study, *Marcion. Das Evangelium vom fremden Gott* (Leipzig: Hinrichs, 1921, 1924); partial ET, *Marcion: The Gospel of the Alien God* (Durham, N.C.: Labyrinth Press, 1990). The best-known English-language study is E. C. Blackman, *Marcion and His Influence* (London: SPCK, 1948). Gerhard May, "Marcion in Contemporary Views," is a valuable analysis of scholarship. For Marcion's theology, see esp. Barbara Aland, "Marcion. Versuch einer neuen Interpretation," *ZTK* 70 (1973): 420-47, who shows serious faults in Harnack's portrait, as does David L. Balás, "Marcion Revisited: A 'Post-Harnack' Perspective," in *Texts and Testaments: Critical Essays on the Bible and Early Church Fathers,* ed. W. Eugene March (San Antonio: Trinity University Press, 1980), 95-108. Also see now Head, "The Foreign God and the Sudden Christ."

sus. As Ernest Evans put it, "Marcion . . . rejected the Old Testament, not as untrue but as non-Christian."[80] Marcion insisted that the highest God was first and solely revealed in Jesus, and that Jesus was not to be interpreted as fulfilling the Old Testament messianic prophecies that played so much a part of the religious beliefs and discourse of proto-orthodox circles. In addition, Marcion's teaching had other identifying features that distinguished it among the various heterodox voices of the time.

Marcion did not espouse the sorts of elaborate mythic schemes that are attributed to Valentinians and gnostics. Related to this, he had a different view of human nature and, consequently, of redemption. In his teaching, humans were *all and entirely* the creation of the inferior deity. Unlike the ideas presented in gnostic schemes, there was no special race of elect whose inner nature made them secretly consubstantial with the high deity, and who carried within themselves the spark of their divine and transcendent nature, origin, and destiny. Consequently, in Marcion's view, and similar to more familiar Christian teaching, redemption was offered to all who would accept it, not simply to an elect. Marcion taught that redemption was effected through Jesus' death, but in his view redemption consisted solely in the deliverance of the souls of those who embraced his message from the power of the creator deity. He made no provision for a bodily resurrection of the redeemed.

That is, in the more typical mythic schemes, the high deity seeks out the elect because they are separated fragments of his own substance; their liberation is a return to their divine origins, which is also the restoration of the alienated bits of the high deity. In actuality, according to this view, redemption serves the needs of the high deity as much as those of the elect. But in Marcion's teaching (which on this point is much closer to proto-orthodox teaching about human nature and redemption), the redemptive overture of the true/high God is purely at his own merciful initiative and solely for the sake of liberating finite/created human souls from the domain of the world creator.

Marcion is also notable for the authority he invoked for his teachings. Various Christian heterodox groups tagged this or that apostolic authority as the source of special, esoteric teachings (e.g., Thomas in *Gos. Thom.*) that were reserved for the elect. On the other hand, proto-orthodox circles claimed to preserve and revere the public traditions of all the apostles. Marcion, however, presented his ideas as simply and solely his restoration of the true and very thoroughgoing Paulinist stance. If *Gos. Truth* reflects a one-sided radicalizing of themes attested particularly in (and possibly derived from) Johannine Chris-

80. Ernest Evans, 1:xiv.

tianity, Marcion more obviously represents a one-sided radicalizing of themes adapted from Paul. Indeed, in Marcion's eyes Paul was the *only* valid apostle, all the others having discredited themselves by diluting Jesus' teaching about the true "alien" God with elements of Judaism.[81]

That is, Marcion did not claim to have a special revelation, and he did not present his teachings as esoteric material reserved for the privileged few. Instead he operated as a radical reformer, and he presented himself as a restorer of the one true Christian faith that stemmed from Jesus and had been authentically elaborated by Paul. In David Balás's apt statement, "Marcion admitted to be an innovator in relation to earlier Christian tradition, though he considered this innovation to be a restoration of the earliest tradition."[82]

Furthermore, unlike some Christian innovators of the time, Marcion did not compose his own gospels, apocalypses, acts, or epistles; nor, in fact, did he promote any of the extracanonical writings of the time. Instead he is best known, and most frequently studied by scholars, on account of his promulgation of a definitive, closed Christian canon of Scripture sometime around 140. This canon consisted solely of his own edited version of the writing we know as the Gospel of Luke, and a collection of ten Pauline epistles.[83] These eleven writings constituted the sum total of what Marcion believed had scriptural force for Christians. They represented an elegantly simple and cohesive collection: one valid Gospel account, and the true text of the genuine writings of the one valid apostle.[84] He even may have been the first to give the title "New Testament" to a canonical collection of Christian texts.[85] In his use of the expression, however,

81. The term "alien" applies to the true God of Marcion as not known or accessible previously or apart from Jesus' revelation of this deity.

82. Balás, 104.

83. E.g., John Knox, *Marcion and the New Testament: An Essay in the Early History of the Canon* (Chicago: University of Chicago Press, 1942); John J. Clabeaux, *A Lost Edition of the Letters of Paul: A Reassessment of the Text of the Pauline Corpus Attested by Marcion* (Washington, D.C.: Catholic Biblical Association, 1989); Ulrich Schmid, *Marcion und sein Apostolos. Rekonstruktion und historische Einordnung der marcionitischen Paulusbriefausgabe*, ANTF 25 (Berlin: de Gruyter, 1995). In Marcion's arrangement of Pauline epistles, Galatians was first, signaling his view of this text as the key for conveying what he saw as Paul's message of redemption as deliverance from the Old Testament deity and his law.

84. The "Pastoral Epistles" of the Pauline traditional corpus were not a part of Marcion's canon, whether because they had not yet become sufficiently well known or because Marcion considered them so obviously and wholly inauthentic that he simply excluded them from consideration.

85. So Wolfram Kinzig, "*Kainē diathēkē*: The Title of the New Testament in the Second and Third Centuries," *JTS*, n.s., 45 (1994): 519-44, who proposes that proto-orthodox circles adopted the term, modifying its connotation from the more antithetical tone that it held for Marcion.

"New Testament" connoted an antithetical contrast between the exclusively valid revelation that had been newly given through Jesus and the "Old Testament" Scriptures with their inferior deity.

It is important to underscore that Marcion's canon represents a *selection* of writings from a larger body, a *narrowed* list of texts to be treated as Scripture. We see this undeniably in his rejection of the Old Testament, which from the earliest years had been treated as Scripture by most circles in the Christian movement. It is also likely that Marcion's canonical list of Christian texts represents a narrowed selection from those that had already begun to win high regard in growing circles of second-century Christianity. For one thing, his restriction of valid apostolic status to Paul alone represents a selective, narrowed view over against the proto-orthodox regard for Paul and the Twelve. Moreover, as we shall see in the next chapter, it is also likely that Marcion's use of Luke as his sole authoritative Gospel represented a choice against the fourfold Gospel that was rapidly gaining favor in the early second century. That is, Marcion rejected Matthew, Mark, and John as inferior, Judaizing, and falsified accounts of Jesus, in favor of a purified version of Luke, which in Marcion's edition was not attributed to the Evangelist but was presented as Jesus' own reliable account of himself.

He not only boldly selected the Christian writings he considered exclusively valid as Scripture, he also produced his own edited versions of them. Convinced that even his chosen New Testament writings had been corrupted with various Judaizing insertions after they were composed, Marcion went through them all, deleting material that went contrary to his own teachings. In Peter Head's memorable phrase, "He criticised with a knife."[86] Sometimes his excisions were words or phrases; in other cases they were more substantial.

For example, he cut out the Lukan birth narrative, in keeping with his conviction that Jesus had not undergone a birth but had miraculously appeared fully formed in the reign of Tiberius. Likewise, of course, he deleted from his Gospel account and his approved Pauline epistles all statements referring to the Old Testament as Scripture, and he modified or removed all statements that identified the God and Father of Jesus as the creator of the world and the deity of the Old Testament. For example, he deleted 3:31–4:25 and most of chapters 9–11 from Romans.

But let us return to his view of Jesus. Barbara Aland has contended that Marcion's Christology was a more important component in his teaching than

---

86. Head, "The Foreign God," 312. Cf. D. S. Williams, "Reconsidering Marcion's Gospel," *JBL* 108 (1989): 477-96, who raised questions about the reliability of patristic citations of Marcion's text of Luke for reconstructing it.

has been commonly recognized by scholars.[87] Indeed, in one sense Jesus was more central in Marcion's teaching than in practically any other kind of early Christianity. For, as we have noted, Marcion taught that Jesus was not simply the highest revelation, but was indeed the *only* revelation of the true God, who was not otherwise known or knowable. Moreover, although we know next to nothing directly about the piety and devotional practices that he followed and promoted, there are reasons to think that in Marcionite piety Jesus was revered warmly and in exalted terms comparable to what we know of proto-orthodox circles of the time.

On the other hand, the Jesus revered in Marcionist Christianity amounts to a significantly different figure from the Jesus of proto-orthodox devotion. As we observed earlier, in any version of Christianity Jesus is characteristically identified with reference to "God," and the view of who "God" is makes a lot of difference to the portrait of Jesus. Consequently, and most importantly, Marcion's total refusal to link Jesus with the God of the Old Testament, and his radical redefinition of the God whom Jesus revealed, constitutes a hugely different standpoint for defining Jesus.

We already noted that in making such a distinction Marcion was not unique, but there were distinguishing elements in his elaboration of matters. To cite one, in his view Jesus was emphatically not the Messiah prophesied in the Old Testament. Unlike some other heterodox Christians, but with proto-orthodox Christians, Marcion affirmed that the Old Testament genuinely predicted a messiah. But unlike proto-orthodox believers, Marcion insisted that the Old Testament messianic figure was purely an earthly savior of the Jewish nation who was still to come. And this messiah predicted in the Old Testament represented the inferior world creator, not the true God of redemption Jesus came to declare.

Balás has observed that the probable time in which Marcion developed his teaching about the strict distinction between the deity of the Old Testament and the Father whom Jesus revealed coincides with "the period of the bloody suppression of the great Jewish revolt" against Roman rule in 132-135. Citing R. M. Grant's proposal from decades earlier, Balás suggested that in this period many Gentile Christians found their previous "association with Jewish history an embarrassing and dangerous liability," and that Marcion offered a way to effect and justify a separation. Precisely by accepting Jewish interpretation of the

---

87. Aland, "Marcion — Marcionites — Marcionism," 523-24. Her complaint about inadequate emphasis on Marcion's view of Jesus has been addressed in the helpful essay by Peter Head referred to in earlier notes, "The Foreign God and the Sudden Christ," which I have gratefully drawn upon here.

Old Testament, Marcion was able to show that the religion and deity of the Scriptures of Israel were totally incompatible with the valid revelation of the true God through Jesus.[88] The more familiar Christian use of the Old Testament was to interpret it typologically and allegorically to show that Jesus and the gospel message were everywhere prefigured and prophesied. But Marcion seized upon the Jewish literalistic interpretation and their rejection of Christian exegesis of the Old Testament "as a liberating insight," on the basis of which he developed "his radical dissociation" of Judaism from Christianity, and of the Old Testament deity from the true/alien God.[89]

Whatever social and historical conditions may have contributed to it, Marcion's evident success in obtaining followers suggests that both the approach and the substance of his teachings were congenial to a good many people (perhaps especially Gentiles) of the time. Also, I repeat the point made earlier that Marcion's views represented an interesting variation on a more widely shared distinction between the creator deity of the Old Testament and the true God. Clearly, numerous Christians found it attractive, for whatever reasons, to define and justify their religious views without reliance on the Old Testament (except to make invidious comparisons between the truth as they saw it and the inferior deity and his laws presented therein).

Also, with some other Christians of his time, Marcion was loath to attribute to Jesus an ordinary mortal nature and body. Thus scholars often say that Marcion held a "docetic" view of Jesus. I trust I need only reiterate the unsatisfactory lack of clarity about what the terms "docetic/docetism" connote, which we considered in the discussion of the Johannine secessionists. In Marcion's case, however, we have some information that allows us to say a bit more precisely what he taught about Jesus as to his earthly appearance, his death and its effects, and his state afterward. Nevertheless, the extant information is frustratingly limited.[90]

According to the ancient reports, as briefly mentioned already, Marcion taught that Jesus was not born, not even miraculously, as, e.g., in the apocryphal *Protevangelium (Infancy Gospel) of James,* discussed in chapter 7. Birth was unworthy of him as divine, for the deity Jesus represents and reveals is not the creator of fleshly bodies.[91] Instead Jesus appeared in Galilee, suddenly and fully

---

88. Balás, 98-99, citing R. M. Grant, *Gnosticism and Early Christianity,* 2nd ed. (New York: Harper and Row, 1966), 122.

89. Balás, 99.

90. In practice, most scholarly descriptions of Marcion's teaching about Jesus are based primarily on Tertullian's five-volume critique *(Adversus Marcionem),* mentioned earlier in this discussion.

91. Tertullian, *Adv. Marc.* 3.8; and see Tertullian's extended critique in 4.21.

formed, in the reign of Tiberius Caesar.[92] Indeed, Marcion's version of Luke opens with the scene where the adult Jesus appears in Capernaum.[93]

Moreover, Marcion is said to have defined Jesus' earthly form repeatedly as a *phantasma* (ghost/specter), by which he meant that Jesus only seemed to have an ordinary human body.[94] The reference to Jesus taking the "form" *(homoiōmati)* and "likeness" *(schēmati)* of a man in Philippians 2:7 was crucial proof for his teaching that Jesus had only *seemed* to have a human nature and an ordinary body.[95] Marcion's text of Colossians 1:22 referred to the reconciliation effected "in [Jesus'] body" rather than "in his body of flesh," for Marcion taught that Jesus' body was not composed of ordinary matter ("flesh") but instead only appeared so.

Interestingly, Marcion is said to have likened Jesus' bodily appearance to the form of the angels who visited Abraham (Gen. 18:1-8), who ate Abraham's food but were obviously not really in mortal nature.[96] This I take as further confirmation of the suggestion I supported in the discussion of docetism in an earlier chapter, that Jewish traditions of angelic appearances in human form may well have contributed a model for some Christians to understand how a divine/heavenly Jesus could appear and function on earth in what appeared to be bodily mode. In any case, for Marcion, as for a good many other Christians of his time and thereafter, it was difficult, perhaps repugnant, to think of Jesus as bearing real human nature.

Actually, for the overwhelming majority of second-century Christians, the question was not whether Jesus was divine; that was widely answered affirmatively. Instead the pressing question about Jesus was in what way, if at all, he could also be thought of as having participated in real human nature. Marcion was simply one of many Christians through the centuries who for the most devout of reasons found that they had to answer negatively. That is, Marcion represents the familiar view that it is incompatible with a reverent view of Jesus as divine to attribute to him mortality and a fleshly body with all its embarrassing characteristics.

In this stance Marcion also reflected a wider discomfort with, or disdain

---

92. Tertullian, *Adv. Marc.* 4.7; 4.21.11; also Hippolytus (ca. 170-236), *Ref.* 7.19 (ANF, 5:113).

93. The opening of Marcion's text of Luke appears to have combined words from 3:1 and 4:31, "In the fifteenth year of Tiberius Caesar, in the time of Pilate, Jesus *came down* [*katēlthen*] to Capernaum," thus connoting a descent from heaven.

94. E.g., Tertullian, *Adv. Marc.* 3.10.11; 4.7.1-5; 3.8.1; 5.8.3; 5.20.3.

95. In Marcion's text the phrase in Phil. 2:7 was *en homoiōmati anthrōpou* ("in the form of a man," also supported by P46), instead of the more widely supported reading, *en homoiōmati anthrōpōn* ("in the form of men").

96. Tertullian, *Adv. Marc.* 3.19.1.

for, the body, its functions (especially sexual relations and procreation), and indeed the whole material order, a discomfort that was echoed in the wider culture of the second century, and still more in later Roman antiquity.[97] Corresponding to this negative view of the body and the material world, Marcion's ethics were rigorously ascetic. In particular, he is said to have forbidden marriage, regarding sexual relations as a degrading act that directly manifested the humiliating situation of humans under the oppressive structures of the creator god.[98]

Given Marcion's view of Jesus as only seeming to have had an ordinary mortal body, it is very interesting that he placed such an emphasis on the efficacy of Jesus' crucifixion.[99] Unlike the view attributed to gnostics and Valentinians, in Marcion's teaching redemption did not come through the disclosure of an esoteric truth to the elect. Instead, Jesus' crucifixion provided for the release of humans from bondage to the creator deity, making it possible for the redeemed to become part of the heavenly body that is the church.[100]

But Jesus' body that was crucified was celestial, not mortal/earthly, and so Jesus did not really undergo the sufferings of mortals, and his body could not have been subject to corruption in the grave.[101] Likewise, in Marcion's teaching Jesus reappeared to disciples after his crucifixion in the form of a *phantasma* (ghost/specter), the same as his precrucifixion mode.[102] Marcion taught that in Jesus' earthly existence he took the *form* of a mortal body, but its substance was spiritual and unique, which could not really suffer corruption in death. Consequently he portrayed the "resurrected" Jesus simply as resuscitated, his "risen" body the same celestial substance as it had always been.[103]

Reflecting another theme widely favored in second-century Christianity, Marcion portrayed Jesus as descending to the realm of the dead after his crucifixion (a theme to which I return in chap. 10). But in Marcion's account the Old Testament "saints," who were revered as fellow members of the redeemed in

---

97. Elaine Pagels, "Adam and Eve, Christ and the Church: A Survey of Second Century Controversies concerning Marriage," in *The New Testament and Gnosis: Essays in Honour of Robert McL. Wilson,* ed. A. H. B. Logan and A. J. M. Wedderburn (Edinburgh: T. & T. Clark, 1983), 146-75; Peter Brown, *The Body and Society: Men, Women, and Sexual Renunciation in Early Christianity* (New York: Columbia University Press, 1988).

98. Tertullian, *Adv. Marc.* 1.29.

99. See esp. Antonio Orbe, *Introduccion a la Teologia de los Siglos II y III,* 2 vols. (Rome: Editrice Pontificia Universita Gregoriana, 1987), 2:724-39.

100. Orbe, 2:739.

101. See Tertullian, *Adv. Marc.* 3.8, where he accuses Marcion of an illogical stance in denying Jesus a mortal body and yet attributing to him a death by crucifixion.

102. E.g., Orbe, 2:852-53.

103. Orbe, 2:852-53.

proto-orthodox circles, rejected Jesus' proclamation of redemption from the creator deity. Instead, those who received Jesus' offer were people classed as disobedient sinners in terms of the Old Testament deity and his law.[104]

Summarizing Reflections

In this chapter we looked closely at the two most important examples of the radical diversity of second-century Christianity over against the emergent proto-orthodox faith of the period. There were, of course, still other variant forms of Christianity of the time, in particular other assorted circles and texts that scholars often lump together as constituting the "gnostics." But to catalogue them here would essentially involve logging comparatively minor variations on the basic patterns of beliefs that we noted as characteristic of Valentinians and Marcionites.[105] These various groups did not differ from one another nearly so much as they all differed from proto-orthodox patterns of belief and practice. The genuinely radical differences in second-century Christianity were over the things that distinguished proto-orthodox Christianity from the kinds of beliefs we have analyzed here. Perhaps the most crucial issue of all, as far as devotion to Jesus was concerned, was whether Jesus was to be identified with reference to the Old Testament and the deity testified to therein. As Daniélou wrote, "The problem of the Old Testament is central to the controversies of the second century."[106]

Marcionites, Valentinians, and the other versions of second-century Christianity that distinguished the true/high/good deity from the world creator of the Old Testament also produced significantly different ways of representing Jesus. Separated from the God of the Old Testament and the story of Israel, and indeed from human history altogether, Jesus was not in any way the fulfillment of human history, the agency, rationale, and goal of creation, as was characteristically claimed in proto-orthodox traditions from the New Testament onward (e.g., John 1:1-18; Heb. 1:1-4; Col. 1:15-20). Despite comparatively minor variations, the portraits of Jesus in the heterodox versions of Christianity examined here (and in other circles not logged here) all disconnected him from the world and its fortunes. In doing so, they advocated a markedly different stance.

In the epic narrative that proto-orthodox Christians derived from the Old Testament, they understood God as the sole creator, ruler, and redeemer of

104. Harnack, *Marcion: The Gospel of the Alien God*, 87.

105. See, e.g., Pheme Perkins, "New Testament Christologies in Gnostic Transformation," in *The Future of Early Christianity*, 433-41.

106. Jean Daniélou, *Gospel Message and Hellenistic Culture*, trans. and ed. J. A. Baker (London: Darton, Longman, Todd; Philadelphia: Westminster, 1973), 199.

all things; the world as God's creation and rightful domain; evil as an intrusion and despoilment that would ultimately be overcome and expelled; themselves as beloved by God, heirs of divine promises recorded in the Old Testament along with spiritual forebears such as Abraham, Moses, David, and the prophets; and Jesus as the Word and Son of God prefigured and promised in the Old Testament, his historical appearance having provided salvation of universal scope.

The mythic schemes preferred by Valentinians and gnostics, however, presented creation as a total tragedy, the world as a vain and pointless realm to be treated with disdain, and the elect as an inner circle of aliens whose only hope could be to escape from the world and return to their true celestial home and status. They defined Jesus (the "Savior") as an alien, heavenly figure with no proper connection with the world and human history, who entered into this worthless domain of stupidity as an intruder who was solely concerned to retrieve from it his fellow divine beings, the elect, whom he came to reawaken to their true identity and destiny.

Marcion's less elaborate scheme, as we noted, includes a variant account of the human predicament and a correspondingly variant definition of redemption. But in undeniable continuity with various other heterodox versions of second-century Christianity, Marcion's portrait of Jesus just as thoroughly dissociated him from the world, its creation, history, and destiny.

For second-century Christianity, the most far-reaching issue was whether to cede the world and human history to a stupid and vain creator deity sharply distinguished from the true God, or to lay claim to them as the creation and rightful property of the true God. Those who urged the first option certainly had their reasons, which were mainly theodicy and the tensions between the Old Testament and the Christian gospel, as well as certain widespread metaphysical assumptions about the incompatibility of the ultimate God and the world of matter.

The world they surveyed was then (as it is now) a less than perfect creation, to put it mildly; it is a classic philosophical difficulty to account for a world so afflicted by natural and moral evil as the creation of an omnipotent and good deity. Moreover, there are undeniable tensions for Christians in treating the Old Testament as their Scriptures: Israel versus church, Torah versus Christ, and the anthropomorphic pictures of God in the Old Testament, to name a few obvious ones. Those who urged a distinction between the Old Testament deity and the true God were not simply trying to be difficult; they were reacting to real issues. But the stakes were high, the issues far-reaching, and the potential consequences of the battle over who the Christian God was were monumental. Those who opposed the advocates of a God different from the world creator were correct, thus, to perceive that they were involved in a struggle over a core issue, and the very soul of Christianity.

In addition to these variant forms of second-century Christianity, however, there were Jewish Christian circles. But once again, we have the same basic source problem. We have no undisputedly direct source from the second century on which to draw. We do, however, have Justin's reply to the Jewish interlocutor in his *Dialogue with Trypho* (46–47), where he distinguishes between two kinds of Jewish Christians. He says both identify themselves as Jewish and both combine faith in Jesus as Messiah and Son of God with full observance of the commandments of Torah (e.g., circumcision of their sons, Sabbath, food laws). But Justin explains that one kind of Jewish Christianity also demands that Gentile Christians observe Torah as a condition for acceptance as fellow members of the redeemed, whereas the other kind does not. With the latter, therefore, Justin says, he and other Gentile Christians can have fellowship, and can recognize them in turn as fellow Christians (though he also grants that some other Gentile Christians do not agree). That is, according to Justin's description, neither of the forms of Jewish Christianity that Justin knew was particularly distinguished from his own preferred circles as to beliefs about Jesus. The tensions with Gentile Christianity were over whether Torah observance was requisite for Gentiles as well as Jewish believers.

This broadly agrees with the analysis offered by Ray Pritz in his study of pre-Nicene Jewish Christianity.[107] Pritz distinguished two types of Jewish Christianity. One type, which he referred to as "Nazarene" Christianity, had a view of Jesus fully compatible with the beliefs favored in proto-orthodox circles (indeed, they could be considered part of the circles that made up proto-orthodox Christianity of the time). Pritz contended that this Nazarene Christianity was the dominant form of Jewish Christian faith in the first and second centuries. Another type of Jewish Christianity, "Ebionites," regarded Jesus as Messiah, but may have balked at according him the divine status reflected in the New Testament and proto-orthodox faith. As Pritz argued, however, this Ebionite Christianity seems to have been a comparatively later form of Jewish Christian expression, and he showed that the key description of the group in the fourth-century Epiphanius seems to constitute a secondary and garbled account.[108] In short, the devotional stance toward Jesus that characterized most

---

107. Ray A. Pritz, *Nazarene Jewish Christianity from the End of the New Testament Period until Its Disappearance in the Fourth Century*, SPB 37 (Leiden: Brill, 1988). A similar conclusion is now supported also by Timo Eskola, *Messiah and the Throne*, WUNT 2/142 (Tübingen: Brill, 2001), 295-321.

108. Similarly, G. A. Koch, "A Critical Investigation of Epiphanius' Knowledge of the Ebionites" (Ph.D. diss., University of Pennsylvania, 1976).

Jewish Christians of the first and second centuries seems to have been essentially congruent with proto-orthodox devotion to Jesus.[109]

I make one further observation to conclude this discussion of early Christian diversity. The versions of belief in Jesus that we have examined in this chapter all had varying degrees of appeal to people of the second century. Whether it was the esoteric teaching of Valentinians and gnostics or Marcion's simpler and stark message, there were obviously those who found these views congenial and attractive. Marcionism in particular seems to have had impressive success both in its geographical spread and its longevity.

But none of the radical innovations represented by Valentinians, Marcionites, or other second-century dissident versions of Christian faith was successful in commending itself to sufficiently large numbers of people to become the dominant, mainstream version of Christianity of the time. Whatever the social, philosophical, and/or existential factors that made these versions of Christianity attractive to some, they did not succeed sufficiently with others. Well before the influence of Constantine and councils of bishops in the fourth century and thereafter, it was clear that proto-orthodox Christianity was ascendant, and represented the emergent mainstream. Proto-orthodox devotion to Jesus of the second century constitutes the pattern of belief and practice that shaped Christian tradition thereafter. In the final chapter we examine more closely this devotional pattern, with particular concern for its key manifestations in the second century.

---

109. Cf. Daniélou, *Theology of Jewish Christianity*, 55-85. But Daniélou uses "Jewish Christianity" to encompass any expression of early Christianity that shows the *influence* of ideas, themes, imagery, and other traditions that may have originated from circles of Christian Jews. That is, for Daniélou, "Jewish Christianity" took in Gentile Christian circles that drew upon traditions of putatively Jewish Christian provenance, both proto-orthodox figures such as Justin and heterodox groups and figures such as Elkesai, Satornil, Basilides, and Carpocrates (about whom in fact we know very little, except for brief, negative summaries in antiheresy writings), and "Egyptian Gnostics" (which takes in "Sethians" and "Ophites," and for which Daniélou had to depend heavily upon fourth-century texts from Nag Hammadi).

CHAPTER TEN

Proto-orthodox Devotion

In this final chapter we focus on expressions of devotion to Jesus that are particularly characteristic of proto-orthodox circles.[1] These phenomena manifest the version of Christianity that was already dominant by the latter half of the second century, and out of which the classical "orthodox" Christian tradition developed.

I emphasize again, however, that second-century proto-orthodox Christianity was not a monolithic entity, but instead comprised an interesting variety in expressions and practices. Also, although there are lines of development and continuity between the two, proto-orthodoxy does not equate with the fully developed orthodoxy of the fourth century and thereafter, with its fixed creeds, established hierarchy, and coercive power to suppress "heresy." In the period we are considering (ca. 70-170), emergent proto-orthodox Christianity is recognized in simpler and more flexible terms that I proposed earlier and reiterate here: a high regard for traditions coupled with a critical suspicion of radical innovations, an exclusivist monotheistic commitment to the Old Testament and its deity, a readiness to accommodate a certain critical diversity.

Proto-orthodox devotion to Jesus honored him as divine within an exclusivist monotheistic stance derived (and adapted) from the biblical/Jewish tradition. This, in particular, is what made the effort to articulate Jesus' divine status so demanding; it largely explains the lengthy and complicated nature of christological debates among Christians in proto-orthodox circles in the first

---

1. In addition to works cited previously, V. A. Spence Little, *The Christology of the Apologists* (London: Duckworth, 1934), is an infrequently cited but valuable study that in fact ranges beyond the second-century writers usually thought of as "the apologists," although it focuses entirely on their doctrines and says little about religious practice.

three centuries of Christianity. Had they been able to revere Jesus as something less than divine, or to accommodate more than one deity — that is, had they opted for either of the two major religious patterns of their time — they would not have required such a struggle to develop a theology adequate to their devotional traditions.

But unlike the many valuable studies that focus almost entirely on the doctrinal developments of this period, my aim here is to set out more broadly the key ways in which proto-orthodox Christians in particular expressed their devotion to Jesus. Because this will involve discussing a number of phenomena, it will be necessary to attempt as economic a treatment of each as we can. But it will also be necessary to convey adequately what these Christians did and what their beliefs and practice meant for them.

Given their commitment to tradition, we should not be surprised to find comparatively little in major innovations in beliefs and devotional practice. In his analysis of second-century beliefs about Jesus, Grillmeier emphasized "the archaic character of its christology, which for the most part is to be attributed to Jewish-Christian influences."[2] In the main, the doctrinal developments identified with proto-orthodox Christianity in this period are most often extensions and elaborations of themes of the New Testament. But along with considerable overlap with the first-century traditions that we have already surveyed, there were certainly further developments, some of them required by the historical conditions of Christianity in the second century. In what follows I first discuss major ways in which proto-orthodox Christians expressed their devotion to Jesus. Then, in the concluding section of this chapter, I focus on some developments in beliefs that emerged in this period in the context of proto-orthodox disputation with other forms of Christian belief and with Jewish and pagan opponents of Christianity.

Finding Jesus in the Old Testament

For those Christians who made up proto-orthodox circles, "The heart of the Christian message lay in the relation between the Old and New Testaments."[3]

---

2. Aloys Grillmeier, *Christ in Christian Tradition*, vol. 1, *From the Apostolic Age to Chalcedon*, rev. and trans. John Bowden, 2nd ed. (London: Mowbray & Co.; Atlanta: John Knox, 1975), 37. Tertullian might be an exception, but he is as often/more often thought of as an early third-century figure (his extant writings commonly dated ca. 196/97 and 212). See, e.g., R. D. Sider, "Tertullian," in *EEC*, 2:1107-9; and for fuller discussion, Eric Osborn, *Tertullian, First Theologian of the West* (Cambridge: Cambridge University Press, 1997).

3. Jean Daniélou, *Gospel Message and Hellenistic Culture*, trans. and ed. J. A. Baker (London: Darton, Longman, Todd; Philadelphia: Westminster, 1973), 198.

We already noted the central place of the controversies over whether to treat the Old Testament as Christian Scripture, and the deity it portrayed as the God Jesus revealed. One of the central features of proto-orthodox circles was the positive answer to these questions, and one of the key expressions of their devotion to Jesus was their use of the Old Testament as testimony to him.[4]

Indeed, from the earliest moments of the Christian movement, believers turned to the scriptures of the Jewish tradition to find resources for understanding Jesus and for expressing and defending their claims about his significance.[5] This wide and deep appropriation of the Old Testament continued through the closing period of earliest Christianity (ca. 70-170), and is one of the key characteristics of proto-orthodox circles. Surveying the Christian use of the Old Testament in the second and third centuries, Skarsaune identified three basic types of exegesis: (1) "proof from prophecy," mainly concerned with demonstrating "from the Old Testament 'proof-texts' that Jesus is the Messiah, that the ritual commandments in the Law are no longer obligatory, and that the Church, not the Jews, is now the people of God"; (2) homiletic use in support of ethical exhortation; and (3) demonstration of the greater antiquity of the Old Testament compared to the Greek philosophers and poets (thereby demonstrating its greater validity).[6]

I want to focus specifically on the use of the Old Testament in support of faith in Jesus, and I propose that second-century proto-orthodox Christians demonstrate three main approaches: (1) Old Testament "proof texts" cited to

---

4. For recent general studies, see especially Oskar Skarsaune, "The Development of Scriptural Interpretation in the Second and Third Centuries — Except Clement and Origen," in *Hebrew Bible/Old Testament: The History of Its Interpretation*, vol. 1, *From the Beginnings to the Middle Ages*, ed. Magne Saebo (Göttingen: Vandenhoeck & Ruprecht, 1996), 373-442 (on which I have drawn repeatedly in this section); William Horbury, "Old Testament Interpretation in the Writings of the Church Fathers," in *Mikra. Text, Translation, Reading, and Interpretation of the Hebrew Bible in Ancient Judaism and Early Christianity*, ed. Martin Jan Mulder, CRINT (Assen: Van Gorcum, 1988), 727-87 (dealing with the first six centuries); Manlio Simonetti, *Biblical Interpretation in the Early Church: An Historical Introduction to Patristic Exegesis*, ed. Anders Berquist and Markus Bockmuehl, trans. J. A. Hughes (Edinburgh: T. & T. Clark, 1994), esp. 1-33. Among previous studies, Daniélou's discussion in *Gospel Message* (197-300) remains particularly useful. The key resource tool is A. Benoit et al., eds., *Biblia Patristica: Index des citations et allusions bibliques dans la littérature patristique*, vol. 1, *Des Origines à Clement d'Alexandrie et Tertullien* (Paris: Éditions du centre nationale de la recherche scientifique, 1975).

5. E.g., Donald Juel, *Messianic Exegesis: Christological Interpretation of the Old Testament in Early Christianity* (Philadelphia: Fortress, 1988); Barnabas Lindars, *New Testament Apologetic* (London: SCM Press, 1961).

6. Skarsaune, "Scriptural Interpretation," 376-77. See also 390-91, on Justin, in whose works "we encounter, for the first time, this 'proof from the Scriptures' in a full-scale presentation" with three foci: Christ, the Torah, and the church.

demonstrate the fulfillment of prophecy in Jesus; (2) a wider "typological" reading of the Old Testament as filled with figures and events that foreshadow Jesus; and (3) the interpretation of Old Testament accounts of theophanies as manifestations of the preincarnate Son of God. All three approaches originated in the first century and are exhibited already in the New Testament.

First we consider Old Testament proof texts presented as prophetic predictions of Jesus. As is clear to any reader of the New Testament, claims that Jesus was prophesied in the Old Testament were part and parcel of first-century Christian proclamation. This is reflected, for example, in Matthew's numerous citations of biblical texts as prophetic words "fulfilled" in Jesus (1:22; 2:15, 17, 23; 4:14; 8:17; 12:17; 13:35; 21:4; 26:54, 56; 27:9); the same standpoint is asserted also in other New Testament writings (e.g., Mark 14:49; 15:28; Luke 4:21; 24:44; John 12:38; 13:18; 15:25; 19:24, 36). That this line of argument goes back to the very earliest years of the Christian movement is asserted in one of our earliest summaries of Christian proclamation, which we noted earlier in our discussion of Pauline Christianity (1 Cor. 15:1-7). Here Jesus' messianic death "for our sins," and his resurrection as well, are both explicitly referred to as "according to the scriptures." Behind these phrases lies a body of early Christian discoveries of Jesus in the Old Testament, which includes numerous texts understood as prophecies of him.

The idea that eschatological events and figures, including the Messiah, were foretold prophetically in the Scriptures was hardly exceptional in the Jewish tradition of the time.[7] But the particular claims that Jesus was the Messiah, that his execution was part of the divine plan and his work as Messiah, and that God had proven Jesus' messianic status by raising him from the dead — these certainly amounted to innovative notions that required energetic effort to validate as fulfillment of Scripture. That is, in addition to appropriating various Old Testament texts that were already treated as referring to a future Messiah in pre-Christian tradition, the earliest believers in Jesus identified many additional passages as predictive of his messianic sufferings and vindication.

The claim that Jesus' appearance (including particularly his death, resurrection, and heavenly exaltation) fulfilled biblical prophecy continued to form a core aspect of Christian use of the Old Testament in the second century and thereafter. Skarsaune judged that the use of Old Testament proof texts, especially to demonstrate that Jesus fulfilled biblical prophecy, constituted "the largest proportion" of the uses of the Old Testament in Christian sources of the

---

7. See, e.g., Daniel Patte, *Early Jewish Hermeneutic in Palestine*, SBLDS 22 (Missoula: Scholars, 1975). On ancient Jewish messianic ideas, see now J. Collins, *The Scepter and the Star: The Messiahs of the Dead Sea Scrolls and Other Ancient Literature* (New York: Doubleday, 1995).

second and third centuries.[8] In Daniélou's words, "The fundamental argument, on which the [early Christian] Fathers based their affirmations about Christ, is that he fulfils the predictions of prophecy."[9] In this argument, second-century Christians were simply perpetuating the widely shared conviction expressed so confidently in 1 Peter 1:10-12, for example, that through "the Spirit of Christ within them" the Old Testament prophets had "testified in advance to the sufferings destined for Christ and the subsequent glory."

Ignatius of Antioch (early second century) quotes the Old Testament explicitly only a few times, and in support of ethical exhortations, but he also affirms the idea that the Old Testament Scriptures prophesy Jesus (Ign. *Philad.* 5.2; Ign. *Smyrn.* 5.1; 7.2).[10] Indeed, all the writings from those known as the "apostolic fathers" reflect this "proof from prophecy" tradition, but their various literary genres require them to employ the Old Testament in different ways. Thus, for example, *1 Clement* (which is addressed to the church in Corinth and primarily concerned with exhortation to peace and harmony) most frequently cites the Old Testament in support of the behavior the author seeks to promote, but 36.1-6 shows a familiarity with the use of Old Testament proofs of Jesus' divine sonship and exalted status. By contrast, citations of the Old Testament in the *Epistle of Barnabas* are mainly used as part of the author's concern to assert the superiority of the church and a particular understanding of the Old Testament commandments, over against Judaism. The author contends that traditional Jewish notions of Torah observance never corresponded to God's intention (e.g., 2.4-10).[11] Yet *Barnabas* also emphasizes that the events of Jesus were predicted by the Old Testament prophets (e.g., 5.1-3 [citing Isa. 53:5, 7]; 5.6; 6.6-

---

8. Skarsaune, "Scriptural Interpretation," 376.

9. Daniélou, *Gospel Message*, 198.

10. The hortatory citations of the Old Testament are in Ign. *Eph.* 5.3 (Prov. 3:24); Ign. *Magn.* 12 (Prov. 18:17); and Ign. *Trall.* 8.2 (Isa. 52:5). Skarsaune persuasively contends that we should not take Ignatius's statement in *Philad.* 8.2, that to him the "archives" are Jesus and his cross, death, and resurrection, to mean that he thought Jesus *replaced* the Old Testament. Instead Ignatius must mean that Jesus' death and resurrection form the key to reading the Old Testament aright. I.e., they *are* what the Old Testament really teaches ("Scriptural Interpretation," 379).

11. "To the author of *Barnabas*, the Scriptures primarily contain ordinances, commandments *(entolai)*" (Skarsaune, "Scriptural Interpretation," 385). Scholars remain divided over the date of *Barnabas* and the exact reason(s) for its sharply anti-Jewish tone. Among recent works, cf. James Carleton Paget, *The "Epistle of Barnabas," Outlook and Background*, WUNT 2/64 (Tübingen: Mohr-Siebeck, 1994); William Horbury, "Jewish-Christian Relations in Barnabas and Justin Martyr," in *Jews and Christians: The Parting of the Ways*, A.D. 70 to 135, ed. J. D. G. Dunn (Tübingen: Mohr-Siebeck, 1992), 315-45; Reidar Hvalvik, *The Struggle for Scripture and Covenant: The Purpose of the "Epistle of Barnabas" and Jewish-Christian Competition in the Second Century*, WUNT 2/82 (Tübingen: Mohr-Siebeck, 1996).

10 [citing Pss. 22:16, 18; 118:12; Isa. 3:9-10]; 11.1). In his recent study, Reidar Hvalvik commented that one of the striking features of *Barnabas* is the large number of Old Testament texts cited in it as dealing with Jesus, his cross, and suffering.[12]

As is the case for the uses of the Old Testament in the period under review here generally, however, Justin gives us the fullest deployment of proof texts to show Jesus as fulfillment of prophecy.[13] However, although Justin employs a huge number of Old Testament proof texts, it is important to note that he essentially transmits a *tradition* of Old Testament passages cited in support of clearly traditional christological claims.[14] Indeed, the predecessor on whom Justin seems to depend most is Paul.[15] Drawing upon a line of argument that originated in the first-century context of proclamation of Jesus especially to fellow Jews, Justin and other second-century Christian writers continue to employ the "proof from prophecy" argument to defend Christian claims, especially against Jewish objections. So a great deal of Justin's *Dialogue with Trypho the Jew* (ca. 160) is given to scriptural predictions of Jesus (e.g., chaps. 32–44; 48–68; 83–87; 98–99; 104–7).

But Justin shows that citing Old Testament proof texts to support christological claims was not simply a tactic in arguing with Jews, but instead a central feature of proto-orthodox proclamation to all. For also in his defense of Christian faith addressed to the emperor Antoninus Pius (*1 Apology*, ca. 150), and for which Justin must have wished a wide readership among educated pagans, he sets forth prominently the argument that the Old Testament predicts Jesus and the redemptive events announced in the Gospel (*1 Apol.* 31–64).

We may cite *1 Apology* 31 as illustrative. After stating that there were "certain men who were prophets of God" through whom "the prophetic Spirit published beforehand things that were to come to pass, ere ever they happened," Justin points out that these prophecies were then preserved by the Jews in the Old Testament books. He then makes the crucial claim: "In these books, then, of the prophets we found Jesus our Christ foretold." More specifically, Justin asserts here that the Old Testament predicts Jesus' coming, his birth of a virgin and his growth to adulthood, his healing sicknesses and raising the

---

12. Hvalvik, 144.

13. Oskar Skarsaune, *The Proof from Prophecy: A Study in Justin Martyr's Proof-Text Tradition: Text-Type, Provenance, Theological Profile*, NovTSup 66 (Leiden: Brill, 1987), gives an exhaustive treatment; and more concisely, Skarsaune, "Scriptural Interpretation," 387-98.

14. See the tables of Justin's Old Testament citations in Skarsaune, *The Proof from Prophecy*, 454-71.

15. As emphasized convincingly by Skarsaune, "Scriptural Interpretation," 391; Skarsaune, *The Proof from Prophecy*, 11, 130-31.

dead, his being hated and rejected and crucified, his dying and rising and ascending into heaven, and his being called the Son of God. In the following chapters Justin presents the biblical passages that support his assertions (esp. 32–35; 48; and 50–53). That is, Justin uses the "proof from prophecy" argument in this presentation of Christian faith, even though he knows he cannot count on his intended pagan readers to accept the Old Testament as divinely inspired Scripture.[16]

Thus in Justin we see an interesting adaptation in the use of this line of argument. Its origins lay in the early first-century efforts to assert the messianic validity of Jesus to those (Jews and "God-fearing" Gentiles) who revered the Old Testament as Scripture. Justin, however, developed a more dialectical line of argument to address a wider audience that did not necessarily treat the Old Testament as prophetic oracles. In *1 Apology* he emphasized the correspondences between the events of Jesus and the Old Testament passages both to accredit these passages as really prophetic predictions which Jesus fulfilled and also to justify the view that in Jesus we really see fulfillment of prophecy.

The second major way in which proto-orthodox circles of the first two centuries used the Old Testament to support claims about Jesus may be termed "typological." In the citation of proof texts, the Old Testament was mined mainly to identify predictive prophecies, for which the books of the prophets and the Psalms were found particularly fruitful.[17] In the typological approach, however, a much wider array of figures, events, and statements from practically all writings of the Old Testament were cited as "types" (from the Greek *typos*), that is, divinely intended models that anticipated and foreshadowed Jesus.[18]

Once again, this approach clearly has its earliest Christian examples in the New Testament, where it is pervasive.[19] The use of the specific term "type" as a characterization of the Old Testament, however, seems to derive particularly from Paul. In 1 Corinthians 10:1-11 Paul illustrates this view of the Old Testament as full of types intended to be recognized with profit by Christians who

16. In reading an earlier draft of this chapter, David Wright reminded me that using the Old Testament in this way was a means for Christians such as Justin to claim ancient roots (and thus, greater validity) for their beliefs, an important apologetic move in the Roman world.

17. Note, e.g., John F. A. Sawyer's discussion of the use of Isaiah in the New Testament and other early Christian writings: *The Fifth Gospel: Isaiah in the History of Christianity* (Cambridge: Cambridge University Press, 1996), 21-64.

18. For the term, see Leonhard Goppelt, "τυπος," in *TDNT*, 8:246-59.

19. The classic study is Leonhard Goppelt, *Typos: The Typological Interpretation of the Old Testament in the New* (Grand Rapids: Eerdmans, 1982; German original, 1939). Also useful is K. J. Woollcombe, "The Biblical Origins and Patristic Development of Typology," in *Essays on Typology*, ed. G. W. H. Lampe and K. J. Woollcombe, SBT 22 (London: SCM Press, 1957), 39-75; and John E. Alsup, "Typology," in *ABD*, 6:682-85.

understand themselves to be living in the time of eschatological fulfillment.[20] Paul treats the biblical narratives of Israel's exodus from Egypt and subsequent behavior in their extended trek toward the Promised Land as intended to provide Christians with prefiguring and warning incidents.

For example, in their flight through the parted Red Sea while overshadowed by the cloud manifestation of divine presence, the Israelites were "baptized into Moses," thus foreshadowing Christian baptism; Paul calls the manna and miraculous supply of water "spiritual" food and drink that anticipated the eucharistic meals his congregations shared (vv. 1-5). Indeed, all the events (including Israel's disobedience and God's judgment in response) "occurred as examples [*typoi*] for us" (v. 6). Paul repeats this point in verse 11, where he also indicates the basic premise of this approach to the Old Testament, which is the conviction that he and his fellow believers are "those upon whom the ends of the ages have come." That is, they are living in the time of eschatological fulfillment of the divine plan that was foreshadowed in the events and figures of the Old Testament.

The relationship of an Old Testament type to the eschatological fulfillment involves a certain recognizable similarity, and a demonstrable superiority, of fulfillment to type. To cite a particularly clear Pauline example of this, in Romans 5:14 Paul refers to Adam as "a type of the one who was to come," Jesus. The similarity lies in each figure being the font of a line of humanity, Adam the source of the biological line and Jesus the source of the new (eschatological) humanity. Jesus' enormous superiority over Adam, however, also amounts to a stark contrast. Whereas Adam's transgression led to condemnation and death for all humanity, Jesus' righteousness produced abundant grace and eschatological life which are now offered to all (5:15-21).

The most extended New Testament typological treatment of the Old Testament appears in Hebrews, although the author does not use the term "type" in this special way. Instead, for example, 10:1 refers to the sacrificial system prescribed in the Old Testament Torah as only a "shadow [*skian*] of the good things to come, and not the true form of these realities [*eikona tōn pragmatōn*]." But it is evident that the author regards the entirety of the Old Testament as valid scripture that records genuinely divine revelations. And yet, also, these revelations were earthly shadows of heavenly realities, and provisional anticipations of their future and final realization, which has now come through Jesus (e.g., 1:1-2; 2:1-4; 3:1-6; 7:18-19, 23-28; 8:1-7).

The underlying logic of the typological approach is based on two convictions. From Jewish tradition of the first century came the conviction that what

---

20. Alsup refers to 1 Cor. 10 as "perhaps the *locus classicus*, along with Romans 5" (Alsup, 6:683).

Christians came to refer to as "the Old Testament" conveyed the reliable account of God's historic revelations and the expression of God's will. But what explosively ignited the particular typological reading of the Old Testament in Christian circles was the conviction that in Jesus God had now decisively inaugurated the final events of world redemption. Prompted by this conviction, early Christians enthusiastically explored their Scriptures (Old Testament), confident that all of God's prior actions (to which these Scriptures bore faithful witness) anticipated and prepared for the final "endgame" of redemption, which was now disclosed in the proclamation of the gospel.

That is, the typological use of the Old Testament in the New Testament and other texts of "earliest Christianity" reflects a strong "eschatological" outlook, and the scope of material that can be used amounts to the entire Old Testament. For the one God who now was bringing about the fulfillment of all things in Jesus had surely done all that was witnessed to in the Old Testament with a view toward this fulfillment, and as preparation for it. As Alsup observed, the typological approach presupposes "that the active involvement of God to save and deliver people in history is consistent," and therefore, that the full significance of the Old Testament is finally disclosed in the gospel.[21]

We should not confuse the typological approach to the Old Testament with allegorizing exegesis, which became more and more dominant in Christian circles in the third century and on into the medieval period.[22] The aim in allegorizing exegesis is to show that the Scriptures encode timeless truths that are already known and accepted, which can be found in a text by treating as symbolic the characters, events, and statements in it.[23] In this approach the biblical characters and events are purely the literary veil beneath which lies the body of philosophical, religious, and moral truths; the actuality of the characters and events is irrelevant. But in the typological approach practiced in earliest Christianity, it is essential that the biblical characters and events be treated as *real*, for the fundamental point is to show that God's prior actions and statements prepared for and foreshadowed the final redemptive events now proclaimed in the gospel.[24] Moreover, the religious truths asserted in typological

---

21. Alsup, 6:683.

22. E.g., R. P. C. Hanson, "Biblical Exegesis in the Early Church," in *CHB*, 1:412-53; Horbury, "Old Testament Interpretation," 766-68.

23. Allegorizing exegesis originated in pre-Christian Greek intellectual tradition, as a device to avoid the embarrassment of the Homeric myths of the gods with their accounts of all-too-anthropomorphic behavior. See, e.g., "Allegory," in *OCD*, 45-46.

24. "Real" here does not mean that characters and events will necessarily satisfy modern criteria of historicity, only that in the typological approach ancient Christians regarded them as historic anticipations of eschatological fulfillments.

exegesis derived entirely from what were proclaimed as further real events in which God had now signaled the fulfillment of the redemptive promises, most importantly, Jesus' appearance, death, resurrection, and heavenly exaltation.

In proto-orthodox texts of earliest Christianity, the typological approach to the Old Testament is used richly to assert claims about Jesus. Indeed, one derives the impression that at least part of the aim was to show that *any* part of the Old Testament prefigured Jesus. We have a first-century instance in the Gospel of John, where the Old Testament account of the bronze serpent (Num. 21:9) is presented as foreshadowing the crucifixion of Jesus (John 3:14-15). In similar fashion *Barnabas* 7.3 presents the account of the offering of Isaac (Gen. 22:1-14) as a "type" *(typos)* now fulfilled in Jesus' crucifixion. Thereafter *Barnabas* 7.6-11 treats extensively the Old Testament ritual of the two goats (Lev. 16:6-10) with the aim of revealing how "the type of Jesus is revealed" (*Barn.* 7.7), followed in 8.1-7 by a similar typological interpretation of the ceremony of the red heifer (Num. 19:1-10), which invites readers to "observe again the type of the cross" (*Barn.* 8.1).[25] In 9.7-9 the author presents the reference to Abraham's 318 servants as prefiguring Jesus and his cross;[26] and in 11.1 the author invites readers to consider still further foreshadowings of "the water [of baptism] and the cross." One of these appears in *Barnabas* 12.2-4, where the outstretched arms of Moses in the battle against the Amalekites (Exod. 17:8-13) is interpreted as a divinely intended type of Jesus' cross.[27]

However far-fetched the author's interpretations may seem to modern readers, I emphasize that these are all examples of Christian typological exegesis primarily shaped by convictions about Jesus.[28] Other Christian writings of the same period reflect the same basic view that the Old Testament is filled with anticipations of Jesus, such as the crimson cord in the story of Rahab and the spies, which *1 Clement* 12.1-8 presents as clearly pointing ahead to the redemptive significance of Jesus' shed blood.[29]

25. Skarsaune ("Scriptural Interpretation," 387) points to studies showing that *Barn.* 7–8 reflect a "close contact with rabbinic halakhah" that is perhaps due more to the nature of the Christian tradition/sources drawn upon in *Barnabas* than to the author of this stridently anti-Jewish writing himself.

26. In the Greek biblical text used by the author of *Barnabas*, 318 was written as the Greek letters ΤΙΗ, the *tau* (= 300) a visual foreshadowing of Jesus' cross, and the *iota-eta* combination (= 18) an abbreviated form of Jesus' name.

27. Cf. Justin's typological reading of the same account in *Dial.* 90. Justin makes the additional claim that Joshua, who led the Israelite army against the Amalekites, prefigured Jesus ("Jesus" and "Joshua" are the same name in Greek, *Iēsous*).

28. The author clearly regards the events and characters in which he sees types of Jesus as real, and it is not correct to characterize him as an allegorizing interpreter.

29. For other instances, see, e.g., the references given by Alsup, 6:684.

In Justin this typological approach is still more amply exhibited, especially, as we should expect, in the *Dialogue with Trypho,* where Justin aims to
show by an exegetical tour de force the validity of the traditional Christian
claims for Jesus. For example, in *Dialogue* 40–41 Justin presents the Passover
lamb, the two goats of the scapegoat ritual, the fine flour of sacrifice prescribed
for those purified from skin diseases, and the commandment to circumcise
male children on the eighth day as types that point to Jesus. Justin recites another series of Old Testament types in *Dialogue* 111, which again includes the
two goats of the scapegoat ritual plus Moses' outstretched hands in the battle
against Amalek (an incident treated also in *Dial.* 90), the blood of the Passover
lamb, and Rahab's crimson cord. That these echo items mentioned in *Barnabas*
shows that there was a common store of Old Testament types deployed in early
Christianity. In 113.1-3 Justin focuses on Joshua, emphasizing that the Old Testament account of him being given this name (Joshua = *Iēsous* in Greek) is to be
understood as pointing ahead to Jesus, who truly succeeded Moses and provided "the eternal possession" that was prefigured in Joshua leading ancient Israel into the Holy Land.

Indeed, in *Dialogue* 75 Justin lays out the argument that *Iēsous* is actually
the name of God referred to in the book of Exodus. Here the crucial text is Exodus 23:20, where God promises to send his "angel/messenger" *(angelos)* to
guard Israel and bring them into the Promised Land; God warns Israel not to
disobey this figure "for my name is in him." Justin then contends that "he who
led your fathers into the land is called by this name 'Jesus' [*Iēsous*]" ("Joshua").
Further, he points out that this name was actually given to the figure (whose
previous name was Hoshea, Num. 13:16), and he contends that the statement
that this figure was given "my name" (i.e., God's name) means that the name Je-
sus/Joshua is the name of God.

Justin also uses the term "symbol" *(symbolon)* with essentially the same
connotation as "type," to characterize figures, events, and items from the Old
Testament as prefiguring Jesus and the gospel. For example, in *Dialogue* 86.1 he
commences a long string of Old Testament symbols that foretold Jesus, including the tree of life and various incidents involving a "rod" and a stone, both of
which symbolize Jesus, and other incidents involving wood *(xylon)*, which
symbolizes Jesus' cross.[30]

These examples are sufficient to make the point that early proto-
orthodox Christians such as Justin were absolutely convinced that the Old Testament was a massive reservoir of characters and events that pointed ahead to

---

30. Justin's other uses of "symbol" for Old Testament people and phenomena include
Dial. 42.1; 90.5; 111.1, 4; 131.4; 138.1.

Jesus. For, as God's Christ and beloved Son, through whom God made the world and in whom God now was bringing about the final redemption of the world, Jesus could not be God's afterthought. Instead, the lofty view of God in the traditions preferred in proto-orthodox circles led them to believe that all that went before Jesus had been divine preparation for his bodily appearance. Seeing in the Old Testament the sacred witness to God's prior actions, they boldly delighted in deploying these Scriptures to justify their christological claims, to celebrate Jesus' high significance, and to affirm that the deity he revealed was the creator God of these Scriptures, whose prior revelations all foreshadowed him.[31]

The third approach to finding (and demonstrating) Jesus in the Old Testament is just as bold, and indeed, may well appear still more bizarre to many moderns. The focus here is on a number of Old Testament passages that narrate manifestations of God (the technical term for such a scene is "theophany"). In this approach these events are presented as manifestations of the "preincarnate" Son of God. Yet again, Justin gives us the most examples from our period of concern.[32]

In *Dialogue* 61.1 Justin makes the general claim to his Jewish dialogue partners that Jesus can be identified in terms of a number of Old Testament manifestations of God. That is, he asserts that "in general the Old Testament theophanies were appearances of the Son, not the Father."[33]

> I shall give to you testimony from the scriptures, my friends, that before all created things God begat from himself a Beginning [*archē*], a certain rational power [*dynamin logikēn*], who is also called by the Holy Spirit "the Glory of the Lord," and sometimes "Son," and "Wisdom," and "Angel," and "God," and "Lord," and "Word"; and he once called himself "Captain" [*architratēgon*] when he appeared in the form of a man to Joshua the son of Nun.[34]

31. As Skarsaune suggested, the fervent linking of Jesus with the Old Testament in Justin and later writers may have been directed, at least in part, against those such as Marcionites who distinguished between the creator deity of the Old Testament and the true God whom Jesus revealed.

32. For a fuller discussion, see Skarsaune, *The Proof from Prophecy*, 409-24, summarized in Skarsaune, "Scriptural Interpretation," 406-9; and Benedict Kominiak, *The Theophanies of the Old Testament in the Writings of St. Justin* (Washington, D.C.: Catholic University of America, 1948).

33. Skarsaune, "Scriptural Interpretation," 408.

34. The Old Testament allusions here are: "Beginning" (Gen. 1:1, "in/by the beginning" taken as a reference to the Son as the divine agent of creation); "Glory of the Lord" (e.g., Exod. 16:7; etc.); "Son" (e.g., Ps. 2:7); "Wisdom" (Prov. 8:22-36; Ps. 104:24 [103:24 LXX]); "Angel [of the

Justin lays out these claims more fully in other parts of the *Dialogue* (especially in 56–62 and 126–29). For example, in 60 he argues that "the Lord" who addressed Moses out of the burning bush (Exod. 3:1-6) was not "the Maker and Father of all things," but instead the figure declared in many places in the Scriptures to be God's principal agent, the preincarnate Word. Then in 61 he engages in a lengthy and detailed analysis of the account of "the Lord" speaking to Abraham (Gen. 18) to show that this also is the same distinguishable figure who is called "Lord" and "God," and is in fact the preincarnate Christ. In these and the other passages where Justin presents this view, he engages in "a closely reasoned argument, based on detailed observations within large passages of the biblical text."[35] That is, Justin's arguments are the fruit of detailed and dedicated mining of the Old Testament.

As Skarsaune has shown, Justin is also probably acquainted with ancient Jewish speculations about whether biblical passages present a second divine figure alongside the creator God.[36] That is, Justin's undeniable familiarity with Jewish tradition of his time appears to have extended to what Alan Segal characterized as "two powers" controversies, debates reflected in rabbinic texts about such a second figure.[37]

Still earlier than the rabbinic sources, Philo of Alexandria (ca. 20 B.C.E.– 50 C.E.) exhibits Jewish speculations about the biblical accounts of manifestations of God.[38] In Philo's case these speculations were motivated at least in part by a concern to reconcile biblical accounts of God's appearances with a sophisticated understanding of God as utterly transcendent and not subject to direct/ ordinary human apprehension. Philo's solution was to identify the biblical manifestations of God as the Logos, in one sense genuinely God but really a distinguishable mode (or "power" [*dynamis*]) of God adapted for human apprehension; the Logos thus represents that of the infinite God which humans as finite creation are capable of perceiving.

Of course, both Philo and Justin drew upon prior Jewish Wisdom tradi-

---

Lord]" (e.g., Gen. 31:11-13); "God" (e.g., Gen. 32:28-30); "Lord" (e.g., Gen. 18:1; 28:13); "Word" (Ps. 33:6 [32:6 LXX]); "Chief Officer" (Josh. 5:14). By "rational power" Justin refers to this divine figure's chief function as expression of the will/mind of God, which is also, of course, conveyed particularly in the epithets "Word" and "Wisdom."

35. Skarsaune, "Scriptural Interpretation," 407-8.

36. Skarsaune, "Scriptural Interpretation," 407-9.

37. Alan F. Segal, *Two Powers in Heaven: Early Rabbinic Reports about Christianity and Gnosticism*, SJLA 25 (Leiden: Brill, 1977).

38. E.g., Segal, 159-81; also Larry W. Hurtado, *One God, One Lord: Early Christian Devotion and Ancient Jewish Monotheism* (Philadelphia: Fortress, 1988; 2nd ed., Edinburgh: T. & T. Clark, 1998), 44-48.

tions (e.g., Prov. 8:22-36; Sir. 24), and they also reflect intellectual currents of their own time stemming from Greek philosophical tradition that made the idea of a transcendent God being manifested seem intellectually naive.[39] In mentioning Philo I do not wish to enter the contentious issue of whether Justin directly drew upon Philo. For the present discussion I propose only that Philo helps us see the sorts of religious and intellectual currents that likely influenced Justin as well.[40] Note, for example, Justin's statement in *Dialogue* 60.2 that even "he who has but the smallest intelligence will not venture to assert that the Maker and Father of all things, having left all supercelestial matters, was visible on a little portion of the earth."[41]

However, in Justin (and the Christian tradition he reflects) it is not simply or primarily an academic debate over what one might make of biblical texts. Instead they explore certain theophanic accounts to confirm and celebrate Jesus' divine status for themselves, and to persuade others to embrace him as divine. For the early Christian handling of these Old Testament texts that Justin exemplifies, the prior and essential basis is the belief that the historic Jesus was the incarnate form of the preexistent and divine Son/Word of God, through and with whom God created all things.[42] This belief certainly goes back early into first-century Christianity, as attested by such passages as 1 Corinthians 8:4-6, Philippians 2:6-8, Colossians 1:15-17, Hebrews 1:1-3, and John 1:1-2. Given this belief, it was not so strange for early Christians such as Justin to look for references to the preincarnate Jesus/Son/Word in their Scriptures.

In fact, the conviction that one could find Old Testament passages in which the preincarnate Jesus was manifested is reflected in first-century Christian texts. Most obviously, of course, the New Testament references to Jesus as the one through whom God created all things (1 Cor. 8:4-6; John 1:1-2; Col. 1:15-17) all reflect such a reading of Old Testament statements about the creation of

---

39. On Philo's links to Jewish Wisdom tradition, see Burton L. Mack, *Logos und Sophia: Untersuchungen zur Weisheitstheologie in hellenistischen Judentum* (Göttingen: Vandenhoeck & Ruprecht, 1973); and on early Christian appropriation of this tradition, see Gottfried Schimanowski, *Weisheit und Messias: Die jüdischen Voraussetzungen der urchristlichen Präexistenzchristologie*, WUNT 2/17 (Tübingen: Mohr [Siebeck], 1985); and Hermann von Lips, *Weisheitliche Traditionen im Neuen Testament*, WMANT 64 (Neukirchen-Vluyn: Neukirchener Verlag, 1990).

40. L. W. Barnard judged there to be "surprisingly little in Justin to suggest a close acquaintance with Philo and Hellenistic Judaism": *Justin Martyr: His Life and Thought* (Cambridge: Cambridge University Press, 1967), 52, also 92-97.

41. I cite here the translation in ANF, 1:227.

42. Demetrios C. Trakatellis, *The Pre-existence of Christ in the Writings of Justin Martyr: An Exegetical Study with Reference to the Humiliation and Exaltation Christology*, HDR 6 (Missoula: Scholars, 1976).

the world. Furthermore, Paul's statement in 1 Corinthians 10:4 that the rock from which Israel drank in their wilderness trek "was Christ" must surely be taken as asserting that in his preincarnate mode Jesus was the divine figure who engaged Israel in the Exodus narrative.[43] Also, whether the original reading in Jude 5 referred to "Jesus" or "the Lord," it is a good bet that this verse likewise portrays the preincarnate Jesus rescuing Israel from Egypt.[44] Further, as we noted in an earlier chapter, John 12:41 asserts that the divine figure seen by the prophet in Isaiah 6:1 was "the Lord" Jesus. These references to passages in Exodus and Isaiah exhibit first-century christological interpretations of Old Testament theophanic passages.

So Justin did not originate the basic idea that the preincarnate Jesus could be found active in certain Old Testament passages. Skarsaune is correct to note that in Justin we have an "enormous widening of the [Old Testament] testimony dossier on Christ's preexistence and divinity."[45] But here, too, Justin was essentially building upon a line of christological argument already available. He reflects an approach to the Old Testament that had been a feature of devotion to Jesus during the first decades of the Christian movement. In turn, his programmatic finding of the preincarnate Jesus in Old Testament passages is probably one of the traditions that helped shape Irenaeus's idea that Jesus is the full and final manifestation of the divine Logos who has been active throughout human history.[46]

Moreover, finding Jesus in the Old Testament — identifying specific prophetic predictions, ubiquitous types of him, and his preincarnate manifestations — was not simply used in arguing with Jews and others. Nor was it solely

43. Gordon D. Fee, *The First Epistle to the Corinthians,* NICNT (Grand Rapids: Eerdmans, 1987), 449, judges this view "far more likely" than a merely figurative meaning; so also Hans Conzelmann, *1 Corinthians,* Hermeneia (Philadelphia: Fortress, 1975), 167 ("real preexistence, not merely symbolic significance"). But see esp. A. T. Hanson, *Jesus Christ in the Old Testament* (London: SPCK, 1965), 10-25. The past-tense verb "was" in 1 Cor. 10:4 can be accounted for only on this view. This statement most likely also reflects the interpretation that "the Rock" of Deut. 32 refers to Christ.

44. There are several variants as to the figure who rescued Israel, the best-supported ones being "Jesus" (Alexandrinus, Vaticanus, 33, and numerous other witnesses) and "(the) Lord" (Sinaiticus, and numerous other witnesses). On the verse, see esp. J. E. Fossum, "Angel Christology in Jude 5-7," in his *The Image of the Invisible God: Essays on the Influence of Jewish Mysticism on Early Christology* (Freiburg: Universitätsverlag Freiburg; Göttingen: Vandenhoeck & Ruprecht, 1995), 41-70.

45. Skarsaune, "Scriptural Interpretation," 407. Curiously, Skarsaune failed to note these New Testament precedents for Justin's exegesis of Old Testament theophanic passages. Cf. also Skarsaune, *The Proof from Prophecy,* 409-24.

46. Albert Houssiau, *La christologie de saint Irénée* (Louvain: Publications universitaires de Louvain; Gembloux: Éditions J. Duculot, 1955).

an academic exercise shared only among those with leisure and inclination to engage in exegesis of texts. From perhaps a bit later than Justin, we have Melito's *Paschal Homily,* a sermon preached (ca. 160-80) to a Christian congregation in Sardis (in modern-day Turkey), which exhibits essentially these same approaches to the Old Testament.[47] Melito's sermon shows us one of the major means by which the sweeping portrayal of the Old Testament as full of references to Jesus was widely disseminated and celebrated in the second-century Christian circles in which the Old Testament was revered as Scripture. In several passages he lyrically proclaims this devotional reading of the Old Testament. For example, in the following excerpt that shows his rhetorical style, he parades a string of Old Testament types of Jesus: "Therefore, if you wish to see the mystery [*mystērion*] of the Lord, look at Abel who is similarly murdered, at Isaac who is similarly bound, at Joseph who is similarly sold, at Moses who is similarly exposed, at David who is similarly persecuted, at the prophets who similarly suffer for the sake of Christ."[48]

As Melito shows us, numerous Christians were made familiar with treating the Old Testament as a collection of writings about Jesus, whether they personally could read it or not, through sermons and other means of sharing the results of the approaches to the Old Testament described here; many were made acquainted with the idea that these Scriptures gave predictions, types, and preincarnate manifestations of Jesus.

The Fourfold Gospel

The collection of, and the preference for, the fourfold Gospel constitutes another major, identifying feature of proto-orthodox Christianity; and it is a remarkable phenomenon.[49] To select several accounts of Jesus, and to affirm them all as valid, allowing their particularities and undeniable differences to re-

47. Stuart George Hall, *Melito of Sardis, "On Pascha"* (Oxford: Clarendon, 1979), gives an introduction, the Greek text, and a translation.

48. *On Pascha* 1.59. I quote here Stuart George Hall's translation (33). Melito engages in similar rhetorical flights elsewhere in the sermon as well (e.g., 69, 83-86). See also G. Racle, "Perspectives christologiques de l'Homélie pascale de Méliton de Sardes," in *Studia Patristica. Vol. IX,* ed. F. L. Cross, TU 94 (Berlin: Akademie-Verlag, 1966), 263-69; cf. D. F. Winslow, "The Polemical Christology of Melito of Sardis," in *Studia Patristica, Vol. XVII,* ed. E. A. Livingstone (Oxford: Pergamon Press, 1982), 765-75, whose psychologizing of Melito, however, is unpersuasive.

49. See also Martin Hengel's review of the various currents in the second century: *The Four Gospels and the One Gospel of Jesus Christ* (London: SCM Press, 2000), 1-33. He characterizes it as "almost a miracle" that the fourfold Gospel became the preferred option (106).

main, was not an inevitable, or even the most obvious, option. There were more predictable moves, and there certainly were other Christians who preferred them. In order to appreciate the significance and likely meaning of the fourfold Gospel as a particular expression of devotion to Jesus, let us consider briefly these other options.

One reasonable alternative was, for instance, for Christians to choose one of the numerous Gospels already available by the second century to serve as the authoritative rendition of Jesus. It is perfectly understandable that, especially amid the multiplicity of renditions of Jesus circulating in the second century, some deemed it wise to select one rendition as the correct one. This is, of course, precisely what Marcion did sometime around 140. As we noted in the previous chapter, Marcion's success shows that his strong distinction between the creator deity of the Old Testament and the true God of Jesus, and also his advocacy of a univocal canon of one Gospel and one apostle, were views many Christians of the time found congenial.

He may well not have been the first, however, to prefer one Gospel as the reliable account of Jesus. The relevant data are too few to be sure, but it is possible that the Gospel of John (perhaps in a previous edition to what we know) was initially used as the sole account of Jesus deemed authoritative by a "Johannine community/circle" from which most scholars think it emerged.[50] Matthew may have been used as the uniquely favored account in some first-century circles, particularly among those who sought to identify themselves strongly with Judaic traditions (perhaps in Roman Judea).[51]

The early Christians who preferred multiple accounts of Jesus had to face up to the differences among them. Even if the four canonical Gospels, for example, are read as the products of friendly colleagues in Christian faith, one cannot fail to note that they differ from one another markedly in contents, arrangement, themes/emphases, order, and even in the ways they present the same incidents and sayings of Jesus. Early Christians were not blind to these matters, and a good many seem to have found them disturbing. For example, in

---

50. Hengel judged that the aim of composing the Gospel of John was to establish it above the Synoptic Gospels, to "correct them and 'surpass' them": *The Johannine Question* (London: SCM Press, 1989), 94.

51. So also, e.g., Oscar Cullmann, "The Plurality of the Gospels as a Theological Problem in Antiquity," in his *The Early Church*, ed. A. J. B. Higgins (London: SCM Press, 1956), 45. Irenaeus refers to "Ebionites" who used only the Gospel of Matthew (*Adv. haer.* 1.26.2). But he may have been confused; the Gospel used by these heterodox Christians may actually have been the *Gospel of the Hebrews*, as proposed by M. R. James, *The Apocryphal New Testament* (Oxford: Clarendon, 1953), 1-8, and accepted by Richard Heard, "The ΑΠΟΜΝΗΜΟΝΕΥΜΑΤΑ in Papias, Justin, and Irenaeus," *NTS* 1 (1954-55): 128 (122-29).

the late second century a presbyter of the church in Rome named Gaius is said to have found features of the Gospel of John so difficult to reconcile with the Synoptics that he attributed it to the heretic Cerinthus.[52] Moreover, pagan critics such as Celsus seized upon the differences among the Gospels to pillory Christianity as a confused, contradictory, and unworthy religion.[53]

This, in part, explains another reasonable stance taken toward the multiplicity of Gospels. We know that very early in the second century some Christians began producing harmonizations of the Gospels, circulated mainly for edification of other believers.[54] More specifically, although there may have been various motives, one of the most important was likely to resolve the differences among the Gospels that were already circulating widely with high regard.[55] In fact, it is practically a historical necessity for particular Gospels to have been held in high regard for Christians to have found the differences among them so troubling as to generate efforts to resolve them. This means, for example, that the steps in the second century to harmonize Gospels count as clear evidence that these particular texts already had acquired a wide circulation and high standing.

The best known of these harmonizing works was Tatian's *Diatessaron*, produced sometime between 160 and 180.[56] As its name indicates (literally, "[one]

52. See, e.g., Hengel, *The Johannine Question*, 5-7.

53. Helmut Merkel, *Die Widersprüche zwischen den Evangelien. Ihre polemische und apologetische Behandlung in der Alten Kirche bis zu Augustin*, WUNT 13 (Tübingen: Mohr, 1971); Merkel, *Die Pluralität der Evangelien als theologisches und exegetisches Problem in der alten Kirche*, Traditio Christiana 3 (Bern and Frankfurt: Peter Lang, 1978); Cullmann, "The Plurality of the Gospels as a Theological Problem in Antiquity."

54. Helmut Koester, *Ancient Christian Gospels: Their History and Development* (Philadelphia: Trinity Press International, 1990), 349-402, discusses some of the evidence. Peter M. Head, "Tatian's Christology and Its Influence on the Composition of the *Diatessaron*," *TB* 43 (1992): 121 n. 3 (121-37), refers to "a harmonistic tendency that was widespread in the early period," pointing to *Gospel of Peter, Gospel of the Ebionites*, and "Secret Mark" as examples, to which I would add the "long ending" of Mark (16:9-20), the Freer Logion of Mark, the Egerton fragment, and P.Oxy. 840.

55. See especially Tjitze Baarda, "ΔΙΑΦΩΝΙΑ-ΣΥΜΦΩΝΙΑ: Factors in the Harmonization of the Gospels, Especially in the *Diatessaron* of Tatian," in *Gospel Traditions in the Second Century: Origins, Recensions, Text, and Transmission*, ed. William L. Petersen (Notre Dame, Ind., and London: University of Notre Dame Press, 1989), 133-54.

56. The *Diatessaron* does not survive except in an array of much later sources from which scholars attempt to reconstruct its text. The key study is William L. Petersen, *Tatian's "Diatessaron": Its Creation, Dissemination, Use, and History in Scholarship*, VCSup 25 (Leiden: Brill, 1994). See also Petersen's contribution on the *Diatessaron* in Koester, *Ancient Christian Gospels* (403-30). Some of Petersen's views, however, are debatable, such as Tatian's supposed use of a fifth (extracanonical) gospel, and the claim that the *Diatessaron* preserves a more ancient form of the text of the Gospels than that preserved in our earliest extant manuscripts. The most widely available English translation is by Hope W. Hogg (in ANF, 9:35-138, from an Arabic text published in 1888, ed. P. Agostino Ciasca).

from four"), this text braided together the four Gospels of the New Testament canon and produced a single, consistent text.[57] But Tatian was not the originator of this genre of text. Various texts in the second century offered harmonistic accounts of Jesus, combining material from more than one of the known Gospels.[58] Recent research has shown that Justin, who for a time was Tatian's teacher in Rome, must have known and used one or more such harmonized texts earlier than the composition of the *Diatessaron*.[59] The sort of harmonizing text he used, however, may have been based only on Matthew and Luke, or perhaps all three Synoptic Gospels; also, it may not have been a harmony of their full contents. Although Justin shows acquaintance with Johannine tradition (especially his elaboration of the Logos seems to presuppose something like the prologue to GJohn), and even one or two possible reminiscences of the Gospel of John itself, overall it is unlikely that he used or regarded John in the same way he did the Synoptic Gospels.[60] Moreover, the harmonistic text(s) he used likely served him essentially as a tool for study and teaching. Such a text was not produced to compete with the Gospels on which it drew, particularly in the public reading of them as part of Christian corporate worship.[61] As a former pupil of Justin,

---

57. Petersen notes that *diatessaron* was also an ancient Greek musical term, and so Tatian may have intended his work as giving a musical-like "harmony" of the four canonical Gospels: *Tatian's "Diatessaron,"* 50-51. Although Tatian may also have included some material from other sources, the only sources used *systematically* in the *Diatessaron* appear to be the four canonical Gospels.

58. Petersen speaks of "a surprising number of gospel harmonies" that circulated in the second century (*Tatian's "Diatessaron,"* 26).

59. The major study is Arthur J. Bellinzoni, *The Sayings of Jesus in the Writings of Justin Martyr*, NovTSup 17 (Leiden: Brill, 1967), esp. 138-42; and also Koester, *Ancient Christian Gospels*, 360-402. Cf. however, Barnard, *Justin Martyr*, 58-66.

60. Barnard, *Justin Martyr*, 60-62; Bellinzoni, 140.

61. Justin's frequently noted summary description of Christian worship of his time (*1 Apol.* 67) includes readings from "the memoirs [*apomnēmoneumata*] of the apostles or the writings of the prophets." The latter are likely Old Testament writings; in *1 Apol.* 66.3 Justin identifies the apostolic "memoirs" as "gospels." Bellinzoni (138) concluded from his study of Justin's citations that they all derive either from one or another of the Synoptic Gospels, or from harmonizing texts composed from the Synoptics and used for instructional purposes. Koester claimed, "Had Justin prevailed, and not Irenaeus, a harmony of the available gospels would have been the answer," and Koester portrayed Tatian as having "fulfilled that task" (*Ancient Christian Gospels*, 402). But Koester is simply incorrect in implying that Justin was interested in replacing the liturgical reading of individual Gospels with a harmony. There is no basis for thinking that Justin ever intended or sought to fashion a harmonized text to use *in lieu of the individual Gospels in church readings*. On Justin's use of the term "memoirs" for the Gospels, see also Luise Abramowski, "The 'Memoirs of the Apostles' in Justin," in *The Gospel and the Gospels*, ed. Peter Stuhlmacher (Grand Rapids: Eerdmans, 1991; German 1983), 323-35.

Tatian would have become acquainted with this sort of harmonizing tool used in teaching.[62]

Tatian's *Diatessaron*, however, appears to have been a much more ambitious project in two important ways. First, it was a systematic effort to weave together the *four* familiar Gospels into one complete account of Jesus, although Tatian in fact also omitted material from the Gospels that he found objectionable, such as the genealogies of Matthew and Luke.[63] That is, one of Tatian's major innovations may have been to make the first programmatic use of the Gospel of John in a harmony.[64] Indeed, the *Diatessaron* appears to have begun with John 1:1 and ended with John 21:25, and the Johannine accounts of Jesus' several Jerusalem visits structured the contents overall.[65]

Second, Tatian's other, and more serious, innovation seems to have been the promotion of his *Diatessaron* in place of the four Gospels, not alongside them as a study tool. In effect, Tatian zealously produced *a new Gospel* that he hoped would fully address internal anxieties about unity of Gospel testimony, and would answer pagan critics as well, by offering what Petersen called "the *single,* the *true* account of what actually happened." Perhaps, as Petersen further proposed, "Tatian saw himself principally as an *historian,* and his *Diatessaron* as a 'scientific' work, the definitive account of Jesus' life."[66] But unlike his teacher Justin, Tatian appears to have wanted the *Diatessaron* to serve as a more accurate and satisfactory account of Jesus, and also to be used in the churches *in lieu of the four Gospels that it harmonized.*[67] As Tjitze Baarda concluded, Tatian aimed "to replace the sources [the Gospels] and their contradictions with a new

62. William L. Petersen, "Textual Evidence of Tatian's Dependence upon Justin's ΑΠΟΜΝΗΜΟΝΕΥΜΑΤΑ," *NTS* 36 (1990): 360-402.

63. Hogg (ANF, 9:39) cites a study of the Arabic text by G. F. Moore ("Tatian's *Diatessaron* and the Analysis of the Pentateuch," *JBL* 9 [1890]: 201-15), showing that the text contains 50 percent of Mark, 66 percent of Luke, 76.5 percent of Matthew, and 96 percent of John. In sum, of a total of 3,780 verses in the four canonical Gospels, Moore found that the Arabic *Diatessaron* includes 2,769 and omits 1,011. Hogg also provides a helpful index listing Gospel material included in the Arabic text.

64. "What is new in Tatian's *Diatessaron* and what is not found in Justin's writings is a full gospel harmony rather than one of limited scope and the incorporation into the gospel harmony of the Gospel of John." Bellinzoni, 142.

65. There is good evidence that the *Diatessaron* commenced with the words from John 1:1, and that it did not include a genealogy (evidence cited by Petersen, *Tatian's "Diatessaron,"* e.g., 45, 62-63). See, e.g., Head, "Tatian's," 129-30; Hengel, *The Johannine Question,* 4, 140 n. 14.

66. Petersen, *Tatian's "Diatessaron,"* 76.

67. This is probably partly why Tatian's work became both notorious and widely used, whereas other harmonies, such as those attributed to Theophilus of Antioch and Ammonius of Alexandria, as well as the harmonizing text(s) that Justin used, have disappeared totally. On these harmonies, see Petersen, *Tatian's "Diatessaron,"* 32-34.

document," and he did not intend this to be another Gospel alongside the others, "but rather, what it actually became in the early Syriac-speaking churches, *the* Gospel."[68]

Part of Tatian's concern may also have been to counter the Marcionite stance that church unity depended upon selecting one, correct Gospel. Ironically, however, in his own way as well, Tatian, like Marcion, obviously held a view that church unity required a *uniformity* of witness to Jesus, a single rendition of Jesus' ministry. They simply had different tactics for achieving this uniformity. Marcion chose one valid witness from among those Gospels whose growing recognition made their differences problematic; a few decades later Tatian created one valid replacement witness by detailed scholarly resolution of these differences.

Although there are conflicting attributions of heresy to Tatian in the ancient heresiologists, the only charge that might have a basis is that he taught an ultrastrict renunciation of sex, treating sexual relations between marriage partners as no less evil than fornication.[69] This negative attitude toward sex is exhibited in a number of readings in the *Diatessaron*. As already mentioned, Tatian omitted the Matthean and Lukan genealogies. He also sought to obscure the relationship between Joseph and Mary, and made other reverentially motivated changes (e.g., omitting the accusation that Jesus was "a glutton and a drunkard," Matt. 11:19). But the religious motivations for such changes (e.g., an ascetic tendency) are simply a stricter version of the anxiety about the body (and sex in particular) that was felt by many Christians in the latter part of the second century.

There is, by contrast, little reason to think Tatian denied the humanity of Jesus, or promoted any other identifiably heretical ideas.[70] As Head noted, this

---

68. Baarda, 154.

69. Statements about Tatian's beliefs rest almost entirely on his defense of Christianity, *Oration to the Greeks*, and a few putative sayings cited in early church writings. For Greek text and translation, see Molly Whittaker, ed. & trans., *Tatian, "Oratio ad Graecos" and Fragments* (Oxford: Clarendon, 1982). The major study of Tatian's thought is Martin Elze, *Tatian und seine Theologie* (Göttingen: Vandenhoeck & Ruprecht, 1960), which is based almost entirely on Tatian's *Oration to the Greeks*. For his view of the Logos, see Elze, 70-83. Also helpful is G. F. Hawthorne, "Tatian and His Discourse to the Greeks," *HTR* 57 (1964): 161-88. On Tatian's asceticism, see now Kathy L. Gaca, "Driving Aphrodite from the World: Tatian's Encratite Principles of Sexual Renunciation," *JTS* 53 (2002): 28-52.

70. Little, 177-93, on Tatian's Logos Christology in the *Oration*, which agrees on the whole with Justin's teaching on the subject, especially as in the *Dialogue*. Little characterized him as "perhaps, the most thoroughly religious of the Apologists" (180). One of the more interesting phrases in Tatian's *Oration* refers to those who were disobedient and rejected "the servant of the suffering God" *(ton diakonon tou peponthotos theou)* in 13.3.

helps explain why the *Diatessaron* was so widely used, even among orthodox circles for several centuries.[71]

In spite of the attractions of Marcion's one-Gospel canon and Tatian's replacement Gospel account, however, the fourfold collection of Gospels won out, as counterintuitive as it may seem. But it took much longer in Syriac Christianity than in the West. As a closed *collection,* the fourfold Gospel represents three affirmations that tell us a good deal about the kind of Christian devotion that it represents. First, it reflects an affirmation of a certain diversity that is represented in multiple witnesses to Jesus, in contrast with the narrower and more exclusivist stance of Marcion, and also with Tatian's own effort to have one "true" account. That is, it illustrates one of the features I have proposed as characteristic of proto-orthodox Christianity in the second century: a certain readiness to find unity of what they deemed essentials beneath obvious diversity.[72]

But second, as a *closed* collection, the fourfold Gospel also certainly represented a refusal to include the numerous other Jesus books that had begun circulating by the second century. In other words, whatever toleration for diversity was represented by the preference for the fourfold Gospel, it was neither mindless nor without limit. Some Jesus books were obviously unacceptable in proto-orthodox circles; their differences were simply too great. Those, such as *Gospel of Thomas,* that showed disdain for the Old Testament, and/or represented major innovations in belief that departed from what proto-orthodox circles regarded as apostolic tradition (e.g., distinguishing between the creator deity and the true God), could not be accommodated.

Thirdly, the fourfold Gospel represents an affirmation of the individual integrity of *each* of the four texts included in the collection, and a refusal to replace them with a homogenized text, such as Tatian's *Diatessaron.* In constructing his new account out of the four Gospels, in one sense Tatian affirmed the general validity of their contents; but at the same time, in promoting the ecclesiastical use of the *Diatessaron,* he also subverted them as specific texts.

We may ask, however, whether the fourfold Gospel was prompted by the other options that we have noted, such as Marcion and Tatian, or whether the latter were reactions subsequent to the fourfold Gospel. I indicated above that Tatian's harmonizing effort practically requires that the sources harmonized

---

71. Head, "Tatian's," 137. See 128-37 for Head's discussion of Diatessaronic passages that may reflect Tatian's beliefs.

72. Hengel points to Bishop Serapion's initially permissive response to questions about the *Gospel of Peter,* as indicative of a generous attitude among proto-orthodox figures of the (late) second century: *The Four Gospels,* 12-15. As we noted earlier (chap. 7), Serapion changed his mind only when it was reported to him that some people were promoting heterodox teachings on the basis of this text.

had already acquired a wide circulation and high standing. Likewise, if Marcion in his own way was seeking to solve the problem of diversity of Christian tradition, then his selection of Luke as the sole valid rendition of Jesus may also indicate that before 140 some or all of the four canonical accounts were sufficiently regarded to make their differences problematic.

In a number of studies of the last few years, several scholars have argued that the fourfold Gospel made its appearance astonishingly early. For example, Graham Stanton gathered up evidence indicating that the present four Gospels functioned as a collection and were highly regarded in an increasing number of churches by about 150.[73] Since Stanton's article appeared, other scholars have underscored this line of argument, contending that the fourfold Gospel was likely circulating in the earliest decades of the second century. It is all the more interesting that these scholars do not agree with one another entirely about which factors are crucial in explaining this, though they agree that what is to be explained must be dated this early.[74]

Most recently, James Kelhoffer's detailed analysis of the "long ending" of Mark shows that this block of material (16:9-20), which represents an attempt to fit Mark with a more "suitable" ending, used elements from the other three canonical Gospels, and these writings only. That is, the prior circulation of these four Gospels as a collection with some sort of special status and validity made it seem appropriate (perhaps even necessary) to give Mark an ending that made it more compatible with the way the other Gospels in the collection ended. In short, a linkage of Mark with the other Gospels is perhaps what made Mark's rather unusual ending seem in need of adjustment. Justin's apparent acquaintance with the Markan long ending (*1 Apol.* 45.5; *Dial.* 76.6) means that it had to have been composed by circa 120-50, which in turn means that these four Gospels must have been circulating with privileged significance earlier still.[75]

73. G. N. Stanton, "The Fourfold Gospel," *NTS* 43 (1997): 317-46. See also William R. Farmer, "Further Reflections on the Fourfold Gospel Canon," in *The Early Church in Its Context: Essays in Honor of Everett Ferguson,* ed. Abraham J. Malherbe, Frederick W. Norris, and James W. Thompson, NovTSup 90 (Leiden: Brill, 1998), 107-13.

74. E.g., Theo K. Heckel, *Vom Evangelium des Markus zum viergestaltigen Evangelium,* WUNT 120 (Tübingen: Mohr-Siebeck, 1999), proposes that the appearance of GJohn in its present form was the crucial factor; but cf. Hengel, *The Four Gospels and the One Gospel of Jesus Christ,* who attributes much to the influence of Mark, along with other factors.

75. James A. Kelhoffer, *Miracle and Mission: The Authentication of Missionaries and Their Message in the Longer Ending of Mark,* WUNT 2/112 (Tübingen: Mohr-Siebeck, 2000), 170-75, on the evidence that Tatian and Justin both knew the Markan "long ending." Kelhoffer (158) sees no evidence that the four canonical Gospels "were *collected* and compared with one another before ca. 110-120." Cf. C.-B. Amphoux, "La finale longue de Marc: un épilogue des quatre évangiles," in

I want to forestall two possible misunderstandings of what I am affirming. To speak of a fourfold Gospel collection in the early second century does not necessarily mean that these four writings all *circulated physically* as a collection. So far as we can tell, the earliest experiments with producing a multiple-Gospel codex began sometime toward the end of the second century.[76] Until then the Gospels seem to have circulated in single-Gospel codices, which is what all our very earliest fragments represent (e.g., P52 of John). So, to posit a "fourfold Gospel" in the early second century is simply to claim that in an increasing number of Christian circles of this time these four renditions of Jesus were all *regarded* and *used* as uniquely valid, or at least as superior to other accounts. Further, the evidence suggests that all through the second century, even after the fourfold Gospel was indisputably becoming the dominant option, Matthew and John were the favorites. They appear to have been copied much more frequently and read more widely in churches than the other two.[77] Indeed, Matthew and John remained the favorites in Christian tradition all through the subsequent centuries, long after all four canonical Gospels were unquestionably recognized as canonical.

Let us wind up this discussion of the fourfold Gospel by underscoring what it represents as a statement of devotion to Jesus. All four Gospels connect Jesus with the God of the Old Testament and with the biblical story of Israel and her messianic hopes. The inclusion of Matthew, in particular, clearly affirms the Old Testament as the interpretive background by which to understand Jesus' appearance, and vividly reflects the proto-orthodox stance that Je-

---

The Synoptic Gospels, Source Criticism, and the New Literary Criticism, ed. C. Focant (Leuven: Peeters/Leuven University Press, 1993), 548-55, who proposes that the Markan long ending was composed precisely for a four Gospel collection arranged in the "Western" order (Matthew-John-Luke-Mark), but agrees that the date for this had to be very early.

76. The Chester Beatty codex, P45 (ca. 250), contained the four Gospels and Acts. In an important recent study, T. C. Skeat has argued that P4, P64, and P67 are all portions of a four Gospel codex, which he dates to the late second century: "The Oldest Manuscript of the Four Gospels?" *NTS* 43 (1997): 1-34. He has also proposed that P75 may be remnants of another four Gospel codex from the early third century: "The Origin of the Christian Codex," *Zeitschrift für Papyrus und Epigraphik* 102 (1994): 263-68; and that Irenaeus (ca. 180) knew of such codices: "Irenaeus and the Four-Gospel Canon," *NovT* 34 (1992): 194-99.

77. The earliest manuscripts of New Testament writings are all from Oxyrhynchus (Egypt). Of those from prior to 300 C.E., the following New Testament writings are found (with the number of copies in parentheses): Matthew (13), John (10), Romans (4), Acts (3), Hebrews (3), James (3), Revelation (3), Luke (2), and one each for 1 Corinthians, Galatians, Philippians, 1-2 Thessalonians, 1 John, Jude. Eldon Jay Epp, "The New Testament Papyri at Oxyrhynchus in Their Social and Intellectual Context," in *Sayings of Jesus: Canonical and Non-Canonical, Essays in Honour of Tjitze Baarda,* ed. William L. Peterson, Johan S. Vos, and Henk J. de Jonge (Leiden: Brill, 1997), 47-68.

sus is Son of the God of the Old Testament who created the world. This sharply contrasts with the stance advocated by Marcion and other heterodox circles of the second century.

Moreover, as we observed in chapter 5, in spite of their variations, all four Gospels are essentially narrative-genre texts that give a *bios*-type account of Jesus. That is, they reflect the proto-orthodox insistence that Jesus' religious significance is tied to his having been a historic figure with a real personal story and circumstances. Although neither Mark nor John has a birth narrative or genealogy, both clearly present Jesus as a member of a family with siblings and a hometown. In particular, all four renditions tell a story of Jesus in which his death and bodily resurrection are the climactic and crucial redemptive events. Obviously, the fourfold Gospel reflects the forms of early Christian devotion in which Jesus' death and resurrection were seen in this way, and were paradigmatic as well for Christian behavior. All this clearly represents a viewpoint that contrasts with the sayings-collection genre of *Gospel of Thomas,* and the characterization of Jesus as essentially a teacher of truths and a revealer of secrets. The Gospels all make the person of Jesus crucial, not simply a body of teachings.

Furthermore, as a collection the four Gospels affirm all of Jesus' disciples (except, of course, for the unfortunate Judas) as truly chosen by Jesus and as valid apostles. That is, the fourfold Gospel represents the view that the valid traditions of Jesus are those that are known to be linked with this full apostolic circle. This view either anticipates or is a reaction against the sort of claim made in some extracanonical Jesus books that this or that figure was uniquely bequeathed the valid (or superior) tradition, and that Jesus' other disciples were discredited or unworthy by comparison.[78] The Jesus of the fourfold Gospel is, in this important sense, a "public" Jesus, the valid teachings and traditions about him those that are presented as resting upon the multiple witness of these texts, not upon esoteric revelations.

To cite another matter, contrary to tendencies toward a univocal witness to Jesus that are represented both in Marcion and Tatian, the fourfold Gospel manifests a preference for a fullness of witnesses to Jesus, with the diversity among the Gospels taken as complementary. For example, the fourfold Gospel gives us a Jesus who is born in a human family, yet who is also the incarnated

---

78. To be sure, Mark unsparingly presents all the disciples (and Peter in particular) as dim during much of Jesus' ministry, and as cowardly in the final test at his arrest in Jerusalem. But, as previously noted, the dominical promise of 14:28 can only signal that readers know them to have been given a postresurrection restoration and revalidation by Jesus. In any case, in a fourfold collection used in churches, each one of the accounts was read in the light of the others, and all three of the other canonical Gospels unambiguously present the body of Jesus' disciples as restored and validated (Matt. 28:16-20; Luke 24:36-53; John 20:19-29).

divine Word and Son of the Father through whom the world was created. The stories of Jesus' human birth in Matthew and Luke are implicitly affirmed in the collection, along with the cosmic scope of Jesus' origins presented in John. Reverent readers almost cannot avoid seeing these sorts of variations in the Gospels in stereoscopic fashion, as combining to offer a multiple witness to Jesus' full nature and significance. It is probably not coincidental that the four-fold Gospel was preferred among those Christian circles that considered it essential to confess Jesus' real humanity as well as his full divinity.

In a sense, Tatian's *Diatessaron* probably presupposes this point of view. And Tatian may well have seen himself as simply carrying through in literary form the sort of combination of the fourfold Gospels that for most Christians, then and subsequently, shaped the Jesus of their imagination and devotion. But, although initially successful in Syriac Christianity for several centuries, and translated and used by many others as a tool for study, the *Diatessaron* was not acceptable to most Christians *as a substitute for the fourfold Gospel* collection. By the time of the *Diatessaron*, the fourfold Gospels had already acquired such wide use and respect as literary witnesses to Jesus that they could not be set aside easily. The practice of reading these writings in corporate worship, already established in a good many churches by the time of Tatian, likely was the key factor that made it difficult to replace them.

Visions and Revelations

From 70 to 170 several Christian writings appeared that present revelatory and visionary experiences as a basis for, and a mode of, expressing devotion to Jesus.[79] In particular, these writings include attempts to express what to make of Jesus vis-à-vis God. The key examples are the book of Revelation (ca. 95), the *Ascension of Isaiah* (variously dated from 70 to ca. 175, and hereafter *Asc. Isa.*), and the *Shepherd of Hermas* (composite of portions written at various dates, ca. 95-150).[80] We concentrate especially on Revelation and *Asc. Isa.* because of the

---

79. David E. Aune, *Prophecy in Early Christianity and the Ancient Mediterranean World* (Grand Rapids: Eerdmans, 1983), esp. 247-316, gives a wider-ranging survey of texts of the sort I discuss here.

80. "The period between the two great Jewish revolts (between 70 and 132 CE) produced the greatest of all the Jewish and Christian apocalypses: the Book of Revelation, 4 Ezra and 2 Baruch — works in which the genre of apocalyptic became the vehicle for truly great literature and truly profound theology." Richard Bauckham, "The *Apocalypse of Peter*: A Jewish Christian Apocalypse from the Time of Bar Kokhba," in his *The Fate of the Dead: Studies on Jewish and Christian Apocalypses* (Leiden: Brill, 1998), 168 (160-258). Other examples from this period in-

pronounced attention they give to Jesus. Among their concerns, both writings exhibit the tandem aims of expressing Jesus' supremely exalted status while also affirming a strong monotheistic stance. Moreover, in both writings Jesus' status is portrayed by visions of heavenly realities, with worship as the key criterion of Jesus' place vis-à-vis other heavenly beings and God.

Given their historical importance, Revelation and *Asc. Isa.* have not really received the amount and quality of scholarly attention they deserve. This is unquestionably true for *Asc. Isa.*, which for a long time was widely ignored by scholars in Christian origins. In recent years, however, this situation has begun to change; there are now some valuable studies of this text that show its importance as an artifact of the devotion to Jesus offered in earliest Christianity.[81] Although Revelation fared somewhat better, this text too has recently been the focus of valuable studies relevant to our discussion.[82] With the benefit of such

---

clude the *Apocalypse of Abraham, Ladder of Jacob, Ascension of Isaiah*, Greek *Apocalypse of Baruch (3 Baruch), Shepherd of Hermas, Apocalypse of Peter*, and probably also the *Parables of Enoch*, the Slavonic *Apocalypse of Enoch (2 Enoch)*, and so-called 5 Ezra.

81. The work of a group of Italian scholars is essential. See the initial volume of studies, Mauro Pesce, ed., *Isaia, il diletto e la chiesa: Visione ed esegesi profetica christiano-primitiva nell' Ascensione di Isaia, Atti del convegno di Roma, 9-10 aprile 1981*, Testi e richerche di Scienze religiose 20 (Brescia: Paideia, 1983), of which Manlio Simonetti, "Note sulla cristologia dell' Ascensione di Isaia" (185-205 in Pesce) is especially relevant here. Out of this group has come an important volume on the text, and the only full-scale commentary: Paolo Bettiolo, Alda Giambelluca Kossova, Claudio Leonardi, Enrico Norelli, and Lorenzo Perrone, eds., *Ascensio Isaiae: Textus*, CCSA 7 (Turnhout: Brepols, 1995); Enrico Norelli, *Ascensio Isaiae: Commentarius*, CCSA 8 (Turnhout: Brepols, 1995). English-language scholars have also made important contributions recently, among which the following are especially relevant: Robert G. Hall, "The *Ascension of Isaiah:* Community Situation, Date, and Place in Early Christianity," *JBL* 109 (1990): 289-306; Jonathan Knight, *Disciples of the Beloved One: The Christology, Social Setting, and Theological Context of the "Ascension of Isaiah,"* JSPSup 18 (Sheffield: Sheffield Academic Press, 1996); Richard Bauckham, "The *Ascension of Isaiah:* Genre, Unity and Date," in *The Fate of the Dead*, 363-90; Darrell D. Hannah, "Isaiah's Vision in the *Ascension of Isaiah* and the Early Church," *JTS* 50 (1999): 80-101; Hannah, "The *Ascension of Isaiah* and Docetic Christology," *VC* 53 (1999): 165-96; Loren T. Stuckenbruck, "Worship and Monotheism in the *Ascension of Isaiah,"* in *The Jewish Roots of Christological Monotheism: Papers from the St. Andrews Conference on the Historical Origins of the Worship of Jesus*, ed. Carey C. Newman, James R. Davila, and Gladys S. Lewis, JSJSup 63 (Leiden: Brill, 1999), 70-89.

82. Earlier studies include Traugott Holtz, *Die Christologie der Apokalypse des Johannes*, TU 85 (Berlin: Akademie-Verlag, 1962); J. Comblin, *Le Christ dans l'apocalypse*, Théologie biblique 3/6 (Tournai: Desclée, 1965). More recently, several further major works have appeared: Richard J. Bauckham, *The Theology of the Book of Revelation* (Cambridge: Cambridge University Press, 1993); M. E. Boring, "Narrative Christology in the Apocalypse," *CBQ* 54 (1992): 702-23; Martin Hengel, "Die Throngemeinschaft des Lammes mit Gott in der Johannesapokalypse," *TBl* 3 (1996): 159-75; Peter Carrell, *Jesus and the Angels: Angelology and the Christology of the Apocalypse of John*, SNTSMS 95 (Cambridge: Cambridge University Press, 1997).

work, I focus on what these texts offer as evidence of how some Christians of the late first and early second centuries sought to honor Jesus within the context of a commitment to the uniqueness of God. I contend that both texts reflect a devotional stance that represents proto-orthodox Christianity of the time.

Revelation

Because it is commonly thought by scholars to be the earliest of the three visonary texts we are considering in the following pages (Revelation, *Ascension of Isaiah,* and *Shepherd of Hermas*), usually dated near the end of the first century, we commence with Revelation.[83] Unusually among the body of ancient Jewish and Christian writings that scholars refer to as "apocalyptic" texts, which are characterized by revelatory visions given to a human seer, Revelation is not pseudonymous. Scholars commonly accept that the actual author of Revelation is the named figure who claims to have received the visions and composed the book, a certain John, who also describes himself as a fellow Christian (1:9) and a prophet (22:8-9). Another unusual feature of Revelation is that it was sent initially to a specific group of seven Christian congregations identified in the Roman province of Asia (2:1–3:21). Our ability to identify the real author and initial recipients makes Revelation particularly valuable for historical purposes as an artifact of early Christianity.

The author's primary concern was not to engage in doctrinal development, but instead to urge perseverance in faith among the intended readers. This perseverance was to be exhibited above all in committed behavior, particularly renunciation of all idolatry, and a readiness to die rather than submit to the blasphemous demands of "the Beast" and participate in the ungodly and cruel system of political and economic power this figure represents. In the refrain in 13:10 and 14:12, the author shows that he issued this text as "a call for the endurance of the saints." I will return to this matter later, but here I want to emphasize that Revelation is also a noteworthy statement of beliefs about Jesus.

At various points Revelation gives us striking portrayals of Jesus. The first three chapters form a unit that opens with a vision of the glorified Jesus (1:12-20), who is described in terms derived from Old Testament scenes such as Daniel 7:9-10, 10:5-6, where the visual manifestation of God or one of his mighty

---

83. Bauckham has offered an interesting case for dating *Asc. Isa.* to 70-80 (*"Ascension of Isaiah,"* 381-90), but I do not think he has sufficiently shown the more widely supported dating in the second century to be less likely. See my brief discussion of the date below.

angels is recounted.[84] The author's point is obviously to portray this vision of Jesus as a theophanic event. The figure seen in this vision is not named, but his self-identification in 1:17-18 gives the crucial information that he is the one who "was dead" and is now "alive for ever and ever," and who now holds "the keys of Death and of Hades." In light of the opening statement that this writing is a "revelation of Jesus Christ" (1:1), and the subsequent characterizations of him as the "firstborn of the dead and the ruler of the kings of the earth," and the one "who loves us and freed us from our sins by his blood" (1:5-6), the identity of the august figure of 1:12-20 is unambiguously clear. He who is encountered here in theophanic glory is the same one whose bloody death was the crucial act that liberates and constitutes the redeemed as a royal priesthood acceptable to God.

This explicitly "high" view of Jesus is further developed in Revelation 2–3, where prophetic oracles are delivered in his name to seven Asian churches. It is utterly remarkable, however, that these oracles all represent the words of the glorified Jesus, for in the biblical tradition that the author obviously reveres the only legitimate source of prophetic inspiration is the one God (e.g., Deut. 13:1-5). Indeed, the prophet John is strongly antagonistic against those whom he regards as false prophets, both in the churches (e.g., 2:20-23) and in the larger religious environment of the time (19:20-21). Therefore, for him unhesitatingly to present his prophetic oracles as the words of Jesus indicates a profound inclusion of Jesus within the sphere of action otherwise restricted to God. Moreover, John's extremely hostile reaction against the religious innovations promoted by people he likens to the Old Testament figures Balaam (2:14) and Jezebel (2:20-24), shows that anything he approves of could hardly be recent. Instead, the view of Jesus depicted in Revelation 2–3 most likely reflects a long-standing tradition in the Christian circles in which John's views and practice were shaped.

But perhaps the most striking passage of all in Revelation is in the two-scene vision recounted in chapters 4–5.[85] This material claims to be an account of a heavenly ascent in which the prophet is allowed to see the inner sanctum where God's throne is. In the religious logic of this author, the scene amounts to the highest, truest reality, in the light of which everything else is to be judged by the readers. Revelation 4–5 in fact governs the whole of the remainder of the

---

84. C. C. Rowland, "The Vision of the Risen Christ in Rev. 1.13ff.: The Debt of an Early Christology to an Aspect of Jewish Angelology," *JTS* 31 (1980): 1-11.

85. L. W. Hurtado, "Revelation 4–5 in the Light of Jewish Apocalyptic Analogies," *JSNT* 25 (1985): 105-24. See also W. C. van Unnik, "'Worthy Is the Lamb': The Background of Apoc 5," in *Mélanges bibliques en hommage au R. P. Beda Rigaux*, ed. Albert Descamps and R. P. André Halleux (Gembloux: Duculot, 1970), 445-61; Russell Morton, "Glory to God and to the Lamb: John's Use of Jewish and Hellenistic/Roman Themes in Formatting His Theology in Revelation 4–5," *JSNT* 83 (2001): 89-109.

book, for readers are to view all the horrific events, the blasphemous demands of the Beast and the violent suffering that faces followers of Jesus, in the light of the vision in these chapters. In Revelation 4 God is pictured as firmly enthroned in the highest level of reality; the ceaseless praise from the heavenly courtiers (the "living creatures" and the twenty-four "elders") reflects the nature of that highest reality: God is supreme.

It is, therefore, all the more arresting that in Revelation 5 something completely unparalleled follows: we see vividly exhibited the radical innovation in monotheistic tradition that we noted as the "binitarian" devotional pattern of earliest Christianity. A second figure is mentioned, "the Lamb," who is acclaimed by the heavenly courtiers as alone worthy to receive and open the scroll that is held by God upon his throne (5:3-5). This scroll can only be the divine program of judgment, redemption, and final victory over evil, and the Lamb is thus designated as uniquely worthy to execute all that is involved.[86] The designation of Jesus as the Lamb reflects the author's emphasis on Jesus' sacrificial death as the key event that both secured the redemption of the elect and also serves as the model for their own commitment (e.g., 1:5-6; 5:9-10).

For our purposes, however, the most important feature of Revelation 5 is that the Lamb *receives heavenly worship* along with God (5:9-14). As Bauckham has shown, Revelation refuses to countenance worship of any other deity, or even of God's own angels (19:10; 22:8-9), a motif that is also attested in Jewish sources of the period.[87] This makes it all the more arresting that Revelation so vividly and jubilantly portrays Jesus as rightfully receiving worship with God. In 5:9-10 the "living creatures" and "elders," first mentioned in Revelation 4 as forming the heavenly circle who offer continuous worship to God, then sing a "new song" lauding the Lamb. Then, in 5:11-14, the entire wider company of heavenly beings joins in a similar song of praise to the Lamb, followed by a hymnic doxology directed jointly to God and the Lamb. In Swete's words, we have here "the roar of the great acclamation" of a vast host.[88]

In the religious values of this author, it would be difficult to imagine a

---

86. E.g., Henry Barclay Swete, *The Apocalypse of St. John,* 3rd ed. (Cambridge: Cambridge University Press, 1908), 75, judged that this scroll "contains no doubt the unknown future," and called it "the Book of Destiny." The description of the scroll seems influenced by Ezek. 2:9-10, but Ezekiel's scroll appears to be the divine plan that he is to pronounce in his prophecies.

87. Richard Bauckham, "The Worship of Jesus," in *The Climax of Prophecy: Studies on the Book of Revelation* (Edinburgh: T. & T. Clark, 1993), 118-49, is a crucially important study of this matter. See esp. 135. (This is an expanded version of his seminal article, "The Worship of Jesus in Apocalyptic Christianity," *NTS* 27 [1981]: 322-41.) See also Loren T. Stuckenbruck, *Angel Veneration and Christology,* WUNT 2/70 (Tübingen: J. C. B. Mohr [Siebeck], 1995).

88. Swete, *Apocalypse,* 83.

more direct and forceful way to express Jesus' divine status. The vision in Revelation 4–5 purports to convey the ultimate and ideal reality against which everything else is to be judged, and in the light of which all of humanity is to see its own proper duty. So, to represent the Lamb as receiving such adoration in Revelation 5 can only mean that this reverence has the highest justification and validity. Revelation 5, therefore, affirms the standard for the proper pattern of worship of the recipients of the book.[89] This does not mean, of course, that first-century readers were expected to use crowns, incense, and thrones, any more than they were expected to imitate the white linen attire of the heavenly beings in dressing for their church meetings! Rather, in this writing which is so concerned with condemning the worship of false and invalid objects of devotion (e.g., 9:20-21; 13:4; 14:9-11), the elaborate description of "binitarian" worship in Revelation 5 surely was intended to reinforce in the strongest terms the early Christian practice of including Jesus with God as recipients of worship on earth.[90]

Elsewhere as well, Revelation affirms the central importance of Jesus and his unique linkage with God. In 7:13-17, for example, we have an anticipatory vision of the elect pictured as redeemed by "the blood of the Lamb," and as having come out of "the great ordeal" that the author predicts will soon break upon the earth. Robed in white and rewarded for their faithfulness, they stand before God's throne and worship him "day and night within his temple" (7:15); "the Lamb at the center of the throne will be their shepherd," guiding them to everlasting life and joy (7:17). 14:1-5 describes the company of the redeemed as those who had the name of the Lamb and the name of the Father written on their foreheads; so the redeemed are identified with God and Jesus.[91] In the vision of final consummation in 21–22 the redeemed are pictured collectively as "the bride, the wife of the Lamb . . . the holy city Jerusalem coming down out of heaven from God" (21:9-10). This "city" has no temple, for "its temple is the Lord God the Almighty and the Lamb" (21:22), and "the glory of God is its light,

---

89. Lucetta Mowry, "Revelation 4–5 and Early Christian Liturgical Usage," *JBL* 71 (1952): 75-84; Otto A. Piper, "The Apocalypse of John and the Liturgy of the Ancient Church," *CH* 20 (1951): 10-22.

90. Swete (*Apocalypse,* 84) rightly notes that Rev. 5 likely reflects "the devotional attitude of the Asiatic Church" of the time of the text, as attested also a few decades later in Pliny's famous report that the Christians he arrested met to sing hymns to Christ as (a) God (Pliny, *Epistles* 10.96). Note also Eusebius, *HE* 5.28.5-6: "All the Psalms and hymns which were written by faithful Christians from the beginning sing of Christ as the Logos of God and treat him as God."

91. It is, in fact, quite plausible that the author refers to the name "Jesus" as both the name of the Lamb and the name of his Father. Note that the participle translated "written" (*gegrammenon*) is singular. We noted earlier that such a view of "Jesus" was touted by Justin and is probably reflected also in the Gospel of John.

and its lamp is the Lamb" (21:23). In the more detailed description of this glorious city in 22:1-5, the author twice refers to "the throne of God and of the Lamb" (22:1, 3). Such language obviously further confirms the point that Revelation reflects and promotes both a view of Jesus as intimately linked with God and a corresponding devotional practice that reveres Jesus along with God.

Neither this binitarian pattern of devotion attested in Revelation, in which Jesus is included with God as rightful recipient of worship, nor the claim to have had visions of heavenly realities in support of this pattern of devotion was a new phenomenon in earliest Christianity. The religious stance portrayed in Revelation reflects the devotional practice that can be traced back to our earliest extant sources of the Christian movement. Likewise, powerful religious experiences, such as visions of the glorified Jesus, are referred to in the earliest extant sources (letters of Paul).

The distinctive note in Revelation is the author's strident emphasis on the completely antithetical relationship between the worship of God and Jesus on the one hand, and the idolatrous demands of the Roman religious environment on the other hand, in particular the pressure of the emperor cult (represented in the "Beast"). This combative thrust surely reflects the actual or anticipated social situation of the author and his intended readers, in which demands that conflict with the rather traditionalist monotheistic stance that the prophet John affirms are made with ever increasing intensity.[92] In this situation, the author warns, Christians must either assent to these demands in order to save their lives or else refuse them, at the risk of forfeiting their lives on account of their commitment to the true God and Jesus. This emphasis on death as testimony to Jesus is taken up in early Christian accounts of martyrs, as we shall see shortly. The points I wish to underscore here are that the presentation of Jesus' exalted status in Revelation is unexcelled among first-century Christian texts, that Revelation presents what it says about Jesus as visions of his glorified and heavenly roles, and that, in particular, the heavenly worship of Jesus is the author's way of claiming the highest validity for the reverence of Jesus that he obviously practices and advocates.

---

92. In Rev. 1:1 the prophet describes his revelation as given to him by Jesus "to show his servants what must soon take place," which indicates that the full force of the ordeal portrayed in Revelation lies in the near future. On the sociopolitical situation, see, e.g., Leonard L. Thompson, *The Book of Revelation: Apocalypse and Empire* (New York: Oxford University Press, 1990).

Ascension of Isaiah

In comparison with Revelation, *Asc. Isa.* is much more difficult to identify with confidence as to time, provenance, and author. It is pseudonymous, presenting itself as written by the biblical prophet Isaiah (active ca. 740-680 B.C.E.), who recounts a vision that describes the transcendent origins of Jesus, and foretells his earthly appearance and subsequent ascent to heavenly glory. This vision involves Isaiah's ascent through the (seven) heavens until he finally sees the glory of God. Darrell Hannah has shown that this elaborate narrative in *Asc. Isa.* 6–11 is probably to be taken as an interpretative expansion of the account of the biblical Isaiah's vision of "the Lord" in Isaiah 6:1-5, a matter to which I return later in this discussion.[93]

The real author of *Asc. Isa.* successfully disguised his actual identity behind the persona of Isaiah, so we know only that he was a Christian. The only basis for scholarly guesswork about the date and provenance of the work is to identify references in the text that might be linked with known historical events and situations. The dates proposed by scholars range from the latter decades of the first century on down into the third century, with most nowadays favoring a date in the second century.[94] Moreover, scholars have differed over whether *Asc. Isa.* is a composite text that incorporates two or more bodies of material or is essentially the product of a single pseudonymous author.[95] In an important recent study of *Asc. Isa.*, however, Jonathan Knight claimed, "The present trend is to see the author as a creative individual who shaped his apocalypse from a variety of sources . . . but who cannot be considered an editor who soldered earlier documents."[96]

In any case, whatever the pseudonymous author drew upon in compos-

93. Hannah, "Isaiah's Vision," 85-90. There are some differences between the vision account in Isa. 6:1-5 and the lengthy ascent of Isaiah through the heavens in *Asc. Isa.* 6–9. But Hannah shows that the interpretative freedom of the author of *Asc. Isa.* in his use of Isa. 6:1-5 has ancient analogies.

94. Although a date sometime in the early decades of the second century enjoys favor in several recent studies, I shall indicate below why I incline toward the middle to late second century as more likely.

95. Cf., e.g., M. A. Knibb, "Martyrdom and Ascension of Isaiah," in *OTP*, 2:143-54 (143-76), who sees *Asc. Isa.* as a composite text; and Bauckham, "*Ascension of Isaiah*," esp. 368-74, who contends that it is a unified text probably from one author.

96. Knight, 28-32, quotation from p. 31. Hannah similarly refers to "the move toward viewing the work as a whole," and an emerging consensus on the probable date as sometime "in the early decades of the second century — or perhaps slightly earlier" ("Isaiah's Vision," 85). Hannah (85 n. 15) cites R. G. Hall, "The *Ascension of Isaiah*," and others who have come to similar views.

ing the work, whether written sources or simply a body of traditional motifs and themes, the text clearly comes from Christian hands; it represents a notable effort to articulate Jesus' high significance. Moreover, whatever the date of its present form, *Asc. Isa.* is deeply rooted in Christian traditions that go back into the first century. But the text also adapts these traditions in interesting ways.

For example, the favorite designation of Jesus in *Asc. Isa.*, "the Beloved One" (Gk. *ho agapētos*), has precedents in first-century Christian usage (e.g., Eph. 1:6), and also appears in Christian writings of the second century (e.g. *Barn.* 3.6; 4.3, 8).[97] The Christian uses constitute appropriations of a term that is found in Old Testament passages, where it was probably seen by early Christians as a messianic epithet (esp. Isa. 5:1; Ps. 45:1 [44:1 LXX]; Zech. 12:10). In all its Christian uses, "the Beloved One" emphasizes Jesus' intimate relationship to God; it signals the unique divine favor enjoyed by Jesus. In *Asc. Isa.*, however, the title more specifically designates Jesus in his heavenly and transcendent mode, both before and after his earthly incarnation; the author uses other epithets for Jesus' earthly existence. In a visionary encounter with an angel sent to reveal to him the future descent of the Beloved One and his heavenly glory, Isaiah is told that when the Beloved One comes into the world, he will be called "Jesus" and "Christ" (9.5, 13; 10.7-8).[98]

One of the recurrent emphases at various points in the text is the descent of the Beloved One from the highest heaven, and his subsequent ascent to share the glory of God. This descent involves his transformation into "the likeness of a man" (3.13). Only after he has accomplished this work will the redeemed be able to receive their future rewards of heavenly garments, thrones, and crowns, which are stored up for them until then (8.26; 9.12, 24-26).

After the account of Isaiah's ascent through the heavens (6–9), we have an extended passage presented as Isaiah's prophetic foretelling of the Beloved One's movement downward, and incognito, through multiple heavens to make his earthly/historic appearance as "Jesus." After being ordered by "the Most High, the Father of my Lord" to descend to the world (10.7-8), the Beloved One then passes through all the seven heavens, one by one. In the fifth heaven and downward, he successively transforms himself to resemble the angelic inhabitants of each level, a motif that receives considerable attention (10.9-10, 18, 20-30); in the third and second heavens he supplies the password required by the angels who guard the gates of these levels (10.27, 29). The purpose for all this se-

---

97. See, e.g., Knight, 153-57.

98. *Asc. Isa.* also refers to Jesus by other terms with roots in earlier Christian and Jewish traditions: "my/the Lord" (e.g., 5.6-7; 8.9-10; 9.4-5, 40; 10.18), "the Son" (8.25), "the Elect One" (8.7).

crecy in his descent is so that the various heavenly powers might not recognize who he is until after he has completed his redemptive work. Then God will announce openly his exaltation, and his appointment as judge over all "the princes and the angels and the gods of that world and the world which is ruled by them" (10.12).[99]

This motif of secrecy continues in 11.1-22, which foretells the human manifestation of Jesus. Here, however, in addition to a virginal conception (11.2-3) is a miraculous birth, with the infant Jesus who had been in her womb suddenly appearing to Mary full-born and without an ordinary delivery process (11.8-10, 14).[100] All of this, too, however, is "hidden from all the heavens and all the princes and every god of this world" (11.16). Indeed, the infant Jesus will suckle Mary's breast as does an ordinary infant, "that he might not be recognized" (11.17). When grown up, Jesus will work miracles in Israel and Jerusalem, and in jealous response Satan will rouse against him "the children of Israel, who did not know who he was" (11.19). This will lead to Jesus being crucified and his descent "to the angel who [is] in *Sheol*" (the realm of the dead). But "after the third day" he rises again, appears to his disciples and sends them out to preach (11.20-22). Thereafter we have a detailed description of Jesus' ascent back through the heavens (11.23-35). But in this upward movement he does not disguise himself, and so at each level the angelic inhabitants offer him praise and worship, now seeing his glory that was previously hidden from them (11.24).

The basic point of this elaborate drama was probably to emphasize for the intended Christian readers the enormity of what it meant for the Beloved One to descend from his supernal state to his earthly manifestation. The sevenfold heavens, the guardians of the three lower heavens, the elaborate effort of the Beloved One to preserve the secret of his identity — all these narrative features contribute to the sense of a redemptive intention in which God and the Beloved One invest a considerable effort. Moreover, the theme of the Beloved One concealing his transcendent nature and identity probably reflects a concern to emphasize that, though transcendent and divine, he had to accomplish human redemption through entering the earthly realm and operating within it as a human being. However unsophisticated, perhaps even crude, one might judge the result, the text likely represents an effort to posit both the true divine status of the Beloved and also the importance of his redemptive actions in the sphere of human existence.

99. Quotes are from the translation by M. A. Knibb in *OTP*, 2:143-76.

100. The motif of Jesus' birth as itself miraculous appears in several Christian texts of the late second century and later. See the review of evidence in Hannah, "The *Ascension of Isaiah*," 181-88.

Clearly, in *Asc. Isa.* the primary work of the Beloved One is to make possible the redemption of the elect through his earthly appearance, death, resurrection, and ascent to glory. This is distinguishable from other Christian texts that present the Savior figure essentially as a revealer of cognitive truths, and it is an important illustration that *Asc. Isa.* most likely emanated from proto-orthodox hands. Although Jonathan Knight judged the work to reflect a "naive docetism," that is, an insufficiently reflective reluctance to attribute full humanity to the incarnate Jesus, I find Hannah's analysis more persuasive. He argues that the emphasis on the reality and efficacy of Jesus' death shows that the text is not really "docetic" (compared to the treatment of Jesus' death in texts such as the *Acts of John*); Hannah also shows that second-century Christian readers would not necessarily have taken the account of Jesus' birth as advancing a docetic stance.[101]

Another important feature of *Asc. Isa.* is a repeated reference to worship as the key means by which to indicate the respective status of the various heavenly figures that Isaiah encounters in his own heavenly ascent. There is a crucial reference early in the narrative of Isaiah's ascent. Upon entering the second heaven Isaiah is so struck with the glory of an enthroned figure that he falls down to offer him worship. But the angel who is conducting Isaiah on the heavenly ascent orders him to desist, and instructs him not to worship any throne or angelic being that he encounters until he reaches the seventh heaven (7.18-23). This prohibition is a variant on the motif in Revelation where the prophet John is likewise forbidden to worship an angelic figure and is instructed to reserve worship for God alone (19:10; 22:8-9). The instance in *Asc. Isa.* shows that this author shares the strict attitude of Revelation about the proper recipient of worship.[102]

This makes it all the more significant that *Asc. Isa.* emphatically includes the Beloved with God in receiving worship in the heavenly spheres. In 7.13-17 the angel guide tells Isaiah that the praise and worship he sees being offered in the first level of heaven is directed to God, who is enthroned in the seventh heaven, "and to the Beloved" (7.17). 10.7-16 prophetically relates the voice of "the Most High" speaking to "my Lord Christ, who will be called Jesus." After telling him to descend to the world and the realm of death so that he may destroy the evil powers who wrongfully exercise rule over the world, God promises the Beloved that, after he ascends back to heavenly glory, "the princes and powers of that world will worship you" (10.15-16). In 8.16-28 the circle of legiti-

---

101. Cf. Knight, 139-41; Hannah, "The *Ascension of Isaiah*," esp. 188-96.

102. See Norelli, 400-406. Note also *Asc. Isa.* 8.3-5, where Isaiah addresses his angel guide as "my lord," and the angel corrects him: "I am not your lord, but your companion."

mate recipients of worship is wider still, as Isaiah joins the inhabitants of the sixth heaven in singing praises to "the primal Father and his Beloved Christ, and the Holy Spirit" (8.17-18), which looks very much like an implicit proto-trinitarian view of the divine. This triadic view is, in fact, signaled as early as 1.7, where Isaiah is pictured invoking in an oath "the Lord," "the Beloved of my Lord," and "the Spirit which speaks in me."

The most extended narrative of heavenly worship is in 9.27-42, however, where a similar triadic view is presented.[103] Having reached the seventh heaven, which is bathed in incomparable light, Isaiah sees innumerable angels and "all the righteous from the time of Adam onwards" (9.6-9). Then, after his angel guide explains how the descent of the Beloved One will make it possible for the righteous to receive their robes, crowns, and thrones (9.10-26), Isaiah sees a figure "whose glory surpassed that of all" being worshiped by Adam, Abel, and all the other righteous and angels (9.27-28). Crucially, at this point the angel guide directs Isaiah to "Worship this one," whom the angel identifies as "the Lord of all the praise which you have seen" (9.31-32), the Beloved One; Isaiah joins in the worship and sung praise directed to this figure. Then another glorious figure approaches, subsequently identified as "the angel of the Holy Spirit who has spoken in you and also in the other righteous" (9.36), and Isaiah is likewise told to join the angels in worshiping this one (9.35-36). Finally, in a carefully prepared climax to this scene, Isaiah sees "the Great Glory" (but with his spirit, for it appears that his eyes are blinded by the light of this glory, 9.37), and he relates how "my Lord" and "the angel of the Spirit" both offered worship to this third figure, along with "all the righteous" and the angels (9.40-42).

In the context of the prohibition in 7.21-22, these references to heavenly worship show that *Asc. Isa.* emphatically includes Jesus ("the Beloved"), and the Holy Spirit as well, with God ("the Father") in the narrowly restricted circle of proper recipients of worship. As in Revelation, the visionary scenes of heavenly worship in *Asc. Isa.* were intended to present the ideal and true realities that declare the proper pattern for corresponding human actions. Furthermore, as in Revelation, relating a vision of heavenly worship directed to Jesus is the favored mode for expressing his surpassing status, aligning him thereby with God and reflecting what amounts to a uniquely Christian revision of the monotheistic scruple inherited from the Jewish tradition of the early Roman period.

Yet, with Revelation (and characteristic of the devotional stance reflected in the earliest Christian texts), *Asc. Isa.* affirms the view that the Beloved (and

---

103. As Norelli noted (487), the scene here is similar to the one in *Apoc. Abr.* 17.1-6, where the angel guide tells Abraham to join in the heavenly worship that he encounters in the highest heaven.

the Holy Spirit) are rightful recipients of worship, and does so with a clear concern to avoid tritheism. As noted already, to refer to the transcendent Jesus as "the Beloved One" is implicitly to identify him with God "the Father." Moreover, *Asc. Isa.* presents the Beloved One's dramatic descent, its earthly consequences, and his glorious ascent as all fulfillment of the wish of the Father, the Beloved thus acting as the uniquely chosen agent of God's purposes.

This affirmation of monotheism (albeit the novel version characteristic of early Christianity) is perhaps most clearly dramatized in the extended scene of triadic worship in 9.27-42. The fully divine status of the Beloved ("the Lord of all the praise which you have seen") and the Holy Spirit is expressed in their being worshiped by all the company of beings in the highest heaven. The portrayal of these two in turn joining in worship of "the Great Glory" must surely signal the author's intention to avoid the idea that there are three gods. This liturgical subordination of the Beloved and the Holy Spirit to God, which could be characterized as a "monarchical monotheism," represents an effort to affirm a fundamental singularity behind the plurality. It also corresponds to the pattern of devotion in the traditions affirmed in proto-orthodox circles. In these traditions, for example, prayer is characteristically offered to God through and/ or in the name of Jesus, and the reverencing of Jesus is done "to the glory of God."[104] We may also recall 1 Corinthians 15:24-28, where Paul likewise asserts both Jesus' uniquely exalted status ("all things" under him) and also the subordination of "the Son" to God. *Asc. Isa.* fits readily within what I term here "proto-orthodox" Christianity, and the earlier suggestions of some scholars that the text has a heterodox or "gnostic" provenance are not tenable.[105]

Indeed, Hannah has proposed that *Asc. Isa.* reflects a primitive effort at what later became trinitarian doctrine. In *Asc. Isa.* this involved affirming the divinity of the Son (Beloved) and the Holy Spirit by distinguishing them from the angels, and yet also subordinating them to the Father to avoid tritheism. Interestingly, Hannah further proposes that *Asc. Isa.* also reflects an early Christian exegetical tradition that is attested in other early Christian sources, in which the vision of "the Lord" flanked by heavenly figures called seraphim in Isaiah 6:1-5 is interpreted as a vision of God flanked by the Son (Logos) and the Holy Spirit.[106] This interpretation of Isaiah 6:1-5 contrasts with the exegesis of

---

104. See Hannah, "Isaiah's Vision," 90-99, for references in Origen and Irenaeus to a similar motif of the subordination of the Son and Holy Spirit to the Father expressed in picturing them joining in the worship of the Father.

105. See esp. Knight, 170-85.

106. Hannah, "Isaiah's Vision," esp. 85-90, 99-101. The idea that there are two seraphim in Isa. 6:1-5 is attested in pre-Christian tradition, where the passage can be interpreted as a vision of God or the Logos, flanked by the two principal attributes or "powers" of God (justice and

the passage alluded to in John 12:41, reflected in a number of other early Christian texts as well, in which Isaiah's vision of "the Lord" is understood as of the preincarnate Jesus (Son, Logos), the seraphim being his heavenly attendants.[107]

Accepting an early second-century date for *Asc. Isa.*, Hannah suggests that this text shows that this trinitarian reading of Isaiah 6:1-5 arose very early, perhaps as early as the other Christian exegesis reflected in John 12:41 (i.e., in the late first century).[108] But Origen (ca. 200-250) gives us the earliest datable attestation of the interpretation of the seraphim of Isaiah 6:1-5 as the Son and the Holy Spirit, whereas the exegesis of Isaiah 6:1-5 as a vision of the Son is attested in unquestionably earlier sources (Gospel of John, Justin, Irenaeus). So I am inclined to suspect that *Asc. Isa.* 9.27-42 may indicate that we should date this important writing a bit later, perhaps in the latter part of the second century, when the early trinitarian exegesis of Isaiah 6:1-5 may have begun to appear.[109]

But, whether composed in the early or later second century, *Asc. Isa.* is an important historical witness to early Christian devotion to Jesus; it also incorporates and develops devotional traditions that are undeniably earlier still, making it a valuable early Christian text.[110] Among the traditions taken up in *Asc. Isa.* is the affirmation of Jesus' divine status through relating visions of him receiving worship in heaven. This phenomenon likely originated in the earliest

---

mercy). See esp. Georg Kretschmar, *Studien zur frühchristlichen Trinitätstheologie*, BHT 21 (Tübingen: Mohr [Siebeck], 1956). The early Christian exegetical tradition cited by Hannah is, thus, almost certainly a distinctive adaptation.

107. Justin (*Dial.* 37.3; 64.4, citing Ps. 98:1-7 LXX) refers to the Logos as "he who sits above the Cherubim," and Irenaeus (*Adv. haer.* 3.11.8, citing Ps. 79:2 LXX) does as well. For these and other references to early Christian texts that reflect the view that Isa. 6:1-5 was a vision of the Son/Logos, see Hannah, "Isaiah's Vision," 80-84.

108. Hannah, "Isaiah's Vision," 99-101.

109. I also wonder if the treatment of Jesus' birth in *Asc. Isa.* 11.1-18 further points to a date in the latter part of the second century. The concern to assert a miraculous *birth* that preserves Mary's virginity has its earliest parallel in the *Infancy Gospel [Protevangelium] of James*, which we noted in a previous chapter, and which is commonly dated no earlier than the late second century. Bauckham, who argues for a late-first-century date for *Asc. Isa.*, does not discuss either the trinitarian motif in 9.27-42 or the account of Jesus' birth: "*Ascension of Isaiah*," 381-90.

110. With *Asc. Isa.* there are problems somewhat similar to those we noted about the texts from Nag Hammadi. Though *Asc. Isa.* was composed in Greek, only one fragmentary manuscript survives (P.Amherst 1.1, fifth or sixth century, provenance unknown), and we are mainly dependent on later translations, especially Ethiopic, but also Latin and Slavonic, preserved in manuscripts from the late medieval period. But where we are able to compare the Ethiopic with the Greek fragments, scholars judge it a relatively faithful translation. Certainly, however, it is clear that its transmission involved the same sort of textual fluidity found in many other writings. For a review of the textual tradition, see Knight, 21-28. But for thorough discussion, see Bettiolo, *Ascensio Isaiae: Textus*.

years of the Christian movement when claims to have had such experiences figured influentially in promoting the view that Jesus had been exalted to a heavenly position that required worship. The Revelation of the prophet John and *Asc. Isa.* probably show us that such claims had become sufficiently familiar in Christian circles that the authors of these texts could expect Christian readers to accept the visionary narratives that they present in support of Jesus' exalted status.

Shepherd of Hermas

The remaining major example of visionary text of the period is the *Shepherd of Hermas* (herafter *Hermas*).[111] This lengthy work is commonly thought today to have been composed (or at least put into its present form) in Rome sometime in the first half of the second century.[112] Compared to Revelation and *Asc. Isa.*, it offers a much more modest amount of material on Jesus. The visions conveyed in *Hermas* are almost entirely concerned with ethical teaching, with particular concerns about forgiveness for postbaptismal sins, and Christian "double-mindedness" (i.e., the inability to match the profession of Christian faith with a consistent ethical effort). Its theology is largely very traditional, and the author seems either little concerned or ill equipped to contribute much toward developing further the beliefs about Jesus that he inherited. Two passages in the *Similitudes* (or *Parables*) are commonly seen as the main places where the text deals with Jesus at any length: *Similitudes* 5 and 9.[113]

The favorite designation for Jesus in *Hermas* is "the Son of God," and he is also referred to as "Lord" *(kyrios).* Neither "Jesus" nor "Christ" appears in the writing. But, indicative of the very traditional Christian faith of its author, *Hermas* emphasizes the unique redemptive significance of the "name" of the Son of God: e.g., "no one will enter the kingdom of God unless he receives the

111. See J. B. Lightfoot, J. R. Harmer, and Michael W. Holmes, *The Apostolic Fathers: Greek Texts and English Translations of Their Writings,* 2nd ed. (Grand Rapids: Baker, 1992), 329-527, for brief introduction, Greek text, and English translation. Carolyn Osiek, *The Shepherd of Hermas,* Hermeneia (Minneapolis: Fortress, 1999), is the most recent commentary on the text.

112. *Hermas* comprises five "Visions," twelve "Mandates," and ten "Parables/Similitudes"; some scholars have suggested multiple authors. Osiek, however, cogently proposes "a theory of sequential composition" (i.e., the three bodies of material composed across a period of time) as "the simplest solution," and rightly sees sufficient thematic unity in *Hermas* to indicate "a guiding hand throughout" (Osiek, 10).

113. Philippe Henne, *La christologie chez Clément de Rome et dans le Pasteur d'Hermas,* Paradosis 33 (Fribourg: Éditions universitaires Fribourg, 1992).

name of his Son" (*Sim.* 9.12.4 [89:4]).[114] In the same passage Jesus is referred to as God's beloved Son (9.12.5 [89:5]), "the door," and "this one entrance to the Lord," through whom all must come if they wish to enter into God (9.12.6 [89:6]). Even the six "glorious angels" who act as an honor guard of the Son "on his right and on his left" cannot enter God's presence without the Son (9.12.8 [89:8]). Referring to the Son of God as "far older than all [God's] creation," and as "the Father's counsellor in his creation," *Hermas* clearly also reflects belief in Jesus' preexistence (9.12.2 [89:2]). In a later passage *Hermas* refers to the name of the Son of God as "great and incomprehensible," sustaining "the whole world." "Those who bear his name" are assured, therefore, that the Son of God will sustain them also, "because they are not ashamed to bear his name" (9.14.5 [91:5]).

Another passage, however, has presented some difficulty for interpreters. When Hermas asks his angel guide to explain the parable he related earlier featuring a master, his son, and a particular slave whom the master places in charge of his vineyard (*Sim.* 5.2 [55:1-11]), the angel guide identifies the son as the Holy Spirit and the slave as the Son of God (5.5 [58:2]). Then, asked by Hermas why the Son of God is presented "in the guise of a slave" *(eis doulou tropon keitai)*, the angel initially emphasizes the "great power and lordship" of the Son of God, whom God has placed over his "vineyard," identified by the angel as God's people (5.6 [59:1-2]). Thereafter the angel explains that "the Son himself cleansed their sins with great labor and enduring much toil" (5.6 [59:2]). Having cleansed their sins, the Son showed the redeemed "the paths of life, giving them the law which he received from his Father"; for he is "Lord of the people, having received all power from his Father" (5.6 [59:3-4]). Here *Hermas* simply echoes traditional beliefs about Jesus as the unique agent of divine redemption, who undergoes sufferings in fulfillment of his obedience to the Father, as a consequence of which he is now the authoritative "Lord" through whose teaching the redeemed are now required to exhibit their obedience to God.

The difficult part of this passage then follows. The angel states that God caused "the pre-existent Holy Spirit, which created the whole creation," to dwell in "the flesh that he wished" (5.6 [59:5]). Being thus indwelt by the Spirit, this flesh "served the Spirit well, living in holiness and purity." Therefore, taking "the Son and the glorious angels as counselors," God rewarded this virtuous

---

114. There are two quite different reference systems used today. In the older system, one cites the number of whichever of these bodies of material is being cited (e.g., *Vis.* 1), whereas the newer system employs a continuous numbering of chapters. I use both here, with the newer reference placed in square brackets.

and obedient "flesh" with "a place to dwell" (5.6 [59:7]). The angel then concludes with the assurance that "all flesh in which the Holy Spirit has lived, if it proves to be undefiled and spotless," will receive a reward from God.

The question scholars have debated is whether the "flesh" here is Jesus.[115] The idea that Jesus was empowered by the Holy Spirit in his earthly life and work is hardly in itself problematic, being well attested in the New Testament (e.g., Acts 10:36-41). Likewise, the notion that, on account of his obedience to God, Jesus was exalted to a glorious status has early roots and is affirmed comfortably by Paul, for example (Rom. 1:3-4; Phil. 2:9-11). But does this passage in *Hermas* reflect a "low" theological view of Jesus as a mere man indwelt by the divine Spirit and subsequently rewarded by God? That is, do we have here an "adoptionist" view of Jesus presented as a revelation by the angel guide, in sharp distinction from the assertions elsewhere in *Hermas* (e.g., *Sim.* 9) about the preexistence of the Son of God?

The phrasing of *Similitude* 5 is not the clearest one could ask for, but I submit that a careful reading will lead to the conclusion that the discussion of the "flesh" indwelt by the Spirit is not really intended to make a christological point of any kind. Instead, as the angel's generalizing statement that all flesh that lives obedient to the Spirit will receive a reward indicates, the passage is really concerned with giving believers an incentive to live virtuous lives. They are to see themselves in the "flesh" indwelt by the Spirit here. This is confirmed in the angel's exhortation to Hermas in the following paragraph to keep his own flesh clean and undefiled so that the Spirit that indwells him may testify to his virtue and Hermas's flesh may be "justified" (*dikaiōthē*; 5.7 [60:1]). So this passage is almost certainly not espousing an "adoptionist" Christology.

In short, though *Hermas* is a visionary text like Revelation and *Asc. Isa.*, the revelations conveyed in it have to do almost entirely with ethical questions; the text essentially presupposes and affirms basic ideas about Jesus as the key agent of divine redemption that are attested in numerous other texts of proto-orthodox circles of the time. As sent forth from God, Jesus can be referred to as God's particular *angelos* (messenger), which surely forms a part of the conceptual categories used in *Hermas*. But Jesus is distinguished as the "*one* angel of ultimate importance," and is not simply one among others.[116] In *Hermas*, and in Christian tradition characteristically, Jesus himself is sent by God, but

---

115. See now the balanced discussion by Osiek, 179-81, with copious references to the scholarly debate.

116. Halvor Moxnes, "God and His Angel in the *Shepherd of Hermas*," *ST* 28 (1974): 55 (49-56). E.g., in *Vis.* 5.1 the shepherd is sent to Hermas by "the revered angel [*tou semnotatou angelou*]"; in *Sim.* 9.3 the same figure is referred to as "the glorious angel [*tou endoxou angelou*]"; and in *Sim.* 10.1, probably the same angel figure addresses Hermas.

Hermas reflects the unique status of Jesus by picturing him also sending angels, a role associated exclusively with God in ancient Jewish tradition.[117]

Worship and Prayer

Both early Christians and contemporaries outside their circles considered worshiping Jesus the distinguishing mark of Christian religion.[118] We have seen that the "binitarian" pattern of devotion in which both God (the "Father") and Jesus are objects of such reverence goes back to the earliest observable stages of the movement that became Christianity. Certainly, in the period under consideration here, treating Jesus as rightful recipient of worship along with God was an uncontested and central feature of the religious life of those varied circles that constituted proto-orthodox Christianity. In Clement of Alexandria's quotations of the early-second-century writing called the *Kerygma Petrou*, Christians are exhorted to "reverence [*sebesthe*] God through Christ in a new way," which surely indicates the tight connection of Jesus with God in Christian worship and reflects an awareness of the innovation it represented in comparison with Jewish devotional traditions.

We have a more extended illustration of this binitarian pattern in Justin's description of Christian worship in *1 Apology* 13. Justin explains that, instead of sacrificial rites of blood and incense, Christians offer thanks to God "by invocations and hymns" *(dia logou pompas kai hymnous)*, and present to God their petitions, doing these things as taught by Jesus. Then Justin indicates that, having been taught that Jesus is God's Son and holds "the second place" (next to God), Christians worship him as well (13.3). Noting that outsiders consider it madness for Christians to give "to a crucified man a place second to the unchangeable and eternal God, the creator of all," Justin then announces his aim: to set forth for his intended pagan readers the divine secret truth *(mystērion)* that critics fail to see, but that is reflected in the pattern of Christian devotion (13.4).

---

117. Moxnes was not quite right, however, to claim that the enfranchising of Jesus with this sending role was "quite new compared to the tradition" (56). Mark 13:26-27 presents "the son of man" (who for Mark is obviously Jesus) sending out angels to "gather his elect," which is only one of a number of ways in which, from the earliest stages onward, Christian tradition pictured Jesus sharing in the attributes and functions otherwise reserved for God alone.

118. Graham N. Stanton, "Aspects of Early Christian and Jewish Worship: Pliny and the *Kerygma Petrou*," in *Worship, Theology, and Ministry in the Early Church: Essays in Honor of Ralph P. Martin*, ed. M. A. Wilkins and T. Paige, JSNTSup 87 (Sheffield: JSOT Press, 1992), 84-98. The discussion of second-century Christian worship by Jules Lebreton (*Histoire du dogme de la Trinité, des origines au concile de Nicée*, 2 vols. [1910; reprint, Paris: G. Beauchesne, 1928], 2:174-247) remains unsurpassed in combining breadth, focus, and sympathetic analysis.

Outsiders and Critics

Moreover, Jewish and pagan critics of early Christianity agreed in seeing the worship of Jesus as one of the most objectionable features of the young faith. The famous report to Trajan from the Roman magistrate Pliny offers valuable early confirmation (Pliny, *Epistles* 10.96-97). As Stanton pointed out, Pliny's letter is "the first report on early Christian worship which we have from an 'outsider.'"[119] From his interrogation of apostate Christians and his torture of two unnamed Christian women "deaconesses" *(ministrae)*, Pliny derived information on what Christians did in their weekly gatherings "on a fixed day" (probably Sunday).[120] The first and most prominent action in Pliny's summary of their regular meetings is that they chant a hymn "to Christ as to a god."[121]

In itself, however, reverencing Jesus as divine would likely not have been such a problem. A sophisticated Roman such as Pliny was quite ready to accept religious diversity, and was well aware that a variety of gods and heroes were reverenced in various religious circles. Nor did recognizing another new deity present a difficulty. What caused Pliny's concern about the Christians in Bithynia was that their reverence of Jesus as divine was accompanied by *a refusal to reverence images of "the gods" and the emperor*. This religious *exclusivity* created a major (indeed, sometimes a mortal) social and political problem for Christians, and it made their worship of Jesus pointedly offensive to pagan outsiders.[122] As Finney observed, "Refusal to worship set a clear boundary between the new [Christian] religionists and their neighbors."[123] Robert Grant proposed that the Romans came to require Christians to offer sacrifice precisely

119. Stanton, "Aspects of Early Christian and Jewish Worship," 85. For a sympathetic sketch of Pliny the man, see Robert L. Wilken, *The Christians as the Romans Saw Them* (New Haven and London: Yale University Press, 1984), 1-30.

120. Stanton, "Aspects of Early Christian and Jewish Worship," 88-89.

121. Pliny also says Christians take an oath *(sacramento)* not to steal, commit adultery, break their word, or deny a deposit when it is demanded of them. J. Stevenson suggested that, if the ex-Christian informers used the word *sacramentum,* they may have meant "sacrament," whereas Pliny took the word in its usual sense of "oath." J. Stevenson, ed., *A New Eusebius: Documents Illustrative of the History of the Church to* A.D. *337* (London: SPCK, 1974), 15. A. N. Sherwin-White, *The Letters of Pliny: A Historical and Social Commentary* (Oxford: Clarendon, 1966), 706-7, discusses more fully such proposals. Stanton suggested, however, that *sacramentum* here refers to "a general list of Christian (and Jewish) ethical teaching" ("Aspects of Early Christian and Jewish Worship," 93).

122. So also Stanton, "Aspects of Early Christian and Jewish Worship," 90.

123. Paul Corby Finney, *The Invisible God: The Earliest Christians on Art* (New York: Oxford University Press, 1994), 105. "So far as I am aware, only two outward marks identified the earliest Christians. . . . One was the name [Christian]. . . . Second, some Christians refused to worship the gods and caesar."

because they had learned that this was a particularly effective way of distinguishing true believers from apostates or people falsely accused of being Christians. That is, the exclusivist devotional stance of Christians seems to have shaped Roman judicial practice toward them.[124]

But this exclusivity of devotion also signals the religious significance that worshiping Jesus had for Christians. They gave the sort of reverence to Jesus that they otherwise reserved for "God the Father" alone, regarding it apostasy to give such reverence to any of the other deities touted in their culture. Pliny wrote that he let anyone accused of being a Christian go free if they reverenced the images of the gods, made supplication to the emperor's image, and "cursed Christ"; for Pliny was reliably informed that these were things that "those who are really Christians cannot be made to do." Reverencing Jesus as uniquely divine, or cursing him — here lies the crucial matter in Pliny's account of how to tell a true Christian from someone falsely accused of being one. As Lebreton noted, "For this magistrate, as for his victims, the characteristic trait of the Christian religion is the rendering of homage to Christ 'as to a god,' and faithful loyalty to his service."[125] Justin (who later had his own opportunity to confirm his words in martyrdom) says, "though threatened with death, we do not deny his [Jesus'] name" (*Dial.* 30.2).

A few decades later, in Justin's account of a disputation with Trypho and a couple of his Jewish compatriots, we see that the Christian reverence of Jesus was clearly a very sensitive issue for Jews as well. The *Dialogue* is a large and invaluable window on the issues under disputation between traditional Jews and early Christians.[126]

Of course, Trypho and the other Jews in the *Dialogue* object to Justin's other claims about Jesus as well, such as his virginal conception and his messianic significance. In particular, Trypho insists that Jesus' accursed death by crucifixion invalidates any claim that he could be Messiah (e.g., *Dial.* 32.1; 89.1; 90.1). But Trypho calls the worship of Jesus the most objectionable matter of all, and for his part, Justin considers the worship of Jesus as divine to be the crucial claim to justify.

For example, Trypho accuses Justin of "many blasphemies" in claiming

---

124. Robert M. Grant, "Sacrifices and Oaths as Required of Early Christians," in *Kyriakon. Festschrift Johannes Quasten,* ed. Patrick Granfield and Josef A. Jungmann, 2 vols. (Münster: Verlag Aschendorff, 1970), 1:12-17.

125. Lebreton, *Histoire,* 2:204 (my translation).

126. Adolf von Harnack noted that Justin's *Dialogue* is the largest Christian writing from the years before Irenaeus (ca. 180), larger than Matthew, Luke, and John combined, and twice the size of the next largest second-century writing, *Hermas* (*Judentum und Judenchristentum in Justins Dialog mit Trypho,* TU 39/1 [Leipzig: Hinrichs, 1913], 47 [47-98]).

that Jesus is the divine "Lord" of Old Testament theophanies, that he became incarnate and was crucified and ascended to heavenly glory, and that he "ought to be worshipped" (*kai proskynēton einai;* 38.1). The climactic position on the list of the claim that Jesus should be worshiped as divine is probably intended to present this as the most outrageous feature of the items under dispute for Trypho and other Jews. Other passages confirm the importance of the matter, both for Justin and for Jewish outsiders of the day (e.g., 63.13-14; 64). On this subject (as on other features of second-century Jewish beliefs and practice referred to in Justin's *Dialogue*) we have reason to take the account as accurate.[127]

Furthermore, in all the reported views of critical outsiders in the first two centuries, whether pagans or Jews, Christian worship is characterized as essentially directed toward Jesus, as Lebreton showed in an incisive analysis that included Pliny, the account of Polycarp's martyrdom, Lucian, and Celsus.[128] In fact, in this early period, outsiders tend to portray Christian worship rather simply as directed to Jesus solely, though the actual pattern of Christian worship appears to have been more what we should call "binitarian," God and Jesus the recipients.

As we have already taken note of Pliny, let us quickly consider these other witnesses, beginning with Lucian of Samosata. Around 170 Lucian complained that Christians reject "the Hellenistic gods [*theous men tous hellēnikous haparnēsōntai*] in order to worship this crucified sophist and to live according to his laws" (*Peregrinus* 13). About the same time as Lucian, and probably with a better knowledge of Christian practice and writings, Celsus pilloried Christians for their "excessive worship" (*hyperthrēskeuousi)* of the one they refer to as "the Son of God" (Origen, *Contra Celsum* 8.12). Though Christians reject the worship of the gods, claiming to revere only the one true God, Celsus says they act inconsistently with this in their unjustified exaltation of the man Jesus. As Lebreton observed, Celsus correctly saw what was central in Christianity: "the adoration of one unique God, rejecting as impiety all polytheism, and uniting in the same worship the Son of God with his Father."[129]

---

127. Of the numerous analyses of Justin's references to Judaism in *Dialogue*, the following are particularly relevant: Harnack, *Judentum und Judenchristentum in Justins Dialog mit Trypho;* A. J. B. Higgins, "Jewish Messianic Belief in Justin Martyr's *Dialogue with Trypho," NovT* 9 (1967): 298-305; Barnard, *Justin Martyr,* 39-52; G. N. Stanton, "Aspects of Early Christian-Jewish Polemic and Apologetics," *NTS* 31 (1985): 377-92. Justin's apparent claim in *Dial.* 68.9 that Jewish teachers actually admit that Messiah "will come to suffer, and to reign, and to be worshipped as (a) God" is either the rhetorical excess claimed by Higgins (305) or else Justin pronouncing what he sees as the logical implications of Jewish messianic exegesis, whether recognized by Jewish teachers or not. In any case, other passages clearly show that Jews such as Trypho were not prepared to worship any figure other than God, the Messiah included (e.g., *Dial.* 68.3-4).

128. Lebreton, *Histoire,* 2:204-8.

129. Lebreton, *Histoire,* 2:206 (my translation).

In the account of the martyrdom of Polycarp in Smyrna (ca. 155-160), the Roman official conducting the hearing repeatedly demands that Polycarp reverence the emperor, and also urges him to "curse Christ" and thereby save himself from death (*Mart. Pol.* 8.2; 9.2-3; 10.1). This echoes the demand Pliny made of Bithynian Christians a few decades earlier. Polycarp's unforgettable reply only confirms that the key issue was reverence of Jesus: "For eighty-six years I have been his servant, and he has done me no wrong. How can I blaspheme my King who saved me?" (9.3).[130] After Polycarp's fiery end, Jewish members of the hostile crowd petition the Roman official not to give the corpse to the Christians, for fear that "they will abandon the crucified one to offer worship to this one" (17.12). The early Christian editors of the account, however, portray this allegation as rank ignorance, and they insist that the worship Christians give Jesus is categorically different from the regard in which they hold martyrs "as disciples and imitators of the Lord" (17.2-3). Even though the account of Polycarp's martyrdom comes from Christian hands and obviously had a propagandistic purpose, the insistent demand of the Roman official and the allegation of the Jews in the narrative are probably authentic indications that in the eyes of second-century outsiders "the object of Christian worship is the crucified one."[131]

Hymnody

The phenomena that constituted the worship of Jesus in proto-orthodox circles of the second century were mainly those we noted in earlier chapters. This is what we should expect, given that a high regard for tradition is a major feature of these circles. As indicated in Pliny's now-famous phrase, one central feature of Christian worship was the chanting/singing of hymns concerned with, and at least in some cases directed to, Jesus. In an analysis that remains essential for scholarship on the subject, Kroll observed that Christian hymnody of the first two centuries was almost entirely concerned with Jesus, a judgment reached later by Deichgräber as well in his study of hymns in the New Testament.[132] The regular inclusion of such hymns in Christian worship clearly signified Jesus' di-

130. Whether authentically Polycarp or the words of those who wrote the account, the reply authentically expresses the point that exclusive devotion to Jesus was the central issue in the second-century conflicts with the state authorities that led to Christian martyrdom.

131. Lebreton, *Histoire*, 2:205 (my translation).

132. Joseph Kroll, *Die christliche Hymnodik bis zu Klemens von Alexandreia* (Königsberg: Hartungsche Buchdruckerei, 1921), 44; Reinhard Deichgräber, *Gotteshymnus und Christushymnus in der frühen Christenheit: Untersuchungen zu Form, Sprache und Stil der frühchristlichen Hymnen*, SUNT 5 (Göttingen: Vandenhoeck & Ruprecht, 1967).

vine status in early Christian circles; the contents of these hymns also likely had a key role in promoting christological teaching in an accessible and influential manner among Christians.

Unfortunately, only hints and fragments survive of what must have been a large body of such hymnody.[133] For example, it is commonly accepted that we have an important allusion to the Christian practice of singing hymns in the letter to Ephesian Christians from Ignatius of Antioch (ca. 110). Developing an extended musical metaphor, Ignatius urges the Ephesian church to act together in harmony with their bishop, so that "taking your pitch from God you may sing in unison with one voice through Jesus Christ to the Father" (Ign. *Eph.* 4.1-2). Ignatius's rhetorical device here practically requires the original readers to be familiar with the practice of congregational singing of praise directed to God through Jesus. There is another allusion to the practice in his letter to the Roman church, where he portrays his looming martyrdom as an offering to God and urges the Roman Christians to "form a chorus and sing to the Father in Jesus Christ," because God has deemed Ignatius worthy of this death (Ign. *Rom.* 2.2).

As we noted in characterizing the worship practices of Pauline Christianity and other first-century circles, the songs of Christian worship included biblical psalms (understood as speaking of Jesus) and also fresh compositions prompted by the religious exaltation attributed to the Holy Spirit. In earliest Christianity these newly composed Christian hymns probably echoed the cadences of the Greek Psalter, rather than conforming to the conventions of Greek poetry of the time.[134] By the later decades of the second century and among Christians more adept at Greek literary style, however, it appears that Christian hymnody was beginning to reflect Greek poetic features, as is illustrated in the oft-cited hymn to Jesus that concludes Clement of Alexandria's *The Instructor*. In this poetic gem, there is an abundance of images celebrating Jesus' significance as, for example, the shaper of Christian conduct; the divine Word of the Father; the Shepherd, Fisher, and King; and Christians are characterized as "those who raise unto God their hymn of praise, Jesus Christ!"[135] From perhaps the same period, the hymn known as the *Phōs Hilaron* lauds Jesus as "Joyous light of the holy glory of the immortal Father," and proclaims it fitting that "at all times you should be praised with auspicious voices, Son of God, Giver of Life." [136]

---

133. See esp. Kroll for an unsurpassed discussion of the evidence. On 35-39 Kroll considers reasons why so little survives.

134. Joseph T. Lienhard, "Poetry," in *EEC*, 2:931-33; Everett Ferguson, "Hymns," in *EEC*, 1:548-51.

135. ANF, 2:295-96.

136. Antonia Tripolitis, "ΦΩΣ ΙΛΑΡΟΝ: Ancient Hymn and Modern Enigma," *VC* 24 (1970): 189-96; E. R. Smothers, "ΦΩΣ ΙΛΑΡΟΝ," *RSR* 19 (1920): 266-83.

Odes of Solomon

If, however, as most scholars contend, the collection of forty-two compositions known as the *Odes of Solomon* can rightly be dated to sometime in the second century, they constitute our earliest extant collection of Christian hymns.[137] James Charlesworth referred to the *Odes* as "a window through which we can occasionally glimpse the earliest Christians at worship."[138] They certainly reflect an impressive religious intensity and memorable poetic imagery. To cite one particularly striking example, 19.1-5 refers to Jesus as the "cup" from which the redeemed drank "the milk of the two breasts of the Father," which were milked by "the Spirit of holiness."[139] David Aune says the *Odes* preserve a distinctive type of early Christian utterance, "the prophetic hymn," in which Jesus speaks in first person, a matter to which I return shortly.[140]

Moreover, whether originally composed in Syriac (or some other Semitic language) or Greek (the other favored option), the *Odes* exhibit similarities in poetic style to the biblical Psalms, and even more closely to the collection of devotional poetry from the Qumran community known as the *Hodayot*.[141] The closest parallels in New Testament writings are probably the Psalm-like passages in the Lukan birth narrative (1:46-55; 68-79). That is, these Christian *Odes* show connections with the poetic patterns of the biblical/Jewish matrix of earliest Christianity.

Although sometimes in the past categorized as "gnostic," nothing in the *Odes* requires, or even really justifies, this view. For example, there is no distinc-

---

137. Dates for the collection vary from the late first to the early third century, with the favored options today being early or late second century. Cf., e.g., Johannes Quasten, *Patrology*, 4 vols. (Westminster, Md.: Christian Classics, 1950-86), 1:160-68; James H. Charlesworth, "Odes of Solomon," in *OTP*, 2:725-71 ("probably sometime around A.D. 100," 725); Majella Franzmann, *The "Odes of Solomon": An Analysis of the Poetical Structure and Form*, NTOA 20 (Göttingen: Vandenhoeck & Ruprecht, 1991), 2 ("the second half of the second century"). Unless otherwise indicated, I quote from Charlesworth's translation. That there are forty-two of these odes (i.e., 3 x 14) may have been intended to connote the Davidic messianic theme, as is signaled in the Matthean genealogy in which scholars commonly recognize the fourteen as the numerical value of "David" in Hebrew (*DWD* = 4 + 6 + 4).

138. Charlesworth, "Odes of Solomon," 728.

139. Somewhat similar imagery, however, also appears in Clement's hymn to Christ at the end of the *Instructor*.

140. Aune, *Prophecy*, 296.

141. Bonnie Kittel, *The Hymns of Qumran*, SBLDS 50 (Chico, Calif.: Scholars, 1981); James H. Charlesworth, "Jewish Hymns, Odes, and Prayers (ca. 167 B.C.E.–135 C.E.)," in *Early Judaism and Its Modern Interpreters*, ed. Robert A. Kraft and G. W. E. Nickelsburg (Atlanta: Scholars, 1986), 411-36; Charlesworth, *Critical Reflections on the "Odes of Solomon"* (Sheffield: Sheffield Academic Press, 1998), 192-231.

tion between the creator and the true God; nor do the *Odes* reflect any other emphasis or idea that was distinctive to any heterodox circle. The intense religious feeling behind them, the strong sense of the present reality of redemption, and the expressions of spiritual union with Jesus were characteristic of a wide spectrum of early Christian circles. We have a clear reflection of the function of these compositions in 16.3, where the speaker announces, "My love is the Lord; hence I shall sing to him." Similarly 26.1-4 refers to pouring forth "a hymn to the Lord," glorifying and exalting him "with all my members." There are repeated claims of divine inspiration producing an overflowing exuberance (e.g., 6.1-2; 21.8-9; 40.2-4). On balance, the pattern of religious ideas of the *Odes* probably corresponds at least as closely with the circles that made up proto-orthodox Christianity as with any other version.[142]

These lyrical compositions are particularly noteworthy as expressions of devotion to Jesus. Though the name Jesus does not appear in the collection, there can be no doubt that he is the figure referred to variously as "the Beloved" (3.7; 7.1; 8.21; 38.11), "the Son" (3.7; 19.2, 8; 23.22), "the Son of God" (36.3), "the Son of the Most High" (41.13), "the Light" (36.3), "the Lord" (37.1; 39.7), "the Word" (37.3), "Messiah" (9.3; 17.17; 24.1; 29.6; 39.11; 41.3, 15), and "our Savior" (42.18).[143] There are references to the incarnation of the Son: e.g., "He became like me, that I might receive him. In form he was considered like me, that I might put him on" (7.4). In 31.4 it is probably the Son who lifted up his voice to the Most High and "offered to him those that had become sons through him."

One of the striking features of the *Odes* is that at certain points the "voice" speaking appears to be that of Jesus (e.g., 8.8-19; 10.4-6; 17.6-17; 31.6-13; 42.3-20).[144] In these passages the speaker recounts in first-person form the actions that almost certainly are the redemptive work of Jesus, as widely celebrated in early Christianity. In 17.6-17, for example, the speaker narrates opening gates that were shut and shattering iron bars (17.8-9), and he tells of giving knowledge and other blessings to those who "became my members"

---

142. See, e.g., Charlesworth's summary of religious ideas in the *Odes,* in *OTP,* 2:728-31; and note a similar judgment by Aune, *Prophecy,* 296-99; and Adalbert Hamman, *La prière I. Le Nouveau Testament* (Tournai: Desclée, 1959), 2:36-51, esp. 38.

143. In Charlesworth's translation, Jesus refers to himself in 36.3 as "the Son of Man," but Franzmann notes that the Syriac expression here is better rendered "a son of man" (i.e., indefinite form), whereas "the Son of God" does have the Syriac marker equivalent to the English definite article, indicating that it is a title (*Odes,* 250-51).

144. Charlesworth inserted headings in his translation (*OTP,* 2:735-71) to signal where he took the voice to be that of Jesus (e.g., after 8.7; and see p. 741 n. e). Note also Franzmann's discussion of the "I" of the *Odes* (*Odes,* 296-98).

and he "their head" (17.16). The doxology that immediately follows, "Glory to you, our Head, O Lord Messiah" (17.17), suggests the identity of the speaker of the preceding verses. In 31.6-13, also, it is probably Jesus who speaks, narrating his endurance of sufferings and rejection, which he underwent in order to fulfill "the promises to the patriarchs, to whom I was promised for the salvation of their offspring" (31.13). The longest of these passages is 42.3-20, which again recounts Jesus' sufferings and rejection, and his descent to the realm of the dead (42.11). Thereupon the dead ran toward him, and cried out, "Son of God, have pity on us . . . and bring us out from the chains of darkness, and open for us the door by which we may go forth to you" (42.15-17), appealing to him as "our Savior" (42.18). Hearing their voice, he set their faith in his heart, and placed his name "upon their head" because they belong to him (42.19-20).[145]

Prayer

Prayer was obviously another characteristic feature of earliest Christians' worship; their prayer practices likewise demonstrate the central place of Jesus in their devotional life. The *Odes* also give us perhaps our earliest explicit references to the devotional action of making the sign of Jesus' cross in the posture of prayer. Indeed, the whole of 27.1-3 appears to describe this liturgical action, which involves standing, for praise and prayer, with outstretched hands as "his sign," this posture portraying "the upright cross [wood]."[146] In 42.1-2 there is a very similar statement about this practice, and in 35.7 and 37.1 the speaker more briefly refers to praising God with outstretched hands. Clearly, for the Christians whose devotion was reflected in the *Odes,* this cross-shaped stance was their characteristic prayer/praise posture. Descriptions in other early Christian texts of praying with hands stretched out to God, such as *1 Clement* 2.3, almost certainly refer to the same posture.

This cruciform stance appears to be an interesting Christian adaptation and reinterpretation of a liturgical posture used in ancient Jewish and pagan religious traditions: standing with hands raised (bent upward at the elbow).[147] In pagan and early Christian art the "orante" figure is frequent, usually a female

145. See also the discussion later in this chapter on Jesus and death.

146. The Syriac word for "wood" here is used with the special early Christian connotation given to the equivalent in Greek *(xylon)*.

147. Standing with hands stretched upward is the prayer/praise posture reflected in biblical references (e.g., 1 Kings 8:22; Pss. 28:2; 44:20; 88:9; 143:6; 1 Tim. 2:8), and in early Christian writings (e.g., *1 Clem.* 2.3; Tertullian, *Apology* 30.4; Origen, *On Prayer* 31).

standing with arms raised, symbolizing piety.[148] The Christian adaptation referred to in the *Odes* and some other early Christian sources involved an obvious shift in meaning, as well as a modification of the physical gesture.[149] Here the arms were stretched out horizontally, for this stance had the distinctively Christian function as a bodily testimony to Jesus' crucifixion. In short, Jesus' crucifixion quite literally shaped this Christian prayer/praise practice.

The contents and forms of prayers in proto-orthodox Christianity are essentially what we have observed to be characteristic in the first-century evidence.[150] We can note references in two early and key writings of different Christian provenances as illustrations. *1 Clement* 59–61 contains an extended prayer that must illustrate the sort of liturgical petition appreciated and practiced in the Roman church in the late first century, and likely in other churches too. It is addressed to "the Creator of the universe" *(ho dēmiourgos tōn hapantōn)*, imploring God to preserve the elect throughout the whole world "through his beloved servant [*paidos*] Jesus Christ, through whom he called us from darkness to light, from ignorance to the knowledge of the glory of his name" (59.2).[151] Following a series of appeals on behalf of various groups of needy people, there is the petition, "Let all the nations know that you are the only God, that Jesus Christ is your servant [*pais*], and that we are your people and the sheep of your pasture" (59.4). In 61.3 the prayer concludes with praise offered to God "through the high priest and guardian of our souls, Jesus Christ,

---

148. Paul C. Finney, "Orant," in *EEC*, 2:831-32; Graydon F. Snyder, *Ante Pacem: Archaeological Evidence of Church Life before Constantine* (Macon, Ga.: Mercer University Press, 1985), 19-20. On the Christian posture, see D. Plooij, "The Attitude of the Outspread Hands ('Orante') in Early Christian Literature and Art," *ExpT* 23 (1912): 199-203, 265-69; Erik Peterson, "Das Kreuz und das Gebet nach Osten," in *Frühkirche, Judentum und Gnosis: Studien und Untersuchungen* (Rome: Herder, 1959), 15-35. Jewish prescriptions about proper prayer posture were perhaps contemporary with the developing Christian practice. See Peterson's essay in the same collection, "Die geschichtliche Bedeutung der jüdischen Gebetsrichtung," 1-14; and Uri Ehrlich, "'When You Pray Know Before Whom You Are Standing,'" *JJS* 49 (2000): 38-50.

149. In at least some early Christian circles, the stance for prayer included facing the east, which was an adaptation of pre-Christian practices that may have originated with sun worship. See esp. Franz J. Dölger, *Sol Salutis: Gebet und Gesang im christlichen Altertum mit besonderer Rücksicht auf die Ostung in Gebet und Liturgie*, 3rd ed., LQF 16/17 (1925; reprint, Münster: Aschendorffsche Verlagsbuchhandlung, 1972).

150. Jacques Marty, "Étude de textes cultuels de prière contenus dans le Nouveau Testament," *RHPR* 9 (1929): 234-63, 366-76; Marty, " Étude de textes cultuels de prière conservés par les 'Pères apostolique,'" *RHPR* 10 (1930): 90-98; Adalbert Hamman, *La prière II. Les trois premiers siècles* (Tournai: Desclée, 1963); Joseph Jungmann, *The Place of Christ in Liturgical Prayer*, 2nd rev. ed. (London and Dublin: Geoffrey Chapman, 1965); Lebreton, *Histoire*, 2:174-247.

151. On the use of *pais* in early Christian prayers, see the discussion of the term in *Didache* below.

through whom be the glory and the majesty to you both now and for all generations for ever and ever" (61.3).[152] Remembering that "the blood of Christ" was "poured out for our salvation," and indeed "won for the whole world the grace of repentance" (7.4), the Christians of *1 Clement* offer their prayer to God through Jesus, their priestly intercessor and redeemer. Note also that in the numerous doxologies of *1 Clement* God is, either unambiguously or arguably, the one to whom glory is ascribed, with Jesus named uniquely in several of them as the one *through whom* glory is given to God.[153] These doxologies are directly indicative of the devotional stance and practice of the Roman Christian circle from whom *1 Clement* came, and these liturgical expressions also likely preserve a very traditional pattern that perhaps stemmed from early Jewish Christian circles.[154]

Didache

The composite writing known as the *Didache* (its full title translated is "The Teaching of the Twelve Apostles") was probably put into its present form around 150, possibly in Egypt or Syria, and was judged by Quasten "the most important document of the subapostolic period."[155] It is commonly accepted that *Didache* incorporates material much older still, among which the prayers are likely some of the oldest.[156] *Didache* 8–10 is a body of very ancient liturgical material that is "without peer in the early period of Christian literature," this

152. I cite the translation in Lightfoot, Harmer, and Holmes, *The Apostolic Fathers*.

153. Glory simply ascribed to God in 38.4; 43.6; 45.7; to God through Jesus in 58.2; 61.3; 64; 65.2. But 20.12 and 50.7 are more ambiguous. In both Jesus is the nearest antecedent of the relative pronoun "to whom," but in each case the doxology concludes a statement about God's actions (God's "compassionate mercies" in 20.11, and God's choice of the redeemed in 50.7). Cf. Henne, 55-56.

154. As noted earlier, the doxology is a liturgical form from Jewish provenance. The word *doxa* does not connote "glory" in ordinary Greek usage, but acquired this connotation in the LXX; from this usage in the LXX it then became part of the religious vocabulary of Jews and Christians. See, e.g., G. Kittel and G. von Rad, "Δόξα," in *TDNT*, 2:233-55; Harold Hegermann, "δόξα," in *EDNT*, 1:344-48.

155. Quasten, *Patrology*, 1:30 (29-39 for his full discussion).

156. Kurt Niederwimmer, *The Didache*, Hermeneia (Minneapolis: Fortress, 1998), deals with all these matters in an extended introduction (1-54), and reviews sources and provenance (42-54). Note also Jonathan A. Draper, ed., *The "Didache" in Modern Research*, AGJU 37 (Leiden: Brill, 1997), esp. Draper's review of research, 1-42; Kenneth J. Harder and Clayton N. Jefford, eds., *The "Didache" in Context: Essays on Its Text, History, and Transmission* (Leiden: Brill, 1995); and most recently, Huub van de Sandt and David Flusser, *The "Didache": Its Jewish Sources and Its Place in Early Judaism and Christianity*, CRINT (Assen: Van Gorcum; Minneapolis: Fortress, 2002).

material including "the oldest formula for the Christian Eucharistic liturgy."[157] After urging Christians to distinguish their fasting days and prayer forms from "the hypocrites" (8.1-2), commonly understood as a pejorative reference to devotional forms being promoted by Jewish authorities of the time, 8.2 directs Christians to pray "just as the Lord commanded in his Gospel." What follows is the well-known "Lord's prayer," in wording almost identical to Matthew 6:9-13, followed by one of the numerous doxologies that regularly conclude prayers in *Didache* and in other early Christian texts. On the authority of Jesus, Christians are to pray "like this" three times a day. The directions in 8.1-3 probably derive from some Jewish Christian group, and clearly Jesus tradition is the authoritative force that shapes their devotional practice.

In *Didache* 9–10 are several prayers proposed for "the Thanksgiving" (*eucharistia*), the precise identity and structure of the meal(s) in question being much debated still.[158] A number of scholars have argued that the prayers in 9.1-5 over "the cup" and "the broken bread" were offered at a distinguishable Christian full meal for the satisfaction of hunger (the so-called *agapē* meal), and that the prayers in 10.1-6 introduce a subsequent part of the meal that corresponds to the Eucharist of subsequent Christian tradition. Among the problems with this view, however, is the consistent use of the noun *eucharistia* and the verb *eucharistein* in all the prayers in *Didache* 9–10. I am not persuaded that two distinguishable meals, or a meal occasion with two separate parts, is really reflected in this part of *Didache*.[159] The absence of the familiar "words of institution" cited by Paul in 1 Corinthians 11:23-25 (and parallels in the Synoptic "last supper" accounts) is no indication that the *Didache* meal is not a Eucharist. We should not presume that the Eucharist meals in all Christian circles included these words. Moreover, in some circles at least, they may have functioned originally not as part of what was said during the meal, but as part of the instructions to converts about the meaning of the meal.[160] In any case, it is the contents of the prayers themselves that concern us here, especially what they tell us about the pattern of devotion to which they testify.

As in *1 Clement,* and as characteristic of early Christian prayers more widely, the recipient of these thanksgivings and petitions is God, variously addressed as "our Father" (*Did.* 9.2, 3), "Holy Father" (10.2), "Almighty Master" (*despota pantokratōr*, 10.3), "Lord" (*Kyrie,* 10.5), and "the God of David" (10.6).

---

157. Niederwimmer, 139. So also, e.g., Lightfoot, Harmer, and Holmes, 247.

158. Niederwimmer, 139-43.

159. See now discussion in van de Sandt and Flusser, 296-329.

160. Andrew Brian McGowan, "'Is There a Liturgical Text in This Gospel?' The Institution Narratives and Their Early Interpretive Communities," *JBL* 118 (1999): 73-87.

Almost equally characteristically, Jesus is portrayed as the one through whom God has made known the blessings of salvation ("the holy vine of David your servant," 9.2; "the life and knowledge," 9.3; "the knowledge and faith and immortality," 10.2; "spiritual food and drink, and eternal life," 10.3). The frequent use of the term *pais* (servant/child) as a title for Jesus in these prayers stems from the most ancient layers of Jewish Christian devotional language, where it had strong messianic connotations deriving from its previous use as a title for David (as also in 9.2).[161]

The regularized references to Jesus as the unique agent of God's redemptive action in these prayers of very antique provenance again attests the important place of Jesus in early Christian devotional practice, a place that has no true antecedent or parallel in the religious environment of the time.[162] Moreover, only those who have been baptized "into the name of the Lord (Jesus)" are to be permitted to partake of the meal (9.5), indicating that Jesus serves as the gateway into the company of the elect who offer these prayers. Furthermore, in the thanks given to God for his "holy name" which God has "caused to dwell [*kateskēnōsas*] in our hearts" (10.2), we probably have another reference to Jesus. As Niederwimmer noted, God's "name" here in this very primitive prayer that derives from Jewish Christian circles represents "God's epiphany, God in person," and it "stands for what the Greeks would call *ousia* [essence, being]."[163] For the Christians from whom this prayer stemmed, Jesus embodied the divine name, and he is the one in whom God's name dwelt among humankind and now dwells in believers.[164]

The conclusion to the eucharistic prayer of 10.1-6 gives us another antique feature of Christian devotional practice, the old Aramaic formula *maranatha*. As we noted earlier in commenting on the use of this expression in 1 Corinthians 16:22, it is an appeal to the exalted Jesus to come in eschatological power. In *Didache* 10.1-6 the appeal forms part of a set of petitions that cumulatively involve the triumph of God's purpose ("May grace come") and kingdom over "this world/age [*kosmos*]." As the climactic component of this series of ap-

---

161. We noted the use of *pais* earlier in prayers in Acts (discussion in "Judean Jewish Christianity"). For further discussion and references to scholarly study of the term, see Niederwimmer, 147.

162. Christian prayer is distinguished from pagan practice in the restriction of prayer to the one God, and in the inclusion of Jesus as his unique Son. In Jewish prayer, no revered figure such as Moses functions in prayer in a way that corresponds to Jesus' place in early Christian practice. See Hurtado, *One God, One Lord*.

163. Niederwimmer, 156, and n. 13.

164. See, e.g., *1 Clem.* 58.1; 59.2-3, where believers "obey," "trust," and "hope" in God's "name," which can only be references to Jesus as embodying the divine name.

peals, the *maranatha* formula exhibits the crucial place of Jesus in early Christian hope and liturgy.

Similar direct appeals to Jesus also feature in the accounts of early Christian martyrs, as we shall see in the following section, the earliest example being Stephen's dying cries, "Lord Jesus, receive my spirit" and "Lord, do not charge them with this sin" (Acts 7:59-60). Ignatius appears to allude to prayers to Jesus (Ign. *Eph.* 20.1). But in the patterns of liturgical prayer preserved in texts of proto-orthodox circles, direct prayer to Jesus is not common. The elegant prayer to Jesus that Clement of Alexandria includes toward the end of *The Instructor* is the more notable because it is unusual in the writings that reflect proto-orthodox devotional practice.[165] By contrast, in apocryphal Christian writings (e.g., *Acts of John*, *Acts of Thomas*), direct prayer to Jesus is much more frequent, and in fact, is typical, including public/liturgical prayer.[166] Direct prayer to Jesus may have been more frequent in "popular" Christian piety, as distinguished from the devotional pattern promoted in liturgical settings in proto-orthodox circles.[167]

The central place given to Jesus in their hymnody and prayer, and at the same time their concern to avoid ditheism by reverencing Jesus rather consistently with reference to "the Father," combine to shape the proto-orthodox "binitarian" pattern of devotion. Jesus is truly reverenced as divine, and the place he is given in the worship of proto-orthodox circles is categorically distinguished from the honor given to any other figure. For example, in *Martyrdom of Polycarp* Polycarp joins all the righteous and apostles in heaven glorifying "the almighty God," and blessing "our Lord Jesus Christ, the Savior of our souls and Helmsman of our bodies and Shepherd of the catholic church throughout the world" (19.3). Dating Polycarp's death by reference to local officials, and with a swipe at the claims of the emperor, the author then refers to Jesus "reigning as king forever," and follows this with a doxology to him (*Mart. Pol.* 21).[168] Yet, in their devotional thought and practice Jesus holds "the second place" to "the Father"; he is reverenced neither merely as a "cult

---

165. ANF, 2:295. Actually, however, this prayer appeals to Jesus to perfect believers that they may give thanks and praise to "the unique Father and Son, Son and Father . . . with the Holy Spirit, all in One," giving us an early expression of trinitarian piety.

166. As noted, e.g., by Jungmann, 165-69; and esp. see Hamman, *La prière*, 2:169-229.

167. After the fourth century, however, there was an increased incorporation of prayers to Jesus in certain areas of Christianity, as described by Jungmann, 213-38. See also Jules Lebreton, "Le désaccord de la foi populaire et de la théologie savante dans l'Église chrétienne du III siècle," *RHE* 19 (1923): 481-506; 20 (1924): 5-27.

168. Cf. *Mart. Pol.* 14.3, where we have a doxology to God, Jesus, and the Holy Spirit, through Jesus!

hero" nor as a "new god" whose worship might impinge upon the honor due "the Father."[169] As well, this pattern of worship demonstrates the link to earlier Christian tradition that constitutes a defining feature of proto-orthodox Christianity.

Martyrdom

We already noted references to martyrs in early Christian writings, but it is appropriate here to devote further, focused attention to martyrdom as a particular, and very influential, expression of devotion to Jesus. Whether one shares the Christian faith of the martyrs or not, it is difficult not to be moved by the accounts of their dedication. The martyrs provide perhaps the most vivid form in which devotion to Jesus was expressed in the earliest centuries.

On the one hand, whereas worship involved the whole Christian congregation, martyrdom was of course restricted to a narrower circle. The total number of martyred Christians was small in absolute terms, at least until the more intense ordeals of the third century and early years of the fourth.[170] In the first two centuries, we are talking about a minority of the total number of members of a still-small minority group in the larger Roman society.[171]

On the other hand, although martyrdom was neither a constant nor a pervasive experience of early Christians in the first two centuries, "it was a possibility with which all had to reckon."[172] Certainly the behavior of those who did undergo martyrdom contributed importantly to the wider sense of who Christians were and what their faith meant, both among insiders and outsiders.[173] Chris-

---

169. See esp. A. Klawek, *Das Gebet zu Jesus. Seine Berechtigung und Übung nach den Schriften des Neuen Testaments: Eine biblisch-theologische Studie*, NTAbh 6/5 (Münster: Aschendorffschen Verlagsbuchhandlung, 1921), 99-116, esp. 107: "We possess, therefore, sufficient historical witnesses that according to the teaching of ancient Christianity *proskynein* [worship] was appropriately given to God and to Jesus with the same meaning" (my translation).

170. See E. C. E. Owen, *Some Authentic Acts of the Early Martyrs* (Oxford: Clarendon, 1927), 21-22, for discussion of ancient references to numbers involved. Wilken (31) proposed that there were fewer than fifty thousand Christians by the early second century.

171. Tacitus (*Annals* 15.44) refers to "vast numbers" arrested in Nero's violent effort to blame Christians for the fire of Rome. But given that the Roman church of Nero's day could not have had "vast numbers" of adherents, this is either a rhetorical exaggeration or many others beyond the Christians were included.

172. Everett Ferguson, "Martyr, Martyrdom," in *EEC*, 2:724-28.

173. Blaise Pascal's epigram aptly captures the effect for many in the ancient world: "I readily believe those stories whose witnesses are slaughtered" [Je croi volontiers les histoires dont les témoins se font égorger]: *Pensées*, #28 (1671 ed.).

tians sought to make much of their martyrs as exemplary disciples of Jesus, thereby to inspire and shape the devotional stance of *all* believers. That is, early Christianity thematized martyrdom heavily, presenting the brutal deaths of believers as inspiring acts of religious devotion.[174] In short, Christians endeavored to make the coercive efforts of the Roman magistrates work to promote the very faith they wanted to destroy! Christians wrote and vigorously disseminated accounts of their martyrs, which formed an important genre of early Christian literature that was circulated to promote courageous faith through the example of those who were lionized.[175] For instance, those who wrote the account of Polycarp's martyrdom expressed the hope that Christians will be able to gather at his tomb "to celebrate the birthday of his martyrdom in commemoration of those who have already fought in the contest, and for the training and preparation of those who will do so in the future" (*Mart. Pol.* 18.3).

The earliest instance of this Christian thematizing of martyrdom is, of course, the account of Stephen's violent death in Acts. From the introductory description of him as "full of grace and power" and endowed with irresistible wisdom and the Spirit (6:8-10) through the rest of the account, readers are to see Stephen as the model for believers who may be arraigned for their faith. 12:1-2 relates the death of another Christian leader as well, James Zebedee, an apostolic figure; but the author of Acts clearly intended the account of Stephen's death in particular to be the inspiring model.

It is really in Revelation, however, that martyrdom for Jesus is made a major theme. Revelation portrays an immediate future of death that Christians will almost certainly face to avoid the only alternative, apostasy. Jesus himself is the paradigmatic "faithful witness [*ho martys ho pistos*]" (1:5) in this book, whose death was not only redemptive but also the pattern for those who bear his name; believers are urged likewise to "be faithful until death" (2:10), that they might have Jesus' reward. In effect, Revelation warns, in the coming crisis the only good Christian will likely be a dead Christian! In 6:9-11, for example, a

---

174. Classic studies of Christian martyrdom include Hans von Campenhausen, *Die Idee des Martyriums in der alten Kirche*, 2nd ed. (Göttingen: Vandenhoeck & Ruprecht, 1964); W. H. C. Frend, *Martyrdom and Persecution in the Early Church: A Study of a Conflict from the Maccabees to Donatus* (Oxford: Blackwell, 1965; reprint, New York: New York University Press, 1967). More recently, Theofried Baumeister, *Die Anfänge der Theologie des Martyriums*, MBT 45 (Münster: Aschendorff, 1980); and B. Dehandschutter, "Example and Discipleship: Some Comments on the Biblical Background of the Early Christian Theology of Martyrdom," in *The Impact of Scripture in Early Christianity*, ed. J. den Boeft and M. L. van de Lisdonk, VCSup 44 (Leiden: Brill, 1999), 20-26.

175. Herbert Musurillo, *The Acts of the Christian Martyrs: Introduction, Texts, and Translations* (Oxford: Clarendon, 1972).

group of martyred Christians are told to wait until the full number of their fellow believers have been killed "as they themselves had been killed."

The oppression of believers is pictured as a war conducted against them by "the dragon" (12:17; 13:7), Revelation thereby anticipating the dominant image of combat used in Christian martyrological accounts in the following two centuries and thereafter.[176] Revelation pronounces special blessings upon all those who will "die in the Lord" (14:13) in the looming maelstrom of evil, and in 15:2-4 characterizes those killed by "the beast" as in reality having conquered him through their death. In 17:6 the author prophetically condemns the evil "Babylon the great" for being "drunk with the blood of the saints and the blood of the witnesses [*martyrōn*] to Jesus," this being the greatest crime of the many that merit its downfall. Here in Revelation are the origins of the new Christian meaning of the term *martys* (witness) as designating a person whose testimony to Jesus can involve death for the faith. In 20:4 those who had been executed by the state (here, beheaded) "for their testimony [*martyria*]" are pictured on thrones reigning with Christ.

Not long after Revelation, Ignatius of Antioch seized upon his own imminent martyrdom as giving him a special basis on which to address the Christians in the cities through which he was taken en route to Rome for execution.[177] It is worth noting how he refers to the ordeal that awaits him. He portrays it as an opportunity to prove his devotion and to achieve a special intimacy with God and Jesus. Through his martyrdom he will "reach God" (Ign. *Smyrn.* 11.1; Ign. *Rom.* 1.2), "reach Jesus Christ" (Ign. *Rom.* 5.3), and "suffer with him" (Ign. *Smyrn.* 4.2). Especially in his epistle to the Roman church he thematizes his death as intense devotion to Jesus. Disdaining "the ends of the world and the kingdoms of this age," Ignatius seeks instead to die for Jesus Christ, and he avows, "Him I seek, who died on our behalf; him I long for, who rose again for our sake" (6.1).[178] Urging the Roman church not to try to interfere on his behalf, he writes, "Allow me to be an imitator of the suffering of my

---

176. Note, e.g., "the noble army of martyrs" who feature in the Te Deum.

177. If the seven commonly accepted letters of Ignatius represent his original epistolary effort, it is likely that the seven churches addressed were collectively intended to represent the whole of the Christian movement, seven being emblematic, as perhaps also the case with the seven churches addressed in Revelation. On the major historical issues, see esp. C. P. Hammond Bammel, "Ignatian Problems," *JTS* 33 (1982): 62-97; L. W. Barnard, *Studies in the Apostolic Fathers and Their Background* (New York: Schocken Books; Oxford: Blackwell, 1966), 19-30.

178. The disdain for universal rule may be a none-too-subtle swipe at imperial grandeur; "kingdoms of this age" may allude to the account of the temptation of Jesus (Matt. 4:8), as noted by William R. Schoedel, *Ignatius of Antioch: A Commentary on the Letters of Ignatius of Antioch*, Hermeneia (Philadelphia: Fortress, 1985), 181-82 n. 1.

God" (6.3). In several passages he says his situation affords him the chance truly to "begin to be a disciple" (Ign. *Eph.* 3.1; Ign. *Rom.* 3), and he says that when executed he "will truly be a disciple of Jesus Christ" (Ign. *Rom.* 4.2). Whatever one's own readiness to contemplate such a fate for any cause, the flame of Ignatius's religious commitment is impressive.[179] In these letters, uniquely in earliest Christianity, we view Christian martyrdom from the standpoint of the victim; Ignatius shows that he very much wanted to make the most of his coming death for the cause of the Christian faith.[180]

The idea that the Christian martyr is given a special, prized opportunity to demonstrate discipleship to Jesus appears in virtually all subsequent accounts of Christian martyrdom. Indeed, martyrs are described as suffering with Jesus, and Jesus is thought of as there with them in the ordeal. For example, in his letter to the church in Philippi (ca. 110), Polycarp (bishop in Smyrna) refers to Christian martyrs (among those named, the recently executed Ignatius) as "now with the Lord, with whom also they suffered together [*synepathon*]" (9.1-2). A few decades later, the account of Polycarp's death refers to him also as being made "a sharer with Christ" (*Mart. Pol.* 6.2), and describes Christian martyrs generally as "disciples and imitators of the Lord" who have demonstrated "matchless devotion to their own King and Teacher" (17.3).[181]

The Christian idea and practice of martyrdom was of course influenced by Jewish martyr traditions, which had developed especially in the time of the Maccabean struggle.[182] The link with the suffering and death of Jesus, however, gives to early Christian understanding of martyrdom its distinctive feature. Whereas ancient Jewish tradition lionized those who died in loyalty to their ancestral religion, their God, and the Torah, in early Christian tradition the aim was to give *witness* to Jesus and to show oneself to be his faithful disciple.[183] In

---

179. Lebreton, *Histoire*, 2:231: "All commentary will appear cold and pale beside this flame."

180. As Schoedel noted, "we do not often see life from the prisoner's point of view in antiquity" (*Ignatius of Antioch*, 11); and see Schoedel's discussion entitled "Ignatius' Journey as History and as Theater," 11-12, where he itemizes the efforts made by Ignatius and other Christians to make as much as possible of this journey to martyrdom.

181. Boudewijn Dehandschutter, "The Martyrdom of Polycarp: A Century of Research," in *ANRW*, 2.27/1:485-522.

182. J. W. van Henten et al., eds., *Die Entstehung der jüdischen Martyrologie*, SPB 38 (Leiden: Brill, 1989).

183. E.g., 2 Macc. 6–7, emphasizing martyrdom out of obedience to Torah; and cf. Josephus's reference to the Jewish captives, after the siege of Jerusalem, who could not be made to confess Caesar as "lord [*despotēs*]" for they held "God alone as their lord" (*War* 7.417-19). Baumeister, 310: "The early church modified Jewish traditional elements in certain points and made them serviceable for their own purposes. Central in early Christian understanding of per-

the early Christian understanding, "The imitation of the suffering Christ, this is the law of the martyr."[184] Both this focus on martyrdom as devotion to Jesus, and the image of death for Jesus as a "testimony" *(martyria)*, mark the Christian treatment of death for one's faith.

The prayers ascribed to early Christian martyrs are a very important body of material that reflects early Christian piety, and was also intended to inspire and shape Christian devotion.[185] As Hamman noted, the Christian accounts of early martyrs were often composed for annual celebrations of their deaths, and this intended use gave the accounts a certain liturgical tone.[186] The prayer of Polycarp, for example, surely reflects both the wider pattern of Christian prayer and also this liturgical usage. It is addressed to the "Lord God Almighty," who is immediately defined further as "Father of your beloved and blessed servant/child [*paidos sou*] Jesus Christ, through whom we have received knowledge of you" (*Mart. Pol.* 14.1). Polycarp then thanks God for being deemed worthy to have "a place among the number of the martyrs in the cup of (your) Christ" (14.2), and prays that his death may be "a rich and acceptable sacrifice" that will also fulfill what God has ordained for him. He concludes in highly liturgical phrasing with a careful trinitarian construction: "I praise you, I bless you, I glorify you, through the eternal and heavenly High Priest, Jesus Christ, your beloved servant/child [*paidos*], through whom to you with him and the Holy Spirit be glory both now and for the ages to come. Amen" (14.3).

As noted previously, however, the accounts of martyrs also frequently feature direct appeals to Jesus. Also, martyrs are portrayed seeing Jesus' glory at the point of death. For example, as he is nailed to a stake for immolation, Carpus claims to have seen "the glory of the Lord"; as the fire is set he prays, "Blessed are you, Lord Jesus Christ, Son of God, because, though I am a sinner, you deemed me worthy of having this share with you."[187] With these direct appeals to Jesus the martyrs invoke "the prince of martyrs, the sole true martyr, from whom all martyrs take their origin and their value."[188] In the motif of visions of the glorified Jesus, and in the exclamatory prayers to him, we probably

---

secution stood the significance of Jesus and the notion of discipleship to him" (translation mine). Also, J. W. van Henten, "Zum Einfluss jüdischer Martyrien auf die Literatur des frühen Christentums, II: Die Apostolischen Väter," in *ANRW*, 2.27/1:700-723.

184. Lebreton, *Histoire*, 2:232.

185. Lebreton, *Histoire*, 2:226-38; Hamman, *La prière*, 2:126-68.

186. Hamman, *La prière*, 2:126-27.

187. *Martyrdom of Saints Carpus, Papylus, and Agathonice* 41, translated from the Greek text in Musurillo, 26.

188. Hamman, *La prière*, 2:165.

again see the influence of the account of Stephen in Acts; these features also obviously show the particularly close association of the martyr with Jesus.

Although only a minority of Christians ever faced martyrdom, the threat was there for everyone. In part, that is how martyrdom shaped the mentality of the wider Christian movement. To judge from the accounts of Roman judicial actions against Christians, when they set their mind to the deed, the Romans were equal-opportunity persecutors and torturers! The early Christian accounts include women as well as men — from the two unnamed deaconesses tortured by Pliny through Charito (ca. 165), Agathonice (ca. 161-69?) and Blandina (martyrs of Lyons, ca. 177) — and also the elderly (e.g., Polycarp at eighty-six) as well as the young (e.g., the fifteen-year-old Ponticus tortured with Blandina), and freeborn as well as slaves. They all got their chance to suffer with Jesus.[189]

There are, however, early proto-orthodox accusations that certain heretical Christians were much more ready to avoid martyrdom by acceding to the demands of Roman interrogators. In a couple intriguing discussions, Elaine Pagels proposed that these accusations reflected a reality. She argued that consistently in second-century Christianity, "the attitude toward martyrdom corresponds to the interpretation of Christ's suffering and death."[190] Those who denied the reality of Jesus' suffering and death attacked martyrdom as foolish.[191] But the proto-orthodox Christians insisted that Jesus really suffered and died, and that his death was powerfully redemptive; these same Christians were the primary ones who thematized martyrdom as a noble service to Jesus and as a glorious victory over their tormentors.

She contended that, behind the doctrinal controversy over the interpretation of Jesus' suffering and death in the first two centuries, there was "an urgent practical question: how are believers to respond to persecution, which raises the imminent possibility of their *own* suffering and death?"[192] As she explains, in the view of proto-orthodox Christians such as Ignatius, Justin, Tertullian,

189. Accounts of these and other martyrs in Musurillo, *The Acts of the Christian Martyrs*, and Owen, *Some Authentic Acts of the Early Martyrs*.

190. Elaine Pagels, *The Gnostic Gospels* (London: Weidenfeld and Nicolson, 1980), 90. She presented the same argument, but directed more to scholars, in "Gnostic and Orthodox Views of Christ's Passion: Paradigms for the Christian's Response to Persecution?" in *The Rediscovery of Gnosticism*, ed. Bentley Layton, 2 vols. (Leiden: Brill, 1980), 1:262-83; and note the debate recorded thereafter, 283-88.

191. See esp. the Nag Hammadi tractate *Testimony of Truth* 31.22–32.8; 32.25–34.26 (*NHLE*, 407-8); *Apocalypse of Peter* 79.11-21 (*NHLE*, 343); and Pagels's discussion, *The Gnostic Gospels*, 91-94.

192. Pagels, "Gnostic and Orthodox Views," 265.

Hippolytus, and Irenaeus, "only if Christ suffered and died in the same way that we do ourselves can our suffering and death imitate his." But if Jesus' experience was not our own experience of pain and death, in that his heavenly/divine nature made it impossible for him truly to suffer, then the suffering of martyrs was meaningless.[193]

Whatever the comparative numbers of proto-orthodox and heterodox martyrs, however, it is certain that early Christian views of the nature of Jesus corresponded to views on right behavior. The way Christians understood Jesus could have powerful implications for how they expressed their devotion to him. For proto-orthodox circles, martyrdom was not necessarily something sought, but when the choice was cursing Jesus or suffering for his sake, they knew where their obligation lay. Scholarly debates about the causes of Roman persecution (i.e., the "crimes" for which they were arraigned), and the legal procedures followed in their trials, are of course interesting historical issues.[194] But they should not obscure the more obvious fact that, rather consistently in the accounts of the martyrs, the demand placed upon them was to compromise their commitment to the exclusive and universal lordship of Jesus. The test before Christians who were brought to the stake or tortured to death by other means was whether they would fit their reverence for Jesus within the larger religious scheme of the Roman environment, or would die as witnesses to his unique status and rights over them.

Moreover, martyrdom was a particularly *public* form of devotion to Jesus.[195] Pagans ordinarily had to go to a meeting of Christians to see their worship, and to watch them pray. But martyrdom was a spectacle of devotion on a platform provided by the state. It vividly indicated to the public at large that at least some Christians were ready to pay any cost to remain Jesus' faithful followers.

The *Nomina Sacra*

An interesting and influential expression of early Christian devotion often overlooked outside specialist circles devoted to the study of early Christian manuscripts is the distinctive phenomenon known as the *nomina sacra*.[196] The

---

193. Pagels, "Gnostic and Orthodox Views," 266.

194. Cf., e.g., G. E. M. de Ste. Croix, "Why Were the Early Christians Persecuted?" *Past and Present* 26 (1963): 6-38; A. N. Sherwin-White, "Why Were the Early Christians Persecuted? An Amendment," *Past and Present* 27 (1964): 23-27; G. E. M. de Ste. Croix, "Why Were the Early Christians Persecuted? A Rejoinder," *Past and Present* 27 (1964): 28-33.

195. I thank David Wright for highlighting this point to me.

196. See, e.g., Bruce M. Metzger, *Manuscripts of the Greek Bible: An Introduction to Palae-*

term refers to a list of words that were written in a curious way by Christian scribes, apparently to mark them off visually as a gesture of piety. The practice is already conventionalized for several key words of the vocabulary of early Christianity in the earliest extant fragments of Christian manuscripts from the second century, and by the Byzantine period some fifteen words had been included among those given this scribal treatment.[197]

Four terms in particular are regularly written as *nomina sacra* in the earliest material, and it is very noteworthy that they refer to God and Jesus: *Iēsous* (Jesus), *Kyrios* (Lord), *Christos* (Christ), and *Theos* (God).[198] That is, as Schuyler Brown noted, these earliest extant *nomina sacra* are *nomina divina* (divine names).[199] At a point still earlier than any of the extant manuscripts, one of these four may have been written in this special manner, from which the subsequent Christian scribal convention developed. In a previous publication I supported the proposal that *Iēsous* may have been the first of the *nomina sacra,* and that special reverence for Jesus' name was the initial motivation that prompted the device of writing "Jesus" in a distinctive manner: abbreviated and with a horizontal stroke over the abbreviated form of the word. Then this scribal practice quickly extended to the other three earliest-attested words, and thereafter to the other words that came to be treated in this manner.[200] We have certainly seen that Jesus' name was regarded as powerful for healings and exorcism, and that it was invoked regularly in liturgical acclamations. In any case, the early conventionalization of the scribal practice

---

ography (New York: Oxford University Press, 1981), 36-37; and fuller discussion in Colin H. Roberts, *Manuscript, Society, and Belief in Christian Egypt* (London: Oxford University Press, 1979), 26-48.

197. In addition to the four earliest-attested words discussed in the next paragraph, the following came to be treated as *nomina sacra:* "Spirit" (referring to the divine Spirit); "Son" and "Savior" (referring to Jesus); "Father" (referring to God); "cross" and "crucify" (referring to Jesus' crucifixion); "mother" (referring to Jesus' mother); "David," "Jerusalem," "Israel," "Man" (referring to Jesus, e.g., as "Son of Man"); and "heaven." These words were predominantly contracted in Christian manuscripts to the first and last letters, and sometimes also a medial letter, with a distinctive horizontal stroke written above the abbreviation. For "Jesus" (*Iēsous*), however, there was also an alternate form of abbreviation by "suspension" involving the first two letters and a stroke over them.

198. Cf. Christopher M. Tuckett, "P52 and *Nomina Sacra*," *NTS* 47 (2001): 544-48, who argues that the Rylands fragment of John usually dated ca. 130 probably did not exhibit the *nomina sacra* forms. But I do not find his claim persuasive. Cf. Charles E. Hill, "Did the Scribe of P52 Use the *Nomina Sacra*? Another Look," *NTS* 48 (2002): 587-92; L. W. Hurtado, "P52 (P. Rylands 457) and the *Nomina Sacra:* Method and Probability," *TB* (forthcoming 2003).

199. Schuyler Brown, "Concerning the Origin of the *Nomina Sacra*," *SPap* 9 (1970): 7-19.

200. L. W. Hurtado, "The Origin of the *Nomina Sacra:* A Proposal," *JBL* 117 (1998): 655-73.

of the *nomina sacra* suggests that it began very early, probably sometime in the first century.

But whenever and however the *nomina sacra* originated, it is particularly striking that the earliest extant pattern was one in which key terms for Jesus and God were consistently given the *equivalent* scribal reverence. Here we see another important instance of the "binitarian" devotional stance of earliest Christianity, with terms that unambiguously designated Jesus *(Iēsous, Christos)* given the same reverence as the terms "God" *(Theos)* and "Lord" *(Kyrios,* in all cases where it refers either to God or to Jesus).

Moreover, although this has not been noticed widely by scholars, along with the early Christian preference for the codex, the *nomina sacra* are the earliest extant manifestations of an emergent "visual and material culture" in early Christianity.[201] The *nomina sacra* were intended to register religious devotion visually. They are textual phenomena with an iconographic function. And, at the earliest stage of this early Christian scribal convention, Jesus figures centrally in the religious devotion that prompted it.

Thus far in this chapter we have concentrated on some features of Christian devotional *practice* in the second century. In what follows I turn to some developments in *beliefs* about Jesus that are characteristic of this period.

Doctrinal Developments

To reiterate a point made in the opening of this chapter, the commitment of proto-orthodox circles to tradition made them generally suspicious of radical innovations in belief and practice. The highly traditional nature of early proto-orthodox beliefs about Jesus is indicated in studies of the Christology of the texts that are associated with proto-orthodox faith. These studies broadly conclude that these texts essentially echo the convictions and beliefs that are reflected in the New Testament.[202] For example, these writings use very tradi-

---

201. L. W. Hurtado, "The Earliest Evidence of an Emerging Christian Material and Visual Culture: The Codex, the *Nomina Sacra* and the Staurogram," in *Text and Artifact in the Religions of Mediterranean Antiquity: Essays in Honour of Peter Richardson,* ed. Stephen G. Wilson and Michel Desjardins (Waterloo, Ontario: Wilfrid Laurier University Press, 2000), 271-88.

202. E.g., the following studies of the christological ideas in texts included among the "apostolic fathers": Alonzo R. Stark, *The Christology of the Apostolic Fathers* (Chicago: University of Chicago Press, 1912); Harold Bertram Bumpus, *The Christological Awareness of Clement of Rome and Its Sources* (Cambridge, Mass.: University Press of Cambridge, 1972); Henne, *La christologie chez Clément de Rome et dans le Pasteur d'Hermas;* M. Mees, "Das Christusbild des ersten Klemensbriefes," *ETL* 66 (1990): 297-318; Michael Rackl, *Die Christologie des heiligen*

tional titles for Jesus (such as "Son of God," "Servant," "Christ"), and they echo beliefs in Jesus' redemptive death and resurrection, his future coming in judgment, his virginal conception, and his priestly-intercessory role on behalf of his followers that are familiar from the New Testament writings as first-century tradition.

But we can identify certain interesting developments in proto-orthodox belief that appear to have become more prominent in the second century. In this final section I focus on three developments that are particularly interesting, although neither individually nor collectively do they amount to a radical innovation. Instead, as with most developments in a religious tradition, whether "radical" or not, they extend and adapt traditional motifs, in these cases, somewhat modestly. I propose, further, that they came about as proto-orthodox believers sought to articulate their faith to, and defend it against, outsiders, and in their disputes with those espousing alternate forms of Christian faith. These three developments were also all "successful" in forming a part of the continuing proto-orthodox tradition; and so, however much we may be able to identify them as further developments in previous belief, they obviously were perceived as congenial by a good many Christians, and as compatible with their traditions.

Jesus' Descent to Hades

The idea that Jesus descended to the realm of the dead (Gk. *hadēs*) and there proclaimed his redemptive work, became perhaps the most widely affirmed and influential development in belief that is first explicitly attested in extracanonical Christian texts of the period under review in this chapter.[203] Indeed, Malcolm Peel judged that in the second century and thereafter, "there was

---

Ignatius von Antiochien, Freiburger Theologische Studien 14 (Freiburg im Breisgau: Herdersche Verlagshandlung, 1914); Wilfred F. Bunge, "The Christology of Ignatius of Antioch" (Ph.D. diss., Harvard University, 1966); Joseph T. Lienhard, "The Christology of the Epistle to Diognetus," *VC* 24 (1970): 280-89.

203. Among important studies, I draw particularly upon the following: Friedrich Loofs, "Descent to Hades (Christ's)," in *Encyclopaedia of Religion and Ethics,* ed. James Hastings (Edinburgh: T. & T. Clark, 1911), 4:654-63; J. A. MacCulloch, *The Harrowing of Hell: A Comparative Study of an Early Christian Doctrine* (Edinburgh: T. & T. Clark, 1930); Werner Bieder, *Die Vorstellung von der Höllenfahrt Jesu Christi: Beitrag zur Entstehungsgeschichte der Vorstellung vom sog. Descensus ad Inferos,* ATANT 19 (Zürich: Zwingli-Verlag, 1949); Jean Daniélou, *The Theology of Jewish Christianity,* trans. and ed. J. A. Baker (London: Darton, Longman and Todd, 1964), 233-48.

no more well-known and popular belief among early Christians."[204] Strangely, however, it does not often figure prominently in scholarly accounts of early beliefs about Jesus. Although there are various versions of the idea in Christian writings of the first several centuries, both orthodox and heterodox, it most likely originated in proto-orthodox circles. The belief in Jesus' descent to the dead came to be included in the classical and well-known confession of orthodox faith, the Apostles' Creed, and has been accepted in all major branches of Christian tradition.[205] Indeed, Jesus' "harrowing of hell" became a major subject in Christian art and medieval plays.[206] It is unlikely the idea would have become so accepted had it originated in heterodox circles, and had it originally served suspect beliefs.

Of course, the New Testament writings affirm that Jesus really died and was buried (e.g., 1 Cor. 15:1-4). Moreover, in Acts 2:24-32 the author draws upon Psalm 16:8-11 to assert that Jesus "was not abandoned to Hades" (Acts 2:31, citing Ps. 16:10), but had been raised by God from death. This obviously implies the idea that at death Jesus "went" to the realm of death/the dead, "hades," which is probably what earliest Christians imagined. But in the plan of God "it was impossible for [Jesus] to be held in its power" (Acts 2:24). Moreover, Christian tradition, and some modern scholars as well, have interpreted a few New Testament texts as alluding to the specific idea that Jesus descended to hades.[207] But it is now more commonly accepted by scholars that references to Jesus' descent in Romans 10:7 and Ephesians 4:9 refer to Jesus descending from heaven to earth.[208]

204. Malcolm L. Peel, "The 'Decensus [*sic*] Ad Inferos' in 'The Teachings of Silvanus' (CG VII, 4)," *Numen* 26 (1979): 23-49, citation 27. Peel helpfully provides a survey of ancient Christian references to Jesus' hades descent (32-48), attempting to distinguish earlier from later developments in the idea.

205. See, e.g., Loofs, 654-58, who reviews Eastern Orthodox, Roman Catholic, Lutheran, and Reformed traditions on the idea.

206. See, e.g., Aloys Grillmeier, "Der Gottessohn im Totenreich," *ZKT* 71 (1949): 1-53, 184-203; F. W. Farrar, *The Life of Christ as Represented in Art* (London: Adam and Charles Black, 1896), 433-37.

207. In addition to the texts discussed here, other New Testament passages have sometimes been suggested as alluding to the idea of Jesus' descent (Matt. 12:40; Rev. 1:18; 5:13; Heb. 13:20); but in none is there any clear basis for this. Harold W. Attridge has proposed that the idea lies behind Heb. 2:10-18, where Jesus is the "pioneer" (*archēgos*) who leads "many children to glory," and through partaking of human nature destroys "the one who has the power of death," freeing those who had been "held in slavery by the fear of death" ("Liberating Death's Captives: Reconsideration of an Early Christian Myth," in *Gnosticism and the Early Christian World*, ed. James E. Goehring, Charles W. Hedrick, Jack T. Sanders, and Hans Dieter Betz [Sonoma, Calif.: Polebridge Press, 1990], 103-15). I return to his proposal later in this discussion.

208. Thus "the lower parts of the earth" (Eph. 4:9) refers to the earthly realm itself as "the lower parts," in distinction from "the heavens" (4:10).

Two passages in 1 Peter have continued to attract the most attention (3:18-20; 4:6) as possible allusions to the idea that Jesus descended to the dead to proclaim his advent and victory.[209] Both passages present interpretative difficulties, especially 3:18-20, which has been judged "the most difficult passage in the entire letter."[210] But it is much more likely that this passage refers to the crucified and risen Jesus announcing to the demonic powers ("the disobedient spirits") his victory and exaltation over them (v. 22).[211] That is, 1 Peter 3:18-20 probably reflects something similar to the idea expressed in Colossians 2:14-15, where Jesus triumphs over demonic powers in his death and resurrection. As for 1 Peter 4:6, the dead here are almost certainly *Christians,* the point being that their death does not cut them off from God's life-giving Spirit and the prospect of future vindication.[212]

Of the ancient Christian sources, the *Gospel of Nicodemus* contains the most elaborate and dramatic narrative of Jesus' descent to hades (which may go back to the fourth century or so); the version of the story in this text probably influenced the subsequent medieval depictions of the harrowing of hell in art and religious plays.[213] But the earliest clear thematizing of Jesus' descent to the dead as having its own part in his redemptive work is probably first alluded to in the epistles of Ignatius (ca. 110). These references in Ignatius also suggest the originating concerns that prompted the thematizing, which were to assert that and how the Old Testament "saints" received the benefits of Jesus' redemptive work, and thus, that he was their Redeemer and Lord just as he was for Christians.

In *Magnesians* 9.2 Ignatius refers to the Old Testament prophets as Jesus' "disciples in the Spirit" who expected him "as their teacher"; because of this, Jesus "raised them from the dead when he came." Ignatius must be referring to the idea that Jesus went to the dead prophets and "raised" them from hades.[214] The same idea is probably presupposed in two passages in his epistle to the Philadelphian church. In one (5.2) Ignatius again refers to the Old Testament prophets, claiming that they "anticipated the gospel in their preaching and set

---

209. E.g., Grillmeier, *Christ in Christian Tradition,* 73-74.

210. Paul J. Achtemeier, *1 Peter,* Hermeneia (Minneapolis: Fortress, 1996), 240. See 244-74 for full discussion of the passage and review of interpretative proposals.

211. For full elaboration of the basis for this view, see now Achtemeier, esp. 258-62.

212. So, e.g., Achtemeier, 286-91.

213. For an introduction and translation, see Felix Scheidweiler, "The Gospel of Nicodemus, Acts of Pilate and Christ's Descent into Hell," in *NTA,* 1:501-36. This writing is often dated to the fifth century, although it may incorporate earlier traditions.

214. So, e.g., Schoedel, *Ignatius of Antioch,* 124; J. B. Lightfoot, *The Apostolic Fathers: Clement, Ignatius, and Polycarp,* 2nd ed., 5 vols. (London: Macmillan, 1889-90; reprint, Grand Rapids: Baker, 1981), 2/2:131-33.

their hope on him [Jesus] and waited for him; in whom they also believed, and were saved."[215] Thereby they are included among those redeemed by, and centered on, Jesus.

In *Philadelphians* 9.1-2 Ignatius calls Jesus "the door of the Father, through which Abraham and Isaac and Jacob and the prophets and the apostles and the church enter" into "the unity of God." In this passage as well, the emphasis is on the inclusion of Old Testament figures into the benefits of Jesus' redemptive work with Christians; but we probably should see here another hint of the idea that their inclusion was effected through Jesus' descent to them in hades to announce and accomplish their deliverance.[216] That Ignatius needed only either to allude to the idea in these two passages or to mention it almost in passing (Ign. *Magn.* 9.2) shows that he presumed his intended readers were acquainted with the theme of Jesus' descent to the Old Testament dead.[217]

The idea is also presumed in the *Gospel of Peter* (41–42), in the scene where Jesus comes forth from the tomb attended by two mighty figures and followed by his cross. A heavenly voice asks, "Have you preached to them that sleep?" and "from the cross there was heard the answer, 'Yes.'" The expression "them that sleep" is found also in Matthew 27:52, with its strange reference to tombs being opened and certain dead people being raised in connection with Jesus' resurrection, and being seen by many "in the holy city." In fact, this Matthean passage may have helped shape the scene in the *Gospel of Peter*. In any case, the latter text certainly reflects the idea that between his death and resurrection Jesus went to hades and proclaimed to the dead his redemptive victory. Unlike some other texts, however, the *Gospel of Peter* does not identify the dead to whom Jesus went.

Additional references to the idea that Jesus went to hades to announce redemption to the righteous of the Old Testament are in Justin (*Dial.* 72.4) and in Irenaeus (*Adv. haer.* 3.20.4; 4.22.1; 4.27.2; 4.33.1; 5.31.1; *Dem.* 78), and both writers treat the idea as familiar tradition.[218] We may take Justin's citation as illustra-

---

215. As Lightfoot proposed (2/2:262), the prophets here are probably to be seen as believing in Jesus when he appeared to them in hades. Of course, the notion that the Old Testament prophets predicted and foresaw the historical appearance of Jesus (as Messiah) is attested as an early tradition (e.g., 1 Pet. 1:10-12).

216. Lightfoot, 2/2:275.

217. Cf. Daniélou, *Theology of Jewish Christianity*, 236-37, who saw *Magn.* 9.2 as the only reference to the doctrine in Ignatius.

218. Justin claims to quote a passage from Jeremiah not found in any known copy, and he accuses Jews of having cut it and other passages from their version of the Scriptures (*Dial.* 72.1-4). Curiously, Irenaeus attributes the same passage to Isaiah in *Adv. haer.* 3.20.4, to Jeremiah in 4.22.1, and to "the prophet" in 5.31.1.

tive: "The Lord God remembered the dead of his Israel who slept in graves of the earth, and he descended to them to preach to them his salvation" (*Dial.* 72.4). Of these early references, however, the most extended is a homilizing passage in Irenaeus (*Adv. haer.* 4.27.2). Irenaeus first affirms that Jesus descended to "the regions beneath the earth" to preach there also his advent, and to offer remission of sins to "all those who believed in Him," those who had also hoped for him and prophesied his coming: "the righteous people, the prophets, and the patriarchs." To these Jesus gave remission of sins "in the same way as he did to us [Gentiles]." Irenaeus then urges that, just as these Old Testament saints did not condemn Gentiles for their sins done before Jesus came, so now Gentile Christians ought not to "lay blame upon those [of Israel] who sinned before Christ's coming."

The *Ascension of Isaiah* refers to Jesus' descent to the dead in several passages presented (pseudonymously) as prophetic predictions. In 9.16-18, when Jesus has "plundered the angel of death, he will rise on the third day," and "many of the righteous will ascend with him." In 10.7-16 we are told that Jesus will descend through the heavens even to "Sheol" (the Hebrew equivalent of hades), and that after he judges and destroys "the princes and the angels and the gods" of the world and the nether regions, he will "ascend from the gods of death" to a glorious place at God's right hand where he will be worshiped by all. There is another, briefer reference to Jesus' descent "to the angel who is in Sheol" in 11.19-21. Interestingly, *Ascension of Isaiah* reflects both the idea of Jesus' descent to hades and also the notion that Old Testament prophets such as Isaiah foresaw and hoped for Jesus' redemptive advent, including his descent to hades/Sheol to liberate them from death.

Earlier in this chapter we noted that the *Odes of Solomon* refer to the idea of Jesus' descent to hades, most extensively and vividly in 42.11-20, which portrays the two themes of Jesus' victory over death and his rescue of the dead who received his redemptive proclamation. 17.6-17 is probably another, but more allusive, reference, where Jesus is said to have shattered "the bars of iron," loosed captives, and made them his "members," with Jesus "their head."[219]

These examples are surely sufficient to confirm the basic meanings of the idea of Jesus' descent to hades in the early circles where it first circulated.[220] Jesus' descent to hades to announce to the Old Testament saints the benefits of his

---

219. "Bars of iron" is likely an allusion to Ps. 107[LXX 106]:16, though similar imagery appears in Isa. 45:2. Ps. 107[LXX 106]:10-16 was likely an influential biblical text in early Christian thematizing of Jesus' hades descent. As Peel notes (40), however, Tartarus is described in pagan sources as having iron gates and a bronze threshold (Homer, *Iliad* 8.15; Virgil, *Aeneid* 6.576); Peel also shows the popularity of this imagery in early Christian sources (40-41).

220. Other references include *Sib. Or.* 8.310-17; and *Ep. Apos.* 27-28.

victorious redemptive work dramatically asserts his lordship over all spheres of creation, vividly illustrating the confession in Philippians 2:9-11 that he is to be acknowledged "in heaven, and on earth and under the earth." The motif also portrays the conviction that "to this end Christ died and lived again, so that he might be Lord of both the dead and the living" (Rom. 14:9). In addition, Jesus' descent asserts that the Old Testament figures to whom he offers deliverance are part of the company of those redeemed through Jesus, being incorporated by Jesus into the salvation he secured. That is, Jesus' hades descent affirms the fundamental unity of divine purpose in the Old Testament and in the churches, with Jesus portrayed as the one savior of all. Clearly, this early form of the idea of Jesus' hades descent carried profound meanings in vividly presenting Jesus' supremacy in all levels of creation and his ultimate standing in redemption.

Variant Forms of the Descent Theme

There are also a couple of very interesting early variant forms of the idea; one is attested in other texts that can be regarded as of proto-orthodox provenance, and the other is favored more in texts that may have a heterodox origin. *Hermas* (*Sim.* 9.16.3-5) explains that after their own death the Christian apostles and teachers "preached to those who had previously fallen asleep," thus providing for the posthumous redemption of those who had died before Jesus' appearance. Clement of Alexandria cites this passage approvingly and, more specifically, portrays this proclamation by Christian apostles as directed to Gentile dead, and as complementing Jesus' prior proclamation to righteous Jews in his own hades descent (*Strom.* 2.9; 6.6 [ANF, 2:357, 490]). Thus, in this scheme all the righteous dead, whether of Israel or of the nations, who had died before Jesus' earthly appearance, are given the opportunity to embrace salvation through him. Obviously, from an initial concern to assert a link between the gospel and the Old Testament, we have here a wider concern that probably reflects both the dominantly Gentile constituency of Christianity in the second century and also a desire by Gentiles such as Hermas and Clement to engage the larger cultural and religious history. Clement in particular shows a concern to offer redemption for those Gentiles who had lived moral lives in accordance with true philosophy, as well as those of pre-Christian Israel who had lived righteously in obedience to Torah. This wider version of the hades-descent motif presents Jesus as the universal redeemer of all righteous dead, of whatever ethnic origin.[221]

Another, very different rendition of Jesus' hades descent interprets it as a

---

221. This form of the idea is reflected also in Hippolytus (*Paschal Homily* 102).

vivid metaphor describing his descent from heaven (or the *plērōma*) to earth.[222] That is, in this adaptation of the hades-descent idea, Jesus' descent to hades is his incarnation. The "dead" are simply his living contemporaries, who are portrayed as spiritually dead, and the earthly domain is taken as "hades," from which the redeemed are offered escape.[223] This metaphorical version may be accounted for historically as a subsequent, revisionist interpretation of a prior form of the hades-descent idea. On the one hand it appears to be one of a number of reinterpretations of traditional terms and categories in heterodox Christianity (e.g., the reinterpretation of resurrection as purely an inward transaction without bodily manifestation). In the *Apocryphon of John*, for example, Jesus' descent into "the midst of darkness and the inside of Hades" is explicitly identified as "the prison of the body" (30.17–31.20; *NHLE*, 122). That is, hades is the world of bodily existence. Jesus' hades descent was his own incarnation in bodily form. And his liberation of captives from hades is accomplished through people heeding his call to arise and throw off the deep sleep of this world of bodily (especially sexual) appetites.

On the other hand, those who flatly identified Jesus' hades descent as his incarnation could also point to earlier texts and traditions for justification and inspiration.[224] To cite one example, in Ephesians 2:1-9 readers are addressed as those who were "dead in trespasses and sins," but subsequently had been "made alive with Christ . . . and raised up and seated in the heavenly realms in Christ Jesus." Attridge has proposed that Hebrews 2:10-18 provides a first-century instance of the adaptation of the idea of hades descent to portray the redemptive significance of Jesus' incarnation.[225] Attridge also contends that this makes Hebrews the earliest witness to the motif of Jesus' hades descent. So the metaphorical version of the hades descent is not so much a totally new concept as it is a

---

222. Peel gathers references to this metaphorical version of the hades-descent motif in various early Christian sources (34-36), showing that it is found both in "gnostic" and in proto-orthodox writings (e.g., Origen).

223. The radical reinterpretation of Jesus' hades descent as the incarnation is reflected in Nag Hammadi writings that are commonly thought to show "gnostic" influences/provenance: e.g., *Trim. Prot.* 40.10–42.2 (*NHLE*, 516-17); *Gos. Truth* 26.5-27 (*NHLE*, 44).

224. Peel says Origen reflects a similar metaphorical interpretation of Jesus' hades descent (*Commentary on John* 6.174-78). But, though Origen here links Jesus' incarnation and hades descent as the two stages/steps by which he procured redemption for all, Origen quite clearly sees *two* distinguishable actions, each with its own redemptive role. So Origen does not in fact give us an instance equivalent to the radical reinterpretation of Jesus' hades descent that we find in some texts of strong heterodox coloring. For the relevant passage in Origen (Greek with French translation), see Cécile Blanc, *Origène: Commentaire sur saint Jean, Tome II*, SC 157 (Paris: Éditions du Cerf, 1970), 260-63.

225. Attridge, "Liberating," esp. 106-9.

selective preference for, and hyperextension of, earlier Christian representations of the status of people apart from and prior to Jesus as spiritually "dead."

Nevertheless, the origins of the theme lie in early Christian circles that were either Jewish Christian or at least heavily shaped by Jewish Christian concerns. In the earliest version, Jesus really descended to the nether regions to proclaim salvation in his name to the prophets and other righteous of pre-Christian Israel. Proto-orthodox Christianity certainly was concerned to affirm that Old Testament saints were part of the same company of redeemed as they were, and that Jesus had provided and bestowed redemption on them all. In this earliest version of Jesus' hades descent, precisely through his own death Jesus had been able to declare deliverance directly to the righteous of pre-Christian Israel who had died in hope of the fulfillment of God's messianic promises.

To be sure, the basic idea of a descent to hades by a human figure is widely attested in pre-Christian and non-Christian traditions.[226] The Christian theme of Jesus' hades descent has to be seen historically as reflecting the worldview in which it can be imagined that someone could go to the realm of the dead and proclaim redemption to them. That is, the motif of Jesus' hades descent obviously reflects the basic "grammar" of such a worldview. But it would be a mistake to fail to see the distinctives of the Christian idea. To cite one central feature, Jesus' proclamation to the dead has no precedents in mythic accounts available to earliest Christians. So, at the least, in Jesus' hades descent we have to see a rather distinctive adaptation of the general idea of descent to the dead.[227]

Jesus, Man and God

We noted that Ignatius testified to his faith with his body, his martyrdom and thematizing of it being highly influential on the developing martyrological tradition of early Christianity. His letters are also noteworthy for expressions of faith that anticipate, and perhaps influenced, subsequent developments in formative orthodox doctrine about Jesus.

Ignatius was at particular pains to emphasize the reality of Jesus' human existence.[228] Earlier traditions reflected in the New Testament writings unambiguously assert Jesus' full participation in human existence, most characteristically, of course, underscoring the reality and significance of his crucifixion

---

226. E.g., J. A. MacCulloch, "Descent to Hades (Ethnic)," in *Encyclopaedia of Religion and Ethics*, 4:648-54; MacCulloch, *The Harrowing of Hell*, chaps. 2–4.

227. See, e.g., Attridge, "Liberating," 109-13.

228. "The special mark of Ignatius' theology is the centrality afforded the incarnation and crucifixion of Jesus Christ." Schoedel, *Ignatius of Antioch*, 17. See also Rackl, 89-144.

and bodily resurrection (e.g., Heb. 2:10-18; 4:14-16). But Ignatius was clearly concerned to affirm Jesus' genuine humanity more broadly. He repeatedly cites key events that represent Jesus' human existence and serve as confessional touchstones: Jesus' birth (of a virgin, from the line of David), his baptism by John, his sufferings and crucifixion (under Pontius Pilate), and his bodily resurrection (Ign. *Magn.* 11.1; Ign. *Trall.* 9.1-2; Ign. *Smyrn.* 1.1-2). These statements almost certainly draw upon confessional traditions such as we find attested in 1 Timothy 6:13 (Jesus' testimony before Pilate) and 2 Timothy 2:8 (Jesus' Davidic descent). But in Ignatius's letters these individual events appear in confessional catenas, as series of events that collectively constitute the statement of Jesus' humanity. In these same passages he also repeatedly (and distinctively) refers to these events as having "truly/really" *(alēthōs)* happened.[229]

It is not difficult to detect the reason for Ignatius's emphasis. He heatedly refers to certain people who say that Jesus "suffered in appearance only" (Ign. *Smyrn.* 2.1; Ign. *Trall.* 10).[230] Much of his letter to Smyrna in particular is concerned with denouncing this view (Ign. *Smyrn.* 2–7). It is more difficult, however, to say exactly what the teaching was, and who the particular Christians he condemns as "unbelievers" were (2.1), "wild beasts in human form" (4.1) who hold "heretical opinions [*tous heterodoxountas*]," and whom he accuses of uncaring and schismatic behavior (6.2). Ignatius openly states his reluctance to give them and their views free publicity by going into detail about their error or even by mentioning their names (5.3; cf. also 7.2). This may well be the same teaching referred to just after Ignatius's death in Polycarp's letter to Philippi. Using phrasing from 1 John 4:2-3, Polycarp condemns as "antichrist" anyone "who does not confess that Jesus Christ has come in the flesh"; he warns against whoever "does not acknowledge the testimony of the cross" and "twists the sayings of the Lord [*ta logia tou kyriou*]" to support claims that "there is neither resurrection nor judgment" (7.1).[231]

The people attacked are, however, obviously fellow Christians. Although Ignatius warns his readers not to receive them in their churches, he does urge prayer for them "if somehow they might repent" (Ign. *Smyrn.* 4.1). Though they

---

229. Of the 23 uses of *alēthōs* in the apostolic fathers, 14 are in Ignatius's letters; the term is used to emphasize the reality of events in Jesus' earthly existence in at least 10 of these latter: Ign. *Magn.* 11.1; Ign. *Trall.* 9.1 (3 occurrences); 9.2; Ign. *Smyrn.* 1.1 (2 occurrences); 1.2; 2.1 (2 occurrences). The term is not so used in any other writer of the period.

230. In Ign. *Trall.* 10.1 and Ign. *Smyrn.* 2.1, Ignatius uses the Greek expression *to dokein peponthenai*, which many historians of early Christianity cite as a basis for the term "docetism/docetics" to refer to teachings and the advocates thereof that deny in some way Jesus' humanity.

231. Cf. the reference in 2 Tim. 2:17-18 to Hymenaeus and Philetus "who have swerved from the truth by claiming that the resurrection has already taken place."

heed "neither the prophecies nor the law of Moses," and are not moved by "the gospel" or the sufferings of Ignatius and fellow believers, he holds out the possibility that they might "change their mind in regard to the Passion [of Jesus], which is our resurrection" (5.1-3). They are "unbelievers" in Ignatius's eyes for refusing to confess Jesus' real humanity, their blasphemy being their refusal to confess that "he was truly clothed in flesh" (5.2); they probably regarded a real human existence incompatible with their belief that Jesus was of heavenly origin and divine.[232] As we noted in previous chapters, there are confirming indications, from 1 John and various extracanonical texts as well, that Ignatius was not jumping at shadows or raising uninformed alarms. There really were various Christians who found it inappropriate to attribute real human existence to Jesus, precisely out of reverence for him as divine; and they in turn probably regarded those who asserted that Jesus was truly human as foolish and ignorant.

For his part, Ignatius, too, certainly affirms Jesus' divinity. Indeed, he is as notable for the way he does this as he is for his emphasis on Jesus' humanity. As preceding chapters of this book have shown, the belief that Jesus is, in some unique and meaningful sense, divine is a feature of Christian devotion from the earliest observable stages. Though the term "god" *(theos)* is applied to Jesus only a few times in New Testament writings (unambiguously in John 1:1; 20:28, only slightly less so in Titus 2:13), in other very eloquent ways first-century Christians treated Jesus as sharing in God's attributes, and as worthy of the sort of reverence otherwise to be reserved for God. The opening statement of *2 Clement* (ca. 120-40) is fully representative of early Christian tradition: "Brothers, we ought to think of Jesus Christ, as we do of God, as 'Judge of the living and the dead.'" Ignatius fully assents to this tradition. For him Jesus was "before the ages with the Father and appeared in the endpoint [*telos*] of time" (Ign. *Magn.* 6.1), and he affirms that Jesus came forth from God, remained with God, and returned to God (Ign. *Magn.* 7.2; also 8.2). Jesus is "the Eternal, the Invisible, who for our sake became visible; the Intangible, the Unsuffering, who for our sake suffered, and who for our sake endured in every way" (Ign. *Poly.* 3.2).

Particularly noteworthy are the numerous places where Ignatius refers to Jesus as "God" *(theos).*[233] In addition to the formulaic expressions "Jesus Christ our God" (the inscriptions to Ign. *Eph.* and Ign. *Rom.*), "our God Jesus Christ"

---

232. Ignatius also accuses them of failing to show concern for the widow, orphan, oppressed, prisoner, and the destitute, and of abstaining from the Eucharist and prayer (*Smyrn.* 6.2). This is probably what he means by accusing them of "contentiousness" (7.1).

233. Demetrios C. Trakatellis, "God Language in Ignatius of Antioch," in *The Future of Early Christianity: Essays in Honor of Helmut Koester*, ed. B. A. Pearson (Minneapolis: Fortress, 1991), 422-30; Schoedel, *Ignatius of Antioch*, 39; and perhaps still the most extensive discussion, Rackl, 152-231, esp. 152-66.

(Ign. *Eph.* 18.2; Ign. *Rom.* 3.3; Ign. *Poly.* 8.3), and "Jesus Christ the God" (Ign. *Smyrn.* 1.1), there are still more striking statements. In Jesus "God appeared in human form" (Ign. *Eph.* 19.3). With Jesus' crucifixion as his model, Ignatius seeks to imitate "the suffering of my God" (Ign. *Rom.* 6.3); he characterizes Ephesian Christians as having taken on new life "through the blood of God" (Ign. *Eph.* 1.1). Of course, these all directly reflect Ignatius's deeply felt piety, but they are not simply emotionally tinged rhetoric. In the context of all that Ignatius attributes to Jesus, his application of the epithet *theos* to him surely signals the view that Jesus is genuinely divine.

An additional factor not reckoned with sufficiently in scholarly discussion of Ignatius's distinctive penchant for referring to Jesus as *theos* is the frequent use of this term as an honorific epithet for the Roman emperor.[234] In fact, Ignatius's phrasings, "our God," "the God," "my God," all mirror the devotional phrasing used in honors given to the emperor, especially and increasingly under the Flavians and thereafter. Given that Ignatius was going to his death as a Christian, quite possibly after refusing to honor the emperor as divine (and closely contemporary with Pliny's practice in the matter), he may well have deliberately appropriated expressions that were familiar in emperor devotion to honor Jesus. Thereby he would have signaled vividly, and pugnaciously, that for him *Jesus,* and not the emperor, was the sole rightful human who could be addressed as *theos*. This would explain why there is this comparatively more frequent application of *theos* to Jesus in Ignatius's letters.

Yet Ignatius refers to Jesus as *theos* while still portraying him as subordinate to "the Father." Jesus is "the mind of the Father" (Ign. *Eph.* 3.2) and "God's knowledge [*theou gnōsin*]" (17.2), and, as we noted earlier, Christians sing "through Jesus Christ to the Father" (4.2). Ignatius confesses that "there is one God who revealed himself through Jesus Christ his Son, who is his Word . . . who in every respect pleased him who sent him" (Ign. *Magn.* 8.2). Just "as the Lord did nothing without the Father" (7.1), and "in the flesh [*kata sarka*]" was subject to the Father (13.2), so Christians are to be united and subject to their bishop and presbyters. To the Romans Ignatius describes Jesus as "the unerring mouth by whom the Father has spoken truly" (Ign. *Rom.* 8.2).

Ignatius emphasizes that the proper stance is to confess *both* Jesus' humanity *and* his divinity, and he shows an obvious relish for compact yet eloquent statements that are also clearly intended to be memorable. Of these, the statement in *Ephesians* 7.2 is perhaps the most artfully constructed: "There is

---

234. I refer again to Lily Ross Taylor, *The Divinity of the Roman Emperor* (Middletown, Conn.: American Philosophical Association, 1931; reprint, Chico, Calif.: Scholars, n.d.), 267-83, who cites numerous inscriptions to various emperors in which *theos* is a frequent epithet.

one physician, who is both enfleshed and spiritual [*sarkikos kai pneumatikos*], born and unborn, God in man, true life in death, both from Mary and from God, first subject to suffering and then beyond suffering [*apathēs*], Jesus Christ our Lord."[235] In other passages as well, he makes similar double-barreled affirmations about Jesus as both human and divine (Ign. *Eph.* 18.2; 20.2; Ign. *Smyrn.* 1.1; Ign. *Poly.* 3.2).

It is also important to note that for Ignatius and this tradition, Jesus *remains* both human and divine. In his earthly suffering and death, Jesus is the model and inspiration for the earthly existence of believers; and in his bodily resurrection, Jesus is the model and guarantee of the resurrection life that believers await for themselves. "The divine plan" has to do with Jesus, "the new man" (Ign. *Eph.* 20.1), and just as the Father truly raised him from death, so will he raise up "in Christ Jesus" those who believe in Jesus, "apart from whom we have no true life" (Ign. *Trall.* 9.2). The incarnation of the divine Word/Son was an irrevocable act that permanently commits Jesus to embodied human destiny.

In addition to attacking the so-called docetics who deny Jesus' full humanity, Ignatius also complains about those who promote *Ioudaïsmos* (Ign. *Magn.* 8–10; Ign. *Philad.* 6–9).[236] The latter also are almost certainly Christians; what they advocate is not conversion from what we today mean by "Christianity" to "Judaism," but instead the observance of Jewish religious practices by (Gentile) Christians.[237] This is most clearly reflected in Ignatius's emphatic statement that "it is utterly absurd to profess [*lalein*] Jesus Christ and to take up Jewish practices [*Ioudaïzein*]" (Ign. *Magn.* 10.3). Whereas Paul defended the freedom of Gentile Christians, in particular, from having to observe the requirements of Torah (though Jewish Christians were equally free to practice Torah, so long as it did not prevent their full acceptance of Gentile believers), Ignatius was simply concerned to differentiate Christian from Jewish religious practices. Convinced that the Old Testament prophets "lived in accordance

235. The rhythm and other poetic features of this statement in Greek are, unfortunately, difficult to convey in translation.

236. Although it remains a disputed matter, I agree with Schoedel (*Ignatius of Antioch,* 118) that the "docetics" are not the same as those who promote *Ioudaïsmos,* and that Ignatius has simply lumped them together, for he sees them both as heterodox (a familiar tactic in antiheresy texts).

237. In the time of Ignatius the Greek term *Ioudaïsmos* consistently designates the system of religious beliefs and practices that characterized Jews, especially observance of Sabbath, food laws, and circumcision. *Ioudaïsmos* is what Ignatius means by "antiquated practices" such as Sabbath observance (Ign. *Magn.* 9.1; cf. 8.1). On the term, and the verb form *ioudaïzein* (to live as a Jew, to take up Jewish religious practices), see, e.g., Otto Betz, "Ἰουδαϊσμός," in *EDNT,* 2:192-93.

with Christ Jesus," Ignatius expects *all* believers now to do the same (9.1), whether Jewish or Gentile. Thus all believers should throw out "the bad leaven, which has become stale and sour [Jewish religious practices]," and reach for "the new leaven, which is Jesus Christ" (10.2). He urges the Philadelphian Christians not to listen to "anyone who expounds *Ioudaïsmos*," for he regards as "tombstones and graves of the dead" those who fail to speak of Jesus Christ (Ign. *Philad.* 6.1). Though Ignatius obviously regards the Old Testament as Scripture, yet for him Jesus' "cross and death and his resurrection and the faith which comes through him" constitute "the inviolable archives" by which all right belief is constituted (8.2). That is, for Ignatius the gospel he affirms is also the hermeneutical key to understanding aright the Old Testament.

In the next couple centuries after Ignatius, the developing orthodox tradition struggled to find conceptual categories for accommodating a fully divine Jesus within their commitment to one God, and also for affirming both Jesus' full divinity and his genuine humanity. We should beware of crediting Ignatius with philosophical developments that came later. But it is fairly clear that he represents the profound commitment to Jesus' divinity and real human existence that demanded those efforts toward the distinctive Christian idea of God, and especially toward the idea of Jesus' "two natures," doctrinal efforts that heavily occupied the developing orthodox/catholic tradition well through the fourth century.[238] Moreover, his penchant for confessional catenas of events of Jesus' human existence prefigures and probably influenced the sort of creedal tradition that received classic expression in the Apostles' Creed.[239]

The Divine Jesus and God

The fully divine status accorded Jesus in proto-orthodox Christianity, and already in the first-century devotional traditions upon which it drew, created an obvious question, especially because proto-orthodox Christians professed to be monotheists. How was this divine Jesus to be understood and reverenced vis-à-vis God "the Father"? In the very "primitive" traditions that we have examined thus far, this question is not explicitly posed and treated. However, it seems to be presupposed, and addressed implicitly, in the attribution of Jesus' divine and exalted status to the will and action of God. That is, not only is Jesus defined

---

238. For a classic review of these issues in the early centuries, see J. N. D. Kelly, *Early Christian Doctrines,* 5th ed. (New York and London: Harper and Row, 1977), 83-162.

239. Philip Schaff, *The Creeds of Christendom,* vol. 1, *The History of the Creeds* (New York: Harper and Row, 1877; reprint, Grand Rapids: Baker, 1977), 14-23.

entirely in relation to God, for example, as God's "Word," "Son," "image," and "Christ," he is also characteristically represented as appointed, exalted, enthroned, and given a "name" above all others by God. Consequently the Christians of the very early years understood their worship of Jesus as obedience to the express will of God, who had exalted Jesus and had designated him as rightful recipient of devotion (e.g., 1 Cor. 15:20-28; Phil. 2:9-11; Heb. 1:3-4). Worshiping Jesus, thus, was for them actually a requisite demonstration of their reverence for God "the Father."

As we have seen, there is an implicit but astonishingly close association of Jesus with God, both in the attributes and functions they share in earliest Christian beliefs (e.g., Jesus as the agent of creation, dispenser of the Holy Spirit, and eschatological judge) and in the reverence accorded to both in early Christian devotional practice. Probably the closest we get to the equivalent of an "ontological" link of Jesus with God is in the notion that Jesus has been given, shares, and embodies the divine "name." This notion obviously reflects the language and conceptual categories of biblical and ancient Jewish tradition, and was meaningful within the terms of reference of this tradition.

But for those Christians of the second century and thereafter who sought to understand and articulate the relationship of Jesus to God in a way that could be made meaningful to the larger intellectual and cultural world, the traditional expressions and categories were not adequate. Nor were these traditional formulations sufficient for the impressively vigorous intra-Christian effort to formulate doctrine about God and Jesus. In the latter half of the second century, Christians found themselves in "one of those brief periods of human invention when earlier concepts become museum pieces."[240] It was not easy, however, to develop adequate doctrines, and to win broad acceptance of them, as is evident from the lengthy and complex efforts to do so that characterized Christianity for a couple of hundred years or more thereafter.[241]

I propose that the writings of Justin Martyr give us the earliest extant example of a proto-orthodox Christian seriously attempting to articulate an understanding of Jesus as divine in terms he hoped to make comprehensible and even persuasive both to Jewish interlocutors and the wider culture.[242] He was

240. Eric Osborn, *The Emergence of Christian Theology* (Cambridge: Cambridge University Press, 1993), 1.

241. R. P. C. Hanson (*The Search for the Christian Doctrine of God* [Edinburgh: T. & T. Clark, 1988]) deals in depth with the fourth-century Arian controversy, which shows how long the issue of Jesus' relationship to God remained alive in early Christianity.

242. The *Apology* by Aristides, sent to Emperor Antoninus Pius (138-61 C.E.), was likely a bit earlier than Justin's main works, but it offers little in the way of doctrine about Jesus, focusing more on monotheism and the validity of Christianity as the "third race" and of its creed. For

educated in philosophy as well as conversant with the Scriptures and traditions of Christianity. According to his own account, after studying the major philosophical traditions of his day (Stoicism, Aristotelianism, Pythagoreanism, and Platonism), he converted to Christian faith (ca. 132), finding in the Old Testament Scriptures and in Christian teachings truth that surpassed what his pagan learning afforded, and regarding himself thereafter as a Christian philosopher (*Dial.* 1–8).[243] The Christian writers who came along later in the proto-orthodox tradition took things much farther, especially in the development of more sophisticated doctrinal categories for expressing Jesus' relationship to God, the creator of all. But in Justin we can already see the broad direction of subsequent doctrinal reflection on this matter, and I propose that he can be treated as the transitional figure between what I am calling "earliest" Christianity and what comes thereafter.[244]

Justin is particularly interesting because <u>he combined a firm loyalty to biblical and Christian traditions with a concern to engage and employ philosophical currents of his day in articulating and defending Christian faith</u>. We can see this, for example, in the pattern of epithets he gives to Jesus. On the one hand he uses many titles drawn from the biblical tradition: e.g., Christ, Son, Captain, Angel, Man, King, Priest, God, Lord, Stone, Child, Angel of the Great Counsel, Jacob, Word (Logos), Wisdom, Israel, and Son of God (*Dial.* 34.2; 59.1; 61.1; 126.1).[245] On the other hand, in his effort to articulate Jesus' relationship for his intended audience of non-Christians, he particularly focuses on the term "Logos," one of the biblical epithets already applied to Jesus in Christian tradition (especially, of course, in the prologue of the Gospel of John), but which also had a rich background in Greek philosophical traditions. Justin

---

English translation, see D. M. Kay, "The Apology of Aristides," in ANF, 9:257-79. Earlier still, Quadratus addressed his *Apology* to Hadrian (117-38), but unfortunately, apart from a single fragment in Eusebius (*HE* 4.3.2), it is lost, as is the *Dialogue of Jason and Papiscus concerning Christ* by Aristo of Pella (ca. 140?). For further introduction, see, e.g., F. L. Cross, *The Early Christian Fathers* (London: Gerald Duckworth, 1960), 45-48; Quasten, *Patrology*, 1:190-96. William R. Schoedel, "Apologetic Literature and Ambassadorial Activities," *HTR* 82 (1989): 55-78, sets Christian apologetic literature in its ancient Roman literary and political context.

243. In Little's view (94), Plato was Justin's favorite philosopher, and he was also respectful of Stoics, but he was contemptuous of Epicureans and Cynics.

244. See, e.g., Eric Osborn, *Justin Martyr*, BZHT 47 (Tübingen: J. C. B. Mohr [Paul Siebeck], 1973), esp. 28-43; Barnard, *Justin Martyr*, esp. 85-100; Little, 90-176; Daniélou, *Gospel Message*, 345-57.

245. Little, 138, gives a full list with references in Justin. He judged that Justin has "the greatest variety by far" in epithets for Jesus among second-century writers. He also notes that Stoics gave many names to the Logos (citing Seneca, *Natural Questions* 2.45), and so did Philo (e.g., *Conf. ling.* 146).

draws upon all sides of the semantic history of this term (Platonic, Stoic, biblical, and Christian) in developing his view of Jesus.

The philosophical background of the term is so rich and diverse that it is difficult, and probably unwise, to try to account for Justin's use of it solely on the basis of any one of the prior traditions. He was, after all, an eclectic thinker living in an eclectic age. It is particularly fallacious and naive to try to account adequately for Justin's use of it on the basis of this or that Greek philosophical tradition, for neither singly nor cumulatively is the body of previous philosophical uses adequate.

One can see some overlap, but for Justin the Logos is defined by *the figure* X *of Jesus.* This human figure is for him, to be sure, also the incarnate Logos, who is the "Lord" mentioned in all Old Testament theophanies, and who was with the Father before all things. But for Justin, the real character of the Logos is derived from what he believes *about Jesus,* and it is Justin's faith in Jesus as unique Son of the Father that gives to his presentation of the Logos a distinctive three-dimensional, person-shaped quality.[246] Indeed, the designation of Jesus as divine Son was of supreme significance to Justin, and "upon its meaning and implications, all other titles, even 'Logos' evidently depend."[247] In Justin's thought, "Jesus is divine and human, the Logos of God; not divine Son because he is the Logos, but Logos because He is the absolute, unique, God the Son."[248] Moreover, as Barnard put it, "For Justin the logos was first and foremost Jesus Christ."[249]

So Justin emphasizes that the Logos is permanently distinguishable from the Father, and he refutes those who teach that the Logos is merely an attribute or power of God that can extend out and then be retracted back, or a creature (*Dial.* 61–62; 128). Particularly in his debate with Jewish rejection of the gospel, Justin develops his emphasis on a real "duality in the heart of the Godhead."[250] He cites biblical passages such as Genesis 1:26-28 to show a genuine conversation between Father and Son/Logos that demands thinking of them as really distinguishable, and able to function as conversation partners (*Dial.* 62). Several times he emphasizes that the Son/Logos is "numerically distinct" from the Father (*arithmō heteron esti; Dial.* 56.11; 62.2; 128.4; 129.1, 4), meaning that the Son/Logos is different in person from the Father.

In this he departs crucially from Stoic or middle Platonist traditions, in

246. For a similar judgment, see M. J. Edwards, "Justin's Logos and the Word of God," *JECS* 3 (1995): 261-80.

247. Little, 104.

248. Little, 105 n. 1. "Justin's whole Christological system rests upon the basic fact that Jesus Christ is the 'only proper Son of God,' the unique Revealing Logos" (95).

249. Barnard, *Justin Martyr,* 91.

250. Barnard, *Justin Martyr,* 89.

which the Logos serves essentially as an explanatory principle of order that made the world a *kosmos* (order) instead of a chaos, and the logical middle principle between the ultimate deity and the world of matter. More than a century before Justin, Philo of Alexandria had appropriated the term as well, seeing the Logos as the "Lord" mentioned in the same biblical passages where Justin finds him. But in Philo's many and varied references to the Logos, the term essentially designates the key mode/medium by which the transcendent, infinite, and ineffable God acts and reveals himself within the confines of a finite world, and to humanity.[251] That is, in Philo, as in Greek philosophical tradition, the Logos was solely an important *logical* category posited to deal with an *intellectual* problem. By contrast, Justin's view was obviously shaped by the fact that he was applying the term to a *real figure* who had appeared in history and was reverenced in Christian worship under his own name along with God the Father.[252] Therefore, in Justin's presentation the Logos certainly has the role of the organizing principle and purpose of the cosmos, which he explicitly acknowledges is in agreement with philosophical tradition (e.g., 2 *Apol.* 6.3). But he insists that on this subject, as on others, the philosophical traditions give but an imperfect and incomplete view of things that are fully disclosed now in Jesus and the Christian gospel (e.g., 1 *Apol.* 60).

A distinctive feature of Justin is his bold and creative adaptation of the Stoic notion of the Logos as the world soul, the organizing principle of the cosmos and the premise of rational truth. Justin refers to the "seed of reason" operative in Greek poets and philosophers (2 *Apol.* 8), and he describes Plato, Stoics, and others as sometimes "able to see realities darkly through the sowing of the implanted Word that was in them" (2 *Apol.* 13.2). True enough, the expression that Justin uses, "spermatic Word [*spermatikos logos*]," had a prior history in middle Platonist and Stoic traditions, where it refers to the presence of wisdom and justice in all human generations, thereby accounting for the love of knowledge, and social mores that are found so widely attested in human history.[253] But in Justin the term features in a new concept that reflects distinctively Christian convictions about the *supremacy and finality* of the revelation of God in *Jesus*.

---

251. E.g., Mack, *Logos und Sophia*. For further references, see Peder Borgen, "Philo of Alexandria: A Critical and Synthetical Survey of Research since World War II," in *ANRW*, 2.21/2:99-154.

252. Barnard (*Justin Martyr*, 92-96) shows persuasively that Philo is not the key to Justin's teaching on the Logos, but that Justin's view is crucially shaped by his view of Jesus.

253. Carl Andresen, "Justin und der mittlere Platonismus," *ZNW* 44 (1952-53): 157-95. Again, predecessors include Philo of Alexandria. See also Barnard, *Justin Martyr*, 97-99; Osborn, *Justin Martyr*, 36-40.

Justin (*2 Apol.* 13) argues that, because their share of the divine Logos was only partial *(apo merous tou spermatikou theiou logou),* the various philosophical traditions contradict one another. But he asserts that Jesus is in fact the direct, full manifestation of the divine Word, who shows thereby that the Logos is most adequately understood as a real person whom Christians engage in *devotion and love,* and not merely an abstract principle or a body of truth. "Next to God, we worship and love the Word who is from the unbegotten and ineffable God, since also He became man for our sakes, that, becoming a partaker of our sufferings, He might also bring us healing."[254] In the light of this full revelation of the Logos, Christians can discriminate among the teachings of philosophers, and can identify those things that correspond to the fullness of truth now known in Jesus. On this basis Justin boldly announces, "Whatever things were rightly said among all people are the property of us Christians" (*2 Apol.* 13.4). That is, Justin both points to the philosophers as partially valid, but incomplete, anticipations of the revelation of the Logos and maintains that the fullness of the Logos in Jesus now completes and surpasses them all. This notion has no precedent in the philosophical traditions about the Logos. Instead, Justin here reflects the early Christian view that the eschatological time of redemption and full revelation of God's purposes had come through Jesus.

Justin is, however, apparently to be credited with this daring and imaginative conception, which proved programmatic in the subsequent efforts of early Christian thinkers to engage intellectual history and the wider culture (particularly in the tradition of "Logos Christology" represented by Clement of Alexandria, Irenaeus, and Origen).[255] But, without detracting from Justin's creativity, it seems likely that his argument may have been inspired and shaped by the similar outlook toward the pre-Christian revelations of God in the Old Testament attested in the first-century Christian traditions that fed Justin's own faith (e.g., Heb. 1:1-4; 1 Pet. 1:10-12). In particular, there is an interesting similarity of thought between Justin's statement that "the seed and imitation imparted according to capacity is one thing, and quite another is the thing itself" (*2 Apol.* 13.6) and the contrast in Hebrews 1:1-2 between God's various and partial revelations in past generations by the Old Testament prophets and his full revelation "to us by the Son." Just as Hebrews portrays the Torah and all its cultic regulations as "only a shadow of the good things to come and not the true form of these realities," so Justin represents pre-Christian philosophy as "the seed and imitation" and not "the thing itself." The previous philosophical speculations

---

254. 2 *Apol.* 13.4 (ANF, 1:193).

255. Daniélou, *Gospel Message,* 345-86; Osborn, *The Emergence of Christian Theology;* Grillmeier, *Christ in Christian Tradition,* 85-149.

about the *spermatikos logos* simply gave Justin a device that he could adapt robustly to serve his aims of commending the superiority of Christian faith to its "cultured despisers" of his time.[256]

As noted already, Justin also emphatically maintains that the Son/Logos is not a creature, but instead shares the same "being" as the Father. Justin is in fact our first witness to the use of new terms in Christian discourse to try to conceive and articulate the unique relationship of Jesus to God, and to accommodate a limited but real plurality within a rigorously monotheistic stance. He refers to one divine *ousia* (being, essence, substance) and distinguishable *prosōpa* ("faces"; *1 Apol.* 36–38). Thereby he makes a prototypical effort that anticipates and shapes references to one divine essence or substance (Lat. *substantia;* Gk. *ousia*) and three "persons" (Lat. *personae;* Gk. *hypostases*) in Tertullian and later Christian thinkers on the road to the developed doctrine of the Trinity.[257]

Moreover, he carefully distinguishes between this view of divine unity and plurality and the views of others. For example, he emphasizes that, though the Son/Logos is distinguishable from the Father and derives in some unique way from the Father, this does not involve any diminution of the Father (*Dial.* 128). That is, attributing divine nature to the Logos/Son does not for Justin involve any reduction or threat to the Father and creator of all. Justin uses the analogy of a torch taken from a fire to illustrate his view. Just as lighting one fire from another does not reduce in volume or intensity the first fire, and yet the second fire is fully the same nature as the first, so the Son/Logos proceeds forth from the Father (61.2). They fully share in the same divine nature, each without minimizing the other, and yet are rightly distinct, both in actuality and in a proper conception of divine things.

As noted already, Justin insists that the Son/Logos is, along with the Father, rightly a recipient of worship, which in Justin's religious stance most eloquently separates the Son/Logos from all creatures (*Dial.* 41; 63.5; 65; 76; *1 Apol.* 6; 13). And yet Justin consistently affirms that the Son/Logos has a second place to the Father (e.g., *1 Apol.* 13) and is the "first power after God" (32.10). That is, Justin unhesitatingly subordinates the Son/Logos to the Father (e.g., *Dial.* 56.11). He refers to the Son as begotten by the will and power of God (61.1) as the "*archē* [beginning, first principle] before all created things" (62.4; cf. 129.4).

---

256. I allude here to Friedrich Schleiermacher's classic work of 1799 addressed to the unbelieving elite of his time: *On Religion: Speeches to Its Cultured Despisers* (New York: Harper and Row, 1958). In doing so, I posit no judgment as to similarities and differences between the efforts of Justin and Schleiermacher.

257. Osborn, *Tertullian*, 7, notes Justin as an important predecessor.

This may well imply that Justin thought of the Son/Logos as "essentially generated for the purpose of creation and revelation," and that the Logos had been begotten "at some point anterior to the creation."[258] If this is a fair inference, then obviously Justin here can be distinguished from the later Nicene-era teaching about the *eternal* generation of the Son. It would be unfair, however, to measure Justin against the issues and developments of the fourth century that he never faced, and on which he never had to take a position. As the Arian crisis had not broken upon Christian thinking in the second century, it is not good historical analysis to manufacture a position on the matter on Justin's behalf.

What Justin did face in his own time was, on the one hand, Jewish accusations that Christians worshiped two gods, and on the other hand, the internal threat of Christian teachings (Marcion, Valentinus, and other demiurgical traditions) that posited a sharp distinction between the creator deity and the God from whom the Son had come forth.[259] Hence, characteristic of proto-orthodox Christianity, he emphasizes one creator of all, and one source and center of all divinity, including the Son/Logos.[260] Justin clearly sought to deny that the Son/Logos was a creature, or an emanation from God like the sun's rays, or represented a partition in God such that the being of the Father was diminished. Yet he also wanted to account for the Son/Logos as a monotheist, and the only way he could do so was by attributing the source of the Son/Logos to the Father.

We also have to recognize that Justin was basically developing terms and conceptions that came to him from prior Christian tradition. In the first two centuries, all texts from, and affirmed in, the developing proto-orthodox tradition, from the New Testament writings onward, reflect subordination Christology, the Son understood as the unique agent of the Father, serving the will of the Father, and leading the redeemed to the Father. In the Johannine prologue the Logos is introduced in close connection with "the beginning" of creation (John 1:1), and in Pauline tradition as well, the preincarnate Son is portrayed as the agent of creation (1 Cor. 8:5-6; Col. 1:15-20). Indeed, it is probably from Colossians 1:15-20 that Justin derives his use of "firstborn" *(prōtotokos)* and "beginning" *(archē)* as important designations of Jesus, although *prōtotokos* in fact is rather widely attested in other first-century texts (Rom. 8:29; Heb. 1:6; Rev.

---

258. Barnard, *Justin Martyr*, 91.

259. Osborn, *Justin Martyr*, 32; Barnard, *Justin Martyr*, 90-91.

260. Joseph Lortz, "Das Christentum als Monotheismus in den Apologien des zweiten Jahrhunderts," in *Beiträge zur Geschichte des christlichen Altertums und der byzantinischen Literatur: Festgabe Albert Ehrhard*, ed. Albert Michael Koeniger (Bonn and Leipzig: Kurt Schroeder, 1922), 301-27.

1:5).²⁶¹ If, in the light of Arius, fourth-century Christians became jittery with anything that smacked of subordinationism, that is irrelevant for understanding Christian thought of the first two centuries.

I want to reiterate that for Justin the Logos is first and foremost *Jesus*, whom Christians worship (*1 Apol.* 66–67), through whose death and resurrection believers are purified of their sins (*Dial.* 13; 41), and through whom now all nations can come to the light of the true God (*Dial.* 26). Whereas for Greek philosophers, and even for Philo, the Logos was essentially an important conceptual category, for Justin the Logos is the Lord Jesus to whom he owes everything. This is an important point that is sometimes missed in intellectual/doctrinal histories of early Christianity. Justin did not merely think about the Logos; Justin worshiped and loved him (*2 Apol.* 13.4).

Finally, in addition to the substance of his ideas about Jesus and their influence upon subsequent Christian doctrine, Justin is also a prototype of the sort of serious intellectual effort to engage and make use of the philosophical categories of his day that features in the following decades and centuries of Christian tradition. As with every prototype, his own particular effort was surpassed and would come to be judged inadequate in comparison to more sophisticated theological developments of later generations. But also, as with every line of development, the subsequent efforts toward the Christian doctrines of God and the Son were dependent upon Justin's prototypical contributions.

---

261. Osborn claims "at least five direct references" to Col. 1:15 (from which Justin derives *prōtotokos*) in the *Dialogue* (84.2; 85.2; 100.2; 125.3; 138.2). Philo prefers the term *prōtogonos* for the Logos (e.g., *Conf. ling.* 63, 146; *Somn.* 1.215). It is, thus, far more likely that Justin's use of *prōtotokos* reflects the term's place in early Christian tradition. "Beginning/first principle" (*archē*) as an epithet for Jesus likely comes from Col. 1:18.

Thereafter

To some readers, perhaps some who are particularly interested in ancient Christian intellectual engagement with culture or the formation of Christian doctrines about the Trinity, to end this analysis with Justin is to break off just when things start getting interesting. But I contend that the period I have characterized here as "earliest Christianity" is not only fascinating in its own right but is also crucial for what comes thereafter.

"What comes thereafter" includes, of course, great figures such as the influential bishop of Lyons, Irenaeus (with whom Bousset concluded his classic study of earliest belief in Jesus); the prolific and broad-minded Clement of Alexandria; Tertullian (that combative father of Latin-writing Christianity); and Origen (who perhaps most fully represents the best of early Christian scholarship). Other interesting, though somewhat less imposing, figures of the same period could be mentioned as well, such as Melito of Sardis and Hippolytus. There were also further noteworthy efforts at religious innovation in the late second and in the third centuries beyond those we studied here, among which Montanism is particularly important.[1]

But I contend that what we have examined in these chapters, "earliest Christianity" (ca. 30-170), provided the major convictions, and the parameters of belief and devotional practice as well, that shaped the subsequent developments in Christian tradition, which in turn came to be dominant and which form our picture of classical Christian faith. The devotional practice of earliest Christianity was particularly foundational for doctrinal developments. Though beliefs, or at least fundamental convictions, were certainly there from the out-

---

1. Most recently, Christine Trevett, *Montanism: Gender, Authority, and the New Prophecy* (Cambridge: Cambridge University Press, 1996).

set, the development of more sophisticated doctrinal formulations that followed was also heavily prompted, and decisively shaped, in the light of earliest Christian devotional practice.

Christians were proclaiming and worshiping Jesus, indeed, living and dying for his sake, well before the doctrinal/creedal developments of the second century and thereafter that have received so much attention in histories of Christian tradition. The early convictions about Jesus and the corresponding devotion offered to him that became so widespread in earliest Christianity were sufficiently robust to nourish the prolonged and vigorous efforts to articulate Christian faith in persuasive doctrinal formulations.

Moreover, devotion to Jesus as divine erupted suddenly and quickly, not gradually and late, among first-century circles of followers. More specifically, the origins lie in Jewish Christian circles of the earliest years. Only a certain wishful thinking continues to attribute the reverence of Jesus as divine decisively to the influence of pagan religion and the influx of Gentile converts, characterizing it as developing late and incrementally. Furthermore, devotion to Jesus as the "Lord," to whom cultic reverence and total obedience were the appropriate response, was widespread, not confined or attributable to particular circles, such as "Hellenists" or Gentile Christians of a supposed Syrian "Christ cult."

Amid the diversity of earliest Christianity, belief in Jesus' divine status was amazingly common. The "heresies" of earliest Christianity largely presuppose the view that Jesus is divine. That is not the issue. The problematic issue, in fact, was whether a genuinely *human* Jesus could be accommodated. Especially in the second century, "proto-orthodox" Christianity comprised those circles that regarded Jesus' human life as crucial in making his redemptive work efficacious.

Additionally, in spite of the diversity, it is equally evident that Jesus was *central* in all the forms of earliest Christianity, proto-orthodox or others, that we can describe with any confidence. This centrality of Jesus, and the uniqueness of his status in the various religious convictions of earliest Christians, also demanded, almost unavoidably, a new view of God.

As we have seen, in the second century, however, there were a few competing options on what view of God was to be widely embraced as best representing what Christians should confess. For example, was Jesus to be seen as an emanation from the divine *plērōma* (the "All"), from which the elect themselves had been separated? Was Jesus the representative of a hitherto unknown, alien God who was not to be associated with the creator deity of the Old Testament? Was it in fact totally inappropriate to link the God from whom Jesus came with this world, creation, and bodily existence? Or was the Christian God properly to be identified as the Old Testament deity who had created all things, had spoken truly through Moses and the prophets, and now was revealed more fully and decisively through Jesus?

The last option was, of course, the one espoused by what I have called "proto-orthodox Christianity," and this constellation of Christians (who, to be sure, exhibited a certain variety of emphases and outlooks) developed across the period of our analysis what amounted to a new and unique view of what the term "God" meant. Granted, they drew freely upon Jewish tradition, as reflected in their insistence that the one God was properly thought of as a personal deity of love, purpose, justice, and faithfulness. The influence of Jewish tradition was also reflected in their critique of pagan polytheism. Furthermore, like their Jewish coreligionists, they came to draw selectively upon philosophical traditions; but in the earliest centuries they did so with considerable caution.

The sum of proto-orthodox Christian teaching about God, however, included critically new elements. Although they stridently professed sole allegiance to the God of the Old Testament, their exclusivist monotheism sometimes being tested by the threat of death, they also posited a real and radical plurality, initially more focused on the "Father" and "Son," as somehow pertaining to the one God they worshiped to the exclusion of all others. That is, earliest Christian faith in Jesus contributed to a literal reshaping of the monotheism inherited from the Jewish/biblical tradition, initially taking things in a "binitarian" direction, though a trinitarian model subsequently became dominant. I emphasize, also, that this reshaping of belief about God was accompanied and expressed by a corresponding "binitarian" pattern of devotional practice, in which the exalted Jesus was included as recipient of reverence along with God "the Father."

The struggle to work out doctrinal formulations that could express in some coherent way this peculiar view of God (as "one" and yet somehow comprising "the Father" and Jesus, thereafter also including the Spirit as the "third Person" of the Trinity) occupied the best minds in early Christian orthodox/catholic tradition for the first several centuries. But the doctrinal problem they worked on was not of their making. It was forced upon them by the earnest convictions and devotional practice of believers from the earliest observable years of the Christian movement.

In addition to demanding this novel endeavor to incorporate plurality within the one God, their faith in Jesus also involved a corresponding view of human nature and hope. This correspondence was, in fact, the case for all the forms of devotion to Jesus that we have surveyed, however various groups understood his divine significance. In proto-orthodox beliefs, historically the most successful of the early options, Jesus is emphatically portrayed as having become human irrevocably, and genuinely and bodily human at that, thereby wedding himself, in an indissoluble union, with the human race. Proto-orthodox Christians believed Jesus had suffered the awful reality of a brutal death (that most fearsome feature of humankind's lot), and that in his resurrection and exaltation he now prefigures and assures the glory that humans can hope for, and for which they can dare to venture their all in the present arena of historical existence.

Whatever one may think personally of the convictions of earliest Christianity, they gripped and moved people to make commitments with far-reaching consequences for them, and for subsequent Christianity as well. To embrace Christian faith in earliest Christianity was to ally oneself with a small, vulnerable religious movement, not with the mighty and venerable (and sometimes oppressive) institution that it became in later centuries. For Jews and Gentiles, such a commitment could jeopardize their relations with their extended families; it almost certainly courted various forms of disapproval, even hostility, from wider social circles. In the second and third centuries in particular, it might mean denunciation to governmental authorities, and the threat of state punishments. For Gentiles, embracing Christian faith certainly meant cutting themselves out of participation in the civic cults and various other facets of the religious environment that functioned so heavily as expressions of social solidarity. There were costs involved in joining this particular "voluntary association" with its exclusivist demands, for which the closest analogies were probably the consequences of proselyte conversion to Judaism. Given these costs, those who did embrace devotion to Jesus must have found sufficient compensation in the fellowship into which they were baptized. Such was the religious power of the message, the new identity, the religious experiences, and the new relational bonding. In this message, this new identity, these religious experiences, and these new relationships, the figure of Jesus was characteristically the center, the inspiration, the example, and the authoritative teacher.

In earliest Christianity powerful dynamics of devotion and belief were propagated with amazing success, then and subsequently, the effects of which form a substantial part of the story of the Christian tradition down through the centuries to the present day. It is remarkable that Jesus was so immediately central in earliest Christian circles. It is perhaps still more remarkable that Jesus has remained the most distinguishing feature of Christianity, many Christians through the ages insisting also that Jesus is the most important and perhaps the most winsome feature of the Christian tradition.

The diversity of views of Jesus evident in the preceding chapters has its counterpart in subsequent centuries, down to our own time. Christians, and many outside Christianity as well, continue to wrestle with the question of what to make of Jesus. The story of devotion to Jesus in earliest Christianity shows that the struggle erupted, volcano-like, at an amazingly early point. Probably, the continuing vitality of Christianity will remain dependent upon how fully Christians engage the question of Jesus, and how radically they are willing to consider what devotion to him means for them.

Given the size and potential impact of Christianity in our world, the question of what Christians will do about these matters could have consequences far beyond the circle of Christian faith. Indeed, in a real sense Jesus is far bigger than Christianity, with an appeal that extends much wider than the global Christian constituency. In our time, as in the famous Galilean scene from the Gospels, for Christians and others as well, Jesus' question remains under lively debate: "Who do you say that I am?" The history of earliest devotion to Jesus shows how answering that question can have profound ramifications.

Bibliography of Works Cited

Aalen, S. "Glory." In *NIDNTT*, 2:44-48.

Aberle, David. "A Note on Relative Deprivation Theory as Applied to Millenarian and Other Cult Movements." In *Reader in Comparative Religion: An Anthropological Approach*, edited by W. A. Lessa and E. A. Vogt, 527-31. 3rd ed. New York: Harper and Row, 1972.

Abramowski, Luise. "The 'Memoirs of the Apostles' in Justin." In *The Gospel and the Gospels*, edited by Peter Stuhlmacher, 323-35. Grand Rapids: Eerdmans, 1991; German trans., 1983.

Achtemeier, Paul J. *1 Peter*. Hermeneia. Minneapolis: Fortress, 1996.

Ackroyd, P. R., and C. F. Evans, eds. *The Cambridge History of the Bible*. Vol. 1, *From the Beginnings to Jerome*. Cambridge: Cambridge University Press, 1975.

Aland, Barbara. "Marcion. Versuch einer neuen Interpretation." *ZTK* 70 (1973): 420-47.

———. "Marcion — Marcionites — Marcionism." In *EECh*, 1:523-24.

Alexander, L. C. A. "Acts and Ancient Intellectual Biography." In *The Book of Acts in Its Ancient Literary Setting*, edited by Bruce W. Winter and Andrew D. Clarke, 31-63. Grand Rapids: Eerdmans, 1993.

———. *The Preface to Luke's Gospel: Literary Convention and Social Context in Luke 1.1-4 and Acts 1.1*. SNTSMS 78. Cambridge: Cambridge University Press, 1993.

Alexander, P. S. "Rabbinic Biography and the Biography of Jesus: A Survey of the Evidence." In *Synoptic Studies: The Ampleforth Conferences of 1982 and 1983*, edited by C. M. Tuckett, 19-50. JSNTSup 7. Sheffield: JSOT Press, 1984.

Alhaus, Paul. "Unser Herr Jesus: Eine neutestamentliche Untersuchung. Zur Auseinandersetzung mit W. Bousset." *NKZ* 26 (1915): 439-57.

Allison, Dale C. "The Pauline Epistles and the Synoptic Gospels: The Pattern of the Parallels." *NTS* 28 (1982): 1-32.

———. *The New Moses: A Matthean Typology*. Minneapolis: Fortress, 1993.

———. *The Jesus Tradition in Q*. Harrisburg, Pa.: Trinity Press International, 1996.

———. *Jesus of Nazareth: Millenarian Prophet*. Minneapolis: Fortress, 1998.

———. *The Intertextual Jesus: Scripture in Q*. Harrisburg, Pa.: Trinity Press International, 2000.

Almond, Philip C. *Mystical Experience and Religious Doctrine: An Investigation of the Study of Mysticism in World Religions.* Berlin: Mouton, 1982.

Alsup, John E. "Typology." In *ABD,* 6:682-85.

Alter, Robert, and Frank Kermode, eds. *The Literary Guide to the Bible.* Cambridge: Harvard University Press, Belknap Press, 1987.

Amphoux, C.-B. "La finale longue de Marc: un épilogue des quatre évangiles." In *The Synoptic Gospels, Source Criticism, and the New Literary Criticism,* edited by C. Focant, 548-55. Leuven: Peeters/Leuven University Press, 1993.

Anderson, Gary A., and Michael E. Stone. *A Synopsis of the Books of Adam and Eve.* 2nd rev. ed. SBLEJL 17. Atlanta: Scholars, 1999.

Anderson, Hugh. "The Old Testament in Mark's Gospel." In *The Use of the Old Testament in the New and Other Essays: Studies in Honor of W. Stinespring,* edited by J. Efird, 280-306. Durham, N.C.: Duke University Press, 1972.

Anderson, Paul N. *The Christology of the Fourth Gospel.* WUNT 2/78. Tübingen: Mohr-Siebeck, 1996.

Anderson, R. Dean, Jr. *Ancient Rhetorical Theory and Paul.* Kampen: Kok Pharos, 1996.

Andresen, Carl. "Justin und der mittlere Platonismus." *ZNW* 44 (1952-53): 157-95.

Arai, Sasagu. *Die Christologie des Evangelium Veritatis: Eine religionsgeschichtliche Untersuchung.* Leiden: Brill, 1964.

Argyle, A. W. "Greek among the Jews of Palestine in New Testament Times." *NTS* 20 (1973-74): 87-90.

Arnold, Clinton E. *The Colossian Syncretism: The Interface between Christianity and Folk Belief at Colossae.* WUNT 2/77. Tübingen: Mohr-Siebeck, 1995.

Ashton, John. *Understanding the Fourth Gospel.* Oxford: Oxford University Press, 1991.

Attridge, Harold W. "The *Gospel of Truth* as an Exoteric Text." In *Nag Hammadi, Gnosticism, and Early Christianity,* edited by Charles W. Hedrick and Robert Hodgson, Jr., 239-56. Peabody, Mass.: Hendrickson, 1986.

———. *The Epistle to the Hebrews.* Hermeneia. Philadelphia: Fortress, 1989.

———. "Liberating Death's Captives: Reconsideration of an Early Christian Myth." In *Gnosticism and the Early Christian World,* edited by James E. Goehring, Charles W. Hedrick, Jack T. Sanders, and Hans Dieter Betz, 103-15. Sonoma, Calif.: Polebridge Press, 1990.

Attridge, Harold W., and George W. MacRae. "The Gospel of Truth." In *Nag Hammadi Codex I (The Jung Codex): Introductions, Texts, Translations, Indices,* edited by H. W. Attridge, 1:55-117, 2:39-135. NHS 22, 23. Leiden: Brill, 1985.

Aune, David E. *The Cultic Setting of Realized Eschatology in Early Christianity.* NovTSup 28. Leiden: Brill, 1972.

———. "Magic in Early Christianity." In *ANRW,* 2.23/2:1507-57.

———. "The Problem of the Genre of the Gospels: A Critique of C. H. Talbert's *What Is a Gospel?*" In *Gospel Perspectives 2,* edited by R. T. France and D. Wenham, 9-60. Sheffield: JSOT, 1981.

———. *Prophecy in Early Christianity and the Ancient Mediterranean World.* Grand Rapids: Eerdmans, 1983.

———. *The New Testament in Its Literary Environment.* Philadelphia: Westminster, 1987.

———. "Charismatic Exegesis in Early Judaism and Early Christianity." In *The Pseudepig-*

rapha and Early Biblical Interpretation, edited by James H. Charlesworth and Craig A. Evans, 126-50. JSPSup 14. Sheffield: Sheffield Academic Press, 1993.

Baarda, Tjitze. "ΔΙΑΦΩΝΙΑ-ΣΥΜΦΩΝΙΑ: Factors in the Harmonization of the Gospels, Especially in the *Diatessaron* of Tatian." In *Gospel Traditions in the Second Century: Origins, Recensions, Text, and Transmission,* edited by William L. Petersen, 133-54. Notre Dame, Ind., and London: University of Notre Dame Press, 1989.

Bailey, James L., and Lyle D. Vander Broek. *Literary Forms in the New Testament: A Handbook.* Louisville: Westminster John Knox, 1992.

Balás, David L. "Marcion Revisited: A 'Post-Harnack' Perspective." In *Texts and Testaments: Critical Essays on the Bible and Early Church Fathers,* edited by W. Eugene March, 95-108. San Antonio: Trinity University Press, 1980.

Ball, David Mark. *"I Am" in John's Gospel: Literary Function, Background, and Theological Implications.* JSNTSup 124. Sheffield: Sheffield Academic Press, 1996.

Balz, Horst R. *Methodische Probleme der neutestamentlichen Christologie.* WMANT 25. Neukirchen-Vluyn: Neukirchener Verlag, 1967.

Balz, Horst, and Gerhard Schneider, eds. *Exegetical Dictionary of the New Testament.* 3 vols. Grand Rapids: Eerdmans, 1990-93.

Bammel, C. P. Hammond. "Ignatian Problems." *JTS* 33 (1982): 62-97.

Barclay, John. *Jews in the Mediterranean Diaspora: From Alexander to Trajan (323 BCE–117 CE).* Edinburgh: T. & T. Clark, 1996.

Barker, Margaret. *The Great Angel: A Study of Israel's Second God.* London: SPCK, 1992.

———. *The Risen Lord: The Jesus of History as the Christ of Faith.* Valley Forge, Pa.: Trinity Press International; Edinburgh: T. & T. Clark, 1996.

———. "The High Priest and the Worship of Jesus." In *The Jewish Roots of Christological Monotheism: Papers from the St. Andrews Conference on the Historical Origins of the Worship of Jesus,* edited by Carey C. Newman, James R. Davila, and Gladys S. Lewis, 93-111. JSJSup 63. Leiden: Brill, 1999.

Barnard, L. W. *Studies in the Apostolic Fathers and Their Background.* New York: Schocken Books; Oxford: Blackwell, 1966.

———. *Justin Martyr: His Life and Thought.* Cambridge: Cambridge University Press, 1967.

———. *Athenagoras: A Study in Second Century Christian Apologetic.* Paris: Beauchesne, 1972.

Barnett, P. W. "Opposition in Corinth." *JSNT* 22 (1984): 3-17.

Barrett, C. K. "The Theological Vocabulary of the Fourth Gospel and the *Gospel of Truth.*" In *Current Issues in New Testament Interpretation: Essays in Honor of Otto A. Piper,* edited by William Klassen and Graydon F. Snyder, 210-23. New York: Harper and Row, 1962.

———. *The Second Epistle to the Corinthians.* London: Adam and Charles Black, 1973.

———. *The Gospel according to St. John.* 2nd ed. Philadelphia: Westminster, 1978.

———. "'The Father Is Greater Than I'. John 14:28: Subordinationist Christology in the New Testament." In his *Essays on John,* 19-36. London: SPCK, 1982.

———. *Luke the Historian in Recent Study.* Philadelphia: Fortress, 1970.

Bauckham, Richard J. "The Worship of Jesus in Apocalyptic Christianity." *NTS* 27 (1981): 322-41.

———. *Jude, 2 Peter.* WBC. Waco, Tex.: Word, 1983.

—————. "The Son of Man: 'A Man in My Position' or 'Someone'?" *JSNT* 23 (1985): 23-33.

—————. *Jude and the Relatives of Jesus in the Early Church.* Edinburgh: T. & T. Clark, 1990.

—————. "Salome the Sister of Jesus, Salome the Disciple of Jesus, and the Secret Gospel of Mark." *NovT* 33 (1991): 245-75.

—————. "Gospels (Apocryphal)." In *DJG,* 286-91.

—————. "Jesus, Worship of." In *ABD,* 3:812-19.

—————. *The Climax of Prophecy: Studies on the Book of Revelation.* Edinburgh: T. & T. Clark, 1993.

—————. *The Theology of the Book of Revelation.* Cambridge: Cambridge University Press, 1993.

—————, ed. *The Book of Acts in Its Palestinian Setting.* Carlisle: Paternoster; Grand Rapids: Eerdmans, 1995.

—————. "The *Apocalypse of Peter:* A Jewish Christian Apocalypse from the Time of Bar Kokhba" and "The *Ascension of Isaiah:* Genre, Unity and Date." In his *The Fate of the Dead: Studies on Jewish and Christian Apocalypses,* 160-258 and 363-90. Leiden: Brill, 1998.

—————. *God Crucified: Monotheism and Christology in the New Testament.* Carlisle: Paternoster, 1998.

—————. "For Whom Were the Gospels Written?" In *The Gospels for All Christians: Rethinking the Gospel Audiences,* edited by Richard Bauckham, 9-48. Grand Rapids: Eerdmans, 1998.

—————. "The Throne of God and the Worship of Jesus." In *The Jewish Roots of Christological Monotheism: Papers from the St. Andrews Conference on the Historical Origins of the Worship of Jesus,* edited by Carey C. Newman, James R. Davila, and Gladys S. Lewis, 43-69. JSJSup 63. Leiden: Brill, 1999.

Bauer, D. R. "Son of God." In *DJG,* 769-75.

Bauer, Walter. *Rechtgläubigkeit und Ketzerei im ältesten Christentum.* Tübingen: Mohr-Siebeck, 1934. ET, *Orthodoxy and Heresy in Earliest Christianity.* Philadelphia: Fortress, 1971.

Baumeister, Theofried. *Die Anfänge der Theologie des Martyriums.* MBT 45. Münster: Aschendorff, 1980.

Beardslee, William A. *Literary Criticism of the New Testament.* Philadelphia: Fortress, 1970.

Bell, H. Idris, and T. C. Skeat. *Fragments of an Unknown Gospel and Other Early Christian Papyri.* London: British Museum, 1935.

Bell, Richard H. "Sacrifice and Christology in Paul." *JTS* 53 (2002): 1-27.

Bellinzoni, Arthur J. *The Sayings of Jesus in the Writings of Justin Martyr.* NovTSup 17. Leiden: Brill, 1967.

Benoit, A., et al., eds. *Biblia Patristica: Index des citations et allusions bibliques dans la littérature patristique.* Vol. 1, *Des Origines à Clement d'Alexandrie et Tertullien.* Paris: Éditions du centre nationale de la recherche scientifique, 1975.

Berger, Klaus. "Zur Diskussion über die Herkunft von I Kor II.9." *NTS* 24 (1978): 270-83.

Berger, Peter L., and Thomas Luckmann. *The Social Construction of Reality.* Garden City, N.Y.: Doubleday, 1966.

Berneker, Erich. "Apotheosis." In *Der Kleine Pauly Lexikon der Antike,* edited by Konrat Ziegler and Walther Sontheimer, 1:458-59. 5 vols. Munich: Deutscher Taschenbuch Verlag, 1979.

Bertrand, Daniel A. *La vie grecque d'Adam et Ève.* Paris: Librairie Adrien Maisonneuve, 1987.

Best, Ernest. *A Commentary on the First and Second Epistles to the Thessalonians.* London: A. and C. Black; New York: Harper and Row, 1972.

———. *Disciples and Discipleship: Studies in the Gospel according to Mark.* Edinburgh: T. & T. Clark, 1986.

———. "Who Used Whom? The Relationship of Ephesians and Colossians." *NTS* 43 (1997): 72-96.

Bettiolo, Paolo, Alda Giambelluca Kossova, Claudio Leonardi, Enrico Norelli, and Lorenzo Perrone, eds. *Ascensio Isaiae: Textus.* CCSA 7. Turnhout: Brepols, 1995.

Betz, Hans Dieter. *Galatians.* Hermeneia. Philadelphia: Fortress, 1979.

———. "Jesus and the Cynics: Survey and Analysis of a Hypothesis." *JR* 74 (1994): 453-75.

———. *The Sermon on the Mount.* Hermeneia. Minneapolis: Fortress, 1995.

Betz, Johannes. "The Eucharist in the Didache." In *The Didache in Modern Research,* edited by Jonathan A. Draper, 244-75. Leiden: Brill, 1996.

Betz, Otto. "Ἰουδαϊσμός." In *EDNT,* 2:192-93.

Beutler, Johannes. "The Use of 'Scripture' in the Gospel of John." In *Exploring the Gospel of John: In Honor of D. Moody Smith,* edited by R. Alan Culpepper and C. Clifton Black, 147-62. Louisville: Westminster John Knox, 1996.

Bevan, E. R. "Deification (Greek and Roman)." In *Encyclopaedia of Religion and Ethics,* edited by James Hastings, 4:525-33. Edinburgh: T. & T. Clark, 1911.

Bickerman, Elias. *From Ezra to the Last of the Maccabees.* New York: Schocken Books, 1962.

Bieder, Werner. *Die Vorstellung von der Höllenfahrt Jesu Christi: Beitrag zur Entstehungsgeschichte der Vorstellung vom sog. Descensus ad Inferos.* ATANT 19. Zürich: Zwingli-Verlag, 1949.

Bieneck, Joachim. *Sohn Gottes als Christusbezeichnung der Synoptiker.* Zürich: Zwingli-Verlag, 1951.

Bietenhard, Hans. *Die himmlische Welt im Urchristentum und Spätjudentum.* Tübingen: J. C. B. Mohr, 1951.

———. "ὄνομα." In *TDNT,* 5:242-81.

Black, Allen. "Women in the Gospel of Luke." In *Essays on Women in Earliest Christianity,* vol. 1, edited by Carroll D. Osborn, 445-68. Joplin, Mo.: College Press Publishing Co., 1993.

Black, Matthew. *An Aramaic Approach to the Gospels and Acts.* 3rd ed. Oxford: Clarendon, 1967.

———. "The Maranatha Invocation and Jude 14, 15 (1 Enoch 1:9)." In *Christ and Spirit in the New Testament,* edited by B. Lindars and S. S. Smalley, 189-96. Cambridge: Cambridge University Press, 1973.

———. *The Book of Enoch or 1 Enoch: A New English Edition with Commentary and Textual Notes.* SVTP 7. Leiden: Brill, 1985.

Blackburn, Barry. *Theios Anēr and the Markan Miracle Traditions: A Critique of the Theios Anēr Concept as an Interpretative Background of the Miracle Traditions Used by Mark.* WUNT 2/40. Tübingen: J. C. B. Mohr (Paul Siebeck), 1991.

Blackman, E. C. *Marcion and His Influence.* London: SPCK, 1948.

Blanc, Cécile. *Origène: Commentaire sur saint Jean, Tome II.* SC 157. Paris: Éditions du Cerf, 1970.

Blasi, Anthony. *Making Charisma: The Social Construction of Paul's Public Image*. New Brunswick, N.J.: Transaction Books, 1991.

Blass, F., and A. Debrunner. *A Greek Grammar of the New Testament and Other Early Christian Literature*. Translated by Robert W. Funk. Chicago: University of Chicago Press, 1961.

Bock, Darrell L. "The Son of Man Seated at God's Right Hand and the Debate over Jesus' 'Blasphemy.'" In *Jesus of Nazareth, Lord and Christ: Essays on the Historical Jesus and New Testament Christology*, edited by Joel B. Green and Max Turner, 181-91. Grand Rapids: Eerdmans, 1994.

―――. *Blasphemy and Exaltation in Judaism and the Final Examination of Jesus: A Philological-Historical Study of the Key Jewish Themes Impacting Mark 14:61-64*. WUNT 2/106. Tübingen: J. C. B. Mohr (Siebeck), 1998.

Bockmuehl, Markus. *Jewish Law in Gentile Churches: Halakhah and the Beginning of Christian Public Ethics*. Edinburgh: T&T Clark, 2000.

Bogart, John. *Orthodox and Heretical Perfectionism*. SBLDS 33. Missoula: Scholars, 1977.

Bonner, Campbell. *Studies in Magical Amulets, Chiefly Graeco-Egyptian*. Ann Arbor: University of Michigan Press; London: Oxford University Press, 1950.

Borg, Marcus J. *Jesus: A New Vision*. San Francisco: Harper and Row, 1987.

Borgen, Peder. "Philo of Alexandria: A Critical and Synthetical Survey of Research since World War II." In *ANRW*, 2.21/2:99-154.

Boring, M. Eugene. "Mark 1:1-15 and the Beginning of the Gospel." *Semeia* 52 (1990): 43-81.

―――. "Narrative Christology in the Apocalypse." *CBQ* 54 (1992): 702-23.

―――. "Prophecy (Early Christian)." In *ABD*, 5:495-502.

Borsch, Frederick H. *The Son of Man in Myth and History*. London: SCM Press, 1967.

Bos, Abraham P. "Basilides as an Aristotelianizing Gnostic." *VC* 54 (2000): 44-60.

Boslooper, Thomas. *The Virgin Birth*. Philadelphia: Westminster, 1962.

Bousset, Wilhelm. *Kyrios Christos: Geschichte des Christusglaubens von den Anfangen des Christentums bis Irenaeus*. Göttingen: Vandenhoeck & Ruprecht, 1913; rev. ed., 1921. ET (from the 4th German ed., 1965), *Kyrios Christos: A History of the Belief in Christ from the Beginnings of Christianity to Irenaeus*. Translated by J. E. Steely. Nashville: Abingdon, 1970.

―――. *Jesus der Herr, Nachträge und Auseinandersetzungen zu Kyrios Christos*. FRLANT 8. Göttingen: Vandenhoeck & Ruprecht, 1916.

Bousset, Wilhelm. *Die Religion des Judentums im späthellenistischen Zeitalter*. Edited by H. Gressmann. HNT 21. Tübingen: J. C. B. Mohr, 1926.

Boyarin, Daniel. *A Radical Jew: Paul and the Politics of Identity*. Berkeley: University of California Press, 1994.

Braumann, G., and H.-G. Link. "I Am." In *NIDNTT*, 2:278-83.

Braun, F.-M. *Jean le théologien et son Évangile dans l'église ancienne*. Ebib. Paris: J. Gabalda, 1959.

―――. *Jean le théologien: Les grandes traditions d'Israël et l'accord des écritures selon le quatrième évangile*. Paris: J. Gabalda, 1964.

Brockington, L. H. "The Greek Translator of Isaiah and His Interest in ΔΟΞΑ." *VT* 1 (1951): 23-32.

Brown, Colin, ed. *New International Dictionary of New Testament Theology*. 3 vols. Grand Rapids: Zondervan, 1975-78.

Brown, J. Pairman. "An Early Revision of the Gospel of Mark." *JBL* 78 (1956): 215-27.

Brown, Peter. *The Body and Society: Men, Women, and Sexual Renunciation in Early Christianity.* New York: Columbia University Press, 1988.

Brown, Raymond E. *The Gospel according to John.* 2 vols. The Anchor Bible. Garden City, N.Y.: Doubleday, 1966, 1970.

———. "The Relation of 'The Secret Gospel of Mark' to the Fourth Gospel." *CBQ* 36 (1974): 466-85.

———. *The Birth of the Messiah.* Garden City, N.Y.: Doubleday, 1977.

———. *The Community of the Beloved Disciple.* New York: Paulist, 1979.

———. *The Epistles of John.* AB. Garden City, N.Y.: Doubleday, 1982.

———. "The *Gospel of Peter* and Canonical Gospel Priority." *NTS* 33 (1987): 321-43.

———. *The Death of the Messiah. From Gethsemane to the Grave: A Commentary on the Passion Narratives in the Four Gospels.* 2 vols. New York: Doubleday, 1994.

Brown, S. Kent. "Sayings of Jesus, Oxyrhynchus." In *ABD,* 5:999-1001.

Brown, Schuyler. "Concerning the Origin of the *Nomina Sacra.*" *SPap* 9 (1970): 7-19.

Browne, G. M., et al., eds. *The Oxyrhynchus Papyri, Vol. 41.* London: Egypt Exploration Society, 1972.

Brox, Norbert. "'Doketismus' — eine Problemanzeige." *ZKG* 95 (1984): 301-14.

Bruce, F. F. *The Epistle to the Hebrews.* NICNT. Grand Rapids: Eerdmans, 1964.

———. *The "Secret" Gospel of Mark.* London: Athlone, 1974.

Bultmann, Rudolf. *Theology of the New Testament.* 2 vols. New York: Charles Scribner's Sons, 1951, 1955.

Bumpus, Harold Bertram. *The Christological Awareness of Clement of Rome and Its Sources.* Cambridge, Mass.: University Press of Cambridge, 1972.

Bundy, David. "Christianity in Syria." In *ABD,* 1:970-79.

Bunge, Wilfred F. "The Christology of Ignatius of Antioch." Ph.D. diss., Harvard University, 1966.

Burger, Christoph. *Jesus als Davidssohn.* FRLANT 98. Göttingen: Vandenhoeck & Ruprecht, 1970.

Burkett, Delbert. *The Son of Man Debate: A History and Evaluation.* SNTSMS 107. Cambridge: Cambridge University Press, 1999.

Burridge, R. A. *What Are the Gospels? A Comparison with Graeco-Roman Biography.* SNTSMS 70. Cambridge: Cambridge University Press, 1992.

———. "Gospel Genre, Christological Controversy and the Absence of Rabbinic Biography: Some Implications of the Biographical Hypothesis." In *Christology, Controversy, and Community: New Testament Essays in Honour of David R. Catchpole,* edited by David G. Horrell and Christopher M. Tuckett, 137-56. Leiden: Brill, 2000.

Buth, Randall. "A More Complete Semitic Background for *Bar-Enasha,* 'Son of Man.'" In *Studies in Scripture in Early Judaism and Christianity,* edited by Craig A. Evans and James A. Sanders, 176-89. Sheffield: Sheffield Academic Press, 1998.

Byrne, Brendan. "The Faith of the Beloved Disciple and the Community in John 20." *JSNT* 23 (1985): 83-97.

Cadbury, Henry J. "Commentary on the Preface of Luke." In *The Beginnings of Christianity,* edited by J. J. Foakes Jackson and Kirsopp Lake, 2:489-510. London: Macmillan, 1920-33.

———. "The Titles of Jesus in Acts." In *The Beginnings of Christianity,* 5:354-75.

Callahan, Allen. "'No Rhyme or Reason': The Hidden Logia of the *Gospel of Thomas*." *HTR* 90 (1997): 411-26.

Cameron, Ron. *Sayings Traditions in the "Apocryphon of James."* HTS 34. Philadelphia: Fortress, 1984.

————. "Hebrews, Gospel of The." In *ABD*, 3:105-6.

————. "Ancient Myths and Modern Theories of the *Gospel of Thomas* and Christian Origins." *Method and Theory in the Study of Religion* 11 (1999): 236-57.

————, ed. *The Other Gospels: Non-Canonical Gospel Texts.* Guildford, Surrey: Lutterworth, 1983.

Camery-Hoggatt, Jerry. *Irony in Mark's Gospel: Text and Subtext.* SNTSMS 72. Cambridge: Cambridge University Press, 1992.

Campbell, W. S. "Israel." In *DPL*, 441-46.

Campenhausen, Hans von. *Die Idee des Martyriums in der alten Kirche.* 2nd ed. Göttingen: Vandenhoeck & Ruprecht, 1964.

————. *The Formation of the Christian Bible.* Philadelphia: Fortress, 1972.

Capes, David B. *Old Testament Yahweh Texts in Paul's Christology.* WUNT 2/47. Tübingen: J. C. B. Mohr (Paul Siebeck), 1992.

Carrell, Peter. *Jesus and the Angels: Angelology and the Christology of the Apocalypse of John.* SNTSMS 95. Cambridge: Cambridge University Press, 1997.

Carrez, Maurice. "Quelques aspects christologiques de l'Évangile de Thomas." In *The Four Gospels 1992: Festschrift for Frans Neirynck,* edited by F. Van Segbroeck, C. M. Tuckett, G. Van Belle, and J. Verheyden, 3:2263-76. 4 vols. Leuven: Leuven University Press, 1992.

Carroll, John T. *Response to the End of History: Eschatology and Situation in Luke-Acts.* SBLDS 92. Atlanta: Scholars, 1986.

Carroll, John T., and Joel B. Green. *The Death of Jesus in Early Christianity.* Peabody, Mass.: Hendrickson, 1995.

Casey, Maurice. *Son of Man: The Interpretation and Influence of Daniel 7.* London: SPCK, 1979.

————. "General, Generic and Indefinite: The Use of the Term 'Son of Man' in Aramaic Sources and in the Teaching of Jesus." *JSNT* 29 (1987): 21-56.

————. *From Jewish Prophet to Gentile God: The Origins and Development of New Testament Christology.* Louisville: Westminster John Knox; Cambridge: James Clarke, 1991.

————. "Method in Our Madness, and Madness in Their Methods: Some Approaches to the Son of Man Problem in Recent Scholarship." *JSNT* 42 (1991): 17-43.

————. *Aramaic Sources of Mark's Gospel.* SNTSMS 102. Cambridge: Cambridge University Press, 1998.

————. "Monotheism, Worship and Christological Developments in the Pauline Churches." In *The Jewish Roots of Christological Monotheism: Papers from the St. Andrews Conference on the Historical Origins of the Worship of Jesus,* edited by Carey C. Newman, James R. Davila, and Gladys S. Lewis, 214-33. JSJSup 63. Leiden: Brill, 1999.

Catchpole, David R. "The Fearful Silence of the Women at the Tomb: A Study in Markan Theology." *Journal of Theology for Southern Africa* 18 (1977): 3-10.

————. *The Quest for Q.* Edinburgh: T. & T. Clark, 1993.

Charlesworth, James H. "A Prolegomenon to a New Study of the Jewish Background of the Hymns and Prayers in the New Testament." *JJS* 33 (1982): 265-85.

———. "Jewish Hymns, Odes, and Prayers (ca. 167 B.C.E.–135 C.E.)." In *Early Judaism and Its Modern Interpreters,* edited by Robert A. Kraft and G. W. E. Nickelsburg, 411-36. Atlanta: Scholars, 1986.

———. *Critical Reflections on the "Odes of Solomon."* Sheffield: Sheffield Academic Press, 1998.

———, ed. *The Old Testament Pseudepigrapha.* 2 vols. Garden City, N.Y.: Doubleday, 1983-85.

Chazon, Esther G. "Hymns and Prayers in the Dead Sea Scrolls." In *The Dead Sea Scrolls after Fifty Years: A Comprehensive Assessment,* edited by Peter Flint, 244-70. Leiden: Brill, 1998.

Chester, Andrew. "Jewish Messianic Expectations and Mediatorial Figures and Pauline Christology." In *Paulus und das antike Judentum,* edited by Martin Hengel and Ulrich Heckel, 17-89. WUNT 58. Tübingen: J. C. B. Mohr (Paul Siebeck), 1991.

Clabeaux, John J. *A Lost Edition of the Letters of Paul: A Reassessment of the Text of the Pauline Corpus Attested by Marcion.* Washington, D.C.: Catholic Biblical Association, 1989.

Clark, W. H., H. N. Malony, J. Daane, and A. R. Tippett. *Religious Experience: Its Nature and Function in the Human Psyche.* Springfield, Ill.: C. C. Thomas, 1973.

Cohen, Shaye J. D. "The Significance of Yavneh: Pharisees, Rabbis, and the End of Jewish Sectarianism." *HUCA* 55 (1984): 27-53.

Coleman-Norton, P. R. *Roman State and Christian Church: A Collection of Legal Documents to A.D. 535.* 3 vols. London: SPCK, 1966.

Collins, Adela Yarbro. "The Worship of Jesus and the Imperial Cult." In *The Jewish Roots of Christological Monotheism: Papers from the St. Andrews Conference on the Historical Origins of the Worship of Jesus,* edited by Carey C. Newman, James R. Davila, and Gladys S. Lewis, 244-70. JSJSup 63. Leiden: Brill, 1999.

———. "Mark and His Readers: The Son of God among Greeks and Romans." *HTR* 93 (2000): 85-100.

Collins, John J. "The Son of Man in First-Century Judaism." *NTS* 38 (1992): 448-66.

———. *The Scepter and the Star: The Messiahs of the Dead Sea Scrolls and Other Ancient Literature.* New York: Doubleday, 1995.

———. "A Throne in the Heavens: Apotheosis in Pre-Christian Judaism." In *Death, Ecstasy, and Other Worldly Journeys,* edited by J. J. Collins and M. A. Fishbane, 43-58. Albany: State University of New York Press, 1995.

Colpe, Carsten. *Die religionsgeschichtliche Schule: Darstellung und Kritik ihres Bildes vom gnostischen Erlösermythus.* Göttingen: Vandenhoeck & Ruprecht, 1961.

Comblin, J. *Le Christ dans l'apocalypse.* Théologie biblique 3/6. Tournai: Desclée, 1965.

Computer-Konkordanz zum Novum Testamentum Graece. Edited by Institut für Neutestamentliche Textforschung. Berlin: De Gruyter, 1985.

Conzelmann, Hans. *Die Mitte der Zeit: Studien zur Theologie des Lukas.* 4th ed. Tübingen: Mohr, 1962.

———. *1 Corinthians.* Hermeneia. Philadelphia: Fortress, 1975.

Corley, Kathleen E. "Women and the Crucifixion and Burial of Jesus." *Forum,* n.s., 1 (1998): 181-225.

Craig, William L. "From Easter to Valentinus and the Apostles' Creed Once More: A Critical Examination of James Robinson's Proposed Resurrection Appearance Trajectories." *JSNT* 52 (1993): 19-39.

Cranfield, C. E. B. *The Epistle to the Romans: Volume 1, Romans 1–8.* ICC. Edinburgh: T. & T. Clark, 1975.

Criddle, A. H. "On the Mar Saba Letter Attributed to Clement of Alexandria." *JECS* 3 (1995): 215-20.

Cross, F. L. *The Early Christian Fathers.* London: Gerald Duckworth, 1960.

Cross, F. L., and E. A. Livingstone, eds. *Oxford Dictionary of the Christian Church.* 3rd ed. Oxford: Oxford University Press, 1997.

Crossan, John Dominic. *Four Other Gospels: Shadows on the Contours of Canon.* Minneapolis: Winston, 1985.

———. *The Cross That Spoke: The Origins of the Passion Narrative.* San Francisco: Harper and Row, 1988.

———. *The Historical Jesus: The Life of a Mediterranean Jewish Peasant.* San Francisco: Harper San Francisco, 1991.

———. *The Birth of Christianity.* New York: Harper Collins, 1998.

———. "The *Gospel of Peter* and the Canonical Gospels." *Forum,* n.s., 1 (1998): 7-51.

Cullmann, Oscar. "The Plurality of the Gospels as a Theological Problem in Antiquity." In his *The Early Church,* edited by A. J. B. Higgins, 43-44. London: SCM Press, 1956.

———. *Die Christologie des Neuen Testament.* Tübingen: J. C. B. Mohr (Paul Siebeck), 1957. ET, *The Christianity of the New Testament.* Philadelphia: Westminster, 1959; rev. ed., 1963.

Cuss, Dominique. *Imperial Cult and Honorary Terms in the New Testament.* Paradosis 23. Fribourg: University of Fribourg, 1974.

Dahl, Nils A. "Christ, Creation and the Church." In *The Background of the New Testament and Its Eschatology: Studies in Honour of C. H. Dodd,* edited by W. D. Davies and D. Daube, 422-43. Cambridge: Cambridge University Press, 1954.

———. *The Crucified Messiah and Other Essays.* Minneapolis: Augsburg, 1974.

———. "The Arrogant Archon and the Lewd Sophia: Jewish Traditions in Gnostic Revolt." In *The Rediscovery of Gnosticism: Volume Two, Sethian Gnosticism,* edited by Bentley Layton, 689-712. Leiden: Brill, 1981.

———. *Jesus the Christ: The Historical Origins of Christological Doctrine.* Edited by D. H. Juel. Minneapolis: Fortress, 1991.

Dalman, Gustaf. *The Words of Jesus.* Translated by D. M. Kay. Edinburgh: T. & T. Clark, 1902.

Daly-Denton, Margaret. "Singing Hymns to Christ as to a God (cf. Pliny *Ep.* X, 96)." In *The Jewish Roots of Christological Monotheism: Papers from the St. Andrews Conference on the Historical Origins of the Worship of Jesus,* edited by Carey C. Newman, James R. Davila, and Gladys S. Lewis, 277-92. JSJSup 63. Leiden: Brill, 1999.

———. *David in the Fourth Gospel: The Johannine Reception of the Psalms.* AGJU 47. Leiden: Brill, 2000.

Daniélou, Jean. *The Theology of Jewish Christianity.* Translated and edited by J. A. Baker. London: Darton, Longman and Todd, 1964.

———. *Gospel Message and Hellenistic Culture.* Translated and edited by J. A. Baker. London: Darton, Longman, Todd; Philadelphia: Westminster, 1973.

Daniels, Jon B. "The Egerton Gospel: Its Place in Early Christianity." Ph.D. diss., Claremont Graduate School, Claremont, Calif., 1989.

Danove, Paul L. *The End of Mark's Story: A Methodological Study.* Biblical Interpretation Series 3. Leiden: Brill, 1993.

Davids, Peter H. *The Epistle of James.* NIGTC. Grand Rapids: Eerdmans, 1982.

Davies, J. G. "The Origins of Docetism." In *Studia Patristica, Vol. VI,* edited by F. L. Cross, 13-34. TU 81. Berlin: Akademie-Verlag, 1962.

Davies, Stevan L. *The "Gospel of Thomas" and Christian Wisdom.* New York: Seabury Press, 1983.

―――. "The Christology and Protology of the *Gospel of Thomas.*" *JBL* 111 (1992): 663-82.

―――. *Jesus the Healer: Possession, Trance, and the Origins of Christianity.* New York: Continuum, 1995.

Davies, W. D. *Paul and Rabbinic Judaism.* New York: Harper and Row, 1948.

Davis, Carl J. *The Name and Way of the Lord.* JSNTSup 129. Sheffield: Sheffield Academic Press, 1996.

Davis, Philip G. "Mark's Christological Paradox." *JSNT* 35 (1989): 3-18.

―――. "Christology, Discipleship, and Self-Understanding in the Gospel of Mark." In *Self-Definition and Self-Discovery in Early Christianity: A Study in Shifting Horizons, Essays in Appreciation of Ben F. Meyer from His Former Students,* edited by David J. Hawkin and Tom Robinson, 101-19. Studies in Bible and Early Christianity 26. Lewiston, N.Y.: Edwin Mellen Press, 1990.

Deakle, David Wayne. "The Fathers against Marcionism: A Study of the Methods and Motives in the Developing Patristic Anti-Marcionite Polemic." Ph.D. diss., Saint Louis University, 1991.

DeConick, April D. *Seek to See Him: Ascent and Vision Mysticism in the "Gospel of Thomas."* VCSup 33. Leiden: Brill, 1996.

―――. "John Rivals Thomas: From Community Conflict to Gospel Narrative." In *Jesus in Johannine Tradition,* edited by Robert T. Fortna and Tom Thatcher, 303-12. Louisville, London, and Leiden: Westminster John Knox, 2001.

―――. "The True Mysteries: Sacramentalism in the *Gospel of Philip.*" *VC* 55 (2001): 225-61.

―――. *Voices of the Mystics: Early Christian Discourse in the Gospels of John and Thomas and Other Ancient Christian Literature.* JSNTSup 157. Sheffield: Sheffield Academic Press, 2001.

―――. "The Original *Gospel of Thomas.*" *VC* 56 (200): 167-99.

Dehandschutter, Boudewijn. "The Martyrdom of Polycarp: A Century of Research." In *ANRW,* 2.27/1:485-522.

―――. "Example and Discipleship: Some Comments on the Biblical Background of the Early Christian Theology of Martyrdom." In *The Impact of Scripture in Early Christianity,* edited by J. den Boeft and M. L. van de Lisdonk, 20-26. VCSup 44. Leiden: Brill, 1999.

Deichgräber, Reinhard. *Gotteshymnus und Christushymnus in der frühen Christenheit: Untersuchungen zu Form, Sprache und Stil der frühchristlichen Hymnen.* SUNT 5. Göttingen: Vandenhoeck & Ruprecht, 1967.

Deissmann, Adolf. *Bible Studies.* Edinburgh: T. & T. Clark, 1901.

―――. *Light from the Ancient East.* 1927. Reprint, Grand Rapids: Baker, 1965.

Delcor, M. "Des diverses manières d'écrire le tetragramme sacré dans les anciens documents hébraïque." *RHR* 147 (1955): 145-73.

Delling, Gerhard. "Die Bezeichnung 'Söhne Gottes' in der jüdischen Literatur der hellenistisch-römischen Zeit." In *God's Christ and His People: Studies in Honour of Nils Alstrup Dahl*, edited by Jacob Jervell and W. A. Meeks, 18-28. Oslo: Universitetsforlaget, 1977.

Denker, Jürgen. *Die theologiegeschichtliche Stellung des Petrusevangeliums.* Europäische Hochschulschriften 23/36. Bern: Herbert Lang; Frankfurt: Peter Lange, 1975.

Desjardins, Michel R. *Sin in Valentinianism.* SBLDS 108. Atlanta: Scholars, 1990.

—————. "Bauer and Beyond: On Recent Scholarly Discussions of *Hairesis* in the Early Christian Era." *SecCent* 8 (1991): 65-82.

De Ste. Croix, G. E. M. "Why Were the Early Christians Persecuted?" *Past and Present* 26 (1963): 6-38.

—————. "Why Were the Early Christians Persecuted? A Rejoinder." *Past and Present* 27 (1964): 28-33.

Dibelius, Martin. *Jungfrauensohn und Krippenkind: Untersuchungen zur Geburtsgeschichte Jesu im Lukas-Evangelium.* Sitzungsberichte der Heidelberger Akademie der Wissenschaften. Heidelberg: Carl Winters Universitätsbuchhandlung, 1932.

Dibelius, Martin, and Hans Conzelmann. *The Pastoral Epistles.* Hermeneia. Philadelphia: Fortress, 1972.

Di Berardino, Angelo, ed. *Encyclopedia of the Early Church.* 2 vols. Translated by Adrian Walford. New York: Oxford University Press, 1992.

Dihle, Albrecht. "The Gospels and Greek Biography." In *The Gospel and the Gospels*, edited by Peter Stuhlmacher, 361-86. Grnad Rapids: Eerdmans, 1991.

Dodd, C. H. *Historical Tradition in the Fourth Gospel.* Cambridge: Cambridge University Press, 1963.

—————. *According to the Scriptures.* London: James Nisbet, 1952. Reprint, London: Collins/Fontana, 1965.

—————. *The Interpretation of the Fourth Gospel.* Cambridge: Cambridge University Press, 1965.

Dölger, Franz J. *Sol Salutis: Gebet und Gesang im christlichen Altertum mit besonderer Rücksicht auf die Ostung in Gebet und Liturgie.* 3rd ed. LQF 16/17. 1925. Reprint, Münster: Aschendorffsche Verlagsbuchhandlung, 1972.

Donahue, John R. "Jesus as the Parable of God in the Gospel of Mark." *Int* 32 (1978): 369-86.

Donaldson, Terence L. *Jesus on the Mountain: A Study in Matthean Theology.* JSNTSup 8. Sheffield: JSOT Press, 1985.

—————. "Zealot and Convert: The Origin of Paul's Christ-Torah Antithesis." *CBQ* 51 (1989): 655-82.

—————. *Paul and the Gentiles: Remapping the Apostle's Convictional World.* Minneapolis: Fortress, 1997.

Donfried, Karl P. *The Setting of Second Clement in Early Christianity.* NovTSup 38. Leiden: Brill, 1974.

Dragas, G. D. "Apostolic Constitutions." In *EEC*, 1:92-93.

Draper, Jonathan A., ed. *The "Didache" in Modern Research.* AGJU 37. Leiden: Brill, 1997.

Dunderberg, Ismo. "John and Thomas in Conflict?" In *The Nag Hammadi Library after*

Fifty Years: Proceedings of the 1995 Society of Biblical Literature Commemoration, edited by John D. Turner and Anne McGuire, 361-80. NHMS 44. Leiden: Brill, 1997.

————. *"Thomas'* I-Sayings and the Gospel of John" and *"Thomas* and the Beloved Disciple." In *Thomas at the Crossroads: Essays on the "Gospel of Thomas,"* edited by Risto Uro, 33-64, 65-88. Edinburgh: T. & T. Clark, 1998.

Dungan, David L. *The Sayings of Jesus in the Churches of Paul.* Philadelphia: Fortress, 1971.

Dunn, J. D. G. "The Messianic Secret in Mark." *TB* 21 (1970): 92-117.

————. *Jesus and the Spirit: A Study of the Religious and Charismatic Experience of Jesus and the First Christians as Reflected in the New Testament.* London: SCM Press; Philadelphia: Westminster, 1975.

————. *Unity and Diversity in the New Testament.* Philadelphia: Westminster, 1977.

————. *Christology in the Making.* London: SCM Press; Philadelphia: Westminster, 1980; 2nd ed., 1989.

————. "Was Christianity a Monotheistic Faith from the Beginning?" *SJT* 35 (1982): 303-36.

————. *Romans 9–16.* WBC 38B. Waco, Tex.: Word, 1988.

————. *The Parting of the Ways between Judaism and Christianity and Their Significance for the Character of Christianity.* London: SCM Press; Philadelphia: Trinity Press International, 1991.

————. "The Making of Christology — Evolution or Unfolding?" In *Jesus of Nazareth: Lord and Christ. Essays on the Historical Jesus and New Testament Christology,* edited by Joel B. Green and Max Turner, 437-52. Grand Rapids: Eerdmans; Carlisle: Paternoster, 1994.

————. "Pseudepigraphy." In *DLNTD,* 977-84.

————. *The Theology of Paul the Apostle.* Grand Rapids: Eerdmans, 1998.

Dwyer, Timothy. "The Motif of Wonder in the Gospel of Mark." *JSNT* 57 (1995): 49-59.

Earhart, H. Byron. "Toward a Theory of the Formation of the Japanese New Religions: A Case Study of the Gedatsu-Kai." *HR* 20 (1981): 175-97.

————. *Gedatsu-kai and Religion in Contemporary Japan: Returning to the Center.* Bloomington and Indianapolis: Indiana University Press, 1989.

Edwards, M. J. "Justin's Logos and the Word of God." *JECS* 3 (1995): 261-80.

Ehrlich, Uri. "'When You Pray Know Before Whom You Are Standing.'" *JJS* 49 (2000): 38-50.

Ehrman, Bart D. *The Orthodox Corruption of Scripture: The Effect of Early Christological Controversies on the Text of the New Testament.* Oxford: Oxford University Press, 1993.

————. *Jesus: Apocalyptic Prophet of the New Millennium.* New York: Oxford University Press, 1999.

Elliott, J. K., ed. *The Apocryphal New Testament: A Collection of Apocryphal Christian Literature in an English Translation.* New York: Oxford University Press, 1993.

Ellis, E. E. *Paul's Use of the Old Testament.* 1957. Reprint, Grand Rapids: Baker, 1981.

————. "Pastoral Letters." In *DPL,* 658-66.

Elze, Martin. *Tatian und seine Theologie.* Göttingen: Vandenhoeck & Ruprecht, 1960.

Emmel, Stephen. "Religious Tradition, Textual Transmission, and the Nag Hammadi Codices." In *The Nag Hammadi Library after Fifty Years: Proceedings of the 1995 Society of Biblical Literature Commemoration*, edited by John D. Turner and Anne McGuire, 34-43. NHMS 44. Leiden: Brill, 1997.

Enermalm-Ogawa, Agneta. *Un langage de prière juif en grec: Le témoinage des deux premiers livres des Maccabées*. ConBNT 17. Uppsala: Almquist and Wiksell, 1987.

Engberg-Pedersen, Troels. *Paul and the Stoics*. Louisville: Westminster John Knox, 2000.

Epp, Eldon Jay. "Wisdom, Torah, Word: The Johannine Prologue and the Purpose of the Fourth Gospel." In *Current Issues in Biblical and Patristic Interpretation: Studies in Honor of M. C. Tenney*, edited by G. F. Hawthorne, 128-46. Grand Rapids: Eerdmans, 1971.

―――. "New Testament Papyrus Manuscripts and Letter Carrying in Greco-Roman Times." In *The Future of Early Christianity: Essays in Honor of Helmut Koester*, edited by Birger A. Pearson, 35-56. Minneapolis: Fortress, 1991.

―――. "Western Text." In *ABD*, 6:909-12.

―――. "The New Testament Papyri at Oxyrhynchus in Their Social and Intellectual Context." In *Sayings of Jesus: Canonical and Non-Canonical, Essays in Honour of Tjitze Baarda*, edited by William L. Peterson, Johan S. Vos, and Henk J. de Jonge, 47-68. Leiden: Brill, 1997.

Epp, Eldon Jay, and Gordon D. Fee. *Studies in the Theory and Method of New Testament Textual Criticism*. SD 45. Grand Rapids: Eerdmans, 1993.

Erickson, R. J. "Flesh." In *DPL*, 303-6.

Eskola, Timo. *Messiah and the Throne*. WUNT 2/142. Tübingen: Brill, 2001.

Evans, Craig A. *Word and Glory: On the Exegetical and Theological Background of John's Prologue*. JSNTSup 89. Sheffield: JSOT Press, 1993.

―――. *Jesus and His Contemporaries: Comparative Studies*. AGJU 25. Leiden: Brill, 1995.

Evans, Craig A., Robert L. Webb, and Richard A. Wiebe. *Nag Hammadi Texts and the Bible: A Synopsis and Index*. NTTS 18. Leiden and New York: Brill, 1993.

Evans, Ernest, ed. and trans. *Tertullian Adversus Marcionem*. 2 vols. Oxford: Clarendon, 1972.

Falk, Daniel K. "Jewish Prayer Literature and the Jerusalem Church in Acts." In *The Book of Acts in Its Palestinian Setting*, edited by Richard J. Bauckham, 267-301. Grand Rapids: Eerdmans; Carlisle: Paternoster, 1995.

―――. *Daily, Sabbath, and Festival Prayers in the Dead Sea Scrolls*. STDJ. Leiden: Brill, 1998.

Fallon, Francis T., and Ron Cameron. "The *Gospel of Thomas*: A *Forschungsbericht* and Analysis." In *ANRW*, 2.25/6 (1988): 4195-4251.

Farmer, William R. "Further Reflections on the Fourfold Gospel Canon." In *The Early Church in Its Context: Essays in Honor of Everett Ferguson*, edited by Abraham J. Malherbe, Frederick W. Norris, and James W. Thompson, 107-13. NovTSup 90. Leiden: Brill, 1998.

Farrar, F. W. *The Life of Christ as Represented in Art*. London: Adam and Charles Black, 1896.

Fee, Gordon D. *The First Epistle to the Corinthians*. NICNT. Grand Rapids: Eerdmans, 1987.

―――. *God's Empowering Presence: The Holy Spirit in the Letters of Paul*. Peabody, Mass.: Hendrickson, 1994.

―――. *Paul's Letter to the Philippians*. NICNT. Grand Rapids: Eerdmans, 1995.

Fenske, Wolfgang. *Und wenn ihr betet . . . (Mt 6,5): Gebete in der zwischenmenschlichen*

Kommunikation der Antike als Ausdruck der Frömmigkeit. SUNT 21. Göttingen: Vandenhoeck & Ruprecht, 1997.

Ferguson, Everett, ed. *Encyclopedia of Early Christianity.* 2nd ed. 2 vols. New York: Garland, 1997. See also his articles "Bishop" (1:182-85), "Hymns" (1:548-51), and "Martyr, Martyrdom" (2:724-28) in these volumes.

Fieger, Michael. *Das Thomasevangelium: Einleitung, Kommentar, und Systematik.* NTAbh 22. Münster: Aschendorff Verlag, 1991.

Finney, Paul Corby. *The Invisible God: The Earliest Christians on Art.* New York: Oxford University Press, 1994.

———. "Orant." In *EEC,* 2:831-32.

Fishwick, Duncan. *The Imperial Cult in the Latin West.* Leiden: Brill, 1987.

Fitzmyer, J. A. "Further Light on Melchizedek from Qumran Cave 11," "'Now This Melchizedek . . .' (Heb 7:1)," and "The Oxyrhynchus Logoi of Jesus and the Coptic Gospel according to Thomas." In *Essays on the Semitic Background of the New Testament.* Missoula: Scholars, 1974.

———. "Jewish Christianity in Acts in the Light of the Qumran Scrolls." In *Essays on the Semitic Background of the New Testament.*

———. "Crucifixion in Ancient Palestine, Qumran Literature, and the New Testament." *CBQ* 40 (1978): 493-513.

———. *A Wandering Aramean: Collected Aramaic Essays.* SBLMS 25. Missoula: Scholars, 1979. See esp. "The Semitic Background of the New Testament *Kyrios*-Title" (115-43) and "The New Testament Title 'Son of Man' Philologically Considered" (143-60).

———. *To Advance the Gospel: New Testament Studies.* New York: Crossroad, 1981.

Fletcher-Louis, Crispin H. T. *Luke-Acts: Angels, Christology, and Soteriology.* WUNT 2/94. Tübingen: Mohr (Siebeck), 1997.

———. "The Worship of Divine Humanity as God's Image and the Worship of Jesus." In *The Jewish Roots of Christological Monotheism: Papers from the St. Andrews Conference on the Historical Origins of the Worship of Jesus,* edited by Carey C. Newman, James R. Davila, and Gladys S. Lewis, 112-28. JSJSup 63. Leiden: Brill, 1999.

Flusser, David. "Psalms, Hymns and Prayers." In *Jewish Writings of the Second Temple Period,* edited by M. E. Stone, 551-77. Assen: Van Gorcum; Philadelphia: Fortress, 1984.

Foerster, Werner, and G. Quell. "κύριος" and "κυριακός." In *TDNT,* 3:1039-98 and 3:1095-96, respectively.

Fossum, Jarl E. "The New *Religionsgeschichtliche Schule:* The Quest for Jewish Christology." In SBLSP, edited by E. Lovering, 638-46. Atlanta: Scholars, 1991.

———. "Angel Christology in Jude 5-7" and "In the Beginning Was the Name: Onomanology as the Key to Johannine Christology." In his *The Image of the Invisible God: Essays on the Influence of Jewish Mysticism on Early Christology,* 41-70 and 109-34, respectively. Freiburg: Universitätsverlag Freiburg; Göttingen: Vandenhoeck & Ruprecht, 1995.

Fowl, S. E. *The Story of Christ in the Ethics of Paul: An Analysis of the Function of the Hymnic Material in the Pauline Corpus.* JSNTSup 36. Sheffield: JSOT Press, 1990.

Fox, Robin Lane. *Pagans and Christians.* New York: Knopf, 1987.

Francis, Fred O. "Humility and Angel Worship in Col. 2:18." In *Conflict at Colossae,* edited by F. O. Francis and Wayne Meeks, 176-81. Missoula: Scholars, 1975.

———. "The Christological Argument of Colossians." In *God's Christ and His People:*

Studies in Honour of Nils Alstrup Dahl, edited by Jacob Jervell and Wayne A. Meeks, 192-208. Oslo: Universitets forlaget, 1977.

Franzmann, Majella. *The "Odes of Solomon": An Analysis of the Poetical Structure and Form.* NTOA 20. Göttingen: Vandenhoeck & Ruprecht, 1991.

————. *Jesus in the Nag Hammadi Writings.* Edinburgh: T. & T. Clark, 1996.

Fredouille, J.-C. *Tertullian. Contre les Valentiniens.* 2 vols. SC 280. Paris: Éditions du Cerf, 1980-81.

Fredriksen, Paula. *From Jesus to Christ: The Origins of the New Testament Images of Jesus.* New Haven: Yale University Press, 1988.

————. *Jesus of Nazareth, King of the Jews: A Jewish Life and the Emergence of Christianity.* New York: Knopf, 2000.

Freedman, D. N., ed. *Anchor Bible Dictionary.* 6 vols. New York: Doubleday, 1992.

Frend, W. H. C. *Martyrdom and Persecution in the Early Church: A Study of a Conflict from the Maccabees to Donatus.* Oxford: Blackwell, 1965. Reprint, New York: New York University Press, 1967.

Frenschkowski, Marco. "Welche biographischen Kenntnisse von Jesus setzt die Logienquelle voraus? Beobachtungen zur Gattung von Q im Kontext antiker Spruchsammlungen." In *From Quest to Q, Festschrift James M. Robinson,* edited by Jon Ma. Asgeirsson, Kristin De Troyer, and Marvin W. Meyer, 3-42. Leuven: Leuven University Press/Peeters, 2000.

Freyne, Sean. *Galilee, Jesus, and the Gospels: Literary Approaches and Historical Investigations.* Philadelphia: Fortress, 1988.

Fuller, Reginald H. *The Foundations of New Testament Christology.* New York: Charles Scribner's Sons, 1965.

Furnish, Victor Paul. "Colossians, Epistle to The." In *ABD,* 1:1090-96.

Gaca, Kathy L. "Driving Aphrodite from the World: Tatian's Encratite Principles of Sexual Renunciation." *JTS* 53 (2002): 28-52.

Gamble, Harry, Jr. *The Textual History of the Letter to the Romans.* SD 42. Grand Rapids: Eerdmans, 1977.

————. *The New Testament Canon: Its Making and Meaning.* Philadelphia: Fortress, 1985.

————. "Egerton Papyrus 2" and "Fayyum Fragment." In *ABD,* 2:317-18 and 2:778-79, respectively.

————. *Books and Readers in the Early Church: A History of Early Christian Texts.* New Haven: Yale University Press, 1995.

García Martínez, Florentino, and Eibert J. C. Tigchelaar. *The Dead Sea Scrolls: Study Edition.* 2 vols. Leiden: Brill; Grand Rapids: Eerdmans, 1997.

Gärtner, Bertil. *The Theology of the Gospel according to Thomas.* London: Collins; New York: Harper and Brothers, 1961.

Gasque, W. Ward. *A History of the Criticism of the Acts of the Apostles.* Grand Rapids: Eerdmans; Tübingen: J. C. B. Mohr (Paul Siebeck), 1975.

Gaston, Lloyd. *Paul and the Torah.* Vancouver: University of British Columbia Press, 1987.

Gero, Stephen. "Apocryphal Gospels: A Survey of Textual and Literary Problems." In *ANRW,* 2.25/5 (1988): 3969-96.

Goldstein, Morris. *Jesus in the Jewish Tradition.* New York: Macmillan, 1950.

Goodspeed, Edgar J. *A History of Early Christian Literature.* Revised and enlarged by Robert M. Grant. Chicago: University of Chicago Press, 1966.

Goppelt, Leonhard. "τύπος." In *TDNT*, 8:246-59.

————. *Typos: The Typological Interpretation of the Old Testament in the New*. Grand Rapids: Eerdmans, 1982; German original, 1939.

Goranson, Stephen. "Ebionites" and "Nazarenes." In *ABD*, 2:260-61 and 4:1049-50, respectively.

Goulder, Michael, ed. *Incarnation and Myth: The Debate Continued*. London: SCM Press; Grand Rapids: Eerdmans, 1979.

Grabbe, Lester L. *Judaism from Cyrus to Hadrian*. 2 vols. Minneapolis: Fortress, 1992.

Graf, Fritz. *Magic in the Ancient World*. Translated by Franklin Philip. Cambridge: Harvard University Press, 1997.

Grant, Robert M. *Gnosticism and Early Christianity*. 2nd ed. New York: Harper and Row, 1966.

————. "Sacrifices and Oaths as Required of Early Christians." In *Kyriakon. Festschrift Johannes Quasten*, edited by Patrick Granfield and Josef A. Jungmann, 1:12-17. 2 vols. Münster: Verlag Aschendorff, 1970.

————. *The Christ of the Second Century: Jesus after the Gospels*. Louisville: Westminster John Knox, 1990.

Grayston, Kenneth. *Dying We Live: A New Enquiry into the Death of Christ in the New Testament*. London: Darton, Longman & Todd, 1970.

Green, Joel B. *The Death of Jesus*. WUNT 2/33. Tübingen: Mohr (Siebeck), 1988.

Green, Joel B., Scot McKnight, and I. H. Marshall, eds. *Dictionary of Jesus and the Gospels*. Downers Grove, Ill.: InterVarsity, 1992.

Grether, Oskar. *Name und Wort Gottes im Alten Testament*. BZAW 64. Giessen: Alfred Töpelmann, 1934.

Grillmeier, Aloys. "Der Gottessohn im Totenreich." ZKT 71 (1949): 1-53, 184-203.

————. *Christ in Christian Tradition*. Vol. 1, *From the Apostolic Age to Chalcedon (451)*. Revised and translated by John Bowden. 2nd ed. London: Mowbray & Co.; Atlanta: John Knox, 1975.

Gronewald, Michael. "Unbekanntes Evangelium oder Evangelienharmonie (Fragment aus dem 'Evangelium Egerton')." In *Kölner Papyri (P. Köln), Vol. VI*, 136-45. Cologne: Rheinisch-Westfälischen Akademischer Wissenschaften unter Universität Köln, 1987.

Grözinger, K. E. *Musik und Gesang in der Theologie der frühen jüdischen Literatur*. Tübingen: Mohr (Siebeck), 1982.

Grundmann, W., et al. "χρίω, χριστός, etc." In *TDNT*, 9:493-580.

Guelich, Robert A. "'The Beginning of the Gospel' — Mark 1:1-15." *BR* 27 (1982): 5-15.

————. "The Gospel Genre." In *The Gospel and the Gospels*, edited by Peter Stuhlmacher, 173-208. Grand Rapids: Eerdmans, 1991.

Gundry, Robert H. *The Use of the Old Testament in St. Matthew's Gospel*. NovTSup 18. Leiden: Brill, 1967.

————. "H. D. Betz's Commentary on the Sermon on the Mount." *CR* 10 (1997): 39-58.

Gunkel, Hermann. *The Influence of the Holy Spirit: The Popular View of the Apostolic Age and the Teaching of the Apostle Paul*. Translated by R. A. Harrisville and Philip A. Quanbeck. Philadelphia: Fortress, 1979; originally Göttingen: Vandenhoeck & Ruprecht, 1888.

Guyot, Peter, and Richard Klein. *Das frühe Christentum bis zum Ende der Verfolgungen.* 2 vols. Darmstadt: Wissenschaftliche Buchgesellschaft, 1993-94.

Habermann, Jürgen. *Präexistenzaussagen im Neuen Testament.* Frankfurt am Main: Peter Lange, 1990.

Haelst, Joseph van. *Catalogue des papyrus littéraires juifs et chrétiens.* Paris: Publications de la Sorbonne, 1976.

Haenchen, Ernst. *The Acts of the Apostles.* Philadelphia: Westminster, 1971. ET from 14th ed., 1965.

Hahn, Ferdinand. *Christologische Hoheitstitel, Ihre Geschichte im frühen Christentum.* Göttingen: Vandenhoeck & Ruprecht, 1963. ET, *The Titles of Jesus in Christology.* New York: World Publishing, 1969.

Hall, Robert G. "The *Ascension of Isaiah:* Community Situation, Date, and Place in Early Christianity." *JBL* 109 (1990): 289-306.

Hall, Stuart George. *Melito of Sardis, "On Pascha."* Oxford: Clarendon, 1979.

Hamerton-Kelly, R. G. "The Idea of Pre-Existence in Early Judaism: A Study in the Background of New Testament Theology." Th.D. diss., Union Theological Seminary, New York, 1966.

Hamman, Adalbert. *La prière I. Le Nouveau Testament.* Tournai: Desclée, 1959.

Hannah, Darrell D. "The *Ascension of Isaiah* and Docetic Christology." *VC* 53 (1999): 165-96.

———. "Isaiah's Vision in the *Ascension of Isaiah* and the Early Church." *JTS* 50 (1999): 80-101.

Hanson, Anthony Tyrrell. *Jesus Christ in the Old Testament.* London: SPCK, 1965.

Hanson, R. P. C. "Biblical Exegesis in the Early Church." In *CHB,* 1:412-53.

———. *The Search for the Christian Doctrine of God.* Edinburgh: T. & T. Clark, 1988.

Harder, Kenneth J., and Clayton N. Jefford, eds. *The "Didache" in Context: Essays on Its Text, History, and Transmission.* Leiden: Brill, 1995.

Hare, Douglas R. A. *The Son of Man Tradition.* Philadelphia: Fortress, 1990.

Hargis, Jeffrey W. *Against the Christians: The Rise of Early Anti-Christian Polemic.* Patristic Studies 1. New York: Peter Lang, 1999.

Harnack, Adolf von. *Judentum und Judenchristentum in Justins Dialog mit Trypho.* TU 39/1. Leipzig: Hinrichs, 1913.

———. *Marcion. Das Evangelium vom fremden Gott.* Leipzig: Hinrichs, 1921, 1924. Partial ET, *Marcion: The Gospel of the Alien God.* Durham, N.C.: Labyrinth Press, 1990.

Harner, Philip B. *The "I Am" of the Fourth Gospel: A Study in Johannine Usage and Thought.* Philadelphia: Fortress, 1970.

Harrington, Daniel J. "The Reception of Walter Bauer's *Orthodoxy and Heresy in Earliest Christianity* during the Last Decade." *HTR* 73 (1980): 289-98.

Harris, Murray J. *Jesus as God: The New Testament Use of Theos in Reference to Jesus.* Grand Rapids: Baker, 1992.

Hartman, Lars. "Baptism 'Into the Name of Jesus' and Early Christology: Some Tentative Considerations." *ST* 28 (1974): 21-48.

———. "'Into the Name of Jesus.'" *NTS* 20 (1974): 432-40.

———. "Baptism." In *ABD,* 1:583-94.

———. "Early Baptism — Early Christology." In *The Future of Christology: Essays in*

Honor of Leander E. Keck, edited by A. J. Malherbe and W. A. Meeks, 191-201. Minneapolis: Fortress, 1993.

———. *"Into the Name of the Lord Jesus": Baptism in the Early Church.* Edinburgh: T. & T. Clark, 1997.

Harvey, A. E. *Jesus and the Constraints of History.* London: Duckworth; Philadelphia: Westminster, 1982.

Hawkin, D. J. "The Incomprehension of the Disciples in the Marcan Redaction." *JBL* 91 (1972): 491-500.

Hawthorne, Gerald F. "Tatian and His Discourse to the Greeks." *HTR* 57 (1964): 161-88.

———. *Philippians.* WBC. Waco, Tex.: Word, 1983.

Hawthorne, Gerald F., R. P. Martin, and D. G. Reid, eds. *Dictionary of Paul and His Letters.* Downers Grove, Ill.: InterVarsity, 1993.

Hay, David M. *Glory at the Right Hand: Psalm 110 in Early Christianity.* SBLMS 18. Nashville: Abingdon, 1973.

Hayman, Peter. "Monotheism — a Misused Word in Jewish Studies?" *JJS* 42 (1991): 1-15.

Hays, Richard B. *The Faith of Jesus Christ: An Investigation of the Narrative Substructure of Galatians 3:1–4:11.* SBLDS 56. Chico, Calif.: Scholars, 1983.

———. *Echoes of Scripture in the Letters of Paul.* New Haven: Yale University Press, 1989.

Hayward, C. T. R. *The Jewish Temple: A Non-Biblical Sourcebook.* London: Routledge, 1996.

Head, Peter M. "A Text-Critical Study of Mark 1:1." *NTS* 37 (1991): 621-29.

———. "On the Christology of the *Gospel of Peter.*" *VC* 46 (1992): 209-24.

———. "Tatian's Christology and Its Influence on the Composition of the *Diatessaron.*" *TB* 43 (1992): 121-37.

———. "The Foreign God and the Sudden Christ: Theology and Christology in Marcion's Gospel Redaction." *TB* 44, no. 2 (1993): 307-21.

———. "Some Recently Published NT Papyri from Oxyrhynchus: An Overview and Preliminary Assessment." *TB* 51 (2000): 1-16.

Heard, Richard. "The ΑΠΟΜΝΗΜΟΝΕΥΜΑΤΑ in Papias, Justin, and Irenaeus." *NTS* 1 (1954-55): 122-29.

Heckel, Theo K. *Vom Evangelium des Markus zum viergestaltigen Evangelium.* WUNT 120. Tübingen: Mohr-Siebeck, 1999.

Hedrick, Charles. "Secret Mark: New Photographs, New Witnesses." *Fourth R* 13, no. 5 (September-October 2000): 3-16.

Hegermann, Harold. "δόξα." In *EDNT,* 1:344-48.

Heitmüller, Wilhelm. *"Im Namen Jesu": Eine sprach-und-religionsgeschichtliche Untersuchung zum Neuen Testament, speziell zur altchristlichen Taufe.* FRLANT 1/2. Göttingen: Vandenhoeck & Ruprecht, 1903.

———. "Zum Problem Paulus und Jesus." *ZNW* 13 (1912): 320-37.

Helderman, J. "Das Evangelium Veritatis in der neueren Forschung." In *ANRW,* 2.25/5 (1988): 4054-4106.

Hengel, Martin. *Judaism and Hellenism: Studies in the Encounter in Palestine during the Early Hellenistic Period.* 2 vols. London: SCM Press, 1974.

———. *The Son of God: The Origin of Christology and the History of Jewish-Hellenistic Religion.* Translated by John Bowden. Philadelphia: Fortress; London: SCM Press, 1976.

————. *Crucifixion in the Ancient World and the Folly of the Message of the Cross.* Philadelphia: Fortress, 1977.

————. *The Charismatic Leader and His Followers.* Translated by J. C. G. Greig. Edinburgh: T. & T. Clark, 1981.

————. *Between Jesus and Paul.* Translated by John Bowden. London: SCM Press, 1983.

————. *The "Hellenization" of Judaea in the First Century after Christ.* London: SCM Press, 1989.

————. *The Johannine Question.* London: SCM Press, 1989.

————. *The Pre-Christian Paul.* London: SCM Press; Philadelphia: Trinity Press International, 1991.

————. "The Geography of Palestine in Acts." In *The Book of Acts in Its Palestinian Setting,* edited by Richard Bauckham, 27-78. Grand Rapids: Eerdmans; Carlisle: Paternoster, 1995.

————. *Studies in Early Christology.* Edinburgh: T. & T. Clark, 1995. See especially "'Sit at My Right Hand!' The Enthronement of Christ at the Right Hand of God and Psalm 110:1" (119-225).

————. "Die Throngemeinschaft des Lammes mit Gott in der Johannesapokalypse." *TBl* 3 (1996): 159-75.

————. *The Four Gospels and the One Gospel of Jesus Christ.* London: SCM Press, 2000.

Hengel, Martin, and Anna Maria Schwemer. *Paul between Damascus and Antioch: The Unknown Years.* Translated by John Bowden. London: SCM Press, 1997.

Henne, Philippe. *La christologie chez Clément de Rome et dans le Pasteur d'Hermas.* Paradosis 33. Fribourg: Éditions universitaires Fribourg, 1992.

Henten, J. W. van. "Zum Einfluss jüdischer Martyrien auf die Literatur des frühen Christentums, II: Die Apostolischen Väter." In *ANRW,* 2.27/1:700-723.

————. "The Tradition-Historical Background of Romans 3.25: A Search for Pagan and Jewish Parallels." In *From Jesus to John: Essays on Jesus and New Testament Christology in Honour of Marinus De Jonge,* edited by Martinus C. De Boer, 101-28. JSNTSup 84. Sheffield: JSOT Press, 1993.

Henten, J. W. van, et al., eds. *Die Entstehung der jüdischen Martyrologie.* SPB 38. Leiden: Brill, 1989.

Herford, R. Travers. *Christianity in Talmud and Midrash.* 1903. Reprint, Clifton, N.J.: Reference Book Publishers, 1966.

————. *The Ethics of the Talmud: Sayings of the Fathers.* 3rd ed. 1945. Reprint, New York: Schocken Books, 1975.

Hick, John, ed. *The Myth of God Incarnate.* London: SCM Press, 1977.

Higgins, A. J. B. "Jewish Messianic Belief in Justin Martyr's *Dialogue with Trypho.*" *NovT* 9 (1967): 298-305.

Hill, Charles E. "Did the Scribe of P⁵² Use the *Nomina Sacra?* Another Look." *NTS* 48 (2002): 587-92.

Hill, Craig C. *Hellenists and Hebrews: Reappraising Division within the Earliest Church.* Minneapolis: Fortress, 1992.

————. "Hellenists, Hellenistic and Hellenistic-Jewish Christianity." In *DLNTD,* 462-69.

Hill, David. *New Testament Prophecy.* Atlanta: John Knox, 1979.

Hills, Julian V. *Tradition and Composition in the "Epistula Apostolorum."* HDR 24. Minneapolis: Fortress, 1990.

Hock, Ronald F. *The Infancy Gospels of James and Thomas.* Scholars Bible 2. Santa Rosa, Calif.: Polebridge Press, 1995.

Hoffmann, R. Joseph. *Marcion: On the Restitution of Christianity, an Essay on the Development of Radical Paulinist Theology in the Second Century.* Chico, Calif.: Scholars, 1984.

———. "How Then Know This Troublous Teacher? Further Reflections on Marcion and His Church." *SecCent* 6 (1987-88): 173-91.

Hogg, Hope W. "The Diatessaron." In ANF, 9:35-138.

Holmberg, Bengt. *Paul and Power.* Philadelphia: Fortress, 1978.

———. *Sociology and the New Testament: An Appraisal.* Minneapolis: Fortress, 1990.

Holtz, Traugott. *Die Christologie der Apokalypse des Johannes.* TU 85. Berlin: Akademie-Verlag, 1962.

Hoover, Roy W. "The Harpagmos Enigma: A Philological Solution." *HTR* 64 (1971): 95-119.

Horbury, William. "The Benediction of the *Minim* and Early Jewish-Christian Controversy." *JTS* 33 (1982): 19-61.

———. "Old Testament Interpretation in the Writings of the Church Fathers." In *Mikra. Text, Translation, Reading, and Interpretation of the Hebrew Bible in Ancient Judaism and Early Christianity,* edited by Martin Jan Mulder, 727-87. CRINT. Assen: Van Gorcum, 1988.

———. "Jewish-Christian Relations in Barnabas and Justin Martyr." In *Jews and Christians: The Parting of the Ways, A.D. 70 to 135,* edited by J. D. G. Dunn, 315-45. Tübingen: Mohr-Siebeck, 1992.

———. *Jewish Messianism and the Cult of Christ.* London: SCM Press, 1998.

Horgan, Maurya P., and Paul J. Kobelski. "The *Hodayot* (1QH) and New Testament Poetry." In *To Touch the Text: Biblical and Related Studies in Honor of Joseph A. Fitzmyer, S.J.,* edited by Maurya P. Horgan and Paul J. Kobelski, 179-93. New York: Crossroad, 1989.

Hornblower, Simon, and Antony Spawforth, eds. *The Oxford Classical Dictionary.* 3rd ed. Oxford: Oxford University Press, 1996.

Hornschuh, M. *Studien zur Epistula Apostolorum.* PTS 5. Berlin: Walter de Gruyter, 1965.

Horsley, Richard A. *Jesus and the Spiral of Violence: Popular Jewish Resistance in Roman Palestine.* San Francisco: Harper and Row, 1987.

Horst, Johannes. *Proskynein: Zur Anbetung im Urchristentum nach ihrer religionsgeschichtlichen Eigenart.* NTF 3/2. Gütersloh: C. Bertelsmann Verlag, 1932.

Horton, Fred L., Jr. *The Melchizedek Tradition: A Critical Examination of the Sources to the Fifth Century A.D. and in the Epistle to the Hebrews.* SNTSMS 30. Cambridge: Cambridge University Press, 1976.

Houssiau, Albert. *La christologie de saint Irénée.* Louvain: Publications universitaires de Louvain; Gembloux: Éditions J. Duculot, 1955.

Howard, George. "The Gospel of the Ebionites." In *ANRW,* 2.25/5 (1988): 4034-53.

———. "The Tetragram and the New Testament." *JBL* 96 (1977): 63-68.

Hubbard, Benjamin J. *The Matthean Redaction of a Primitive Apostolic Commissioning: An Exegesis of Matthew 28:16-20.* SBLDS 19. Missoula: Scholars, 1974.

Hübner, Hans. "πλήρωμα." In *EDNT,* 3:110-11.

Hultgren, Arland J. *The Rise of Normative Christianity.* Minneapolis: Fortress, 1994.

———. *Christ and His Benefits: Christology and Redemption in the New Testament.* Philadelphia: Fortress, 1987.

Hultgren, Arland J., and Steven A. Haggmark. *The Earliest Christian Heretics: Readings from Their Opponents.* Minneapolis: Fortress, 1996.

Hunter, A. M. *Paul and His Predecessors.* Rev. ed. London: SCM Press; Philadelphia: Westminster, 1961.

Hurst, Lincoln D. *The Epistle to the Hebrews: Its Background of Thought.* SNTSMS 65. Cambridge: Cambridge University Press, 1990.

Hurtado, Larry W. "New Testament Christology: A Critique of Bousset's Influence." *TS* 40 (1979): 306-17.

————. *Text-Critical Methodology and the Pre-Caesarean Text: Codex W in the Gospel of Mark.* SD 43. Grand Rapids: Eerdmans, 1981.

————. "Jesus as Lordly Example in Philippians 2:5-11." In *From Jesus to Paul: Studies in Honour of Francis Wright Beare,* edited by P. Richardson and J. C. Hurd, 113-26. Waterloo, Ontario: Wilfrid Laurier University Press, 1984.

————. "New Testament Christology: Retrospect and Prospect." *Semeia* 30 (1984): 15-27.

————. "Revelation 4–5 in the Light of Jewish Apocalyptic Analogies." *JSNT* 25 (1985): 105-24.

————. *One God, One Lord: Early Christian Devotion and Ancient Jewish Monotheism.* Philadelphia: Fortress, 1988; 2nd ed., Edinburgh: T. & T. Clark, 1998.

————. "The Gospel of Mark: Evolutionary or Revolutionary Document?" *JSNT* 40 (1990): 15-32.

————. "Christ," "God," and "Gospel (Genre)." In *DJG,* 106-17, 270-76, and 276-82, respectively.

————. "Convert, Apostate or Apostle to the Nations? The 'Conversion' of Paul in Recent Scholarship." *SR* 22 (1993): 273-84.

————. "Lord" and "Son of God." In *DPL,* 560-69 and 900-906 respectively.

————. "What Do We Mean by 'First-Century Jewish Monotheism'?" In SBLSP, edited by Eugene H. Lovering, 348-68. Atlanta: Scholars, 1993.

————. "Christ-Devotion in the First Two Centuries: Reflections and a Proposal." *TJT* 12, no. 1 (1996): 17-33.

————. "Following Jesus in the Gospel of Mark — and Beyond." In *Patterns of Discipleship in the New Testament,* edited by Richard N. Longenecker, 9-29. Grand Rapids: Eerdmans, 1996.

————. "Christology." In *DLNTD,* 170-84.

————. "Philippians 2:6-11." In *Prayer from Alexander to Constantine: A Critical Anthology,* edited by Mark Kiley, 235-39. London: Routledge, 1997.

————. "A Taxonomy of Recent Historical-Jesus Work." In *Whose Historical Jesus?* edited by William E. Arnal and Michel Desjardins, 272-95. ESCJ 7. Waterloo, Ontario: Wilfrid Laurier University Press, 1997.

————. "First-Century Jewish Monotheism." *JSNT* 71 (1998): 3-26.

————. "The Origin of the *Nomina Sacra:* A Proposal." *JBL* 117 (1998): 655-73.

————. "Beyond the Interlude? Developments and Directions in New Testament Textual Criticism." In *Studies in the Early Text of the Gospels and Acts,* edited by D. G. K. Taylor, 26-48. Birmingham: University of Birmingham Press, 1999.

————. "The Binitarian Shape of Early Christian Worship." In *The Jewish Roots of Christological Monotheism: Papers from the St. Andrews Conference on the Historical*

Origins of the Worship of Jesus, edited by Carey C. Newman, James R. Davila, and Gladys S. Lewis, 187-213. JSJSup 63. Leiden: Brill, 1999.

————. "Jesus' Divine Sonship in Paul's Epistle to the Romans." In *Romans and the People of God,* edited by Sven K. Soderlund and N. T. Wright, 217-33. Grand Rapids: Eerdmans, 1999.

————. "Pre–70 C.E. Jewish Opposition to Christ-Devotion." *JTS* 50 (1999): 35-58.

————. *At the Origins of Christian Worship: The Context and Character of Earliest Christian Devotion.* Carlisle: Paternoster, 1999; U.S. ed., Grand Rapids: Eerdmans, 2000.

————. "The Earliest Evidence of an Emerging Christian Material and Visual Culture: The Codex, the *Nomina Sacra* and the Staurogram." In *Text and Artifact in the Religions of Mediterranean Antiquity: Essays in Honour of Peter Richardson,* edited by Stephen G. Wilson and Michel Desjardins, 271-88. Waterloo, Ontario: Wilfrid Laurier University Press, 2000.

————. "Religious Experience and Religious Innovation in the New Testament." *JR* 80 (2000): 183-205.

————. "Paul's Christology." In *The Cambridge Companion to Paul,* edited by J. D. G. Dunn. Cambridge: Cambridge University Press, 2003.

————. "P^{52} (P. Rylands 457) and the *Nomina Sacra:* Method and Probability." *TB* (forthcoming 2003).

Hvalvik, Reidar. *The Struggle for Scripture and Covenant: The Purpose of the "Epistle of Barnabas" and Jewish-Christian Competition in the Second Century.* WUNT 2/82. Tübingen: Mohr-Siebeck, 1996.

Ilan, Tal. "'Man Born of Woman . . .' (Job 14:1), the Phenomenon of Men Bearing Metronymes at the Time of Jesus." *NovT* 34 (1992): 23-45.

Jacobson, Arland D. *The First Gospel: An Introduction to Q.* Sonoma, Calif.: Polebridge Press, 1992.

James, M. R. *The Apocryphal New Testament.* Oxford: Clarendon, 1953.

Jeremias, Joachim. *New Testament Theology: The Proclamation of Jesus.* Translated by John Bowden. New York: Charles Scribner's Sons, 1971.

————. "ποιμήν." In *TDNT,* 6:485-502.

Jervell, Jacob. *Luke and the People of God.* Minneapolis: Augsburg, 1972.

Jewett, Robert. "The Agitators and the Galatian Congregation." *NTS* 17 (1971): 198-212.

Johnson, Earl S. "Is Mark 15:39 the Key to Mark's Christology?" *JSNT* 31 (1987): 3-22.

Johnson, Luke T. *The Letter of James.* AB 37A. New York: Doubleday, 1995.

————. *Religious Experience in Earliest Christianity: A Missing Dimension in New Testament Studies.* Minneapolis: Fortress, 1998.

Johnson, Marshall D. *The Purpose of the Biblical Genealogies.* SNTSMS 8. Cambridge: Cambridge University Press, 1969.

————. "The Life of Adam and Eve." In *OTP,* 2:249-95.

Johnson, Norman B. *Prayer in the Apocrypha and Pseudepigrapha: A Study of the Jewish Concept of God.* SBLMS 2. Philadelphia: SBL, 1948.

Jones, F. Stanley. "Ebionites." In *EEC,* 1:357-58.

Jonge, Marinus de. *Christology in Context: The Earliest Christian Response to Jesus.* Philadelphia: Westminster, 1988.

Judge, Edwin A. "The Early Christians as a Scholastic Community." *JRH* 1 (1961): 4-15, 125-37.

———. "Papyri." In *EEC*, 2:867-72.

Juel, Donald. *Messiah and Temple*. SBLDS 31. Missoula: Scholars, 1977.

———. *Messianic Exegesis: Christological Interpretation of the Old Testament in Early Christianity*. Philadelphia: Fortress, 1988.

Jungmann, Joseph. *The Place of Christ in Liturgical Prayer*. 2nd rev. ed. London and Dublin: Geoffrey Chapman, 1965.

Käsemann, Ernst. *The Testament of Jesus: A Study of the Gospel of John in the Light of Chapter 17*. Translated by Gerhard Krodel. Philadelphia: Fortress, 1968.

Kay, D. M. "The Apology of Aristides." In ANF, 9:257-79.

Kee, Howard Clark. "The Function of Scriptural Quotations and Allusions in Mark 11–16." In *Jesus und Paulus: Festschrift für Werner Georg Kümmel*, edited by E. E. Ellis and E. Grässer, 165-88. Göttingen: Vandenhoeck & Ruprecht, 1975.

Keener, Craig S. *A Commentary on the Gospel of Matthew*. Grand Rapids: Eerdmans, 1999.

Kelhoffer, James A. *Miracle and Mission: The Authentication of Missionaries and Their Message in the Longer Ending of Mark*. WUNT 2/112. Tübingen: Mohr-Siebeck, 2000.

Kelly, J. N. D. *Early Christian Doctrines*. 5th ed. New York and London: Harper and Row, 1977.

Kempson, Ruth M. *Semantic Theory*. Cambridge Textbooks in Linguistics. Cambridge: Cambridge University Press, 1977.

Kennedy, H. A. A. *Sources of New Testament Greek or the Influence of the Septuagint on the Vocabulary of the New Testament*. Edinburgh: T. & T. Clark, 1895.

Kennel, Gunter. *Frühchristliche Hymnen? Gattungskritische Studien zur Frage nach den Liedern der frühen Christenheit*. WMANT 71. Neukirchen-Vluyn: Neukirchener Verlag, 1995.

Kieffer, René. "Les premiers indices d'une réception de L'Évangile de saint Jean." In *The Four Gospels 1992: Festschrift Frans Neirynck*, edited by F. Van Segbroeck, C. M. Tuckett, G. Van Belle, and J. Verheyden, 3:2225-38. Leuven: Leuven University Press/ Peeters, 1992.

Kiley, Mark C. *Colossians as Pseudepigraphy*. Sheffield: JSOT Press, 1986.

———, ed. *Prayer from Alexander to Constantine: A Critical Anthology*. London: Routledge, 1997.

Kimelman, Reuven. "The *Birkat Ha-Minim* and the Lack of Evidence for an Anti-Christian Prayer in Late Antiquity." In *Jewish and Christian Self-Definition*, vol. 2, edited by E. P. Sanders, A. I. Baumgarten, and A. Mendelson, 226-44. Philadelphia: Fortress, 1981.

King, Karen L. "Approaching the Variants of the *Apocryphon of John*." In *The Nag Hammadi Library after Fifty Years: Proceedings of the 1995 Society of Biblical Literature Commemoration*, edited by John D. Turner and Anne McGuire, 105-37. NHMS 44. Leiden: Brill, 1997.

Kingsbury, Jack D. *Matthew: Structure, Christology, Kingdom*. Philadelphia: Fortress, 1975.

———. "The Title 'Son of David' in Matthew's Gospel." *JBL* 95 (1976): 591-602.

———. *The Christology of Mark's Gospel*. Philadelphia: Fortress, 1983.

———. "The Figure of Jesus in Matthew's Story: A Literary-Critical Probe." *JSNT* 21 (1984): 3-36.

Kinzig, Wolfram. "*Kainē diathēkē*: The Title of the New Testament in the Second and Third Centuries." *JTS*, n.s., 45 (1994): 519-44.

Kirchner, Dankwart. *Epistula Jacobi Apocrypha: Die zweite Schrift aus Nag-Hammadi-Codex I.* TU 136. Berlin: Akademie-Verlag, 1989.

———. "The Apocryphon of James." In *NTA*, 1:285-99.

Kirk, Alan. "Examining Priorities: Another Look at the *Gospel of Peter's* Relationship to the New Testament Gospels." *NTS* 40 (1994): 572-95.

———. *The Composition of the Sayings Source: Genre, Synchrony, and Wisdom Redaction in Q.* NovTSup 91. Leiden: Brill, 1998.

———. "The Johannine Jesus in the *Gospel of Peter:* A Social Memory Approach." In *Jesus in Johannine Tradition,* edited by Robert T. Fortna and Tom Thatcher, 313-22. Louisville, London, and Leiden: Westminster John Knox, 2001.

Kistemaker, Simon J. *The Psalm Citations in the Epistle to the Hebrews.* Amsterdam: Van Soest, 1961.

Kittel, Bonnie. *The Hymns of Qumran.* SBLDS 50. Chico, Calif.: Scholars, 1981.

Kittel, Gerhard, and Gerhard Friedrich, eds. *Theological Dictionary of the New Testament.* Translated by G. M. Bromiley. 10 vols. Grand Rapids: Eerdmans, 1964-76.

Kittel, Gerhard, and G. von Rad. "Δόξα." In *TDNT*, 2:233-55.

Klauck, H.-J. *Herrenmahl und hellenistischer Kult.* NTAbh 15. Münster: Aschendorffsche Verlagsbuchhandlung, 1982.

———. "Lord's Supper." In *ABD*, 4:362-72.

———. "Presence in the Lord's Supper: 1 Corinthians 11:23-26 in the Context of Hellenistic Religious History." In *One Loaf, One Cup: Ecumenical Studies of 1 Cor 11 and Other Eucharistic Texts,* edited by B. F. Meyer, 57-74. Macon, Ga.: Mercer University Press, 1993.

Klawek, A. *Das Gebet zu Jesus. Seine Berechtigung und Übung nach den Schriften des Neuen Testaments: Eine biblisch-theologische Studie.* NTAbh 6/5. Münster: Aschendorffsche Verlagsbuchhandlung, 1921.

Klijn, A. F. J. "Das Hebräer- und das Nazoräerevangelium." In *ANRW*, 2.25/5 (1988): 3997-4033.

———. *Jewish-Christian Gospel Tradition.* VCSup 17. Leiden: Brill, 1992.

Klijn, A. F. J., and G. J. Reinink. *Patristic Evidence for Jewish-Christian Sects.* NovTSup 36. Leiden: Brill, 1973.

Kloppenborg, John S. "Wisdom Christology in Q." *LTP* 34 (1978): 129-47.

———. *The Formation of Q: Trajectories in Ancient Wisdom Collections.* Philadelphia: Fortress, 1987.

———. *Q Parallels: Synopsis, Critical Notes, and Concordance.* FFNT. Sonoma, Calif.: Polebridge Press, 1988.

———. *Excavating Q: The History and Setting of the Sayings Gospel.* Minneapolis: Fortress, 2000.

Knibb, M. A. "Martyrdom and Ascension of Isaiah." In *OTP*, 2:143-76.

Knight, Jonathan. *Disciples of the Beloved One: The Christology, Social Setting, and Theological Context of the "Ascension of Isaiah."* JSPSup 18. Sheffield: Sheffield Academic Press, 1996.

Knox, John. *Marcion and the New Testament: An Essay in the Early History of the Canon.* Chicago: University of Chicago Press, 1942.

Kobelski, Paul J. *Melchizedek and Melchiresa'.* CBQMS 10. Washington, D.C.: Catholic Biblical Association, 1981.

Koch, G. A. "A Critical Investigation of Epiphanius' Knowledge of the Ebionites." Ph.D. diss., University of Pennsylvania, 1976.

Koch, Klaus. *The Rediscovery of Apocalyptic.* SBTss 22. London: SCM Press, 1972.

Kodell, Jerome. *The Eucharist in the New Testament.* Wilmington, Del.: Michael Glazier, 1988.

Koenig, John. *The Feast of the World's Redemption: Eucharistic Origins and Christian Mission.* Harrisburg, Pa.: Trinity Press International, 2000.

Koester, Craig R. "The Epistle to the Hebrews in Recent Study." *CRBS* 2 (1994): 123-46.

Koester, Helmut. "One Jesus and Four Primitive Gospels." *HTR* 61 (1968): 203-47; also in James M. Robinson and Helmut Koester, *Trajectories through Early Christianity* (Philadelphia: Fortress, 1971), 158-204.

————. *Introduction to the New Testament.* 2 vols. Philadelphia: Fortress, 1982.

————. "History and Development of Mark's Gospel: From Mark to Secret Mark and 'Canonical' Mark." In *Colloquy on New Testament Studies: A Time for Reappraisal and Fresh Approaches,* edited by Bruce C. Corley, 35-57. Macon, Ga.: Mercer University Press, 1983.

————. "Überlieferung und Geschichte der frühchristlichen Evangelienliteratur." In *ANRW,* 2.25.2:1463-1542.

————. "The Text of the Synoptic Gospels in the Second Century." In *Gospel Traditions in the Second Century: Origins, Recensions, Text, and Transmission,* edited by William L. Petersen, 19-37. Notre Dame, Ind., and London: University of Notre Dame Press, 1989.

————. "Introduction." In *Nag Hammadi Codex II.2-7,* edited by Bentley Layton, 38-49. NHS 20. Leiden: Brill, 1989.

————. *Ancient Christian Gospels: Their History and Development.* Philadelphia: Trinity Press International, 1990.

————. "Epilogue: Current Issues in New Testament Scholarship." In *The Future of Early Christianity: Essays in Honor of Helmut Koester,* edited by Birger A. Pearson, 467-76. Minneapolis: Fortress, 1991.

Kominiak, Benedict. *The Theophanies of the Old Testament in the Writings of St. Justin.* Washington, D.C.: Catholic University of America, 1948.

Krämer, H. "μυστήριον." In *EDNT,* 2:446-49.

Kramer, Werner. *Christ, Lord, Son of God.* SBT 50. London: SCM Press, 1966; German, 1963.

Krauss, Wolfgang. *Zwischen Jerusalem und Antiochia: Die "Hellenisten," Paulus, und die Aufnahme der Heiden in das endzeitliche Gottesvolk.* SBS 179. Stuttgart: Verlag Katholisches Bibelwerk, 1999.

Kreitzer, Larry J. *Jesus and God in Paul's Eschatology.* JSNTSup 19. Sheffield: JSOT Press, 1987.

————. "Kingdom of God/Christ." In *DPL,* 524-26.

————. "The Apotheosis of the Roman Emperor." In *Striking New Images: Roman Imperial Coinage of the New Testament World,* 69-98. JSNTSup 134. Sheffield: Sheffield Academic Press, 1996.

Kretschmar, Georg. *Studien zur frühchristlichen Trinitätstheologie.* BHT 21. Tübingen: Mohr (Siebeck), 1956.

Kroll, Joseph. *Die christliche Hymnodik bis zu Klemens von Alexandreia.* Königsberg: Hartungsche Buchdruckerei, 1921.

Kruger, Michael J. "P.Oxy. 840: Amulet or Miniature Codex?" *JTS* 53 (2002): 81-94.

Kuhn, Hans Georg. "μαραναθά." In *TDNT*, 4:471-72.

Kuhn, H.-W. "ξύλον." In *EDNT*, 2:487.

Kuhn, K. G. "The Lord's Supper and the Communal Meal at Qumran." In *The Scrolls and the New Testament*, edited by Krister Stendahl, 65-93. London: SCM Press, 1958. Reprint, New York: Crossroad, 1992.

Kümmel, Werner Georg. *The New Testament: The History of the Investigation of Its Problems*. Translated by S. M. Gilmour and H. C. Kee. Nashville: Abingdon, 1972.

———. *Introduction to the New Testament*. Edited and translated by H. C. Kee. Rev. ed. Nashville: Abingdon, 1975.

Kuschel, Karl-Josef. *Before All Time? The Dispute over Christ's Origin*. New York: Crossroad, 1992.

Kysar, Robert. *The Fourth Evangelist and His Gospel: An Examination of Contemporary Scholarship*. Minneapolis: Augsburg, 1975.

———. "John, Epistles Of." In *ABD*, 3:900-912.

Laible, Heinrich. "Jesus Christ in the Talmud." In *Jesus Christ in the Talmud, Midrash, Zohar, and the Liturgy of the Synagogue*, by Gustav Dalman, 1-98. Cambridge: Deighton, Bell, 1893. Reprint, New York: Arno, 1973.

Lampe, G. W. H. "Church Discipline and the Interpretation of the Epistles to the Corinthians." In *Christian History and Interpretation: Studies Presented to John Knox*, edited by W. R. Farmer, C. F. D. Moule, and R. R. Niebuhr, 337-61. Cambridge: Cambridge University Press, 1967.

Lane, William L. *Hebrews*. 2 vols. WBC. Dallas: Word, 1991.

———. "Hebrews." In *DLNTD*, 443-58.

Lang, Bernhard. *Monotheism and the Prophetic Minority*. Sheffield: Almond Press, 1983.

———, ed. *Der einzige Gott: Die Geburt des biblischen Monotheismus*. Munich: Köselverlag, 1981.

La Potterie, Ignace de. "Le titre Kyrios appliqué à Jésus dans l'Évangile de Luc." In *Mélanges biblique en hommage au R. P. Béda Rigaux*, edited by Albert Descamps and R. P. André Halleux, 117-46. Gembloux: Duculot, 1970.

Lattke, Michael. *Hymnus: Materialien zu einer Geschichte der antiken Hymnologie*. NTOA 19. Göttingen: Vandenhoeck & Ruprecht; Fribourg: Editions universitaires, 1991.

Lau, Andrew Y. *Manifest in Flesh: The Epiphany Christology of the Pastoral Epistles*. WUNT 2/86. Tübingen: Mohr Siebeck, 1996.

LaVerdiere, Eugene. "Mary." In *EEC*, 2:733-36.

Laws, Sophie. *A Commentary on the Epistle of James*. London: Adam and Charles Black, 1980.

Layton, Bentley. "The Recovery of Gnosticism: The Philologist's Task in the Investigation of Nag Hammadi." *SecCent* 1 (1981): 85-99.

———. *The Gnostic Scriptures*. Garden City, N.Y.: Doubleday, 1987.

———, ed. *Nag Hammadi Codex II.2-7, Together with XIII, 2*, British Library Or. 4926(1), and P.Oxy. 1, 654, 655: With Contributions by Many Scholars, Volume One*. NHS 20. Leiden: Brill, 1989.

Lebreton, Jules, *Histoire du dogme de la Trinité, des origines au concile de Nicée*. 2 vols. 1910. Reprint, Paris: G. Beauchesne, 1928. ET of vol. 1, *History of the Dogma of the Trinity from Its Origins to the Council of Nicaea.* London: Burns, Oates, and Washbourne, 1939.

——. "Le désaccord de la foi populaire et de la théologie savante dans l'Église chrétienne du III siècle." *RHE* 19 (1923): 481-506; 20 (1924): 5-27.

Lehmkühler, Karsten. *Kultus und Theologie: Dogmatik und Exegese in der religionsgeschichtliche Schule.* Forschungen zur systematischen und ökumenischen Theologie 76. Göttingen: Vandenhoeck & Ruprecht, 1996.

Leivestad, Ragnar. "Der apokalyptische Menschensohn ein theologisches Phantom." *ASTI* 6 (1968): 49-105.

——. "Exit the Apocalyptic Son of Man." *NTS* 18 (1971-72): 243-67.

Levin, Saul. "The Early History of Christianity in the Light of the 'Secret Gospel' of Mark." In *ANRW*, 2.25/6 (1988): 4270-92.

Lieberman, Saul. *Hellenism in Jewish Palestine: Studies in the Literary Transmission, Beliefs, and Manners of Palestine in the I Century B.C.E.–IV Century C.E.* 2nd ed. Texts and Studies of JTSA 18. 1950. Reprint, New York: Jewish Theological Seminary, 1962.

——. *Greek in Jewish Palestine.* New York: Jewish Theological Seminary, 1962.

Lienhard, Joseph T. "The Christology of the Epistle to Diognetus." *VC* 24 (1970): 280-89.

——. "Poetry." In *EEC*, 2:931-33.

Lietzmann, Hans. *Mass and Lord's Supper: A Study in the History of the Liturgy.* ET, Leiden: Brill, 1979.

Lieu, Judith. *The Theology of the Johannine Epistles.* Cambridge: Cambridge University Press, 1991.

Lightfoot, J. B. *The Apostolic Fathers: Clement, Ignatius, and Polycarp.* 2nd ed. 5 vols. London: Macmillan, 1889-90. Reprint, Grand Rapids: Baker, 1981.

Lightfoot, J. B., J. R. Harmer, and Michael W. Holmes. *The Apostolic Fathers: Greek Texts and English Translations of Their Writings.* 2nd ed. Grand Rapids: Baker, 1992.

Lim, Timothy. *Holy Scripture in the Qumran Commentaries and Pauline Letters.* Oxford: Clarendon, 1997.

Lindars, Barnabas. *New Testament Apologetic.* London: SCM Press, 1961.

——. *Jesus Son of Man.* London: SPCK, 1983.

——. *The Theology of the Letter to the Hebrews.* Cambridge: Cambridge University Press, 1991.

Linton, Olaf. "Evidences of a Second-Century Revised Edition of St. Mark's Gospel." *NTS* 14 (1968): 321-55.

Lips, Hermann von. *Weisheitliche Traditionen im Neuen Testament.* WMANT 64. Neukirchen-Vluyn: Neukirchener Verlag, 1990.

Little, V. A. Spence. *The Christology of the Apologists.* London: Duckworth, 1934.

Loader, William R. G. "Christ at the Right Hand — Ps. CX.1 in the New Testament." *NTS* 24 (1977): 199-217.

——. *Sohn und Hoherpriester: Eine traditionsgeschichtliche Untersuchung zur Christologie des Hebräerbriefes.* WMANT 53. Neukirchen: Neukirchener Verlag, 1981.

——. *The Christology of the Fourth Gospel: Structure and Issues.* 2nd rev. ed. BBET 23. Frankfurt am Main: Peter Lang, 1992.

Logan, Alistair H. B. *Gnostic Truth and Christian Heresy: A Study in the History of Gnosticism.* Edinburgh: T. & T. Clark, 1996.

Lohfink, Gerhard. *Die Himmelfahrt Jesu: Untersuchungen zu den Himmelfahrts- und Erhöhungstexten bei Lukas.* SANT 26. Munich: Kösel, 1971.

Löhr, Winrich A. *Basilides und seine Schule: Eine Studie zur Theologie- und Kirchengeschichte des zweiten Jahrhunderts.* WUNT 83. Tübingen: Mohr-Siebeck, 1995.

Lohse, Eduard. *Colossians and Philemon.* Hermeneia. Philadelphia: Fortress, 1971.

Longenecker, Richard. *The Christology of Early Jewish Christianity.* SBTss 17. London: SCM, 1970.

Loofs, Friedrich. "Descent to Hades (Christ's)." In *Encyclopaedia of Religion and Ethics,* edited by James Hastings, 4:654-63. Edinburgh: T. & T. Clark, 1911.

Lortz, Joseph. "Das Christentum als Monotheismus in den Apologien des zweiten Jahrhunderts." In *Beiträge zur Geschichte des christlichen Altertums und der byzantinischen Literatur: Festgabe Albert Ehrhard,* edited by Albert Michael Koeniger, 301-27. Bonn and Leipzig: Kurt Schroeder, 1922.

Lösch, Stephan. *Deitas Jesu und Antike Apotheose.* Rottenburg: Bader'sche Verlagsbuchhandlung, 1933.

Lüdemann, Gerd. *Virgin Birth? The Real Story of Mary and Her Son Jesus.* London: SCM Press, 1998; German original, 1997.

———. *Early Christianity according to the Traditions in Acts: A Commentary.* London: SCM, 1989; German, 1987.

Lüdemann, Gerd, and Martin Schröder. *Die Religionsgeschichtliche Schule in Göttingen: Eine Dokumentation.* Göttingen: Vandenhoeck & Ruprecht, 1987.

Lührmann, Dieter. "POx 2949: EvPet 3-5 in einer Handschrift des 2/3 Jahrhunderts." *ZNW* 72 (1981): 216-26.

———. "Das neue Fragment des P Egerton 2 (P Köln 255)." In *The Four Gospels 1992: Festschrift Frans Neirynck,* edited by F. Van Segbroeck, C. M. Tuckett, G. Van Belle, and J. Verheyden, 3:2239-55. Leuven: Leuven University Press/Peeters, 1992.

———. "POx 4009: Ein neues Fragment des Petrusevangeliums?" *NovT* 35 (1993): 390-410.

Lührmann, Dieter, and P. J. Parsons, "P.Oxy. LX 4009." In *The Oxyrhynchus Papyri, Vol. 60,* edited by R. A. Coles et al., 1-5. London: Egypt Exploration Society for the British Academy, 1994.

Luz, Ulrich. "Eine thetische Skizze der matthäischen Christologie." In *Anfänge der Christologie,* edited by Cillers Breytenbach and Henning Paulsen, 221-36. Göttingen: Vandenhoeck & Ruprecht, 1991.

———. *The Theology of the Gospel of Matthew.* Cambridge: Cambridge University Press, 1995.

Lyons, George. *Pauline Autobiography: Toward a New Understanding.* SBLDS 73. Atlanta: Scholars, 1985.

Lyons, John. *Language and Linguistics: An Introduction.* Cambridge: Cambridge University Press, 1981.

MacArthur, Harvey K. "Son of Mary." *NovT* 15 (1973): 38-58.

Maccoby, Hyam. *The Mythmaker: Paul and the Invention of Christianity.* New York: Harper and Row, 1986.

MacCulloch, J. A. "Descent to Hades (Ethnic)." In *Encyclopaedia of Religion and Ethics,* edited by James Hastings, 4:648-54. Edinburgh: T. & T. Clark, 1911.

———. *The Harrowing of Hell: A Comparative Study of an Early Christian Doctrine.* Edinburgh: T. & T. Clark, 1930.

Mach, Michael. *Entwicklungsstudien des jüdischen Engelglaubens in vorrabbinischer Zeit.* TSAJ 34. Tübingen: J. C. B. Mohr, 1992.

Machen, J. Gresham. *The Origin of Paul's Religion.* 1925. Reprint, Grand Rapids: Eerdmans, 1965.

————. *The Virgin Birth of Christ.* New York: Harper and Row, 1932. Reprint, Grand Rapids: Baker, 1965.

Mack, Burton L. *Logos und Sophia: Untersuchungen zur Weisheitstheologie in hellenistischen Judentum.* Göttingen: Vandenhoeck & Ruprecht, 1973.

————. *A Myth of Innocence: Mark and Christian Origins.* Philadelphia: Fortress, 1988.

————. *The Lost Gospel: The Book of Q and Christian Origins.* San Francisco: Harper Collins, 1993.

MacRae, George W. "The Ego-Proclamation in Gnostic Sources." In *The Trial of Jesus: Cambridge Studies in Honour of C. F. D. Moule,* edited by Ernst Bammel, 123-29. SBT 2/13. London: SCM Press, 1970.

Maier, Johann. *Jesus von Nazareth in der talmudischen Überlieferung.* Darmstadt: Wissenschaftliche Buchgesellschaft, 1978.

Malbon, Elizabeth S. "Fallible Followers: Women and Men in the Gospel of Mark." *Semeia* 28 (1983): 29-48; reprinted in Malbon, *In the Company of Jesus,* 41-69.

————. "Disciples/Crowds/Whoever: Markan Characters and Readers." *NovT* 18 (1986): 104-30.

————. *In the Company of Jesus: Characters in Mark's Gospel.* Louisville: Westminster John Knox, 2000.

Malherbe, Abraham J. *Moral Exhortation, a Greco-Roman Sourcebook.* Library of Early Christianity. Louisville: Westminster John Knox, 1986.

————. *Social Aspects of Early Christianity.* Baton Rouge: Louisiana State University Press, 1977.

Mansfeld, Jaap. "Bad World and Demiurge: A 'Gnostic' Motif from Parmenides and Empedocles to Lucretius and Philo." In *Studies in Gnosticism and Hellenistic Religions,* edited by R. Van Den Broek, 261-314. Leiden: Brill, 1981.

Mara, M. G. *Évangile de Pierre: Introduction, Text critique, traduction, commentaire et index.* SC 201. Paris: Éditions du Cerf, 1973.

Marcus, Joel. *The Way of the Lord: Christological Exegesis of the Old Testament in the Gospel of Mark.* Louisville: Westminster John Knox, 1992.

————. *Mark 1–8: A New Translation with Introduction and Commentary.* AB. New York: Doubleday, 2000.

Markschies, Christoph. *Valentinus Gnosticus? Untersuchungen zur Valentinianischen Gnosis mit einem Kommentar zu den Fragmenten Valentinus.* WUNT 65. Tübingen: Mohr-Siebeck, 1992.

————. "Das Problem des historischen Valentin — Neue Forschungen zu Valentinus Gnosticus." In *Studia Patristica, Vol. 24,* edited by Elizabeth A. Livingstone, 382-89. Leuven: Peeters, 1993.

————. "Nochmals: Valentinus und die Gnostikoi, Beobachtungen zu Irenaeus, Haer. I 30,15 und Tertullian, Val. 4.3." *VC* 51 (1997): 179-87.

————. "Valentinian Gnosticism: Toward the Anatomy of a School." In *The Nag Hammadi Library after Fifty Years: Proceedings of the 1995 Society of Biblical Literature Com-*

memoration, edited by John D. Turner and Anne McGuire, 401-38. NHMS 44. Leiden: Brill, 1997.

Marshall, I. Howard. "Palestinian and Hellenistic Christianity: Some Critical Comments." *NTS* 19 (1972-73): 271-87.

―――. *Luke: Historian and Theologian.* Grand Rapids: Zondervan, 1970.

―――. *The Gospel of Luke.* NIGTC. Grand Rapids: Eerdmans, 1978.

―――. *Last Supper and Lord's Supper.* Grand Rapids: Eerdmans, 1980.

―――. "Son of Man." In *DJG*, 775-81.

―――. "Acts and the 'Former Treatise.'" In *The Book of Acts in Its First-Century Setting*, edited by Bruce W. Winter and Andrew D. Clarke, 163-82. Grand Rapids: Eerdmans, 1993.

Marshall, John W. "The *Gospel of Thomas* and the Cynic Jesus." In *Whose Historical Jesus?* edited by William E. Arnal and Michel Desjardins, 37-60. Waterloo, Ontario: Wilfrid Laurier University Press, 1997.

Martin, R. P. *Carmen Christi: Philippians 2:5-11 in Recent Interpretation and in the Setting of Early Christian Worship.* Cambridge: Cambridge University Press, 1967. Rev. ed., Grand Rapids: Eerdmans, 1983.

―――. "Some Reflections on New Testament Hymns." In *Christ the Lord: Studies Presented to Donald Guthrie,* edited by H. H. Rowdon, 37-49. Leicester: InterVarsity, 1982.

Martin, R. P., and Peter H. Davids, eds. *Dictionary of the Later New Testament and Its Developments.* Downers Grove, Ill.: InterVarsity, 1997.

Martin, R. P., and Brian J. Dodd, eds. *Where Christology Began: Essays on Philippians 2.* Louisville: Westminster John Knox, 1998.

Martin, Thomas W. "Hellenists." In *ABD*, 3:135-36.

Marty, Jacques. "Étude de textes cultuels de prière contenus dans le Nouveau Testament." *RHPR* 9 (1929): 234-63, 366-76.

―――. " Étude de textes cultuels de prière conservés par les 'Pères apostolique.'" *RHPR* 10 (1930): 90-98.

Martyn, J. Louis. *History and Theology in the Fourth Gospel.* 2nd ed. Nashville: Abingdon, 1979; original ed., 1968.

―――. *Theological Issues in the Letters of Paul.* Edinburgh: T. & T. Clark, 1997.

Massoux, Edouard. *The Influence of the Gospel of Saint Matthew on Christian Literature before Saint Irenaeus.* Edited by Arthur J. Bellinzoni. Translated by Norman J. Belval and Suzanne Hecht. 2 vols. Macon, Ga.: Mercer University Press, 1990.

Matera, Frank J. *New Testament Christology.* Louisville: Westminster John Knox, 1999.

May, Gerhard. "Ein neues Marcionbild?" *TRu* 51 (1986): 404-13.

―――. "Marcion in Contemporary Views: Results and Open Questions." *SecCent* 6 (1987-88): 129-51.

McCant, J. W. "The *Gospel of Peter:* Docetism Reconsidered." *NTS* 30 (1984): 258-73.

McCue, James. "Orthodoxy and Heresy: Walter Bauer and the Valentinians." *VC* 33 (1970): 118-30.

McDonald, J. I. H. *The Crucible of Christian Morality.* London: Routledge, 1998.

McDonald, Lee Martin. *The Formation of the Christian Biblical Canon.* Rev. ed. Peabody, Mass.: Hendrickson, 1995.

McKnight, Edgar V. "Literary Criticism." In *DJG*, 473-81.

McKnight, Scot. "Collection for the Saints." In *DPL*, 143-47.

Meade, David G. *Pseudonymity and Canon*. Grand Rapids: Eerdmans, 1987.

Meadors, Edward P. "The Orthodoxy of the 'Q' Sayings of Jesus." *TB* 43 (1992): 233-57.

———. "The 'Messianic' Implications of the Q Material." *JBL* 118 (1999): 253-77.

Mealand, David L. "The Christology of the Fourth Gospel." *SJT* 31 (1978): 449-67.

Mearns, C. L. "Dating the Similitudes of Enoch." *NTS* 25 (1979): 360-69.

Meeks, Wayne A. "The Man from Heaven in Johannine Sectarianism." *JBL* 91 (1972): 44-72.

———. *The First Urban Christians: The Social World of the Apostle Paul*. New Haven: Yale University Press, 1983.

———. *The Moral World of the First Christians*. Library of Early Christianity. Philadelphia: Westminster, 1986.

———. "Equal to God." In *The Conversation Continues: Studies in Paul and John in Honor of J. Louis Martyn*, edited by Robert T. Fortna and Beverly R. Gaventa, 309-21. Nashville: Abingdon, 1990.

Mees, M. "Das Christusbild des ersten Klemensbriefes." *ETL* 66 (1990): 297-318.

Meier, John P. *A Marginal Jew*. Vol. 1, *Rethinking the Historical Jesus*. New York: Doubleday, 1991.

———. "Matthew, Gospel Of." In *ABD*, 4:622-41.

———. *A Marginal Jew*. Vol. 2, *Mentor, Message, and Miracles*. New York: Doubleday, 1994.

Meissner, W. W. *The Cultic Origins of Christianity: The Dynamics of Religious Development*. Collegeville, Minn.: Liturgical Press, 2000.

Ménard, Jacques-É. *L'Évangile selon Philippe: Introduction, texte, traduction, commentaire*. Paris: Letouzey & Ané, 1967.

———. *L'Évangile de Vérité*. NHS 2. Leiden: Brill, 1972.

———. *L'Évangile selon Thomas*. NHS 5. Leiden: Brill, 1975.

———. "*Pais Theou* as Messianic Title in the Book of Acts." *CBQ* 19 (1957): 83-92.

Menken, M. J. J. *Old Testament Quotations in the Fourth Gospel*. CBET 15. Kampen: Kok Pharos, 1996.

Merkel, Helmut. *Die Widersprüche zwischen den Evangelien. Ihre polemische und apologetische Behandlung in der Alten Kirche bis zu Augustin*. WUNT 13. Tübingen: Mohr (Siebeck), 1971.

———. *Die Pluralität der Evangelien als theologisches und exegetisches Problem in der alten Kirche*. Traditio Christiana 3. Bern and Frankfurt: Peter Lang, 1978.

Metzger, Bruce M. *Manuscripts of the Greek Bible: An Introduction to Palaeography*. New York: Oxford University Press, 1981.

———. *The Canon of the New Testament: Its Origin, Development, and Significance*. Oxford: Clarendon, 1987.

Metzger, Bruce M., et al. *A Textual Commentary on the Greek New Testament*. London and New York: United Bible Societies, 1971.

Meye, Robert P. *Jesus and the Twelve: Discipleship and Revelation in Mark's Gospel*. Grand Rapids: Eerdmans, 1968.

Meyer, Marvin W. *The Letter of Peter to Philip: Text, Translation, and Commentary*. SBLDS 53. Chico, Calif.: Scholars, 1981.

———. "The Beginning of the *Gospel of Thomas*." *Semeia* 52 (1990): 161-73.

———. *The "Gospel of Thomas": Hidden Sayings of Jesus*. San Francisco: Harper San Francisco, 1992.

Meyers, Eric M. "Synagogue." In *ABD*, 6:251-60.

Michel, Otto, and I. H. Marshall. "Son of Man." In *NIDNTT,* 3:613-34.

Moore, Carey A. "Tobit, Book Of." In *ABD*, 6:585-94.

Moore, G. F. "Tatian's *Diatessaron* and the Analysis of the Pentateuch." *JBL* 9 (1890): 201-15.

Moore, Richard Kingsley. "Right with God: Paul and His English Translators." Ph.D. diss., University of Queensland, 1978.

Morgenthaler, Robert. *Statistik des neutestamentlichen Wortschatzes.* Zürich: Gotthelf-Verlag, 1958.

Morton, Russell. "Glory to God and to the Lamb: John's Use of Jewish and Hellenistic/Roman Themes in Formatting His Theology in Revelation 4–5." *JSNT* 83 (2001): 89-109.

Moule, C. F. D. *An Idiom Book of New Testament Greek.* Cambridge: Cambridge University Press, 1963.

———. "Neglected Features in the Problem of 'the Son of Man.'" In *Neues Testament und Kirche,* edited by Joachim Gnilka, 413-28. Freiburg: Herder, 1974.

Moulton, James Hope, Wilbert Francis Howard, and Nigel Turner. *A Grammar of New Testament Greek.* 4 vols. Edinburgh: T. & T. Clark, 1908-79.

Mowinckel, Sigmund. *He That Cometh.* Translated by G. W. Anderson. New York: Abingdon, 1954.

Mowry, Lucetta. "Revelation 4–5 and Early Christian Liturgical Usage." *JBL* 71 (1952): 75-84.

Moxnes, Halvor. "God and His Angel in the *Shepherd of Hermas.*" *ST* 28 (1974): 49-56.

Müller, P.-G. "ἐπιφάνεια." In *EDNT,* 2:44-45.

———. *ΧΡΙΣΤΟΣ ΑΡΧΗΓΟΣ. Der religionsgeschichtliche und theologische Hintergrund einer neutestamentlichen Christusprädikation.* Frankfurt/Bern: Peter Lang, 1973.

Mullins, Mark R. "Christianity as a New Religion: Charisma, Minor Founders, and Indigenous Movements." In *Religion and Society in Modern Japan,* edited by Mark R. Mullins, Shimazono Susumu, and Paul Swanson, 257-72. Berkeley: Asian Humanities Press, 1993.

Munck, Johannes. *Paul and the Salvation of Mankind.* Richmond: John Knox, 1959; German ed., 1954.

Murgia, Charles E. "Secret Mark: Real or Fake?" In *Longer Mark: Forgery, Interpolation, or Old Tradition? Colloquy 18 of the Center for Hermeneutical Studies in Hellenistic and Modern Culture,* edited by Wilhelm Wuellner, 35-40. Berkeley: Center for Hermeneutical Studies, 1975.

Murphy-O'Connor, Jerome. "Christological Anthropology in Phil. II, 6-11." *RevB* 83 (1976): 25-50.

Musurillo, Herbert. *The Acts of the Christian Martyrs: Introduction, Texts, and Translations.* Oxford: Clarendon, 1972.

Nagata, Takeshi. "Philippians 2:5-11: A Case Study in the Contextual Shaping of Early Christology." Ph.D. diss., Princeton Theological Seminary, 1981.

Naluparayil, Jacob Chacko. "Jesus of the Gospel of Mark: Present State of Research." *CRBS* 8 (2000): 191-226.

Neirynck, Frans. "The Apocryphal Gospels and the Gospel of Mark." In *The New Testament in Early Christianity,* edited by Jean-Marie Sevrin, 123-75. Leuven: Leuven University Press, 1989.

Neufeld, V. H. *The Earliest Christian Confessions.* NTTS 5. Grand Rapids: Eerdmans, 1963.

Neusner, Jacob. *Why No Gospels in Talmudic Judaism?* BJS 135. Atlanta: Scholars, 1988.

New, Silva. "The Name, Baptism, and the Laying On of Hands." In *The Beginnings of Christianity,* edited by F. J. Foakes Jackson and Kirsopp Lake, 5:121-40. 1933. Reprint, Grand Rapids: Baker, 1966.

Newman, Carey C. *Paul's Glory-Christology: Tradition and Rhetoric.* NovTSup 69. Leiden: Brill, 1992.

———. "Glory." In *DLNTD,* 395-400.

Newman, Carey C., James R. Davila, and Gladys S. Lewis, eds. *The Jewish Roots of Christological Monotheism: Papers from the St. Andrews Conference on the Historical Origins of the Worship of Jesus.* JSJSup 63. Leiden: Brill, 1999.

Niebuhr, Karl-Wilhelm. *Heidenapostel aus Israel: Die jüdische Identität des Paulus nach ihrer Darstellung in seinen Briefen.* WUNT 62. Tübingen: Mohr (Siebeck), 1992.

Niederwimmer, Kurt. *The Didache.* Hermeneia. Minneapolis: Fortress, 1998.

Nock, A. D. *Conversion: The Old and the New in Religion from Alexander the Great to Augustine of Hippo.* London: Oxford University Press, 1933.

———. *Early Christianity and Its Hellenistic Background.* New York: Harper and Row, 1964.

———. "'Son of God' in Pauline and Hellenistic Thought." In *Essays on Religion and the Ancient World,* edited by Z. Stewart, 2:928-39. 2 vols. Oxford: Clarendon, 1972.

Nolan, Brian M. *The Royal Son of God: The Christology of Matthew 1–2 in the Setting of the Gospel.* Göttingen: Vandenhoeck & Ruprecht, 1979.

Norelli, Enrico. *Ascensio Isaiae: Commentarius.* CCSA 8. Turnhout: Brepols, 1995.

Obermann, Andreas. *Die christologische Erfüllung der Schrift im Johannesevangelium.* WUNT 2/83. Tübingen: Mohr-Siebeck, 1996.

O'Brien, Peter T. *Introductory Thanksgivings in the Letters of Paul.* NovTSup 49. Leiden: Brill, 1977.

———. "Benediction, Blessing, Doxology, Thanksgiving" and "Colossians, Letter to the." In *DPL,* 68-71 and 147-53, respectively.

O'Connor, Daniel W. *Peter in Rome: The Literary, Liturgical, and Archaeological Evidence.* New York: Columbia University Press, 1969.

Old, H. O. "The Psalms of Praise in the Worship of the New Testament Church." *Int* 39 (1985): 20-33.

Olyan, Saul M. *Asherah and the Cult of Yahweh in Israel.* SBLMS 34. Atlanta: Scholars, 1988.

Onuki, Takashi. "Traditionsgeschichte von Thomasevangelium 17 und ihre christologische Relevanz." In *Anfänge der Christologie,* edited by Cilliers Breytenbach and H. Paulsen, 399-415. Göttingen: Vandenhoeck & Ruprecht, 1991.

Orbe, Antonio. *Introducción a la Teología de los Siglos II y III.* 2 vols. Rome: Editrice Pontificia Universita Gregoriana, 1987.

Osborn, Eric. *The Philosophy of Clement of Alexandria.* TS, n.s., 3. Cambridge: Cambridge University Press, 1957.

———. *Justin Martyr.* BZHT 47. Tübingen: J. C. B. Mohr (Paul Siebeck), 1973.

———. *The Beginning of Christian Philosophy.* Cambridge: Cambridge University Press, 1981.

———. *The Emergence of Christian Theology.* Cambridge: Cambridge University Press, 1993.

―――. *Tertullian, First Theologian of the West*. Cambridge: Cambridge University Press, 1997.

Osiek, Carolyn. *The Shepherd of Hermas*. Hermeneia. Minneapolis: Fortress, 1999.

Oster, Richard. "Christianity in Asia Minor." In *ABD*, 1:938-54.

Overman, J. Andrew. *Matthew's Gospel and Formative Judaism*. Minneapolis: Fortress, 1990.

Owen, E. C. E. *Some Authentic Acts of the Early Martyrs*. Oxford: Clarendon, 1927.

Owen, Paul, and David Shepherd. "Speaking Up for Qumran, Dalman and the Son of Man: Was *Bar Enasha* a Common Term for 'Man' in the Time of Jesus?" *JSNT* 81 (2001): 81-122.

Pagels, Elaine. "Gnostic and Orthodox Views of Christ's Passion: Paradigms for the Christian's Response to Persecution?" In *The Rediscovery of Gnosticism*, edited by Bentley Layton, 1:262-83. 2 vols. Leiden: Brill, 1980.

―――. *The Gnostic Gospels*. London: Weidenfeld and Nicolson, 1980.

―――. "Adam and Eve, Christ and the Church: A Survey of Second Century Controversies concerning Marriage." In *The New Testament and Gnosis: Essays in Honour of Robert McL. Wilson*, edited by A. H. B. Logan and A. J. M. Wedderburn, 146-75. Edinburgh: T. & T. Clark, 1983.

―――. "Ritual in the *Gospel of Philip*." In *The Nag Hammadi Library after Fifty Years: Proceedings of the 1995 Society of Biblical Literature Commemoration*, edited by John D. Turner and Anne McGuire, 280-91. NHMS 44. Leiden: Brill, 1997.

Paget, James Carleton. *The "Epistle of Barnabas," Outlook and Background*. WUNT 2/64. Tübingen: Mohr-Siebeck, 1994.

Painter, John. *Just James: The Brother of Jesus in History and Tradition*. Columbia: University of South Carolina Press, 1991.

―――. *The Quest for the Messiah: The History, Literature, and Theology of the Johannine Community*. 2nd ed. Edinburgh: T. & T. Clark; Nashville: Abingdon, 1993.

Palmer, Darryl W. "Acts and the Ancient Historical Monograph." In *The Book of Acts in Its Ancient Literary Setting*, edited by Bruce W. Winter and Andrew D. Clarke, 1-29. Grand Rapids: Eerdmans, 1993.

Pamment, Margaret. "The Meaning of *Doxa* in the Fourth Gospel." *ZNW* 74 (1983): 12-16.

Parke-Taylor, G. H. *Yahweh: The Divine Name in the Bible*. Waterloo, Ontario: Wilfrid Laurier University Press, 1975.

Parsons, Mikeal C. *The Departure of Jesus in Luke-Acts*. JSNTSup 21. Sheffield: Sheffield Academic Press, 1987.

Patsch, H. "εὐλογέω." In *EDNT*, 2:79-80.

Patte, Daniel. *Early Jewish Hermeneutic in Palestine*. SBLDS 22. Missoula: Scholars, 1975.

Patterson, Stephen J. "The *Gospel of Thomas* and the Synoptic Tradition: A *Forschungsbericht* and Critique." *Forum* 8 (1992): 45-97.

―――. "Gospels, Apocryphal." In *ABD*, 2:1079-81.

―――. *The "Gospel of Thomas" and Jesus*. Sonoma, Calif.: Polebridge Press, 1993.

Patton, Corrine L. "Adam as the Image of God: An Exploration of the Fall of Satan in the *Life of Adam and Eve*." In SBLSP 33, edited by E. H. Lovering, 294-300. Atlanta: Scholars, 1994.

Pearson, Birger A. "Use, Authority and Exegesis of *Mikra* in Gnostic Literature." In *Mikra: Text, Translation, Reading, and Interpretation of the Hebrew Bible in Ancient Judaism and Early Christianity,* edited by Martin Jan Mulder, 635-52. CRINT. Assen: Van Gorcum; Philadelphia: Fortress, 1988.

————. "Pre-Valentinian Gnosticism in Alexandria." In *The Future of Early Christianity: Essays in Honor of Helmut Koester,* edited by B. A. Pearson, 455-66. Minneapolis: Fortress, 1991.

————. "Christianity in Egypt." In *ABD,* 1:954-60.

Peel, Malcolm L. "The 'Decensus [*sic*] Ad Inferos' in 'The Teachings of Silvanus' (CG VII, 4)." *Numen* 26 (1979): 23-49.

Penner, Todd C. *The Epistle of James and Eschatology: Re-Reading an Ancient Christian Letter.* JSNTSup 121. Sheffield: Sheffield Academic Press, 1996.

————. "In Praise of Christian Origins: Stephen and the Hellenists in Lukan Apologetic Historiography." Ph.D. diss., Emory University, 2000.

Perkins, Pheme. *The Gnostic Dialogue: The Early Church and the Crisis of Gnosticism.* New York: Paulist, 1980.

————. "New Testament Christologies in Gnostic Transformation." In *The Future of Early Christianity: Essays in Honor of Helmut Koester,* edited by Birger A. Pearson, 433-41. Minneapolis: Fortress, 1991.

Perrin, Nicholas. *Thomas and Tatian: The Relationship between the Gospel of Thomas and the Diatessaron.* Atlanta: Society of Biblical Literature, 2002.

Perrin, Norman. "Mark 14:62: The End Product of a Christian Pesher Tradition?" *NTS* 12 (1965-66): 150-55.

Pervo, Richard. *Profit with Delight.* Philadelphia: Fortress, 1987.

Pesce, Mauro, ed. *Isaia, il deletto e la chiesa: Visione ed esegesi profetica christiano-primitiva nell' Ascensione di Isaia, Atti del convegno di Roma, 9-10 aprile 1981.* Testi e richerche di Scienze religiose 20. Brescia: Paideia, 1983.

Petersen, William L. "Textual Evidence of Tatian's Dependence upon Justin's ΑΠΟΜΝΗΜΟΝΕΥΜΑΤΑ." *NTS* 36 (1990): 360-402.

————. "Ebionites, Gospel of The" and "Nazoraeans, Gospel of The." In *ABD,* 2:261-62 and 4:1051-52, respectively.

————. *Tatian's "Diatessaron": Its Creation, Dissemination, Use, and History in Scholarship.* VCSup 25. Leiden: Brill, 1994.

Peterson, David. "The Worship of the New Community." In *Witness to the Gospel: The Theology of Acts,* edited by I. Howard Marshall and David Peterson, 373-95. Grand Rapids and Cambridge: Eerdmans, 1998.

Peterson, Erik. *Heis Theos: epigraphische, formgeschichtliche und religionsgeschichtliche Untersuchungen.* FRLANT, n.s., 24. Göttingen: Vandenhoeck & Ruprecht, 1926.

————. "Die geschichtliche Bedeutung der jüdischen Gebetsrichtung" and "Das Kreuz und das Gebet nach Osten." In his *Frühkirche, Judentum und Gnosis: Studien und Untersuchungen,* 1-14 and 15-35, respectively. Rome: Herder, 1959.

Pickering, S. R. "Transmission of Gospel Materials in the Second Century: Evidence of a New Fragment from Oxyrhynchus." *New Testament Textual Research Update* 2 (1994): 105-10.

Pietersma, Albert. "Kyrios or Tetragram: A Renewed Quest for the Original Septuagint." In *Studies in Honour of John W. Wevers on His Sixty-Fifth Birthday,* edited by Albert Pietersma and Claude Cox, 85-101. Mississauga, Ontario: Benben Publishers, 1984.

Piper, Otto A. "The Apocalypse of John and the Liturgy of the Ancient Church." *CH* 20 (1951): 10-22.

Piper, Ronald A. *Wisdom in the Q-Tradition: The Aphoristic Teaching of Jesus.* SNTSMS 61. Cambridge: Cambridge University Press, 1989.

Plooij, D. "The Attitude of the Outspread Hands ('Orante') in Early Christian Literature and Art." *ExpT* 23 (1912): 199-203, 265-69.

Pokorny, Petr. *The Genesis of Christology.* Edinburgh: T. & T. Clark, 1987; German ed., 1985.

Polag, Athanasius. *Die Christologie der Logienquelle.* WMANT 45. Neukirchen-Vluyn: Neukirchener Verlag, 1977.

———. "The Theological Center of the Sayings Source." In *The Gospel and the Gospels,* edited by Peter Stuhlmacher, 97-105. Grand Rapids: Eerdmans, 1991.

Pollard, T. E. *Johannine Christology and the Early Church.* SNTSMS 13. Cambridge: Cambridge University Press, 1970.

Price, S. R. F. *Rituals and Power: The Roman Imperial Cult in Asia Minor.* Cambridge: Cambridge University Press, 1984.

Pritz, Ray A. *Nazarene Jewish Christianity from the End of the New Testament Period until Its Disappearance in the Fourth Century.* SPB 37. Leiden: Brill, 1988.

Quasten, Johannes. *Patrology.* 4 vols. Westminster, Md.: Christian Classics, 1950-86.

———. *Musik und Gesang in den Kulten der heidnischen Antike und christlichen Frühzeit.* 2nd ed. Münster: Aschendorffsche Verlagsbuchhandlung, 1973 [1930].

Quesnell, Quentin. "The Mar Saba Clementine: A Question of Evidence." *CBQ* 37 (1975): 48-67.

Quinn, Jerome D. "Timothy and Titus, Epistles To." In *ABD,* 6:560-71.

Quispel, Gilles. "The Original Doctrine of Valentinus the Gnostic." *VC* 50 (1996): 327-52.

———. "Valentinus and the Gnostikoi." *VC* 50 (1996): 1-4.

Rackl, Michael. *Die Christologie des heiligen Ignatius von Antiochien.* Freiburger Theologische Studien 14. Freiburg im Breisgau: Herdersche Verlagshandlung, 1914.

Racle, G. "Perspectives christologiques de l'Homélie pascale de Méliton de Sardes." In *Studia Patristica. Vol. IX,* edited by F. L. Cross, 263-69. TU 94. Berlin: Akademie-Verlag, 1966.

Rainbow, Paul A. "Monotheism and Christology in 1 Corinthians 8:4-6." D.Phil. thesis, Oxford, 1987.

Räisänen, Heikki. "Die 'Hellenisten' der Urgemeinde." In *ANRW,* 2.26/2:1468-1514.

Ramsey, George W., Stanley E. Porter, and William Scott Green. "Joshua." In *ABD,* 3:999-1002.

Raschke, Carl. "Revelation and Conversion: A Semantic Appraisal." *ATR* 60 (1978): 420-36.

Rawlinson, A. E. J. *The New Testament Doctrine of the Christ: The Bampton Lectures for 1926.* London: Longmans, Green, 1926.

Reed, Jonathan L. *Archaeology and the Galilean Jesus: A Re-examination of the Evidence.* Harrisburg, Pa.: Trinity Press International, 2000.

Reif, Stefan. *Judaism and Hebrew Prayer.* Cambridge: Cambridge University Press, 1993.

Reijners, G. Q. *The Terminology of the Holy Cross in Early Christian Literature.* Nijmegen: Dekker & Van De Vegt, 1965.

Reim, Günter. *Studien zum Alttestamentlichen Hintergrund des Johannesevangeliums.* SNTSMS 22. Cambridge: Cambridge University Press, 1974.

Rhoads, David M., and Donald Mitchie. *Mark as Story: An Introduction to the Narrative of a Gospel.* Philadelphia: Fortress, 1982.

Richard, Earl. *Jesus: One and Many: The Christological Concept of New Testament Authors.* Wilmington, Del.: Michael Glazier, 1988.

Richardson, Neil. *Paul's Language about God.* JSNTSup 99. Sheffield: Sheffield Academic Press, 1994.

Richardson, Peter. *Israel in the Apostolic Church.* SNTSMS 10. Cambridge: Cambridge University Press, 1969.

Riesner, Rainer. "Archeology and Geography." In *DJG*, 33-46.

―――. *Paul's Early Period: Chronology, Mission Strategy, Theology.* Grand Rapids: Eerdmans; Carlisle: Paternoster, 1998.

Riley, Gregory J. "The *Gospel of Thomas* in Recent Scholarship." *CRBS* 2 (1994): 227-52.

―――. *Resurrection Reconsidered: Thomas and John in Controversy.* Minneapolis: Fortress, 1995.

Rissi, Matthias. *Die Theologie des Hebräerbriefs.* WUNT 41. Tübingen: Mohr (Siebeck), 1987.

Roberts, Alexander, and James Donaldson, eds. *The Ante-Nicene Fathers.* 10 vols. Edinburgh: T. & T. Clark, 1885. Reprint with "Annotated Index of Authors and Works of the Ante-Nicene, Nicene, and Post-Nicene Fathers," Peabody, Mass.: Hendrickson, 1994.

Roberts, Colin H. *Manuscript, Society, and Belief in Christian Egypt.* London: Oxford University Press, 1979.

Robinson, James M. "Die Hodajot-Formel in Gebet und Hymnus des Frühchristentums." In *Apophoreta: Festschrift für E. Haenchen zu seinem siebzigsten Geburtstag am 10 Dezember 1964,* edited by W. Eltester and F. H. Kettler, 194-235. Berlin: A. Töpelmann, 1964.

―――. *The Problem of History in Mark.* London: SCM Press, 1968.

―――. "LOGOI SOPHON: On the Gattung of Q." In *Trajectories through Early Christianity,* by James M. Robinson and Helmut Koester, 71-113. Philadelphia: Fortress, 1971.

―――. "Jesus — from Easter to Valentinus (or to the Apostles' Creed)." *JBL* 101 (1982): 5-37.

―――. "On Bridging the Gulf from Q to the *Gospel of Thomas* (or Vice Versa)." In *Nag Hammadi Gnosticism and Early Christianity,* edited by Charles W. Hedrick and Robert Hodgen, Jr., 127-75. Peabody, Mass.: Hendrickson, 1986.

―――, ed. *The Nag Hammadi Library in English.* 3rd rev. ed. New York and Leiden: Brill, 1988.

Robinson, James M., and Helmut Koester. *Trajectories through Early Christianity.* Philadelphia: Fortress, 1971.

Robinson, James M., Paul Hoffmann, and John S. Kloppenborg, eds. *The Critical Edition of Q.* Leuven: Peeters; Minneapolis: Fortress, 2000.

Robinson, Thomas A. *The Bauer Thesis Examined: The Geography of Heresy in the Early Christian Church.* Lewiston, N.Y.: Edwin Mellen Press, 1988.

Rose, Martin. "Names of God in the OT." In *ABD,* 4:1001-11.

Rowland, Christopher. "The Vision of the Risen Christ in Rev. 1.13ff.: The Debt of an Early Christology to an Aspect of Jewish Angelology." *JTS* 31 (1980): 1-11.

————. "Apocalyptic Visions and the Exaltation of Christ in the Letter to the Colossians." *JSNT* 19 (1983): 73-83.

Royse, James R. "Philo, Kyrios, and the Tetragrammaton." *Studia Philonica Annual* 3 (1991): 167-83.

Ruck-Schröder, Adelheid. *Der Name Gottes und der Name Jesu: Eine neutestamentliche Studie.* WMANT 80. Neukirchen-Vluyn: Neukirchener-Verlag, 1999.

Rudolph, Kurt. *Gnosis: The Nature and History of Gnosticism.* San Francisco: Harper and Row, 1983.

————. "Early Christianity as a Religious-Historical Phenomenon." In *The Future of Early Christianity: Essays in Honor of Helmut Koester,* edited by B. A. Pearson, 9-19. Minneapolis: Fortress, 1991.

Runnalls, Donna R. "The King as Temple Builder: A Messianic Typology." In *Spirit within Structure (Festschrift for George Johnston),* edited by E. J. Furcha, 15-37. Allison Park, Pa.: Pickwick, 1983.

Saldarini, Anthony J. *Matthew's Christian-Jewish Community.* Chicago Studies in the History of Judaism. Chicago: University of Chicago Press, 1994.

Sanders, E. P. *Paul and Palestinian Judaism.* Philadelphia: Fortress, 1977.

————. *Paul, the Law, and the Jewish People.* Philadelphia: Fortress, 1983.

————. *Jesus and Judaism.* London: SCM Press, 1985.

Sanders, Jack T. *The New Testament Christological Hymns: Their Historical Religious Background.* SNTSMS 15. Cambridge: Cambridge University Press, 1971.

Sandmel, Samuel. "Parallelomania." *JBL* 81 (1962): 1-13.

Sandnes, Karl Olav. *Paul — One of the Prophets?* WUNT 2/43. Tübingen: Mohr (Siebeck), 1991.

Sandt, Huub van de, and David Flusser. *The "Didache": Its Jewish Sources and Its Place in Early Judaism and Christianity.* CRINT. Assen: Van Gorcum; Minneapolis: Fortress, 2002.

Sänger, Dieter. "'Verflucht ist jeder, der am Holze hängt' (Gal. 3,13b): Zur Rezeption einer frühen antichristlichen Polemik." *ZNW* 85 (1994): 279-85.

Sawyer, John F. A. *The Fifth Gospel: Isaiah in the History of Christianity.* Cambridge: Cambridge University Press, 1996.

Schaberg, Jane. *The Illegitimacy of Jesus: A Feminist Theological Interpretation of the Infancy Narratives.* New York: Crossroad, 1990. Reprint, Sheffield: Sheffield Academic Press, 1995.

Schaff, Philip. *The Creeds of Christendom.* Vol. 1, *The History of the Creeds.* New York: Harper and Row, 1877. Reprint, Grand Rapids: Baker, 1977.

Schaper, Joachim. *The Eschatology of the Greek Psalter.* WUNT 2/71. Tübingen: Mohr-Siebeck, 1995.

Scheidweiler, Felix. "The Gospel of Nicodemus, Acts of Pilate and Christ's Descent into Hell." In *NTA,* 1:501-36.

Schelkle, K. H. "Σωτήρ." In *EDNT,* 3:325-27.

Schille, Gottfried. *Frühchristliche Hymnen.* Berlin: Evangelische Verlagsanstalt, 1965.

Schimanowski, Gottfried. *Weisheit und Messias: Die jüdischen Voraussetzungen der urchristlichen Präexistenzchristologie.* WUNT 2/17. Tübingen: Mohr (Siebeck), 1985.

Schmahl, Günter. *Die Zwölf im Markusevangelium. Eine redaktionsgeschichtliche Untersuchung.* TTS 30. Trier: Paulinus Verlag, 1974.

Schmid, Ulrich. *Marcion und sein Apostolos. Rekonstruktion und historische Einordnung der marcionitischen Paulusbriefausgabe.* ANTF 25. Berlin: de Gruyter, 1995.

Schmidt, A. "Zwei Anmerkungen zu P.Ryl. III." *Archiv für Papyrusforschung* 35 (1989): 11-12.

Schmidt, Karl Ludwig. "Die Stellung der Evangelien in der allgemeinen Literaturgeschichte." In *Eucharisterion: Studien zur Religion und Literatur des Alten und Neuen Testaments. Hermann Gunkel zum 60. Geburtstag,* edited by Hans Schmidt, 50-134. Göttingen: Vandenhoeck & Ruprecht, 1923.

―――. "επικαλεω." In *TDNT,* 3:496-500.

Schnackenburg, Rudolf. *The Gospel according to St. John.* 3 vols. New York: Seabury Press, 1980-82.

―――. *Jesus in the Gospels: A Biblical Christology.* Translated by O. C. Dean, Jr. Louisville: Westminster John Knox, 1995.

Schneemelcher, Wilhelm, ed. *New Testament Apocrypha.* 2 vols. Translated and edited by R. McL. Wilson. Rev. ed. Louisville: Westminster John Knox; Cambridge: James Clarke, 1991-92.

Schneider, Johannes. "ξύλον." In *TDNT,* 5:37-41.

Schoedel, William R. *Ignatius of Antioch: A Commentary on the Letters of Ignatius of Antioch.* Hermeneia. Philadelphia: Fortress, 1985.

―――. "Apologetic Literature and Ambassadorial Activities." *HTR* 82 (1989): 55-78.

Schoeps, Hans Joachim. *Paul: The Theology of the Apostle in the Light of Jewish Religious History.* Philadelphia: Westminster, 1961.

Schröter, Jens. *Erinnerung an Jesu Worte: Studien zur Rezeption der Logienüberlieferung in Markus, Q, und Thomas.* WMANT 76. Neukirchen-Vluyn: Neukirchener Verlag, 1997.

Schubert, Paul. *Form and Function of the Pauline Thanksgivings.* Berlin: Töpelmann, 1939.

Schulz, Siegfried. "Markus und das Alte Testament." *ZTK* 58 (1961): 184-97.

―――. "Maranatha und Kyrios Jesus." *ZNW* 53 (1962): 125-44.

Schweizer, Eduard. *Egō Eimi. Die religionsgeschichtliche Herkunft und theologische Bedeutung der johanneischen Bildreden, zugleich ein Beitrag zur Quellenfrage des vierten Evangeliums.* 2nd ed. FRLANT 56. Göttingen: Vandenhoeck & Ruprecht, 1965 [1939].

Scott, Kenneth. *The Imperial Cult under the Flavians.* Stuttgart: W. Kohlhammer, 1936. Reprint, New York: Arno Press, 1975.

Scott, Martin. *Sophia and the Johannine Jesus.* JSNTSup 71. Sheffield: Sheffield Academic Press, 1992.

Segal, Alan F. *Two Powers in Heaven: Early Rabbinic Reports about Christianity and Gnosticism.* SJLA 25. Leiden: Brill, 1977.

―――. "Heavenly Ascent in Hellenistic Judaism, Early Christianity and Their Environment." In *ANRW,* 2.23/2:1333-94.

―――. "Hellenistic Magic: Some Questions of Definition." In *Studies in Gnosticism and Hellenistic Religions (FS G. Quispel),* edited by R. Van Den Broek and M. J. Vermaseren, 349-75. Leiden: Brill, 1981.

―――. *Paul the Convert: The Apostolate and Apostasy of Saul the Pharisee.* New Haven: Yale University Press, 1990.

Seland, Torrey. *Establishment Violence in Philo and Luke: A Study of Non-Conformity to the Torah and Jewish Vigilante Reactions.* Leiden: Brill, 1995.

Sellew, Philip. "Secret Mark and the History of Canonical Mark." In *The Future of Early Christianity: Essays in Honor of Helmut Koester*, edited by Birger A. Pearson, 242-57. Minneapolis: Fortress, 1991.

―――. "The *Gospel of Thomas*: Prospects for Future Research." In *The Nag Hammadi Library after Fifty Years: Proceedings of the 1995 Society of Biblical Literature Commemoration*, edited by John D. Turner and Anne McGuire, 327-46. NHMS 44. Leiden: Brill, 1997.

Selwyn, E. G. *The First Epistle of St. Peter*. London: Macmillan, 1964.

Setzer, Claudia J. *Jewish Responses to Early Christians: History and Polemics, 30-150 C.E.* Minneapolis: Fortress, 1994.

Sevenster, J. N. *Do You Know Greek? How Much Greek Could the First Jewish Christians Have Known?* NovTSup 19. Leiden: Brill, 1968.

Sevrin, Jean-Marie. "L'interprétation de l'*Évangile selon Thomas*, entre tradition et rédaction." In *The Nag Hammadi Library after Fifty Years: Proceedings of the 1995 Society of Biblical Literature Commemoration*, edited by John D. Turner and Anne McGuire, 347-60. NHMS 44. Leiden: Brill, 1997.

Shatkin, Margaret A. "Virgins." In *EEC*, 2:1165-67.

Sherwin-White, A. N. "Why Were the Early Christians Persecuted? An Amendment." *Past and Present* 27 (1964): 23-27.

―――. *The Letters of Pliny: A Historical and Social Commentary*. Oxford: Clarendon, 1966.

―――. *Roman Society and Roman Law in the New Testament (The Sarum Lectures, 1960-61)*. Oxford: Oxford University Press, 1963. Reprint, Grand Rapids: Baker, 1978.

Shuler, P. L. *A Genre for the Gospels: The Biographical Character of Matthew*. Philadelphia: Fortress, 1982.

Sider, R. D. "Tertullian." In *EEC*, 2:1107-9.

Siegel, Jonathan P. "The Employment of Paleo-Hebrew Characters for the Divine Names at Qumran in the Light of Tannaitic Sources." *HUCA* 42 (1971): 159-72.

Siker, Jeffrey S. *Disinheriting the Jews: Abraham in Early Christian Controversy*. Louisville: John Knox, 1991.

Silva, Moisés. *Biblical Words and Their Meaning*. Grand Rapids: Zondervan, 1983.

Simon, Marcel. *Verus Israel*. Paris: Editions E. de Boccard, 1964. ET, Oxford: Oxford University Press, 1986. Reprint, London: Littman Library of Jewish Civilization, 1996.

Simonetti, Manlio. "Note sulla cristologia dell' Ascensione di Isaia." In *Isaia, il deletto e la chiesa: Visione ed esegesi profetica christiano-primitiva nell' Ascensione di Isaia, Atti del convegno di Roma, 9-10 aprile 1981*, edited by Mauro Pesce, 185-205. Testi e richerche di Scienze religiose 20. Brescia: Paideia, 1983.

―――. *Biblical Interpretation in the Early Church: An Historical Introduction to Patristic Exegesis*. Edited by Anders Berquist and Markus Bockmuehl. Translated by J. A. Hughes. Edinburgh: T. & T. Clark, 1994.

Skarsaune, Oskar. *The Proof from Prophecy: A Study in Justin Martyr's Proof-Text Tradition: Text-Type, Provenance, Theological Profile*. NovTSup 66. Leiden: Brill, 1987.

―――. "The Development of Scriptural Interpretation in the Second and Third Centuries — Except Clement and Origen." In *Hebrew Bible/Old Testament: The History of Its Interpretation*, vol. 1, *From the Beginnings to the Middle Ages*, edited by Magne Saebo, 373-442. Göttingen: Vandenhoeck & Ruprecht, 1996.

Skeat, T. C. "Irenaeus and the Four-Gospel Canon." *NovT* 34 (1992): 194-99.

———. "The Origin of the Christian Codex." *Zeitschrift für Papyrus und Epigraphik* 102 (1994): 263-68.

———. "The Oldest Manuscript of the Four Gospels?" *NTS* 43 (1997): 1-34.

Skehan, Patrick W. "The Divine Name at Qumran, in the Masada Scroll, and in the Septuagint." *BIOSCS* 13 (1980): 14-44.

Skehan, Patrick W., and Alexander A. Di Lella. *The Wisdom of Ben Sira.* AB 39. New York: Doubleday, 1987.

Slusser, Michael. "Docetism: A Historical Definition." *SecCent* 1 (1981): 163-72.

Smith, D. Moody. *John among the Gospels: The Relationship in Twentieth-Century Research.* Minneapolis: Fortress, 1992.

———. *John: Abingdon New Testament Commentaries.* Nashville: Abingdon, 1999.

Smith, J. Z. *Drudgery Divine.* Chicago: University of Chicago Press, 1990.

Smith, Mark S. *The Early History of God.* San Francisco: Harper and Row, 1987.

Smith, Morton. *Palestinian Parties and Politics That Shaped the Old Testament.* New York: Columbia University Press, 1971. Reprint, London: SCM Press, 1987.

———. *Clement of Alexandria and a Secret Gospel of Mark.* Cambridge: Harvard University Press, 1973.

———. *The Secret Gospel: The Discovery and Interpretation of the Secret Gospel according to Mark.* New York: Harper and Row, 1973.

———. "Clement of Alexandria and the Secret Mark: The Score at the End of the First Decade." *HTR* 75 (1982): 449-61.

———. "Ascent to the Heavens and Deification in 4QMᵃ." In *Archaeology and History in the Dead Sea Scrolls,* edited by L. H. Schiffman, 181-88. Sheffield: Sheffield Academic Press, 1990.

Smothers, E. R. "ΦΩΣ ΙΛΑΡΟΝ." *RSR* 19 (1920): 266-83.

Snyder, Graydon F. *Ante Pacem: Archaeological Evidence of Church Life before Constantine.* Macon, Ga.: Mercer University Press, 1985.

Soards, Marion L. "Appendix IX: The Question of a PreMarcan Passion Narrative." In *The Death of the Messiah,* by Raymond E. Brown, 2:1492-1524. New York: Doubleday, 1994.

———. *The Speeches in Acts: Their Content, Context, and Concerns.* Louisville: Westminster John Knox, 1994.

Sproston, Wendy E. "'Is Not This Jesus, the Son of Joseph . . . ?' (John 6.42): Johannine Christology as a Challenge to Faith." *JSNT* 24 (1985): 77-97.

Standaert, Benoit. "L'Évangile de Vérité: critique et lecture." *NTS* 22 (1975-76): 243-75.

———. "'Evangelium Veritatis' et 'Veritatis Evangelium': La question du titre et les témoins patristiques." *VC* 30 (1976): 138-50.

Stanley, David. "Imitation in Paul's Letters: Its Significance for His Relationship to Jesus and to His Own Christian Foundations." In *From Jesus to Paul: Studies in Honour of Francis Wright Beare,* edited by Peter Richardson and John C. Hurd, 127-41. Waterloo, Ontario: Wilfrid Laurier University Press, 1984.

Stanton, G. N. "On the Christology of Q." In *Christ and Spirit in the New Testament,* edited by S. S. Smalley and B. Lindars, 27-42. Cambridge: Cambridge University Press, 1973.

————. *Jesus of Nazareth in New Testament Preaching.* SNTSMS 27. Cambridge: Cambridge University Press, 1974.

————. "Aspects of Early Christian-Jewish Polemic and Apologetics." *NTS* 31 (1985): 377-92.

————. *The Gospels and Jesus.* Oxford: Oxford University Press, 1989.

————. *A Gospel for a New People: Studies in Matthew.* Edinburgh: T. & T. Clark, 1992.

————. "Aspects of Early Christian and Jewish Worship: Pliny and the *Kerygma Petrou.*" In *Worship, Theology, and Ministry in the Early Church: Essays in Honor of Ralph P. Martin,* edited by M. A. Wilkins and T. Paige, 84-98. JSNTSup 87. Sheffield: JSOT Press, 1992.

————. "Jesus of Nazareth: A Magician and a False Prophet Who Deceived God's People?" In *Jesus of Nazareth, Lord and Christ: Essays on the Historical Jesus and New Testament Christology,* edited by Joel B. Green and Max Turner, 164-80. Carlisle: Paternoster; Grand Rapids: Eerdmans, 1994.

————. "The Fourfold Gospel." *NTS* 43 (1997): 317-46.

Stark, Alonzo R. *The Christology of the Apostolic Fathers.* Chicago: University of Chicago Press, 1912.

Stark, Rodney. "A Taxonomy of Religious Experience." *JSSR* 5 (1965): 97-116.

————. "How New Religions Succeed: A Theoretical Model." In *The Future of New Religious Movements,* edited by David G. Bromley and Phillip E. Hammond, 11-29. Macon, Ga.: Mercer University Press, 1987.

————. "Normal Revelations: A Rational Model of 'Mystical' Experiences." In *Religion and the Social Order,* vol. 1, *New Developments in Theory and Research,* edited by David G. Bromley, 239-51. Greenwich, Conn.: JAI Press, 1991.

————. *The Rise of Christianity.* Princeton: Princeton University Press, 1996.

Stark, Rodney, and William Sims Bainbridge. *The Future of Religion: Secularization, Revival, and Cult Formation.* Berkeley, Los Angeles, and London: University of California Press, 1985.

Stark, Werner. *The Sociology of Religion: A Study of Christendom.* Vol. 4. New York: Fordham University Press, 1970.

Stauffer, Ethelbert. "Jeschu ben Mirjam: Kontrovergeschichtliche Anmerkungen zu Mk 6:3." In *Neotestamentica et Semitica: Studies in Honour of Matthew Black,* edited by E. Earle Ellis and Max Wilcox, 119-28. Edinburgh: T. & T. Clark, 1969.

Stead, G. C. "In Search of Valentinus." In *The Rediscovery of Gnosticism,* vol. 1, *The School of Valentinus,* edited by Bentley Layton, 75-102. Leiden: Brill, 1980.

Steenburg, David. "The Case against the Synonymity of *Morphē* and *Eikōn.*" *JSNT* 34 (1988): 77-86.

————. "The Worship of Adam and Christ as the Image of God." *JSNT* 39 (1990): 95-109.

Stendahl, Krister. *The School of St. Matthew and Its Use of the Old Testament.* Philadelphia: Fortress, 1968.

————. *Paul among Jews and Gentiles.* Philadelphia: Fortress, 1976.

Stern, M. "The Province of Judaea." In *The Jewish People in the First Century: Historical Geography, Political History, Social, Cultural, and Religious Life and Institutions,* edited by S. Safrai and M. Stern, 1:308-76. CRINT 1/1. Philadelphia: Fortress, 1974.

Stettler, Christian. *Der Kolosserhymnus: Untersuchungen zu Form, traditionsgeschichtlichem*

Hintergrund und Aussage von Kol 1,15-20. WUNT 2/131. Tübingen: Mohr Siebeck, 2000.

Stettler, Hanna. *Die Christologie der Pastoralbriefe*. WUNT 2/103. Tübingen: Mohr Siebeck, 1998.

Stevenson, J., ed. *A New Eusebius: Documents Illustrative of the History of the Church to A.D. 337*. London: SPCK, 1974.

Stone, Michael E. *A History of the Literature of Adam and Eve*. SBLEJL 3. Atlanta: Scholars, 1992.

Story, C. I. K. *The Nature of Truth in "The Gospel of Truth" and in the Writings of Justin Martyr*. NovTSup 25. Leiden: Brill, 1970.

Strack, H. L., and G. Stemberger. *Introduction to the Talmud and Midrash*. Translated by Markus Bockmuehl. Minneapolis: Fortress, 1992.

Strange, James F. "First-Century Galilee from Archaeology and from the Texts." In SBLSP 33, edited by E. H. Lovering, Jr., 81-90. Atlanta: Scholars, 1994.

Strecker, Georg. *The Johannine Epistles*. Hermeneia. Minneapolis: Fortress, 1996.

Stuckenbruck, Loren T. *Angel Veneration and Christology*. WUNT 2/70. Tübingen: J. C. B. Mohr (Siebeck), 1995.

————. "Worship and Monotheism in the *Ascension of Isaiah*." In *The Jewish Roots of Christological Monotheism: Papers from the St. Andrews Conference on the Historical Origins of the Worship of Jesus*, edited by Carey C. Newman, James R. Davila, and Gladys S. Lewis, 70-89. JSJSup 63. Leiden: Brill, 1999.

Stuhlmacher, Peter. "Das Christusbild der Paulus-Schule — eine Skizze." In *Jews and Christians, the Parting of the Ways, A.D. 70 to 135*, edited by J. D. G. Dunn, 159-75. WUNT 66. Tübingen: Mohr-Siebeck, 1992.

Swete, H. B. *The Akhmîm Fragment of the Apocryphal Gospel of St. Peter*. London: Macmillan, 1893.

————. *The Apocalypse of St. John*. 3rd ed. Cambridge: Cambridge University Press, 1908.

Talbert, Charles H. *What Is a Gospel? The Genre of the Canonical Gospels*. Philadelphia: Fortress, 1977.

————. "Biographies of Philosophers and Rulers as Instruments of Religious Propaganda in Mediterranean Antiquity." In *ANRW*, 2.16/2:1619-57.

Talley, Thomas. "Liturgical Time in the Ancient Church: The State of Research." *Studia Liturgica* 14 (1982): 34-51.

Tannehill, Robert C. "The Disciples in Mark: The Function of a Narrative Role." *JR* 57 (1977): 386-405.

Tarja, Harry W. *The Martyrdom of St. Paul: Historical and Judicial Context, Traditions, and Legends*. WUNT 2/67. Tübingen: Mohr-Siebeck, 1994.

Taylor, Lily Ross. *The Divinity of the Roman Emperor*. Middletown, Conn.: American Philosophical Association, 1931. Reprint, Chico, Calif.: Scholars, n.d.

Taylor, Nicholas. *Paul, Antioch, and Jerusalem: A Study in Relationships and Authority in Earliest Christianity*. JSNTSup 66. Sheffield: Sheffield Academic Press, 1992.

Taylor, Vincent. *The Historical Evidence for the Virgin Birth*. Oxford: Clarendon, 1920.

————. *The Gospel according to St. Mark*. 2nd ed. London: Macmillan, 1966.

Temporini, H., and W. Haase, eds. *Aufstieg und Niedergang der römischen Welt, Teil II: Prinzipat*. Berlin: De Gruyter, 1978-.

Thomassen, Einar. "How Valentinian Is *The Gospel of Philip*?" In *The Nag Hammadi Li-*

brary after Fifty Years: Proceedings of the 1995 Society of Biblical Literature Commemoration, edited by John D. Turner and Anne McGuire, 251-79. NHMS 44. Leiden: Brill, 1997.

Thompson, Leonard. "Hymns in Early Christian Worship." *ATR* 55 (1973): 458-72.

———. *The Book of Revelation: Apocalypse and Empire.* New York: Oxford University Press, 1990.

Thompson, Marianne Meye. *The Humanity of Jesus in the Fourth Gospel.* Philadelphia: Fortress, 1988.

———. "John, Gospel Of." In *DJG,* 368-83.

Thompson, Michael B. *Clothed with Christ: The Example and Teaching of Jesus in Romans 12:1–15:13.* JSNTSup 59. Sheffield: JSOT Press, 1991.

———. "The Holy Internet: Communication between Churches in the First Christian Generation." In *The Gospels for All Christians: Rethinking the Gospel Audiences,* edited by Richard Bauckham, 49-70. Grand Rapids: Eerdmans, 1998.

Tödt, Heinz-Edward. *The Son of Man in the Synoptic Tradition.* ET, London: SCM Press, 1965; German, Gütersloh: Gerd Mohn, 1959.

Tomson, Peter J. *Paul and the Jewish Law: Halakha in the Letters of the Apostle to the Gentiles.* CRINT 3/1. Assen: Van Gorcum; Philadelphia: Fortress, 1990.

Towner, P. H. "Households and Household Codes." In *DPL,* 417-19.

———. "Household Codes." In *DLNTD,* 513-20.

Trakatellis, Demetrios C. *The Pre-existence of Christ in the Writings of Justin Martyr: An Exegetical Study with Reference to the Humiliation and Exaltation Christology.* HDR 6. Missoula: Scholars, 1976.

———. "Justin Martyr's Trypho." In *Christians among Jews and Gentiles,* edited by G. W. E. Nickelsburg and G. W. McCrae, 287-97. Philadelphia: Fortress, 1986.

———. "God Language in Ignatius of Antioch." In *The Future of Early Christianity: Essays in Honor of Helmut Koester,* edited by B. A. Pearson, 422-30. Minneapolis: Fortress, 1991.

Trevett, Christine. *Montanism: Gender, Authority, and the New Prophecy.* Cambridge: Cambridge University Press, 1996.

Tripolitis, Antonia. "ΦΩΣ ΙΛΑΡΟΝ: Ancient Hymn and Modern Enigma." *VC* 24 (1970): 189-96.

Trobisch, David. *Die Endredaktion des Neuen Testaments. Eine Untersuchung zur Entstehung der christlichen Bibel.* Freiburg: Universitätsverlag Freiburg; Göttingen: Vandenhoeck & Ruprecht, 1996. ET, *The First Edition of the New Testament.* New York: Oxford University Press, 2000.

Tuckett, Christopher M. *Q and the History of Early Christianity: Studies on Q.* Edinburgh: T. & T. Clark, 1996.

———. "P52 and *Nomina Sacra.*" *NTS* 47 (2001): 544-48.

Turner, Martha L. "On the Coherence of the *Gospel according to Philip.*" In *The Nag Hammadi Library after Fifty Years: Proceedings of the 1995 Society of Biblical Literature Commemoration,* edited by John D. Turner and Anne McGuire, 223-50. NHMS 44. Leiden: Brill, 1997.

Turner, Max. "The Spirit of Christ and 'Divine' Christology." In *Jesus of Nazareth: Lord and Christ: Essays on the Historical Jesus and New Testament Christology,* edited by Joel B. Green and Max Turner, 413-36. Grand Rapids: Eerdmans; Carlisle: Paternoster, 1994.

Twelftree, Graham H. *Jesus the Exorcist: A Contribution to the Study of the Historical Jesus.* WUNT 2/54. Tübingen: J. C. B. Mohr (Siebeck), 1993.

Unnik, W. C. van. "'The Gospel of Truth' and the New Testament." In *The Jung Codex,* edited by F. L. Cross, 79-129. London: A. R. Mowbray, 1955.

———. "'Worthy Is the Lamb': The Background of Apoc 5." In *Mélanges bibliques en hommage au R. P. Beda Rigaux,* edited by Albert Descamps and R. P. André Halleux, 445-61. Gembloux: Duculot, 1970.

Untergassmair, Franz Georg. *Im Namen Jesu — Der Namensbegriff im Johannesevangelium: eine exegetisch-religionsgeschichtliche Studie zu den johanneischen Namenaussagen.* Stuttgart: Katholisches Bibelwerk, 1974.

Urbach, Ephraim E. *The Sages: Their Concepts and Beliefs.* Translated by Israel Abrahams. 2 vols. Jerusalem: Magnes Press, 1979.

Uro, Risto, ed. *Thomas at the Crossroads: Essays on the "Gospel of Thomas."* Edinburgh: T. & T. Clark, 1998. See Risto, "Is *Thomas* an Encratite Gospel?" (140-62).

Valantasis, Richard. *The Gospel of Thomas.* London: Routledge, 1997.

Vermes, Geza. "The Use of *Bar Nasha/Bar Nash* in Jewish Aramaic." In *An Aramaic Approach to the Gospels and Acts,* by Matthew Black, 310-30. 3rd ed. Oxford: Oxford University Press, 1967.

———. *Jesus the Jew: A Historian's Reading of the Gospels.* London: Collins, 1973.

———. *Jesus and the World of Judaism.* Philadelphia: Fortress, 1983.

———. *The Religion of Jesus the Jew.* Minneapolis: Fortress, 1993.

Verseput, D. J. "The Role and Meaning of the 'Son of God' Title in Matthew's Gospel." *NTS* 33 (1987): 532-56.

Von Rad, Gerhard. *Old Testament Theology.* 2 vols. ET, New York: Harper and Row, 1962.

Vorster, Willem S. "The Growth and Making of John 21." In *The Four Gospels 1992: Festschrift Frans Neirynck,* edited by F. Van Segbroeck, C. M. Tuckett, G. Van Belle, and J. Verheyden, 3:2207-21. Leuven: Leuven University Press/Peeters, 1992.

Vos, Geerhardus. "The Kyrios Christos Controversy." *PTR* 15 (1917): 21-89.

Votaw, Clyde Weber. *The Gospels and Contemporary Biographies in the Greco-Roman World.* Philadelphia: Fortress, 1970.

Wainwright, Arthur W. *The Trinity in the New Testament.* London: SPCK, 1962.

Waldman, Marilyn Robinson, and Robert M. Baum. "Innovation as Renovation: The 'Prophet' as an Agent of Change." In *Innovation in Religious Traditions,* edited by Michael A. Williams, Collette Cox, and Martin S. Jaffee, 241-84. Berlin and New York: Mouton de Gruyter, 1992.

Waldstein, Michael, and Frederik Wisse. *The "Apocryphon of John": Synopsis of Nag Hammadi Codices II,1; III,1; and IV,1 with BG 8502,2.* NHMS 33. Leiden: Brill, 1995.

Wallace, A. F. C. "Revitalization Movements." *American Anthropologist* 58 (1956): 264-81.

Wedderburn, A. J. M. *Baptism and Resurrection: Studies in Pauline Theology against Its Graeco-Roman Background.* WUNT 44. Tübingen: Mohr (Siebeck), 1987.

Weder, Hans. "The Hermeneutics of Christology in the Johannine Writings." In *Exploring the Gospel of John: In Honor of D. Moody Smith,* edited by R. Alan Culpepper and C. Clifton Black, 325-45. Louisville: Westminster John Knox, 1996.

Weeden, Theodore J. "The Heresy That Necessitated Mark's Gospel." *ZNW* 59 (1968): 145-58.

———. *Mark — Traditions in Conflict.* Philadelphia: Fortress, 1971.

Weinfeld, Moshe. *Organizational Pattern and the Penal Code of the Qumran Sect: A Comparison with Guilds and Religious Associations of the Hellenistic-Roman Period.* NTOA 2. Göttingen: Vandenhoeck & Ruprecht, 1986.

Wendling, Emil. *Ur-Marcus: Versuch einer Wiederherstellung der ältesten Mitteilungen über das Leben Jesu.* Tübingen: Mohr-Siebeck, 1905.

Wengst, Klaus. *Christologische Formeln und Lieder des Urchristentums.* SNT 7. Gütersloh: Gerd Mohn, 1972.

Werner, Martin. *Die Entstehung des christlichen Dogmas.* 2nd ed. 1941. Reprint, Bern: Paul Haupt, 1954. ET, *The Formation of Christian Dogma.* New York: Harper and Brothers, 1957.

Wernle, Paul. "Jesus und Paulus: Antitheses zu Bousset's Kyrios Christos." *ZTK* 25 (1915): 1-92.

White, Hugh G. Evelyn. *The Sayings of Jesus from Oxyrhynchus.* Cambridge: Cambridge University Press, 1920.

White, John L. "New Testament Epistolary Literature in the Framework of Ancient Epistolography." In *ANRW*, 2.25/2:1730-56.

Whittaker, Molly. *Jews and Christians: Graeco-Roman Views.* Cambridge: Cambridge University Press, 1984.

―――, ed. and trans. *Tatian, "Oratio ad Graecos" and Fragments.* Oxford: Clarendon, 1982.

Whybray, R. N. *The Second Isaiah.* Sheffield: JSOT Press, 1983.

Wiles, Maurice. *The Spiritual Gospel: The Interpretation of the Fourth Gospel in the Early Church.* Cambridge: Cambridge University Press, 1960.

―――. *The Divine Apostle: The Interpretation of St. Paul's Epistles in the Early Church.* Cambridge: Cambridge University Press, 1967.

Wilken, Robert L. *The Christians as the Romans Saw Them.* New Haven and London: Yale University Press, 1984.

Williams, Catrin H. *I Am He.* WUNT 2/113. Tübingen: Mohr-Siebeck, 2000.

―――. "'I Am' or 'I Am He'? Self-Declaratory Pronouncements in the Fourth Gospel and Rabbinic Tradition." In *Jesus in Johannine Tradition,* edited by Robert T. Fortna and Tom Thatcher, 343-52. Louisville, London, and Leiden: Westminster John Knox, 2001.

Williams, D. S. "Reconsidering Marcion's Gospel." *JBL* 108 (1989): 477-96.

Williams, Jacqueline A. *Biblical Interpretation in the Gnostic "Gospel of Truth" from Nag Hammadi.* SBLDS 79. Atlanta: Scholars, 1988.

Williams, Michael Allen. *Rethinking "Gnosticism": An Argument for Dismantling a Dubious Category.* Princeton: Princeton University Press, 1996.

Wilson, R. McL. *The Gospel of Philip, Translated from the Coptic Text, with an Introduction and Commentary.* London: A. R. Mowbray, 1962.

―――. "Valentinianism and the *Gospel of Truth.*" In *The Rediscovery of Gnosticism,* vol. 1, *The School of Valentinus,* edited by Bentley Layton, 133-41. Leiden: Brill, 1980.

Wilson, Stephen G. *Related Strangers: Jews and Christians, 70-170 C.E.* Minneapolis: Fortress, 1995.

Winslow, D. F. "The Polemical Christology of Melito of Sardis." In *Studia Patristica, Vol. XVII,* edited by E. A. Livingstone, 765-75. Oxford: Pergamon Press, 1982.

Winter, Bruce. "The Imperial Cult." In *The Book of Acts in Its Graeco-Roman Setting,* edited by D. W. J. Gill and C. Gempf, 93-103. Carlisle: Paternoster; Grand Rapids: Eerdmans, 1994.

Winter, Bruce W., and Andrew D. Clarke, eds. *The Book of Acts in Its Ancient Literary Setting*. The Book of Acts in Its First-Century Setting 1. Grand Rapids: Eerdmans; Carlisle: Paternoster, 1993.

Wise, Michael O. "Languages of Palestine." In *DJG*, 434-44.

Wisse, Frederik. "Prolegomena to the Study of the New Testament and Gnosis." In *The New Testament and Gnosis: Essays in Honour of Robert McL. Wilson*, edited by A. H. B. Logan and A. J. M. Wedderburn, 138-45. Edinburgh: T. & T. Clark, 1983.

————. "The Use of Early Christian Literature as Evidence for Inner Diversity and Conflict." In *Nag Hammadi, Gnosticism, and Early Christianity*, edited by Charles W. Hedrick and Robert Hodgson, Jr., 177-90. Peabody, Mass.: Hendrickson, 1986.

————. "Egyptians, Gospel Of." In *ABD*, 2:413-14.

————. "After the *Synopsis*: Prospects and Problems in Establishing a Critical Text of the *Apocryphon of John* and in Defining Its Historical Location." In *The Nag Hammadi Library after Fifty Years: Proceedings of the 1995 Society of Biblical Liteature Commemoration*, edited by John D. Turner and Anne McGuire, 138-53. NHMS 44. Leiden: Brill, 1997.

Witherington, Ben, III. *The Christology of Jesus*. Minneapolis: Fortress, 1990.

————. "Birth of Jesus." In *DJG*, 60-74.

Woollcombe, K. J. "The Biblical Origins and Patristic Development of Typology." In *Essays on Typology*, by G. W. H. Lampe and K. J. Woollcombe, 39-75. SBT 22. London: SCM Press, 1957.

Wrede, William. *The Messianic Secret*. Cambridge: James Clark, 1971; German ed., 1901.

Wright, David F. "Apocryphal Gospels: The 'Unknown Gospel' (Pap. Egerton 2) and the *Gospel of Peter*." In *The Jesus Tradition Outside the Gospels*, edited by David Wenham, 207-32. Sheffield: JSOT Press, 1985.

————. "Papyrus Egerton 2 (the Unknown Gospel) — Part of the *Gospel of Peter*?" *SecCent* 5 (1985-86): 129-50.

————. "Docetism" and "Ebionites." In *DLNTD*, 306-9 and 313-17, respectively.

Wright, N. T. *The Climax of the Covenant*. Edinburgh: T. & T. Clark, 1991.

————. *Jesus and the Victory of God*. Minneapolis: Fortress, 1996.

Wu, J. L. "Liturgical Elements." In *DPL*, 557-60.

Young, Frances. *The Theology of the Pastoral Letters*. Cambridge: Cambridge University Press, 1994.

Young, Franklin W. "A Study of the Relation of Isaiah to the Fourth Gospel." *ZNW* 46 (1955): 215-33.

Ziegler, Konrat, and Walther Sontheimer, eds. *Der Kleine Pauly Lexikon der Antike*. 5 vols. Munich: Deutscher Taschenbuch Verlag, 1979.

Zimmermann, Heinrich. "Das absolute Εγω ειμι als die neutestamentliche Offenbarungsformel." *BZ* 4 (1960): 54-69, 266-76.

Zwiep, A. W. *The Ascension of the Messiah in Lukan Christology*. NovTSup 87. Leiden: Brill, 1997.

Index of Modern Authors

Aalen, S., 376n.54
Aberle, David, 67n.114
Abramowski, Luise, 581n.61
Achtemeier, Paul J., 518n.76, 630nn.210-12
Aland, Barbara, 554n.87, 550n.79, 553
Alexander, Loveday C. A., 280n.46, 341n.205
Alexander, Philip, 274, 275
Alhaus, Paul, 13n.20
Allegro, J. M., 193n.74
Allison, Dale C., 54n.76, 220n.11, 226n.23, 234n.47, 235, 240n.57, 246n.68, 250n.80, 268n.19, 290n.75, 333n.189
Almond, Philip C., 66, 67
Alsup, John E., 569n.19, 570n.20, 571, 572n.29
Amphoux, C.-B., 585n.75
Anderson, Gary A., 39n.40
Anderson, Hugh, 307n.124
Anderson, Paul N., 52n.73, 350n.3, 353n.10, 392n.92, 393-94, 416-17
Anderson, R. Dean, Jr., 90n.26
Andresen, Carl, 644n.253
Arai, Sasagu, 541n.55
Argyle, A. W., 23n.56
Arnold, Clinton E., 34n.20, 199n.86, 203n.98, 509n.53
Ashton, John, 350n.3, 353n.10
Attridge, Harold W., 189n.61, 452n.76, 453nn.79-80, 457n.94, 467n.128,

497nn.24-25, 498nn.26,27,29, 499, 501n.34, 503nn.38,40, 539nn.46,49, 540n.53, 542nn.58,60, 629n.207, 634, 635n.227
Aune, David E., 73n.130, 114n.84, 135, 142n.149, 150nn.173-74, 177n.39, 185n.51, 203n.98, 262n.8, 270, 272n.29, 274, 278, 280, 401, 588n.79, 611, 612n.142
Aus, R., 158n.6

Baarda, Tjitze, 580n.55, 582, 583n.68
Bailey, James L., 261n.6
Bainbridge, William Sims, 522n.5
Balás, David L., 550n.79, 552, 554, 555nn.88-89
Ball, David Mark, 370n.39, 371n.41, 372n.43
Balz, Horst, 13n.21
Bammel, C. P. Hammond, 621n.177
Barclay, John, 228n.27
Barker, Margaret, 33-34, 37n.32, 42n.49, 71n.126
Barnard, L. W., 491, 492n.15, 576n.40, 581nn.59-60, 608n.127, 621n.177, 642n.244, 643, 644nn.252-53, 647nn.258-59
Barnett, P. W., 164n.21
Barrett, C. K., 52n.73, 136n.131, 158n.6, 165n.22, 166nn.24-25, 177n.37, 212n.116,

Index of Subjects

Index of Ancient Sources